THE VICTORIA HISTORY
OF THE
COUNTIES OF ENGLAND

———

A HISTORY OF
STAFFORDSHIRE

VOLUME XX

THE VICTORIA HISTORY
OF THE
COUNTIES OF ENGLAND

EDITED BY C. R. ELRINGTON

THE UNIVERSITY OF LONDON
INSTITUTE OF
HISTORICAL RESEARCH

Oxford University Press, Walton Street, Oxford OX2 6DP
London New York Toronto
Delhi Bombay Calcutta Madras Karachi
Kuala Lumpur Singapore Hong Kong Tokyo
Nairobi Dar es Salaam Cape Town
Melbourne Auckland

and associated companies in
Beirut Berlin Ibadan Mexico City Nicosia

Oxford is a trade mark of Oxford University Press

Published in the United States by
Oxford University Press, New York

ISBN 0 19 722765 1

Printed in Great Britain
at the University Press, Oxford
by David Stanford
Printer to the University

INSCRIBED TO THE

MEMORY OF HER LATE MAJESTY

QUEEN VICTORIA

WHO GRACIOUSLY GAVE THE TITLE TO

AND ACCEPTED THE DEDICATION

OF THIS HISTORY

A HISTORY OF THE COUNTY OF STAFFORD

EDITED BY M. W. GREENSLADE

VOLUME XX

SEISDON HUNDRED (PART)

PUBLISHED FOR

THE INSTITUTE OF HISTORICAL RESEARCH

BY

OXFORD UNIVERSITY PRESS

1984

Distributed by Oxford University Press until 1 January 1987
thereafter by Dawsons of Pall Mall

CONTENTS OF VOLUME TWENTY

PAGE

Dedication v

Contents ix

List of Illustrations x

List of Maps and Plans xii

Editorial Note xiii

Staffordshire Victoria History Committee xiv

Classes of Documents in the Public Record Office xv

Note on Abbreviations xvi

Analysis of Sources in *Collections for a History of Staffordshire* . . . xviii

Topography . . . Architectural descriptions prepared in
collaboration with A. P. BAGGS

Seisdon Hundred, Northern Division (part)

    Tettenhall . . By M. W. GREENSLADE, D. A. JOHNSON,
and N. J. TRINGHAM 1

Seisdon Hundred, Southern Division

    Amblecote . . By M. W. GREENSLADE . . . 49

    Bobbington . . By N. J. TRINGHAM 64

    Codsall . . . By N. J. TRINGHAM, D. A. JOHNSON,
and ANN J. KETTLE 76

    Enville . . . By D. A. JOHNSON and N. J. TRINGHAM . 91

    Kinver . . . By M. W. GREENSLADE, D. A. JOHNSON,
and N. J. TRINGHAM . . . 118

    Patshull . . . By M. W. GREENSLADE . . . 161

    Pattingham . . By M. W. GREENSLADE and N. J. TRINGHAM 172

    Trysull . . . By M. W. GREENSLADE and N. J. TRINGHAM 185

    Wombourne . . By M. W. GREENSLADE, D. A. JOHNSON,
and N. J. TRINGHAM . . . 197

    Woodford Grange . By N. J. TRINGHAM . . . 225

Index 227

LIST OF ILLUSTRATIONS

Grateful acknowledgement is made to the following for permission to use material: the British Geological Survey; *Country Life*; Mr. H. J. Haden; the Hereford and Worcester County Record Office; the National Monuments Record of the Royal Commission on Historical Monuments (England); the National Trust; Mr. J. W. Phillips of the Wodehouse, Wombourne; the Staffordshire Record Office; the Trustees of the William Salt Library, Stafford; and Wolverhampton Central Library. Photographs dated 1980-3 are by A. P. Baggs.

Tettenhall: Wightwick Manor from the south-east. Photograph by A. Starkey in the possession of *Country Life* . . . . *facing page* 16

The Wodehouse, Wombourne. The drawing room. Photograph, 1982 . . ,, 16

Tettenhall: Compton Hall. The drawing room decorated by Morris & Co. *c.* 1896. Photograph, 1981 . . . . ,, 17

Tettenhall: The Mount, Tettenhall Wood. The entrance hall. Photograph, 1983 ,, 17

Tettenhall Towers in 1880. Engraving in *The Builder*, 24 January 1880 . . *page* 22

Tettenhall Towers. The Music Room. Photolithograph in *The Builder*, 24 January 1880, from a drawing by D. A. Warry . . . . . ,, 23

Tettenhall: Wrottesley Hall from the south-west in the later 19th century. Photograph in Wolverhampton Central Library, P/N2 . . . . *facing page* 32

Tettenhall: Wrottesley Hall and village in 1634. Facsimile 61 at the William Salt Library, Stafford . . . . ,, 32

Enville: Mere Farm from the south-west in 1857 with clementing in progress. Engraving in *Illustrated London News*, 26 December 1857, based on a drawing by 'Cuthbert Bede' (the Revd. E. Bradley) . . . . . ,, 33

Tettenhall: Pendeford Hall from the south *c.* 1835. Drawing by J. R. Fernyhough, in Staffordshire Views, viii. 6, at the William Salt Library, Stafford . ,, 33

Amblecote: Holy Trinity Church from the north-west in the mid 19th century. Engraving in the Staffordshire Record Office, D. 716/5/2 . . . ,, 64

Amblecote: the National school at Coalbournbrook in 1858. Engraving in *Views of Stourbridge* (n.d.; copy at the Hereford and Worcester Record Office, Worcester) . . . . ,, 64

Bobbington: Bobbington Hall from the north-east. Photograph, *c.* 1960, by R. J. Sherlock, in the possession of the National Monuments Record . . ,, 65

Bobbington: Blakelands from the north-west. Photograph, 1982 . . . ,, 65

Tettenhall: Barnhurst Farm, demolished *c.* 1962. Photograph, 1960, by R. J. Sherlock, in the possession of the National Monuments Record . . ,, 65

Kinver: Whittington Manor Farm. Photograph, 1983 . . . . ,, 65

Tettenhall: view of Wolverhampton from the Rock in 1837. Drawing by R. Noyes, in Staffordshire Views, xii. 84, at the William Salt Library, Stafford ,, 80

Wombourne: canal locks at the Bratch. Photograph, 1981 . . . ,, 80

Tettenhall: the church from the south in 1822. Drawing by R. Noyes, in Staffordshire Views, x. 116, at the William Salt Library, Stafford . . ,, 81

Wombourne: waterworks at the Bratch. Photograph, 1982 . . . ,, 81

Wombourne: the church from the south in 1837. Drawing by T. P. Wood, in Staffordshire Views, xii. 136, at the William Salt Library, Stafford . . ,, 81

Enville Hall: the south front in the 1680s. Engraving by M. Burghers (from his own drawing) in R. Plot, *A Natural History of Staffordshire* (Oxford, 1686), plate VII . . . . ,, 96

Enville Hall: the south front in the later 18th century. Drawing in the possession of the National Trust at Dunham Massey, Cheshire . . . . ,, 96

Enville Hall: the conservatory of 1855. Photograph, later 19th century, in private possession . . . . ,, 96

Harry Grey, earl of Stamford (d. 1768). Unlocated painting by Thomas Hudson; photograph in the possession of the National Trust at Dunham Massey, Cheshire . . . . ,, 97

George Harry Grey, earl of Stamford and Warrington (d. 1883). Lithograph in the possession of the National Trust at Dunham Massey, Cheshire . . ,, 97

LIST OF ILLUSTRATIONS

Enville: Lyndon in the later 18th century. Drawing in private possession   .   *facing page* 112

Kinver Edge: Holy Austin Rock with former cave dwellings. Photograph, 1983   ,,   112

Enville Church: misericords. Photograph, 1982 .   .   .   .   .   ,,   113

Kinver: High Street in 1836. Drawing by R. Noyes, in Staffordshire Views, v. 76, at the William Salt Library, Stafford   .   .   .   .   ,,   128

Kinver Edge from the north-west. Photograph in the possession of the British Geological Survey, London (NERC copyright)   .   .   .   ,,   128

Kinver: Stourton Castle c. 1800. Drawing by S. Shaw, in Staffordshire Views, x. 37, at the William Salt Library, Stafford   .   .   .   .   ,,   129

Kinver: the Stewponey inn in 1828. Drawing by R. Noyes, in Staffordshire Views, x. 38, at the William Salt Library, Stafford   .   .   .   ,,   129

Kinver: the Hyde ironworks c. 1870. Engraving from J. Griffiths, *Guide to the Iron Trade of Great Britain* (1873)   .   .   .   .   .   ,,   144

Amblecote: Coalbournbrook from the north c. 1900, with glassworks. Photograph in the possession of Mr. H. J. Haden of Stourbridge   .   .   ,,   144

Kinver: the Old Grammar School. Photograph, 1982   .   .   .   .   ,,   145

Kinver: the school-chapel at Halfcot in 1846. Drawing by J. Buckler, in Staffordshire Views, v. 83, at the William Salt Library, Stafford   .   .   .   ,,   145

Enville: Lady Dorothy's Cottage. Photograph, 1983   .   .   .   .   ,,   145

Enville: Countess of Stamford and Warrington School. Photograph, 1982   .   ,,   145

Patshull Church: Astley Monuments. Engraving from a drawing by T. Carter in S. Shaw, *History and Antiquities of Staffordshire*, ii (1801), plate facing p. 286 .   .   .   .   *page* 171

Patshull House. The south front in the late 18th century. Drawing in Staffordshire Views, vii. 135, at the William Salt Library, Stafford   .   .   *facing page* 176

Patshull House. The north front. Photograph, 1980   .   .   .   .   ,,   176

Pattingham: the church from the north-east and the east front of the vicarage house c. 1793. Drawing by R. Paddey, in Staffordshire Views, vii. 160, at the William Salt Library, Stafford   .   .   .   .   .   ,,   177

Patshull: the church from the south-east c. 1800. Engraving from a drawing by S. Shaw in S. Shaw, *History and Antiquities of Staffordshire*, ii (1801), plate facing p. 279   .   .   .   .   .   .   ,,   177

Trysull: the church from the north-east in 1837. Drawing by T. P. Wood, in Staffordshire Views, xi. 66, at the William Salt Library, Stafford   .   ,,   192

Enville: the church from the south-east in 1837. Drawing by T. P. Wood, in Staffordshire Views, iv. 175, at the William Salt Library, Stafford   .   ,,   192

The Wodehouse, Wombourne. Prospects and garden features in 1773. Drawings by J. Hughes at the Wodehouse, Wombourne   .   .   .   .   ,,   193

LIST OF MAPS AND PLANS

The maps facing page 1 and on pages 4, 6, 66, 78, 92, 120, 162, 174, 186, and 198 were drawn by Mary Edwards and Joan Hill from drafts prepared by M. W. Greenslade and N. J. Tringham. The plans were drawn by A. P. Baggs. Owners of source material are thanked for making it available.

Seisdon Hundred *c.* 1850. Based on Ordnance Survey Map 1″, index to the Tithe Survey . . . . *facing page* 1

Yates's Map of 1775 (part). From W. Yates, *A Map of the County of Stafford* (1775) . . . . *page* 2

Tettenhall, 1980. Based on Ordnance Survey Map 6″ (1883–90 edn.) . . ,, 4

Tettenhall: central area, 1980. Based on Ordnance Survey Map 6″ (1889–90 edn.) . . . . ,, 6

Amblecote, 1882. From Ordnance Survey Map 6″ (1886–8 edn.) . . ,, 50

Bobbington, 1981. Based on Ordnance Survey Map 6″ (1884–9 edn.) . . ,, 66

Codsall, 1983. Based on Ordnance Survey Map 6″ (1883–9 edn.) . . ,, 78

Enville, 1982. Based on Ordnance Survey Map 6″ (1887–9 edn.) . . ,, 92

Plan of Enville Hall. Based on a plan of 1981 by M. J. Scott-Bolton, agent for the Enville estate . . . . ,, 98

Enville Hall: plan of the grounds *c.* 1750. Based on a plan in the Staffordshire Record Office, Tp. 1273/54 . . . . ,, 100

Enville Hall: plan of the grounds *c.* 1880. Based on Ordnance Survey Map 6″ (1887–8 edn.) . . . . ,, 101

Plan of the Home Farm, Enville. Based on an undated plan in the Staffordshire Record Office, Tp. 1273 . . . . ,, 102

Kinver, 1982. Based on Ordnance Survey Map 6″ (1887–8 edn.) . . ,, 120

Patshull, 1921. Based on Ordnance Survey Map 6″ (1924 edn.) . . . ,, 162

Plan of Patshull House. Based on a plan of 1956 in the possession of Wolverhampton Area Health Authority . . . . ,, 166

Pattingham, 1979. Based on Ordnance Survey Map 6″ (1884–6 edn.) . . ,, 174

Trysull, 1979. Based on Ordnance Survey Map 6″ (1884–6 edn.) . . ,, 186

Wombourne, 1981. Based on Ordnance Survey Map 6″ (1884–9 edn.) . . ,, 198

Plan of the Wodehouse, Wombourne. Based on a plan of 1912 by J. and H. E. Lavender at the Wodehouse . . . . ,, 205

EDITORIAL NOTE

This volume is the ninth to appear in the Staffordshire set of the Victoria History of the Counties of England. Like its seven immediate predecessors it has been produced by the Staffordshire Victoria History Committee, which represents a partnership between the university of London and several local authorities in Staffordshire and the County of West Midlands. The nature of the partnership is described in the Editorial Note to volume IV of the Staffordshire set, and the membership of the Committee is set out on p. xiv below. The university of London thanks the Staffordshire County Council and the metropolitan boroughs of Dudley, Sandwell, Walsall, and Wolverhampton for their continued support and generous financial help.

In 1979 Dr. N. J. Tringham was appointed to the staff of the Staffordshire Victoria History as assistant editor, a post which had been vacant since 1978.

Many people and organizations have helped in the preparation of the present volume. Several are acknowledged in the lists of illustrations and of maps and plans and in the footnotes to the articles on which their help was given. Thanks are also offered to Mrs. K. H. Atkins, archivist at Dudley Central Library; Mr. G. C. Baugh, editor of the Shropshire Victoria History, and his staff; Miss B. J. Cousens of the Mercia Region of the National Trust; Mr. M. B. S. Exham, registrar of Lichfield Diocese; Mr. L. J. Livesey, Staffordshire County Librarian, and his staff; Mr. R. A. Meeson of the Staffordshire County Planning and Development Department; Miss Liz Rees, archivist to Wolverhampton Metropolitan Borough; Mr. F. B. Stitt, Staffordshire County Archivist and William Salt Librarian, and his staff, especially Mrs. J. Hampartumian, archivist at the Lichfield Joint Record Office; and Mr. A. G. Taylor of the Staffordshire County Planning and Development Department.

The structure and aims of the Victoria History as a whole are outlined in the *General Introduction* (1970).

STAFFORDSHIRE
VICTORIA COUNTY HISTORY COMMITTEE

as at 1 January 1984

LIST OF CLASSES OF DOCUMENTS IN THE PUBLIC RECORD OFFICE
USED IN THIS VOLUME
WITH THEIR CLASS NUMBERS

Chancery

	Proceedings	
C 1	Early	
C 2	Series I	
C 3	Series II	
	Six Clerks Series	
C 5	Bridges	
C 7	Hamilton	
C 8	Mitford	
	Enrolments	
C 54	Close Rolls	
C 60	Fine Rolls	
C 66	Patent Rolls	
C 88	Records upon Outlawries	
C 93	Proceedings of Commissioners for Charitable Uses, Inquisitions and Decrees	
C 103	Masters' Exhibits, Blunt	
	Inquisitions post mortem	
	Series I	
C 137	Henry IV	
C 140	Edward IV	
C 142	Series II	
C 143	Inquisitions ad quod damnum	

Court of Common Pleas

CP 25(1)	Feet of Fines, Series I
CP 25(2)	Feet of Fines, Series II
CP 34	King's Silver Books, Series I
CP 43	Recovery Rolls

Exchequer, Treasury of the Receipt

E 32	Forest Proceedings
E 42	Deeds, Series AS

Exchequer, King's Remembrancer

E 101	Accounts, Various
E 134	Depositions taken by Commission
E 150	Inquisitions post mortem, Series II
E 178	Special Commissions of Inquiry
E 179	Subsidy Rolls, etc.

Exchequer, Augmentation Office

E 301	Certificates of Colleges and Chantries
E 303	Conventional Leases
E 310	Particulars for Leases

E 315	Miscellaneous Books
E 318	Particulars for Grants
E 321	Proceedings of Court of Augmentations
E 326	Ancient Deeds, Series B
E 328	Ancient Deeds, Series B

Ministry of Education

ED 7	Elementary Education, Public Elementary Schools, Preliminary Statements

Home Office

HO 107	Census Papers, Population Returns, 1841 and 1851
HO 129	Census Papers, Ecclesiastical Returns

Indexes

IND	Indexes (various classes)

Auditors of Land Revenue (Exchequer)

LR 2	Miscellaneous Books

Ministry of Agriculture, Fisheries, and Food

MAF 9	Deeds and Awards of Enfranchisement

Maps and Plans

MR 308	Map of part of Tettenhall, 1613

Prerogative Court of Canterbury

PROB 11	Registered Copies of Wills proved in P.C.C.

British Transport Historical Records

RAIL 874	Canal Companies, Stourbridge Navigation

Registrar General

RG 9	Census Returns, 1861
RG 10	Census Returns, 1871

Court of Requests

REQ 2	Proceedings

Special Collections

SC 6	Ministers' Accounts

State Paper Office

	State Papers Domestic
SP 14	Jas. I

Court of Star Chamber

STAC 4	Mary
STAC 8	Jas. I

NOTE ON ABBREVIATIONS

Among the abbreviations and short titles used the following, in addition to those listed in the Victoria History's *Handbook for Editors and Authors*, may require elucidation:

B.R.L.	Birmingham Central Library, Reference Library
Bennett, 'Kinver'	A. J. Bennett, 'A History of Kinver' (typescript, 1977; copy in W.S.L.)
Brighton, *Pattingham*	F. Brighton, *Pattingham* (Dudley, 1942)
Brook, *Ind. Arch. W. Midlands*	F. Brook, *The Industrial Archaeology of the British Isles: 1 The West Midlands* (London, 1977)
Char. Digest Staffs.	*General Digest of Endowed Charities of the County of Stafford*, H.C. 91 (5) (1868–9), xlv (3)
Char. Dons. 1786–88	*Abstract of the Returns of Charitable Donations for the Benefit of Poor Persons 1786–1788*, H.C. 511 (1816), xvi (2)
Colvin, *Brit. Architects*	H. Colvin, *A Biographical Dictionary of British Architects 1600–1840* (1978)
D.C.L.	Dudley Central Library
Ekwall, *Eng. Place-Names*	E. Ekwall, *Concise Oxford Dictionary of English Place-Names* (4th edn.)
Erdeswick, *Staffs.*	S. Erdeswick, *A Survey of Staffordshire*, ed. T. Harwood (1844)
Greenwood, *Map of Staffs.* (1820)	C. and J. Greenwood, *Map of Staffordshire* (1820)
Hodgson, *Queen Anne's Bounty*	C. Hodgson, *An Account of the Augmentation of Small Livings by the Governors of the Bounty of Queen Anne* (1845, 1856)
H. W. R. O. (H.)	Hereford and Worcester Record Office (Hereford)
H. W. R. O. (W.)	Hereford and Worcester Record Office (Worcester)
Jay, 'Bobbington'	Archibald Jay, 'A short history of Bobbington, Enville, Kinver, Claverley, and adjoining hamlets' (MS. written mainly in the mid 1950s; in the possession of the author's daughter, Mrs. Mary Crump of Clair Hayes, Bobbington)
Jennings, *Staffs. Bells*	T. S. Jennings, *A History of Staffordshire Bells* (priv. print. 1968; copy in W.S.L.)
Jones, *Tettenhall*	J. P. Jones, *A History of the Parish of Tettenhall in the County of Stafford* (1894)
Lynam, *Church Bells*	C. Lynam, *The Church Bells of the County of Stafford* (1889)
M.A.F.F.	Ministry of Agriculture, Fisheries, and Food (Crewe Divisional Office)
Matthews, *Cong. Churches of Staffs.*	A. G. Matthews, *The Congregational Churches of Staffordshire* (n.d.; preface 1924)
N.S.J.F.S.	*North Staffordshire Journal of Field Studies*
Parson and Bradshaw, *Dir. Staffs.* (1818)	W. Parson and T. Bradshaw, *Staffordshire General and Commercial Directory* (1818)
Pevsner, *Staffs.*	N. Pevsner, *The Buildings of England: Staffordshire* (Harmondsworth, 1974)
Pitt, *Staffs.*	W. Pitt, *A Topographical History of Staffordshire* (Newcastle-under-Lyme, 1817)
Plot, *Staffs.*	R. Plot, *A Natural History of Staffordshire* (Oxford, 1686)
4th Rep. Com. Char.	*Fourth Report of the Charity Commissioners for England and Wales*, H.C. 312 (1820), v
5th Rep. Com. Char.	*Fifth Report of the Charity Commissioners for England and Wales*, H.C. 159 (1821), xii
9th Rep. Com. Char.	*Ninth Report of the Charity Commissioners for England and Wales*, H.C. 258 (1823), ix
Rep. Com. Eccl. Revenues	*Report of the Commissioners appointed by His Majesty to inquire into the Ecclesiastical Revenues of England and Wales* (2 vols., 1835)

S.H.C.	Staffordshire Record Society (formerly William Salt Archaeological Society), *Collections for a History of Staffordshire*
S.R.O.	Staffordshire Record Office (including Tp. for Temporary Deposits)
Scott, *Stourbridge*	W. Scott, *Stourbridge and its Vicinity* (Stourbridge, 1833)
Shaw, *Staffs.*	Stebbing Shaw, *The History and Antiquities of Staffordshire* (2 vols., 1798, 1801; reprinted with additions, Wakefield, 1976)
Sherlock, *Ind. Arch. Staffs.*	R. Sherlock, *The Industrial Archaeology of Staffordshire* (1976)
Staffs. Cath. Hist.	*Staffordshire Catholic History* (Journal of the Staffordshire Catholic History Society)
Staffs. Endowed Chars.	*Report on Charitable Endowments appropriated to purposes of Elementary Education in the County of Stafford* [Cd. 2729], H.C. (1906), xc
T.B.A.S.	Birmingham and Midland Institute: Birmingham Archaeological Society, *Transactions and Proceedings*
W.S.L.	William Salt Library, Stafford
White, *Dir. Staffs.*	W. White, *History, Gazetteer, and Directory of Staffordshire* (1834; 1851)
Wolv. C.L.	Wolverhampton Central Library
Yates, *Map of Staffs.* (1775; 1799)	W. Yates, *A Map of the County of Stafford* (1775; revised edition by W. Faden, 1799)

ANALYSIS OF SOURCES PRINTED IN
COLLECTIONS FOR A HISTORY OF STAFFORDSHIRE
(STAFFORDSHIRE RECORD SOCIETY)
AND USED IN THIS VOLUME

Vol.	*Pages*	*Subject-matter or title of article*
i	1-143	Pipe Rolls, 1130, 1155-89
	145-240	Liber Niger Scaccarii, 1166
	290-384	Manor and Parish of Blymhill
ii (1)	1-177	Pipe Rolls, 1189-1216
	178-276	Staffordshire Chartulary, 1072-*c.* 1237
iii (1)	1-163	Plea Rolls, 1194-1215
	166-77	Final Concords, 1196-1213
	178-231	Staffordshire Chartulary, *c.* 1120-*c.* 1272
iii (2)		Visitation of Staffordshire, 1583
iv (1)	1-215	Plea Rolls, 1219-72
	218-63	Final Concords, 1218-72
iv (2)	1-124	Parish of Church Eaton
v (1)	1-101	Burton Chartulary
	105-21	Staffordshire Hundred Rolls
	123-80	Pleas of the Forest, 1262-1300
v (2)		Visitations of Staffordshire, 1614 and 1663-4
vi (1)	37-300	Plea Rolls, 1271-94
vii (1)	1-191	Plea Rolls, 1293-1307
	195-255	Subsidy Roll, 1327
viii (1)	1-122	Military Service performed by Staffordshire Tenants
viii (2)		History of Castle Church
ix (1)	3-118	Plea Rolls, 1308-26
	119-32	Fine Rolls, 1307-26
ix (2)		The Barons of Dudley
x (1)	3-75	Plea Rolls, 1308-26
	79-132	Subsidy Roll, 1332-3
x (2)		Family of Sutton, alias Dudley
xi	3-123	Plea Rolls, 1327-41
	127-292	Final Concords, 1327-1546
xii (1)	3-173	Plea Rolls, 1341-59
	177-239	Final Concords, Hen. VII–Philip and Mary
xiii	3-204	Plea Rolls, 1360-87
	207-300	Final Concords, 1559-73
xiv (1)	3-162	Plea Rolls, 1327-83
	165-217	Final Concords, 1573-80
xv	3-126	Plea Rolls, 1387-1412
	129-98	Final Concords, 1580-9
xvi	3-93	Plea Rolls, Edw. III–Hen. IV
	97-225	Final Concords, 1589-1603
xvii	3-153	Plea Rolls, 1413-35
	209-36	Final Concords, 1558-88
xviii (1)	3-21	Final Concords, 1589-1602
New Series i		The Gresleys of Drakelowe
New Series ii		History of Weston-under-Lizard
New Series iii	3-70	Final Concords, 1607-12
	123-229	Plea Rolls, 1423-57, with 1392 and 1401
New Series iv	3-28	Final Concords, 1603-25
	31-91	Final Concords, 1613-16
	95-212	Plea Rolls, 1456-74
New Series v	3-232	History of the Giffard Family
New Series vi (1)	63-87	Muster Roll, Staffordshire, 1539
	91-164	Plea Rolls, 1475-85, with 1427
	167-90	Inventory of Church Goods and Ornaments, 1552

ANALYSIS OF SOURCES

Vol.	Pages	Subject-matter or title of article
New Series vi (2)		History of the Wrottesley Family
New Series viii		Second Register of Bishop Robert de Stretton, 1360-85
New Series x (1)	13-70	Final Concords, 1622-5
	73-188	Star Chamber Proceedings, Hen. VII and Hen. VIII
New Series x (2)		First Register of Bishop Robert de Stretton, 1358-85
New Series xi	3-224	History of the Bagot Family
1910	3-85	Star Chamber Proceedings, Hen VIII and Edw. VI
1911	28-111	Final Concords, 1272-1307
	115-375	Inquisitions post mortem, ad quod damnum, etc., 1223-1326
	379-414	Testa de Nevill and other Feodaries
1912	3-207	Star Chamber Proceedings, Hen. VII-Eliz. I
	272-94	Sheriffs of Staffordshire, 1086-1912
	303-44	Keepers and Justices of the Peace for Staffordshire
1913	3-178	Inquisitions post mortem, ad quod damnum, etc., 1327-66
1915		Staffordshire Incumbents and Parochial Records (1530-1680)
1916	69-137	Staffordshire Pre-Conquest Charters
1917-18		Staffordshire Parliamentary History (1213-1603)
1919	182-4	Notes on Seisdon Hundred, etc.
1920 and 1922		Staffordshire Parliamentary History (1603-1780)
1921	1-39	Calendar of Salt MSS.
1923	47-116	Hearth Tax, 1666, Seisdon Hundred
1927	119-81	Staffordshire Quarter Sessions Rolls
1928	3-134	Ancient Deeds preserved at the Wodehouse, Wombourne
	137-71	Calendar of Early Charters in the possession of Lord Hatherton
1929		Staffordshire Quarter Sessions Rolls, 1581-9
1930		Staffordshire Quarter Sessions Rolls, 1590-3
1931	61-99	Enclosure of Open Fields and Commons in Staffordshire
	123-231	Chancery Proceedings, 1558-79 (H-P)
1932		Staffordshire Quarter Sessions Rolls, 1594-7
1933(1)		Staffordshire Members of Parliament, 1780-1841
1934(1)	1-157	Transport and the pottery industry during the 18th century
1934(2)	3-52	Staffordshire Quarter Sessions Rolls: Enrolment of Deeds, 1579-1622
	55-94	History from the Wolseley Charters
1935		Staffordshire Quarter Sessions Rolls, 1598-1602
1938	3-201	Chancery Proceedings, 1558-79 (P-Y)
1939	177-220	Priory of the Black Ladies of Brewood
1940		Staffordshire Quarter Sessions Rolls, 1603-6
1941	3-20	A Hand List of English Enclosure Acts and Awards. Staffordshire
	23-80	Additions to Grazebrook's 'The Barons of Dudley'
1945-6		The Manor of Tyrley
1948-9		Staffordshire Quarter Sessions Rolls, 1608-9
1950-1	109-35	William Baker of Audlem, Architect
	231-42	The 1801 Crop Returns for Staffordshire
4th Series ii	44-70	List of Active Parliamentarians during the Civil Wars
	72-99	List of Staffordshire Recusants, 1657
4th Series iii		Dissenting Chapels and Meeting Houses in Staffordshire, 1689-1852
4th Series vi	1-25	Some Staffordshire Poll Tax Returns
	26-65	Church Lighting in Staffordshire since the Reformation
	136-70	Sir Edward Littleton's Fox-Hunting Diary, 1774-89
	209-23	Staffordshire and the Voluntary Contribution, 1798
4th Series viii		A List of Families in the Archdeaconry of Stafford, 1532-3
4th Series x		Visitations of the Archdeaconry of Stafford, 1829-41

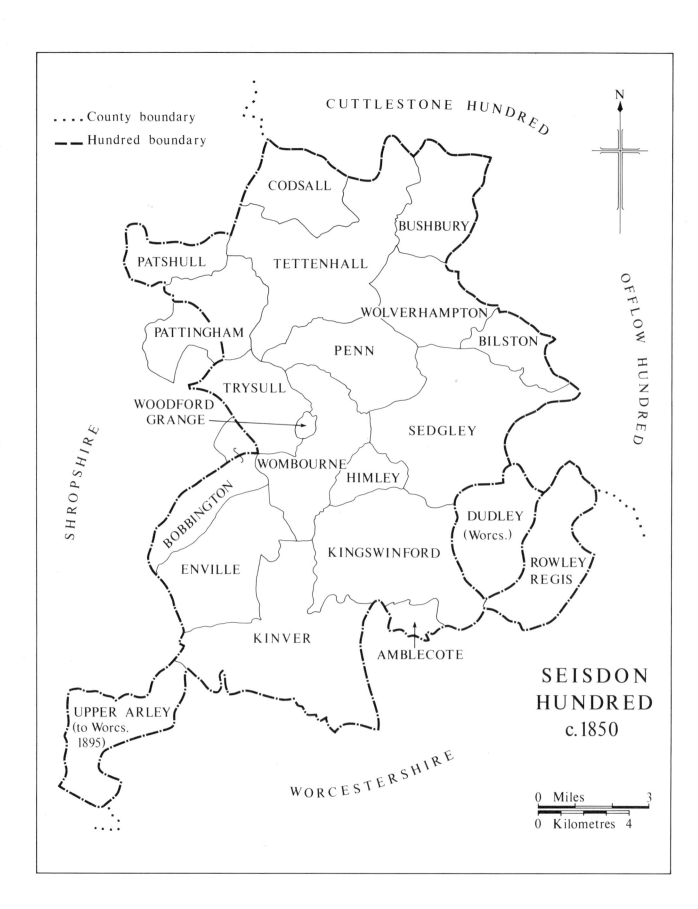

CUTTLESTONE HUNDRED

N

OFFLOW HUNDRED

.... County boundary
— — Hundred boundary

CODSALL

BUSHBURY

PATSHULL

TETTENHALL

WOLVERHAMPTON

BILSTON

PATTINGHAM

PENN

TRYSULL

WOODFORD
GRANGE

SEDGLEY

WOMBOURNE

HIMLEY

DUDLEY
(Worcs.)

BOBBINGTON

ROWLEY
REGIS

ENVILLE

KINGSWINFORD

SHROPSHIRE

KINVER

AMBLECOTE

SEISDON
HUNDRED
c.1850

UPPER ARLEY
(to Worcs.
1895)

WORCESTERSHIRE

0   Miles   3

0   Kilometres 4

SEISDON HUNDRED
NORTHERN DIVISION
(part)

TETTENHALL

TETTENHALL adjoins Wolverhampton, and the south-eastern part of the former ancient parish has become a residential suburb of that town. The rest is mainly agricultural land with some residential areas.

The ancient parish of Tettenhall, 8,306 a. (3,361 ha.) in area,[1] was divided between the northern and southern divisions of Seisdon hundred until 1845. In that year the Pendeford and Wrottesley portions of the parish were transferred from the south to the north so that the whole parish then lay in the northern division.[2] The urban district of Tettenhall, 1,531 a. in area, was formed in 1894 to include Tettenhall village, Tettenhall Wood, Compton, Finchfield, Wightwick, and Wergs. The remaining 6,775 a. of the ancient parish became the civil parish of Wrottesley, divided into two detached parts by the Wergs area of the urban district; nearly two thirds (4,240½ a.) occupied the western part of the ancient parish, and 2,534½ a. lay in the north-east. In 1927 an area of 556 a. around Barnhurst and Blakeley Green in the north-east part of Wrottesley was transferred to Wolverhampton county borough, and in 1934 another 972 a. of Wrottesley west of Tettenhall Wood and Wightwick were added to the urban district.[3] In 1966 two thirds of the urban district became part of Wolverhampton; most of the remainder was transferred to Wrottesley, but the Wergs Hall area was added to Codsall. The built-up Aldersley and Codsall Road district of Wrottesley was transferred to Wolverhampton. The area of Wrottesley was increased to 2,286 ha. (5,649 a.).[4] Codsall was originally part of Tettenhall parish but had become independent by the mid 16th century; its history is treated elsewhere in the present volume.

The rock is sandstone, and a feature of the district is the outcrop which forms an escarpment running south-west and west from Tettenhall village through Tettenhall Wood and Perton to Dadnall Hill on the Pattingham boundary and beyond. Lying around 450 ft. (137 m.) in Tetten-hall itself, the ridge reaches 500 ft. (152 m.) at Tettenhall Wood and drops to 432 ft. (132 m.) at Perton and 388 ft. (118 m.) at Dadnall Hill. A plateau extends north from the top of the ridge, rising to 541 ft. (165 m.) in Wrottesley Old Park in the north-west but dropping to 325 ft. (99 m.) at Pendeford in the north-east. South of the ridge the ground drops to 350 ft. (107 m.) and below along Smestow brook and 294 ft. (90 m.) by Black brook in the south-west. It rises sharply to 400 ft. (122 m.) at Finchfield south of Smestow brook. There is an outcrop of marl in the Wrottesley area. In the north-west there is glacial boulder clay, with some sand in the Cranmoor area south of Wrottesley; there is also sand at Bilbrook and in Sandy Lane at Claregate in the north-east and between Compton and Wightwick in the south.[5] There is a variety of soils.

The village of Tettenhall lies on the watershed between Smestow brook flowing south towards the Stour and the Severn and the headwaters of the Penk flowing north towards the Trent. Smestow brook rises in Bushbury and enters Tettenhall at Aldersley, forming much of the southern boundary of Tettenhall ancient parish and Wrottesley civil parish. A tributary stream once formed the boundary north from Aldersley, but it evidently disappeared when the Stafford-shire and Worcestershire Canal was built. Graiseley brook, also a tributary, formed the boundary between Tettenhall and Wolverhampton east of Compton. Another tributary, Black brook, is for a short distance the south-western boundary of Wrottesley. The Penk rises in the area between Yew Tree Lane and Wrottesley Road formerly occupied by meadow called Penkridge Well; the southern end of the meadow is marked by the modern street named Penk Rise. The stream flows south-west before turning north to the Wergs area and then forms the boundary with Codsall as far as Dam Mill. At Pendeford it is joined by Pendeford brook from the Barnhurst area and by Moat brook from Codsall; at Bilbrook, Moat brook forms the

[1] *Census*, 1901. This article was written mainly in 1980. Mr. K. Parker, editor of the *Express & Star*, and his staff (especially Miss I. Grainger), Mr. K. Williams, chief executive and town clerk of Wolverhampton metropolitan borough, and his staff (especially Mr. R. A. Yeomans), and others named in footnotes are thanked for their help.

[2] S.R.O., Q/SO 35, ff. 25, 139v., 163v.

[3] *Census*, 1901, 1931, 1951; Staffs. Review Order, 1934, p. 61 (copy in S.R.O.); S.R.O., L.G.O. 36, map 8.

[4] W. Midlands Order 1965, S.I. 1965, no. 2139; *Census*, 1971. One ha. of the urban district was added to Penn, and 6 ha. were added to Wrottesley from Wolverhampton.

[5] T. H. Whitehead and others, *Memoirs of Geol. Surv., the Country between Wolverhampton and Oakengates*, 5, 119, 135–6, 189–91; below, econ. hist.

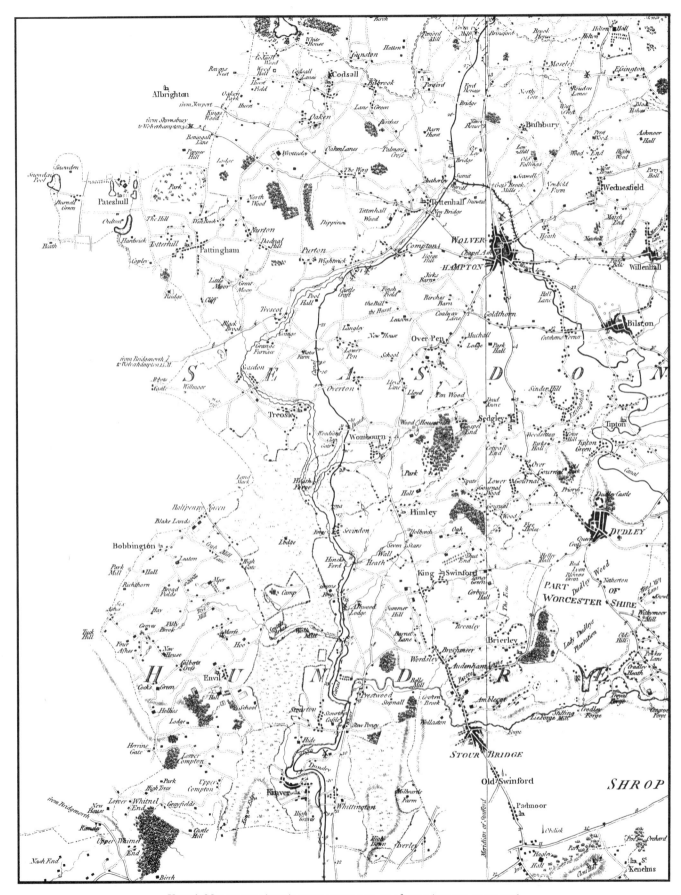

YATES'S MAP OF 1775 (PART): SCALE ABOUT 1 IN. TO 1¾ MILE (APPROX. 1:110,000)

boundary with Brewood. The Penk then continues the boundary before entering the Coven area of Brewood.[6]

Traces of early settlement have been found on the high ground in the north-west. In the 1680s Robert Plot recorded the remains there of 'several partitions, yet visible, running divers ways like the sides of streets' and also the discovery of large hinges, an antique dagger, and squared stones. The area concerned was mostly in Wrottesley Old Park, but it extended to Kingswood and into Pattingham, Patshull, and Boningale (Salop.). Plot considered it to be the site of a British fortification or city. By the mid 18th century most of the stone had been used to repair buildings and to make the coping of the wall round Patshull park. While Plot's interpretation is no longer accepted, there have been mesolithic, neolithic, and possibly Bronze Age finds in Wrottesley Old Park. Nearby in Boningale there are a neolithic or Bronze Age site and two Romano-British sites.[7] A Bronze Age palstave has been found at Perton.[8] There seems formerly to have been a barrow north of Wergs Road in the open field called Low field.[9] The place name Bilbrook is thought to be Celtic.[10] A Roman road from Pennocrucium on Watling Street at Stretton can be traced south-east of the site of Pendeford Hall. There is no surviving evidence of its southward continuation, but a possible terminus was the camp near Ashwood in Kingswinford.[11]

Tettenhall first appears by name in the year 910 as the scene of a battle in which the Anglo-Saxon forces defeated the Danes; it began the process by which the Danes were pushed eastwards. The battle is also described as at Wednesfield, 3 miles to the east.[12] There was a church by 1086 and possibly by 975.

The recorded population of the area in 1086 was 48; there may also have been 4 priests serving the church.[13] For the 1327 subsidy 97 people were assessed.[14] For that of the mid 1520s there were 94; Bilbrook was included with Codsall, the two having 21.[15] The muster roll of 1539 listed 69 people.[16] In the mid 16th century the number of communicants was given as 1,000.[17] The poll-tax assessment of 1641 listed 457 people in the constablewicks of Tettenhall Regis, Tettenhall Clericorum, Pendeford, Perton and Trescott, and Wrottesley.[18] In 1666 a total of 153 people were assessed for hearth tax in those constable-

wicks; a further 52 were too poor to pay.[19] In 1780 there were 332 houses, over two thirds of them cottages or small houses with no land except gardens.[20] The population was 1,570 in 1801 and had risen to 3,396 by 1851 and 6,459 in 1901, with a particularly sharp rise in the 1870s. The new urban district accounted for 5,337 of the 1901 total and the new civil parish of Wrottesley for the remaining 1,222. In 1911 the population of the urban district was 5,381 and of Wrottesley 1,275. It was 5,488 and 1,405 in 1921, 5,769 and 1,635 in 1931, 7,743 and 5,451 in 1951, and 14,867 and 8,510 in 1961. Most of the populous parts of the urban district and of Wrottesley were added to Wolverhampton in 1966; in 1971 Wrottesley, although increased in area, had a population of only 4,189.[21]

Tettenhall parish remained rural until the 19th century. By the later 18th century its rural character was coming to be appreciated as a contrast with the growing industrialism of Wolverhampton. In the 1750s and 1760s people in Wolverhampton seem to have been putting their children out to nurse in Tettenhall.[22] In 1776 Arthur Young, after travelling from Birmingham through Wolverhampton, marvelled at the change of scene when he reached Tettenhall, finding it by comparison 'as retired as the Ohio'.[23] William Pitt the agronomist noted 'many pleasant houses and genteel families' in 1791.[24] Tettenhall was also the goal of excursions from Wolverhampton. In 1789 the Revd. William Fernyhough celebrated the charms of the 'sweet, peaceful place' in a poem which ended with the couplet:

Here Hampton's sons in vacant hours repair,
Taste rural joys, and breathe a purer air.

There was a 'pleasure room' in the village in 1780, and pleasure gardens were opened on Old Hill in 1843.[25]

The inclosure of much of Tettenhall Wood common in 1809 was followed by a concentration of lockmaking in the new village of Tettenhall Wood,[26] but Tettenhall's development was mainly as a residential district, attracting especially businessmen working in Wolverhampton.[27] Already in 1812 the 'delightful view of Wolverhampton and the adjoining country' was used as a selling point for a house on the ridge south-west of the village.[28] The notice of an auction in 1838

[6] Whitehead, *Country between Wolverhampton and Oakengates*, 3, 190; Jones, *Tettenhall*, 2; Shaw, *Staffs.* ii. 198; Erdeswick, *Staffs.* 157, 346; *Express & Star*, 26 Oct. 1933, 14 Nov. 1944; B.L. Add. Ch. 71088 (deed of 1462); H.W.R.O. (H.), B 47/S22, S25; W.S.L., Fac. 12; T. Congreve, *Scheme or Proposal for making a navigable communication between rivers of Trent and Severn* (1717; copy in W.S.L., S.663). For the Smestow brook tributary at Aldersley see H.W.R.O. (H.), B 47/S3 (1413); P.R.O., MR 308.
[7] Plot, *Staffs.* 394–5; Shaw, *Staffs.* ii. 194; W.S.L., S.MS. 468, f. 29 (2nd nos.); *S.H.C.* 1919, 184; *Trans. Salop. Arch. Soc.* lix. 209–13.   [8] *N.S.J.F.S.* iv. 45.
[9] Shaw, *Staffs.* ii. 194; below, econ. hist. (agric.).
[10] Below.
[11] I. D. Margary, *Roman Roads in Britain* (1973 edn.), 294–5 and map 17.
[12] *V.C.H. Staffs.* i. 219; F. M. Stenton, *Anglo-Saxon Eng.* (1971 edn.), 323; Jones, *Tettenhall*, 8–9.
[13] *V.C.H. Staffs.* iv. 38, 43, 45, 52, 55. For the possibility of 4 priests see ibid. iii. 316.

[14] *S.H.C.* vii (1), 251, 253–5.
[15] P.R.O., E 179/177/96.
[16] *S.H.C.* n.s. vi (1), 64–7, 75.
[17] *S.H.C.* 1915, 285.
[18] H.L., Main Papers, box 178.
[19] *S.H.C.* 1923, 76, 85, 103–6, 111, 113–14.
[20] W. Pitt, 'Particulars of par. of Tettenhall', *Annals of Agric.* vii. 459.
[21] *V.C.H. Staffs.* i. 326; *Census*, 1901–71.
[22] S.R.O., D. 1364/1/2, burials of 30 June 1754, 12 Apr., 4 May, 2 June 1766.
[23] *Tours in Eng. and Wales by Arthur Young* (London Sch. of Economics, Reprints of Scarce Tracts in Econ. and Pol. Science, no. 14, 1932), 143.
[24] Shaw, *Staffs.* ii. 198.
[25] *Gent. Mag.* lxvi (2), 633; F. Mason, *Book of Wolverhampton*, 10; S.R.O., D. 1018/2; below, social and cultural activities.   [26] Below, econ. hist.
[27] White, *Dir. Staffs.* (1834), 287.
[28] *Wolverhampton Chron.* 23 Dec. 1812.

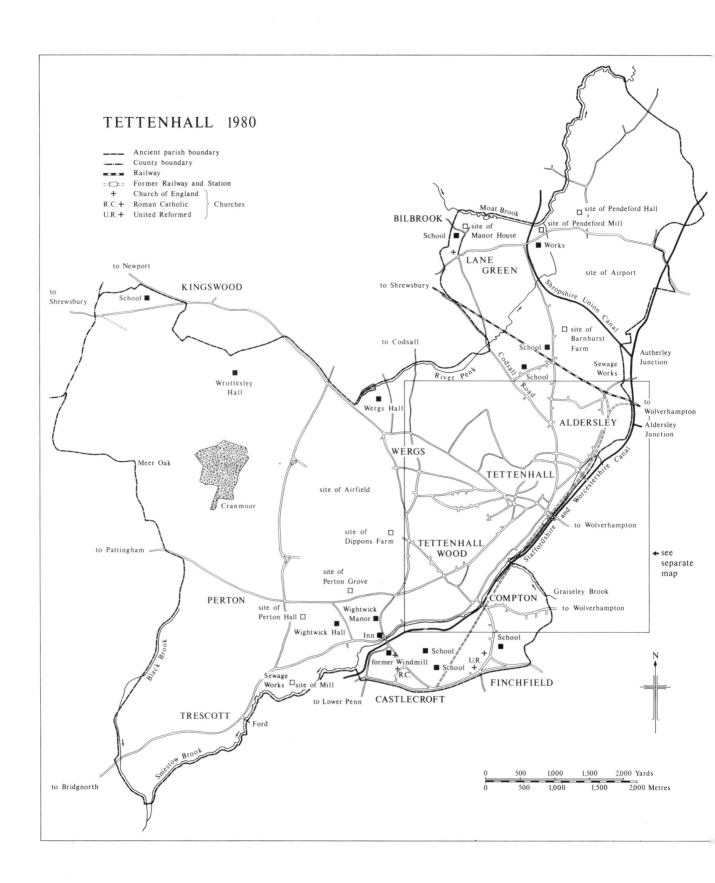

TETTENHALL 1980

- - - - Ancient parish boundary
- · - · - County boundary
■ ■ ■ Railway
═□═ Former Railway and Station
+ Church of England ⎫
R.C.+ Roman Catholic ⎬ Churches
U.R.+ United Reformed ⎭

to Newport

to Shrewsbury

KINGSWOOD

School ■

BILBROOK

Moat Brook

School ■

site of Manor House

+ LANE GREEN

Works ■

site of Pendeford Hall

site of Pendeford Mill

site of Airport

Shropshire Union Canal

to Shrewsbury

to Codsall

River Penk

Codsall Road

School ■

School

Sewage Works

site of Barnhurst Farm

Autherley Junction

Wrottesley Hall ■

Wergs Hall ■

ALDERSLEY

to Wolverhampton

Aldersley Junction

Meer Oak

Cranmoor

WERGS

TETTENHALL

site of Airfield

TETTENHALL WOOD

Staffordshire and Worcestershire Canal

to Wolverhampton

to Pattingham

site of Dippons Farm

site of Perton Grove

PERTON

site of Perton Hall

Wightwick Manor ■

Wightwick Hall ■

Inn ■

COMPTON

Graiseley Brook

to Wolverhampton

see separate map

N

School ■

former Windmill +
R.C.

■ School

■ School
U.R. +

FINCHFIELD

Sewage Works

site of Mill

to Lower Penn

CASTLECROFT

Black Brook

TRESCOTT

Ford

Smestow Brook

to Bridgnorth

| 0 | 500 | 1,000 | 1,500 | 2,000 Yards |
| 0 | 500 | 1,000 | 1,500 | 2,000 Metres |

4

of houses and building land in Tettenhall Wood stressed the 'extensive, picturesque, and panoramic views', the healthy situation, and the opportunity for building 'casines or villas'.[29] The ridge has continued to attract the building of large houses all the way to the Pattingham boundary. In 1846[30] Tettenhall village was described as

daily more intruded upon by clumsy proprietors of scraps of ground, by imported shopkeepers, and by those architectural affectations, termed 'country houses', in which the hardware gentility of Wolverhampton carries on its evening and Sabbath masquerade, at a convenient distance of a mile and three quarters from the locks, nails, and frying-pans of the productive emporium.

A list of 84 substantial residents in the parish in 1851 included 16 with businesses in Wolverhampton; many others had business and professional interests elsewhere outside the parish.[31] In 1853 the Pearson family's estate extending from the village to Compton was advertised for auction as 'forming remarkably choice and delightful sites for the erection of mansions and villas, perfectly removed from the bustle of the town and every local objection'.[32] Large houses continued to be built in the later 19th century, particularly along the ridge, along Wergs Road, and on the high ground south of Compton. In 1928 it was possible to bracket Tettenhall and Clifton as the two finest suburbs possessed by any large manufacturing town.[33] After the Second World War houses and blocks of flats were built in the grounds of villas which had been demolished or put to new uses. In addition two notably large estates were under construction in 1980 on former airfields at Perton and Pendeford and nearby farmland.

Several notable people have been born in or associated with the parish. Distinguished members of the Wrottesley family of Wrottesley Hall included Sir Hugh Wrottesley, K.G. (d. 1381).[34] His descendant John, Baron Wrottesley (1798–1867), assisted in the foundation of the Royal Astronomical Society in 1820 and was president from 1841 to 1843; after succeeding to the Wrottesley estate in 1841 he built an observatory on the Codsall part of the estate, the base of which still stands. He was also president of the Royal Society from 1854 to 1857 and of the British Association in 1860.[35] Lord Wrottesley's son Major-General George Wrottesley (1827–1909) served in the Crimean War under John (later Sir John) Burgoyne, his father-in-law, and later wrote Sir John's biography. In 1863 Wrottesley was chairman of the War Office committee on army signalling which introduced

the use of the Morse Code. After his retirement from the Army in 1881 he devoted his time to historical research. In 1879 he had been instrumental in founding the William Salt Archaeological Society (from 1936 the Staffordshire Record Society), and he served as its secretary until his death, also contributing extensively to its publications. After his death he was mourned by J. H. Round as 'the Nestor of genealogists', who through his use of the public records had helped to put genealogical research on a modern footing.[36]

Mary Fitton (1578–1641), possibly the 'Dark Lady of the Sonnets', lived for many years at Perton Hall.[37] Sir John Wollaston (1595–1658), lord mayor of London in 1643–4, was a native of Tettenhall, being the son of Edward Wollaston of Perton.[38]

Francis Smith (1672–1738), architect and builder, was born at Wergs, the son of a bricklayer; he sometimes worked with his brother William (1661–1724), who was buried at Tettenhall.[39] William Pitt (1749–1823), a writer on agriculture and author of A Topographical History of Staffordshire (1817), was born at Tettenhall. From 1780 to 1894 he was tenant of New House farm at Pendeford, which had been held by members of his family from c. 1725. He then moved to Edgbaston (Warws.) but was buried at Tettenhall.[40] Henry Hartley Fowler, 1st Viscount Wolverhampton (1830–1911), built Woodthorne in Wergs Road c. 1867 and lived there until his death. A Wolverhampton solicitor and a Liberal in politics, he was one of the M.P.s for the borough from 1880 until he was raised to the peerage in 1908; from 1884 he held various government posts, becoming secretary of state for India in 1894. He has been claimed as the first Wesleyan Methodist to hold government office and to be created a peer.[41] His daughter, Ellen Thorneycroft Felkin (1860–1922), who wrote novels under her maiden name, lived at Woodthorne until her marriage in 1903.[42] Her novel Fuel of Fire (1902) is set in Tettenhall, which is disguised at Tetleigh, and the central event is the burning of Wrottesley Hall in 1897. A. G. Matthews (1881–1962), the ecclesiastical historian, was Congregational minister at Tettenhall Wood from 1907 to 1922, having been ordained there in 1907.[43]

Charles II, on his was from Boscobel to Moseley in 1651, dismounted at Pendeford mill and walked the rest of the way for safety.[44]

GROWTH OF SETTLEMENT. Tettenhall village developed round two centres. One lies below the escarpment by Lower Green and along Lower Street; the other is around Upper Green on the top of the ridge. The first is probably the older

[29] H.W.R.O. (H.), E 12/S, Tettenhall.
[30] F. P. Palmer and A. Crowquill, Wanderings of a Pen and Pencil, 33–4.
[31] White, Dir. Staffs. (1851), 207–8.
[32] S.R.O., D. 755/4/15.
[33] H. V. Morton, The Call of Eng. (1928 edn.), 198.
[34] Below, manors and other estates.
[35] D.N.B.; S.H.C. n.s. vi (2), 377–82.
[36] D.N.B. 1901–11; S.H.C. n.s. vi (2), 382–4; n.s xii, appreciation of Wrottesley's work by J. H. Round.
[37] Below, manors and other estates.

[38] A. B. Beaven, Aldermen of City of London, i. 6; ii. 64; S.H.C. v (2), 321.
[39] Colvin, Brit. Architects, 747–53; Shaw, Staffs. ii. 197.
[40] D.N.B.; Annals of Agric. xlii. 107, 204; below, econ. hist.
[41] D.N.B. 1901–11; E. H. Fowler, Life of Henry Hartley Fowler, First Viscount Wolverhampton, 687.
[42] D.N.B. 1922–30. Her mother Ellen was the sister of Thomas Thorneycroft of Tettenhall Towers.
[43] Cong. Year Bk. (1963–4), 436–7.
[44] Boscobel (1660), 39.

TETTENHALL : central area 1980

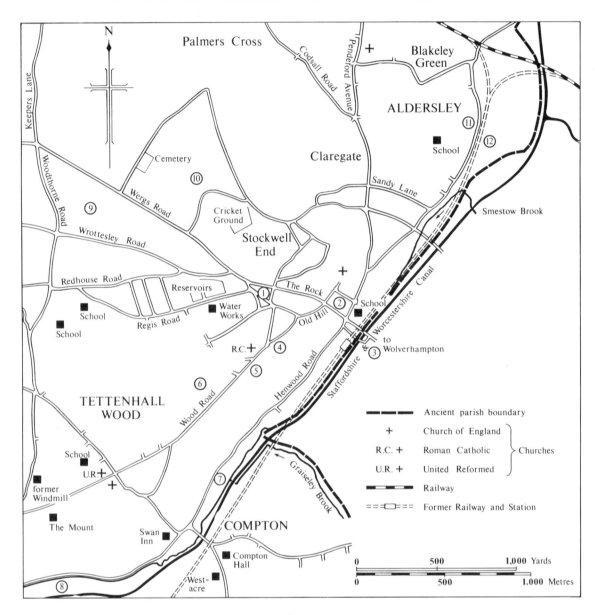

Palmers Cross

Blakeley Green

ALDERSLEY

Claregate

Keepers Lane

Codsall Road

Pendeford Avenue

Cemetery

⑩

Wergs Road

Woodthorne Road

⑨

Wrottesley Road

Cricket Ground

Sandy Lane

School

⑪

⑫

Smestow Brook

Stockwell End

Redhouse Road

Reservoirs

The Rock

Regis Road

Water Works

Old Hill

School

School

R.C. ✝

④

⑤

Henwood Road

②

School

③

to Wolverhampton

Staffordshire & Worcestershire Canal

⑥

TETTENHALL WOOD

Wood Road

⑦

Graiseley Brook

School

U.R. ✝

former Windmill

The Mount

Swan Inn

COMPTON

Compton Hall

West-acre

⑧

	Ancient parish boundary
✝	Church of England
R.C. ✝	Roman Catholic
U.R. ✝	United Reformed

Churches

Railway

Former Railway and Station

0   500   1,000 Yards

0   500   1,000 Metres

① Upper Green   ④ Tettenhall College   ⑦ Site of Compton Mill   ⑩ Site of Danes Court

② Lower Green   ⑤ Former Tettenhall Towers   ⑧ Former Wightwick Mill   ⑪ Site of Aldersley Upper Farm

③ Newbridge   ⑥ Site of Tettenhall Wood Ho.   ⑨ Site of Woodthorne   ⑫ Aldersley Lower Farm

settlement. The name Tettenhall is thought to mean Teota's (or Teotta's) valley[45] and suggests a settlement by Smestow brook. It is probably represented by the hide at Tettenhall held in 1086 by the priests of the collegiate church. The church, founded in the 10th or 11th century, stands on sloping ground below the ridge north of Lower Green. The college buildings seem, in part at least, to have stood east of the church; the house of the vicars choral, mentioned at the Dissolution, was probably the college house newly built in 1517 and mentioned in 1576.[46] Lower Green may be the green mentioned in 1327 when Thomas in the Green was a tenant of the canons. In 1613 it was known as Old Tettenhall Green and later simply as Tettenhall Green. Although it was called Lower Green in 1695 the name was not in regular use until the mid or later 19th century. The green originally straddled the Wolverhampton road and in 1613 covered just over 14 a. In 1707 some 4 a. were inclosed to compensate Jonas Grosvenor for a house which he gave for the minister of Tettenhall. In 1980 the green consisted of 3 a. lying on the north side of the Wolverhampton road and preserved as an open space.[47] Lower Street was so named by 1710 and was presumably the street in the manor of Tettenhall Clericorum near the College croft mentioned in 1665.[48] Henwood Road continuing Lower Street southwards was mentioned in 1517 as the road from Tettenhall to Compton; a field called Henwood lay at its northern end adjoining Lower Green.[49] Tettenhall Hill mentioned in the late 14th century may be the Church Hill of the 18th century; the 63 yd. on Church Hill which were paved in the early 1720s were probably part of the present path up the hill from the churchyard.[50] Claregate to the north was probably an inhabited area by 1327 when Nicholas le Clare was a tenant of the canons of Tettenhall; Richard Clare was a tenant in 1333.[51] There was at least one house there in 1699 when Alexander Stanley of Claregate was appointed churchwarden.[52] There was a house of that name in Lothians Road in the late 19th century; it was demolished between the two World Wars and the site built over.[53] Malthouse Lane running up the hill from Lower Street past Claregate existed by the early 17th century.[54] Sandy Lane running west from Lower Street to Aldersley Road existed by the later 18th century.[55] New Bridge to the south of Lower Green carrying the main road from Wolverhampton over Smestow brook existed by the early 16th century; the course of the road

along Meadow View was realigned to the north in the earlier 1820s.[56]

In 1086 the part of Tettenhall belonging to the church had 1 villein, 3 bordars, and possibly 4 priests.[57] Most of the 19 tenants of the church assessed for the subsidy of 1327 and of the 13 inhabitants of Tettenhall Clericorum assessed in the mid 1520s probably lived in the Lower Green area.[58] The poll-tax assessment of 1641 listed 73 people.[59] In 1666 there were 27 inhabitants assessed for hearth tax, with a further 13 too poor to pay.[60] Most of the 98 houses and cottages recorded in Tettenhall in 1780 were probably in the Lower Street area.[61] By the mid 19th century the population of the area was largely artisan; spectacle-frame making was carried on as a domestic industry, but many of the inhabitants probably worked in Wolverhampton.[62]

Settlement began to spread northwards in the late 19th century when terraced cottages were built along Aldersley Road. In the last years of the century the first houses were built in Sandy Lane; they were Danesbury House (later St. Joseph's Convent preparatory school) and the two cottages opposite. Sand pits were being worked at that time north and south of the road. A terrace of cottages was built in Meadow View in the late 19th century, and Tettenhall station was opened to the south in 1925.[63] During the 20th century the area has continued to develop mainly as a suburb of smaller houses.

The village on the top of the ridge grew around Upper Green, which may be the surviving northern end of the waste called Kingsley Wood and later Tettenhall Wood common. The settlement is presumably represented by the hide at Tettenhall held by the king in 1086. Four villeins and 3 bordars were then recorded there.[64] Eleven people there were assessed for the subsidy of 1327, and 10 appeared in the muster roll of 1539.[65] By the early 17th century there was building along Old Hill, where the main road from Wolverhampton climbed the ridge, and in the present Upper Street and High Street; there were three houses along the ridge and a house on the eastern edge of Kingsley Wood on or near the site of the 17th-century house later known as Gorsty Hayes Cottage. There were also several houses north-east of Upper Green at Stockwell End, so named by the 1640s. The main road continued along the present Wrottesley and Woodthorne Roads, and the present Redhouse and Regis Roads already existed as lanes.[66] Upper Green, 11 a. in area in 1613, was known as Marsh

[45] Ekwall, *Eng. Place-names.*
[46] *V.C.H. Staffs.* iii. 320; H.W.R.O. (H.), B 47/S3, 1517 terrier; S.R.O., D. 593/J/22/4.
[47] *S.H.C.* vii (1), 255; P.R.O., MR 308; S.R.O., D. 3160/9/1; Act for support of minister of Tettenhall, 6 Anne, c.28 (Priv. Act; TS. copy in S.R.O., D. 366/M/1); H.W.R.O. (H.), E 12/S, Kingsley terrier, 1831; O.S. Map 6″, Staffs. LXII. NW. (1889 edn.); inf. from W. Midlands C.C., legal dept.
[48] S.R.O., D. 1018/3/1; S.R.O., Tp. 1226, parcel A.
[49] H.W.R.O. (H.), B 47/S3, 1517 terrier; below, econ. hist. Its existence in 1300 may be implied in the reference then to the road from Wightwick towards Stafford: below, p. 13.
[50] H.W.R.O. (H.), B 47/S3, S24; S.R.O., D. 571/A/PK/1, p. 18.   [51] *S.H.C.* vii (1), 254; x (1), 131.
[52] S.R.O., D. 1364/6/1.
[53] O.S. Map 6″, Staffs. LXII. NW. (1889 edn. and prov. edn. with addns. of 1938).

[54] P.R.O., MR 308.
[55] Yates, *Map of Staffs.* (1775).
[56] Below, communications.
[57] *V.C.H. Staffs.* iv. 45.
[58] *S.H.C.* vii (1), 254-5; P.R.O., E 179/177/96.
[59] H.L., Main Papers, box 178.
[60] *S.H.C.* 1923, 111.
[61] S.R.O., D. 1018/2.
[62] P.R.O., HO 107/715/998; HO 107/2017(1); RG 9/1984; RG 10/2927; below, econ. hist.
[63] Date stones 1878-81 in Aldersley Rd.; O.S. Map 6″, Staffs. LXII. NW. (1889 edn.); O.S. Map 1/2,500, Staffs. LXII.2 (1902 edn.); W.S.L., Sale Cat. F/3/20; below, communications.   [64] *V.C.H. Staffs.* iv. 38.
[65] *S.H.C.* vii (1), 254; *S.H.C.* n.s. vi (1), 66.
[66] P.R.O., MR 308; S.R.O., Tp. 1226, parcel A, answers of jury; below, Roman Catholicism.

Green in the early 18th century; the adjoining pool, which still exists, was known as Marsh Pool.[67] The name Upper Green was coming into use by 1780. There were then 20 houses and cottages there and 6 or 7 houses at Stockwell End.[68] Three large houses had been built along the ridge by 1791, all on or near the sites of the three houses existing in 1613. One was a predecessor of the later 19th-century Manor House, on the site of which the flats called Woodfield Heights were built in the 1960s. To the south-west was the mid 18th-century house in which Tettenhall College was opened in 1863 and which is now the headmaster's house. Further south-west was the house later called Tettenhall Towers, which was built before 1763. To the west there was also by the 1780s a house on or near the site of the later Tettenhall Wood House, which stood near the end of the present Grange Road.[69]

The village grew in the 19th century, developing particularly as a residential area. In 1810 the straight line of the new Wergs Road across Upper Green replaced the old course of the main road; in the earlier 1820s a new and less steep ascent up the ridge was cut to the north of Old Hill.[70] The Red House at the west end of Redhouse Road, demolished in the earlier 1970s, was on the site of, or another name for, the New House mentioned in 1813. In 1834 the New House was the home of John Roaf, minister of Queen Street Congregational chapel in Wolverhampton. The Red House itself was mentioned in 1871.[71] The Pearson family's estate along the ridge was sold in 1853 and 1854 mainly as building land, and four large houses had been built on it by 1886.[72] North-west of the village two large houses were built in the 1860s, Danes Court at Stockwell End and Woodthorne in Wergs Road. Edward Perry, a Wolverhampton japanner, bought 116 a. at Stockwell End in the earlier 1860s, and in 1864 he built Danes Court there, a villa in a Gothic style with a four-storey tower. In 1874 it was bought with most of the estate by Samuel Loveridge, a Wolverhampton ironmaster, and in 1908, after the break-up of the estate, it was sold to Edward Hickman, a prominent South Staffordshire industrialist. After his death in 1941 it was occupied by troops and then by the territorial army. It was demolished in 1958.[73] Woodthorne was built c. 1867 for H. H. Fowler, later created Viscount Wolverhampton. It was taken over in

1946 by the Ministry of Agriculture and Fisheries (from 1955 the Ministry of Agriculture, Fisheries, and Food) and was demolished in 1978; the ministry was building offices on the site in 1980.[74]

Many smaller villas and houses were built at Stockwell End in the later 19th and early 20th century.[75] An area of small houses, known as New Village by 1871, developed north-west of High Street. Already in 1845 the Wolverhampton Waterworks Co. had built a pumping station in Regis Road (known as Waterworks Road until the early 20th century). A few terraces were built at the east end of Limes Road in the earlier 1870s. Several were built in Regis Road in the later 1870s, in Nursery Walk in the mid 1880s, and in Limes Road in the 1890s. The area was extended with council housing around Regis Road soon after the First World War and in the 1960s and around Grange Road in the 1950s.[76] The roads to the north as far as Wergs were developed with privately built houses in the years between the two World Wars and after 1945; others have been built over the grounds of older houses at Stockwell End since 1945. In 1980 Upper Green consisted of 7 a. preserved as an open space.[77]

The village of Tettenhall Wood south-west of Tettenhall dates mainly from the inclosure in 1809 of most of Tettenhall Wood common, formerly Kingsley Wood. By 1586 there was settlement in the Holloway, then known as Compton Holloways. The name Tettenhall Wood was in use by 1613.[78] Dippons Farm to the north-west, demolished in 1974, dated from the early 18th century.[79] By 1733 there was an inn at Tettenhall Wood known as the Blue Boar; it was renamed the King's Head in the earlier 1740s.[80] In 1780 Tettenhall Wood had 42 houses and cottages. The most populous part was around the junction of the Holloway and Ormes Lane; by 1809 there was an inn, the Prince of Wales, in Ormes Lane. Wood Road, Mount Road, the southern end of School Road, and the northern end of Church Road evidently date from the inclosure.[81] A petition for the inclosure of the common c. 1805 mentioned extensive encroachment and also described it as the haunt of gypsies, thieves, and other disreputable people.[82] By the 1830s a large number of cottages had been built in the new Tettenhall Wood village and were occupied mainly by lockmakers; there were also

[67] P.R.O., MR 308; Wolv. C.L., D/MAN/38.
[68] S.R.O., D. 1018/2.
[69] Shaw, Staffs. ii. 198; R. Baugh, Map of Salop. (1808); P.R.O., MR 308; S.R.O., D. 755/4/16; O.S. Map 6″, Staffs. LXII. NW. (1889 edn.); Express & Star, 31 May 1962; G. V. Hancock, Hist. of Tettenhall Coll. (Tettenhall, priv. print. 1963), 12–13; below, manors and other estates. For a photograph of the Manor House see National Monuments Record, AA 66/1830.
[70] Below, communications.
[71] Wolv. C.L., D/MAN/8 and map 308 (R. Timmis, Map of par. of Tettenhall, 1837); White, Dir. Staffs. (1834), 289; Lond. Gaz. 31 Jan. 1871, p. 346; inf. from Mr. G. V. Hancock of Tettenhall College.
[72] S.R.O., D. 755/4/15–16; Staffs. Advertiser, 26 Aug. 1854; O.S. Map 6″, Staffs. LXII. NW. (1889 edn.).
[73] Wolv. Civic Centre, deed bdle. C 5/22; Staffs. Advertiser, 6 Mar. 1869, 15 Aug. 1874, 11 Jan. 1941; W.S.L., Sale Cat. E/1/5; Express & Star, 11 Apr. 1958.
[74] Inf. from the Min. of Agric., Fisheries, and Food (1980).

For Fowler see above.
[75] O.S. Map 6″, Staffs. LXII. NW. (edns. of 1889 and 1903); O.S. Map 1/2,500, Staffs. LXII.1 (1919 edn.); Wolv. C.L., D/MAN/38.
[76] P.R.O., RG 10/2927; dates on terraces; O.S. Map 6″, Staffs. LXII. NW. (edns. of 1889 and 1903); O.S. Map 1/2,500, Staffs. LXII.5 (1919 edn., rev. 1914, showing Regis Rd.); below, p. 38.
[77] Inf. from W. Midlands C.C., legal dept.
[78] S.H.C. 1929, 161, 261; P.R.O., MR 308; below, p. 29.
[79] Below, manors and other estates (Tettenhall Regis).
[80] H.W.R.O. (H.), E 12/S, Kingsley Manor, ct. of 9 Apr. 1733; E 12/S, Kinver, Compton Hallows, and Kingsley ct. bk. 1734–61, Kingsley cts. of 14 Feb. 1739/40, 7 Oct. 1744; E 12/S, Tettenhall, deed of 21 Aug. 1745.
[81] S.R.O., D. 1018/2 (listing Dippons Farm under Wergs); S.R.O., Q/RDc 66. A new road was being made in 1800: S.R.O., D. 571/A/PS/1.
[82] J. P. Jones, 'The Enclosure of Tettenhall Wood', A. Webb's Annual (1908; copy in Wolv. C.L.).

'several handsome houses'.[83] A school was opened in the village in 1844; a mission was started from St. Michael's, Tettenhall, at the same time, using the school, and a church was opened in 1866.[84] The population in the immediate vicinity of the village centre was given as upwards of 800 in 1856.[85] Of the several large houses dating from the later 19th century the most notable is the Mount. It was built c. 1865, on the site of an earlier house of the same name, by C. B. Mander, of the Wolverhampton paint and varnish firm of Mander Bros.; it was enlarged to the west and south-west in 1891, and a large ballroom was added in 1908. Part at least of the new work was by Edward Ould, who also worked for another branch of the Mander family at Wightwick. Later there was further enlargement. After the death of C. B. Mander's grandson Sir Charles Mander, Bt., in 1951, the house was sold in 1952 and converted into a hotel.[86] The Dippons on the opposite side of Wood Road was built for Sir Charles's brother G. P. Mander a year or so after his marriage in 1913. Extensive additions include a stable court dated 1927. G. P. Mander died in 1951 and his widow in 1960; the house and 10 a. were sold in 1962. Houses and flats were built over the grounds, the house itself being converted into flats.[87] The development reflects the continuing growth of Tettenhall Wood during the 20th century as a residential area. Most of the development has been private, but a council estate was built east of School Road in the 1920s, and two more were built on either side of School Road soon after the Second World War.[88] The private building of houses and flats has been particularly marked since the 1950s.

Compton occupies the area where the Wolverhampton–Bridgnorth road is met by Finchfield Hill and, having crossed Smestow brook, is joined by Henwood Road and by the Holloway running down the ridge from Tettenhall Wood. Compton takes its name from its position in the valley of Smestow brook, the name meaning a settlement in a coomb or narrow valley.[89] In 1086 it was in the portion of the royal manor of Tettenhall which extended up the high ground south of Compton to Finchfield, with Graiseley brook and the Wolverhampton–Trescott road (now Castlecroft Road) forming the boundary of both manor and parish; the Compton–Finchfield area was part of Kinver forest.[90] Domesday Book does not mention any inhabitants, but Compton was an inhabited area by the later 13th century.[91] Seven people there were assessed for the subsidy of 1327.[92] Six people from what was described as the hamlet of Compton appeared in the muster roll of 1539.[93] In the early 17th century settle-

ment was concentrated in Compton Road West and Finchfield Hill near their junction. There were then a few houses and a mill at the end of Henwood Road, and there was also a building on the site of the present Swan inn on the corner of the Holloway and Bridgnorth Road.[94] There was a nailer at Compton in 1654, and in the 18th century there was some hingemaking and lockmaking.[95] In 1780 there were 33 houses in Compton, including the Swan inn and a tollhouse on the Wolverhampton–Bridgnorth road. There was also a wharf on the Staffordshire and Worcestershire Canal; it was at Compton that work on the first part of the canal had begun in 1766. In 1780 there were two houses at Cuckolds Corner, evidently the Oak Hill area of Finchfield.[96] In 1817 Compton was described as a small village consisting of several farms and other houses with a wharf and warehouses on the canal.[97] The population of Compton and the Tettenhall part of Finchfield in 1841 was 621. Around the mid 19th century much of it was artisan, engaged particularly in lockmaking; at Compton there was also key stamping and digging of sand.[98]

Later development has been residential. A number of villas had been built throughout the area by 1880.[99] A notable example is Compton Hall in Compton Road West, a mid 19th-century rebuilding of a house which Thomas Elwell, a Wolverhampton hardware merchant, bought from John Evans in 1828. On Elwell's death in 1856 Compton Hall passed to his second son Charles John, who was succeeded by his younger brother Paul in 1875. Paul died in 1880, and later that year the Hall was put up for sale. In 1884 it was occupied by Sir John Morris. By 1888 it was the home of William Hodson, a partner in the Springfield Brewery at Wolverhampton. He died in 1890, and by the mid 1890s Compton Hall was the home of his son Laurence, a connoisseur and a director of the Springfield Brewery Co. Ltd. formed in 1891. The entrance hall and principal rooms were redecorated by Morris & Co. c. 1896, William Morris's last wall-paper design being named Compton after the house. Hodson fell into financial difficulties, and the contents of the house were sold in 1906; tapestries designed by Sir Edward Burne-Jones are in the Birmingham Museum and Art Gallery. Fittings, however, survived at the house in 1981, including panelling, stained glass, a painted ceiling, and fireplaces with tiles by William de Morgan. From c. 1907 until his death in 1938 the Hall was the home of T. B. Adams; his widow continued to live there. After the Second World War it became a nurses' home. In 1982 it was

[83] White, *Dir Staffs.* (1834), 288.
[84] Below, churches; educ.
[85] S.R.O., D. 1364/4/30.
[86] Pevsner, *Staffs.* 311; *Express & Star*, 13 June 1962; Burke, *Peerage* (1967), 1639; dates on the building. The earlier house was occupied by the Pretty family in 1834 and 1841: White, *Dir. Staffs.* (1834), 289; P.R.O., HO 107/715/998; below, pl. facing p. 17. Mr. D. Galbraith, general manager of the Mount Hotel, and his staff are thanked for their help.
[87] W.S.L., Sale Cat. E/3/33; list of members in *S.H.C.* 1914 and *S.H.C.* 1915; *Express & Star*, 23 Feb., 30 Mar. 1962, 4 Mar., 16 May 1964, 16 Aug. 1966.
[88] Below, p. 38.

[89] Ekwall, *Eng. Place-names.*
[90] P.R.O., MR 308; below, manors and other estates. Before the 19th century the name Finchfield was evidently restricted to the adjoining part of Penn: Yates, *Map of Staffs.* (1775).
[91] *S.H.C.* v (1), 144.
[92] *S.H.C.* vii (1), 254.
[93] *S.H.C.* n.s. vi (1), 64.
[94] P.R.O., MR 308.
[95] Below, econ. hist.; S.R.O., D. 284/M/1–4.
[96] S.R.O., D. 1018/2; Yates, *Map of Staffs.* (1775).
[97] Pitt, *Staffs.* i. 185.
[98] P.R.O., HO 107/715/998; below, econ. hist.
[99] G. Stevens, *Dir. Wolverhampton 1879–80*; O.S. Map 6", Staffs. LXII. NW. (1889 edn.), SW. (1890 edn.).

opened as a Macmillan Home for Continuing Care.[1]

By the end of the 19th century terraces of cottages had been built in the centre of Compton, with larger houses on Finchfield Hill and on Ash Hill to the east. In the years between the two World Wars council houses were built in the Terrace off Finchfield Hill, and there was private building in Henwood Road and in Windmill Lane at Castlecroft west of Finchfield.[2] The urban district council built an estate of prefabricated bungalows in Henwood Road in 1946. Wolverhampton corporation bought land at Castlecroft and Finchfield in 1948 and had built some 1,000 dwellings there by 1965.[3] There has also been extensive private building throughout the area since the Second World War. When the house called Westacre with some 11½ a. on Finchfield Hill was put up for sale in 1963, the site was noted as one of the few sizeable pieces of building land remaining in the Wolverhampton area.[4]

Wightwick lies on Bridgnorth Road beside Smestow brook downstream from Compton and extends northwards up the ridge along Wightwick Bank. The name is Old English and may mean a place (wic) at a bend (wiht) in the brook; the first element may, however, derive from a personal name.[5] In 1086 Wightwick was part of the royal manor of Tettenhall, and there was one villein there. Wightwick Hall on Wightwick Bank was the centre of an estate held by the Wightwick family at least from the 13th century.[6] Several inhabitants were mentioned in 1271.[7] Eight were assessed for the subsidy of 1327.[8] Seven names appeared in the muster roll of 1539.[9] In 1780 there were 23 houses, including the Mermaid and another inn; there was also a boat house on the canal.[10] The second inn may have been the Field House in Perton Road, which existed by 1834.[11] In 1841 there were limekilns west of the canal bridge in Windmill Lane, and by the mid 1880s sand was dug nearby.[12] Perton Grove, a villa in Perton Road on the top of the ridge, was built c. 1855 for Henry Underhill, a Wolverhampton solicitor; it was demolished c. 1964.[13] In 1863 Theodosia Hinckes sold 11 a. of her Wightwick estate for the building of 'villa residences', and three were built on Wightwick

Bank soon afterwards.[14] Wightwick Manor, also on Wightwick Bank, was built by Theodore Mander after his purchase of Wightwick Hall and the surrounding land in 1887.[15] He also built some smaller houses in a similar style on Bridgnorth Road.[16] In addition he bought the Mermaid inn with a view to rebuilding it and running part of it on the lines of the People's Refreshment House Association, a temperance group.[17] Since the Second World War there has been extensive private building of houses and flats, largely in the grounds of villas.

Perton, lying below the top of the ridge west of Wightwick, is thought to derive its name from 'pear tun'.[18] It lay round a green where the present Jenny Walkers Lane was joined by a road running north-west from Tinacre Hill and passing in front of the moated Perton Hall. In 1364 Sir John Perton, lord of Perton, received licence to close the road where it passed his 'court' on condition that he substituted another road. The new route evidently followed Tinacre Hill to the top of the ridge where it joined the Pattingham road.[19] In 1086 Perton was the most populous area in the parish, with 1 free man, 13 villeins, and 2 bordars.[20] Northwood near Meer Oak on the Pattingham boundary north of the Pattingham road was inhabited by 1257.[21] The oak tree itself was mentioned in 1298 as the boundary mark between the manors of Pattingham, Wrottesley, and Perton; the road which runs south from it along the parish boundary was called 'le Mere Way'.[22] Nineteen people were assessed for the subsidy of 1327, but the figure evidently included Trescott also. By then Netherton at the foot of the present Tinacre Hill was an inhabited place.[23] Twenty-seven people from Perton and Trescott were assessed for the subsidy of the mid 1520s, and 13 appeared in the muster roll of 1539.[24] The poll-tax assessment of 1641 listed 87 people.[25] A map of 1663 shows a cluster of seven houses round the green with another house nearer the hall; there was a house at Netherton, two houses and a cottage at Dadnall Hill on the Pattingham road near the Pattingham boundary, and a house at Northwood.[26] In Perton and Trescott constablewick 27 people were assessed for hearth tax in 1666, and another 4 were too poor to pay.[27] There were 11

[1] Pevsner, Staffs. 326; C. J. L. Elwell, The Iron Elwells (Ilfracombe, 1964), 57, 60-1, 63-5; S.R.O., D. 284/M/6, no. 97; D. 660/14/6, sale partics. 1880; Wolv. C.L., D/MAN/38; Kelly's Dir. Staffs. (1888 and later edns.); Victoria and Albert Mus. Cat. of Exhibition of Victorian and Edwardian Decorative Arts (1952), 49; inf. on the Hodsons from Mr. A. Crawford of the Victorian Soc. (1980), including details from a TS. hist. of Springfield Brewery by S. Fellows; Staffs. C.C. Yearbook 1907-8, 188; Staffs. Advertiser, 22 Oct. 1938; Express & Star, 3 Mar. 1982; inf. from Mr. M. W. Domoney, administrator of Compton Hall Home, who is thanked for his help; below, pl. facing p. 17.
[2] O.S. Map 6″, Staffs. LXII. NW., SW. (edns. of 1889, 1890, 1903, and prov. edn. with addns. of 1938); date stone of 1881 on cottage in Henwood Rd.; below, p. 38.
[3] Below, p. 38.
[4] Express & Star, 16 Aug. 1963, 4 Mar. 1964.
[5] Eng. Place-name Elements (E.P.N.S.), ii. 265; W. H. Duignan, Notes on Staffs. Place-names, 173.
[6] Below, manors and other estates (Tettenhall Regis).
[7] S.H.C. v (1), 144.
[8] S.H.C. vii (1), 254.
[9] S.H.C. n.s. vi (1), 64.
[10] S.R.O., D. 1018/2.

[11] White, Dir. Staffs. (1834), 289 (giving it as Fields); P.O. Dir. Staffs. (1845), giving it as Field House.
[12] Below, econ. hist.
[13] Wolv. C.L., D/MAN/8; Sir Arthur Underhill, Change and Decay, 18-19; Express & Star, 7 Jan. 1965. For a photograph see Wolv. C.L., P/N3.
[14] S.R.O., D. 3160/10/7, deeds of 6 Aug. and 28 Sept. 1863; P.O. Dir. Staffs. (1868; 1872; 1876); O.S. Map 6″, Staffs. LXII. NW. (1889 edn.), SW. (1890 edn.).
[15] Below, manors and other estates.
[16] Inf. from Mr. S. J. Ponder of Burnhill Green, Patshull (1980).
[17] Express & Star, 10 Sept. 1898.
[18] Below, econ. hist.
[19] S.R.O., D. 3548/2 (printed in S.H.C. 1931); Cal. Pat. 1361-4, 476.
[20] V.C.H. Staffs. iv. 43.
[21] S.H.C. 1911, 128.
[22] S.H.C. n.s. vi (2), 55.
[23] S.H.C. vii (1), 253.
[24] P.R.O., E 179/177/96; S.H.C. n.s. vi (1), 67.
[25] H. L. Main Papers, box 178.
[26] S.R.O., D. 3548/2.
[27] S.H.C. 1923, 85.

houses at Perton in 1780, one at Dadnall Hill, and 3 at the Hollies on the Pattingham boundary to the north.[28] Wightwick Hall on Tinacre Hill was built in the mid 1890s for Sir Alfred Hickman, a South Staffordshire coal and iron master who was Conservative M.P. for Wolverhampton West 1885–6 and 1892–1906; knighted in 1901 and made a baronet in 1903, he died in 1910. The Hall has been a special school since 1956.[29] In the early 20th century houses were built on the north side of Pattingham Road at the corner with Wrottesley Park Road,[30] and along the ridge on the south side of Pattingham Road there are privately built houses dating from the period between the two World Wars and the years after 1945. Others have been built in Tinacre Hill and on the opposite side of Bridgnorth Road since 1945. To the north of Perton Road a large private estate has been laid out over the former Perton airfield and adjoining farmland. A landing ground there was used in 1916 and 1917, and an airfield was opened for the R.A.F. in 1941. It was closed probably late in 1945 and was abandoned in 1947, the land being returned to agriculture.[31] Permission to build a housing estate covering the area was sought in 1963 by Sir Charles Mander, who owned the greater part of the land. The scheme was delayed by the opposition of local authorities wishing to keep the area within the green belt. Work on the estate, claimed as one of the largest private developments in the country, began in 1974, and the first houses were finished in 1976.[32]

Trescott lies on Bridgnorth Road beside Smestow brook south-west of Perton. The name means a settlement by the 'Tresel', an early name for the brook.[33] A free man was recorded there in 1086.[34] The subsidy assessment for Perton in 1327 probably included people living at Trescott, such as William and Thomas of Mareford; they presumably lived by the ford through Smestow brook which was mentioned in 1648 and still exists.[35] Nine people from Trescott appeared in the muster roll of 1539, and in 1663 there were nine houses and a cottage strung out on either side of the main road.[36] The houses included the present Old Trescott Farm and possibly the timber-framed cottage to the west. In 1780 there were seven houses and a cottage, including a public house; in the mid 19th century there was an inn called the Holly Bush.[37] A mission room was opened in the later 1880s.[38] Houses were built on the north side of Bridgnorth Road in the period between the two World Wars.

The north-west part of the parish is occupied by the former Wrottesley Hall estate, which includes the site of a lost village. The name Wrottesley probably means Wrot's glade or wood.[39] One villein and one bordar were recorded in 1086, besides Glodoen, the tenant of the manor.[40] An alehouse and a graveyard were mentioned in 1294 and a green in 1332.[41] Twelve people were assessed for the subsidy of 1327 and 10 for that of the mid 1520s.[42] In 1634 there were several houses grouped round an open space, evidently the green, south of Wrottesley Hall and along the Wolverhampton–Shrewsbury road which ran through the village. More houses stood at a crossroads west of the village, and there was another house at Meer Oak.[43] The poll-tax assessment of 1641 listed 48 people in Wrottesley constablewick.[44] A parliamentary garrison occupied the Hall in 1645 and improved its defences by pulling down tenants' houses.[45] In 1666 eleven people in the constablewick were assessed for hearth tax and another two were too poor to pay.[46] A new Hall was built on the west side of the village in the 1690s, and any surviving houses probably disappeared then. The later history of the area is that of the estate.[47] A hutted army camp was established along the south-east edge of the park for Dutch troops in 1941 and was taken over from the Dutch in 1947 by the Civil Resettlement Unit. In 1950 the camp was converted into dwellings by Seisdon rural district council and was occupied until 1962.[48] Tracks still preserve the earlier pattern of lanes. One of them, Deers Leap south of the Old Park, forms the boundary with Pattingham; a place called 'Dersprynge' was mentioned in the bounds of Wrottesley in 1088. About 1800, when the lane was known as the Bucks Leap, it was in dispute between the lords of Wrottesley and Pattingham manors; it was finally agreed to be in Tettenhall with the boundary running along its southern side, as it still does.[49]

Kingswood, straddling the boundary with Codsall in the north-west corner of the parish, probably lay within Brewood forest, which was disafforested in 1204. The Tettenhall part became part of the common waste of the royal manor of Tettenhall. Kingswood House on the site of the present Kingswood Bank Farm existed by 1634, and there were a few families living on the common in the later 17th century. In 1707 most of the common was inclosed.[50] The Tettenhall part of Kingswood contained four houses and a cottage in 1780.[51] The new line of the Shrewsbury road was run from the Newport road through it in 1810.[52] By 1836 there were a few houses in the fork of the roads and along the

[28] S.R.O., D. 1018/2.
[29] Kelly's Dir. Staffs. (1896); Burke, Peerage (1967), 1251–2; Staffs. Advertiser, 12 Mar. 1910; below, educ.
[30] O.S. Map 1/2,500, Staffs. LXI.8 (1924 edn.).
[31] D. J. Smith, Action Stations: 3, 141.
[32] Express & Star, 28 Oct. 1963, 18 Sept. 1969, 12 and 14 Oct. 1970, 28 June, 20 July 1972, 15 May, 25 Nov. 1974, 23 Aug. 1976.
[33] Ekwall, Eng. Place-names; below, Trysull.
[34] V.C.H. Staffs. iv. 45.
[35] S.H.C. vii (1), 253; S.R.O., D. 593/J/3/1, 5 Apr. 1648.
[36] S.H.C. n.s. vi (1), 67; S.R.O., D. 3548/2.
[37] S.R.O., D. 1018/2; P.O. Dir. Staffs. (1845; 1850; 1860).
[38] Below, churches.   [39] Ekwall, Eng. Place-names.
[40] V.C.H. Staffs. iv. 52.

[41] S.H.C. n.s. vi (2), 71; S.H.C. x (1), 131.
[42] S.H.C. vii (1), 251; P.R.O., E 179/177/96.
[43] S.R.O., D. 3548/1, partly reproduced below, facing p. 32.
[44] H. L. Main Papers, box 178.
[45] S.H.C. n.s. vi (2),325; S.H.C. 4th ser. i. 338.
[46] S.H.C. 1923, 113–14.
[47] Below, manors and other estates; econ. hist.
[48] Express & Star, 14 May, 2 Oct. 1947, 16 July 1962; Wolverhampton Chron. 2 Dec. 1949, 29 Sept. 1950.
[49] S.H.C. ii (1), 183; S.H.C. 1934 (2), 87 n.; S.R.O., D. 1018/2.
[50] Below, econ. hist.; S.R.O., D. 3548/1; Tettenhall Par. Reg. i (Staffs. Par. Reg. Soc. 1930), 65, 68, 76, 80.
[51] S.R.O., D. 1018/2.   [52] Below, communications.

parish boundary north of the Shrewsbury road.[53] The present Junction inn at the fork was opened c. 1880.[54] Houses were built on the north side of the Shrewsbury road between the two World Wars.

Wergs, north-west of Tettenhall, was an inhabited area by 1304.[55] The name means willows, growing presumably along the Penk which flows through the area.[56] Wergs lies on the Shrewsbury road, which originally ran along Woodthorne Road and then turned west on to Wergs Road; the south-eastern extension of Wergs Road was of local significance only until the early 19th century when it became part of the new course of the main road. In 1613 there was still a cross, Bell Cross, at the crossroads formed by Wergs Road, Woodthorne Road, and Keepers Lane.[57] Eight people at Wergs were assessed for the subsidy of 1327, and eight appeared in the muster roll of 1539.[58] In 1780 there were 23 houses and a cottage.[59] There was an inn, the Crown, on the north side of Wergs Road by 1834 and a post office by 1860.[60] Wergs Hall to the north-west on Wergs Hall Road dates from c. 1860.[61] There are privately built houses dating from the period between the two World Wars and since 1945 along Wergs Road, Wergs Hall Road, and Keepers Lane.

Bilbrook in the north-east of the parish evidently derives its name from what is now Moat brook which forms the boundary there. The name is thought to be Celtic and to mean the brook in which 'billers' (water plants such as watercress) grow.[62] In 1086 the recorded population consisted of 2 free men, 1 villein, and 2 bordars.[63] Two main settlements developed, at Bilbrook itself where Bilbrook Road turns west towards Codsall and at Lane Green to the south. The green, which survives at the top of Lane Green Road, was mentioned in the early 1640s; a lane called Lane Green, mentioned in 1648, is perhaps Lane Green Road.[64] The road runs south to Dam Mill; the mill there was on the Codsall side of the Penk, but there were people living on the Tettenhall side by the 1680s.[65] In 1780 there were 11 houses at Bilbrook, 9 at Lane Green, and a cottage at Dam Mill.[66] The Woodman inn on the north side of the green existed by 1834.[67] The house called Bilbrook Manor House by the 1880s, on the north side of Bilbrook Road where it turns west, was probably the 'capital messuage or mansion house' which was the home

of John Lowe in the early 18th century. It was the home of Lt.-Col. H. E. Twentyman in the earlier 20th century and was demolished after his death in 1945. There was a mission room in Bilbrook Road by 1894.[68] In 1921 ten smallholdings were created in the south-east part of the area.[69] Between the two World Wars many houses were built in the north-east part, some of them for workers at Boulton Paul Aircraft Ltd.'s factory opened at Pendeford in 1936.[70] After 1945 there was extensive building of council as well as private houses, and Bilbrook and Lane Green now merge into Codsall with its similar development.

Like Bilbrook the north-eastern corner of the ancient parish, covering Pendeford and the Barnhurst area, became populous only in the 20th century. Pendeford is thought to mean Penda's ford,[71] presumably a crossing of the Penk. In 1086 it had 4 villeins, 5 bordars, and 3 slaves besides Almar, the tenant of the manor.[72] Barnhurst farm can be traced from the later 13th century.[73] Cronkhall (originally Cronkwall) on the present Windermere Road between Barnhurst Lane and Codsall Road was an inhabited area by the 1220s; the path from Cronkhall Green to Barnhurst was mentioned in 1419.[74] Eleven people in Pendeford were assessed for the subsidy of 1327 and 8 for that of the mid 1520s. The poll-tax assessment of 1641 listed 48 people in Pendeford constablewick. In 1666 nine people in the constablewick were assessed for hearth tax and three more were too poor to pay.[75] Palmers Cross, a farm in Codsall Road opposite the end of Windermere Road, existed by the mid 18th century; it was amalgamated with Cronkhall farm after the sale of both in 1873.[76] In 1780 there were 14 houses at Pendeford, including the Hall, 3 at Barnhurst, and the 2 farms at Cronkhall and Palmers Cross.[77] Wolverhampton corporation's sewage works at Barnhurst dates from the late 1860s.[78] In the period between the two World Wars privately built houses were erected along Pendeford Avenue and Codsall Road. Boulton Paul Aircraft Ltd.'s factory in Wobaston Road, Pendeford, was opened in 1936 and the airport to the east in 1938. The privately built estate around Windermere Road, although begun by 1938, dates mainly from c. 1960; similarly the private Tyninghame estate south of Codsall Road is mainly of c. 1960, but Knights Avenue had been built by 1938.[79] An industrial estate was opened on part of the airport in the early 1970s; it was

[53] Wolv. C.L., map 133.
[54] Kelly's Dir. Staffs. (1880).
[55] S.H.C. vii (1), 157.   [56] Ekwall, Eng. Place-names.
[57] P.R.O., MR 308; below, communications.
[58] S.H.C. vii (1), 254; N.S. vi (1), 75.
[59] S.R.O., D. 1018/2; Yates, Map of Staffs. (1775).
[60] White, Dir. Staffs. (1834), 290; P.O. Dir. Staffs. (1860).
[61] Below, manors and other estates (Tettenhall Regis).
[62] Ekwall, Eng. Place-names; Eng. Place-name Elements (E.P.N.S.), i. 35.   [63] V.C.H. Staffs. iv. 45.
[64] Below, econ. hist.; S.R.O., Tp. 1226, parcel A, ct. baron of Pendeford prebend, Jan. 1647/8.
[65] Tettenhall Par. Reg. i. 83, 236; below, Codsall.
[66] S.R.O., D. 1018/2.
[67] White, Dir. Staffs. (1834), 290; P.O. Dir. Staffs. (1845).
[68] O.S. Map 6", Staffs. LVI. SW. (1889 edn.); S.R.O., D. 571/A/PK/1, p. 5; S.R.O., Tp. 1226, parcel A, ct. of prebends of Bovenhill and Pendeford, 2 July 1734; Kelly's Dir. Staffs. (1912 and later edns. to 1940); below, churches.

[69] Below, econ. hist.
[70] O.S. Map 6", Staffs. LVI. SW. (prov. edn. with addns. of 1938); inf. from the priest-in-charge, Holy Cross, Bilbrook.
[71] Ekwall, Eng. Place-names.
[72] V.C.H. Staffs. iv. 55.
[73] Below, manors and other estates (Tettenhall Clericorum).
[74] S.H.C. iv (1), 45; S.R.O., D. 593/A/2/16/6; Yates, Map of Staffs. (1775).
[75] S.H.C. vii (1), 251; S.H.C. 1923, 76; P.R.O., E 179/177/96; H. L. Main Papers, box 178. Other inhabitants of the area may have been included under Tettenhall Clericorum.
[76] W.S.L., S.MS. 467, p. 219; W.S.L., Sale Cat. E/1/7. For a field nearby called Palmers Cross Corner in 1613 see P.R.O., MR 308.
[77] S.R.O., D. 1018/2.
[78] Below, manors and other estates.
[79] O.S. Map 6", Staffs. LXII. NW. (prov. edn. with addns. of 1938); Express & Star, 1 Mar. 1961, 2 July 1964; below, communications; econ. hist.

closed in the late 1970s.[80] Work began on large estates of council and privately built houses at Barnhurst and Pendeford, including the site of the airport, in the mid 1970s[81] and was still in progress in 1980. An area along the Penk incorporating pools and woodland formerly attached to Pendeford mill and Pendeford Hall was being maintained in 1980 as a nature reserve by Wolverhampton corporation.[82]

Aldersley to the south, part of the manor of Tettenhall Clericorum, was mentioned in 1294 and was an inhabited area at the beginning of the 14th century.[83] The road thence to Tettenhall, later Aldersley Road, existed by 1377; Green Lane running east from Pendeford Avenue was mentioned as the lane to Oxley, in Bushbury, in 1418.[84] The medieval name of the settlement was Allerley, with Alderley, found in 1471, coming into use by the late 15th century. The form Autherley was also used by 1588 and became the normal usage from the later 17th century. The present Aldersley was used in the late 18th century and became usual in the 19th century, with Autherley being used as the name of the northern of the two canal junctions there.[85] In 1780 there were two farms, with a house and cottage at Blakeway (later Blakeley) Green.[86] The whole district was developed between the two World Wars as a residential area consisting of smaller houses,[87] and there was further development after the Second World War.

COMMUNICATIONS. Two main roads cross the parish, that from Wolverhampton to Shrewsbury and to Newport (Salop.) and Chester, and that from Wolverhampton to Bridgnorth via Compton. The first was mentioned in 1296 as the road from Tettenhall to Shrewsbury.[88] In 1551 Walter Leveson of Wolverhampton left money 'towards the amending of the evil highways at the Wirges and between Tetnall and Wolverhampton'.[89] In the early 18th century the road became part of the main route between London and Holyhead.[90] It originally followed a course south of its present line and ran along Meadow View, up Old Hill, and along Upper Street, Upper Green, Wrottesley Road, and Woodthorne Road to Wergs. There it forked, the Shrewsbury road running south of Wrottesley Hall to the county boundary and the Newport road running to Kingswood.[91] In the early 19th century the whole Tettenhall stretch was re-aligned. In 1810 a more direct line was brought into use between Upper Green and Wergs. In addition the course of the Shrewsbury road south of Wrottesley Hall was abandoned; instead the road followed the Newport branch to Kingswood and there branched off to follow a new line which joined the old road at the county boundary.[92] In the earlier 1820s the steep course up Old Hill was altered as one of Thomas Telford's improvements to the Holyhead post route. A new road was made running along an embankment north of Meadow View and cutting through the rock north of Old Hill with a much reduced gradient.[93] The work involved the building of a bridge over Smestow brook. The bridge in Meadow View carrying the old road over the brook existed as New Bridge by 1517. It was the joint responsibility of Tettenhall and Wolverhampton in 1581 and 1629, but it had evidently become a county bridge by 1710. It was a two-arch stone structure c. 1880 and was later rebuilt.[94]

The Wolverhampton–Bridgnorth road runs along Compton Road to Compton where a bridge carrying it over Smestow brook existed by 1613.[95] It then becomes Bridgnorth Road, part of which was mentioned in 1300 as the road leading from Wightwick towards Stafford.[96]

Both the main roads from Wolverhampton were turnpiked in 1748.[97] By 1780 there was a tollhouse north of New Bridge; it was advertised for sale in 1820 and was converted into a cottage. Another tollhouse was built on the new line of road to the north.[98] In 1780 there was also a tollhouse at Compton, and there was still a tollbar at the junction of Compton Road and Finchfield Hill in 1880.[99] Both main roads were disturnpiked that year.[1]

The Staffordshire and Worcestershire Canal, built under an Act of 1766 between the Severn at Stourport, in Kidderminster (Worcs.), and the Trent and Mersey Canal at Great Haywood, in Colwich, runs through the Smestow valley. James Brindley started work on the canal at Compton in September 1766, at the southern end of the summit level which extends north to Gailey, in Penkridge. Brindley built his first lock at Compton, setting the standard for all other narrow locks in the Midlands. The two bridges

[80] *Express & Star*, 16, 20–1, 23 June, 28 Sept. 1978.
[81] Ibid. 22 July 1970, 26 June, 6 Dec. 1973, 4 Apr. 1974, 10 Nov. 1975, 5 Oct., 19 Dec. 1977, 13 and 30 Mar., 23 Aug. 1979.
[82] Inf. from Mr. R. G. A. Stringer, Wolverhampton Boro. Dept. of Environmental and Technical Services.
[83] H.W.R.O. (H.), B 47/S3; *S.H.C.* vii (1), 100, 254.
[84] H.W.R.O. (H.), B 47/S3 (1417/18); ibid. S24 (1377); Yates, *Map of Staffs.* (1775).
[85] e.g. H.W.R.O. (H.), B 47/S3; *S.H.C.* vii (1), 254; x (1), 131; S.R.O., Tp. 1226, folder 12 (1506); S.R.O., D. 593/B/1/26/38/11; D. 678/15/1; *Tettenhall Par. Reg.* i. 216 sqq.; Shaw, *Staffs.* ii. 201; Pitt, *Staffs.* i. 185; below, communications.
[86] S.R.O., D. 1018/2. For the 2 farms see below, manors and other estates (Tettenhall Clericorum).
[87] O.S. Map 6″, Staffs. LXII. NW. (prov. edn. with addns. of 1938).
[88] H.W.R.O. (H.), E 12/S, Kinver VI, rents from waste in Kinver forest temp. Edw. I.
[89] G. P. Mander and N. W. Tildesley, *Hist. of Wolverhampton*, 48.
[90] Below, Wombourne.

[91] J. P. Jones, 'Old Tettenhall', *Wolverhampton Jnl.* iv. 182; Yates, *Map of Staffs.* (1775); S.R.O., D. 3548/1; S.R.O., D. 755/4/13.
[92] 50 Geo. III, c. 56 (Local and Personal). The new course is shown on R. Baugh, *Map of Salop.* (1808).
[93] *Rep. Com. Holyhead Road*, H.C. 126, pp. 5, 11, 21 (1820), vi; ibid. H.C. 575, pp. 13, 20 (1821), x; *Rep. Com. Shrewsbury and Holyhead Road*, H.C. 151, p. 4 (1823), x; *1st Rep. Com. Road from London to Holyhead*, H.C. 305, p. 22 (1824), ix.
[94] H.W.R.O. (H.), B 47/S3, 1517 terrier, mentioning 'Newbrugecroft'; B.L. Stowe Ch. 631; *S.H.C.* 1948–9, 83; S.R.O., D. 641/2/C/5/2D; *S.H.C.* 1934 (1), 81; J. Fullwood and E.B., *Remnants of Old Wolverhampton and its Environs* (1880), vol. i.
[95] P.R.O., MR 308.
[96] *S.H.C.* v (1), 180.
[97] 21 Geo. II, c. 25.
[98] S.R.O., D. 755/4/13; D. 1018/2; *Wolverhampton Chron.* 23 Feb. 1820; below, pl. facing p. 80.
[99] S.R.O., D 660/14/6, sale partics. 1880; D. 1018/2.
[1] 40 & 41 Vic. c. 64, sched. 3.

there were the first on the canal and thus among the oldest canal bridges in the country; that on the Bridgnorth road was rebuilt in 1974. The canal was opened south from Compton in 1770 and north in 1772. By 1780 there was a wharf at Compton and a boat house at Wightwick.[2]

The Birmingham and Liverpool Junction Canal (later the Shropshire Union Canal), begun in 1830 and finished in 1835, runs through the Pendeford area. It leaves the Staffordshire and Worcestershire Canal at Autherley Junction, just over the parish boundary in Bushbury.[3]

The railway from Wolverhampton to Shrewsbury, opened in 1849,[4] runs through the northeast part of the parish, but the nearest station has always been in Codsall. The Wolverhampton and Kingswinford Railway, opened in 1925 with a station at Tettenhall and a halt at Compton, ran through the south-east, following the Smestow valley like the canal. Tettenhall station south of Meadow View was closed for passenger traffic in 1932 when passenger services were withdrawn from the line; it remained open for goods traffic until 1964. Temporary passenger facilities were provided in July 1937 for the Royal Show in Wrottesley Park. Compton halt was closed completely in 1932. The line was closed in 1965 and the track lifted in 1967–8.[5] The derelict station buildings at Tettenhall and a goods depot still stood in 1980, and the railway bed through Tettenhall had been made into a walkway by Wolverhampton corporation.

A tramway was opened in 1878 from Queen's Square, Wolverhampton, to Newbridge on the Tettenhall boundary. It had been extended up the hill to Wergs Road by 1908 after the introduction of electric power. By then there was also an omnibus from Queen's Square to Compton, and the Great Western Railway ran a motor omnibus from the Wolverhampton Low Level station to Bridgnorth via Wightwick. The trams were replaced in 1927 by trolley buses and they by motor buses in 1963.[6]

An airport was opened at Pendeford by Wolverhampton corporation in 1938. It was used by the nearby Boulton Paul Aircraft Ltd.'s factory and by private fliers. In 1941 the Air Ministry converted it into a training station for pilots. The flying school was closed in 1953, but civil flying had begun again in 1946. In 1953 Don Everall Aviation Ltd. and Wolverhampton Aviation Ltd., who were then managing the airport for the corporation, were granted licences for scheduled flights to the Isle of Man and Jersey respectively. Don Everall Aviation Ltd. became sole managers

in 1956. Facilities were provided for private users and members of the Air Training Corps, and the field was also used for flying displays. From the later 1950s there was growing local opposition to the continuation of the airport, and competition from Halfpenny Green airfield in Bobbington led to a decline. After an accident in 1970 the corporation closed Pendeford. An industrial estate was opened on part of it soon afterwards, and in the mid 1970s work began on a large housing estate on the site.[7]

SOCIAL AND CULTURAL ACTIVITIES. A Michaelmas wake was held at Tettenhall, the church being dedicated to St. Michael. It was mentioned in 1686, and after the adoption of the Gregorian calendar in 1752 it was held on the Sunday and Monday after old Michaelmas day. In the late 18th century it was held on Tettenhall Wood common. In 1815 the constables were ordered to prevent the bull baiting which had usually taken place at the wake; fines were imposed for bull baiting in 1818, but the sport was still practised in the early 1830s. The wake continued to be held in the 1860s.[8] Well dressing took place at Bilbrook on Maundy Thursday in the later 17th century.[9]

There was pony racing on a course on Tettenhall Wood common near the site of Tettenhall Towers in the later 18th century. Horse races were held at Compton in the early 19th century on what was called the new course.[10] A cricket club was established in 1809 with plans to use alternately a field in front of Wrottesley Hall and a ground in Tettenhall village.[11] The present cricket ground at Stockwell End existed by the early 1880s. In 1910 it was leased to the Wolverhampton Cricket Club. Ann Swindley of the Cedars, Stockwell Road (d. 1940), devised the ground to the club.[12] There was a football club at Tettenhall Wood in the later 1880s and early 1890s, another at Tettenhall itself in the late 1880s, and one at Compton in the early 1890s.[13] The present golf course north of Stockwell End was opened on part of the Danes Court estate in 1908 for the South Staffordshire Golf Club, which moved that year from Penn.[14]

An association of Loyal Volunteer Cavalry was formed in 1798 for Tettenhall and the surrounding district. The company was disbanded in the early 19th century. A rifle volunteer company was established in 1860; it first met at the former workhouse in Wrottesley Road and then moved to a drill hall on Old Hill, built apparently in 1864. The volunteers became a territorial army company in 1908.[15]

[2] V.C.H. Staffs. ii. 288; J. I. Langford, Towpath Guide to Staffs. and Worcs. Canal, 106–8; Shaw, Staffs. ii. 200; S.R.O., D. 1018/2.
[3] V.C.H. Staffs. ii. 295. Aldersley Juntion to the south, where the Birmingham Canal joins the Staffs. and Worcs. Canal, is also just in Bushbury. [4] Ibid. 313.
[5] Ibid. 325, 328; J. N. Williams, By Rail to Wombourne (Wolverhampton, 1977 edn.); C. R. Clinker, Clinker's Reg. of Closed Passenger Stns. and Goods Depots, 144, 146.
[6] J. S. Webb, Black Country Tramways, i (Bloxwich, 1974), 6, 10, and plans at end; A. Webb's Annual (1908); Kelly's Dir. Staffs. (1908); Express & Star, 25 June 1963, 1 July 1965.
[7] The Blackcountryman (Spring, 1971), 66–9; D. Gregory, Green Belts and Development Control (Univ. of Birmingham, 1970), 46; D. J. Smith, Action Stations: 3, 206–7; Express &

Star, 28 Feb. 1973; above, pp. 12–13.
[8] W.S.L. 244/79; A. Webb's Parish Almanack for Tettenhall and Tettenhall Wood (1892; copy in Wolv. C.L.); Wolverhampton Chron. 4 Oct. 1815, 18 Nov. 1818; White, Dir. Staffs. (1834), 168; (1851), 205; White's Dir. Wolverhampton (1869). [9] Plot, Staffs. 318.
[10] Webb's Par. Almanack (1892); Wolverhampton Chron. 14 Oct. 1812.
[11] Staffs. Advertiser, 17 June 1809.
[12] O.S. Map 1/2,500, Staffs. LXII. 1 (1902 edn.); Wolv. Civic Centre, deed bdle. C5/18, 22; Birmingham Post, 31 May 1940. [13] Webb's Par. Almanack (1886; 1888; 1892).
[14] Express & Star, 30 Nov. 1934.
[15] Jones, Tettenhall, 286–8; Hist. of Volunteer Force of Staffs. 1859–1908 (Stafford, 1909), 5, 30, 71; below, pp. 44, 46.

Payment for thatching an alehouse in Wrottesley was made in 1294.[16] In the late 16th century there were five licensed alehouse-keepers in Tettenhall Regis.[17] The Angel inn, mentioned in 1754, was one of three public houses in Tettenhall in 1780; the other two were the Wrottesley's Arms, which had a bowling green, and the Crown. There were also inns at Compton (the Swan), Perton, and Trescott, and two at Wightwick (one of them the Mermaid).[18] The Crown was probably the inn on Old Hill known as the Rose and Crown by 1804 and the Old Rose and Crown by 1814. By 1851 it had been renamed the Rock Villa and in 1980 was the Rock Hotel.[19] In 1843 the landlord, George Spink, opened the Rock Villa Gardens next to the inn. There was a bandstand and a bowling green, and in the early 1890s on Monday evenings in the summer there were firework displays and balloon ascents which attracted artisans from Wolverhampton.[20]

The 'great room' at the post office was used for concerts and dances in the early 19th century. Dances were also held at the Old Rose and Crown.[21] In 1877 the Tettenhall Negro Minstrels performed in Wolverhampton as well as at the Lower Street school in Tettenhall; they performed at the drill hall in 1882. There was a Tettenhall Amateur Dramatic Society by 1883, also using the drill hall.[22] A driving club was formed in 1883 by Thomas Thorneycroft and was still meeting in 1893. Limited to 40 members, it met every week during the summer, usually on Saturdays, to 'drive to some appointed place'.[23]

A young men's institute, with a library and reading and smoking rooms, was established in Tettenhall in 1872. It was presumably used in the late 1880s for the twice-weekly meetings of the Young Men's Friendly Society.[24] A working men's institute was opened on the corner of Upper Street and Upper Green, Tettenhall, c. 1876; by 1894 it had a subscription library and reading, bagatelle, and smoking rooms.[25] A similar institute for Tettenhall Wood was opened in 1887; it moved to a building erected at the corner of Wood Road and School Road in 1893. In the early 20th century it had a lending library, reading, bagatelle, and smoking rooms, a large room for concerts, and a bowling green and alley. By the early 1960s the building was run as a community centre.[26] A branch of the county library was opened at Tettenhall Wood in 1950. Branch libraries were opened at Finchfield in 1960 and Pendeford in 1981.[27]

The Tettenhall Union Friendly Society, established in 1804, was still meeting in the mid 1870s. Other friendly societies were the Loyal Regis Lodge of the Independent Order of Odd Fellows, founded in 1826 and still meeting in 1912; the Tettenhall Perseverance Friendly Society, founded in 1844 and still meeting in 1876; the Compton Volunteer Society, established by 1860 and still meeting in 1912; a court of the Ancient Order of Foresters, established in 1861 and still meeting in 1912; and a lodge of the United Order of Free Gardeners, formed in 1867 and still meeting in 1905. In 1905 a branch of the Independent Order of Rechabites, including a Juvenile Tent, was meeting on alternate Mondays in the Holloway, Compton.[28]

MANORS AND OTHER ESTATES. In 1086 the king held 2½ hides in Tettenhall in demesne; one hide was at Tettenhall itself, one was at Compton, and the half hide was at Wightwick.[29] The manor, later known as *TETTENHALL REGIS* or *KING'S TETTENHALL*, consisted of two detached parts. One extended north from Old Hill and the ridge above the church to the later Woodthorne Road South, Keepers Lane at Wergs, the Penk as far east as Dam Mill, the Cronkhall area, and the later Pendeford Avenue. The other extended south-west from Lower Green to include Compton, the Finchfield area on the high ground to the south, and Wightwick.[30]

Under Henry II and Richard I the manor was on occasion farmed by the tenants: aids and tallages were sometimes accounted for by the sheriff and sometimes by the men of the manor.[31] In 1193 Richard I granted the manor to his aunt Emma, wife of David, prince of Gwynedd.[32] That was apparently a temporary measure, and there is no evidence that she had any further connexion with Tettenhall. In 1198 Matthew de Gamage (or de Gamages) was granted £4 a year from the manor.[33] He held lands in both England and Normandy, and the grant was probably intended to preserve his loyalty in Normandy. Nevertheless, when the duchy fell he was one of those who transferred their allegiance to the French king. His English lands were confiscated and at Easter 1204 his annuity from Tettenhall was cancelled.[34] Instead, from midsummer 1204 Hubert Walter, archbishop of Canterbury, received the income towards the endowment of a Cistercian house which he was establishing at

[16] *S.H.C.* n.s. vi (2), 71.
[17] *S.H.C.* 1929, 320; 1935, 101.
[18] S.R.O., D. 1018/2; D. 1364/1/2.
[19] S.R.O., D. 1018/2; *Wolverhampton Chron.* 23 Nov. 1814; White, *Dir. Staffs.* (1851), 208. For the use of the name Rock Villa until c. 1890 see e.g. *P.O. Dir. Staffs.* (1860); *Kelly's Dir. Staffs.* (1880; 1892); *Webb's Par. Almanack* (1888; 1892).
[20] *Webb's Par. Almanack* (1892).
[21] *Wolverhampton Chron.* 12 Jan., 23 Nov. 1814; below, educ.   [22] W.S.L., M.1051.
[23] Jones, *Tettenhall*, 275; *A Day with the Tettenhall Driving Club, Aug. 12th 1893* (copy in W.S.L. Pamphs.).
[24] *P.O. Dir. Staffs.* (1872; 1876); *Webb's Par. Almanack* (1888).
[25] *Webb's Par. Almanack* (1888); O.S. Map 6″, Staffs. LXII. NW. (1889 edn.).
[26] *Webb's Par. Almanack* (1888); *Webb's Annual* (1905); *Tettenhall Official Guide* [1961], 27; date on foundation stone.
[27] Inf. from Staffs. County Libr. H.Q. and Miss Monica Green, Wolverhampton Educ. Dept.
[28] *Reps. of Chief Registrar of Friendly Socs. 1876*, H.C. 429, p. 409 (1877), lxxvii; *Webb's Par. Almanack* (1888); *Webb's Annual* (1905); *Rules of the Friendly Volunteer Society of Tradesmen* (Birmingham, 1860; copy in W.S.L. Pamphs.).
[29] *V.C.H. Staffs.* iv. 38.
[30] P.R.O., MR 308; *S.H.C.* v (1), 180.
[31] *S.H.C.* i. 56, 68, 87; ii (1), 3, 12, 46.
[32] *S.H.C.* ii (1), 24–5, 27–8. For Emma see J. E. Lloyd, *Hist. of Wales from earliest times to Edwardian Conquest* (1912 edn.), ii. 551.
[33] *S.H.C.* ii (1), 74, 77.
[34] R. W. Eyton, *Antiquities of Shropshire*, iv. 143–4; *Pipe R. 1204* (P.R.S. n.s. xviii), pp. xxxviii–xxxix, 209.

Wolverhampton. In September the king informed the sheriff of Staffordshire that he had given the manor to the archbishop.[35] William de Gamage, Matthew's younger brother, had also held estates in both England and Normandy but had remained loyal to King John.[36] Within the next few months he had established a claim to Tettenhall: in May 1205, when John confirmed the archbishop in possession of the manor with permission to grant it to the Cistercians in free alms, it was stated that William had quitclaimed Tettenhall to the archbishop, receiving compensation in the archiepiscopal manor of Salt-wood (Kent).[37] In July 1205 Hubert Walter died. In October the exchange was cancelled and the sheriff was ordered to give William his land at Tettenhall.[38] William remained lessee[39] of the manor until his death, probably in 1240.[40] In 1241–2 the sheriff accounted for the manor.[41] In 1249 it was being leased to the tenants.[42] In 1256 it was leased for seven years to John Chishull, a royal clerk.[43] In the earlier 14th century it was regularly leased, generally to local landowners or their relatives.[44]

In 1338 Edward III granted the manor to his chamberlain, Henry, Lord Ferrers of Groby, in tail male.[45] It descended with the barony until the death in 1445 of William, Lord Ferrers. The barony then passed to his grand-daughter Elizabeth, child of his deceased elder son;[46] under the terms of the 1338 grant Tettenhall went to William's second son, Thomas Ferrers, *jure uxoris* lord of Tamworth. Thomas died in 1459 and his son and heir, Sir Thomas, in 1498.[47] Sir Thomas's heir, his grandson Sir John Ferrers, died in 1512. Thereafter the manor descended from father to son until the late 17th century: Sir Humphrey (d. 1554); John (d. 1576); Sir Humphrey (d. 1608); Sir John (d. 1633); Sir Humphrey (also d. 1633); and John (d. 1680), who came of age in 1650.[48] John included the manor in a family settlement of 1671, and in 1679 he bought a confirmation of his title from the Crown. The confirmation stipulated that a 6s. 8d. rent charge was to be paid to the Crown by the

lord; the payment was commuted in 1787.[49] Later in 1679 Ferrers sold the manor to three tenants: Francis Wightwick of Wightwick, who bought a half share, and William Hayward of Tettenhall and Humphrey Fleeming of Wergs, who each bought a quarter share.[50] The three men may have bought the copyhold rights in 1665.[51]

The Wightwick moiety passed from Francis (d. 1692) to his son Francis (d. *c.* 1697) and to that Francis's son Francis (d. 1714), whose widow Elizabeth held it, presumably in dower, until her death in 1736. It then passed to her only surviving son James. On his death in 1749 it passed to his nephew John Wightwick, later of Sandgates, in Chertsey (Surr.), who died in 1816. John's son Francis, also of Sandgates, died childless in 1843 and the moiety passed to his elder surviving sister, Winifred Wightwick. On her death in 1851 the main line of the family became extinct. In 1852 Francis's executors conveyed the moiety to George Robinson, a Wolverhampton solicitor. From him it passed in 1862 to Charles Neve, in whose hands the manor was reunited.[52]

William Hayward's quarter share[53] passed on his death in 1709[54] to his son John (d. 1718) and then to John's son, the Revd. John Hayward (d. 1729).[55] In 1729 another grandson, William Wilkes, a London distiller and a relative of the Wilkes family of Aldersley, inherited it. In 1737 he went bankrupt and his relative Israel Wilkes (d. 1745), also a London distiller, bought the share.[56] In 1738 Israel sold it to Gen. Thomas Howard of Great Bookham (Surr.), who died in 1753. Howard's widow Mary then held it until her death in 1782.[57] She was succeeded by her son Sir George (later Field Marshal) Howard of Stoke Place, in Stoke Poges (Bucks.), who died in 1796 leaving his estates to his grandson Richard William Howard Vyse, from 1812 Richard William Howard Howard-Vyse (d. 1853).[58] In 1818 Howard-Vyse sold his share of the manor to William Mott (d. 1826), a Lichfield solicitor and registrar of Tettenhall peculiar.[59] In 1862 Mott's son John sold it to Charles Neve.[60]

[35] *Rot. Litt. Claus.* (Rec. Com.), i. 8; *Pipe R.* 1204, 209; *V.C.H. Staffs.* iii. 322–3.
[36] Eyton, *Shropshire*, iv. 145.
[37] *Rot. Chart.* (Rec. Com.), 152.
[38] *Rot. Litt. Claus.* i. 56.
[39] *Bk. of Fees*, i. 143, 384; *Rot. Litt. Claus.* i. 495; *S.H.C.* iv (1), 70; W.S.L., S. MS. 327, p. 11. But see *S.H.C.* ii (1), 141, 147, 153, 160, 166; *Pipe R.* 1218 (P.R.S. N.S. xxxix), 1; *Pipe R.* 1219 (P.R.S. N.S. xlii), 3; *Pipe R.* 1230 (P.R.S. N.S. iv), 232.
[40] Eyton, *Shropshire*, iv. 148; *Close R.* 1237–42, 171.
[41] *Pipe R.* 1242 (ed. H. L. Cannon), 9.
[42] *Cal. Inq. Misc.* i, p. 18.
[43] Below, churches.
[44] See e.g. *Cal. Fine R.* 1307–19, 90, 376; 1319–27, 387; 1337–47, 7.
[45] *Complete Peerage*, v. 345 n.
[46] Ibid. 358.
[47] Ibid. 357 n.
[48] C. F. Palmer, *Hist. of Town and Castle of Tamworth* (Tamworth, 1845), 368–9, 372–5.
[49] Ibid. 374; *Cal. Treas. Bks.* 1679–80, 139; S.R.O., D. 284/M/5, 19 Oct. 1787.
[50] S.R.O., D. 546/M/25, sched. of deeds belonging to R. W. H. Vyse, f. 4; Shaw, *Staffs.* ii. 193, giving Hayward's Christian name as Robert.
[51] Jones, *Tettenhall*, 35, citing no authority, wrongly states that they bought the manor in 1665. His further statement that they then 'became joint owners of the copyhold rights'

may explain what they bought, if there was a purchase in 1665.
[52] G. P. Mander, *Wolverhampton Antiquary*, i. 302–4; H. D. Wightwick, *The Wightwicks: a Family Hist.* (priv. print. 1934), 'Wightwicks of Staffs.'; S.R.O., D. 284/M/1–7 (Tettenhall Regis manor ct. bks.); S.R.O., D. 1364/1/2, burial 28 Nov. 1736. Jones, *Tettenhall*, 45, states that the Wightwicks' interest in the manor ceased in 1834 when they sold their copyhold rights to the Foley fam. The ct. bks. do not support the statement.
[53] For this para. see, unless otherwise stated, S.R.O., D. 284/M/1–7; S.R.O., D. 546/M/25, sched. of deeds belonging to R. W. H. Vyse.
[54] L.J.R.O., P/C/11, Wm. Hayward (1709).
[55] *Tettenhall Par. Reg.* i. 261, 270.
[56] S.R.O., D. 546/M/26, deed of 23 Sept. 1818, f. 1; C.D. Wilkes, *Wilkes Chronology* (Vevey, Switzerland, priv. print. 1959), 31, 52.
[57] S.R.O., D. 546/M/25, abstract of title to lands in Tettenhall, and copy of will of Lt.-Gen. Thos. Howard; *D.N.B.* s.v. Howard, Sir Geo.; Burke, *Peerage* (1871), 396; *Gent. Mag.* lii. 95.
[58] *D.N.B.* s.v. Howard, Sir Geo.; *V.C.H. Bucks.* iii. 304; Burke, *Land Gent.* (1871), i. 655; *Gent. Mag.* N.S. xl. 200.
[59] S.R.O., D. 546/M/27, pedigree; A. L. Reade, *Johnsonian Gleanings*, viii (priv. print. 1937), 154–5; L.J.R.O., PTe/A/28.
[60] S.R.O., D. 260/M/F/5/20, deed of 10 Oct. 1861; Wolv. Civic Centre, deed bdle. C 5/22, abstract of title 1889.

TETTENHALL: WIGHTWICK MANOR FROM THE SOUTH-EAST

THE WODEHOUSE, WOMBOURNE: THE DRAWING ROOM

The Mount, Tettenhall Wood: the entrance hall

Compton Hall: the drawing room decorated by Morris & Co. c. 1896

TETTENHALL

The quarter share bought by Humphrey Fleeming (d. 1705) descended with the Wergs estate. When Wergs passed to Mary Fryer in 1810 her husband Richard became one of the joint lords of Tettenhall Regis in her right. In 1829 or 1830 the Fryers conveyed their interest in the manor to their son William Fleeming Fryer, from whom it passed in 1862 to Charles Neve.[61]

The reunited manor had passed by 1866 to John Neve of Oaken, in Codsall. He died in 1914 and was succeeded by his son Edward John Neve, who in 1944 conveyed the lordship to Geoffrey (later Sir Geoffrey) Mander of Wightwick Manor.[62]

In 1371 and 1388 there was no capital messuage belonging to the manor,[63] and the site of the manor was stated in 1498 to be worth nothing.[64] A building described as the manor house in 1760 was an inn used for meetings of the court.[65]

In the 1810s and 1820s a fee-farm rent of £1 19s. 7½d., known as frith silver, was being collected from properties in the liberty of Tettenhall Regis by the constable for payment to John, Baron Somers, from 1821 Earl Somers. A rent charge was due to Charles, Earl Somers, from one of the properties in 1878.[66]

DIPPONS FARM in Tettenhall Regis manor was formed in the early 18th century, when John Stokes of Bushbury established his son John as a farmer in Tettenhall. In 1709, 1711, and 1712 they bought land at Wightwick and Wergs from Richard Cresswell (d. 1743). The 1711 purchase included several adjoining closes called Dipping or Dippings, and by 1717 a farmhouse, the later Dippons Farm, had been built on one of them.[67] John Stokes the elder died in 1724; his son, the occupant of the new house, died at Tettenhall in 1752 and was succeeded by his eldest son William.[68] William, who had settled at Roughton, in Worfield (Salop.), died in 1779 and was succeeded by his son William, who died childless in 1784. In 1785 the younger William's widow Nancy and his uncle John Stokes were admitted to the estate. John Stokes had been holding the farm as his nephew's tenant in 1779; he died in 1786.[69] In that year Nancy married her late husband's cousin William Smith Stokes of Roughton. In 1809 Francis Smith Stokes of Kinver, elder brother of W. S. Stokes, conveyed to him all rights which he had to the farm under a settlement of 1717.[70] W. S. Stokes died in 1812,

and later that year the property, consisting of the farmhouse and 128 a., was put up for sale. It was bought, apart from 16 a., by James Perry of Graiseley, in Wolverhampton.[71] Perry died in 1837 and was succeeded by his brother Thomas, who in 1843 sold the farm to Theodosia Hinckes of Tettenhall Wood House.[72] When the Hinckes Trust Estate was put up for sale in 1895 Dippons Farm was offered with 87 a.[73] The farmhouse was demolished in 1974 as part of the redevelopment of the area of the former Perton airfield.[74]

In the 16th century the Fleeming family held a farm at *WERGS* in Tettenhall Regis manor. The family had settled in the parish by the later 13th century and had, according to tradition, moved to Wergs from Wightwick in the earlier 14th century.[75] A Henry Flemyng of Wergs, yeoman, who was living in 1529, may be the man of that name who was described in 1551 as of Aldersley.[76] A Thomas Fleeming of Wergs was a presentment juror for Seisdon hundred from 1586 to 1590.[77] Another Thomas Fleeming of Wergs, yeoman, died in 1658;[78] he may have been the father of Humphrey Fleeming, described in 1659 as 'of the Wergs, yeoman'.[79] Humphrey, who later bought a quarter share of the lordship of Tettenhall Regis, died in 1705.[80] He was succeeded by his son John (d. 1740), his grandson John (d. 1764), and his great-grandson, another John. Grandson and great-grandson added to the family estate, which in 1780 amounted to 301 a. in the parish.[81] On the death of the great-grandson in 1810 the estate passed to his niece Mary, whose husband Richard Fryer (d. 1846) was a Wolverhampton banker and a Radical M.P. for that borough from 1832 to 1834.[82] On Mary's death in 1852 the property passed to her son William Fleeming Fryer (d. 1891), a Walsall ironmaster.[83] He added to and improved the estate. The improvements included a new house. In 1834 the Fryers' seat at Wergs was described as possessing no architectural beauties, and in 1851 it was merely 'pleasant'.[84] The new Wergs Hall, a large Italianate house, 'capacious and handsome', was built upon 'an eminence bordered by pleasure grounds' at the foot of which was a park with a lake and a trout stream. In the early 1870s the estate amounted to some 1,210 a. in Tettenhall and Codsall. From 1872 it was sold off in parcels. The hall was sold with almost 700 acres.[85] The purchaser, T. J. Perry, a Bilston ironmaster, died in 1885, leaving the property to his brother F. C.

[61] S.R.O., D. 284/M/5, 23 Mar. 1811, 6, 28 Oct. 1829, 19 Feb. 1830, 7, 30 Sept. 1862; Jones, *Tettenhall*, 54–5; below, (Wergs).
[62] S.R.O. D. 284/M/7, 30 Sept., 19 Dec. 1862, 17 Mar. 1866, and notes at end of vol.
[63] Jones, *Tettenhall*, 33; *Cal. Inq. p.m.* xvi, p. 212.
[64] *Cal. Inq. p.m. Hen. VII*, ii, p. 159.
[65] S.R.O., D. 284/M/3, 21 Oct. 1760; below, p. 36.
[66] S.R.O., D. 1364/6/2 (giving amount at £1 18s. 3½d. on one occasion); S.R.O., D. 1018/2; S.R.O., D. 3160/12/5; II.W.R.O. (H.), B 47/S46.
[67] H.W.R.O. (H.), B 47/S25.
[68] *Bushbury Par. Reg.* (Staffs. Par. Reg. Soc. 1956–7), 58; S.R.O., D. 284/M/2, no. 137; D. 1364/1/2.
[69] Salop. R.O. 1374/6; S.R.O., D. 284/M/4, nos. 55–6; M/5, no. 2; D. 1364/1/2.
[70] Local Studies Libr., Shrewsbury, MS. 4645, p. 208, and MS. 4646, p. 121; S.R.O., D. 284/M/5, nos. 166–9.
[71] S.R.O., D. 284/M/5, nos. 204–9; D. 1364/1/4, p. 75; *Wolverhampton Chron.* 15 Apr. 1812.

[72] *Staffs. Advertiser*, 29 Apr. 1837; S.R.O., D. 284/M/7, nos. 176, 195.   [73] W.S.L., Sale Cat. F/3/20.
[74] *Express & Star*, 12 June, 1 Oct. 1974.
[75] Jones, *Tettenhall*, 54–5.
[76] S.R.O., D. 593/A/2/18/10–14.
[77] *S.H.C.* 1927, 131, 133, 136, 160; 1929, 112, 117, 119, 201, 211, 272; 1930, 8.
[78] *Tettenhall Par. Reg.* i. 224.
[79] Ibid. 60. Jones, *Tettenhall*, 55, states that he was the son of a Hen. Fleeming.
[80] *Tettenhall Par. Reg.* i. 251.
[81] S.R.O., D. 1018/2; D. 1364/1/2.
[82] *Staffs. Advertiser*, 29 Dec. 1810; Jones, *Tettenhall*, 54–5; *S.H.C.* 1933 (1), 84–5.
[83] Jones, *Tettenhall*, 55–6, 313; *V.C.H. Staffs.* xvii. 193.
[84] *Wolverhampton Chron.* 28 Aug. 1872; White, *Dir. Staffs.* (1834), 289; (1851), 207.
[85] W.S.L., Sale Cats. E/1/4 and F/5/28; *Wolverhampton Chron.* 28 Aug. 1872. For 2 farms on the estate sold by W. F. Fryer in 1872–3 see W.S.L., Sale Cat. E/1/7.

Perry of Dunston Hall in Penkridge, who died in 1900.[86] The estate then passed to the Perrys' sister Helen (d. 1907), who had lived at Wergs Hall since T. J. Perry's death.[87] In 1908 or 1909 the estate was acquired by Col. T. E. Hickman (d. 1930), a younger son of another ironmaster, Sir Alfred Hickman, Bt., of Wightwick Hall on Tinacre Hill, and Conservative M.P. for Wolverhampton South (1910–18) and Bilston (1918–22).[88] His widow was still living at the Hall in 1932.[89] From the mid 1930s until 1961 it was owned by J. L. Swanson (d. 1974), a director of Wolverhampton and Dudley Breweries Ltd.[90] The Hall and c. 7 a., after being sold in 1961 for conversion into a hotel, were bought in 1963 by Sir Alfred McAlpine & Son Ltd., builders and civil engineers. The firm moved its Wolverhampton office there in 1964 and 1965 and bought c. 47 a. of adjoining land in stages.[91]

In 1086 a villein held ½ hide at *WIGHTWICK* in the king's manor of Tettenhall.[92] The ½ hide may have formed the nucleus of the small estate centred on Wightwick which was held from the 13th century or earlier by a family which took its name from Wightwick.[93] Although Humphrey Wightwick was declared 'ignobilis' by the heralds in 1583, his son Francis styled himself gentleman in 1586 and was accepted as such by the heralds in 1614.[94] He died in 1616 and his son Alexander in 1659. Alexander's son Francis had bought an estate at Dunstall, in Wolverhampton, and after 1659 no head of the family lived at Wightwick. Francis was succeeded in 1692 by his son Francis and he c. 1697 by his son, another Francis (d. 1714), whose son, another Francis, died while still a minor in 1715 and was succeeded by his brothers Hancox (d. 1731) and James in turn. James died unmarried in 1749, leaving his property to a nephew, John Wightwick.[95] In 1780 John held 485 a. on the high ground north of Smestow brook and along the road from Wightwick to Wergs.[96] He had already sold land in Tettenhall in the 1760s;[97] following a family settlement of 1814 John, by then of Sandgates, in Chertsey (Surr.), and his son Francis disposed of most of their remaining property in the parish.[98] Wightwick Hall on Wightwick Bank was bought with 98 a. in 1815 by P. T. and Josiah Hinckes and became part of the Hinckes estate in Tettenhall.[99]

In 1887 Wightwick Hall and some surround-ing land was bought by Theodore Mander, a partner in Mander Bros., a Wolverhampton firm which made paint, varnish, and printing-inks.[1] Near the Hall Mander built a large new house, Wightwick Manor. He was succeeded in 1900 by his son Geoffrey, who in 1937 presented Wightwick Manor and 17 a. of land to the National Trust. Geoffrey (later Sir Geoffrey), who was Liberal M.P. for Wolverhampton East 1929–45, continued to live at the Manor until his death in 1962. His widow was living there in 1980.

Wightwick Manor is a timber-framed house designed by Edward Ould; the range facing the entrance drive and the west end of the garden front date from 1887 and the east end of the garden front from 1893. Theodore Mander furnished and decorated the house under the influence of Ruskin and Morris; many of the furnishings were supplied by Morris's own firm, and there is work by C. E. Kempe and L. A. Shuffrey. Pictures and furnishings, mostly by Morris and the Pre-Raphaelites or reflecting their taste, have been added to Theodore's collections by Sir Geoffrey and Lady Mander and by the National Trust. The gardens were laid out by Alfred Parsons; the terrace on the south front was added c. 1910 to the design of T. H. Mawson.

Wightwick Hall was a brick house of the late 16th or early 17th century and probably had a central range and two cross wings. Only the western portion, containing one wing and part of the centre, survives. Behind there is a range of the same period which may have contained stables. Both buildings were heavily restored by Ould when he built the Manor.

The manor of *TETTENHALL CLERICORUM* belonged to the college of Tettenhall in the Middle Ages with the dean as lord of the manor. The name, however, seems to have come into use only in the early 16th century; the previous style was the fee of the church or of the clerks of Tettenhall.[2] A local jury stated in 1401 that King Edgar (957–75) had endowed the college with 100 a. and 10s. rent in Tettenhall.[3] The earliest reference to its property is in 1086 when the priests held a hide in Tettenhall and another in Bilbrook.[4] The manor extended north and north-east from the area round the church to include Aldersley and Barnhurst as well as Bilbrook; a stone on Old Hill still marked the

[86] Jones, *Tettenhall*, 56–7; G. T. Lawley, *Hist. of Bilston* (Bilston, 1893), 153; *Staffs. Advertiser*, 4 Apr. 1885; *V.C.H. Staffs.* v. 147.

[87] Jones, *Tettenhall*, 57; *Kelly's Dir. Staffs.* (1888 and later edns. to 1904); *Staffs. Advertiser*, 22 Feb. 1890, 4 May 1907.

[88] *Kelly's Dir. Staffs.* (1908; 1912); *Staffs. and some neighbouring records: historical, biographical, and pictorial* [1910], 197–9; Burke, *Peerage* (1970), 1332.

[89] *Kelly's Dir. Staffs.* (1932).

[90] Ibid. (1936); *Express & Star*, 31 Jan. 1963; *Who's Who* (1974); ibid. (1975), intro. p. 36.

[91] *Express & Star*, 9 Nov. 1961, 31 Jan. 1963; inf. from Sir Alfred McAlpine & Son (Southern) Ltd. (1981).

[92] *V.C.H. Staffs.* iv. 38. The royal manor of 'Wightwick' to which Kingswood belonged in 1271 (*S.H.C.* v (1), 144) was evidently Tettenhall; in 1371 Wightwick and Kingswood apparently formed together a recognized fiscal or administrative unit in the manor: *Cal. Close*, 1369–74, 356.

[93] Shaw, *Staffs.* ii. 201; Jones, *Tettenhall*, 46–9. Neither gives a completely satisfactory pedigree of the Wightwick family: Mander, *Wolverhampton Antiquary*, i. 298.

[94] S.R.O., D. 593/C/8/2/4; *S.H.C.* iii (2), 16; v (2), 313.

[95] Mander, *Wolverhampton Antiquary*, i. 298–304.

[96] S.R.O., D. 1018/2; W.S.L., Fac. 112 (copy of lost map of John Wightwick's estate in Tettenhall and Penn, 1762).

[97] S.R.O., D. 3160/10/8.

[98] Mander, *Wolverhampton Antiquary*, i. 302; S.R.O., D. 3160/10/7.

[99] S.R.O., D. 3160/12/5; below (Tettenhall Wood House).

[1] For the next three paras. see M. Girouard, *Victorian Country House* (1979 edn.), 375–80; Pevsner, *Staffs.* 310–11; *Wightwick Manor* (National Trust, 1973 edn.); *Country Life* (1963), 1242–5, 1316–19; above, pl. facing p. 16. Lady Mander is thanked for her help.

[2] e.g. *S.H.C.* v (1), 168–9; S.R.O., D. 593/A/2/16/3, 6; D. 3160/9/6. The heading 'Tettenhale Clericorum' in *S.H.C.* vii (1), 254, should read 'Tenentes Clericorum' or 'Tenentibus Clericorum': *S.H.C.* 4th ser. vi. 25.

[3] *Cal. Inq. Misc.* vii, p. 82.

[4] *V.C.H. Staffs.* iv. 28, 45. The entries appear under the land of the clerks of Wolverhampton, but clearly the clerks of Tettenhall are meant.

boundary with Tettenhall Regis manor in 1804.[5] The college was dissolved in 1548, and in 1549 Tettenhall Clericorum was sold with most of its property to Walter Wrottesley.[6] The manor then descended in the Wrottesley family with Wrottesley manor, a court still being held in 1814.[7]

Five prebends were mentioned in the mid 1250s; four were named in 1269 as Tettenhall, Pendeford, Perton, and Wrottesley, and the fifth in 1304 as Codsall. Tettenhall prebend was later called Tettenhall and Compton and was known simply as Compton by 1373. Although the name Compton was still in use in 1401, the prebend was also styled Bovenhill by 1398 and that became its accepted name.[8] The prebendal estates lay intermingled and not confined to the part of the parish from which they were named; thus the prebendaries of Pendeford, Wrottesley, and Codsall all had land in Aldersley.[9] All prebendaries had manorial jurisdiction by the late Middle Ages, but the dean as lord of Tettenhall Clericorum exercised a superior jurisdiction over the prebendal manors.[10] In 1535 the prebends of Bovenhill and Perton each possessed a manor house.[11] All five manors passed to Walter Wrottesley in 1549.[12]

In the same year Walter Wrottesley received licence to convey the prebendal manors of *BOVENHILL* and *PENDEFORD* to Henry Southwick and to Richard Cresswell of Barnhurst, who was already the lessee of both prebends. Nothing further is known of the Southwick share. Cresswell held the manor courts in 1553 and had half of both manors at his death in 1559. His son held a joint court for the two manors in 1576. The manors remained in the Cresswell family until the 1720s, descending with Barnhurst. At some time between 1723 and 1726 Richard Cresswell of Rudge and Sidbury (Salop.) sold them to Samuel Hellier of the Wodehouse in Wombourne. They then descended with the Wodehouse, and a joint court was still held for the two prebendal manors in 1912.[13]

In 1549 Walter Wrottesley sold the prebendal manor of *PERTON* to his nephew Edward Leveson, lord of half the other manor of Perton. The prebendal estate then descended with that manor but was apparently retained by the Levesons when the main manor was sold to Sir Walter Wrottesley in 1664. The Leveson-Gowers continued to hold the tithes of Perton until 1795 when the marquess of Stafford exchanged them with Sir John Wrottesley for those of Codsall.[14]

The prebendal manors of *CODSALL* and *WROTTESLEY* were already held by Walter

Wrottesley as tenant when he bought the college estate in 1549. They seem thereafter to have been administered as part of Tettenhall Clericorum manor.[15]

In 1535 each of the prebendaries enjoyed the great and small tithes of his prebend.[16] After the Dissolution the tithes descended with the prebendal estates, but by the 19th century much had been sold. In 1840 the great and small tithes of Wightwick, Bilbrook, and Kingswood, owned by Lord Wrottesley, were commuted for rent charges of £110, £60 5s., and £32 10s. respectively. In 1849 the townships of Tettenhall, Perton, and Wrottesley were stated to be by prescription subject to the payment of great tithes only. By then much of the great tithe had been merged with the lands from which it arose; the rest was owned by 27 people and was that year commuted for rent charges ranging from £150 to 12s. 6d. In 1850 and 1852 twenty-five of the owners merged the rent charges with their lands, and in 1853 rent charges of £10 and £6 2s. 6d. were assigned to the two remaining owners.[17]

The holding in Tettenhall Clericorum manor known in the later 18th century as *ALDERSLEY UPPER FARM* or Aldersley Large Farm (to distinguish it from the nearby Lower or Small Farm)[18] seems to have originated between 1367 and 1385, when members of the Wilkes family acquired land at Aldersley and moved there from Wightwick. The early descent of the property is obscure; at least two households were involved, and their lands were intermingled. A Roger Wilkes of Aldersley occurs from 1385 to 1398 and his son Henry from 1410 to 1414, a William Wilkes of Aldersley from 1398 to 1411 and his son Roger from 1410 to 1418.[19] There was a John Wilkes of Aldersley in 1444,[20] possibly the John Wilkes who acted as an attorney for two Staffordshire landowners in 1469 and 1480.[21] A Richard Wilkes of Willenhall married the daughter and heir of a Wilkes of Aldersley and held land in Tettenhall in 1444.[22] His son William, also of Willenhall, held land at Aldersley in 1460.[23] He was active as an advocate from the 1460s, was a J.P. from 1484, and was almost certainly the William Wilkes who was second prothonotary of the court of Common Pleas from 1487 to 1498. In his will, proved in 1507, he devised land at Aldersley to his son Richard.[24] The land was presumably that which in 1483–4 William leased to Thomas Wilkes of Aldersley, probably a cousin. Thomas, who had held land in the prebends of Perton and Bovenhill in 1473 and

[5] For Aldersley and Barnhurst see below; for the stone see S.R.O., D. 3160/9/6.
[6] V.C.H. Staffs. iii. 319–20.
[7] Below, local govt.
[8] V.C.H. Staffs. iii. 317–18 and nn. For a canon of Tettenhall described as rector of Codsall about the mid 13th century see S.H.C. n.s. vi (2), 36; S.R.O., D. 593/A/2/18/1.
[9] H.W.R.O. (H.), B 47/S24; S.R.O., D. 3160/9/6, deeds of 26 Apr. 1507, 26 Aug. 1508, 19 Nov. 1532.
[10] Below, local govt.
[11] Valor Eccl. iii. 105.
[12] V.C.H. Staffs. iii. 320.
[13] Ibid.; P.R.O., C 142/127/49; S.R.O., Tp. 1226, folder 2 and parcel A; Wolv. C.L., D/MAN/15 and DX/49; below (Barnhurst); Wombourne, manors and other estates.
[14] S.R.O., D. 593/A/2/14/4, 5, 8; D. 593/C/6/1/6; D. 593/

C/8/1/3; D. 593/C/8/2/16; D. 593/G/1/1/13, 18; D. 593/1/2/ 4A; below (Perton); Codsall, manors and other estates.
[15] V.C.H. Staffs. iii. 320; S.R.O., D. 3160/9/6, deed of 5 Apr. 1576.   [16] Valor Eccl. iii. 105.
[17] L.J.R.O., B/A/15/Tettenhall.
[18] Shaw, Staffs. ii. 201; S.R.O., D. 678/15/3.
[19] H.W.R.O. (H.), B 47/S3.
[20] S.H.C. n.s. vi (2), 211.
[21] S.H.C. n.s. iv. 167; S.H.C. n.s. vi (1), 130.
[22] Shaw, Staffs. ii. 149; S.H.C. n.s. vi (2), 211.
[23] S.H.C. n.s. iv. 116–17.
[24] Ibid. 120, 145; S.H.C. n.s. vi (1), 92, 106, 128–9, 134, 138, 143, 155–6, 160–1; S.H.C. 1912, 316, 318; Spelman's Reps. ii (Selden Soc. xciv), 377; Mander, Wolverhampton Antiquary, i. 34–7, modifying the biography of Wm. given in S.H.C. 1917–18, 270–1.

1481, died in or before 1507; he was succeeded by his son William, to whom in 1508 and 1509 George, another son of the justice, conveyed land at Aldersley, probably that mentioned in his father's will.[25] William died in 1521 and was succeeded by his son Thomas, who held land at Aldersley in 1547.[26] It seems that by 1569 Thomas had been succeeded by his son Richard, who made a feoffment of part of the property in 1576.[27] By 1589 land at Aldersley was held by Thomas Wilkes, perhaps Richard's brother Thomas who occurs in settlements of 1539 and 1547. Thomas, who was a presentment juror for Seisdon hundred regularly between 1589 and 1606,[28] died in 1612 and was succeeded by his son Richard.[29] Richard died in 1655, and his eldest son Thomas inherited the Aldersley property;[30] he was assessed on seven hearths there in 1666.[31] A younger son, Edward, who moved to Albrighton (Salop.), was great-grandfather of John Wilkes the politician.[32] Thomas Wilkes died in 1694[33] and was succeeded by his son William. In 1710 William purchased 27 a. at Aldersley and Pendeford and bought exemption from tithes on all his property in the parish.[34] He died in 1726 and was succeeded by his son William, who died in 1734.[35] The younger William was described in 1734 as 'of Aldersley, yeoman'. His daughter Elizabeth Booth was grandmother of the actor Junius Brutus Booth; the actor cherished his Wilkes ancestry and his relationship to the politician, after whom he named his son John Wilkes Booth, the assassin of Abraham Lincoln.[36] Before 1750 William's widow Elizabeth, although apparently still living in Tettenhall, had leased the family farm to Richard and Barnet Wilkes, possibly her brothers-in-law Richard and Bernard Wilkes. In 1751 she and her son William sold their Tettenhall property, which then consisted of the farmhouse at Aldersley and 138 a. of land, part freehold and part copyhold, to Peter Hinckes of Wolverhampton.[37] In 1761 Hinckes bought the other farm at Aldersley,[38] and in 1780 his property in the parish, which included several smaller purchases, amounted to some 222 a.[39] In 1781 Hinckes was succeeded by his nephew Peter Tichborne Hinckes, who settled at Tettenhall Wood. The land at Aldersley remained in the Hinckes family until the late 19th century.[40] In 1980 the house belonging to Lower Farm still stood on the east side of Aldersley Road; the

house of Upper Farm on the opposite side had been demolished.

An estate at *BARNHURST* held of the canons of Tettenhall existed by the later 13th century, when a William son of Alfred of Barnhurst held land in the fields of Cronkhall.[41] William may have been the father of the Henry of Barnhurst who was a juror for Tettenhall liberty in 1307.[42] He or another Henry of Barnhurst was one of the principal tenants of the canons in 1327 and 1332;[43] he may have been the father of the John Barnhurst who was in the entourage of Sir Hugh Wrottesley in 1337 and 1344.[44] A John son of John Barnhurst witnessed a Wrottesley charter in 1349 and bought land at Barnhurst and elsewhere in the parish in 1353.[45] A John Barnhurst was a poll-tax collector for Tettenhall in 1377;[46] he may be the John Barnhurst the elder who occurs in 1391.[47] Another John Barnhurst, aged thirty or more in 1388, was the nephew of Sir John Perton, lord of Perton, from whom he inherited the manor of Trysull; when he alienated it in 1396 he did so as John Barnhurst the younger, so presumably John the elder was still alive.[48] The two men may have been uncle and nephew: in 1391 it was stated that during the minority of John the younger John the elder had held his socage lands, while John the younger was probably the John Barnhurst, son of Richard Barnhurst, who executed feoffments of property at Barnhurst between 1407 and 1419.[49] A John Barnhurst, probably the son of John son of Richard, held Barnhurst in 1442 and may be the John Barnhurst who was alive in 1463.[50] By 1512 Barnhurst was held by Joan Milston, daughter and heir of a John Barnhurst.[51] In 1521 she sold her manor or messuage of Barnhurst, consisting of a house and 70 a. of land held of the prebendaries of Perton and Bovenhill, to James Leveson of Wolverhampton.[52] Leveson also acquired other land in the parish which had formerly been held with Barnhurst,[53] and at his death in 1547 he held a house and c. 150 a. at Barnhurst of the canons of Tettenhall.[54]

In 1524 Richard Cresswell of Bilbrook quit-claimed to James Leveson all his rights in the Barnhurst property.[55] The nature of those rights is not clear. The Levesons later granted the Barnhurst estate to the Cresswells, who were paying James's descendants a fee-farm rent of £2 for it in the late 16th century and in the 1650s.[56] The date

---

[25] H.W.R.O. (H.), B 47/S3; S.R.O., D. 3160/9/6.
[26] B.L. Stowe Ch. 631; H.W.R.O. (H.), B 47/S3.
[27] H.W.R.O. (H.), B 47/S3; S.R.O., D. 3160/9/6.
[28] *S.H.C.* 1929, 344, 349–50; *S.H.C.* 1930, 1932, 1935, 1940, *passim*; *S.H.C.* 1948–9, 90, 118. For the settlements see S.R.O., D. 3160/9/6; H.W.R.O. (H.), B 47/S3.
[29] *Tettenhall Par. Reg.* i. 195; S.R.O., D. 3160/9/6.
[30] *Tettenhall Par. Reg.* i. 223. For the relationship see ibid. 6; S.R.O., D. 3160/9/6.   [31] *S.H.C.* 1923, 104.
[32] C. Chenevix Trench, *Portrait of a Patriot*, 375, correcting the account of John Wilkes's ancestry given in *D.N.B.*
[33] *Tettenhall Par. Reg.* i. 245.
[34] S.R.O., D. 3160/10/3.
[35] *Tettenhall Par. Reg.* i. 266; S.R.O., D. 1364/1/2.
[36] S.R.O., D. 3160/10/3; A. F. Booth, *The Elder and the Younger Booth* (Boston, U.S.A. [1882]), 3–8; *D.N.B.* s.v. Booth, Junius Brutus.
[37] S.R.O., D. 3160/10/3.
[38] S.R.O., D. 3160/10/1.
[39] S.R.O., D. 1018/2. For smaller purchases see e.g. S.R.O., D. 3160/10/8.

[40] Shaw, *Staffs.* ii. 201; W.S.L., Sale Cat. F/3/20; below (Tettenhall Wood House).
[41] S.R.O., D. 593/A/2/16/1.
[42] *S.H.C.* vii (1), 173.
[43] Ibid. 255; *S.H.C.* x (1), 131.
[44] *S.H.C.* N.S. vi (2), 157–8, 160. The suggestion (Jones, *Tettenhall*, 84) that John was steward of the deanery manor and that Barnhurst was the manor house and tithe barn of that manor is unlikely.
[45] *S.H.C.* N.S. vi (2), 162; S.R.O., D. 593/A/2/16/3.
[46] *S.H.C.* 4th ser. vi. 8.
[47] *S.H.C.* xv. 32, 41.
[48] *Cal. Inq. p.m.* xvi, p. 293; *S.H.C.* xi. 202.
[49] *S.H.C.* xv. 32, 41; S.R.O., D. 593/A/2/16/6–7.
[50] S.R.O., D. 593/A/2/16/2; *S.H.C.* N.S. vi (2), 209.
[51] S.R.O., D. 593/A/2/16/12; A/2/17/2.
[52] Ibid. A/2/17/2, 4–7, 12.
[53] Ibid. A/2/17/3, 8.
[54] S.R.O., D. 593/C/4, inq. p.m. of Jas. Leveson (Staffs.), ff. 9–10.   [55] S.R.O., D. 593/A/2/17/9.
[56] S.R.O., D. 593/G/1/1/14, f. 26; G/1/1/15, f. 26; P/3/2.

of the grant is uncertain; it may have been the lease of Barnhurst dated 1559 which Richard Cresswell of Barnhurst, a merchant of the staple, bequeathed to his wife on his death that year.[57] Richard's son, also Richard and a merchant of the staple, died in 1612,[58] and the younger Richard's son Richard in 1625.[59] In 1658 the third Richard's son, another Richard, married Anne Lee, heir of Roland Purslow of Sidbury (Salop.),[60] and thereafter the Cresswell family's interests lay chiefly outside Staffordshire.[61] Some of Richard Cresswell's relatives seem to have lived at the house at Barnhurst until the 1680s or 1690s, perhaps as tenants; afterwards no member of the family lived there.[62] Richard Cresswell was succeeded in 1708 by his second son Richard (d. 1723), whose son Richard (d. 1743) sold Barnhurst to Samuel Hellier of the Wodehouse in Wombourne, probably between 1723 and 1726 when he sold him Bovenhill and Pendeford prebends.[63] The estate, 273 a. in 1780,[64] descended with the Wodehouse until 1867, when Wolverhampton corporation bought what was described as the Barnhurst estate and Little Barnhurst, in all c. 300 a., from Thomas Shaw-Hellier. The corporation bought the land in connexion with its first major sewerage scheme, and by 1870 a sewage works had been opened on part of the land.[65] The corporation farmed the other land until 1975.[66]

The present Barnhurst Farm dates from 1963 and replaced a house on a nearby moated site which was then demolished. The older house included a brick block of six bays, evidently dating from the 18th century; a lower service range may have been the remains of a timber-framed house.[67] In 1666 the house was assessed at 11 hearths.[68] A three-bay brick gatehouse dated 1602, with two storeys and attics, was demolished in 1961.[69] A large octagonal brick dovecot of the 16th or 17th century remained in 1980, although derelict.

The manor of *KINGSLEY*, known by the 17th century as Kingsley otherwise Kinfare, extended south-west from Old Hill to Mill Lane, Wightwick Bank, and Smestow brook between Wightwick and Compton. The area included Kingsley Wood, a detached portion of Kinver forest, and the manor seems to have originated as an outlying part of Kinver manor. In 1293 John FitzPhilip, lord of Kinver and keeper of Kinver forest, successfully asserted his right to 5 a. in Tettenhall as part of Kinver manor. Kingsley descended with Kinver manor. In 1831 the area was 219 a., of which 157 a. were copyhold. Courts were held until 1919; by then most of the copyhold land had been enfranchised.[70]

Before 1763 Thomas Pearson bought land on the edge of the waste south-west of Tettenhall village within Kingsley manor; he was the son and heir of Edward Pearson of Wolverhampton who held land in the manor. By 1763 Thomas had built a house there, the later *TETTENHALL TOWERS*, said to incorporate part of an inn called the Holly Bush.[71] By 1853 the estate consisted of 104 a. lying along the slope south-west of Tettenhall as far as Compton and extending across Henwood Road to the canal and Smestow brook.[72] Pearson died in 1796. His son John (d. 1841) was advocate-general of Bengal 1824–40, and John's son Lt.-Gen. Thomas Hooke Pearson (d. 1892), a distinguished cavalry officer, spent his active military career in India.[73] The house meanwhile was let.[74] T. H. Pearson sold most of the estate in 1853 and 1854, but at his death in 1892 he still owned property around Compton, which passed to his son G. J. H. Pearson. In 1854 the house was bought by Thomas Thorneycroft, a Wolverhampton ironmaster, who had been tenant from 1851 and became one of the most influential residents of Tettenhall.[75] After his death in 1903 his widow and daughters continued to live in the house.[76] In 1944 Florence Thorneycroft, his surviving daughter, sold it with 26½ a. to Tettenhall College, which had been opened in a neighbouring villa in 1863.[77]

The house built for Thomas Pearson by 1763 was described as Grecian in style; the grounds were planted to take advantage of the landscape.[78] Apparently remodelled in the earlier 19th century, the house was greatly extended by Thomas Thorneycroft. By 1880 it had a four-storeyed tower and a private theatre with 500 seats and various special effects. By 1888 the house was called Tettenhall Towers. In the grounds Thorneycroft built racquet courts, a swimming

---

[57] W.S.L. 45/24/56, will of Ric. Cresswell.
[58] Burke, *Land. Gent.* (1969), ii. 119.
[59] *Tettenhall Par. Reg.* i. 203. Burke, op. cit. 119, wrongly gives 1626 as date of death.
[60] Burke, op. cit. 119, wrongly dating marriage 1657; *Tettenhall Par. Reg.* i. 159.
[61] See e.g. Burke, op. cit. 119; *V.C.H. Salop.* iii. 258, 277.
[62] *S.H.C.* 1923, 111; Wolv. C.L., D/MAN/15.
[63] Burke, op. cit. 119; Wolv. C.L., D/MAN/15; above (Bovenhill and Pendeford prebends).
[64] S.R.O., D. 1018/2.
[65] J. P. Barnes, 'Sewage Disposal in Wolverhampton' (duplicated 1963; copy in Wolv. C.L.), pp. 5–6; *Staffs. Advertiser*, 15 June, 14 Sept., 19 Oct., 14 Dec. 1867; Wolverhampton Civic Centre, deed bdle. A/27, deed of 22 Mar. 1870.
[66] Inf. from Mr. A. Hodgkins of Wolverhampton, formerly farm manager (1980).
[67] Below, pl. facing p. 65; Jones, *Tettenhall*, 89; inf. from Mr. Hodgkins.
[68] *S.H.C.* 1923, 111.
[69] Shaw, *Staffs.* ii. 202; J. P. Jones, *Heart of the Midlands* (Wolverhampton, n.d. but 1906), 90, with photograph.

[70] P.R.O., MR 308; H.W.R.O. (H.), E 12/S, Kinver Manor; ibid. Kingsley ct. bk. 1861–1930 and 1831 terrier; *V.C.H. Staffs.* ii. 344; *S.H.C.* v (1), 258; below, econ. hist.; local govt.
[71] Jones, *Tettenhall*, 268–9; *St. James's Chron.* 17–19 Feb. 1763; 'Old Inns and Beerhouses', *A. Webb's Parish Almanack for Tettenhall and Tettenhall Wood* (1892); H.W.R.O. (H.), E 12/S, Kinver and Kingsley ct. bk. 1767–1801, cts. of 12 Dec. 1767, 25 Aug. 1795. Mr. G. V. Hancock of Tettenhall College is thanked for his help with this section.
[72] S.R.O., D. 755/4/15–16.
[73] B. Robinson, *Genealog. Memoirs of Fam. of Brooke Robinson of Dudley* (priv. print. 1896), 121–3; *D.N.B.* s.v. Pearson, T. H.
[74] Jones, *Tettenhall*, 269–70, 274–8.
[75] S.R.O., D. 755/4/15, 16, 21; *Staffs. Advertiser*, 26 Aug. 1854; Jones, *Tettenhall*, 270.
[76] *Kelly's Dir. Staffs.* (1904 and later edns.); Thorneycroft gravestone in St. Michael's churchyard.
[77] G. V. Hancock, *Hist. of Tettenhall Coll.* (Tettenhall, priv. print. 1963), 12–13, 179.
[78] R. Warner, *Tour through the Northern Counties of Eng. and the Borders of Scotland* (1802), ii. 200.

TETTENHALL TOWERS IN 1880

bath, and Turkish and salt-water baths. He was an amateur technologist, and his inventions, of which he listed thirty in 1902, were largely domestic and sanitary. The devices in his house included a lift, telegraphic communication between the dining room and the smoking room in the tower, and signalling equipment at the top of the tower.[79] Tettenhall College adapted the house for school purposes and used the grounds for new playing fields and new buildings. In 1970 the stables were converted into a library.[80]

Peter Tichborne Hinckes, who inherited property at Aldersley and elsewhere in Tettenhall from his uncle Peter Hinckes in 1781, had settled by 1784 at a house in Tettenhall Wood in Kingsley manor.[81] He died in 1822, and his property passed to his brother the Revd. Josiah Hinckes (d. 1830), whose daughter Theodosia inherited *c.* 390 a. in Tettenhall.[82] In 1835 she built a new house at Tettenhall Wood, a castellated Gothic villa designed by Thomas Rickman which became known as *TETTENHALL WOOD HOUSE.* [83] Theodosia, a traveller and collector and the founder of St. Mary's church in Wolverhampton,[84] died in 1874. She settled her property in trust for the children of her third cousin, John Davenport (d. 1862) of Westwood,

in Leek,[85] and left the house for life to her friends and travelling companions Henry Moore (d. 1876), archdeacon of Stafford, and his wife Rebecca (d. 1883).[86] The house and grounds then passed to H. T. Davenport, John Davenport's second surviving son. Davenport, Conservative M.P. for North Staffordshire (1880–5) and Leek (1886–92), changed his surname to Hinckes in 1890. On his death in 1895 the Hinckes estate in Tettenhall and Bushbury, excluding the house and its grounds, was put up for auction.[87] By 1900 Samuel Bayliss, a Wolverhampton industrialist, was living at the house, which he still occupied in 1912.[88] By 1915 it had passed to V. E. Hickman, a younger son of Sir Alfred Hickman, Bt., of Wightwick Hall.[89] He died in 1935, leaving his widow Ethel Margaret a life tenancy of the house and 91 a. or more. Tettenhall urban district council bought 24 a. in 1946 and built a housing estate there. In 1953 it bought another 51 a. for housing, with an option on the house and a further 16 a. when Mrs. Hickman died or left.[90] She died aged 103 in 1969 and the house and land passed to Wolverhampton corporation as successor to the urban district council.[91] The house was demolished, and houses and a school were built on the land.

[79] Pevsner, *Staffs.* 326; *The Builder*, 24 Jan. 1880; *Kelly's Dir. Staffs.* (1888); booklet of 1902 issued to the press on the occasion of a visit to Tettenhall Towers (copy in W.S.L. Pamphs.). For his fire brigade see below, p. 39.
[80] *V.C.H. Staffs.* vi. 172.
[81] Shaw, *Staffs.* ii. 201; S.R.O., D. 678/15/2–3; D. 3160/10/2.
[82] S.R.O., D. 678/15/4; D. 3160/13/1.
[83] W.S.L., Sale Cat. F/3/16; *Staffs. Advertiser*, 13 Aug. 1836.
[84] *Lich. Dioc. Mag.* 1887, 110; G. P. Mander and N. W. Tildesley, *Hist. of Wolverhampton*, 178.
[85] *Staffs. Advertiser*, 9 May 1874; S.R.O., D. 678/19. For the relationship see S.R.O., D. 3160/13/1; Burke, *Land. Gent.*

(1952), 641; *Staffs. Advertiser*, 22 June 1895.
[86] *Staffs. Advertiser*, 22 July 1876; *Lich. Dioc. Ch. Cal.* (1884), 355; *Lich. Dioc. Mag.* 1887, 110; *Trans. Lich. Arch. & Hist. Soc.* ii. 7–29.
[87] *Staffs. Advertiser*, 22 Nov. 1890, 30 June 1894, 23 Mar., 22 June 1895; W.S.L., Sale Cats. F/3/16, 20.
[88] *Kelly's Dir. Staffs.* (1900; 1912); obituary in *Staffs. Advertiser*, 26 Mar. 1932.
[89] *Kelly's Handbk. to Titled, Landed, and Official Classes* (1915), 741. For Hickman and his wife see Burke, *Peerage* (1970), 1333.
[90] Wolv. Civic Centre, deed bdle. Tett./79, deed of 5 Jan. 1955; *Express & Star*, 4 Mar. 1952, 7 July 1953.
[91] *Express & Star*, 1 Apr., 13 June 1969.

In 1066 *PENDEFORD* was held by two free men, Ulstan and Godwin. In 1086 William Fitz-Ansculf, lord of Dudley, held 2 hides there.[92] The overlordship then descended with the barony of Dudley. By the later 13th century the overlords treated the manor administratively as belonging to their manor of Sedgley.[93] In 1323 the barony was divided after the death of John, Lord Somery: Sedgley and the overlordship of Pendeford fell to his elder sister Margaret and her husband, John de Sutton.[94] The overlordship then descended in the Sutton (later Sutton or Dudley) family until 1538.[95]

In the 1250s there was a mesne tenant, Alan of Erdington.[96] He was probably a member of the family which held Erdington, in Aston (Warws.), of the lords of Dudley;[97] he may, however, have been the Alan of Eardington (or de Haya) who in the earlier 13th century was a minor landowner in Eardington (Salop.).[98] About 1250 Alan was receiving 20s. a year from the terre tenant at Pendeford in lieu of all services; by the early 1260s the tenant had redeemed all but 12d. of the rent.[99] A further payment may have extinguished Alan's interest in the manor; there is no further reference to a mesne tenancy.

Almar held the manor of William FitzAnsculf in 1086.[1] In the 1250s the terre tenant was Robert of Pendeford. He was the son of another Robert of Pendeford,[2] probably the man of that name living in the early 1220s.[3] By 1271, and probably by 1268, the younger Robert had been succeeded by his son John.[4] John got into financial difficulties,[5] and in 1277 he sold Pendeford to the priory of St. Thomas near Stafford.[6] The priory's interest in Pendeford may have come through the Warwickshire Erdingtons: Giles of Erdington, dean of the collegiate church of Wolverhampton, and lord of Erdington from the early 13th century until his death in 1268, was a benefactor to the priory.[7]

The priory was surrendered to the Crown in 1538. In 1539 its property was granted in fee to Rowland Lee, bishop of Coventry and Lichfield, and on his death in 1543 it was divided among the sons of his sister Sibyl Fowler. Pendeford fell to James Fowler (d. 1584), M.P. for Stafford in 1558.[8] He was succeeded by his son Walter (d. 1647), and the estate continued to pass from father to son until 1752: Walter (d. 1668); Walter (d. 1711); Charles (d. 1731); and Richard (d. 1752).[9] It was held by Richard's widow Dorothy until her death in 1764 and then passed to his nephew Thomas Fowler (d. 1796); Thomas was succeeded by his son Thomas Leversage Fowler (d. 1815).[10] The estate covered 917 a. in 1780 and 937 a. in 1813.[11] T. L. Fowler's eldest son,

TETTENHALL TOWERS: THE MUSIC ROOM

Thomas, died unmarried in 1851 and Pendeford passed to his brother Richard (d. 1864), who had taken the surname Fowler-Butler in 1824 on succeeding to the Barton Hall estate in Tatenhill. Richard's elder son, Richard Owen Wynne Fowler-Butler, was succeeded in 1865 by his half-brother Robert Henry Fowler-Butler (d. 1919), later a major-general, who in 1893 sold c. 160 a. of the estate lying south and east of Pendeford Farm to Wolverhampton corporation for the enlargement of its sewage farm. The major-general's son Lt.-Col. Richard Fowler-Butler died in 1931, leaving a widow Caroline Anne who sold the rest of the estate to Wolverhampton corporation in 1935. The estate then covered c. 734 a., mostly in the parishes of Brewood and Bushbury. After the Second World War the corporation sold some of the land.[12]

Pendeford Hall stood west of the present Pendeford Hall Lane. The house of eight hearths which was there in 1666 was rebuilt in 1670. The new house, for which the local sandstone was

[92] *V.C.H. Staffs.* iv. 55.
[93] *S.H.C.* ix (2), 28; W.S.L. 35/2/49, no. 16.
[94] *Complete Peerage*, xii (1), 114–15; *S.H.C.* ix (2), 52–3.
[95] *S.H.C.* 1913, 120; *Valor Eccl.* iii. 111; below.
[96] *S.H.C.* v (1), 109.
[97] *V.C.H. Warws.* vii. 63; W. Dugdale, *Antiquities of Warws.* (1730 edn.), ii. 889–90. Neither, however, mentions an Alan in the Erdington pedigree.
[98] Eyton, *Shropshire*, i. 63–4, 123–4.
[99] W.S.L. 35/2/49, nos. 1–2.
[1] *V.C.H. Staffs.* iv. 55.
[2] *S.H.C.* v (1), 109; W.S.L. 35/2/49, nos. 1–2.
[3] *S.H.C.* iv (1), 10, 19.
[4] Ibid. 186; *S.H.C.* v (1), 152; *S.H.C.* N.S. vi (2), 43.
[5] W.S.L. 35/1/49, no. 23; 35/2/49, no. 6.

[6] W.S.L. 35/2/49, nos. 7, 8B, 16; *V.C.H. Staffs.* iii. 263.
[7] *V.C.H. Staffs.* iii. 263; *V.C.H. Warws.* vii. 63; Dugdale, *Warws.* ii. 889–90.
[8] *V.C.H. Staffs.* iii. 266; P.R.O., C 142/208, no. 209; W.S.L. 35/3A/49; Shaw, *Staffs.* ii. 202; *S.H.C.* 1917–18, 351 (wrongly dating his death 1585).
[9] *Tettenhall Par. Reg.* i. 216, 229, 256, 271; S.R.O., D. 1364/1/2; Jones, *Tettenhall*, 98–9.
[10] W.S.L. 35/4/49, deeds of 9 and 10 June 1764; S.R.O., D. 1364/1/2; Jones, *Tettenhall*, 97.
[11] S.R.O., D. 1018/2; W.S.L. 35/7/49.
[12] Burke, *Land. Gent.* (1894), i. 699; *Kelly's Handbk. to Titled, Landed, and Official Classes* (1915; 1931; 1935); Wolv. Civic Centre, deed bdles. D/5 and AA12; inf. from Wolv. Boro. Dept. of Environmental and Technical Services (1980).

used, was a two-storeyed, double-depth building in a semi-classical style, with a south façade of five bays with a central pedimented doorway and Dutch gables. It was altered *c.* 1800 when the roof was raised and the gables were removed.[13] After being requisitioned during the Second World War it was partly demolished in 1953; what remained was demolished in 1968.[14]

Between 1062 and 1066, probably in 1065, Edward the Confessor gave *PERTON* to Westminster abbey; the grant may have confirmed or extended an earlier gift to the abbey by the king's chamberlain Hugelin. Before 1068 William I confirmed the monks' title.[15] In 1086 the manor was assessed at 3 hides; it was one of 13 manors on the abbey's estates where a demesne existed.[16] The abbey still held Perton in 1162.[17] It was afterwards lost, presumably to the Crown. In 1189–90 Richard I restored it to the monks, who immediately leased it for life to Hugh de Nonant, bishop of Coventry (d. 1198), probably as part of a bargain with the king.[18] The practical consequences of the lease are obscure. Apparently, however, the Crown had already granted the manor to a tenant who held in chief by military serjeanty, and he and his heirs remained in possession. There is no evidence of any further connexion between the abbey and Perton until 1356, when the abbot sued the then lord, William Perton, for the manor. Although the plea failed, the abbot had meanwhile come to an agreement with William's heir, Sir John Perton, under which the abbey dropped its claims in return for a £5 rent charge. Royal licence was obtained in 1360 and the agreement was ratified. Sir John promptly tried to break it, but without success. In 1413 the rent charge from Perton formed part of the income of one of the abbey's central officials, the monk-bailiff.[19] The king granted it to Trinity College, Cambridge, in 1546, and it was paid to the college until 1938.[20]

A certain John held Perton in 1166 and as John of Perton was fined in 1186–7 for having dogs in the forest without warranty.[21] He was succeeded in or before 1193 by his son Ranulph.[22] Ranulph, and evidently John, held in chief by military serjeanty. In 1198 the serjeanty was described as archer service and the holding was stated to be 2 carucates.[23] In 1212 and thereafter the tenant was required to provide an armed horseman; detailed

requirements varied from time to time. The tenant was paid for all save his first eight days' service.[24] It is one of the few cases in which the king paid for all or part of a military serjeant's service.[25] Ranulph was succeeded in 1241 by his son John,[26] who died in 1257 and was followed by his son Ralph.[27] Ralph died in 1259, probably killed on campaign in Wales, and was succeeded by his brother William.[28] William died in 1279 or 1280, leaving as heir his son John.[29] John was a knight of the shire in 1315 and held various offices in the county. He died in 1331 and was succeeded by his son William. William died in 1360,[30] having already, without licence, conveyed Perton to his son, Sir John Perton.[31] Sir John fought in Edward III's French wars and was a prominent figure among the Staffordshire gentry, serving six times as a knight of the shire and twice as sheriff. He died in 1388.[32]

Sir John left as his heir his nephew John Barnhurst, who in 1369 or 1370 had conveyed his rights in Perton to Sir John's uncle Leo (or Lionel) Perton.[33] In or before 1362 Sir John had settled the manor on his bastard son John, to whom the escheator was ordered in 1388 to deliver Perton[34] and who in 1389, as John Perton, conveyed his right in the manor to feoffees acting for Sir Humphrey Stafford of Southwick, in North Bradley (Wilts.). At the same time John Barnhurst granted some of the same feoffees what he described as his manor of Perton with Trescott.[35] In 1390 the Crown ratified the feoffees' acquisition of Perton and licensed them to convey the manor to Sir Humphrey, who obtained seisin in 1397 after other claims had been extinguished.[36]

In 1398 Sir Humphrey (d. 1413) granted the manor to his second son, Sir Humphrey 'with the silver hand', for 50 marks a year payable to the elder Sir Humphrey during his lifetime.[37] In 1406 John Barnhurst quitclaimed the manor to the younger Sir Humphrey.[38] Sir Humphrey, who was sheriff of Staffordshire in 1403–4 and a knight of the shire in 1406, was at Perton in 1413.[39] In 1414 he leased the manor, retaining only the house.[40] In 1419 Leo Perton's son William, having seized the manor, settled it on feoffees, but Sir Humphrey had recovered it by 1421.[41] It then descended with Littywood, in Bradley, until 1519, when Robert Willoughby,

[13] *S.H.C.* 1923, 76; Shaw, *Staffs.* ii. 202; below, pl. facing p. 33.
[14] Inf. from Wolv. Boro. Dept. of Environmental and Technical Services and from Mr. G. Hooper of Pendeford (1980).
[15] F. E. Harmer, *Anglo-Saxon Writs*, 324–6, 360–1, 516; *Reg. Regum Anglo-Norm.* i, no. 25.
[16] *V.C.H. Staffs.* iv. 43; B. Harvey, *Westminster Abbey and its Estates in the Middle Ages*, 102.   [17] *S.H.C.* i. 35–6.
[18] Harvey, *Westminster Abbey*, 357 n.
[19] *S.H.C.* xii (1), 145, 152; *S.H.C.* xiii. 15; *Cal. Pat.* 1358–61, 436–7; H. F. Westlake, *Westminster Abbey*, i. 114; ii. 404.
[20] *L. & P. Hen. VIII*, xxi (2), pp. 342–3; inf. from the senior bursar, Trinity Coll. (1979).
[21] *S.H.C.* i. 48, 51, 130, 132.
[22] *S.H.C.* ii (1), 26–7; iii (1), 222. The name is also given as Randle and Ralph: *S.H.C.* iii (1), 39, 62, 393; *Bk. of Fees*, i. 142, 384.   [23] *Bk. of Fees*, i. 7.
[24] e.g. ibid. 142, 384, 594; ii. 1185; *Cal. Inq. p.m.* i, pp. 110, 118; ii, pp. 200–1, 298–9.
[25] E. G. Kimball, *Serjeanty Tenure in Medieval Eng.* 71

and n. 10, citing Perton though not by name.
[26] *Ex. e Rot. Fin.* (Rec. Com.), i. 353.
[27] *Cal. Inq. p.m.* i, p. 110.
[28] Ibid. p. 118; *S.H.C.* N.S. vi (2), 39.
[29] *Cal. Inq. p.m.* ii, pp. 200–1, 298–9.
[30] *S.H.C.* 1917–18, 32, 93.
[31] *Cal. Pat.* 1361–4, 257; *S.H.C.* xii (1), 170.
[32] *S.H.C.* 1917–18, 93; *Cal. Inq. p.m.* xvi, p. 293.
[33] *Cal. Inq. p.m.* xvi, p. 293; Jones, *Tettenhall*, 126. For Leo see *S.H.C.* N.S. vi (2), 159 n.
[34] *Cal. Pat.* 1361–4, 257. For the relationship see *S.H.C.* xv. 54 n.
[35] *Cal. Close*, 1385–9, 511; S.R.O., D. 593/A/2/10/1–5; Warws. R.O., CR 1886/Bloom 517–19.
[36] *Cal. Pat.* 1388–92, 191; S.R.O., D. 593/A/2/10/6–8; Warws. R.O., CR 1886/Bloom 521A and B.
[37] Warws. R.O., CR 1886/Bloom 522–3; *S.H.C.* 1917–18, 165.   [38] Warws. R.O., CR 1886/Bloom 526.
[39] *S.H.C.* xvii. 18, 26; *S.H.C.* 1917–18, 166.
[40] Warws. R.O., CR 1886/Bloom 526.
[41] S.R.O., D. 593/A/2/10/10–11; *Cal. Inq. Misc.* vii, p. 343; *Cal. Close*, 1419–22, 28–9.

Lord Willoughby de Broke, sold it to a prominent courtier, Sir William Compton.[42]

In 1523 Compton sold the manor to James Leveson, a Wolverhampton merchant of the staple and a brother-in-law of Walter Wrottesley of Wrottesley.[43] Leveson settled half the manor on his younger son Edward in 1546 and died in 1547. He left the other half to his elder son Richard, later Sir Richard (d. 1560), of Lilleshall (Salop.) and Trentham, who in 1550 gave it to Edward. Edward settled at Perton. He died childless in 1569. His heir was his nephew Walter, later Sir Walter, Leveson (d. 1602), Sir Richard's son and heir.[44] Edward's widow Elizabeth lived at Perton until her death in 1576.[45]

Sir Walter's son and heir, Sir Richard, who was appointed Vice-Admiral of England in 1604, died in 1605 without legitimate children.[46] He had settled Perton on a distant cousin Richard Leveson (b. 1598) as prospective husband of his bastard daughter Anne Fitton, and Richard's father, Sir John Leveson of Halling (Kent), took possession of the manor.[47] Rival claimants appeared,[48] and Perton was secured by William, Lord Howard of Effingham, the brother and guardian of Sir Richard's lunatic widow Margaret; her guardians held it until her death in 1641.[49] It passed to Richard (by then Sir Richard) Leveson,[50] although the marriage with Anne Fitton had not taken place. It was agreed in 1652 that he should retain the manor for life with remainder to the earl of Dorset, who had married Mary, niece and heir at law of Sir Walter Leveson (d. 1602).[51] Sir Richard died in 1661.[52] In 1664 Mary's son Richard, earl of Dorset, sold Perton to Sir Walter Wrottesley; the manor then covered 1,895 a., including 570 a. of demesne.[53] It descended with Wrottesley.

After the death of Elizabeth Leveson in 1576 the Levesons continued to use the manor house, Perton Hall, as an appendage to their principal seats at Trentham and Lilleshall.[54] It has been suggested that Vice-Admiral Leveson may have installed his mistress and cousin Mary Fitton there shortly before his death. A former maid of honour to Elizabeth I, Mary (1578–1641) is a candidate for identification as the 'dark lady' of Shakespeare's sonnets. In 1606 she married William Polwhele, who had served under the vice-admiral, and later in 1606 Lord Howard of Effingham granted Polwhele a lease of the Hall for the lifetime of the insane Lady Margaret. Polwhele died in 1609; the lease passed to Mary, who c. 1612 married John Lougher (d. 1635 or 1636). She bequeathed the lease to her son William Polwhele. Although Polwhele was still living at Tettenhall a few years later, he was said to be of Wolverhampton at the time of his death in 1654.[55] A Robert Granger was probably living in the Hall in 1666.[56] In 1685 Sir Walter Wrottesley was living at Perton, and from 1739 until her death in 1769 Frances, dowager Lady Wrottesley, lived there. The house was still inhabited in the early 19th century, but by 1820 most of it had been demolished.[57]

The Hall stood south-east of the junction of the Pattingham road and Jenny Walkers Lane.[58] It was probably enlarged in or soon after 1364 by Sir John Perton.[59] It stood within a square moat, which remained in 1663.[60] Two arms of the moat, still wet, survived in 1982.[61] In the early 1630s the out-buildings included a chapel, 'very ruinous and propped up', which had been used as a barn for 20 years or more.[62] In 1661 the house, much out of repair, consisted 'below stairs' of a hall, a kitchen with two little rooms adjoining it, a 'day house', a nursery, a little pantry, and a cellar, and 'above stairs' of a dining room with a little closet adjoining it, a chamber, two little rooms, three small chambers over the dayhouse and nursery, and several cocklofts.[63] A map of 1663 shows the house as a two-storeyed building with a gable at each end and what may be a third gable for a dormer window above a central door.[64] By the 1680s there had probably been some rebuilding, partly at least with stone from a quarry in the park. In the late 18th century the façade was described as 'modern', but much of an earlier house remained, including two octagonal stone turrets facing the road.[65] By 1820 all that remained was a derelict gabled end of the mid 17th century and one of the turrets, capped with a pepperpot roof which may have been Tudor.[66]

In 985 King Ethelred granted the Lady Wulfrun 9 hides at what became Wolverhampton and 1 at *TRESCOTT*. The land at Trescott was not mentioned in the charter of 994 by which Wulfrun founded or re-endowed the minster

[42] *S.H.C.* N.S. iv. 204–6; N.S. vi (2), 98, 149–50; *Cal. Close, 1485–1500*, p. 21; *Cal. Inq. p.m. Hen. VII*, ii, pp. 402–3; *V.C.H. Staffs.* iv. 79; S.R.O., D. 593/A/2/13/1–2. For Compton see *D.N.B.*

[43] S.R.O., D. 593/A/2/13/1–2. For Leveson see *S.H.C.* N.S. vi (2), 257; *S.H.C.* 1917–18, 306 n., which wrongly dates his death as 1546.

[44] S.R.O., D. 593/C/5, will of Sir Ric. Leveson; C/6/1/6, inq. p.m. of Edw. Leveson (Staffs.). For refs. to Edw. as 'of Perton' see e.g. *Cal. Pat.* 1558–60, 150; *S.H.C.* 1938, 139. For Sir Wal. see *S.H.C.* 1917–18, 404.

[45] S.R.O., D. 593/C/6/1/5B, 10.

[46] *D.N.B.* s.v. Leveson, Sir Ric.; S.R.O., D. 593/C/9/4/21.

[47] S.R.O., D. 593/C/9/3, Sir John Leveson's accts.; D. 593/E/6/12, breviate; *S.H.C.* 1920 & 1922, 31–2.

[48] S.R.O., D. 593/C/9/4/2–3, 13; G. P. Mander, *Wolverhampton Antiquary*, i. 371–2.

[49] S.R.O., D. 593/C/9/4/21; D. 593/E/4/6, breviate; D. 593/J/3/2, 30 Sept. 1636, 2 Oct. 1637, 1 Oct. 1638; Mander, *Woverhampton Antiquary*, i. 369; *S.H.C.* 1928, 103–5.

[50] S.R.O., D. 593/C/9/4/21; D. 593/J/3/1, ct. of survey 5 Oct. 1642.

[51] *S.H.C.* N.S. vi (2), 336; S.R.O., D. 868/2, no. 11. For Mary, ctss. of Dorset, see *Complete Peerage*, iv. 425, which

wrongly states that her mother Dame Mary Curzon was Sir Wal. Leveson's daughter.

[52] *S.H.C.* 1920 & 1922, 33.

[53] *S.H.C.* N.S. vi (2), 336; S.R.O., D. 3548/2.

[54] e.g. S.R.O., D. 593/C/9/2/7; C/9/3, p. [2].

[55] Mander, *Wolverhampton Antiquary*, i. 369–70, 374–5; Lady [A. E.] Newdigate-Newdegate, *Gossip from a Muniment-room* (1898 edn.), 82–3, 159; S.R.O., D. 593/E/4/6, breviate.

[56] *S.H.C.* 1923, 85.

[57] *S.H.C.* N.S. vi (2), 337, 345–6; Shaw, *Staffs.* ii. 207; *Woverhampton Chron.* 10 May 1815; W.S.L., Staffs. Views, x. 117–18.

[58] S.R.O., D. 3548/2.

[59] *Cal. Pat.* 1361–4, 476.

[60] S.R.O., D. 3548/2.

[61] Staffs. C.C. Planning Dept., Sites and Monuments Rec. 1138.

[62] S.R.O., D. 593/E/4/6, breviate.

[63] Kent A.O., U269/T144/A511, f. 1.

[64] S.R.O., D. 3548/2. Although the drawing may be partly conventional it tallies with what else is known of the house.

[65] Plot, *Staffs.* 168; Shaw, *Staffs.* ii. 207.

[66] W.S.L., Staffs. Views, x. 117–18.

which later became the collegiate church of St. Peter, Wolverhampton, but among the minster's property in 1086 was 1 virgate at Trescott, held by a free man.[67] It was probably the land granted in 985. In 1236, and probably by the 1190s, Trescott formed part of Perton manor,[68] and it thereafter descended with that manor; between the 14th and 17th centuries the manor was sometimes called Perton and Trescott.[69]

In the late 10th century *WROTTESLEY* was held by Elfhild. She had apparently agreed with her kinsman Wulfgeat of Donington (Salop.) that he should inherit the estate if he outlived her.[70] Hunta, a free man, held it in 1066. It was one of the manors given by William I to Robert de Stafford.[71]

In 1072 Robert, with the king's consent, granted the manor to Evesham abbey (Worcs.).[72] Domesday Book lists Wrottesley as one of Robert's manors,[73] possibly because Robert either neglected to fulfil his grant or resumed the manor after the death in 1077 of the abbot to whom he had conveyed it. In 1088 the abbey obtained from Robert, then a monk in the house and probably on his death-bed, a confirmation of the earlier grant. The property was granted in free alms as mensal land, assessed at 2 hides and covering *c.* 1,600 a.[74] The 1088 charter was confirmed by Robert's son Nicholas and *c.* 1163 by Nicholas's son Robert.[75] In 1166, however, Robert claimed that the abbot held Wrottesley of him as 1 knight's fee of the old feoffment.[76] In 1199 Robert's daughter Millicent, who inherited the Stafford barony, and her husband Hervey Bagot warranted his charter of confirmation.[77] Wrottesley was again stated to be held by knight service of the Stafford barony in 1221, and Evesham abbey was said to hold it of Nicholas, baron of Stafford, in 1284–5.[78] There seems to be no later mention of a Stafford overlordship.

Evesham abbey held Wrottesley until its dissolution in 1539.[79] The chief rent of 1 mark which it received from the 1160s from a terre tenant was assigned to the infirmarer or pittancer.[80] In 1539 the rent was said to be annexed to the abbey's manor of Oldberrow (Worcs.).[81]

Wrottesley was held in 1086 by Glodoen.[82] Between 1160 and 1167, probably in 1163–4, Adam, abbot of Evesham, granted it in fee to Simon of Coughton (Warws.) or de Verdun, a younger son of William of Coughton. The family was descended from the brother of the first Norman abbot of Evesham; it already held property of the abbey, and the grant of Wrottesley was apparently in exchange for Simon's sur-

render of his claims to various other abbey lands elsewhere. The grant stipulated that he was to pay a rent of 1 mark for Wrottesley and to perform the service due to the king.[83] Simon may have leased Wrottesley to the Adam of Wrottesley who was stated to be the abbey's tenant in 1166 and was still alive in 1176.[84]

Before 1199 Simon was succeeded by his son William of Wrottesley or de Verdun. William died between 1241 and 1248 and was succeeded by his son Hugh, later Sir Hugh, of Wrottesley. In the 1260s Sir Hugh supported Simon de Montfort, and after the battle of Evesham in 1265 his lands were seized and given to Roger Sprenchose, lord of Longnor (Salop.). Under the Dictum of Kenilworth in 1266 Hugh redeemed his property from Sprenchose and by July 1268 was again in possession of Wrottesley. He died in 1275 or 1276. The family's fortunes were restored and augmented by his son William, knighted in 1298, who at various times held most of the posts in the county normally filled by men of knightly rank. Thereafter the Wrottesleys generally stood among the leading Staffordshire gentry. Sir William died in 1313.[85]

He was succeeded by his son Sir William, who died in 1319 or 1320 leaving as heir his son Hugh, a minor.[86] The abbot of Evesham sued Hugh's mother, Joan, for the boy's wardship, claiming that Wrottesley was held of the abbey by knight service. Hugh's grandfather had successfully claimed in 1284–5 that he held the manor in socage, but in 1320 Joan acknowledged that the abbot was the rightful guardian. In 1325 he sold custody of the manor and Hugh's marriage to the abbey's steward, John de Hampton. John was apparently living at Wrottesley in 1327 but seems later to have relinquished the manor and wardship to Joan and her second husband, John of Tetbury. In 1331 they were sued on Hugh's behalf to render an account for the time they had occupied Wrottesley, which, it was again claimed, was held in socage. In the autumn of 1333 Hugh was suing them himself and had evidently been given livery of his lands, although still a minor. Hugh had, however, been knighted by January 1334, possibly before the battle of Halidon Hill (19 July 1333), and he was therefore qualified to receive his estates before coming of age. He served in many of Edward III's and the Black Prince's campaigns, and in 1348 he was created one of the original Knights of the Garter. He died in 1381, leaving as heir his son Hugh, a minor.[87] The boy died still a minor, possibly in 1385, and his rights passed to his brother John, who came of

[67] C. R. Hart, *Early Charters of Northern Eng. and N. Midlands*, 97; *S.H.C.* 1916, 101–3; *V.C.H. Staffs.* iii. 321 n., 322; iv. 45.
[68] *Bk. of Fees*, i. 594; *S.H.C.* iii (1), 222.
[69] e.g. above, Perton; S.R.O., D. 593/C/4, inq. p.m. of Jas. Leveson (Staffs.), 1547; C/5, inq. p.m. of Sir Ric. Leveson (Staffs.), 1561; D. 593/J/3/1, 5 Apr. 1648.
[70] D. Whitelock, *Anglo-Saxon Wills*, 54–7, 163–7; *S.H.C.* 1916, 120–1.   [71] *V.C.H. Staffs.* iv. 52.
[72] *S.H.C.* ii (1), 178–82; *S.H.C.* N.S. vi (2), 4–6.
[73] *V.C.H. Staffs.* iv. 52.
[74] *S.H.C.* ii (1), 182–5; *S.H.C.* N.S. vi (2), 6–7.
[75] *S.H.C.* ii (1), 193–4.
[76] *Red Bk. Exch.* (Rolls Ser.), i. 268; *S.H.C.* ii (1), 185; N.S. vi (2), 31–2.
[77] *S.H.C.* iii (1), 168–9.

[78] *S.H.C.* N.S. vi (2), 31–2; *Feud. Aids*, v. 10. In 1221 the mesne tenancy of Evesham was not mentioned.
[79] *Valor Eccl.* iii. 253; *V.C.H. Worcs.* ii. 425 n.
[80] Dugdale, *Mon.* ii. 24, 29; *Tax. Eccl.* (Rec. Com.), 253.
[81] *V.C.H. Worcs.* ii. 425 n.
[82] *V.C.H. Staffs.* iv. 52.
[83] *S.H.C.* N.S. vi (2), 8–21, 177, 249–50; *V.C.H. Staffs.* iv. 158.
[84] *S.H.C.* N.S. vi (2), 21–2. The later dispute over the nature of the tenure by which Wrottesley was held of Evesham (below) has led to the suggestion that the abbey had divided Wrottesley into two estates, later reunited, one held by knight service and one in socage: *S.H.C.* ii (1), 191–3.
[85] *S.H.C.* N.S. vi (2), 25, 35, 37–46, 51–64.
[86] Ibid. 73–81.
[87] Ibid. 52, 83–144, 153–4.

age in 1400. Between 1381 and 1400, under the terms of a grant by the abbot of Evesham, the manor was held by Sir Nicholas Stafford (d. 1394) and then by Sir Nicholas's widow, Elizabeth. John died in 1402, and another minority followed. Wrottesley passed to John's widow Elizabeth for life. In 1403 she married Sir William Butler of Warrington (Lancs.), who held Wrottesley until his death in 1415. In 1416 Elizabeth married William, Lord Ferrers of Groby, lord of Tettenhall Regis. John Wrottesley's son and heir Hugh was apparently living at Wrottesley by the 1430s and may have held the manor as his mother's tenant until her death in 1441. He died in 1463 or 1464, leaving as heir his son Sir Walter; his widow Thomasine held Wrottesley for life,[88] and outlived Sir Walter, who died in 1473.[89] He was one of the leading retainers of Richard Neville, earl of Warwick, and had been sheriff of Staffordshire in 1460–1.[90] His son and heir Richard came of age in 1478. Thomasine Wrottesley died in 1480, and in 1481 Richard obtained possession of the manor after a dispute with his mother, who also claimed it. He died in 1521, having served three times as sheriff of Staffordshire. His son Walter (d. 1562 or 1563) was sheriff in 1531–2 and held other offices in the county. Walter's son John died in 1578, and John's son Walter (sheriff 1597–8) in 1630. Walter's son Sir Hugh (sheriff 1617–18) died in 1633.[91] Sir Hugh's son Walter was created a baronet in 1642.[92]

In 1643 and 1644 Wrottesley Hall, strong and defensible, was apparently regarded by both royalists and parliamentarians as a royalist post, though Sir Walter Wrottesley later claimed that it had been in a state of armed neutrality and had never become a garrison for the king. In 1645 he handed it over to the parliamentarians and took in a garrison. His estate was nevertheless sequestrated later that year. He compounded in 1647 for a small fine which took into account the fact that since 1645 royalist troops had plundered his property and burnt the outbuildings of the Hall.[93]

Wrottesley descended with the baronetcy until 1838, when Sir John Wrottesley, the 9th baronet, was created Baron Wrottesley. It then descended with the barony until 1963, when the family's remaining Staffordshire property was sold to a syndicate of tenants and broken up.[94]

There was a moated manor house at Wrottesley in the Middle Ages. Sir Hugh Wrottesley in 1349 apparently moved to Pillaton in Penkridge, and the house at Wrottesley fell into disrepair.[95] A dovecot recorded at Wrottesley in 1294 alone

remained in good order in 1353 and 1382.[96] It is not known when the family moved back and how far the house was rebuilt. In 1634 a large moat enclosed a long house with a central hall, two-storeyed cross wings, and extensions to the east; the entrance was through a two-storeyed gatehouse range. The area within the moat was encircled by a palisade, and another palisade ringed the outer bank of the moat.[97] In 1635 and 1647 the house contained a hall, gallery, dining room, great parlour, and some 20 chambers. In 1647 the gatehouse contained Sir Walter Wrottesley's chamber and study and other living accommodation; the range had recently been extended.[98]

In 1666 the Hall was assessed at 20 hearths.[99] In 1685 Sir Walter Wrottesley, 2nd baronet, was living at Perton; it has been suggested that Wrottesley Hall had become uninhabitable.[1] In the mid 1690s Sir Walter Wrottesley, 3rd baronet, demolished the house and built a new one some distance to the south-west.[2] The builders were William Smith of Tettenhall and his elder brother Richard; William was probably also the architect.[3] The new Hall, dated 1696, had three storeys and attics and was of brick with stone dressings over a stone basement on the plan of an **H**. The south front of eleven bays had projecting wings of two bays at each end; the three central bays projected slightly and were capped with a pediment within which was an achievement of arms flanked by swags. The ground floor of the north side of the central range was open, and above there was a long gallery. The Hall was altered between 1769 and 1787 by Sir John Wrottesley, 8th baronet; he removed dormer windows, bricked up the arcade, and divided the long gallery into bedrooms; a bayed projection on the north side was probably also his. The dormer windows were restored in the later 19th century.[4]

In 1897 the Hall was gutted by fire and thereafter stood derelict.[5] In 1923 the 4th Lord Wrottesley built on its foundations a smaller house of brick with stone dressings, designed in a Queen Anne style by F. T. Beck of Wolverhampton and J. A. Swan of Birmingham. Much material from the earlier house was used, including the achievement from the pediment. The new house followed the pattern of the old but on a reduced scale: the centre was two-storeyed and the wings single-storeyed.[6]

In 1964 the syndicate of tenants which had bought the estate sold the Hall with c. 50 a., and in 1965 the buyer opened it as a country club, which was closed in 1970. Most of the 50 a. were converted into a golf course, still in use in 1980.

[88] Ibid. 173–8, 183–4, 186, 188, 191–2, 196, 201–2, 207.
[89] Ibid. 216, 237.   [90] D.N.B.
[91] S.H.C. n.s. vi (2), 244–6, 250, 253–4, 266–74, 277–82, 284–92, 295–8.
[92] Burke, Peerage (1967), 2712.
[93] S.H.C. n.s. vi (2), 319, 322–8.
[94] Burke, Peerage (1967), 2712–13; W.S.L., Sale Cat. C/3/17; Birmingham Post, 6 Nov. 1963; inf. from Mr. D. C. Hartill of Wrottesley Hall Grange (1980).
[95] S.H.C. n.s. vi (2), 110–11; V.C.H. Staffs. v. 119.
[96] S.H.C. n.s. vi (2), 70–1, 120; Jones, Tettenhall, 194–5.
[97] Below, pl. facing p. 32. A drawing of the view in S.H.C. n.s. vi (2), pl. facing p. 301, misdates the map and adds details with no apparent justification.
[98] S.H.C. n.s. vi (2), 301–5, 333.
[99] S.H.C. 1923, 113.

[1] S.H.C. n.s. vi (2), 337.
[2] Ibid. 338–9, stating that the new Hall was on the site of the earlier building, there being a 'Tudor window with stone mullions and transoms covered by the stone work of the new house, on the east side'. A comparison of the 1634 map with modern maps reveals the change of site.
[3] S.R.O., Tp. 1226/folder 17, 'Moneys paid by my Lady'. Dr. A. H. Gomme of Keele University is thanked for his comments on this document. For the Smith family see Colvin, Brit. Architects, 747; above, introduction.
[4] S.H.C. n.s. vi (2), 339–40 and pl. facing p. 340; W.S.L., Staffs. Views, xii. 142–5, 149; below, pl. facing p. 32.
[5] S.H.C. n.s. vi (2), 387–8; Kelly's Dir. Staffs. (1900 and later edns.); W.S.L. 8/00, photos. of Hall after fire.
[6] Pevsner, Staffs. 329; W.S.L., Sale Cat. C/3/16; Country Life, 1 Nov. 1924, pp. 691–2.

The house passed through various hands and after a sale in 1976 was converted into three self-contained houses.[7]

In 1780 Lincoln College, Oxford, owned a 22-a. field called the *DEEPS* south-east of Barnhurst. In 1868 the Deeps was part of Ford Mill farm, Bushbury, one of two farms in Bushbury which had been given to the college in 1508 by William Smyth, bishop of Lincoln; the field had probably formed part of the bishop's benefaction. In 1892 Wolverhampton corporation bought it to enlarge Barnhurst sewage works.[8]

ECONOMIC HISTORY. AGRICULTURE. The king's manor of Tettenhall had land for 2 ploughteams in 1086. Two ploughteams were in demesne, and there were 4 villeins and 3 bordars with another team. The manor, which included woodland, was valued with Compton and had been worth 20s. in 1066; in 1086 it was worth 30s. The Wightwick portion of the manor was described separately in Domesday Book. There was ½ ploughteam there with 1 villein in 1086, and it was worth 4s., the same value as before the Conquest.[9] The priests of Tettenhall had land at Tettenhall for 2½ ploughs in 1086, and there were 1 villein and 3 bordars with 3 ploughs. The priests also had an estate at Bilbrook in 1086, where there were 2 free men, 1 villein, and 2 bordars with 2½ ploughteams.[10] At Pendeford in 1086 there was land for 3 ploughteams. One plough was in demesne with 3 slaves, and there were 4 villeins and 5 bordars with one team. The manor, which included 4 a. of meadow, was worth 20s. in 1086, the same value as before the Conquest.[11] Perton manor had the greatest area of arable cultivation in 1086. There was land for 6 ploughteams; 1 team was in demesne, and there were 1 free man, 13 villeins, and 2 bordars with 5 teams. The manor, which also had 8 a. of meadow and woodland, was worth 40s., the same value as before the Conquest.[12] There was 1 virgate at Trescott in 1086, and a free man held ½ ploughteam there. The manor was then valued at 12d.[13] At Wrottesley there was land for 2 ploughs in 1086; 1 team was in demesne. There were 1 villein and 1 bordar. The manor, which included woodland, was worth 4s.[14]

The open fields of Tettenhall Regis manor lay at Tettenhall village, Wergs, Compton, and Wightwick. In 1613 there were two large fields north of Stockwell End. Caldercroft field, 101 a. in area, extended across Codsall Road to the later Pendeford Avenue, and Middle field, 105 a. in area, adjoined it on the west. Further west again, on the opposite side of the later Coppice Lane

and extending to Wergs Road, was Low field, mentioned in 1518 and 99 a. in area in 1613; it was common to Tettenhall and Wergs.[15] A field called Arrowsland, also mentioned in 1518, consisted in 1613 of 19 a. on the north side of Wrottesley Road; it was common to Tettenhall and Wergs and had probably extended as far as Wergs in earlier times. It still existed in 1740. Two other open fields at Wergs were mentioned in 1518, Hollygreave field and New field. In 1709 inclosures out of Hollygreave field were mentioned. New field still existed in 1740.[16] At Compton there were three open fields by the 16th century, Nether field north of Compton Road West, Middle field between Compton Road West and Finchfield Hill, and Egars field west of Finchfield Hill. Egars field was shown as Wightwick field on a map of 1613 which described it as common to Wightwick and Compton; by 1726 it was known as Windmill or Egars field. There had evidently been encroachment on all three fields by 1613, but they were still extensive, Nether field being 45 a. in area, Middle field 76 a., and Wightwick field 98 a. Piecemeal inclosure continued, but all three fields survived in 1775.[17] At Wightwick an open field, Wightwick field, was mentioned in 1367. In 1613 there were two pieces of open field on the east side of Wightwick Bank, but there had been inclosure by then. In 1614 arable lands in the open field of Wightwick called Underwood were mentioned. An open field called Wightwick Upper Field in 1712 lay north of Perton Road on the Wightwick–Perton boundary, and there was still a Wightwick field in 1775.[18] Another open field, Snape field, in the same area was mentioned in 1712 and 1718.[19]

There were at least three, and possibly four, open fields for the tenants of Tettenhall Clericorum at Aldersley. Autherley field between the later Lower Street and its continuation Pendeford Avenue on the west and Aldersley Road on the east existed in 1377; by the late 15th century it was also known as Caldercroft (or Calvercroft) field. It was 87 a. in area in 1613 and still existed in the early 18th century.[20] It was adjoined on the north by Soland field, in 1411 called Senelondes field. As Sollom field in 1613 it was 18 a. in area and was common to Aldersley and Barnhurst. It still existed in 1710.[21] Adjoining Soland field on the north was Birch field, which was called Broche field in 1483–4 and was also common to Aldersley and Barnhurst. It was 36 a. in 1613 and still existed in 1710. It may be identifiable with a field called New Land in 1371, New field in 1411, and Newebruche in 1412 and 1413.[22] There may have been another field, Mawe field: selions there were mentioned in 1518.[23]

[7] *Express & Star*, 23 Jan. 1964, 1 July 1965, 28 Aug., 11 Sept. 1970, 19 Mar., 22 Apr., 20 Nov. 1971, 13 Mar. 1974, 26 Apr., 25 Aug. 1976; inf. from Mr. Hartill.
[8] S.R.O., D. 1018/2; Wolverhampton Civic Centre, deed bdle. C/60; inf. from the Revd. V. H. H. Green, Lincoln Coll. (1980). [9] *V.C.H. Staffs.* iv. 38.
[10] Ibid. 45. [11] Ibid. 55. [12] Ibid. 43.
[13] Ibid. 45.
[14] Ibid. 52.
[15] P.R.O., MR 308; H.W.R.O. (H.), E 12/S, Tettenhall, Tettenhall Regis cts. of 12 Nov. 1685, 10 Feb. 1709/10; S.R.O., D. 593/A/2/18/7.
[16] S.R.O., D. 284/M/2; D. 593/A/2/18/7; H.W.R.O. (H.), B 47/S25; P.R.O., MR 308.

[17] H.W.R.O. (H.), B 47/S3, 22; P.R.O., MR 308; S.R.O., D. 284/M/1, 4.
[18] H.W.R.O. (H.), B 47/S3, 25; S.R.O., D. 593/J/3/1; P.R.O., MR 308; P.R.O., SP 14/196, nos. 2, 3; S.R.O., D. 284/M/4.
[19] H.W.R.O. (H.), B 47/S25; Wolv. C.L., D/MAN/8. It lay on the north side of Tettenhall Wood.
[20] H.W.R.O. (H.), B 47/S3, 24; P.R.O., MR 308; S.R.O., D. 3160/10/1, 3, 9.
[21] H.W.R.O. (H.), B 47/S3; P.R.O., MR 308; S.R.O., D. 3160/10/3.
[22] H.W.R.O. (H.), B 47/S3; S.R.O., D. 593/A/2/16/11; D. 3160/10/3; P.R.O., MR 308.
[23] H.W.R.O. (H.), B 47/S3.

Bilbrook had four open fields. Three were mentioned in 1506, Stanford, Longford, and Stubb fields. Stanford field, also known as Stonall and Townsend field in the 17th century, lay south of Bilbrook near the green. Longford field, also called Hurr field in the 17th century, was apparently bounded on the south by the road from Pendeford and probably stretched down to Moat brook on the north. An open field called the Hampitts was mentioned in 1648. All four fields still existed in 1712.[24]

There was farming at Cronkhall in Tettenhall Clericorum manor by the later 13th century when two fields there were mentioned, Long furlong and Forte furlong. It seems that the arable at Cronkhall became part of the fields of Barnhurst. Smalebrome field north-west of Barnhurst is mentioned in 1419, and some inclosure was in progress there by 1512. Two other fields were mentioned in the early 16th century, Wall (or Cronkwall) field and Barnhurst field. All had been inclosed by 1613; the names Wall field and Long furlong then survived at Cronkhall.[25] As already seen, Barnhurst also shared two fields with Aldersley.

An open field called Henwood south-west of Lower Green was divided between Tettenhall Regis and Tettenhall Clericorum. It was mentioned in 1517, and in 1613 it consisted of c. 7 a. on the Tettenhall side of Henwood Road in Tettenhall Regis and c. 5 a. between the road and Smestow brook in Tettenhall Clericorum. The first part had been inclosed by the early 18th century, but in 1710 the other part was still open-field arable known as Lower Henwood.[26]

At Pendeford Dude or Dodecroftes field near the Penk was mentioned c. 1275.[27] Open fields called Middle and Nether fields were mentioned in 1565 and 1595. Netherfield still existed in 1657, but part of it had been inclosed by then.[28]

Three open fields survived at Perton in 1661, Windlane field lying north of the village, Over (or Upper) field west of Windlane field, and Lower (or Nether) field south of the village.[29]

An open field at Trescott was mentioned in the 1270s.[30] Fomer field was mentioned in 1649 and Copgreen field in 1650. In 1663 three fields lay around the village, Nether field to the west, Copgreen field to the north, and a third field, evidently Fomer field, to the north-east.[31]

The open fields of Wrottesley were mentioned in 1403, though not by name. There were evidently three, lying round the village: Upper field to the south-west, Hyndall to the south, and Nether field to the east. They had been inclosed by 1634.[32]

In the early 17th century there were two open meadows in Tettenhall Regis, the 16-a. Kings meadow by the Penk west of Dam Mill and the 1½-a. Long meadow along Graiseley brook north of Compton Road West.[33] Meadow called Bunn meadows along the west bank of the Penk in Wrottesley was still held in strips in the mid 1630s.[34] Open meadow survived in Perton in 1661, in Longford field in Bilbrook in 1712, and at the Dippons in the 1780s.[35]

By the later 1160s Perton, Wrottesley, and Bilbrook may have lain in Brewood forest, disafforested in 1204.[36] A hay called Harewood in Perton manor, mentioned in 1258, was apparently waste later in the 13th century; an assart in Harewood was recorded in the early 14th century.[37] There were a number of assarts in the south-west of Wrottesley manor by 1298.[38] Kingswood, an area of waste straddling the border with Codsall and so called by 1403, had presumably lain in the forest. Part of it was held in common by the tenants of Tettenhall Regis, who still maintained a forester there in 1604. They also appointed four men to protect their rights to timber.[39] In 1707 c. 49 a. of Kingswood were inclosed to provide an endowment for the minister of Tettenhall parish; c. 5 a. more on the southern edge of the common bordering Wrottesley Park were vested in Thomas Astley of Hinnington, in Shifnal (Salop.).[40] In 1820 there were still c. 10 a. of uninclosed land at Kingswood; it was then uncertain whether the land lay in Tettenhall or with the rest of Kingswood in Codsall parish.[41]

Kingsley Wood, mentioned in 1205, was a detached portion of Kinver forest centring on the later Tettenhall Wood area; it was administered as part of the forest and in 1306 still had its own forester.[42] The forest eyres of 1271 and 1286 recorded assarting, notably in the Wightwick area,[43] and the process of reducing the forest land continued in the later Middle Ages: 17 selions of new assart in pasture called Hemebroche, probably on the west side of Kingsley Wood and thus in Wightwick, were mentioned in 1462.[44] By 1498 Kingsley Wood was an area of waste,[45] also known as Tettenhall Wood by 1613; encroachment was recorded there in the early 17th century.[46] In 1809 it was inclosed under an Act of 1806.[47]

[24] S.R.O., Tp. 1226, folder 12 and parcel A. There was also mention of selions in Heath field in 1712.
[25] S.R.O., D. 593/A/2/16/1, 6, 11; H.W.R.O. (H.), B 47/S3, 1517 terrier; P.R.O., MR 308.
[26] H.W.R.O. (H.), B 47/S3; ibid., E 12/S, Tettenhall, deed of 24 Mar. 1714/15; P.R.O., MR 308; Act for support of minister of Tettenhall, 6 Anne, c. 28 (Priv. Act; TS copy in S.R.O., D. 366/M/1); S.R.O., Tp. 1226, parcel A.
[27] W.S.L. 35/1/49, nos. 23, 30.
[28] Ibid. no. 47; S.H.C. 1934 (2), 13–14; S.R.O., D. 562/5.
[29] S.R.O., D. 593/J/3/1; D. 3548/2 (printed in S.H.C. 1931); Kent A.O., U269/T144/A511, f. 3.
[30] W.S.L., S.MS. 350A/40, p. 99.
[31] S.R.O., D. 593/J/3/1; D. 3548/2 (where 'Ssow Sen field' appears to be a copying error).
[32] S.H.C. N.S. vi (2), 200; S.R.O., D. 3548/1.
[33] P.R.O., MR 308.
[34] S.R.O., D. 3548/1.
[35] Kent A.O., U269/T144/A511, f. 2; S.R.O., Tp. 1226, parcel A; Wolv. C.L., D/MAN/8.
[36] S.H.C. i. 47–8; V.C.H. Staffs. ii. 337.
[37] S.H.C. iv (1), 138; W.S.L. 350A/40, p. 99.
[38] S.H.C. N.S. vi (2), 55.
[39] Ibid. 200; Jones, Tettenhall, 39–40.
[40] Act for support of minister of Tettenhall, 6 Anne, c. 28 (Priv. Act; TS. copy in S.R.O., D. 366/M/1).
[41] 5th Rep. Com. Char. 585–6.
[42] Rot. Chart. (Rec. Com.), i. 152–3; S.H.C. v (1), 113, 144, 150, 168, 180; vii (1), 157; P.R.O., MR 308.
[43] S.H.C. v (1), 144, 168, 180.
[44] B.L. Add. Ch. 71088.
[45] Cal. Inq. p.m. Hen. VII, ii, p. 159.
[46] P.R.O., MR 308; Tettenhall Par. Reg. i. 52–3, 60; H.W.R.O. (H.), E12/S, Tettenhall, deed of 28 Mar. 1613 and Kingsley accts. 1672–9.
[47] 46 Geo. III, c. 16 (Priv. Act); S.R.O., Q/RDc 66.

Pendeford lay in Cannock forest by the later 13th century. In 1271 John Pendeford was fined for assarting ½ a. there, and much of the inclosure in the later 13th century was encroachment on the forest.[48]

There were several greens in the parish. Two survive in Tettenhall village. Lower Green south of the church may be the green mentioned in 1327. It originally lay on both sides of the Wolverhampton road and in 1613 was 14 a. in area. Some 4 a. were inclosed in 1707. It survives as 3 a. of common north of the main road. Upper Green on top of the ridge was 11 a. in area in 1613. It was cut in two by the new Wergs Road in the early 19th century, and encroachments were mentioned in 1856. It survives as 7 a. of common.[49] A green at Wrottesley was mentioned in 1332, and it evidently survived in the 17th century.[50] A green at Cronkhall was mentioned in 1419.[51] There was a green at Bilbrook in the early 1640s, presumably the waste there known as Town Green in 1665;[52] it evidently lay south of Bilbrook at Lane Green, where a small green survived in 1980. Penkridge Well Green north of the present Tettenhall Wood was mentioned in 1761.[53] Compton Green at the junction of Henwood Road and Bridgnorth Road was inclosed in 1809 along with Tettenhall Wood.[54]

Wheat, barley, rye, oats, beans, and peas were being grown at Wightwick in 1337. The same crops, except beans, were sown on the demesne of Perton manor at the time of its lease in 1423.[55]

In 1198–9 the sheriff was allowed 85s. for restocking the king's manor of Tettenhall; the stock comprised 8 oxen and 10 cows worth 54s., and 30 pigs and a boar worth 31s.[56] There was a shepherd at Pendeford in 1278. He was possibly the same man as Richard the shepherd whose ½ virgate in Pendeford in 1304 gave him the right to pasture 6 oxen, 12 cattle with their young, 2 plough beasts, 24 sheep, and 2 sows with their young; the young had to be moved off when a year old.[57] In 1362 Sir Hugh Wrottesley sued for the theft of 6 oxen, 6 steers, and 4 cows at Wergs.[58] At Perton a sow, 4 piglets, and a small boar were included in the lease of 1423.[59]

Arable farming came to predominate. In the late 18th century arable accounted for over three quarters of agricultural land in Tettenhall Regis and Perton. In the 1840s there was almost six times as much arable as pasture in Kingswood township and four times as much in Wightwick;

the proportion was smaller in Bilbrook, where arable was less than two thirds of the area of pasture.[60] In 1979 in Wrottesley civil parish 1,091.4 ha. (2,697 a.) of arable were recorded, and only 371.2 ha. (892½ a.) of pasture.[61]

The main crops in the later 17th and early 18th century were rye, barley, wheat, peas, and oats;[62] some clover was also grown then.[63] In the later 18th century clover lying 3 or 4 years was used as fallow at Wrottesley, where a four-course system of Norfolk rotation had been adopted. Turnips, which were part of the course, were used as winter feed for sheep and cattle. Cabbages and potatoes were also grown.[64] When William Pitt, the agronomist, took the lease of New House farm in Pendeford in 1780, he set about improving the arable by dressing it with lime; in three years he burnt 1,200 qrs. of lime for the purpose. He also dressed thin soils with marl. In the early 19th century he experimented with mangolds as a cattle feed.[65] There was also innovation in sowing and harvesting the crops. In the early 1790s seed-drills were used on at least six farms around Pendeford, and threshing machines were used at Wrottesley and Pendeford in 1814. A farm at Wightwick had drills and winnowing, straw, and turnip machines in 1815.[66] Another improvement was the extensive drainage by Sir John Wrottesley of his land at Wrottesley in the early 19th century.[67] Grain crops still predominated in the late 19th century.[68] In 1918 oats and barley were the main crops on Pendeford Mill farm. Mangolds, swedes, potatoes, and cabbages were also grown; the cabbages were for the Wolverhampton market.[69]

Hemp and flax were grown in small quantities in the later 17th and the earlier 18th century.[70] At Bilbrook in 1741 there was a towdresser with tools and hemp worth £3 10s., and in 1745 John Becket of Wightwick, a hatcheller, owned £5 worth of rough hemp. In 1748 Humphrey Lloyd of Wergs had £50 worth of tow and £20 worth of flax; his widow was described as a flaxdresser in 1749.[71] At Aldersley in 1751 a tenant taking a lease of a farm was forbidden to sow flax without the landlord's consent.[72]

The name Perton is thought to mean 'pear *tun*', but it is not known whether the fruit was wild or cultivated. In the late 18th century the Tettenhall pear was grown in considerable quantities and supplied to local markets; by the early 19th century it was also taken by canal as far as Lanca-

[48] *S.H.C.* v (1), 152, 166, 178; W.S.L. 35/1/49, no. 23; 35/2/49, no. 18.
[49] Above, p. 8; S.R.O., D. 366/M/1.
[50] Above, p. 11.
[51] S.R.O., D. 593/A/2/16/6.
[52] S.R.O., Tp. 1226, parcel A.
[53] H.W.R.O. (H.), B 47/S22; above, p. 12.
[54] S.R.O., Q/RDc 66.
[55] *S.H.C.* N.S. vi (2), 93; *V.C.H. Staffs.* vi. 45.
[56] *S.H.C.* ii (1), 79.
[57] W.S.L. 35/1/49, no. 37; 35/2/49, no. 5.
[58] *S.H.C.* xiii. 25.
[59] *V.C.H. Staffs.* vi. 43.
[60] S.R.O., D. 1364/6/2; L.J.R.O., B/A/15/Tettenhall: Bilbrook, Kingswood, and Wightwick.
[61] M.A.F.F., agric. returns 1979.
[62] L.J.R.O., P/C/11, John Bull (1661), Hen. Clempson (1661), Ric. Mott (1677), Wm. Lowe (1704), Thos. Perry (1716), Ric. Green (1723), John Jewkes (1733).
[63] Ibid., Alice Croft (1694), Wm. Fleeming (1699),

Humph. Ryley (1711), John Michell (1722), John Lowe (1728), John Foxall (1744).
[64] *Tours in Eng. and Wales by Arthur Young* (London Sch. of Econ. Reprints of Scarce Tracts in Econ. and Pol. Science, no. 14, 1932), 142; Shaw, *Staffs.* ii. 199; *Annals of Agric.* iii. 131–3.
[65] *Annals of Agric.* xlii. 205; *V.C.H. Staffs.* vi. 107; letter of W. Pitt in unident. periodical, 1789 (copy in W.S.L. Pamphs. *sub* Pendeford).
[66] *V.C.H. Staffs.* vi. 108; *Wolverhampton Chron.* 23 Feb., 2 Mar. 1814; 22 Feb. 1815.
[67] Pitt, *Staffs.* ii. 95.
[68] *Kelly's Dir. Staffs.* (1880; 1900),
[69] *Staffs. Advertiser*, 15 Feb. 1919, p. 2.
[70] L.J.R.O., P/C/11, John Bull (1661), Hen. Clempson (1661) and (1684), Wm. Lowe (1704), Joseph Illedge (1720).
[71] Ibid., Wm. Latham (1742), John Beckett (1745), Humph. Lloyd (1748), Eleanor Lloyd (1749).
[72] S.R.O., D. 3160/10/3, deed of 10 Dec. 1750.

shire. The fruit, still grown in the later 20th century, is suitable for cooking only.[73] Sir Walter Wrottesley had a plantation of fruit trees at Perton in the late 17th century, but the kind of fruit is not known.[74]

Cattle were an important item of livestock in the parish. At Barnhurst in 1662 John Cresswell had 18 cows, a bull, 6 heifers, 9 young beeves, and 8 calves, together worth £119 4s., as well as 8 oxen worth £48. William Hinckes of Perton had 5 cows, 4 oxen, and 10 young beasts, worth £48, in 1688, and in 1732 Thomas Brookes of Palmers Cross had 15 cows, 5 twinters, 8 yearlings, and 3 calves, worth £59 10s. One of the largest herds recorded was that at Wrottesley where in 1737 Thomas Faulkner had 17 cows, 6 heifers, a bullock, 8 stirks, and 10 calves, worth £83 10s.; what was probably the same herd was kept by his widow Judith in 1746 and then numbered 21 cows, 16 stirks, 11 yearlings, and a bull, worth £100.[75] Smaller herds of 5 cows and under with yearlings and calves were common in the same period.[76] Longhorns were the chief breed of cattle in the late 18th century, some of them brought into the parish for fattening.[77] In May 1815 and 1816 a farmer at Perton, H. Owen, advertised fat cows for sale, as well as sheep and pigs. William Owen of Pendeford held spring sales of fat cows in 1818, 1819, and 1820; his herd included a Longhorn bull. Another farmer at Pendeford had Hereford and Devon cows in 1819.[78] In 1861 four out of the six cowmen recorded in the parish were living at Pendeford; none was mentioned there in 1871.[79] In 1918 on Pendeford Mill farm calves and bullocks were reared and fattened for early sale.[80]

There was evidently an early emphasis on dairy farming. Among goods stolen from a house at Wightwick in 1599 were 12 cheeses.[81] Cheese and butter were often recorded among household possessions in the late 17th and earlier 18th century.[82] At Perton in 1708 Samuel Bradeney had 5 tubs, a cheese press, and a kneading tub, besides cheese and butter, and in 1729 Jervis Anson of Pendeford had a milk house with barrels, tubs, and a churn. John Lees of Tettenhall had cheese, butter, and bacon worth £20 in 1730; he also had 10 milking cows worth £35. In 1737 Thomas Faulkner of Wrottesley had £10 worth of cheese in a cheese chamber and 17 cows

worth £46.[83] Dairying continued to be important in the early 19th century. A farmer at Pendeford advertised 100 milk cheeses and 10 family cheeses for sale in 1814, and in 1815 at Compton a farmer, who was also a hingemaker, had 24 cheeses, a cheese press, and tubs in his house.[84] In 1918 there was a large dairy herd on Pendeford Mill farm.[85]

Sheep farming also was important. James Leveson, who bought Perton manor in 1523, was a Wolverhampton wool merchant; there was a wool house among the out-buildings at the Hall in 1576 and a sheepcot in 1661.[86] A flock of white sheep was grazed at the Wightwick end of Kingsley Wood in 1596.[87] Small flocks of around 20 sheep were common in the parish in the later 17th and earlier 18th century; their value was little more and often less than that of pigs kept.[88] A flock of 90 sheep worth £15 belonging to John Cresswell of Barnhurst in 1662 was exceptionally large. Roger Mulliner had a flock of 60 in 1663, but the sheep, valued at only £7 10s., were probably of poor quality. A flock of 47 worth £20 belonged to Thomas Brookes of Palmers Cross in 1732.[89] By the late 18th century Tettenhall Wood was described as an excellent sheep walk, and the sheep bred there, some of them Leicesters, were noted as being of good size and producing fine wool. Sheep were brought into the parish from Shropshire and other counties including Wiltshire and Dorset to be fattened.[90] In 1804 William Pitt had a flock of 136 sheep, half of them lambs or yearlings.[91] Other large flocks in the early 19th century included fattened sheep: at Wrottesley in 1814 a flock of 225 included 93 fat sheep, and on a farm at Wightwick 45 fat wethers out of a flock of 126 were advertised for sale in 1815.[92] The spring sales of livestock by H. Owen and William Owen included large numbers of sheep: 220 in 1815 and 200 in 1816, 1818, 1819, and 1820. A farmer at Pendeford advertised between 200 and 400 Leicesters for sale in 1819.[93] In the late 1860s R. H. Massen had a flock of 200 Shropshire ewes on his farm at Pendeford (formerly Pitt's farm).[94] In 1871 there were 10 shepherds living in the parish, 3 of them at Pendeford.[95] In the early 20th century on Pendeford Mill farm sheep were brought in for fattening and early sale; a flock there in 1918 consisted of 318 ewes and 348 lambs.[96]

[73] Eng. Place-Name Elements, ii (E.P.N.S. xxvi), 63; Annals of Agric. vii. 465–6; Pitt, Staffs. ii. 55; J. I. Langford, Towpath Guide to Staffs. and Worcs. Canal, 104–5.
[74] Plot, Staffs. 384.
[75] L.J.R.O., P/C/11, John Creswell (1662), Wm. Hinckes (1688), Thos. Brookes (1732), Thos. Faulkner (1737), Judith Faulkner (1746).
[76] Ibid., John Bull (1661), Roger Mulliner (1663), Ric. Bradley (1675), Thos. Addenbrooke (1681), Alice Croft (1694), John Handson (1709), Joseph Foxall (1718), John Lowe (1728), John Billingsley (1737).
[77] Shaw, Staffs. ii. 199.
[78] Wolverhampton Chron. 24 May 1815; 8 May 1816; 8 Apr. 1818; 31 Mar., 5 May 1819; 19 Apr. 1820.
[79] P.R.O., RG 9/1984; RG 10/2927.
[80] Staffs. Advertiser, 15 Feb. 1919, p. 2.
[81] S.H.C. 1935, 149.
[82] L.J.R.O., P/C/11, Ellen Owen (1678), John Bull (1661), Ric. Bradney (1675), Sam. Foxall (1683), Thos. Kempson (1685), Alice Croft (1694), John Perry (1697), Wm. Lowe (1704), Thos. Higgs (1733), John Perry (1737).

[83] Ibid., Sam. Bradeney (1708), Jervis Anson (1729), John Lees (1731), Thos. Faulkner (1737).
[84] Wolverhampton Chron. 2 Mar. 1814; 15 Mar., 10 May 1815.
[85] Staffs. Advertiser, 15 Feb. 1919, p. 2.
[86] S.R.O., D. 593/C/6/1/5(B); Kent A.O., U269/T144/A511, f. 1.
[87] S.H.C. 1932, 263.
[88] L.J.R.O., P/C/11, Alex. Bache (1661), Ric. Bradley (1675), Ric. Chamberlain (1676), Thos. Addenbrooke (1681), John Cauldwell (1686), Alice Croft (1694), Wm. Fleeming (1699), John Handson (1709), Thos. Perry (1716), John Michell (1722), Thos. Hipwood (1733).
[89] Ibid., John Creswell (1662), Roger Mulliner (1663), Thos. Brookes (1732).
[90] Annals of Agric. vii. 465; Shaw, Staffs. ii. 199.
[91] Annals of Agric. xlii. 109–10.
[92] Wolverhampton Chron. 23 Feb. 1814; 22 Feb. 1815.
[93] Ibid. 5 May 1819.
[94] Jnl. Royal Agric. Soc. of Eng. 2nd ser. v. 293.
[95] P.R.O., RG 10/2927.
[96] Staffs. Advertiser, 15 Feb. 1919, p. 2.

Herds of 7 pigs and fewer were widely kept in the later 17th and earlier 18th century;[97] normally worth c. £1 or £2, some of the small herds were valued at £4 or more.[98] John Cresswell of Barnhurst had a herd of 23 pigs worth £12 in 1662, and in 1721 John Michell of Trescott had 3 large pigs and 13 small, together worth £7. The herd kept by John Lees of Tettenhall, 2 large pigs and 13 stores worth £14 in 1730, was the most valuable recorded in the period. Two pigs worth £8 were kept by John Foxall of Wightwick in 1744.[99] Flitches of bacon were often among household goods recorded in the late 17th and earlier 18th century.[1] In the late 18th century pigs were allowed to feed on the large quantities of fallen pears found in the parish.[2] At Pendeford in 1814 a farmer had 7 sows in pig and 63 stores, and at Aldersley in 1815 there was a herd of 4 sows and 10 small pigs. Sales of around 30 pigs, including sows in pig, were advertised at Perton in 1815 and 1816 and at Pendeford in 1819 and 1820.[3] A boar offered for sale at Compton mill in 1815 was claimed as one of the best in the country.[4]

Geese, ducks, and hens were kept in the later 17th and earlier 18th century. In 1684 Thomas Onions of Compton had a flock of 16 geese, 3 hens, and a cock, together worth 6s. Poultry owned by Thomas Brookes of Palmers Cross and worth £1 in 1732 included turkeys.[5] Four stalls of bees worth £1 were mentioned at Tettenhall in 1661.[6]

The main crops recorded in Wrottesley civil parish in 1979 were barley and wheat; sugar beet and potatoes were also grown. There were 148 ha. (367 a.) devoted to fruit growing; cooking apples, strawberries, and blackcurrants predominated, but there were also gooseberries and raspberries. Livestock recorded in 1979 comprised some 430 cattle and 120 sheep; no pigs were recorded. Poultry was still kept in 1979 when nearly 700 birds were recorded in the civil parish.[7]

By 1837 land at Tettenhall Wood, in the angle of Mount Road and Mill Lane, was owned by the trustees of Tettenhall Club and let as 21 gardens.[8] There were two market gardeners at Compton in 1841, and in 1871 there were three at Tettenhall Wood and two at Upper Green.[9] In 1921 ten smallholdings centring on five pairs of cottages were created for ex-servicemen by Wolverhampton corporation in the area between Lane Green Road, Pendeford Mill Lane, and Barn-

hurst Lane. The administration was taken over by Staffordshire county council after the Second World War and by West Midlands county council in 1980. The cottages were still occupied in 1980, although the number of smallholdings had decreased.[10]

Copyhold land amounted to c. five sixths of Tettenhall Regis manor in 1615; the remaining sixth was freehold.[11] There were 11 copyhold and customary tenants and only 1 freeholder on the prebendal manors of Bovenhill and Pendeford in 1642–3; another 9 were tenants at will and 3 were described as under-tenants.[12] Inheritance of copyhold land on the manors was by primogeniture in the mid 17th century.[13] Copyhold land in Tettenhall Regis and Tettenhall Clericorum was being enfranchised in the later 19th century.[14]

Labour services at harvest time were still owed at Wrottesley in the late 14th century.[15]

Rack rents had been introduced on the Leveson manor of Perton by the later 17th century. In 1661 twelve tenements, amounting to 600 a., were held on long leases of 3 lives and yielded £25 5s. in rents; 6 tenements, amounting to c. 400 a., were rack-rented and produced £105 a year. Some of the 376 a. of demesne was also held at rack rent. Most of the holdings were between 40 a. and 60 a. in area.[16] In the late 18th century a policy of severe rack-renting at Pendeford forced William Pitt to vacate his farm there. Entering on the 230-a. New House farm at a rent of £131 10s. in 1780, Pitt improved the land and had his rent raised to £203 in 1783. He left the farm in 1804, when it was leased out for £350 to a tenant at will who had only 6 months' notice of dismissal.[17] Small farms were characteristic of the parish in the earlier 19th century.[18] Of the 20 farms recorded in Wrottesley civil parish in 1979, 12 were under 50 ha. (123 a.) and 3 were over 200 ha.[19]

WOODLAND AND PARKS. The parish was well wooded in 1086; there was woodland ½ league in length and breadth in both Tettenhall and Perton, and ½ league in length and 2 furlongs in breadth in Wrottesley.[20]

The wood of Wrottesley was mentioned in 1334 when housebote and haybote there were included in a grant of land. In 1347 Sir Hugh Wrottesley was licensed to impark his wood there.[21] By 1353 there were three parks stocked with game; a survey of 1382 identifies them as

[97] L.J.R.O., P/C/11, Ellen Owen (1678), Roger Mulliner (1663), Thos. Barnesley (1675), Ric. Mott (1677), Wm. Gunston (1681), Thos. Onions (1684), Alice Croft (1694), Wm. Fleeming (1699), Wm. Lowe (1704), Sam. Bradeney (1708), Thos. Hipwood (1733), Thos. Faulkner (1737), Humph. Lloyd (1748).

[98] Ibid., Wal. Croft (1688), Wm. Dix (1695), John Lowe (1728), John Michael (1728), Silvanus Davies (1742).

[99] Ibid., John Creswell (1662), John Michell (1722), John Lees (1731), John Foxall (1744).

[1] Ibid., Thos. Hand (1677), Roger Chaundless (1689), Joseph Foxall (1718), John Lees (1731).

[2] Shaw, Staffs. ii. 199.

[3] Wolverhampton Chron. 2 Mar. 1814; 22 Feb., 24 May 1815; 8 May 1816; 5 May 1819; 19 Apr. 1820.

[4] Ibid. 24 May 1815.

[5] L.J.R.O., P/C/11, John Bull (1661), Ric. Chamberlain (1676), Thos. Onions (1684), Wm. Lowe (1704), Thos. Brookes (1732).

[6] L.J.R.O., P/C/11, Hen. Clempson (1661).

[7] M.A.F.F., agric. returns 1979.

[8] Wolv. C.L., map 308; L.J.R.O., B/A/15/Tettenhall: Wightwick.

[9] P.R.O., HO 107/715/998; P.R.O., RG 10/2927.

[10] Inf. from the deputy land agent, Staffs. C.C. (1980).

[11] P.R.O., E 134/13 Jas. I Mich./32, f. 5.

[12] S.R.O., Tp. 1226/parcel A, ct. of 22 Apr. 1642.

[13] S.R.O., D. 3160/9/6, deed of 13 Oct. 1656.

[14] S.R.O., D. 678/17, deed of 18 Jan. 1877; P.R.O., MAF 9/275/12609–14.

[15] Jones, Tettenhall, 194–8; S.H.C. n.s. vi (2), 182.

[16] S.R.O., D. 593/G/1/1/9; Kent A.O., U269/T144/A511.

[17] Annals of Agric. iii. 192; xlii. 204–9.

[18] App. 1st Rep. Com. Poor Laws, H.C. 44, p. 445 (1834), xxx.

[19] M.A.F.F., agric. returns 1979.

[20] V.C.H. Staffs. iv. 38, 43, 52.

[21] S.H.C. 1928, 138–9; Cal. Pat. 1345–8, 529, 559.

Wrottesley Hall from the south-west in the later 19th century

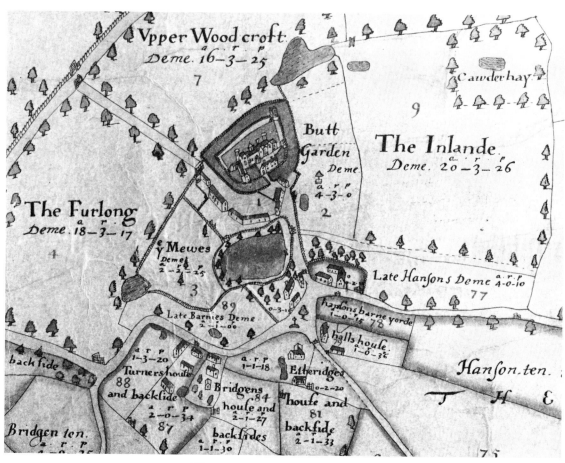

Wrottesley Hall and village in 1634

TETTENHALL

ENVILLE: MERE FARM FROM THE SOUTH-WEST IN 1857
with clementing in progress

TETTENHALL: PENDEFORD HALL FROM THE SOUTH *c.* 1835

Lodge Park (later Wrottesley Park) which lay west of the village and was the principal park until the 18th century, the Lea north-west of the village, and Cranmoor to the south.[22] In 1634 Wrottesley Park comprised some 450 a. within a pale; on the west the pale ran along the parish boundary with Patshull and Pattingham. There was a small moated lodge in the park and north-west of the lodge a conduit head, possibly supplying water to the Hall. The Lea, some 43 a., was also surrounded by a pale; it too was well wooded and included 10 a. of meadow. Much of the Cranmoor area was apparently used for grazing, and part of it seems to have consisted of a formal plantation.[23] During the Civil War the parkland suffered from the ravages of the garrison, who burned the pales and felled timber.[24] A charcoal burner was living at Cranmoor in 1684.[25] Wrottesley Park still existed in the 1740s, but by the end of the 18th century there was a new park stretching south-east from the Hall.[26] In the later 19th century the old Wrottesley Park was farm-land and plantations, and Wrottesley Lodge Farm stood on the site of the moated lodge.[27] The new Wrottesley Park contained deer in the 1860s but not in the 1890s.[28]

The wood of Pendeford was mentioned in the later 13th century; it was evidently known as Hurst Wood in 1302 and as Pendeford Wood in 1565.[29]

There was a park at Perton by 1423; it may have been created by Sir John Perton, who probably enlarged his house in the mid 1360s.[30] It lay west of Perton hamlet and extended almost to the parish boundary.[31] By 1654 it had been divided into six portions which were leased to tenants, but in the earlier 1660s the 50-a. park was held by a single tenant.[32]

In the later 18th century there were c. 250 a. of woodland at Wrottesley, Wergs, and Pendeford, and south of Lane Green.[33] There were 80 elm trees on Upper Green in 1817.[34] In 1979 Wrottesley civil parish contained 61.7 ha. (152½ a.) of woodland.[35]

FREE WARREN AND FISHERIES. Free warren was granted to the lord of Pendeford in 1284, of Perton in 1307, and of Wrottesley in 1347.[36] In 1230 the dean of Wolverhampton collegiate church sued William the chaplain of Tettenhall for building a stank in Tettenhall which had harmed the dean's property at Codsall.[37] The stank was possibly a fish pond on the Penk north-west of Wergs Hall where there was later a mill. There was a fishery at Wrottesley in 1333; pike, perch, bream, and roach were stolen from the lord's fishpond then.[38] The pond was no longer stocked by 1382.[39]

MILLS. When John of Pendeford sold Pendeford manor to the Augustinian priory of St. Thomas near Stafford in 1277 a mill there was excluded from the sale. In that year or shortly before John granted it at a nominal rent to Ralph de Burgh, perhaps one of his creditors. He expressed the wish that if Ralph were to grant it to the priory he should make the grant in free alms. Ralph duly did so, John confirming the grant as lord of Pendeford.[40] The mill then descended with the manor, of which it was still held in the 1720s.[41] In 1711 the copyhold was sold to Thomas Higgs, a miller of Penn. Thomas's son John sold the mill in 1739 to John Taylor, a Wolverhampton iron-monger. In 1794, after the death of Taylor's son John, a London ironmonger, his executors sold it to the Staffordshire and Worcestershire Canal Co., which wished to ensure that the mill did not interfere with the supply of water to the canal. In 1826 the company sold the mill to T. W. Giffard of Chillington Hall in Brewood, reserving its rights to water.[42] The mill remained part of the Chillington estate until 1893, when it was sold to Wolverhampton corporation. By 1909 the flow of water was becoming inadequate, and in 1911 the mill was closed.[43] It had stood on the same site at the confluence of the Penk and Moat brook at least since the 1650s. Between then and the 19th century it was known variously as New, Barn-hurst, or Pendeford mill.[44] In the 18th century it had three sets of stones.[45] When it was closed some of the buildings were converted to house cattle from Wolverhampton corporation's farm at Barnhurst; they were demolished in 1916.[46] The mill house was converted into two cottages in 1912.[47] The mill itself was demolished in 1961.[48]

In 1411 the prior of St. Thomas near Stafford sued Roger Fleming, who had built a water mill in the vill of Tettenhall upstream from Pendeford

[22] *S.H.C.* N.S. vi (2), 120; Jones, *Tettenhall*, 195.
[23] S.R.O., D. 3548/1.
[24] *S.H.C.* N.S. vi (2), 325.
[25] *Tettenhall Par. Reg.* i. 83.
[26] E. Bowen, *Improved Map of County of Stafford* [1749]; Shaw, *Staffs.* ii, pl. facing p. 204; C. and J. Greenwood, *Map of Staffs.* (1820). Yates, *Map of Staffs.* (1775 and 1799 edns.) shows neither old nor new park.
[27] O.S. Map 6", Staffs. LV. SE. (1886 edn.); LXI. NE. (1884 edn.).
[28] J. Whitaker, *Deer-Parks and Paddocks of Eng.* (1892), 4.
[29] W.S.L. 35/1/49, nos. 47, 50; 35/2/49, no. 13.
[30] S.R.O., D. 593/A/2/10/12; above, p. 25.
[31] S.R.O., D. 3548/2.
[32] S.R.O., D. 593/G/1/1/14, f. 24; S.R.O., D. 3548/2; Kent A.O., U269/T144/A511, f. [14].
[33] *Annals of Agric.* vii. 458; Yates, *Map of Staffs.* (1775).
[34] Pitt, *Staffs.* ii. 59.
[35] M.A.F.F., agric. returns 1979.
[36] *Cal. Chart. R.* 1257–1300, 272; 1300–26, 108; *Cal. Pat. 1345–8*, 529.
[37] *Pat. R.* 1225–32, 356.
[38] *S.H.C.* vi (2), 90; xiv (1), 29.

[39] Jones, *Tettenhall*, 195.
[40] W.S.L. 35/1/49, no. 15; 35/2/49, nos. 11–14.
[41] *S.H.C.* xv. 124; Shaw, *Staffs.* ii. 202; S.R.O., D. 590/10/6.
[42] S.R.O., D. 590/10/1, 20, 22, 27, 29, 33, 45, 47.
[43] Wolv. Civic Centre, deed bdle. D/1; Wolv. C.L., Wolv. Corp. sewerage cttee. min. bk. 30, pp. 31–2, 37, 39–40.
[44] S.R.O., D. (W.) 1766/4, ct. of 22 Apr. 1657; *Tettenhall Par. Reg.* ii. 73, 75, 164, 227 (entries mentioning the New Mill(s) 1664–76; earlier and later entries mention Pendeford mill). For the identification of the New Mill and Barnhurst mill with Pendeford mill see e.g. S.R.O., D. 590/10, *passim*, especially plan of 1826 in D. 590/10/47B. Yates, *Map of Staffs.* (1775 and 1799 edns.) shows 2 water mills at Pende-ford; the northern one, although labelled Pendeford mill, has not been identified.
[45] S.R.O., D. 590/10/1–2; *Aris's Birmingham Gaz.* 12 Aug. 1765.
[46] Wolv. C.L., sewerage cttee. min. bk. 30, pp. 31–2, 67, 96; min. bk. 32, p. 28.
[47] Ibid. min. bk. 30, pp. 80, 150, 165.
[48] Inf. from Wolv. Boro. Dept. of Environmental and Technical Services (1980).

mill; the prior alleged that Pendeford mill's grinding capacity had been cut from 10 qr. to 10 bu. a day. Fleming was ordered to restore the flow of water to its previous rate. His mill stood on a stream called Stanford brook, which flowed into another stream called Longmeadow brook to power Pendeford mill. The streams were probably the Penk and Moat brook.[49]

Sir Hugh Wrottesley (d. 1381) held a water mill known as the New Mills at Wergs in Tettenhall Regis manor. It was presumably the mill there known as Burdon (or Burdun's) mill, held of that manor, which was mentioned in Wrottesley family settlements of 1441 and 1501–2, and the water mill called Rodesford mill which stood at Wergs in 1613. The mill pool is identifiable with the dammed fishpond on the Penk north-west of Wergs Hall.[50]

Ranulph, lord of Perton, had a water mill there on Smestow brook in the mid 1190s, possibly newly built. It descended with the Perton estate. The last mill at Perton was worked as a corn mill until about the early 1920s. Part of the derelict brick building which remained at Perton Mill Farm in the 1970s was apparently built or repaired in 1766; a mill had stood on the same site at least since the 17th century.[51]

Wightwick mill on Smestow brook was probably one of two mills which in 1249 formed part of the royal manor of Tettenhall; it was still held as copyhold of Tettenhall Regis manor in the early 19th century.[52] In 1294 the bailiff of Wrottesley manor collected rent from Wightwick mill, and in or shortly before 1316 William, son of Henry atte Mulne of Wightwick, conveyed the mill to Sir William Wrottesley. Ownership was later disputed by the Pertons of Perton, but Sir Hugh Wrottesley's rights were finally recognized in 1343. The Wrottesleys still held the mill in the later 15th century.[53] In 1744 John Grove of Rugby, son and heir of Edward Grove, a Birmingham tallow chandler, conveyed the copyhold of the mill to Richard Fryer of Wolverhampton.[54] Fryer died in 1774 and was succeeded by his son John, also of Wolverhampton.[55] On John's death in 1780 the mill passed to his nephew Richard Fryer of Wergs and in 1828 to Richard's son John, of Islington (Mdx.).[56] It was worked as a corn mill until the late 19th or early 20th

century.[57] In 1980 the 19th-century building survived as part of Wightwick Mill Farm. In 1744 the mill had two sets of stones.[58] By 1888 it had been converted into a steam mill.[59]

Compton mill on Smestow brook was probably the other water mill on the king's manor in 1249, and is almost certainly the mill of Rodesford mentioned in 1300.[60] In 1326 John, son of William of Compton, was licensed to grant Roger, son of Nicholas of Trescott, property which he held in chief in Compton, including a mill, stated in 1325 to be dilapidated, and a house; they were evidently Compton mill and the miller's house.[61] Roger held the mill and the house in 1338.[62] The mill was still held of Tettenhall Regis manor in the 19th century. Between c. 1709 and 1717 the copyhold was sold by Richard Cresswell (d. 1743) to John Shelton. The mill was held by members of the Allen family in the later 18th century, and in 1843 and 1892 it formed part of the Pearsons' estate at Tettenhall Wood.[63] In 1743 it was described as a corn mill or a blade mill.[64] Described as an old-established flour mill in 1853, it was still so used in 1894 but by 1900 had gone out of use.[65] By the late 1860s the premises were occupied by members of the Bate family, millwrights and machinists, still the occupants in 1939.[66] In 1853 the buildings comprised a house and a two-storey mill with an overshot wheel and two sets of stones.[67] They were no longer standing in 1980.

In 1613 a windmill stood on the east side of the later Pendeford Avenue south of its junction with Green Lane.[68] A windmill was built in 1720 on the west side of what became Windmill Lane on the high ground south of Wightwick; it ceased work in the 1880s and was converted into a house, probably by 1905, surviving as such in 1980.[69] In the later 18th and early 19th century there was another windmill east of Windmill Lane.[70] A windmill east of Mill Lane in Tettenhall Wood was worked in the late 18th and earlier 19th century; it was converted into a house, probably by the 1880s, and survived as such in 1980.[71] In the earlier 19th century there was a windmill at Pendeford ¼ mile west of the water mill.[72]

INDUSTRIES. There was a sandstone quarry at Tettenhall Wood by 1613, and quarrying was

[49] S.H.C. xv. 124.
[50] Jones, Tettenhall, 195; S.H.C. N.S. vi (2), 140, 178, 207–8, 251; P.R.O., MR 308; J. P. Jones, 'The Village Mill', A. Webb's Annual (1912; copy in Wolv. C.L.).
[51] S.H.C. iii (1), 222–3; S.R.O., D. 593/J/3/1, ct. of survey 25 Feb. 1647/8; D. 3548/2; Soc. for Protection of Ancient Buildings, Watermill Survey (1967); Brook, Ind. Arch. W. Midlands, 208.
[52] Cal. Inq. Misc. i, p. 18; S.R.O., D. 284/M/6, 27 May 1828.
[53] S.H.C. N.S. vi (2), 70, 76, 104, 207–8; P.R.O., C 140.
[54] S.R.O., D. 284/M/2.
[55] S.R.O., D. 284/M/4, 27 Oct. 1775; D. 1157/1/1/64, 10 Mar. 1774.
[56] S.R.O., D. 284/M/6, 27 May 1828; D. 1157/1/1/64, 10 Apr. 1780.
[57] Jones, Tettenhall, 2, mentions it as still in use in 1894, and O.S. Map 1/2,500, Staffs. LXII. 9 (1919 edn., rev. 1914), shows it as a working mill. It is not, however, listed in Kelly's Dir. Staffs. after 1888.
[58] S.R.O., D. 284/M/2.
[59] Kelly's Dir. Staffs. (1888).
[60] Cal. Inq. Misc. i, p. 18; S.H.C. v (1), 180.

[61] S.H.C. 1911, 368–9; Cal. Pat. 1324–7, 252.
[62] S.H.C. xi. 86.
[63] S.R.O., D. 284/M/2, 28 July 1743; 3, 17 Feb. 1769; 4, 22 Mar. 1776; S.R.O., D. 755/4/13, 21; D. 1018/2. For the date of the sale of the copyhold see Burke, Land. Gent. (1969), ii. 119.
[64] S.R.O., D. 284/M/2.
[65] S.R.O., D. 755/4/15; Jones, Tettenhall, 2; O.S. Map 1/2,500, Staffs. LXII. 5 (1902 edn.). It does not, however, appear in directories from the 1830s as a corn or flour mill.
[66] W. White, Dir. Wolverhampton (1869); P.O. Dir. Staffs. (1872; 1876); Kelly's Dir. Staffs. (1880 and later edns.).
[67] S.R.O., D. 755/4/15.
[68] P.R.O., MR 308.
[69] W. A. Seaby and A. C. Smith, Windmills in Staffs. (Stafford County Mus. 1980), 13, 22.
[70] Yates, Map of Staffs. (1775); R. Baugh, Map of Salop. (1808).
[71] S.R.O., D. 1018/2; W.S.L. 67/3/41; Seaby and Smith, Windmills in Staffs. 13, 23.
[72] Wolverhampton Chron. 5 Jan. 1820; S.R.O., D. 590/10/47B; O.S. Map 1″, LXII. NW. (1834 edn.).

still in progress there in the 1670s.[73] About 1680 a large quarry near Pendeford Farm was producing good weatherstone, and there was still quarrying at Pendeford in 1717.[74] A quarry at Perton south of Pattingham Road near Dadnall Hill was producing weatherstone, firestone, and grindstone c. 1680. About the same time Perton stone was used for the new Perton Hall, and it provided the facing for St. John's church at Wolverhampton, completed in 1776.[75] There was still a quarry at Perton in 1822, but it was disused by the 1880s.[76]

Sand was dug at Compton by the mid 1830s, probably at the bottom of the Holloway where there is evidence of former working. It was used in iron foundries and for making mortar. By 1850 sand was also dug at Wightwick and near Tettenhall village. In the mid 1880s there were pits on the south side of the canal between Compton and Wightwick; those east of Wightwick bridge were being worked c. 1900 but were disused by 1914, when other pits east of Wightwick Mill bridge were being worked. Canal wharves connected with the pits were still in use in the 1930s. The sand workings near Tettenhall village were probably those being worked on either side of Sandy Lane c. 1900; they were disused by 1914.[77]

In the late 18th century William Pitt had a limekiln beside the Staffordshire and Worcestershire Canal on his farm at Pendeford.[78] There were limekilns at Wightwick wharf west of the canal bridge in Windmill Lane in 1841. Stone brought from the quarries around Dudley was burnt there for sale to farmers.[79]

A brickmaker named Thomas Tranter was living in the parish in 1604.[80] In 1636 the lord of Kingsley granted a Thomas Tranter a lease of ½ a. in Kingsley Wood with a brickyard and garden and the right to dig clay in the waste for making bricks and tiles; the terms included a consideration of 1,000 tiles and a rent of 1,000 tiles a year. Thomas was succeeded by his son William who in 1647 was granted a new lease; it included a further ½ a. and a cottage newly built by William. He continued to make bricks and tiles and may have been the brickmaker of the same name who died in 1694 and was then described as of Compton. Later that year a brickmaker named Thomas Tranter was granted a lease of his house

in Kingsley manor, and he was still active in the late 1690s.[81] There was a brick kiln and yard at Tettenhall Wood in 1780 and a brickworks at Stockwell End in the early 19th century.[82] In 1861 three brickmakers were living at Tettenhall Wood.[83]

Metal workers are found in the parish from the late 16th century. Thomas Carter, a scythesmith, was described as late of Bilbrook in 1591.[84] Adam Moseley, a nailer, was living in Kingsley manor in 1647 and 1655, and a Tettenhall nailer named Andrew Palmer took a lease of a plot of land there in 1708.[85] Another nailer, Edward Greene, was living at Compton in 1654 and was still working there at his death in 1689.[86] Two locksmiths were living at Perton and Trescott in 1658, and there were several locksmiths in the parish in the early 18th century. Besides locks, metal goods produced in the parish in the 18th century included hinges, buckles, toys, rings, swivels, nails, files, and watch-chains.[87]

Lockmaking had become the chief trade by the late 18th century, with Wolverhampton providing a market.[88] Large numbers of locksmiths settled at Tettenhall Wood after the inclosure of the common in 1809.[89] There were 55 in the parish in 1841, of whom 31 lived at Tettenhall Wood; the others lived at Compton and Finchfield and around Lower Street. In 1871 there were still some 40 in the parish, nearly half of them in Tettenhall Wood.[90] By the end of the century the domestic trade had almost ceased, but there was at least one lockworks in the 1890s, James Whitehouse & Sons at Finchfield. The firm had presumably been founded by the James Whitehouse who was living there by 1851.[91]

Keys were made in the parish from the early 19th century. In 1810 a Compton man named Hope produced keys of high quality by stamping them, a method of production invented in Birmingham c. 1806.[92] He was probably the Thomas Hope who was keystamping at Compton in 1834. Thomas was one of 5 keystampers in 1841, 4 of them at Compton and 1 in Lower Street; there were also 8 keymakers, 5 at Tettenhall Wood and 3 in Lower Street. By 1871 there were only 2 keystampers and 2 keymakers. By 1850 Thomas Hope had evidently been succeeded by another Thomas, who combined keystamping and the

[73] H.W.R.O. (H.), E 12/S, Tettenhall, deed of 28 Mar. 1613 and Tettenhall Wood accts. 1672-9, 1679-80; T. H. Whitehead and others, *Memoirs of Geol. Surv.*, *Country between Wolverhampton and Oakengates*, 135.

[74] T. Congreve, *Scheme or Proposal for making a Navigable Communication between the Rivers of Trent and Severn in the County of Stafford* (1717), 7.

[75] *V.C.H. Staffs.* ii. 191 (which wrongly gives Perton Hall as 16th-cent.); Plot, *Staffs.* 167-8; Whitehead, *Country between Wolverhampton and Oakengates*, 136, 205; above, manors and other estates (Perton).

[76] S.R.O., D. 1364/4/14A (1822); O.S. Map 6″, Staffs. LXI. NE. (1884 edn.).

[77] White, *Dir. Staffs.* (1834), 288; Whitehead, *Country between Wolverhampton and Oakengates*, 130; P.O. Dir. *Staffs.* (1850); O.S. Map 1/2,500, Staffs. LXII. 2, 9 (1887, 1902, and 1919 edns.); J. I. Langford, *Towpath Guide to Staffs. and Worcs. Canal*, 110, 112.

[78] *Annals of Agric.* xlii. 205.

[79] P.R.O., HO 107/715/998; Brook, *Ind. Arch. W. Midlands*, 208; O.S. Map 1/2,500, Staffs. LXII. 9 (1887 edn.).

[80] *S.H.C.* 1940, 60.

[81] H.W.R.O. (H.), E 12/S, Tettenhall, deeds of 10 Nov.

1647, 3 Nov. 1694, and Tettenhall Wood accts. 1672-9; ibid. Staffs. legal papers, breviate 3 Aug. 1663 and draft deed 1698-9; *Tettenhall Par. Reg.* i. 60; L.J.R.O., P/C/11, Wm. Tranter (1694).

[82] S.R.O., D. 1018/2; *Rep. Com. Holyhead Road*, H.C. 126, p. 21 (1820), vi.

[83] P.R.O., RG 9/1984.

[84] *S.H.C.* 1930, 155.

[85] H.W.R.O. (H.), E 12/S, Tettenhall, deed of 10 Nov. 1647; ibid. Prestwood leases, deed of 5 June 1708; *Tettenhall Par. Reg.* i. 52.

[86] *Tettenhall Par. Reg.* i. 50, 58, 242; L.J.R.O., P/C/11, Edw. Greene (1689).

[87] *Tettenhall Par. Reg.* i. 58-60, 103-5, 253; ii. 12-36; S.R.O., D. 284/M/1-4; L.J.R.O., P/C/11, Thos. Brown (1735); Jones, *Tettenhall*, 2.

[88] Shaw, *Staffs.* ii. 198.

[89] White, *Dir. Staffs.* (1834), 288, 290.

[90] P.R.O., HO 107/715/998; P.R.O., RG 10/2927.

[91] Jones, *Tettenhall*, 2; *Kelly's Dir. Staffs.* (1892; 1896; 1900); P.R.O., HO 107/2017(1); P.R.O., RG 9/1984; RG 10/2927.

[92] *V.C.H. Staffs.* ii. 252.

keeping of a beerhouse at Compton; he was still working as a keystamper in 1879.[93]

Other 19th-century metal trades included hingemaking and spectacle-frame making. In 1841 there were 10 hingemakers, 8 of them at Tettenhall Wood; by 1871 there were only 2. There were 2 spectacle-frame makers in 1841 and 10 by 1871 when most of them were living in Lower Street and Aldersley. A few survived in the earlier 1890s.[94]

There was an agricultural-implement manufacturer at Compton in the late 19th and early 20th century.[95] In the later 1950s Aldersley Engineers Ltd. made agricultural equipment at Tettenhall.[96]

In 1936 Boulton Paul Aircraft Ltd. opened a factory adjoining the site of the projected airfield at Pendeford, itself opened in 1938. The firm has been part of the Dowty Group Ltd. since 1961 and specializes in light training aircraft.[97]

In 1840 the Ballincolig Royal Gunpowder Mills Co. of Liverpool had a powder warehouse on the Shropshire Union Canal at Barnhurst. The company was still in occupation in 1877 and probably in 1883.[98] By the late 19th century Gaunt & Hickman, gunpowder manufacturers of Horseley Fields, Wolverhampton, had a powder house nearby in Barnhurst Lane, which was evidently still in use in 1921.[99]

LOCAL GOVERNMENT. There was mention of a court and a leet for Tettenhall Regis in 1371. From 1720 the court leet was held once a year only, normally in October, and it still met in 1856. In 1709 it met at a dwelling house at Wergs. The meeting place was an inn by the early 19th century and evidently by 1744; it was moved from the Old Rose and Crown to the Rose and Crown in 1840. Court baron business was still transacted in 1922 at the office of the lord of the manor, a Wolverhampton solicitor.[1] By the early 17th century a bailiff was elected annually, clerks and smiths being ineligible. A lord's bailiff was still appointed in 1764 but was not recorded thereafter. In the 18th century the office was attached to certain properties in rotation.[2] A pinner was still appointed at the leet in 1856.[3] In 1837 the pinfold stood on Upper Green at the east end of the later Clifton Road.[4]

The manor of Kingsley had its own court leet and court baron by the later 16th century. The court baron still existed in 1919. A tree called Court Oak which stood at the top of the Holloway in the early 17th century may have been a meeting place of the court. In 1647 the lord of Kingsley granted a lease of a house subject to his right to hold the manor court in it. In the later 18th century the courts met in private houses and inns in Tettenhall, Compton, and Tettenhall Wood; the Wrottesley's Arms in Tettenhall was a frequent meeting place. By 1861 the courts met at the Swan in Compton and were still held there in 1917. The last court was held in the offices of Bernard, King & Sons, a firm of Stourbridge solicitors.[5] A stone pound was built for the manor in the 1670s.[6]

The lords of Pendeford, Perton, and Wrottesley each held views of frankpledge by the mid 1250s, paying respectively 2s., 3s., and 12d. for the right.[7] In 1293 the lord of Perton successfully claimed a twice-yearly view and waif by ancestral right from time immemorial; he also claimed assize of bread and of ale.[8] A court leet was still held for the manor of Perton and Trescott in October 1656. The manorial pinfold was mentioned then.[9] The lord of Wrottesley held courts in August and November 1294, and at the beginning of the 15th century two reeves, a constable, and two aletasters were elected at the Wrottesley leet.[10] The stocks of Wrottesley township were mentioned in 1593.[11]

The dean of Tettenhall had view of frankpledge by the mid 1250s, paying $\frac{1}{2}$ mark for it.[12] As lord of Tettenhall Clericorum he had leet jurisdiction over the five prebendal manors, and his paramount jurisdiction passed to the Wrottesleys with the manor of Tettenhall Clericorum after the Dissolution. In the early 18th century tenants on the prebendal lands attended the Tettenhall Clericorum courts and chose the constables there.[13] A court leet was still held for the manor in 1784; it met in a house on Lower Green where the court baron too met in the later 18th century.[14] The court baron still met at Lower Green in 1814,[15] and in 1839, 1840, and 1841 the meeting for choosing the constable was held at the Mitre there.[16] Stocks were made in 1723–4 and probably stood on Lower Green.[17] About 1860 stocks were moved there from out-

[93] White, *Dir. Staffs.* (1834), 290; *P.O. Dir. Staffs.* (1845 and later edns.); P.R.O., HO 107/715/998; G. Stevens, *Dir. Wolverhampton* (1879–80).

[94] P.R.O., HO 107/715/998; P.R.O., RG 10/2927; Jones, *Tettenhall*, 2.

[95] Kelly's *Dir. Staffs.* (1892 and later edns. to 1908).

[96] *V.C.H. Staffs.* ii. 145.

[97] Ibid. 171; Brook, *Ind. Arch. W. Midlands*, 207.

[98] L.J.R.O., B/A/15/Tettenhall: Bilbrook; *Gore's Dir. Liverpool* (1841); Wolv. Civic Centre, D/1, deed of 29 Aug. 1874; *Staffs. Advertiser*, 5 May 1877; O.S. Map 6″, Staffs. LVI. SW. (1888 edn.).

[99] Kelly's *Dir. Staffs.* (1896; 1900; 1904); O.S. Map 6″, Staffs. LVI. SW. (1888, 1903, and 1924 edns.).

[1] S.R.O., D. 284/M/1–7; H.W.R.O. (H.), B 47/S25; White, *Dir. Staffs.* (1834), 290. For a reference to a 1762 map showing the Tettenhall Regis court house near Upper Green see S.R.O., D. 366/M/28.

[2] Jones, *Tettenhall*, 36; S.R.O., D. 284/M/2–3.

[3] S.R.O., D. 284/M/7.

[4] Wolv. C.L., Map 308 (R. Timmis, Map of par. of Tettenhall, 1837).

[5] H.W.R.O. (H.), E 12/S, Kingsley Manor; ibid. Kinver, Compton Hallows, and Kingsley ct. bk. 1734–61; Kinver and Kingsley ct. bk. 1767–1801; Kingsley ct. bk. 1861–1930; Tettenhall, deed of 10 Nov. 1647. For Court Oak see P.R.O., MR 308.

[6] H.W.R.O. (H.), E 12/S, Tettenhall, Tettenhall Wood accts. 1672–9.

[7] *S.H.C.* v (1), 112, 114.

[8] *S.H.C.* vi (1), 248, 261; *Plac. de Quo Warr.* (Rec. Com.), 716.

[9] S.R.O., D. 593/J/3/1.

[10] *S.H.C.* n.s. vi (2), 173, 184, 186, 199. In 1402 only one reeve was appointed. A constable existed in 1377: *S.H.C.* 4th ser. vi. 9.

[11] *S.H.C.* 1930, 296.

[12] *S.H.C.* v (1), 113.

[13] S.R.O., D. 3160/9/2, 6; *S.H.C.* n.s. vi (2), 285; P.R.O., E 134/5 Geo. I East./14.

[14] S.R.O., D. 1018/3/1; D. 3160/10/2, deed of 8 Oct. 1784.

[15] S.R.O., D 1018/3/2.

[16] S.R.O., D. 571/A/PK/1, pp. 96–7.

[17] Ibid. p. 21; Jones, *Tettenhall*, 292–3.

side the police station in High Street and later were broken up.[18]

A court was held for each subordinate prebendal manor. The court for Bovenhill prebend was recorded from 1398, and despite the right of the dean alone to leet jurisdiction within Tettenhall Clericorum the prebendary had a view of frankpledge with the court in 1506. The court was held in the church in 1546. There was reference to the court of the prebendary of Pendeford in 1377. In 1506 his tenants acknowledged that they owed suit at his three-weekly courts and also at two great courts a year, besides being liable for service as reeve and aletaster. The court baron was held at Tettenhall that year, apparently at Pendeford in 1540, 1541, and 1553, at Bilbrook in 1648, at Tettenhall Clericorum in 1650, 1652, and 1665, and at Tettenhall in 1710. From the later 16th century, however, with both prebendal manors held by a single lord, the Bovenhill and Pendeford courts were usually held jointly. In 1642 the joint court was held in the churchyard by the east end of the chancel. Thereafter the meeting place was stated to be Tettenhall Clericorum, but in the earlier 18th century it was usually given simply as Tettenhall. The house of Thomas Chapman in Tettenhall Clericorum was the meeting place between 1787 and 1799. In 1705 and 1786 the jury stated that both prebends had view of frankpledge and leet jurisdiction by immemorial right, and what were described as views and courts leet were held several times in the late 18th century. A court baron was still held in 1912, at the office of a Wolverhampton solicitor who was steward of the manors.[19] A court was held for the prebend of Perton in 1463 and a court leet in 1487. In 1507 a court for the prebend was held at the college. It was stated c. 1700 that the Levesons occasionally held a court after buying the prebendal manor in 1549.[20] A court was held for the prebend of Wrottesley in 1503, with view of frankpledge as well in 1506.[21] A court baron for the prebend of Codsall was held in Tettenhall church in 1508. A court leet was held for the prebend in 1521 and a court with view of frankpledge in 1532.[22]

The five main manorial divisions were used for taxation by the earlier 14th century and persisted into the 19th century as constablewicks—Tettenhall Regis, Tettenhall Clericorum, Pendeford, Perton and Trescott, and Wrottesley.[23] At Perton and Trescott in the mid 17th century a constable and a headborough were appointed at the autumn leet.[24] At Tettenhall Clericorum a constable was

appointed at the leet in October 1695.[25] By 1714 his accounts were being passed and his successor appointed at a meeting in October. The duty of serving the office was attached to certain houses in rotation.[26] Probably the office rotated at Perton and Trescott also: in 1650 a woman chosen as constable had to find a man to act for her; the previous year a woman was chosen as headborough and her servant was sworn in her place.[27]

For poor-law purposes the parish was divided into four areas named after four of the prebends: Bovenhill (or Tettenhall), covering Tettenhall village, Tettenhall Wood, Compton, and Aldersley; Pendeford, covering Pendeford, Bilbrook, and Barnhurst; Perton, covering Perton, Trescott, and Wightwick; and Wrottesley covering Wrottesley, Kingswood, and Wergs.[28] The Tettenhall vestry was appointing an overseer for each of the four divisions at its Easter meeting by the later 1660s; that office too rotated by property.[29] The four divisions continued for rating purposes after Tettenhall had become part of Seisdon poor-law union in 1836.[30] A select vestry was appointed in 1827 but abandoned after a year.[31] Brych House in Wrottesley Road west of the junction with Redhouse Road was bought with charity money in 1714 for the benefit of the poor. By 1746 it had been turned into a workhouse. It was extended in or before 1787. It was enlarged in 1836 to hold 80 inmates and used as the union workhouse until a new house was opened at Trysull in 1860.[32]

In the late 17th century the vestry appointed a varying number of surveyors of the highways: the lowest was 4, but 8 were appointed in 1684 and in 1687 (when a woman was included). The areas for which they served were named from 1684. The 8 of that year were Trescott, Perton, Wergs, Tettenhall Regis, Tettenhall Clericorum, Bilbrook, Wrottesley, and Wightwick; Compton was among the 6 of 1685.[33] In the earlier 19th century Tettenhall Regis had 2 surveyors instead of its previous one,[34] Wightwick had 2 in 1819,[35] and Tettenhall Clericorum had 2 in the late 1820s.[36] It was stated in 1832 that the parish was divided into a number of liberties for the repair of the roads.[37]

There were two churchwardens in 1553,[38] and the election of two wardens and two sidesmen was recorded from 1669, the churchwarden's office rotating by property.[39] In 1802 the curate stated that he nominated one warden and the parishioners the other.[40] By 1770 there was a

[18] R. A. Jones, 'Ancient Punishments', *A. Webb's Annual* (1912; copy in Wolv. C.L.).

[19] H.W.R.O. (H.), B 47/S24; S.R.O., Tp. 1226, folder 12 and parcel A; Wolv. C.L., DX/49.

[20] H.W.R.O. (H.), B 47/S3; S.R.O., D. 593/H/14/1/4, f. 46v.; D. 3160/9/6.

[21] S.R.O., Tp. 1226, folder 12.

[22] S.R.O., D. 3160/9/6, deeds of 26 Aug. 1508, 19 Nov. 1532; H.W.R.O. (H.), B 47/S3, deed of 14 Feb. 1520/1.

[23] R. E. Glasscock, *Lay subsidy of 1334*, 277, 282–3; *S.H.C.* 1923, 76, 85, 103, 111, 113; S.R.O., D. 571/A/PO/3–5.

[24] S.R.O., D. 593/J/3/1.

[25] S.R.O., D. 3160/9/1.

[26] S.R.O., D. 571/A/PK/1.

[27] S.R.O., D. 593/J/3/1.

[28] S.R.O., D. 1018/2.

[29] S.R.O., D. 1364/6/1. The assignment of an overseer to a

division is given only from 1679; Wightwick is given instead of Wrottesley in 1679 and 1680.

[30] S.R.O., D. 571/A/PO/88; D. 1364/6/1; *3rd Ann. Rep. Poor Law Com.* H.C. 546, p. 164 (1837), xxxi.

[31] S.R.O., D. 571/A/PO/5.

[32] S.R.O., D. 1018/1; D. 1364/1/2; White, *Dir. Staffs.* (1851), 62; below, chars. for the poor; below, Trysull.

[33] S.R.O., D. 1364/6/1, covering 1682–90 and 1692.

[34] S.R.O., D. 571/A/PS/1, showing an increase to 2 in 1802 and 1804 and 2 from 1806.

[35] Ibid. PS/6.   [36] Ibid. PS/7.

[37] S.R.O., D. 571/A/PO/5.

[38] *S.H.C.* 1915, 282.

[39] S.R.O., D. 1364/6/1 (not mentioning sidesmen after 1711); L.J.R.O., PTe/V/5, presentments (Tettenhall and Codsall) 1828–46, showing sidesmen from 1830.

[40] L.J.R.O., PTe/A/19.

nobbler who acted as dog-whipper and sexton and was paid 10s. a year by the churchwardens.[41]

In 1880 a lighting district under a board of 12 inspectors was formed covering the populous part of the parish. In 1883 the district became a local government district under a local board of 12 members.[42] At first the board met at the drill hall on Old Hill. In 1886 a lease was taken of a house on Upper Green which was adapted to provide a board room and offices; the board met there from January 1887.[43] In 1894 the local board was replaced by an urban district council of 12 members, and the rest of the ancient parish was formed into the civil parish of Wrottesley in Seisdon rural district.[44] In 1961 the urban district was divided into five wards and the number of councillors was increased to 15.[45] The urban district was abolished in 1966; most of it was added to Wolverhampton borough, and the rest was divided between Wrottesley and Codsall parishes.[46] In 1974 Wrottesley became part of South Staffordshire district.[47]

PUBLIC SERVICES. The town well of Tettenhall was mentioned in 1679–80 when it was repaired with stone from Tettenhall Wood. In 1804 there were wells in Lower Street and at the top of Old Hill and a pump house on the western boundary of the parish south of the Shrewsbury road.[48] The Wolverhampton Waterworks Co. began building a pumping station in the later Regis Road in 1845 and supplied water to Wolverhampton from 1847. Under an Act of 1850, authorizing a new works at Goldthorn Hill in Wolverhampton, Tettenhall was included in the company's area of supply. In 1884 the Tettenhall medical officer of health reported that although the better houses were well supplied, too many small houses depended on wells of doubtful purity. The works at Tettenhall was extended in the later 1850s and c. 1910.[49]

Although Wolverhampton corporation had opened a sewage farm at Barnhurst by 1870, Tettenhall's sewage continued to discharge into Smestow brook. In 1890 the local board opened a sewage works in Bennett's Lane by Black brook on the south-western boundary. It was replaced in 1930 by a new works on an adjoining site, itself replaced in 1961 when the urban district council opened a works by Smestow brook west of Perton Mill Farm.[50] In 1933 the rural district council completed a sewerage scheme for Wrottesley civil parish, and most of the houses were connected by the end of the year.[51]

The first houses built by the urban district council were completed in 1922, 40 around Regis Road, Tettenhall, and 14 in the Terrace, Finchfield. The next were 78 on the Woodland Avenue estate between School Road and Wood Road at Tettenhall Wood, finished in 1927. Those were followed by six more in the Terrace. Towards the end of the Second World War the council began laying out the Long Lake site at Tettenhall Wood between Mill Lane and School Road, using prisoners of war for the work; the estate was finished in 1948. Thirty-six prefabricated bungalows were built in Henwood Road in 1946. The Woodhouse estate east of School Road was started in 1948; the final stage was begun in 1952.[52] Also in 1952 the council started work on the Grange estate to the east; it was built in three stages and includes flats. It was finished in 1960.[53] The council announced its first slum clearance scheme, in Lower Street, in 1955; the redevelopment of the cleared area was in its last stage in 1960.[54] In 1963 work started on six three-storeyed blocks of flats in Regis Road, and in 1964 a tender was accepted for 60 maisonettes in Aldersley Road.[55] The council owned 1,050 houses and flats by 1964, of which some 900 had been built since the end of the Second World War.[56] Wolverhampton corporation had also built some 1,000 dwellings by 1965 on land at Castlecroft and Finchfield which it had acquired by compulsory purchase in 1948 for overspill housing.[57] In the mid 1970s the corporation began work on a large estate at Barnhurst and Pendeford.[58] Council houses were built at Lane Green in Wrottesley civil parish after 1945.

Danes Court cemetery in Coppice Lane was opened in 1959 by the Tettenhall, Wrottesley, and Codsall joint cemetery board.[59]

The watchmen of Tettenhall Regis were mentioned in 1592 after being beaten and ill treated.[60] In 1738 a public meeting for Tettenhall Clericorum agreed that felons should be prosecuted at the expense of the constablewick.[61] That may be the origin of the Tettenhall association for the prosecution of felons which existed by 1790; it had twenty members in 1816 and was meeting in 1818 at the Old Rose and Crown.[62] By 1790 there were so many robberies at night in Tettenhall

[41] S.R.O., D. 1018/1.
[42] Jones, *Tettenhall*, 294–5; *Kelly's Dir. Staffs.* (1884); Wolv. C.L., C/UD/TET/D1, copy of Local Govt. Bd. Order 1883.
[43] Wolv. C.L., C/UD/TET/D1, pp. 1, 243–4, 252–3, 258–9, 273, 280.
[44] Ibid. TET/D3, pp. 294, 306; Counties of Stafford and Salop (Tettenhall) Conf. Order, 1894 (Local Govt. Bd. Order no. 31,893; copy in S.R.O., C/C/O/1).
[45] *Express & Star*, 13 Jan. 1961; Wolv. C.L., C/UD/TET/D29, p. 46; S.R.O., L.G.O. 16/12.
[46] Above, introduction.
[47] O.S. Map 1/100,000, Staffs. Admin. Areas (1974 edn.).
[48] H.W.R.O. (H.), E 12/S, Tettenhall, Kingsley accts. 1679–80; S.R.O., D. 1018/2.
[49] B. L. McMillan, *Hist. of Water Supply of Wolverhampton 1847–1947* (Wolverhampton, 1947); *Evening Express*, 12 Jan. 1884.
[50] N. Mutton, 'The Blackbrook Sewage Works of the Tettenhall U.D.C.', *Ind. Arch.* Nov. 1966, 261–7; U.D. of Tettenhall, *Ann. Rep. of M.O.H. for 1952*, 5 (copy in S.R.O., C/H/1/2/2/50).
[51] Seisdon R.D.C., *Rep. of M.O.H. for 1933*, 8 (copy in S.R.O., C/H/1/2/2/36).
[52] Brochure for opening of first house on Woodhouse estate Nov. 1949 (copy in W.S.L. Pamphs.); U.D. of Tettenhall, *Ann. Rep. of M.O.H. for 1946*, 15; *1952*, 22.
[53] *Ann. Rep. of M.O.H. for 1952*, 23; *1960*, 33; *Express & Star*, 23 June 1953, 26 Jan. 1954, 29 Nov. 1955, 3 Feb. 1961.
[54] *Express & Star*, 26 Apr. 1955, 19 Dec. 1958; *Ann. Rep. of M.O.H. for 1959*, 32; *1960*, 33.
[55] *Express & Star*, 27 Feb., 26 Apr. 1963, 1 May 1964; *Tettenhall Observer and Advertiser*, 5 Nov. 1964.
[56] *Tettenhall Official Guide* [1964], 17.
[57] *Express & Star*, 29 Jan. 1952, 2 July 1965; *Wolverhampton Chron.* 28 Mar. 1958; *Ann. Rep. of M.O.H. for 1955*, 22.
[58] Above, p. 13.
[59] *Ann. Rep. of M.O.H. for 1959*, 41; Wolv. C.L., C/UD/TET/F.
[60] *S.H.C.* 1930, 255.
[61] S.R.O., D. 571/A/PK/1, p. 50.
[62] G. P. Mander, *Wolverhampton Antiquary*, ii. 61 n.; *Wolverhampton Chron.* 23 Oct. 1816, 28 Jan., 18 Mar. 1818.

that in December the inhabitants gave notice of their intention to fire upon anyone seen lurking about their houses after 10 p.m.[63] In 1839 the vestry resolved to appoint five police inspectors, although limiting expenditure to £30 14s. a year.[64] There was a police officer in Lower Street in 1841 and one at Tettenhall Wood in 1849. There was an officer at each place in 1851.[65] In 1861 there were an inspector and a constable in Tettenhall village, probably in High Street where there were two officers in 1871.[66] The police station in High Street dates from the 1970s, replacing one on the corner of High Street and Upper Green.[67]

Thomas Thorneycroft of Tettenhall Towers had his own fire brigade by 1889 when it turned out to a fire at a house adjoining the drill hall on Old Hill. A fire station was opened in Wergs Road in the early 1940s. It was replaced by a station in Regis Road in 1970.[68]

There was a post office at Tettenhall by 1811; it was on Lower Green in 1841. By 1860 there were two others at Compton and Wergs.[69]

CHURCHES. During the Middle Ages Tettenhall parish was served by the collegiate church. Codsall, where there was a chapel by the 12th century, was originally part of Tettenhall parish but had become independent by the mid 16th century. There was at least one other chapel in Tettenhall parish during the Middle Ages. In the 1860s the first of several new churches was built for the growing population.

The history of the college, reputedly founded by King Edgar (957–75) and recorded from 1086, is given elsewhere. The dean's peculiar jurisdiction, which passed with most of the college property to Walter Wrottesley in 1549, was exercised by the Wrottesleys until such jurisdictions were brought under the bishop's control in 1846; their testamentary and marriage jurisdiction survived until 1858.[70]

In 1548 the chantry commissioners appointed Francis Hill vicar of Tettenhall. Within a few, months Henry Wollaston, the last prebendary of Perton in the college, had replaced him, but Wollaston was removed for being of small learning and hostile to the king's proceedings. In 1549 John Sheldon, vicar choral of the last prebendary of Bovenhill, was appointed vicar; he soon became an absentee pluralist, and the parishioners complained that he appointed unsuitable people

as curates. As a result his stipend was ordered to be suspended until he became resident or appointed a fit substitute.[71] There was a curate in the late 1590s,[72] and during the 17th and 18th centuries his successors were described variously as minister or curate; as a result of an endowment in the early 18th century the incumbent became a perpetual curate.[73] The living was called a vicarage from 1868.[74] The Wrottesleys were patrons by the 1740s and had presumably appointed earlier curates.[75] In 1653 and 1655, however, the curates were appointed by the government.[76] When the curacy was endowed with land on Kingswood common in 1707, it was stipulated that the lords and tenants of the manor of Tettenhall Regis should have the right of approving appointments to the cure.[77] In 1968 the patronage was vested jointly in Lord Wrottesley and the bishop of Lichfield. In 1980 a team ministry was formed, with the vicar becoming the team rector; the patronage of the living remained with Lord Wrottesley and the bishop.[78]

The vicars appointed in 1548 and 1549 received a stipend of £13 6s. 8d., and the curate received the same in 1604.[79] In 1646 Sir Walter Wrottesley and Sir Richard Leveson of Trentham were allowed reductions in their compositions for their sequestrated estates provided that they each settled £20 a year on the curate, and in 1649 Richard Cresswell of Barnhurst was ordered to settle £30 a year on him. By c. 1659 the curate was receiving an augmentation of £73 a year, but by 1661 part certainly, and presumably all, of the augmentation had lapsed.[80] In 1707 the curacy was endowed with c. 49 a. on Kingswood common, the inhabitants being anxious to attract a minister 'of learning and ability'.[81] In 1716 a grant of £200 was made from Queen Anne's Bounty to meet a benefaction, apparently from Charles Fowler of Pendeford Hall.[82] By 1830 the incumbent's net annual income averaged £196.[83] In 1888 the income was £273 14s. made up of £50 a year given by Lord Wrottesley (d. 1867), £50 a year granted by the Ecclesiastical Commissioners in 1867 to meet Wrottesley's benefaction, £75 from glebe, £10 from tithes, £9 14s. from the Consolidated Fund, £55 from fees, and £24 interest on the money raised from the sale of the former vicarage house.[84] The glebe consisted of 58 a. in Tettenhall and in Beamhurst, in Checkley; part of the Kingswood land had been sold for the new turnpike road brought into use in 1810 and the money used to buy 1 a. near the church.[85]

[63] Mander, *Wolverhampton Antiquary*, ii. 62.
[64] S.R.O., D. 571/A/PC/36.
[65] P.R.O., HO 107/715/998; HO 107/2017(1); *Wolverhampton Dir. for 1849.*
[66] P.R.O., RG 9/1984; RG 10/2927.
[67] *Express & Star*, 19 July 1972; O.S. Map 1/2,500, Staffs. LXXI. 5 (1919 edn.).
[68] *Midland Counties Express*, 14 Sept. 1889; inf. from Tettenhall fire station (1980).
[69] *Wolverhampton Chron.* 11 Dec. 1811; P.R.O., HO 107/715/998; *P.O. Dir. Staffs.* (1860).
[70] *V.C.H. Staffs.* iii. 315–21.
[71] *S.H.C.* 1915, 281–3, 285.
[72] S.R.O., D. 743/1, burial of 5 June 1599.
[73] *Tettenhall Par. Reg.* i. 2; S.R.O., D. 743/1, burial of 14 July 1615; D. 1364/6/1; L.J.R.O., PPe/A/4A.
[74] *Lich. Dioc. Ch. Cal.* (1869).
[75] J. Ecton, *Thesaurus Rerum Ecclesiasticarum* (1742 edn.), 110.

[76] *Walker Revised*, ed. A. G. Matthews, 323; *S.H.C.* 1915, 287.
[77] Below, n. 81.
[78] Lich. Dioc. Regy., Reg. of Transfer of Patronage, f. 161; *Lich. Dioc. Dir.* (1981); inf. from the Lichfield diocesan registrar.
[79] *S.H.C.* 1915, 281, 285–6.
[80] Ibid. 287; *S.H.C.* N.S. vi (2), 327–8; S.R.O., D. 868/2, no. 54A; Kent A.O., U269/T144/A511, f. [14].
[81] Act for support of minister of Tettenhall, 6 Anne, c. 28 (Priv. Act; TS. copy in S.R.O., D. 366/M/1).
[82] Hodgson, *Queen Anne's Bounty*, p. ccxcviii; Jones, *Tettenhall*, 97, 313.
[83] *Rep. Com. Eccl. Revenues*, 503.
[84] S.R.O., D. 1364/3/11; *Lond. Gaz.* 1 Jan. 1867, p. 35.
[85] *Returns relating to Glebe Lands in Eng. and Wales*, H.C. 307, p. 67 (1887), lxiv; White, *Dir. Staffs.* (1834), 287.

In 1893 the Ecclesiastical Commissioners granted £700 to the benefice to meet a benefaction, presumably the £1,000 given shortly before by Jane Margaret Perry (d. 1890) or her sister Helen Perry of Wergs Hall.[86] In 1894 Lord Wrottesley gave a tithe rent charge of £12 15s. 10d.[87] The glebe at Kingswood and Beamhurst was sold in 1921.[88]

The endowment of the curacy in 1707 included a house and garden on the east side of Lower Street where the curate was already living.[89] Another house was bought in 1856, apparently the house south-west of the churchyard which was the vicarage in the 1880s.[90] It was sold to Lord Wrottesley in 1888. In 1889 land in Church Hill Road was bought as the site for a new house, later Eynsham House.[91] It was given up in the later 1920s, being too large.[92] Various houses were then occupied. In 1978 a house in Grotto Lane was bought as a house for the rector of the team ministry.[93]

Thomas Beiston acted as assistant curate in the early 1620s, probably because the curate was non-resident; he subsequently became curate.[94] Richard Harrison was appointed assistant to Beiston in 1649 and succeeded as curate on Beiston's death in 1653.[95] There was again an assistant curate by the early 1830s, the incumbent being non-resident; his stipend was £150.[96] Helen Perry, by will proved in 1907, left £5,000 to support a second curate, who was duly appointed.[97]

A chantry of the Blessed Virgin was founded before 1265 by John Chishull, a royal clerk who became bishop of London in 1274; he had been granted a seven-year lease of the king's manor of Tettenhall in 1256. He endowed it with land in Tettenhall and farm stock. Others added new endowments, and by 1548 the chantry possessed lands in Tettenhall, Compton, and Bilbrook. In 1535 it was evidently served by one of the vicars choral. In 1548 the stipend of the priest was £5 0s. 8d. He received a pension of £5 and died at Tettenhall c. 1559. Richard Cronkhall founded a chantry in 1528 or 1529, endowing it with lands in Tettenhall. In 1548 it was served by William Wyatt, the vicar choral of the prebendary of Pendeford, who was paid £4 7s. 2d. as chantry priest. He too received a pension of £5, dying at Tettenhall in 1552. The chantry was revived during the reign of Mary I.[98]

A Jesus mass was being celebrated by 1521: in his will of that year William Wilkes directed his wife to provide a light to burn during the mass.[99] By 1548 there was a light in honour of Our Lady endowed with two cows. The villagers of Codsall were making a customary payment of 1s. 3d. to maintain a lamp in the church. Seven obits were being kept by 1548.[1]

Puritan influence was felt in the mid 17th century. In the 1630s Richard Lee, a prebendary of St. Peter's, Wolverhampton, was one of several 'inconformable' ministers who regularly preached at Tettenhall, drawing people from Wolverhampton.[2] Richard Harrison, although appointed curate in 1653 under the Great Seal, was found unacceptable by the committee for the approbation of ministers in 1654. He remained in possession, and in April 1655 ten parishioners petitioned for his removal by force. In July 1655 Thomas Buxton was admitted on Cromwell's presentation. Harrison, despite his enforced absence, continued to act as registrar until January 1657.[3] Buxton was evidently ejected in 1662.[4] Continuing puritanism may be evident in the attitude of Thomas Addams, who was rebuked at a visitation in 1670 'for not kneeling in time of prayer'.[5]

In 1776 and 1777 payments were made to a singing master,[6] and psalm singers were mentioned in 1810.[7] A collection of 25 hymns was printed for the congregation in 1826.[8]

A parish magazine was started in 1874.[9]

A reference in 1294 to a graveyard at Wrottesley[10] may indicate the existence of a chapel there. By 1521 there was a chapel at Aldersley. Mass was celebrated there four times a year, presumably by priests from the parish church.[11]

A mission was established at Tettenhall Wood in 1844 and a church built there in 1866. A parish was formed in 1868.[12]

By 1894 there was a mission room at Bilbrook where 'a short bright service with instruction' was held on Monday evenings; there was also a Sunday school.[13] The first part of the present church of Holy Cross in Bilbrook Road was built in 1898 to the design of F. T. Beck of Wolverhampton, with a bell and bellcot at the east end. In 1951 a vestry and porch were added at the south-west end in memory of Lt.-Col. H. E. Twentyman (d. 1945) of Bilbrook Manor House. In 1965 the church was extended eastwards and the bellcot placed over the new east end; the architects were Alan Young & Partners of Dudley. A house next to the church was bought c. 1958 for the first resident priest-in-charge. In 1959 the

[86] Lich. Dioc. Regy., B/A/2(i)/T, p. 514; Lich. Dioc. Mag. (1893), 28; Jones, Tettenhall, 57, 262.
[87] Lich. Dioc. Regy., B/A/2(i)/U, p. 2.
[88] S.R.O., D. 1364/3/12.
[89] Above, n. 81.
[90] Lich. Dioc. Regy., B/A/2(i)/P, p. 550; O.S. Map 1/2,500, Staffs. LXII. 5 (1887 edn.).
[91] Lich. Dioc. Regy., B/A/2(i)/T, pp. 225-6, 239-41, 246; Lond. Gaz. 9 Nov. 1888, p. 6082.
[92] S.R.O., D. 1364/4/26.
[93] Lich. Dioc. Regy., B/A/2(i)/Y, p. 240.
[94] Tettenhall Par. Reg. i. 14-17, 200; S.H.C. 1915, 234, 282.
[95] Tettenhall Par. Reg. i. 43, 47, 220; S.H.C. n.s. vi (2), 328.
[96] Rep. Com. Eccl. Revenues, 503; White, Dir. Staffs. (1834), 287; L.J.R.O., PTe/V/4.
[97] S.R.O., D. 1364/9/11; Lich. Dioc. Ch. Cal. (1909).
[98] V.C.H. Staffs. iii. 316, 319; Jones, Tettenhall, 25;

S.H.C. 1915, 282-4, 286; P.R.O., E 178/3239, m.10.
[99] B.L. Stowe Ch. 631.
[1] S.H.C. 1915, 284.
[2] A. G. Matthews, Cong. Churches of Staffs. 8-11; S.H.C. 1915, 331-2.
[3] Cal. S.P. Dom. 1655, 124-5; Walker Revised, ed. Matthews, 323; S.H.C. 1915, 287; Tettenhall Par. Reg. i. 55.
[4] Calamy Revised, ed. A. G. Matthews, 95.
[5] L.J.R.O., D/C/1/1.
[6] S.R.O., D. 1018/1.
[7] L.J.R.O., PTe/C/5, faculty of 29 Dec. 1810.
[8] Colln. of Hymns for use of the Congregation of Tettenhall (Wolverhampton, 1826; copy in Wolv. C.L.).
[9] The issue for Aug. 1874 is no. 4 (copy in S.R.O., D. 1364/6/9).
[10] S.H.C. n.s. vi (2), 70.
[11] B.L. Stowe Ch. 631.
[12] Below.
[13] Lich. Dioc. Mag. (1894).

church was transferred to the parish of St. Nicholas, Codsall.[14]

In 1939 land on the Aldersley side of Pendeford Avenue was bought as the site for a mission church, but plans were interrupted by the Second World War.[15] From 1946 there was a succession of temporary churches on the site until the consecration of the church of Christ the King there in 1956. On a free-standing frame outside the main entrance of the church is a bell of 1604 originally at St. Michael's.[16]

In 1978 an open-air service was held at the dovecot, Barnhurst, for the residents of the new housing estate. From 1979 monthly services were held in Dovecotes infants' school and from 1980 in the nearby community centre. In 1981 St. Paul's church centre was established in St. Paul's primary school at Pendeford.[17]

The present church of *ST. MICHAEL AND ALL ANGELS*[18] dates from 1955. The former church, except for the porch and west tower, was gutted by fire in 1950.[19]

The medieval church, built of pink sandstone, consisted of a chancel with north and south chapels, an aisled and clerestoried nave of three bays with a south porch, and a west tower.[20] The oldest parts were later 12th-century responds at both ends of the nave arcade. In the 13th century the chancel was extended eastwards and a south chapel of four bays, a south aisle, and a two-storeyed porch were added. The north chapel was also a 13th-century addition. The south chapel and the south aisle were rebuilt in the 14th century when the north arcade was also rebuilt between the earlier responds. The west tower was added in the 15th century when a clerestory was inserted in the nave and the south aisle windows were replaced. There were choir stalls with misericords dating from c. 1500.[21]

A wooden screen which may have dated from the early 15th century divided the north chapel from the north aisle.[22] In the early 16th century the chapel had an altar of St. Thomas and was known as the St. Thomas chancel. The west end was used as a burial place by the Wrottesley family. Richard Wrottesley (d. 1521) left a cow and 'a pair' of vestments to the altar and money for his burial. Monuments included an incised alabaster floor slab to Richard and to his wife Dorothy (d. 1518), and an alabaster table tomb erected in 1580 for John Wrottesley (d. 1578) by his wife Elizabeth.[23] The east end of the north chapel became the vestry. In the later 18th

century it was also used as a schoolroom; access was through a door on the north side.[24]

The south chapel was used as a burial place by the Levesons of Perton. There was an alabaster table tomb depicting Edward Leveson (d. 1569) and his wife Elizabeth; it had been removed by the later 19th century. In 1671 William Leveson-Gower of Sheriff Hales (Salop.) gave what was then called the Perton chancel to Sir Walter Wrottesley, who had recently acquired the Perton prebendal estate. By the later 18th century the chapel had been divided. The west end was used by the Wightwick family and named after them. The east end was used by the Fowlers of Pendeford.[25] Around 1800 the middle window of three in the south wall was converted into a doorway.[26] Glass in one of the remaining windows depicting a chalice with the sun or a host and bearing the legend 'Orate pro anima Henrici Southwycke', commemorated a 16th-century prebendary of Bovenhill. In 1882–3 fragments of medieval glass from the east window of the church were inserted into a window in the chapel.[27]

In the early 19th century there were galleries at the west end of the nave against the tower opening, at the west end of the north aisle, and between the south chapel and aisle. There was a pulpit and reading desk in the north-east of the nave.[28] A new north gallery was built in 1810 extending the length of the aisle. The door at the west end of the aisle was then removed and the space converted into a window; the other windows on the north side were lowered to provide light for the occupants of seats under the gallery.[29] An organ, made by G. P. England, was installed in the west gallery at the same time.[30] The seating was still insufficient, and in 1825 the south aisle was doubled in width and a gallery erected. The 13th-century porch, which had a sundial over the entrance, was replaced as part of the work. An imitation clerestory of lath and plaster was inserted on the north side of the nave. It may also have been at that time that a new pulpit was erected on the south side of the chancel arch and the earlier pulpit and reading desk were placed on the north side. The architect was Edward Haycock of Shrewsbury.[31] His work was unsatisfactory, and in 1833 the roof had to be repaired under the direction of Robert Ebbels of Trysull.[32] The church was repewed in 1841. More seating was provided in the later 1850s when the south chancel chapel was made available. At the same

[14] Lich. Dioc. Regy., B/A/2(i)/U, pp. 323–9; Tettenhall par. mag. for Jan. 1948; inf. from the team vicar (1980).
[15] S.R.O., D. 1364/4/34.
[16] Inf. from Mr. J. Hayward of Aldersley (1980). For the bell see below.
[17] Inf. from Miss Monica Green, Wolverhampton Educ. Dept., and the diocesan registrar.
[18] Called St. Michael's in 1247: V.C.H. Staffs. iii. 316.
[19] Express & Star, 3 Feb. 1950.
[20] This para. is based on W.S.L., Staffs. Views, x. 113, 116 (reproduced below, facing p. 81); photographs in Wolv. C.L.; S.R.O., D. 1364/4/5; Jones, Tettenhall, 245–50; Tettenhall Collegiate Church (1975; copy in W.S.L. Pamphs.).
[21] T.B.A.S. lxvii. 51.
[22] Ibid. 44–5; Jones, Tettenhall, pl. facing p. 251; Tettenhall Coll. Ch. (1975).
[23] S.H.C. N.S. vi (2), 254–5 and pls. facing pp. 256, 282;

T.B.A.S. lxx. 29–30; Shaw, Staffs. ii. 197; Jones, Tettenhall, 258.
[24] S.R.O., D. 571/A/PC/29; W.S.L., Staffs. Views, x. 115; below, p. 44.
[25] Shaw, Staffs. ii. 197; Jones, Tettenhall, 248, 257; S.R.O., D. 571/A/PC/29; D. 593/B/1/5/1.
[26] W.S.L., Staffs. Views, x. 111; S.R.O., D. 571/A/PC/29.
[27] Shaw, Staffs. ii. 196; Jones, Tettenhall, 249–50.
[28] S.R.O., D. 571/A/PC/29.
[29] L.J.R.O., PTe/C/5, faculty of 29 Dec. 1810; W.S.L., Staffs. Views, x. 116; Jones, Tettenhall, 246–7.
[30] S.R.O., D. 571/A/PC/30; D. 1018/1; Lich. Dioc. Mag. (1883), 74. For England see D.N.B. s.v. England, Geo.
[31] L.J.R.O., PTe/A/19, Revd. C. Wrottesley to Wm. Mott, 25 Feb. 1823; Jones, Tettenhall, 248; Lich. Dioc. Mag. (1883), 74; S.R.O., D. 571/A/PC/31; D. 1018/1; W.S.L., Staffs. Views, x. 116; Tettenhall Coll. Ch. (1975), early view of interior.   [32] S.R.O., D. 571/A/PC/32; D. 1018/1.

time the west gallery was removed and the stone-work of the west window restored. A new organ by Messrs. Hill of London was placed in the east end of the north chapel.[33]

In 1882–3 the church was restored by A. E. Street to the design of his father G. E. Street (d. 1881). The stone used was Codsall stone, matching that in the older parts of the building. The south aisle and porch of 1825 were replaced and the outer aisle was extended half way along the south chapel. A clerestory was inserted on the north side of the nave in the same style as that on the south. The north and south galleries and the Wrottesley family's gallery above the screen of the Wrottesley chapel were removed. The pews were replaced by benches. A new pulpit of Caen stone was presented by Joseph Walker; it was itself replaced in 1924 by an oak pulpit made from beams taken out of the belfry at the rehanging of the bells in 1923.[34]

The present church was built to the design of Bernard Miller of Liverpool and consecrated in 1955. It incorporates the medieval tower and Street's south porch, which survived the fire of 1950. In keeping with modern views of the liturgy the high altar is at the east end of the nave. A low wall separates the sanctuary from a Lady chapel which occupies the normal site of the chancel. The nave arcades have exceptionally short columns; the aisles are cross-gabled and have windows which are traceried in a modern reticulated style. The light fittings are of polished copper and resemble inverted chalices.[35]

The Norman font had been removed from the church by the early 19th century. It was taken to St. Mary's, Wolverhampton, built in the early 1840s, and in 1948 it was returned to Tettenhall, where it was kept in the churchyard. In 1982 the font was placed in the newly built St. Paul's church centre at Pendeford.[36]

The plate in 1552 and 1553 consisted of two silver chalices with patens; there was also a copper cross. Apart from vestments and bells the rest of the church goods had been sold for £6 3s. 4d., most of which had been spent on church repairs.[37] By 1672 the only plate was a large silver bowl with a silver cover, a silver plate for bread, and a pewter flagon.[38] All the plate was stolen in 1794 from the parish chest, which was kept in the schoolroom behind the Wrottesley chapel.[39] None of the present plate is earlier than 1850.[40] The chest, over 13 ft. long, was made from the trunk of an oak and was strapped with

bands of iron. It was in two sections, each with its own lid. It was moved to the belfry in the 19th century and broken up during the restoration of 1882–3.[41]

There were four bells and a sanctus bell in 1553. A peal of five was installed in 1604 and replaced in 1841 by a peal of six cast by Thomas Mears of Whitechapel. Two more were presented by Thomas Gilbert in 1911. The eight bells were recast by Gillett & Johnston of Croydon in 1923 and survived the fire of 1950. A new bell, cast in 1955 by Taylor of Loughborough, was placed in a bellcot at the south-east end of the rebuilt church.[42] One of the 1604 bells was taken to St. Mary's, Wolverhampton, built in the early 1840s; it was returned to Tettenhall for the premises used as a church while St. Michael's was being rebuilt after the fire of 1950 and was later given to the mission church of Christ the King opened at Aldersley in 1956.[43]

The churchyard, described in 1826 as inadequate because of the great increase in population, was extended that year by the addition of land east of Church Lane bought for the purpose in 1819.[44] There were further extensions in 1848 and 1888.[45] In 1890 the churchyard was extended southwards, with the demolition of eight cottages in the lane leading to the church; the lichgate at the south entrance was erected in 1891.[46] In 1897 two houses and gardens in Lower Street east of the churchyard were given by Thomas Thorney-croft of Tettenhall Towers; the profits were to be paid to the vicar until the site was needed as an additional burial ground.[47] The churchyard was closed for burials in 1979.[48]

The registers date from 1602 and are complete.[49]

CHRIST CHURCH in Church Road, Tettenhall Wood, originated in a mission established from St. Michael's in 1844 in the infants' school-room.[50] In 1853 an offer by Lord Wrottesley to endow a church for the inhabitants of Compton, Wightwick, Perton, and Trescott with an annual £100, was accepted by the parishioners.[51] Land was bought in 1856 and a church opened in 1866. The cost was met largely by voluntary contributions.[52] An ecclesiastical district was assigned in 1868.[53] The living, a vicarage, was in the gift of Lord Wrottesley until 1968 when the patronage was vested jointly in Lord Wrottesley and the bishop of Lichfield, still patrons in 1980.[54] In 1867 and 1870 the Ecclesiastical Commissioners made two grants of £50 to meet benefactions of

[33] Jones, *Tettenhall*, 248–9; *Lich. Dioc. Mag.* (1883), 74.
[34] S.R.O., D. 1364/4/5; *Lich. Dioc. Mag.* (1883), 74; Jones, *Tettenhall*, 260–1. For the 1924 pulpit see S.R.O., D. 1364/4/18–19; printed notes on Tettenhall ch. loose in copy of Jones, *Tettenhall*, in W.S.L. 8/oo.
[35] *Tettenhall Coll. Ch.* (1975); *S.H.C.* 4th ser. vi. 35, 65.
[36] *Outlook* (Tettenhall Par. Mag., Sept. 1979; copy in W.S.L. Pamphs.).
[37] *S.H.C.* N.S. vi (1), 190; *S.H.C.* 1915, 281–2.
[38] S.R.O., D. 1364/6/1.
[39] Shaw, *Staffs.* ii. 197; S.R.O., D. 1018/1.
[40] *T.B.A.S.* lxxiii. 1, 48–9, 52–3.
[41] Jones, *Tettenhall*, 248; W.S.L., Staffs. Views, x. 113b, 114b; S.R.O., D. 1364/6/1.
[42] *S.H.C.* 1915, 282; Jones, *Tettenhall*, 251–2; *Lich. Dioc. Mag.* (1911), 158; Jennings, *Staffs. Bells*, 96; inscription on 1955 bell.
[43] Lynam, *Church Bells*, 36; White, *Dir. Staffs.* (1851), 84; inf. from Mr. Hayward.

[44] *Lich. Dioc. Regy.*, B/A/2(i)/H, pp. 139–43, 190–206; S.R.O., D. 1364/4/2.
[45] *Lich. Dioc. Regy.*, B/A/2(i)/O, pp. 246–56; T, pp. 226, 237–8.
[46] Ibid. T, pp. 308–14; *Lich. Dioc. Mag.* (1891), 201–2; Jones, *Tettenhall*, 276; W.S.L. 8/oo.
[47] *Lich. Dioc. Regy.*, B/A/2(i)/U, pp. 230–5.
[48] *Lond. Gaz.* 27 Mar. 1979, pp. 4059–60.
[49] All except those in current use are in S.R.O., D. 1364/1; they have been printed for burials to 1732, baptisms to 1741, and marriages to 1839 by the Staffs. Par. Reg. Soc. (1930 and 1966–7).
[50] S.R.O., D. 1018/1, p. 195; D. 1364/4/30.
[51] S.R.O., D. 1364/4/4.
[52] Jones, *Tettenhall*, 267; Lich. Dioc. Regy., B/A/2(i)/R, pp. 282–6.
[53] *Lond. Gaz.* 23 June 1868, pp. 3513–14.
[54] *Lich. Dioc. Ch. Cal.* (1869); Lich. Dioc. Regy., Reg. of Transfer of Patronage, ff. 104, 160; *Lich. Dioc. Dir.* (1981).

£50 and £55 7s. 4d., evidently those made by Lord Wrottesley out of the great tithes of Tettenhall and by the incumbent of St. Michael's. The Commissioners also assigned pew rents to the minister in 1867.[55] In the early 1870s the living was worth £235 net.[56] A house in Church Road was bought as a vicarage house in 1875 by voluntary subscription.[57] The vicar moved into a newly built house in Broxwood Park in 1969 and the old vicarage was sold and demolished.[58] The church, which is of Codsall stone, was designed in a Decorated style by Bateman & Corser of Birmingham.[59] It consists of a chancel with north chapel and south organ chamber, a broad aisled nave, and north and south porches. In 1910 a porch was built at the west end; a vestibule was added in 1975.[60]

By c. 1873 there was a mission room at Finchfield served from Christ Church. The present church of St. Thomas in Oak Hill dates from 1875; it was still used during the week as a school in the early 20th century.[61] It is built of pink stone and has a bellcot on the south side.

There was a mission room at Trescott from the later 1880s. A mission church was opened in 1931 and continued in use until 1972.[62]

The mission church of the Good Shepherd, Windmill Lane, Castlecroft, a brick building designed by Lavender, Twentyman & Percy of Wolverhampton, was opened in 1955.[63] A bell hangs on the north wall. There is a house for an assistant curate nearby.

Interdenominational services were held by a deaconess in houses on the Perton estate from Christmas 1976. From 1977 they were held in the control tower of the former airfield and from 1980 in the community centre. An ecumenical centre called the Church at Perton and served by the deaconess was opened in 1982 under the sponsorship of the Church of England and the United Reformed Church.[64]

ROMAN CATHOLICISM. One recusant was returned in Tettenhall Regis in 1641, three in 1657, and eight c. 1670.[65] In 1715 Thomas Higgs of Barnhurst mill was a papist.[66] Seven papists were listed in 1767.[67]

A church dedicated to St. Thomas of Canterbury was opened in 1931 in the former ballroom at Rock House on Old Hill. The house, which had been rejected as a new vicarage for St. Michael's in 1928, was given to the Roman

Catholic archdiocese of Birmingham by J. F. Myatt of Red Hill Lodge, Compton. The church was at first served from the church of St. Mary and St. John, Wolverhampton, but a priest lived at Rock House from 1932. He was responsible for a mass centre at Codsall until 1961 and another at Pattingham until c. 1959. A site for a new church was bought in Sandy Lane, Claregate, in the mid 1950s, and the priest moved to Danesbury House there; the church at Rock House meanwhile continued in use, but the house itself was used for a short time as a Roman Catholic private school. In 1957 the property in Sandy Lane was handed over to the Sisters of St. Joseph of Tarbes, who opened a school there; Rock House again became the presbytery. In 1962 Gorsty Hayes Cottage in Grange Road was bought, with adjoining land. A church was opened there in 1965 in place of that at Rock House. It is a square building of pale brick surmounted by slender twin towers with a cross between them; the architects were Jennings, Homer & Lynch of Brierley Hill. A parish hall was added in 1978.[68] Gorsty Hayes Cottage, which was owned by the Thorneycroft family from 1886 to 1956, became the presbytery. It is a 17th-century structure, possibly incorporating re-used materials; it contains intruded and imitation 17th-century panelling.[69]

The church of St. Pius X, a small brick building in Castlecroft Avenue, dates from 1956 and is served from St. Michael's, Wolverhampton.[70]

PROTESTANT NONCONFORMITY. Baptisms were performed by dissenting ministers in 1704 and 1706.[71] A house in Compton was registered for protestant dissenters in 1720 and served by itinerant ministers.[72] Paul Russel, a dissenting minister, was buried at Tettenhall in 1751.[73] John Wesley visited Bilbrook nine times between 1751 and 1770, forming a society of 20 people in 1757.[74] There is also a tradition that he preached in Wood Road.[75] Two houses in Tettenhall were registered for protestant dissenters in 1798 and one at Moors Lane in 1827.[76]

A Wesleyan Methodist cause was established at Tettenhall Wood in 1824, and a chapel was built in the later Mount Road in 1825. On Census Sunday 1851 there were congregations of 57 in the morning and 94 in the evening. The chapel was leased to the Congregationalists in 1867. Preaching at Kingswood was organized from Tettenhall Wood for a short time.[77] In 1860 a

[55] Lond. Gaz. 1 Jan. 1867, p. 35; ibid. 25 Feb. 1870, p. 1031; Lich. Dioc. Regy., B/A/2(i)/R, pp. 149–53, 284.
[56] P.O. Dir. Staffs. (1876).
[57] S.R.O., D. 3363/2/34–9; P.R.O., C 54/17734, m. 9.
[58] Inf. from the vicar (1980); Lich. Dioc. Regy., B/A/2(i)/Y, p. 97.
[59] The Builder, 20 May 1865, p. 360.
[60] Lich. Dioc. Mag. (1910), 94; inf. from the vicar.
[61] Lich. Dioc. Ch. Cal. (1874); P.R.O., ED 7/113/324.
[62] Lich. Dioc. Ch. Cal. (1888; 1928); S.R.O., D. 3363/2/8–9.
[63] Printed order of service for dedication, 5 Feb. 1955 (copy in Wolv. C.L.).
[64] Inf. from Deaconess Sheila Finn of Perton.
[65] Staffs. Cath. Hist. v. 18; S.H.C. 4th ser. ii. 84; Cath. Rec. Soc. vi. 310.
[66] Eng. Cath. Nonjurors of 1715, ed. E. E. Estcourt and J. O. Payne, 249.
[67] Staffs. Cath. Hist. xvii. 43.

[68] Inf. (1980) from the Revd. M. F. McGrath, parish priest 1948–77, his successor the Revd. T. J. Rock, and the nuns of the Sandy Lane convent; Express & Star, 5 and 13 Jan. 1931. For the plan to buy Rock Ho. as St. Michael's vicarage see S.R.O., D. 1364/4/26.
[69] Warws. and Worcs. Life, Jan. 1980, 46–7; P.R.O., MR 308, showing a house on or near the site in 1613; deed of 26 Nov. 1956 (copy in W.S.L., C.B./Tettenhall/2).
[70] Archdioc. of Birmingham Dir. (1980).
[71] Tettenhall Par. Reg. i. 135.
[72] S.H.C. 4th ser. iii. 118–19; A. G. Matthews, Cong. Churches of Staffs. 129.   [73] S.R.O., D. 1364/1/2.
[74] Jnl. of Rev. John Wesley, A.M. ed. N. Curnock, iii. 519; iv. 14, 36, 56, 203, 442; v. 87, 357, 449.
[75] Tettenhall Official Guide [1964], 14.
[76] S.H.C. 4th ser. iii. 71, 136.
[77] H. A. May, Queen St. Cong. Church, Wolverhampton, 102; P.R.O., HO 129/379/1/2; A. C. Pratt, Black Country Methodism, 82.

private house at Compton was registered as a place of worship for Primitive Methodists. It was still a place of worship in the late 1860s but had ceased to be used by 1879.[78] For a few months in 1865 Primitive Methodist meetings were held in the drill hall on Old Hill.[79]

In 1837 John Roaf, minister at Queen Street Congregational chapel in Wolverhampton, organized the building of a chapel at Stockwell End. Anglican hostility was such that it was abandoned after a few years and converted into cottages. In 1865 through the efforts of S. S. Mander of Glen Bank, Tettenhall, a leading member of Queen Street, the drill hall on Old Hill was taken over from the Primitive Methodists and opened as a preaching station under the auspices of Queen Street. In 1867 Mander took a lease of the Wesleyan chapel at Tettenhall Wood instead; it was bought in 1869. A new chapel on an adjoining site was begun in 1872 and opened in 1873. Designed in a Gothic style by George Bidlake of Wolverhampton, it is of Codsall stone and has a north-east turret and spire. The former chapel became the Sunday school. By 1874 the church had 54 members, and in that year it was made independent of Queen Street. In 1882, however, it again became a branch church, remaining one until 1949. A new Sunday school building was opened in 1911. In 1914 a mission room was opened in Henwood Road at Compton, but it was soon closed for lack of support. A church hall and ancillary buildings were erected behind the church in 1974. In the late 1970s Tettenhall Wood United Reformed Church had a membership of 157.[80] The ecumenical centre at Perton opened in 1982 was sponsored by the United Reformed Church jointly with the Church of England.[81]

The Presbyterian Church of England began work on a church in Castlecroft Road, Finchfield, in 1965, registering it for worship in 1966. As St. Columba's United Reformed Church it had a membership of 243 in the late 1970s.[82]

A Pentecostal Gospel Mission at Compton was registered in 1939 and had been closed by 1954.[83] The Christian Believers' Meeting Room in Castlecroft Road, Finchfield, was registered in 1970[84] and was still in use in 1980.

EDUCATION. In 1668 Thomas Carr was summoned before the Tettenhall peculiar court for teaching school without a licence.[85] A schoolmaster named William Rudge was living in the parish in 1712.[86] In 1750 there was a newly erected schoolhouse in Compton with an adjoining cottage; both were described as lately erected. The school may have been the one which stood on the south side of Ormes Lane in 1806.[87]

By 1774 a charity school was held in the vestry of the parish church. It was run by Job Price from 1776 until his death in 1824 at the age of 65; he was also parish clerk.[88] In 1818 there were 64 boys at the school, which was supported entirely by voluntary contributions and collections at charity sermons. There was also a parish Sunday school by 1815.[89]

The charity school was replaced by a National school in Lower Street, built in 1827 by subscription and with a grant from the National Society. In 1828 there were 101 boys and 90 girls under a master and a mistress. The school was supported mainly by subscriptions and collections; there was also an income from £20 left c. 1825 by Phoebe Rogers of Tettenhall, from £13 left in 1832 by Thomas Hand, and from a share in the Wyrley and Essington canal company given by Henry Granger of Tettenhall Wood by will proved in 1837. School pence of 1d. and 2d. a week were charged by 1858.[90] The school received a government grant by 1869.[91] A separate infants' school, also supported by subscriptions and by the National Society, was opened in 1856. In 1860 the average attendance was 65 and the children were charged 1d. a week. In 1865 the infants' school moved into a building erected in 1864 and leased for the school until 1871 from the Tettenhall rifle volunteers, apparently the new drill hall on Old Hill.[92] It moved to the Lower Street National school probably when the lease expired. The Lower Street building was enlarged in 1873, and the average attendance there in 1875-6 was 80 boys, 60 girls, and 40 infants.[93] In 1888 the school was rebuilt on a larger scale on the same site.[94] Average attendance in 1905-6 was 207 boys, 191 girls, and 138 infants.[95] The building was enlarged in 1911.[96] By the late 1970s the school was St. Michael's C. of E. controlled primary school, with an average attendance of 200.[97]

[78] G.R.O. Worship Reg. no. 9681; White's Dir. Wolverhampton (1869), mentioning a Methodist chapel at Compton.
[79] S.R.O., D. 1206, box B, mins. of village preachers' meetings 1863-74.
[80] May, Queen St. Cong. Ch. 102-3; Matthews, Cong. Churches of Staffs. 231, 242-3, 246, 262-3; S.H.C. 4th ser. iii. 85; F. H. Lamb, 'Notes on Hist. of Tettenhall Wood Cong. Church, Wolverhampton', Tettenhall Wood Cong. Ch. Yr. Bk. 1968-69 (copy in Wolv. C.L.); S.R.O., D. 1206, box B, mins. of village preachers' meetings 1863-74; Manual of Queen St. Chapel, Wolverhampton (1911), 74; (1912), 79; (1915), 93; (1916), 62; inf. from Mr. K. Cattell of Tettenhall (1980); United Reformed Ch. Yr. Bk. (1980), 72. For Mander see May, op. cit. 34-6.
[81] Above, churches.
[82] Date on church; G.R.O. Worship Reg. no. 70509; United Reformed Ch. Yr. Bk. (1980), 71.
[83] G.R.O. Worship Reg. no. 58775.
[84] Ibid. no. 72317.
[85] L.J.R.O., D/C/1/1. Another schoolmaster who was in trouble at the same time seems to have come from Codsall.
[86] Tettenhall Par. Reg. i. 257; ii. 28.
[87] H.W.R.O. (H.), E 12/S, Kingsley Manor, ct. of 5 May

1750; ibid. Kingsley ct. bk. 1767-1801, p. 21; ibid. plan of Tettenhall Wood common 1806.
[88] S.R.O., D. 1018/1, Dec. 1771; D. 1018/2, note on title page; Jones, Tettenhall, 283.
[89] Digest of Returns to Sel. Cttee. on Educ. of Poor, H.C. 224, p. 868 (1819), ix (2); Wolverhampton Chron. 11 Oct. 1815, 9 Oct. 1816.
[90] S.R.O., D. 571/A/PZ/3; D. 1364/6/1; White, Dir. Staffs. (1834), 288; Staffs. Endowed Chars. 121; L.J.R.O., PTe/A/19, Revd. R. Wrottesley to Wm. Mott, 22 Nov. 1825; P.R.O., ED 7/110/322; O.S. Map 1/2,500, Staffs. LXII. 5 (1887 edn.); below, p. 47.
[91] Rep. Educ. Cttee. of Council, 1869-70 [C. 165], p. 644, H.C. (1870), xxii.
[92] P.R.O., ED 7/110/322.
[93] Jones, Tettenhall, 284; Rep. Parochial Chars. of Tettenhall, 1876 (1877; copy in Wolv. C.L.).
[94] Lich. Dioc. Mag. (1889), 14; O.S. Map 1/2,500, Staffs. LXII. 5 (1902 edn.).
[95] Public Elem. Schs. 1907 [Cd. 3901], p. 572, H.C. (1908), lxxxiv.
[96] Kelly's Dir. Staffs. (1916).
[97] Lich. Dioc. Dir. (1980).

A National school for infants was opened at Tettenhall Wood in what became School Road in 1844; it was given an endowment of £45 a year from the Poor's Land by the freeholders of the parish. In 1846–7 there were 40 boys and 50 girls. By the late 1860s it had an average attendance of 71 and received a government grant.[98] The average attendance in 1905–6 was 98.[99] The school was rebuilt on a site to the west in Shaw Lane in 1963, and as Christ Church C. of E. controlled infants' school it had an average attendance of 150 in the late 1970s.[1] The former building was then used as a branch library.

A National school connected with Christ Church was built on the opposite side of School Road from the infants' school in 1874. Within a few weeks of opening it had 80 boys and 60 girls under a master and a mistress. School pence of 2d. a week were charged.[2] The school received a government grant, and the average attendance in 1879–80 was 231.[3] In 1905–6 it was 283.[4] A new building was opened in Woodcote Road in 1974, and as Christ Church C. of E. controlled junior school it had an average attendance of 230 in the late 1970s. The former building was taken over for a special school in 1976.[5]

The mission church opened at Finchfield in 1875 was used as a school for boys, girls, and infants from 1876; the desks were constructed to be used also as seats for the church. It was run by a mistress and was under government inspection; the children were charged 2d. a week.[6] By 1893 it had become an infants' school only.[7] The average attendance was 49 in 1893–4 and 29 in 1905–6.[8] It was closed c. 1920 but was used as a temporary junior school in the earlier 1940s.[9]

The development of the area after the Second World War was reflected in the number of new schools.[10] In 1980 there were three comprehensive schools, Regis in Regis Road (1955), Smestow in Windmill Crescent, Castlecroft, opened in 1963[11] and brought into full use in 1964, and Aldersley in Barnhurst Lane (1977). Bilbrook Church of England middle school in Bilbrook Road was opened in 1976 in part of the premises of the former Bilbrook county primary, opened in 1950.[12] Perton middle school in Gainsborough Drive was opened in 1982.[13] The other new primary schools were Castlecroft junior and infants' in Windmill Crescent (1952), Palmers Cross junior and infants' in Windermere Road

(1952), Westacre infants' in Finchfield Hill, opened in 1954 as a county primary school, Claregate junior and infants' in Chester Avenue (1958), Woodthorne junior in Woodthorne Road South (1958), Uplands junior in Finchfield Road West (1970), Woodthorne infants' in Woodthorne Road South (1973), Lane Green first school, opened in part of the former Bilbrook country primary school in 1976,[14] Dovecotes infants', Ryefield, Barnhurst (1978), Dovecotes junior (1979), Perton first school, Manston Drive (1979), St. Paul's C. of E. primary, Pendeford (1981), Priory Green nursery, infants', and junior, Pendeford (1981), and Sandown first school, Perton (1982).[15] A nursery school was opened in Martham Drive off Bridgnorth Road, Compton, in 1975. There were five special schools in 1980, Wightwick Hall (1956),[16] Kingswood (1960), Uplands Intermediate Unit in Finchfield Road West (1975), Tettenhall Wood in the former National school in School Road (1976), and Castlecroft in Windmill Crescent (1978).

There have also been a number of private schools in Tettenhall. By 1811 Mrs. Hill ran a girls' boarding school there. In 1814 she offered a finishing-school education for a few young ladies, in addition to her general school which in 1815 had 8 little boys and about 30 girls. Dancing was taught by William Hill, who gave lessons there and at other schools in the neighbourhood accompanied on the pedal harp by his daughter Charlotte. Annual balls were held in the 'great room' of the post office. In 1816 William Hill advertised lessons in the waltz. He also gave private tuition in astronomy, geography, and shorthand and in 1818 was running the ladies' boarding school.[17] In 1835 and 1845 there were four private schools, two at Compton and one each at Tettenhall and Tettenhall Wood. The ladies' school run in 1845 by Ann Wright at Mount Pleasant, Tettenhall Wood, was still open in 1861; by 1871 her daughter, also Ann Wright, had moved it to Clifton Road. There was one other private school in 1861, a mixed school at Finchfield, which by 1871 had moved to Compton.[18] Tettenhall Proprietary School was opened in the house called the Hall in 1863 as a Free Church boarding school for boys and was renamed Tettenhall College in 1869; its history is given elsewhere.[19] There was a boys' school at Wergs in 1904

[98] S.R.O., D. 571/A/PZ/2; D. 1364/4/30; Nat. Soc. Inquiry, 1846–7, Staffs. 10–11; Rep. Educ. Cttee. of Council 1869–70 [C. 165], p. 644, H.C. (1870), xxii.
[99] Public Elem. Schs. 1907, 572.
[1] Inf. from the director of educ., Wolverhampton metropolitan boro. (1980); Lich. Dioc. Dir. (1980).
[2] P.R.O., ED 7/110/323.
[3] Rep. Educ. Cttee. of Council, 1879–80 [C. 2562-I], p. 231, H.C. (1880), xxii.
[4] Public Elem. Schs. 1907, 572.
[5] Lich. Dioc. Dir. (1980); inf. from the director of educ., Wolverhampton.
[6] P.R.O., ED 7/113/324; S.R.O., D. 3363/2/43.
[7] S.R.O., D. 3363/2/43, pp. 161, 168; Jones, Tettenhall, 267. It was described as mixed in Rep. Educ. Cttee. of Council, 1894–95 [C. 7776-I], p. 994, H.C. (1895), and as an infants' school in Schs. in receipt of Parl. Grants, 1899–1900 [Cd. 332], p. 225, H.C. (1900), lxiv.
[8] Rep. Educ. Cttee. of Council, 1894–95, 994; Public Elem. Schs. 1907, 572.
[9] Kelly's Dir. Staffs. (1916; 1924); Express & Star, 29

Aug. 1944.
[10] Para. based, unless otherwise stated, on Tettenhall Official Guide [1964], 18, 20, and inf. from the director of educ., Wolverhampton (1980).
[11] Express & Star, 2 Nov. 1965.
[12] Inf. from the headmaster, Bilbrook C. of E. middle sch.
[13] Inf. from the sec., Perton first sch.
[14] Inf. from the headmaster, Bilbrook C. of E. middle sch.
[15] Inf. on the 2 Pendeford schs. from Miss Monica Green, Wolverhampton Educ. Dept., and on the 2 Perton schs. from the sec., Perton first sch.
[16] Inf. from the headmaster.
[17] Wolverhampton Chron. 11 Dec. 1811, 15 Jan. 1812, 13 Jan., 14 Apr. 1813, 9 Mar. 1814, 6 Sept. 1815, 12 June 1816; Parson and Bradshaw, Dir. Staffs. (1818).
[18] Pigot, Nat. Com. Dir. (1835), 482; P.O. Dir. Staffs. (1845); Wolverhampton Dir. for 1849; P.R.O., HO 107/2017; P.R.O., RG 9/1984; RG 10/2927.
[19] V.C.H. Staffs. vi. 171–2.

preparing boys for public schools and the Navy.[20] The Sisters of St. Joseph of Tarbes opened a girls' preparatory school in Sandy Lane in 1957 with 50 pupils; in 1980 there were 188 pupils.[21]

CHARITIES FOR THE POOR. CRESSWELL'S ALMSHOUSE. By will dated 1707 Richard Cresswell, the owner of Barnhurst, devised to trustees an almshouse in Tettenhall with the intention that it should be divided into six apartments, each for a retired servant of his family. Cresswell died in 1708, and the building seems to have remained uncompleted: in the later 1780s it consisted of only four dwellings. Cresswell also left a house at Bilbrook to provide £30 a year for distribution among the almspeople. After the Cresswell family had sold their property in the parish, probably in the mid 1720s, the beneficiaries lived at a distance and let the dwellings at £1 a year each. The rents ceased to be collected after 1776 and the cottages were occupied by anyone who could obtain possession. About 1800 payment of the £30 from the Bilbrook property had ceased; by 1820, however, the owner was prepared to resume payment provided that the annuitants once more resided in the almshouse. It appears that the charity was revived and that the income was still paid in the mid 1860s.[22]

THE PAROCHIAL CHARITIES. William Wollaston (d. 1595) gave £2 12s. a year, charged on land at Trescott, to be distributed in bread each week to 12 poor of the parish. By 1820 penny loaves were distributed every Sunday to widows, the aged, and persons with large families.[23]

Matthew Wightwick (d. probably 1621) left an annual 20s. from land at Wightwick to the poor of the parish. The charge was redeemed in 1896 and the proceeds were invested in stock.[24]

In 1630 £50 given by Walter Wrottesley and £10 given by Francis Tunck for the poor was used to buy land in Albrighton (Salop.). The annual income in 1820 was £13 11s.[25]

Sir John Wollaston (d. 1658), a native of Tettenhall and a lord mayor of London, gave £5 10s. a year, charged on land at Trescott, and by 1820 the income was distributed among 12 poor widows. In addition he gave £2 12s. a year, also charged on land at Trescott, to be distributed each week in bread. By the later 1780s the recipients were widows, and by 1820 the bread was distributed with William Wollaston's charity.[26]

Mary Dobson (d. 1674) left to the parishes of

Tettenhall and Wolverhampton £60, of which £10 was used towards the purchase of Brych House (see below). The rest was used to buy meadow in Brewood from which in the later 1780s the poor of Tettenhall received an annual £1, a two-fifths share of the income.[27]

In 1709 Thomas Croffts of Tettenhall Wood and his wife Anne gave meadow in Wolverhampton, the income to be paid to the poor of Tettenhall parish at Michaelmas. In 1820 the income was £5 a year.[28]

In 1714 Brych House and the adjoining 8 a. of land between Wrottesley Road and Redhouse Road were bought for the benefit of the poor of Tettenhall parish; its use was to be decided by a special annual meeting of parishioners.[29] The cost was met with the capital of 14 bequests to the poor:[30] £10 from Walter Fleeming (d. 1617 or 1652);[31] £10 each from Ralph Lovat and Thomas Farmer (both dead by 1630);[32] £6 13s. 4d. from John Addenbrooke (d. 1634);[33] £5 from Francis Morris (d. 1635); £10 from John Croft (d. 1641); £10 from Thomas Southwick (d. 1650); £2 from Henry Southwick (d. 1650 or 1700); £10 from Mary Robson (d. 1674); £20 from Dame Mary Wrottesley (d. 1711); £10 from Walter Fowler (d. probably 1711);[34] £5 from Francis Wightwick (d. probably 1714);[35] £5 from Francis Tomkins and £2 from Richard Garret (dates of death unknown). By 1746 the house was used as a workhouse, and in 1820 the rent received from the property was £19 6s. 4½d. a year.[36] In 1860 a new workhouse was opened in Trysull; Brych House was used as an arms store and drill hall by the rifle volunteer company for some four years and was then converted into cottages. The annual income had risen to £57 10s. by the mid 1860s and to £113 1s. by 1924–5. In 1926 the cottages, old and dilapidated, were put up for sale.[37]

Henrietta Wrottesley (d. 1720) left £100, the interest to be paid to the poor of the parish. The money, augmented by £15 out of William Smith's bequest (see below), was invested in land at Wightwick, a lease of which was granted in 1730 at £5 5s. a year. The annual income was £16 10s. in 1820 and £18 14s. by the mid 1860s. The land was sold in 1899 and the proceeds were invested in stock which produced £21 2s. 6d. a year in the early 20th century.[38]

Dame Frances Wrottesley (d. 1769) left £100, the interest to be paid to the poor of the parish. In 1770 a distribution of £23 10s. was made from the capital and the remainder invested in stock, the interest to be distributed at Candlemas. The

[20] Kelly's Dir. Staffs. (1904).
[21] Inf. from the nuns (1980).
[22] 5th Rep. Com. Char. 582–4; Char. Dons. 1786–88, 1150–1; Char. Digest Staffs. 54–5; above, manors and other estates.
[23] Shaw, Staffs. ii. 197; S.H.C. v (2), 320 n.; Char. Dons. 1786–88, 1150–1; 5th Rep. Com. Char. 581–2.
[24] Shaw, Staffs. ii. 197; Tettenhall Par. Reg. i. 200.
[25] S.R.O., D. 1364/2/16; 5th Rep. Com. Char. 579.
[26] Shaw, Staffs. ii. 197; Char. Dons. 1786–88, 1150–1; 5th Rep. Com. Char. 581–2; above, introduction.
[27] Shaw, Staffs. ii. 196–7; Char. Dons. 1786–88, 1150–1.
[28] S.R.O., D. 1364/2/22; 5th Rep. Com. Char. 580.
[29] S.R.O., D. 1364/2/28–31; J. Phillips and W. F. Hutchings, Map of Staffs. (1832); 5th Rep. Com. Char. 579.

[30] Shaw, Staffs. ii. 197. The figure of £123 4s. 6d. given in 5th Rep. Com. Char. 579, includes £5 left by Catherine Fowler and used to repair the house.
[31] Dates of death, unless stated otherwise, are derived from burial dates in Tettenhall Par. Reg. i.
[32] S.R.O., D. 1364/2/16.
[33] Omitted by Shaw but given in S.R.O., D. 1018/2.
[34] Above, manors and other estates (Pendeford).
[35] Above, manors and other estates (Tettenhall Regis; Wightwick).
[36] Above, local government; 5th Rep. Com. Char. 579–80.
[37] Jones, Tettenhall, 287; Char. Digest Staffs. 54–5; S.R.O., D. 1364/9/12.
[38] Shaw, Staffs. ii. 198; S.H.C. N.S. vi (2), 341; S.R.O., D. 1364/2/25, 27; 5th Rep. Com. Char. 580–1; Char. Digest Staffs. 54–5; Staffs. Endowed Chars. 120.

income, £3 in the later 1780s, was distributed in bread in 1820.[39]

Phoebe Rogers (d. c. 1825) left £40, half the interest to be spent on the National school and half on the poor who regularly attended the parish church, preferably widows. The bequest was augmented by the sale of timber in 1827 and 1831, and the aggregate of £178 18s. 6d. was invested in stock. In the mid 1860s the annual income was £5 7s. 4d., of which £2 7s. 4d. was distributed to the poor at Christmas.[40]

By will dated 1832 Thomas Hand left £100, the interest to be divided between the National school and the poor of the parish. Only £26 was received, and it was invested in stock. In the mid 1860s an annual 8s. 8d. was paid to the poor in cash.[41]

By 1820 the charities of Matthew Wightwick, Mary Dobson, and Thomas and Anne Croffts and the income from the Albrighton poor's land, Brych House, and the Wightwick poor's land were distributed together twice a year to the poor not receiving parish relief. In 1820 the combined income was £56 7s. 4d.[42] In 1844 the income from what was called the Poor's Land in Tettenhall (presumably the above six charities) amounted to £76 4s. 6d.; it was then decided to spend £45 a year on the infants' school at Tettenhall Wood and the rest on the poor.[43]

By a scheme of 1888 the six charities were consolidated with those of William and Sir John Wollaston, Dame Frances Wrottesley, Phoebe Rogers, and Thomas Hand, under the name of the Parochial Charities. The income of the consolidated charity, which also included Henry Granger's bequest of 1837 for the National school, was to be divided into five equal parts, three of them to be used for medical purposes, in providing apprentices with tools, in supplying clothing, food, and fuel for the sick, and in giving financial help in urgent cases. The remaining two fifths were to be spent on children attending the National schools in the parish. In 1971–2 the income was £343.21, of which £100 was distributed in 16 cash doles, £118.75 in 125 food parcels, and £30 in 10 £3 coal vouchers.[44]

OTHER CHARITIES. Sir Walter Wrottesley (d. 1686) left £5 for the poor of the parish. In 1701, with the consent of his son Sir Walter, the charity was raised to £8 by the addition of £3 from the poor's land in Albrighton. It was then agreed to spend £6 on apprenticing boys and girls outside the parish and to distribute the income from the remaining £2 among the poor. The charity may have been amalgamated with the Albrighton poor's land, since Sir Walter Wrottesley's charity was listed with Walter Wrottesley's in the charity abstracts of the later 1780s.[45]

Catherine Fowler (d. 1715) left £5 for the poor of the parish. The capital was used to repair Brych House.[46]

William Smith of Wergs (d. 1724), builder and architect, left £40, the interest to be paid to the poor of the parish. In 1729 £15 was spent with Henrietta Wrottesley's £100 on land at Wightwick. The remaining £25 was lent on bond; some time before 1787 the bond was called in and the charity spent on enlarging Brych House, by then the workhouse.[47]

Richard Smith of Tettenhall Wood (d. 1730) left £20, the interest to be distributed, after small payments to the minister and clerk, to poor attending prayers on Midsummer Day. The money was lent on bond; before 1787 the bond was called in and the money spent on enlarging the workhouse. In 1820 the overseers continued to pay an annual 20s. which was considered to be the interest on the charity money. It was apparently no longer paid in the mid 1860s.[48]

By will of 1757 Elizabeth Russell left £20, the interest to be distributed in bread on the first Sunday in each month. In 1786 the money was lent on bond; the holder defaulted in 1800, but the parish held itself responsible to maintain the charity. In 1820 the overseers were distributing 18s. in monthly bread doles. In 1856 the money was paid as a donation by the minister and churchwardens out of the offertory. The charity was still paid in the mid 1860s, but nothing further is known of it.[49]

Dorothy Fowler (d. 1791) left £50, the interest to be spent on copies of the Bible, the Book of Common Prayer, and the *Whole Duty of Man* for poor children of the parish. In 1820 an annual £2 10s. was due to the vicar out of the poor's rate for the books, probably because the charity money had been spent on repairs to the workhouse, but it was paid irregularly.[50] Nothing further is known of the charity.

In 1859 and 1865 Thomas Thorneycroft established charities to provide blankets and flannel for the poor of Wolverhampton and Tettenhall. In 1970 they were amalgamated with a Wolverhampton blanket charity, founded by G. B. Thorneycroft, to form the Thorneycroft Charity. It was to provide help in cash and kind for people in Wolverhampton borough, Tettenhall urban district, and Wrottesley civil parish. In 1973 the income was £101, and £109 was spent on blankets.[51]

By will proved 1895 Henry Owen left £100 to the vicar of Tettenhall Wood for the poor of that parish. In 1982 the income of £5 was distributed in gifts at Christmas.[52]

By will proved 1907 Helen Perry of Wergs Hall left £3,000, two thirds of the interest to be laid out in coal and one third in blankets for the poor

[39] Shaw, *Staffs.* ii. 198; *S.H.C.* n.s. vi (2), 345–6; *Char. Dons. 1786–88*, 1150–1; *5th Rep. Com. Char.* 582.
[40] S.R.O., D. 571/A/PZ/1; D. 1364/6/1; D. 1364/9/1, 8; *Char. Digest Staffs.* 54–5.
[41] *Staffs. Endowed Chars.* 121; *Char. Digest Staffs.* 54–5.
[42] *5th Rep. Com. Char.* 581.
[43] S.R.O., D. 571/A/PZ/2.
[44] *Staffs. Endowed Chars.* 121–2; Jones, *Tettenhall*, 301; Char. Com. files.
[45] S.R.O., D. 1364/6/1; *S.H.C.* n.s. vi (2), 337; *Char. Dons. 1786–88*, 1150–1.

[46] Shaw, *Staffs.* ii. 197; *Tettenhall Par. Reg.* i. 259.
[47] Shaw, *Staffs.* ii. 197; *Tettenhall Par. Reg.* i. 264; *5th Rep. Com. Char.* 580–2.
[48] Shaw, *Staffs.* ii. 197–8; S.R.O., D. 284/M/1; *Tettenhall Par. Reg.* i. 271; *5th Rep. Com. Char.* 582; *Char. Digest Staffs.* 54–5.
[49] *5th Rep. Com. Char.* 582; S.R.O., D. 1364/9/1; *Char. Digest Staffs.* 54–5.
[50] S.R.O., D. 1364/1/2; *5th Rep. Com. Char.* 582.
[51] Char. Com. files.
[52] Ibid.; inf. from the vicar of Tettenhall Wood.

of Tettenhall parish. Under a Scheme of 1974 the terms of the charity were widened to cover payments in cash and kind to those in need.[53]

By will proved 1928 Dr. John Lycett of Leamington (Warws.), formerly of Tettenhall, left £3,000 stock, the income to be spent by the parochial church council of St. Michael's on needy members of the congregation not in receipt of parish relief. The income also provided an annual 2 guineas for the vicar to preach a sermon on the Sunday nearest 10 May, the birthday of Lycett's wife Ann, after whom the charity was named. In 1972 the income was £94.43, and £105 was distributed in six doles of £10 and nine of £5.[54]

By will proved 1930 Mary Bruford left £105, the income to buy groceries for the poor of Tettenhall Wood at the beginning of each year. In 1982 the income of £5.30 was distributed in gifts at Christmas.[55]

[53] S.R.O., D. 1364/9/11; Char. Com. files.
[54] S.R.O., D. 1364/9/13; *Express & Star*, 11 Mar. 1929; Char. Com. files.
[55] Char. Com. files; inf. from the vicar of Tettenhall Wood.

SEISDON HUNDRED
SOUTHERN DIVISION

AMBLECOTE

THE town of Amblecote lies in an angle of the river Stour, which there formed the county boundary with Worcestershire until 1966.[1] Amblecote was the Staffordshire portion of the ancient parish of Old Swinford; the rest of the parish was in Worcestershire and included the town of Stourbridge, which adjoins Amblecote on the south. In 1898 what had previously been styled the hamlet of Amblecote was made an urban district, 665 a. in area. In 1966 it was divided between the boroughs of Stourbridge and Dudley, and from 1974 it was wholly within Dudley.[2]

Most of Amblecote lies on a spur of high ground bounded by the Stour on the south and west; there is also a low-lying area in the south-west which has attracted ironworks, a canal basin, and a railway goods depot. The ground rises from 215 ft. (66 m.) in that corner and 238 ft. (73 m.) at Bagleys Road in the south-east corner to 426 ft. (130 m.) at Amblecote Bank halfway along the former eastern boundary; it drops to below 300 ft. (91 m.) along Coalbourn brook in the north-east.[3] The brook, which flows west into the Stour, formed the boundary on the north-east. It was mentioned by name in 1510[4] and apparently in 1295.[5] The rock is sandstone in the west; the eastern part of Amblecote lies on the Coal Measures, and there are also beds of fire-clay.[6] Both coal and clay were worked until the 1970s. The soil is marl.[7]

In 1086 the recorded population was seven.[8] Two tax assessments of the mid 1520s listed 10 and 12 people,[9] and 11 names appeared on the muster roll of 1539.[10] A survey of the manor c. 1600 listed 21 houses.[11] The poll-tax assessment of 1641 listed 118 people.[12] In 1666 there were 31 people assessed for hearth tax with a further 31 too poor to pay.[13] The population in 1801 was

1,002, and it rose steadily to 1,236 in 1831; it then increased more rapidly, with particularly sharp rises in the 1850s, 1860s, and 1890s, and had reached 3,128 by 1901.[14] The sharp increases then ceased, the population being 3,155 in 1911 and 3,182 in 1921. It had dropped to 3,099 by 1931, and although it had risen to 3,165 by 1951, it was down to 3,009 in 1961.[15]

The name Amblecote, deriving perhaps from Amela's cot, suggests Anglo-Saxon settlement.[16] The original centre was probably on the high ground in the north-east where the manor house stood. Settlement, however, became concentrated along the main Stourbridge–Wolverhampton road which runs through the west of Amblecote. The Platts in the north-west was an inhabited area by the later 12th or early 13th century. There was then a local family called Platte, which was still living at the Platts in the early 15th century.[17] Holloway End along the southern part of the main road was inhabited by 1540; Amblecote Lane (later Vicarage Road) running from Amblecote Bank in the east and past the manor house to join the main road at Holloway End, was mentioned by name in 1589.[18] One of the first glasshouses in Amblecote was built at Holloway End in the earlier 17th century.[19] In 1642 there were four houses, a horse mill, and a mill house in the sandstone outcrop on the east side of the main road.[20] In the 1680s the cave dwellings were described as consisting of 'partitions and offices, with holes forth at the top instead of chimneys, wherein several people of meaner rank have their constant habitations'.[21] By the late 17th century the name Coalbourn-brook was in use[22] for the area north of Holloway End lying around the junction of the main road and the road to Wollaston, in Old Swinford, and crossed by Coalbourn brook; there were then at

[1] This article was written mainly in 1981. Mr. H. J. Haden of Stourbridge is thanked for generously providing much information and for reading and commenting on the article in draft. Miss M. Henderson, assistant county archivist at Worcester, Mr. D. C. Hickman, area librarian at Stourbridge, Mr. N. R. Perry of Old Swinford, the Revd. P. Tongue, vicar of Amblecote, and others named in footnotes are also thanked for their help.
[2] Below, local govt.
[3] O.S. Map 6″, Staffs. LXXI. NW. (1887 edn.); SW. (1888 edn.).
[4] S.R.O., Tp. 1273/13.
[5] W.S.L., S.D. Pearson 286, mentioning Colebourne meadow.
[6] T. H. Whitehead and others, Memoirs of Geol. Surv., Geol. of Southern Part of S. Staffs. Coalfield, 60, 132, 173, 193–4; Memoirs of Geol. Surv., Special Reps. on Mineral

Resources of Gt. Brit. vol. xiv: Refractory Materials: Fire-clays, 106–7; V.C.H. Staffs. i, map before p. 1.
[7] Kelly's Dir. Staffs. (1940).
[8] Below, econ. hist. (agric.).
[9] P.R.O., E 179/177/96, 106.
[10] S.H.C. N.S. vi (1), 72.
[11] S.R.O., Tp. 1273/13.
[12] H.L., Main Papers, box 178.
[13] S.H.C. 1923, 56–7.
[14] V.C.H. Staffs. i. 326.
[15] Census, 1911–61.
[16] Ekwall, Eng. Place-names.
[17] H.W.R.O. (H.), E 12/S, Early Deeds.
[18] S.R.O., Tp. 1273/13.
[19] Below, econ. hist.
[20] D.C.L., D/OH/I/1/22.
[21] Plot, Staffs. 172.
[22] Ibid. 122.

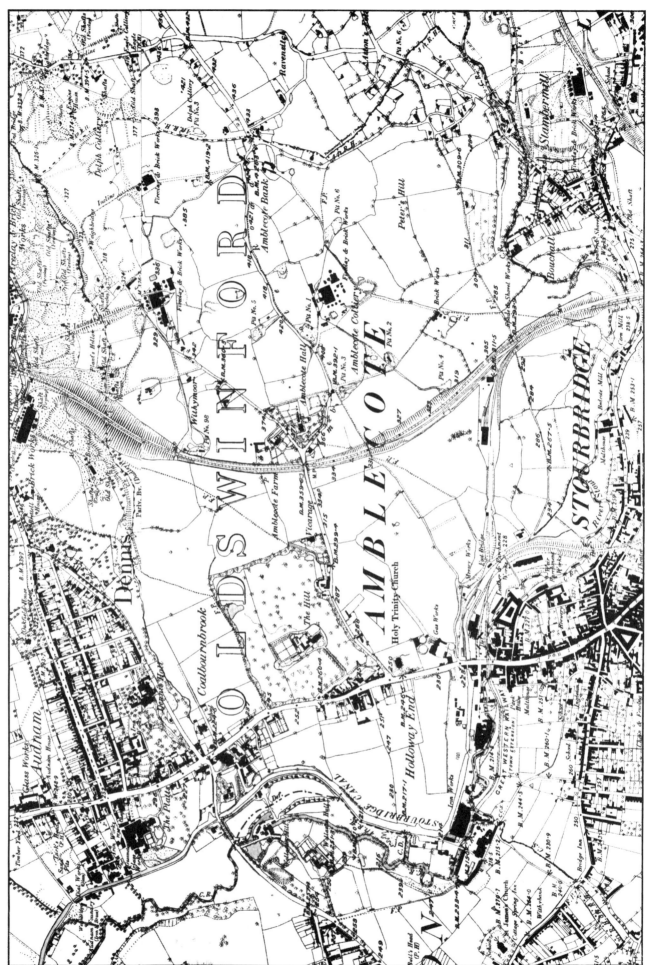

AMBLECOTE 1882: SCALE 6 IN. TO 1 MILE (1:10,560)

least two glasshouses there.[23] In 1718 there was a public house there called the Royal Oak; it had been renamed the Green Dragon by 1722.[24] A public house called the Fish, presumably a predecessor of the inn of that name in the south-west angle of the road junction, existed by the late 1770s.[25] The name Coalbournhill was in use for the area south-west of the road junction by the late 18th century.[26] Brettell Lane, running east to Brierley Hill, in Kingswinford, and forming part of the northern boundary of Amblecote, was so named by 1727.[27] The area immediately south of its junction with the main road was known as Tobacco Box Hill by the late 18th century, when there was a small glasshouse there. The name was still in use in 1871 and survived into the 20th century as Box Hill and Bacca Box.[28]

The eastern part of Amblecote was the scene of extensive coal and clay mining from the 16th century. In the later 17th century there were houses and a glasshouse on the waste called Withymoor north-east of the manor house; there was further settlement at the east end of Amblecote Lane in the area known as Amblecote Bank by 1733, down the south-eastern boundary, and along the Stour.[29] The road from the river to Amblecote Bank, the later Stamford Road, was mentioned in 1739.[30] The name Babylon was in use for an area in the north-east corner in 1774 when there were two houses there; the name was still in use in the earlier 19th century.[31] The Birch Tree inn at the eastern end of Vicarage Road is probably an 18th-century building, although much altered. The former Pear Tree inn nearby in Stamford Road was stated in 1896 to be over a century old.[32] Peter's Hill, the area south-west of Amblecote Bank, evidently derives its name from Peter Hill who held a house and 8½ a. there in 1805.[33]

Three large houses were built near the Stourbridge–Wolverhampton road in the 18th century. The Hill, from 1893 Corbett Hospital, north-east of the junction of the road with Amblecote Lane was the home of a John Grove in 1724 and later of Thomas Rogers, who owned the Holloway End glasshouse and was grandfather of the poet Samuel Rogers. In 1769 its grounds covered 18½ a.[34] Dennis House (later Hall) to the north was built on land which was called Dennis by the 1380s, taking its name from the family of the 12th-century Denis of Amblecote.[35] The house was built by Thomas Hill in the 1760s when he

inherited the property, including a glasshouse. In 1769 the house stood in 27 a. The grounds were built over in the mid 19th century, but in 1981 the house survived as part of the glassworks built in the earlier 1850s; a lodge still stood on the main road.[36] The Platts on the opposite side of the main road was the home in the early 18th century of Joshua Henzey, who ran a glasshouse to the north of it. A new house was built c. 1760; in 1769 it stood in 26 a. which was built over in the mid and late 19th century. The house, which survived as 66 Platts Crescent, was divided into two residences. It was demolished in 1967 after part of it had been occupied for some years by the Ducat Heating Co. with the rest standing empty; houses were then built over the site.[37]

The opening of the Stourbridge Canal in 1779 led to the building of a number of ironworks in the south-west of Amblecote in the early 19th century; at the same time the scale of mining in the east began to grow. Increased industrialization did not at first lead to a great increase in population; although the new ironworks employed large numbers, the workers lived mostly in Stourbridge and other neighbouring parts.[38] Nevertheless some houses were built north of the bridge over the Stour;[39] a National school was opened at Holloway End in 1815 and a church in 1842. Extensive development took place from the late 1830s north of Coalbournbrook. In 1838 part of the Dennis estate consisting of 40 building lots fronting Brettell Lane was offered for sale with 17 tenements on Tobacco Box Hill to the south. In 1839 another 40 building lots on the Platts estate were for sale together with three houses there. The first area, which became known as Dennis Park, was apparently bought by William Blow Collis, a Stourbridge solicitor. By 1846 a new street had been laid out parallel to Brettell Lane and many houses built; the street had been named King William Street by 1861 after William King of Amblecote Hall, a clay master who died in 1850. Two side streets, later Hill Street and Vale Street, linked it with Brettell Lane. The rest of the Dennis estate was sold in the earlier 1850s, and most of it was bought by a land society. Collis Street was completed in 1853; two side streets, later Vale Street and Villa Street, connected it with King William Street by 1856, and a third, Dennis Street, had been built by 1861. A National school replacing that at Holloway End was built south of Collis Street in 1856.[40] Old Wharf Road

[23] Below, pp. 58–9.
[24] S.R.O., Tp. 1273/4, deed of 4 Dec. 1745; 10, deeds of 24 June 1718 and 14 May 1722.
[25] H.W.R.O. (W.), 899:31 BA4380/42(ii), Old Swinford Road Order Bk. 1768–79, 25 Jan. 1779; S.R.O., D. 356A, no. 64.
[26] Stourbridge Libr., list of glass manufacturers in Stourbridge and Dudley 1796; Scott, *Stourbridge*, 108.
[27] Below, p. 52.
[28] Stourbridge Libr., list of glass manufacturers 1796; P.R.O., RG 10/3021; inf. from Mr. H. J. Haden.
[29] Below, econ. hist.; S.R.O. 1392; R. L. Chambers, *Oldswinford, Bedcote, and Stourbridge Manors and Boundaries* (Dudley Teachers' Centre, 1978), 43.
[30] S.R.O., Q/SO 14, f. 51v.
[31] *Plan for Navigable Canal from Stourbridge surveyed in 1774 by Rob. Whitworth* (1775; copy in W.S.L.); S.R.O., Tp. 1273/25, rate bk. 1784, p. 41; S.R.O., D.356A, nos. 330, 333.
[32] S.R.O., Tp. 1273/32.
[33] Ibid. 25, particular of Amblecote estates of earl of

Stamford and Warrington 1805; S.R.O., D. 356A, no. 287, giving 'Petre' Hill as a field name in the later 1830s.
[34] D. R. Guttery, *From Broad-glass to Cut Crystal*, 112; *D.N.B.* s.v. Rogers, Sam.; S.R.O., Tp. 1273, map of Amblecote 1769; below, pp. 58, 62.
[35] H.W.R.O. (H.), E 12/S, Early Deeds.
[36] Below, econ. hist.; S.R.O., Tp. 1273, map of Amblecote 1769.
[37] Below, econ. hist.; S.R.O., C/P/14/2; S.R.O., Tp. 1273, map of Amblecote 1769; *County Express*, 7 Oct. 1967; inf. from Mr. Haden.
[38] Scott, *Stourbridge*, 111.
[39] Ibid. 106; S.R.O., Tp. 1273/33, deed of 29 Sept. 1852.
[40] Stourbridge Libr., case 21, sale particulars 1838 and 1839; H.W.R.O. (W.), b 850 Old Swinford BA5214/5, church rate bk. 1846, openings 69, 70; H. W. Woodward, 'Art, Feat and Mystery': the story of Thos. Webb & Sons, glassmakers (Stourbridge, 1978), 12–13; S.R.O., Q/SB, T. 1853, Amblecote and Kingswinford; S.R.O., D. 648/1/16; below, educ.

running west from the main road near the canal evidently dates from the late 1850s.[41] Stamford Street off the west side of the main road between Holloway End and Coalbournbrook was cut in 1899 by the earl of Stamford's trustees.[42] Holly-bush Road, running north from Stamford Street and consisting of bungalows and flats, was built after the Second World War; it took its name from a nearby inn.[43] A terrace of large houses to the north on the main road dates from a few years later. Streets had been built over the southern part of the Platts estate by the beginning of the 20th century, while the northern part has remained industrialized.[44] Most of the cottages on Tobacco Box Hill were demolished in the 1930s and after the Second World War. Piper Place to the south dates from 1952 and consists of flats built on the site of old cottages; it was named after Harold Piper, clerk and formerly surveyor to the urban district council.[45] In the south the area along the river south-east of the bridge, where an ironworks, a canal basin, and a railway depot were built in the 19th century, was developed as a trading estate in the 1970s.

The eastern part of Amblecote, where settlement had remained scattered, was developed as a residential district mainly after the Second World War, with the end of mining and the restoration of the land. In the years between the two World Wars there was some private building along the west end of Vicarage Road and a council estate was laid out to the south. The Penfield area further south still was developed privately in the 1960s. The Trinity Road estate north of Vicarage Road was built in the same period. A third private estate was built in the 1960s and 1970s in the Peter's Hill area.[46] In the late 1960s most of the eastern half of Vicarage Road was stopped up to allow opencast mining in the area and was replaced by the new Hillfields Road to the south. The restoration of the land was completed in 1978, and the building of private housing estates on either side of the new road was still in progress in 1981.[47]

COMMUNICATIONS. Three fords listed in a charter of 957-8 relating to the Old Swinford area have been tentatively identified to the stretch of the Stour south of Amblecote. The first, the ford of the swine, may have been near the present bridge on the Stourbridge-Wolverhampton road. The second, the pig's ford, may have been

upstream near the railway viaduct where stepping stones are known to have existed later. The third, thief's or deep ford, may have been further upstream where Bagley Street crosses the river.[48]

The stretch of the Stourbridge-Wolverhampton road through Amblecote was mentioned in 1295.[49] A bridge carrying the road over the Stour must have existed by 1255 when Stourbridge itself was mentioned.[50] Brettell Lane, which joins the Stourbridge-Wolverhampton road in the north of Amblecote, was turnpiked in 1727 as part of the road from Dudley and was among the first roads in the Black Country to be turnpiked.[51] The Stourbridge-Wolverhampton road was turnpiked as far north as Wordsley, in Kingswinford, in 1753 and to Wolverhampton in 1761.[52] A road leaving the main road at Coalbournbrook to run southwest through Wollaston, in Old Swinford, and Iverley, in Kinver, to the Stourbridge-Kidderminster road in Churchill parish (Worcs.) was turnpiked in 1789.[53] Brettell Lane was disturnpiked in 1871 and the other two roads in 1877.[54] By 1822 there was a tollgate on the Stourbridge-Wolverhampton road at Coalbournbrook between Wollaston Road and Brettell Lane. A tollbar was erected on the same road in 1828 at Holloway End south of Amblecote Lane (later Vicarage Road). Both still existed in 1871.[55] The bridge over the Stour consisted of four arches in the 1660s. It was rebuilt in 1840 and again in the late 1960s when the Stourbridge ring road was constructed.[56]

As part of the abortive scheme for making the Stour navigable from Stourbridge to the Severn under an Act of 1662 a new line was cut in Amblecote. There was also a plan for a railway from the coal pits in the north of Amblecote and nearby in Kingswinford to a wharf in the Coalbournbrook area.[57] An arm of the Stourbridge Canal runs close to the Stour through the western part of Amblecote to Wordsley, in Kingswinford; there it joins the main canal, which runs from Brierley Hill, in Kingswinford, to the Staffordshire and Worcestershire Canal at Stewponey, in Kinver. Built under an Act of 1776, the canal was opened throughout in 1779. The promoters included a number of glassmakers, and several ironworks were opened at the southern end of the Amblecote arm in the 19th century.[58] The arm originally ended west of the Stourbridge-Wolverhampton road, where a former bonded

---

[41] S.R.O., Tp. 1273/41, deed of 28 Mar. 1857.
[42] Amblecote U.D.C. *Ann. Rep. of M.O.H. 1899*, 10 (copy in S.R.O., C/H/1/2/1/10).
[43] Inf. from Mr. Haden.
[44] O.S. Map 6″, Staffs. LXXI. NW. (1903 edn.); below, pp. 60-1.
[45] Inf. from Mr. Haden; Guttery, *From Broad-glass to Cut Crystal*, 93 n.
[46] *Geographia* street atlases of Birmingham and W. Midlands *c.* 1960, *c.* 1975, *c.* 1980; *Geographers' A to Z Street Atlas of Birmingham and W. Midlands* [*c.* 1970]; D.C.L., Amblecote U.D.C. Mins. 1965-6, p. 19.
[47] *County Express*, 10 and 24 May, 5 July 1968, 14 Feb., 1 Aug., 24 Oct. 1969, 24 July 1970, 4 Jan. 1980; below, p. 57.
[48] *T.B.A.S.* liii. 72; C. R. Hart, *Early Charters of Northern Eng. and N. Midlands*, p. 21 n.; below, p. 55.
[49] W.S.L., S.D. Pearson 286.
[50] Chambers, *Oldswinford, Bedcote, and Stourbridge*, 27.
[51] 13 Geo. I, c. 14; *V.C.H. Staffs.* ii. 280.

[52] 26 Geo. II, c. 47; below, p. 200.
[53] 29 Geo. III, c. 95; *C.J.* xliv. 134.
[54] 34 & 35 Vic. c. 115; 40 & 41 Vic. c. 64.
[55] H.W.R.O. (W.), 899:31 BA3762/4 (iv), Stourbridge Roads Order Bk. 1821-30, 8 Jan. 1822, 6 Aug., 3 Sept. 1828; P.R.O., RG 10/3021.
[56] Guttery, *From Broad-glass to Cut Crystal*, 92 n., 93; H.W.R.O. (W.), 899:31 BA3762/4 (iv), Stourbridge Roads Order Bk. 1830-42, 27 July 1838, 29 Apr., 20 and 25 June 1840; *County Express*, 2 Feb., 8 Nov. 1968, 7 Nov. 1969.
[57] J. H. Parker Oxspring, 'Andrew Yarranton' (TS. in Worcester City Branch Libr., microfilm in S.R.O.), i, pp. 215-18, 324-6; ii, pp. 29, 45-6, 49, 193, 195.
[58] C. Hadfield, *Canals of W. Midlands* (1969), 73-4; *V.C.H. Staffs.* ii. 293; Scott, *Stourbridge*, 368; H. J. Haden, *Notes on Stourbridge Glass Trade* (Dudley Public Libraries, 1977 edn.), 22; P.R.O., RAIL 874/3, 2 Mar., 30 Nov. 1779 (refs. supplied by Mr. D. C. Hickman).

warehouse still stands. In the early 1830s William Foster and William Orme extended the arm through a tunnel under the road to a basin to serve their timber yard and ironworks.[59] In 1973 the tunnel was filled in, and despite a campaign to turn the basin into a boating centre, it too was filled in.[60]

A railway carrying coal into Amblecote was built in 1829 by Messrs. Wheeley, ironmasters in the Kingswinford part of Brettell Lane. It ran from a point in Brettell Lane near the Stourbridge Canal down to the valley of Coalbourn brook; it then followed the brook to a coal wharf on the site occupied from 1856 by the new National school. The railway still existed in 1846.[61]

The Oxford, Worcester, and Wolverhampton Railway was opened through Amblecote in 1852 and completed in 1854. It crossed the Stour on a wooden viaduct, rebuilt in brick in 1882. The nearest stations to Amblecote were Stourbridge (from 1879 Stourbridge Junction) at Old Swinford and Brettell Lane just over the Kingswinford boundary, both opened in 1852. Stourbridge Junction was rebuilt on a new site in 1901; Brettell Lane was closed to passengers in 1962 and to goods traffic in 1965.[62] An engine shed was built in the Penfield area in 1870; a second and larger shed was built nearby in 1926. Both were demolished in 1969.[63] A branch from the main line at Stourbridge Junction was opened to Stourbridge Town in 1879, continuing to a goods depot in Amblecote south-east of the canal basin, to the basin itself, and to the works on either side of the main road; the Stour was culverted east of the bridge. The depot was closed in 1965, and the buildings were demolished and the tracks on both sides of the road taken up.[64]

Amblecote lay on the route of the steam trams which ran between Stourbridge and Dudley from 1884. They were replaced by electric trams in 1899.[65] A tramway known as the Kinver Light Railway, which ran from the Fish inn at Coalbournbrook via Wollaston to Kinver, was opened in 1901. A tram depot was built at Coalbournbrook on the Stourbridge road south of its junction with Collis Street in 1905; it was enlarged in 1908.[66] The trams on both routes were replaced by buses in 1930.[67]

SOCIAL AND CULTURAL ACTIVITIES. In the earlier 19th century bull baiting took place at the west end of Amblecote Lane on ground which later became part of the churchyard.[68] Stourbridge Cricket Club, which was in being by 1842 but had a continuous existence only from 1868, moved in 1857 to a ground in Amblecote on the west side of the Stourbridge road opposite the church; the land was owned by Lord Stamford, a cricket enthusiast. The club's activities also included rugby football by the 1870s; in the 1880s lawn tennis became popular, and there was also a bowling green. From 1882 the club organized an athletics meeting each summer.[69] From 1888 the ground was used also by Stourbridge Football Club.[70] It became the Stourbridge War Memorial athletic ground after being bought from Lady Grey (d. 1925) by the War Memorial Committee.[71] Amblecote Cricket Club was founded in 1908 and used a ground off Stamford Road at Peter's Hill. With the building of Hillfields Road over the ground in 1969 the club moved to a ground at Blackheath, in Rowley Regis, and in 1979 to another at Wall Heath, in Kingswinford.[72] A field at Coalbournbrook east of School Drive was acquired by the urban district council in 1925 and made into a recreation ground.[73]

In the earlier 1840s the Church of England Young Men's Association was formed under the presidency of J. W. Grier, the first incumbent of Holy Trinity, and provided classes, lectures, essay writing, and a library. It was still active in 1860 and may be identifiable as the evening school which met at the Coalbournbrook National school in 1869 with an average attendance of 19.[74] W. O. Foster opened a workmen's lending library and reading room at his Stourbridge ironworks in 1856; the library continued until 1908.[75] In 1901 the vicar, E. G. J. Moore, started a workmen's club in the mission room in King William Street. It was replaced by the Amblecote Institute in Collis Street, which was opened in 1908.[76] A branch library was opened in the former National school in School Drive in 1962.[77]

MANOR AND OTHER ESTATES. In 1086 *AMBLECOTE* was held as 1 hide by William FitzAnsculf with Pain as the sub-tenant; before the Conquest it was held by two men of Earl

[59] H.W.R.O. (W.), 899:31 BA 3762/4 (iv), Stourbridge Roads Order Bk. 1830–42, 15 Sept. 1830; P.R.O., RAIL 874/9, 7 Nov., 15 Dec. 1833 (refs. supplied by Mr. Hickman); S.R.O., D. 356A.
[60] *County Express*, 29 June, 17 Aug. 1973.
[61] Scott, *Stourbridge*, 362; Guttery, *From Broad-glass to Cut Crystal*, 114; S.R.O., D. 356A, no. 66; *County Express*, 7 July 1917; H.W.R.O. (W.), b 850 Old Swinford BA 5214/5, church rate bk. 1846, opening 69.
[62] C. R. Clinker, *Rlwys. of W. Midlands*, 21–3, 40, 50; C. R. Clinker, *Clinker's Reg. of Closed Passenger Stations and Goods Depots*, 144; H. J. Haden, *Stourbridge in Times Past*, 33–5.
[63] H. Hardwick, *Magic of Steam* (Dudley Teachers' Centre, 1981), 17; *County Express*, 4 July 1969; O.S. Map 6", Staffs. LXXI. SW. (1888 edn.).
[64] Clinker, *Rlwys. of W. Midlands*, 40, 50, 56, 58; Haden, *Stourbridge in Times Past*, 34; Hardwick, *Magic of Steam*, 17; O.S. Map 1/2,500, Staffs. LXXI. 10 (1885 edn.).
[65] J. S. Webb, *Black Country Tramways*, i (Bloxwich, 1974), 84–5, 212.
[66] Ibid. 220–32, 251, 255; ii (Bloxwich, 1976), 15–18, 21.
[67] Ibid. ii. 94.
[68] *County Express*, 7 July 1917.
[69] H. J. Haden, *Stourbridge Cricket Club* (Stourbridge, 1957), 1–3 (copy in possession of Mr. Haden); Stourbridge Libr., Stourbridge Cricket Club Min. Bks. 1879–87; inf. from Mr. Haden.
[70] *Stourbridge F.C. Official Handbk. Centenary Edn.* (1976), 26 (copy in possession of Mr. Haden).
[71] *Stourbridge Official Guide* (1970–1), 41.
[72] *County Express*, 26 Apr., 6 Sept. 1968; inf. from Mr. Haden.
[73] *Stourbridge Official Guide* (1970–1), 43; S.R.O., Tp. 1273/32, deed of 30 Mar. 1925.
[74] *P.O. Dir. Staffs.* (1845), 543; *P.O. Dir. Worcs.* (1860), 1255; *Rep. of Educ. Cttee. of Council, 1869–70* [C.165], p. 640, H.C. (1870), xxii.
[75] N. Mutton, 'The Foster Family' (London Univ. Ph.D. thesis, 1974), 152.
[76] *Stourbridge Official Guide* (1970–1), 67. For Moore see *Kelly's Dir. Staffs.* (1904).
[77] Below, educ.

Alfgar without soc.[78] The descent of the manor is treated elsewhere under Old Swinford parish.[79] From 1540 the manor was held by the Greys of Enville (later earls of Stamford), who owned nearly five sixths of the township in the later 1830s.[80] Nearly all the property was sold in stages after the Second World War.[81]

The hall of Sir William de Stafford, lord of Amblecote, was mentioned in 1292.[82] The seven hearths in Amblecote on which Henry Grey was assessed for tax in 1666 presumably belonged to the hall.[83] A map of 1688 shows a house in the fork of Amblecote Lane (later Vicarage Road) and Withymoor Lane and another to the north; in the late 19th century those were the sites respectively of Amblecote Hall and Amblecote Farm.[84] By 1723 the hall was leased, and it was occupied as a farm at the end of the century.[85] It was demolished c. 1820 and rebuilt in 1831.[86] In 1838 it was leased to William King, a coal and clay master, who lived at the hall until 1850. In 1949 the hall and the farmhouse (then known as Amblecote House) were included in the property sold by Mrs. Eileen Bissill to John Hall & Co. (of Stourbridge) Ltd.[87] Amblecote Hall was demolished c. 1960 and Amblecote House c. 1965.[88]

The endowments of Old Swinford Hospital included c. 8 a. in Amblecote lying east of the Stourbridge road near the southern boundary. The land was bought by the founder Thomas Foley in 1672 and then consisted of a close called Culverhouse field and a parcel called Powkmore Hill Lane. It was leased by 1743 and was sold to the earl of Stamford in 1853.[89]

The rector of Old Swinford owned the great and small tithes of Amblecote. In 1839 they were commuted for a rent charge of £220.[90]

ECONOMIC HISTORY. AGRICULTURE. In 1086 Amblecote had land for 2 ploughteams, and there were 4 villeins, 2 bordars, and 1 slave with 2 teams; meadow occupied 4 a., and there was woodland. The value was 10s., the same as before the Conquest.[91] Part of Amblecote was added to Kinver forest after 1154; in 1300 only the north-western corner was in the forest.[92] There is

evidence of sheep farming in the later 16th and early 17th century.[93] Although the area became increasingly industrialized in the 19th century, over a third of the land, 222 a., was arable in 1839 and most of the remainder was pasture.[94] In 1851 there were three farms in the south-east; one was of 90 a. at Amblecote Bank, one of 79 a. at Bagley's mill, and one of 14 a. in the Penfield area. Amblecote Hall farm covered 150 a. in 1861.[95] Farming continued in the Vicarage Road area until the mid 20th century.[96]

Three open fields were mentioned from the 15th century: Little field lying along the south side of Coalbourn brook, Hanbury field adjoining it on the south-east and extending at least as far as Vicarage Road, and Water field by the Stour in the south-west.[97] In 1574 the lord of the manor and the tenants agreed that the three fields of Amblecote should be inclosed by 25 March 1576; inclosure was still in progress in the autumn of that year.[98] The New Leasow in the south was mentioned from 1494 as open-field arable, although it is not clear that it was a separate field; acres there were still mentioned in 1592 and 1623.[99]

There was open meadow along the Stour. King's meadow lay in the south-west corner of Amblecote, and a dole there called Stafford dole still existed in 1623; dole meadow survived to the north in 1769.[1] The tenants of Amblecote manor had aftermath in King's meadow before Lammas, and from Lammas to Candlemas they had pasture rights.[2] In 1613, in recognition of the expense incurred by Ambrose Grey, the lord of the manor, in a lawsuit, the tenants agreed that the lord should have the right to aftermath for ever provided that he would always let it to them 'if they will give as any other will give'. It was then stated that the foremath had been granted by Lord Dudley to Alice Madstard.[3] Penn meadow lay near King's meadow, and dole meadow there was mentioned in 1607.[4] By 1615 it had been inclosed by Roger Perrott of Wollaston by agreement with the tenants of Amblecote in return for his renunciation of common rights in King's meadow.[5] Mill meadow, also known as Broad meadow, lay east of the Stourbridge road; it was still an open meadow in 1624.[6]

[78] V.C.H. Staffs. iv. 54.
[79] V.C.H. Worcs. iii. 217–18. The account mentions several lords in the late 13th and early 14th centuries named William de Stafford and Sir William de Stafford, the references are in fact to the same person: S.H.C. 1917–18, 9–11, 52. For the Greys see below, Enville, manors and other estates.   [80] S.R.O., D. 356A.
[81] Inf. from Mr. M. J. Scott-Bolton, agent for the Enville estate (1981).   [82] Cal. Inq. Misc. i, p. 445.
[83] S.H.C. 1923, 56.
[84] S.R.O. 1392; O.S. Map 1/2,500, Staffs. LXXI. 10 (1885 edn.).
[85] S.R.O., Tp. 1273/2, deed of 13 June 1798; Tp. 1273/39, rental of early 1760s, f. 21; Scott, Stourbridge, 105.
[86] S.R.O., Tp. 1273/5, outgoings from Staffs. estate 1831; 50, Amblecote Misc.
[87] Below, econ. hist. (clay); copy deed of 22 June 1949 in poss. of Johnson, Poole & Bloomer, Brierley Hill.
[88] Inf. from Mr. B. E. Poole of Johnson, Poole & Bloomer, tenant of Amblecote Ho. from 1949.
[89] D.C.L., D/OH/I/1/22; D/OH/II/5/1/1; plans of estates belonging to feoffees of Old Swinford Hosp. (1828; in poss. of Old Swinford Hosp.); 25th Rep. Com. Char. H.C. 60, pp. 577–9 (1833), xviii; S.R.O., D. 356A; S.R.O., Tp. 1273/25, numerical ref. bk. 1841; Tp. 1273/37, deed of 29 Sept. 1853.

[90] State of Bpric. of Worcester 1782–1808 (Worcs. Hist. Soc. N.S. vi), 45; S.R.O., D. 356A.
[91] V.C.H. Staffs. iv. 54.
[92] S.H.C. v (1), 179–80.
[93] S.R.O., Tp. 1273/6, ct. of 5 Nov. 1566; 11, 1623 survey; 13, ct. of 5 Apr. 1613 and undated survey.
[94] S.R.O., D. 356A.
[95] P.R.O., HO 107/2035; P.R.O., RG 9/2068.
[96] Inf. from Mr. B. E. Poole of Johnson, Poole & Bloomer, Brierley Hill.
[97] S.R.O., Tp. 1273/13; S.R.O. 1392.
[98] S.R.O., Tp. 1273/6, ct. of 2 Dec. 1574; 13, ct. of 24 Sept. 1576.
[99] S.R.O., Tp. 1273/11, 1623 survey; 13.
[1] Ibid. 11, 1623 survey; 13; Tp. 1273, map of Amblecote 1769; S.R.O. 1392. For the extent of King's meadow see Tp. 1273/4, deeds of 25 Feb. 1687/8, 28 Aug. 1710; S.R.O., D. 695/1/39/55.
[2] S.R.O., Tp. 1273/13, cts. of 23 Aug. 1597, 25 Oct. 1606.
[3] Ibid. 13, ct. of 5 Apr. 1613.
[4] Ibid. 4, deed of 28 May 1576; 13, ct. of 24 Oct. 1607.
[5] Ibid. 13, ct. of 7 Aug. 1615, which, however, dated the agreement to 'some lx score years past or thereabouts'.
[6] Ibid. 4, deed of 15 Mar. 1623/4; 11, 1623 survey; 13, ct. of 24 Apr. 1541; S.R.O. 1392.

In the late 17th century there was an area in the south-east known as the Waste; Withymoor in the north-east was evidently another area of waste. Several cottages had been built on each by then, and there was also a glasshouse on Withymoor.[7] In 1806 Withymoor consisted of 45 a. of uninclosed land with a further 7½ a. inclosed; by 1828 the 45 a. lay in six inclosures.[8]

The Stewponey Association for the Improvement of the Labouring Classes held 7 a. in Amblecote as tenant of Lord Stamford in 1845 and let it to the poor. By 1853 the land was divided into 27 allotment gardens, and there were still that number in 1879.[9]

PARK. There may have been a park at Amblecote in the late 13th century: William the parker of Amblecote was accused in 1292 of having several times brought venison stolen from Dudley park to the hall of Sir William de Stafford at Amblecote.[10] There was mention of the park of the lord of Amblecote in the earlier 1570s.[11]

FISHERY. The lord of the manor asserted exclusive fishing rights in the Stour. Presentments and fines for fishing in the river occur in the court rolls from 1463, and ordinances against fishing there were issued by the court in the early 16th century. Coalbourn brook was also included in an ordinance of 1517. Bans on fishing in the Stour continued during the 16th century, while in 1593 the court ordered that no one from Stourbridge should bathe, fish, or set a trap in the Stour between the stepping stones (near the modern railway viaduct) and Wollaston mill on the Worcestershire side of the boundary south of the Wollaston road.[12]

MILLS. The manorial mill stood on the Stour south-east of the bridge on the Stourbridge road.[13] A lease, with tenants' multure, was granted to Leonard Clare in 1518. In 1530 Robert Clare was granted a lease for three lives of two water mills, presumably two mills under one roof; he still held them in 1541, having apparently rebuilt the whole mill.[14] The mills were in the hands of the lord of the manor in 1623 but were again leased by 1648.[15] By the 1730s they had been converted into a 'forge, battering mill, or slitting mill' known as the Town Mills. In 1734 they were leased to William Scott, a Stourbridge clothier, for conversion into a fulling mill.

In 1771 a further lease of what were described as the corn and fulling mills commonly called the Town Mills was made to William and John Scott, clothiers of Stourbridge.[16] The lease was renewed for 14 years in 1792, but corn grinding ceased in 1793 because of the scarcity of water.[17] Although still held by the Scotts in 1805 the mills were then little used.[18] In 1811 the fulling mill was leased to James Pitman, a Stourbridge leather dresser, who converted it into a leather mill; he was granted a further lease in 1821. In 1836 the leather mill was leased to Joseph Pitman, also a Stourbridge leather dresser, but although still held by him in 1837 it evidently ceased operation about then.[19]

A second mill stood upstream in the south-east corner of Amblecote. It was built at the beginning of the 17th century as a blade mill,[20] but by 1688 it was a fulling mill.[21] It continued as a fulling mill until 1719 and was then converted into a corn mill, which was worked from 1720 by Robert Richards, who moved there from Cradley, in Halesowen (Worcs.). The Richards family held the lease until 1785, when the mill was let to Dudley Bagley.[22] Known as Lye mill by 1791, it then had three wheels, but there was not enough water to keep them in constant operation.[23] Water power was still a problem in 1805 when Bagley was working the mill as a corn and blade mill.[24] He continued to use it in that way until 1822 when it was leased to Littlewood, King & Co., clay merchants.[25] The interior was remodelled in 1831, when the tenants were Joseph and William King, coal and clay masters.[26] They still held Lye mill in 1844; it then had one wheel and was well supplied with water.[27] It was no longer in operation in 1851.[28] It was worked in 1871 by John Silvester, a miller and brewer, and for a few years afterwards by Mrs. Elizabeth Silvester.[29] It was leased to the South Staffordshire Mines Drainage Commissioners in 1875 and again went out of use; the commissioners took the lease in order to prevent the water from being pounded and so flooding the mines of the vicinity.[30]

The site of a windmill east of the main road at Coalbournbrook may be indicated by land there known as Windmill Hill by 1466.[31]

COAL. In 1372–3 a lease of land called Wolfordsford partly in Amblecote manor and partly in Old Swinford manor stipulated that if any coal

[7] S.R.O. 1392; below (glass).
[8] S.R.O., Tp. 1273/4, deed of 29 Dec. 1806; 7, deed of 30 Apr. 1828.
[9] H.W.R.O. (H.), E 12/S, Stewponey Becher Club II, ann. reps. of the assoc. For the assoc. see below, Kinver, econ. hist. (agric.).
[10] Cal. Inq. Misc. i, p. 445.
[11] S.R.O., Tp. 1273/13, cts. of 12 May 1573, 7 Nov. 1575.
[12] S.R.O., Tp. 1273/13. For the stepping stones see Guttery, From Broad-glass to Cut Crystal, 6 and pl. facing p. 2; for the mill see O.S. Map 6″, Staffs. LXXI. SW. (1888 edn.).
[13] S.R.O. 1392; S.R.O., Tp. 1273, map of Amblecote 1769.
[14] S.R.O., Tp. 1273/13.
[15] Ibid. 2, deed of 9 July 1648; 11, 1623 survey.
[16] Ibid. 10.
[17] Ibid. 2; 18, rent roll 1800.
[18] Ibid. 25, partic. of Amblecote estates of earl of Stamford and Warrington 1805.
[19] Ibid. 2; 7, deed of 20 Aug. 1821; 33, deed of 25 July 1836;

D. 585/159/1/1, p. 13. The mill does not appear on the tithe map (1837) and apportionment (1839) in S.R.O., D. 536A.
[20] S.R.O., Tp. 1273/4, doc. headed 'Concerning the mills at Amelcote' and deed of 28 July 1719; 11, 1623 survey.
[21] S.R.O. 1392.
[22] S.R.O., Tp. 1273/4 and 12.
[23] Ibid. 18, rent roll 1800.
[24] Ibid. 25, partic. of Amblecote estates of earl of Stamford and Warrington 1805.
[25] Ibid. 33, deed of 19 Apr. 1822.
[26] Ibid. 5, outgoings 1831; below, p. 57.
[27] S.R.O., Tp. 1273/18, loose paper in 1808 rent roll.
[28] P.R.O., HO 107/2035.
[29] S.R.O., RG 10/3021; P.O. Dir. Staffs. (1872; 1876).
[30] S.R.O., Tp. 1273/33, deed of 31 July 1875 and letter from F. B. Punchard to H. G. Hall 30 July 1896; O.S. Map 1/2,500, Staffs. LXXI. 10 (1885 edn.).
[31] S.R.O., Tp. 1273/13, 22 Dec. 1466, 29 Apr. 1532; 39, rental of early 1760s, f. 24; S.R.O. 1392; S.R.O., D. 356A, no. 85.

or ironstone were mined half the profits should go to the lessor.[32] That division was described as the custom in the mines of Amblecote in 1382 in a lease of the land called Dennis north-east of Coal-bournbrook. In 1426, however, a lease of the same property included permission to dig and sell sea coal for the lessees' own profit.[33] A Richard Collier was living in Amblecote in 1449, and there was a Coalpit leasow by 1494. A house called Colliers House in 1501 and 1541 was probably the Colliers tenement south-east of Withymoor which was leased in 1565 with adjoining land and liberty to dig coal and ironstone; by then there was mining at Withymoor itself.[34] In 1549 the jury of the manor court stated that from the early 16th century the lord had had the right to enter any copyhold land to dig coal and ironstone; compensation was to be assessed by two tenants, one chosen by the lord and the other by the tenant. The jury went on to mention a lease of the demesne early in the century which gave the tenant complete freedom to mine coal and ironstone.[35]

The scale of coal mining was evidently increasing by the 1530s.[36] In 1536 a tenant was licensed to lease out his coal pit for 20 years; in 1538 two tenants were permitted to work a pit in a pasture which they held. In 1540 tenants were paying 5s. rent a year for each man whom they employed in the pits. Seven payments of between 5s. and 25s. were listed in July, amounting to 110s.; one of the pits was held by two tenants and another by three. From the later 1530s the court regularly made orders for the filling of coal pits, and it was also concerned to control the amount of coal worked. In 1540, having fined two men 20d. each for selling coals beyond the amount stipulated, the court went on to fix 40d. as the fine for each infraction. The amount allowed came to be called a turn. In 1550 the court ordered that everyone with a coal pit should 'load six wains for a turn and six horses for another turn thereafter and take them as they come, little and much, without refusing, upon pain for every wain 2s. and for every horse 12d.' In 1552 Roger Perrott was duly fined 12d. for breaking the turn with a horse and John Solmore £4 for breaking 40 turns with carts and 12d. for breaking one with a horse. In 1563 the court ordered that every master collier and anyone with a share in a pit should be allowed 'to sell a dozen or two beforehand and to set them down in the turn as the turn comes to, and no man to load no more until the turn be up under pain of every wain 20s.' It was further ordered 'for the turn of great horses that if they will not load at one pit let him then load at the next and set them down in the turn . . . also that no man shall turn neither wain nor horses away so long as they have any coals upon the hill, upon pain of 20s.' In

1566 the court ordered one collier from each pit in the manor to attend the next court in order to present all offences committed by the colliers in their turns. The turn to be kept was increased in 1573 to eight carts and eight horseloads; anyone selling over those limits was to be fined 3s. 4d. for every cart and 12d. for every horseload.[37]

The court's close involvement seems to have ceased after the mid 1570s, but mining continued. In a conveyance of property in Enville and Kinver in 1589 one of the parties agreed to provide a wagon and six oxen every year to bring coal from Amblecote to the home of the other party in Enville.[38] A lease of 1590 made by John Grey reserved all mines of coal and ironstone and the right to sink pits,[39] and in 1623 the tenants of four pits were paying Ambrose Grey weekly sums of between 20s. and 24s. a pit.[40] In 1677 Lord Ward and Henry Grey made an agreement for draining coal mines in Rough Withymoor and other land in Amblecote and Kingswinford belonging to them and for entering into a 21-year partnership to work the coal; by 1692 there were four partners, and John Grey, Henry's heir, then assigned his interest to the other three for a rent of £85.[41] Robert Plot, describing the coal strata at Amblecote c. 1680, stated that the coal lay deep and that over 25 yards of earth and rock had to be penetrated to reach it; he also noted the cheapness of coal in the area.[42] By the early 19th century coal mining had become subsidiary to clay working,[43] but in the mid century there were coal miners living at Amblecote Bank on the eastern boundary.[44] Because of the subsidiary nature of the mining, Amblecote coal was excepted from nationalization. Mining ceased when clay working ceased.[45]

CLAY. The fireclay found in the Amblecote area was considered in the late 17th century to be the best in England for the manufacture of pots for the glass industry.[46] Even before the establishment of that industry in the area the clay seems to have been dug extensively. In 1566 the manor court forbade anyone living outside Amblecote to dig clay in the manor. In 1593 it repeated the ban, with reference to the inhabitants of Stourbridge and Wollaston, and in 1596 it fined a Stourbridge man for flouting the ordinance. In 1593 it also forbade the digging of clay unless the holes were filled within ten days.[47] When Sir Robert Mansell started a glassworks at Newcastle upon Tyne, probably in 1617, he at first used clay from the Stourbridge area. He claimed that jealous glass-makers in Staffordshire corrupted it and made it useless so that he had to import clay from abroad.[48] The lord of Amblecote was receiving £10 a year for clay in 1623.[49] About 1680 Amblecote clay was sold for 7d. a bushel, the lord receiving 6d.

[32] T. R. Nash, *Collns. for Hist. of Worcs.* ii. 208. Mr. B. E. Poole of Johnson, Poole & Bloomer, Brierley Hill, is thanked for his help with the following section and that on clay.
[33] H.W.R.O. (H.), E 12/S, Early Deeds.
[34] S.R.O., Tp. 1273/11, 1623 survey; 13; S.R.O. 1392.
[35] S.R.O., Tp. 1273/13.
[36] For this para. see ibid.
[37] Although the roll is endorsed with a memorandum that the old fines were 'to be utterly void and frustrate', a court of 1575 imposed a 2s. fine on each excess cartload sold.
[38] S.R.O., Tp. 1273/11.
[39] Ibid. 13.

[40] Ibid. 11, 1623 survey.
[41] Ibid. 4.
[42] Plot, *Staffs.* 122, 132.
[43] S.R.O., Tp. 1273/22, clay and coal royalty books 1802–1913.
[44] P.R.O., HO 107/2035; P.R.O., RG 9/2068.
[45] Inf. from Mr. Poole.
[46] Plot, *Staffs.* 121.
[47] S.R.O., Tp. 1273/13.
[48] E. S. Godfrey, *Development of Glassmaking 1560–1640*, 87–8.
[49] S.R.O., Tp. 1273/11, 1623 survey.

and the workmen 1d. It was sent as far as London either by road or by water via Bewdley (Worcs.); it was used in both the glass and the iron industries. Firebricks were being made from the clay by the early 18th century.[50] About 1780 mining was concentrated in an area of 200 a. in and near Amblecote, with the best clay found in some 48 a. The clay was raised in hundredweight lumps, which were washed, picked, and scraped by women. Output was about 4,000 tons a year. The clay was sent via Stourport, in Kidderminster (Worcs.), all over the British Isles, and a large amount was exported from Bristol.[51] In 1784 William Waldron, who mined 21 a. of the best clay, also had pot rooms in Amblecote; in addition he had a glassworks there. Scott, Jones & Co. had two clay mills, pot rooms, and two glassworks.[52]

With the increased demand for refractories in the 19th century the industry expanded. In 1802 Lord Stamford leased mining rights in and near Withymoor to Wastel Cliffe of West Bromwich lodge for 21 years. Cliffe mined clay and coal, but in 1806 he was succeeded by John Pidcock of the Platts, to whom Lord Stamford leased 45 a. of uninclosed land at Withymoor, two clay mills there, and mining rights in the area. The lease was renewed for seven years from 1827. In 1834 a 21-year lease was granted to two coal and clay masters, Joseph King of Cradley, in Halesowen (Worcs.), and William King of Holloway End in Amblecote; in the later 1830s they also had a firebrick works at Withymoor.[53] In 1838 William King took a lease of the nearby Amblecote Hall, and he lived there until his death in 1850.[54] Hill, Hampton & Co. had a firebrick works adjoining its Coalbournbrook glassworks in 1837, and both had passed to Joseph Stevens by 1839. John Henzey Pidcock and William Henry Cope had a clay room on the north-west boundary in 1839.[55] The Withymoor lease was surrendered in 1852 by Joseph King, then of Hagley (Worcs.), and by William's executors.[56]

In the same year the Withymoor works and pits were taken over by Peter Harris and George Pearson. The firm of Harris & Pearson continued working at Withymoor until the 1920s. In 1930 a new 35-year lease was taken by E. J. & J. Pearson Ltd. Founded in 1860 with mines and works at Brierley Hill and at the Lye in Old Swinford, E. J. & J. Pearson had opened the Crown works in Amblecote east of the Withymoor works in the early 1900s and also mined nearby; the works and mines were included with Withymoor in the 1930

lease. Although the Withymoor works was not reopened mining was started again.[57] Henry Hall, a Kingswinford ironmaster, and John Hall, an ironmaster of Corngreaves, in Rowley Regis, began mining at Amblecote in 1853, with a lease of 148 a. south of the area worked by Harris & Pearson; they also opened a brick works south of Vicarage Road. In 1949 John Hall & Co. (of Stourbridge) Ltd., then operating under a 30-year lease of 1929, bought 103 a. of the land already leased to it and most of the mineral rights.[58] A fourth firm, Timmis & Co. of Stamber Mill on the Worcestershire side of the Stour, took a 21-year lease of coal and clay on Amblecote Bank in 1915; the lease was renewed for a further 23 years in 1934.[59]

Underground mining declined from the later 1950s and was replaced by opencast working. Opencast pits were worked for a few years and then filled ready for building development. The last area to be restored was at Withymoor where filling was completed in 1978.[60]

Amblecote clay has also been used for making domestic earthenware. In 1769 Caleb Moreton had a potworks in the south-east of the area near what is now the junction of Penfield Road and Stamford Road.[61] He continued to hold a life tenancy when in 1771 a 21-year lease of the works was granted to Thomas Compson of Amblecote, a potter; the lease included a house and 11½ a. 'with the mughouses, kilns, and hovels thereupon erected' and the right to dig clay there for making mugs, pots, and other sorts of earthenware.[62] Compson held the property in 1784, but by 1785 it had passed to John Hart.[63] Hart continued in occupation until 1805, when he also had a nail shop there. In 1791 much of the clay used in the works was said to come from elsewhere.[64] There were several potters living in Amblecote in the mid and later 19th century.[65] About 1939 there was a firm making earthenware and another producing porcelain enamel.[66]

GLASS. Most of the so-called Stourbridge glass industry has always been sited on the Staffordshire side of the Stour, with a large part of it in Amblecote.[67] Glassmaking was started in Amblecote in the early 17th century by members of the Lorrainer glassmaking families who had settled in central Staffordshire in the late 16th century. Robert Plot stated that they were attracted to the Amblecote area by the existence of cheap coal and the best clay in England for making glasshouse pots. The royal proclamation of 1615 banning the

[50] Plot, *Staffs.* 121-2, 374; *V.C.H. Staffs.* ii. 269.
[51] Nash, *Worcs.* ii. 212.
[52] S.R.O., Tp. 1273/25, rate bk. 1784, pp. 3, 5, 7.
[53] S.R.O., Tp. 1273/4; ibid. 7; ibid. 22; S.R.O., D. 356A, nos. 312, 356.
[54] S.R.O., D. 648/3/4/2 and 3; memorial in Amblecote ch.
[55] S.R.O., D. 356A, nos. 62-3; D. 585/159/1/1, p. 5.
[56] S.R.O., Tp. 1273/7.
[57] Ibid. 22; S.R.O., D. 695/1/26/11; D. 1222; *P.O. Dir. Worcs.* (1860), 1253; copy deeds of 5 Feb. 1930 and 24 Feb. 1932 in poss. of Johnson, Poole & Bloomer. For E. J. & J. Pearson see also *P.O. Dir. Staffs.* (1864); *Kelly's Dir. Staffs.* (1904); letterheads in poss. of Johnson, Poole & Bloomer.
[58] S.R.O., Tp. 1273/22; 36, deed of 21 Feb. 1853; *P.O. Dir. Worcs.* (1860), 1253; copy deeds of 1 Oct. 1929 and 22 June 1949 in poss. of Johnson, Poole & Bloomer.
[59] Sched. of mining tenancies on the Amblecote estate in

poss. of Johnson, Poole & Bloomer.
[60] C. Knipe, 'Comparison of settlement rates on back filled opencast mining sites', *Procs. of Conference on Engineering Behaviour of Industrial and Urban Fill Apr. 1979* (Midland Geotechnical Soc. 1979).
[61] S.R.O., Tp. 1273, map of Amblecote 1769.
[62] S.R.O., Tp. 1273/10, deed of 23 Mar. 1771.
[63] Ibid. 25, rate bk. 1784, pp. 27-9; 43, Staffs. rentals.
[64] Ibid. 18, rent roll 1800; 25, partic. of Amblecote estates of earl of Stamford and Warrington 1805; 43, Staffs. rentals.
[65] P.R.O., HO 107/2035; RG 9/2068; RG 10/3021.
[66] *Kelly's Dir. Staffs.* (1940).
[67] D. R. Guttery, *From Broad-glass to Cut Crystal*, p. viii. Mr. J. Byrne of Webb Corbett Ltd. and Mr. S. R. Eveson of Thomas Webb & Sons Ltd. are thanked for their help with the following section. For a general account of the Staffs. glass industry see *V.C.H. Staffs.* ii. 224-30.

use of timber in glass furnaces presumably encouraged the migration. It seems too that natives of nearby Kingswinford had shortly before started to make glass there, using local coal; that may have been a further encouragement.[68] Paul Tyzack, of the Lorrainer family which settled in Eccleshall, was living in Kingswinford by 1612; in 1613 he and a Mr. de Houx were digging sand in Amblecote manor.[69] Tyzack built the first identifiable glasshouse in the area c. 1618 in the Worcestershire part of Old Swinford;[70] at some date de Houx had a glasshouse in Amblecote.[71] Jacob Henzey, also of a Lorrainer family, was living in Old Swinford parish by 1615, and Edward Henzey, a glassmaker, was living in Amblecote in 1621.[72]

One of two glasshouses in Amblecote in 1623[73] was probably at Holloway End, where a glasshouse was mentioned in 1639.[74] It was known as Hoo in the 1660s.[75] Although it has been suggested that the name derives from the de Houx family,[76] the name may well have been taken from land called Who Place, held in 1541 by Leonard Beare.[77] The land passed to the family of Tompson, otherwise Beare;[78] in 1650 Anne Tompson, otherwise Beare, was living at Holloway End House and owned the nearby glasshouse.[79] Her daughter Anne had married Daniel Tittery, of another Lorrainer family (d. 1641), and in 1650 their son Daniel was a glassmaker living in Amblecote. The Holloway End glasshouse and house passed to Thomas Rogers (d. 1680), who married Anne Tittery, apparently a daughter of Anne and Daniel the elder.[80] The glasshouse remained in the Rogers family until the later 18th century. Thomas, son of Thomas and Anne, made flint glass, bottles, and by 1718 drinking glasses. His grandson Thomas, who lived at the Hill on the opposite side of the Stourbridge road, was producing broad and flint glass, bottles, and phials in 1760. In 1768 Thomas advertised the works for letting, but he still held it in 1769; there were then two cones.[81] From 1772 it was held by James Keir (1738–1820), the chemist, in partnership with John Taylor, Samuel Skey of Bewdley (Worcs.), and others; Keir acted as manager of the works and lived at the nearby Holloway End House (later Harring-

ton House). Initially at least he made only flint glass, although he had plans for expansion and conducted experiments at the works. He supplied glassware, probably including tubes for thermometers, to Boulton and Watt's Soho manufactory in Handsworth. In 1778 he left Amblecote to become manager at Soho. In 1783 the works was listed as held by Scott, Keir, Jones & Co.[82] In 1784, however, the firm was Scott, Jones & Co.; it then had two glasshouses in Amblecote as well as clay interests.[83] Benjamin Littlewood was making flint glass at Holloway End in 1809 and was still living and working there in the early 1830s. Although his son Thomas was running the works in 1834, he or another Benjamin was owner in the later 1830s. John Berry had joined the firm by 1835, and the partnership of Littlewood & Berry was still working at Holloway End in 1841.[84] Benjamin died in 1844[85] and the works was sold. It was run by Edward and Joseph Webb in 1845 and by Edward alone in 1852. Richardson, Mills & Smith were making flint glass there in 1860 and Richardson & Smith in 1868 and 1872. Castrey & Gee moved there from Wordsley c. 1874 and continued until c. 1894. The works was then closed until c. 1900 when Joseph Fleming & Co. moved there from the Platts. Production ceased c. 1930. In the later 1940s the premises were occupied by Amblecote Glass Co. Ltd., a firm of glass decorators. The buildings were pulled down soon afterwards, the surviving cone being demolished in 1955.[86]

The other glasshouse in Amblecote in 1623 may have been at Withymoor. A glasshouse there north-east of Amblecote Hall was run in 1670 by Paul Tyzack, his nephew Zachariah, and Abraham Bigoe. The furnace still stood in 1688, and the works may have continued to operate until the early 18th century.[87]

A glasshouse had been built on Fimbrell leasow north-east of Coalbournbrook by 1691 and probably by the early 1680s. In 1691 it was leased for 999 years by Thomas Bradley of Old Swinford, a glassmaker, to Benjamin Batchelor of Coalbournbrook, also a glassmaker, with a house formerly occupied by Bradley and 35 a. called Dennis.[88] Thomas Batchelor was making bottles there in the late 1690s,[89] but his son Humphrey

[68] V.C.H. Staffs. ii. 224–5; Godfrey, Eng. Glassmaking 1560–1640, 59–65; above, coal, clay.
[69] Guttery, From Broad-glass to Cut Crystal, 4, 6; S.R.O., Tp. 1273/13, ct. of 21 Sept. 1613.
[70] Guttery, From Broad-glass to Cut Crystal, 6–9.
[71] S.R.O., Tp. 1273/13, rental of 5 Sept. 1598 with addns.
[72] Guttery, From Broad-glass to Cut Crystal, 12–14; H. S. Grazebrook, Collns. for Genealogy of Noble Families of Henzey, Tyttery, and Tyzack (Stourbridge, 1877), 34, 102–3, 127.
[73] S.R.O., Tp. 1273/11, 1623 survey.
[74] Ibid. 4, deed of 27 Feb. 1638/9.
[75] P.R.O., E 134/19 Chas. II East./8.
[76] Guttery, From Broad-glass to Cut Crystal, 20.
[77] S.R.O., Tp. 1273/13, cts. of 26 Apr. 1541, 22 Oct. 1570.
[78] Ibid. 11, 1623 survey.
[79] Ibid. 4, deed of 11 Nov. 1650.
[80] Ibid., abstract of John Newbrough's writings and title, and deeds of 27 Feb. 1638/9 and 3 May 1650; Grazebrook, Fams. of Henzey, Tyttery, and Tyzack, 16–17; Guttery, From Broad-glass to Cut Crystal, 20.
[81] Grazebrook, Fams. of Henzey, Tyttery, and Tyzack, 17–18; H. J. Haden, Notes on Stourbridge Glass Trade (Dudley Public Libraries, 1977 edn.), 25; Guttery, From Broad-glass to Cut Crystal, 34, 61–2, 77, 109–10, 112–13; S.R.O. 1392; S.R.O., Tp. 1273/10, deed of 28 Feb. 1721/2;

Tp. 1273/39, rental of early 1760s, f. 19; Tp. 1273, map of Amblecote 1769.
[82] R. E. Schofield, Lunar Soc. of Birmingham, 80–2, 153–4; Scott, Stourbridge, 107; Haden, Stourbridge Glass Trade, 26; Guttery, From Broad-glass to Cut Crystal, 112–13. For Keir see also V.C.H. Staffs. xvii. 4. For Harrington House see below, church.
[83] Above (clay).
[84] Haden, Stourbridge Glass Trade, 26; Scott, Stourbridge, 107; White, Dir. Staffs. (1834), 247; Pigot, Nat. Com. Dir. (1835), 657; Stourbridge Libr., newspaper cuttings, p. 37.
[85] S.R.O., Tp. 1273/41, will of Benj. Littlewood.
[86] Haden, Stourbridge Glass Trade (1949 edn.), 26; (1977 edn.), pl. facing p. 29; Stourbridge Libr., newspaper cuttings, p. 37; P.O. Dir. Worcs. (1860), 1254; P.O. Dir. Staffs. (1868; 1872); Kelly's Dir. Staffs. (1896 and later edns. to 1928); H. J. Haden, The 'Stourbridge Glass' Ind. in the 19th cent. (Black Country Soc. 1971), 8, 21; Guttery, From Broad-glass to Cut Crystal, 38 n., 146, and pl. facing p. 19.
[87] Guttery, From Broad-glass to Cut Crystal, 9–10, 24, 53, 62; S.R.O. 1392.
[88] Deed of 1 Mar. 1738/9 at Dennis glassworks (copy in W.S.L. 254/2/81); Plot, Staffs. 122; Guttery, From Broad-glass to Cut Crystal, 39 n., 47, 49.
[89] Guttery, From Broad-glass to Cut Crystal, 37.

had evidently taken over by 1703, probably in partnership with Elijah, another son, and Benjamin Batchelor.[90] Humphrey and Elijah were described as partners and broad-glass makers in 1714, and Humphrey was again described as a broad-glass maker in 1725 when he had added clay working in Kingswinford to his interests. In 1728 his products at Fimbrell included flint glass, 'common green glass', and also crown glass, then recorded for the first time in the district; he also made bottles, drinking glasses, cruets, and apothecaries' phials. He took a new 999-year lease of the works, house, and land in 1739.[91] A Thomas Batchelor was running the works in 1749.[92] Under the will of Humphrey's widow Elizabeth dated 1762 the property passed to her nephew Thomas Hill, who built Dennis House there. Production appears to have ceased by 1769, and by 1777 the glasshouse was in ruins.[93] After Hill's death in 1824 the Dennis estate passed to W. S. Wheeley, and from 1838 it was broken up. The house and a few acres were bought in the earlier 1850s by Thomas Webb of the Platts, who moved there and opened the new Dennis glassworks adjoining the hall in 1855. By 1860 there was also an iron foundry.[94] The firm became Thomas Webb & Sons in 1859 when Thomas's son Thomas Wilkes Webb became a partner. His developments included coloured and cameo glass, crystal, and engraving. At the Paris Exhibition of 1878 the firm was awarded the Grand Prix for glass and T. W. Webb received the Legion of Honour. The firm became a public company in 1886. In 1920 it was incorporated as a limited company and became part of Webb's Crystal Glass Co. Ltd. which in 1964 was acquired by Crown House Ltd. and in 1971 was merged with Dema Glass Ltd. The works was extended and modernized in 1967.[95] In 1981 the house was used for offices and a museum.

In 1692 Thomas Henzey took a lease of Harlestones field west of the Stourbridge road at Coalbournbrook and built a glasshouse there for his second son John (d. 1719). John produced flint glass, bottles, and vessels there besides broad glass and lived in a large house nearby.[96] By 1760 the works was run by Elijah Barrar, making flint glass and phials; he was declared bankrupt in 1767.[97] In 1768 the glasshouse was let by Oliver Dixon, John Henzey's grandson, to John Pidcock, George Ensell, and Richard Bradley. In 1769 they were engaged in glass engraving there.

Ensell acted as manager. In 1778 he was awarded a prize by the Society for the Encouragement of Arts, Manufactures, and Commerce for his sheet glass, the secret of which he is said to have found out in Germany by stealth; he also perfected a new tunnel-type annealing furnace, or leer, at the works in 1780. The partnership was still in possession in 1784, but in 1785 the buildings collapsed.[98] It is not clear whether the glasshouse was rebuilt.

A second glasshouse west of the Stourbridge road at Coalbournbrook existed by the early 18th century. After being occupied by Jeremiah Minors and Edward Bradley, it was used by John Bradley for making flint glass. In 1714 John let it, with a house formerly occupied by him, to Elijah and Humphrey Batchelor. In 1739 Humphrey took a new lease of the works and house along with the Dennis property.[99] The glasshouse passed like that at Dennis to Thomas Hill under his aunt's will of 1762. He concentrated his operations at Coalbournbrook, and it was probably there that already in 1760 he was making broad glass, bottles, and phials.[1] By 1771 he was in partnership there with his father Waldron Hill and with William Waldron.[2] They were evidently still working there in 1774,[3] but William Waldron alone was listed in 1784; he was then involved in the clay industry also. By 1809 Hill, Waldron, Littlewood & Hampton were producing bottles at Coalbournbrook, and the members of the partnership had interests outside the glass industry—in banking, clay mining, brickmaking, and metal working. By 1818 the firm had become Hill, Hampton, Harrison & Wheeley and by 1829 Hill, Hampton & Co. which in 1834 was making bottles at the works. In 1837 the firm also had a firebrick works on an adjoining site. By 1839 both had been taken over by Joseph Stevens.[4] By 1852 he had been succeeded by Joseph Webb, who moved from Holloway End and made flint, coloured, and pressed glass at Coalbournbrook. After his death in 1869 the Coalbournbrook works was run by his executors until c. 1892. It was then little used for many years apart from a short occupation around the turn of the century by the British Lens & Wall Glazing Co. In 1914 the works was taken over by Thomas Webb & Corbett Ltd. after a fire at its White House works in Wordsley. The firm was renamed Webb Corbett Ltd. in 1952 and became part of the Royal Doulton Group in 1969.[5]

Early in the 18th century Thomas Henzey

[90] Ibid. 48, 52–3; Haden, *Stourbridge Glass Trade* (1977), 16.
[91] Deed of 1739 at Dennis glassworks; Guttery, *From Broad-glass to Cut Crystal*, 43–4, 63–5.
[92] Guttery, *From Broad-glass to Cut Crystal*, 37.
[93] Grazebrook, *Fams. of Henzey, Tyttery, and Tyzack*, 20; Haden, *Stourbridge Glass Trade* (1977 edn.), 20–1. No glasshouse is shown at Dennis on S.R.O., Tp. 1273, map of Amblecote 1769.
[94] H. W. Woodward, '*Art, Feat and Mystery': the story of Thos. Webb & Sons, glassmakers* (Stourbridge, 1978), 12–15; Guttery, *From Broad-glass to Cut Crystal*, 114; Haden, *Stourbridge Glass Trade*, 23; Scott, *Stourbridge*, 108.
[95] Woodward, '*Art, Feat and Mystery*', 14, 17 sqq.
[96] Guttery, *From Broad-glass to Cut Crystal*, 52, 56; Grazebrook, *Fams. of Henzey, Tyttery, and Tyzack*, 43–5, 131–3.
[97] Guttery, *From Broad-glass to Cut Crystal*, 80 n.; J. A. Langford, *Staffs. and Warws. Past and Present*, i (2), p. lxviii.

[98] Guttery, *From Broad-glass to Cut Crystal*, 96–9, 152; *V.C.H. Staffs.* ii. 228; Haden, *Stourbridge Glass Trade*, 27; S.R.O., Tp. 1273/25, pp. 7, 9, 13, listing each partner separately as a tenant of Lord Foley. Guttery (p. 80) states that Thos. Hill bought the works from Dixon in 1779.
[99] Deed of 1739 at Dennis glassworks.
[1] Langford, *Staffs. and Warws.* i (2), p. lxviii.
[2] Guttery, *From Broad-glass to Cut Crystal*, 84, 113.
[3] *Plan for Navigable Canal from Stourbridge surveyed in 1774 by Rob. Whitworth* (1775; copy in W.S.L.).
[4] Above, clay; Haden, *Stourbridge Glass Trade*, 23; White, *Dir. Staffs.* (1834), 247, 270; Pigot, *Nat. Com. Dir.* (1835), 657; Stourbridge Libr., newspaper cuttings, p. 33.
[5] Stourbridge Libr., newspaper cuttings, p. 33; Haden, *Stourbridge Glass Trade*, 23–4; D. and J. Byrne, *Webb Corbett and Royal Doulton English Full Lead Crystal* (Royal Doulton Tableware Ltd. 1978), 6–7 (copy in W.S.L. Pamphs.); inf. from Mr. J. Byrne; below, pl. facing p. 144.

built a glasshouse at the Platts in the north-west corner of Amblecote for his eldest son Joshua, who later lived in an adjoining house. Joshua was succeeded in 1737 by his nephew John Pidcock. In 1747 Pidcock was working the nearby Dial glasshouse just over the Kingswinford boundary; the Platts, described as a bottle house, was then advertised for letting.[6] In 1769 Pidcock was working the Platts and living in the house.[7] His son, also John, who succeeded in 1791, lived there until his death in 1834, but the works had by then ceased operation.[8] The house was briefly occupied by the Misses Pidcock[9] and was then bought by Thomas Webb, who was living there in 1836.[10] He built a new works, moving to it from his Wordsley works in 1840. By 1846 his main product was flint glass. By 1851 he was also making coloured glass, and his products were represented that year at the Great Exhibition, where he won a medal for cut glass. By then he was also engaged in ironfounding.[11] After his move to Dennis in 1855 the Platts passed through various hands. It was run by the Harbridge Crystal Glass Co. from 1924. Production there ceased in 1955, but the company then leased two furnaces at Webb Corbett's works and continued to cut glass at the Platts until 1966 when the site was sold.[12]

The number of firms making glass in Amblecote increased in the later 19th century, and by the end of the century there were evidently seven.[13] In 1921 glassmaking accounted for 219 out of every 1,000 males aged over 12, the highest figure in Staffordshire for the industry.[14] The 20th century, however, brought a steady decline in the industry, and the closure of the Platts reduced the number of glassworks in Amblecote to two, Dennis and Coalbournbrook.

IRON. The ironstone which is found in association with the Thick Coal was being dug by 1540 and probably by the later 14th century.[15] Some was still being mined at the beginning of the 19th century.[16]

The ironstone was also worked locally about the mid 16th century when a bloomsmithy was built in Amblecote.[17] It was probably on the Stour in the south-east corner on or near the site of the blade mill which was built at the beginning of the 17th century, converted into a fulling mill by 1688, and again used as a blade mill in the early 19th century.[18] There was mention in 1605

of a nailer late of Amblecote.[19] A locksmith was living there in 1654[20] and an ironmonger in 1672.[21] An ironworks on the Stour in the south-west was conveyed in 1680 by John Newbrough and his wife Mary to Joshua Bradley and others.[22] As the Royal forge it was sold in 1688 by Joshua Bradley, then of Stourbridge, and his wife Hannah to Ambrose Crowley of Stourbridge (d. 1720). The sale also included a steelhouse on the Stourbridge side of the river which Crowley held in 1682.[23] The forge was later worked by Francis Homfray, who was living in Old Swinford at the time of his death in 1737.[24] John Wyatt, a scythesmith of Amblecote, took a lease of the Royal Oak inn in 1718 and was living there in 1722; another scythesmith was living in Amblecote a few years later.[25] By the 1730s the manorial mill on the Stour south-east of the Stourbridge road was used as a 'forge, battering mill, or slitting mill', but it was converted into a fulling mill in or soon after 1734.[26] Thomas and Waldron Hill and William Waldron had a blade mill by the Stour on the Coalbournbrook glasshouse premises which they occupied in the 1770s, and in 1784 Waldron Hill had four scythesmiths' workshops in Amblecote.[27] The Town forge worked by Thomas Hill in 1784 was evidently the Royal forge; it included a steel furnace.[28] The nailing which was then the main feature of ironworking in the Stourbridge area had extended to Amblecote by the mid 1830s when there were two nail manufacturers, George Bates in the south-west by the canal and Arthur Harrison & Co. at Coalbournbrook; the second also made scythes.[29] There was a nail shop in the south-east corner in the later 1830s, occupied by the Griffiths family; it was presumably the nail shop held by J. Griffiths in 1857.[30] The population included many nailers in 1841.[31]

The Stourbridge ironworks in the south-west between the Stour and the canal was built in the early 19th century. In 1800 John Bradley, a Stourbridge ironmaster, took a lease of a site west of the Royal forge and built a forge there with a slitting and rolling mill. He acted in association with the trustees of his step-brothers and -sisters named Foster, who were all minors, and in 1802 the group went into formal partnership as John Bradley & Co. The company bought King's meadow east of the Royal forge in 1808 and built a second works. In 1813 it bought the glass-cutting and -engraving works which stood west

[6] Guttery, *From Broad-glass to Cut Crystal*, 56–61; Grazebrook, *Fams. of Henzey, Tyttery, and Tyzack*, 81; Haden, *Stourbridge Glass Trade*, 24.
[7] S.R.O., Tp. 1273, map of Amblecote 1769.
[8] Grazebrook, *Fams. of Henzey, Tyttery, and Tyzack*, 83; White, *Dir. Staffs.* (1834), 246.
[9] Pigot, *Nat. Com. Dir.* (1835), 655.
[10] S.R.O., D. 356A; D. 585/159/1/1, p. 1; H.W.R.O. (H.), E 12/S, Iverley II, deed of 26 Dec. 1836.
[11] Woodward, '*Art, Feat and Mystery*', 8–10, 29.
[12] Ibid. 10; Guttery, *From Broad-glass to Cut Crystal*, 147; *Kelly's Dir. Staffs.* (1928); inf. from Mr. Byrne.
[13] Haden, *Stourbridge Glass Trade*, 8; *Kelly's Dir. Staffs.* (1900).
[14] *Census*, 1921.
[15] S.R.O., Tp. 1273/13; above, coal.
[16] S.R.O., Tp. 1273/22, clay and coal royalty bk. 1802–52.
[17] H.W.R.O. (H.), E 12/S, Early Deeds, deed of 2 Feb. 1549/50; S.R.O., Tp. 1273/11, 1623 survey.
[18] Above (mills).

[19] *S.H.C.* 1940, 266–7.
[20] S.R.O., Tp. 1273/4, deed of 18 Mar. 1653/4.
[21] D.C.L., D/OH/I/1/22.
[22] P.R.O., CP 25(2)/726/32 Chas. II Mich. no. 9; ibid. 36 Chas. II Trin. no. 18.
[23] S.R.O., Tp. 1273/4, deed of 25 Feb. 1687/8; M. W. Flinn, *Men of Iron*, 10 sqq.
[24] Grazebrook, *Fams. of Henzey, Tyttery and Tyzack*, 53 n.
[25] S.R.O., Tp. 1273/10, deeds of 24 June 1718, 14 May 1722, 17 Mar. 1733/4.
[26] Above, mills.
[27] Guttery, *From Broad-glass to Cut Crystal*, 108; S.R.O., Tp. 1273/25, p. 13.
[28] S.R.O., Tp. 1273/25, p. 15; Tp. 1273, map of Amblecote 1769; *Plan for Navigable canal from Stourbridge surveyed in 1774 by Rob. Whitworth* (1775; copy in W.S.L.).
[29] Nash, *Worcs.* ii. 212; White, *Dir. Staffs.* (1834), 247; S.R.O., D. 585/159/1/1, pp. 2, 4, 10.
[30] S.R.O., D. 356A, no. 263; S.R.O., Tp. 1273/42, deed of 15 June 1857.
[31] P.R.O., HO 107/996.

of the company's first works and dated from the early 1790s. Bradley, who moved his home from Stourbridge to Coalbournhill, died in 1816, and James Foster, one of his step-brothers, was left in sole control of the undertaking, which retained the name of John Bradley & Co. From 1827 to 1837 Foster was in partnership with Bradley's son Henry, but from 1837 he was again the sole proprietor. In 1847 he bought the Royal forge from J. A. Addenbrooke of Hagley (Worcs.); it had been held from 1837 by Thomas and John Siddaway on a 21-year lease. In 1848 Foster bought the ironworks between the river and the canal east of the Stourbridge road which had been built c. 1830 by his brother William and William's brother-in-law William Orme. James moved from Stourbridge to Stourton Castle in Kinver in 1833 and lived there until his death in 1853. His heir was his nephew William Orme Foster, who was succeeded by his son William Henry in 1899. In 1919 W. H. Foster sold the Stourbridge ironworks to a company which adopted the name John Bradley & Co. (Stourbridge) Ltd. and whose successors in title were operating the John Bradley Rolling Mills in 1981.[32]

The iron industry spread to the Platts Road area in the north-east of Amblecote, but the concentration has remained in the south-west. In the later 1830s there was a steelworks on the north side of the canal west of the Stourbridge road worked by Young & Son.[33] In 1893 Jones & Attwood, a firm making water heating apparatus, moved from Stourbridge to the newly erected Titan works in Old Wharf Road off the Stourbridge road north of the canal. A foundry there began operation in 1896. In 1914 the firm bought 3 a. for a new foundry; work on it began in 1920, and it came into use in 1922.[34] The Titan works was still in operation in 1981. In 1921 the iron industry was the main employer in Amblecote: metal workers accounted for 203 of every 1,000 males aged over 12, and foundry workers made up another 35.[35]

CLOTH. By 1688 the mill on the Stour in the south-east of Amblecote was used as a fulling mill. It continued as such until 1719. The Town Mills south-east of the bridge on the Stourbridge road were leased to William Scott, a Stourbridge clothier, in 1734 for conversion into a fulling mill. The Scott family ran a fulling mill there until the early 19th century when it was converted into a leather mill.[36]

ROPE. There was a ropewalk in Amblecote in 1784 in the hands of Richard Grovenor.[37] A ropewalk beside the Stour south-east of the Stourbridge road was occupied by Richard Barney in the later 1830s.[38] A ropewalk existed further north in 1882.[39] In the early 1860s Thomas Guest was making rope at Coalbournbrook.[40]

LOCAL GOVERNMENT. Cecily de Stafford, lady of the manor in the mid 13th century, held view of frankpledge, paying 12d. for the right.[41] A court baron was normally held each year in the spring or autumn in the 16th and early 17th century; that was probably the custom by the mid 15th century.[42]

There was frequent mention of the constable in the 17th century.[43] In 1613 the court was concerned at the extensive theft of timber by outsiders, mostly 'very poor and beggarly people of whom nothing can be expected but a strict punishment to be inflicted upon them for reformation of such misdemeanours'; those caught were to be taken to the constable who was to put them in the stocks. In 1563, when a new pound was being made, the court laid down the procedure for having animals released from it. In 1613 the pound was broken into several times, and in 1615 cattle being driven there were intercepted. In 1612, 1614, and 1621 the court took action to control the settlement of strangers in the manor.[44]

Parochially Amblecote was part of Old Swinford until the 19th century. As the hamlet of Amblecote it formed a division of the parish for rating purposes. By 1744 it contributed to levies at a lower rate in the £ than the other two divisions, Stourbridge and the rest of Old Swinford.[45] It became part of Stourbridge poor-law union in 1836.[46]

A parish council was established in 1894. It had 11 members and met at the National school.[47] It continued until 1898 when Amblecote became an urban district with 9 councillors. They too at first met at the National school but by 1924 had moved to 131 High Street. The urban district's area of 665 a. was increased in 1936 by the addition of 1 a. at the junction of Brettell Lane and Collis Street from Brierley Hill urban district.[48]

In 1966 the 158 ha. west of the railway line were added to Stourbridge borough and the 111 ha. east of the line to Dudley borough.[49] In 1974

[32] N. Mutton, 'The Foster Family' (London Univ. Ph.D. thesis, 1974), esp. chaps. 3–6; S.R.O., D. 356A, nos. 134, 136, 146; D. 695/1/39/55. For the Foster and Orme works see Scott, Stourbridge, 106; S.R.O., D. 356A, no. 160; S.R.O., Tp. 1273/41, deed of 10 Mar. 1833; above, introduction (communications). Dr. Mutton is thanked for his help.

[33] S.R.O., D. 356A, no. 142.

[34] Mr. Walter Jones (souvenir of his retirement from chairmanship of Jones & Attwood Ltd. 1922), 16 (copy in possession of Mr. H. J. Haden).

[35] Census, 1921.

[36] Above (mills).

[37] S.R.O., Tp. 1273/25, rate book 1784, p. 7.

[38] S.R.O., D. 356A, no. 197. Pigot, Nat. Com. Dir. (1835), 659, listed him in High St., Stourbridge.

[39] O.S. Map 1/2,500, Staffs. LXXI. 10 (1885 edn.).

[40] P.O. Dir. Worcs. (1860), 1253; P.R.O., RG 9/2068.

[41] S.H.C. iv (2), 202; v (1), 111.

[42] S.R.O., Tp. 1273/13, broken run of ct. rolls 1445–1621.

[43] See e.g. S.H.C. 1923, 56; 1935, 449, 466; 1940, 228.

[44] S.R.O., Tp. 1273/13.

[45] Inf. supplied by Mr. N. R. Perry of Old Swinford from the Old Swinford churchwardens' accts. 1603–67; H.W.R.O. (W.), b 850 Old Swinford BA5214/4, churchwardens' and overseers' accts. 1667–1878, vestry meeting 2 Apr. 1744; ibid. 5, churchwardens' accts. 1767–1852 and church rate bk. 1846; Scott, Stourbridge, 111.

[46] 3rd Ann. Rep. Poor Law Com. H.C. 546, p. 166 (1837), xxxi.

[47] D.C.L., Amblecote Par. Council Min. Bk. 1894–8.

[48] D.C.L., Amblecote U.D. Min. Bks. 1898–1900, 1965–6; Kelly's Dir. Staffs. (1924; 1936); Census, 1901, 1951; O.S. Map 6″, Staffs. LXXI. NW. (1921 edn.; prov. edn. with addns. of 1938).

[49] Census, 1971.

both portions became part of the new metropolitan borough of Dudley in the new county of West Midlands.[50]

PUBLIC SERVICES. When the Stourbridge Waterworks Co. was established in 1854, Amblecote was included in the area of supply. A reservoir and pumping station were built in Mill meadow in the south of Amblecote, and a supply became available from 1857. The present pumping station north of Wollaston Road was built in 1880.[51]

By the later 1950s the urban district council was providing 203 houses and 48 flats. Eight of the houses and all the flats had been built since 1945.[52]

In 1845 there was an unsuccessful plan for making Dennis House into a hospital.[53] By 1891 efforts were being made to provide a cottage hospital for the Stourbridge district. In 1892 John Corbett of Impney, in Dodderhill (Worcs.), a retired Worcestershire salt manufacturer and M.P., vested the Hill and its 31-a. estate in trustees for conversion into a hospital for the poor of the area. He gave money for the conversion, and a public appeal was also launched. The 18-bed Corbett Hospital was opened in 1893. A children's ward was added in 1896, towards which Corbett gave £1,500. He also gave £10,000 as an endowment fund. Many more additions were later made, notably in the 1930s and 1960s–70s, and after the early 1970s little remained of the original house.[54]

A gasworks was built in 1835 on the 2-a. Coney Close east of the Stourbridge road at Holloway End by John Swift, a Stourbridge ironfounder, and five other shareholders. The company, the Stourbridge Gas Co., was incorporated in 1855. The undertaking was bought by the Stourbridge improvement commissioners in 1893.[55] The works was demolished in 1966 except for one gasholder.[56] In 1835 the trustees of the Stourbridge turnpike roads decided to enter into an agreement with the gas company for the lighting of the main road through Amblecote with fifteen lamps.[57]

There was a post office in Brettell Lane by 1850.[58]

CHURCH. For ecclesiastical purposes Amblecote was part of the parish of Old Swinford in Worcester diocese until 1845 when it became a separate parish in the same diocese; the Wollaston area of Old Swinford was part of the new parish until 1860.[59] The building of a church was begun in 1841 at Holloway End. It was opened in 1842 and consecrated in 1844. The site was given by the earl of Stamford, who also made an endowment of £100 a year, charged on Hermitage farm, then in Coningsby but later in Langriville (Lincs.); the rent charge was redeemed in 1968. The building costs were met by subscription. The largest subscribers were Lord Stamford, the ironmaster James Foster who also gave the railings for the churchyard, and Lord Ward. Adelaide, the queen dowager, who was living at Witley Court (Worcs.), gave £20, and the Diocesan Church Building Society made a grant. Foster, having bought the tithes from land at Compton, in Kinver, assigned the commuted rent charge of £10 for the maintenance of the church and churchyard on condition that 500 of the sittings should be free.[60]

The living was at first a perpetual curacy and from 1868 a vicarage. The first minister, J. W. Grier, was chosen in 1842 by the subscribers to the building fund, who received one vote for every £10 subscribed; he was then recommended to Lord Stamford. By the subscribers' wish the patronage was assigned to Lord Stamford and his heirs, and it descended with the Enville estate until 1928 when Sir John Grey transferred it to the bishop of Worcester.[61] By 1846 the incumbent was living at Dennis House and was still there in 1851.[62] A house was built for him in 1860 on a site in Amblecote Lane given by Lord Stamford and later occupied by Queen's Crescent; the cost was met by subscription and a grant from the Ecclesiastical Commissioners. In 1925 the house was sold and Harrington House (formerly Holloway End House) in High Street north of the church was bought instead. A new vicarage house was built in 1976, one of several houses then built on the site of Harrington House in a new street named the Holloway.[63] After Wollaston had become a separate parish in 1860 J. W. Grier was assigned £10 a year during his incumbency to compensate for loss of income.[64] In 1877, after the vicar had abolished pew rents worth £150 a year, an appeal was launched for £1,000 to augment his stipend; the sum was increased in stages to 1881 and matched by grants from the Ecclesiastical Commissioners. The Commissioners made further grants of £25 a year in 1928

[50] Dudley Metropolitan Boro. Official Guide (1975 edn.), 37.
[51] A Century of Water Supply in Stourbridge District (1957; copy in possession of Mr. H. J. Haden).
[52] Amblecote U.D.C. Reps. of M.O.H. and Pub. Health Insp. 1956 and 1957 (copies in S.R.O., C/H/1/2/2).
[53] Woodward, 'Art, Feat and Mystery', 12.
[54] Stourbridge Libr., case 13, rep. of 1st A.G.M. of Governors and Subscribers 1893, 8–9; ibid. rep. of 2nd A.G.M. 1894, 8–9; ibid. appeals for the hosp. and the children's ward; V.C.H. Worcs. iii. 222; County Express, 14 July 1917; 4 Nov. 1967; 19 Feb. 1971; Stourbridge Official Guide (1970–1), 51; D.N.B. 1901–11; inf. from Mr. Haden.
[55] Boro. of Stourbridge Gas Dept. Brief Descrip. of Gas Works (1948), 3 (copy in S.R.O., D. 734/19/1); S.R.O., Tp. 1273/8, deed of 23 June 1834; S.R.O., D. 356A, no. 166; Stourbridge Gas Act, 1855, 18 & 19 Vic. c. 37 (Local and Personal).
[56] Inf. from Mr. Haden.
[57] H.W.R.O. (W.) 899:31 BA3762/4 (iv), Stourbridge Roads Order Bk. 1830–42, 4 Sept. 1835.
[58] P.O. Dir. Staffs. (1850), 477.
[59] H.W.R.O. (W.), 728 Amblecote BA2968 (consulted by kind permission of the Revd. J. A. Dale, Worcester diocesan registrar); Lond. Gaz. 25 Jan. 1860, pp. 284–5.
[60] S. Pritt, Holy Trinity Church, Amblecote, 1842–1942, 5–7 (copy in Stourbridge Libr.); County Express, 30 June 1917; H.W.R.O. (W.), 728 Amblecote BA2968.
[61] Pritt, Holy Trinity Ch. 6; White, Dir. Staffs. (1851), 167; P.O. Dir. Staffs. (1868; 1872); Worcester Dioc. Dir. (1980); H.W.R.O. (W.), 728 Amblecote BA2968.
[62] H.W.R.O. (W.), b 850 Old Swinford BA5214/5, church rate bk. 1846; P.R.O., HO 107/2035.
[63] P.O. Dir. Worcs. (1860), 1250; Pritt, Holy Trinity Ch. 4, 12; County Express, 15 Sept. 1972, 14 July 1975, 2 July 1976; S.R.O., Tp. 1273/36, deed of 18 Feb. 1860; inf. from the vicar (1981).
[64] Lond. Gaz. 2 May 1862, p. 2286.

and £2 a year in 1929.[65] From the time of the second incumbent, J. S. Boldero, 1866–1900, services were conducted in the high-church tradition.[66]

A mission room was opened in King William Street in 1889. It continued in use until 1921 when it was sold. The proceeds of the sale were put towards the cost of the parish hall opened in 1922 on a site in Vicarage Road adjoining the churchyard.[67]

The church of *THE HOLY TRINITY* was designed in an Early English style by Samuel Heming and built of yellow firebricks supplied at cost by William King of Amblecote Hall from his Withymoor works. It consists of an aisleless nave with a shallow sanctuary, south-east vestries, and a west gallery; there is a west tower with three porches. The sanctuary was originally the chancel, but in 1900 the stalls were moved into the body of the church to create a new chancel. The east window is a memorial to James Foster (d. 1853). A bell was installed in 1859 to replace one lent by the governors of Stourbridge grammar school; it was itself removed when a peal of eight cast by John Taylor & Co. of Loughborough was installed in 1965–6. An organ built by J. Nicholson and paid for by subscription was installed in 1849 in the west gallery. In 1873 it was moved to the vestry on the south-east, the south-west porch being made into a vestry; it was moved to its present position in the north-east corner of the church in 1900. The south-east vestry was re-occupied, and a priest's vestry was added to it in 1906. In that year too the original box pews were replaced by chairs. A lichgate was dedicated in 1921 as a war memorial.[68]

NONCONFORMITY. In the mid 18th century there was a Wesleyan meeting place in Brettell Lane, thought to be the forerunner of the chapel in Stourbridge. John Wesley is said to have preached at the house on Amblecote Bank later known as Stamford House, perhaps during his visit to Stourbridge in 1770. Land was bought on the south side of Brettell Lane in 1831 and a Wesleyan Methodist chapel built there. As a result of a schism in the Stourbridge circuit in 1836 the chapel was taken over by those members who joined the Methodist New Connexion, and the few remaining Wesleyans had to worship in private houses. Their numbers grew. In 1839 they bought a piece of land in High Street

opposite the end of Brettell Lane and opened a church there in 1840. Despite the change of site the chapel continued to be called Brettell Lane until 1905 when the name was changed to Amblecote Wesleyan Methodist Church.[69] A school was opened behind the chapel in 1841. On Census Sunday 1851 the congregation numbered 45 in the morning, with 34 Sunday school children, 30 in the afternoon, with 47 children, and 75 in the evening.[70] Improvements were made in the early 1870s, including the erection of a gallery in place of a small singers' loft over the entrance. A new school was built in 1872. In 1876 the chapel was extended at the rear, more galleries were inserted, the box pews were replaced with benches, and a new organ and organ chamber were installed.[71] In 1932 two new school buildings were opened behind the chapel in place of the 1872 school.[72] In 1958, as part of the renovation of the church, the side galleries were removed, that over the entrance surviving.[73]

On Census Sunday 1851 the New Connexion chapel in Brettell Lane had attendances of 25 in the morning, with 50 Sunday school children, 50 in the afternoon, with 61 children, and 50 in the evening. It was closed in 1958 after the amalgamation of its society with that of the High Street church.[74] In 1959 it was opened as a Christian Science church.[75] In 1980 it was bought by the Full Gospel Church which occupied the former Anglican mission church in King William Street; the building was renovated, and services were begun in 1981.[76]

EDUCATION. A National school for boys and girls was built in 1815 on the east side of the Stourbridge road at Holloway End by one of the Lee family of the Hill and Thomas Hill of Dennis House; the site was leased by Lord Stamford at a nominal rent. A house for the master was built on an adjoining site c. 1819. The school was known as the Madras school from the system of education followed there.[77] In 1834 it was run by a master and a mistress.[78] A new school was built in 1856 at Coalbournbrook in the later School Drive; it included houses for a master and a mistress. The cost was met by subscription and a government grant.[79] The earlier building became part of the gasworks.[80] The new school was enlarged apparently in 1871.[81] Average attendance was 230 in 1869 and 341 in 1905–6.[82] The school was closed in 1939.[83] The building was

[65] Pritt, *Holy Trinity Ch.* 10; *Lond. Gaz.* 25 May 1877, p. 3344; 19 July 1879, p. 4209; 13 May 1881, pp. 2500–1; H.W.R.O. (W.), 728 Amblecote BA2968.
[66] Pritt, *Holy Trinity Ch.* 10, 12; *Amblecote Par. Ch. of Holy Trinity: the story of its beginning,* 6–7 (copy in B.L.).
[67] Pritt, *Holy Trinity Ch.* 11–12.
[68] Ibid. 8–12; Pevsner, *Staffs.* 60; *P.O. Dir. Worcs.* (1845), 543; *County Express,* 30 June 1917; H.W.R.O. (W.), 728 Amblecote BA2968; below, pl. facing p. 64.
[69] J. H. Mees, *Story of a Hundred Years: Handbk. of Wesleyan Methodist Church Stourbridge Circuit* (Stourbridge, 1928), 51–5 (copy in Stourbridge Libr.); P.R.O., HO 129/383/2/6, gives the date of the chapel as 1833.
[70] P.R.O., HO 129/383/2/6.
[71] Mees, *Hundred Years,* 56–7.
[72] J. H. Mees and L. A. Watson, *Handbk. of Methodist Sunday Schs., High St., Amblecote,* 42 (copy in possession of Mr. H. J. Haden).
[73] *County Express,* 11 Oct. 1958.

[74] P.R.O., HO 129/383/2/6; D.C.L., envelope of misc. Methodist leaflets, brochure of Amblecote Meth. Ch. direct giving campaign; G.R.O., Worship Reg. no. 64343; *County Express,* 11 Oct. 1956.
[75] *County Express,* 7 and 10 Oct. 1967; G.R.O., Worship Reg. no. 67759.   [76] Inf. from Mr. Haden.
[77] Scott, *Stourbridge,* 108–10; *P.O. Dir. Staffs.* (1845), 543; S.R.O., Tp. 1273/50, Amblecote Sch.; S.R.O., D. 356A, no. 164.
[78] Scott, *Stourbridge,* 106; White, *Dir. Staffs.* (1834), 246.
[79] *P.O. Dir. Worcs.* (1860), 1250; *Kelly's Dir. Staffs.* (1884); S.R.O., D. 812/1/19, 20, 22; below, pl. facing p. 64.
[80] Pritt, *Holy Trinity Ch.* 4.
[81] S.R.O., D. 812/1/27–8; O.S. Map 1/2,500, Staffs. LXXI. 10 (1885 edn.).
[82] *Rep. of Educ. Cttee. of Council, 1869–70,* 640; *Public Elem. Schs. 1907* [Cd. 3901], p. 562, H.C. (1908), lxxxiv.
[83] Inf. from Mrs. L. M. Wass, headmistress, Amblecote primary school (1981).

used as an emergency feeding centre during the Second World War and as a school canteen in the 1950s; in 1962 it became a civic hall and public library.[84]

A National school for girls and infants was built in 1846 on the corner of King William Street and Hill Street; there was also a house for the mistress. In 1851 the mistress had two assistants. In 1860 the children paid 2d. or 1½d. a week according to the number in the family; average attendance was 110.[85] By 1880 the school was for infants only.[86] In 1905–6 attendance averaged 141.[87] A new infants' school was opened in School Drive in 1962 and extended in 1974; it became a primary school in 1971. The old building was demolished.[88]

Peter's Hill primary school in Peter's Hill Road was opened in 1974. The building was extended in 1976–7.[89]

There was a private school in 1834 run by Eliza and Maria Hopkins,[90] and a dame school held in the Wesleyan Methodist Sunday school was recorded between 1848 and 1867.[91] In 1853 Amblecote Training School was opened in a building on the corner of High Street and Vicarage Road opposite Holy Trinity church. In 1856, with Philip Marks as principal, the school claimed to be educating 'upwards of 100 of the most respectable youth residing in the neigh-bourhood' and advertised arrangements for a limited number of young gentlemen as boarders. In 1861 there were 24 boarders, aged between 8 and 15. The school had closed by 1868. Part of the building became the Royal Oak inn, which was rebuilt in the late 1950s; the other part, the High House, was demolished in 1949.[92]

CHARITIES FOR THE POOR. By will proved 1825 James Batson of Stourbridge left £100 to the overseers of Amblecote and Kingswinford, the interest to be spent on the poor of both places. In the earlier 1970s the Amblecote part of the charity was distributed in 50p vouchers.[93]

By will proved 1866 Joseph Cole, a Stourbridge grocer, left money to provide food and clothing for the poor of Amblecote. In 1982 the charity was distributed in six sums of £5.[94]

Holy Trinity parish shares in the charity established under the will of Henry Bate, proved 1866, for the benefit of the poor of the ecclesiastical districts within Old Swinford parish.[95]

By the will proved 1936 Mabel Janet Booth left stock to provide a distribution every Christmas to poor members of the congregation of Holy Trinity. In 1982 the charity was distributed in 14 sums of £5 and 2 of £10.[96]

BOBBINGTON

THE ancient parish of Bobbington, which lies on the county boundary with Shropshire, is 2,681 a. (1,085 ha.) in area.[97] The northern part around Whittimere was in Shropshire until 1895 when it was transferred to Staffordshire.[98] The parish remains predominantly agricultural in character.

Along Brantley brook, which forms part of the county boundary in the west, the land lies at its lowest, 258 ft. (80 m.); it rises to around 375 ft. (114 m.) on the ridge known as Abbot's Castle Hill in the north-east, 363 ft. (111 m.) in the south, and 533 ft. (162 m.) in the south-west. The county boundary on the west near Blakelands is marked by granite stones.[99] At Six Ashes in the south-west the boundary was marked by six ash trees, still standing in 1793.[1] An arm of Philley brook forms part of the parish boundary with Enville on the south. At least since the earlier 19th century the boundary east of Lutley Lane has been marked by tumps or mounds of earth.[2] Before the transfer of Whittimere to Staffordshire in 1895 the county boundary ran eastwards from Halfpenny Green along the Wombourne road, past the War Stone on the boundary with Wombourne, and north along Abbot's Castle Hill. The underlying rock is breccia and sandstone, and the soil is a mixture of sand, gravel, and clay.[3]

Prehistoric settlement in the area is suggested by Mesolithic and post-Mesolithic flint artifacts found at Leaton Hall south of the village and at Tuckhill in the south-west.[4] A Roman road from Ashwood, in Kingswinford, to Bridgnorth and Wales ran through the Whittimere area, entering the parish east of the War Stone and passing below Abbot's Castle Hill.[5] What were described as two small camps near the stone were noted in the mid 18th century.[6]

[84] County Express, 29 Mar. 1968.
[85] P.R.O., ED 7/108/12; P.R.O., HO 107/2035; S.R.O., D. 812/1/29.
[86] Kelly's Dir. Staffs. (1880); O.S. Map 1/2,500, Staffs. LXXI. 6 (1884 edn.).
[87] Public Elem. Schs. 1907, 562.
[88] Inf. from Mrs. Wass; County Express, 29 Mar. 1968.
[89] Inf. from the head teacher (1981).
[90] White, Dir. Staffs. (1834), 246.
[91] Mees, Hundred Years, 55.
[92] County Express, 29 Mar. 1968; P.R.O., RG 9/2068; S.R.O., D. 416/5/1; Stourbridge Libr., photograph 1457. The school is not listed in P.O. Dir. Staffs. (1868).
[93] Tablet in Amblecote ch.; V.C.H. Worcs. iii. 223; Char. Com. files.
[94] H.W.R.O. (W.), 728 Amblecote BA2968, terrier of 1908; V.C.H. Worcs. iii. 223; inf. from the vicar and Mr. Haden.
[95] V.C.H. Worcs. iii. 223; inf. from Bannister, King & Rigbeys, Stourbridge.
[96] Inf. from the vicar.
[97] Census, 1971. This article was written in 1981–2. Miss L. B. Amphlett of Four Ashes Hall, Enville, Mrs. Mary Crump of Clair Hayes, Bobbington, the Revd. J. Gibbons, vicar of Bobbington, Brig. C. Goulbourn of Ewdness, Bridgnorth (Salop.), and others named in footnotes are thanked for their help.
[98] V.C.H. Salop. ii. 220.
[99] D.C.L., A 610.
[1] Torrington Diaries, ed. C. Bruyn Andrews, iii. 226.
[2] S.R.O., Q/RDc 87.
[3] T. H. Whitehead and R. W. Pocock, Memoirs of Geol. Surv., Dudley and Bridgnorth, 157–8, 169–70; V.C.H. Staffs. i, map before p. 1.
[4] Trans. Salop. Arch. Soc. lix. 204.
[5] Ibid. lvi. 237.   [6] Shaw, Staffs. ii. 278.

Holy Trinity Church from the north-west in the mid 19th century

The National school at Coalbournbrook in 1858 with the
Dennis glassworks in the background on the left

AMBLECOTE

TETTENHALL: BARNHURST FARM, DEMOLISHED c. 1962

KINVER: WHITTINGTON MANOR FARM

BOBBINGTON: BOBBINGTON HALL FROM THE NORTH-EAST

BOBBINGTON: BLAKELANDS FROM THE NORTH-WEST

In 1086 the recorded population was 12.[7] There were 17 people assessed for tax in 1327 and 19 in the mid 1520s.[8] The muster roll of 1539 also recorded 19 people.[9] The poll-tax assessment of 1641 listed 121.[10] In 1666 there were 31 people assessed for hearth tax in the Staffordshire part of the parish, and a further 17 were too poor to pay.[11] At Whittimere 5 people were assessed for the hearth tax of 1672.[12] The population of the Staffordshire and the Shropshire parts together was 381 in 1801 and 393 in 1821. It rose to 426 in 1831, remaining around that figure until the later 19th century. Between 1871 and 1881 it fell from 413 to 404; it continued to fall, reaching 367 in 1891, 337 in 1901, 332 in 1911, and 325 in 1921, but had risen to 376 by 1931. It was 560 in 1951, 478 in 1961, and 548 in 1971.[13]

Bobbington, meaning the *tun* of Bubba's people,[14] was presumably the site of the present village, where there was a church by the 12th century. In 1775 settlement was concentrated near the church,[15] and the village remained small until the 20th century. An inn, the Red Lion, existed by 1825, and probably by 1797. It stood on a site south of the church by 1883 when the vicarage was built there; Mill Farm, an 18th-century building to the east, then became the inn.[16] In the early 1880s the only buildings apart from the church, the vicarage, and the inn, were cottages at the corner of Six Ashes Road and Church Lane and three houses to the east.[17] Four council houses were built on the south side of Six Ashes Road opposite the Red Lion in 1926, and a private house named Bannockburn was built nearby in the mid 1930s. The village hall on the north side of the road was opened in 1947.[18] An estate of 22 council houses in Brantley Crescent at the western end of the village dates from the 1950s, and 4 pensioners' bungalows opposite the vicarage and another 2 to the east were built *c.* 1970. There are privately built houses on the south side of Six Ashes Road dating from the 1960s and 1970s. From 1960, when a Green Belt policy was applied to the village, there were restrictions on new building.[19]

There was an early settlement at Whittimere: land there called Wulfhamton in the later 13th century has been identified as the later Whittimere farm. The farmhouse stands on a knoll west of the road from Halfpenny Green to Upper Aston, in Claverley (Salop.). A vill of Whittimere existed by the later 13th century.[20] It may have

lain east of Whittimere Farm at Upper Whittimere: Thom or Tom Street, mentioned in the vill in the 15th century, may have been the name of a stretch of the Roman road near Upper Whittimere.[21]

Settlement was scattered by an early date; that pattern is characteristic of a forest area, Bobbington formerly lying in Kinver forest.[22] Leaton south of Bobbington village and Rickthorn to the south-west were inhabited by the later 13th century. Tuckhill south-west of Rickthorn was settled by the 1290s.[23] By the earlier 14th century there was a settlement at Hay, presumably the later Hay Farm near the southern boundary.[24] Blacklands north-east of Bobbington was inhabited by the earlier 15th century, and Bobbington Hall south of the village dates from *c.* 1600. There was a farmhouse at Blakelands north-east of Blacklands by the earlier 17th century. Bobbington Farm south-west of the village existed by 1691; the house was rebuilt in 1841, and the name was changed to College Farm about that time. Bobbington House Farm nearer the village was built in 1695 apparently by William and Frances Pratt.[25]

Much of the eastern part of the parish was formerly waste and marsh. By the mid 15th century the marsh was being drained: the repair of a dike near Halfpenny lake was ordered in 1448, and similar orders were made between the mid 15th and later 16th century.[26] The word lake suggests a drainage channel. Dikes and channels at Halfpenny Green were mentioned in 1532 and 1536.[27] The name Halfpenny presumably derived from rents and not, as has been suggested, from the cost of water from a well on the green.[28] There was a cottage at Halfpenny Green by 1662, evidently the result of encroachment on the waste. Manor farm south-east of Halfpenny Green dates from the later 17th century.[29] By 1775 there were scattered dwellings on the edge of the waste along Gospelash Road.[30] As Chester Way the road formed part of the medieval route between south-west England and Chester which continued in use until *c.* 1800. It was included in the stretch of the route turnpiked in 1762.[31] By 1775 a small settlement had also grown up at Halfpenny Green itself.[32] An inn, the Royal Oak, existed there by 1821.[33] Nailers were living in Gospelash Road in 1841 and 1851,[34] while in 1857 Halfpenny Green was said to contain houses of the better class.[35] In 1941 the Air

[7] *V.C.H. Staffs.* iv. 52.
[8] *S.H.C.* vii (1), 252; P.R.O., E 179/177/96.
[9] *S.H.C.* N.S. vi (1), 68.
[10] H.L., Main Papers, box 178.
[11] *S.H.C.* 1923, 70–1.
[12] *Salop. Hearth-Tax Roll of 1672* (Salop. Arch. Soc. 1949), 109.
[13] *V.C.H. Staffs.* i. 326; *V.C.H. Salop.* ii. 220; *Census,* 1911–71.   [14] Ekwall, *Eng. Place-Names.*
[15] Yates, *Map of Staffs.* (1775).
[16] S.R.O., Q/RSf; D. 833/6/2; O.S. Map 6″, Staffs. LXVI. SW. (1889 edn.); below, church.
[17] O.S. Map 6″, Staffs. LXVI. SW. (1889 edn.).
[18] Note in poss. of Bobbington History Group.
[19] Inf. from Mrs. M. Jones, clerk to Bobbington par. council (1981).
[20] Below, pp. 70–1.
[21] Apley Estate Office, Bridgnorth (Salop.), transcript of Claverley ct. rolls 1377–1461, p. 166; 1461–1546, pp. 14, 89; ibid. ct. roll C.20 (21 Oct. 1483).

[22] For this para. see, unless otherwise stated, below, manor and other estates; econ. hist.
[23] Salop. R.O. 52/3–5; *S.H.C.* 1911, 204, 207.
[24] *S.H.C.* vii (1), 252.
[25] Tablet on house; S.R.O., D. 3373/1, burial of 1717.
[26] Apley Estate Off., transcript Claverley ct. rolls 1377–1461, pp. 282, 306; 1461–1546, pp. 91, 140, 144, 268, 294; 1509–89, pp. 75, 86, 135.
[27] Ibid. 1461–1546, pp. 264, 279.
[28] *N. & Q.* 2nd ser. iv. 147; Jay, 'Bobbington', 22.
[29] S.R.O., D. 1287/6/8/1; below, manor and other estates.
[30] Yates, *Map of Staffs.* (1775).
[31] Apley Estate Off., transcript Claverley ct. rolls 1461–1546, p. 294; below, Patshull, introduction.
[32] Yates, *Map of Staffs.* (1775).
[33] S.R.O., Tp. 1273/5, doc. recording meeting for inclosure of Bobbington common (1821).
[34] Below, p. 73; P.R.O., HO 107/2017(1).
[35] *N. & Q.* 2nd ser. iv. 147.

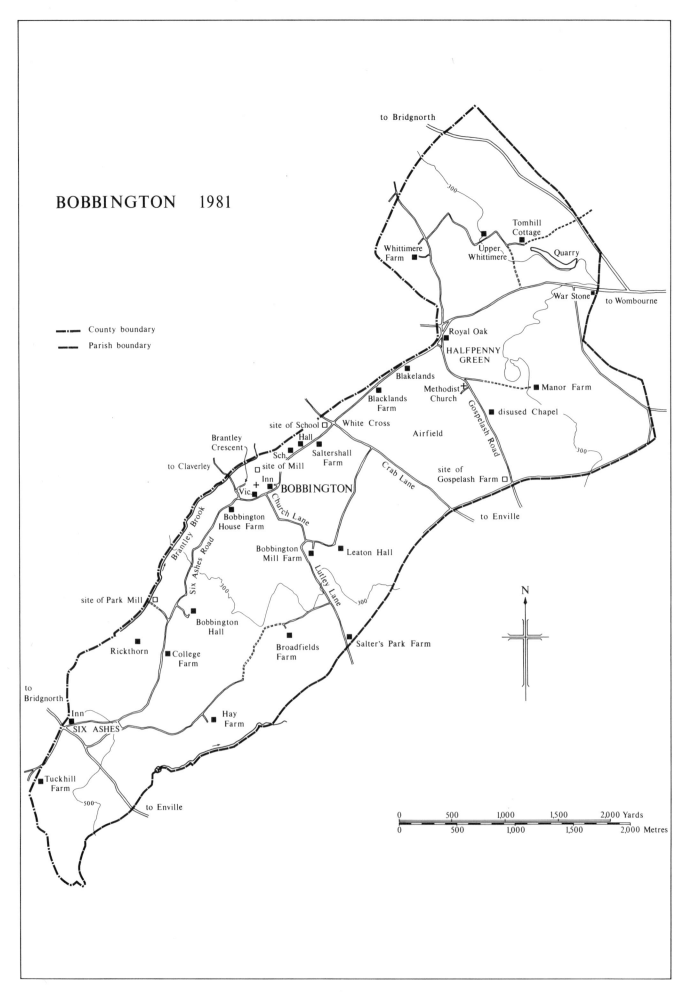

BOBBINGTON 1981

County boundary
Parish boundary

to Bridgnorth

Tomhill
Cottage

Whittimere
Farm

Upper
Whittimere

Quarry

War Stone

to Wombourne

Royal Oak

HALFPENNY
GREEN

Blakelands

Blacklands
Farm

Methodist
Church

Manor Farm

disused Chapel

site of School

White Cross

Airfield

Brantley
Crescent

Hall

Sch.

Saltershall
Farm

Crab Lane

site of
Gospelash Farm

to Claverley

site of Mill

Inn

Vic.

BOBBINGTON

to Enville

Bobbington
House Farm

Church Lane

Bobbington
Mill Farm

Leaton Hall

site of Park Mill

Six Ashes Road

Brantley Brook

Bobbington
Hall

Lutley Lane

300

300

N

Rickthorn

College
Farm

Broadfields
Farm

Salter's Park Farm

to
Bridgnorth

Inn

SIX ASHES

Hay
Farm

Tuckhill
Farm

500

to Enville

0	500	1,000	1,500	2,000 Yards
0	500	1,000	1,500	2,000 Metres

Ministry opened an airfield at Halfpenny Green for use as a training station. Buildings near the edge of the airfield were demolished, notably the timber-framed Gospelash Farm at the southern end of Gospelash Road and in 1944 the school buildings at White Cross. In 1963 the airfield was transferred to private ownership for civilian flying. In 1972 Prince William of Gloucester was killed in an aircrash there. From 1974 the airfield was also used for holding 14 markets a year on Sundays and bank holidays.[36]

The settlement which straddles the county boundary at Six Ashes existed by 1775.[37] It lay along the Stourbridge–Bridgnorth road, turnpiked in 1816.[38] A family of nailers was living there in 1841,[39] and the present Six Ashes inn existed by 1845.[40]

There was a post office in Bobbington village by 1892; it was probably housed in a cottage, demolished in 1981, at the corner of Six Ashes Road and Church Lane. By the mid 1960s the post office had moved to Bannockburn, where it remained until c. 1976; it then moved to a garage on the south side of Six Ashes Road.[41] From 1923 water was supplied by the South Staffordshire Water Works Co. The parish had electricity by 1935. A sewerage scheme for the village was completed in the mid 1950s.[42]

There were donkey and greyhound races in the parish in the early 19th century. A cup was awarded to the winner of a donkey race on 27 September 1813, possibly on the occasion of a wake.[43] Coursing took place on the waste in 1811.[44] The Bobbington Friendly Society was established in 1825, meeting at the Red Lion. The Friendly Society of Tradesmen was founded in 1827; by 1876 it met at the Royal Oak. The Yew Tree Lodge of the United Order of Free Gardeners, established in 1870, also met at the Royal Oak in 1876.[45] The custom of gooding on St. Thomas's day (21 December), when the poor were given alms by the wealthier parishioners, was practised in the mid 19th century.[46] The Bobbington History Group was established in 1974.[47] A quarterly news-sheet, the *Bobbington Bulletin*, financed by the parish council, was started in 1976.[48]

Henry III was at Bobbington in 1238 and 1245. In June 1256 he ordered the sheriff to send four pipes of wine there, to await his arrival *en route* to Bridgnorth.[49] Royal justices held an assize at Bobbington in 1274.[50]

The Revd. Edward Bradley ('Cuthbert Bede'), 1827–89, author of *Mr. Verdant Green*, was vicar of Bobbington from 1857 to 1859.[51] His novel *The Curate of Cranston* (1862) was set in Bobbington.

MANOR AND OTHER ESTATES. Before the Conquest *BOBBINGTON* was held by Wifare with sac and soc; in 1086 Robert de Stafford held 5 hides there.[52] The overlordship descended with the barony of Stafford at least until 1621.[53]

Helgot held the manor of Robert de Stafford in 1086.[54] Philip son of Helgot, evidently a grandson of the Helgot of 1086, held Bobbington in 1166.[55] The manor then descended with Kinver until the early 14th century. In 1287 John Fitz-Philip granted it to John son of John de Wauton, probably his nephew, and received it back for life.[56] On his death between 1306 and 1309 the manor passed to Joan, daughter of the younger John de Wauton, and her husband Hugh de Hepham.[57] Although Hugh fought at Bannockburn in 1314 as one of the retinue of Hugh le Despenser,[58] by 1318 he had become a retainer of John, Lord Somery.[59] After Hugh's murder in 1318 or 1319 Lord Somery acquired the manor, probably by purchase from Hugh's widow Joan, who is known to have alienated other estates which she had by inheritance.[60] Lord Somery died in 1322, and Bobbington was assigned to his younger sister Joan Botetourt.[61] She died in 1338 and was succeeded by her son John Botetourt.[62] John died in 1386 leaving as his heir a granddaughter Joyce, wife of Hugh, Lord Burnell. She died in 1407.[63] Lord Burnell retained a life interest in the manor but later surrendered it, the manor being assigned in 1415 to Joyce's aunt Joyce and her husband Sir Adam de Peshale of Weston under Lizard. Adam died in 1419 and Joyce in 1420. The manor then passed to her grandson William Mytton, a minor.[64] William Mytton came of age in 1436. He also held the manor of Weston under Lizard, inherited from his grandfather Sir Adam de Peshale, and Bobbington descended with Weston until 1763 and then with Walsall until 1766.[65] In that year Diana, countess of Mountrath, left Bobbington

[36] D. Gregory, *Green Belts and Development Control* (Univ. of Birmingham, 1970), 58–60; Jay, 'Bobbington', 22, 24–5, 42; inf. from Mrs. Jones; below, church.
[37] Yates, *Map of Staffs.* (1775).
[38] Below, Kinver, introduction (communications).
[39] Below, econ. hist.
[40] *P.O. Dir. Staffs.* (1845).
[41] *Kelly's Dir. Staffs.* (1892); O.S. Map 1/2,500, Staffs. LXVI. 10 (1923 edn.); inf. from Mrs. A. Smellie, Japonica Cottage, Bobbington (1981).
[42] Seisdon R.D.C. *Rep. of M.O.H. 1921*, 8; *1923*, 8; *1935*, 10; *1953*, 18; *1955*, 18 (copies in S.R.O., C/H/1/2/2/36).
[43] Letter c. 1976 in poss. of Bobbington History Group (1981).
[44] S.R.O., Tp. 1273/58, Stour water, Dan. Clarke to Lord Stamford 14 Oct. 1811.
[45] S.R.O., Q/RSf; *Reps. of Chief Registrar of Friendly Socs. 1876*, H.C. 429, pp. 393, 401 (1877), lxxvii.
[46] *N. & Q.* 2nd ser. iv. 487–8.   [47] Mins. of group.
[48] Inf. from Mrs. J. Phillips, the editor.
[49] *Close R.* 1237–42, 104, 146; 1242–7, 333; *Cal. Pat.* 1232–47, 233, 466; *Cal. Lib.* 1251–60, 307.

[50] *S.H.C.* vi (1), 54–5.
[51] *D.N.B.* (*Suppl.*).
[52] *V.C.H. Staffs.* iv. 52.
[53] *S.H.C.* i. 177; *S.H.C.* N.S. ii. 135; *S.H.C.* 1911, 352; *Bk. of Fees*, i. 543; *Cal. Close*, 1419–22, 32.
[54] *V.C.H. Staffs.* iv. 52.
[55] R. W. Eyton, *Antiquities of Shropshire*, iii. 161; *S.H.C.* i. 177.
[56] *S.H.C.* 1911, 42–3; Eyton, *Shropshire*, iii. 183.
[57] *S.H.C.* vii (1), 143, 145–6, 151; *S.H.C.* 1911, 78–9; P.R.O., C 143/76, no. 17; *V.C.H. Yorks. N.R.* i. 324.
[58] *S.H.C.* viii (1), 33–4.
[59] *S.H.C.* N.S. vi (2), 80.
[60] *S.H.C.* ix (1), 77; Eyton, *Shropshire*, iii. 168–9.
[61] *S.H.C.* 1911, 352–4; *Cal. Inq. p.m.* vi, pp. 255, 259; *Cal. Fine R.* 1319–27, 191.
[62] *Cal. Inq. p.m.* viii, pp. 113–14; *V.C.H. Worcs.* iii. 194.
[63] *Cal. Inq. p.m.* xvi, p. 79; *Complete Peerage*, ii. 435.
[64] *S.H.C.* N.S. ii. 89, 91, 93, 96; *V.C.H. Staffs.* iv. 172.
[65] *V.C.H. Staffs.* iv. 172–3; xvii. 170; *S.H.C.* i. 371, 373, 376; *S.H.C.* N.S. ii. 121–3, 129–30.

to Lionel Damer, third son of Joseph, Lord Milton, later earl of Dorchester. Lionel died childless in 1807, and the manor passed to his sister Lady Caroline Damer, who sold it in 1818 to Lord George Cavendish.[66] He sold it to Walter Henry Moseley of Leaton Hall in 1821, and the manor then remained in the Moseley family with Leaton.[67]

In 1234 Henry III granted John son of Philip six oaks from Worfield (Salop.) to make a barn at Bobbington.[68] The barn may have adjoined a manor house. In 1244 John's widow Parnel was allowed to take timber to repair houses at Stourton and Bobbington.[69] The house at Stourton was evidently the royal hunting lodge known as Kinver (later Stourton) castle,[70] and it is likely that there was also a lodge at Bobbington. Henry III is known to have stayed more than once in Bobbington.[71]

An estate centred on *BOBBINGTON HALL* may have originated in land attached to the capital messuage of the manor. In the later 14th century the capital messuage was held with 3 virgates of land by Edward atte Lowe, possibly a relation of the Lowes of Whittington, in Kinver, later lords of Enville.[72] In 1576 John Grey, lord of Enville, held a messuage and land in Bobbington,[73] and in the late 17th century the Grey family owned a small estate centred on Bobbington Hall, so called by 1717.[74] In 1733 the estate comprised 67 a.[75] It remained part of the Enville Hall estate until 1864, when it was sold to Isaac Downing. Downing died in 1874 and his estate passed to John Herbert Crump (d. 1924).[76] In 1979 Mr. M. J. Hickman bought the house with some 8 a. from Mr. R. Poole; Mr. Hickman was still the owner in 1981.[77]

The building is a tall brick house of c. 1600 which incorporates a less substantial and possibly earlier timber-framed building. It has a main range which is divided from a northern cross wing by a passage. The gables are stepped throughout and the window surrounds are of mounted brick which is plastered to resemble stone. In the 17th century small additions were made in similar style to the west of the main range and a porch was added to the eastern doorway.[78] It was evidently the house assessed at 12 hearths in 1666 and then occupied by Ferdinand Hastings, a younger son of Sir Henry Hastings of Braunston (Leics.).[79] In 1701 the house con-

tained a hall, parlour, withdrawing room, and kitchen, each with a chamber above, garrets over the hall and parlour chambers, and a study.[80] By the early 19th century the house was in a poor condition, having been occupied by labourers for many years.[81] A tenant farmer was living there by the early 1820s.[82] The extensive 19th-century farm buildings north-east of the house were probably constructed as part of a programme of improvements on the Enville Hall estate.[83]

BOBBINGTON MANOR FARM, later *MANOR FARM*, was owned by Thomas Dickins of Leaton in 1662. He died in 1674, and in 1675 the property, comprising a house, tithe barn, and 45 a., passed to his nephew Tomyns Dickins the elder. In 1684 Sir Thomas Wilbraham of Woodhey, in Faddiley (Ches.), the lord of Bobbington, bought the property from Nathaniel Hulton, citizen and salter of London, who may have been acting for Tomyns Dickins.[84] The property then descended with the manor. In 1763 it was 40 a. in extent.[85] It was sold in 1821, at the same time as the manor, and bought by Thomas Bowen of Bradney, in Worfield.[86] By 1840 William Moseley of Leaton Hall owned the farm.[87] Land awarded to William's uncle out of the waste, inclosed in 1827, was added to the farm, which comprised 216 a. in 1851.[88] Moseley sold the property to the earl of Dudley in 1877.[89] About 1946 the farm was bought by Godfrey Booth, whose father George had been tenant c. 1900.[90] In 1978 the house and 4 a. were bought by Mr. H. J. Amies, the owner in 1981.[91]

An estate called *BLACKLANDS*, formerly *BLAKELAND*, existed by the earlier 15th century. John Brooke, a member of the Brooke family of Claverley (Salop.), was described as of Bobbington in the mid 1420s and in 1431 and 1438, and as of Blakeland in 1433, 1434, and 1446.[92] He is probably identifiable as the John Brooke to whom Thomas Brooke confirmed Blakeland in 1446–7 with ½ virgate nearby at Broughton, in Claverley.[93] Although John named his son Richard as his heir in his will of 1477, by 1479 another son John had evidently inherited the estate.[94] John Brooke the younger was churchwarden of Bobbington in 1500 and 1513.[95] He held the estate by 1536. He died in 1543 and was probably succeeded by his son Ralph (d. 1577).[96] A John Brooke was living at Blakeland by 1596 and died in 1640.[97] Edward

[66] S.R.O., D.(W.) 1854/6; *S.H.C.* iv (2), 95–6; *Hist. Parl., Commons, 1754–90*, ii. 298.
[67] S.R.O., D.(W.) 1746/T/5; below (Leaton).
[68] *Close R.* 1231–4, 469.   [69] Ibid. 1242–7, 209.
[70] Below, Kinver, manors and other estates.
[71] Above, introduction.
[72] Nottingham Univ. Libr., Mi. 6/173/252.
[73] *S.H.C.* xiv (1), 183.
[74] S.R.O. 1392; S.R.O., Tp. 1273/10, deed of 20 Nov. 1717.
[75] S.R.O., Tp. 1273/54, map of Ld. Stamford's lands in Bobbington 1733.
[76] Bobbington ch., vestry bk., sched. of new seats in par. ch. 1828; S.R.O., D. 695/1/5/4.
[77] Inf. from Mr. Hickman.
[78] Above, pl. facing p. 65.
[79] *S.H.C.* 1923, 70; J. Nichols, *Hist. and Antiquities of County of Leicester*, iv (2), 627; S.R.O., Tp. 1273/8, deeds of 26 Nov. 1672, 10 June 1677.
[80] L.J.R.O., Bridgnorth peculiar, Tomyns Dickins (1701).
[81] S.R.O., Tp. 1273/25, partic. of Enville estates 1792.

[82] Ibid. 5, acct. of Ld. Stamford's property in Bobbington; Bobbington ch., vestry bk., sched. of new seats in par. ch. 1828.   [83] Below, Enville, econ. hist.
[84] S.R.O., D. 1287/6/8/1–3.
[85] S.R.O., D. 1287/1/3.
[86] S.R.O., D.(W.) 1746/E/38; T/6.
[87] S.R.O., D. 3373/5.
[88] P.R.O., HO 107/2017 (1); below, econ. hist.
[89] Sale cat. in poss. of Mrs. M. Crump.
[90] Hist. notes in poss. of Bobbington History Group (1981).   [91] Inf. from Mrs. Amies.
[92] W.S.L., S.MS. 386/2, no. 268; *Cal. Fine R.* 1430–7, 68; 1445–52, 38; Apley Estate Off., transcript Claverley ct. rolls 1377–1461, pp. 238, 240, 252.
[93] W.S.L., S.MS. 386/2, no. 251.
[94] B.L. Add. MS. 31932, f. 19; Apley Estate Off., transcript Claverley ct. rolls 1461–1546, p. 74.
[95] Shrewsbury Pub. Libr. MS. 112, ff. 46, 79A.
[96] Apley Estate Off., transcript Claverley ct. rolls 1461–1546, pp. 277, 305; S.R.O., D. 3373/1.
[97] P.R.O., REQ 2/405/85; S.R.O., D. 3373/1.

Brooke, probably his son, succeeded. He died in 1674 and was followed successively by his sons Richard (d. 1677) and Leigh (d. 1718).[98] About 1690 the house, then known as Blacklands, was occupied by Edward Careswell, evidently a relative of Leigh.[99] Leigh's son Richard, vicar of Shifnal (Salop.), died in 1752, leaving a son John, who was also vicar of Shifnal until 1772. He died in 1786 and was succeeded by his nephew George Townshend, who in 1797 adopted the surname Brooke.[1] George Brooke sold Blacklands in 1800.[2] By 1828 William Moseley of Leaton Hall had acquired the estate.[3] In 1861 Moseley's tenant farmed 283 a. there.[4] The Moseley family sold Blacklands some time before the break-up of their estate in 1916. In 1969 the farmhouse with 5 a. was bought from Mr. E. E. Marsh by Mr. Brian Taylor, the owner in 1981.[5]

Blacklands incorporates at its south end a wing of a 17th-century timber-framed house; in 1666 the house was assessed at nine hearths.[6] The wing was encased in brick and extended eastwards in the early 19th century. The main range is probably of the 18th century and has a brick front but may have been partly timber-framed at the back. The back wall has been largely rebuilt.

An estate called *BLAKELANDS* was occupied by the Corbett family in the earlier 17th century. A wooden plaque reset in the roof of the house bears the initials R. C. and the date 1638. The initials presumably belonged to Roger Corbett of Bobbington (d. 1656); he was described as late of Blakelands in 1666.[7] In that year a Mrs. Corbett, possibly Roger's widow, occupied a house in Bobbington assessed at five hearths.[8] By 1716 the estate was held by Edward Corbett, who died in 1719 leaving a son, also Edward. He died in 1752, leaving a son Charles. Charles died in 1786, and the property passed jointly to his sisters Mary (d. 1792) and Hannah (d. 1799). Both were unmarried, and on Hannah's death the estate passed to John Charles Beckingham, the son of a cousin, Catherine Beckingham. In March 1801 Beckingham, then of Bishopsbourne (Kent), sold Blakelands to Sherington Sparkes, formerly of Bridgnorth (Salop.) but then living at Blakelands. The estate comprised the house and 119 a.[9] By 1811 the owner was Thomas Bowen of Bradney, in Worfield (Salop.).[10] The Bowen family remained owners until at least 1936. The owner in 1953 was L. W. Eveson of Tipton, who sold it to C. P. Bolland of Bobbington in 1956. Ownership subsequently passed to Mr. Norman Holland, who sold the house and 4½ a. to Mr. John Morgan in 1981.[11]

The house incorporates at its south end part of a timber-framed building of the 17th century. Its plan may underlie the main range which is of red brick with stone dressings; the rainwater heads are dated 1722 and bear the initials of Edward Corbett and his wife Mary.[12] The range has a symmetrical west front of seven bays in brick, and there is a contemporary walled forecourt, entered from the road through a wrought-iron gate set between 20th-century railings.[13] Some 17th-century panelling and staircase balusters are reset in the interior, where there is a staircase of the early 18th century. The entrance hall on the west front has a stone fireplace contemporary with the front. In the mid 18th century the northern end of the interior was remodelled, a new staircase being put in and the main rooms panelled. At the same time the entrance hall was replastered and given an enriched cornice, panelled walls, and rococo decoration above the earlier fireplace. To the east and south of the house are a large malting and a stable and coachhouse, all of the 19th century.

BOBBINGTON FARM, later *COLLEGE FARM*, was one of the estates with which Edward Careswell of Blacklands (d. 1691) endowed exhibitions at Christ Church, Oxford.[14] It comprised 161½ a. in 1769.[15] The farmhouse was rebuilt in 1841, and the name was changed to College Farm about that time.[16] Ownership remained with the trustees of the exhibitions until 1920, when the farm was sold to the tenant, Frank Whitehouse.[17] Soon after the Second World War the farm was bought by Sir Edward Thompson of Gatacre Park, in Claverley (Salop.), the owner in 1982.[18]

The estate later known as *HAY FARM* may be identifiable as the messuage, ½ virgate, ½ nook, and 5 a. held by William atte Hay in the later 14th century.[19] It was evidently the property which Lancelot Shadwell acquired from the Dickins family of Leaton in 1674.[20] The estate remained in the Shadwell family, formerly of Lyndon in Enville, until 1855 when the house and 162½ a. were sold to Benjamin Gibbons of Shut End, in Kingswinford.[21] In 1903 Gibbons's trustees sold the estate to Charles Amphlett of Four Ashes Hall in Enville, in whose family it remained in 1981.[22]

The house has an east wing of rubble with dressings of ashlar and red brick, probably dating from the early 17th century. The west wing is of brick and was probably built early in the 19th century, but it may have replaced an earlier wing on the same site.

[98] W.S.L. 6/27; S.R.O., D. 3373/1; B.L. Add. MS. 31932, f. 215.
[99] B.L. Add. MS. 31932, f. 215; tablet in church.
[1] Burke, *Land. Gent.* (1952), 271; Salop. R.O. 1335/1/2.
[2] T. F. Dukes, *Antiquities of Shropshire*, 206.
[3] Bobbington ch., vestry bk., sched. of new seats in par. ch. 1828.
[4] P.R.O., RG 9/1985.
[5] Inf. from Mr. Taylor.
[6] *S.H.C.* 1923, 70.
[7] Apley Estate Off., Original Deeds on Paper 1559–1829, no. 14; S.R.O., D. 3373/1.
[8] *S.H.C.* 1923, 70.
[9] S.R.O., D.(W.) 1854/2; tablet in church.
[10] S.R.O., D.(W.) 1854/4; S.R.O., Tp. 1273/58/Stour water, Dan. Clarke to Lord Stamford 14 Oct. 1811.

[11] *Kelly's Dir. Staffs.* (1936); inf. from Mr. and Mrs. Morgan.
[12] S.R.O., D. 1854/2.
[13] Above, pl. facing p. 65.
[14] *V.C.H. Salop.* ii. 164; below, chars. for the poor.
[15] Christ Church Archives, Oxford, viii. a. 53, ff. 12v.–14.
[16] *N. & Q.* 2nd ser. iv. 204–5; Jay, 'Bobbington', 61.
[17] Inf. from Dr. J. F. A. Mason of Christ Church, Oxford.
[18] Inf. from Messrs. Burd & Evans of Shrewsbury; inf. from the farm manager.
[19] Nottingham Univ. Libr., Mi. 6/173/252.
[20] P.R.O., CP 25(2)/725/26 Chas. II Trin. no. 13.
[21] S.R.O. 392/M 5; Shaw, *Staffs.* ii. 278; MSS. at Four Ashes Hall, bdle. 44, abstract of title to Hay Farm and deed of 25 Mar. 1855; below, Enville, manors and other estates (Enville).
[22] Jay, 'Bobbington', 64.

The estate at *LEATON* may have originated in the later 13th century: land there once held by William of Leaton was then confirmed to his daughter Emma by John FitzPhilip, lord of Bobbington, who also granted her further land 'in the Lee' and elsewhere. Emma married John's (probably illegitimate) son Gilbert.[23] A Hugh de la Lee and a William de la Lee were recorded at Bobbington in 1327 and 1332–3;[24] one of them may have held the land at Leaton. The estate later passed to the Dickins family. A William Dicones was poll-tax collector for Bobbington in 1377.[25] John son of William Dykon of Bobbington held land there in 1379.[26] Thomas Dickins of Bobbington, lord of Churchill (Worcs.), recorded in 1429, 1432, and 1440, may have been the Thomas Dickins who was bailiff of William Mytton, lord of Bobbington, in 1440.[27] A Thomas Dickins, lord of Churchill, recorded at Bobbington in 1471 and dead by 1483, may have been the same man.[28] John Dickins of Bobbington, Thomas's son, was alive in 1496.[29] By 1533 he had been succeeded by his son Hugh, who was described as of Leaton in 1540 and died in 1575, leaving a son Humphrey.[30] Humphrey's son William had succeeded by 1583, and probably by 1581.[31] He was dead by 1604, leaving a son John.[32] John died in 1656 and was succeeded by his son Thomas (d. 1674).[33] Thomas's son John was succeeded in 1679 by his son Thomas (d. 1710). Thomas's heir, his son John (d. 1760), mortgaged the house at Leaton and 200 a. of land in 1712. In 1749 the mortgagees sold the estate to James Moseley, younger son of Acton Moseley of the Mere, in Enville.[34] James died in 1786 and was succeeded by his son Walter Henry, who became lord of Bobbington manor in 1821.[35] He died in 1827[36] and was succeeded by his nephew William, son of James Moseley of Ludlow (Salop.). By 1840 William was the most substantial landowner in the parish with 1,508½ a. He died in 1869 and was succeeded by his son William Henry (d. 1919).[37] In 1916 the estate was broken up. The owner of the hall in 1918 was Thomas Woodhouse, who lived there until *c.* 1943, when it was taken over by the Air Ministry and used as a hostel. In 1946 the hall was acquired by the family of Ernest King; they sold the hall and outbuildings *c.* 1976. The hall and 3½ a. were bought by Unifurnaces Ltd., later

Unifurnaces (Overseas) Ltd., the owners in 1981.[38]

Nothing survives of the house assessed at twelve hearths in 1666.[39] The present Leaton Hall is of 18th-century origin but was refronted with stucco and enlarged to the rear in the early 19th century. Some of the later additions were demolished *c.* 1977, and internal remodelling was taking place in 1981. The former washhouse to the west is of brick with stepped gables; the date 1751 on the weather vane may refer to the remodelling of the house after the building of the hall. The washhouse, coachhouse, and stables were converted into private houses *c.* 1976.

The farm known as *TUCKHILL* straddles the county boundary, with the house situated in Bobbington. It may be identifiable as the 3 messuages and 3 half virgates in Bobbington held by John Tuk in the later 14th century.[40] A Richard Tuk of Bobbington, described as a franklin, was recorded in 1420 and was still alive in 1449.[41] A Thomas Pratt was living at Tuckhill in 1541 and 1551. He was presumably the Thomas Pratt who died in 1556.[42] A Hugh Pratt of Bobbington and presumably of Tuckhill was mentioned *c.* 1631; he died in 1646.[43] Hugh's son William was evidently dead before 1666, when his son John was taxed on a house of five hearths in Bobbington. When John died in 1678 he was described as of Tuckhill.[44] He was succeeded by his son William, still alive in 1718 but dead by 1732, when his son John was living at Tuckhill.[45] John died in 1742, leaving a son William.[46] William was succeeded by Henry Pratt, vicar of Orpington (Kent) and possibly a brother. Henry died in 1802 leaving his son John, later rector of Sedlescombe (Suss.), as heir. John still owned Tuckhill in the later 1840s.[47] In 1851 Thomas Nicholls, possibly a tenant of the Pratts, farmed 300 a. there,[48] much of the land evidently lying in Shropshire. The later ownership of the estate until the mid 20th century is uncertain. Members of the Nicholls family lived at Tuckhill as tenants until *c.* 1940. The next tenant, R. A. England, bought the farm in 1956; it soon afterwards passed to Sir Edward Thompson of Gatacre Park, in Claverley (Salop.), the owner in 1982.[49]

An estate centring on *WHITTIMERE FARM* appears to have originated in the hide at Whittimere which John FitzPhilip, lord of Bobbington,

[23] Eyton, *Shropshire*, iii. 169–70.
[24] *S.H.C.* vii (1), 252; x (1), 129.
[25] *S.H.C.* 4th ser. vi. 8.
[26] Apley Estate Off., transcript Claverley ct. rolls 1377–1461, p. 3.
[27] I. H. Jeayes, *Descriptive Cat. of Charters and Muniments of Lyttelton Fam.* pp. 81–3, 86; *S.H.C.* N.S. ii. 118; *V.C.H. Worcs.* iii. 44. For the Dickins pedigree see, unless otherwise stated, *S.H.C.* iii (2), 67–8; v (2), 107–9.
[28] Jeayes, *Lyttelton Charters*, pp. 99, 104–5; *V.C.H. Worcs.* iii. 44.
[29] S.R.O., D. 593/J/15.
[30] *S.H.C.* 4th ser. viii. 122; S.R.O., D. 3373/1.
[31] *S.H.C.* xv. 185; below, manor and other estates (tithes).
[32] B.R.L. 351713.
[33] S.R.O., D. 3373/1.
[34] S.R.O., D. 833/1/3; A. Sparrow, *Hist. of Church Preen* (priv. print. 1898), 44–6; Burke, *Commoners* (1833–8), i. 321.
[35] Inf. from Lt.-Col. C. M. Townsend of Denbury Manor, Devon; Burke, *Commoners*, i. 321.
[36] *Staffs. Advertiser*, 4 Aug. 1827.
[37] Inf. from Lt.-Col. Townsend; below, econ. hist.

[38] Jay, 'Bobbington', 50–1; inf. from Mr. S. R. Shelton of Unifurnaces (Overseas) Ltd.
[39] *S.H.C.* 1923, 70.
[40] Nottingham Univ. Libr., Mi. 6/173/252.
[41] *S.H.C.* xvii. 37; *Cal. Fine R.* 1445–52, 127.
[42] S.R.O., Tp. 1273/8, deed of 30 Mar. 1541; P.R.O., E 315/129, f. 124; L.J.R.O., B/c/11, Thos. Pratt (1556).
[43] *S.H.C.* ii (2), 16; *S.H.C.* N.S. x (1), 34; Salop. R.O. 2089/ADD, Lutley ct. of 14 Apr. 1635; S.R.O., D. 3373/1, burial of 1646.
[44] J. and J. B. Burke, *General and Heraldic Dict. of Landed Gentry*, ii (1846), 1066; *S.H.C.* 1923, 70; S.R.O., D. 3373/1, burial of 1678.
[45] Salop. R.O. 2089/9, deed of 14 Jan. 1730/1; 2089/ADD, Lutley ct. of 30 Oct. 1690; S.R.O., Tp. 1273/32, deed of 9 May 1718.
[46] S.R.O., D. 3373/1, burial of 1742; H.W.R.O. (H.), E 12/S, Kinver ct. bk. 1734–61, p. 30.
[47] Burke, *Gen. and Heraldic Dict.* 1066.
[48] P.R.O., HO 107/2017(2).
[49] Inf. from Mr. J. E. Brown of Binde House, Wootton, Bridgnorth.

held in the mid 13th century; it was then part of the manor of Claverley.[50] In the later 13th century he gave William of Claverley, chaplain, ½ virgate of land in the vill of Whittimere with increase (*acrescum*). The land, called Wulfhamton, had been held previously by William de Haselwall.[51] William of Claverley was possibly the William son of Agatha who in 1323 held ½ virgate with a messuage extending 'from the way in Whittimere up to the heath'. The land, however, was said to be in the manor of Bobbington.[52] William of Claverley sold his rights in the ½ virgate called Wulfhamton to Richard son of Richard of the Hill of Bobbington, also known as of the Hill of Whittimere.[53] The land continued to be held of the lord of Bobbington, and in 1317 it was granted by Hugh de Hepham to Bertram son of Bertram of Rickthorn. In 1323 Bertram gave seisin of the land to William son of Richard of the Fieldhouse of Whittimere.[54] William was still alive in 1347.[55] Roger Fieldhouse held ½ virgate of the lord of Bobbington in the later 14th century,[56] and the property evidently descended in the same family until 1466, when William Fieldhouse of Whittimere granted a messuage and 33 a. at the Fieldhouse to Richard Wood, son of William Wood of Aston, in Claverley.[57] Later in 1466 Wood conveyed the property to Richard Bulwardine and John Ryce. In 1470 Bulwardine resigned his interest in the estate, which became vested in Ryce alone.[58] In 1520 John Ryce's son William granted it to John Grosvenor, or Gravenor.[59] A William Gravenor was living at Whittimere in 1524.[60] When he died in 1544, leaving a son Nicholas as his heir, William was described as of 'Schowle'.[61] The name 'le Scholle' was in use for land in the area in 1443, and by the late 16th century the estate was known as the Scholle or Whittimere Hall.[62] It was later acquired by Walter James of Corbyn's Hall, in Kingswinford, who sold it to Humphrey Brigg of Haughton, in Shifnal (Salop.), in 1596.[63] Humphrey's son Moreton sold it to Sir William Whitmore of Apley, in Stockton (Salop.), in 1628.[64] Whitmore leased the house and estate to William Warham in 1635, and Warham's widow Jane was still living there in 1672 in a house assessed at seven hearths. She died c. 1673.[65] A William Warham was tenant before 1738, when Thomas Whitmore of Apley re-let the house and estate, then some 160 a.[66] By 1828 William Moseley of Leaton Hall had acquired the property.[67] When the Moseley estate was broken up in 1916 Whittimere, consisting of 263 a., was sold

together with a farm of 221 a. at Upper Whittimere. The owner in 1928 was J. J. Snelson, whose son Mr. J. Snelson, was in possession in 1981.[68]

The house, which has a **U**-shaped plan, appears to have been built in 1731.[69] It was refronted, rerooofed, and largely refitted early in the 19th century. The farm buildings are mostly of the 19th century and later but include part of an 18th-century timber-framed barn against which there was formerly a horse mill.[70]

The tithes of Bobbington belonged to the rectory of Claverley, which itself formed part of the endowment of Quatford college (Salop.), founded by Roger, earl of Shrewsbury, in 1086. They were transferred to Bridgnorth college (Salop.) which replaced Quatford in the early 12th century. The dean of Bridgnorth held the tithes until the dissolution of the college in 1548.[71] In that year the Crown leased to John Seymour for 21 years the great tithes of Bobbington with Easter offerings and oblations, and half the great and all the small tithes of Whittimere.[72] The same tithes were leased to William Whitmore of Apley, in Stockton (Salop.), in 1565.[73] The Whitmore family continued to hold tithes in Bobbington until the early 19th century when they were bought by William Moseley.[74] The other moiety of the great tithes of Whittimere was owned by William Dickins of Leaton in 1581; he also had the small tithes. In 1675 the Dickins family had a tithe barn at Halfpenny Green.[75] By 1840 some of the tithes had been merged by the owners of the land from which they arose. Most of the remainder were owned by William Moseley, who that year was granted a rent charge of £328 5s. 6d. in lieu of them. There were seven other tithe owners, who were granted rent charges of between £55 1s. 7d. and £1 10s.[76]

ECONOMIC HISTORY. There was land for 6 ploughteams in 1086. Four slaves worked the demesne with 2 teams, and there were 5 villeins and 3 bordars with another team. The manor, which included woodland, was then worth 40s.[77] By the later 12th century the manor lay in Kinver forest, and assarts were recorded in the later 13th and early 14th century.[78] In 1309 the lord of the manor inclosed 60 a. out of the forest for his own use.[79] As late as 1496 a grant of land at Saltershill (later Salter's Park farm) on the southern boundary and at Broadfields nearby included the right to cut down and uproot brambles, underwood,

[50] Eyton, *Shropshire*, iii. 166.
[51] Apley Estate Off., Charters Box 1, no. 1.
[52] Ibid. no. 10.
[53] Ibid. no. 3; Shaw, *Staffs*. ii. 208.
[54] Apley Estate Off., Charters Box 1, nos. 5, 6, 8.
[55] B.L. Add. MS. 31932, f. 209.
[56] Nottingham Univ. Libr., Mi. 6/173/252.
[57] Apley Estate Off., Charters Box 2, nos. 75–6.
[58] Ibid. Box 3, nos. 78, 81–2.
[59] Ibid. no. 98.
[60] Apley Estate Off., transcript Claverley ct. rolls 1461–1546, p. 230.
[61] Ibid. p. 308.
[62] Apley Estate Off., Charters Box 2, no. 61; Box 5, no. 221.
[63] Ibid. Box 5, no. 221.
[64] Ibid. Box 9, nos. 375–6.
[65] Ibid. Box 10, no. 400; *Salop. Hearth-Tax Roll of 1672*

(Salop. Arch. Soc. 1949), 109; L.J.R.O., Bridgnorth peculiar, Jane Warham (1675).
[66] Apley Estate Off., Charters Box 15, no. 552.
[67] Bobbington ch., vestry bk., sched. of new seats in par. ch. 1828.
[68] Sale cat. in poss. of Bobbington History Group; inf. from Mr. J. Snelson.   [69] Jay, 'Bobbington', 15.
[70] Inf. from Mr. Snelson.
[71] *V.C.H. Salop*. ii. 123–4, 130; *S.II.C*. iv (1), 163–4, 168.
[72] *Cal. Pat.* 1563–6, pp. 96, 367.
[73] Ibid. p. 366.
[74] S.R.O., Q/RDc 87; White, *Dir. Staffs*. (1834), 248.
[75] S.R.O., D. 1287/6/8/3; D. 1854/2.
[76] S.R.O., D. 3373/5.
[77] *V.C.H. Staffs*. iv. 52.
[78] *S.H.C.* v (1), 144, 168, 180.
[79] P.R.O., C 143/76, no. 17.

ashes, and oaks, as long as enough was left to provide haybote.[80] There is no surviving reference to open-field cultivation in the parish.

Much of the eastern part of the parish was waste. In 1343 the lord of the manor agreed not to inclose any part of his waste in Bobbington and Whittimere and confirmed the grazing rights of free tenants.[81] By the early 17th century part of the waste had been inclosed.[82] In 1827 the remaining 411 a., chiefly between Gospelash Road and the parish boundary to the north, was inclosed under an Act of 1822; a further 5 a. mentioned in the Act had been inclosed prior to the award.[83]

There was woodland pasture 1 league in length and $\frac{1}{2}$ league in breadth in 1086.[84] Woods called the Hay and the Lee existed in the later 13th century.[85] Joan Botetourt, lady of the manor, had woodland in demesne in 1326, when she sued for the theft of six young sparrow hawks there.[86] In 1840 the parish contained 91$\frac{1}{2}$ a. of woodland; 49$\frac{1}{2}$ a. (20 ha.) were recorded in 1979.[87]

In the later 14th century the capital messuage and 3 virgates of demesne were occupied by a lessee. A further 3 lessees occupied the remaining 2 half virgates and 2 nooks of demesne. The lord had recently enfranchised 22 tenants, most of whom held single messuages, each with a half virgate; 5 tenants held 2 or 3 messuages with half virgates, and there was one cottager. Six neifs had also been manumitted by the same lord.[88] When the manor was sold in 1821 the only land owned by the lord was the 40-a. Manor farm.[89] By 1840, however, William Moseley, who succeeded to the manor in 1827, had added considerably to his family's original estate at Leaton Hall. With 1,508$\frac{1}{2}$ a. covering Blacklands farm, Leaton, Manor farm, Saltershall farm, and Whittimere, Moseley was the most considerable landowner in the parish; a further 850 a. were held by the owners of Blakelands, Bobbington Hall farm, College farm, Hay farm, and Tuckhill.[90] Manor farm was sold in 1877 and Saltershall and Blacklands farms some time before 1916. The remaining 757 a. belonging to the Moseley family were sold when the estate was broken up in 1916.[91]

The soil, being partly sand and partly clay,[92] has produced a variety of crops. A lease of 1650 stipulated a six-year course of wheat and other grain, preceded by liming.[93] In the mid 1670s rye, wheat, barley, oats, and peas were being grown at Leaton, and rye, wheat, barley, and peas at Whittimere.[94] The existence of Hopyard meadow on the Bobbington Hall estate in 1688 suggests the growing of hops in the area.[95] Flax was grown in large quantities in the late 18th century,[96] and clover, rye, oats, barley, peas, and root crops such as turnips in the earlier 19th century.[97] Swedes were grown in the late 1860s, and mangolds together with grain crops in the early 20th century.[98] In 1979 over half the land in the parish was devoted to crop farming, the main crops being wheat and barley; lettuce also was grown. Of the 12 farms recorded only 3 were engaged in full-time crop farming.[99]

A shepherd was living in the parish in the earlier 14th entury.[1] In the mid 1550s Thomas Pratt of Tuckhill had a flock of over 100 sheep, and there were other flocks of between 40 and 80. In 1559 each tenant at Whittimere holding a virgate of land was limited to pasturing 80 sheep on the waste there.[2] Thomas Knocker, a weaver of Bobbington, had 30 sheep and a store of wool in 1638, and at Whittimere c. 1673 Jane Warham had a flock of 84 wethers, 54 ewes, and 28 lambs.[3] There was still some sheep farming in 1979.[4]

There has also been other pastoral farming. A cow and two calves were stolen from William Gravenor's fold-yard at Whittimere in 1524.[5] Jane Warham of Whittimere had 5 cows in calf and 5 yearling calves c. 1673; she also had 10 pigs then. Thomas Dickins of Leaton had £80 worth of cattle, including weaning calves, in 1674; his sheep and pigs were worth only £15. At Bobbington Hall Tomyns Dickins had 6 cows, a heifer, and 2 calves in 1701; his widow Martha had 5 cows, 3 yearling heifers, and 2 weaning calves in 1717. Both had pigs as well.[6] In 1979, out of 12 farms recorded, 4 dealt in cattle, one of them for dairying and the others for rearing and fattening. There was also some poultry and pig farming.[7]

The lady of the manor received a grant of free warren in her demesne lands in Bobbington in 1334.[8]

The lord of the manor had two mills in Bobbington in the later 13th century.[9] Two water mills were assigned as dower to the widow of John FitzPhilip, lord of the manor, in 1317, and in the later 14th century a water mill was held with the capital messuage of the manor by a tenant.[10] A water mill was still owned by the lord in 1686.[11] One of the mills stood on Brantley

[80] S.R.O., D. 593/J/15.
[81] B.L. Add. MS. 28732, f. 1.
[82] Salop. R.O. 3662/D/5, ff. 122, 125v.
[83] S.H.C. 1931, 97; S.R.O., Q/RDc 87; D. 833/1/4; S.R.O., Tp. 1273, map of Bobbington inclosure, 1823.
[84] V.C.H. Staffs. iv. 52.   [85] Eyton, Shropshire, iii. 170.
[86] S.H.C. ix (1), 112.
[87] S.R.O., D. 3373/5; M.A.F.F., agric. returns 1979.
[88] Nottingham Univ. Libr., Mi. 6/173/252.
[89] S.R.O., D.(W.) 1746/E/38.
[90] S.R.O., D. 3373/5.
[91] Sale cat. in poss. of Bobbington History Group; above, manor and other estates (Manor Farm).
[92] Pitt, Staffs. i. 35–6, 201; P.O. Dir. Staffs. (1868), 484.
[93] S.R.O., Tp. 1273/8.
[94] L.J.R.O., Bridgnorth peculiar, Thos. Dickins (1674), Jane Warham (1675).   [95] S.R.O. 1392.
[96] S.R.O., Q/SO 18, f. 199v.; 19, ff. 49v., 97.
[97] S.R.O., D.(W.) 1746/E/38; T/4; N.S.J.F.S. xiii. 46, 48; S.R.O., Tp. 1273/18, Enville and Bobbington tenants c. 1840.

[98] P.O. Dir. Staffs. (1868), 484; Kelly's Dir. Staffs. (1912; 1916).   [99] M.A.F.F., agric. returns 1979.
[1] S.H.C. vii (1), 252; x (1), 129.
[2] L.J.R.O., B/C/11, Thos. Pratt (1556), Wm. Mache (1558), Gillian Pratt (1558), Hen. Clemson (1559); Apley Estate Off., transcript Claverley ct. rolls 1509–89, p. 110.
[3] L.J.R.O., Bridgnorth peculiar, Thos. Knocker (1639), Jane Warham (1675).
[4] M.A.F.F., agric. returns 1979.
[5] Apley Estate Off., transcript Claverley ct. rolls 1461–1546, p. 230.
[6] L.J.R.O., Bridgnorth peculiar, Thomas Dickins (1674), Jane Warham (1675), Tomyns Dickins (1701), Martha Dickins (1717).   [7] M.A.F.F., agric. returns 1979.
[8] Cal. Chart. R. 1327–41, 310.
[9] Eyton, Shropshire, iii. 70.
[10] S.H.C. 1911, 92–3, 352; Nottingham Univ. Libr., Mi. 6/173/252.
[11] John Rylands Univ. Libr. of Manchester, Ryl. Ch. 130; S.R.O., D.(W.) 1854/6.

brook near the church. A mill there had been pulled down by 1767 but was rebuilt by William Marrian (d. 1801), who diverted part of a stream flowing into Brantley brook in order to increase the water supply.[12] The diversion created an extensive mill pool north of the church, with the mill itself on the eastern edge of the pool.[13] The mill was still worked in 1851[14] but had probably stopped by the late 19th century when the farm buildings there were converted into the present Red Lion inn.[15] The mill survived in the early 20th century but had been dismantled by the late 1930s. The pool was then dredged and used for a time for fishing,[16] but it later dried up.

The other manorial mill may have been at Bobbington Mill Farm in the present Church Lane on the stream which rises near the farm and flows past the church into Brantley brook. In the 20th century a mill there ground meal for animal feed; it ceased work c. 1939.[17]

In 1574 Thomas Rickthorn held a water mill in Bobbington; it was held by another Thomas Rickthorn in 1620.[18] It may have been the Park mill which stood on Brantley brook north of Rickthorn Farm in the early 19th century. By 1839 only the pool remained.[19]

The lord of the manor had a windmill in 1686.[20] A windmill was built on Bobbington common c. 1769; it evidently stood north of Manor Farm where the site of a windmill has been identified.[21]

There was reputedly a cider mill worked by a horse at Crab Mill Farm on the southern boundary, probably in the 19th century; the presence of crab apples there is suggested by Crab Tree field, mentioned in 1573.[22] There was formerly a horse mill at Whittimere.[23]

Ellis Wannerton, a locksmith, was living in Bobbington in 1693.[24] Nine nailers were living in the parish in 1841, 5 of them at Common Side (later Gospelash Road), 2 at Six Ashes, and 2 in Crab Lane. In 1851 there were 4 nailers, 3 of them also working as agricultural labourers. Nailers' cottages in Naylors Lane off Gospelash Road were demolished by the Air Ministry in the 1940s.[25]

A brickmaker lived in Gospelash Road in 1851. By 1861 he was employing 7 men.[26] There was sand working east of Upper Whittimere Farm in 1981.

A grass-drying business was established at Bobbington Mill Farm in the early 1950s. By the late 1960s the company working there, Everest Frozen Foods, specialized in making frozen potato chips.[27]

LOCAL GOVERNMENT. The lord of Bobbington had view of frankpledge by the mid 1250s, paying 18d. for the right.[28] Great courts were held after Easter and Michaelmas in the earlier 14th century.[29] Bobbington manor did not cover the whole parish. Part of Whittimere lay in the manor of Claverley by 1277, and it continued to make presentments at the Claverley court until 1741.[30] Another part of the parish appears to have belonged to the manor of Lutley in Enville; in 1496 land at Saltershill (later Salter's Park farm), Broadfields, and 'le More' in Bobbington was confirmed to tenants at the Lutley court.[31]

The constable of Bobbington was mentioned c. 1540. The office still existed in 1826.[32]

Two churchwardens were recorded in 1487, and two continued to be appointed until 1733. From that year a single churchwarden was appointed until 1811 when the number was again raised to two. Thereafter two was the usual number.[33] There was at least one overseer of the poor in 1666.[34] Two were recorded in the early 18th and earlier 19th century.[35]

In 1836 Bobbington became part of Seisdon poor-law union.[36] It was in Seisdon rural district until 1974, when it became part of South Staffordshire district.[37]

CHURCH. Architectural evidence shows that there was a church on the present site by the 12th century. It originated as a dependent chapel of Claverley and remained a dependency until the Reformation. The parish was in the diocese of Lichfield as part of Bridgnorth peculiar until 1846, when it was transferred with Bridgnorth to Hereford diocese; in 1905 it returned to Lichfield diocese.[38] The present invocation of the church, Holy Cross, is not ancient; it was noted in 1756,[39] but an invocation to St. Nicholas was recorded in 1477, 1500–1, and 1559.[40] St. Mary was given as the invocation in 1742 and again in the 19th century, when Holy Cross and St. Ruth are also

[12] S.R.O., D. 833/1/4.
[13] G. Lipscomb, *Journey into South Wales in the year 1799* (1802), 281; S.R.O., D. 3373/5, nos. 7–8; D.C.L., A 610.
[14] White, *Dir. Staffs.* (1851), 169.
[15] S.R.O., D. 833/1/4; above, introduction.
[16] Jay, 'Bobbington', 43.
[17] Inf. from the vicar (1981).
[18] *S.H.C.* vi (1), 40; xiv (1), 171; N.S. iv. 25–6; S.R.O., D. 3373/1, burials of 1586, 1642.
[19] B.L. Maps, O.S.D. 214; O.S. Map 1", sheet LXI SE. (1834 edn.); S.R.O., D. 3373/5, no. 417; D.C.L., A 610.
[20] S.R.O., D.(W.) 1854/6.
[21] Indenture of 21 Mar. 1814 between Jas. Sparry and Wm. Moseley (in possession of Bobbington History Group); Jay, 'Bobbington', 29–31.
[22] Inf. from Mr. J. Snelson (1981); S.R.O., Tp. 1273/8, deed of 31 January 1572/3.
[23] Above, manor and other estates.
[24] Salop. R.O. 4001/Mar/1, toll bks.
[25] P.R.O., HO 107/1001; HO 107/2017(1); RG 10/2928; Jay, 'Bobbington', 24–5.
[26] P.R.O., HO 107/2017(1); RG 9/1985.
[27] Inf. from Mr. R. Smellie (1981).
[28] *S.H.C.* v (1), 110; Eyton, *Shropshire*, iii. 170–1.
[29] Apley Estate Off., Charters Box 1, no. 6.
[30] Ibid. Claverley ct. rolls 1277–1608, C.2; Bk. of Misc. Records, Presentments etc. 1711–1850, vol. 2.
[31] S.R.O., D. 593/J/15.
[32] P.R.O., C 1/987/25–6; S.R.O., D. 3451/2/2; *S.H.C.* 1935, 353; 1940, 231; Bobbington ch., vestry bk., overseers' accts. 2 Apr. 1826.
[33] Shrewsbury Pub. Libr. MS. 112, ff. 17, 46, 67v., 73, 79A, 103AV., 106; Salop. R.O. 3662/D/1–2; D/5, ff. 12, 51, 52, 67; Bobbington ch., vestry bk.
[34] *S.H.C.* 1923, 71.
[35] S.R.O., D. 42/A/PO/95; Bobbington ch., vestry bk.
[36] *3rd Ann. Rep. Poor Law Com.* H.C. 546, p. 164 (1837), xxxi.
[37] O.S. Map 1/100,000, Staffs. Admin. Areas (1967 and 1974 edns.).
[38] *V.C.H. Staffs.* iii. 95; *Lich. Dioc. Ch. Cal.* (1906), 3.
[39] Shaw, *Staffs.* ii. 278.
[40] B.L. Add. MS. 31932, f. 19; Shrewsbury Pub. Libr. MS. 112, ff. 46, 55; L.J.R.O., B/C/11, Hen. Clemson (1559).

found. Holy Cross was used consistently only from the late 1880s.[41]

The right of appointing a chaplain in the Middle Ages lay with the dean of the royal free chapel of Bridgnorth as rector of Claverley. The dean's failure to find a chaplain in the early 13th century led to the intrusion of Leo, evidently the brother of John son of Philip, lord of the manor. In 1222 the king sued John for the right to appoint and John failed to defend his claim. His son John FitzPhilip later intruded a clerk of his own, but in 1267 he renounced his claim to appoint.[42] After the dissolution of Bridgnorth college in 1548 Bobbington became independent of Claverley. In 1562 Benedict Shokeborough presented to what was described as the perpetual vicarage of the parish church of Bobbington.[43] In 1600 John and William Hewett acquired the advowson of what was called Bobbington vicarage from Nicholas and Elizabeth Moseley, Rowland and Anne Moseley, and John Haughton.[44] In 1606 Anthony Moseley conveyed a moiety of the advowson to William (later Sir William) Whitmore of Apley, in Stockton (Salop.), who acquired the whole advowson in 1616.[45] The living, however, was a curacy and not a vicarage: Humphrey Morten was described as curate of Bobbington at his death in 1609 and so was William Darbey in 1669.[46] The living became a perpetual curacy as a result of a grant from Queen Anne's Bounty in 1726 and a vicarage in 1868. The patronage remained with the Whitmore family until the later 19th century. Thomas Whitmore presented in 1862, but in 1871 the patron was William Henry Moseley of Leaton Hall.[47] Moseley transferred the patronage to Charles Stone in 1916, and in 1917 Stone transferred it to trustees, who in 1939 vested it in the Martyrs Memorial Trust, still the patron in 1981.[48]

In 1553 the curate of Bobbington had a house and garden worth an annual 6s.[49] By 1649 he was receiving £6 13s. 4d. a year from the patron;[50] the income probably represented the stipend previously paid by the deans of Bridgnorth. The income was augmented by Edward Careswell of Blacklands who by will proved in 1691 left an annual £10 to the minister of Bobbington; the income, which came from property known as Bobbington (later College) farm, was to be paid after the death of Edward's wife, which occurred in 1700.[51] In 1726 a grant of £200 was made out of Queen Anne's Bounty to meet a benefaction

made, apparently by will of 1718, by William Whitmore of Apley. The curate's income was £17 3s. 4d. in 1735. Queen Anne's Bounty provided a further £200 in 1792.[52] About 1830 the living was worth £97, of which £40 came from the Careswell trust, the land devised having increased in value.[53] The curate had glebe of nearly 2 r. in 1840. By 1887 the glebe had been increased to 1½ a. yielding an annual £3 10s. The living was then worth £110 a year.[54] A bequest of £400 was made by Catherine Moseley (d. 1926) for the augmentation of the living.[55]

There was a house for the curate by the later 13th century, when there was mention of land next to the curtilage of the pastor of Bobbington.[56] In 1553 the endowments of the church consisted of a house and garden.[57] By 1802 there was no longer a glebe house.[58] In 1861 the incumbent was living at Four Ashes in Enville; in 1871, however, he was lodging in Bobbington village with the former schoolmistress.[59] A vicarage house was built in 1883 on a site south of the church given by W. H. Moseley.[60]

A chantry priest was celebrating in the church at the Dissolution.[61] Lights at the high altar and in honour of the Virgin Mary and of St. Catherine were mentioned in 1477.[62]

In 1369 the parish had been without a curate for seven years, and there were deficiencies in the church's vestments and ornaments.[63] John Brown, who was instituted in 1778, intended to reside but later made over his life interest in the curacy to Henry Downing. In order to encourage Downing to reside the parishioners entered into a subscription to augment the living; they withdrew it, however, c. 1783 after Downing began to employ stipendiary curates to perform morning services only.[64] A stipendiary curate was again employed at least from 1794 to 1813, and there were assistant curates in the 1830s and 1840s during the incumbency of George Gabert, who was also perpetual curate of Claverley.[65] In the mid 19th century both morning and afternoon services were held on Sundays.[66]

The church of *HOLY CROSS* is mostly of ashlar and consists of a chancel, north-east vestry, four-bayed nave with north aisle, and south porch surmounted by a tower. The nave, which has walls of rubble, is probably contemporary with the 12th-century north arcade and aisle. There is a 13th-century effigy of a civilian in the south porch. The chancel arch and chancel were rebuilt early in the 14th century.

[41] J. Ecton, *Thesaurus Rerum Ecclesiasticarum* (1742), 104; *P.O. Dir. Birm.* (1845), 508; *P.O. Dir. Staffs.* (1850; 1860; 1868); White, *Dir. Staffs.* (1851), 169; Harrison, Harrod & Co. *Dir. Staffs.* (1861), 79; *Kelly's Dir. Staffs.* (1880 and later edns.).
[42] *S.H.C.* iv (1), 21-2, 162-3, 165; *Cal. Pat. 1232-47*, 120.
[43] L.J.R.O., B/A/1/15, f. 30.
[44] *S.H.C.* xviii (1), 17.
[45] *S.H.C.* n.s. iv. 6-7, 22.
[46] S.R.O., D. 3373/1.
[47] Shaw, *Staffs.* ii. 278; Salop. R.O. 3662/D/2; A. T. Bannister, *Dioc. of Heref. Institutions, etc.* (A.D. *1539-1900*), 176, 184.
[48] Lich. Dioc. Regy., Reg. of Transfers of Patronage, ff. 24, 30, 89; *Lich. Dioc. Dir.* (1981).
[49] *S.H.C. 1915*, 33.
[50] W.S.L., S.MS. 339 (vi), p. 465.
[51] Bobbington ch., copy of Edw. Careswell's will; S.R.O., D. 3373/1.

[52] Hodgson, *Queen Anne's Bounty*, p. ccxcv; *Return made by Governors of Bounty of Queen Anne* (1736), 38, 103.
[53] *Rep. Com. Eccl. Revenues*, 464-5; White, *Dir. Staffs.* (1834), 248-9.
[54] S.R.O., D. 3373/5; *Returns relating to Glebe Lands in Eng. and Wales*, H.C. 307, p. 57 (1887), lxiv; *Kelly's Dir. Staffs.* (1888).
[55] Bobbington ch., terrier of 1927.
[56] Eyton, *Shropshire*, iii. 170.
[57] *S.H.C. 1915*, 33.
[58] *Salop. N. & Q.* viii (1), 87.
[59] P.R.O., RG 9/1985; RG 10/2928.
[60] *Kelly's Dir. Staffs.* (1884).
[61] P.R.O., C 66/917, m. 27.
[62] B.L. Add. MS. 31932, f. 19.
[63] *Cal. Inq. Misc.* iii, p. 279.
[64] L.J.R.O., D. 30; Salop. R.O. 3662/D/2.
[65] Salop. R.O. 3662/D/2-3; *Rep. Com. Eccl. Revenues*, 464-5. [66] P.R.O., HO 129/379/2/1.

About the same time new windows were put into the south side of the nave and into the north wall of the aisle, which was probably then faced with ashlar.[67] The font is 14th-century,[68] and there is a pre-Reformation wooden chest. A tower had been built by the mid 16th century[69]. By the earlier 19th century the church had dormer windows in the south side of the nave roof and a square, wooden tower over the west end of the nave. In 1828 a new pulpit and reading desk and new pews were installed. A singers' and children's gallery, which may have been in the chancel, was removed and a new gallery erected at the west end. Additional free sittings were provided under the tower.[70] The vestry was added in 1858. The church was restored in 1878 by A. W. (later Sir Arthur) Blomfield. The dormer windows were removed, the east window replaced, and new windows inserted in the south wall of the nave. The south chancel door, still used in 1846, was blocked up probably during the restoration. The wooden tower was removed, and a stone one with a pyramidal roof was built over the south porch; the roof was later removed, probably at the beginning of the 20th century.[71]

The plate in 1552 consisted of a silver chalice with paten; there was also a brass cross and a brass pax.[72] In 1840 George Whitmore, the assistant curate, presented a cup, flagon, and paten.[73] A wrought-iron flower stand in the north aisle was given by H.R.H. Princess Alice in memory of her son Prince William of Gloucester, whose death in an aircrash at Halfpenny Green in 1972 is also commemorated by a tablet in the aisle. There were three bells in 1552; they were recast as four by Abraham Rudhall of Gloucester in 1699.[74]

The churchyard was mentioned in 1555. In the early 19th century there was a wall along its east side and hedges on the south and west sides.[75] It was extended to the north in 1896 and westwards in 1971.[76]

The registers date from 1571 and are complete.[77]

NONCONFORMITY. In 1827 a house at Gospel Ash belonging to John Southall was registered for Protestant dissenting worship.[78] A Wesleyan Methodist chapel was built on the east side of Gospelash Road opposite the later Yew Tree Farm in 1830. The congregation on Census Sunday 1851 numbered 34; the service was then held in the afternoon.[79] New members came from the Enville congregation, disbanded c. 1857.[80] The chapel was rebuilt in 1884 on a site to the north on the opposite side of Gospelash Road given by Thomas Bowen of Blakelands.[81] The older chapel was used as a cowshed in 1981.

EDUCATION. There may have been an early school associated with the church. Property known as the School House with a croft called Priest Croft lay north of the church in 1654.[82]

A school was established at White Cross northeast of the village in 1792 by Hannah Corbett of Blakelands, fulfilling the intention of herself and her sister Mary Corbett (d. 1792). It was for 20 boys and 12 girls between the ages of 8 and 15. They were to be chosen from among the poorest in the parish, with preference given to orphans and to children whose parents, through age or sickness, were unable to provide for them. If the number from Bobbington was insufficient children from Claverley and adjoining parishes were to be chosen. All children were to be catechized and were to learn to sing the psalms; in addition, boys were to be taught the elements, and girls reading, knitting, spinning, and plain needlework. Out of the annual income of £42 the master was assigned £15 and the mistress £5; £22 was to be spent on providing clothes for the children and on books, pens, ink, and paper. On leaving school each child was to keep the clothes provided and receive a New Testament and Prayer Book. A house between two schoolrooms was provided for a master and mistress.[83] In 1820 there were 8 boys and 6 girls from Claverley among the pupils. By the mid 1840s 10 boys not on the foundation were being taught. They were presumably charged fees, and in 1858 the trustees amended the foundation to allow fee-paying pupils. In or before 1860 the master, William Cox, was dismissed after complaints about his excessive discipline and the poor scholastic achievement of the children. It was also alleged that the admittance of the sons of well-to-do parents deprived poorer boys of places in the school.[84] By the late 1860s a further £14 18s. was received in rent from 2½ a. formerly occupied by the master.[85] In 1891 average attendance was 17 boys and 28 girls and infants. School pence were 2d. and 3d. for those who could afford to pay.[86] In 1892 the schoolrooms were incorporated into the teacher's house and a new school

[67] W.S.L., Staffs. Views, ii. 101–2; T.B.A.S. lxix. 20.
[68] T.B.A.S. lxviii. 18.
[69] S.H.C. n.s. vi (1), 189.
[70] W.S.L., Staffs. Views, ii. 101–2; Bobbington ch., churchwardens' accts. 3 Oct., 16 Nov. 1828, 18 Apr. 1830; Salop. R.O. 3662/D/3.
[71] Kelly's Dir. Staffs. (1880); S.R.O., D. 833/6/2; Bobbington ch., churchwardens' accts. 31 Aug. 1874.
[72] S.H.C. n.s. vi (1), 189.
[73] Bobbington ch., vestry bk.; Salop. R.O. 3662/D/3.
[74] S.H.C. n.s. vi (1), 189; Salop. R.O. 3662/D/15, Sept. 1906; Lynam, Church Bells, 65.
[75] L.J.R.O., B/C/11, Ellen Foxall (1567); S.R.O., D. 833/6/2.
[76] Bobbington ch., churchwardens' accts. 25 July 1896; doc. relating to 1971 extension.
[77] All except those in current use are in S.R.O., D. 3373/1–4.
[78] S.H.C. 4th ser. iii. 70.
[79] Tablet on chapel; P.R.O., HO 129/379/2/1, giving 1831 as date of erection; S.R.O., D. 3373/5, no. 211; D.C.L., A 610.
[80] Below, Enville, nonconformity.
[81] G.R.O., Worship Reg. no. 28248; J. H. Mees, Story of a Hundred Years: Handbk. of Wesleyan Methodist Church Stourbridge Circuit (Stourbridge, 1928), 114 (copy in Stourbridge Libr.).
[82] MSS. at Four Ashes Hall, Enville, deed of 10 Apr. 1654; S.R.O., D. 833/1/4.
[83] G. Griffith, Free Schools of Staffs. 442–3; P.R.O., ED 7/108/37.
[84] 5th Rep. Com. Char. 606–7; Nat. Soc. Inquiry, 1846–7, Staffs. 2–3; Jay, 'Bobbington', 40–1; Griffith, Free Schools, 628.
[85] Char. Digest Staffs. 8–9.
[86] P.R.O., ED 7/108/37.

was built nearby by public subscription.[87] By a scheme of 1896 the school, known as the Free School of Hannah and Mary Corbett, or White Cross School, became a public elementary school, retaining its association with the Church of England. Most of the endowment income was to be spent on prizes for children at the school or other Church of England schools, preference being given to those who lived in Bobbington parish, and on outfits and technical exhibitions for leavers.[88] The school and school house, being on the edge of Halfpenny Green airfield, were demolished in 1944.[89] Children were taught in temporary buildings on a site to the south-west until a school was built there in 1957. A house for the master was built in Gospelash Road in 1955. In the late 1970s the school, then known as the Corbett primary (aided) school, had an average attendance of 75.[90]

A Sunday school existed by 1845.[91] There was a dame school in the mid 1840s. In the later 19th century a Mrs. Gretton ran a private school

called the Marigolds at Broadfields Farm south of the village.[92] By 1860 William Cox, formerly master at White Cross, had established a private school. He was still running it in 1868, but by 1872 Mrs. Elizabeth Cox had the school. Another member of the family, Mr. J. Cox, continued it in Bobbington House Farm.[93]

CHARITIES FOR THE POOR. By will proved 1691 Edward Careswell of Blacklands gave £10 for the poor of the parish. In the late 1780s the charity produced an annual 10s. In 1820 it was distributed annually on a sacrament Sunday.[94] In 1981 the income was £1.37, but no distribution was made that year.[95]

Eliza Rogers of Halfpenny Green (d. 1905) left £500, the interest to be distributed annually in coal to the poor. The first distribution was made in 1907.[96] In 1980 the income was £37.25; there were 13 distributions of coal and two small grants towards the cost of electricity.[97]

CODSALL

THE ancient parish of Codsall lies on the county boundary with Shropshire. Although it is still partly rural, there has been extensive residential development, mainly for people working in the Wolverhampton area. Consisting of the townships of Codsall and Oaken, the parish was 2,994 a. in extent. In 1966 part of Wergs was added from Wrottesley civil parish, and the area was increased to 3,044 a. (1,232 ha.).[98] In 1845 Codsall township was transferred from the southern to the northern division of Seisdon hundred, in which Oaken already lay.[99]

Part of the parish boundary on the north is formed by Moat brook and part of that on the south by the river Penk. The western boundary runs along County Lane and part of the southern boundary along Holyhead Road. North-east of the church on Moat brook the land lies at its lowest, 344 ft. (105 m.). At Dam Mill in the south-eastern corner the land lies at 354 ft. (108 m.); south of Greenhills it rises to 412 ft. (125 m.). Oaken hamlet stands on a spur around 450 ft. (137 m.) overlooking Moat brook, which there formed the boundary between the two townships.[1] The level gradually rises to 484 ft. (148 m.) at Codsall Wood in the north-west and 462 ft.

(131 m.) at Kingswood in the south-west. The underlying rock is sandstone and was formerly quarried. A strip of Keuper Marl runs down the west side of the parish.[2]

Six persons were recorded at Codsall and eight at Oaken in 1086.[3] In 1327 the number of people assessed for tax at Codsall was 11 and at Oaken 10.[4] In the mid 1520s 21 people were assessed at Codsall and Bilbrook and 7 at Oaken,[5] while the muster roll of 1539 recorded 12 at Codsall and 15 at Oaken.[6] In 1554 the number of communicants in the parish was given as 200.[7] The poll-tax assessment of 1641 listed 105 people in Codsall and 53 in Oaken.[8] In 1666 there were 38 people assessed for hearth tax at Codsall, with 30 too poor to pay, and 22 at Oaken, with 7 too poor.[9] The population of the parish was 589 in 1801 and rose to 1,115 by 1831. It fell to 1,096 by 1841 but rose again, reaching 1,195 by 1851 and 1,204 by 1861. It then increased steadily, reaching 1,452 by 1901. There were larger increases in the early 20th century as Codsall became a residential area. The population was 1,634 in 1911, 1,805 in 1921, and 2,172 in 1931. It was 2,868 in 1951, increasing to 6,745 by 1961 and 9,027 by 1971.[10]

The early settlement at Codsall probably lay

[87] Kelly's Dir. Staffs. (1896); Jay, 'Bobbington', 41.
[88] Bobbington ch., Scheme of 1896; Staffs. Endowed Chars. 18–19.
[89] Above, introduction.
[90] Express & Star, 14 Oct. 1959; Lich. Dioc. Dir. (1980); inf. from Mr. Snelson (1981).
[91] P.O. Dir. Staffs. (1845).
[92] Ibid.; Nat. Soc. Inquiry, 1846–7, Staffs. 2–3; Jay, 'Bobbington', 49; P.R.O., RG 10/2928.
[93] Griffith, Free Schools, 628; P.O. Dir. Staffs. (1868; 1872); Jay, 'Bobbington', 59.
[94] Bobbington ch., copy of will; Char. Dons. 1786–88, ii. 1144–5; 5th Rep. Com. Char. 605; tablet in church.
[95] Char. Com. files.
[96] Bobbington ch., copy of will and vestry bk.; tablet in church.
[97] Char. Com. files.

[98] Census, 1891, 1971. This article was written in 1983. Mr. J. Blamire Brown of the Mount, Codsall Wood, Mr. E. H. Gaskell of the Cottage, Codsall Wood, Mr. D. Whitehead of Codsall Civic Society, and others named in footnotes are thanked for their help.
[99] S.R.O., Q/SO 35, f. 25.
[1] S.R.O., D. 743/15.
[2] T. H. Whitehead and others, Memoirs of Geol. Surv., Country between Wolverhampton and Oakengates, 146, 162–3; below, econ. hist.   [3] V.C.H. Staffs. iv. 52, 57.
[4] S.H.C. vii (1), 250–1.
[5] P.R.O., E 179/177/96.
[6] S.H.C. n.s. vi (1), 74–5.
[7] P.R.O., STAC 4/4/36.
[8] H.L., Main Papers, box 178.
[9] S.H.C. 1923, 74–6, 81.
[10] V.C.H. Staffs. i. 326; Census, 1911–71.

near the church, which stands on a hill north of the present village. The open space on the south side of the churchyard may be the remains of a green. By the later 18th century the village was spread out along Church Road leading south from the church.[11] Codsall House, on the site of what was probably Codsall manor house,[12] then marked the southern limit of settlement. The oldest buildings which survived at Codsall in 1983 were a 16th-century timber-framed house, then a restaurant, in the centre of the village,[13] and a 17th-century timber-framed cottage east of the church. The site of Codsall Hall in Church Road was occupied by the mid 17th century.[14] A brick house dated 1720 and bearing the initials T/IE stood opposite Codsall Hall; it was demolished in the early 1970s.[15] A road from Wolverhampton originally entered the village opposite Codsall House, following the route of the present Wilkes Road. In the first decade of the 19th century the road was realigned to the north, forming a crossroads with Church Road.[16] The Bull inn mentioned in 1791[17] probably stood on the site of the present inn of that name in the south-east corner of the crossroads. It was possibly the inn called the Lord Nelson in 1818. Another inn, the Holly Bush, also mentioned in 1818, may have stood south of the church on the site of the vicarage built in 1848.[18] The Bull was again mentioned in 1834, when the Crown in the north-west corner of the crossroads also existed; both still stood in 1983.[19] There were a few cottages in Sandy Lane east of the church in the mid 19th century; the Wheel inn on Wolverhampton Road also existed then.[20]

In the later 18th century there were scattered houses along Moatbrook Lane west of Codsall village, an area then known as Codsall Lanes.[21] In 1851 there were six families living at what by then was called Moatbrook, and 10 families at 'Merriden', probably near Merridale, later Moatbrook, House.[22]

From the 1840s Codsall village became a residential area favoured by people working in the Wolverhampton area. Three villas were built in the village in the 1840s, the Mount in Wolverhampton Road, demolished in 1968, the Firs in Wood Road, and Clifton House (later Manor Court) in Church Road. The Mount was probably built for Thomas Harley, a Wolverhampton wine merchant, who was living there in 1849; his son, also Thomas, then lived at the Firs.[23] A railway station on the Wolverhampton-Shrewsbury

line south of the village was opened c. 1850[24] and encouraged more residential development. On the west side of the village Wood Road had been laid out by 1850, replacing the eastern part of Moatbrook Lane as the route of the Newport road.[25] Wheatstone Park, a villa at the west end of Wood Road, dates from the 1850s. It was probably built for Thomas White, a Bilston chemist and druggist, who was living there in 1861.[26] By the earlier 1880s other villas included the Shrubbery in Wood Road, Brabourne east of the church, and several in Elliots Lane, Oaken Lanes, and Histons Hill.[27] Flemmyng House west of Codsall House was built in the late 19th century; it was demolished in the early 1960s.[28] In the late 19th and early 20th century semi-detached and terraced houses were built on both sides of Wood Road for tradesmen and clerks working in Wolverhampton, Bilston, and Wednesbury.[29] Twelve council houses were built in Station Road in the early 1920s.[30] Houses and bungalows were built from the 1930s between Oaken Lanes and Histons Hill.

After the Second World War extensive housing estates were laid out around the village. The first was a council estate in Moat Brook Avenue south of Wood Road built shortly after the war. A private estate to the south, partly in the grounds of the former Flemmyng House, dates from the 1960s and 1970s.[31] Further west houses and bungalows were built in Moatbrook Lane and in Slate Lane opposite Moatbrook House in the 1960s and 1970s. In the late 1950s and early 1960s a large council estate was built in the Wilkes Road area east of the village; most of the houses were for people from Wolverhampton.[32] To the north a small estate of privately built houses was laid out over the grounds of the Mount in the late 1960s.[33] A bypass, Bakers Way, was constructed north of the village centre in the early 1970s; two estates, one of privately built houses and the other of old people's bungalows, were then laid out on its north side. A 40-a. site between Sandy Lane and Wolverhampton Road was developed privately in the mid 1960s.[34] Privately built houses in the grounds of Brabourne House date from the late 1970s.[35] A private estate east of Histons Hill dates from the 1950s.[36] From the 1970s houses were built further south in Histons Hill, some of them in the grounds of former villas.

Dam Mill in the south-east corner of the parish took its name from a medieval mill. The area

[11] Yates, *Map of Staffs.* (1775).
[12] Below, manors and other estates.
[13] Often mistakenly described as the former manor house.
[14] Below, manors and other estates (Codsall).
[15] Staffs. C.C. Planning Dept., Conservation Section photographs, 153/70 to 155/70; inf. from Mr. Gaskell.
[16] Yates, *Map of Staffs.* (1775; 1799); R. Baugh, *Map of Salop.* (1808); S.R.O., D. 743/17.
[17] S.R.O., D.(W.) 1766/13, ct. of 31 May 1791.
[18] Parson and Bradshaw, *Dir. Staffs.* (1818); R. H. Gaskell, *St. Nicholas' Church, Codsall* (2nd edn.); below, church.
[19] White, *Dir. Staffs.* (1834), 255; S.R.O., D. 743/16–17, nos. 32, 50.
[20] S.R.O., D. 743/16–17, nos. 68–70, 128, 135.
[21] Yates, *Map of Staffs.* (1775).
[22] P.R.O., HO 107/1002; HO 107/2016; O.S. Map 6", Staffs. LV. SE. (1886 edn.).

[23] S.R.O., D. 660/24/1, sale partics. 3 Apr. 1845; D. 743/16–17, nos. 9, 37, 51–2; White, *Dir. Staffs.* (1834), 217; (1851), 136, 174; *Express & Star*, 24 Aug. 1968.
[24] Below.   [25] S.R.O., D. 743/17.
[26] Ibid.; P.R.O., RG 9/1984; *P.O. Dir. Staffs.* (1850), 207; (1860), 498; Harrison, Harrod & Co., *Dir. Staffs.* (1861), 100.
[27] O.S. Map 6", Staffs. LV. SE. (1886 edn.).
[28] Ibid.; O.S. Map 1/2,500, Staffs. LV. 12 (1903 edn.).
[29] O.S. Map 1/2,500 Staffs. LV. 12 (1903 and 1924 edns.); Wolv. C.L., DX/86/3, 5; T.C.T. [D. Plant], *Life's Realities* [1922], 150.
[30] Inf. from Mr. Blamire Brown.
[31] Inf. from Mr. Blamire Brown and Mr. Whitehead.
[32] *Express & Star*, 5 June, 30 July 1959.
[33] Ibid. 24 Aug. 1968.
[34] Ibid. 30 Nov. 1963; inf. from Mr. Whitehead.
[35] *Express & Star*, 2 Mar. 1978.
[36] Ibid. 26 Mar. 1953.

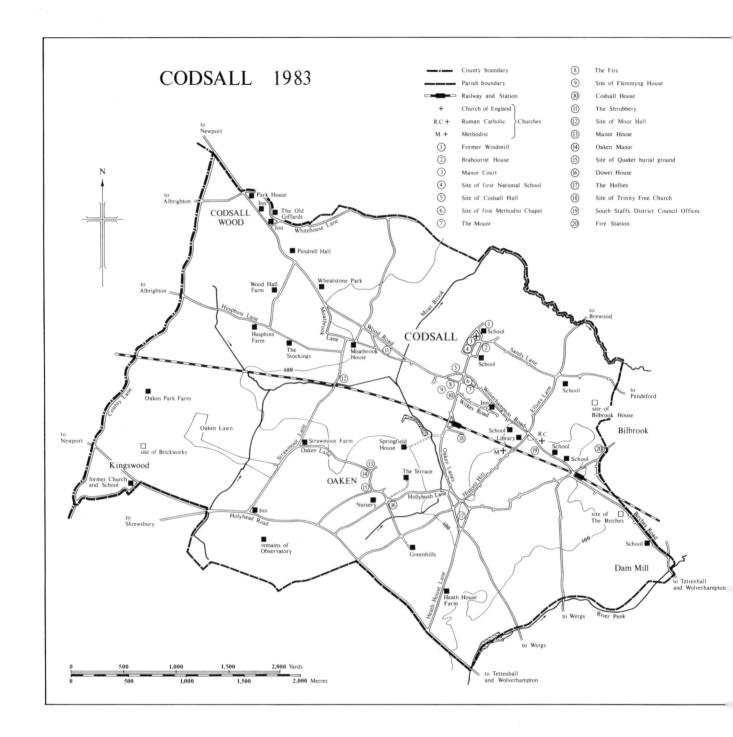

CODSALL 1983

	County boundary	⑧	The Firs
	Parish boundary	⑨	Site of Flemmyng House
	Railway and Station	⑩	Codsall House
+	Church of England	⑪	The Shrubbery
R.C.+	Roman Catholic	Churches	⑫ Site of Moor Hall
M.+	Methodist		⑬ Manor House
①	Former Windmill	⑭	Oaken Manor
②	Brabourne House	⑮	Site of Quaker burial ground
③	Manor Court	⑯	Dower House
④	Site of first National School	⑰	The Hollies
⑤	Site of Codsall Hall	⑱	Site of Trinity Free Church
⑥	Site of first Methodist Chapel	⑲	South Staffs. District Council Offices
⑦	The Mount	⑳	Fire Station

remained inhabited after the mill was first demolished in the 17th century.[37] A house to the north-west called the Birches was inhabited by 1716. An estate of privately built houses was laid out in the grounds c. 1970.[38] Houses along Birches Road date mainly from the later 20th century. To the north the settlement of Bilbrook extended into Codsall parish by the mid 17th century.[39] Bilbrook House was built for John Egginton of Oxley, in Bushbury, probably c. 1805.[40] In 1841 and 1851 it was occupied by Joseph Tarratt, a Wolverhampton iron merchant.[41] It was demolished in the late 1960s and an estate built over the grounds.[42]

Moor Hall west of Codsall village stood on a medieval moated site where Strawmoor Lane crosses Moat brook; it was still occupied in 1690.[43] The brook, so called by 1652,[44] presumably took its name from the moat. Wood Hall Farm to the north-west, also standing on a moated site, was inhabited probably by the early 14th century.[45] Stocking (later Husphins) Lane leading to Albrighton (Salop.) was mentioned in 1308–9.[46] In the late 17th century there was a farmhouse, the Stockings, at the east end of the lane,[47] and a cottage, known as Dead Woman's Grave, at the west end.[48] Husphins Farm between them was inhabited by the earlier 18th century.[49]

There was a sulphur spring by the Newport road north of Wood Hall Farm. The medicinal properties of the water were recorded c. 1680, and the spring continued to attract visitors until the later 19th century.[50] In the mid 19th century there was an inn on or near the site of the later Pendrell Hall lodge; water from the spring was obtained from a well in the inn's courtyard.[51] Pendrell (formerly Pendryl) Hall was built c. 1870 for Edward Viles of Bilston, editor of the Gentlewoman's Journal. In 1910 the estate was bought by Frank Gaskell, the son of a Lancashire industrialist. Gaskell remodelled the house and built the lodge by the main road. In 1955 his family sold the property to Staffordshire county council, which opened the hall as a residential college of adult education in 1961.[52]

Codsall Wood, an area of waste in the north-west corner of the parish, may have been inhabited as early as the 14th century: William at

the wood was among those assessed for tax in Codsall in 1327 and 1332–3.[53] Several families lived there by the 17th century.[54] By 1834 there was an inn, the Giffard Arms, on the Newport road near the parish boundary.[55] Another inn, the Cross Guns, to the south-east existed by 1849.[56] In 1851 there were 45 people living in Codsall Wood, mostly at the east end of the former waste and along Whitehouse Lane to the north.[57] There was then a third inn, the Old Giffard's Arms, in Whitehouse Lane.[58] The Giffard Arms ceased to be an inn in the early 1860s and the Old Giffard's Arms in the mid 1920s; both buildings survived in 1983 as private houses, respectively Park House and the Old Giffards. The Crown, first mentioned in 1940, and the Cross Guns remained in 1983.[59]

Oaken township occupies the southern part of the parish. The name is of Old English origin,[60] and the main settlement lies on the spur overlooking Moat brook. Oaken Manor at the top of Oaken Lane dates from the earlier 19th century but evidently stands on the site of an earlier house: a stone dated 1677 is set into a barn in the grounds. Manor House, opposite Oaken Manor, dates from the early 19th century. The hamlet lay to the south and evidently stood round a green: three families were living at Oaken green in 1841.[61] Dower House nearby in Hollybush Lane dates from the later 18th century. The Terrace, standing in its own grounds east of the hamlet, was built in the early 19th century for Henry Wood, a Wolverhampton distiller.[62] His nephew Christopher Wood sold the house in 1849. It was probably bought by William Bailey, a manufacturing chemist from Wolverhampton, who was living there in 1851.[63] In 1983 the house was owned by the National Coal Board and occupied as a residential training centre by its subsidiary Compower Ltd. Springfield House to the north was built c. 1850 for William Woodall, a nail and iron merchant.[64]

The area east of Oaken hamlet was inhabited by the earlier 17th century when it was known as Oaken Lanes. Heath House on the east side of Heath House Lane may have existed then; it certainly stood there in the later 18th century.[65] The present farmhouse on the site dates from the 19th century. There was an inn, the Bull, on Holyhead

[37] Codsall Par. Reg. (Staffs. Par. Reg. Soc. 1962-3), 80-1, 89, 144, 152, 226, 231; below, econ. hist.
[38] Below, manors and other estates (Codsall).
[39] S.R.O., D.(W.) 1766/3, ct. of 6 July 1646.
[40] Pitt, Staffs. i. 186; Staffs. Advertiser, 25 May 1805; Codsall Par. Reg. 236; S.R.O., D.(W.) 2766/18, ct. of 12 July 1838.
[41] P.R.O., HO 107/1002; HO 107/2016; White, Dir. Staffs. (1834), 207; (1851), 130.
[42] Inf. from Mr. Whitehead.
[43] Below, manors and other estates.
[44] S.R.O., D.(W.) 1766/3, ct. of 18 May 1662.
[45] Below, manors and other estates.
[46] S.R.O., D. 593/J/5/4/1.
[47] S.H.C. 1923, 74.
[48] Codsall Par. Reg. 78, 91, 94; O.S. Map 1″, sheet LXII. NW. (1834 edn.).
[49] Codsall Par. Reg. 126.
[50] Plot, Staffs. 101; F. P. Palmer and A. Crowquill, Wanderings of a Pen and Pencil (1846), 36-7; Trans. S. Mid. Inst. of Mining, Civil, and Mechanical Engineers, iii (1871-3), 16-17; W.S.L., Staffs. Views, iii. 133b; Wolv. C.L., maps 24 and 53.

[51] S.R.O., D. 743/16-17, no. 421; Mara [Mary S. Wakefield], Ancient Brewood (1932), 51 (copy in W.S.L.).
[52] P.O. Dir. Staffs. (1868; 1872); S.R.O., C.229; Pendrell Hall prospectus 1974 (copy in W.S.L. Pamphs.).
[53] S.H.C. vii (1), 250; x (1), 128.
[54] Codsall Par. Reg. 21-86 passim.
[55] Yates, Map of Staffs. (1775); White, Dir. Staffs. (1834), 255; S.R.O., D. 590/684; D. 743/16-17, no. 461.
[56] S.R.O., D. 743/16-17, no. 454.
[57] P.R.O., HO 107/2016; P.R.O., RG 9/1984; S.R.O., D. 743/17.
[58] P.O. Dir. Staffs. (1850); inf. from Mr. Blamire Brown.
[59] P.O. Dir. Staffs. (1860 and later edns.); Kelly's Dir. Staffs. (1880 and later edns.).
[60] Ekwall, Eng. Place-Names.
[61] Yates, Map of Staffs. (1775); P.R.O., HO 107/1002.
[62] W.S.L., C.B./Codsall/2; Baugh, Map of Salop. (1808).
[63] S.R.O., D. 1492/9/2; W.S.L., C.B./Codsall/2; White, Dir. Staffs. (1851), 115, 174.
[64] S.R.O., D. 1492/9/2; Reg. of persons entitled to vote ... for southern div. of county of Stafford 1852-3 (Stafford, 1852), 304.
[65] Codsall Par. Reg. 58; Yates, Map of Staffs. (1775).

Road south of Heath House in the 1730s; it still existed in 1779.[66] Greenhills, a large house west of Heath House, was built in the later 1850s for Thomas Bolton, a Wolverhampton lawyer.[67] The stables along Heath House Lane are dated 1860. The Hollies, north-east of Greenhills, was built c. 1870 apparently for Henry Anslow, a Wolverhampton grocer.[68]

Strawmoor Farm west of Oaken hamlet appears to date from the early 19th century. There were a few houses to the south at the corner of Strawmoor Lane and Holyhead Road in 1850; one of them had been converted into an inn, the Foaming Jug, by the early 1880s.[69] Houses at the southern end of Strawmoor Lane date from before and after the Second World War. An observatory, the base of which still stands, was built south of Holyhead Road in the 1840s.[70]

Oaken Lawn, an area of waste west of Strawmoor Farm, was being encroached upon by the later 17th century.[71] There were at least two cottages along the edge in the later 18th century and six in 1850.[72] A few cottages survived there in 1983. Further west there was an area of parkland in the Middle Ages.[73] It was still known as Oaken park in the 17th century, when several families were described as living in the park.[74] The Cooper family, described as being of Oaken Park in the late 17th and early 18th century,[75] may have been living at Oaken Park Farm, which existed in the later 18th century.[76] The present house dates from the early 19th century.

Kingswood, straddling the boundary with Tettenhall in the south-west, was formerly an area of common, part of which survived in 1983.[77] Some families may have been living on the Codsall side in the 17th century.[78] In 1850 there were a few houses along the boundary; in the early 1880s others stood to the north along the edge of the surviving common.[79] A church and a school were built in the later 19th century.[80]

The road from Wolverhampton to Newport (Salop.) and Chester runs through the south of the parish; that stretch was mentioned as the mere way in 1393.[81] The road was turnpiked in 1748, and there was a tollhouse at its junction with County Lane c. 1840. The road was disturnpiked in 1880. From 1810 the Wolverhampton–Shrewsbury road (the Holyhead road) followed

the same course as far as Kingswood.[82] The railway from Wolverhampton to Shrewsbury was opened through the parish in 1849 with a station at Codsall village by 1851.[83] A halt was opened at Bilbrook in 1934. Codsall station was closed for goods traffic in 1964[84] but was still open for passengers in 1983.

A police officer was living in Codsall by 1851.[85] By 1881 the number of 'turbulent people from the Black Country' visiting the parish, especially in the summer, was causing local concern. In 1882 the trustees of the Codsall charities, having first sought the approval of the Charity Commissioners, built a police house with a cell on charity land north of the railway station. From 1883 the house was leased rent-free to the county, which provided a full-time police officer. The arrangement lasted until 1924, when the county council bought the house.[86] A new police station was built on Wolverhampton Road in the early 1950s.[87]

There was a post office at Codsall by 1851; by 1864 there were also post offices at Codsall Wood and Oaken.[88] From 1855 Codsall parish was included in the area supplied by the Wolverhampton Waterworks Co. Oaken was supplied from 1895, and in 1927, after eight samples from wells in Codsall Wood were found to be polluted, arrangements were made for supplying that area also.[89] A sewerage scheme for the parish was completed in 1933. Electricity was available by 1935.[90] A fire station was opened in Duck Lane in 1972.[91]

Codsall wake was held on 6 May in 1821 and on 5–6 May in 1823; bull baiting and bear baiting were among the entertainments.[92] By the earlier 1880s Codsall had become a popular resort for day trippers, especially from Wolverhampton.[93] There was a refreshment room in the village by 1880; by 1908 there were three rooms, one of them at Codsall Wood. There were still three in 1916 but only two in 1924 and one in 1928.[94]

In the early 1820s there was a club in Codsall village, meeting in the evenings.[95] In 1896 there was an institute, probably meeting in the parish room in Church Road.[96] A village hall on the north side of Wolverhampton Road was opened in 1964.[97] There was a working men's club, evidently in Sandy Lane, in 1908; it still existed

[66] Codsall Par. Reg. 119, 132, 151; S.R.O., Q/SO, A. 1779.
[67] P.R.O., RG 9/1984; White, Dir. Staffs. (1851), 111, 174.
[68] P.R.O., RG 10/2927; White, Dir. Staffs. (1851), 119.
[69] S.R.O., D. 743/15; O.S. Map 6", Staffs. LV. SE. (1886 edn.).
[70] Above, Tettenhall, introduction.
[71] Codsall Par. Reg. 70-1, 91, 94, 97-8.
[72] Yates, Map of Staffs. (1775); S.R.O., D. 743/15.
[73] Below, econ. hist.
[74] Codsall Par. Reg. 44, 47, 50-4, 70.
[75] Ibid. 95-6, 99, 102, 141.
[76] Yates, Map of Staffs. (1775).
[77] Below, econ. hist.
[78] Codsall Par. Reg. 24, 58, 64, 72, 98.
[79] S.R.O., D. 743/15; O.S. Map 6", Staffs. LV. SE. (1886 edn.).
[80] Below, church; educ.
[81] S.R.O., D. 593/A/2/5/11.
[82] S.R.O., D. 743/15, no. 65; above, Tettenhall, communications.
[83] V.C.H. Staffs. ii. 313; White, Dir. Staffs. (1851), 173.
[84] C. R. Clinker, Clinker's Reg. of Closed Passenger Stns.

and Goods Depots, 31; inf. from British Railways, London Midland Region.
[85] P.R.O., HO 107/2016; P.R.O., RG 9/1984; RG 10/2927.
[86] S.R.O., D. 3793/7/4, 9, 15.
[87] S.R.O., C. 744.
[88] White, Dir. Staffs. (1851), 174; P.O. Dir. Staffs. (1864).
[89] B. L. McMillan, Hist. of Water Supply of Wolverhampton 1847-1947 (Wolverhampton, 1947), 33, 35; Seisdon R.D.C. Rep. of M.O.H. for 1895, 9 (copy in S.R.O., C/H/1/2/1/6); 1927, 8 (copy in S.R.O., C/H/1/2/236).
[90] Seisdon R.D.C. Rep. of M.O.H. for 1933, 8; 1935, 10 (copies in S.R.O., C/H/1/2/2/36).
[91] Inf. from the sec. to the Staffs. county fire officer.
[92] Wolv. C.L., DX/37/1, p. 57; 2, pp. 114-15.
[93] A. Hinde, Hist. of Wolverhampton and Guide to the District (Wolverhampton, 1884), 77-8; above.
[94] Kelly's Dir. Staffs. (edns. from 1880 to 1928).
[95] Wolv. C.L., DX/37/2, p. 4; 3, p. 6.
[96] Kelly's Dir. Staffs. (1896 and later edns.); S.R.O., D. 3793/6, acct. for par. room 1911-12; S.R.O., D.(W.) 1766/27, ct. of 14 Oct. 1907.
[97] Express & Star, 1 Feb. 1964.

TETTENHALL: VIEW OF WOLVERHAMPTON FROM THE ROCK IN 1837
with New Bridge tollhouse in the middle distance

WOMBOURNE: CANAL LOCKS AT THE BRATCH

WOMBOURNE: THE CHURCH FROM THE SOUTH IN 1837

TETTENHALL: THE CHURCH FROM THE SOUTH IN 1822

WOMBOURNE: WATERWORKS AT THE BRATCH

in 1939.[98] In 1873 penny readings under the patronage of the vicar were given at a house in Codsall Wood.[99]

A lending library was kept at the National school in 1833. It was still at the school in 1911, when it was open once a week. A branch of the county library was opened in Histons Hill in 1961.[1]

A cricket club was established in the early 20th century, and a football club in 1945. Playing fields near the village hall were opened in 1963, and a sports centre at Codsall high school in Elliots Lane was opened in 1976. Numerous social clubs and branches of national societies have been established in the village, especially since the Second World War, reflecting an active community life among the increased population.[2]

Charles (later Sir Charles) Wheeler (1892–1974), sculptor and president of the Royal Academy 1956–66, was born at no. 12, Church Road. His bronze sculpture, *The Lone Singer*, was presented to the village by his daughter in 1974; in 1975 it was erected in a public garden south of Bakers Way.[3]

MANORS AND OTHER ESTATES. Before the Conquest *CODSALL* was held by Chenvin; in 1086 he held 3 hides there as a king's thegn.[4] His successors as lords of the manor in the late 11th and the 12th century are unknown. William of Codsall, who was living in the early 13th century, may have been lord then, but it appears that by 1248 much, if not all, of the manor had passed to the collegiate church of Wolverhampton.[5] Giles of Erdington then held land in Codsall as dean of Wolverhampton, and the deans continued to hold an estate there until 1848 when the college was dissolved and its possessions transferred to the Ecclesiastical Commissioners. The Church Commissioners, as successors of the Ecclesiastical Commissioners, still held Codsall as part of the deanery manor in 1983.[6]

There was evidently a manor house in the earlier 14th century when William at the hall gate was living in Codsall.[7] It may have been the Hall House, described in 1608 as the capital messuage of the dean of Wolverhampton.[8] That house

stood on the site of the later Codsall House, so called by the early 19th century.[9] Between 1659 and 1676 it was occupied by John Danynell, the dean's steward.[10] Known by the late 1650s as the Old Hall or Lower House, it was assessed at nine hearths in 1666.[11] It was occupied by Francis Steward in 1691; when he died in 1705 it comprised a hall, two parlours, and seven chambers.[12] It was rebuilt in the late 18th century, presumably by members of the Stuart family who then occupied the house.[13] From 1815 until at least 1851 the house was run as a private school.[14] In 1861 and 1871 it was the home of William Dent, a lawyer formerly of Wolverhampton.[15] In 1931 the house was bought by R. S. Carr; his trustees sold it to Seisdon rural district council in 1966. In 1972 the council leased the house to Staffordshire county council, which established an office for the social services department in it. It was still used for that purpose in 1983.[16]

By 1758 Codsall House had been replaced as the capital messuage by Codsall Hall in Church Road.[17] There was a house on the site by 1659 known as New Hall or Upper House.[18] Codsall Hall was leased in 1748 with *c.* 70 a. to Henry Wood, a Wolverhampton distiller.[19] Wood died in 1775[20] and was succeeded by another Henry Wood, possibly his son. In the early 19th century the younger Henry, also a Wolverhampton distiller, moved to the Terrace in Oaken, and in 1809 he gave the lease of Codsall Hall to his nephew, William Wenman of Gorsebrook, in Bushbury.[21] In 1860 Wenman's son, also William, of Rolstone (Herefs.), acquired the freehold of the estate, then 87 a. in extent.[22] In the early 20th century at least part of the farm was converted into a nursery, which closed in the later 1960s.[23]

THE BIRCHES in the south-east corner of the parish existed as an estate by 1716 when Richard Stubbs was living there.[24] Richard's son Samuel had succeeded by 1760. He died in 1764 leaving a son John who succeeded to an estate of *c.* 153 a.[25] John died in 1816, and his heir was his nephew Thomas Bedford, a Wolverhampton liquor merchant, who died probably in 1829. He was succeeded by his son Thomas Stubbs Bedford.[26] In 1872 the estate was conveyed to William Fleeming Fryer of Wergs Hall in Tettenhall;

[98] *Kelly's Dir. Staffs.* (1908 and later edns.); S.R.O., D.(W.) 1766/28, ct. of 17 Feb. 1921.
[99] *Wolverhampton Chron.* 3 Dec. 1873; *P.O. Dir. Staffs.* (1876), 81, 418.
[1] *Educ. Enq. Abstract*, H.C. 62, p. 874 (1835), xlii; S.R.O., D. 3793/6, accts. for 1889–90, 1911–12; *Codsall Par. Mag.* (Jan. 1911); inf. from Mr. G. L. King, deputy divisional librarian (1980).
[2] *Codsall* (coronation brochure, 1953; copy in W.S.L. Pamphs.); *Official Guide: Codsall and Wrottesley* [1968]; plaque in sports centre.
[3] Plaques on house and sculpture; *Express & Star*, 12 Dec. 1974.
[4] *V.C.H. Staffs.* iv. 57.
[5] *S.H.C.* ii (1), 149, 154; ix (1), 62; *Close R.* 1247–51, 50.
[6] S.R.O., D.(W.) 1766/1–28; *V.C.H. Staffs.* iii. 330; inf. from the records officer of the Church Commissioners.
[7] *S.H.C.* vii (1), 250; x (1), 128.
[8] S.R.O., D.(W.) 1766/1, ct. of 26 July 1608.
[9] *Staffs. Cath. Hist.* xx. 32.
[10] S.R.O., D.(W.) 1766/4, ct. of 2 June 1659; 5, ct. of 11 July 1676; Wolv. C.L., D/MAN/33, pedigree and notes on the Andrewes family.

[11] S.R.O., D.(W.), 1766/4, ct. of 2 June 1659; *S.H.C.* 1923, 74.
[12] S.R.O., D.(W.) 1766/7, ct. of 9 June 1691; L.J.R.O., P/C/11, Fra. Steward (1705).
[13] S.R.O., D.(W.) 1766/12, ct. of 18 Feb. 1772; plaque in Codsall church.
[14] Below, educ.
[15] P.R.O., RG 9/1984; RG 10/2927.
[16] Inf. from the clerk to S. Staffs. dist. council.
[17] S.R.O., D.(W.) 1766/10, ct. of 16 Feb. 1747/8.
[18] Ibid. 4, ct. of 2 June 1659.
[19] Ibid. 10, ct. of 16 Feb. 1747/8; S.R.O., D. 628/37.
[20] G. P. Mander, *Wolverhampton Antiquary*, i. 320.
[21] *Bailey's Brit. Dir.* (1784), 482; S.R.O., D.(W.) 1766/18, ct. of 29 Oct. 1833; W.S.L., C.B./Codsall/2; above, introduction.
[22] S.R.O., D.(W.) 1766/21, ct. of 15 Apr. 1861.
[23] Below, econ. hist.
[24] S.R.O., D.(W.) 1766/9, ct. of 19 May 1716.
[25] Ibid. 12, ct. of 10 Sept. 1765; S.R.O., D. 284/M/3, 10 Apr. 1760; *Codsall Par. Reg.* 172.
[26] S.R.O., D.(W.) 1766/16, ct. of 2 Sept. 1817; 17, ct. of 15 June 1829.

Fryer had held the property, evidently as mortgagee, in 1849 and was living there in 1851.[27] It descended with the Wergs Hall estate until its sale in 1907, when it comprised 225 a.[28] The house was sold in the late 1960s by Mr. A. Johnstone; it was then demolished and an estate of privately built houses laid out over the grounds.[29]

MOOR HALL, on a medieval moated site east of Strawmoor Lane, was mentioned in 1538, when John Ashwood gave a moiety of his messuage there to James Leveson of Wolverhampton.[30] Allan Brook was living at Moor Hall in the late 1580s and in 1596 as a tenant of the Leveson family.[31] In 1691 the estate was held by William Grosvenor of the Stockings; it appears to have been incorporated into Stockings farm about that time.[32] The house was still occupied in 1690.[33] It had been demolished by 1796, but the moat survived in 1849.[34]

WOOD HALL, so named by the early 17th century,[35] stood on a moated site in the northwest of Codsall. The estate may have originated in land granted by Nicholas Fitzherbert, lord of Somersall Herbert (Derb.), to John de Dene in 1317.[36] Martin de Dene was living in Codsall in 1332–3, and in 1362 he held land there of the dean of Wolverhampton.[37] Richard Dene held land in Codsall in 1393 and John Dene in 1434.[38] By 1530 the family was known as Wood otherwise Dene, and their estate was evidently freehold. William Wood otherwise Dene, alive in 1530, had been succeeded by his son Richard by 1564.[39] Richard died in 1591 and was succeeded by his son Walter. In 1598 Walter conveyed his estate in Codsall to his brother Edward, who continued to live in the parish until his death in 1635.[40] On Edward's death Wood Hall passed to his daughter Mary and her husband Alexander Persehouse.[41] Alexander died in 1639 and his son Edward succeeded. Edward died in 1700 and, being childless, left his estate to his distant cousin Peter Persehouse of Sedgley.[42] Peter died in 1731. It appears that his children predeceased him, and by 1739 Wood Hall was the property of William Persehouse of Reynolds Hall in Walsall.[43] William died in 1749, leaving a son Richard (d. 1771).[44] The estate, 173 a. in extent in 1774, probably passed with the rest of Richard Persehouse's property in trust to John Walhouse of

Hatherton, in St. Peter's, Wolverhampton.[45] In the later 19th century it was part of the Wergs Hall estate, in Tettenhall. It was sold in 1872, and in 1896 it belonged to Henry Ward of Rodbaston, in Penkridge.[46] It was sold by the Ward family in the late 1920s to Frank Gaskell of Pendrell Hall. His family sold it with 235 a. in 1976 to two brothers, K. J. and R. G. Shropshire; Mr. K. J. Shropshire was farming there in 1983.[47]

The hall was assessed at seven hearths in 1666.[48] A house still stood within the four arms of a moat in the early 19th century, but by 1835 it had been demolished and a brick house built to the north. The northern arm of the moat had also been filled in.[49] The remaining three arms, still wet, survived in 1983.

The prebend of *CODSALL* in the collegiate church of Tettenhall, in existence by the 1250s, had land in the parish. Land held by the 'rector of Codsall' near Dam Mill in 1433 was evidently prebendal: land within the prebend at Dam Mill was mentioned in 1679. In 1549, after the dissolution of the college, most of its property, including the prebendal manor of Codsall, was sold to Walter Wrottesley of Wrottesley, in Tettenhall. The prebend thereafter seems to have been administered as part of Tettenhall Clericorum manor.[50]

In 1535 most of the £6 income enjoyed by the prebendary of Codsall came from the great and small tithes of his prebend.[51] The tithes passed with the prebendal estate to the Wrottesley family. In 1626 Walter Wrottesley had a tithe barn in Codsall.[52] In 1795 Sir John Wrottesley exchanged the tithes of Codsall, but not those of Oaken, with the marquess of Stafford for those of Perton.[53] In 1796 tithes from 187 a. in Codsall were merged with the lands from which they arose, leaving the marquess an average income of £181 from Codsall tithes in the later 1820s. There were further mergers in 1831.[54] In 1849 it was stated that by prescription great tithes only were paid. They were commuted that year for a rent charge of £272 0s. 4d., of which the duke of Sutherland (as the successor of the marquess of Stafford) received £169 18s. 6d.[55] The tithes of Oaken, both great and small, were still owned by the Wrottesley family in 1838; they were commuted for a rent charge of £212 in 1841.[56]

[27] S.R.O., D.(W.) 1766/22, ct. of 23 Sept. 1872; D. 743/16–17, no. 175; White, *Dir. Staffs.* (1851), 174.
[28] W.S.L., Sale Cat. E/1/4; above, Tettenhall, manors and other estates.
[29] Inf. from Mr. J. Blamire Brown.
[30] S.R.O., D. 593/J/5/4/3. Remains of medieval pottery from the site are in the possession of Mr. R. M. Iliff of Oaken Manor.
[31] P.R.O., C 3/261/28; S.R.O., D. 593/H/14/4/11, 1596 surv.
[32] S.R.O., D.(W.) 1766/7, ct. of 5 Aug. 1691; S.R.O., D. 593/T/2/18, deed of 12 Aug. 1796.
[33] *Codsall Par. Reg.* 36–7, 82, 92.
[34] S.R.O., D. 593/T/2/18, deed of 12 Aug. 1796; S.R.O., D.(W.) 1766/19, ct. of 31 July 1849.
[35] W.S.L. 40/277/52 (giving it as the Hall of the Wood, 1601); *Codsall Par. Reg.* 45 (the Wood Hall, 1625).
[36] P.R.O., E 326/5189.
[37] *S.H.C.* x (1), 128; S.R.O., D. 593/J/5/4/1, ct. of 23 Aug. 1362.
[38] S.R.O., D. 593/A/2/5/11; D. 593/J/5/1/2, ct. of 15 June 1434.
[39] *S.H.C.* xi. 270; xiii. 232.
[40] Ibid. xiii. 232; xvi. 180; *Codsall Par. Reg.* 12, 54.

[41] P.R.O., C 142/529, no. 104.
[42] Brooke Robinson, *Geneal. Memoirs of Fam. of Brooke Robinson, of Dudley* (priv. print. 1896), 201–2; *S.H.C.* v (2), 237 n., 238; *S.H.C.* 1923, 74.
[43] Robinson, *Fam. of Brooke Robinson*, 233–4; S.R.O., D. 260/M/T/2/73.
[44] *V.C.H. Staffs.* xvii. 177.
[45] Wolv. C.L., map 24; S.R.O., D. 260/M/T/1/123, copy of deed of 7 Feb. 1780.
[46] W.S.L., Sale Cat. F/5/28; Robinson, *Fam. of Brooke Robinson*, 201 n. 4; *V.C.H. Staffs.* v. 122.
[47] Inf. from Mr. E. H. Gaskell and Mr. K. J. Shropshire.
[48] *S.H.C.* 1923, 74.
[49] Wolv. C.L., maps 24 and 53; S.R.O., D. 593/H/3/74.
[50] S.R.O., D. 593/J/5/1/2, ct. of 22 Oct. 1433; *Codsall Par. Reg.*. 81; above, Tettenhall, manors and other estates (Tettenhall Clericorum).
[51] *Valor Eccl.* iii. 105.
[52] S.R.O., D.(W.) 1766/1, ct. of 28 Feb. 1625/6.
[53] S.R.O., D. 593/B/1/5/1, deed of 4 June 1795; D. 593/T/2/16, abstract of duke of Sutherland's title to Codsall tithes 1831.
[54] S.R.O., D. 593/T/2/17–18.
[55] S.R.O., D. 743/16.
[56] Ibid. 15.

Before the Conquest *OAKEN* was held by Brodor, a free man; in 1086 Robert de Stafford held 5 hides there.[57] The overlordship of most of the estate was still held by the Stafford family in 1242–3, but there seems to be no further mention of their rights. The overlordship of the remainder was held in the mid 1250s by the Crown, which retained it until 1327.[58]

In 1086 the 5 hides were held of Robert de Stafford by Hugh.[59] Part at least came into the possession of Bertram de Verdun, lord of Alton, in Farley, and he granted an estate at Oaken to Croxden abbey when he endowed it in the later 1170s.[60] The monks held the estate as 1 knight's fee in 1220–1, and it was described in the mid 1250s as consisting of 4 hides. The remaining hide was then held of the king by Nicholas of Oaken and Adam son of Robert Dole.[61] In 1327 the hide was held with two messuages by Ralph and Hervey Freman, who owed suit at the court of the royal manor of Tettenhall Regis for the property. In that year Edward III made an exchange of rents with Croxden abbey, which received a 2s. rent from Ralph and Hervey's land; the abbey was not required to attend the Tettenhall Regis court but agreed to celebrate an obit for the king's father.[62] The whole manor was then held by Croxden abbey until its dissolution in 1538.[63]

Croxden abbey had established a grange at Oaken by 1291, and there was evidently a resident monk in the 1390s.[64] By the early 16th century the abbey was leasing the grange.[65] In the 1530s it had a steward and a rent-collector, both laymen, at Oaken.[66]

In 1540 the Crown granted the manor to William Whorwood of Putney (Surr.) and his wife Margaret. William, who was a member of the Whorwood family of Compton, in Kinver, died in 1545, and his widow continued to hold a life interest. Whorwood's heirs were his daughters Anne, wife of Ambrose Dudley by 1546, and Margaret, a minor who later married Thomas Throckmorton of Coughton (Warws.). Anne died childless in 1552; her heir was Thomas Whorwood of Compton.[67] In 1578 Thomas agreed to convey his interest in Oaken to Thomas and Margaret Throckmorton.[68] In 1591 the Throckmortons sold Oaken to Robert Chamberlayne.[69] Robert died in 1607. He was succeeded by his brother Richard (d. 1624) and Richard by another brother John (d. 1628).

Oaken then passed to Sir Thomas Stukeley of Hinton (Hants) and Thomas Windham of Kensford (Som.).[70] Stukeley's share of Oaken appears to have been acquired by Windham, who in 1631 sold the manor to Henry Fareley of Codsall and William Smith, Robert Hayward, and Richard Hickmans (later Hickman), all of Oaken.[71]

Henry Fareley died in 1638 and was succeeded by his son Richard, a royalist whose estate was confiscated in 1651.[72] William Smith died in 1645. His son, also William, was still living at Oaken in 1726 and died in 1734.[73] Robert Hayward was probably still alive in 1666 when a man of that name occupied a house in Oaken assessed at five hearths.[74] He died in 1680 and may have been succeeded by John Hayward, still alive in 1703.[75] None of the houses or lands owned by any of the three families has been identified, but the families' interest in the manor was evidently acquired by the Wrottesley family. In 1678 Sir Walter Wrottesley owned what was described as a moiety of Oaken, and in 1725 Sir John Wrottesley was named as one of the two lords of Oaken.[76]

Richard Hickman died in 1662. In 1666 his son Roger lived in a house in Oaken assessed at five hearths;[77] it may be identifiable as the later Oaken (or Dower) House. Roger died in 1672, leaving a son Nathan, who in 1725 was named as one of the two lords of Oaken. Nathan was dead by 1752, when John Hickman was lord.[78] In 1754 John conveyed his portion of the manor, described as a two-thirds part, to Nathaniel Barrett, apparently a relation: Nathaniel's mother Anne was formerly the wife of a William Hickman.[79] Nathaniel, who was high sheriff of Staffordshire in 1764, was living at Oaken in 1774; he was evidently responsible for building the present house, which is of brick with three storeys and shaped parapets to the gable ends.[80] He died childless in 1793. His heirs were the children of his brother William, one of whom, Anne, married Walter Mansell of London in 1793. She may have inherited the estate at Oaken: Walter Mansell was living at Oaken House in the 1790s.[81] It later passed to the Wrottesley family. By 1817 it was the home of the dowager Lady Wrottesley.[82] A later dowager Lady Wrottesley was living at the house in the 1870s with her son Charles, who still lived there in 1904.[83] During the First World War the house, by then also known as the Dower House, was occupied by Belgian refugees.[84] In 1956 Lord

[57] *V.C.H. Staffs.* iv. 52.
[58] *Bk. of Fees*, ii. 974; *S.H.C.* v (1), 115; *Cal. Pat.* 1327–30, 177–8.   [59] *V.C.H. Staffs.* iv. 52.
[60] Ibid. iii. 226; *Cartae Antiquae* (Pipe R. Soc. N.S. xxxiii), no. 528.
[61] Jones, *Tettenhall*, 147; *S.H.C.* v (1), 115.
[62] *Cal. Pat.* 1327–30, 177–8; *Cal. Close*, 1327–30, 228.
[63] *Valor Eccl.* (Rec. Com.), iii. 125; *V.C.H. Staffs.* iii. 228.
[64] *Tax. Eccl.* (Rec. Com.), 253; *S.H.C.* N.S. vi (2), 182–3; S.R.O., D.(W.) 1807/39, ct. of 26 Jan. 1394/5.
[65] *L. & P. Hen. VIII*, xv, pp. 287–8.
[66] *Valor Eccl.* iii. 125.
[67] *L. & P. Hen. VIII*, xv, p. 287; below, Kinver, manors and other estates (Kinver).
[68] H.W.R.O. (H.), E 12/S, Whorwood inheritance, deed of 6 Apr. 1578.   [69] *S.H.C.* xvi. 111.
[70] P.R.O., C 142/305, no. 131; C 142/450, no. 84; Burke, *Ext. & Dorm. Baronetcies* (1838), 511–12.
[71] P.R.O., CP 25 (2)/485/7 Chas. I East., no. 31; Wolv. C.L., DX/67/68, deed of 2 July 1631.

[72] *Codsall Par. Reg.* 41, 58; *Cal. Cttee. for Money*, iii, p. 1252.
[73] *Codsall Par. Reg.* 51, 60, 88, 93, 151; P.R.O., C 103/40/5.
[74] *S.H.C.* 1923, 81.
[75] *Codsall Par. Reg.* 81, 103.
[76] W.S.L. 574B/38; S.R.O., list of gamekeepers' deputations.
[77] *Codsall Par. Reg.* 40, 65; *S.H.C.* 1923, 81.
[78] *Codsall Par. Reg.* 68, 75; S.R.O., list of gamekeepers' deputations.
[79] P.R.O., CP 34/191, p. 111; *Codsall Par. Reg.* 103, 108.
[80] Pevsner, *Staffs.* 106.
[81] *S.H.C.* 1912, 291; *Codsall Par. Reg.* 208; Shaw, *Staffs.* ii. 289; memorial tablet to Wm. Barrett in Codsall ch.; Yates, *Map of Staffs.* (1799).
[82] Pitt, *Staffs.* 186; S.R.O., D. 743/15, no. 228.
[83] P.R.O., RG 10/2927; *P.O. Dir. Staffs.* (1872; 1876); *Kelly's Dir. Staffs.* (edns. from 1880 to 1908).
[84] *Codsall Par. Mag.* Nov. 1914, Apr. 1919 (copies in Codsall Libr.).

Wrottesley sold the house to Mrs. R. J. L. Maitland, and she and her husband were living there in 1983.[85]

ECONOMIC HISTORY. AGRICULTURE. There was land for 3 ploughteams at Codsall in 1086; there were 6 villeins with 2 teams. At Oaken there was also land for 3 teams; 1 team was in demesne, and there were 4 villeins and 4 bordars with 1½ team. With woodland, Oaken was then worth 8s.[86]

There were three open fields for Codsall in the Middle Ages. Histons field, mentioned as Uchestones field in the later 14th and early 15th century[87] and known as Hall field from the early 17th century,[88] lay east of Codsall village. Moor field, mentioned in the later 14th and early 15th century[89] and known as Church field by the mid 17th century,[90] evidently lay north-west of the church. Caldwall field, mentioned in 1399 and 1425,[91] lay north-east of the church.[92] There were closes in Church field in 1659, in Hall field in 1682, and in Caldwall field in 1709.[93] Butts in the three fields were still recorded, however, in 1779.[94] There was an open field at Dam Mill in 1433.[95] Selions in what was called Dam Mill Brych still existed in 1644. The field appears to have been inclosed by 1656.[96] There is no record of any open field at Oaken.

Doles of meadow along Moat brook north of the church were mentioned during the 17th century. There were still doles there called Broad Doles in 1752.[97]

Kingswood, an area of waste straddling the border with Tettenhall and so called by 1403, may have formerly lain in Brewood forest, disafforested in 1204.[98] There were nearly 20 a. of waste on the Codsall side of the boundary c. 1840. At the same date there were 16 a. of waste at Oaken Lawn north of Kingswood; shortly before 1849 the land there was drained.[99] There was still 16 a. (6.5 ha.) of waste at Oaken Lawn in 1983.[1] Codsall wood in the north-west corner of the parish may also have once formed part of Brewood forest. It was described as common in the mid 17th century.[2] In 1824 42 a. were inclosed under an Act of 1820.[3]

Leighting green apparently north of Moat-

brook House was mentioned in 1671.[4] There were probably once greens in both Codsall and Oaken.[5]

Wheat, peas, and oats were being grown at Bilbrook in 1659, and barley, wheat, and rye at Codsall in 1705. In 1659 William Mountford of Bilbrook had a herd of 3 cows with calves, 4 twinters, and 4 yearlings. In 1705 Francis Steward of Codsall House had 6 cows, 7 heifers, and 5 calves; he also had a cheese press and 80 cheeses. Margaret Simcox of Bilbrook had a herd of 6 cows with calves and 17 heifers in 1721. Flocks of sheep, the largest numbering only 35, were recorded in the later 17th and early 18th century.[6]

The main crops in 1801 were wheat, barley, and oats; turnips and peas were also important, and small acreages of potatoes and beans were grown.[7] In the 1840s there was nearly three times as much arable as pasture in Codsall and twice as much in Oaken.[8] In 1979 arable farming was less important. Barley and oats, the main crops, covered only 290.4 ha. (717½ a.) of the 1,059.9 ha. (2,619 a.) returned for the parish.[9]

In contrast pastoral farming, especially cattle, and nurseries and market gardening had become a feature of the parish, possibly reflecting demand from Wolverhampton. There was a flock of 93 sheep with 6 rams on a farm at Oaken in 1811, and in 1812 a farmer at Codsall advertised the sale of 128 Wiltshire sheep crossed with New Leicesters. A mixed farm at Oaken in 1814 had 70 sheep and lambs; it also had a herd of 10 cows in calf, 7 fat cows, and 2 calves.[10] Much of the 97-a. farm on the northern edge of Oaken Lawn was described as excellent water meadow in 1849; the lawn had recently been drained and manured.[11] A cattle dealer was living at Oaken Lawn in the earlier 20th century, and there was a dairy farm at Oaken in the later 1930s.[12] A cattle pen by the railway east of Codsall station in 1921 suggests a trade in cattle then.[13] In 1979 recorded livestock numbered 1,257 cattle and 430 sheep, and there were 5 dairy farms and 3 farms rearing and fattening livestock. Nearly half the farming land returned then was grass, 480.3 ha. (1,189 a.).[14]

There was a nursery at the Birches in 1860. It was owned by William Thomas, by 1868 a Wolverhampton nurseryman and seed merchant.

[85] Inf. from Mr. Maitland.
[86] V.C.H. Staffs. iv. 52, 57.
[87] S.R.O., D. 593/J/4/1, ct. of 23 Aug. 1362; D. 593/J/5/1/ 1, ct. of 16 Sept. 1399; 2, ct. of 9 Jan. 1424/5.
[88] S.R.O., D. 593/J/5/1/2, ct. of 12 Jan. 1433/4; D.(W.) 1766/1, cts. of 16 July 1622, 30 Sept. 1623, 26 May 1624; 4, ct. of 1 July 1662; 5, ct. of 17 Oct. 1676; 13, ct. of 29 June 1779.
[89] S.R.O., D. 593/A/2/5/13; D. 593/J/5/1/2, ct. of 9 Jan. 1424/5; D. 593/J/5/4/1, ct. of 23 Aug. 1362; S.R.O., D.(W.) 1766/13, ct. of 29 June 1779.
[90] S.R.O., D.(W.) 1766/3, ct. of 12 Mar. 1648/9; 4, ct. of 13 Aug. 1656; 8, ct. of 9 May 1709; 11, ct. of 9 June 1751.
[91] S.R.O., D. 593/J/5/1/1, ct. of 16 Sept. 1399; 2, ct. of 9 Jan. 1424/5.
[92] S.R.O., D.(W.) 1766/1, ct. of 30 Sept. 1623; 2, cts. of 9 May 1638, 9 Feb. 1640/1; 6, ct. of 29 Nov. 1682.
[93] Ibid. 4, ct. of 2 June 1659; 6, ct. of 20 Apr. 1682; 8, ct. of 9 May 1709.
[94] Ibid. 13, ct. of 29 June 1779.
[95] S.R.O., D. 593/J/5/1/2, ct. of 22 Oct. 1433.
[96] S.R.O., D.(W.) 1766/1, ct. of 12 Apr. 1608; 2, ct. of 20 May 1634; 3, ct. of 9 Apr. 1644; 4, ct. of 21 Oct. 1656.
[97] Ibid. 1, cts. of 30 Sept. 1623, 26 May 1624; 3, cts. of 2

Oct. 1643, 21 Oct. 1651; 6, ct. of 13 Sept. 1683; 11, ct. of 24 Aug. 1752; 25, ct. of 25 Sept. 1895.
[98] Above, Tettenhall, econ. hist.
[99] S.R.O., D. 743/15, nos. 34, 63; below.
[1] Inf. from South Staffs. district council, clerk's dept.
[2] S.R.O., D.(W.) 1766/3, ct. of 16 Mar. 1650/1; 4, ct. of 4 Mar. 1656/7.
[3] S.R.O., D. 590/684.
[4] S.R.O., D.(W.) 1766/5, ct. of 16 Oct. 1671; S.R.O., D. 743/16–17, nos. 371, 373, 391.
[5] Above, introduction.
[6] L.J.R.O., P/C/11, Wm. Mountford (1661), John Smith (1700), Fra. Steward (1705), Marg. Simcox (1722).
[7] S.H.C. 1950–1, table facing p. 242.
[8] S.R.O., D. 743/15–16.
[9] M.A.F.F., agric. returns 1979.
[10] Wolverhampton Chron. 6 Mar. 1811; 15 Jan. 1812; 2 Mar. 1814.
[11] S.R.O., D. 1492/9/2.
[12] Kelly's Dir. Staffs. (edns. from 1912 to 1924; 1936; 1940).
[13] O.S. Map 1/2,500, Staffs. LV. 16 (1923 edn.).
[14] M.A.F.F., agric. returns 1979.

He still ran the Codsall nursery in 1872. By 1876 he appears to have been replaced by Richard Lowe, another Wolverhampton nurseryman, who still had a nursery in Codsall in 1888.[15] A nursery was established at Codsall Hall farm by Baker's of Wolverhampton between 1900 and 1904; it closed in the later 1960s.[16] A nursery in Shop Lane, Oaken, established by 1921,[17] was still trading in 1983.

There was a market gardener living at Oaken in 1851 and one at Kingswood in 1861. In the early 20th century there were 3 market gardens in the parish, 2 at Kingswood and 1 at Codsall.[18] In 1979 there were 11.7 ha. (29 a.) of orchards and small fruit recorded in the parish, and 3.1 ha. (8 a.) of vegetables. One farm specialized in horticulture.[19]

In 1921 John Matthews established a poultry farm in Sandy Lane. By 1935 he was experimenting with the battery farming of hens and then had some 500 hens, apparently Rhode Island Reds, each in its own cage.[20] In 1979 that farm was one of two in the parish, together having nearly 58,400 birds.[21]

WOODLAND AND PARKS. There was woodland ½ league in length and 2 furlongs in breadth at Oaken in 1086.[22] The wood of Oaken was mentioned in the mid 13th century.[23] The wood of Codsall was mentioned in 1293; it may have lain in the north-west corner of the parish where the name Codsall wood was used for common there by the mid 17th century. In 1774 there was a 12-a. wood along County Lane south of the common and a 4-a. wood to the east; both survived in 1835.[24] In the later 18th century there was woodland at the Birches in the south-east corner of the parish.[25] Two woodmen were living at Codsall Wood in 1831; in 1841 there were 9 there and another 2 in Codsall village.[26] In 1851 there were 8 woodcutters living at Codsall Wood, 3 at Codsall, and 2 at Oaken. By 1861 there was only one at Codsall Wood, with 3 timber fellers at Codsall. Only 3 woodmen were living in the parish in 1871.[27] In 1979 there was 12.4 ha. (31 a.) of woodland recorded in the parish.[28]

Croxden abbey had a park in its manor of Oaken by 1329.[29] The park evidently lay at the west end of Oaken Lane in the area of the later

Oaken Park Farm.[30] There was a parker in 1337.[31] It seems that in the late 17th century at least part of the dean of Wolverhampton's property at Codsall Wood was a park: a warden of the park of Codsall was chosen at the dean's leet court in 1683 and 1684.[32]

MILLS. The dean of Wolverhampton may have had a mill in Oaken as early as 1230. He certainly had one there by 1255, given to him with its fishpool by Nicholas son of Adam of Oaken.[33] It may have stood on Moat brook north of Springfield House: land there was called Mill field c. 1840,[34] and a large pool survived in 1983. In 1317 the ownership of the mill was disputed, evidently because of its position on the boundary of Oaken and Codsall manors: the dean and chapter of Wolverhampton claimed to hold the mill, as part of its estate in Codsall, against Richard Burdun, whose defence that the mill was in Oaken, not Codsall, was upheld.[35] Nothing further is known of the mill.

The loss of Oaken mill by the dean may have led to the construction of Dam mill on the river Penk at the south-eastern tip of the parish. The dean had a mill there by 1341, and in 1412 it was one of several mills in the area attacked by rioters.[36] The mill was evidently working in 1559, and a miller was living there in 1616.[37] The mill had been demolished by 1653 but had evidently been rebuilt by 1717.[38] Nothing further is known of it.

There was a windmill north of Codsall church by 1775.[39] It was still working in 1850[40] but was converted into a house in the later 19th century.[41] The house still stood in 1983.

A horse mill at Oaken manor house was mentioned in 1509; it was still working c. 1539.[42]

INDUSTRIES. A sandstone quarry at the east end of Sandy Lane may have been worked in 1852.[43] A quarry on the west side of Histons Hill was being worked in 1849; it then provided stone for the rebuilding of the parish church. Still worked in the early 1880s, the quarry was disused by 1900.[44] A quarry on the south side of the Wolverhampton Road, also worked in the early 1880s, was still open in the late 1930s;[45] from 1976 the site was occupied by the offices of the South

[15] P.O. Dir. Staffs. (edns. from 1860 to 1876); Kelly's Dir. Staffs. (1880; 1884; 1888); O.S. Map 6″, Staffs. LVI. SW. (1888 edn.).
[16] P.O. Dir. Staffs. (1904); Kelly's Dir. Staffs. (edns. from 1928 to 1940); S.R.O., D. 3035/1, loose letter of 24 Mar. 1940; O.S. Map 6″, Staffs. LV. SE. (1903 and 1924 edns.); Official Guide: Codsall and Wrottesley [1968], 11.
[17] O.S. Map 6″, Staffs. LV. SE. (1924 edn.); Kelly's Dir. Staffs. (1932; 1936; 1940).
[18] P.R.O., HO 107/2017; P.R.O., RG 9/1984; Kelly's Dir. Staffs. (edns. from 1900 to 1924).
[19] M.A.F.F., agric. returns 1979.
[20] W. F. Crane, Codsall Christmas Annual, 1935, 25 (copy in Wolv. C.L.).
[21] M.A.F.F., agric. returns 1979.
[22] V.C.H. Staffs. iv. 52.
[23] S.H.C. v (1), 115.
[24] S.H.C. 1911, 230; Wolv. C.L., maps 24 and 53; above (agric.).   [25] Yates, Map of Staffs. (1775).
[26] S.R.O., D. 593/T/2/18, memo. of sale of tithes, 2 Aug. 1831; P.R.O., HO 107/1002.
[27] P.R.O., HO 107/2016; P.R.O., RG 9/1984; RG 10/2927.
[28] M.A.F.F., agric. returns 1979.
[29] V.C.H. Staffs. iii. 227.

[30] S.R.O., D. 1492/4/7, deed of 13 Sept. 1809.
[31] S.H.C. xiv (1), 49.
[32] S.R.O., D.(W.) 1766/6, cts. of 16 Oct. 1683, 9 Oct. 1684.
[33] Pat. R. 1225-32, 356; S.H.C. v (1), 115; S.R.O. 3764/95.
[34] S.R.O., D. 743/15, nos. 214, 216.
[35] S.H.C. ix (1), 50.
[36] S.H.C. xvii. 17-18; S.H.C. 1913, 82.
[37] W.S.L. 45/24/56; Codsall Par. Reg. 35.
[38] G. P. Mander and N. W. Tildesley, Hist. of Wolverhampton, 94-5; T. Congreve, Scheme or Proposal for making a Navigable Communication between the Rivers of Trent and Severn in the County of Stafford (1717), 10.
[39] Yates, Map of Staffs. (1775).
[40] S.R.O., D. 743/16-17, no. 1.
[41] Jnl. Staffs. Ind. Arch. Soc. ix. 37.
[42] L. & P. Hen. VIII, xv, p. 287; P.R.O., SC 6/Hen. VIII/3353, m. 46.
[43] W.S.L., D. 1758/506.
[44] S.R.O., D. 1492/9/2; O.S. Map. 6″, Staffs. LV. SE. (edns. of 1886 and 1903).
[45] O.S. Map 6″, Staffs. LVI. SW. (prov. edn. with addns. of 1938); T. H. Whitehead and others, Memoirs of Geol. Surv., Country between Wolverhampton and Oakengates, 137.

Staffordshire district council. At Kingswood a quarry worked in the early 1880s was disused by 1900. There was a quarry, disused in the early 1880s, on the north side of Holyhead Road southwest of Oaken.[46] There were four quarrymen living in Codsall in 1861 and two in 1871.[47] By 1876 there was a stone merchant's firm at Codsall run by Charles Hardware; it was still run by the same family in the late 1930s. Another stone merchant lived at Oaken in the 1880s.[48] Sand was dug at the north end of Codsall Wood and at Kingswood in the early 1880s. Both pits were disused by 1900.[49]

Two brickmakers were living in the parish in 1851 and 1861.[50] A brickworks north of Kingswood common, where there was an exposure of till, existed c. 1900. In 1904 a brick manufacturer named William Collins was living at Oaken. Bricks were probably still being made there in 1915, but the works was apparently disused by 1921.[51]

There may have been a scythesmith living at Bilbrook in the late 16th century, and there was a nailer at Codsall in 1604.[52] Locksmiths at Codsall were recorded during the 18th century, and one lived at Bilbrook in the 1780s.[53] There was a locksmith at Codsall Wood in 1841, one at Codsall in 1861, and one at Oaken in 1871.[54]

There was a ropemaker in the parish in the later 18th century,[55] and a basket maker was living at Codsall Wood in 1841.[56]

There was a soap works in Station Road in the earlier 1920s.[57]

LOCAL GOVERNMENT. Codsall manor was administered as part of the deanery manor of Wolverhampton. From the mid 17th century some deanery courts were held at Codsall to deal with transfers of land there.[58] An aletaster was appointed in 1425 and 1434.[59] A constable was appointed at the October court by the early 1680s; the last appointment recorded was in 1738.[60] A pound was mentioned in 1596. It may have stood against the south wall of the churchyard, where there was a pound in 1850. In the earlier 1880s the pound stood north-west of the churchyard; it had been removed by 1900.[61] A

pinner was appointed in 1699, 1704, and 1738.[62] Stocks in Codsall were still used in 1833.[63]

Courts for the prebendal manor of Codsall were held in the earlier 16th century.[64]

The right of the abbot of Croxden to hold view of frankpledge in his manor of Oaken was confirmed in 1293.[65] No court rolls are known to have survived.

Two churchwardens were recorded in 1553 and 1666 and from the earlier 19th century.[66] There were two overseers of the poor in 1756.[67] There was a poorhouse on the Wolverhampton road east of Codsall village by the late 18th century. The workhouse mentioned in 1823 was presumably the same building. It evidently stood near the Wheel inn where there was a house called the Old Workhouse in 1861.[68]

The parish became part of Seisdon poor-law union in 1836.[69] It was in Seisdon rural district until 1974 when it became part of South Staffordshire district.[70] In 1976 the district council's offices were moved from Wombourne to a new building in Wolverhampton Road, Codsall, designed by the Mason Richards Partnership of Wolverhampton.[71]

CHURCH. Architectural evidence shows that there was a church on the present site by the 12th century. By the later 13th century it was a dependent chapel of the collegiate church of St. Michael in Tettenhall, and belonged to one of the canons as prebendary of Codsall.[72] It was served by a curate, who by custom still went to the mother church at Tettenhall with his cross on the Tuesday in Whitsun week in the earlier 1550s. It was then claimed, however, that weddings, christenings, and burials were conducted at Codsall as in any parish church; burials were evidently conducted there in the 15th century.[73] Codsall remained a parish within the peculiar jurisdiction of Tettenhall until 1846, when such jurisdictions were brought under the bishop's control. Tettenhall's right of probate survived until 1858.[74]

In 1548 the chantry commissioners retained Nicholas Webb as curate.[75] Although Webb claimed in 1554 that he had been admitted c. 1520

[46] O.S. Map 6″, Staffs. LV. SE. (1886 and 1903 edns.).
[47] P.R.O., RG 9/1984; RG 10/2927.
[48] P.O. Dir. Staffs. (1876); Kelly's Dir. Staffs. (edns. from 1880 to 1940).
[49] O.S. Map 6″, Staffs. LV. NE., SE. (1883 and 1903 edns.).
[50] P.R.O., HO 107/2016; P.R.O., RG 9/1984.
[51] O.S. Map 6″, Staffs. LV. SE. (1903 and 1924 edns.); Kelly's Dir. Staffs. (1904); Whitehead, Wolverhampton and Oakengates, 188.
[52] Above, p. 35; S.R.O., D.(W.) 1766/1, ct. of 7 Aug. 1604.
[53] L.J.R.O., P/C/11, John Tonks (1704); S.R.O., D.(W.) 1766/12, ct. of 12 Dec. 1769; 13, ct. of 29 Nov. 1790; Codsall Par. Reg. 205.
[54] P.R.O., HO 107/1002; P.R.O., RG 9/1984; RG 10/2927.
[55] Codsall Par. Reg. 204.
[56] P.R.O., HO 107/1002.
[57] Kelly's Dir. Staffs. (1924).
[58] S.R.O., D. 593/J/5/1/2; D.(W.) 1766/1–28; above, manors and other estates.
[59] S.R.O., D. 593/J/5/1/2, cts. of 18 Sept. 1425, 5 Oct. 1434.
[60] S.R.O., D.(W.) 1766/6–10.
[61] S.H.C. 1932, 227; S.R.O., D. 743/16–17, no. 11; O.S. Map 1/2,500, Staffs. LV. 12 (1884 and 1903 edns.).
[62] S.R.O., D.(W.) 1766/8, cts. of 23 Oct. 1699, 24 Oct. 1704; 10, ct. of 19 Oct. 1738.
[63] Wolv. C.L., DX/37/6, p. 25.
[64] Above, Tettenhall, local govt.
[65] S.H.C. vi (1), 261.
[66] S.H.C. 1915, 72; 1923, 76, 81; L.J.R.O., PTe/V/5.
[67] S.R.O., D. 21/A/PO/72, cert. of 5 Feb. 1756.
[68] Wolv. C.L., DX/37/3, p. 29; P.R.O., RG 9/1984; below, educ.
[69] 3rd Ann. Rep. Poor Law Com. H.C. 546, p. 164 (1837), xxxi.
[70] O.S. Map 1/100,000, Staffs. Admin. Areas (1967 and 1974 edns.).
[71] Express & Star, 20 Jan. 1976; Architecture West Midlands (Sept. 1978), 23.
[72] Above, Tettenhall, manors and other estates (Tettenhall Clericorum).
[73] P.R.O., STAC 4/4/36; S.R.O., D. 593/A/2/5/14. For the customary payment by the inhabitants of Codsall to maintain a lamp in Tettenhall church see above, Tettenhall.
[74] V.C.H. Staffs. iii. 74, 319–20.
[75] S.H.C. 1915, 71–2.

as vicar, he and his successors were described variously as curate or minister.[76] With its endowment from Queen Anne's Bounty in 1756 the living became a perpetual curacy, and from 1868 it was called a vicarage.[77] The patronage was held by the Wrottesley family of Wrottesley in Tettenhall, which acquired most of the property of Tettenhall college in 1549, including the prebend of Codsall. In 1968 the patronage was vested jointly in Lord Wrottesley and the bishop of Lichfield.[78]

In 1548 the prebendary of Codsall was paying Webb £5 a year for serving Codsall; the chantry commissioners gave him the same salary from Crown revenues.[79] No further provision was made when Codsall prebend was sold to Walter Wrottesley. A few years later Webb, who claimed that his stipend before the Dissolution had been £9 or £10, refused to hold services and stated that poverty forced him to abandon the cure. In 1554 a group of his supporters at Codsall sued Wrottesley for an annual contribution out of the tithes. Wrottesley denied any liability, but he was probably compelled to reach some accommodation since Webb was back as curate in 1556.[80] In 1646 Sir Walter Wrottesley stated that he was bound to pay the curate of Codsall £15 a year from the tithes of Codsall and Oaken to augment the £5 stipend paid by the Crown. The government was still paying the curate £5 a year in 1650 and apparently in the early 1660s.[81] In the earlier 18th century the net annual value of the living was £19 10s. 4d.[82] In 1756 a £200 grant was made out of Queen Anne's Bounty by lot; in 1808 a further £200 grant was made to meet a benefaction. A parliamentary grant of £1,200 was made by lot in 1815, and parliamentary grants to meet benefactions were made in 1817 (£300), 1819 (£300), and 1820 (two grants of £300 each). About 1830 the average net income of the living was £146. In 1849 there was a further grant of £200 from Queen Anne's Bounty to meet a benefaction.[83] In 1869 the Ecclesiastical Commissioners granted the benefice £16 13s. 4d. a year out of the Common Fund, and in 1874 the impropriator, the duke of Sutherland, granted the Commissioners a £25 1s. 3d. tithe rent charge to augment the endowment of the living.[84] In 1887 there were 16½ a. of glebe with a gross estimated rental of £49 10s. The living was then worth £260 a year.[85] In 1902 the Ecclesiastical Commissioners granted it a further £125 out of the Common Fund.[86]

In the 1480s and in 1554 there was a house in Codsall known as the parsonage.[87] There was no glebe house in the early 1830s.[88] A house was built south of the church in 1848. It was reduced in size in 1951 and sold in 1979, a new vicarage house having been built in its garden.[89]

Several curates were pluralists. The only one known to have employed an assistant was Matthew Kemsey (1800–46), and then only from 1831 to 1833 or 1834.[90] In the mid 19th century morning and afternoon services were held on Sundays.[91] There was a parish magazine by the early 20th century.[92]

The mission church of St. John the Baptist, a building of stone with a bellcot at the west end, was built on Kingswood common in 1861. The site was given by Lord Wrottesley to the incumbents of Codsall, Tettenhall, Albrighton (Salop.), and Boningale (Salop.), each of whom was responsible for services every fourth Sunday or on other agreed days. From the beginning of the Second World War it was served from Tettenhall. The church was closed c. 1979.[93] In 1983 it was being converted into a private house.

Services were being held in a house at Codsall Wood by 1873.[94] St. Peter's church in Whitehouse Lane was built as a mission room in 1885 on land given by W. T. C. Giffard of Chillington Hall in Brewood. In 1906 it was licensed for the celebration of Holy Communion. In 1925–6 a chancel was added at the expense of Frank Gaskell of Pendrell Hall.[95] The church is a building of red brick with a south-west bellcot.

The mission church of Holy Cross in Bilbrook Road, Bilbrook, was transferred from Tettenhall parish to Codsall in 1959. It became a district church in 1979.[96]

The present church of *ST. NICHOLAS*, an invocation in use by the 15th century,[97] dates from 1849. The former church was rebuilt that year, with the exception of the tower.

The medieval church consisted of a chancel, a nave of five bays with a north aisle, a west tower, and probably a south porch. The nave evidently dated from the 12th century: the present south doorway is Norman and was re-used in 1849. The chancel was of the 12th or early 13th century. The tower was built in the 14th century, and the north aisle was probably added in that century also. The east window of the chancel and the windows on the south side of the nave were enlarged in the 14th or 15th century. It was probably then, and certainly after the building of the tower, that the church was reroofed; the massive carved timbers were noted in the 18th

[76] P.R.O., STAC 4/4/36; *Codsall Par. Reg.* 7–9.
[77] L.J.R.O., PPe/A/4A, 28 Dec. 1797; *Lich. Dioc. Ch. Cal.* (1869), 90.
[78] Lich. Dioc. Regy., Reg. of Transfer of Patronage, ff. 160, 170; above, Tettenhall, manors and other estates (Tettenhall Clericorum).
[79] *V.C.H. Staffs.* iii. 319; *S.H.C.* 1915, 72.
[80] P.R.O., STAC 4/4/36.
[81] *S.H.C.* 1915, 72; W.S.L., S.MS. 339 (transcripts of Royalist Composition Papers), vi, pp. 658, 660–1; P.R.O., E 134/17 Chas. II Mich./2.
[82] J. Ecton, *Thesaurus Rerum Ecclesiasticarum* (1742), 110.
[83] Hodgson, *Queen Anne's Bounty*, p. ccxcvi; ibid. *Supplement*, p. lxvii; *Rep. Com. Eccl. Revenues*, 470–1.
[84] Lich. Dioc. Regy., B/A/2i/R, p. 375; S, p. 88.
[85] *Returns relating to Glebe Lands in Eng. and Wales*, H.C. 307, p. 63 (1887), lxiv.
[86] Lich. Dioc. Regy., B/A/2i/U, p. 528.
[87] P.R.O., STAC 4/4/36.
[88] *Rep. Com. Eccl. Revenues*, 470–1.
[89] R. H. Gaskell, *St. Nicholas' Church, Codsall* (2nd edn.); S.R.O., D. 743/16–17, no. 8; inf. from the diocesan registrar.
[90] *Codsall Par. Reg.* 6–8; L.J.R.O., PTe/V/4.
[91] P.R.O., HO 129/379/1/1.
[92] The earliest surviving copy in the set in Codsall Libr. is for Apr. 1907.
[93] S.R.O., D. 1364/4/31–2; inf. from the vicar. It last appears in *Lich. Dioc. Dir.* in the 1978 edn., p. 144.
[94] *Wolverhampton Chron.* 3 Dec. 1873.
[95] *Codsall Par. Mag.* (Apr., Sept. 1925, July 1926).
[96] Inf. from the dioc. registrar; above, Tettenhall, churches.
[97] S.R.O., D. 593/A/2/5/14.

century. At an indeterminate date a south porch was added.[98] There was an octagonal font, probably of the 14th century. It was moved from the church, probably in 1849, and in 1908 was placed in the churchyard, where it remained in 1983.[99] In the late 16th and earlier 17th century part of the church was known as the Wrottesley chapel; it may have been the chancel, on the north side of which the altar tomb of Walter Wrottesley (d. 1630) was erected. The monument was replaced in the same position in the church of 1849.[1] A new pulpit was installed in 1627.[2] Briefs for rebuilding the church were issued in 1803 and 1806,[3] but the only work known to have been done in the early 19th century was the restoration of the lancet windows in the south wall of the nave and the removal of the south porch.[4]

In 1849 the body of the church was rebuilt in local sandstone to the design of Edward Banks of Wolverhampton. It consists of a chancel with north-east vestries, a nave of five bays with north and south aisles, and a south porch; the west tower was repaired.[5] A ringers' gallery was installed in the tower in 1936. In 1958 the church was restored by Bernard Miller of Liverpool. At the same time the vestry was made into a choir vestry and a new vestry was constructed. The gallery was removed and the chancel repaired.[6]

There were three bells and a sanctus bell in 1552 and 1553. In the late 18th century there were six bells, of which four had been cast in 1637 and two in 1638. Two were recast in 1815 and 1867. All six were recast in 1936, and at the same time two new bells were added.[7] In 1552 and 1553 the plate consisted of a silver chalice and paten; there were also a brass cross and a brass censer. In 1983 the plate included a silver chalice dated 1592, a silver tray of 1767, and a silver cup and lid of 1771-2 given in 1786 by William Barrett of Westminster.[8]

The churchyard was mentioned in the 15th century.[9] Extensions were consecrated in 1868, 1894, 1937, 1960, and 1982.[10]

The registers date from 1587 and are complete.[11]

ROMAN CATHOLICISM. Four recusants in Codsall were returned in 1641.[12] There were five c. 1670, three of them at Codsall and two at Oaken.[13] Thirteen adults and three children were listed in 1705 and 1706, all 'tenants or paupers'. There were 29 papists in 1767.[14]

From 1931 mass was said on alternate Sundays at a Codsall teashop. Initially the mass centre was served from the church of St. Mary and St. John, Wolverhampton, but in 1932 it became the responsibility of the priest at Tettenhall.[15] In 1934 the church of St. Christopher was opened in Wolverhampton Road, Codsall. It was built by Louis Connolly of Wolverhampton as a memorial to his wife Henrietta. It was served from Tettenhall until 1961 when it was given a resident priest. The church was extended in the early 1960s.[16]

PROTESTANT NONCONFORMITY. In 1672 Henry Osland, who had been ejected from Bewdley (Worcs.), was licensed as a Presbyterian teacher at Oaken, and the house of Roger Hickman at Oaken was licensed for Presbyterian worship. Richard Mase's house at Oaken may have been licensed for Congregational worship.[17]

In 1691 a Wolverhampton woman was buried at 'the Quakers' place near Oaken'. Presumably it was the small piece of land at Oaken which Richard Chandler or Chandless offered to the Friends in 1692 for use as a burial ground. In 1695 the land, which lay in Middle Lane next to the donor's house, was conveyed to Quaker trustees. A weekly meeting of Friends was being held at Oaken, perhaps in the house adjoining the burial ground, in 1696. That year the Friends' Staffordshire Quarterly Meeting discussed moving it elsewhere and left the final decision to the Wolverhampton weekly meeting. No further reference to a meeting at Oaken has been found. The burial ground continued to be held in trust until 1851 when it was sold. Burials may have ceased in 1704, when the Friends at Wolverhampton acquired their own burial ground.[18]

The dwelling house at Codsall Wood registered for dissenting worship in 1791[19] may have been for Methodists. By 1823 Primitive Methodist preachers were visiting Codsall,[20] and in 1825 the Primitive Methodists built a small chapel in Codsall village east of the crossroads.[21] The cause subsequently lapsed. The Wesleyan Methodists preached for a short time at Kingswood in the early 1820s but had no success until a preacher

[98] W.S.L., Staffs. Views, iii. 131-4; Shaw, Staffs. ii. 288.
[99] W.S.L., Staffs. Views, iii. 130; Codsall Par. Mag. (Mar. 1908); Gaskell, St. Nicholas' Church.
[1] Codsall Par. Reg. 14-56 passim; Shaw, Staffs. ii. 288; T.B.A.S. lxxi. 21-2.
[2] Shaw, Staffs. ii. 289.
[3] W. A. Bewes, Church Briefs, 349, 351; B.L., Ch. Br. B. xliii. 4; xlvii. 4.
[4] Gent. Mag. lxvii (1), pl. facing p. 17.
[5] P.R.O., HO 129/379/1/1; L.J.R.O., B/C/5/1849, Codsall; S.R.O., D. 1353/13; Gaskell, St. Nicholas' Church; above, econ. hist.
[6] Gaskell, St. Nicholas' Church.
[7] S.H.C. N.S. vi (1), 188; S.H.C. 1915, 72; Shaw, Staffs. ii. 289; plaque in tower.
[8] S.H.C. N.S. vi (1), 188; S.H.C. 1915, 72; T.B.A.S. lxxiii. 8-9, 34-5.
[9] S.R.O., D. 593/A/2/5/14.
[10] Lich. Dioc. Regy., B/A/2i/R, pp. 351-4; T, pp. 528, 562-5; W, pp. 376, 596; X, pp. 464-5; inf. from the vicar.
[11] All except those in current use are in S.R.O., D. 743, D. 1353, D. 3793; they have been printed for baptisms and burials to 1812 and for marriages to 1843 by the Staffs. Par. Reg. Soc. (1962-3).
[12] Staffs. Cath. Hist. v. 18.
[13] Miscellanea, v (Cath. Rec. Soc. vi), 310.
[14] Staffs. Cath. Hist. xiii. 16-17; xvii. 15-16.
[15] Archdioc. of Birmingham Dir. (1932), 85; (1933), 85; (1934), 93; Express & Star, 5 Jan. 1931.
[16] Archdioc. of Birmingham Dir. (1935), 96, 170; W. F. Crane, Codsall Christmas Annual, 1935, 39 (copy in Wolv. C.L.); Archdioc. of Birmingham Dir. (1966), 190-1.
[17] G. L. Turner, Orig. Rec. of Early Nonconf. ii. 747 (giving 'Gickmaw' where Hickman is presumably meant), 751; A. G. Matthews, Cong. Churches of Staffs. 91 (giving 'Gukman'), 93; above, p. 83.
[18] S.R.O., D. 1157/1/1/61, 27 Apr. 1691; S.R.O., D. 3159/1/1, nos. 271-2, 276, 280, 286, 293, 296, 302, 321, and 'Abstract of Public Writings'; Trans. S. Staffs. Arch. & Hist. Soc. xii. 43, 47.
[19] S.H.C. 4th ser. iii. 131.
[20] Wolv. C.L., DX/37/2, p. 169.
[21] P.R.O., HO 129/379/1/1; S.R.O., D. 743/16-17, no. 57; Wesley Hist. Soc., W. Midlands Branch, Bulletin, i. 45.

from Bilston, William Hackett, visited Codsall in 1823. It was not until 1841 that a Wesleyan cause was established, served from Wolverhampton. The former Primitive Methodist chapel was leased, and in the 1850s and 1860s there were afternoon and evening services on Sundays, with one weekday service a month.[22] In 1851 average attendance was 12 on Sunday afternoon and 26 in the evening.[23] The cause did not flourish, and in 1876, when the Wesleyans could no longer afford the rent, the chapel was given up.[24]

In 1872 a group of local Free Churchmen meeting at Codsall decided to build in the village a chapel open to all nonconformists.[25] Trinity Free Church was built in 1873-4 on the corner of Broadway and Chapel Lane to the design of J. R. Veall, a Wolverhampton architect who lived at Codsall Wood.[26] Among those responsible for the scheme was S. S. Mander of Tettenhall, a leading member of Queen Street Congregational church, Wolverhampton, who in the mid 1860s had been involved in an attempt to set up a Congregational mission at Codsall.[27] Trinity Church was conveyed to trustees and its management given to a committee, annually elected by the members; admission to membership was by a majority vote of the existing members. There was no ordained minister in charge, preaching was by laymen, and the Sacrament was available to all Christians. The church remained without a minister until 1936, when a retired Methodist missionary became full-time minister on the committee's appointment. When he retired from Trinity Church in 1951 he was succeeded by another Methodist minister, and in 1956 the church joined the Wolverhampton (Trinity) circuit and became Trinity Methodist Church. In 1967 the congregation moved to a new church in Histons Hill designed by J. Seymour Harris & Partners of Edgbaston, Birmingham.[28] The former chapel was demolished in 1968.[29]

EDUCATION. In 1554 Sir John Giffard of Chillington, in Brewood, stated that he had known Codsall church since the 1480s, when he went to school there.[30] Presumably the curate kept a school or took private pupils. William Tonks, an unlicensed schoolmaster in 1668, seems to have taught in Codsall.[31]

Dorothy Derby (d. 1720), the daughter of Alexander Persehouse of Wood Hall, left £20,

the interest to be used for teaching poor children in Codsall to read the Bible.[32] A similar bequest was made by Margaret Somerford (d. 1730).[33] In 1770 trustees used Dorothy Derby's legacy and the Revd. John Hellman's bequest to the poor to buy a cottage and land on the Wolverhampton road. The cottage was burnt down c. 1790 and rebuilt as a poorhouse. It was leased to the parish for £6 10s. of which £3 was paid to a master for teaching six poor children to read. Margaret Somerford's legacy remained at interest in private hands until 1787, when principal and interest were vested in trustees and used to buy stock. The income, 16s. 8d., was paid to a mistress who taught four poor children to read. On the death of the managing trustee in 1815 the charity lapsed for several years.[34]

In 1818 a National school was built by subscription at the corner of Church Road and Church Lane. Within a year there were 129 pupils. Most of the school's income came from subscriptions and school pence, but c. £4 from Derby's and Somerford's charities was used to provide a free education for eight poor children.[35] In 1833 there were 45 boys and 66 girls, taught by a master and a mistress. There was an average of 110 pupils in 1861; fees were then 2d. a week for one child and 4d. for two or more children from the same family.[36] A new school was built in 1864 on a site north of the church bought in 1863. The cost was met by subscription, government grant, the sale of the former site, and half the proceeds of the sale of cottages belonging to Derby's and Hellman's charities.[37] The school was receiving an annual government grant by 1869-70. The average attendance was 178 in 1879-80 and 219 in 1884-5.[38] An infants' department was built c. 1885 and extended in 1913.[39] The average attendance at the school was 248 in 1907.[40] The school moved to new buildings in Chillington Drive in 1965. As St. Nicholas's C. of E. controlled first school it had an average attendance of 199 in 1983.[41] From 1944 a moiety of Derby and Hellman's charities, £1.20 in the early 1980s, and Margaret Somerford's charity, then 68p, were paid to the Sunday school.[42]

A mixed National school for 50 children, with a mistress's house, was added to the mission church at Kingswood c. 1874. In the mid 1890s there was an average attendance of 30. There were only 10 children on the roll when Mrs. M. L. Shaw, who had been mistress since 1911,

[22] A. C. Pratt, *Black Country Methodism*, 82; Wolv. C.L., MC/DS/5B-0, 51.
[23] P.R.O., HO 129/379/1/1.
[24] Pratt, *Black Country Methodism*, 82-3; Wolv. C.L., MC/DS/55; G.R.O., Worship Reg. 3704.
[25] Para. based on Wesley Hist. Soc., W. Midlands Branch, *Bulletin*, i. 45-6; *Codsall* (coronation brochure, 1953), 27-8 (copy in W.S.L. Pamphs.).
[26] *Builder*, 24 Jan. 1874; *Wolverhampton Chron.* 3 Dec. 1873.
[27] S.R.O., D. 1206/1/41, 24 Nov. 1865, 10 Dec. 1866, 17 June 1867.
[28] *Wolverhampton Mag.* (Dec. 1967), 16.
[29] Inf. from the minister.
[30] P.R.O., STAC 4/4/36.
[31] L.J.R.O., D/C/1/1, *acta* of 15 Oct. 1668, 7 June 1669.
[32] *5th Rep. Com. Char.* 615, stating that the bequest was made by will in 1716; *Codsall Par. Reg.* 145; Brooke Robinson, *Geneal. Memoirs of Fam. of Brooke Robinson, of Dudley* (priv. print. 1896), 205.

[33] *5th Rep. Com. Char.* 615; *Codsall Par. Reg.* 149.
[34] *5th Rep. Com. Char.* 615; S.R.O., D.(W.) 1766/21, ct. of 3 Oct. 1864.
[35] *5th Rep. Com. Char.* 615; *Digest of Returns to Sel. Cttee. on Educ. of Poor*, H.C. 224, p. 858 (1819), ix (2); White, *Dir. Staffs.* (1834), 255; S.R.O., D. 743/16-17, no. 20.
[36] *Educ. Enq. Abstract*, H.C. 62, p. 874 (1835), xlii; P.R.O., ED 7/108/98.
[37] *Codsall Chars. Scheme* (1860), 13 (copy in S.R.O., D. 660/24/16); *Rep. of Educ. Cttee. of Council, 1864-5* [3533], p. 510, H.C. (1865), xlii; S.R.O., D. 812/2/66-8; *Staffs. Endowed Chars.* 41.
[38] *Rep. of Educ. Cttee. of Council, 1869-70* [C. 165], p. 641, H.C. (1870), xxii; *1879-80* [C. 2562-I], p. 688, H.C. (1880), xxii; *1884-5* [C. 4483-I], p. 623, H.C. (1884-5), xxiii.
[39] S.R.O., D. 3793/8-9; P.R.O., C 54/18937, no. 7, m. 8; *Codsall Par. Mag.* Jan., Apr., July 1913.
[40] *Public Elem. Schs. 1907* [Cd. 3901], p. 565, H.C. (1908), lxxiv.   [41] Inf. from the headmaster.
[42] Inf. from Mr. Blamire Brown.

retired in 1947, and the school was then closed.[43] There was a National school with a mistress at Codsall Wood in 1851.[44]

A secondary school, later Codsall high school, was opened in Eliotts Lane in 1940. The buildings were extended in the later 1950s.[45] The residential development in Codsall after the Second World War has resulted in the opening of new schools: the Birches first school in Birches Avenue (1959), Histons Hill first school in Histons Hill (1962), St. Christopher's R.C. (aided) primary school (1972), and Codsall middle school in Wolverhampton Road (1976).[46]

Thomas Richmond and his wife Mary, who had kept a school at Albrighton (Salop.) since 1800, moved it to Codsall House in 1815. It was mainly, but not exclusively, for Roman Catholic children; it was principally a boarding school for girls, although day girls were also accepted, and by 1819 the Richmonds were advertising for boys aged 5–10. Richmond was the author of a French grammar and translated devotional works from the French. In 1822 the school adopted the system of teaching devised by the educational reformer James Perry. It had 35 pupils in 1823 and 31 in 1833. In 1834 Richmond sold the school to a Mrs. Perry and her two daughters, who had run a Roman Catholic school at Bloxwich, in Walsall, since 1829.[47] The Misses Perry gave up the school to the sisters Maryann and Emma Fairbanks some time between 1835 and 1841. In 1841 the Fairbanks sisters had 11 girl boarders; in 1851 there were 13, and the sisters employed three resident teachers.[48] The school had closed by 1861.[49]

There was another day and boarding school in the parish in 1833, with 12 boys and 7 girls.[50] In the later 1870s there was a girls' school at Oaken, and in the late 1890s and early 1900s one in a house near the church.[51] A private school in Mill Lane called Clare College existed in the 1930s and 1940s.[52] In the late 1960s there were two private nursery schools. There was also a preparatory school in Histons Hill, which closed c. 1980.[53]

CHARITIES FOR THE POOR. In 1602 Walter Wrottesley gave the parish £30. A cottage and land in Codsall were bought, the income from

which was distributed to the poor. In 1726 it was found that for some years the trustees and churchwardens had been retaining or misapplying the income. In 1820 the endowment consisted of two cottages, in which paupers were placed by the parish rent free, and land producing £27 16s. 6d. a year, which was distributed to the poor in cash.[54]

John Brooke of Blakeland, in Bobbington, perhaps the man of that name who died in 1640, gave a cottage and land in Codsall, the income to be used for repairs to the church, the relief of the poor, or other useful purposes. By 1820 the £9 income went into the churchwardens' general account, none being used for the poor.[55]

William Greasley (d. 1705) gave £2 a year, charged on land in Codsall, for the use of the poor. In 1820 it was distributed with Wrottesley's charity.[56]

The Revd. John Hellman or Hillman (d. 1726) left £20 to buy land, the income to be used for the relief of the poor. In 1770 the money, with £20 left by Dorothy Derby to endow an educational charity, was laid out on a cottage and land in Codsall. By 1820 £3 10s. of the income was distributed with Wrottesley's charity.[57]

William Barrett of Westminster (d. 1801) left £400 stock, the interest to be used to provide bread for the poor on Sundays. In 1820 twenty-eight poor each received a 2d. loaf.[58]

A scheme of 1860 established a body of trustees for the parochial charities. The income from the charities of Wrottesley and Greasley and half that from the charity of Derby and Hellman was to be distributed to the poor of Codsall in cash or in kind. The income from Barrett's charity was to be spent on bread as before. That from Brooke's charity was to be paid into the general funds of the church. In the early 1980s the income from the eleemosynary charities was distributed among some 20 elderly men and women in cash at Christmas and Easter. The income of Walter Wrottesley's charity was then £60, that of Greasley's £2, and that of Barrett's £10. A moiety of Derby and Hellman's charity amounted to £1.20.[59]

Charles Wrottesley (d. 1907) left £200 to establish a charity for the benefit of widows and the aged in Oaken. In the early 1980s the income was £6.08.[60]

[43] Kelly's Dir. Staffs. (1896); S.R.O., D. 1364/6/13, copy of Tettenhall par. mag. Jan. 1948 and enclosed press-cutting.
[44] White, Dir. Staffs. (1851), 174.
[45] S.R.O., CEK/10/1. [46] Inf. from the headteachers.
[47] Staffs. Cath. Hist. xx. 32–9.
[48] Pigot, Nat. Com. Dir. (1835), 482; P.R.O., HO 107/1002 and 2017. [49] Above, manors and other estates (Codsall).
[50] Educ. Enq. Abstract, 874.
[51] P.O. Dir. Staffs. (1876); Kelly's Dir. Staffs. (edns. from 1896 to 1908).
[52] Kelly's Dir. Staffs. (1932; 1936; 1940); W. F. Crane, Codsall Christmas Annual, 1935, 25 (copy in Wolv. C.L.); local inf.

[53] Official Guide: Codsall and Wrottesley [1968], 4, 19; inf. from the headmaster of St. Nicholas's first school.
[54] 5th Rep. Com. Char. 613–14; P.R.O., C 93/54, no. 10.
[55] 5th Rep. Com. Char. 616; above, Bobbington, manor and other estates.
[56] 5th Rep. Com. Char. 614–15; S.H.C. ns. i. 211.
[57] 5th Rep. Com. Char. 615; Codsall Par. Reg. 7; above, educ.
[58] 5th Rep. Com. Char. 616; memorial to Barrett in church.
[59] Codsall Charities Scheme (1860; copy in S.R.O., D. 660/24/16); inf. from Mr. Blamire Brown.
[60] Codsall Par. Mag. (July 1907); inf. from Mr. Blamire Brown.

ENVILLE

THE ancient parish of Enville, 4,986 a. (2,018 ha.) in area,[61] lies on the county boundary with Shropshire. It is rural in character with the grounds of Enville Hall a major feature. The spellings Enfeld, Enveld, and other variants, in use until the late 18th century,[62] derive from Old English words meaning 'smooth field',[63] presumably a reference to the flat ground in the east of the parish. The spelling Envill was used by Christopher Saxton (1577) and some later mapmakers. From the late 18th century the spelling Enville was adopted.[64]

A fault runs diagonally through the parish from north-east to south-west. East of the fault the land is flat, lying between 279 ft. (85 m.) and 216 ft. (66 m.). To the west it is undulating, its height falling from 361 ft. (110 m.) in the north-eastern corner to 321 ft. (98 m.) at Lutley in the north and to 288 ft. (88 m.) at Enville village in the centre of the parish. It rises to 484 ft. (147 m.) at Coxgreen in the west and to 670 ft. (204 m.) at No Man's Green in the south-west. Much of the parish boundary with Bobbington is marked by tumps or mounds of earth which existed by the earlier 19th century.[65] An arm of Philley brook forms part of the north-west boundary. In the east the boundary follows Spittle brook and the line of a dried-up tributary. Mill brook forms part of the south-east boundary. Much of the eastern boundary follows Chester Road. The underlying rock is sandstone and breccia. East of the fault the soil is clay; to the west it is generally sandy.[66]

The parish lay in Kinver forest,[67] and the pattern of settlement, a small village and numerous scattered farmhouses, is characteristic of a forest area. Three manors covered the parish: Enville and Morfe, which were settlements in the Anglo-Saxon period, and Lutley, which existed by the mid 12th century. Enville manor lay in the southern half of the parish. To the north of it lay Morfe; the name is of Celtic origin.[68] A tongue of land in the south-western corner of the parish, which included the Hollies, also belonged to Morfe manor. Part of the boundary between Enville and Morfe manors was marked by Sneyd's brook. By the later 12th century the land along the boundary with Bobbington in the north formed Lutley manor. The name Lutley means a small clearing or open space in woodland,[69] and

the area may have been originally part of the extensive woodland in Morfe manor recorded in 1086.[70] Part of Philley brook west of Mere mill divided Morfe and Lutley manors.[71]

In 1086 the recorded population of Enville was 7. There was no recorded population at Morfe, which was then waste.[72] In 1327 Enville had 22 people assessed for tax, Morfe 17, and Lutley 14.[73] In the mid 1520s 57 people in the parish were assessed for tax, and 36 names appeared on the muster roll of 1539.[74] In 1563 there were 41 households.[75] The poll-tax assessment of 1641 listed 219 people.[76] In 1666 ninety-five people were assessed for hearth tax, and a further 29 were too poor to pay.[77] The Compton Census of 1676 returned 500 parishioners.[78] The population was 799 in 1801 and 842 in 1821. It had fallen to 766 by 1831 but risen to 814 by 1841. After reaching 850 in 1861, it declined steadily to 645 in 1901. A rise to 712 in 1911 gave way to another steady decline, the population falling to 657 in 1921, 642 in 1931, 605 in 1951, 515 in 1961, and 468 in 1971.[79]

Enville village lies on the Stourbridge-Bridgnorth road at the foot of a steep ridge. The church stands on top of the ridge. In 1688 the village comprised four houses on the main road, including the Crown inn which existed by 1642 and possibly by 1582, and a further four houses around a green called Bar green on a road running south to Enville Hall from the main road. Another house stood at the foot of the ridge in Blundies Lane.[80] By the later 18th century Bar green had been taken into the hall grounds and most of the houses in the village lay on either side of the main road.[81] The village then had two inns: the Swan, mentioned in 1752,[82] and the Cat, mentioned in 1777.[83] In 1841 there were 15 households in the village and another two on the road to the hall.[84] There was little change until the period between the two World Wars when 10 council houses were built on the north side of Blundies Lane; six privately built houses on the north side of the lane date from the 1960s.[85]

Leigh House farm west of Enville Hall existed by the mid 15th century.[86] It stood on Legh Lane which in the late 17th century ran south-west from Bar green. The lane, although realigned, still existed in the later 18th century but was soon

[61] *Census*, 1971. This article was written in 1981-2. Miss L. Amphlett of Four Ashes Hall, Mrs. E. Bissill of Enville Hall, the Revd. A. A. Collins, rector of Enville, Mr. J. A. Gloss of Whitegates, Enville, Mr. M. J. Scott-Bolton, agent for the Enville Estate, and others named in footnotes are thanked for their help.

[62] S.R.O., Tp. 1273/12; S.R.O., D. 42/A/PZ/18-54.

[63] Ekwall, *Eng. Place-Names*.

[64] *Companion to the Leasowes, Hagley, and Enville* (1789); Shaw, *Staffs*. ii. 268 sqq.; Pitt, *Staffs*. i. 199.

[65] Above, Bobbington, introduction.

[66] T. H. Whitehead and R. W. Pocock, *Memoirs of Geol. Surv., Dudley and Bridgnorth*, 97, 101-2, 128, 166, 180; *P.O. Dir. Staffs*. (1872).

[67] Below, econ. hist.

[68] *Eng. Place-Name Elements* (E.P.N.S.), ii. 37, 185.

[69] Ekwall, *Eng. Place-Names*.

[70] Below, econ. hist. (agric.).

[71] Salop. R.O. 2089/ADD, descrip. of Lutley manor bounds 1744.   [72] *V.C.H. Staffs*. iv. 54.

[73] *S.H.C.* vii (1), 252.

[74] P.R.O., E 179/177/106; *S.H.C.* n.s. vi (1), 69-70.

[75] *S.H.C.* 1915, p. lxx.

[76] H.L., Main Papers, box 178.

[77] *S.H.C.* 1923, 77-9.

[78] W.S.L., S.MS. 33, p. 371.

[79] *V.C.H. Staffs*. i. 326; *Census*, 1911-71.

[80] S.R.O. 1392; S.R.O., Tp. 1273/8, deed of 7 June 1642; Tp. 1273/12/5, nos. 3, 8.

[81] S.R.O., Tp 1273/54, plan of Enville Hall grounds *c.* 1750 (redrawn below, p. 100); Yates, *Map of Staffs.* (1775).

[82] *Aris's Birmingham Gaz*. 6 Apr. 1752.

[83] S.R.O., D. 42/A/PC/1.

[84] P.R.O., HO 107/1002.

[85] Inf. from Mr. Scott-Bolton.

[86] Below, manors and other estates.

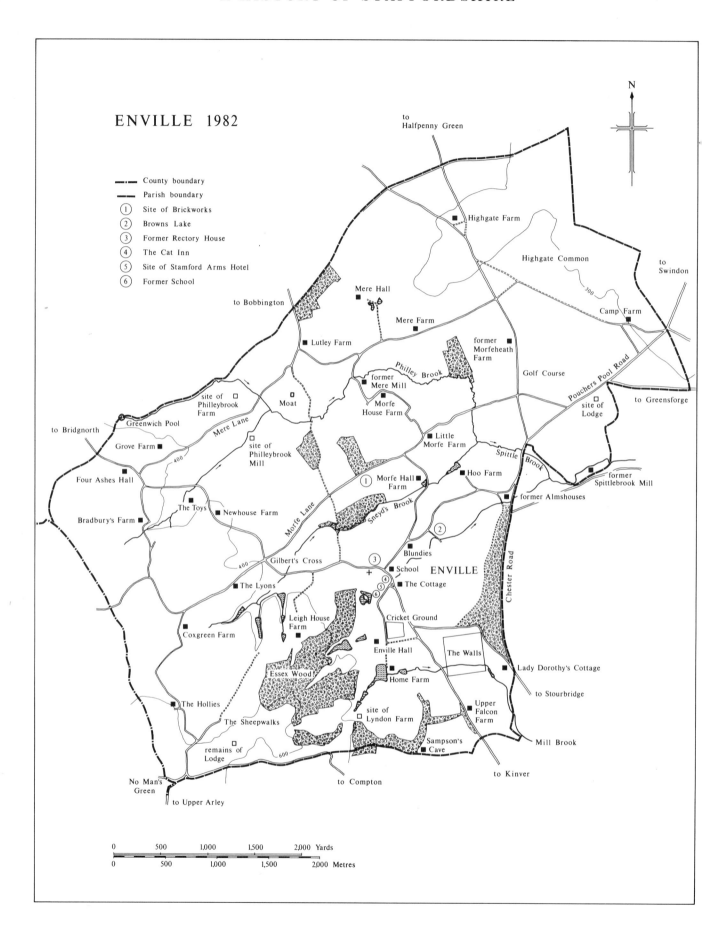

ENVILLE 1982

-·-·— County boundary
——— Parish boundary
① Site of Brickworks
② Browns Lake
③ Former Rectory House
④ The Cat Inn
⑤ Site of Stamford Arms Hotel
⑥ Former School

N

to Halfpenny Green

Highgate Farm

Highgate Common

to Swindon

Camp Farm

to Bobbington

Mere Hall

Mere Farm

former Morfeheath Farm

Golf Course

Pouchers Pool Road

Lutley Farm

Philley Brook

former Mere Mill

300

site of Philleybrook Farm

Moat

Morfe House Farm

site of Lodge

to Greensforge

Mere Lane

Greenwich Pool

to Bridgnorth

Grove Farm

site of Philleybrook Mill

Little Morfe Farm

Spittle Brook

former Spittlebrook Mill

400

① Morfe Hall Farm

Hoo Farm

former Almshouses

Four Ashes Hall

The Toys

Newhouse Farm

Morfe Lane

Sneyd's Brook

②

Bradbury's Farm

Blundies

Chester Road

400

Gilbert's Cross

③

School

ENVILLE

The Lyons

④
⑤
⑥ The Cottage

Coxgreen Farm

Leigh House Farm

Cricket Ground

Enville Hall

The Walls

Lady Dorothy's Cottage

Essex Wood

Home Farm

to Stourbridge

The Hollies

The Sheepwalks

site of Lyndon Farm

Upper Falcon Farm

Mill Brook

remains of Lodge

600

Sampson's Cave

to Kinver

No Man's Green

to Compton

to Upper Arley

| 0 | 500 | 1,000 | 1,500 | 2,000 Yards |

| 0 | 500 | 1,000 | 1,500 | 2,000 Metres |

after taken into Enville Hall grounds.[87] South of Leigh House it passed over an area of high ground known as the Sheepwalks. Because of its name the area has been suggested as a possible site for the pre-Conquest settlement of 'Cippemore', which was waste in 1086; the name probably means sheep moor or shepherd moor.[88] The name Sheepwalks, however, is not found until *c.* 1800,[89] and in the 17th century the area was known simply as 'the hills'.[90] None the less there was settlement on the Sheepwalks by 1327 when a William de la Hull was mentioned.[91] The Hull, later Hillhouse, was still inhabited in 1692.[92] There was also a warrener's lodge on the southern edge of the Sheepwalks, probably by 1623.[93]

There was settlement at Lyndon south of Enville Hall by 1312.[94] Lyndon Farm was one of five houses there in 1663;[95] it was demolished *c.* 1961.[96] A rock house called Sampson's Cave on the parish boundary south of Lyndon was constructed by Sampson Allen, who was alive in 1768; in 1770 it was occupied by Thomas Brook. It was still inhabited in 1861 and evidently remained in use into the 20th century.[97] Upper Falcon Farm east of Lyndon had been built by 1688.[98] Lady Dorothy's Cottage north-east of the farm was built in 1755 as a charity school.[99] The area known as the Walls, north of the farm, takes its name from a retreat created by Harry Grey, earl of Stamford (d. 1739), on what was then part of the common. The earl, believing lime unwholesome, built a small wooden house there; it was struck by lightning in 1728, and he built another house with several rooms and a cellar. He enclosed it with a high brick wall forming a square with sides of 400 yd.[1] The site is on a ridge overlooking a small valley to the south and the hills beyond. In 1982 the house no longer stood, but much of the wall survived.

A settlement called Hoo in the later 13th century[2] may be identified with Blundies north-east of Enville village: the Blundel family, from whom the name Blundies evidently derives, was living in Enville parish at that date, and land once held by a Walter Blundel was recorded in the hamlet of 'la Hoo' in 1323.[3] A messuage called Blundells *c.* 1527[4] may have been the present Blundies farmhouse, which incorporates one wing of a 16th- or 17th-century timber-framed house; the rest of the house was rebuilt in brick in the 18th and 19th centuries. Another partly timber-framed farmhouse stood north of Blundies

Farm in the late 18th century;[5] it was probably demolished soon after Lord Stamford bought it in 1811.[6] There were other houses along, and to the south of, the road to Hoo Farm in the late 18th century.[7] Those to the south may have made up a subsidiary settlement called Over Hoo; land at Over Hoo was recorded in 1313, and there was a messuage there by 1446.[8] The houses were probably demolished in the early 19th century after property in that area had been bought up by Lord Stamford.[9] In 1841 there were eight families living at Blundies, one of them at Blundies Farm and the others presumably in the cottages around the junction of the roads to Morfe and Hoo Farm.[10] In the mid 1950s 12 council houses were built in Browns Lake and at its junction with Blundies Lane. A further four council bungalows in Blundies Lane and four council houses in Brookside off Browns Lake date from 1963.[11]

Hoo Farm north-east of Blundies incorporates one wing of a 16th- or 17th-century timber-framed house; the brick front was added in the early 19th century. Further east there was a house on Chester Road south of Spittle brook by 1775;[12] in the late 18th and early 19th century it was occupied as the Cock inn and subsequently used as the workhouse. The three council houses further south were originally built as poorhouses in the early 19th century.[13]

Although the manor of Morfe was described as waste in 1086, the area may not have been depopulated. Mere mill on Philley brook may have existed by 1222,[14] and Morfe Hall Farm to the south on Sneyd's brook may stand on or near the site of the medieval manor house.[15] A small settlement grew up around the junction of Morfe Lane and the road from Enville: two timber-framed cottages, dating probably from the 17th century, survive there, and there were a few houses nearby in 1775.[16] In 1841 there were 19 families living at Morfe, evidently at Morfe House Farm and to the south; a further eight families lived near Morfe Hall Farm.[17] Little Morfe Farm at the junction of Morfe Lane and the road from Enville was built in 1852.[18] There was little subsequent change: the farmhouses and most of the cottages, or their 20th-century replacements, still stood in 1982. The part of Morfe manor east of Chester Road was waste land until the 17th century. A warrener's lodge stood on the waste near Pouchers Pool, probably by 1623.[19] After the waste was inclosed in 1683, two farms

[87] S.R.O., Tp. 1273/54, plan of Enville Hall grounds *c.* 1750; Yates, *Map of Staffs.* (1775); R. Baugh, *Map of Salop.* (1808).
[88] *V.C.H. Staffs.* iv. 54; *Eng. Place-Name Elements*, ii. 42–3, 100–1.
[89] Shaw, *Staffs.* ii. 271 (calling it the Sheep Walk); B.L. Maps, O.S.D. 214 (calling it Sheepwalks).
[90] S.R.O., Tp. 1273/6, undated survey of Enville manor; 11, 1623 survey; 40, deed of 23 Mar. 1691/2.
[91] *S.H.C.* vii (1), 252.
[92] S.R.O., Tp. 1273/11, Enville cts. of 14 Mar. 1593/4 and 15 Oct. 1603, and 1623 survey; 40, deed of 23 Mar. 1691/2.
[93] Below, econ. hist. (agric.).   [94] B.R.L. 452871.
[95] S.R.O., Tp. 1273/6, deed of 12 Sept. 1663.
[96] Below, manors and other estates.
[97] S.R.O., Tp. 1273/58, charity papers; P.R.O., HO 107/1002; P.R.O., RG 9/1985; D. M. Bills and E. and W. R. Griffiths, *Kinver Rock Houses* (Kinver, n.d.), 21.
[98] S.R.O. 1392.   [99] Below, educ.
[1] Shaw, *Staffs.* ii. 269–70.

[2] *S.H.C.* v (1), 141.
[3] Ibid.; S.R.O., Tp. 1273/8, deed of 17 July 1323.
[4] S.R.O., Tp. 1273/11, Enville ct. of survey *c.* 1527.
[5] Ibid. 58, Yorke, valuation of 1791 and undated plan.
[6] Ibid. 3, bdle. 29, case for counsel Mar. 1811.
[7] Ibid. 54, map of John Downing's estate *c.* 1781; 58, Yorke, valuation of 1791 and undated plan.
[8] Ibid. 8, deed of 14 Aug. 1446; 12/6, no. 2.
[9] Below, econ. hist. (agric.).
[10] P.R.O., HO 107/1002.
[11] Inf. from Mr. Scott-Bolton.
[12] Yates, *Map of Staffs.* (1775).
[13] S.R.O., Tp. 1273/42, deeds of 29 Mar. 1793, 19 Dec. 1818; below, local govt.
[14] Below, econ. hist. (mills).
[15] Below, manors and other estates.
[16] Yates, *Map of Staffs.* (1775).
[17] P.R.O., HO 107/1002.
[18] S.R.O., Tp. 1273/27, cash bk. Mar. and Apr. 1852.
[19] Below, econ. hist. (agric.).

were established: Morfeheath farm existed by 1723, and Camp farm to the east by 1744.[20]

Gilbert's Cross, where Morfe Lane meets the Stourbridge–Bridgnorth road, was an inhabited area by the 17th century.[21] The cross, which possibly took its name from the Domesday lord of Enville, may have served as a boundary mark between Enville and Morfe manors.[22] There were at least three cottages at Gilbert's Cross in the later 18th century;[23] only one survived in 1982. Newhouse Farm on the main road to the north existed by 1688.[24] Woodhouse, mentioned in 1326 and presumably an inhabited site, stood on the other side of the road from Newhouse Farm. The site was inhabited in 1688 but not in the late 18th century.[25] The boundary with Lutley manor lay immediately to the north.[26] A farmhouse called Lyons west of Gilbert's Cross existed by 1704.[27] The name may have been taken from Lions meadow, mentioned in 1300.[28] The present tall white-brick villa in Tudor style known as the Lyons was built in 1847 for Job Bissell, formerly of Tipton.[29] Coxgreen Farm further west was inhabited by the late 16th century, and probably earlier. The Hollies in the south-west corner of the parish was inhabited by the 16th century.[30]

The earliest settlement in Lutley probably lay near the point where Mere Lane was crossed by a road between Enville and Bobbington.[31] The medieval manor house stood south of the road junction; a moated site survived there in 1982. Lutley Farm at the junction dates from the late 15th century or earlier.[32] There was an inhabited area called Philleybrook west of the moated site in the early 14th century.[33] A house there was known as Philleybrook Hall in the late 17th and earlier 18th century;[34] by the late 18th century it was occupied by farm labourers, and it was demolished in the 19th century.[35] Poolhouse Farm, a 19th-century building of red brick, stands near Mere mill east of the moated site. There was settlement at Mere east of Lutley by the early 14th century, probably near the present Mere Hall which stands north of Mere Lane. The nearby Mere Farm dates from the later 16th century.[36] Further east lies Highgate common, formerly the northern part of the waste which

covered the eastern edge of the parish. Highgate Farm on the edge of the common was inhabited by 1693.[37] The waste was inclosed in 1746[38] but remained uncultivated. A golf course was laid out over the southern part of the common in the later 1930s.[39] In the mid 1950s Staffordshire county council bought 331 a. (134 ha.) north of the golf course and opened most of it as a country park.[40]

Grove Farm west of Lutley was inhabited by the late 14th century.[41] The present farmhouse of red brick dates from the early 18th century.[42] A tenement called Groundwyns on the Bobbington boundary north of Grove Farm existed by 1391.[43] It was probably inhabited then, and there was still a farmhouse there in 1770, when it was also known as Greenage.[44] Nothing more is known of the house which evidently lay near Greenwich Pool. The point where Mere Lane crosses the Stourbridge–Bridgnorth road was marked by four ash trees, mentioned in 1496.[45] There were still four trees standing there in 1817.[46] The site of Four Ashes Hall on the west side of the main road was inhabited by 1680.[47] In 1775 there were at least five cottages near the hall on a lane to Coxgreen Farm;[48] most of them survived in 1982. Toys Farm south-east of Four Ashes Hall existed by 1496.[49] Bradbury's Farm south of the hall is a partly timber-framed building dating from the 17th century.

The main road through the parish, the Stourbridge–Bridgnorth road, was mentioned in 1391.[50] It was turnpiked in 1816 and disturnpiked in 1877.[51] Chester Road, which runs north from the Stourbridge–Bridgnorth road in the south-east corner of the parish, was known in 1300 as Chester Way, being part of the route between the south-west of England and Chester, which continued in use until c. 1800. When Sir John Dugdale inquired about travelling from London to Enville to attend Henry Grey's funeral in 1687, he was advised to take first a coach to Worcester; there he was presumably to take the Chester road to Enville. The stretch running north from Highgate towards Halfpenny Green in Bobbington was turnpiked in 1762.[52]

A coach service between Stourbridge and Bridgnorth stopped at the Cat inn three times a week in 1834. There was only a Saturday omni-

[20] S.R.O., Tp. 1273/8, will of Gravenor Dyson 1725; 38, licence to appropriate pew in Enville ch. 18 June 1723; Salop. R.O. 2089/25, plan of Enville ch. pews 1744.
[21] S.R.O., Tp. 1273/8, deed of 13 Apr. 1629; S.R.O. 1392.
[22] P.R.O., E 318/39/2101; S.R.O., Tp. 1273/11, Enville ct. of 7 Apr. 1614; below, manors and other estates.
[23] Yates, Map of Staffs. (1775).
[24] S.R.O. 1392.
[25] Ibid.; S.R.O., Tp. 1273/12/8, nos. 1, 3, 7; Tp. 1273/12/10, no. 2; S.R.O., Tp. 1273/54, undated map of Newhouse farm.
[26] Salop. R.O. 2089/ADD, descrip. of Lutley manor bounds 1744.
[27] S.R.O., Tp. 1273/12, deed of 21 Dec. 1704.
[28] S.H.C. v (1), 180; S.R.O., Tp. 1273/10, deed of 17 Feb. 1673/4.   [29] P.O. Dir. Staffs. (1845); date on house.
[30] Below, manors and other estates.
[31] S.R.O., Tp. 1273/54, undated map of Newhouse and Fillibrook farms.   [32] Below, manors and other estates.
[33] P.R.O., C 143/76, no. 17; S.H.C. 1911, 329.
[34] S.R.O., Tp. 1273/8, deeds of 28 Sept. 1632, 26 Aug. 1674; 10, deed of 5 Oct. 1743; 54, undated map of Fillibrook farm.
[35] Ibid. 25, partics. and valuation of Ld. Stamford's Enville estates 1792; L.J.R.O., B/A/15/Enville.

[36] Below, manors and other estates.
[37] S.R.O., D. 3578/1/6, burial of 24 Nov. 1693.
[38] Below, econ. hist. (agric.).
[39] Below, social and cultural activities.
[40] Inf. from Staffs. C.C. Planning Dept. (1982).
[41] S.R.O., Tp. 1273/12/6, nos. 16, 19.
[42] MSS. at Four Ashes Hall, bdle. 6, deed of 20 Jan. 1721/2.
[43] S.R.O., Tp. 1273/8, deed of 11 Nov. 1391.
[44] MSS. at Four Ashes Hall, bdle. 22, deed of 26 June 1770.
[45] S.R.O., D. 593/J/15, ct. of 1 Nov. 1496.
[46] MSS. at Four Ashes Hall, deed of 7 Apr. 1817 relating to diversion of road.
[47] Below, manors and other estates.
[48] Yates, Map of Staffs. (1775).
[49] Salop. R.O. 2089/ADD, deed of 1 Oct. 1396 and Lutley ct. of 30 Oct. 1610; S.R.O., D. 593/J/15, ct. of 1 Nov. 1496.
[50] S.R.O., Tp. 1273/8, deed of 11 Nov. 1391.
[51] Below, p. 127.
[52] S.H.C. v (1), 180; Salop. R.O. 2089/ADD, deeds of 6 Nov. 1440, 24 Mar. 1540/1, 1 May 1673; S.R.O., Tp. 1226, folder 8, Sir John Dugdale to John Huntbach 8 and 15 Jan. 1686/7; Tp. 1273/11, Enville ct. of 28 Oct. 1609; below, Patshull, introduction.

bus service in 1845 and 1850. Omnibuses from Kinver to Wolverhampton stopped in Enville in 1860. Letters were brought by carrier from Stourbridge daily by 1845; by 1850 there was a post office in Enville village.[53]

A gasworks was built south of Home Farm probably in the late 1850s. It served the hall and its outbuildings and was able to provide gas to houses in the village. Still working in 1901, it had ceased to operate by 1921.[54] Water was supplied by the South Staffordshire Water Works Co. by the mid 1920s, and electricity was available by 1935.[55]

The parish had an association for the prosecution of felons in 1811 and 1833.[56] There was a police officer living in the parish by 1846, when repairs were made to a police cottage provided by Lord Stamford.[57] The officer was living in Blundies Lane in 1851 and 1871.[58]

There was a children's convalescent home known as the Cottage in Enville village in 1888. It was still there in 1892, but by 1896 it had moved elsewhere in the parish.[59] Nothing further is known about it.

SOCIAL AND CULTURAL ACTIVITIES. The black cherries for which Enville was noted had given rise by the early 19th century to what were called cherry wakes, held on three consecutive Sundays in late July and early August.[60] The wakes were tourist events rather than simply parish festivities; they attracted large crowds from the neighbouring towns and were accompanied by cock-fighting, boxing, and general unruliness.[61] In July 1821 a parish celebration for the coronation of George IV was marred by a disturbance created by men from Wordsley supporting his estranged wife, Queen Caroline. Although the subsequent wakes that year were quieter than usual, Lord Stamford's agent at Enville Hall suggested replacing them with a single Monday wake.[62] The change was soon implemented, and by the mid 1840s organized games and sports were a principal feature of the wake, then held at the end of July or beginning of August.[63] Nothing further is known of the wake.

In 1853 Lord Stamford opened the gardens of Enville Hall to the public.[64] In 1856 he staged a three-day fête in connexion with a cricket festival; there were bands and balloon ascents, and a firework display on the evening of the last day attracted a crowd estimated at between 60,000 and 80,000 people.[65] In the mid 1850s, when the gardens were open twice-weekly from the beginning of May to the end of September, an average of between 6,000 and 8,000 visited them each week; most came from Birmingham, Wolverhampton, Dudley, and Stourbridge. In order to accommodate the visitors in time for the 1857 season the earl built the Stamford Arms hotel on a site behind the Cat inn; the hotel could serve 300 people in its two refreshment rooms and had stables for 50 horses.[66] An evening concert of music was held in the hotel in 1882.[67] After the closure of the gardens to casual visitors in 1892 the hotel too was closed. The building survived as a private house, Stamford House, until its demolition in 1950.[68]

Other aspects of social life in the parish reflected the tastes and activities of the owners of Enville Hall. There was a hunt at Enville c. 1790 with the earl as master. In the late 1840s Lord Stamford hunted the Albrighton country at his own expense, keeping the dogs in kennels on the Sheepwalks. He again took the Albrighton Hunt in 1855.[69] By 1800 there was a racecourse east of Enville village on the Kinver side of the parish boundary.[70] It was used for racing and training horses stabled at Enville Hall.[71] The course was maintained until the late 19th century, and its outline still survived in 1982. Race horses were again kept at the hall then, but they were trained mostly on a new ground south of Home Farm.[72]

By 1821 cricket was played on a ground east of Enville Hall.[73] A team was raised by Lord Stamford employing as coaches F. W. Lillywhite, the M.C.C. bowler, and one of his sons in 1846,[74] and R. C. Tinley, another bowler, in 1853.[75] The earl, who was elected president of the M.C.C. in 1851, held cricket festivals at Enville in the 1850s. An All England XI and a United England XI played Lord Stamford's Twenty-Two, made up of professionals and local players, including the earl himself. In 1856 a three-day match attracted a crowd estimated at over 10,000 on the second day.[76] An XI led by the earl played the Free Foresters in 1858, and in 1872 a county team played the M.C.C. at Enville.[77] The ground, which covered 6½ a., was exceptionally smooth and was regarded as superior to that at Lord's.[78]

[53] White, *Dir. Staffs.* (1834), 258; *P.O. Dir. Staffs.* (1845; 1850; 1860).

[54] S.R.O., Tp. 1273/35, John Ewnson to Mr. Hackett 30 Mar. 1858; 54, plan of proposed Enville hall gasworks 1858; O.S. Map 1/2,500, Staffs. LXX. 7 (1883 edn.).

[55] Seisdon R.D.C. *Reps. of M.O.H. 1921*, 8; *1925*, 8; *1935*, 10 (copies in S.R.O., C/H/1/2/2/36).

[56] S.R.O., Tp. 1273/5, outgoings from Staffs. estate, 1833 acct.; 50, letter of John Beckett to Ld. Grey 28 Dec. 1818.

[57] Ibid. 39, guardian's accts. (Staffs.) 1846.

[58] P.R.O., HO 107/2017(1); P.R.O., RG 10/2928.

[59] *Kelly's Dir. Staffs.* (1888; 1892; 1896).

[60] White, *Dir. Staffs.* (1834), 256.

[61] E. Burritt, *Walks in the Black Country and its Green Border-land* (1869 edn.), 285-6, 288. For a main of cocks held at Enville in 1752 see *Aris's Birmingham Gaz.* 6 Apr. 1752.

[62] S.R.O., Tp. 1273/50, John Beckett to Ld. Stamford 21 and 30 July, 6 Aug. 1821.

[63] Notices of the wake 1845, 1847, and 1850, displayed at the Cat inn, Enville.   [64] *Illus. London News*, 2 Aug. 1856.

[65] Ibid.; Burritt, *Walks in Black Country*, 284-5; W. G. Watson, *Staffs. Cricket*, 21.

[66] S.R.O., Tp. 1273/43, memo. to Com. of Inland Revenue re Swan Hotel, 1857; Burritt, *Walks in Black Country*, 282-3.

[67] H.W.R.O. (H.), E 12/S, Bobbington and Enville, notice of concert.

[68] *Gardeners' Chron.* 15 Feb. 1896, p. 200; inf. from Mr. M. J. Scott-Bolton.

[69] *V.C.H. Staffs.* ii. 359-60; J. E. Auden, *Short Hist. of Albrighton Hunt*, 15, 72-3, 77; S.R.O., Tp. 1273/39, guardian's accts. (Staffs.) 1846-8.

[70] S.R.O., D. 1140/2.

[71] S.R.O., Tp. 1273/31, racing accts.; 39, guardian's accts. (Staffs.) 1846.

[72] Inf. from Mr. Scott-Bolton.

[73] S.R.O., Tp. 1273/50, John Beckett to Ld. Stamford 16 July 1821.

[74] Ibid. 39, guardian's accts. (Staffs.) 1846; *D.N.B. s.v.* Lillywhite.

[75] S.R.O., Tp. 1273/27, Enville estate cash bk., 19 Oct. 1853; H. S. Altham, *Hist. of Cricket*, 92-3.

[76] Watson, *Staffs. Cricket*, 18-21.

[77] Ibid. 22, 67.

[78] *Illus. London News*, 1 Aug. 1857.

In 1979 it was used for one of the qualifying matches for that year's cricket world cup.[79] Enville Cricket Club, established in 1850,[80] was still using the ground in 1983.

Enville Golf Club was founded in 1933. A golf course covering 118 a. was laid out over the southern part of Highgate common in the later 1930s; it was extended in 1971 and again in 1981 when it covered 243 a. The first clubhouse stood on the east side of Chester Road. In 1968 the club moved into Morfeheath Farm.[81]

The custom of clementing, when children sang as they begged for apples and money on St. Clement's day (23 November), was followed at Enville by the mid 1840s.[82] It survived c. 1930 but later died out. It was revived in 1961.[83]

Penny readings at which there was poetry and music were begun by Lady Stamford in the mid 1860s. First held in the school, meetings were later held at Enville Hall. That of 1867 had an attendance of 450.[84]

Two friendly societies, the Enville Amicable Society and the Swan Club, apparently existed by the mid 1780s. They still functioned in the mid 1840s.[85] A sick club existed in 1847.[86] By 1848 there was a coal club, which continued until 1925 or shortly afterwards.[87] Rules for a clothing club were drawn up in 1862.[88]

MANORS AND OTHER ESTATES. Before the Conquest *ENVILLE* was held by Alric, a king's thegn. In 1086 William FitzAnsculf held 3 hides there.[89] The overlordship then descended with the barony of Dudley. When the barony was divided in 1323 after the death of John, Lord Somery, the overlordship of 1 knight's fee in Enville was allotted to his elder sister Margaret and her husband John de Sutton.[90] There seems to be no later mention of it.

By the 1250s a mesne lordship of Enville was held by William of Birmingham, lord of Birmingham.[91] In the later 13th and earlier 14th century Enville was held of the Birmingham family as 1 knight's fee.[92] In 1386 Sir John Birmingham conveyed his estates in Enville and Morfe to John Horewood of Kinver.[93] The lordship then descended in the Horewood (later Whorwood)

family with Compton Hallows, in Kinver, until at least 1581, when Enville was held of Thomas Whorwood.[94]

The terre tenant of Enville in 1086 was Gilbert.[95] Ralph of Enville held the manor in 1176 and 1183.[96] He was evidently succeeded by William of Enville,[97] and William by Richard of Enville, who was living in 1207.[98] He or another Richard held Enville in 1227.[99] The manor was later held by John of Enville. He was dead by 1242 when his widow Margery recovered her dower of ⅓ knight's fee in Enville, seized by the sheriff when her second husband killed a man and fled the realm.[1] John's heir, a minor when the mesne lord had custody of the manor in the mid 1250s,[2] was probably the Richard of Enville who was lord in the mid 1260s.[3] He was a verderer of Kinver forest in 1271 and was alive in 1276.[4] He was succeeded, probably in that year, by his son William, who was alive in 1286[5] but may have died that year or in 1287.[6] Andrew of Enville was lord in 1291 and still held the manor in 1317.[7] Ralph of Enville, possibly his brother, was lord in 1323 and 1333.[8] Richard of Enville, probably Ralph's son, was lord in 1342[9] and was probably the man of that name recorded in 1355.[10] A Ralph of Enville, one of the foresters of Kinver forest, was killed in Iverley hay in the forest in 1354 or 1355.[11] He was evidently Richard's son. In 1363 Sir Fulk Birmingham granted the wardship and marriage of Joan, daughter and heir of Ralph, son of Richard of Enville, to Thomas Dunclent, rector of Tredington (Worcs., later Warws.), who in 1364 conveyed them to Thomas Lowe of Whittington, in Kinver.[12] It seems that Joan later married into the Lowe family.

Roger Lowe was lord of Enville in 1428 and may already have held the manor in 1421.[13] William Lowe, lord in 1437–8, was probably the William Lowe of Enville who was alive in 1452.[14] Richard Lowe, probably William's immediate heir, forfeited his manor of Milton (Cambs.), and presumably Enville also, when Edward IV was restored in 1471; as Richard Lowe late of Enville he was being sought for various high treasons and felonies in 1472. He was pardoned in 1473; later that year he and his wife Eleanor settled Enville and Milton on themselves and their issue, with

[79] *Wisden Cricketer's Almanack* (117th edn.), 314.
[80] Centenary score card in possession of Mr. J. A. Gloss.
[81] Inf. from Mr. Scott-Bolton.
[82] S.R.O., Tp. 1273–39, guardian's accts. (Staffs.) 1846; *N. & Q.* 2nd ser. iv (1857), 495; above, pl. facing p. 33.
[83] S.R.O., D. 1359/8/2.
[84] Burritt, *Walks in Black Country*, 288, 290.
[85] *Rules and Regulations of Stewponey Agric. Soc. for 1846*, 13 (copy in S.R.O., D. 1273/31); S.R.O., Tp. 1273/39, guardian's accts. (Staffs.) 1846.
[86] S.R.O., Tp. 1273/39, guardian's accts. (Staffs.) Sept. 1847.
[87] Ibid. May 1848; Tp. 1273/24, Enville Coal Club accts. 1868–1925.
[88] Copy in possession of Mr. Gloss.
[89] *V.C.H. Staffs.* iv. 54.
[90] *Cal. Inq. p.m.* vi, p. 258; *Cal. Close, 1318–23*, 630.
[91] *Cal. Pat. 1247–58*, 338; *S.H.C.* v (1), 109–10. For the Birminghams see *V.C.H. Warws.* vii. 58–9.
[92] *S.H.C.* iv (1), 154; *Feud. Aids*, v. 10; *Cal. Inq. p.m.* ii, p. 496; vi, p. 258.
[93] S.R.O., Tp. 1273/12/3, no. 1. *V.C.H. Warws.* vii. 59, wrongly gives Sir John's date of death as 1380.
[94] H.W.R.O. (H.), E 12/S, Bobbington and Enville, valor of lands of John Grey 1581.   [95] *V.C.H. Staffs.* iv. 54.

[96] *S.H.C.* i. 78–9, 112.
[97] *S.H.C.* iii (1), 218; *Sir Christopher Hatton's Book of Seals*, ed. L. C. Loyd and D. M. Stenton, p. 34.
[98] *Hatton's Bk. of Seals*, p. 32; *S.H.C.* iii (1), 139.
[99] *S.H.C.* iv (1), 47–8, 59.
[1] *Close R. 1237–42*, 387.
[2] *Bk. of Fees*, ii. 968; *S.H.C.* v (1), 110.
[3] *Close R. (Suppl.), 1244–66*, p. 48; *Ex. e Rot. Fin.* (Rec. Com.), ii. 442; *S.H.C.* N.S. vi (2), 43.
[4] *S.H.C.* v (1), 140; *S.H.C. 1911*, 167.
[5] *S.H.C.* v (1), 174; *Feud. Aids*, v. 10. The Wm. of Enville whose widow Alice brought a plea of dower in 1279 (*S.H.C.* vi (1), 96) may have been a younger brother of Ric.
[6] *S.H.C.* vi (1), 169, plea of dower by Joan, widow of Wal. (? recte Wm.) of Enville, 1287.
[7] *Cal. Inq. p.m.* ii, p. 496; S.R.O., Tp. 1273/12/6, no. 4.
[8] S.R.O., Tp. 1273/11, Enville ct. of 17 Oct. 1623; *S.H.C.* N.S. v. 219, 225–6.
[9] S.R.O., Tp. 1273/12/2, no. 1; ibid. 12/4, nos. 5–6.
[10] *S.H.C.* xii (1), 134.   [11] *Cal. Pat. 1354–8*, 232.
[12] S.R.O., Tp. 1273/12/4, nos. 7A, 7B, 8. For Dunclent see *V.C.H. Worcs.* iii. 550.
[13] *Feud. Aids*, v. 22; *Cal. Close, 1419–22*, 206.
[14] S.R.O., Tp. 1273/11, Enville ct. of 17 Oct. 1623; *S.H.C.* N.S. iii. 206.

The south front in the 1680s

The south front in the later 18th century

The conservatory of 1855

ENVILLE HALL

GEORGE HARRY GREY, EARL OF STAMFORD AND WARRINGTON (d. 1883)

HARRY GREY, EARL OF STAMFORD (d. 1768)

remainder to Richard's heirs.[15] He died in or shortly before 1479, with his two sisters Constance and Elizabeth as his heirs. His widow Eleanor, who remarried twice, held a life interest in a moiety of the manor and was still living in 1497. In that year Thomas Arnold and his wife Margaret, daughter and heir of Richard Lowe's sister Elizabeth, conveyed to John Whichcot the elder and two others the reversion of that moiety. In or before 1510 Whichcot's son John conveyed the moiety to Edward (from 1513 Sir Edward) Grey of Whittington, in Kinver.[16] By 1527 the other moiety had passed to Edward Sutton, Lord Dudley; in 1528 he and his son Sir John Dudley sold it to Grey.[17]

Sir Edward Grey died in 1529 and was succeeded by his eldest son Thomas. Under Sir Edward's will a younger son Francis was to have a moiety of Enville for life when he came of age; it is not clear whether the provision took effect.[18] Thomas, who moved from Whittington to Enville before 1548, was M.P. for Staffordshire in 1554. He died in 1559 in possession of the whole manor and was succeeded by his son John, aged nine.[19] John, who was three times M.P. for the county, died childless in 1594,[20] and Enville passed to his widow Jane as dower; she was still alive in 1608.[21] Under settlements made by John and his brother Edward, John's estates passed to Ambrose Grey. He was a younger son of a distant cousin, Sir Henry Grey of Pyrgo, in Havering-atte-Bower (Essex), from 1603 Lord Grey of Groby.[22] Jane conveyed her interest in the manor house to Ambrose c. 1605, and he took possession of the house shortly thereafter. Although he was living at Lutley in 1608, he had moved to Enville by 1614.[23] He died in 1636 and was succeeded by his son Henry.[24]

Henry Grey died in 1687, having devised his estates to John Grey, a younger son of his cousin Henry, earl of Stamford.[25] John, three times M.P. for Staffordshire, died in 1709. He was succeeded by his son Harry, who in 1720 became 3rd earl of Stamford on the death of his cousin Thomas. Enville then descended with the earldom. Harry died in 1739. His son Harry (d. 1768) married Lady Mary Booth (d. 1772), daughter and heir of the wealthy George, earl of Warrington (d. 1758), and their son George Harry, the 5th earl, was created earl of Warrington in 1796. The style 'earl of Stamford and Warrington' was used until the death of George Harry, the 7th earl, in 1883, but the shortened form 'earl of

Stamford' was still commonly employed.[26] The 7th earl left all his English estates to his widow Katherine for life; on her death in 1905 the Staffordshire estates passed, under the earl's will, to her grandniece Catherine, daughter of the Revd. Henry Payne, rector of Enville, and wife of Sir Henry Foley Lambert, Bt. The Lamberts took the name Grey later in 1905. Sir Henry died in 1914 and Lady Catherine in 1925. Their son Sir John Foley Grey, Bt., died in 1938 and was succeeded by his daughter Eileen, who married the earl of Harrington in 1942 and Mr. J. P. Bissill in 1947.[27]

Nothing survives of a medieval manor house unless fragments of one were incorporated in the brick house which Thomas Grey built at Enville before 1548.[28] The new house contained hall, parlour, chapel, armoury, kitchen and other service rooms, and at least 18 chambers.[29] It faced south and lay round three sides of a courtyard which was a little under 40 ft. square; the fourth side was closed by a wall with a central gateway. The hall occupied the ground floor of the central range. There were octagonal turrets in the angles between the ranges. In the 1680s short wings extended outwards from the south ends of the side ranges, and a long two-storeyed service wing extended east from the hall range. Amenities in the house then included water-powered spits in the kitchen.[30]

By the mid 18th century the wall closing the courtyard had been removed, small additions had been built on the west side of the house, and there was a large outer entrance court flanked by walls. On the east side of the house an enclosed court had been created in the early 18th century. Beyond it the stables are of similar date.[31] They have been attributed to William Baker of Audlem (Ches.), who was at Enville in 1748 and was paid for plans in 1750,[32] but they have architectural details which appear to be earlier than the mid 18th century. Baker's work was perhaps on the nearby Home Farm.

The accession of the 5th earl in 1768 was followed by increased building activity; the death of his mother in 1772 no doubt substantially increased his income. Sir William Chambers produced designs for a large new house, probably in or before 1772,[33] but they were not used. In 1773-4 Robert Mylne also designed a new house for Enville which was not built.[34] Instead the earl enlarged and remodelled the old building. A pedimented classical wing of three storeys and nine

[15] Cal. Pat. 1467-77, 276, 398; S.H.C. xi. 251; S.H.C. N.S. iv. 186.

[16] S.H.C. xi. 252; xii (1), 178; S.H.C. 1917-18, 290 n.; P.R.O., C 1/174, no. 24; P.R.O., C 140/69, no. 12; S.R.O., Tp. 1273/12, deed of 12 Mar. 1509/10; below, Kinver, manors and other estates.

[17] S.R.O., Tp. 1273/11, Enville cts. of 8 July 1527, 26 Oct. 1528; 12, deed of 14 Dec. 1528.

[18] P.R.O., C 142/49, no. 53.

[19] Ibid. 127, no. 46; P.R.O., E 150/1054, no. 2; S.H.C. 1917-18, 339-40; below.

[20] S.H.C. 1917-18, 359. The date of his death is given as 1593 and 1594 in P.R.O., REQ 2/42/70, and as 1595 in P.R.O., C 142/517, no. 4.

[21] S.R.O., Tp. 1273/11, deed of 1 Aug. 1608; 12, deed of 12 Dec. 1591; P.R.O., C 2/Eliz. I/G 3/56.

[22] V.C.H. Worcs. iii. 218.

[23] S.R.O., Tp. 1273/11, deed of 1 Aug. 1608; S.H.C. v (2), 339.

[24] P.R.O., C 142/554, no. 64.

[25] For this para. see, unless otherwise stated, Staffs. Pedigrees 1664-1700 (Harl. Soc. lxiii), 111-12; S.H.C. 1920 and 1922, 166-7; Complete Peerage, xii (1), 224-8; xii (2), 356; S.R.O., Tp. 1273/6, deed of 9 Nov. 1683.

[26] The shortened form has normally been used in the present volume.

[27] Burke, Peerage (1970), 1531.

[28] P.R.O., E 326/11298; Erdeswick, Staffs. 381.

[29] L.J.R.O., B/C/11, Thos. Grey (1566).

[30] Plot, Staffs. 40-1, 121, 337, and pl. VII (reproduced above, facing p. 96), pl. XXXII fig. 1.

[31] S.R.O., Tp. 1273/54, plan of Enville Hall grounds c. 1750.

[32] S.H.C. 1950-1, 119; Pevsner, Staffs. 130-1; Colvin, Biog. Dict. Brit. Architects, 431.

[33] S.R.O., Tp. 1273/55, plans by Chambers; Archit. Review (1953), 190.

[34] A. E. Richardson, Robert Mylne, 94-5, 97-9.

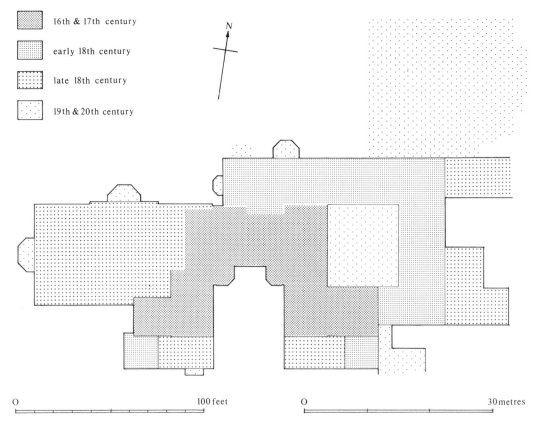

16th & 17th century

early 18th century

late 18th century

19th & 20th century

N

0   100 feet   0   30 metres

PLAN OF ENVILLE HALL

bays was added to the west end of the north front by John Hope of Liverpool. Hope also produced a design for gothicizing the south front, but it was not adopted.[35] Instead the side ranges were enlarged and given embattled parapets, and the front of the hall range and the turrets were gothicized in a style unrelated to Hope's surviving design. The brickwork was rendered. Most of the work on the south front had been completed by 1773. A view of it, showing the alterations, appears on the dinner service decorated with views of English country houses which Josiah Wedgwood made for Catherine II of Russia in 1773–4. The view of Enville is evidently based on a picture which Lord Stamford offered to lend Wedgwood in 1773.[36] An entrance screen had been added by 1796.[37] In 1776 Mylne sent Lord Stamford drawings for cornices in three rooms at Enville and for a dining-room ceiling.[38]

There is no evidence of further major work on the house until the 1870s. In 1875–6 Thomas Smith of Stourbridge (Worcs.), the estate architect, produced designs for remodelling some of the principal rooms. He died in 1876; the work which was carried out was principally from

designs produced in 1876–7 by Andrew Heiton the younger of Perth. Heiton added bays to the north and west fronts and altered and redecorated the principal rooms.[39] In 1904 the house was badly damaged by a fire, although at the west end only the upper floors seem to have been affected.[40] The rebuilding was from designs by Richard Creed of London. The kitchen area was extensively rebuilt, the enclosed court was glazed over, and the remains of a ballroom, perhaps added by Heiton, at the north-east corner of the house were demolished. A new main entrance was made through the former library in the original west range, to the south front of which a porte-cochère was added.[41]

There was a park within a pale at Enville in 1548; it was timbered and was stocked with deer.[42] In 1634 the demesne included a 177-a. park, adjoining the Hall, and the 30-a. Essex Wood.[43] The park was then described as pasture; land within the pale was being cultivated in the early 17th century, and by the 1640s there were no deer in the park.[44] By 1688 the area within the pale had been divided into closes. The demesne was bounded on the north and west by Legh

[35] S.R.O., Tp. 1273/55, elevations by Hope; *Archit. Review* (1953), 190, dating elevations 1773.
[36] Hermitage, Leningrad, 'Frog' service, piece no. 709 (photograph supplied by Mr. J. Harris of the R.I.B.A.); *Burlington Mag.* (Aug. 1980), 557; J. Wedgwood, *Personal Life of Josiah Wedgwood*, 152. The picture has not been found. For another view of the house, see above, pl. facing p. 96.
[37] W.S.L., Staffs. Views, iv. 169.
[38] Richardson, *Mylne*, 107–8.
[39] S.R.O., Tp. 1273/31, specifications of addns. and altera-

tions 1875; 54, plans by Smith and Heiton; *Brierley Hill Advertiser*, 15 July 1876. For views of the S. front *c.* 1900 see W.S.L. 16/1/77; *Country Life*, 16 Mar. 1901, p. 339.
[40] *Blackcountryman* (Autumn 1979), 44–50; W.S.L. 16/5/77; S.R.O., Tp. 1273/31, sched. of claim for fire damage 1904.
[41] Plans by Creed in S.R.O., D. 3929 and Tp. 1273; plaque dated 1906 on S. front of Enville Hall.
[42] P.R.O., E 326/11298.
[43] S.R.O., Tp. 1273/8, deed of 3 Jan. 1633/4.
[44] Ibid. 11, Enville ct. of 12 Apr. 1610; W.S.L., S.MS. 467, p. 91.

Lane, on the east by Mill Lane, and on the south by the slopes leading up to the ridge on which stood Lyndon Farm. Within that area the woodland was concentrated on the tops of the hills along the western boundary. Two streams, one west of the house and the other running down from Lyndon, fed several man-made pools. The garden lay north of the house. The stables and malthouse were some distance south of it and were reached by a drive, on the axis of the south front, which ran across an intervening paddock. Immediately west of the garden and paddock were orchards. From them a track led up into the hills and ultimately to a warrener's lodge a mile to the south-west.[45]

The first planned landscaping was apparently undertaken in the early 18th century.[46] By c. 1750 the park had been enlarged, chiefly by the 4th earl (1739–68), who took in the Leigh House and Lyndon estates; contemporaries noted that having married an heiress he could afford to buy property adjoining his demesne and to spend large sums on beautifying his estate.[47] A double avenue was planted from the Kinver road to the south forecourt of the Hall. Parallel to it a single avenue was made from the Kinver road to Lyndon Farm, aligned with a rotunda at the head of the valley above Lyndon. South of Lyndon the extended park was bounded by a long wood with a winding drive along its inner edge. A rectangular lake, Temple Pool, was made on the site of the old stables, and in 1747–8 a new Home Farm was built below the dam at the east end of the lake, perhaps to designs by William Baker.[48] At the centre of the lake was a Chinese temple on an island; it had been built before 1750 and was one of the earliest recorded chinoiserie garden buildings in England.[49] In the woods along the western edge of the park there were sinuous paths, picturesque buildings, and viewpoints with vistas along cleared alleys. Closer to the Hall the walled garden was enlarged westward, taking in one of the orchards and the lowest of the old pools. The pool was reshaped as a regular trapezoid, and the embankment between it and the next pool upstream was extended to form a terrace which ended at a summerhouse in the north-west corner of the enlarged garden.

The names of the designers of the earlier 18th-century landscaping are not known. Sanderson Miller designed a greenhouse built in 1750 and a castellated gateway south-west of the Hall,[50] and he may have been responsible for gothicizing Lyndon Farm and the warrener's lodge in the outer park.[51] In 1754 a friend of Miller found that one of the Gothic buildings, perhaps the greenhouse, had been altered by 'some Shrewsbury man',[52] probably T. F. Pritchard. By then the poet and landscape gardener William Shenstone had become Lord Stamford's adviser at Enville. He first visited the estate in 1750 and continued to do so until his death in 1763.[53] His work was carried on by, among others, Booth Grey (d. 1802), second son of the 4th earl.[54] As a result of their influence remaining elements of the formal landscaping were altered. Straight avenues were broken up; Temple Pool was given an irregular outline, its island and temple being removed and a new classical boat house being built at its southeast corner; the regular clumps of trees on the Lyndon ridge were joined into a single wood. The pools on the stream from Lyndon were remodelled to form a cascade, below which the stream wound through a glade and was crossed by a simple wooden bridge.[55] Shenstone was commemorated by Shenstone's Chapel on the edge of a wood below the rotunda.[56] Enville, with the other Shenstonian gardens at Hagley (Worcs.) and the Leasowes, in Halesowen (Worcs.), became a place of pilgrimage for cognoscenti. To make visits easier a carriage road was laid out round the park.[57]

By the early 19th century the type of landscaping represented at Enville was out of fashion.[58] Interest in the surroundings of the Hall did not revive until the accession of the 7th earl in 1845 and the arrival in 1847 of a new head gardener, John Aiton, almost certainly one of the distinguished family of horticulturists.[59] In 1848 John Pope & Sons, Smethwick nurserymen, submitted plans for 'new grounds' to Lord Stamford,[60] perhaps for the enlargement of the north garden, which was to be the main area of activity in the late 1840s and 1850s. A large workforce was employed to produce some of the most spectacular gardens in the Midlands.[61] The 18th-century walls on the north and west sides of the old garden were removed, and by the mid

---

[45] S.R.O. 1392.

[46] For the following para. see, unless otherwise stated, S.R.O., Tp. 1273/54, plan of Enville Hall grounds c. 1750 (redrawn below, p. 100).

[47] Shaw, Staffs. ii. 270; W. Shenstone, Letters, ed. M. Williams, 488.

[48] Plaque on building. For Baker see above.

[49] Travels of Dr. Pococke, ii (Camd. Soc. N.S. xliv), 231; Shenstone, Letters, 284; H. Honour, Chinoiserie, 150–1; S.R.O., Tp. 1273/18, survey of part of Enville 1750.

[50] Shenstone, Letters, 256–62.

[51] A. C. Wood and W. Hawkes, Sanderson Miller of Radway (Banbury Hist. Soc. 1969), 109.

[52] An Eighteenth-Century Correspondence, ed. L. Dickins and M. Stanton, 306. It has long been assumed that the greenhouse was the same building as that now known as the Gothic summerhouse, in the 1770s as the billiard room, and in the 19th century as the museum. Mr. T. Mowl, however, has suggested that the greenhouse was short-lived and that the surviving summerhouse was designed by Henry Keene: Jnl. of Garden Hist. iii (2), 134–43.

[53] Shenstone, Letters, 256 n., 284, 448–9, 486, 488, 494, 496–7, 528, 649–51.

[54] Shaw, Staffs. ii. 271; Gent. Mag. lxxii (1), 377.

[55] Shaw, Staffs. ii. 271, where it is attributed to Shenstone.

[56] Ibid. where the design of the chapel is attributed to Shenstone; [J. Heely], Description of Hagley, Envil and the Leasowes (Birmingham, n.d. but earlier than 1777), 126, apparently rejecting the idea.

[57] See e.g. Companion to the Leasowes, Hagley, and Enville (1789), 95–7, 108. See also [Heely], Description; J. Heely, Letters on the Beauties of Hagley, Envil, and the Leasowes (1777). A German translation of Heely's Letters was published in Leipzig in 1779.

[58] J. C. Loudon, Encyclopaedia of Gardening (1830 edn.), 1076, noting that Enville grounds were 'formerly celebrated'.

[59] S.R.O., Tp. 1273/31, garden acct. bks. 1827–54. Aiton was born at Richmond (Surr.) in 1810, the son of a Hugh Aiton: P.R.O., HO 107/2017(2), p. 227; Surr. R.O., Richmond par. regs. For the horticulturists Wm. and Wm. T. Aiton, both with Richmond connexions, see D.N.B.

[60] S.R.O., Tp. 1273/27, Enville estate cash bks., 5 Apr. 1848. For the firm see V.C.H. Staffs. xvii. 108.

[61] Rest of para. based on Florist (1855), 325–9; E. A. Brooke, Gardens of Eng. (1857), Enville; Jnl. of Horticulture, xxxii (1864), 353–6, 372–6, 393–6; E. Burritt, Walks in the Black Country and its Green Border-Land (1869 edn.), 279–82.

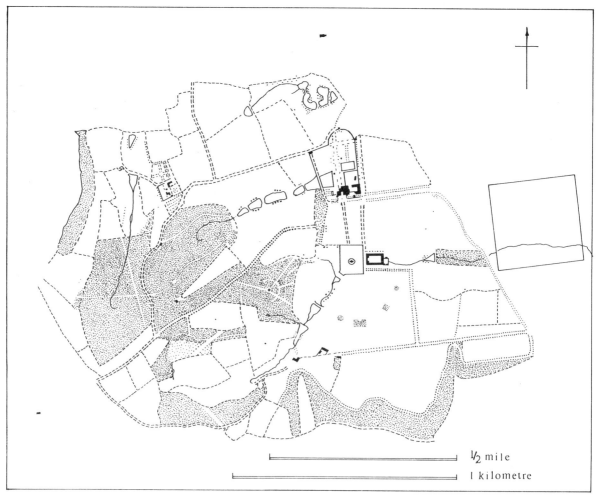

ENVILLE HALL: PLAN OF THE GROUNDS *c.* 1750

1850s flower and ornamental gardens had been created which covered over 70 a.[62] Fountains were installed in two large pools north-east of the house; one of them threw up a jet 180 ft. To feed them a reservoir holding over 4 million gallons was constructed at Batch north of Essex Wood; water was raised to it by two steam-pumps. At the centre of the new gardens stood a large conservatory, mixed Gothic and Moorish in style, erected in 1855[63] to designs by Gray & Ormson of London. Within the gardens were a Chinese pagoda, an aviary (1850–1),[64] an eaglery (1856),[65] more pools and fountains, many specimen trees, large shrubberies, extensive lawns, ribbon borders, and ornamental flower-beds. In 1855 one ribbon border was 400 yd. long and there were 102 flower-beds; in 1864 there were 160 flower-beds, and over 100,000 bedding plants were used during the season. New nurseries and kitchen gardens, including a walled area of 4 a., were laid out in the 1850s. Between the walled area and the Enville Hall cricket ground was an

orchard, where by 1864 there was another large conservatory. From 1853 the pleasure grounds were open to the public.[66]

Once he had created the gardens Lord Stamford seems to have made few alterations. In 1896 a gardening journal recommended Enville's 'large old-fashioned garden' in which ribbon borders and carpet bedding could still be seen. The gardens were still maintained to a high standard, though less lavishly cared for than formerly.[67] After the division of the Grey estates in 1905 the elaborate flower gardens were gradually abandoned. The pumps for the reservoir were sold for scrap during the First World War.[68] The kitchen gardens were leased in the early 1920s.[69] The conservatory of 1855 was partly taken down *c.* 1928 and demolished in 1938. The house and a portion of the grounds were requisitioned by the army during the Second World War, and as a result many of the park monuments were neglected. Several, including the boat house on Temple Pool, were afterwards demolished, as

[62] *Florist* (1855), 325, says *c.* 100 a., which may be an exaggeration.
[63] S.R.O., Tp. 1273/47, Enville Hall vouchers Dec. 1855, sub-bdle. 27. For a view see above, pl. facing p. 96.
[64] S.R.O., Tp. 1273/27, Enville estate cash bks., 20 Nov. 1850–25 Dec. 1851.

[65] Ibid. 5 and 7 Apr., 24 May 1856.
[66] Above, introduction (social and cultural activities).
[67] *Gardeners' Chron.* 15 Feb. 1896, 199; *Country Life*, 16 Mar. 1901, 336–40.
[68] Jay, 'Bobbington', 96.
[69] S.R.O., Tp. 1273/31, kitchen garden accts.

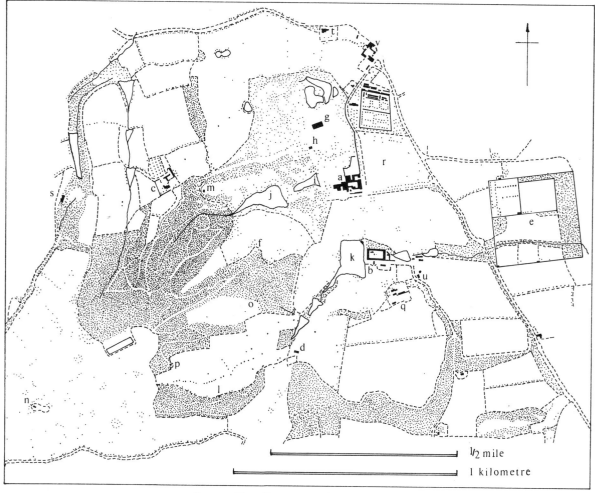

ENVILLE HALL: PLAN OF THE GROUNDS *c.* 1880

a Hall   b Home Farm   c Leigh House Farm   d Lyndon Farm   e The Walls   f Gothic Gate   g Conservatory   h Museum
i Haha Pool   j Jordan Pool   k Temple Pool   l Shenstone's Chapel   m Pagoda   n Sheepwalks House   o Round Hill
p Rotunda   q Pheasantry   r Cricket Ground   s Engine House   t Enville Church   u Gasworks   v Stamford Arms Hotel

was Lyndon Farm. The castellated gateway was restored *c.* 1980, and the restoration of the Gothic summerhouse was begun in 1982.[70]

LEIGH HOUSE in the manor of Enville, so named by the early 17th century,[71] was held by the Leigh family probably by the mid 15th century. John Leigh and his son William held land in the parish in 1440 and 1453.[72] William had probably succeeded his father by 1462 and was still alive in 1478.[73] About 1527 his son Robert's estate in Enville manor comprised a freehold house and virgate and a pasture held at will.[74] Robert was succeeded by his son John, whose son Richard died before 1577. Richard's son Thomas made his career in London and in 1596 or 1597 was appointed to be a clerk sitter in the Wood Street Counter, a London prison. In or

before 1621 he conveyed his estate in Enville manor to his son John in return for an annuity. He may have been the Thomas Leigh who was buried at Enville in 1629.[75] His son John, secondary of the Poultry Counter, another London prison, went to London for the law terms but lived at Leigh House during the vacations; it was later recalled that 'getting a place in London and growing rich thereby, [he] set up for a gentleman'. In the 1620s he bought land at Hoo.[76] He died in 1642 and was succeeded by his son John, who was succeeded in or shortly before 1645 by his brother Richard.[77] Richard was succeeded in 1674 or 1675 by his son John (d. 1700).[78] By 1704 the estate had passed to Richard Leigh, by 1721 rector of Eastham (Worcs.). In 1712–13 he sold his estate at Hoo, and in 1739 his son John sold

[70] Inf. from Mr. Scott-Bolton.
[71] S.R.O., Tp. 1273/12, deed of 20 May 1609.
[72] Ibid. 11, deed of 4 Apr. 1440; 12, deed of 8 Jan. 1452/3. For the descent of the estate to 1687 see, unless otherwise stated, *Heraldic Cases in Ct. of Chivalry 1623-1732* (Harl. Soc. cvii), 52–9.
[73] S.R.O., Tp. 1273/12, deed of 18 Sept. 1462; *S.H.C.* N.S. vi (1), 113.
[74] S.R.O., Tp. 1273/11, Enville ct. of survey *c.* 1527.

[75] Ibid. Enville ct. of 20 Nov. 1621; S.R.O., D. 3578/1/1, 30 Dec. 1629, which may in fact record the burial of Thos. Lee of Hoo.
[76] S.R.O., Tp. 1273/10, deeds of 21 June 1620, 30 Sept. 1624, 11 Dec. 1640.
[77] Ibid. deeds of 17, 18, 19 Oct. 1645; S.R.O., D. 3578/1/1, burial of 12 June 1642.
[78] S.R.O., Tp. 1273/11, deed of 10 Mar. 1673/4; *Index of P.C.C. Wills*, ix (Index Libr. lxvii), 129; S.R.O., D. 3578/1/6, 10 Oct. 1700.

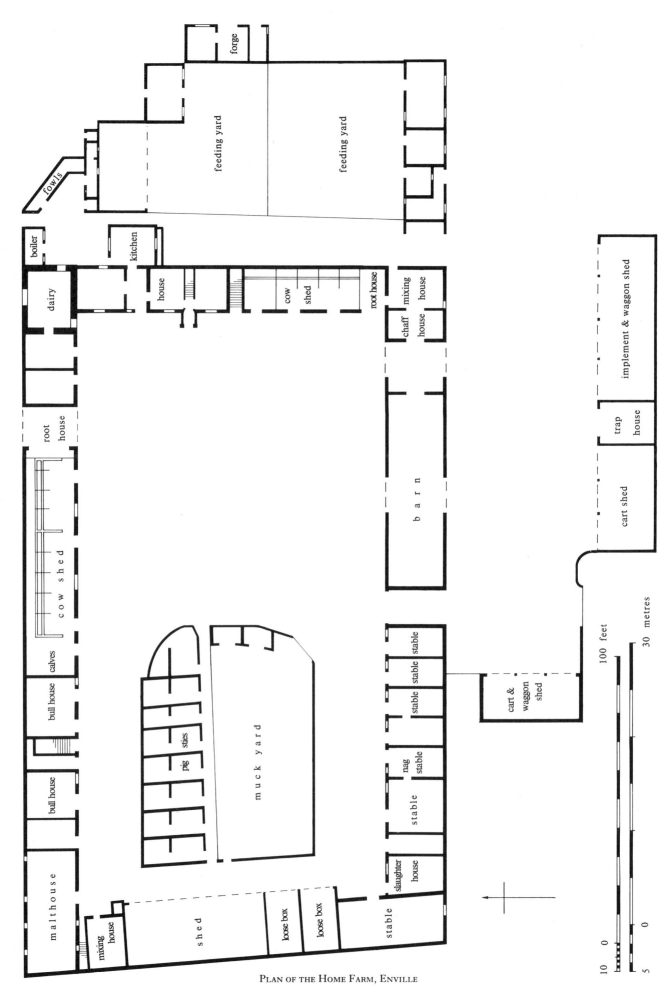

PLAN OF THE HOME FARM, ENVILLE

the reversion of Leigh House and the rest of the estate to Thomas Robbins of Enville, who was probably acting on behalf of Lord Stamford. Richard died in 1740. In 1741 Lord Stamford advanced the money which enabled Robbins to pay off a mortgage on the property and to extinguish any claims on the estate which might be made by Richard's surviving son, Thomas Leigh of Bradninch (Devon). In 1744, in return for a further payment, Robbins conveyed Leigh House to Lord Stamford.[79] In 1982 it was part of the Enville Hall estate.

The low brick buildings which form the south-west portion of the present Leigh House incorporate part of a timber-framed building which may be of late medieval origin. A tall brick building was built against the older range c. 1700. The new work had an irregular cruciform plan. The shortest arm houses a fine staircase with corkscrew-twist ballusters. The south-eastern arm was removed in the later 18th century, possibly at the same time as the earliest buildings were rebuilt or encased in brick.[80]

The Shadwells of *LYNDON*, from whom the dramatist and poet Thomas Shadwell (d. 1692) claimed descent,[81] held land in Enville manor in the early 14th century. In the 1520s a Thomas Shadwell held a messuage and a virgate in the manor as a free tenant and 3 crofts at will.[82] He was granted arms in 1537 and died c. 1553.[83] In 1544, when he sold land at Lutley, he was apparently living at Worcester.[84] His estate passed to his younger son Edward; in the early 17th century Edward and his son John were buying more land in the parish.[85] Edward died in 1630 and was succeeded by John, who died in 1653.[86] The estate then passed to John Shadwell's son Thomas, an Exchequer clerk. In 1666 his house at Lyndon, assessed at seven hearths, was occupied by two of his relatives, a John Shadwell and Thomas's brother-in-law John Wilcox. In 1668 Thomas bought the Beamish Hall estate in Albrighton (Salop.), and thereafter neither he nor his descendants lived at Lyndon. Thomas was succeeded in 1682 or 1683 by his son Lancelot (d. 1713), whose son and heir Thomas died in 1731, heavily in debt, leaving as his heir a son Lancelot, a minor. The younger Lancelot, a London chemist, sold the Lyndon estate in 1747

to the tenant, Lord Stamford.[87] In 1982 it was part of the Enville Hall estate. The house was demolished c. 1961.[88]

The manor of *LUTLEY* existed by 1166 when it was held of Gervase Paynel, lord of Dudley. The overlordship descended with that of Enville until the 14th century, passing in 1323 after Lord Somery's death to his sister Margaret and her husband John de Sutton.[89] In 1365 Philip Lutley, the lord of Lutley, agreed to hold the manor of Sir John Botetourt of Weoley castle, in Northfield (Worcs.), the son and heir of Margaret de Sutton's younger sister and coheir Joan.[90] About the same time Philip married a kinswoman of Sir John.[91] In 1506 it was held of John Mytton, one of the heirs of the Botetourts, as of his manor of Bobbington.[92]

William of Hagley held 1 knight's fee in Hagley (Worcs.) and Lutley of Gervase Paynel in 1166.[93] He was probably the William of Hagley who witnessed a charter of Paynel c. 1154,[94] and may have been the William of Hagley who held land in Staffordshire in 1130.[95] The tenant of 1166 may have been succeeded by Roger of Hagley.[96] In 1183 Lutley was held by Philip of Lutley,[97] probably the Philip of Hagley who witnessed another of Paynel's charters in 1187.[98] He was perhaps the Philip of Lutley who was alive in 1213,[99] but a William of Lutley was active between 1202 and 1208.[1]

The lords of Hagley created a mesne lordship, presumably by settling Lutley on a younger son. A Philip of Lutley held the manor in the 1220s, and about the same time a Robert of Hagley seems to have held Hagley.[2] In 1242-3 Lutley was held as ¼ knight's fee of the lord of Hagley,[3] who still held the mesne lordship in 1323.[4]

From the early 13th century until c. 1369 all the known lords of Lutley were named Philip Lutley.[5] One was a Staffordshire M.P. in 1332; he, or more probably a son and successor, was killed in 1352 by the men of Sir Hugh Wrottesley of Wrottesley, in Tettenhall.[6] The son of the man killed, another Philip Lutley, was escheator, sheriff, and three times an M.P. for the county. He was succeeded c. 1369 by his brother John.[7] In 1415 John, who was childless, sold the manor to Sir Humphrey Stafford 'with the silver hand',

[79] S.R.O., Tp. 1273/3; 36, deeds of 11 Feb. 1711/12, 28 Mar. 1712; 38, abstract of title to Hoo; 39, abstract of title to John Cherrington's estate; 44A, deed of 5 June 1741; S.R.O., D. 3578/1/6, burial of 11 May 1740.
[80] The plan of the house is shown on S.R.O., Tp. 1273/54, plan of Enville Hall grounds c. 1750; for a view of the house before the demolition of the S.E. arm see W.S.L., Fac. 360.
[81] D.N.B.
[82] S.H.C. vii (1), 252; S.R.O., Tp. 1273/11, Enville ct. of survey c. 1527.
[83] Trans. Salop. Arch. Soc. 3rd ser. ix. 90.
[84] S.R.O., Tp. 1273/11, deed of 11 Oct. 1544; 12, deed of 10 Oct. 1544.
[85] Trans. Salop. Arch. Soc. 3rd ser. ix. 90; S.H.C. N.S. iii. 28; N.S. iv. 60; S.R.O., Tp. 1273/11, Enville ct. of 28 Oct. 1609.
[86] Trans. Salop. Arch. Soc. 3rd ser. ix. 90, corrected from S.R.O., D. 3578/1/1, 27 July 1653.
[87] Trans. Salop. Arch. Soc. 3rd ser. ix. 90-1, misdating sale of Lyndon; S.H.C. 1923, 77; S.R.O., Tp. 1273/10, abstract of title to Lyndon.
[88] Inf. from Mr. Scott-Bolton. For a view see below, pl. facing p. 112.

[89] S.H.C. i. 201; Cal. Inq. p.m. vi, p. 258; Cal. Close, 1318-23, 630.
[90] Charters and Muniments of Lyttelton Fam. ed. I. H. Jeayes, p. 46.
[91] Cal. Pat. 1361-4, 267; 1364-7, 400; S.H.C. xiv (1), 121.
[92] Cal. Inq. p.m. Hen. VII, iii, p. 565; above, Bobbington, manor and other estates.
[93] S.H.C. i. 201.   [94] S.H.C. 1941, 61.
[95] S.H.C. i. 4, 12.
[96] S.H.C. iii (1), 216.
[97] S.H.C. i. 112.
[98] Dugdale, Mon. v. 204.
[99] S.H.C. ii (1), 84, 94; iii (1), 44, 64, 142-3, 161.
[1] S.H.C. iii (1), 75, 87, 143.
[2] S.H.C. iv (1), 47, 220-1; Cal. Inq. Misc. i, p. 1; V.C.H. Worcs. iii. 133.
[3] Bk. of Fees, ii. 968.
[4] Cal. Inq. p.m. vi, p. 258; Cal. Close, 1318-23, 630.
[5] For the period from 1242-3 to 1327 see Bk. of Fees, ii. 968; Cal. Inq. p.m. ii, p. 496; Feud. Aids, v. 15; S.H.C. v (1), 144; vii (1), 252.
[6] S.H.C. 1917-18, 60, arguing, however, that the M.P. was the man killed in 1352.
[7] Ibid. 104.

retaining a life interest.[8] He died in 1416, before payment for the manor had been made in full, and was succeeded by a relative, Catherine Cole. In 1422 she and her husband Robert agreed to complete the sale, but it was not until 1427 that they did so.[9] Lutley then descended with Amblecote, being disputed after the execution of Humphrey Stafford, earl of Devon, in 1469 between his three cousins and coheirs and Humphrey Stafford of Grafton. Unlike Amblecote it was held by the earl's widow Isabel from 1483–4 until her death in 1489. It was then allotted to Eleanor Strangeways, one of the coheirs, passing to her son Henry Strangeways in 1502 and to his son Giles (later Sir Giles) in 1504.[10] In 1540 Sir Giles sold it to Walter Wrottesley of Wrottesley.[11] In 1560 Wrottesley granted a 50-year lease of the house and demesne lands to Richard Whorwood, a younger son of the Whorwoods of Compton, in Kinver, and in 1590 Walter's grandson Walter Wrottesley sold the manor to Michael Moseley of the Mere.[12] It then descended with the Mere and was part of the Enville Hall estate in 1982.

The medieval manor house evidently stood on a moated site in Moat field, between Philley brook and a lane leading from a meadow known as Chapel Yard to Mere Lane. The house is said to have had a chapel, and there are earthworks in Chapel Yard. Stonework was visible on the moat platform in the early 1970s. Coins and other artifacts, including what was said to be a stone font, were dug up in the area in the early 19th century.[13] A manor house which was included in the lease of 1560 to Richard Whorwood may have been the house in the vill of Mere which William and Francis Whorwood quitclaimed to Michael Moseley in 1590 with their other property in the vill; it was possibly the house at Lutley in which Ambrose Grey was living in 1608.[14] It is not clear whether that house was the moated building or, as seems possible, the present Lutley Farm. Lutley Farm stands near the moated site and is a late medieval house consisting of a hall and cross-wing, retaining its original plan and some of the timber framing of both wings. An upper floor was inserted in the hall in the earlier 17th century and its walls were rebuilt in brick in the 18th century, but it still has its low medieval roofline. The south-east cross-wing was partly rebuilt in brick and heightened in the 19th century, and a long dormer was put into the roof of the hall c. 1952.[15]

An estate in Lutley manor known as *FOUR ASHES* existed by 1680, when Henry Wollaston (d. 1720) was living there.[16] Henry was succeeded

by his son Thomas (d. 1722), whose property in Enville was inherited by his daughter Elizabeth. In 1725 she married Joseph Amphlett of Woodhampton, in Astley (Worcs.), who died in 1758. Their son Joseph died unmarried in 1811. His nephew and heir James Amphlett Grove died unmarried in 1854. He left the estate in the first instance to Ann Dunne, a great-granddaughter of Thomas Wollaston.[17] She failed to make Four Ashes Hall her principal residence, one of the provisos in Grove's will, and in 1855 the estate consequently passed to her younger son Charles Dunne. Charles changed his surname to Amphlett, in accordance with the will.[18] The estate then comprised Four Ashes Hall with 39 a. attached, the 98-a. Crump Hillocks farm, the 73-a. Lutley Mill farm, and Grove farm, of which 187 a. lay in Enville parish.[19] Charles Amphlett was succeeded in 1891 by his son Charles (d. 1921). Charles's heir was his brother the Revd. George Amphlett (d. 1944), whose eldest daughter Miss Leila Amphlett occupied the Hall in 1982.[20]

A mid 18th-century drawing at the house, which is labelled in a later hand as a plan of Four Ashes Hall, shows a house apparently of the late 16th or early 17th century, with a centre range and two long wings. Nothing in the present house can be identified as forming part of the building shown on the plan. The appearance of the house is dominated by additions and alterations of the mid and late 19th century, but some of the walling towards the back courtyard is probably of the later 18th century. A contract for building work in 1814[21] makes it clear that additions were being made to an older house. The main work under the contract consisted of the present dining room and drawing room, but some earlier features, notably the 18th-century mahogany doors, were re-used.[22] The kitchen wing was rebuilt in the mid 19th century, and a number of 18th-century fittings were re-used. Perhaps at the same time the large bay windows were added to the dining room and drawing room. The library and the study were added to the west end of the house in two stages in the late 19th century. North and west of the kitchen yard there are extensive brick outbuildings of the 18th and 19th centuries. At some distance north-west of the house is a large late 18th-century stable and farm building; it has a symmetrical main elevation with a central pediment and a roof-top cupola.

The estate known as *THE MERE* was built around a virgater's holding in the manor of Lutley. A family which took its name from the

[8] Salop. R.O. 2089/ADD, deed of 13 Dec. 1415.
[9] *S.H.C.* xi. 229; xvii. 56, 58; B.L. Eg. Ch. 1682.
[10] *V.C.H. Worcs.* iii. 217–18; Shaw, *Staffs.* ii. 276; *Complete Peerage*, iv. 328; *Cal. Inq. p.m. Hen. VII*, iii, p. 565; above, Amblecote.
[11] *S.H.C.* xi. 282; Salop. R.O. 2089/ADD, deed of 30 June 1540.
[12] Salop. R.O. 2089/ADD, deeds of 20 July 1560, 27 Sept. 1590; below (the Mere).
[13] Shaw, *Staffs.* ii. 276; Scott, *Stourbridge*, 282–3; Stour and Smestow Arch. Research Group, *Field Survey Reps.* i (1970–3), 3.
[14] Salop. R.O. 2089/ADD, deeds of 20 July 1560, 9 June 1590; S.R.O., Tp. 1273/11, deed of 1 Aug. 1608.
[15] Local inf.
[16] H.W.R.O. (H.), E 12/S, Tettenhall, John Shawe to

Daniel Rowley 1680; S.R.O., D. 3578/1/6, burial of 1 July 1720.
[17] MSS. at Four Ashes Hall, family tree and bdle. 4, abstract of title to Lutley farm and mill; Burke, *Land. Gent.* (1952), 36.
[18] MSS. at Four Ashes Hall, copy of will of James Amphlett Grove; Burke, *Land. Gent.* 36.
[19] MSS. at Four Ashes Hall, abstract of valuation of estate of James Amphlett Grove.
[20] Burke, *Land. Gent.* 36.
[21] MSS. at Four Ashes Hall, draft contract between James Amphlett Grove and John Smallman of Quatford (Salop.) 1814.
[22] The 18th-century fireplace and ornaments in the drawing room were introduced in the 20th century: inf. from Miss Amphlett.

Mere held land there by the early 14th century. Philip atte Mere acquired lands in Lutley and Bobbington in 1391 and 1392, and in 1398 his father Roger atte Mere conveyed to him the family's estate in Lutley.[23] A Thomas atte Mere held the land by 1422 and was alive in 1446.[24] Humphrey Mere died in or before 1496.[25] In 1509 Humphrey's house and virgate at the Mere passed to John Moseley of Whittington, in Kinver, and to Moseley's brother-in-law Henry Longmore of Upper Arley (Staffs., later Worcs.). Moseley was alive in 1511 but had died by December 1513, when Longmore conveyed his own interest in the estate at the Mere to his sister, Moseley's widow Agnes, for life, with remainder to her son Nicholas Moseley of the Mere and his heirs.[26] Nicholas was still alive in 1552, but his son John had succeeded by 1568, when he made a settlement of the estate.[27] John was succeeded by his youngest brother Michael, a Londoner, who is said to have bought the Mere from him shortly after 1568.[28] Michael bought land in the parish from 1568 and Lutley manor in 1590.[29] He was succeeded in 1592 or 1593 by his son Nicholas, who was still alive in 1638.[30] The estate continued to pass from father to son: Walter (d. 1656); Walter, high sheriff in 1711 (d. 1712); Acton (d. 1745); Walter Acton, high sheriff in 1757 (d. 1793); Walter Michael (d. 1827); Walter.[31] W. A. Moseley left the Mere some time between 1765 and 1778, and it seems that thereafter no member of the family lived in the parish. In 1849 Walter Moseley sold the estate with Lutley manor to Lord Stamford. It then included 738 a. in Enville.[32] The land was part of the Enville Hall estate in 1982.

Two houses at Mere formed part of the estate sold to Lord Stamford in 1849. Both survived in 1982. The older and more substantial, known in the earlier 19th century as the Mere[33] and in 1982 as Mere Farm, stands on the north side of Mere Lane. Part of a later 16th-century wing survives at the back of the house, and the eastern or service wing probably incorporates a structure of similar date. Early in the 17th century the house was largely rebuilt in brick to give it a tall front range with gables and a projecting porch and bays with canted sides.[34] North-west of it is the house known by 1838 as Mere House[35] and in 1982 as Mere Hall. It is the east end of the mid 18th-century stable block of a vanished house. Behind are barns of the same period, laid out symmetric-

ally. The stables were originally approached from the south through a tall central doorway; beyond them the barns formed the north side of the rickyard and foldyard.

The buildings at Mere Hall comprise the sole visible remains of the house which in the mid 18th century was the seat of the Moseleys and was known as the Mere. It stood south-east of Mere Hall, and a modern farm reservoir covers the site. The house was L-shaped and was approached from Mere Lane along a tree-lined avenue. West of the house were gardens, ponds, and an orchard, and north of those were the stables and barns which survived in 1982 as Mere Hall.[36] The house was demolished or destroyed by fire in the early 19th century,[37] and it was presumably then that part of the stables were converted into a farmhouse.

Before the Conquest *MORFE* was held by three free men. In 1086 William FitzAnsculf held 5 hides there, which were waste, in demesne.[38] By 1167 the manor had been subinfeudated, and the overlordship descended with that of Enville, passing in 1323 to Margaret de Sutton and her husband John. Morfe was still held of the Suttons in 1432, and in 1504 Edward Sutton, Lord Dudley, arbitrated in a dispute over possession of the manor, perhaps as overlord.[39]

In 1166-7 Peter son of William (Peter of Birmingham) held the manor, and Hugh of Morfe who *c.* 1154 witnessed a charter of Gervase Paynel, lord of Dudley, probably held it of him;[40] Hugh may have been Peter's son but is unlikely to have been the Hugh son of Peter recorded in 1175-6 and 1213-14.[41] After 1171 William son of Peter of Birmingham, with the assent of his son Brian, granted Morfe to Roger, another of his sons, to hold as ½ knight's fee.[42] Roger was possibly the Roger son of William recorded in 1177-8 and presumably the Roger of Morfe whose gravestone was discovered at Enville church in 1762.[43] Morfe had escheated or reverted to the senior branch of the Birminghams by 1221, and in 1222 William of Birmingham, Peter's son or grandson, granted Henry of Birmingham a moiety of 2 hides at Morfe to hold as ¼ knight's fee. William retained the other moiety.[44]

The moiety which William retained and a mesne lordship over the other moiety descended in the Birmingham family with the mesne lordship of Enville.[45] In 1263 the Birminghams'

[23] Salop. R.O. 2089/ADD, deeds of 5 July 1310, 1 May 1321, 24 Feb. 1390/1, 24 Dec. 1392, 15 Sept. 1398.
[24] Ibid. deed of 1 May 1422; *S.H.C.* 1928, 48.
[25] S.R.O., D. 593/J/15, 1 Nov. 1496.
[26] Salop. R.O. 2089/ADD, deeds of 15 Nov. 1509, 11 Nov. 1511, 4 Dec. 1513.
[27] Salop. R.O. 2089/ADD, deeds of 3 Apr. 1552, 9 Oct. 1568. [28] Ibid. commonplace bk., p. 180.
[29] Ibid. deed of 20 Oct. 1568; *S.H.C.* xiv (1), 197; xv. 165, 167, 192; xvi. 105, 126.
[30] P.R.O., PROB 11/82 (P.C.C. 59 Nevell); Salop. R.O. 2089/ADD, deed of 20 Mar. 1637/8.
[31] Burke, *Land. Gent.* (1952), 1834; *Gent. Mag.* xcvii (2), 367-70; *Trans. Worcs. Arch. Soc.* N.S. xxxi. 44-8, misdating sale of estate; S.R.O., D. 3578/1/1, burial of 30 Dec. 1656.
[32] Nat. Libr. Wales, *Cal. of Deeds and Docs.* iii, pp. 308-9; S.R.O., Tp. 1273/32, deeds of 9 Sept. 1778, 15 Feb. 1849; L.J.R.O., B/A/15/Enville.
[33] O.S. Map 1", sheet LXI. SE. (1833 edn.); S.R.O., Tp. 1273/32, partics. and plan of Mere estate 1848.

[34] Above, pl. facing p. 33.
[35] L.J.R.O., B/A/15/Enville.
[36] Yates, *Map of Staffs.* (1775; 1799); Salop. R.O. 2089/27, map of 'The Meer Farm', n.d.
[37] It seems to be the Mere Hall shown on B.L. Maps, O.S.D. 214 (*c.* 1815), but it does not appear on L.J.R.O., B/A/15/Enville. Burnt material, apparently from the house, was discovered when the farm reservoir was excavated: local inf. (1982).
[38] *V.C.H. Staffs.* iv. 54.
[39] *Cal. Fine R.* 1430-7, 132; below.
[40] *S.H.C.* 1941, 48-9, 60, 67. For the Birmingham family see above.
[41] *S.H.C.* i. 79, 191-2. The identification is suggested in *S.H.C.* 1941, 67.
[42] S.R.O., Tp. 1273/12/10, no. 1.
[43] *S.H.C.* i. 90; Shaw, *Staffs.* ii. 275.
[44] W.S.L., S.MS. 327, p. 9; *S.H.C.* iv (1), 218-19.
[45] For the mesne lordship see *Cal. Inq. p.m.* ii, p. 496; vi, p. 258; S.R.O., Tp. 1273/12/6, nos. 8, 18.

demesne moiety seems to have amounted to 44s. rent, 12 a. of wood, and 12 villein holdings;[46] in 1346-7 there were at least 10 tenants who held 276 a., 3 more who paid 20s. rent, and a mill.[47] In 1386 Sir John Birmingham granted his estate in Morfe to John Horewood of Kinver.[48] The mesne lordship of the whole of Morfe then descended in the Whorwood family until at least 1581.[49]

Henry of Birmingham, who received the other moiety, became known as Henry of Morfe.[50] He was dead by 1256.[51] His successor, Henry, died between 1296 and 1302.[52] The second Henry's son Henry made a settlement of the manor in 1327 and died in or shortly before 1330. His son Henry, a minor, died in or before 1332 leaving a widow Joan, who was holding a third of what was described as Morfe manor in dower in 1347.[53] Under the settlement of 1327 Henry was succeeded by his brother John Morfe, who came of age in 1335.[54] John died in 1355 and was succeeded by his son Henry, who came of age in 1375.[55] Henry was still alive in 1408 but was dead by 1411 when his daughter and heir Catherine and her husband John Corbyn quitclaimed the manor to Edmund Lowe, lord of Whittington in Kinver, Richard Leveson, and Nicholas Russell.[56] The manor then descended in the main with Whittington. In 1482, however, it was held by Humphrey Lowe's widow Alice, who that year made a settlement of it. On her death it was to go to her daughter Eleanor's son John Grey, with remainder to his brothers Robert and Henry.[57] In 1504 Lord Dudley cited the settlement when, acting as arbitrator between Henry Grey's son George and George's cousin Edward (later Sir Edward) Grey, he awarded the manor to George. Edward, who was already in possession, ignored the award, and in 1507 George formally abandoned his claim.[58] Sir Edward died in 1529, leaving a life interest in Morfe to one of his younger sons, William.[59] William was still in possession of the manor in 1581.[60] By 1588 it had passed to his nephew John Grey.[61] It then descended with Enville and was part of the Enville Hall estate in 1982.

There was a manor house at Morfe in the 14th century, probably the hall which in 1295 stood at the end of a green way leading from Morfe wood. It may have had a chapel.[62] About 1530 William Grey leased the manor house to John Watkins and his wife. It was burnt down soon afterwards and rebuilt by Watkins at his own expense.[63]

There was a small estate in the manor of Morfe, known as *COXGREEN* by 1593.[64] It took its name from the Cox family, members of which held land in the parish by the 15th century. They were then generally described as yeomen or husbandmen.[65] A John Cox was one of the wealthier parishioners in 1539.[66] He was perhaps the John Cox, gentleman, who in 1572 settled a house and land in Morfe on Francis Cox and Francis's son Thomas. Francis was alive in 1584 but had presumably died by 1593 when Thomas settled the house and land on himself and his heirs.[67] Thomas was probably the Thomas Cox the elder who, with Thomas Cox the younger, executed a further settlement of the estate in 1618.[68] The younger Thomas died in 1621. His widow Frances held the Coxes' estate in Morfe and Enville after his death, but c. 1625 it passed to Richard Leigh, a London haberdasher and brother of John Leigh (d. 1642) of Leigh House. Richard's son Thomas may have been a minor when Richard died in 1650; it was Richard's widow Mary who opposed demands for heriot and held Coxgreen in 1654.[69] Thomas Leigh was described as a London merchant when he bought more land in the parish in 1664. He died at Worcester in 1692 and was succeeded by his son Richard.[70] Richard apparently moved from Coxgreen to Worcester. By will dated 1725 he devised a life interest in his property in Enville, Kinver, and Alveley (Salop.) to his sister Ann, wife of the Revd. Richard Leigh of Leigh House, with remainder to Ann's son Richard Leigh. In 1735 the younger Richard sold part of the estate to the Revd. John Downing of Enville. Coxgreen itself seems to have passed to the Hale family of the Hollies.[71] In 1982 it was part of the Enville Hall estate.

The oldest part of the present building is the timber-framed ground floor of the north-west wing, the central part of the service cross-wing of a late-medieval house whose plan is preserved in later rebuilding. The parlour cross-wing appears to have been extended south-eastwards by a timber-framed range in the later 16th or early 17th century. In the mid 17th century the older part of that cross-wing and the hall range were rebuilt in brick, a fine open staircase being put into the cross-wing. Later alterations included

[46] *S.H.C.* iv (1), 154.
[47] Ibid. xii (1), 50-1, 55, 64; S.R.O., Tp. 1273/12/6, nos. 9-10.
[48] Above, p. 96.
[49] H.W.R.O. (H.), E 12/S, Bobbington and Enville, valor of lands of John Grey 1581.
[50] *Bk. of Fees*, ii. 968.
[51] R. W. Eyton, *Antiquities of Shropshire*, iii. 141 n.
[52] Ibid. 143.
[53] *S.H.C.* xi. 38, 128; *Cal. Fine R. 1327-37*, 196; S.R.O., Tp. 1273/12/9, no. 3.
[54] *Cal. Inq. p.m.* viii, pp. 33-4.
[55] Ibid. x, p. 279; xiv, p. 179.
[56] S.R.O., Tp. 1273/12/6, no. 18.
[57] S.R.O., Tp. 1273/12/9, no. 9.
[58] Ibid. no. 10; Tp. 1273/12, bk. of deeds and evidences, p. 10.
[59] P.R.O., C 142/49, no. 53.
[60] H.W.R.O. (H.), E 12/S, Bobbington and Enville, valor of lands of John Grey 1581.
[61] *S.H.C.* xvii. 235-6.

[62] B.L. Add. Ch. 27651; *S.H.C.* xi. 128; *Cal. Inq. p.m.* viii, p. 33; x, p. 279; S.R.O., Tp. 1273/12, deed of 2 Feb. 1294/5.
[63] P.R.O., C 1/1294, nos. 21, 24.
[64] *S.H.C.* 1930, 344.
[65] P.R.O., C 88/114, no. 64; *Cal. Pat. 1429/36*, 325; *S.H.C.* xvii. 123; *S.H.C.* N.S. iii. 222, 224; N.S. iv. 95, 107-8, 131, 196; N.S. vi (1), 158, 160.
[66] *S.H.C.* 1923, 69.
[67] *S.H.C.* xiii. 291; xv. 152; xvi. 126; S.R.O., Tp. 1273/11, deed of 25 Mar. 1593.   [68] *S.H.C.* N.S. iv. 25.
[69] S.R.O., Tp. 1273/11, will of Ric. Leigh; ibid. Morfe ct. of 20 Nov. 1621, lists of suitors 27 Oct. 1625, 18 Jan. 1633/4, and 19 May 1654, and papers in case Leigh v. Grey, draft receipt 1650; *Heraldic Cases in Ct. of Chivalry 1623-1732* (Harl. Soc. cvii), 53, 56.
[70] S.R.O., Tp. 1273/10/Wilmott's, deed of 1 Apr. 1664; Tp. 1273/11, deed of 6 Feb. 1666/7 and will of Susanna Leigh; S.R.O., D. 3578/1/6, burial of 3 Nov. 1692; *Index of P.C.C. Wills*, xi (Index Libr. lxxvii), 171.
[71] S.R.O., Tp. 1273/3, deed of 26 Mar. 1718; Tp. 1273/10/ Wilmott's; below.

the division of the hall into two rooms, the demolition of both ends of the service cross-wing and the rebuilding of its upper storey in brick, and the removal of a south-eastern block. The house was restored in 1981.

Two estates at *THE HOLLIES* in the manor of Morfe existed by the 16th century, held by yeomen whose families later rose to gentility. Both estates eventually descended to non-resident proprietors and were sold to the Greys of Enville Hall.

A William Gravenor was one of the free tenants of the manor of Enville in the late 1520s.[72] By 1550 he had been succeeded by a John Gravenor, who was dead by 1559. His son and heir Edward was in 1574 described as of the Hollies and was styled gentleman. In 1575 Edward held a freehold estate in the manor of Morfe as well as another in Enville manor. He died c. 1580 and was succeeded by his son John, a minor.[73] John was succeeded in or shortly before 1621 by his son Edward, who died in 1654, having devised his estate to his nephew Henry Dyson of Inkberrow (Worcs.). Henry died in 1659 and was succeeded by his son Gravenor, then a minor. Gravenor Dyson died in 1726, leaving the estate to his grandson William Holmer.[74] Holmer, who was living in Kinver by the 1740s, died in 1744, having devised the estate to trustees for sale. Most of the land was added in 1747–8 and 1776 to the Enville Hall estate,[75] of which it was part in 1982.

The house, which was assessed at seven hearths in 1666,[76] was sold by William Holmer's widow to Thomas Brettell of Stourbridge in 1759.[77] The present house, a plain 18th-century brick building, was remodelled in the earlier 19th century, probably soon after 1802 when Brettell's son, also Thomas, sold it to John Hale, the owner of the other estate at the Hollies.[78] It was known as the New House by 1845.[79]

The other estate at the Hollies, said in the 18th century to have been originally 1½ yardland,[80] was held in the 16th century by the Hale family. Thomas Hale of the Hollies, yeoman, was a presentment juror from 1586 to 1606.[81] A Thomas Hale the elder died in 1627; his son, another Thomas Hale, died in 1630 or 1632.[82] William Hale of the Hollies, son of the last-named Thomas, styled himself gentleman and claimed to bear arms.[83] He died in 1681 and was succeeded by his son John (d. 1710). John's son

and heir, another John, was succeeded in 1745 by his son Corbett.[84] In 1750 and 1752 Corbett sold land in Enville and Morfe to Lord Stamford but retained the bulk of the estate.[85] He died in 1794 and was succeeded by his son John (d. 1808). John devised all his property not settled on his wife Polly to his mother Mary, who already held part of the estate in dower, with remainders to his wife and his daughter Mary.[86] In 1821, at the time of Mary's marriage to Hugh Montgomery Campbell (d. 1846), the two widows settled the Hollies itself (69 a.) and Coxgreen farm (218 a.) on her. In 1849 her son and heir Capt. H. J. M. Campbell, a regular soldier then serving in Canada, sold all his property in the parish to Lord Stamford; it comprised the land settled in 1821 and the 119-a. New House farm lying north of the Hollies.[87] In 1982 it was part of the Enville Hall estate.

William Hale's house was assessed at eight hearths in 1666.[88] It stood south of the Dyson house and was evidently the more substantial of the two in the later 18th century, when it had an enclosed garden. It was known as Hollies House in the late 1830s.[89] The house still stood in 1858 but had been demolished by 1882.[90] Part of what may have been the house survived in 1982, incorporated into farm buildings.

Edwin, a free man, held 3 hides at *CIPPE-MORE* in 1066. In 1086 Roger held the land of William FitzAnsculf, but it was evidently abandoned soon afterwards. The site of the settlement may have been in the Sheepwalks area in the south-west corner of the parish.[91]

The *RECTORY* manor is discussed below.[92]

ECONOMIC HISTORY. AGRICULTURE. Cultivation in the parish was not extensive in 1086. Enville manor, which lay in the forest, had land for 4 ploughteams; 1 team was in demesne with 1 slave, and a further 1½ team was worked by 5 villeins and 1 bordar. With meadow and woodland Enville was worth 24s., the same value as before the Conquest. Morfe, where there was land for 6 teams, was waste. At 'Cippemore', possibly in the south-west of the parish, there was land for 4 teams; 2 teams were in demesne with 3 slaves, and there were 5 bordars. With woodland the manor was worth 10s., the same value as before the Conquest.[93] By 1300 the whole parish lay in Kinver forest.[94] Assarts in

---

[72] S.R.O., Tp. 1273/11, Enville ct. of survey c. 1527, Enville ct. of 26 Oct. 1528.

[73] Ibid. Enville ct. of 18 Apr. 1550; Tp. 1273/12, deed of 10 Feb. 1574/5; L.J.R.O., B/C/11, John Gravenor (1559), Edw. Gravenor (1580); *S.H.C.* xiv (1), 179–80.

[74] S.R.O., Tp. 1273/11, Enville and Morfe cts. of 20 Nov. 1621; *S.H.C.* v (2), 120–1; Nat. Libr. of Wales, *Cal. of Deeds and Docs.* iii, p. 203.

[75] S.R.O., D. 3578/1/6, burial of 22 Mar. 1743/4; S.R.O., Tp. 1273/8, deeds of 1 Sept. 1747, 11 Feb. 1747/8; Tp. 1273/11, deed of 2 Sept. 1747; Tp. 1273/41, will of Wm. Holmer and deeds of 27 and 28 Dec. 1744, 15 Jan. 1776.

[76] *S.H.C.* 1923, 77.

[77] S.R.O., Tp. 1273/41, deeds of 24 and 25 Mar. 1759.

[78] Ibid. deed of 25 Mar. 1802.

[79] S.R.O., Tp. 1273/40, deed of 8 Apr. 1845.

[80] S.R.O., Tp. 1273/11, deed of 23 Jan. 1749/50.

[81] *S.H.C.* 1929, 1930, 1932, 1935, and 1940, *passim*.

[82] S.R.O., D. 3578/1/1, burials of 17 May 1627, 1 Mar. 1629/30, 29 July 1632; *S.H.C.* v (2), 165.

[83] S.R.O., Tp. 1273/11, deeds of 29 Sept. 1638, 18 Dec. 1648; *S.H.C.* v (2), 165–6.

[84] *S.H.C.* v (2), 166; S.R.O., D. 3578/1/6, burials of 21 June 1681, 22 Aug. 1710, 29 Sept. 1745; S.R.O., Tp. 1273/11, deed of 23 Jan. 1749/50.

[85] S.R.O., Tp. 1273/11, deeds of 23 Jan. 1749/50, 25 Jan. 1751/2.

[86] S.R.O., D. 3578/1/6, burial of 20 Feb. 1794; S.R.O., Tp. 1273/35, wills of Corbett and John Hale.

[87] S.R.O., Tp. 1273/40, deeds of 7 and 8 June 1821, 8 Apr. 1845, 21 Aug. 1846, 14 May 1847, 3 Sept. 1849, and declaration on title to Hollies.

[88] *S.H.C.* 1923, 77.

[89] Yates, *Map of Staffs.* (1775); L.J.R.O., B/A/15/Enville, no. 119.

[90] S.R.O., Tp. 1273/18, partics. of tithe on Hollies Estate 1858; O.S. Map 1/2,500, Staffs. LXX.10 (1883 edn.).

[91] *V.C.H. Staffs.* iv. 54; above, introduction.

[92] Below, church.

[93] *V.C.H. Staffs.* iv. 54.

[94] *S.H.C.* v (1), 180.

Morfe and Lutley were recorded in the later 13th and early 14th century.[95]

The number and distribution of open fields in the parish reflects a gradual process of bringing forest woodland into cultivation. Each of the three manors had its own set of fields, and there was in addition, within Enville manor, a separate set for Lyndon. Cross (later Cress) field, mentioned the early 14th century,[96] lay north of Enville village on the west side of Blundies Lane.[97] It was still open in 1648.[98] An open field called Moorland lay in the same area near Blundies in the early 14th and early 15th century.[99] There was evidently a field north of Blundies between the lanes to Morfe Hall Farm and Hoo Farm in the early 14th century; it may have been called Middle field.[1] By the late 16th century there was an open field in that area lay called Mill field, evidently named after the mill at Morfe Hall Farm.[2] Mill field was still open in the late 18th century.[3] Hale field, mentioned in 1333, lay east of Browns Lake. It had 17 a. in strips in the early 18th century and was still open in 1773.[4] Brook field, probably lying further east where there is a tributary of Spittle brook, may have existed by 1331, when Smallbrook field was recorded. Brook field was still open in 1662.[5] Nether field and Hell field, both mentioned in 1589, lay in the same area as Brook field. Nether field was still open in 1612 and Hell field in 1662.[6] Ast field, mentioned in 1327, lay south of Browns Lake; it was known as Heath field by 1713 and was still open in 1756.[7] Horestone (later Whetstone) field, mentioned in 1333,[8] probably lay south-west of Ast field. Although a close called Whetstone field was mentioned in 1704, the surviving open land may have been renamed Crown field. Crown field was still open in 1791.[9] Hall field, mentioned in 1569, lay to the south. Still open in 1676, it had been inclosed by the late 18th century.[10]

There were three open fields at Lyndon. Deepdale field, mentioned in 1458, lay south of Lyndon and stretched into Kinver; it was described as an open field of Lyndon in 1543.[11] Mill field, mentioned in 1543, evidently lay near Mill brook.[12] Lyndon (later Old) field existed in 1594; it lay next to Mill field and stretched eastwards from Lyndon as far as the Enville–Kinver road.[13] The three fields were inclosed in 1672.[14]

There were at least three open fields for Morfe manor. Bosenhill field, mentioned in 1316, lay west of Morfe House Farm.[15] It contained inclosed land by 1622.[16] Whittenhill field, mentioned in 1385, lay east of Morfe House Farm; it was mostly inclosed by 1688.[17] Street field, lying further east and bounded by Chester Road, was mentioned in 1610;[18] it was partly inclosed by 1622.[19]

Selions in Holywall field and Chelwastre field in Lutley were mentioned in 1385.[20] The position of the fields is unkown. There were two open fields at Mere in 1605: Lee or Level field, which lay north of Mere, and Bold field, which stretched east of Mere as far as Chester Road. Both fields contained open land in 1711.[21]

There were 4 a. of meadow in Enville manor in 1086.[22] Three doles in Dole meadow at Hoo were mentioned in 1624; doles still existed there in 1756.[23]

The eastern part of the parish was waste in the Middle Ages. In the early 16th century Sir Giles Strangeways, lord of Lutley, tried to inclose Clare Hays, commmon to Lutley and Mere. In 1535 local people pulled down hedges which he had erected round 200 a. of waste there.[24] Clare Hays appears to have remained open until 1746, when it was inclosed by agreement. The lord of Lutley received 100 a., and the remaining 172 a. were shared among the lord and the freeholders.[25] Morfe heath to the south was inclosed by agreement in 1683, when it covered 500 a.[26] Waste at Lyndon was inclosed in 1663.[27] Inhabitants of Morfe, Enville, and Lyndon had pasture rights in Checkhill waste over the eastern boundary in Kinver.[28]

There were a number of greens in the parish. Church green was mentioned in 1342[29] and presumably lay near Enville church. Bar green between Enville village and the hall existed by

[95] *S.H.C.* v (1), 110, 114; B.L. Add. Ch. 27651.

[96] S.R.O., Tp. 1273/12, undated grant by Phil. of the Mere and his w. Lucy to Phil. Bryd.

[97] Ibid. 35, undated partics. of Wm. Kay's land; 54, map of John Downing's estate *c*. 1781.

[98] Ibid. 11, deed of 18 Dec. 1648.

[99] Ibid. 12, undated grant by Phil. of the Mere and his w. Lucy to Phil. Bryd, and deed of 7 Oct. 1409; 58, Yorke, valuation of 1791 and undated plan.

[1] Ibid. 12, undated grant by Phil. of the Mere and his w. Lucy to Phil. Bryd; 12/4, nos. 3, 5, 13.

[2] Ibid. 11, deeds of 9 Jan. 1579/80, 1 Mar. 1588/9.

[3] Ibid. 58, Yorke, undated partics. and plan.

[4] Ibid. 12/4, no. 4; 54, map of John Downing's estate *c*. 1781; 58, Yorke, undated partics. and plan.

[5] Ibid. 11, deed of 29 Sept. 1662; 12/4, nos. 3, 13.

[6] Ibid. 11, deeds of 1 Mar. 1588/9, 29 Sept. 1662, and Enville cts. of 14 Mar. 1593/4, 27 Oct. 1612.

[7] Ibid. 12/4, no. 1; 12/5, no. 3; 12, deed of 10 Feb. 1712/13; 33, deed of 17 Apr. 1756; 58, Yorke, undated partics. and plan.

[8] Ibid. 11, deed of 21 June 1620; 12/4, no. 4; 12, deed of 10 Feb. 1578/9.

[9] Ibid. 8, deed of 10 June 1704; 35, undated partics. of Wm. Kay's land; 58, Yorke, undated partics. and plan and 1791 valuation.

[10] Ibid. 6, deed of 4 Dec. 1676; 12, deed of 10 Feb. 1578/9; 54, map of John Downing's estate *c*. 1781.

[11] H.W.R.O. (H.), E 12/S, Kinver ct. rolls 1387–1498, bdle. 24, ct. of 27 Apr. 1458; E 12/S, Kinver copyhold estates, 1831 survey and map, no. 199; S.R.O., Tp. 1273/12/1, no. 8.

[12] S.R.O., Tp. 1273/12/1, no. 8.

[13] S.R.O., Tp. 1273/11, Enville cts. of 16 Oct. 1594, 25 Apr. 1601.

[14] Ibid. 44A, partics. of lands in Lyndon fields 18 Jan. 1671/2.

[15] Ibid. 6, no. 3; 54, undated map of John Downing's estate.

[16] Salop. R.O. 2089/ADD, deed of 28 July 1622.

[17] S.R.O., Tp. 1273/12/6, no. 17; S.R.O. 1392.

[18] S.R.O., Tp. 1273/11, Morfe ct. of 12 Apr. 1610; S.R.O. 1392.

[19] Salop. R.O. 2089/ADD, deed of 28 July 1622.

[20] S.R.O., Tp. 1273/12/6, no. 17.

[21] Salop. R.O. 2089/ADD, deeds of 14 May 1605, 26 May 1711.

[22] *V.C.H. Staffs.* iv. 54.

[23] S.R.O., Tp. 1273/10, deed of 30 Sept. 1624; 33, deed of 17 Apr. 1756.

[24] *S.H.C.* n.s. x (1), 141–3; *S.H.C.* 1912, 71–5.

[25] Salop. R.O. 2089/ADD, deed of 28 May 1746.

[26] S.R.O., Tp. 1273/38, deed of 3 Mar. 1681/2 and memo. of 25 June 1683.

[27] Ibid. 6, deed of 12 Sept. 1663.

[28] Below, Kinver, econ. hist. (agric.).

[29] S.R.O., Tp. 1273/4, no. 6.

the late 14th century; it was taken into the hall grounds during the 18th century.[30] There was evidently a green near Coxgreen Farm in 1593;[31] a triangle of waste ground survived west of the farmhouse in 1982. No Man's green in the south-west corner of the parish on the county boundary was mentioned in 1601 and 1624.[32] In the north of the parish a green at Hoo was enclosed c. 1550,[33] while Bendey's green west of Morfe House Farm and Careley green north of Mere mill still existed in the late 18th century.[34]

There was extensive woodland in the parish in 1086, 1 league in length and ½ league in breadth at Enville, 2 leagues in both length and breadth at Morfe, and 1 league in length and breadth at 'Cippemore'.[35] Some of the woodland evidently lay south-west of Enville Hall in the area of what was later called Essex Wood: in the earlier 14th century it was called 'Evezetowode', a name of Old English origin.[36] Assarts had been made there by the earlier 14th century, but there was still a 30-a. wood there in 1634.[37] Lutley wood was mentioned in 1271, and the wood of the lord of Enville in 1330.[38] Morfe wood was mentioned in 1295. Trees cut down there in 1355 included oak, ash, and pear; there was probably no timber left by 1366, when the wood was described as an assart.[39] Trees were planted by the earls of Stamford on Highgate common in the east of the parish in the earlier and late 18th century. Lord Stamford had 168 a. of woodland in the parish in 1798 and 200 a. in 1800.[40] By 1840 there were 299 a. of woodland, including the 90-a. Essex Wood.[41] Regular sales of timber from the Enville Hall estate were made in the 19th century.[42] In 1982 there were at least 173.6 ha. (429 a.) of woodland in the parish.[43]

Barley was grown at Enville in 1342, and barley, beans, and peas at Morfe in 1377.[44] Rye, wheat, and barley were grown at Enville in 1566. Thomas Cox of Coxgreen had wheat, peas, barley, and oats in his barns in 1621, and in 1625 the same crops, with wheat and barley predominating, were growing in fields north-east of Enville village. On a farm at Lyndon in 1634 the main crops were rye and peas. Wheat and barley were the chief crops on a farm at Enville in 1670 and on another at Philleybrook in 1689; oats and peas were grown in smaller quantities on both farms.[45] There was a hopyard west of Enville Hall

in the late 1680s.[46] Surviving inventories for the later 16th and the 17th century suggest that arable farming did not predominate in the parish; on many farms animals, especially sheep and cows, were notably more valuable than crops.

Grazing for 200 sheep was included in a grant of land in Morfe in 1316.[47] Three shepherds were among those taxed in Enville manor in 1332–3.[48] In 1551 virgaters in Enville manor were limited to pasturing 100 sheep, half-virgaters 60, and those holding a nook 30.[49] In Lutley manor half-virgaters were limited to pasturing 10 sheep in 1560.[50] John Wilcox of Lutley had 80 sheep and 26 lambs in 1558, and Thomas Grey of Enville had 100 sheep in 1566. Richard Garbett, rector of Enville, had a flock of 114 sheep in 1592, and had 13 tods of wool in his house.[51] By 1603 the number of sheep that a virgater in Enville manor was allowed to pasture had risen to 120.[52] A flock of 112 sheep was recorded at Enville in 1625, and one of 75 at Lyndon in 1634. There was a flock of 130 sheep at Morfe in 1668 and one of 160 at Enville in 1690.[53] A sheepcot at Lyndon was mentioned in 1743.[54]

Tithe on dairy produce was paid to the rector of Enville in 1535.[55] In 1558 John Wilcox of Lutley had 6 cows and 4 calves, and in 1566 Thomas Grey of Enville had 14 cows. The herd of Thomas Cox of Mere in 1615 included a cow and calf, 6 cows in calf, and 2 yearling calves. Richard Pratt of Enville had 9 cows, 1 heifer, and 1 calf in 1632. At Philleybrook in 1688 Francis Devey had 10 cows and 1 bull, and at Enville in 1690 Elizabeth Hodgetts had 7 milch cows; both had cheese and cheese presses in their houses.[56]

Herds of 14 pigs were kept at Morfe in 1556 and at Mere in 1563. Thomas Cox of Coxgreen had 12 pigs in 1621, and there was a herd of 12 at Four Ashes in 1678. At Philleybrook in 1688 Francis Devey had 3 sows with 20 young and 6 hogs; the herd was the largest recorded in the period.[57] Turkeys were among the poultry kept by Richard Garbett in 1592. In 1621 Thomas Cox of Coxgreen had 10 turkeys, 8 geese, and a gander as well as other poultry. A gaggle of 28 geese belonged to Francis Devey of Philleybrook in 1688.[58] In 1544 Thomas Deysse of Lyndon left a hive of bees to endow a light in the parish church. Richard Garbett had 10s. worth of bees in 1592, and in 1634 John Pitchford of Lyndon

[30] Ibid. 54, map of Enville Hall grounds c. 1750 (redrawn above, p. 100); below, p. 115.
[31] S.H.C. 1930, 344.
[32] S.R.O., Tp. 1273/11, Enville ct. of 25 Apr. 1601; 12, deed of 10 Oct. 1624.
[33] Ibid. 11, Enville ct. of 18 Apr. 1550.
[34] Ibid. 54, undated map of Morfe manor; L.J.R.O., B/A/15/Enville, no. 783.
[35] V.C.H. Staffs. iv. 54.
[36] S.R.O., Tp. 1273/12/4, no. 2; Eng. Place-Name Elements (E.P.N.S.), i. 147, 198; ii. 279–80.
[37] S.R.O., Tp. 1273/8, deed of 3 Jan. 1633/4; Tp. 1273/12/4, no. 2.
[38] S.R.O., Tp. 1273/12/4, no. 2; S.H.C. v (1), 144.
[39] S.R.O., Tp. 1273/12, deed of 2 Feb. 1294/5; S.H.C. xii (1), 136, 143–4; Shaw, Staffs. ii. 275.
[40] S.R.O., Tp. 1273/18, rent roll of Ld. Stamford's Staffs. and Worcs. estates 1798, 1800; Express & Star, 12 Feb. 1971.
[41] L.J.R.O., B/A/15/Enville.
[42] S.R.O., Tp. 1273/21.
[43] Inf. from Mr. Scott-Bolton.
[44] S.R.O., Tp. 1273/12/4, no. 5; S.H.C. xiv (1), 147.
[45] L.J.R.O., B/C/11, Thos. Gray (1566), Thos. Cox (1621), John Spittal (1625), John Pitchford (1634), Ric. Elliott (1670), Fra. Devey (1689).   [46] S.R.O. 1392.
[47] S.R.O., Tp. 1273/12/6, no. 3.
[48] S.H.C. x (1), 129.
[49] S.R.O., Tp. 1273/11, Enville ct. of 15 June 1551.
[50] Salop. R.O. 2089/ADD, ct. of 29 Apr. 1560.
[51] L.J.R.O., B/C/11, John Wylcockis (1558), Thos. Gray (1566), Ric. Garbett (1592).
[52] S.R.O., Tp. 1273/11, Enville ct. of 15 Oct. 1603.
[53] L.J.R.O., B/C/11, John Spittal (1625), John Pitchford (1634), Humph. Toy (1668), Eliz. Hodgetts (1690).
[54] S.R.O., Tp. 1273/44A, deed of 19 May 1743.
[55] Valor Eccl. (Rec. Com.), iii. 103.
[56] L.J.R.O., B/C/11, John Wylcockis (1558), Thos. Gray (1566), Thos. Cox (1615), Ric. Pratt (1632), Fra. Devey (1689), Eliz. Hodgetts (1690).
[57] L.J.R.O., B/C/11, Humph. Hale (1556), Hugh Clare (1563), Thos. Cox (1621), Kath. Ellyotts (1678), Fra. Devey (1689).
[58] Ibid. Ric. Garbett (1592), Thos. Cox (1621), Fra. Devey (1689).

had 3 hives. In 1638 Humphrey Jevon of Enville had a half share in 10 hives, which were placed out in different parts of the parish.[59]

The chief crops in 1801 were barley and wheat; turnips, oats, and peas were also grown.[60] At Newhouse farm c. 1840 wheat, barley, and peas were grown.[61] In the later 19th century barley, rye, and turnips were the main crops in the parish.[62] Oats, wheat, and barley were the chief crops on the home farm in 1918, but turnips, swedes, and mangolds were also grown.[63]

Nearly a third of the parish was pasture in 1840, and at Newhouse farm nearly half the cultivated land was sown with grass.[64] A herd of over 160 cattle belonging to the home farm were grazed on the Sheepwalks in 1826,[65] and by the late 1830s the farm was producing large quantities of milk.[66] The purchase of an Ayrshire bull in 1839 and of Channel Island cows in 1851 and 1853 was evidently an attempt to improve dairy stock. Indian cows were also introduced.[67] In 1853 the farm won a prize from the Worcestershire Agricultural Society for the best milking cow.[68] There was a dairy herd at Newhouse farm c. 1840.[69] In the mid 1880s the herd at Coxgreen farm included Channel Island and Ayrshire milking cows; cattle were also being raised for meat.[70] In 1919 there were 19 milking cows, 66 one- and two-year olds, and 17 calves on the home farm.[71]

There was a flock of 316 sheep on the home farm in 1844.[72] At Coxgreen farm in 1885 there was a flock of 46 Shropshire ewes with lambs, and at Mere farm in 1898 there were 150 Shropshire sheep.[73] Pigs were an important item of stock on the home farm in the 1840s, and bacon pigs were regularly sold.[74] There were also sales of hens, ducks, geese, turkeys, and guinea fowls in the 1830s and 1840s; the turkeys were apparently kept on the Sheepwalks.[75] A bee-hive maker was living on Highgate common in 1871.[76] In the early 1920s a new stock of Italian bees was introduced at the home farm.[77]

Crops were grown on 832 ha. (2,056 a.) of the 1,455.3 ha. (3,956 a.) of farmland returned in 1979. Barley predominated, with sugar beet and wheat also being grown. One farm specialized in vegetables. There were 5 dairy farms and nearly 1,500 cattle in the parish. Another farm specialized in pigs, of which there were over 1,400.

There was also some sheep and poultry farming.[78] On the heavier soil in the west of the parish the farms were mainly dairying mixed with arable; arable was predominant on the lighter soil in the east.[79]

A 'fruiteress' was living on Highgate common in 1841.[80] In 1979 two farms specialized in fruit and horticulture; most of the 9 ha. (22 a.) of fruit was under strawberries.[81]

Until the early 16th century there were no large landowners in the parish. About that time the Greys of Whittington, in Kinver, acquired the manors of Morfe and Enville. In 1533 Thomas Grey, who had moved to Enville from Whittington, bought the estate which had belonged to the chantry of Our Lady in Enville church. In the late 16th century another Whittington family, the Moseleys, who had acquired the Mere estate earlier in the century, bought the manor of Lutley and other land in the parish. From the late 17th century the Greys of Enville Hall pursued a policy of buying up property in the parish, often from landowners who were no longer resident. Philleybrook farm was bought in 1683, and Newhouse farm was part of the Greys' estate by 1688.[82] The Leigh House estate was bought in 1744, and the estate at Lyndon in 1747. One of the two estates at the Hollies was bought piecemeal in the mid and later 18th century.[83] Estates at Hoo, evidently the later Hoo farm and Blundies farm, were bought between 1763 and 1811; the land bought in 1811 overlooked Lord Stamford's pleasure grounds and was 'so great an object . . . that he took long and infinite pains in obtaining it'.[84] In 1840 Lord Stamford owned 2,538½ a. in the parish; the other chief landowners were Walter Moseley of the Mere with 738 a., James Amphlett Grove of Four Ashes Hall with 402½ a., and Polly Hale of the Hollies with 234½ a.[85] Most of the farms on the Grey estate were then of medium size, c. 150 a.; Newhouse farm (247 a.) was by far the largest.[86] The Hale estate, which included Coxgreen farm, and the Moseley estate were both bought by Lord Stamford in 1849.[87] In 1982 nearly four fifths of the parish, 1,561 ha. (3,857 a.), belonged to the Enville Hall estate. Medium-sized farms were still characteristic. Of the 15 farms recorded in 1979 only 2 were over 200 ha. and 3 were under 50 ha.[88]

[59] L.J.R.O., B/C/11, Thos. Deysse (1544), Ric. Garbett (1592), Humph. Jevon (1638).
[60] S.H.C. 1950–1, table facing p. 242.
[61] S.R.O., Tp. 1273/18, Enville and Bobbington tenants c. 1840.   [62] P.O. Dir. Staffs. (1868; 1872).
[63] S.R.O., Tp. 1273/27, Enville estate acct. bk. 1919, return to Bd. of Agric. and Fisheries for 1918.
[64] L.J.R.O., B/A/15/Enville; S.R.O., Tp. 1273/18, Enville and Bobbington tenants c. 1840.
[65] S.R.O., Tp. 1273/50, John Davenport to Ld. Stamford 20 May 1826.
[66] Ibid. 27, home farm stock bk.
[67] Ibid. stock bk. Nov. 1839; cash bks. Mar. 1851, Oct. and Nov. 1853; J. P. Sheldon, Dairying, 134, 143.
[68] S.R.O., Tp. 1273/27, cash bk. Nov. 1853.
[69] Ibid. 18, Enville and Bobbington tenants c. 1840.
[70] Ibid. 53, Coxgreen farm sale cat. 1885.
[71] S.R.O., Tp. 1273/27, Enville estate acct. bk. 1919, return to Bd. of Agric. and Fisheries for 1918.
[72] Ibid. 25, stock valuation 1843–4; 50, John Davenport to Ld. Stamford 20 May 1856.
[73] Ibid. 53, farm sale cats.

[74] Ibid. 25, stock valuation 1843–4; 27, stock bk.
[75] Ibid. 27, stock bk.; cash bk. Dec. 1853.
[76] P.R.O., RG 10/2928.
[77] S.R.O., Tp. 1273/27, corresp. of Geo. Mytton of Lyncroft Apiary, Lichfield, in acct. bk. for 1919.
[78] M.A.F.F., agric. returns 1979.
[79] Staffs. C.C. Planning Dept. Farm Open Day: Blundies Farm, Enville, 13 July 1980 (copy in W.S.L. Pamphs. sub Enville).   [80] P.R.O., HO 102/1007.
[81] M.A.F.F., agric. returns 1979.
[82] S.R.O., Tp. 1273/8, deed of 7 Mar. 1682/3; S.R.O. 1392.   [83] Above, manors and other estates.
[84] S.R.O., Tp. 1273/35, deeds of 21 and 22 Jan. 1763; 37, Dan. Clarke to Hugo Worthington 19 July 1824; 38, abstract of title to Hoo; 39, abstract of title to John Cherrington's estate; 41, deeds of 18, 22, and 23 Feb. 1773; Staffs. Advertiser, 18 Mar. 1809.
[85] L.J.R.O., B/A/15/Enville.
[86] S.R.O., Tp. 1273/18, Enville and Bobbington tenants c. 1840.   [87] Above, manors and other estates.
[88] Inf. from Mr. Scott-Bolton; M.A.F.F., agric. returns 1979.

In the later 19th century Lord Stamford carried out extensive rebuilding of farm buildings on his estate, notably on Home farm, Morfe House farm, and Morfeheath farm. The bricks were made at the brickworks in Morfe.[89]

Permission to construct a rabbit warren in the north-east part of the parish was given by Walter Wrottesley, lord of Lutley, to Nicholas Moseley of the Mere and his son John in 1543.[90] A warrener lived near Four Ashes in 1629, and there was a warrener's lodge at Mere in 1711.[91] When Clare Hays was inclosed in 1746, the lord was allowed to kill as many rabbits as he wished within 10 months; thereafter the tenants were free to kill any which remained.[92] The lord of Enville had a warrener's house known as Enville lodge by 1623; it probably stood near the southern edge of the Sheepwalks.[93] The ruins of a late 17th-century building stood there in 1982. A warrener was living on Morfe common in 1623.[94] He may have lived in the lodge which in 1688 stood south of Pouchers Pool Road. The lodge was still standing in 1747.[95]

FAIR. In 1254 the Crown granted William of Birmingham a fair in Enville manor on the eve, feast, and morrow of the finding of the Holy Cross (2–4 May).[96] Nothing further is known of it.

MILLS. The mill recorded at Morfe in 1222[97] may have been on the site of the present Mere mill on Philley brook. In 1321 Philip Lutley, lord of Lutley, had a mill on the boundary between Lutley and Morfe manors. An agreement made that year with Henry Morfe, lord of a moiety of Morfe, allowed Philip to extend the mill pond over Henry's land.[98] Although Philip worked the mill, it evidently belonged to the manor of Morfe: in 1332 Henry's widow claimed from Philip dower in what were described as two mills,[99] and in 1346, 1349, and 1362 Sir Fulk Birmingham, lord of the other moiety of Morfe, made leases of the mill, then called Aylewynes mill, to the lords of Lutley.[1] In 1356 the mill at Morfe was described as ruinous, but it was working again by 1403.[2] A corn mill and a fulling mill, evidently under the same roof, were stated in 1442 to be held of Lutley manor.[3] In 1496 Eleanor Strangeways, lady of Lutley, leased the mill, then called

Aldwyns mill, to Stephen Toy, with land called Walkmill pool.[4] Humphrey Toy held the mill in 1570, and it remained in the Toy family until 1778, when it was bought from the family by W. A. Moseley, owner of the Mere estate.[5] Known as Toys mill in 1775 and 1834,[6] it was called Mere mill by 1841.[7] The mill, a two-storeyed brick building, continued to work until c. 1935;[8] it still stood in 1982.

A mill on Philley brook upstream from Mere mill may have been the mill belonging to Lutley manor in the 15th and 16th centuries.[9] It probably stood south-west of the original site of Lutley manor house: in 1632 a corn mill there was held with Philleybrook Hall farm.[10] By 1727 the mill was owned by Joseph Amphlett of Four Ashes Hall, whose family still held it in 1840.[11] The owner in 1848 was Walter Moseley, who sold it the following year to Lord Stamford.[12] The mill was probably dismantled soon after.

The mill which belonged to Henry Wilcox of Lutley at his death in 1603 may have been the mill on Philley brook at Hay House (later Toys Farm): Wilcox's property, which included land called Walkmill pool, lay in that area.[13] In 1638 John Toy of Lutley assigned a moiety of a mill at Hay House to his son Edward; it was then worked as a corn mill.[14] By 1704 the other moiety was held by Henry Wollaston of Four Ashes Hall.[15] Wollaston had evidently acquired the Toys' moiety by 1712, when he settled on his second son what were described as two corn mills under one roof. They were known as Lutley or Lower mills in 1746, but there was only a single mill by 1797. In 1829 it was sold to J. A. Grove of Four Ashes Hall.[16] It was still working in 1845.[17]

There was probably a mill on Sneyd's brook at Hoo Farm by the mid 1840s. James Parrish, who farmed there, was described as a miller in 1845 and 1850.[18] In 1982 traces of a building survived at the northern corner of a pool near the farmhouse.

There was a mill on Sneyd's brook at Morfe Hall Farm probably by 1507, and certainly by 1609.[19] Edward Hawkes held it in 1698 and 1730, and it was known as Hawkes's mill in 1760.[20] A mill pool survived south of the house in 1982.

In 1574 the mill later known as Spittlebrook mill was granted by John Grey, lord of Enville, to Richard Lee of the Hoo.[21] It was probably the

[89] Below, industries.
[90] Salop. R.O. 2089/ADD, deed of 20 Oct. 1543.
[91] S.R.O., Tp. 1273/8, deed of 26 Sept. 1629; Salop. R.O. 2089/11, deed of 26 May 1711.
[92] Salop. R.O. 2089/ADD, deed of 28 May 1746.
[93] S.R.O., Tp. 1273/11, 1623 survey; Yates, *Map of Staffs.* (1775).   [94] S.R.O., Tp. 1273/11, 1623 survey.
[95] Ibid. 54, map of Heath farm 1747; S.R.O. 1392.
[96] *Cal. Pat.* 1247–58, 338.
[97] P.R.O., CP 25(1)/208/3, no. 27.
[98] S.R.O., Tp. 1273/12/6, no. 5.
[99] *S.H.C.* xi. 38.
[1] S.R.O., Tp. 1273/12/6, no. 10; S.R.O. 1485/1/10; Salop. R.O. 2089/ADD, 17th-cent. copy of deed of 8 Mar. 1361/2.
[2] *S.H.C.* 1913, 162–3; S.R.O., Tp. 1273/12/6, no. 18.
[3] S.R.O., Tp. 1273/12/8, no. 1.
[4] S.R.O., D. 593/J/15.
[5] Salop. R.O. 2089/ADD, Lutley cts. of 4 Oct. 1570, 1 June 1654, 30 Oct. 1690, 27 Apr. 1713, and descrip. of Lutley manor bounds 1744; S.R.O., D. 1021/1/12.
[6] Yates, *Map of Staffs.* (1775); White, *Dir. Staffs.* (1834), 258.   [7] P.R.O., HO 107/1002.

[8] Sherlock, *Ind. Arch. Staffs.* 166.
[9] *S.H.C.* xi. 229, 282; xvii. 35–6.
[10] S.R.O., Tp. 1273/8, deeds of 28 Sept. 1632, 17 June 1670; B.L. Maps, O.S.D. 214.
[11] MSS. at Four Ashes Hall, bdle. A, deed of 17 Jan. 1726/7; L.J.R.O., B/A/15/Enville, no. 702.
[12] S.R.O., Tp. 1273/32, partics. and plan of Mere estate 1848 and deed of 15 Feb. 1849.
[13] L.J.R.O., B/C/11, Hen. Wilcox otherwise Taylor (1603); Salop. R.O. 2089/ADD, Lutley ct. of 30 Oct. 1610.
[14] H.W.R.O. (H.), E 12/F/P/3, deed of 30 June 1638.
[15] S.R.O., D. 740/9/1.
[16] MSS. at Four Ashes Hall, bdle. 4, abstract of title to Lutley farm and mill, and valuation of Smith estate 1797.
[17] P.R.O., HO 107/1002; *P.O. Dir. Staffs.* (1845).
[18] P.R.O., HO 107/1002; *P.O. Dir. Staffs.* (1845; 1850).
[19] S.R.O., Tp. 1273/11, Enville ct. of 17 Oct. 1623, and 1623 survey; 12, bk of deeds and evidences, p. 10.
[20] L.J.R.O., B/V/6/Enville; S.R.O., Tp. 1273/3, deed of 29 Sept. 1760.
[21] S.R.O., Tp. 1273/11, deed of 1 Mar. 1579/80 (spelling Lee as Leigh).

fulling mill held by a Roger Higgs in 1516:[22] the name Higgs mill was used for the mill on Spittle brook in 1679, 1681, and 1728.[23] In 1580 Richard Lee granted his mill to Thomas Leigh of Leigh House, who seems to have converted it to a blade mill by 1603.[24] It was probably a corn mill again by 1656[25] but was working as a fulling mill in 1704 and 1773.[26] By 1817 it was a corn mill once more.[27] Bought by Lord Stamford in 1849 when it was known as Spittlebrook mill,[28] it was rebuilt and continued to work until c. 1920; the machinery was removed c. 1967.[29] The five-bayed, three-storeyed brick mill still stood in 1982; the miller's house, dating from c. 1750,[30] stood nearby over the Kinver boundary.

There was a mill on Mill brook at Lyndon c. 1527 and in 1594.[31] It was probably the mill leased by Ambrose Grey to John Pitchford in 1609; when John Pitchford, presumably the same man, died in 1634, he was living at Lyndon.[32] Lord Stamford still had a mill there in 1753. Its working was presumably affected by the creation of Temple Pool, and it was later demolished.[33]

There were two windmills in the parish in 1808. One was south of Mere Lane and east of Four Ashes and still stood in 1820. The other was at Woodcock Hill south of Morfeheath Farm and still stood in 1840.[34]

INDUSTRIES. Fulling was done at Mere mill by 1442, at Spittlebrook mill probably in 1516 and certainly in 1704 and 1773, and possibly at Toys Farm mill in or before 1603.[35]

There was a glover living in the parish in 1563.[36] In 1712 Henry Wollaston of Four Ashes settled a tanhouse, barkhouse, and tanpits at Lutley farm on his son Henry, a tanner. The buildings had been demolished by 1829.[37]

In addition to the possible use of Spittlebrook mill as a blade mill in 1603,[38] a scythesmith was living at Mere in 1662 and a locksmith at Enville in 1688.[39] John Collings, a bucklemaker and spectacle maker, was living in the parish in 1756; he and his son were both working as spectacle makers in 1772.[40] Land called Nailer's meadow west of Little Morfe Farm suggests nail making there before 1838.[41] There was a nailer at Gilbert's Cross in 1841 and two at Highgate common in 1861.[42]

A brickmaker lived at Four Ashes in 1674.[43] Enville brickworks west of Morfe Hall Farm was established c. 1850 by Lord Stamford. It produced bricks for the extensive reconstruction of farm buildings on his estate in the later 19th century. Still operating in 1888, the works had closed by 1901.[44] Two brickmakers, father and son, were living near Gilbert's Cross in 1851; both were still working in 1861, but only one in 1871.[45]

LOCAL GOVERNMENT. In the mid 1250s the lords of Enville, Morfe, and Lutley all held view of frankpledge. The lords of Enville and Morfe paid 2s. each for it, the lord of Lutley 12d.[46] Michaelmas and Easter great courts were being held at Enville in the late 13th century and at Morfe in the early 14th century.[47] By 1603 small courts for Enville and Morfe were held on the same day, and by 1621 it was the practice to hold the court for Morfe in the morning and that for Enville in the afternoon.[48] At Lutley in the later 1490s there was an annual Michaelmas court, apparently concerned only with small court business.[49] By 1560 and until at least 1788 small courts for Lutley were held at irregular intervals; the court was held at Four Ashes in 1654 and 1657; in 1713 and 1728 the meeting place was William Aingworth's house at Mere, probably the present Mere Farm. The court met at the Mere in 1738, 1744, and 1774.[50] A court for the rectory manor was held in 1458; the only other known courts were held in 1624 and 1691, when the rectory house was the meeting place.[51]

There was a constable for Enville and another for Morfe in 1377.[52] By 1666 the parish formed a single constablewick.[53] A pound was mentioned in 1612 and 1615[54] and stocks in 1827.[55] By 1784 a biennial rent of 4s. for frith silver was paid to the

[22] H.W.R.O.(H.), E 12/S, Early Deeds, deed of 22 Apr. 1516.
[23] Ibid. E 12/S, Bobbington and Enville, deed of 18 July 1681; S.R.O., Tp. 1273/32, abstract of title to Spittlebrook mill 1846 reciting deed of 18 July 1679; 42, will of John Barker 16 Mar. 1727/8.
[24] S.R.O., Tp. 1273/11, deed of 1 Mar. 1579/80 and Morfe ct. roll of 15 Oct. 1603.
[25] H.W.R.O.(H.), E 12/S, Whorwood inheritance, rental of Lady Whorwood's lands 1656.
[26] S.R.O., Tp. 1273/36, deeds of 24 and 25 June 1709; 42, deed of 14 Dec. 1773.
[27] Ibid. 37, 'Mr. Gilbert Brown's papers', Aug. 1817.
[28] Ibid. 36, deed of 11 May 1849.
[29] Kelly's Dir. Staffs. (1916; 1924); Staffs. C.C. Planning Dept., Water Mills (South) file.
[30] S.R.O., Tp. 1273/7, deed of 10 Dec. 1824.
[31] Ibid. 11, Enville ct. of survey c. 1527 and ct. of 16 Oct. 1594.
[32] Ibid. ct. of 17 Oct. 1623; L.J.R.O., B/C/11, John Pitchford (1634).
[33] S.R.O., Tp. 1273/58, Enville tithes, draft claim for tithe exemption c. 1810. It is not shown by Yates, Map of Staffs. (1775).
[34] R. Baugh, Map of Salop. (1808); C. and J. Greenwood, Map of Staffs. (1820); B.L. Maps, O.S.D. 214; L.J.R.O., B/A/15/Enville, no. 419.
[35] Above, mills.
[36] S.R.O., Tp. 1273/11, deed of 31 Mar. 1563.

[37] MSS. at Four Ashes Hall, bdle. 4, abstract of title to Lutley farm and mill.
[38] Above, mills.
[39] H.W.R.O.(H.), E 12/S, Bobbington and Enville, deed of 2 June 1662; Heraldic Cases in Ct. of Chivalry 1623–1732 (Harl. Soc. cvii), 55.
[40] S.R.O., Tp. 1273/33, deeds of 17 Apr. 1756, 17 Dec. 1772.
[41] L.J.R.O., B/A/15/Enville, no. 520.
[42] P.R.O., HO 107/1002; P.R.O., RG 9/1985.
[43] L.J.R.O., B/C/11, Thos. Sallaway (1674).
[44] S.R.O., Tp. 1273, plans for Enville Brick Works 1848; Tp. 1273/27, Enville estate cash bk.; O.S. Map 1/2,500, Staffs. LXX. 3 (1883 and 1903 edns.).
[45] P.R.O., HO 107/2017(1); P.R.O., RG 10/2928.
[46] S.H.C. v (1), 110.
[47] S.R.O., Tp. 1273/6/1/1; Tp. 1273/12/6, nos. 1, 4.
[48] S.R.O., Tp. 1273/11, Enville cts. of 15 Oct. 1603, 12 Apr. 1610, 20 Nov. 1620, 20 Nov. 1621, 23 Apr. 1636.
[49] S.R.O., D. 593/J/15.
[50] Salop. R.O. 2089/ADD, ct. rolls, and deed of 29 Nov. 1744.
[51] S.R.O., Tp. 1273/12, deeds of 29 May 1458, 26 Oct. 1624; 38, deed of 19 May 1691.
[52] S.H.C. 4th ser. vi. 9.
[53] S.H.C. 1923, 77–9.
[54] S.R.O., Tp. 1273/11, Enville cts. of 18 Apr. and 27 Oct. 1612, 27 Apr. 1615.
[55] S.R.O., D. 42/A/PK/17.

ENVILLE: LYNDON IN THE LATER 18TH CENTURY

KINVER EDGE: HOLY AUSTIN ROCK
with former cave dwellings

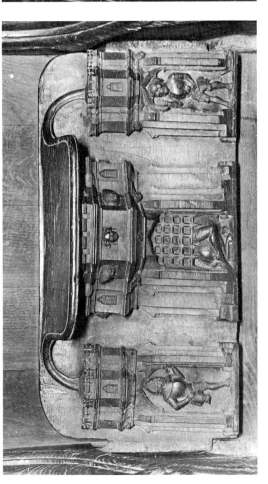

earl of Stamford by the constable of Enville.[56] It was still being paid c. 1840.[57]

There were two churchwardens by the mid 16th century.[58] There was a parish clerk by 1640.[59] In 1698 he received wages of 18s. 8d., made up partly from payments by the principal landowners in the parish and partly from fees, which included 1s. for ringing the bell every hour.[60] By 1769 he was paid by the churchwardens; his salary was £5 10s. by 1784.[61] In the mid 1740s there was a nobbler, responsible for keeping people awake in church.[62]

There were two overseers of the poor by 1699.[63] The poor were badged by 1769.[64] In the early 19th century the former Cock inn was used as a workhouse.[65] Poorhouses were evidently built in 1718, when Henry Wollaston gave £6 towards the cost.[66] They may have replaced an earlier poorhouse. In 1745 what was described as an old house called the parish house was leased, together with poor's land in Enville village, to the earl of Stamford; the following year the earl agreed to provide a road to the 'new erected houses', presumably the poorhouses.[67] Although maintained by the parish, the houses were called almshouses from the later 18th century.[68] In 1810 the houses, of which there were then eight, were ruinous; it was decided to demolish them and build six houses on waste ground by Chester Road at the joint expense of the parish, the rector, and Lord Stamford. They had been built by 1818 and appear to have been refurbished by Lord Stamford in the later 1830s.[69] At least one of the houses was still an almshouse in 1863, when the vestry appointed a new occupant.[70] In 1960 the parish council sold the houses to Seisdon rural district council for £500, which was invested as the capital of the Almshouse Trust. Under a Scheme of 1978 the trust was amalgamated with several charities to form the Enville Poor Charity.[71] In 1982 the houses were occupied as three council houses.

In 1836 the parish became part of Seisdon poor-law union.[72] It was in Seisdon rural district until 1974, when it became part of South Staffordshire district.[73]

CHURCH. Architectural evidence shows that there was a church on the present site on the ridge north of Enville village by the 12th century. The patronage of the rectory was evidently held by the lord of Enville manor by the earlier 13th century: during a minority in the lordship in the mid 1250s William of Birmingham, the mesne lord, held the patronage as guardian.[74] The lord of Enville was patron in 1291.[75] In the 1360s, during another minority, Sir Fulk Birmingham presented to the church. His son Sir John Birmingham presented in 1382, and the patronage continued to be held by the Birmingham family.[76] By 1522 it descended with an acre in Ast field.[77] The acre was known as the Advowson acre by 1698.[78] By the mid 17th century, however, it appears that the land was regarded as descending with the patronage.[79] In 1522 Edward Birmingham sold the acre, and with it the patronage, to John Whorwood of Compton Hallows in Kinver.[80] John's grandson Thomas Whorwood presented in 1571.[81] In 1604 Thomas granted the next turn to John Fowke of Gunstone, in Brewood, one of his creditors. Fowke acted as patron in 1619, when he presented his son Anthony.[82] The patronage reverted to Thomas Whorwood's son Gerard, who died in 1627.[83] It remained in his family until 1677 when his great-grandson, Wortley Whorwood, sold it to Richard Avenant of Shelsley Walsh (Worcs.), an ironmaster.[84] Avenant presented in 1681 and 1682.[85] The patron in 1685 was George Palmer; in 1686 Henry Palmer presented George Southall, also rector of Pedmore (Worcs.). In 1687 Thomas Tyrer, perhaps the Halesowen lawyer of that name, presented Southall's son-in-law William Bowles.[86] Bowles died in 1705, having by then acquired the patronage himself.[87] In 1706 Tryer and Thomas Bowles, possibly acting as trustees, presented Henry Bowles, probably William's brother. In 1718 William's sister, Bridget Downing, presented her son John Downing, who by 1736 held the patronage in his own right. He died in 1737, leaving the patronage to trustees who were to present one of his sons when qualified. Henry Bowles Downing, John's second son, was duly presented in 1743, acquiring the patronage at the same time.[88] Henry died in 1765 leaving the patronage to one of his younger sons, John, who presented himself in 1770.[89] In 1794 John sold the patronage to Richard Wilkes of Chapel Ash, in Wolverhampton

[56] S.R.O., Tp. 1273/43, Staffs. rentals.
[57] Ibid. 18, Enville and Bobbington tenants c. 1840.
[58] S.H.C. N.S. vi (1), 188; S.H.C. 1915, 98.
[59] S.R.O., D. 3578/1/1, burial of 5 June 1640.
[60] L.J.R.O., B/V/6/Enville.
[61] S.R.O., D. 42/A/PC/1, churchwardens' accts.
[62] S.R.O., D. 3578/1/6, burial of 6 Dec. 1746.
[63] S.R.O., D. 42/A/PO/90.
[64] S.R.O., D. 42/A/PC/1, overseers' accts.
[65] S.R.O., Tp. 1273/42, declaration of Ann Nicholls 12 June 1861; above, introduction.
[66] Enville ch., char. boards.
[67] S.R.O., Tp. 1273/10, deed of 20 Aug. 1745.
[68] S.R.O., D. 42/A/PC/1, overseers' accts. 1771, 1782.
[69] S.R.O., Tp. 1273/50, John Beckett to Ld. Grey 24 Apr. 1810, John Davenport to Ld. Stamford 14 Sept. 1839; L.J.R.O., B/A/15/Enville, no. 304; Poor Law Abstract, H.C. 82, pp. 420-1 (1818), xix.
[70] S.R.O., D. 3578/4, 16 Mar. 1863.
[71] Inf. from Mr. J. A. Gloss; below, chars. for the poor.
[72] 3rd Ann. Rep. Poor Law Com. H.C. 546, p. 164 (1837), xxxi.

[73] O.S. Map 1/100,000, Staffs. Admin. Areas (1967 and 1974 edns.).
[74] S.H.C. v (1), 110.   [75] S.H.C. 1911, 204.
[76] S.H.C. N.S. iv. 133-4, 141; N.S. vi (1) 91; N.S. x (2), 115, 118, 151.   [77] S.R.O., Tp. 1273/12/3, no. 8.
[78] S.H.C. xiii. 287; L.J.R.O., B/V/6/Enville, 1698.
[79] S.R.O., Tp. 1273/6, deed of 26 May 1658.
[80] S.R.O., Tp. 1273/12/3, no. 8.
[81] S.H.C. 1915, 98.
[82] H.W.R.O. (H.), E 12/S, Whorwood inheritance, deed of 2 Nov. 1604; P.R.O., IND 17003, p. 21.
[83] P.R.O., C 142/354, no. 104.
[84] P.R.O., CP 25(2)/725/28 and 29 Chas. II Hil. no. 14; below, Kinver, econ. hist.
[85] P.R.O., IND 17008, p. 91b.
[86] Ibid.; J. Ball, William Caslon, 52, 64.
[87] Shaw, Staffs. ii. 274.
[88] P.R.O., IND 17009, p. 156; 17012, p. 80; S.R.O., Tp. 1273/42, release of Jane Downing 26 Mar. 1745; Caslon, 52, 54.
[89] S.R.O., Tp. 1273/42, copy of Hen. Downing's will; P.R.O., IND 17012, p. 80.

(d. 1797). Wilkes's second son, also Richard, inherited it and presented himself in 1800.[90] He died in 1824 leaving it to a cousin, Thomas Price, a minor canon of Worcester cathedral, who presented himself. Price died in 1836, and the patronage descended to the younger Richard Wilkes's sister Sarah, wife of Henry Jesson of Trysull. In 1841 Sarah gave it to her son Cornelius, himself rector of Enville since 1837.[91] In 1859 he sold it to Lord Stamford; it then descended with Enville manor, and the patron in 1981 was Mrs. Eileen Bissill.[92]

The rectory was worth £8 in 1291.[93] In 1535 the income was £28 gross (£27 3s. net), from glebe, tithes, oblations, and Easter offerings.[94] In 1598 the tithes and oblations, except those from the Hale estate at the Hollies and the tithes of hemp and flax, were leased, with barns at the rectory house, for £120 a year. In 1633 the rectory was valued at £160.[95] In 1636 the glebe comprised a house, 3 a. of garden and orchard, 37½ a. of closes adjoining the curtilage and the churchyard, 24 a. in the open fields of Enville township, and a dole of meadow; the tithe of hay was leased for £6 6s. 8d. a year and the remaining tithes, offerings, and oblations for £120 a year. By 1698 most of the tithe of hay had been replaced by moduses; other tithes were generally paid in kind.[96] The rector was one of the inhabitants of Enville who had pasture rights in Checkhill waste in Kinver, and when the waste was inclosed in 1804 he was allotted 78 a. there.[97] The average income of the rectory c. 1830 was £1,084 gross (£979 net).[98] In 1840 tithes and moduses were commuted for a rent charge of £900.[99] In 1841 there were 124 a. of glebe, including the 78 a. at Checkhill.[1] The Checkhill land was exchanged with Lord Stamford for 35 a. at Compton in Kinver in 1854.[2] In the later 1880s the glebe comprised 77 a. with a gross estimated rental of £114.[3]

A rectory manor, known in 1546 as the Parson's manor, existed by 1458, when a tenement on the Bobbington boundary called Groundwyns, apparently part of Lutley manor in 1391, was surrendered and regranted in the rector's court.[4] Chief rents totalling 11s. 6d. were paid to the rector by four tenants at or near Groundwyns in 1698; they were still paid in 1776 and seem to have been, with heriots, the rector's only source of income from the manor.[5]

A rectory house east of the church was recorded in 1342.[6] In 1592 it included a parlour, hall, seven chambers, offices, and a newly built study or library in which the rector, Richard Garbett, had books worth £4. There was also a dovecot; barns, approached from the main road through a gate-house, were mentioned in 1598.[7] In 1666 the rectory house was assessed at seven hearths.[8] In 1698 the house, partly rebuilt by William Bowles, rector from 1688, consisted of four bays; there were nine bays of barns and two of stabling, with a large foldyard covering c. 1½ a. Bowles also replanted the garden and orchard.[9] The house was rebuilt by Richard Wilkes, rector 1800–24;[10] he may have retained parts of the earlier building. The principal rooms, at the east end, have early 19th-century decorations, as have the small library and staircase. At the west end are additions in a later 19th-century plain Gothic style, probably built by Lord Stamford for the Revd. Henry Payne. The house ceased to be the rectory in 1975 and was empty in 1982, when the rector was living in West Cottage in Enville village.[11]

There was a curate in 1533, the rector being a pluralist and evidently non-resident, and another in 1558.[12] About 1619 John Evans was curate. He had practised magical arts in the neighbourhood for some five years and lived with the rector, John Colombyne, who encouraged his activities. Evans resigned the curacy c. 1620 apparently because of growing local hostility when his spells and cures failed to work. He then set up as a teacher in the parish.[13] Edward Archer was appointed curate in 1632, the rector being a lunatic. Archer left Enville in 1640, but there was another curate in 1651.[14] There was a curate in 1730; he was then also teaching grammar at Enville free school.[15] A curate was appointed in the later 1850s, and there was normally one until the early 1890s.[16]

A chantry at the altar of Our Lady was founded by Philip Lutley in 1362 and ordained in 1372.[17] The right to appoint a priest descended with Lutley manor.[18] The chantry was endowed with an assart called Morfe wood in 1366.[19] By 1369 the endowment was worth £4 in rents, and the reversion of a 20s. rent had also been given. The rents, paid by parishioners in Enville, Morfe, and Lutley, were mostly 1s. or less.[20] In 1535 the chantry was worth £6 13s. 4d.[21] When it was suppressed in 1548 it had an income of £8 17s. 11d.

[90] S.R.O., Tp. 1273/42, sched. of title deeds to advowson and copy of Ric. Wilkes's will; P.R.O., IND 17012, p. 81.
[91] S.R.O., Tp. 1273/42, sched. of title deeds to advowson and copy of will of Revd. Ric. Wilkes.
[92] S.R.O., Tp. 1273/42, deed of 8 July 1859; Lich. Dioc. Dir. (1982).   [93] Tax. Eccl. (Rec. Com.), 243.
[94] Valor Eccl. (Rec. Com.), iii. 103.
[95] S.H.C. 1934(2), 8; Cal. S.P. Dom. 1633–4, 344. For the Hale estate see above, manors and other estates.
[96] L.J.R.O., B/V/6/Enville.
[97] S.R.O., Q/RDc 59; below, p. 138.
[98] Rep. Com. Eccl. Revenues, 476–7.
[99] L.J.R.O., B/A/15/Enville.
[1] Ibid.; L.J.R.O., B/V/6/Enville.
[2] W.S.L., M. 1018.
[3] Returns of Glebe Lands, H.C. 307, p. 64 (1887), lxiv.
[4] S.R.O., Tp. 1273/8, deed of 11 Nov. 1391; 12, deed of 29 May 1458; S.H.C. 1910, 56–8.
[5] L.J.R.O., B/V/6/Enville; S.R.O., Tp. 1273/12, deeds of 29 May 1458, 26 Oct. 1624; above, local govt.
[6] S.R.O., Tp. 1273/12/4, no. 6.

[7] L.J.R.O., B/C/11, Ric. Garbett (1592); S.H.C. 1934 (2), 8.   [8] S.H.C. 1923, 77.
[9] L.J.R.O., B/V/6/Enville.
[10] S.H.C. 4th ser. x. 10, stating, in 1830, that house had been rebuilt by late rector.
[11] Inf. from the rector and Mr. Scott-Bolton.
[12] S.H.C. 1915, 99; L.J.R.O., B/C/11, John Wylcockis (1558).
[13] P.R.O., STAC 8/255/24; printed sheet relating to Evans in W.S.L. Pamphs. sub Enville; below, educ.
[14] Alum. Cantab. to 1751, ed. Venn, i. 37; Calamy Revised, ed. A. G. Matthews, 14, 414; Cal. S.P. Dom. 1633–4, 344; S.H.C. 1915, 65, 67, 99.   [15] Below, educ.
[16] Lich. Dioc. Ch. Cal. (1858 and edns. to 1892).
[17] Cal. Pat. 1361–4, 267; Shaw, Staffs. ii. 275; Salop. R.O. 2089/ADD, deed of 12 July 1372.
[18] Salop. R.O. 2089/ADD, deeds of 12 July 1372, 30 June 1540.
[19] Shaw, Staffs. ii. 275.
[20] Salop. R.O. 2089/ADD, deed of 24 Aug. 1375.
[21] Valor Eccl. (Rec. Com.), iii. 101.

and the priest was granted a pension of £6.[22] In 1553 the Crown gave the chantry estate to two speculators, who sold it immediately to Thomas Grey of Enville.[23] It then consisted of the former priest's house and another house, ½ virgate at Enville, a house and ½ virgate at Lyndon, a cottage, several crofts, and rents in Enville parish, and a mill in Kinver.[24] The property was incorporated into the Grey estate.[25] The chantry priest's house may have been the newly built cottage at Bar green mentioned in 1375.[26] His house certainly stood at Bar green at the Dissolution.[27]

There was evidently an altar dedicated to St. Nicholas in the Middle Ages: in 1556 the St. Nicholas aisle of the parish church was mentioned.[28] There were lights on the rood screen in 1503 and one at the Lady altar in 1544.[29] By 1549 a paschal light had been endowed by Isabel Brauntley.[30]

Edward Archer, curate in the 1630s, was a puritan.[31] In the mid 1630s the wife of Ambrose Grey, lord of Enville, attended puritan lectures in neighbouring parishes.[32]

In 1830 there were two services on Sunday and a monthly communion service.[33] In 1892 there were daily communion services early in the morning and one at noon on the first Sunday in the month.[34]

There was a chapel of St. Michael at Lutley by 1367; there was also an altar of St. Michael there, possibly served by a chantry priest. What may be the remains of the building were visible in 1982 in a field near the site of Lutley manor house. The chapel recorded at Morfe in the 14th century may have been in the manor house.[35]

The church of *ST. MARY*, an invocation in use by 1742 although St. Laurence was used in the 16th century,[36] is built of red sandstone and consists of a chancel, a four-bayed nave with north and south aisles, north and south porches, and a south-west tower. The nave and south aisle date from the 12th century, and two contemporary sculptures are reset on either side of the arcade. One is of a priest with his right hand raised in blessing and his left hand holding a fan; the other is of a bishop.[37] The north arcade and aisle were added in the 13th century, and the chancel was rebuilt to its present size. A 13th-century effigy of a priest survives in a canopied niche on the north side of the chancel.[38] A new east window was inserted in the earlier 14th century, and the south aisle was evidently remodelled at the same time. The unbuttressed south-west tower was probably there by that date.[39] Glass dating from the 14th century survives in the east window of the chancel and the east window of the south aisle.[40] Four misericords in the chancel date from the later 15th century;[41] they may be 'the long seats formerly belonging to the chantry' which were on the north side of the chancel in 1697.[42] An alabaster table tomb raised by Anne Grey as a memorial to her husband Edward Grey (d. 1559), herself, and their children, formerly stood on the north side of the chancel. It was moved to its present position at the east end of the south aisle c. 1872.[43]

The chancel was remodelled in the 18th century, the lateral walls being given exterior classical pilasters and round-headed windows. The south porch too was built or rebuilt in the 18th century.[44] By 1756 there was a gallery in the south aisle lit by two dormer windows.[45] In 1820 the gallery, then used by the singers, was replaced by one in the north aisle for singers and Sunday-school children. The lower part of the tower was converted into a vestry.[46] A new vestry on the north side of the chancel was built in 1825. At the same time the two-decker pulpit, which stood on the south side of the nave by 1744, was moved to the south side of the chancel arch.[47] A later pulpit stood in the same position in 1982.

The church was restored by G. G. (later Sir Gilbert) Scott in 1872–4. The tower, west end, north and south porches, and lateral walls of the chancel were rebuilt; the plaster was removed from the interior walls, and the capitals of the arcade piers were recut. The north gallery, the aisle dormers, and the box pews were removed. The vestry was converted into an organ chamber and a new vestry created by screening off the east end of the north aisle.[48] The south wall was rebuilt in 1968.[49]

The plate in 1552 consisted of a silver chalice and paten and four cruets; there were also two brass crosses. A piece of silver at the foot of the rood had been removed. In 1553 only two cruets were mentioned.[50] Mary Grey (d. 1690) gave a silver chalice in memory of her son Thomas.[51] A silver-guilt chalice and paten, silver flagons, and a silver almsdish were given by Lord Stamford in 1763.[52]

[22] *S.H.C.* 1915, 99, 101; P.R.O., E 318/39/2101.
[23] *Cal. Pat.* 1553, 218–19; S.R.O., Tp. 1273/12, deed of 12 Feb. 1552/3.
[24] P.R.O., E 318/39/2101.
[25] H.W.R.O. (H.), E 12/S, Bobbington and Enville, valor of lands of John Grey 1581.
[26] Salop. R.O. 2089/ADD, deed of 24 Aug. 1375.
[27] S.R.O., Tp. 1273/8, undated survey of chantry rents.
[28] L.J.R.O., B/C/11, Humph. Hale (1556).
[29] Ibid. John Wilcox (1533), Thos. Deysse (1544).
[30] *S.H.C.* 1915, 99.
[31] *Calamy Revised*, ed. Matthews, 14, 414; *S.H.C.* 1915, 67.   [32] L.J.R.O., B/V/1/55, p. 7.
[33] *S.H.C.* 4th ser. x. 10.
[34] S.R.O., D. 3578/3/1, reg. of services.
[35] *Cal. Pat.* 1364–7, 400; above, manors and other estates.
[36] J. Ecton, *Thesaurus* (1742), 108; L.J.R.O., B/C/11, Thos. Tomyns (1540), Thos. Deysse (1544), John Wylcockis (1558), Eliz. Bradney (1592).
[37] *T.B.A.S.* lxix. 17.
[38] Ibid. 17–18.   [39] Below, plate facing p. 192.

[40] *T.B.A.S.* lxviii. 50–1; *Torrington Diaries*, ed. C. Bruyn Andrews, iii. 226.
[41] *T.B.A.S.* lxvii. 50–1; above, plate facing p. 113.
[42] MSS. at Four Ashes Hall, bdle. A, deed of 14 Oct. 1697.
[43] *T.B.A.S.* lxx. 20–1; W.S.L., Staffs. Views, iv. 183; *P.O. Dir. Staffs.* (1868; 1872).
[44] Below, plate facing p. 192.
[45] Salop. R.O. 2089/25, plan of Enville ch. pews 1744, endorsement.
[46] L.J.R.O., B/C/2/1820–3, pp. 73–5; S.R.O., Tp. 1273/50, Enville ch. bdle.
[47] Salop. R.O. 2089/25, plan of Enville ch. pews 1744; L.J.R.O., B/C/5/1825, Enville; Lichfield Cathedral Libr., Moore and Hinckes drawings, ix, no. 16.
[48] L.J.R.O., B/C/5/1871, Enville; *Kelly's Dir. Staffs.* (1884).
[49] Note in show case in church.
[50] *S.H.C.* N.S. vi (1), 188; *S.H.C.* 1915, 98, describing the chalice as partly gilt.
[51] Enville ch., char. boards.
[52] *T.B.A.S.* lxxiii. 34–5.

There were four bells and a sanctus bell in 1552 and 1553.[53] Michael Moseley gave a bell in 1626, and four bells, possibly those which existed in 1552, were recast by Abraham Rudhall of Gloucester in 1718. A further three bells were cast by John Taylor & Co. of Loughborough in 1876.[54] A tower clock was given by Thomas Shadwell, son of Edward Shadwell of Lyndon, in 1659. A second dial was added by Harry Grey c. 1700. In 1769 a caretaker was paid £1 11s. 6d. a year for looking after the clock. A new clock, in memory of Lord Stamford (d. 1883), was installed c. 1884.[55]

The shaft and base of an ancient cross stand in the churchyard south of the church. The burial ground was extended in 1857 and 1915.[56]

The surviving registers date from 1627 and are complete except for 1686–8.[57]

NONCONFORMITY. In 1845 a house at Four Ashes occupied by John Standon was registered for protestant dissenting worship.[58] In 1855–6 Richard Smallman opened his house in Enville for worship by Wesleyan Methodists. On Sundays there were morning and evening services, the latter taken by a preacher from Gospel Ash chapel in Bobbington. The cause flourished but was abandoned c. 1857 because of opposition from the rector, Cornelius Jesson.[59]

EDUCATION. There may have been a school in the parish in the late 16th century: John Key, a schoolmaster, was described as formerly of Enville in 1598.[60] In 1625 John Evans of Four Ashes, formerly curate of Enville, offered tuition in Latin, Greek, Hebrew, and mathematics.[61]

A free school for six poor boys of the parish was established by Edward Gravenor of the Hollies, who by will of 1654 endowed it with an annual £5 from land at Swindon, in Wombourne. The boys were to be chosen by the churchwardens and overseers and by the owner of Gravenor's house at the Hollies, who was to have two votes.[62] Latin was apparently taught by 1666, when the foundation was called Enville grammar school. By 1710 the master gave an English education alone, although in 1730 Latin was taught by the curate of Enville.[63] By the early 19th century the schoolhouse was the building now known as Swinford Cottage, standing in the village on the road leading to Enville Hall. The

rector, Richard Wilkes, added a Sunday school to the free school c. 1807, and Lord Stamford built a separate schoolroom, now the garage of the cottage, which enabled the schoolhouse to be used solely as the master's residence.[64] The master received an annual £30, raised by subscription, for teaching the Sunday school. There were 35 weekday pupils c. 1818, of whom 6, still appointed in accordance with Gravenor's wishes, were supported by the foundation and 15 by Lord Stamford, his family, and other individuals.[65] There were 35 boys and 5 girls at the school in the mid 1830s.[66] By the mid 1840s it was a National school with 43 boys and 20 girls.[67] In 1860–1 there were two teachers, a married couple, who received a salary of £69 13s. 6d. from the endowment, voluntary contributions, and school pence.[68] In 1861 a new school was built opposite the Cat inn by Lady Stamford.[69] It received a government grant by 1869.[70] There was an average attendance of 97 boys and girls and 36 infants in 1907.[71] The school, which was extended c. 1957,[72] was known as Enville parochial school by the late 1860s; in 1959 it was renamed the Countess of Stamford and Warrington primary school. In 1981 it was a C. of E. junior (controlled) school with an average attendance of 27.[73]

Under a Scheme of 1978 the foundation was amalgamated with the charity of Henry Grey for apprentices and the charity of Peter Lafargue to form the Enville Education Charity. The income was to be spent on grants to Enville schoolchildren and to young people starting on a trade or profession, and also on grants to provide books at schools attended by Enville children. The income in 1980 was £157, of which £40 was spent on a grant to an apprentice.[74]

A charity boarding school to prepare 12 girls for domestice service was established in 1755 by Lady Dorothy Grey (d. 1781), a daughter of the 3rd earl of Stamford.[75] The girls, admitted between 5 and 7 years old, remained at the school until they were 17 or went into service, whichever was the sooner. Entrance was restricted to girls from Enville and any other Staffordshire parish where the Grey family had property. Each girl on leaving was to receive a Bible, a prayer book, and copies of *The Whole Duty of Man* and *Wilson on the Sacrament*, funds permitting. The mistress was to be an Anglican, over 30, and unmarried. To support the school Lady Dorothy settled a rent charge of £50 from land in

[53] *S.H.C.* n.s. vi. (1), 188; *S.H.C.* 1915, 98.
[54] Lynam, *Ch. Bells Staffs.* 11.
[55] Bennett, *Enville*, 30; S.R.O., D. 42/A/PC/1.
[56] Lich. Dioc. Regy., B/A/2(i)/P, pp. 635–40; V, p. 511.
[57] All except those in current use are in S.R.O., D. 3578/1.
[58] *S.H.C.* 4th ser. iii. 99.
[59] J. H. Mees, *Story of a Hundred Years: Handbk. of Wesleyan Methodist Church Stourbridge Circuit* (Stourbridge, 1928), 112–13 (copy in Stourbridge Libr.).
[60] *S.H.C.* 1935, 55.
[61] B. Capp, *Astrology and the Popular Press*, 235, 305.
[62] *5th Rep. Com. Char.* 616; P.R.O., ED 7/108/132.
[63] L.J.R.O., B/A/4/5; S.R.O., D. 3578/1/2.
[64] *Digest of Returns to Sel. Cttee. on Educ. of Poor*, H.C. 224, p. 859 (1819), ix (2); P.R.O., ED 7/108/132; L.J.R.O., B/A/15/Enville, no. 11; B/V/6/Enville, 1841.
[65] *Digest of Returns to Sel. Cttee. on Educ. of Poor*, 859; *5th Rep. Com. Char.* 617.
[66] *Educ. Enq. Abstract*, H.C. 62, p. 876 (1835), xlii.
[67] Nat. Soc. *Inquiry, 1846–7*, Staffs. 4–5.
[68] P.R.O., ED 7/108/132.
[69] *Kelly's Dir. Staffs.* (1888); below, plate facing p. 145.
[70] *Rep. of Educ. Cttee. of Council, 1869–70* [C.165], p. 641, H.C. (1870), xxii.
[71] *Public Elem. Schs. 1907* [Cd. 3901], p. 565, H.C. (1908), lxxxiv.
[72] S.R.O., D. 1359/7/1.
[73] *Rep. Educ. Cttee. of Council, 1869–70*, 641; S.R.O., surv. of sch. records 1965, Enville; inf. from the headmistress (1981).
[74] Below, chars. for the poor; inf. from Mr. J. A. Gloss.
[75] For this para. see *5th Rep. Com. Char.* 617–18; *Digest of Returns to Sel. Cttee. on Educ. of Poor*, 859; J. Heely, *Letters on the Beauties of Hagley, Envil, and the Leasowes* (1777), ii. 63–4; Shaw, *Staffs.* ii. 274.

Lincolnshire; of the income £2 10s. was set aside for the rent of the school land and for repairs to the building. In 1757 Lady Dorothy gave a further £20 a year from the same property in Lincolnshire. Lord Stamford gave £100 in 1764, and Thomas Evans, archdeacon of Worcester, gave £100 in 1815. The income, however, was insufficient to maintain a full complement of 12 girls, and the number had fallen to six by 1806; it was then further reduced to four. There continued to be an annual deficiency of c. £20, met by Lord Stamford. By will proved 1819 he left £450 to the school, and its annual income c. 1820 was £101 2s. 10d., of which the mistress received £7. There were only three girls at the school in the mid 1830s and five in 1860.[76] The school still functioned in 1925 but was closed soon afterwards. From c. 1930 the building, in the south-east corner of the parish, was occupied as a private house known as Lady Dorothy's Cottage.[77]

Under a Scheme of 1978 the foundation was opened to both girls and boys in the parishes of Enville, Bobbington, and Kinver, preference being given to those from Enville. The income was to be spent on grants to children attending secondary schools, to students at places of further education, including universities, and to young people starting on a trade or profession; on travel bursaries; and on grants to students studying music or other arts. In 1981–2 the income was £3,186.95, from which two grants of £100 and £158 were made.[78]

There was a dancing master living in Enville in 1759; by 1766 he had moved to Kinver.[79] There was a private school at Four Ashes in 1778.[80] There was a girls' boarding school in the parish in 1819; a drawing master then living in Enville may have taught there.[81] A private school with nine boys and nine girls existed in the mid 1830s.[82] Mary and Sarah Norris ran a school in Enville village in 1841 and 1851.[83] In 1860 and 1864 Jane and Ellen Harcourt ran a school, probably in Moos Cottage near the church where they were living in 1861.[84] By 1888 a Miss Buraston was running a private school at Four Ashes; she continued it to c. 1900.[85]

CHARITIES FOR THE POOR. By deed of 1667 Henry Grey of Enville Hall gave a rent charge of 56s. from 12 a. in Enville. The gift was evidently in consideration of £56 given to him by the parish officers. The money was accumulated poor's stock,[86] of which £46 16s. 8d. was pre-sumably made up of the benefactions of 14 people named on the charity boards in the church.

By deed of 1690 Tomyns Dickins the elder of Morfe gave c. 10 a. in Enville, the income to be distributed among the poor of the parish six days before Christmas and at Easter. The income from the land and from £30 raised by the sale of timber was £6 in the late 1780s. In 1819 the income was £10 10s., disbursed in doles of between 1s. and 5s. on St. Thomas's day (21 December); there were 96 recipients that year.[87]

By 1727 Abigail Watts, widow of a rector of Enville, had given £10, the interest to be divided between two poor widows. There was an income of 10s. in the late 1780s, but distribution stopped c. 1802. In 1819 the accumulated arrears were distributed by the rector among 19 widows.[88]

By will of 1773 John Elcock left £6, the interest to be distributed in 3d. loaves to the poor on Whitsunday. About 1820 the income of 5s. was supplemented by bread bought with 'sacrament money'.[89]

By deed of 1807 Lord Stamford invested £518 15s. to produce an income of £25 for the relief of the poor. The distribution, made by the earl and his successor, was in the form of sheets, blankets, and clothing.[90]

Under a Scheme of 1978 the above five charities were united as the Enville Poor Charity, which also included the Almshouse Trust established in 1960. The income in 1981 was £472.39, of which £100 was spent in a grant to one family.[91]

Edward Gravenor of the Hollies (d. 1654) left £10 to produce an annual 10s. which was to be distributed at Michaelmas in 3d. doles to 40 poor parishioners, chosen by the churchwardens and overseers and by the owner of Gravenor's house. An owner of the other Hollies estate, Corbett Hale (d. 1794), doubled each share to 6d. The increased distribution was still paid c. 1820.[92] Nothing further is known of the charity.

Henry Grey (d. 1687) also left £100, the interest to be used each year in apprenticing two poor boys from the parish. In 1732 the money, together with the charity of Peter Lafargue, was used to buy 8 a. in King's Norton (Worcs., later Birmingham).[93] The income was £5 in 1737 and had increased to £5 5s. by the late 1780s.[94] There was a limited demand for the charity: only nine apprenticeship indentures survive between 1724 and 1782, and by 1820 there was an accumulated surplus of £31 1s. 2d. The income c. 1820 was £12 12s., of which 10s. was paid in respect of Lafargue's charity.[95]

[76] Educ. Enquiry Abstract, 876; G. Griffith, Free Schs. of Staffs. 627.
[77] Staffs. Endowed Chars. 57; Kelly's Dir. Staffs. (1916; 1924; 1928; 1932); S.R.O., Tp. 1273/52, bdles. of sch. accts.; below, plate facing p. 145.
[78] Inf. from Mr. Gloss.
[79] H.W.R.O. (H.), E 12/S, Kinver X, deeds of 20 Feb. 1759, 3 July 1766.
[80] A. L. Reade, Reades of Blackwood Hill (priv. print. 1906), 187 n.
[81] Digest of Returns to Sel. Cttee. on Educ. of Poor, 859; S.R.O., Tp. 1273/24, Enville reg. of apprentices 1802–19, no. 52.   [82] Educ. Enq. Abstract, 876.
[83] P.R.O., HO 107/1002; HO 107/2017(1).
[84] P.O. Dir. Staffs. (1860; 1864); P.R.O., RG 9/1985.
[85] Kelly's Dir. Staffs. (1888 to 1904).

[86] S.R.O., Tp. 1273/6, deed of 20 Oct. 1667; 5th Rep. Com. Char. 620.
[87] 5th Rep. Com. Char. 620; Char. Dons. 1786–8, ii. 1144–5; S.R.O., Tp. 1273/44A, deed of 20 June 1691.
[88] 5th Rep. Com. Char. 621; Char. Dons. 1786–8, ii. 1144–5.
[89] 5th Rep. Com. Char. 621; Char. Dons. 1786–8, ii. 1144–5; Enville ch., char. board.
[90] 5th Rep. Com. Char. 621–2; S.R.O., Tp. 1273/24, char. accts. 1807–23; Tp. 1273/50, bdle. marked 'Poor at Enville'.
[91] Inf. from Mr. J. A. Gloss. For the Almshouse Trust see above, local govt.
[92] 5th Rep. Com. Char. 621; above, manors and other estates.
[93] 5th Rep. Com. Char. 619.
[94] S.R.O., D. 3578/1/6; Char. Dons. 1786–8, ii. 1144–5.
[95] 5th Rep. Com. Char. 619; S.R.O., D. 42/A/PZ/19–27.

Peter Lafargue (d. 1711), a refugee Huguenot doctor who became tutor to Harry Grey, left £10, the interest to be spent on copies of *The Whole Duty of Man* which the rector of Enville was to distribute among poor communicants. The first distribution, of six books, was made in 1713; four books were distributed in 1714 and annually thereafter until at least 1766. In 1732

the endowment was laid out, together with Henry Grey's charity, in land in King's Norton. No books were distributed between *c.* 1801 and 1817, but the charity was evidently revived in 1818.[96]

Under a scheme of 1978 Grey's and Lafargue's charities were united to form part of the Enville Education Charity.[97]

KINVER

KINVER[98] occupies the south-west corner of Staffordshire adjoining Shropshire and Worcestershire.[99] It is mainly rural with extensive hilly scenery, notably the escarpment known as Kinver Edge, and *c.* 1900 it was known as 'the Switzerland of the Midlands'.[1] In the Middle Ages it lay in the centre of Kinver forest, so named by 1168. A borough was created in the 13th century. Between the 17th and 19th centuries Kinver had a flourishing iron industry, and cloth working was important in the 17th and 18th centuries. Kinver's scenery has attracted visitors since the later 19th century, and in the 20th century there has been extensive residential building for people working in the nearby towns. The centre of the parish can be described as a large village, but even in the late 19th century one writer found description difficult: 'if we call it a town we flatter it, if we speak of it as a village we insult it.'[2] The ancient parish was 9,011 a. (3,647 ha.) in area. In 1934 the Prestwood and Ashwood parts of Kingswinford parish were transferred to Kinver, and in 1966 a small part of Brierley Hill was added.[3] This article deals only with the ancient parish.

The general use of the spelling Kinver is recent. The form Kinfare evolved from medieval usage and remained the normal spelling until the 19th century.[4] The spelling Kinver was used by Christopher Saxton (1577) and later mapmakers until Robert Plot adopted Kinfare on his map of 1682; thereafter usage on maps varied.[5] Kinver appeared as an alternative to Kinfare in documents and books from the later 18th century and

had become established by the 1840s.[6] The use of Kinfare, however, lingered for many years.[7]

The river Stour and its tributary Smestow brook formed the boundary of the ancient parish in the north-east. The Stour then flows south through the centre of the parish with Kinver village on its west bank. Short stretches of the northern boundary are formed by Spittle brook and the line of a dried-up tributary stream and by Mill brook. The level of the ground drops to below 200 ft. (61 m.) along the Stour and the Smestow and to 160 ft. (49 m.) where the Kidderminster–Wolverhampton road crosses the southern boundary. It rises steeply west of Kinver village to 543 ft. (166 m.) near the north end of Kinver Edge, and it reaches 670 ft. (204 m.) at No Man's Green on the boundary in the north-west. On the high ground which forms the northern extension of the parish the level reaches 443 ft. (135 m.). An escarpment runs down the east side of the parish, reaching 478 ft. (146 m.) at Iverley at its southern end. The rock is mainly sandstone, with Bunter Pebble Beds forming the Kinver Edge escarpment and that on the eastern boundary. Rock dwellings have been numerous. The Compton area in the west lies on the Coal Measures, and there is an outcrop of coal in Roughpark Wood north of Park Farm.[8] The soil is mainly light sand; there is also some sandy loam and, around Compton, clay.[9] Sand pits have been worked in the east since the 17th century or earlier.[10]

Mesolithic and Neolithic flints have been found in various parts of the parish.[11] A barrow

[96] *5th Rep. Com. Char.* 619; Shaw, *Staffs.* ii. 275; S.R.O., D. 3578/1/6.   [97] Above, educ.

[98] This article was written mainly in 1982. Mr. A. T. Foley, of Stoke Edith, Herefs., Mr. A. M. Wherry, county archivist of Hereford and Worcester, and Miss S. Hubbard, assistant county archivist at Hereford, are thanked for their kindness in placing the relevant part of the Foley family's extensive archives on temporary deposit at the Staffs. Record Office for the writers' use. Mr. J. W. and Mrs. L. E. King of Rockmount, Kinver, and their son Mr. P. W. King are thanked for their generosity in making available the results of their extensive research into Kinver's history and for reading and commenting on the article in draft. Mr. D. M. Bills of Kinver, Mrs. E. Griffiths of Kinver Library, Mr. J. G. Smith of Kinver, Prebendary D. W. Watson, vicar of Kinver until 1982, and Mrs. J. Watson, and others named in footnotes are also thanked for their help.

[99] Until its transfer to Worcs. in 1895 the parish of Upper Arley formed the south-western extremity of Staffs.

[1] Birmingham and Midland Tramways, *Illustrated Guide to Kinver* (1904), 1 (copy in W.S.L. Pamphs.).

[2] S. Baring-Gould, *Bladys of the Stewponey* (1897), 1.

[3] *Census*, 1891, 1951, 1971; Staffs. Review Order, 1934, p. 64 (copy in S.R.O.).

[4] Ekwall, *Eng. Place-names*; H.W.R.O. (H.), E 12/S, Kinver ct. rolls.

[5] The 1st edn. of O.S. 1″ used Kinver on sheet LXI SE. (1833) and Kinfare on sheet LXII. SW. (1834).

[6] W.S.L., S.MS. 468, p. 114; L.J.R.O., B/A/3/Kinver from 1779; S.R.O., Q/RDc 42; Shaw, *Staffs.* ii. 262; Pitt, *Staffs.* i. 196; White, *Dir. Staffs.* (1834), 259; *P.O. Dir. Staffs.* (1845).

[7] Both spellings were used in the 1861 Census (P.R.O., RG 9/1985); *Kelly's Dir Staffs.* used Kinver as the preferred spelling only from 1884.

[8] T. H. Whitehead and R. W. Pocock, *Memoirs of Geol. Surv.*, *Dudley and Bridgnorth*, 5, 57, 80, 106–7, 111–12.

[9] *Kelly's Dir. Staffs.* (1940); Bennett, *Kinver*, 7–8; Scott, *Stourbridge*, 172.

[10] Below, econ. hist.

[11] *Worcs. Arch. Newsletter*, iv. 2; *W. Midlands Arch. News Sheet*, xvii. 20–1; xx. 31–2; xxii. 39–41.

has been recorded near the northern end of Kinver Edge,[12] and there may have been another on the ridge between Dunsley and Whittington east of Kinver village.[13] A standing stone east of Bannut Tree Road in Compton may have had prehistoric significance or may simply have been a glacial erratic. In the later 17th century it was variously known as the Boltstone and the Battlestone. It was destroyed c. 1840.[14] There is an Iron Age promontory fort at the northern end of Kinver Edge, 11 a. (4.5 ha.) in over-all area with an internal area of 8¾ a. (3.5 ha.). On the southwest and south-east it is defended by a substantial bank and ditch; the other two sides follow the edge of the escarpment, with traces of a bank on the north-west side.[15] There are indications of Romano-British settlement in the parish.[16] The line of a Roman road from Ashwood, in Kingswinford, to Droitwich (Worcs.) is followed by County Lane, which forms part of the eastern boundary of the parish.[17]

References to the wood of Cynibre in 736 and to Cynefares Stane in 964[18] preserve early forms of the name Kinver, which is Celtic. Although the meaning of the first element is obscure, the second means a hill.[19] It may refer to the hillfort or to a settlement near the church east of the fort; a church existed by 1086. Anglo-Saxon settlement on the rivers is indicated by place names. It has been suggested that the southern boundary of the parish west of the Stour is partly that recorded as the northern boundary of land in Wolverley (Worcs.) in 964; it ran from Cynefares Stane, perhaps Vale's Rock on the Wolverley side of the parish boundary, and reached the Stour evidently along the line of what is now Gipsy Lane.[20]

In 1086 Kinver had a recorded population of 28. In 1293 there were 26 freeholders, 63 customary tenants, and 22 burgesses; two of the burgesses appear also among the freeholders.[21] In 1327 there were 52 people assessed for tax.[22] In the mid 1520s 81 were assessed,[23] and there were 79 names on the muster roll of 1539.[24] In 1563 the parish had 75 households.[25] A poll-tax assessment of 1641 listed 421 people.[26] In 1666 there were 125 people assessed for hearth tax with a further 105 too poor to pay.[27] The Compton Census of 1676 recorded 957 people.[28] In 1755 there were 249 people in the parish owing

suit at Kinver manor court, and in 1789 there were 299 suitors.[29] In the earlier 1770s there were stated to be between 200 and 300 houses in the parish.[30] The population in 1801 was 1,665. By 1831 it was 1,831, and by 1841 the prosperity of the iron trade had increased it to 2,207. It continued to rise, reaching 3,551 by 1861.[31] The drop to 3,194 by 1871 was blamed on the closure of the screw works at Kinver mill and the slackness of the iron trade in the district. The population was down to 2,842 in 1881, and the further decline of the iron trade, notably the closure of the works at the Hyde about the end of 1882, caused a fall to 2,160 by 1891 as well as much distress.[32] The population had risen to 2,176 by 1901 and thereafter increased steadily. It was 2,348 in 1911, 2,886 in 1921, and 3,220 in 1931. Although the area added in 1934 was not populous, numbers were 4,490 in 1951, 5,352 in 1961, and 6,376 in 1971.[33]

By 1086 there was evidently a church on the high ground south of the present village centre, and it is likely that the main settlement was near the church. In 1221 the lord of the manor was granted a market, and it was probably about then that a borough was laid out on the low ground between the Stour and the steep slope up to the church. A further grant added a fair in 1257. About 1270 the lord of Kinver issued a charter of liberties to his burgesses, of whom there were 22 in 1293.[34] The borough occupied a constricted site on either side of High Street stretching from the area later known as the Burgesses northward almost as far as Stone Lane; the long narrow burgage plots are still distinguishable.[35] In the late 1750s Richard Wilkes, the Staffordshire antiquary, stated that 'the town . . . consists chiefly of one long spacious street well paved with pebbles, and the houses are many of them handsome and well built'.[36] Surviving timber-framed buildings, some with timbers still exposed but others with them hidden behind later façades, suggest that by the early 17th century the street was continuously built up or nearly so. From that time rebuilding or refronting in brick was a regular occurrence. There were 52 people in the borough owing suit of court in 1662; the number was 69 in 1755 and 86 in 1789.[37]

[12] Shaw, Staffs. ii. 263; Bennett, Kinver, 11.
[13] Inf. from Mrs. King, citing the occurrence there of the name Low Hill. She doubts the barrows mentioned by Plot, Staffs. 413-14.
[14] Plot, Staffs. 397-8; Bennett, Kinver, 9-10; Trans. Worcs. Arch. Soc. N.S. vi. 143-4; V.C.H. Staffs. i. 191, writing as though the stone still (1908) existed; H.W.R.O. (H.), E 12/S, Kinver ct. papers 17th and 18th cents., cts. of 18 Apr., 30 May 1665; W.S.L.; Staffs. Views, v. 87; below, econ. hist. (agric.: open fields). For the story, mentioned by Plot, that it was hurled from Kinver Edge by a giant see J. Raven, Folklore of Staffs. 42.
[15] V.C.H. Staffs. i. 338, 340; inf. from Mr. R. A. Meeson of the Conservation and Archaeology Section of the Staffs. C.C. Planning Dept.
[16] Staffs. C.C. Planning Dept., Sites and Monuments Rec. 1714-17, 1724.
[17] I. D. Margary, Roman Roads in Brit. (1973), 295-6; Staffs. C.C. Planning Dept., Sites and Monuments Rec. 1725.
[18] Below for Cynefares Stane; below, econ. hist., for wood of Cynibre.
[19] A. L. F. Rivet and C. Smith, Place-names of Roman Brit. 328-9; Ekwall, Eng. Place-names.
[20] T.B.A.S. liii. 108-9. It is there suggested that Cynefares

Stane was at Start's Green on the south-west boundary of Kinver; Mr. P. W. King argues that that is too far west and suggests that the stone was Vale's Rock or a vanished hoarstone.   [21] Below, econ. hist. (agric., borough).
[22] S.H.C. vii (1), 246-7.
[23] P.R.O., E 179/177/96.
[24] S.H.C. N.S. vi (1), 73-4.   [25] S.H.C. 1915, p. lxx.
[26] H.L., Main Papers, box 178.
[27] S.H.C. 1923, 106-10. Two of those assessed in the borough were assessed jointly on one house.
[28] W.S.L., S.MS. 33, p. 371.
[29] H.W.R.O. (H.), E 12/S, Kinver manor misc. papers, suitors rolls 1755, 1789.
[30] L.J.R.O., B/V/5/Kinver, 1772.
[31] V.C.H. Staffs. i. 326; S.R.O., Tp. 1273/24, Kinver sch., G. Wharton to Lord Stamford 10 May 1834.
[32] Census, 1871-91; Lich. Dioc. Mag. (1885), 143; (1886), 168-70; Bennett, Kinver, 125.
[33] Census, 1901-71.
[34] Below, econ. hist.   [35] W. Midlands Arch. xxiii. 96-7.
[36] W.S.L., S.MS. 468, p. 115.
[37] H.W.R.O. (H.), E 12/S, Kinver ct. papers 17th and 18th cents., ct. of 4 May 1663; Kinver manor misc. papers, suitors rolls 1755, 1789.

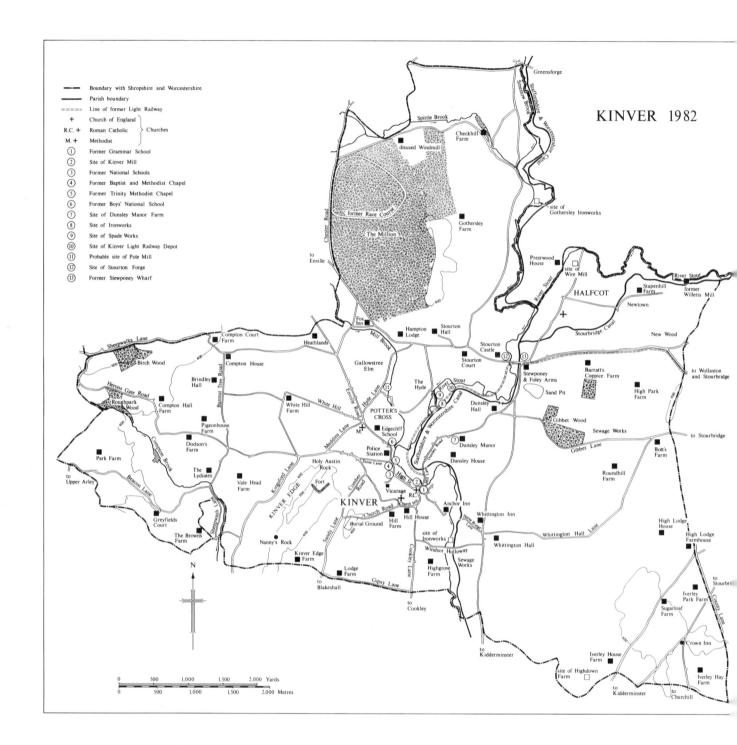

KINVER 1982

Boundary with Shropshire and Worcestershire
Parish boundary
Line of former Light Railway
+ Church of England
R.C. + Roman Catholic ⎫ Churches
M. + Methodist
① Former Grammar School
② Site of Kinver Mill
③ Former National Schools
④ Former Baptist and Methodist Chapel
⑤ Former Trinity Methodist Chapel
⑥ Former Boys' National School
⑦ Site of Dunsley Manor Farm
⑧ Site of Ironworks
⑨ Site of Spade Works
⑩ Site of Kinver Light Railway Depot
⑪ Probable site of Pole Mill
⑫ Site of Stourton Forge
⑬ Former Stewponey Wharf

The village, which stood on the old route between the south-west of England and Chester, was noted in the mid 18th century as providing good accommodation for travellers on that road.[38] The Cock inn within the borough was mentioned in 1555.[39] The White Hart inn existed by 1605,[40] and at the beginning of the 18th century it occupied two burgages.[41] It was used for meetings by the earlier 18th century and had become the regular meeting place of the borough and manor courts by the earlier 19th century.[42] In the later 18th century it was known as the White Hart and Angel.[43] The Red Lion was mentioned in 1672,[44] the Green Dragon in 1718,[45] and the Swan in the later 1740s.[46] In 1830, besides the White Hart, the Green Dragon, and the Swan, there were two public houses in High Street, the Unicorn and the George and Dragon.[47]

There was early suburban development at both ends of the borough. The southern area, known as the Overend in the 15th century and Kinver Hill by the 17th,[48] may have contained survivals of an early settlement by the church. On the low ground by the Stour there was a medieval mill,[49] and a bridge by the mill carried Mill Lane over the river by 1461.[50] A wayside cross in Mill Lane was mentioned in 1440.[51] A grammar school was established at the junction of Church Hill and Dark Lane in the 16th century.[52] An inn called the Plough existed in the area in 1648 and was probably the inn of that name mentioned in 1555.[53] A house was built in Dark Lane east of the grammar school in or shortly before 1624; it was known as the Stone House by 1672 and as Rockmount by the 1860s, having been remodelled probably in the 1840s.[54] A group of timber-framed cottages survives south of the church; a house there was mentioned in 1635.[55] In 1662 there were 24 people at Kinver Hill who owed suit to the manor court, 30 in 1755, and 31 in 1789.[56] Church Hill House on the west side of Church Hill and Hill House south-east of the church date from the 18th century. In 1830 there were cottages around the junction of High Street, Mill Lane, and Church Hill and also along the south side of Mill Lane where they

included a rock house. Kinver mill was then used as a rolling mill. East of the canal bridge further north stood Kinfare Lock public house. At the junction of Church Hill and the Holloway running up from Mill Lane was the Cross public house; on the opposite side of Church Hill was the parish workhouse.[57] A school was opened in the Holloway in 1835.[58] By 1841 there were several houses in Brockley's Walk north of Dark Lane and at Penhole to the south.[59] Council houses were built in the same area before and after the Second World War, and there are a large number of privately built houses of the later 20th century.

The area immediately north of the borough around the junction of High Street and Stone Lane became known as Kinver town's end or the lower end of the town. Stone Lane was so named by 1610.[60] In 1662 there were 16 people in the area owing suit to the manor court. The number was 22 in 1755 and 28 in 1789.[61] The inclosure of the nearby Kinver common in 1774 brought no immediate expansion. Building north along Enville Road began only in the mid 19th century, when a working-class district developed. Foster Street on the west side existed by 1851 and the parallel James Street by 1856; the Kinver Benefit Building Society was involved in both.[62] Castle and Foley Streets on the east side of Enville Road had been laid out by 1861.[63] Potter's Cross to the north, where a cottage was mentioned in the early 1620s,[64] had many artisan dwellings by 1841, as did Gallowstree Elm still further north in 1851; both areas continued to grow. Potter's Cross Farm and White Hill Farm to the west date from the mid 19th century; Stonelane Farm existed by the 1880s but has been built over. In the Comber area south-east of Stone Lane both villas and artisans' houses were built in the mid 19th century.[65] Near the parish boundary to the north Heathlands, a villa on the Enville road, existed by 1850 and the Fox inn on the Stourbridge-Bridgnorth road at Clambrook (later Clanbrook) by 1851.[66] The growth of the area was halted by the industrial decline of the later 19th century, but in the early 20th century many

[38] W.S.L., S.MS. 468, p. 115; below (communications).
[39] Cal. Pat. 1554–5, 167–8.
[40] S.H.C. 1940, 229; H.W.R.O. (H.), E 12/S, Kinver IX, deed of 26 Nov. 1613.
[41] H.W.R.O. (H.), E 12/S, Prestwood leases, deed of 31 Jan. 1703/4.
[42] Lond. Gaz. 4–7 Nov. 1727; S.R.O., D. 1197/4/1, 1747–8; S.R.O., D. 3162/2/1, 23 Dec. 1751, 24 Jan. 1758; below, local govt.
[43] S.R.O., D. 3162/2/1; S.R.O., Q/RDc 36.
[44] W.S.L,. notes on Kinver par., envelope labelled 'Stourton Castle'.
[45] L.J.R.O., B/C/11, Eliz. White (1718).
[46] S.R.O., D. 1197/4/1, 1747–8.
[47] S.R.O., D. 891/3, nos. 922, 925, 933, 1021; ibid. 4, pp. 38, 40, 49, 51.
[48] Below, local govt.; H.W.R.O. (H.), Kinver ct. rolls 1387–1498, bdle. 9, ct. of 17 Apr. 1434.
[49] Below, econ. hist.
[50] H.W.R.O. (H.), E 12/S, Kinver ct. rolls 1387–1498, bdle. 26, ct. of 10 Jan. 1460/1.
[51] Ibid. bdle. 14, ct. of 11 Apr. 1440.
[52] Below, educ.
[53] Cal. Pat. 1554–5, 167–8; H.W.R.O. (H.), E 12/S, Kinver I, deed of 18 May 1648.
[54] H.W.R.O. (H.), E 12/S, Kinver ct. rolls 1590–1629, ct. of 26 Jan. 1623/4 and ct. of survey 24 Oct. 1625; Kinver ct.

papers 17th and 18th cents., ct. of 14 Apr. 1673; S.R.O., D. 3579, 13 Dec. 1866, 17 Dec. 1868, 20 Dec. 1869; P.R.O., RG 10/2928; P.O. Dir. Staffs. (1876). Mr. J. W. King suggests that the change of name may have followed the remodelling which was probably carried out by T. M. Woodyatt after his purchase of the house in 1840.
[55] L.J.R.O., B/V/6/Kinver.
[56] H.W.R.O. (H.), E 12/S, Kinver ct. papers 17th and 18th cents., ct. of 4 May 1663; Kinver manor misc. papers, suitors rolls 1755, 1789.
[57] S.R.O., D. 891/4, pp. 52–4; below, econ. hist. (iron); local govt.   [58] Below, educ.
[59] P.R.O., HO 107/1002.
[60] H.W.R.O. (H.), E 12/S, Kinver ct. rolls 1590–1629, ct. of 22 Oct. 1610.
[61] Ibid., Kinver ct. papers 17th and 18th cents., ct. of 4 May 1663; Kinver manor misc. papers, suitors rolls 1755, 1789.
[62] P.R.O., HO 107/2017; S.R.O., D. 1493/1; inf. from Mr. J. W. King, citing deeds mentioning the building soc.
[63] S.R.O., D. 1493/1; P.R.O., RG 9/1985.
[64] S.R.O., Tp. 1273/11, 1623 survey, Whittington; 12, bk. of 17th-cent. surveys of Whittington, 1621.
[65] P.R.O., HO 107/1002 and 2017; P.R.O., RG 9/1985; date stone of 1848 on cottage at Gallowstree Elm; O.S. Map 6″, Staffs. LXX. SE. (1888 edn.).
[66] P.O. Dir. Staffs. (1850); White, Dir. Staffs. (1851), 180.

houses were built in Stone Lane, Enville Road, and Meddins Lane.[67] By 1939 a council estate had been begun south of White Hill, and there were some privately built houses in Hyde Lane. The council estate was completed in the early 1950s, and another was then built north of White Hill. Private building continued over the following decades, filling in undeveloped spaces and also expanding the village west and north.[68] As a result the village extends as far as Kinver Edge.

Kinver Edge, so named by the later 17th century,[69] was formerly a separate area of settlement. John atte Bury, mentioned in 1293, was presumably living at or near the hillfort.[70] A cave called Mag-a-Fox Hole c. 1680 may have derived its name from Margaret of the Fox Earth who died in 1617.[71] In the late 1750s it was stated that a few years before a poor man had converted the cave into a dwelling house for himself and his family; it is said that the date 1726 was once legible in one of the rooms.[72] Known as Nanny's Rock by the 1880s, it was occupied by Sarah Evans c. 1820 and Nancy Evans in 1830; a woman recluse was living there c. 1890.[73] Holy Austin Rock at the north end of Kinver Edge, so named by 1801, possibly derived its name from a former hermitage.[74] There were several cottages in Holy Austin Rock by 1801 and evidently by 1774; there were seven by 1830.[75] In 1851 there were 10 households there.[76] Families occupying rock houses were rehoused c. 1950, but a café in the rock continued in use until 1967.[77] There were two houses in Astle's Rock at Comber in 1830 and three in 1841. Early in the 20th century a rock dwelling there was turned into a museum which remained open for over 20 years.[78] Kinver Edge Farm and Lodge Farm on the southern boundary, respectively west and east of Sandy Lane, existed by the early 19th century;[79] the former was rebuilt later in the century.

Compton, covering the rural western part of the parish and the present residential area north-west of Kinver village, was mentioned in 1167 as belonging to the lord of Kinver.[80] Robert son of

William of Compton was mentioned in 1227–8.[81] Twenty-five tenants of the lord of Kinver were listed in 1293,[82] but only nine people were assessed for tax in 1332–3.[83] By 1293 the main settlement probably centred on a green in the bend of the present Herons Gate Road (formerly Compton Lane).[84] There was by then a sub-manor centring on Horewood near the western boundary where a moated site survives; the manor came to cover the whole of the Compton area. In the 15th century the lord moved from Horewood to Compton, and Compton Hall north-west of the green was mentioned in 1538.[85] The house east of the green known as Pigeonhouse Farm by the 19th century can be traced from the mid 17th; it was rebuilt in 1979.[86] Compton Court Farm in Sheepwalks Lane is probably 17th century, being once timber-framed and having a large central stack of sandstone with brick chimneys; the external walls were rebuilt in brick perhaps in the later 18th century, and in the 19th century a new front block was added on the east. In 1772 it was sold to Lord Stamford of Enville Hall by the Shadwell family of Albrighton (Salop.) and formerly of Enville, who owned it by the later 17th century.[87] In 1662 there were 15 inhabitants in Compton owing suit at Kinver manor court. The number was 18 in 1755 and 20 in 1789.[88] By the 1730s there was an isolated house in the area east of Compton known as Britch by the early 19th century;[89] the present farmhouse there dates from the 20th century. By 1775 the area round the green was known as Lower Compton. Upper Compton was the area to the south round the Lydiates, an 18th-century farmhouse off the present Beacon Lane (formerly Bacons Lane and possibly in existence by 1310); to the south-west there was a farmhouse called Greyfields on the site of the later Greyfields Court.[90] Brown's Farm, so named by 1841 and now called the Brown's Farm, dates from the late 17th century, and the rear wing retains elements of the original timber-framing; the house was refaced in brick in the early 19th century and extended c. 1900.[91] In

[67] O.S. Map 6″, Staffs. LXX. SE. (1888, 1903, 1925 edns.).

[68] D. M. Bills and E. and W. R. Griffiths, *Kinver: a closer look* (Kinver, 1981), 9.

[69] Plot, *Staffs.* 398.

[70] P.R.O., SC 6/202/64; *Eng. Place-name Elements* (E.P.N.S.), i. 60.

[71] Plot, *Staffs.* 172; D. M. Bills and E. and W. R. Griffiths, *Kinver Rock Houses* (Kinver, n.d.), 6. Ric. Wilkes in the 1750s calls it both Meg a Fox Hole and Meg o' Fox Hole; W.S.L., S.MS. 468, f. 8 and p. 117. Shaw, *Staffs.* ii. 263 reprints the second spelling, which was repeated by Pitt, *Staffs.* i. 197, and White, *Dir. Staffs.* (1834), 260, and (1851), 178.

[72] W.S.L., S.MS. 468, f. 8; J. Heeley, *Letters on Beauties of Hagley, Envil, and the Leasowes* (1777), ii. 19–20; *Trans. Worcs. Arch. Soc.* N.S. vi. 144; Yates, *Map of Staffs.* (1775).

[73] O.S. Map 6″, Staffs. LXX. SE. (1888 edn.); H.W.R.O. (H.), E 12/S, undated plan of estate called Kinfare Edge; S.R.O., D. 891/3, no. 844; ibid. 4, p. 61; Bills and Griffiths, *Kinver Rock Houses*, 14–15.

[74] *V.C.H. Staffs.* iii. 136; H.W.R.O. (H.), E 12/S, Kinver I, deed of 29 June 1801. For a view see above, pl. facing p. 112. For a holding called 'le Ostyn redyng' in 1444 see ibid. Kinver ct. rolls 1387–1498, bdle. 17, ct. of 12 Oct. 1444.

[75] H.W.R.O. (H.), E 12/S, Kinver I, deed of 29 June 1801; S.R.O., Q/RDc 36; S.R.O., D. 891/3, no. 834; ibid. 4, p. 59.

[76] P.R.O., HO 107/2017.

[77] Bills and Griffiths, *Kinver Rock Houses*, 6.

[78] Ibid. 16; S.R.O., D. 891/3, nos. 823–4; ibid. 4, p. 59.

[79] R. Baugh, *Map of Salop.* (1808); H.W.R.O. (H.), E 12/

S, undated plan of estate called Kinfare Edge; S.R.O., D. 891/3.　　　　[80] *S.H.C.* i. 48.

[81] *S.H.C.* iv (1), 69.

[82] P.R.O., SC 6/202/64.　　　　[83] *S.H.C.* x (1), 86.

[84] Below, econ. hist. (agric.: open fields; waste); H.W.R.O. (H.), E 12/S, vol. of 18th- and 19th-cent. plans; ibid. Early Deeds, deed of 1 Dec. 1353; ibid. Compton II, deeds of 20 Sept. 1538, 24 June 1562.

[85] Below, manors and other estates. The bounds are given in H.W.R.O. (H.), E 12/S, Compton I, deed of 7 July 1650.

[86] Deeds of Pigeonhouse Farm, in the possession of the owner, Mr. T. R. Brown; inf. from Mr. Brown, who is thanked for his help.

[87] S.R.O., Tp. 1273/58, Shadwell estates; above, Enville, manors and other estates (Lyndon). Mr. and Mrs. S. Morley of Compton Court Farm are thanked for their help.

[88] H.W.R.O. (H.), E 12/S, Kinver ct. papers 17th and 18th cents., ct. of 4 May 1663; Kinver manor misc. papers, suitors rolls 1755, 1789.

[89] Ibid. vol. of 18th- and 19th-cent. plans.

[90] Yates, *Map of Staffs.* (1775). For Greyfields farm see H.W.R.O. (H.), E 12/S, Compton I, partics. and valuation of Compton estates 23 Aug. 1790. For Bacons Lane see ibid. Compton I, survey of Compton Park 29 July 1654; Kinver ct. papers 17th and 18th cents., ct. of 18 Apr. 1665; vol. of 18th- and 19th-cent. plans; for Ric. atte Bacun in 1310 and 1327 see H.W.R.O. (H.), E 12/F/P3, deed of 6 Apr. 1310; *S.H.C.* vii (1), 246.

[91] For the name see P.R.O., HO 107/1002. Mrs. M. Timmington of the Brown's Farm is thanked for her help.

the north the farmhouse at the junction of Bannut Tree Road and Sheepwalks Lane existed by 1775.[92] Union Hall to the south in Bannut Tree Road was built c. 1790 by William Hodgetts, brother of John Hodgetts of Prestwood, in Kingswinford. In 1798 he fell to his death while riding along Kinver Edge, and the same year his son John sold the house.[93] It was the home of the Brindley family for much of the 19th century and was known as Brindley Hall by the end of the century.[94] By 1815 there was a house south of the road from Compton to Kinver on the site of Vale Head Farm, so named by 1861; the present house dates from the early 1970s.[95] By the 1820s there was a house at the north end of Bannut Tree Road at its junction with Compton Road (formerly Wigley Lane); known as Compton House by 1836, it was enlarged in stages during the 19th century.[96]

A royal hunting lodge was built at Stourton in the late 12th century on the site above the Stour still occupied by Stourton Castle; the first reference to it, however, as at Stourton rather than Kinver was in 1207.[97] Adam, John, and Walter of Stourton were mentioned in 1227–8,[98] and 15 tenants there were listed in 1293.[99] The area north of Stourton was occupied by Checkhill common and included Gothersley, mentioned in the mid 1290s in connexion with a ford on Smestow brook.[1] Gothersley may have been the site of the hermitage of Gutheresburn in Kinver forest granted by Henry III in 1248 to Brother Walerund of Kidderminster.[2] There was a warrener's lodge on the northern part of the common by 1601, and the part immediately north of Stourton was brought into cultivation in the 17th century. There were blade mills at Gothersley and Checkhill by the 17th century, and a corn mill near the castle was turned into a forge in 1670–1 and a slitting mill in 1698.[3] There were 35 people at Stourton and Checkhill and at the Hyde south-west of Stourton owing suit at the manor court in 1662.[4] In 1755 there were 36 suitors at Stourton and 8 at Checkhill; in 1789 the numbers were 35 and 9.[5] By the earlier 18th century settlement was mainly along Stourton Street, the southern end of the road to Gothersley and Checkhill. There was also settlement along the lane to the west leading from the

Bridgnorth road to the southern part of the common, probably the old road to Enville; buildings included the Rock tavern, which still existed in 1830.[6] Checkhill common was inclosed in 1804, but little expansion of settlement followed. Stourton Fields farm (later Gothersley farm) had been created by 1830.[7] Hampton House (later Hampton Lodge) was built on 4 a. at the south-west corner of the former waste in 1846 by Jane Mary Davenport; what seems originally to have been a service wing was added by William Bennitt of Stourton Hall a few years later.[8] Stourton Hall stands to the east on or near a site where there had been a house by the 1730s. It was built c. 1850 by William Bennitt, who was living there in 1851 and also laid out the grounds; the house was later extended.[9] Stourton Court on the Bridgnorth road in Stourton itself was built in 1850, burnt in 1877, and rebuilt in 1883.[10] The mill at Stourton had been demolished by 1830. That at Checkhill, having become a fulling mill and later a corn mill, had ceased operation by the 1880s, but a farm survived. Gothersley mill, to which an industrial hamlet was attached, closed in the early 1890s.[11]

The Hyde on the Stour south-west of Stourton was evidently an inhabited area by 1293.[12] A fulling mill erected there c. 1590 was rebuilt as a slitting mill in the late 1620s. The Hyde remained an industrial centre until the closure of its two ironworks in the early 1880s and c. 1910.[13] There were seven people there owing suit at the manor court in 1755 and five in 1789.[14] The 18th-century Hyde House was demolished in the 1920s,[15] but an 18th-century octagonal pigeon house and 18th-century garden walls survive. The nearby farm buildings date from the 19th century. The Staffordshire and Worcestershire Canal was opened through the area in 1770, and a late 18th-century lock-keeper's cottage is still occupied. In 1830 there was a rock house in the hillside east of the cottage.[16] To the north a row of five houses stood beside the canal by 1830,[17] one of which survives. Several small houses were built in the area in the 20th century.

Halfcot, covering the north-east corner of the ancient parish, had nine tenants in 1293.[18] Stapenhill, mentioned then as an area of pasture, was the name of a farm by the 1630s; the present

[92] Yates, *Map of Staffs.* (1775); S.R.O., Tp. 1273/58, sale partics. 1855.

[93] K. C. Hodgson, *Out of the Mahogany Desk*, 47, 50–1.

[94] *Wolverhampton Chron.* 11 Jan. 1815; S.R.O., D. 891/4, p. 5; S.R.O., Tp. 1273/36, deed of 17 July 1899; 40, extracts from ct. rolls 1826–69 and deeds of 3 Oct. 1888, 5 June 1896.

[95] B.L. Maps, O.S.D. 214; P.R.O., RG 10/2928; local inf.

[96] It is not shown on C. and J. Greenwood, *Map of Staffs.* (1820) but had been built by 1830: S.R.O., D. 891/3, no. 180. See also S.R.O., Tp. 1273/35, deed of 29 July 1896; 41, deed of 16 June 1836; 58, sale partics. 1855. For the name Wigley Lane see H.W.R.O. (H.), vol. of 18th- and 19th-cent. plans, Compton.

[97] Below, manors and other estates.

[98] *S.H.C.* iv (1), 51, 69.

[99] P.R.O., SC 6/202/64.

[1] H.W.R.O. (H.), E 12/S, Kinver VI, rents from waste in Kinver forest temp. Edw. I.

[2] *V.C.H. Staffs.* iii. 137.

[3] Below, econ. hist.

[4] H.W.R.O. (H.), E 12/S, Kinver ct. papers 17th and 18th cents., ct. of 4 May 1663.

[5] Ibid. Kinver manor misc. papers, suitors rolls 1755, 1789.

[6] Ibid. vol. of 18th- and 19th-cent. plans; S.R.O., D. 891/3, no. 508; ibid. 4, p. 32; Bills and Griffiths, *Kinver Rock Houses*, 23.   [7] S.R.O., D. 891/3, no. 635.

[8] S.R.O., D. 3162/1/10; S.R.O., Tp. 1273/35, bdle. of 6 June 1864. Mrs. K. Durrant of Hampton Lodge is thanked for her help.

[9] H.W.R.O. (H.), E 12/S, vol. of 18th- and 19th-cent. plans, Stourton, no. 75; ibid. Kinver and Compton ct. bk. 1800–53, ct. of 24 Oct. 1848; S.R.O., D. 891/3, no. 539; D. 1493/1; P.R.O., HO 107/2017; inf. from Mr. J. H. Folkes, formerly of Stourton Hall, who is thanked for his help.

[10] Inscription on house.

[11] Below, econ. hist.

[12] P.R.O., SC 6/202/64, listing Felicity atte Hyde among the tenants of Compton. In 1387 Wal. and Rog. atte Hyde each held a burgage in Kinver: H.W.R.O. (H.), E 12/S, Kinver ct. rolls 1387–1498, bdle. 1.

[13] Below, econ. hist.

[14] H.W.R.O. (H.), E 12/S, Kinver manor misc. papers, suitors rolls 1755, 1789.

[15] Below, econ. hist. (iron); educ.

[16] S.R.O., D. 891/3, nos. 1578–9; ibid. 4, p. 96.

[17] Ibid. 3, nos. 414–18; ibid. 4, pp. 28–9.

[18] P.R.O., SC 6/202/64.

house appears to date from *c.* 1840.[19] In 1662 there were 11 people at Halfcot owing suit at the manor court; the number was 22 in 1755 and 27 in 1789.[20] By the earlier 18th century settlement was concentrated along the Wolverhampton road south of the parish boundary, with two wire mills west of the road; the mills ceased working in the 1820s, and there was some decline in the number of houses about then.[21] Meanwhile the Stourbridge Canal was opened through the area in 1779, joining the Staffordshire and Worcestershire Canal west of the main road; Stewponey wharf south of the junction became the hub of the system.[22] By *c.* 1830 sandworking was in progress in the Stapenhill area, using the Stourbridge Canal for transport, and the small hamlet of Newtown had grown up near a wharf there.[23] New Wood farm to the east existed by the 1880s.[24] The farmhouse survived in 1982 on the edge of a privately built housing estate dating from the years before the Second World War and the later 20th century; Hyperion Road on the earlier part of the estate was named after the 1933 Derby winner.[25] There is similar residential development on the Wolverhampton road and along the Stourbridge road. Stourbridge Rugby Football Club has its ground south of the road.

Stewponey, the area around the junction of the Wolverhampton–Kidderminster and Stourbridge–Bridgnorth roads, takes its name from an inn called the Stewponey which stood there by the earlier 18th century. It then had a bowling green attached and was described in 1744 as 'the house of Benjamin Hallen, being the sign of the Green Man and called the Stewponey'.[26] Thereafter it was known simply as the Stewponey until *c.* 1840 when it became the Stewponey and Foley Arms. It was then a posting house.[27] The 18th-century house was extended in the 19th century and rebuilt in the later 1930s when the road junction was improved.[28] Various explanations of the name have been put forward, deriving it from the nearby bridge over the Stour ('Stouri pons'),[29] from an inn called the Pony and a nearby stew or fishpond,[30] from Estepona in Spain where a tenant of the inn was said to have been quartered as a soldier during the reign of

Anne,[31] and from stepony, either a kind of ale or a kind of raisin wine.[32]

Dunsley was an inhabited area *c.* 1200,[33] and in 1293 the lord of Kinver had nine tenants there.[34] Dunsley later became a sub-manor with Dunsley Hall as its manor house.[35] In 1662 six people at Dunsley owed suit at Kinver manor court; the number was nine in 1755 and 17 in 1789.[36] Four of those listed in 1662 were assessed for hearth tax in 1666, in addition to the tenant of the hall.[37] Edward Jorden, who was assessed on six hearths, was a member of a family which was living at Dunsley by the 1530s.[38] He may have lived at the house now known as Dunsley Manor where one range survives from a late 16th-century timber-framed house; by the early 19th century it had been encased in brick and the interior remodelled. In the mid and later 19th century the exterior was remodelled in Tudor style and the house partly rebuilt. Richard Bird, who died in the early 1690s, was assessed on five hearths; in 1625 John Bird had a house and land in Dunsley described as 'his ancestors' land', and the family was living at Dunsley by 1595.[39] Thomas and John Hillman lived at the Hill, which was assessed at three hearths; the family was living at Dunsley by the earlier 15th century. The house remained in the Hillman family and passed in 1775 by marriage to Benjamin Brooke, who still lived there in 1780. A villa called Dunsley Hill was advertised for letting in 1820.[40] Dunsley Manor Farm to the east of Dunsley Manor existed by 1775. In 1817 it was sold by Edmund Wells Grove, a Dunsley farmer, to George Burgess of Checkhill; the Burgess family farmed there until the mid 1860s.[41] Farm buildings of the 18th and 19th centuries survive, although the house has been demolished. Dunsley House to the south-west dates from the early 19th century and as Dunsley Villa was the home of the Hancox family until the mid 1860s.[42] By 1912 it was occupied as a home of rest by the Girls' Friendly Society, which used it until the later 1930s.[43] The area at the southern end of the Dunsley Road became residential in the later 20th century.

By 1780 the area along the canal south of Dunsley was known as Gibraltar and had several

[19] P.R.O., SC 6/202/64; below, econ. hist. (agric.: sheep farming). Mrs. G. Jones of Stapenhill Farm is thanked for her help.
[20] H.W.R.O. (H.), E 12/S, Kinver ct. papers 17th and 18th cents., ct. of 4 May 1663; Kinver manor misc. papers, suitors rolls 1755, 1789.
[21] Ibid. vol. of 18th- and 19th-cent. plans; Yates, *Map of Staffs.* (1775); C. and J. Greenwood, *Map of Staffs.* (1820); S.R.O., D. 891/3.   [22] Below, communications.
[23] Below, econ. hist.; Scott, *Stourbridge*, 182.
[24] O.S. Map 6", Staffs. LXXI. SW. (1888 edn.).
[25] Inf. from Mr. J. W. King.
[26] H.W.R.O. (H.), E 12/S, vol. of 18th- and 19th-cent. plans, Halfcot, no. 45; *Lond. Gaz.* 1–5 May 1744; S.R.O., D. 1197/4/1.
[27] *P.O. Dir. Staffs.* (1845), giving it the new name.
[28] Below, pl. facing p. 129; W.S.L., Sale Cats. Q/3, p. 75; J. I. Langford, *Towpath Guide to Staffs. and Worcs. Canal*, 145–6.
[29] *N. & Q.* 3rd ser. vi. 298; P. M. Grazebrook, *Short Hist. of Stourton Castle and Royal Forest of Kinver*, 42–3.
[30] Scott, *Stourbridge*, 173.
[31] S. Baring-Gould, *Bladys of the Stewponey*, 14–15.
[32] *N. & Q.* 6th ser. ii. 308–9, 334; iii. 97–8, 130; iv. 155, 457; vii. 131.
[33] S.R.O., Tp. 1273/12, bk. of deeds and evidences, p. 13.

[34] P.R.O., SC 6/202/64.
[35] Below, manors and other estates.
[36] H.W.R.O. (H.), E 12/S, Kinver ct. papers 18th and 19th cents., ct. of 4 May 1663; Kinver manor misc. papers, suitors rolls 1755, 1789.
[37] *S.H.C.* 1923, 107.
[38] *S.H.C.* 4th ser. viii. 14. For the family see below, p. 208.
[39] L.J.R.O., B/C/11, Ric. Bird (1692); H.W.R.O. (H.), E 12/S, Kinver ct. rolls 1590–1629, ct. of 15 Apr. 1595 and ct. of survey 24 Oct. 1625.
[40] *Cal. Cttee. for Money*, iii, p. 1184; H.W.R.O. (H.), E 12/S, Kinver ct. rolls 1387–1498, bdle. 9, ct. of 17 Apr. 1434; ibid. Dunsley I, deed of 9 Apr. 1694; Dunsley II, deeds of 9 Oct. 1711, 12 Apr. 1769; Kinver and Kingsley ct. bk. 1767–1801, cts. of 20 Oct. 1773, 21 Mar. 1774, 9 Jan. 1775; S.R.O., Q/RDc 42; *Wolverhampton Chron.* 19 Apr. 1820.
[41] Yates, *Map of Staffs.* (1775); H.W.R.O. (H.), E 12/S, Dunsley III, abstract of title to Dunsley farm 1866, conditions of sale 1866, and sale partics. 1866; ibid. Halfcot III, deed of 7 Aug. 1817; White, *Dir. Staffs.* (1851), 180; *P.O. Dir. Staffs.* (1864); below, econ. hist. (mills).
[42] Parson and Bradshaw, *Dir. Staffs.* (1818); S.R.O., D. 891/3, no. 1508; ibid. 4, p. 98; P.R.O., HO 107/1002; P.R.O., RG 9/1985; *P.O. Dir. Staffs.* (1864).
[43] *Kelly's Dir. Staffs.* (1912 and edns. to 1936).

rock houses in the hillside.[44] There were 12 such dwellings by 1830 and 17 households there in 1851.[45] During the 19th century occupants included labourers employed at the nearby wharf. The dwellings had ceased to be let by the 1880s because they were unhealthy, but they apparently continued to be occupied for a time by boatmen.[46]

The common east of Dunsley and south of the Stourbridge road was inclosed in 1780.[47] By 1815 Park Farm and the house known as Bott's Farm by 1871 had been built respectively north and south of the junction of Gibbet Lane and Whittington Hall Lane; the farms were probably laid out in the late 18th century.[48] Round Hill Farm south-west of Bott's Farm existed by 1851.[49] By 1856 High Park Farm had been built north of Park Farm, and there was a farm to the northwest at Barratt's Coppice.[50] Park Farm had disappeared by the 1880s.[51]

Gibbet Wood and Gibbet Lane running from Dunsley to Stourbridge derive their names from the gibbeting of William Howe, otherwise John Wood, in 1813. In December 1812 Howe murdered Benjamin Robins of Dunsley Hall who was returning home from Stourbridge. Howe was arrested in London and executed at Stafford. His corpse was hung in chains at the scene of his crime for twelve months, but the gibbet remained for several years.[52]

Whittington was an inhabited area by the 1180s and became a sub-manor of Kinver c. 1200; by the 17th century the manor house stood south of Whittington Hall Lane. High Grove Farm on the high ground west of the Stour is probably the successor of Haygreve, in existence c. 1200.[53] The Whittington Inn, a large timber-framed building on the Wolverhampton–Kidderminster road, was a private house until Lord Stamford turned it into an inn in 1788. It dates probably from the later 16th century; the range on the north was added in the 18th century. As an inn it is said to have replaced the timber-framed house to the west in Horse Bridge Lane now known as Whittington Old House (formerly Bathpool Cottages).[54] The road or lane from Whittington to Kinver mentioned from 1598 evidently ran from Horse Bridge Lane across the Stour to Dark Lane.[55] The footpath from Whittington to Kinver church also mentioned from 1598[56] may have followed the course of the present footpath from the river to Cookley Lane. The footbridge at Whittington for the repair of which William Moseley of London left £5 in 1617[57] must have carried one or both of those ways over the river. East of the Stour Horse Bridge Lane formerly continued south as a road which crossed the river at Windsor bridge, mentioned in 1621, and then followed Windsor Holloway to Cookley Lane. It was evidently with the building of the Staffordshire and Worcestershire Canal through that part of Whittington in the later 1760s that the stretch of road east of the river disappeared; by 1775 Windsor Holloway had been extended east to the Wolverhampton–Kidderminster road, turnpiked in 1760.[58] A mill stood on the Stour c. 1200, and in 1515 there was a fulling mill as well as a corn mill. In 1619 Whittington mill was converted into an ironworks, and an industrial hamlet was created. The works continued until 1893, and part of it survives as a private house.[59] There are two short rows of early 19th-century brick cottages on the canal to the north at the end of Horse Bridge Lane. In 1662 there were 18 people at Whittington owing suit at Kinver manor court.[60] They included Thomas Moseley, whose family was living in Whittington by 1446; he was assessed for tax on three hearths in 1666.[61] Another of the suitors was Thomas Jukes, who was assessed on six hearths; in 1691 he occupied a freehold house and was leasing another to a tenant.[62] The number of suitors was 19 in 1755 and 28 in 1789.[63] In the later 18th century settlement was concentrated along the Wolverhampton–Kidderminster road and Horse Bridge Lane.[64] The house known in 1754 as the Talbot and formerly as Bird's tenement[65] was presumably an inn. The house called Windsor Castle by the 1780s may have been an inn in Windsor Holloway; in 1861 it was occupied by a labourer and his family.[66] Whittington Lower Farm at the junction of the Wolverhampton–Kidderminster road and Windsor Holloway is an 18th-century building. A row of four 18th-century brick cottages at the southern end of Dark Lane on the west side of the river had been extended and turned into the Anchor inn by 1851.[67] The open country east of Whittington

[44] S.R.O., Q/RDc 42.

[45] S.R.O., D. 891/4, pp. 96, 98–100; P.R.O., HO 107/2017.

[46] Bills and Griffiths, *Kinver Rock Houses*, 19–20.

[47] Below, econ. hist.

[48] B.L. Maps, O.S.D. 214; S.R.O., Q/RDc 42; H.W.R.O. (H.), E 12/S, Halfcot III, deeds of 24 Dec. 1791, 19 Mar. 1795; P.R.O., RG 9/2928.

[49] P.R.O., HO 107/2017.

[50] S.R.O., D. 1493/1.

[51] O.S. Map 6″, Staffs. LXXI. SW. (1888 edn.).

[52] L. Radzinowicz, *Hist. of Eng. Criminal Law from 1750*, i. 218 n., 219; *Staffs. Advertiser*, 26 Dec. 1812; 2 Jan., 20 Mar. 1813. It is wrongly stated in 'The Manor House of the de Whittingtons' (copy at Staffs. County Libr. H.Q.) that Howe, arrested at the Whittington Inn and hanged in Gallows Wood, was the last man to be gibbeted in England; for the last man, in Leics. in 1832, see Radzinowicz, op. cit. 219–20.

[53] Below, manors and other estates.

[54] D. M. Palliser, *Staffs. Landscape*, 96–7 (although the present inn was not, as there stated, the manor house); sale partics. of Bathpool Cottages 1974 (giving date of change as 1798) among the deeds of the property in the possession of the Staffs. Building Soc., Wolverhampton. Mr. T. M. J. Oldnall of the Staffs. Building Soc. and Dr. A. B. Clymo of Whittington Old House are thanked for their help.

[55] S.R.O., Tp. 1273/12, deed of 22 Dec. 1598; H.W.R.O. (H.), E 12/S, Kinver ct. rolls 1590–1629, ct. of 26 Jan. 1623/4; ibid. Kinver I, deed of 4 Oct. 1634.

[56] S.R.O., Tp. 1273/12, deed of 22 Dec. 1598; H.W.R.O. (H.), E 12/S, Kinver ct. papers 17th and 18th cents., ct. of 20 Oct. 1681.

[57] P.R.O., PROB 11/130, f. 173v.

[58] S.R.O., 1392; H.W.R.O. (H.), E 12/S, Whittington, deed of 4 Aug. 1621; Yates, *Map of Staffs.* (1775); below (communications).

[59] Below, econ. hist.

[60] H.W.R.O. (H.), E 12/S, Kinver ct. papers 17th and 18th cents., ct. of 4 May 1663.

[61] Ibid. E 12/F/P3, deed of 23 Dec. 1446; S.R.O., Tp. 1273/11, 1623 survey; *S.H.C.* 1923, 107.

[62] *S.H.C.* 1923, 107; S.R.O., Tp. 1273/38, survey of Whittington 1691.

[63] H.W.R.O. (H.), E 12/S, Kinver manor misc. papers, suitors rolls 1755, 1789.

[64] Yates, *Map of Staffs.* (1775).

[65] S.R.O., Tp. 1273/10, deed of 25 Dec. 1754.

[66] S.R.O., D. 1197/5/1; P.R.O., RG 9/1985.

[67] S.R.O., D. 891/3, no. 1085; ibid. 4, p. 64; White, *Dir. Staffs.* (1851), 180.

was used for laying out three sewage farms in the late 19th and early 20th century.[68]

Iverley in the south-east part of the parish gave its name to one of the hays of Kinver forest and has remained sparsely inhabited. The mention in 1293 of Nicholas of Iverley[69] indicates some settlement by then. The keeper of the hay built himself a house there at the beginning of the 17th century.[70] Inclosure of the common began in the 1630s,[71] and farms were created from the late 17th century. Tristram's farm, later Iverley Park farm, originated in a lease to William Tristram of Old Swinford (Worcs.) in 1676 of c. 50 a. north of the Stourbridge–Kidderminster road near the eastern boundary.[72] Nash's farm, later Iverley Hay farm, was formed out of c. 70 a. east of the road to Churchill (Worcs.) leased to Thomas Nash of Clent (Staffs., later Worcs.) in 1698; he built a house there shortly afterwards.[73] Another house and smaller estate on the west side of the Churchill road was leased with it in 1719, having originated apparently in a lease of 1710.[74] Iverley House farm on the southern boundary between the Stourbridge–Kidderminster road and Sugarloaf Lane may have existed by 1676 and was certainly created by the early 18th century. The house there was probably that mentioned as in the area in 1712. It was rebuilt in the mid 18th century on the opposite side of Sugarloaf Lane,[75] but the present house dates from the 19th century. Known as Bum Hall in the 1850s, it had regained its former name by the early 1880s.[76] High Down farm to the west existed by 1712. A lease of it in 1722 obliged the tenant to take down a five-bayed barn recently built on Iverley House farm and use the materials for building a farmhouse for High Down within 20 months. There was still a farmhouse there in 1901, but by 1924 High Down had become part of Iverley House farm.[77] There was a house on the site of Sugarloaf Farm by the 1730s,[78] but the present house appears to date from later in the century. The Crown inn at the junction of the Stourbridge–Kidderminster road and the road to Churchill existed by 1753.[79] High House near the eastern boundary north of Sugarloaf Lane was built about the mid 18th century. It was described in 1832 as 'of grotesque architecture'. High Lodge was built on the site

later in the 19th century and was opened as a private nursing home in 1983. High House Farm (later High Lodge Farmhouse) to the east dates from the 19th century; the farm buildings incorporate 18th-century bricks.[80] There were four people at Iverley owing suit at Kinver manor court in 1735, nine in 1755, and 14 in 1789.[81] In the 20th century several sandpits were opened in the Iverley area.[82] The large houses along the Stourbridge–Kidderminster road near the Stourbridge boundary date mainly from the period between the two World Wars. There are also several detached houses dating from before and after the Second World War towards the southern end of Sugarloaf Lane. Stourbridge Lawn Tennis Club in Sugarloaf Lane occupies the site of a former sandpit.

Between the late 11th and early 13th century kings visited Kinver on several occasions, probably when hunting in the forest.[83] Edward I stayed at Stourton in 1277, perhaps also when hunting; in 1294 he was at Horewood on his way to Wales.[84] Royal justices were at Kinver in 1276 and 1277.[85] Charles II road over Kinver common to Stourbridge during his escape after the battle of Worcester in 1651.[86]

Cardinal Pole (d. 1558) is said to have been born at Stourton Castle, and Bishop Talbot (d. 1730) was evidently born at Whittington Hall.[87] The physician Richard Moreton (1637–98) was curate of Kinver.[88] The Revd. Sabine Baring-Gould (1834–1924), folklorist, author, and hymn writer, visited Kinver in the late 19th century. He wrote the hymn 'Now the day is over' there, and much of his novel *Bladys of the Stewponey* (1897) was set in the parish. In 1919 the novel was made into a film shot mainly in Kinver.[89] Nancy Price (1880–1970), stage and film actress and novelist, was born at Rockmount in Dark Lane.[90] Her autobiography *Into an Hour-glass* (1953) records her early life in Kinver.

COMMUNICATIONS. The parish was crossed by the medieval route between the south-west of England and Chester, which continued in use until c. 1800. It ran along Cookley Lane, Kinver High Street, Enville Road, and Chester Road.[91]

The road to the east between Kidderminster

[68] Below, p. 152.
[69] P.R.O., SC 6/202/64.
[70] V.C.H. Staffs. ii. 348.
[71] Below, econ. hist. (agric.).
[72] H.W.R.O. (H.), E 12/S, Iverley I, deed of 4 Mar. 1675/6; vol. of 18th- and 19th-cent. plans. For Nash see S. Grazebrook, *Heraldry of Worcs.* 580–1.
[73] H.W.R.O. (H.), E 12/S, Iverley I, deed of 20 Oct. 1698; Iverley V, deed of 2 May 1707; vol. of 18th- and 19th-cent. plans.
[74] Ibid. Iverley I, deed of 21 Mar. 1709/10; Iverley V, deed giving date 17 Feb. 1718; vol. of 18th- and 19th-cent. plans.
[75] Ibid. Iverley I, deed of 10 Oct. 1676; Iverley Heath, deeds of 23 Jan. 1679/80, 15 Oct. 1712, 29 Jan. 1721/2; vol. of 18th- and 19th-cent. plans; Yates, *Map of Staffs.* (1775).
[76] H.W.R.O. (H.), E 12/S, Iverley II, deed of 17 Mar. 1855 and plan of Iverley est. c. 1860; O.S. Map 6", Staffs. LXXV. NW. (1888 edn.).
[77] H.W.R.O. (H.), E 12/S, Iverley Heath, deeds of 15 Oct. 1712, 29 Jan. 1721/2; Iverley IV, sale cat. of Iverley House farm 1924; O.S. Map 6", Staffs. LXXV. NW. (1904 edn.).
[78] H.W.R.O. (H.), E 12/S, vol. of 18th- and 19th-cent. plans.
[79] Below, communications.
[80] Yates, *Map of Staffs.* (1775); Scott, *Stourbridge*, 183;

O.S. Map 6", Staffs. LXXI. SW. (1888 edn.), showing High House Farm as Iverley Farm; sale cats. at High Lodge Farmhouse; inf. from Mr. and Mrs. T. S. Mangat of High Lodge Farmhouse, who are thanked for their help.
[81] H.W.R.O. (H.), E 12/S, Kinver manor misc. papers, suitors rolls 1735, 1755, 1789.
[82] Below, econ. hist.
[83] Below, manors and other estates.
[84] Cal. Fine. R. 1272–1307, 80, 86; *Book of Prests*, ed. E. B. Fryde, 222.
[85] S.H.C. vi (1), 77, 91.
[86] *Boscobel* (1660), 14.
[87] Below, manors and other estates.
[88] Below, church.
[89] D.N.B. 1922–30; F. E. Campbell, *Royal Kinver*, 27 (copy in W.S.L. Pamphs.); Bills and Griffiths, *Kinver Rock Houses*, 11.
[90] *Who was Who*, 1961–70.
[91] Scott, *Stourbridge*, 170–1; H.W.R.O. (H.), E 12/S, Kinver ct. rolls 1387–1498, bdle. 8, cts. of 20 Apr. 1433, 4 Apr. 1435; bdle. 16, ct. of 2 or 9 Apr. 1442; ibid. Whorwood inheritance, deed of 18 Jan. 1669/70; L.J.R.O., B/V/6/ Kinver, 1635; S.R.O., D. 1197/1/2, burial of 10 July 1689 of 'Serjeant Lambeth in his march to Ireland'; below, Patshull, introduction.

and Wolverhampton carried much traffic in the mid 17th century. Halfcot bridge, by which the road crosses the Stour on the parish boundary, was described in 1647 as 'a great thoroughfare for carts and packhorses 'twixt Worcester and Wolverhampton and to Stafford and the usual passage for the judges at their circuits'.[92] It had been the joint responsibility of the parishes of Kinver and Kingswinford in 1631, but by 1647 it had become a county bridge.[93] The present bridge dates from the 19th century and is a brick structure with a tall arch. The Wolverhampton–Kidderminster road was turnpiked in 1760 and disturnpiked in 1873.[94] There was a tollhouse at Halfcot by 1815 near the junction with the road from Stapenhill; it remained in use until the main road was disturnpiked.[95]

The Stourbridge–Bridgnorth road crosses the Wolverhampton–Kidderminster road by the Stewponey inn. Stourton bridge carrying it over the Stour west of the inn existed by 1387 and was a county bridge by 1647.[96] The present structure is of engineering brick. The road was turnpiked in 1816 and disturnpiked in 1877.[97] There was a tollhouse at New Wood near the eastern boundary by 1820, and it continued in use until the road was disturnpiked.[98] By 1830 there was another tollhouse between the Stewponey and Stourton bridge; it was still in use in 1871.[99] The old route between Kinver and Stourbridge ran along Mill Lane, Dunsley Road, and Gibbet Lane.[1]

The road from Stourbridge to Kidderminster runs through Iverley. The stretch from Stourbridge as far as the Crown inn at Iverley was turnpiked in 1753 and disturnpiked in 1877; the rest was turnpiked in 1760 and disturnpiked in 1873.[2] Sugarloaf Lane to the west, which continues into Churchill parish (Worcs.) to join the Stourbridge–Kidderminster road at Five Ways, was turnpiked in 1789 as part of the road from Coalbournbrook in Amblecote; it was disturnpiked in 1877.[3]

As part of the abortive scheme for making the Stour navigable from Stourbridge to the Severn under an Act of 1662 a trench was cut in the north-east corner of the parish from Willett's mill to Prestwood.[4] It was known in the 18th century as the Navigation Cut and survived into the 20th century as Trench brook. In 1983 the cut, though dry, was visible for most of its course.[5]

The work under the 1662 Act also included the widening of the river below the Hyde.[6]

The Staffordshire and Worcestershire Canal, which follows the Stour valley through Kinver, was built by James Brindley under an Act of 1766; the Kinver stretch was opened in 1770 and the whole canal in 1772.[7] North-east of Dunsley Hall it passes through a tunnel which, because it is short and cut through soft rock, was provided with a towpath at the time of its construction.[8] North of Stewponey it is joined by the Stourbridge Canal built under an Act of 1776 and opened in 1779.[9] The wharf at Stewponey was the hub of the system, and the toll office there remained the busiest on the canal.[10] The tollhouse and other buildings still stood in 1982. A boat hire business, Dawncraft, was started by George and Ralph Wilson in 1958 with a yard on the canal off Mill Lane in Kinver. They later turned to boat building, and in 1971 the hire fleet was sold. In 1972 the boat building was moved to Kidderminster. The Kinver yard was then used for repairs and display, and a marina was later built nearby. The firm also had a showroom at Stewponey wharf.[11] In the early 1980s the firm moved to Stourport, but the marina was still in use in 1982.

By the earlier 1830s a carrier was running a service from Kinver to Stourbridge and back each day.[12] A tramway known as the Kinver Light Railway was opened in 1901 running from Coalbournbrook in Amblecote via Wollaston to a terminus in Mill Lane in Kinver. West of Stewponey the track left the road to follow a course close to the Stour and the canal; much of it was embanked because of the risk of flooding. A depot was built at the Hyde and used between Good Friday and October to serve the excursion traffic to Kinver. The tramway was closed in 1930 and replaced by a bus service.[13]

SOCIAL AND CULTURAL ACTIVITIES. In 1719 Kinver wake was held on Monday and Tuesday, 14 and 15 September. The entertainment included bull baiting.[14] In 1814 bulls were baited near the junction of High Street and Stone Lane.[15] In 1851 land near the National school in High Street was known as the Bull Ring.[16] Land near Halfcot wire mills called the Cockpit in 1733 may indicate that cock fighting took place there.[17] There was a racecourse on Checkhill

[92] S.R.O., Q/SR, E. 1647, no. 8.
[93] Ibid.; H.W.R.O. (H.), E 12/S, Kingswinford, memo. of 26 May 1631.
[94] 33 Geo. II, c. 50; 36 & 37 Vic. c. 90.
[95] B.L., O.S.D. 214; H.W.R.O. (H.), E 12/S, Prestwood sales, list of title deeds.
[96] H.W.R.O. (H.), E 12/S, Kinver ct. rolls 1387–1498, bdle. 1; S.R.O., Q/SR, E 1647, no. 8.
[97] 56 Geo. III, c. 16 (Local and Personal); 39 & 40 Vic. c. 39.
[98] H.W.R.O. (H.), E 12/S, Prestwood Estate surveys I; Kinver II, deed of 7 Mar. 1877.
[99] S.R.O., D. 891/3, no. 1616; ibid. 4, p. 89; P.R.O., RG 10/2928.   [1] Above, p. 125.
[2] 26 Geo. II, c.47; 33 Geo. II, c.50; 36 & 37 Vic. c.90; 40 & 41 Vic. c.64.   [3] Above, p. 52.
[4] J. H. Parker Oxspring, 'Andrew Yarranton' (TS. in Worcester City Branch Libr.; microfilm in S.R.O.), ii, pp. 11–12, 28–9, 159–64, 282; H.W.R.O. (H.), E 12/S, Halfcot I, deed of 1 Jan. 1664/5; Halfcot II, deed of 14 Sept. 1663.
[5] H.W.R.O. (H.), E 12/S, Kinver VII, deed of 17 Jan.

1759; Halfcot I, deed of 22 Mar. 1781; inf. from Mr. P. W. King.
[6] Oxspring, 'Yarranton', ii, p. 282.
[7] Above, pp. 13–14.
[8] J. I. Langford, Towpath Guide to Staffs. and Worcs. Canal, 147.
[9] Above, p. 52.
[10] Langford, Staffs. and Worcs. Canal, 142–3, 146.
[11] Ibid. 146, 151.
[12] Below, p. 153.
[13] J. S. Webb, Black Country Tramways, i (Bloxwich, 1974), 220–32, 261, 265; ii (Bloxwich, 1976), 17–19, 21, 94, and frontispiece; D. M. Bills and E. and W. R. Griffiths, By Tram to Kinver (Kinver, 1980).
[14] V.C.H. Worcs. iii. 216.
[15] J. H. Mees, Story of a Hundred Years: Handbk. of Wesleyan Methodist Church Stourbridge Circuit (Stourbridge, 1928), 93–4 (copy in Stourbridge Libr.).
[16] P.R.O., HO 107/2017.
[17] H.W.R.O. (H.), E 12/S, Kinver VII, deed of 23 Feb. 1732/3.

common near the Enville boundary by 1800; it belonged to the owners of Enville Hall.[18] A two-day meeting at Kinver advertised for October 1816 may have taken place on the Checkhill course.[19] Another possible site is a field east of Kinver Edge Farm called Lower Racecourse in 1830.[20] Kinver cricket club, which had been formed by 1847 with Lord Stamford of Enville Hall and J. H. Hodgetts-Foley of Prestwood House in Kingswinford as patrons, probably played on the ground at Enville Hall. It still existed in 1852.[21] In the 1960s a new club was established. In 1982 it used a ground near Kinver community centre at the north end of the village.[22]

A company of rifle volunteers for Kinver was formed in 1860. It had ceased to exist by 1871.[23]

Strolling players may have given performances at Kinver in 1774.[24] An amateur theatrical company existed in 1870.[25] A choral society advertised a concert in the grammar school on New Year's Day 1883.[26] An operatic and dramatic society had been formed by 1928 and as Kinver Light Operatic Society still existed in 1982. There was a cinema at the junction of High Street and Vicarage Drive by 1924. During the Second World War the building was used as a fire station; it reopened as a cinema in the mid 1950s but later closed.[27]

There was a library and reading room in High Street by 1861. In 1865 it was in a house next to the Wesleyan chapel at the corner of Stone Lane and High Street; it was evidently still there in 1871.[28] It fell heavily into debt and was closed c. 1900.[29] A branch of the county library was opened in the former girls' National school in Vicarage Drive in 1967.[30]

Kinver and District Horticultural Society existed by 1928.[31] Kinver Historical Society was established in 1955.[32] In the mid 1960s the Kinver Community Association opened a hall, the Edward Marsh Centre, east of High Street at the north end of the village.[33] A village hall for the Stourton area was opened east of Stewponey in 1969.[34]

Kinver Edge has attracted summer visitors from the neighbouring towns since the later 19th century. Until the opening of a tramway to Kinver in 1901 visitors either walked or travelled by wagonette from Stourbridge. The tramway greatly increased the number of visitors, many of them in school or society outings; some 14,000 passengers travelled to Kinver by tram on Whit Monday in 1903 and 16,700 on the same day in 1905.[35] Refreshment rooms were opened to cater for the visitors. There was a coffee house in the 1880s and in 1892. A temperance hotel in Comber Road called Edge View had been opened by 1900; it was still open in 1904 but closed soon after.[36] There were 6 tea rooms and coffee houses in 1904; the number dropped to 3 in 1908 and 1912 but had risen to 9 by 1924, 12 by 1928, and 15 by 1936. Most visitors seem to have been day trippers, but some evidently stayed in apartments or boarding houses, of which there were 2 or 3 in the years before and after the First World War.[37] In 1917 the National Trust was given 198 a. on Kinver Edge by the children of Thomas Grosvenor Lee, a Birmingham solicitor who was born at Kinver and died in 1916; the gift was in memory of Lee and his wife. The area owned by the Trust was increased to 283 a. by three purchases between 1964 and 1980.[38] Kinver Edge remained a popular resort in 1982.

An attempt was made in 1821 to establish a benevolent society in Kinver, to provide money and other help for women at their confinement. The organizer seems to have been Thomas Housman, the assistant curate.[39] In 1842 George Wharton, the minister of Kinver, together with J. H. Hodgetts-Foley, helped to establish the Stewponey Becher Club, to provide pensions, money and medical help during illness, and also death grants. The club, which was at first a branch of the Stewponey Agricultural Society, covered the area within 12 miles of the Stewponey inn. It held Whitsuntide meetings at the inn.[40] Members paid monthly subscriptions which were graduated according to their age, a system of insurance devised by Canon John Becher.[41] The club was dissolved in 1912.[42]

The White Hart Club mentioned in 1830[43] may have been a friendly society meeting at the White Hart in High Street. The Vanguard Lodge of Nelsonic Crimson Oaks was established in 1833; it still existed in 1876 with an office in Foster Street. There were three other friendly societies in 1876. The Earl of Stamford Society, established in 1840, met at the Swan in High Street. The Robert Burns Society, established in

[18] Above, p. 95.
[19] *Wolverhampton Chron.* 25 Sept. 1816.
[20] S.R.O., D. 891/3, no. 851; ibid. 4, p. 60.
[21] H.W.R.O. (H.), E 12/S, Kinver III, printed list of club members 1847; S.R.O., Tp. 1273/27, Enville estate cash bk., 10 Mar. 1852; above, p. 95.
[22] Inf. from the club secretary.
[23] *Hist. of Volunteer Force of Staffs. 1859–1908* (Stafford, 1909), 6, 14–15.
[24] Birmingham Univ. Libr., accts. of Kinver schoolmaster (photocopy in S.R.O. 1401).
[25] S.R.O., CEH/76/1, 4 Feb. 1870.
[26] H.W.R.O. (H.), E 12/S, Kinver III, concert handbill.
[27] *Kelly's Dir. Staffs.* (1924; 1928); inf. from Mrs. E. Griffiths, Kinver Libr.; below, p. 153.
[28] P.R.O., RG 9/1985; RG 10/2928; S.R.O., Tp. 1273/32, sale notice.
[29] *Kelly's Dir. Staffs.* (1900); Bennett, *Kinver*, 124.
[30] Inf. from Mr. G. L. King, deputy divisional librarian (1980).
[31] *Kelly's Dir. Staffs.* (1928).
[32] Inf. from the chairman.
[33] Local inf.

[34] Plaque at the entrance.
[35] Bennett, *Kinver*, 123; Birmingham and Midland Tramways, *Illustrated Guide to Kinver* (1904), 1 (copy in W.S.L. Pamphs.); Webb, *Black Country Tramways*, i. 220, 230, 241, 252; above, communications.
[36] *Kelly's Dir. Staffs.* (edns. from 1884 to 1908); Bennett, *Kinver*, 123.
[37] *Kelly's Dir. Staffs.* (edns. from 1904 to 1940).
[38] W. and A. W. Sutton, 'Kinver and Neighbourhood', 36 (copy in Kinver Libr.); Bennett, *Kinver*, 46; inf. from the National Trust.
[39] S.R.O., Tp 1273/50, Thos. Housman to Ld. Stamford 3 Mar. 1821, and draft plan for society.
[40] H.W.R.O. (H.), E 12/S, Stewponey Becher Club II, bk. of rules; III, min. bk. 1842–59, 7 Mar. 1842; below, econ. hist. (agric.).
[41] R. Seymour, *Old and New Friendly Socs.* (1839; copy in H.W.R.O. (H.), E 12/S, Stewponey Becher Club II). For Becher see *D.N.B.*
[42] H.W.R.O. (H.), E 12/S, Stewponey Becher Club I, instrument of dissolution 20 Aug. 1912.
[43] S.R.O., D. 891/4, p. 36.

High Street in 1836; the White Hart inn is in the centre with curvilinear gables

Kinver Edge from the north-west

KINVER

Stourton Castle *c.* 1800

The Stewponey inn in 1828

KINVER

1845, met at the Stag in Mill Lane. A court of the Ancient Order of Foresters, established in 1858, met at the Lock, also in Mill Lane.[44] There was a clothing club in the later 1840s.[45]

MANORS AND OTHER ESTATES. Before the Conquest *KINVER* was held by Alfgar, earl of Mercia; it evidently passed to his son Earl Edwin and was confiscated after the rebellion of 1069.[46] In 1086 the 5½ hides there were held by the king but were farmed for 100s. by the sheriff of Worcestershire, Urse d'Abetot.[47] On his death in 1108 Urse was succeeded in the shrievalty by his son Roger, who held it until his banishment a few years later; they may also have continued to farm Kinver.[48] Henry II granted the manor with the keepership of Kinver forest to Philip son of Helgot, also known as Philip of Kinver.[49] The grant had evidently been made by 1168 when Philip accounted for the pannage of Kinver. He had been deprived of the manor and keepership, apparently for a forest offence, by 1176 when he owed 100 marks for the king's favour and the restoration of his forfeited office and land. It took him several years to pay the sum. Meanwhile the chief justice of the forests, Thomas FitzBernard, accounted for the pannage of Kinver in 1177 and for the proceeds from land at Kinver. In 1183 he was farming Kinver, probably both forest and manor, for £9. From the beginning of 1184 the farm was held by Geoffrey FitzPeter. In the middle of the year it passed to Philip of Kinver, who held it for the rest of his life. He received a new grant of the manor and the keepership of the forest in fee farm on Richard I's accession in 1189, still at a rent of £9. King John renewed the grant when he came to the throne in 1199, and Philip had to pay £100 for the renewal. He was succeeded by his son John in 1213 and the grant was again renewed, John paying 38 marks.[50] He was dead by December 1238, and his heir was his son John, a minor, who came of age between 1248 and 1250.[51] In 1293 the king resumed possession of the manor and the keepership of the forest and in November granted them back to John for life only, still at a rent of £9.[52]

Although John was still alive in 1306,[53] the keepership was granted to Richard son of Richard of Cleobury for life in 1304 at the request of Prince Edward.[54] In 1307 Edward as king granted Richard of Cleobury, described as his cook, 'the king's manor of Kinver which is called Stourton', to be held at the royal pleasure.[55]

There followed a number of grants of the keepership and the manor, all apparently at a rent of £9.[56] The estate was regularly called the manors of Kinver and *STOURTON* until the 17th century, perhaps a reflection of its division into a borough and a foreign.[57] In 1339 the king granted the reversion of the keepership to Hugh Tyrel in fee, adding the reversion of the manors of Kinver and Stourton in 1340 for the support of his knighthood; the life tenant of the keepership and the manors was Henry Mortimer, who in 1340 surrendered them to Tyrel and received them back for life.[58] Sir Hugh died in 1343 with a son John, a minor, as his heir. The king thereupon granted the keepership to Edward Atwood during the minority. In 1344 Mortimer granted his life interest in the keepership and the manors to Atwood. On Atwood's death in 1346 his interest passed to his infant daughter. His executor John Atwood subsequently secured the keepership and the manors and still held them in the earlier 1360s.[59] Meanwhile John Tyrel, having come of age in 1360, died the same year before taking possession. His heir was his brother Hugh, who came of age in 1362 and was given possession of Kinver and Stourton and the keepership of the forest in 1364. Hugh was later knighted. He died in 1381, and by 1382 his widow Catherine had conveyed her life interest in the property to Richard Hampton; Hugh's heirs too had renounced their interest.[60] It was done without royal licence, but in 1385 the king granted that the manors and keepership should be held by Richard for life at a fee-farm rent of £9 and should then become hereditary in his family.[61] Richard died in 1388 and his son John succeeded. John died in 1433 and was succeeded by his son, another John. The younger John had already been granted the £9 rent during the king's pleasure in 1427, and in 1437 he received it for life; from 1466 to 1540, however, it was granted to various members of the royal family. John held many offices under the Crown both in Staffordshire and elsewhere and was M.P. for Staffordshire seven times between 1437 and 1459. He died in 1472, with his brother Bevis as his heir.[62]

By 1475 the manors had been conveyed, evidently by trustees, to George, duke of Clarence, who that year gave them to Tewkesbury abbey (Glos.).[63] In 1495 the monks conveyed them to the Crown, which in return granted that they should in future have to act as collectors of clerical subsidies in Worcester diocese only.[64] A 40-year lease was granted to Charles Somerset,

---

[44] *Reps. of Chief Registrar of Friendly Socs. 1876*, H.C. 429, p. 404 (1877), lxxvii.

[45] S.R.O., Tp. 1273/39, guardian's accts. (Staffs.) 1846, 1848.

[46] *V.C.H. Staffs.* iv. 6, 40; R. W. Eyton, *Domesday Studies*, 26–30, 39.

[47] *V.C.H. Staffs.* iv. 40; *V.C.H. Worcs.* i. 262–5, 287; Eyton, *Domesday Studies*, 66–7.

[48] *Beauchamp Cartulary* (P.R.S. N.S. xliii), pp. xviii–xxi.

[49] *Bk. of Fees*, i. 142; *S.H.C.* i. 53–102 *passim*.

[50] *V.C.H. Staffs.* ii. 344. For the renewal of 1189 see *Cartae Antiquae* (Pipe R. Soc. N.S. xxxiii), no. 510.

[51] R. W. Eyton, *Antiquities of Shropshire*, iii. 164–6.

[52] *Cal. Pat.* 1292–1301, 23, 42.

[53] Above, Bobbington, manor and other estates.

[54] *Cal. Pat.* 1301–7, 247, describing John as deceased.

[55] Ibid. 1307–13, 1; *Abbrev. Rot. Orig.* (Rec. Com.), i. 155.

[56] *V.C.H. Staffs.* ii. 344–5. This wrongly states that the rent was not specifically mentioned again until 1347; for mentions see *Cal. Pat.* 1307–13, 349; *Cal. Close*, 1339–41, 380; *Cal. Inq. p.m.* xi, p. 466.

[57] Below, local govt.

[58] *Cal. Pat.* 1338–40, 399; 1340–3, 11, 15–16, 512.

[59] *Cal. Fine R.* 1337–47, 321, 395; *Cal. Close*, 1346–9, 106–7, 216; 1364–8, 37–8; *Cal. Inq. p.m.* ix, p. 17; *Cal. Pat.* 1358–61, 10; 1361–4, 469.

[60] *V.C.H. Staffs.* ii. 345; *Cal. Inq. p.m.* xv, p. 171. The *V.C.H.* wrongly gives 1359 as the year when John Tyrel came of age; in n. 48 'p. 466' should read 'p. 483'.

[61] *Cal. Pat.* 1381–5, 153; 1385–9, 72.

[62] *V.C.H. Staffs.* ii. 345; *S.H.C.* 1917–18, 221–3.

[63] *Cal. Pat.* 1461–7, 379; 1467–77, 346–7, 513, 530; H.W.R.O. (H.), E 12/S, Kinver ct. rolls 1387–1498, bdle. 27, ct. of 25 Sept. 1466.   [64] *Cal. Pat.* 1494–1509, 54.

Baron Herbert, later earl of Worcester, at £20 a year in 1504.[65] In 1522, after his surrender of the lease, one of 21 years was granted at the same rent to Edward Sutton, Baron Dudley.[66] A new 21-year lease, to take effect in 1543, was made in 1528 to Humphrey Bowland, an Exchequer clerk retained by the duchy of Lancaster.[67]

In 1537 the reversion of the manors was granted to William Whorwood and his second wife Margaret in fee; William, then solicitor general and later attorney general, was a younger son of the Whorwoods of Compton. The grant evidently took effect in 1543.[68] William Whorwood died in 1545, and his widow, who later married William Sheldon, continued to hold a life interest in the manors.[69] Whorwood's heirs were his daughters Anne, by 1546 wife of Ambrose Dudley, later earl of Warwick, and Margaret, a minor who later married Thomas Throckmorton of Coughton (Warws.). Anne died childless in 1552, and her heir was Thomas Whorwood of Compton, her first cousin once removed and a minor.[70] In 1578 Thomas and Margaret Throckmorton agreed to convey their interest to him.[71] In 1580 he joined with the Throckmortons and Margaret Sheldon in making a settlement of Kinver and Stourton, evidently in trust.[72] The manor court was held in Margaret Sheldon's name in 1584. She died in 1589, and the court was held in Thomas Whorwood's name in 1590.[73] He was M.P. for Staffordshire from 1572 to 1583, was twice sheriff, and was knighted in 1604. He died in 1616, having settled Kinver and Stourton in 1613 on his son Gerard in return for the payment of his debts and for the marriage portion of Gerard's wife.[74] The manor court was then held in Gerard's name.[75] Gerard was succeeded in 1627 by his son John.[76] In 1650 John made over his property to his son Sir William in return for William's agreement to the sale of Compton manor to pay John's debts.[77] John moved between Stourton Castle and Dunsley Hall in the

1650s and evidently lived until 1669.[78] Sir William was still alive in 1653 but was dead by 1657 with a son Wortley, a minor, as his heir.[79] Sir William's widow Catherine retained a life interest in Kinver and Stourton; by 1661 she had married William Hamerton, and they held the manors in Catherine's right by reason of her jointure.[80] Wortley, still a minor in 1668, was of age in 1669.[81] In 1672 he sold the manors to Philip Foley of Prestwood, in Kingswinford, a younger son of Thomas Foley, the ironmaster.[82]

Philip died in 1716 and was succeeded by a younger son Paul, who died in 1718 with a son William, a minor, as his heir. William died in 1735, also leaving a son William, a minor, as his heir. The younger William was succeeded in 1755 by his sister Elizabeth, who married John Hodgetts of Shut End, in Kingswinford. She died in 1759, leaving an infant daughter Eliza Maria.[83] Hodgetts, who lived at Prestwood, held Kinver manor until his death in 1789 when it passed to Eliza Maria.[84] In 1790 she married Edward Foley of Stoke Edith (Herefs.), a distant cousin; he died in 1803 and she in 1805. Kinver passed with Prestwood to their younger son John Hodgetts Foley (b. 1797), who changed his surname to Hodgetts-Foley in 1820 or 1821. He was succeeded in 1861 by his son H. J. W. Hodgetts-Foley, who was followed in 1894 by his son Paul Henry.[85] Paul changed his surname back to Foley.[86] He sold his Staffordshire property in the early 20th century, mainly in 1913 and the years following.[87]

The fee-farm rent of £9 was still paid to the sheriff in 1625.[88] A rent from Kinver was among the fee-farm rents sold by the Crown in 1672 and owned by Lord Boston in the late 18th century. In 1872 H. J. W. Hodgetts-Foley bought from the 5th Baron Boston what were described as the Kinver reeve rents with a view to selling them to the tenants, who paid them through the Kinver reeve.[89]

Stourton Castle, which became the home of

[65] *Cal. Pat.* 1494–1509, 389.
[66] H.W.R.O. (H.), E 12/S, Stourton VI, brief in case Rex v. Whorwood 1615; S.R.O., D. 593/O/3/5; *L. & P. Hen. VIII*, iii (2), p. 1315.
[67] *L. & P. Hen. VIII*, iv (2), p. 1898; R. Somerville, *Hist. of Duchy of Lancaster*, i. 458–9.
[68] *L. & P. Hen. VIII*, xii (2), 350; *S.H.C.* 1917–18, 304–5. He received a grant of a market and 2 fairs at Kinver in 1544: below, econ. hist.
[69] H.W.R.O. (H.), E 12/S, Staffs. legal papers, inq. p.m. of Anne Dudley 1555; E 12/S, Bobbington and Enville, valor of lands of John Grey 1581 (which, however, mentions Wm. Sheldon as still alive although Marg. Sheldon was described as a widow in 1577: E 12/S, Kingsley, ct. of 19 Sept. 1577).
[70] P. M. Grazebrook, *Short Hist. of Stourton Castle and Royal Forest of Kinver*, 33; *Complete Peerage*, xii (2), 402; H.W.R.O. (H.), E 12/S, Staffs. legal papers, inq. p.m. of Anne Dudley 1555.
[71] H.W.R.O. (H.), E 12/S, Whorwood inheritance, deed of 6 Apr. 1578.
[72] P.R.O., C 66/1194, m. 26; P.R.O., CP 25 (2)/260/22 Eliz. I East. no. 7.
[73] *S.H.C.* 1930, 72–3; 1945–6, 98; H.W.R.O. (H.), E 12/S, Kinver ct. rolls 1590–1629, ct. of 31 Mar. 1590.
[74] *S.H.C.* 1917–18, 371–2; P.R.O., C 3/389/13; P.R.O., C 142/354, no. 104.
[75] H.W.R.O. (H.), E 12/S, Kinver ct. rolls 1590–1629.
[76] P.R.O., C 142/432, no. 109.
[77] H.W.R.O. (H.), E 12/S, Whorwood inheritance, articles between John and Sir Wm. Whorwood 6 Aug. 1650.
[78] Below (Stourton Castle; Dunsley); S.R.O., D. 1197/1/2,

[78] burial of 'Mr. John Whorwood Esq.' 22 Sept. 1669.
[79] H.W.R.O. (H.), E 12/S, Kinver ct. papers 17th and 18th cents., ct. of 17 Oct. 1653; E 12/S, Stourton I, deeds of 1 Feb. 1656/7, 17 June 1657; E 12/S, Staffs. legal papers, bill in Chancery (Grey and others v. Whorwood and others).
[80] Ibid. E 12/S, Kingsley manor, ct. of 11 Apr. 1661; Kinver ct. papers 17th and 18th cents., ct. of 16 Oct. 1662.
[81] Ibid. Kinver ct. papers 17th and 18th cents., cts. of 20 Jan. 1667/8, 26 Oct. 1669.
[82] Ibid. Whorwood inheritance, deed of 24 Feb. 1671/2; P.R.O., CP 25 (2)/725/24 Chas. II Trin. no. 12.
[83] Shaw, *Staffs.* ii. 232, 235, 264; S.R.O., D. 1197/1/3, burials 30 Nov. 1716, 4 Apr. 1718.
[84] H.W.R.O. (H.), E 12/S, Kinver, Compton Hallows, and Kingsley ct. bk. 1734–61, Kinver ct. of 23 Apr. 1760; Kinver and Kingsley ct. bk. 1767–1801; Shaw, *Staffs.* ii. 264.
[85] Shaw, *Staffs.* ii. 235; Grazebrook, *Stourton Castle*, 39, wrongly giving Edw.'s date of death as 1808; *Staffs. Advertiser*, 2 July 1803, 20 July 1805; Bennett, *Kinver*, 100. For the change of name see H.W.R.O. (H.), E 12/S, Kinver and Compton Hallows ct. bk. 1800–36, ct. of 19 Oct. 1820; ibid. Kinver VIII, deed of 15 Sept. 1821.
[86] H.W.R.O. (H.), E 12/S, Prestwood sales, H. T. F. King to P. H. Foley 23 and 25 Oct. 1917.
[87] Ibid. Prestwood sales.
[88] Ibid. Kinver ct. rolls. 1590–1629, ct. of survey 24 Oct. 1625.
[89] S.R.O., Tp. 1273/21, notebook 1797–1814; ibid. 41, Staffs. fee-farm rents, showing also a separate reeve rent due to Lord Boston from Lord Stamford for Whittington manor and other land in Kinver.

the lords of Kinver, originated as a royal hunting lodge. There was probably a lodge in the area in the late 11th century when William II was at Kinver. Henry II may have been at Kinver in 1176 and 1186. In 1184–5 the sheriff accounted for making a ditch round the king's houses at Kinver, in 1185–6 for enclosing the court round them, and in 1187–8 for work on the king's chamber at Kinver. There was further work on the buildings in 1190–1. In 1195–6 a new set of buildings, evidently of timber, was erected at Stourton. They included a hall and offices, a kitchen, a chamber, a gaol, and a gate with a brattice. The surrounding palisade was 16 perches in circumference and 16 ft. high. There was also a fishpond. King John was at Kinver in 1200, 1206, and 1207 and at Stourton in 1207 and 1215.[90] By 1222 the lodge was known as the castle of Kinver and was the home of John son of Philip, the keeper of Kinver forest and lord of Kinver manor. He fortified it in 1222–3, the king providing money and also timber from the forest.[91] In 1244 John's widow, who had custody of his heir and lands, was given timber to repair the buildings at Stourton.[92] In the mid 1250s the heir held what was called the castle of Stourton with a wood assigned for the maintenance of its kitchen.[93]

The castle was included in the grant for life of Stourton manor and the keepership of Kinver forest which the king made to Sir John de Vaux in 1310.[94] He was accused of taking part in the murder at the castle in 1316 of Sir Thomas Murdak, whose widow, Gillian, Vaux married a few days after the murder; she too was implicated and was sentenced to be burnt, but Vaux was acquitted.[95] The gaol at the castle was used in 1360 when the prior of Dudley was held there for a forest offence before being granted bail.[96] The Hamptons were evidently living at Stourton by 1391 when John Hampton was licensed to have an oratory in his manor of Stourton.[97] His son John was living there in 1441 and was buried in Kinver church in 1472.[98] About 1500 the castle may have been the home of Sir Richard Pole and his wife Margaret, daughter of George, duke of Clarence: according to an early tradition their son

Reginald (d. 1558), cardinal and archbishop of Canterbury, was born there in 1500 or 1501.[99]

Sir Thomas Whorwood had moved from Compton to Stourton Castle by 1602 and died at the castle in 1616;[1] his son-in-law was living there in 1604.[2] Sir Thomas's son Gerard was there in 1625 but had moved to Compton by 1626.[3] Gerard's son John lived at Stourton Castle at least until 1642.[4] Although John seems to have been neutral in the Civil War, the castle was taken by the parliamentarian Col. Thomas Fox in 1644. Sir Gilbert Gerard, the royalist governor of Worcester, promptly marched against it, and after he had routed Fox on Stourbridge heath, the castle surrendered to him.[5] In 1647 John and his son Sir William were living at Compton. Sir William moved to Stourton Castle later that year, evidently on his marriage.[6] With the sale of Compton in 1650 it was agreed that John should have for life the use of part of the castle 'commonly called the new building, the tower and cellars with the closet, and other necessary use of the parlour'.[7] He was living at the castle in 1651,[8] but by 1655 he was at Dunsley Hall, his granddaughter's home. He was again at the castle in 1656 but had moved back to Dunsley by 1657.[9] Meanwhile in 1657 the castle was granted to Sir Francis Lawley of Spoonhill, in Much Wenlock (Salop.), for the duration of Wortley Whorwood's minority. Sir Francis agreed to carry out the repairs needed to make the castle fit to live in, although the Whorwoods' bailiff was to reimburse him.[10] Sir William Whorwood's widow, however, was living at the castle in 1658,[11] and it was presumably the house in Stourton where Thomas Brettle was assessed for tax on 13 hearths in 1666.[12] The castle was known as one of Sir Francis Lawley's residences in the late 1660s.[13] It was leased with the mill to John Finch of Dudley in 1670 but was not included in a new lease of the forge granted to Finch in 1672.[14] The Foleys continued to let the castle, their home being at Prestwood. William Talbot had moved there from Whittington by 1676, and he died there in 1686.[15] In 1692 it was occupied by Richard Oliver.[16] After the conversion of the mill into a forge in 1670 or 1671 it was suggested that

[90] *V.C.H. Staffs.* ii. 346–7.
[91] *Rot. Litt. Claus.* (Rec. Com.), i. 520, 523, 548, 556, 596.
[92] *Close R.* 1242–7, 209.
[93] *S.H.C.* v (1), 116.
[94] *Cal. Chanc. Wts.* i. 328; *Cal. Fine R.* 1307–19, 75, 84.
[95] *S.H.C.* x (1), 27–8, 34–9; xiv (1), 4, 18.
[96] *V.C.H. Staffs.* ii. 347, where in n. 22 '*Cal. Close, 1360–5*' should read '*Cal. Close, 1360–4*'.
[97] L.J.R.O., B/A/1/6, f. 127.
[98] *S.H.C.* N.S. vi (2), 209; below, church.
[99] Leland, *Itin.* ed. Toulmin Smith, v. 20; Camden, *Britannia* (1610 edn.), 581; *D.N.B.* s.v. Pole, Marg., and Pole, Reg.; Wood, *Athenae Oxonienses*, i (1813 edn.), 278–9, wrongly states that London is given as Pole's birthplace by L. Beccatelli, *Vita Reginaldi Poli* (Venice, 1563), 7v.; Beccatelli, Pole's secretary and first biographer, does not identify the birthplace.
[1] H.W.R.O. (H.), E 12/S, Kinver XIII, Bill in Chancery 29 Jan. 1601/2; ibid. Compton I, deed of 20 Nov. 1605; P.R.O., C 142/432, no. 109; *S.H.C.* v (2), 339.
[2] Oxspring, 'Yarranton', 55; *S.H.C.* ix (2), 108.
[3] H.W.R.O. (H.), E 12/S, Whorwood inheritance, deed of 1 Dec. 1625; below (Compton Hallows).
[4] H.W.R.O. (H.), E 12/S, Dunsley I, deed of 23 Mar. 1634/5; Compton I, deeds of 3 Apr. 1635, 29 May 1639;

Whorwood inheritance, deed of 15 Feb. 1639/40; Stourton III, deed of 26 Mar. 1642.
[5] Grazebrook, *Stourton Castle*, 34–5; Hist. MSS. Com. 3, *4th Rep.* p. 265; *S.H.C.* N.S. vi (2), 332.
[6] H.W.R.O. (H.), E 12/S, Whorwood inheritance, articles of agreement June 1647 and articles between John and Sir Wm. Whorwood 6 Aug. 1650; E 12/S, Tettenhall, deed of 10 Nov. 1647.
[7] Ibid. Whorwood inheritance, articles between John and Sir Wm. Whorwood 6 Aug. 1650.
[8] Ibid. tithe and inclosure papers, deed of 20 Feb. 1650/1; Stourton II, deed of 10 Oct. 1651.
[9] Below (Dunsley).
[10] H.W.R.O. (H.), E 12/S, Stourton I, deeds of 1 Feb. 1656/7, 17 June 1657; Whorwood inheritance, Lawley v. Jolley and others 1657.
[11] Ibid. Whorwood inheritance, deed of 16 Nov. 1658.
[12] *S.H.C.* 1923, 106.
[13] Erdeswick, *Staffs.* p. lvii.
[14] H.W.R.O. (H.), E 12/S, Whorwood inheritance, deed of 7 Dec. 1672.
[15] Ibid. Stourton II, deed of 21 July 1676; Shaw, *Staffs.* ii. 264–5.
[16] H.W.R.O. (H.), E 12/S, Stourton II, deed of 30 Sept. 1692.

the castle had become unfit to be the residence of a person of quality as well as having its foundations threatened by vibration from the forge.[17] For much of the 18th century it was the home of the Hollins family, which occupied it as a farmhouse.[18] In 1805 T. W. Grazebrook, who owned much of the land in the vicinity, moved from Audnam, in Kingswinford, to Stourton Castle and died there in 1816. His widow Elizabeth continued to live there until 1832.[19] In 1833 James Foster, an ironmaster with interests in Amblecote and elsewhere, moved to the castle from Stourbridge. He died at the castle in 1853, and his nephew and heir W. O. Foster lived there until 1868.[20] In 1869 he assigned the residue of the lease to G. R. Collis, an electro-plate manufacturer of Birmingham, who lived at the castle until 1877 or 1878. George Arkle, a Liverpool banker, took a lease in 1878 and lived there until his death in 1885 or 1886. His family moved out, and the castle remained empty until its sale to Francis Grazebrook on the break-up of the Foley estate in 1913.[21] A great-great-great-nephew of T. W. Grazebrook, he lived there from 1915 until his death in 1945. His son O. F. Grazebrook, who revived the prosperity of the family ironworks at Netherton, in Dudley, moved to the castle and remained there until his death in 1974.[22] It was bought in that year with 107 a. by Mr. M. Fellows, the owner in 1982.[23]

Stourton Castle stands on a rocky outcrop with the Stour to the east and steep natural slopes to the north and south.[24] The present buildings evidently occupy the site of a keep, and the discovery in 1832-3 of the foundations of two round towers some distance to the north-west may indicate that there was a bailey or outer court on that side. The earliest surviving part of the house is the late-medieval stone gate-tower on the west side of a formerly open court which is surrounded by brick ranges of the mid to later 16th century. The hall was on the east side of the court, the parlour and main staircase on the north, and the service rooms on the south, where there was also a porch tower. In the mid 17th century the exterior was remodelled, perhaps after damage during the Civil War. Shaped gables were added to the roofline, and a walled square court was made in front of the gate-tower.

By the early 19th century there were a service court and an assortment of out-buildings south of the gate-tower. In 1832 and 1833 extensive alterations and additions were made by James Foster from designs by Sir Robert Smirke. The ground floor was lowered by c. 4 ft. throughout. The porch tower and a staircase in the courtyard were demolished, and a top-lit hall was created there, a new staircase being made between the hall and the south range. The interior was redecorated. Wings were added on either side of the gate-tower to make a new front in a Jacobean style, the tower being rendered and the new work being in red brick. On the south side an existing terrace was extended along both the old and the new work, and on the north it was continued as a bridge above outhouses which were connected with the lower floor of kitchens in the new north wing. In 1838 a gothic lodge of red brick was built at the entrance to the drive from the Bridgnorth road.

The manor of *COMPTON HALLOWS* was known in the late 13th century as the manor of *HOREWOOD*. It was referred to as Haulowe in 1387,[25] presumably after the Haudlo family who held it earlier in the century, but Horewood was still the usual name in the 15th century.[26] The normal usage was Halowes in Compton by the end of that century,[27] but 'le Horewood otherwise le Halowes' is found in 1527.[28] By the later 16th century the name used was Compton Hallowes.[29] Whorwood and Compton Whorwood were also used in the 17th and 18th centuries.[30]

The manor probably originated in the 8½-a. wood in Kinver manor called Horewood which Leo of Romsley, rector of Kinver, was licensed to inclose and assart in 1269; in 1286 Leo son of Leo received permission to assart 20 a. of his waste in Kinver manor.[31] A manor of Horewood existed by 1292. The overlordship was held by the lord of Kinver, who in the late 13th and the 14th century received a rent for it, variously given as 1d., 22s., and 21s. 9d.[32] The tenant was stated in 1315 to perform suit twice a year at Kinver court.[33] The manor was still described as within Kinver manor in 1800. In the early 19th century it became united with Kinver.[34]

The manor was held by Robert Burnell, bishop

[17] H.W.R.O. (H.), E 12/S, Whorwood inheritance, annot. copy of partic. of Stourton Castle estate; below, econ. hist.
[18] H.W.R.O. (H.), E 12/S, Stourton I, draft deed of 1712; E 12/S, vol. of 18th- and 19th-cent. plans; S.R.O., D. 1021/2/4; D. 1197/1/3, baptism of 11 Oct. 1711, burials of 6 Nov. 1730, 2 Jan. 1764; Shaw, *Staffs.* ii. 267.
[19] Grazebrook, *Stourton Castle*, 40.
[20] Ibid. 40-1; H.W.R.O. (H.), E 12/S, Stourton II, notice of auction of contents of Stourton Castle, Aug. 1868; above, Amblecote, econ. hist.
[21] Grazebrook, *Stourton Castle*, 41; B. Robinson, *Genealogical Memoirs of Fam. of Brooke Robinson, of Dudley* (priv. print. 1896), 38-9; H.W.R.O. (H.), E 12/S, Prestwood leases, list of Stourton Castle fixtures 22 Jan. 1877, deed of 26 Aug. 1878.
[22] *Blackcountryman* (Summer 1974), 30-1; Grazebrook, *Stourton Castle*, 41.
[23] Inf. from Mr. Fellows (1982); *Stourton Castle Est. Sale Cat.* (copy in possession of Staffs. C.C. Planning Dept., Conservation Section).
[24] For this para. see Grazebrook, *Stourton Castle*, 42-7; Colvin, *Brit. Architects*, 746; H.W.R.O. (H.), E 12/F/P7; above, pl. facing p. 129.
[25] H.W.R.O. (H.), E 12/S, Kinver ct. rolls 1387-1498, bdle. 1.
[26] Ibid. E 12/S, Early Deeds, notification of receipt of rent 4 Oct. 1425, deed of 1 Apr. 1439; Compton I, deeds of 17 May 1437; P.R.O., C 140/488, no. 27.
[27] *Cal. Pat.* 1485-94, 336; *L. & P. Hen. VIII*, i (2), p. 1114; H.W.R.O. (H.), E 12/S, Compton Hallows ct. rolls, ct. of 21 Oct. 1504.
[28] H.W.R.O. (H.), E 12/S, Compton I, inq. p.m. of John Whorwood 1527.
[29] Ibid. Compton Hallows ct. rolls.
[30] P.R.O., C 142/354, no. 104; H.W.R.O. (H.), E 12/S, Compton I, deeds of 7 July 1650, 17 June 1657, 9 Feb. 1758; S.R.O., index to gamekeepers' deputations.
[31] *S.H.C.* 1911, 140-1; *Cal. Pat.* 1266-72, 335, 381; 1281-92, 220.
[32] *S.H.C.* 1911, 214, 222, 263, 331; 1913, 113; *Cal. Inq. p.m.* xv, p. 289; H.W.R.O. (H.), E 12/S, Kinver ct. rolls 1387-1498, bdle. 1.
[33] *Cal. Inq. p.m.* v, p. 390.
[34] H.W.R.O. (H.), E 12/S, Kinver and Kingsley ct. bk. 1767-1801, Compton Hallows cts. of 12 Nov. 1778, 1 Sept. 1791, 25 Mar. 1800; below, p. 151.

of Bath and Wells, at his death in 1292.[35] It then descended with Acton Burnell (Salop.), passing to Robert's nephew Philip Burnell (d. 1294), Philip's son Edward (d. 1315), Edward's sister Maud (d. 1341) and her second husband John de Haudlo (d. 1346), and their son Nicholas, later Sir Nicholas (d. 1383), who took the name Burnell,[36] Although Nicholas's son Sir Hugh Burnell was given as heir, he does not appear to have held Horewood.[37] Apparently the same lordship was held in 1425 by William, Lord Lovel, great-great-grandson of Maud Haudlo by her first husband John, Lord Lovel. In that year William received from the tenant a rent of £4 (and by 1437 two running dogs also). On William's death in 1455 the mesne lordship passed to his son John, who was succeeded by his son Francis in 1465.[38] On Francis's attainder in 1485 the rent passed to the Crown, which was still receiving it in 1662.[39]

In 1387 the manor was held by John Horewood, who was paying the lord of Kinver a rent of 21s. 9d. for the demesne lands.[40] His family was living at Horewood by 1295[41] and may have been terre tenants of the manor before the statute of *Quia Emptores*. In 1425 a John Horewood held the manor of Lord Lovel, who in 1437 made a grant of it to the same or another John Horewood.[42] A John Horewood the elder was living in the earlier 1460s and was succeeded by a son John.[43] It is not clear whether that younger John or a son of the same name was the John who held the manor at his death in 1527, with a son John, a minor, as his heir. By then the family name was spelled Whorwood.[44] The manor eventually passed, probably by 1538, to a younger son Edward, who died in 1547 with a son Thomas, a minor, as his heir.[45] In 1559 the manor court was held by Edward's widow Dorothy and her husband Hugh Shadwell; they were living in Compton in 1562 and were evidently still in possession of the manor, but Thomas held it by 1569.[46] The manor then descended in the Whorwood family with Kinver until 1650. In 1625, however, Gerard Whorwood settled it on his wife Anne as

her jointure, and her trustee Nicholas Moseley was still described as lord in 1641.[47] In 1650 John Whorwood, being in financial difficulties, sold the manor to Thomas Foley.[48] By 1671 it was held by Thomas's son Philip,[49] and it descended with Kinver. By 1806 the two were treated as a single manor.[50] In 1830, however, J. H. Hodgetts-Foley owned no land in Compton; the land there had been sold evidently in the late 18th and early 19th century.[51]

There was a manor house with a garden at Horewood by 1294,[52] presumably on the moated site now occupied by Park Farm, near which a field named Whorwood still exists.[53] In 1346 the house was said to be worth nothing beyond reprises.[54] John Horewood was described as of Horewood in 1425, but by 1429 he was of Compton.[55] The family then continued to be so described.[56] Park Farm, which stands within the remains of a rectangular moat, dates from the earlier 17th century and was originally timber-framed. It has an L-shaped plan with a large internal stack and a lobby entrance. Almost all the original external walling was cased in or replaced by brick in the 18th and 19th centuries. There was extensive reconstruction during the restoration of the house after its sale in 1980 by Mr. C. Parkes to Mr. R. J. Fletcher.[57] A large barn to the east, now mainly of brick, may be of 17th-century origin.

The Whorwoods' capital messuage at Compton was mentioned in 1527 and was called Compton Hall by 1538.[58] Thomas Whorwood was still living at Compton in 1584,[59] but by 1605 he had moved to Stourton Castle. In that year he conveyed the manor house at Compton to his son and heir Gerard, who was living there in 1626.[60] In 1640 the hall was held by Gerard's widow Anne.[61] Gerard's son John was living there by 1647, and it was still his home at the time of the sale of the manor to Thomas Foley in 1650. John's son Sir William too was described as of Compton in 1647, but he moved to Stourton Castle later that year.[62] In 1650 the hall stood in grounds of *c.* 9 a. including gardens and an orchard.[63] Foley

[35] *S.H.C.* 1911, 214.
[36] *V.C.H. Salop.* viii. 7 and refs. given there.
[37] *Cal. Inq. p.m.* xv, p. 289. In 1387 the tenant paid rent direct to the lord of Kinver: below.
[38] H.W.R.O. (H.), E 12/S, Early Deeds, notification of receipt of rent 4 Oct. 1425; Compton I, deed of 17 May 1437; P.R.O., C 140/488, no. 27; *Complete Peerage*, viii. 221–5.
[39] *Cal. Pat.* 1485–94, 336; *L. & P. Hen. VIII*, i (2), p. 1114; iii (2), p. 889; xiii (1), p. 567; H.W.R.O. (H.), E 12/S, Compton I, inq. p.m. of John Whorwood 1527, and receipt for rent 18 Oct. 1648; Compton II, deed of 16 Dec. 1651; Halfcot I, deed of 16 Mar. 1661/2.
[40] H.W.R.O. (H.), E 12/S, Kinver ct. rolls 1387–1498, bdle. 1.
[41] *Charters and Muniments of Lyttelton Fam.* ed. I. H. Jeayes, p. 14. For later refs. see e.g. *S.H.C.* vii (1), 247; x (1), 86; H.W.R.O. (H.), Early Deeds, deeds of 27 May 1309, 30 June 1312, 2 Mar. 1374/5.
[42] H.W.R.O. (H.), E 12/S, Early Deeds, notification of receipt of rent 4 Oct. 1425; Compton I, deed of 17 May 1437.
[43] Ibid. Early Deeds, 13 Jan. 1459/60; S.R.O., Tp. 1273/12/3, nos. 4, 5; Grazebrook, *Stourton Castle*, 33.
[44] H.W.R.O. (H.), E 12/S, Compton I, deed of 30 Sept. 1527; Grazebrook, *Stourton Castle*, 33.
[45] H.W.R.O. (H.), E 12/S, Compton II, deed of 20 Sept. 1538; E 12/S, Staffs. misc., deed of 20 Sept. 1542; P.R.O., C 142/104, no. 87.
[46] H.W.R.O. (H.), E 12/S, Compton Hallows ct. rolls; Compton II, deed of 24 June 1562.

[47] Ibid. Whorwood inheritance, deed of 1 Dec. 1625; Compton Hallows ct. rolls.
[48] Ibid. Compton I, deed of 7 July 1650; ibid. Compton inheritance, articles between John and Sir Wm. Whorwood 6 Aug. 1650.
[49] Ibid. Compton Hallows ct. rolls; Shaw, *Staffs.* ii. 235.
[50] Below, local govt.
[51] S.R.O., D. 891/4; H.W.R.O. (H.), E 12/S, Compton I, sale partic. of freehold estates in Compton 1790; below (Compton Hall).   [52] *S.H.C.* 1911, 222.
[53] H.W.R.O. (H.), E 12/S, vol. of 18th- and 19th-cent. plans; inf. from Mr. C. Parkes.   [54] *S.H.C.* 1913, 113.
[55] H.W.R.O. (H.), E 12/S, Early Deeds, receipt of 4 Oct. 1425; *Cal. Fine R.* 1422–30, 292.
[56] *Cal. Fine R.* 1422–30, 332; *S.H.C.* N.S. iii. 191; H.W.R.O. (H.), E 12/S, Early Deeds, 6 Oct. 1491.
[57] Inf. from Mr. Fletcher, who is thanked for his help.
[58] H.W.R.O. (H.), E 12/S, Compton I, inq. p.m. of John Whorwood 1527; Compton II, deed of 20 Sept. 1538.
[59] Ibid. Stourton VI, inf. of Thos. Whorwood 1584.
[60] Ibid. Compton I, deed of 20 Nov. 1605; Stourton I, deed of 3 May 1626.
[61] H.W.R.O. (H.), E 12/S, Whorwood inheritance, deed of 15 Feb. 1639/40.
[62] Ibid. deed of 1648 and articles between John and Sir Wm. Whorwood 6 Aug. 1650; Compton I, deed of 7 July 1650; above (Stourton Castle).
[63] H.W.R.O. (H.), E 12/S, Compton I, survey of 6 July 1650 and deed of 7 July 1650.

let it from 1651,[64] but it was presumably the house in Compton where he was assessed for tax on 15 hearths in 1666.[65] In 1803 the trustees of Eliza Maria Foley sold the hall as a farmhouse to John Holt, a glassmaker of Wordsley, in Kingswinford. On his death c. 1820 it passed to his daughter Mary, and in 1849, some six years after her death, her husband G. W. Wainwright sold the 214-a. Compton Hall farm to Lord Stamford.[66] In 1982 the farm was part of the Enville Hall estate and was held by Mr. T. R. Brown, owner of the adjoining Pigeon House farm. Compton Hall Farm is a brick house of the earlier 18th century with an early 19th-century addition on the north. There are farm buildings of the 18th and early 19th century.

An estate at *DUNSLEY* in Kinver manor consisting of a house, 1 virgate, 4 a. of meadow, and a water mill was held in the early 14th century by Robert Throckmorton of Throckmorton, in Fladbury (Worcs.). Gilbert of Dunsley, who was active in the area by 1304, held the estate of Robert in the mid 1320s. Gilbert died in, or shortly before, 1326; he was a bastard and had no legal heir.[67] In 1327 Throckmorton was licensed to enfeoff Richard Atwell of 'Overdon', evidently Orton in Wombourne.[68] The estate was probably the origin of the manor of Dunsley, held in 1440 by William Everdon, lord of Orton. The manor was granted by his trustees to his son Thomas in 1458.[69] A Humphrey Everdon, who had probably succeeded by 1479, made a settlement of the manor in 1504.[70] He was still living in 1515.[71] The manor was disputed between his son John and William Whorwood and in 1532 was assigned by arbitrators to Whorwood.[72] By his death in 1545 Whorwood was also lord of Kinver, with two daughters, Anne and Margaret, as his heirs. Anne (d. 1552) married Ambrose Dudley, and in 1555, after his attainder, Dudley's life interest in half of Dunsley manor was granted to William Rice. The reversion lay with Anne's heir, Thomas Whorwood.[73] In 1578 Margaret and her husband Thomas Throckmorton agreed to convey their share to Thomas Whorwood, and the three of them made a settlement of the manor in 1580.[74] Whorwood evidently held the whole manor in 1584.[75] Dunsley

descended with Kinver until 1651. In that year John Whorwood and his son Sir William conveyed the manor to John's son-in-law William Carter under the terms of a mortgage made in 1635.[76] Carter died in 1651, leaving a daughter Catherine, a minor.[77] She was presumably the Catherine who with her husband John Hamerton held the manor in 1665. John died in 1669 with a son John as his heir. In 1709 Catherine Hamerton and the younger John sold Dunsley to Philip Foley.[78] It then descended with Kinver. In 1918 P. H. Foley sold c. 270 a. at Dunsley to Alfred Marsh, the tenant of part of the estate from 1894. Marsh died soon afterwards, and his executors sold the estate later in 1918 to Marsh & Baxter Ltd., a Brierley Hill firm of bacon and ham curers and pork butchers founded by Marsh. His son A. E. Marsh bought the estate in 1929 and died in 1938. His son Mr E. E. Marsh owned 635 a. at Dunsley in 1982.[79]

Gilbert of Dunsley's estate in 1326 included a house.[80] Humphrey Everdon was evidently living at Dunsley in 1504[81] and William Whorwood in 1536.[82] John Whorwood was described as of Dunsley in 1629 and 1631.[83] In the early 1640s Dunsley Hall was leased to a scythesmith.[84] It was the home of John Whorwood's son-in-law William Carter in 1651, and Carter's daughter Catherine lived there after his death in that year.[85] As her guardian John Whorwood was living there in 1655 and 1657, although in 1656 he was described as of Stourton Castle.[86] In 1657 he leased the house to one of his creditors, reserving for himself the hall, three upper chambers, and the main offices.[87] In 1658 he surrendered the guardianship to his daughter-in-law Dame Catherine Whorwood, who paid some of his debts and reduced his rooms at Dunsley to the kitchen, the chamber over it, and his study adjoining the chamber, with use of half the garden.[88] In 1666 John Hamerton and his wife, described as of Dunsley Hall, leased the house to William Hamerton in consideration of the amount which he had spent on it.[89] He was assessed on nine hearths there that year.[90] John and Catherine moved back there from Worcester c. 1693,[91] and it was still Catherine's home in 1707.[92] Later the house was regularly let; for

[64] H.W.R.O. (H.), E 12/S, Compton I, deeds of 25 Apr. 1651, 24 Dec. 1652, 22 Oct. 1655; Compton II, 4 Oct. 1652.
[65] *S.H.C.* 1923, 107.
[66] S.R.O., Tp. 1273/33, deeds of 12 Mar. 1803, 12 July 1849, 6 July 1854, and copy will of John Holt; G. R. Guttery, *From Broad Glass to Cut Crystal*, 100.
[67] *S.H.C.* 1911, 329, 362, 370–1; *V.C.H. Worcs.* iii. 356 (misdating Gilbert's death); H.W.R.O. (H.), E 12/S, Kinver VI, rents from waste in Kinver forest temp. Edw. I; ibid. E 12/F/P3, deed of 6 Apr. 1310.
[68] *S.H.C.* 1911, 371; *Cal. Pat.* 1327–30, 10.
[69] S.R.O., D. 593/B/1/26/7B/1 and 3.
[70] *S.H.C.* N.S. vi (1), 118; *S.H.C.* 1928, 89–90.
[71] Below, econ. hist. (mills).
[72] H.W.R.O. (H.), E 12/S, Dunsley I, deed of 12 Nov. 1532.
[73] Above (Kinver manor); *Cal. Pat.* 1553, 1; 1554–5, 167–8.
[74] H.W.R.O. (H.), E 12/S, Whorwood inheritance, deed of 6 Apr. 1578; P.R.O., CP 25 (2)/260/22 Eliz. I East. no. 7.
[75] *S.H.C.* xv. 159.
[76] H.W.R.O. (H.), E 12/S, Dunsley I, deeds of 23 Mar. 1634/5, 27 Mar. 1651; P.R.O., C 3/437/54.
[77] P.R.O., C 3/437/54; H.W.R.O. (H.), E 12/S, Whorwood inheritance, legal opinion 21 Nov. 1653.
[78] H.W.R.O. (H.), E 12/S, Dunsley II, sched. of deeds

relating to estate at Dunsley purchased by Philip Foley; S.R.O., D. 1197/1/2, burial of 15 or 16 Aug. 1699.
[79] H.W.R.O. (H.), E 12/S, Prestwood leases, deed of 12 Apr. 1894; ibid. Prestwood sale, Bernard, King & Sons' accts. 1917–18; copy of *Prestwood Est. Sale Cat.* in poss. of Bannister, King & Rigbeys, Stourbridge, sched. of purchasers made 1922; inf. from Mr. E. E. Marsh, who is thanked for his help with this section. For the firm see *P.O. Dir. Staffs.* (1872; 1876); *Kelly's Dir. Staffs.* (1880 and later edns.).
[80] *S.H.C.* 1911, 370; *Cal. Pat.* 1327–30, 10.
[81] *S.H.C.* 1928, 90. [82] *L. & P. Hen. VIII*, xi, p. 158.
[83] H.W.R.O. (H.), E 12/S, Stourton II, deed of 25 Aug. 1629; ibid. Kingswinford I, memo. of 26 May 1631.
[84] L.J.R.O., B/C/11, Wm. Penn (1646).
[85] H.W.R.O. (H.), E 12/S, Dunsley I, deed of 27 Mar. 1651; P.R.O., C 3/437/54.
[86] H.W.R.O. (H.), E 12/S, Whorwood inheritance, deeds of 3 Oct. 1655, 26 Feb. 1655/6; Dunsley V, deed of 10 Apr. 1657. [87] Ibid. Dunsley V, deed of 10 Apr. 1657.
[88] Ibid. Whorwood inheritance, deed of 16 Nov. 1658.
[89] Ibid. Dunsley I, deed of 15 Sept. 1666.
[90] *S.H.C.* 1923, 107.
[91] H.W.R.O. (H.), E 12/S, Dunsley I, deeds of 25 Mar., 20 and 21 Apr., 13 July 1692, 29 Jan. 1693/4, 2 Aug. 1697.
[92] Ibid. deed of 9 Apr. 1707; below, Roman Catholicism.

much of the 19th century it was the home of the Robins family.[93] It was included in the sale to Alfred Marsh, whose son A. E. Marsh was living there by 1916.[94] His widow lived there until her death in 1951. Mr. E. E. Marsh then moved to the Hall, which was his home in 1982.[95]

The hall range and parlour cross wing survive from a substantial timber-framed house of the later 16th century. The hall, which has a heavily timbered and moulded ceiling, was entered from a screens passage at its east end and was separated from the parlour by a large chimney stack. The parlour wing is of a substantial size and build. Along its east side there was a passage with an enclosed first-floor gallery above, and there may have been a garderobe turret projecting from the west side. The replacement or casing of some of the outer walls in brick probably began in the 17th century, and in the 18th century a two-storeyed brick range was built on the north side of the court formed by the cross wings. The service wing was demolished in the late 18th or early 19th century, and the kitchens were moved to the north end of the parlour cross wing. It was presumably then that the screens wall was removed and the entrance moved to the centre of the hall range. In the later 19th century a wing containing drawing rooms was built on the site of the old service wing, a staircase was added behind the hall, much of the exterior walling was renewed in dark red brick, and the front was given symmetrical gables and a central porch. In the earlier 20th century the drawing rooms were combined and panelled and a room was added on their north side.

The farm buildings, on the south side of the road, are of brick and mostly 19th-century.

About 1200 Philip of Kinver granted *WHITTINGTON* to Peter de Hurech and his heirs in fee at a rent of 20s.[96] The manor was still held of Kinver at that rent in the late 16th century, and inhabitants of Whittington owed suit at Kinver court in 1662.[97] The rent was paid to the Crown as a fee-farm rent by 1672 when it was sold. It was owned by Lord Boston by the late 18th century and was sold by the 5th baron to Lord Stamford in 1872.[98]

Peter de Hurech may have been the Peter of Whittington who was alive in 1187-8.[99] At least one person named William of Whittington was

active in the area in the later 13th century,[1] and a William was lord of the manor in 1304 and 1310.[2] He was probably the Sir William Whittington whose son, also Sir William, sold the manor to Thomas Lowe in 1351-2.[3] Thomas's father William had been acquiring property in Whittington, Kinver, and Dunsley in the 1320s.[4] Thomas was evidently still alive in 1364[5] but was probably dead by 1377 when Adam Lowe made a grant of lands in Whittington.[6] In 1387 the manor was held by Edmund Lowe,[7] who with his wife Eleanor made a settlement of it in 1397.[8] He died in 1428 and was succeeded by his son Humphrey, who was sheriff in 1440-1.[9] Humphrey was succeeded in 1447 by his daughter Eleanor, wife of Robert Grey, a younger son of Reynold, Lord Grey of Ruthin; it was, however, Humphrey's widow who paid the heriot due for the manor.[10] In 1475 Eleanor, by then a widow, granted the manor to her son Humphrey Grey and his wife Anne.[11] Humphrey died in 1499 or 1500 and was succeeded by his son Edward.[12] Knighted in 1513, Sir Edward Grey held Enville too at his death in 1529.[13] Whittington then descended in the Grey family with Enville. There were several sales of land in the late 19th and early 20th century, including that of the 650-a. Whittington Hall farm to the Upper Stour Valley Main Sewerage Board in 1895. In 1982 Mrs. Eileen Bissill of Enville Hall owned no land in Whittington.[14]

The Whittington family presumably had a house at Whittington. Edmund Lowe was living at Whittington at the time of his death in 1428,[15] and it was the home of his son and successor Humphrey in 1444.[16] Humphrey Grey and his son Edward also lived there.[17] Thomas Grey was described as of Whittington in 1538, but he later moved to Enville.[18] In 1621 Whittington manor house was let for life to Mary Overton, widow of William Overton, bishop of Coventry and Lichfield, with reversion to her son Richard Kettleby and his wife. In 1639 Mary and her son granted a lease to Richard Foley, along with a lease of Whittington forge which he was already working. In 1640, after Mary's death, Richard made over his interest to his son Thomas. In 1649 Henry Grey leased the house to Thomas for life.[19] Thomas let it to Mary Talbot of Wolverhampton in 1652, and her husband William was living at

[93] S.R.O., D. 740/17/3; Robins fam. tombs at E. end of Kinver churchyard; *Kelly's Dir. Staffs.* (1880); above, introduction.   [94] *Kelly's Dir. Staffs.* (1916).
[95] Inf. from Mr. E. E. Marsh.
[96] S.R.O., Tp. 1273/12, bk. of deeds and evidences, p. 13.
[97] *S.H.C.* 1911, 362; H.W.R.O. (H.), E 12/F/P3, deed of 2 Apr. 1377; ibid. E 12/S, Kinver ct. rolls 1387-1498, bdles. 1, 19; E 12/S, Bobbington and Enville, valor of lands of John Grey 1581; P.R.O., C 142/517, no. 4; above, introduction.
[98] S.R.O., Tp. 1273/21, notebook 1797-1814; ibid. 41, Staffs. fee farm rents.
[99] *S.H.C.* i. 138.
[1] *S.H.C.* v (1), 110, 157, 159; vi (1), 255; *Charters and Muniments of Lyttelton Fam.* ed. I. H. Jeayes, p. 14.
[2] S.R.O., Tp. 1273/12, bk. of deeds and evidences, p. 2; H.W.R.O. (H.), E 12/F/P3, deed of 6 Apr. 1310.
[3] W.S.L., S.MS. 201 (i), p. 308.
[4] *S.H.C.* ix (1), 132; *S.H.C.* 1911, 361-2; *Cal. Pat.* 1324-7, 38; S.R.O., Tp. 1273/12, bk. of deeds and evidences, p. 3.
[5] *S.H.C.* 1928, 79; above, Enville, manors and other estates (Enville).

[6] H.W.R.O. (H.), E 12/F/P3, deed of 2 Apr. 1377.
[7] Ibid. E 12/S, Kinver ct. rolls 1387-1498, bdle. 1.
[8] *S.H.C.* xi. 203.
[9] Shaw, *Staffs.* ii. 185, 267; *Feud. Aids.* v. 22; *S.H.C.* 1912, 281; S.R.O., Tp. 1273/12/2, no. 5.
[10] H.W.R.O. (H.), E 12/S, Kinver ct. rolls 1387-1498, bdle. 19, view of frankpledge spring 1447 and ct. of 6 Dec. 1447; Shaw, *Staffs.* ii. 268.
[11] S.R.O., Tp. 1273/12, bk of deeds and evidences, p. 8.
[12] *S.H.C.* 1917-18, 290 n.
[13] Above, Enville, manors and other estates.
[14] Inf. from Mr. M. J. Scott-Bolton, Enville Estates Office; below, p. 152.
[15] Shaw, *Staffs.* ii. 185.
[16] *Cal. Pat.* 1441-6, 227.
[17] *S.H.C.* 1917-18, 290 n.; S.R.O., Tp. 1273/12/1, no. 6.
[18] H.W.R.O. (H.), E 12/S, Early Deeds, 10 Dec. 1538; above, Enville, manors and other estates.
[19] H.W.R.O. (H.), E 12/S, Whittington, deeds of 20 Dec. 1606, 4 Aug. 1621, 11 May 1635, 13 Mar. 1638/9, 28 Sept. 1640, 29 Oct. 1649.

Whittington Hall later that year. He was assessed for tax on 13 hearths there in 1666. By 1676 he had moved to Stourton Castle.[20] It was presumably at Whittington that his son Thomas (d. 1730), bishop successively of Oxford, Salisbury, and Durham, was born in 1658 or 1659.[21] In 1683 Henry Grey settled Whittington Hall on his cousin and heir John Grey on the occasion of John's marriage, and John was living there in 1684. Having succeeded Henry in 1687, he was still living at Whittington in 1692.[22] The hall was later occupied as a farmhouse[23] and was still such in 1982.

In 1688 the hall, on the south side of Whittington Hall Lane, was evidently a timber-framed building.[24] The present Whittington Manor Farm on the same site is a brick house dating from the earlier 18th century. It has an impressive west front of three storeys and seven bays approached from the Wolverhampton–Kidderminster road along an avenue of trees.[25] To the south there is a circular stone pigeon house. The farm buildings to the north included a large barn, dating perhaps from the 16th century, which was demolished in 1969. It had heavy timber framing of high quality, and although brick-nogged, it may formerly have had plank infilling between the studs.[26]

HIGH GROVE FARM on the high ground west of the Stour is probably the medieval Haygreve. A priest named Alfred lived at 'Heygrewe' c. 1200.[27] A Robert of Heygreve was a regarder of Kinver forest in 1262[28] and may be the man of that name listed among the tenants of Kinver manor in 1293.[29] Robert's daughters Emma and Felice had succeeded by 1309[30] and had granted a house and land, presumably Haygreve, to William Lowe by 1324.[31] In 1387 the lord of Whittington held a house and land called Haygreve land, and tenements called Haygreve were held with Whittington manor in 1447.[32] A farm called High Greaves formed part of the Grey family's estate at Whittington in 1683.[33] High Grove farm, so named by 1796, remained in the family until its sale in 1911 to Edward Webb of Studley Court, Stourbridge; the Brown family occupied it at least between 1739 and the earlier 1830s.[34] The interest of Edward's son Charles

was sold apparently in 1921 to his cousin W. H. Webb, who was succeeded by 1968 by his son Major M. J. Webb, the owner in 1982.[35] The farmhouse was extensively remodelled c. 1970;[36] it is probably 19th century, but it incorporates older materials, especially ceiling beams.

After the appropriation of Kinver church to Bordesley abbey in 1380 the *RECTORY* remained with the monks until the abbey's surrender to the Crown in 1538.[37] They were leasing the estate by the early 1420s and were still doing so at the Dissolution. Heriots were payable to Bordesley in the 1530s.[38] In 1535 the net value of the great and small tithes and Easter offerings was £25 6s. 8d. (£27 4s. 1d. gross).[39]

In 1543 the Crown granted the rectory to William Whorwood,[40] lord of Kinver manor at his death in 1545. It then descended with Dunsley, passing eventually to William's great-nephew Thomas Whorwood.[41] In the 1620s the inhabitants of Kinver, wanting a good preacher and a schoolmaster, approached the puritan group known as the Feoffees for the Purchase of Impropriations. Using £560 given for Kinver church and school by several London merchants and by Edward Jorden of Dunsley, the feoffees in 1630 took a 1,000-year lease from John Whorwood of the great tithes of Kinver and Whittington townships, most of those of Halfcot, and nearly all the small tithes of the parish. They then leased the tithes back to Whorwood for 999 years at a rent of £50 to be paid to the lecturer (£33 6s. 8d.), the curate (£10), and the schoolmaster (£6 13s. 4d.). The lease passed with the manor and the rest of the rectory from the Whorwoods to the Foleys in 1672.[42] In 1650 John Whorwood sold the tithes of Compton with the manor of Compton Hallows to Thomas Foley, who in 1659 sold much of them to John Nurthall of Compton.[43] By 1742 the rectory was divided among three owners, but the Foleys' share amounted to over three fifths.[44] Sales of tithe by J. H. Hodgetts-Foley in 1824 and 1825 included one to Lord Stamford of the tithe arising from 1,320 a. of his land; Lord Stamford then became responsible for paying the £50 to the minister and the master of the grammar school.[45] The Foleys continued to be partly responsible for the repair

[20] H.W.R.O. (H.), E 12/S, Compton II, deed of 4 Oct. 1652; *Severall Procs. in Parl.* 4–11 Nov. 1652; *S.H.C.* 1923, 107; above (Stourton Castle).

[21] Shaw, *Staffs.* ii. 266–7, stating that he was born at Stourton Castle.

[22] S.R.O., Tp. 1273/4, deeds of 21 Apr. 1688, 25 Mar. 1692; 6, deed of 9 Nov. 1683; 12, deeds of 1 May, 7 June 1684; above, Enville, manors and other estates.

[23] e.g. S.R.O., Tp. 1273/33, deed of 30 June 1802; D. 891/4, pp. 73–4.

[24] S.R.O. 1392.

[25] Above, pl. facing p. 65.

[26] Photographs and survey in possession of Staffs. C.C. Planning Dept., Conservation Section; inf. from Mr. J. W. King.

[27] S.R.O., Tp. 1273/12, bk. of deeds and evidences, p. 13.

[28] *S.H.C.* v (1), 139.

[29] P.R.O., SC 6/202/64.

[30] S.R.O., Tp. 1273/12, bk of deeds and evidences, p. 2.

[31] *S.H.C.* 1911, 362; *Cal. Pat.* 1324–7, 38.

[32] H.W.R.O. (H.), E 12/S, Kinver ct. rolls 1387–1498, bdle. 1; bdle. 19, view of frankpledge spring 1447 and ct. of 6 Dec. 1447.

[33] S.R.O., Tp. 1273/6, deed of 9 Nov. 1683.

[34] Ibid. 33, deed of 20 Apr. 1796; 35, deed of 12 Dec. 1911;

S.R.O., D. 695/4/17/2; S.R.O., D. 891/4, p. 69; H.W.R.O. (H.), E 12/S, Iverley I, deed of 25 Sept. 1739; White, *Dir. Staffs.* (1834), 262.

[35] Inf. from Major M. J. Webb, who is thanked for his help.

[36] Inf. from Major Webb.

[37] Below, church; *V.C.H. Worcs.* ii. 153.

[38] P.R.O., C 1/612, no. 41; ibid. E 321/2, no. 59.

[39] *Valor Eccl.* (Rec. Com.), iii. 102, 273.

[40] *L. & P. Hen. VIII*, xviii (1), pp. 531–2.

[41] H.W.R.O. (H.), E 12/S, Staffs. legal papers, inq. p.m. of Anne Dudley 1555; E 12/S, Whorwood inheritance, deed of 6 Apr. 1578; P.R.O., C 66/1194, m. 26; *Cal. Pat.* 1553, 1; 1554–5, 167–8.

[42] *V.C.H. Staffs.* iii. 58; S.R.O., D. 1197/13/17, printed copy of appellant's and respondents' cases 1721; *L.J.* xxi. 617; *5th Rep. Com. Char.* 630–1.

[43] H.W.R.O. (H.), E 12/S, Compton I, deed of 7 July 1650; Halfcot I, deed of 3 Aug. 1659.

[44] Board in vestry giving proportion due from each owner towards repair of chancel 19 Mar. 1741.

[45] H.W.R.O. (H.), E 12/S, vol. relating to valuation of tithes in Kinver belonging to J. H. Hodgetts-Foley 1824; ibid. reg. of Kinver tithes sold 1824–5; S.R.O., Tp. 1273/43, deeds of 7 Feb., 31 Dec. 1824.

of the chancel and raised objections in 1902 and 1937 when its repair was under consideration.[46]

By the mid 19th century much of the parish was tithe-free by prescription and by the merging of tithes in the freehold of the lands from which they arose. Certain lands were subject to the payment of only small tithes under the inclosure Acts of 1773, 1779, and 1801. The ownership of the surviving tithes remained in many different hands. In 1850 various rent charges were assigned in lieu of tithes to the many tithe owners. There were several more mergers in 1851 and 1852, and in 1853 rent charges totalling £102 6s. 9½d. were assigned to the remaining 13 owners.[47]

In 1189 the Hospitallers were granted 6 a. in Kinver free of forest customs by Richard I.[48] The land may have lain in the Checkhill area which is crossed by Spittle brook, so named by 1300.[49]

About 1200 Combermere abbey (Ches.) owned 1 virgate of land apparently in the Whittington area.[50] Monks green in Whittington, recorded in 1574,[51] may have derived its name from a connexion with the abbey.

In 1485 the property of Dodford priory (Worcs.) included Lady meadow in Kinver.[52] There was a Lady meadow beside the Stour in Dunsley in 1638,[53] and a 2½-a. meadow of the same name was described as in Kinver parish in 1694.[54]

Rents of £3 2s. 6d. from Iverley wood and of £2 4s. 2d. from Kinver rectory were among the rents settled on trustees by Charles II in 1675 to provide pensions for members of the Penderel family and their descendants as a reward for helping him to escape after the battle of Worcester in 1651.[55] Both rents were redeemed in 1970.[56]

ECONOMIC HISTORY. AGRICULTURE. There was only one manor in the parish in 1086, and it had land for 16 ploughteams. One team was in demesne with 3 slaves; there were 17 villeins, 7 bordars, and a priest; and they had 10 teams.

With woodland, meadow, and two mills Kinver manor was then worth 100s., the same value as before the Conquest.[57] The parish lay in the centre of Kinver forest, in existence by 1086 and so named by 1168; Iverley gave its name to one of the hays.[58]

Kinver field was mentioned in 1310.[59] By the earlier 15th century there were open fields for people living to the north and south of the borough and one field for the burgesses. Stone field, mentioned in 1431, lay in the area of Stone Lane; it was still open in 1739.[60] Oathill field and Nether field, both mentioned in 1435,[61] lay south-east of the church. Nether field was last recorded in 1515.[62] Oathill field was still open in the early 1620s but was inclosed by the early 18th century.[63] Dekon field, mentioned in 1456, lay to the east of Kinver Hill near the river; it was last recorded as an open field in 1498.[64] Burgage field, mentioned in 1431, lay west of the borough; it was at least partly inclosed by 1601.[65]

At Compton there were three open fields in 1423, Clareland and Boston (later Botstone or Boltstone) field, both on the east side of Bannut Tree Road, and Middle field north of Boston field.[66] Clareland was inclosed in 1607.[67] It was evidently replaced as an open field by Wigley field, which was first mentioned in 1610; it lay north of Middle field and extended to the Enville boundary.[68] Inclosures in Boston field were recorded from the earlier 1620s; the rest of the field was still open in 1665.[69] Closes in Middle and Wigley fields were mentioned in 1761.[70]

There were three open fields at Stourton in the 15th century. Castle field, mentioned in 1437, lay west of Stourton Castle.[71] Moreyate field, mentioned in 1448, lay further west beyond the Stourton–Gothersley road.[72] Hyde field between Stourton and the Hyde was mentioned in 1498.[73] In 1629 the lord and freeholders of Stourton agreed to inclose Castle field. In its place c. 180 a. of Checkhill common north of Stourton were converted into two open fields.[74] By 1674 they were known as Hithermost and Further New

[46] S.H.C. 4th ser. x. 15; L.J.R.O., B/C/5/Kinver, 1902; ibid. B/V/6/Kinver, 1841; H.W.R.O. (H.), E 12/S, vol. relating to valuation of tithes in Kinver 1824, with letter of 1937 from G. M. King to H. T. H. Foley.
[47] L.J.R.O., B/A/15/Kinver.
[48] Cartae Antiquae (Pipe R. Soc. N.S. xxxiii), no. 611.
[49] S.H.C. v. (1), 180.
[50] S.R.O., Tp. 1273/12, bk. of deeds and evidences, p. 13.
[51] Below, econ. hist.
[52] T. R. Nash, Collns. for Hist. of Worcs. ii, App. p. xxxvii.
[53] S.R.O., Tp. 1273/8, deed of 10 Nov. 1638.
[54] H.W.R.O. (H.), E 12/S, Prestwood leases, deed of 12 Nov. 1694.
[55] S.R.O., D. 590/699A; Salop Arch. Soc. 4th ser. vii. 31–2, listing smaller sums granted in 1664.
[56] Inf. from Mr. K. S. P. Swayne, of Fowler, Langley & Wright, Wolverhampton.
[57] V.C.H. Staffs. iv. 40.
[58] Ibid. ii. 343–8.
[59] H.W.R.O. (H.), E 12/F/P3, deed of 6 Apr. 1310.
[60] Ibid. E 12/S, Kinver ct. rolls 1387–1498, bdle. 6, ct. of 16 Apr. 1431; 1590–1629, cts. of 11 Apr. 1614, 14 Oct. 1616; Kinver, Compton Hallows, and Kingsley ct. bk. 1734–61, Kinver ct. of Dec. 1739; Kinver and Kingsley ct. bk. 1767–1801, ct. of 22 Oct. 1792.
[61] Ibid. Kinver ct. rolls 1387–1498, bdle. 9, ct. of 9 May 1435.
[62] S.R.O., Tp. 1273/12, bk. of deeds and evidences, p. 11; 12, deed of 22 Dec. 1598; S.R.O., D. 891/3, no. 1087; ibid. 4, p. 62.

[63] H.W.R.O. (H.), E 12/S, Kinver ct. rolls 1590–1629, cts. of 12 Apr. 1620, 9 Apr. 1621; Kinver ct. papers 17th and 18th cents., cts. of 15 Sept. 1701, 27 Apr. 1703.
[64] Ibid. Kinver ct. rolls 1387–1498, bdle. 23, ct. of 19 Apr. 1456; Kinver I, deed of 30 Aug. 1498.
[65] Ibid. Kinver ct. rolls 1387–1498, bdle. 6, ct. of 16 Apr. 1431; 1590–1629, ct. of 2 Apr. 1601; S.R.O., D. 891/3, no. 883; ibid. 4, p. 12.
[66] H.W.R.O. (H.), Kinver ct. rolls 1387–1498, bdle. 2, ct. of 18 Jan. 1422/3; S.R.O., D. 891/3, nos. 224, 232–4; ibid. 4, p. 10.
[67] H.W.R.O. (H.), E 12/S, Compton I, agreement of 10 Sept. 1607.
[68] Ibid. Kinver ct. rolls 1590–1629, ct. of 1 Oct. 1610; vol. of 18th- and 19th-cent. plans; S.R.O., D. 891/3, nos. 191–2; ibid. 4, p. 7.
[69] S.R.O., D. 660/19/1; H.W.R.O. (H.), E 12/S, Kinver ct. rolls 1590–1629, ct. of 6 Feb. 1623/4; Kinver ct. papers 17th and 18th cents., ct. of 18 Apr. 1665; Compton Hallows ct. rolls, ct. of 8 Oct. 1659.
[70] H.W.R.O. (H.), E 12/S, Kinver, Compton Hallows, and Kingsley ct. bk. 1734–61, Compton ct. of 27 May 1761.
[71] Ibid. Kinver ct. rolls 1387–1498, bdle. 11, ct. of Thurs. in (? before) St. Alphege 1437; S.R.O., D. 891/3, no. 577; ibid. 4, p. 33.
[72] H.W.R.O. (H.), Kinver ct. rolls 1387–1498, bdle. 19, ct. of 22 Apr. 1448; S.R.O., D. 891/3, no. 531; ibid. 4, p. 31.
[73] H.W.R.O. (H.), E 12/S, Kinver ct. rolls 1387–1498, ct. of 19 Feb. 1497/8; S.R.O., D. 891/3, nos. 389, 395; ibid. 4, p. 27.
[74] H.W.R.O. (H.), Stourton III, deed of 26 Aug. 1629; S.R.O., Tp. 1273/6, deed of 14 Jan. 1635/6.

fields.[75] In 1681 the recent inclosure of Moreyate and Hyde fields was confirmed.[76] The two new fields had been inclosed by the 1730s.[77]

A selion near Stapenhill north-east of Halfcot was mentioned in 1423.[78] Dale field or Dalelond was mentioned in the 1440s and 1450; it lay on the south side of the lane from Halfcot to Stapenhill.[79] There were evidently three open fields for Halfcot in 1608.[80] Besides Dale field, they were presumably Wheatstone field, mentioned in 1633 and lying west of Dale field, and Moresell field, mentioned between 1648 and 1672. Dale field was at least partly inclosed by 1680.[81] Temporary cultivation of the waste at Halfcot took place in the early 18th century. In 1705 it was agreed that part of it which had already been inclosed should remain so for seven years; it would then be returned to the waste and another part inclosed, the process continuing on a seven-year basis.[82]

'The field of Dunsley' was mentioned in 1303–4.[83] Arable called Drake furlong in 1498 probably lay in Dregnall field, which in 1635 occupied the north-east angle of the Kidderminster–Wolverhampton road and Gibbet Lane. There were two other open fields, Pitt field south of Dregnall field and Mercers field south of Dunsley Hall, both mentioned in 1609.[84] Dregnall and Mercers field, still open in 1665, had been inclosed by 1680; that year it was agreed to inclose Pitt field also.[85]

'The field of Whittington' was mentioned in 1303–4.[86] In the 17th century there were three open fields. Mercers field was mentioned in 1613 as belonging to Whittington.[87] Roundhill field north-east of Whittington Hall and Windsor field west of the Hall were mentioned in 1634.[88] Windsor field was partly inclosed in 1657.[89] All three fields were inclosed by agreement in 1680.[90]

There were 6 a. of meadow in Kinver in 1086.[91] Heath meadow, mentioned in 1360, may have lain on Spittle brook in the north of the parish: a dole in a meadow of the same name there was mentioned in 1549.[92] Dole meadow existed at Whittington in the earlier 17th century.[93] Two

open meadows called Stockbridge meadows on the Stour near the Hyde were mentioned in 1629.[94]

Kinver heath was mentioned in 1352.[95] It was probably the area of waste later known as Kinver common which lay north and west of the village and extended into Compton. Mill brook formed its northern limit, and on the south it included Kinver Edge. It was common to both Kinver and Compton.[96] In 1774 the 1,157-a. common was inclosed under an Act of 1773.[97]

Checkhill waste was mentioned in 1190–1.[98] It was used by the inhabitants of Stourton. By the early 16th century it was shared with the inhabitants of Enville manor, and by the 17th century with those of Morfe also.[99] Encroachments were recorded in the 1590s, and c. 1630 some 180 a. at the southern end of the waste were converted into two open fields.[1] In 1682 c. 245 a. at the northern end of the waste were inclosed.[2] There remained 1,294 a. of waste which as Stourton common, Great Checkhill, and Little Checkhill were inclosed in 1804 under an Act of 1801.[3]

Halfcot common extended south from Stapenhill across the Stourbridge road and beyond Gibbet Lane. The common north of the road was being inclosed in the late 17th and early 18th century, and in 1705 it was agreed that parts of it should be cultivated on a seven-year basis.[4] In 1780 the rest of the common was inclosed along with Dunsley common, in all an area of 676 a.[5]

The waste in Whittington was mentioned in 1606.[6] Part of it had been inclosed by 1681, possibly in the previous year, when the open fields were inclosed.[7] In 1797 Lord Stamford was proposing to inclose 180 a. on the north-east side of the remaining waste, then called Whittington common.[8] It appears that most, if not all, of the waste was in fact inclosed about that time: an inclosure made by Lord Stamford in 1800–1 amounted to 329 a. He acquired a further 67 a., possibly by an exchange, in 1808.[9]

Rights of common in the forest at Iverley were enjoyed by the inhabitants of settlements on either side of the Staffordshire–Worcestershire

[75] H.W.R.O. (H.), E 12/S, Prestwood leases, deed of 24 Oct. 1674.
[76] Ibid. Stourton III, deed of 17 Mar. 1680/1.
[77] Ibid. vol. of 18th- and 19th-cent. plans.
[78] Ibid. Kinver ct. rolls 1387–1498, bdle. 3, ct. of 26 Oct. 1423.
[79] Ibid. bdle. 16, ct. of 7 May 1442; bdle. 19, ct. of 5 Feb. 1447/8; bdle. 20, ct. of 27 Apr. 1450; vol. of 18th- and 19th-cent. plans.
[80] Ibid. Kinver ct. rolls 1590–1629, ct. of 11 Oct. 1608.
[81] Ibid. Halfcot I, deeds of 18 Mar. 1632/3, 9 Oct. 1648; Halfcot II, valuation of Halfcot est. 1680; Kinver ct. papers 17th and 18th cents., ct. of 16 Sept. 1672; vol. of 18th- and 19th-cent. plans.
[82] Ibid. Halfcot I, deed of 29 Aug. 1705.
[83] Ibid. Kinver VI, rents from waste in Kinver forest temp. Edw. I.
[84] Ibid. Kinver I, deed of 30 Aug. 1498; Dunsley I, deed of 23 Mar. 1634/5; vol. of 18th- and 19th-cent. plans; S.R.O., Tp. 1273/1, 20 Apr. 1609; S.R.O., D. 891/3, nos. 1475–7, 1496, 1637–9; ibid. 4, pp. 87–8, 95.
[85] H.W.R.O. (H.), E 12/S, Dunsley I, deeds of 28 Sept. 1665, 6 Sept. 1680.
[86] Ibid. Kinver VI, rents from waste in Kinver forest temp. Edw. I.
[87] Ibid. Kinver ct. rolls 1590–1629, ct. of 12 Oct. 1613; S.R.O., D. 891/3, no. 1496; ibid. 4, p. 95.
[88] S.R.O., Tp. 1273/36, deed of 1 Jan. 1633/4; S.R.O., D. 891/3, nos. 1211, 1263–5; ibid. 4, pp. 72, 74.

[89] S.R.O., Tp. 1273/12, copy ct. roll of 8 Aug. 1657.
[90] Ibid. 2, deeds of 21 and 24 Mar. 1704/5.
[91] V.C.H. Staffs. iv. 40.
[92] H.W.R.O. (H.), E 12/S, Early Deeds, deed of 30 Nov. 1360; S.R.O., Tp. 1273/13, acquittance of 22 Dec. 1549.
[93] S.R.O., Tp. 1273/2, deed of 14 May 1635, 7 May 1638; 11, 1623 survey.
[94] H.W.R.O. (H.), E 12/S, Kinver ct. rolls 1590–1629, ct. of 2 Feb. 1628/9.
[95] Cal. Pat. 1350–4, 336.
[96] S.R.O., Q/RDc 36.
[97] S.R.O., Q/RDc 36; S.H.C. 1941, 16.
[98] S.H.C. ii (1), 11; S.H.C. 1925, 244–5.
[99] S.R.O., D. 593/O/3/5; S.R.O., Tp. 1273/6, deed of 14 Jan. 1635/6; H.W.R.O. (H.), E 12/S, Checkhill II, deed of 13 June 1683.
[1] H.W.R.O. (H.), E 12/S, Kinver ct. rolls 1590–1629, cts. of 28 Sept. 1590, 20 Mar. 1591/2, 15 Apr. 1595; above.
[2] H.W.R.O. (H.), E 12/S, Checkhill I, deed of 14 Mar. 1669/70; Checkhill II, deed of 13 June 1683.
[3] S.R.O., Q/RDc 59.
[4] H.W.R.O. (H.), E 12/S, Halfcot I, deeds of 6 Nov. 1686, 29 Aug. 1705; above.
[5] S.R.O., Q/RDc 42; S.H.C. 1941, 16.
[6] H.W.R.O. (H.), E 12/S, Whittington, deed of 20 Dec. 1606.
[7] S.R.O., Tp. 1273/58, Whittington, deed of 1 June 1681.
[8] Ibid. Whittington correspondence, Dan. Clarke to Booth Grey 7 Jan. 1797.
[9] Ibid. 54, plan of inclosure at Whittington 1801.

boundary.[10] In 1630 John Whorwood of Stourton acquired a lease of 300 a. of waste and woodland at Iverley made by the Crown in 1629, and he inclosed part of the land. There was also some piecemeal inclosure by commoners by the 1640s.[11] Iverley was included in the sale of Kinver manor to Philip Foley in 1672.[12] In the later 17th century Foley made leases of waste, amounting in all to c. 120 a., south-east from Sugarloaf Lane to the county boundary; the land was inclosed and farms were laid out.[13] A further 450 a. west of Sugarloaf Lane was leased for inclosure to Richard Bradley of Whittington in 1712.[14] Inhabitants of Whittington who had common rights in that part of the waste objected to the lease, but Bradley's right to inclose the land, later occupied by Iverley House and Sugarloaf farms, was upheld in 1718.[15]

There were several greens in the parish. Simon of the green was recorded among the Compton tenants in 1293, and Compton green was mentioned in 1353.[16] It probably extended west from Pigeonhouse Farm as far as Herons Gate Road. By the 1730s, however, there was only a small green immediately west of the farmhouse.[17] It still existed in 1830 but had been inclosed by 1856, probably soon after roads giving access to it had been stopped up in 1830.[18] Medenale or Medall green in Compton was mentioned in 1453 and 1562.[19] Stocking green in Kinver manor existed in 1434.[20] There was evidently a green at Stourton: Green close on the east side of the Stourton–Gothersley road existed in the 1730s.[21] Dunsley green, on Dunsley Road ¼ mile south-west of Dunsley Hall, was mentioned in 1780 and had been inclosed by 1830.[22] There was evidently a green at Whittington in the 14th century: a tenement there was stated in 1377 to have been formerly held by Maud of the green.[23] Monks green at Whittington was mentioned in 1574.[24]

Barley and rye were the main crops grown in the parish in the 17th century; oats, barley, and peas were also grown.[25] Wheat was grown on a farm at Kinver in 1682 and on a farm at Compton c. 1712; it was also the chief crop stored at Compton Hall farm in 1780.[26] A lease of Sugar-

loaf farm at Iverley in 1776 stipulated that turnips were to be grown.[27]

Before the inclosure of the extensive waste in the parish sheep farming appears to have been more important than arable farming. Sheeps Way near Gothersley was mentioned in the mid 1290s;[28] it was possibly a route for driving sheep across the waste at Checkhill. A sheep pen held by Thomas Comber in 1387 probably stood on Kinver common.[29] There was a sheepfold on the southern part of Checkhill waste in 1448, and a sheepcot at Compton in 1527 and 1538.[30] Flocks of 50 sheep and more were common in the 16th and 17th centuries. Thomas Hawys had a flock of 200 sheep in 1539, Richard Atkys of the Hyde one of 120, including 40 lambs, in 1559, Thomas Longmore of Stourton one of 150 in 1583, and John Clarke of Halfcot one of 125 in 1588. At Dunsley in 1622 Thomas Hillman had a flock of 80 sheep.[31] The holder of a nook of land at Kinver Hill had commoning rights for 50 sheep in 1626.[32] The lease of Stapenhill farm in 1633 included the right to pasture some 260 sheep on the neighbouring waste.[33] About 1671 the farm buildings included a sheepcot, and there was right of pasture for 300 sheep.[34] Sheepcots were mentioned at Compton in 1603, 1610, and 1648,[35] at Kinver in 1617 and 1626,[36] and at Checkhill in 1640 when there was also a sheepwalk there.[37] A sheepcot was built on the newly inclosed part of Iverley in or soon after 1630, and permission to build one was included in a lease of a house at Kinver in 1659.[38] William Penn of Dunsley Hall, although described as a scythesmith at his death in 1642, ran a large mixed farm which included a flock of 284 sheep; not all were grazed at Dunsley, 70 of them being described as away 'at wintering' in November 1642. Edward Jorden, also of Dunsley, had some 150 sheep in 1667, and Richard Ketly of Stourton had 262 in 1670. John Lowe of Whittington had 52 sheep in 1684, and a flock of 127 owned by Richard Bird of Dunsley in 1692 was grazed at Whittington. There was a flock of 90 at Compton in 1674 and one of 134 at Kinver in 1681.[39]

It is likely that in the early 1560s wool from

[10] V.C.H. Staffs. ii. 344, 348; H.W.R.O. (H.), E 12/S, Whittington, deed of 20 Dec. 1606; Kinver ct. papers 17th and 18th cents., cts. of 6 Oct. 1662, 18 Apr. 1665.
[11] V.C.H. Staffs. ii. 348; H.W.R.O. (H.), E 12/S, Iverley I, deed of 12 July 1630.
[12] H.W.R.O. (H.), E 12/S, Whorwood inheritance, deed of 24 Feb. 1671/2.   [13] Above, introduction.
[14] H.W.R.O.(H.), E 12/S, Iverley I, deed of 1 Jan. 1711/12.
[15] Ibid. Iverley II, plan of Iverley estate c. 1860; S.R.O., Tp. 1273/8, deed of 22 Nov. 1718.
[16] P.R.O., SC 6/202/64; H.W.R.O. (H.), E 12/S, Early Deeds, deed of 1 Dec. 1353.
[17] H.W.R.O. (H.), E 12/S, Compton I, deed of 2 Sept. 1693; vol. of 18th- and 19th-cent. plans.
[18] S.R.O., D. 891/3; D. 1490/1; S.R.O., Q/RDc 36; Q/RHd 5; Q/SO 30, ff. 244v.–245v.
[19] H.W.R.O. (H.), E 12/S, Kinver ct. rolls 1387–1498, ct. given as on Monday in the feast of St. Philip and St. James (1 May) 1453; Compton II, deed of 24 June 1562.
[20] Ibid. Kinver ct. rolls 1387–1498, bdle. 9, ct. of 5 Apr. 1434.
[21] Ibid. vol. of 18th- and 19th-cent. plans.
[22] S.R.O., Q/RDc 42; S.R.O., D. 891/3, nos. 1585–7; ibid. 4, pp. 96, 98, 101.
[23] H.W.R.O. (H.), E 12/F/P3, deed of 2 Apr. 1377.
[24] S.R.O., Tp. 1273/1, deed of 20 June 1574.
[25] L.J.R.O., B/C/11, Thos. Hillman (1622), Edw. Comber

(1637), Wm. Penn (1646), Alice Lye (1676).
[26] Ibid. Ric. Bradley (1682); H.W.R.O. (H.), E 12/S, Compton I, memo. relating to Compton tithe dispute, and Mr. Grove's inventory 1780.
[27] H.W.R.O. (H.), E 12/S, Iverley II, deed of 4 July 1776.
[28] Ibid. Kinver VI, rents from waste in Kinver forest temp. Edw. I.   [29] Ibid. Kinver ct. rolls 1387–1498, bdle. 1.
[30] Ibid. Kinver ct. rolls 1387–1498, bdle. 19, ct. of 5 Aug. 1448; Compton I, deed of 30 Sept. 1527; Compton II, 20 Sept. 1538.
[31] L.J.R.O., B/C/11, Thos. Hawys (1539), Ric. Atkys (1559), Thos. Longmore (1584), John Clarke (1588), Thos. Hillman (1622).
[32] H.W.R.O. (H.), E 12/S, Kinver I, deed of 31 July 1626.
[33] Ibid. Halfcot I, deed of 18 Mar. 1632/3, mentioning pasture rights for 13 or 14 score sheep.
[34] Ibid. Whorwood inheritance, Stapenhill rental c. 1671.
[35] Ibid. Kinver ct. rolls 1590–1629, cts. of 7 Nov. 1603, 20 Aug. 1610; Compton I, deed of 18 May 1648.
[36] Ibid. Kinver ct. rolls 1590–1629, cts. of 14 Apr. 1617, 26 Apr. and 26 Sept. 1626.
[37] Ibid. Stourton I, deed of 1 Feb. 1656/7.
[38] Ibid. Kinver IX, deed of 28 Apr. 1659; V.C.H. Staffs. ii. 348.
[39] L.J.R.O., B/C/11, Wm. Penn (1646), Edw. Jorden (1668), Ric. Ketly (1670), John Ley (1675), Roger Bradley (1681), John Lowe (1684), Ric. Bird (1692).

sheep in Kinver was being sold at Wolverhampton: in 1564 Humphrey Hope of Stourton, who had a flock of 60 sheep at Checkhill, was owed money for wool from John Harwale of Wolverhampton. Kinver's own cloth industry was presumably another market for the wool; some clothiers and weavers had their own flocks, such as Thomas Hazelwood with 26 sheep in 1568 and Richard Luce of Stourton with 60 in 1662.[40]

Cattle farming was on a much smaller scale than sheep farming in the 16th and 17th centuries. Richard Atkys of the Hyde had a herd of 20 cows and 3 young beasts in 1558, Thomas Bird of Compton had one of 5 cows, a heifer, 4 two-year olds, and 2 calves in 1565, and John Clarke of Halfcot had 6 cows and 2 calves in 1588.[41] On other farms smaller herds were common.[42] At Dunsley in 1642 William Penn had 5 milch cows, 3 heifers, and a bull; at Compton in 1674 John Ley had 7 cows and 4 young beasts; and at Stourton in 1682 John Worrall had 3 cows, 3 young beasts, and 3 calves. For all three farmers cattle were less important than sheep or crops.[43]

Pig farming too was conducted on a small scale in the 16th and 17th centuries. Among the largest herds recorded in the period were herds of 18 in 1539, 9 in 1559, 10 in 1584, 14 in 1642, 7 in 1670, and 10 in 1674.[44]

The chief crops on farms at Checkhill, Stourton, and Halfcot in the late 1830s and early 1840s were wheat, barley, and turnips; they were also the main crops at Iverley in the 1850s and early 1860s.[45] Fertilizers were probably being used in the parish in the mid 1840s: John Nock of Kinver was then advertising the sale of Peruvian and African guano. He was also advertising agricultural implements, such as winnowing machines, threshing machines, and turnip cutters.[46] By 1850 there were 5,603 a. of arable and 1,882 a. of pasture in the parish.[47] The proportion of arable later declined, and by 1979 there were 1,676.7 ha. (4,141½ a.) of arable and 1,180.9 ha. (2,918 a.) of pasture recorded in the parish.[48]

In 1812 a flock of 233 sheep at Stourton, mainly New Leicesters and Southdowns, was advertised for sale; in 1816 a flock of 50 best quality New Leicesters at Compton was advertised.[49] There were seven shepherds living at the parish in 1861, two of them at Compton; there were six shepherds in 1871.[50] A flock of 181 sheep on a farm at Halfcot in 1916 included an Oxford ram, 60 Shropshire ewes, and 80 lambs.[51]

A specialist seed farm covering 1,200 a. was established at Hill farm in the later 1870s by Edward Webb & Sons of Wordsley, in Kingswinford. It was enlarged to 1,500 a. between 1904 and 1908. There were some 50 a. of breeding and trial ground for plants in the 1960s. The seed farm was closed c. 1970.[52]

The main crop in the parish recorded in 1979 was barley; sugar beet, potatoes, and wheat were also grown. Vegetables were grown on 48.2 ha. (119 a.). There were three dairy farms and over 1,300 cattle in the parish. Over 5,000 sheep were recorded in 1979 and were evidently kept on the small, mixed farms that were characteristic of Kinver. Over 2,700 pigs and over 18,000 poultry were also recorded.[53]

In 1841 the Stewponey Agricultural Society was established, meeting at the Stewponey inn and taking its membership from an area covering a 12-mile radius around the inn. By 1844 the society had 225 members and a library of books on agricultural subjects. It also employed a consulting chemist to analyse soil and manure for members.[54] A farmers' club was formed as a branch of the society in 1843; discussions were held at its monthly meetings. The first chairman was John Robins of Dunsley, and the first secretary and treasurer was John Nock who had the farm-implement and fertilizer business in Kinver.[55] The society was dissolved in 1849 or 1850.[56] Annual shows organized by the Enville and Kinver Farmers' Club began in 1911; the club still existed in 1933 when the show was held at Dunsley.[57]

Fifteen allotment gardens were being let to the poor of Kinver between 1832 and 1847;[58] the owner is unknown. In 1844 the Stewponey Association for the Improvement of the Labouring Classes was established as a branch of the Stewponey Agricultural Society mainly to provide allotment gardens. In its first year the society had 100 a., of which 12 a. were in Kinver. In 1854 the Kinver allotments, then in the angle between Meddins Lane and Compton Road, were let to 50 tenants. In 1887 there were 47 tenants, and thereafter the number steadily declined; by 1906 there were 21 tenants, with 22 allotments vacant.[59] Nothing further is known of the society.

There were 26 freeholders and 63 customary tenants on Kinver manor in 1293.[60] By 1447 copyhold land on the manor held by a tenant who

[40] L.J.R.O., B/C/11, Humph. Hope (1564), Thos. Haselwod (1568), Ric. Luce (1662); below (cloth).
[41] Ibid. Ric. Atkys (1559), Thos. Byrde (1565), John Clarke (1588).
[42] e.g. ibid. Geo. Watkys (1586), Isabella Fisher (1610), Ric. Hill (1620), Edw. Comber (1637).
[43] Ibid. Wm. Penn (1646), John Key (1675), John Worrall (1682).
[44] Ibid. Thos. Hawys (1539), John Browne (1559), Geo. Watkys (1586), Wm. Penn (1646), Ric. Ketly (1670), John Ley (1675).
[45] H.W.R.O. (H.), E 12/S, Prestwood Estate I, cultivation book 1837–65.
[46] Essays on various subjects by members of the Stewponey Farmers' Club, 1844 (Stourbridge, 1845), advert. (copy in H.W.R.O. (H.), E 12/S, Stewponey Becher Club II).
[47] L.J.R.O., B/A/15/Kinver.
[48] M.A.F.F., agric. returns 1979.
[49] Wolverhampton Chron. 18 Mar. 1812; 13 Mar. 1816.

[50] P.R.O., RG 9/1985; RG 10/2928.
[51] H.W.R.O. (H.), E 12/S, Halfcot II, cat. of stock on Stewponey and Halfcot farms 1916.
[52] V.C.H. Staffs. vi. 127; Staffs. Advertiser, 23 Nov. 1878; inf. from Major M. J. Webb (1982).
[53] M.A.F.F., agric. returns 1979.
[54] H.W.R.O. (H.), E 12/S, Stewponey Becher Club II, ann. reps. 1844, 1845; P.O. Dir. Staffs. (1845), 543.
[55] H.W.R.O. (H.), E 12/S, Stewponey Becher Club II, farmers' club rules; above.
[56] H.W.R.O. (H.), E 12/S, Stewponey Becher Club III, min. bk. 1842–59, 1 Apr. 1850.
[57] S.R.O., Tp. 1273/27, Enville home farm acct. bk. 1932–3, brochure advertising show.
[58] H.W.R.O. (H.), E 12/S, Kinver III, Poor Gardens acct. bk.
[59] Ibid. Stewponey Becher Club II, ann. reps. 1845, 1854; Allotments bks. 1887–1906; O.S. Map 1/2,500, Staffs. LXX. 15 (1883 edn.).
[60] P.R.O., SC 6/202/64.

died leaving daughters but no son was inherited by the eldest daughter and not divided.[61] In 1625 and 1674 it was stated that copyholders by inheritance could lease their holdings for up to 99 years without licence. In 1625 most of the land on the manor was copyhold.[62] At Whittington in 1623 there were 6 freeholds and 5 copyholds; a further 10 holdings were on leases for three lives.[63] In 1831 there were 602 a. of copyhold land on the Foley estate in the parish. Small amounts of copyhold were still being enfranchised in the early 20th century.[64]

The labour services owed by tenants on most of Kinver manor in 1387 were ploughing for two days, reaping, mowing, haymaking, and carrying. Services from what was called Mondayland or 'beleland' at Kinver Hill were limited to haymaking and threshing; the other services had been commuted.[65] After John Hampton's succession to the manor in 1388 all services were withdrawn by the tenants, who numbered 41 in 1400. The tenants were later released from their obligations by agreement with John.[66] The next lord, John's son John, entered into a new agreement at his first great court in April 1434, declaring it to be the same as that made with his father; all labour services, heriots, chevage, and payments for permission to marry were commuted for an annual 37s.[67] A contemporary sealed copy of the agreement added a further clause by which the tenants agreed not to ask anything from the lord for acting as reeve.[68] Labour services on Whittington manor may have been retained longer: ploughing, reaping, and weeding services were still recorded in the 17th century, although by then probably only as a matter of form.[69]

The rights of the inhabitants of Kinver as dwellers on ancient demesne of the Crown were confirmed by Henry VIII in 1526.[70] Further confirmations were granted by Mary I,[71] by Elizabeth I in 1559,[72] and by Charles I in 1628.[73] The privileges and exemptions granted, such as freedom from toll and stallage throughout England, were those customarily given to inhabitants of ancient demesne.

Parts of the large manor of Kinver were established as separate estates in the 13th and 14th centuries: Whittington c. 1200, Compton in the late 13th century, and Dunsley by the 1320s. From the later 16th century, with brief interruptions in the 17th and 18th centuries, Kinver, Compton and Dunsley manors were in the same ownership, first of the Whorwoods and then of the Foleys.[74] By the mid 1730s the Foleys' estate in the parish comprised 4,361 a.[75] The only other substantial estate was at Whittington, where Lord Stamford had 584 a. c. 1790.[76] In 1830 J. H. Hodgetts-Foley owned no land in Compton. What remained of the Foley estate was sold in the early 20th century.[77]

WOODLAND AND PARK. The wood called Cynibre mentioned in 736 lay in the Kinver area.[78] In 1086 there was woodland 3 leagues in length and 1 league in breadth in Kinver manor.[79] Kinver wood, mentioned c. 1270, probably lay in the area of Kinver Edge: the burning of oaks at 'le Bury', presumably the hillfort, was mentioned in 1456.[80] By at least 1434 the wood was administered, together with Checkhill wood, by a keeper, called a woodward in the 1440s and in 1460.[81] Kinver wood was being felled in the late 16th century.[82]

There was an 8½-a. wood in Compton called Horewood in 1268.[83] In 1269 Leo of Romsley was licensed to inclose it, although only with a small ditch and low hedge so that the deer could pass in and out; a new ditch was mentioned in 1312.[84] There was a park along the south-western boundary of Compton by the earlier 16th century.[85] Greyfield gate in the south-east corner of the park was mentioned in 1616.[86] The park contained some 80 deer c. 1650.[87] In 1651 Thomas Foley leased the 232-a. park with the rest of his Compton estate to John Bridges of Hurcott Hall in Kidderminster (Worcs.). By the terms of the lease Foley was to cut down much of the timber; Bridges was then allowed to remove the pale and divide the park into several inclosures. By 1654 it had been divided into six parcels, one of them of 133 a. and the other five of between 12 a. and 30 a.[88] By 1672 Compton Park farm had been laid out over the largest parcel. It was leased that year by Philip Foley, who reserved the right to cut trees and turves and to coal the timber.[89] In

[61] H.W.R.O. (H.), E 12/S, Kinver ct. rolls 1387–1498, bdle. 19, ct. of 1447.
[62] Ibid. Kinver ct. rolls 1590–1629, ct. of survey of 24 Oct. 1625; E 12/F/P3, articles relating to rights of Kinver manor copyholders 1674.
[63] S.R.O., Tp. 1273/11, 1623 survey.
[64] H.W.R.O. (H.), E 12/S, Kinver copyhold estates 1831; P.R.O., MAF 9/270/12608, 21473; S.R.O., D. 695/4/17/1.
[65] H.W.R.O. (H.), E 12/S, Kinver ct. rolls 1387–1498, bdle. 1; bdle. 9, ct. of 5 Apr. 1434.
[66] Cal. Pat. 1396–9, 365; Cal. Close, 1396–9, 502; 1399–1402, 109–10.
[67] H.W.R.O. (H.), E 12/S, Kinver ct. rolls 1387–1498, bdle. 9, ct. of 5 Apr. 1434.
[68] S.R.O., D. 1197/8/1; R. H. Hilton, Eng. Peasantry in Later Middle Ages, 65–6, 74 5 (where the document is printed).
[69] S.R.O., Tp. 1273/12, survey of 18 May 1665; 38, survey of 1691; 44A, 'Mr. Willett's rents and services', n.d. but c. 1600.
[70] An 18th-century translation (S.R.O., D. 1197/8/2) is printed with some inaccuracies in H. Grainger, Hist. of Church of St. Peter, Kinver (1951). Shaw, Staffs. ii. 262–3, prints a similar translation.
[71] S.R.O., D. 1197/8/3.

[72] Translation in Grainger, Church of St. Peter.
[73] S.R.O., D. 1197/8/3. Misdated translations are printed in Grainger, Church of St. Peter; Bennett, Kinver, 134.
[74] Above, manors and other estates.
[75] H.W.R.O.(H.),E12/S,vol. of 17th- and 18th-cent. plans.
[76] S.R.O., Tp. 1273/25, survey of Whittington c. 1790.
[77] Above, manors and other estates.
[78] T.B.A.S. liii. 110.   [79] V.C.H. Staffs. iv. 40.
[80] H.W.R.O. (H.), E 12/S, Kinver ct. rolls 1387–1498, bdle. 23, ct. of 19 Apr. 1456; below (borough).
[81] H.W.R.O. (H.), E 12/S, Kinver ct. rolls 1387–1498, bdle. 9, cts. of 5 Apr. 1434, 16 Oct. 1441, 5 Apr. 1445, 21 Jan. 1459/60.   [82] P.R.O., E 134/37 and 38 Eliz. I Mich./56.
[83] S.H.C. 1911, 140–1.
[84] Cal. Pat. 1266–72, 335–81; H.W.R.O. (H.), E 12/S, Early Deeds, deed of 30 June 1312.
[85] H.W.R.O. (H.), E 12/S, Compton I, deed of 30 Sept. 1527; Compton II, deed of 20 Sept. 1538.
[86] Ibid. Kinver ct. rolls 1590–1629, ct. of 14 Oct. 1616.
[87] Ibid. Compton I, partic. of Compton manor n.d.; Compton II, deed of 23 June 1649.
[88] Ibid. Compton I, memo. of 25 Apr. 1651, agreement of 24 Dec. 1652, partic. of 29 Apr. 1654.
[89] Ibid. Compton I, agreement of 26 Dec. 1653, deed of 25 Mar. 1672.

the 1730s there were two woods in Compton, the 17-a. Roughpark Wood in the area of the former park and the 20-a. Birch Wood to the north on the Enville boundary.[90] Both survived in 1982.

Checkhill wood was mentioned in the late 1270s.[91] In the 15th century it was administered with Kinver wood. Although there was extensive felling in the late 16th century,[92] there was 140 a. of woodland near the Enville boundary in the early 19th century, including a coppice called the Million.[93] In 1948 the Enville Hall estate leased 567 a. at Checkhill, the whole of it then known as the Million, to the Forestry Commission.[94]

In 1232 the Crown made a grant of 60 oaks from Iverley hay to the bishop of Worcester.[95] In the earlier 16th century timber in Iverley wood was felled on a large scale, and in 1609 the Crown sold 1,560 trees growing there.[96] There was a keeper of Iverley wood in the 1560s and 1570s appointed by the Crown for life. There was still a keeper in 1604.[97] All the timber had been felled by the early 1670s.[98]

New Wood on the north-eastern boundary originated as a 35-a. plantation made in the early 18th century on land taken out of Halfcot common. It comprised 74 a. in the 1730s, when there was also a 24-a. wood called Barratt's Coppice to the south-west.[99] By 1982 much of New Wood had been replaced by a housing estate,[1] but Barratt's Coppice survived.

In 1446 John Hampton was licensed to impark 300 a. at Stourton and Halfcot including arable and wood.[2] There is, however, no record that a park was created.

WARRENS AND FISHERIES. There was a warren in Kinver manor in 1395 and 1457.[3] It was presumably on Kinver common where a rabbit warren was mentioned in 1605. By 1627 the warrener lived in Compey lodge, presumably at Comber where there was a lodge in the 1730s.[4] The warren was destroyed in the late 17th century during a dispute between the lord and the commoners of Kinver.[5] It was later restocked and survived until the waste was inclosed in 1774.[6]

In 1461 John Hampton sued a group of men

for stealing 1,000 rabbits at Stourton; the warren evidently lay south of Stourton Castle.[7] There was a warren and lodge on Checkhill common by 1601.[8] When the southern part of the common was brought into cultivation c. 1630 the warren was reduced to the area between Spittle brook and the parish boundary to the north. It was destroyed in 1682 when that part of the waste was inclosed.[9] In 1689, however, the area of the former warren was leased with liberty to restock it.[10] In the 1730s there was a 250-a. warren with the tenant living in a house north-east of Checkhill Farm.[11]

A warren at Whittington existed c. 1600.[12] It was destroyed in 1681, after the inclosure of the open fields there.[13]

The hunting lodge built at Stourton in 1195-6 included a fishpond.[14] In 1231 John son of Philip was instructed to stock the pond with 200 bream from the royal pond at Feckenham (Worcs.).[15] The royal fishpond at 'Flederith' in Kinver forest which John was ordered to repair and stock in 1232[16] was probably at Flatheridge on Smestow brook north of Stourton. John Hampton's fishery at Kinver, mentioned in 1402, may have been at Stourton; in 1422 perch, trout, and other fish were stolen from it.[17] There is no later reference to a fishpond at Stourton, but the lords of Kinver maintained fishing rights in the Stour and other streams in the manor.[18] In 1672 it was stated that the lords had punished fishing offences privately without recourse to the manor court; in 1686 and the 1690s, however, ordinances regulating fishing were made by the court.[19]

A fishery at Horewood in Compton was mentioned in 1294.[20] Two pools in Compton Park farm were leased as fishponds in 1688.[21] There was a fishery in the pool at Pole mill north of Kinver village in 1471; it was still described as a fishpool in 1615.[22] There was a fishery in the pool at Checkhill mill in the 1680s. When Philip Foley leased the mill in 1683 he excluded fishing rights; he also required the tenant to set eel traps at times of flood and deliver the eels to Prestwood.[23]

Fishing rights in the Stour at Whittington mills were sold to Sir Edward Grey, lord of Whittington, in 1515.[24] By the mid 1840s Lord

[90] H.W.R.O. (H.), E 12/S, vol. of 18th- and 19th-cent. plans.
[91] Cal. Fine R. 1272-1307, 106, 109.
[92] P.R.O., E 134/37 and 38 Eliz. I Mich./56.
[93] S.R.O., Q/RDc 59; S.R.O., D. 1140/2.
[94] Inf. from Mr. M. J. Scott-Bolton.
[95] Close R. 1231-4, 64. [96] V.C.H. Staffs. ii. 347-8.
[97] Cal. Pat. 1563-6, pp. 118, 323; 1572-5, p. 563; P.R.O., E 134/2 Jas. I Trin./4.
[98] H.W.R.O. (H.), E 12/S, Whorwood inheritance, annotated copy of partic. of Stourton Castle estate 1671.
[99] Ibid. Halfcot I, deed of 29 Aug. 1705; vol. of 18th- and 19th-cent. plans.
[1] Above, introduction.
[2] Cal. Chart. R. 1427-1516, 59-60.
[3] S.H.C. xv. 72; S.H.C. N.S. iv. 102.
[4] H.W.R.O. (H.), E 12/S, Compton I, deed of 20 Nov. 1605; Kinver I, deed of 20 Aug. 1627; vol. of 18th- and 19th-cent. plans, Kinver.
[5] Ibid. Kinver IV, acct. of dispute between Mr. Foley and the commoners of Kinver 1698-1700.
[6] Ibid. Compton III, deed of 30 Aug. 1739; S.R.O., Q/RDc 36.
[7] S.H.C. N.S. iv. 121; H.W.R.O. (H.), E 12/S, vol. of 18th- and 19th-cent. plans, Stourton, nos. 54-5.
[8] H.W.R.O. (H.), E 12/S, Checkhill I, deed of 2 Apr. 1620.
[9] Ibid. Stourton III, deed of 26 Aug. 1629; Checkhill I, copy deed of 14 Mar. 1669/70, wrongly given as 25 Chas. II; Checkhill II, deed of 13 June 1683.
[10] Ibid. Checkhill I, agreement of 24 Apr. 1689.
[11] Ibid. vol. of 18th- and 19th-cent. plans, Stourton, nos. 115-16.
[12] Ibid. Whittington, deed of 20 Dec. 1606; S.R.O., Tp. 1273/44A, 'Mr. Willett's rents and services' n.d. but c. 1600.
[13] S.R.O., Tp. 1273/10, deed of 7 June 1681.
[14] Above, manors and other estates (Stourton Castle).
[15] Close R. 1227-31, 515.
[16] Ibid. 1231-4, 82, 176.
[17] S.H.C. xv. 106; xvii. 119.
[18] H.W.R.O. (H.), E 12/S, Kinver ct. rolls 1387-1498, bdle. 6, ct. of 16 Apr. 1431; bdle. 14, ct. of 11 Apr. 1440; bdle. 19, ct. of 1 Apr. 1448; Kinver ct. rolls 1590-1629, ct. of 10 Oct. 1615.
[19] Ibid. Kinver ct. papers 17th and 18th cents., cts. of 22 Apr. 1672, 13 Apr. 1691, 9 May 1698; Kinver ct. rolls 1681-1702, ct. of 3 May 1686.
[20] S.H.C. 1911, 222.
[21] H.W.R.O. (H.), E 12/S, Compton I, deed of 2 Nov. 1688.
[22] Ibid. Kinver ct. rolls 1387-1498, bdle. 28, ct. of 28 Jan. 1470/1; 1590-1629, ct. of 9 Apr. 1615.
[23] Ibid. Checkhill I, deed of 8 Mar. 1682/3.
[24] S.R.O., Tp. 1273/2, deed of 12 Nov. 1515.

Stamford had an eel trap there; in 1911 it was sold to Edward Webb of Studley Court, in Stourbridge.[25]

MARKETS AND FAIRS. In 1221 John son of Philip was granted a Tuesday market in his manor of Kinver during the minority of Henry III.[26] There is no record of renewal after Henry declared himself of age in 1227, but in 1257 John's son John was granted a Wednesday market.[27] His right was upheld in 1293.[28] The market was still held in the mid 15th century,[29] but nothing further is known of it. In 1544 William Whorwood was granted a Tuesday market.[30] The market place was presumably south of the junction of High Street and Vicarage Drive where the street widens and where a town hall was built in 1619.[31] The market was mentioned in 1717,[32] but it had been discontinued by the mid 18th century.[33]

A fair in Kinver manor on the vigil, feast, and morrow of St. Peter and St. Paul (28–30 June) was granted to the lord in 1257.[34] That right too was upheld in 1293,[35] but nothing further is known of the fair. In 1544 William Whorwood was granted two fairs at Kinver, on 1 May and 8 December, with a court of piepowder.[36] The second was held on 14 December by the late 1750s.[37] By 1850 fairs dealing mainly in pigs were held on the last Tuesday in February, the second Tuesday in May, and the first Tuesday in December.[38] All were held until the later 1880s.[39]

BOROUGH. A borough was probably established about the time of the grant of a market in 1221. Richard Beneit 'de novo burgo' appeared among a group of local men in 1227–8.[40] About 1270 the lord of the manor issued a charter granting his burgesses of Kinver the same liberties in holding their burgages as those enjoyed by the burgesses of Kidderminster (Worcs.). The burgesses were also granted rights of pasture in Kinver wood, except at times of the lord's pannage, and of cutting brushwood and fern outside the wood all the year round. The rent for each burgage was 10d. a year.[41] In 1293 there were 23 or 24

burgages in the borough. Of the 22 burgesses then recorded, 13 held a single burgage and 6 held double burgages; another burgess paid 16d., and two others 6d. and 4d.[42] In 1387 there were 28 burgages; 14 were each held by a single burgess, and 7 were each shared by two burgesses. The remaining burgages were held by individual burgesses as holdings of 3, 2, 1½, or ½. It appears that burgages had not been laid out over the whole borough: in 1387 the borough contained an assart held at a rent of 3d. and a cottage at a rent of 2d.[43] A heriot of 4d. was due from the holders of a single burgage in 1387; in 1422 a heriot of 4d. was paid from each of two half burgages.[44] A standard 4d. heriot was last taken in 1791.[45] A standard 10d. rent was still paid in the early 1830s.[46]

MILLS. A newly built mill on the Stour where it formed the north-eastern boundary of the parish was held with adjoining land on both sides of the river by John Willetts of Halfcot in 1573. In that year he settled the reversion after his death on his son Richard.[47] It was known as Willetts mill by 1617 when there was a house adjoining.[48] By 1629 the estate, including two corn mills under one roof, was sold by John Brettell of Kingswinford, the successor of a John Willett (so spelled), to Richard Nashe of Halfcot.[49] Nashe sold it to George Brindley of the Hyde in 1631.[50] George settled it on his son Richard and Richard's wife Hester in 1641, and they sold it in 1654 to Richard's cousin, Thomas Foley the ironmaster.[51] By the 1670s Willetts mills were owned by Thomas's son Philip.[52] In 1701 Philip leased the mills as three corn mills called Stapenhill mills to Margaret Willett of Kinver.[53] By 1716 Willetts mills were worked by Thomas White, who that year received permission to use one of the wheels and materials from the mills for a new mill at Halfcot.[54] In 1733 William Foley granted a lease of 'a mill house in which lately were corn mills called Willetts mills'.[55] The building was known as Bells mill by 1775.[56] The remains of a 19th-century mill building survive on the site.

[25] Ibid. 23, Crowther Bros. & Co. to Lord Stamford 19 Nov. 1883; 35, deed of 12 Dec. 1911; 39, guardian's accts. (Staffs.), Dec. 1846 and 1847.
[26] Rot. Litt. Claus. (Rec. Com.), i. 464.
[27] Cal. Chart. R. 1226–57, 474.
[28] Plac. de Quo Warr. (Rec. Com.), 705–6.
[29] H.W.R.O. (H.), E 12/S, Kinver ct. rolls 1387–1498, bdle. 19, ct. of 1 Apr. 1448; bdle. 20, cts. of 19 Sept. 1449, 27 Apr. 1450.
[30] L. & P. Hen. VIII, xix (1), p. 377.
[31] Below, local govt. (borough).
[32] H.W.R.O. (H.), Kinver ct. papers 17th and 18th cents., boro. ct. of 18 May 1717.
[33] W.S.L., S.MS. 466/16, P. White to R. Wilkes.
[34] Cal. Chart. R. 1226–57, 474.
[35] Plac. de Quo Warr. 705–6.
[36] L. & P. Hen. VIII, xix (1), p. 377; H.W.R.O. (H.), E 12/S, addenda to portfolios, writ of 19 May 1544.
[37] W.S.L., S.MS. 466/16, White to Wilkes; S.R.O. 1401, 14 Dec. 1774. Pitt, Staffs. i. 196, stated (1817) that the second was held on 15 Dec.; Scott, Stourbridge, 170, stated (1832) that the fairs were held on 14 May and 14 Dec. White, Dir. Staffs. (1834), 259, stated that they were long obsolete.
[38] White, Dir. Staffs. (1851), 177.
[39] Rep. Com. Mkt. Rights and Tolls [C. 5550], p. 202, H.C. (1888), liii; Kelly's Dir. Staffs. (1888).
[40] S.H.C. iv (1), 69–70.

[41] H.W.R.O. (H.), E 12/S, Kinver XIII, transcript of borough charter; Shaw, Staffs. ii. 262, printing a less accurate version; Brit. Boro. Charters 1216–1307, ed. A. Ballard and J. Tait, p. xlii. No evidence survives of the 13th-century liberties of Kidderminster; in the 14th century it enjoyed privileges such as freedom from relief and heriot never acquired by the burgesses of Kinver: V.C.H. Worcs. iii. 163–4.
[42] P.R.O., SC 6/202/64.
[43] H.W.R.O. (H.), E 12/S, Kinver ct. rolls 1387–1498, bdle. 1.   [44] Ibid.; bdle. 2, ct. of 19 Oct. 1422.
[45] H.W.R.O. (H.), E 12/S, Kinver boro. ct. bk. 1763–1841, ct. of 25 Oct. 1791.
[46] Ibid. list of boro. rents between cts. of 22 Oct. 1831 and 27 Oct. 1832.
[47] H.W.R.O. (H.), E 12/S, Kinver VII, deed of 31 Oct. 1573; S.H.C. xiv (1), 171.
[48] P.R.O., E 178/4984.
[49] H.W.R.O. (H.), E 12/S, Kinver VII, deed of 14 July 1629.
[50] Ibid. Kinver II, deed of 16 May 1631; Kinver VII, deed of 15 June 1631.
[51] Ibid. Kinver VII, deeds of 1 July 1641, 7 Nov. 1654, and Ric. Brinley's receipt to Thos. Foley 7 Nov. 1654.
[52] Ibid. acct. of rent of Phil. Foley.
[53] Ibid. deed of 26 Feb. 1700/1.
[54] Ibid. deed of 29 Feb. 1715/16.
[55] Ibid. deed of 23 Feb. 1732/3.
[56] Yates, Map of Staffs. (1775).

In 1716 a new corn mill at Halfcot on the Navigation Cut west of the Wolverhampton–Kidderminster road was leased to Thomas White of Willetts mills. By 1733 it had been turned into a wire mill.[57]

There was a mill at Stourton by 1293.[58] By 1330 it had fallen down, and that year the king ordered the sheriff to have it rebuilt; the keeper of Kinver forest was ordered to provide the timber needed.[59] By 1640 what were known as the Castle mills consisted of three corn mills under one roof on the Stour adjoining the castle.[60] They were converted into a forge in 1670 or 1671.[61]

From the 1790s there was a corn mill at the Hyde. It was still in existence in 1839.[62]

A water mill formed part of Gilbert of Dunsley's estate at Dunsley at his death in 1326.[63] In 1327 it was found to be ruinous.[64]

One of the two mills in Kinver in 1086[65] may have been on the Stour on the north side of the present Mill Lane. There was a mill there by 1439,[66] and it remained part of Kinver manor until 1648.[67] In that year John Whorwood and his son Sir William sold three water corn mills called Kinver mills to William Kimberley, the curate of Kinver, and Samuel Jukes of Wolverley (Worcs.) in two equal shares. In 1675 Kimberley and his wife Elizabeth and Jukes's son Samuel and widow Margaret sold it to Philip Foley.[68] In the earlier 18th century Kinver mills, owned by the Foleys, consisted of three corn mills and a malt mill.[69] There was still a corn mill there in 1783, but the rest had been converted into a slitting mill by the late 1760s.[70]

There was a mill on the Stour at Whittington c. 1200,[71] possibly the second mill mentioned in 1086. It evidently descended with the manor until the 15th century. In 1423 Edmund Lowe, lord of Whittington, exchanged land in Kinver, including some next to the mill, with William Everdon,[72] and in 1458 the mill passed with Dunsley manor to William's son Thomas.[73] In 1515 Humphrey Everdon, the lord of Dunsley, and his son and heir John sold a corn mill and a fulling mill on the Stour at Whittington to Sir Edward Grey, lord of Whittington.[74] Sir

Edward's grandson John Grey held three water mills at Whittington in 1581.[75] In 1619 Whittington mill, south of what is now the end of Horse Bridge Lane, was converted into an ironworks.[76]

A fulling mill on Spittle brook at Checkhill[77] became a corn mill probably when it was rebuilt in the late 18th century. George Burgess had a farm and mill at Checkhill at his death in 1824. He was succeeded by his son George, who was working a corn mill there in 1830 as tenant of J. H. Hodgetts-Foley and still had the farm and mill in the early 1860s.[78] The mill had evidently ceased to work as a corn mill by the early 1880s.[79] By 1913 it was used to work farm machinery,[80] and it was supplying electricity for the farm in the mid 1930s, when it ceased to operate.[81] The small late 18th-century building and the machinery survived in 1982.[82]

Pole or Pool mill was mentioned in 1460 and was still in existence in 1617 when it was described as on the heath.[83] It may have stood on Mill (or Clam) brook east of Hyde Lane.[84]

By 1294 the manor of Horewood included a water mill, mentioned again in 1315.[85] It was presumably the predecessor of Compton mill in Compton park mentioned in 1585[86] and apparently held by John Whorwood in 1639.[87] The mill site was evidently on Compton brook east of Compton Park Farm.[88]

The endowments of Our Lady's chantry in Enville church included a water mill in Kinver by 1535. It was bought with the rest of the chantry's property by Thomas Grey in 1553 and was owned by John Grey in 1581.[89] Its site is not known.

There was a windmill west of Dunsley Hall c. 1770.[90] In 1780 John Hodgetts leased to Benjamin Warren of Enville a plot of waste at Checkhill on which Warren was to build a windmill within a year.[91] The mill was in operation by 1784.[92] J. H. Hodgetts-Foley sold it in 1830 to Gilbert Brown of Shifnal (Salop.).[93] Brown was declared bankrupt in 1846 and died in 1847; in 1849 the mill was sold to Lord Stamford, whose tenant was working it in 1854.[94] The tower still stood in 1982. Land west of White Hill Farm near Comp-

[57] H.W.R.O. (H.), E 12/S, Kinver VIII, deed of 29 Feb. 1715/16; below (iron).

[58] P.R.O., SC 6/202/64.

[59] Cal. Close, 1330-3, 37.

[60] H.W.R.O. (H.), E 12/S, Whorwood inheritance, deed of 15 Feb. 1639/40; P. M. Grazebrook, Short Hist. of Stourton Castle and Royal Forest of Kinver, plan facing p. 47.

[61] Below (iron).

[62] Below (iron); M. V. Cooksley, 'Iron Ind. of Kinver' (copy in W.S.L.), 66-7; S.R.O., D. 695/4/17/5.

[63] Above, manors and other estates.

[64] P.R.O., C 143/191, no. 15.

[65] V.C.H. Staffs. iv. 40.

[66] H.W.R.O. (H.), E 12/S, Kinver ct. rolls 1387-1498, bdle. 13, ct. of 20 Apr. 1439; bdle. 14, ct. of 11 Apr. 1440.

[67] Ibid. addenda to portfolios, Lord Dudley to steward of Kinver manor 24 June 1522; Kinver ct. rolls 1590-1629, boro. ct. of 31 Mar. 1590; Kinver XIII, bill in Chancery 29 Jan. 1601/2.

[68] Ibid. Kinver VII, deeds of 18 May 1648, 26 Mar. 1675.

[69] Ibid. Prestwood leases, deed of 1 May 1719; Halfcot II, deed of 2 July 1735; vol. of 18th- and 19th-cent. plans.

[70] Ibid. Kinver II, deed of 7 June 1783; below (iron).

[71] S.R.O., Tp. 1273/12, bk. of deeds and evidences, p. 13.

[72] S.R.O., Tp. 1273/12/6, no. 21.

[73] S.R.O., D. 593/B/1/26/7B/3.

[74] S.R.O., Tp. 1273/2, deeds of 12, 15, 24 Nov. 1515.

[75] H.W.R.O. (H.), E 12/S, Bobbington and Enville, valor of lands of John Grey 1581.

[76] Below (iron).

[77] Below (cloth).

[78] H.W.R.O. (H.), E 12/S, Dunsley III, abstract of title to Dunsley farm 1866; S.R.O., D. 891/4, p. 23; Harrison, Harrod & Co. Dir. Staffs. (1861), 83.

[79] O.S. Map 6", Staffs. LXX. NE. (1889 edn.), showing 'old mill pond'.

[80] W.S.L., Sale Cats. G/3, p. 47.

[81] Local inf. (1982).

[82] Staffs. C.C. Planning Dept., Ind. Arch. Survey.

[83] H.W.R.O. (H.), E 12/S, Kinver ct. rolls 1387-1498, bdle. 25, 8 Jan. 1459/60; bdle. 28, 29 Jan. 1470/1; Kinver ct. rolls 1590-1629, 7 Apr. 1613, 6 Oct. 1617.

[84] There are traces of a dam there: inf. from Mr. J. W. King.

[85] S.H.C. 1911, 222, 330-1.

[86] H.W.R.O. (H.), E 12/S, Compton I, deed of 18 Oct. 1588.

[87] P.R.O., CP 25(2)/486/15 Chas. I Trin. no. 8.

[88] H.W.R.O. (H.), E 12/S, vol. of 18th- and 19th-cent. plans, Compton, nos. 56, 130.

[89] Ibid. Bobbington and Enville, valor of lands of John Grey 1581; Valor Eccl. (Rec. Com.), iii. 101; above, pp. 114-15.

[90] Yates, Map of Staffs. (1775).

[91] H.W.R.O. (H.), E 12/S, Checkhill I, deed of 28 Oct. 1780.

[92] S.R.O., D. 1197/5/1.

[93] S.R.O., Tp. 1273/32, abstract of title to Spittal Brook mill etc. 1846.

[94] Ibid. 27, Enville estate cash bks.; 36, deed of 11 May 1849.

KINVER: THE HYDE IRONWORKS *c.* 1870

AMBLECOTE: COALBOURNBROOK FROM THE NORTH *c.* 1900, WITH GLASSWORKS

ENVILLE: LADY DOROTHY'S COTTAGE

KINVER: THE OLD GRAMMAR SCHOOL HOUSE

ENVILLE: COUNTESS OF STAMFORD AND WARRINGTON SCHOOL

KINVER: THE SCHOOL-CHAPEL AT HALFCOT IN 1846

ton was known as Windmill Hill in the earlier 19th century[95] and may be the site of a windmill.

IRON. There was a forge (*fabrica*) in the borough in 1387,[96] but otherwise the first evidence of ironmaking dates from the early 17th century. In 1619 George Taylor was granted a lease of Whittington mill and converted it into a forge. He was presented at the Kinver manor court for establishing a number of men and a woman in the mill house without indemnifying the parish; in 1620 he gave the necessary undertaking in respect of the workers 'at the hammer'.[97] Richard Foley had taken over the forge by 1628,[98] and in 1629 he too was presented for not indemnifying the parish in respect of his workers there.[99] In 1640 Foley conveyed his interest to his son Thomas, who was granted a lease for life by Henry Grey, lord of Whittington, in 1649.[1] The forge was taken over by Thomas's son Philip in 1669 with Thomas Jukes as manager.[2] By 1683 it was held by Richard Avenant, John Wheeler, and Andrew Bentley.[3] From 1692 until 1705 it was run by the Ironworks in Partnership, a company which included Philip Foley, Avenant, and Wheeler. From 1725 the forge was run by the Stour Valley Partnership, in which the Knight family was prominent. Production rose from 200 tons in 1717 to 300 tons in 1750.[4] New workers' houses were built in 1766. In 1770 Edward Knight secured permission from Lord Stamford to convert the forge into a slitting mill, and the conversion was duly carried out.[5] Edward's son John succeeded in 1784 and was followed in 1797 by his own son John, who continued to work the mill until 1810.[6] In that year it was leased to Jacob Turner of Park Hall, in Kidderminster (Worcs.).[7] A wire mill was added in 1818.[8] Jacob's son Henry had succeeded by 1826.[9] Henry was a lunatic by 1838 and the lease was assigned that year to Thomas Webb, who in 1839 sublet the ironworks to George Hartshorn of Old Swinford and Benedict Neale of Wall Heath, in Kingswinford. They were soon in financial difficulties, and in 1840 the works was taken over by Benjamin and James Williams, who con-

siderably extended it.[10] In 1851 the workforce numbered 120 men and 24 boys, and in 1871 it consisted of 150 men and boys.[11] James Williams & Co. retained the works until 1882, although operations appear to have ceased *c.* 1879.[12] The Whittington Patent Horse Nail Co. Ltd. was in occupation from 1883 until 1893, and the works then closed.[13]

In 1670 Stourton mills were leased by Wortley Whorwood to John Finch of Dudley with liberty to convert them into a furnace or forge.[14] Finch had a forge there by 1671.[15] Philip Foley granted a new lease in 1672, but Finch surrendered it in 1673; the forge was stated to be a cause of flooding and also, 'by reason of the extreme knocking and continual beating forth of iron', a threat to the foundations of Stourton Castle.[16] In 1672, however, Foley had agreed to lease it to Sir Clement Clerke and John Forth, and in 1676, after that partnership had broken up, it was leased to Henry Cornish, John Langworth, and Thomas Sergeant for five years.[17] John Wheeler and Richard Avenant held it probably from 1681 and ran it until 1692 when it became part of the Ironworks in Partnership. It was turned into a slitting mill in 1698.[18] In that year Philip Foley leased it to Richard Wheeler, a member of the partnership. In 1703, after Wheeler's bankruptcy and death, Foley granted a 40-year lease to John Cook of Stourton.[19] A Thomas Cook, who died in 1699, was then described as head workman at the mill, and John lived at the mill house.[20] In 1752 William Foley granted John a lease of the house and mill for life.[21] John died in 1762 and was succeeded by Richard Marston, although in 1756 the reversion of the lease had been granted to Thomas Hodgetts of Ashwood Lodge, in Kingswinford.[22] In 1781 Francis Homfray was living at Stourton, having moved there shortly before from the nearby Wollaston Hall, in Old Swinford (Worcs.),[23] and in 1783 he was granted a 20-year lease of the house and mill.[24] He turned the mill into a rolling mill *c.* 1792. He was succeeded by his son Jeston of Broadwaters in Kidderminster, who took a 21-year lease in 1804.[25] Jeston died in 1816, but his executors

[95] S.R.O., D. 891/3, no. 201; ibid. 4, p. 8.
[96] H.W.R.O. (H.), E 12/S, Kinver ct. rolls 1387–1498, bdle. 1.
[97] Ibid. E 12/F, box 1119, deed of 15 Dec. 1628; E 12/S, Kinver ct. rolls 1590–1629, cts. of 19 Oct. 1619, 10 Oct. 1620; S.R.O., Tp. 1273/11, 1623 survey.
[98] H.W.R.O. (H.), E 12/F, box 1119, deed of 15 Dec. 1628.
[99] Ibid. E 12/S, Kinver ct. rolls 1590–1629, cts. of 28 Apr., 20 Oct. 1629.
[1] Above, manors and other estates (Whittington) and refs. given there.
[2] M. V. Cooksley, 'Iron Ind. of Kinver', 75 (copy in W.S.L.); *Records of Phil. Foley's Stour Valley Iron Works 1668–74* (Worcs. Hist. Soc. N.S. ix).
[3] S.R.O., Tp. 1273/6, deed of 9 Nov. 1683.
[4] Cooksley, 'Iron Ind. of Kinver', 29–32, 76–7; *V.C.H. Staffs.* ii. 120.
[5] Cooksley, 'Iron Ind. of Kinver', 80–2.
[6] Ibid. 82; S.R.O., Tp. 1273/41, deeds of 9 July 1784, 5 Aug. 1797.
[7] S.R.O., Tp. 1273/41, deed of 23 Aug. 1810.
[8] Ibid. 50, Dan. Clarke to Lord Grey 25 Jan., 25 Apr. 1818.
[9] Cooksley, 'Iron Ind. of Kinver', 83.
[10] S.R.O., Tp. 1273/23, sale partics.; Cooksley, 'Iron Ind. of Kinver', 83–4.
[11] P.R.O., HO 107/2017; P.R.O., RG 10/2928.

[12] S.R.O., Tp. 1273/23; R. Hunt, *Memoirs of Geol. Surv., Mineral Statistics of U.K. 1879,* 92; *1880,* 96; *1881,* 88.
[13] S.R.O., Tp. 1273/23; Cooksley, 'Iron Ind. of Kinver', 85–6.
[14] Cooksley, 'Iron Ind. of Kinver', 90.
[15] H.W.R.O. (H.), E 12/S, Whorwood inheritance, partic. of Stourton Castle estate 1671; Kinver ct. papers 17th and 18th cents., ct. of 10 Apr. 1671.
[16] Ibid. E 12/F/VI/KE/32, 37; E 12/S, Whorwood inheritance, deed of 7 Dec. 1672; E 12/S, Kinver ct. papers 17th and 18th cents., ct. of 14 Apr. 1673.
[17] *Business Hist.* xiii. 29.
[18] Cooksley, 'Iron Ind. of Kinver', 91; H.W.R.O. (H.), E 12/S, Whorwood inheritance, deed of 20 Sept. 1686.
[19] H.W.R.O. (H.), E 12/S, Prestwood leases, deed of 11 Nov. 1703.
[20] Ibid. Kinver VII, deed of 21 May 1756; Cooksley, 'Iron Ind. of Kinver', 92–3.
[21] H.W.R.O. (H.), E 12/S, Kinver VII, deed of 29 Sept. 1752.
[22] Ibid. deed of 21 May 1756; Cooksley, 'Iron Ind. of Kinver', 93–4.
[23] S.R.O., Tp. 1226, bdle. xl, deed of 12 May 1781; Cooksley, 'Iron Ind. of Kinver', 94.
[24] H.W.R.O. (H.), E 12/S, Kinver VII, 12 June 1782.
[25] Ibid. Stourton I, deed of 16 Feb. 1804; Cooksley, 'Iron Ind. of Kinver', 96.

continued to pay the rent until 1828. By 1830 the mill had been demolished.[26]

In 1627 a fulling mill on the Stour at the Hyde was leased by Gerard and John Whorwood for 21 years to trustees, with a view to their subletting it to Richard Foley of Dudley.[27] He had taken possession by 1628 and had rebuilt the mill as a slitting mill to serve his ironworks elsewhere.[28] About the same time he moved to Stourbridge.[29] By the later 1630s the mill was worked by Foley's brother-in-law George Brindley of the nearby Hyde House.[30] George's son Richard bought the mill in 1647,[31] but it continued to work in association with the Foleys. Thus in 1651 Richard Brindley agreed to slit 8 tons of iron a week supplied by Richard Foley's son Thomas up to a total of 300 tons a year; Thomas was to pay Brindley 30s. a ton.[32] In 1653–4 the mill also slit iron from Sir Thomas Middleton's Shropshire forges.[33] The Brindleys were soon mortgaging the Hyde estate, and £72 was due to Thomas Foley in 1669–70 as interest on the mortgage of the mill.[34] The Brindleys continued to work it until 1731, when Richard's grandson John was declared bankrupt; he died later the same year. Meanwhile, at the time of his marriage in 1726, he had built a new house at the Hyde. In 1733 the mill was bought by George Draper, whose son George sold it in 1741 to Jeremiah Caswell, the tenant since 1736. Caswell died in 1769, and his daughter Eleanor then ran the mill at least until her marriage in 1776 to Paul White, the curate of Kinver. She was running it in 1780, the year after her husband's death, and in 1781 she went into partnership with her nephew Francis Homfray of Gothersley, son of Francis Homfray of Stourton. She withdrew in 1793, making over the property to Francis, who moved to the Hyde. By 1791 he had already converted the mill into a rolling mill, and by 1797 he had installed a steam hammer; by then he had also turned the original house into a corn mill. On his death in 1809 he was succeeded by his son Jeremiah.[35] In 1810 Jeremiah offered the works for sale; it consisted of a steam engine, a forge, rolling and slitting mills, and 12 workmen's cottages, as well as the 18th-century Hyde House. The eventual buyer was his uncle Thomas Homfray, who moved to the Hyde and was still living there in 1818.[36] He was declared bankrupt in 1819, and in 1821 the works was bought by the Stourbridge banking firm of Thomas Hill, Thomas Bate, and William Robins.

They sold it in 1831 to Benjamin Littlewood, an Amblecote glassmaker. His family retained the ownership until 1912 when the Revd. H. C. Littlewood sold it to T. L. Downing of Stourton Hall.[37]

In the meantime two separate works were developed by tenants. In the late 1820s Joseph and Thomas Parkes started a spade and shovel manufactory, which the Parkes family was still running in the 1860s. It passed to other tenants, including Isaac Nash & Sons from c. 1886 until its closure c. 1910.[38] In 1830 the ironworks was vacant, but in 1831 a lease was taken by John Hunt and William Brown who proceeded to enlarge it. In 1838 they sublet it to Thomas Bolton of Whittington. He and his partner J. F. Lee further expanded the works. By the early 1870s they were evidently producing steel. In 1851 the workforce consisted of 135 men, 1 woman, and 15 boys; by 1861, when Bolton was living at Hyde House, the workers numbered 292 men and 21 boys. The firm, however, was in financial difficulties by the mid 1860s and operations ceased in 1877. The works was taken over the same year by H. O. Firmstone, who continued to run it until about the end of 1882. It was then finally closed.[39]

By the mid 1730s a blade mill on Smestow brook at Gothersley had been rebuilt as a slitting mill worked by Francis Homfray of Old Swinford (Worcs.). After his death in 1737 his widow Mary ran the mill. In 1788 John Hodgetts leased it with Swindon forge in Wombourne to Francis's son Francis, who lived at Stourton, and his two sons, Francis of Gothersley and Jeston of Broadwaters, in Kidderminster.[40] In 1793 the last Francis moved from Gothersley to the Hyde, where he was already involved in the ironworks.[41] The house and mill at Gothersley were leased in 1798 to John Hodgetts's nephew, also John Hodgetts.[42] In 1799 he went into partnership with John Thompson and John Scale to run Gothersley and other ironworks, but he died in 1800. His widow Elizabeth continued to run Gothersley mill, buying out the other partners in 1802. In 1812, when the works consisted of a rolling and slitting mill and workmen's houses, she sublet it to John Bradley & Co. of Amblecote. She continued to live at Gothersley, and in 1821 J. H. Hodgetts-Foley granted her a new lease; she was apparently acting for her future son-in-law, Henry Hodgson.[43] By 1830 Gothersley rolling mill was

[26] P. M. Grazebrook, *Short Hist. of Stourton Castle and Royal Forest of Kinver*, 43; Cooksley, 'Iron Ind. of Kinver', 96; H.W.R.O. (H.), E 12/S, Prestwood Estate surveys I.
[27] H.W.R.O. (H.), E 12/S, Kinver VII, deed of 1 Feb. 1626/7.
[28] Cooksley, 'Iron Ind. of Kinver', 43–6; H.W.R.O. (H.), E 12/F, box 1119, deed of 4 Dec. 1628.
[29] *Trans. Worcs. Arch. Soc.* N.S. xxi. 2.
[30] H.W.R.O. (H.), E 12/S, Compton I, deed of 29 May 1639.
[31] Cooksley, 'Iron Ind. of Kinver', 47, 50.
[32] H.W.R.O. (H.), E 12/S, Kinver VI, agreements of 22 Mar. 1650/1, Apr. 1651. For an agreement between Thos. Foley and Geo. Brindley see ibid. 20 June 1646.
[33] Cooksley, 'Iron Ind. of Kinver', 51.
[34] Ibid. 50–1; *Records of Phil. Foley's Stour Valley Iron Works*, 96.
[35] Cooksley, 'Iron Ind. of Kinver', 53–63, 95.
[36] Ibid. 64–5; S.R.O., Tp. 1273/50, bdle. marked 'Enville Letters and Papers', newspaper extract announcing sale in letter of 7 Apr. 1810.

[37] Cooksley, 'Iron Ind. of Kinver', 65–7, 74; H.W.R.O. (H.), E 12/S, reg. of Kinver tithes sold 1824–5.
[38] Cooksley, 'Iron Ind. of Kinver', 66, 73–4; H.W.R.O. (H.), E 12/S, Prestwood rent bk. 1882–6.
[39] Cooksley, 'Iron Ind. of Kinver', 66–73; S.R.O., D. 695/4/17/4; P.R.O., HO 107/2017; P.R.O., RG 9/1985; Hunt, *Mineral Statistics 1878*, 90; *1881*, 88; Kinver Libr., Kinver Hist. Soc. archives, dismissal notice of 9 Dec. 1882; above, pl. facing p. 144.
[40] H. S. Grazebrook, *Collns. for Genealogy of Noble Fams. of Henzey, Tyttery, and Tyzack* (Stourbridge, 1877), 53 n.; H.W.R.O. (H.), E 12/S, vol. of 18th- and 19th-cent. plans, Stourton; ibid. Kinver VIII, deed of 27 Sept. 1788.
[41] Cooksley, 'Iron Ind. of Kinver', 98–9; H.W.R.O. (H.), Kinver and Kingsley ct. bk. 1767–1801, ct. of 28 Sept. 1793.
[42] H.W.R.O. (H.), E 12/S, Kinver VIII, deed of 31 Aug. 1798; Cooksley, 'Iron Ind. of Kinver', 99.
[43] Cooksley, 'Iron Ind. of Kinver', 99–108; H.W.R.O. (H.), E 12/S, Kinver VIII, deed of 15 Sept. 1821; K. C. Hodgson, *Out of the Mahogany Desk*, 104.

occupied by George and Edward Thorneycroft.[44] Arrangements were made in 1833 for a lease to John Hunt and William Brown, with the proviso that the mill should be used solely as a rolling mill.[45] In 1836 it was leased to Joseph Maybury of Bilston, who took a new lease in 1840 and was at the works until 1849. From then it was held on a 21-year lease by E. B. Dimmock and John Thompson of Bilston, who were joined in 1856 by William Hatton of Bilston. By 1861 it was worked by S. W. Bunn, who lived at Gothersley House. In 1870 a 21-year lease was made to Bunn and to William Hatton of Kidderminster.[46] In 1871 the workforce consisted of 15 men and 9 boys.[47] From 1876 the works was run by William Finnemore of Small Heath, Birmingham, and Richard Titley of Sutton Coldfield (Warws.), with Finnemore alone from 1877. The works was closed c. 1890, and the contents were offered for sale in 1891.[48]

By the late 1760s part of Kinver mills in Mill Lane was worked as a slitting mill by George Stokes.[49] In 1783, as tenant of John Hodgetts, he was working a rolling and slitting mill as well as a corn mill.[50] The Stokes family was still there in 1814,[51] but by 1830 what was called Kinver rolling mill was owned and occupied by Henry Turner, the lessee of Whittington ironworks.[52] In 1837 there were complaints about the noise from the newly installed hammer and fears about the effects of the vibration on the grammar school building.[53] Turner was a lunatic by 1838, and the mill was then unoccupied.[54] By 1845 T. M. Woodyatt had converted it into a screw manufactory. In the 1860s his executors sold it to Nettlefold & Chamberlain, a Smethwick screwmaking firm, which closed it; some 20 men were then employed there. In 1868 the mill was run by S. F. Bolton, a maker of iron and steel ware. In the late 19th century it was a spade and shovel works. Thomas Timmings made agricultural implements there by 1896. He was followed in the early 20th century by C. H. Timmings, who was still working there in 1912. A water works was opened on part of the site in 1908. The rest of the mill was converted into a saw mill; electric power was substituted for water in 1929. The mill was closed in 1978, and much of it was demolished in 1980.[55]

By 1733 the mill on the west side of the main road at Halfcot had been turned into a wire mill, and a second wire mill had been built nearby. They were leased that year to John Turton of Rowley Regis and John Webster of Birmingham, both ironmongers, for 21 years.[56] In 1759 John Webster, then described as a Shrewsbury ironmaster, took a new 21-year lease and assigned it to John Ryland, a wiredrawer, Joseph Smith, a merchant, and John Kettle, a steel merchant and manufacturer, all of Birmingham.[57] About that time Richard Wilkes, the antiquary, stated that iron wire was 'made to perfection' there.[58] In 1781 Ryland took a 21-year lease from John Hodgetts of the two wire mills; the lease was renewed for another 21 years in 1801.[59] In the early 1820s, when the more southerly was described as a block mill, the mills were held by J. W. Phipson.[60] They had been dismantled by 1830.[61]

In 1601 a blade mill formerly held by Francis Penn and Edward Meeke or one of them was surrendered by Richard Bate to the use of Humphrey Jorden.[62] In 1625 Jorden held two blade mills.[63] They evidently stood on Spittle brook at Checkhill. A scythegrinder named Richard Burneford was living at Checkhill in 1628,[64] and blade mills at Checkhill were mentioned in 1636.[65] Francis Bennett was working as a scythegrinder at Checkhill at his death in 1666, presumably at the blade mills which were held by the widow Bennett in 1670. William Bennett was evidently working there c. 1680.[66] In 1683 Philip Foley granted a 21-year lease of a house and two blade mills at Checkhill to Thomas Wannerton, a scythegrinder, who was evidently still working there in 1689.[67] By 1698 the mill had been turned into a fulling mill.[68]

There was evidently a blade mill on Smestow brook at Gothersley by 1685. A scythesmith named James Raybold then held land in the area, and in 1691 a blade mill there was described as newly built and as lately held by him.[69] It may have been built by Philip Foley in the early 1670s.[70] In 1691 Foley leased it for 99 years to William Webb, a scythegrinder of Kingswinford. Webb built himself a house near the mill. For the convenience of his customers he had laid out a road from Ashwood Lane, in Kingswinford, by

[44] Cooksley, 'Iron Ind. of Kinver' 108.

[45] H.W.R.O. (H.), E 12/S, Prestwood leases.

[46] Ibid. Kinver VIII, agreements of 1836 and 1840, deeds of 24 Mar. 1843, 26 May 1849, 11 Apr. 1856, 3 Aug. 1870; P.R.O., RG 9/1985.

[47] P.R.O., RG 10/2928.

[48] H.W.R.O. (H.), E 12/S, Kinver VIII, deed of 9 June 1877; Prestwood leases, cat. of sale of Gothersley mills Sept. 1891; Hunt, *Mineral Statistics 1876*, 8; *1877*, 86; Cooksley, 'Iron Ind. of Kinver', 108–9.

[49] Cooksley, 'Iron Ind. of Kinver', 110.

[50] H.W.R.O. (H.), E 12/S, Kinver II, deed of 7 June 1783.

[51] Cooksley, 'Iron Ind. of Kinver', 110–11.

[52] S.R.O., D. 891/4, p. 54.

[53] S.R.O., Tp. 1273/24/Kinver Sch., Lord Stamford to Geo. Wharton 4 Feb. 1837 and Wharton to Stamford 6 Feb. 1837.

[54] S.R.O., Tp. 1273/23, sale partics.; Cooksley, 'Iron Ind. of Kinver', 111.

[55] Cooksley, 'Iron Ind. of Kinver', 111–12A; Sherlock, *Ind. Arch. Staffs.* 174–5; R. Benbow, 'Story of Kinver Volunteer Fire Brigade' (TS. in Kinver Libr.), 6, 8; D. M. Bills and E. and W. R. Griffiths, *Kinver: a closer look* (Kinver, 1981), 8;

Kinver Village Trail (Kinver Civic Soc. 1981 edn.); O.S. Map 1/2,500, Staffs. LXX. 16 (1924 edn.).

[56] H.W.R.O. (H.), E 12/S, Kinver VII, deed of 23 Feb. 1732/3; vol. of 18th- and 19th-cent. plans, Halfcot, no. 129.

[57] Ibid. Kinver VII, deed of 17 Jan. 1759; S.R.O., D. (W.) 1921/4.   [58] W.S.L. S.MS. 468, p. 118.

[59] H.W.R.O. (H.), E 12/S, Halfcot I, deeds of 22 Mar. 1781, 1 Aug. 1801.

[60] Ibid. Prestwood Estate surveys I.

[61] Cooksley, 'Iron Ind. of Kinver', 116.

[62] H.W.R.O. (H.), E 12/S, Kinver ct. rolls 1590–1629, ct. of 2 April 1601.   [63] Ibid. ct. of survey 24 Oct. 1625.

[64] L.J.R.O., B/C/11, Ric. Burneford (1628).

[65] S.R.O., Tp. 1273/6, deed of 14 Jan. 1635/6.

[66] L.J.R.O., B/C/11, Fra. Bennett (1669), Wm. Bennett (1681); H.W.R.O. (H.), E 12/S, Checkhill I, copy deed of 14 Mar. 1669/70.

[67] H.W.R.O. (H.), E 12/S, Checkhill I, deed of 24 Apr. 1689; Checkhill III, deed of 8 Mar. 1682/3.

[68] Below (cloth).

[69] S.R.O., D. 648/22/1/1; H.W.R.O. (H.), E 12/S, Prestwood leases, deed of 23 Mar. 1690/1.

[70] H.W.R.O. (H.), E 12/F/VI/KBC/10.

1706 and built a bridge over Smestow brook. By 1716 his widow Jane was running the mill.[71] By the mid 1730s it had been rebuilt as a slitting mill.

A nailshop in the borough was described as a fire hazard in 1672,[72] and there was evidently a nailer working in the borough in 1696.[73] Three nailers were recorded in the Stourton area in 1683. One of them was working there in 1681, and another was there at his death in 1696.[74] There was a nailer at Iverley in 1706 and 1710,[75] and in 1714 Esdras Poole of Kinver was described as a nailer and brickmaker.[76] There was a nail-shop in Stone Lane in 1760.[77] In 1829–30 there were 5 nailshops in High Street, 1 at Stourton, 2 near Dunsley, 2 at Whittington, and 2 at Iverley.[78] In 1841 there were 4 nailers living in Kinver village, 3 of them in Nailers Row off High Street; there was also a nailer at Stourton and another at Dunsley.[79] There was still a nailer in High Street in 1851 and a nailshop at Iverley in 1883.[80] The ironworks at Whittington was occupied by the Whittington Patent Horse Nail Co. Ltd. from 1883 to 1893.[81]

CLOTH. There is some evidence that a local cloth industry existed by the 14th century. Thomas the comber ('combere') of Kinver and William the walker of Whittington were mentioned in 1327,[82] and heriots due from tenants of Kinver manor in 1387 included an uncut length of cloth.[83] There was a fulling mill at Whittington in 1515.[84] The tenement in the borough called the 'tuke' house in 1544 was presumably connected with tucking, or cloth working.[85] Thomas Hazelwood, who lived in the borough, was working as a clothier at his death in 1568.[86] A fulling mill was built on the Stour at the Hyde c. 1590; it was converted into a slitting mill in the later 1620s.[87] There was land called Tenter furlong at Kinver Hill in the early 17th century.[88] Thomas Hackett of Kinver was a wool carrier when he died in 1622,[89] and several clothiers were again recorded from 1640.[90] By 1698 the blade

mill at Checkhill had been converted into a fulling mill and was worked by John Heath.[91] It was held by John Insall in the 1730s and by Thomas Arnott in 1789.[92] It became a corn mill soon afterwards.[93] In the mid 18th century Kinver was producing both coarse and fine narrow cloth; according to Richard Wilkes, the latter was comparable in quality to western broad cloth.[94] By the 1830s the industry was only a memory.[95]

LEATHER. Two glovers were recorded at Kinver in 1414.[96] There was a tanner there in 1571.[97] The appointment of leather searchers for the borough was recorded four times between 1619 and 1624 and again in 1662 and 1669.[98] Glovers and tanners were recorded during the 17th century, including a glover at Compton. In 1632 the warehouse of the deceased John Catteroll, or Catheralle, a glover of the borough, contained some 300 sheep pelts, another 95 skins with the wool on, 100 sheep's 'leather', 19 calf skins, other leather, and wool.[99] There was a skinner living at Stourton in the earlier 1680s.[1]

STONE, SAND, AND GRAVEL. A quarry in the Comber area was mentioned in 1498.[2] In the early 1520s there was a quarry at 'Hygley' within the manor of Stourton and Kinver.[3] A waste called Quarry hill was mentioned in 1601, and stone was dug at Copton hill in the early 1620s.[4] In 1631 stone from Stapenhill was assigned for the rebuilding of Halfcot bridge.[5] A quarry of red sandstone on Checkhill common was worked by the Foleys in the earlier 18th century.[6] There were two disused quarries in Compton in 1882, one north-west of Greyfields Court and the other north-west of Compton Court Farm. There was also a working quarry north of the Hyde, itself disused by 1901.[7]

A sand pit in Castle field west of Stourton Castle was mentioned in 1619, although it is not clear that it was then being worked.[8] The existence

[71] H.W.R.O. (H.), E 12/S, Prestwood leases, deeds of 23 Mar. 1690/1, 4 July 1706, 15 Sept. 1716.
[72] Below, p. 153.
[73] H.W.R.O. (H.), E 12/S, Kinver I, deed of 15 Sept. 1696.
[74] Ibid. Stourton III, deed of 17 Mar. 1680/1; Checkhill II, deed of 13 June 1683; L.J.R.O., B/C/11, Wm. Lyne (1696).
[75] H.W.R.O. (H.), E 12/S, Iverley I, deed of 21 Mar. 1709/10; Iverley V, deed of 29 Mar. 1706.
[76] S.R.O., D. 1197/5/25.
[77] H.W.R.O. (H.), E 12/S, Kinver copyhold estates 1831, W. Bright's sched., opening 15.
[78] Ibid. Stourton I, deed of 1830; S.R.O., D. 891/4, pp. 40, 47, 51, 76, 82–3, 100–1.
[79] P.R.O., HO 107/1002.
[80] P.R.O., HO 107/2017; H.W.R.O. (H.), E 12/S, Iverley II, deed of 10 Feb. 1883. [81] Above.
[82] S.H.C. vii (1), 246; S.R.O., Tp. 1273/12, bk. of deeds and evidences, p. 3.
[83] H.W.R.O. (H.), E 12/S, Kinver ct. rolls 1387–1498, bdle. 1. [84] Above (mills).
[85] H.W.R.O. (H.), E 12/S, Kinver IX, deed of 16 Jan. 1543/4.
[86] L.J.R.O., B/C/11, Thos. Haselwod (1568).
[87] Cooksley, 'Iron Ind. of Kinver', 45–6; S.H.C. 1930, 358; above (iron).
[88] H.W.R.O. (H.), E 12/S, Kinver ct. rolls 1590–1629, ct. of 12 Oct. 1613.
[89] L.J.R.O., B/C/11, Thos. Hackett (1622).
[90] e.g. ibid. John Cooke (1640); H.W.R.O. (H.), E 12/S, Kinver ct. papers 17th and 18th cents., boro. cts. of 6 Oct.

1662, 20 Oct. 1681, 3 May 1729; Kinver VII, deed of 7 Mar. 1731/2; S.R.O., D. 1197/1/2, burials of 1684/5, 1698 sqq.; B.R.L. 338247 (1723); below, chars. for the poor.
[91] S.R.O., D. 1197/1/2, burial of 15 July 1698.
[92] H.W.R.O. (H.), E 12/S, vol. of 18th- and 19th-cent. plans; ibid. Kingsley Manor, deeds of 2 and 3 Dec. 1789.
[93] Above (mills). [94] Shaw, Staffs. ii. 263.
[95] White, Dir. Staffs. (1834), 259.
[96] S.H.C. xvii. 52. [97] S.R.O., D. 3162/4/1.
[98] H.W.R.O. (H.), E 12/S, Kinver ct. rolls 1590–1629 and ct. papers 17th and 18th cents.
[99] e.g. L.J.R.O., B/C/11, John Willett (1625), Ric. White (1630), John Catteroll (1632), Rob. Dickens (1633), Geof. Cooke (1636); H.W.R.O. (H.), E 12/S, Compton Hallows ct. rolls, ct. of 3 Nov. 1647; S.R.O., D. 1197/1/2, burials of 14 Aug. 1691, 7 Aug. 1696, 21 June 1698.
[1] H.W.R.O. (H.), E 12/S, Stourton III, deed of 17 Mar. 1680/1; Checkhill II, deed of 13 June 1683.
[2] Ibid. Kinver I, deed of 30 Aug. 1498.
[3] S.R.O., D. 593/O/3/5.
[4] H.W.R.O. (H.), E 12/S, Kinver ct. rolls 1590–1629, cts. of 2 Apr. 1601, 21 Oct. 1622, 21 Apr., 10 Oct. 1623.
[5] Ibid. Kingswinford I, memo. of 26 May 1631.
[6] Ibid. Staffs. legal papers, Foley v. Powell, prosecution brief.
[7] O.S. Map 6", Staffs. LXX. SE. (1888 edn.), SW. (1887 and 1904 edns.). A quarry shown at the north end of Kinver Edge in 1888 was apparently a gravel pit: below.
[8] H.W.R.O. (H.), E 12/S, Kinver ct. rolls 1590–1629, ct. of 18 Jan. 1618/19.

of land called Sand Pit Piece in Dunsley in 1797 indicates sand working there at some date.[9] Sand was being dug near Stapenhill *c.* 1830 and was worked in the 20th century at various places on both sides of the Stourbridge Canal, which was used to transport it.[10] A pit opened at Stewponey in 1934[11] was still worked in 1982. Pits were worked in the Whittington area in the late 19th and the 20th century, the last being abandoned in the late 1970s.[12] Several were worked at Iverley in the 20th century.[13]

There was a gravel pit on the site of the present Comber Ridge burial ground in Church Road in the later 18th century; disused by 1901, it was worked again by 1921. A pit south-west of the hillfort on Kinver Edge in the later 18th century was still worked in the early 20th century.[14] There was gravel working south of Checkhill Farm in the later 19th century, and it was still in progress in 1921.[15]

BRICKS. In 1671 Wortley Whorwood leased a brick kiln at Checkhill, with the right to get clay, sand, and turf there, to Richard Smallman, a brickmaker of Kinver, and his family. The lease also included land on the common on which Richard agreed to build a house.[16] The Smallmans continued to live and work at Checkhill until 1722, receiving payment for 13,000 bricks in 1674 and giving 40,000 bricks as a consideration for a new lease in 1691.[17] On the death of William Smallman in 1722 the residue of a further lease passed to his cousin William Powell of Checkhill, one of another family of brickmakers. The lease passed through various hands before being sold back to John Hodgetts of Prestwood in 1782.[18]

GLASS. The Kinver Crystal Glass Co.'s works in Fairfield Drive south of Stone Lane was opened in 1978.[19]

LOCAL GOVERNMENT. From the 13th century Kinver manor was divided between the borough and the foreign. Three sub-manors also developed. By 1622 the parish formed a single constablewick divided into seven areas: Kinver town, Kinver Hill, Stourton, Halfcot, Dunsley, Whittington, and Compton. The manor court

ordered that two men from the town and one from each of the other townships were to receive officials' accounts that year.[20] The same seven divisions were shown in the hearth tax assessment of 1666.[21] By the 1780s Kinver Hill had disappeared and Iverley had appeared; from 1806 the Hyde formed an eighth division. From 1830 the Hyde was joined with Stourton, and Dunsley with Halfcot.[22] By the mid 19th century the six divisions had become four, Kinver, Stourton with the Hyde, Whittington, and Compton.[23]

BOROUGH. About 1270 the lord of Kinver manor granted his burgesses at Kinver the same liberties as the burgesses of Kidderminster, but the only rights detailed in his charter were economic privileges.[24] By 1293 the lord of the manor held a separate borough court, called the hundred of Kinver until 1432; a great hundred was held in the spring and autumn by the 1420s. The rolls surviving from 1422 show that the borough courts, great and small, were normally held with the foreign courts. After the 15th century there are few instances of the holding of the small court. As with the foreign the spring court ceased in the 1750s. The autumn court continued to be held with the foreign court until 1906; it was discontinued in 1907.[25]

There was a bailiff of the borough by 1293. By 1422 a bailiff and two tasters were elected at the autumn court, a practice which continued until 1906. The bailiff was styled the high bailiff from 1808. A town crier was appointed at the court from 1877.[26] In 1592 the court ordered that borough officials should present their accounts to the bailiff 'and others appointed for receiving thereof' within two months of going out of office.[27] The bailiff's office evidently rotated among certain property holders. In September 1626 John Eaton of London was chosen in respect of a house occupied by Richard Wolverley; the following March the court ordered Wolverley to serve for the rest of the term, Eaton being unable to do so since he was 'the king's servant and a trained soldier'.[28]

A town hall was built in 1619 in High Street south of its junction with the lane later called Vicarage Drive.[29] It was taken down *c.* 1825 and its timber frame re-erected near Barratt's

[9] S.R.O., Tp. 1273/10, deed of 6 Feb. 1797.
[10] Scott, *Stourbridge*, 182; O.S. Map 6″, Staffs. LXX. SE. (1888, 1903, 1925 edns.); LXXI. NW. (1887, 1903, 1925 edns.), SW. (1888, 1903, 1925 edns.); H.W.R.O. (H.), E 12/S, Prestwood leases, draft deed of 1858; Prestwood sales, rep. on part of estate 1905 and letters from H. T. F. King and C. W. Roberts to P. H. Foley 22 and 24 Oct. 1917.
[11] Inf. from Staffs. C.C. Planning Dept.; T. H. Whitehead and R. W. Pocock, *Memoirs of Geol. Surv., Dudley and Bridgnorth*, 153.
[12] O.S. Map 6″, Staffs. LXX. SE. (1888, 1903, 1925 edns.); LXXIV. NE. (1903 edn.); Whitehead and Pocock, *Dudley and Bridgnorth*, 150; inf. from Mr. J. W. King.
[13] O.S. Map 6″, Staffs. LXXV. NW. (1925 edn.), with the 1903 edn. showing 2 pits on the Worcs. side of the boundary; O.S. Map 1/2,500, SO 88 (1961 edn.); Whitehead and Pocock, *Dudley and Bridgnorth*, 150, 181.
[14] S.R.O., Q/RDc 36; O.S. Map 6″, Staffs. LXX. NW. (1888, 1903, 1925 edns.).
[15] O.S. Map 6″, Staffs. LXX. NE. (1889, 1903, 1925 edns.).
[16] H.W.R.O. (H.), E 12/S, Whorwood inheritance, deed of 23 Feb. 1670/1.

[17] Ibid. Checkhill I, deed of 14 Apr. 1691; Checkhill III, acct. 25 July 1674; Stourton III, deed of 26 Mar. 1705.
[18] Ibid. Checkhill I, will of Wm. Smallman 25 July 1722; Checkhill III, deeds of 26 Sept. 1730, 22 Feb. 1744/5, 1 May 1747, 24 Apr. 1782.
[19] Inf. from Mr. D. M. Bills.
[20] H.W.R.O. (H.), E 12/S, Kinver ct. rolls 1590–1629, foreign ct. of 21 Oct. 1622. For Kingsley, a detached part of the manor in Tettenhall, see above, Tettenhall.
[21] *S.H.C.* 1923, 106–10.
[22] S.R.O., D. 1197/4/1 and 2; D. 1197/5/1.
[23] L.J.R.O., B/A/15/Kinver, 3rd sched.
[24] Above, econ. hist.
[25] P.R.O., SC 6/202/64; H.W.R.O. (H.), E 12/S, Kinver ct. rolls; ibid. Kinver boro. ct. bks. 1763–1840, 1841–1906.
[26] See refs. in preceding note.
[27] H.W.R.O. (H.), E 12/S, Kinver ct. rolls 1590–1629, ct. of 18 Sept. 1592.
[28] Ibid. cts. of 26 Sept. 1626, 27 Mar. 1627.
[29] Ibid. cts. of 19 Oct. 1619, 21 Oct. 1622.

Coppice south of the Stourbridge road.[30] Nothing further is known of it. In 1460 the borough court fined a group of men for breaking the gumblestool and the pillory.[31]

MANORIAL GOVERNMENT. By the mid 1250s the lord of Kinver had a free court and view of frankpledge.[32] In 1293 he claimed two free courts a year.[33] A three-weekly court was held in June and July that year while the manor was in the king's hands.[34] There was mention of the twice-yearly court in 1315,[35] and record survives of a meeting of the great court in October 1388 and meetings of the small court in November and December 1407.[36] Court rolls survive, with gaps, from 1422 and show great courts regularly held in the spring and autumn with intermediate small courts of varying frequency.[37] The duty of suit every three weeks was mentioned several times in the mid 15th century.[38] The spring court ceased in the 1750s,[39] but an October court continued until 1918, although by then there had long ceased to be any business. Separate small courts (or courts baron) continued until December 1860, and special courts baron were held in February 1888 and February 1889. Surrenders and admissions took place before the steward of the manor in the offices of Bernard, King & Sons, a firm of Stourbridge solicitors, until 1920.[40]

In the later 17th century the town hall in the borough seems to have been the usual meeting place of the manor court. A court of November 1681, however, met at Stourton, one of April 1700 at Halfcot, and another of July 1734 at Stourton. From 1740 the meeting place was frequently stated to be a dwelling house or an inn, notably the Stewponey.[41] From 1818 to 1918 the White Hart in High Street was the normal meeting place, although the Stewponey was used in 1822 and 1836.[42]

A reeve was elected at a small court in 1293 while the manor was in the king's hands.[43] By the 15th century he was normally appointed at the October great court, and elections were recorded until 1749.[44] The person chosen was sometimes stated to be serving in respect of certain property; in 1745 William Foley, the lord of Kinver, was appointed in respect of land bought from Edward Oliver.[45] A woman was elected in 1681 and 1708.[46]

A beadle was elected at a small court in 1293,[47] but by the 15th century he was normally chosen at the October great court.[48] His election had ceased to be recorded by the late 16th century, although a beadle continued to be appointed; he was styled a bailiff from the later 19th century.[49]

The lord of Kinver claimed assize of bread and ale in 1293, and two tasters were elected for the manor in June that year.[50] Two were regularly appointed at the October great court by the 15th century and were last recorded for the foreign in 1713.[51]

The election of a constable was recorded at the October great court for the foreign in 1422, 1434, and 1441, and the appointment was recorded annually in surviving court rolls from 1446. From 1457 the constable was sometimes appointed at the borough court.[52] By the late 16th century it had become the custom for the foreign to appoint two years out of three and the borough one, a practice which continued evidently until the late 1830s. The borough then began to appoint more frequently and from 1843 made the appointment every year until the discontinuance of its court in 1907. Between 1614 and 1621 the court not appointing the constable appointed a tithingman. Between 1826 and 1841 one or two deputy constables were normally appointed by the borough. In October 1619 Thomas Bate was granted exemption from ever serving as constable in consideration of his having contributed 20s. towards the building of the town hall.[53]

The lord of Kinver claimed gallows, pillory, and infangthief in 1293.[54] Gallowstree hill west of Potter's Cross was mentioned in 1650.[55] The name Gallowstree Elm was used for land north of Potter's Cross and had given its name to that area by the mid 19th century.[56]

In 1634 sheep found grazing in Checkhill coppice were put in the common pound of Kinver.[57] It stood in Mill Lane, still its site in the 19th century.[58] In 1730 it was stated in the manor court to be out of repair and to be the lord's responsibility.[59] In 1837, however, the vestry

[30] Pitt, *Staffs.* i. 196; W. Pinnock, *Hist. and Topog. of Staffs.* (1823), 46; Scott, *Stourbridge*, 170.
[31] H.W.R.O. (H.), E 12/S, Kinver ct. rolls 1387–1498, bdle. 25, ct. of 7 Jan. 1459/60.
[32] *S.H.C.* v (1), 116.
[33] *S.H.C.* vi (1), 241.   [34] P.R.O., SC 6/202/64.
[35] Above, manors and other estates (Compton Hallows).
[36] H.W.R.O. (H.), E 12/S, Kinver ct. rolls 1387–1498, copies of ct. rolls; Salop. R.O. 1781/2/337 (ref. supplied by Mr. J. W. King).
[37] In H.W.R.O. (H.), E 12/S. The main gap is from 1498 to 1590.
[38] Ibid. Kinver ct. rolls 1387–1498, bdle. 13, ct. of 6 Oct. 1438; bdle. 14, cts. of 28 Dec. 1439, 29 Feb. 1439/40; bdle. 26, ct. of 18 May 1461.
[39] The last recorded was on 18 Apr. 1750: ibid. Kinver ct. papers 17th and 18th cents.
[40] Ibid. Kinver and Compton Hallows ct. bk. 1888–1920.
[41] Ibid. Kinver ct. rolls 17th and 18th cents. (from Oct. 1662); Kinver ct. rolls 1681–1702; Kinver, Compton Hallows, and Kingsley ct. bk. 1734–61; Kinver and Kingsley ct. bk. 1767–1801; S.R.O., D. 695/1/40/1.
[42] H.W.R.O. (H.), E 12/S, Kinver and Compton Hallows ct. bks. 1800–1920.   [43] P.R.O., SC 6/202/64.
[44] H.W.R.O. (H.), E 12/S, Kinver ct. rolls 1387–1498; Kinver ct. papers 17th and 18th cents.

[45] Ibid. Kinver ct. rolls 1387–1498, bdle. 24, ct. of 5 Oct. 1457; 1681–1702, ct. of 21 Oct. 1686; Kinver ct. papers 17th and 18th cents., cts. of 26 Oct. 1726, 28 Oct. 1730, 16 Oct. 1745.
[46] Ibid. Kinver ct. papers 17th and 18th cents., cts. of 20 Oct. 1681, 26 Oct. 1708.
[47] P.R.O., SC 6/202/64.
[48] H.W.R.O. (H.), E 12/S, Kinver ct. rolls 1387–1498.
[49] Ibid. Kinver ct. rolls 1590–1629, cts. of 12 Oct. 1613, 5 May, 21 Oct. 1628, 20 Oct. 1629; Kinver etc. ct. bks. 1734–1920.
[50] P.R.O., SC 6/202/64.
[51] H.W.R.O. (H.), E 12/S, Kinver ct. rolls 1387–1498; Kinver ct. rolls 17th and 18th cents.
[52] Ibid. Kinver ct. rolls 1387–1498.
[53] Ibid. Kinver ct. rolls 1590–1629; Kinver ct. rolls 17th and 18th cents.; Kinver boro. ct. bks. 1763–1840, 1841–1906.
[54] *S.H.C.* vi (1), 257.
[55] H.W.R.O. (H.), E 12/S, Compton I, deed of 7 July 1650.
[56] L.J.R.O., B/A/15/Kinver, nos. 771, 788; P.R.O., HO 107/2017.
[57] S.R.O., Tp. 1273/6, exemplification of verdict 1634.
[58] H.W.R.O. (H.), E 12/S, Kinver VII, deed of 18 May 1648; S.R.O., D. 891/4, p. 54.
[59] H.W.R.O. (H.), E 12/S, Kinver ct. papers 17th and 18th cents., ct. of 25 Apr. 1730.

ordered its repair with the cost allowed in the accounts of the highway surveyors. In 1853 the vestry ordered the surveyors to appoint a pinner.[60]

A court was held for Horewood (later Compton Hallows) manor by 1294 when pleas and perquisites were valued at 5s. a year.[61] Although in 1346 it was stated that there were no pleas and perquisites,[62] a court baron was held at Horewood in 1363.[63] Records survive of courts in 1492, 1504, and 1510 and (with gaps) from 1559 to 1575.[64] Early in the 17th century Compton Hallows was described as 'an obscure manor within which there has been no court baron holden for many years past'.[65] Although the lord of Compton was usually the lord of Kinver from the late 16th century, separate courts baron were again held for Compton at varying intervals from 1610 until at least 1800.[66] About that time the Foleys sold all their land in Compton.[67] From 1806 the name Kinver and Compton Hallows was used for the nominally joint manors.[68] The Compton court was held somewhere within the manor in 1633 and 1635 and at Compton Hall in 1647. Earlier in 1647 and in 1657 it was held at Kinver, which was again given as the meeting place in 1755, 1764, and 1765. The last recorded courts, in 1791 and 1800, were held at the Stewponey inn.[69] A pound keeper for Compton manor was mentioned in 1569.[70]

Records survive of a court baron held by the Greys for the manor of Whittington at intervals between 1618 and 1705.[71] No court records are known for Dunsley manor.

PARISH GOVERNMENT. The Kinver churchwardens were mentioned in 1498,[72] and there were two in 1553.[73] In 1830 it was stated that they were appointed alternately by the minister and the parishioners.[74] In the earlier 18th century the parish clerk received, in addition to fees, £2 9s. a year from the churchwardens, 2d. from every householder, and 4d. from everyone keeping a plough.[75] In 1830 his salary was £8 8s. and he was appointed by the minister.[76] There was a nobbler by 1743, receiving 2s. 6d. a quarter; by 1799 he received 3s. 9d.[77] In the 1880s his office of rousing sleepers during the sermon was performed by the beadle, who also acted as sexton.[78]

There were two overseers of the poor in the 18th century and three in 1831.[79] Three houses in

Swan Lane, later Vicarage Drive, were leased to the parish in 1739 for 21 years and converted into a workhouse.[80] By 1830 the workhouse was at the foot of Church Hill adjoining the house known in 1982 as Clifford Cottage.[81] By 1758 there was a parish house at Whittington.[82] It had presumably been formed out of three cottages on the south side of Horse Bridge Lane which had been sold to trustees by Mary Newey in 1717 and which formed the endowment of a charity for the poor. By 1812 the cottages had been converted into five dwellings known as the almshouses and let to poor persons rent free.[83] In 1830 they were occupied by three men and two women; two of the holdings included nailshops.[84] There were still five so-called almshouses in 1861; in 1871 they were described as parish houses and only four were occupied.[85] In 1906 there were only four houses, evidently no longer used as poorhouses.[86] In 1835 the vestry gave permission for a pauper to move into a house owned by the parish at the Rock, probably Holy Austin Rock, and in 1836 it ordered the repair of houses at the Rock.[87] In the 1750s and in 1786 the vestry appointed a surgeon to provide medical care for the poor.[88]

The manor court continued to exercise control over parish affairs into the 18th century. In 1592 it ordered the constable, churchwardens, highway surveyors, 'and all other officers within this manor' to present their accounts within 40 days of leaving office and at the same time to hand over any money in their keeping. Similar orders continued until the early 1620s and fines were imposed on defaulters. In 1623 the court left the constable or churchwardens to fix the time and place for accounting and to issue the summons.[89] The two highway surveyors were frequently presented in the borough and foreign courts in the 17th and earlier 18th century for failing to maintain roads.[90] By the 1740s, however, the vestry was passing the churchwardens' accounts and administering poor relief.[91]

Kinver became part of Seisdon poor-law union in 1836.[92] It was in Seisdon rural district until 1974 when it became part of South Staffordshire district.[93]

PUBLIC SERVICES. The Giant's Well near the junction of Compton Road and Stone Lane provided a water supply for many centuries; so

[60] W.S.L., notes on Kinver par., notes from vestry min. bk.

[61] S.H.C. 1911, 222.   [62] Ibid. 1913, 114.

[63] Salop. R.O. 1781/2/336 (ref. supplied by Mr. J. W. King).

[64] Ibid. 338; H.W.R.O. (H.), E 12/S, Compton Hallows ct. rolls.   [65] P.R.O., REQ 2/404/10.

[66] H.W.R.O. (H.), E 12/S, Compton Hallows ct. rolls; Kinver ct. rolls 1590–1629, cts. of 1610; Kinver, Compton Hallows, and Kingsley ct. bk. 1734–61; Kinver and Kingsley ct. bk. 1767–1801.

[67] Above, manors and other estates.

[68] H.W.R.O. (H.), E 12/S, Kinver and Compton Hallows ct. bk. 1800–36.

[69] Ibid. Compton Hallows ct. rolls; S.R.O., D. 801/2/1.

[70] H.W.R.O. (H.), E 12/S, Compton Hallows ct. rolls.

[71] S.R.O., Tp. 1273/12.

[72] H.W.R.O. (H.), E 12/S, Kinver I, deed of 30 Aug. 1498.

[73] S.H.C. 1915, 141.

[74] S.H.C. 4th ser. x. 15.

[75] L.J.R.O., B/V/6/Kinver.

[76] S.H.C. 4th ser. x. 15.

[77] S.R.O., D. 1197/4/1.

[78] N. Price, Into an Hour-glass, 44.

[79] S.R.O., D. 1197/4/1 and 7.

[80] S.R.O., D. 1197/4/1; D. 1197/5/31.

[81] S.R.O., D. 891/3, no. 907; ibid. 4, p. 36; inf. from Mr. J. W. King.   [82] S.R.O., D. 1197/4/1.

[83] S.R.O., D. 1197/5/2; below, charities for the poor.

[84] S.R.O., D. 891/3, no. 1183; ibid. 4, p. 76.

[85] P.R.O., RG 9/1985; RG 10/2928.

[86] Staffs. Endowed Chars. 76–7.

[87] W.S.L., notes on Kinver par., extracts from vestry min. bk. 21 Nov. 1835, 30 July 1836.

[88] S.R.O., D. 1197/4/1.

[89] H.W.R.O. (H.), E 12/S, Kinver ct. rolls 1590–1629, cts. of 18 Sept. 1592, 16 Apr., 1 Oct. 1610, 5 Oct. 1618, 13 Apr. 1619, 21 Oct. 1622, 21 Apr., 13 Oct. 1623.

[90] Ibid. cts. of e.g. 5 Oct. 1618, 11 Oct. 1625; Kinver ct. papers 17th and 18th cents.   [91] S.R.O., D. 1197/4/1.

[92] 3rd Ann. Rep. Poor Law Com. H.C. 546, p. 164 (1837), xxxi.

[93] O.S. Map 1/100,000, Staffs. Admin. Areas (1967 and 1974 edns.).

named by 1774, it survived until the Heath Drive estate was built in 1956.[94] In the early 17th century there was a public washing place called Lady Well pool near Pigeonhouse Farm in Compton.[95] In the early 19th century there was a public watering place at the Hole on the Wolverhampton–Kidderminster road north of Whittington.[96] A cistern, probably of the 19th century, still stands at the junction of Bannut Tree Road and Sheepwalks Lane in Compton. In 1900 the medical officer of health for Seisdon rural district reported that many people in Kinver dared not use their wells. Between 1898 and 1901 water from 14 wells in the parish was analysed; six, all in Kinver High Street, were found to be polluted. In 1902 the medical officer stressed that the matter was serious because of the thousands of visitors who came to Kinver each year.[97] In 1901 the Stourbridge Water Works Co. (from 1909 the Stourbridge and District Water Board) agreed to lay pipes to supply Iverley.[98] In 1908 Seisdon rural district council opened a water works in Mill Lane, and by 1912 nearly all the houses in Kinver village had mains water. Mains were laid to Dunsley in 1914 and to Whittington in 1918.[99] A new works was opened north of the 1908 works in 1939.[1] Prestwood water works in Gothersley Lane is dated 1926.

Stourbridge Main Drainage Board opened a 129-a. sewage works in Whittington Hall Lane in 1884; by 1899 its Whittington sewage farm covered c. 250 a., and it bought another 44 a. in 1908.[2] The Upper Stour Valley Main Sewerage Board opened the 650-a. Whittington Hall sewage farm to the west and south-west in 1898.[3] In the early 20th century Kingswinford rural district council opened a works on Round Hill farm north of the Stourbridge Board's farm despite local opposition. P. H. Foley objected that the works would cut his estate in two. Kinver parish council objected that one tenth of the parish was already taken up for outsiders' sewage.[4] None of the works served Kinver itself, which by the late 1890s badly needed drainage. In 1914 the rural district council built the present sewage works between the canal and the Stour south of Windsor Holloway. The connexion of house drains with the sewerage system was delayed by the First

World War but was completed in 1921.[5] At Round Hill a new works was built north of Gibbet Lane in the 1960s.[6]

In 1849 the vestry ordered two of three cottages on the corner of High Street and Vicarage Drive to be converted into a temporary hospital in case of a cholera outbreak.[7] There was a cottage hospital for infectious diseases at Potter's Cross by 1880, serving Seisdon union; it was closed in 1895 shortly after the opening of an isolation hospital at the Bratch, in Wombourne.[8] Edge View in Comber Road had been taken over as a sanatorium for men by the Staffordshire, Wolverhampton, and Dudley Joint Committee for Tuberculosis by 1920; from the early 1970s it was used as a home for spastic children.[9]

The cemetery at the west end of Church Road was opened in 1980.[10]

The Kinver Gas Light Co. opened a works in the early 1860s on the south side of the canal east of Mill Lane. Gas was made there until 1917 when the company was merged with the Brierley Hill Gas Co.; gas was then supplied from Brierley Hill and later from Dudley. The holder was rebuilt in 1923, and a second was added later to meet increasing demand in the area. Both were demolished c. 1970.[11]

In 1592 the borough court ordered every burgess to keep 16 staves in his house, and in 1619 it ordered every householder in the borough to keep a club at least 6 ft. long for the assistance of the king's officers.[12] The churchwardens paid 2s. 6d. for a pair of handcuffs in 1756–7.[13] A curfew was rung from October to March by the later 1820s, and it continued until the outbreak of the Second World War in 1939.[14] There was a police officer living in High Street in 1851 and in Mill Lane in 1861. By 1871 a house in High Street was occupied by a sergeant and a constable.[15] In the late 19th century a rented house 'in an exceedingly out of the way part of the village' was used as a police station; it had accommodation for a sergeant and a constable with a lock-up which was 'nothing more than a cupboard'.[16] In the earlier 1890s property in Mill Lane was bought and converted into a station.[17] A new station was opened at the north end of High Street in 1908 and rebuilt in 1968.[18]

[94] Plaque on drinking fountain at junction of Compton Rd. and Heather Drive; S.R.O., Q/RDc 36.
[95] H.W.R.O. (H.), E 12/S, Kinver ct. rolls 1590–1629, cts. of 11 Apr. 1614, 10 Apr. 1615. Lady Well Lane bounded a close called Wall croft on Pigeonhouse farm: deeds of 22 Oct. 1647 and 15 Oct. 1659 in the possession of Mr. T. R. Brown of Pigeonhouse Farm.
[96] S.R.O., D. 891/4, p. 102.
[97] Seisdon R.D.C. Rep. of M.O.H. for 1900, 7 (copy in S.R.O., C/H/1/2/1/11); 1901, 6 (copy in C/H/1/2/1/13); 1902, 6 (copy in C/H/1/2/1/15).
[98] H.W.R.O. (H.), E 12/S, Iverley III.
[99] Seisdon R.D.C. Rep. of M.O.H. for 1908, 7 (copy in S.R.O., C/H/1/2/1/27); 1912, 6 (copy in C/H/1/2/1/35); 1914, 5; 1918, 7 (copies in C/H/1/2/2/36).
[1] F. E. Campbell, Royal Kinver, 31 (copy in W.S.L. Pamphs.). The building is dated 1938.
[2] County Express, 18 Feb. 1899; S.R.O., Tp. 1273/35, deeds of 25 Mar. 1885, 23 Dec. 1908; O.S. Map 6″, Staffs. LXX. SE. (1903 edn.).
[3] County Express, 18 Feb. 1899; O.S. Map 6″, Staffs. LXX. SE. (1903 edn.); LXXIV. NE. (1903 edn.).
[4] County Express, 18 Feb., 17 June 1899; 9 Aug. 1913; H.W.R.O. (H.), E 12/S, Prestwood sales, notes on Prestwood 1905.

[5] Seisdon R.D.C. Rep. of M.O.H. for 1898, 7 (copy in S.R.O., C/H/1/2/1/9); 1914, 5; 1918, 5; 1921, 7; 1925, 9 (copies in C/H/1/2/2/36); O.S. Map 6″, Staffs. LXXIV. NE. (1925 edn.).
[6] Express & Star, 24 Jan. 1960.
[7] W.S.L., notes on Kinver par., extracts from vestry min. bk.
[8] Kelly's Dir. Staffs. (1880); Seisdon R.D.C. Rep. of M.O.H. for 1895, 7 (copy in S.R.O., C/H/1/2/1/6); below, Wombourne.
[9] Seisdon R.D.C. Rep. of M.O.H. for 1920, 5; 1923, 6–7 (copies in S.R.O., C/H/1/2/2/36); inf. from Mr. D. M. Bills.
[10] Below, church.
[11] Campbell, Royal Kinver, 31–2; S.R.O., D. 3579/1/1, 12 Nov., 13 Dec. 1860; inf. from Mr. Bills.
[12] H.W.R.O. (H.), E 12/S, Kinver ct. rolls 1590–1629, cts. of 20 Mar. 1591/2, 19 Oct. 1619.
[13] S.R.O., D. 1197/4/1.
[14] Ibid. 4/2; T. S. Jennings, Hist. of Staffs. Bells. 8; N. Price, Into an Hour-glass, 45.
[15] P.R.O., HO 107/2017; P.R.O., RG 9/1985 and 2928.
[16] S.R.O., C/PC/VIII/2/3, p. 207.
[17] Ibid. pp. 214, 217, 249, 306; inf. from Mr. Bills.
[18] Inf. from Mr. Bills; Express & Star, 11 Oct. 1968.

In the 17th century the courts of the borough and the foreign concerned themselves with precautions against fire. The borough court was particularly active. In 1620 it appointed two inspectors to check every house in the borough for fire risks,[19] and in the later 17th century it made orders against dangerous chimneys and the storage of combustible materials.[20] In 1672 it found William Tyrer's nailshop 'very dangerous for fire' and ordered him to remove it or put it in order.[21] In 1673 the foreign court forbade John Powell and 'any of his company' to carry fire or candles into his outhouses.[22]

Kinver was served by the Stourbridge volunteer fire brigade from 1899 until 1915 when it formed its own volunteer brigade with a station in Mill Lane adjoining the pumping station. The brigade was presented with its first motor fire engine by the Stourbridge brigade in 1936. The engine was replaced in 1938 with a Lanchester limousine given by H. J. Folkes of Stourton Hall; the cost of conversion was met from the surplus of money collected for the coronation celebrations in 1937. Early in the Second World War the cinema in High Street was turned into the central fire station. In 1948 a temporary station was built in the Acre on the south side of High Street and the part-time brigade, replaced during the war, was restored. A new station was opened in Fairfield Drive in 1957 with a full-time resident fireman. In 1980, with reductions in public spending, the service became part-time again.[23]

In 1818 Edward Green, a wheelwright of Kinver, was organizing a daily 'bye post' to Stourbridge.[24] In the earlier 1830s Benjamin Fieldhouse, keeper of the White Hart and a carrier, took letters to and from Stourbridge each day.[25] By the mid 1840s James Bennett was running a post office in Kinver to which letters were brought from Stourbridge by foot post in the morning and from which they were dispatched in the late afternoon.[26] There was a post office at Stourton also by 1861.[27] In 1908 the Kinver village post and telegraph office moved from no. 33 High Street to no. 28, and later a telephone exchange was installed there. In 1960 an automatic exchange was built at Dunsley, and the post office moved to the opposite side of High Street, where it remained in 1982.[28]

CHURCH. The presence of a priest at Kinver in 1086[29] indicates the existence of a church. By the time of Richard I the patronage was held by the Crown. In 1228 Henry III recognized that it had been granted by King John to Philip son of Helgot as an appurtenance of the manor and that Philip's son John was the patron.[30] The patronage descended with the manor to John's son John.[31] His right was challenged by the Crown in 1293, and when he was granted the manor for life that year the advowson was withheld.[32] The Crown presented in 1324 and continued to do so until the 1360s.[33] In 1363 the king granted the advowson to the Cistercian abbey of Bordesley (Worcs.) with licence to appropriate the church.[34] The licence was renewed in 1380, and the same year Bishop Stretton appropriated the church to Bordesley, stipulating that on the cession or death of the existing rector the church was to be served by a chaplain removable at the will of the abbot.[35] The abbey granted pensions of 6s. 8d. each to the bishop and to the chapters of Lichfield and of Coventry; the pensions were still paid to the bishop and the dean and chapter of Lichfield by the Foley family as the impropriators in 1806.[36] The appropriation had become effective by 1390.[37] Despite the new arrangements the Crown presented twice in 1403,[38] and in 1423 it sued the abbot for the next presentation.[39] The appropriation was confirmed by Bishop Smith in 1492.[40]

Bordesley abbey was surrendered to the Crown in 1538, and in 1543 the king granted Kinver church to William Whorwood, and the right of nominating a curate then descended with the rectory until 1630. The lease of part of the tithes secured that year from John Whorwood by the Feoffees for the Purchase of Impropriations included the right to nominate the curate. It was considered to be held in trust for the parishioners, who exercised it several times in the mid 17th century. In July 1662, however, William and Catherine Hamerton, lords of Kinver manor, described themselves as true patrons and conveyed what they called 'the next advowson' to William Talbot of Whittington Hall; similarly Wortley Whorwood conveyed the advowson with the manor and part of the rectory to Philip Foley in 1672. Meanwhile, in the autumn of 1662, the curacy being vacant after the ejection of William Moreton, some 20 leading parishioners met at William Talbot's home and nominated Jonathan Newey. When Newey died in 1716, a dispute arose between the Foleys and the parishioners, both sides claiming the right to appoint a successor. Rival candidates were nominated. In 1721, after two Chancery decrees

[19] H.W.R.O. (H.), E 12/S, Kinver ct. rolls 1590–1629, ct. of 12 Apr. 1620.
[20] Ibid. Kinver ct. papers 17th and 18th cents., cts. of e.g. 16 Oct. 1662, 18 Apr. 1665, 10 and 22 Apr. 1671, 10 Apr. 1676, 3 May 1686.
[21] Ibid. ct. of 22 Apr. 1672.
[22] Ibid. ct. of 14 Apr. 1673.
[23] R. Benbow, 'Story of Kinver Volunteer Fire Brigade' (TS. in Kinver Libr.); D. M. Bills and W. R. Griffiths, Kinver, 9.
[24] Parson and Bradshaw, Dir. Staffs. (1818).
[25] White, Dir. Staffs. (1834), 263; Pigot, Nat. Com. Dir. (1835), 654.
[26] P.O. Dir. Staffs. (1845).
[27] P.R.O., RG 9/1985.
[28] D. M. Bills, A House in Kinver High St. (copy in W.S.L. Pamphs.).

[29] V.C.H. Staffs. iv. 40.
[30] Pat. R. 1225-32, 176.
[31] S.H.C. v (1), 116.
[32] Abbrev. Rot. Orig. (Rec. Com.), i. 78.
[33] Cal. Pat. 1324-7, 36, 124, 190; 1327-30, 169, 174; 1334-8, 98; 1348-50, 354; 1361-4, 54, 125.
[34] Ibid. 1361-4, 438; 1377-81, 435.
[35] Ibid. 1377-81, 435; S.H.C. N.S. viii. 141; N.S. x (2), 148; P.R.O., E 326/B 9008.
[36] P.R.O., E 42/411; E 326/B 6655; Cat. Anct. D. i, B 1713; Valor Eccl. (Rec. Com.), iii. 273; P.R.O., SC 6/Hen. VIII/ 3737, m. 53; H.W.R.O. (H.), E 12/S, Stourton VI, receipts of 1627 and 1640; ibid. Foley Fam. I, receipts 1806-7.
[37] P.R.O., E 326/B 9001.
[38] Cal. Pat. 1401-5, 207, 217.
[39] P.R.O., E 328/36; S.H.C. N.S. iii. 123.
[40] P.R.O., E 326/B 9078.

in favour of the parishioners, the House of Lords ordered the right to be vested in 13 trustees appointed by Chancery, the same number as in 1630. The Lords also recommended that the parishioners' candidate Richard Bate, the master of the grammar school, should be nominated, directing that he should officiate in the meantime. The trustees were appointed in 1723 and duly nominated Bate in 1724.[41] The curacy was called a perpetual curacy from the later 18th century and a vicarage from the early 1860s.[42] The patronage remained with trustees until 1935 when it was transferred to the Lichfield Diocesan Board of Patronage, still the patron in 1981.[43]

In the mid 1250s the church was worth 20 marks a year, and it was valued at £8 in 1291.[44] The curate's stipend in 1604 was £10.[45] In 1630 he was assigned £10 a year from the rent due for the tithes to the Feoffees for the Purchase of Impropriations. An annual £33 6s. 8d. was assigned to a lecturer who was to be allowed to act as curate also if he wished.[46] After the next vacancy, in the later 1630s, it evidently became normal for the two offices to be combined.[47] The curate thereby enjoyed in addition the proceeds of a bequest made by William Moseley, a citizen and leatherseller of London, who by his will proved in 1617 settled £200 on the Leathersellers' Company to be invested in land; two thirds of the rents were to be paid to a preacher who was to give a sermon in Kinver church every Sunday, and the rest was to go to the schoolmaster. Land was bought in 1627.[48] In 1646, however, the minister's income was only £40 a year, and the committee for plundered ministers granted him an augmentation of £70 from the property of the dean and chapter of Lichfield. In 1652 the committee granted £25 a year from the impropriated tithes of Penkridge. In 1655 the augmentation was reduced to £10 a year.[49] By 1699 the curate received the £43 6s. 8d. from the tithes and £6 13s. 4d. from the Leathersellers' Company. A house in Wapping (Mdx.) had been given for his maintenance some years before by the widow of a Dr. Whitchcote, but the income was small and uncertain; in 1732 it was £7 10s. By the early 19th century the gift was represented by a house in Shadwell (Mdx.). By will proved 1715 Edward Barton of London gave £30 a year to the curate.[50] Several curates also acted as school-

master between 1563 and the 1720s.[51] In 1812 a grant of £600 was made from Queen Anne's Bounty to meet a benefaction.[52] The curate's average income c. 1830 was £140 net.[53] In 1872 and 1873 the Ecclesiastical Commissioners made two grants of £100 to meet benefactions.[54] The payment from the Leathersellers' Company, which had risen to £30 by 1841,[55] was augmented by a bequest of £1,000 from John Hodgson, vicar from 1867 until his death in 1901; nine tenths of the income was to be paid to the preacher.[56]

There was a rectory house in 1370 when the rector was granted licence for an oratory there.[57] About the mid 17th century, since the minister then had no house, the parishioners and others of the neighbourhood bought an old house at the junction of High Street and the later Vicarage Drive and repaired it for him.[58] It had been leased out by the earlier 1770s; by the early 19th century it had been divided into three cottages, and it was conveyed as the site for a National school in 1851.[59] A vicarage house was built c. 1870 at the western end of Vicarage Drive.[60] It still stood in 1981 but had been replaced in 1957 by a new house on a nearby site.[61]

Mention in 1387 of the chamber of St. Mary[62] may indicate the existence of a chantry of St. Mary by then. There was a warden of St. Mary in 1454, and a house belonging to St. Mary was mentioned in 1457.[63] John Hampton, lord of Kinver, by his will of 1472 left money to a chaplain celebrating at the altar of St. Mary in Kinver church,[64] probably in the south chancel aisle. In 1514 John Perot assigned to the chantry the income from land in Kinver for 90 years; after that the money was to be used 'in the maintenance of God's service' and other charitable works. More land was later given by other people. In 1535 the chantry's income was £8 10s. and in 1546 £5 16s. 5d. net. The priest's stipend in 1546 was £4 19s. 5d., and he was also provided with a house.[65] In 1548 William Pole, the last chantry priest, was given a pension of £2 13s. 4d., and he may have become vicar of Chebsey in 1558.[66]

By 1328 there was a lamp before an image of St. Peter in the church endowed with a rent of 6d.[67] In 1472 John Hampton left 20d. to 'the high light before the cross' in the church and 6s. 8d. to the light of St. Mary.[68] By the Reformation there was

[41] S.R.O., D. 1197/13/17, printed copy of appellant's and respondents' cases 1721; L.J. xxi. 597, 617; L.J.R.O., B/A/3/Kinver, 1718, 1724; H.W.R.O. (H.), E 12/S, Kinver III, deed of 1 July 1662 and account of the dispute 1719; Kinver VI, bill in Chancery 26 Nov. 1716; P.R.O., CP 25(2)/725, 24 Chas. II Trin. no. 12; above, manors and other estates (rectory).

[42] L.J.R.O., B/A/3/Kinver, 1759, 1779; Lich. Dioc. Ch. Cal. (1861).

[43] Lich. Dioc. Regy., Reg. of Transfer of Patronage, f. 86; Lich. Dioc. Dir. (1982).

[44] S.H.C. v (1), 116; Tax. Eccl. (Rec. Com.), 243.

[45] S.H.C. 1915, 143.

[46] Above, manors and other estates (rectory); S.R.O., D. 1197/13/17, printed copy of appellant's and respondents' cases 1721.

[47] Below (John Cross as reader); L.J.R.O., B/V/6/Kinver; 5th Rep. Com. Char. 631.

[48] P.R.O., PROB 11/130, ff. 172, 174; S.R.O., D. 1197/6/4; D. 3162/4/1.

[49] S.H.C. 1915, 143; W. A. Shaw, Hist. of Eng. Church 1640–60, ii. 505; Cal. S.P. Dom. 1657–8, 242.

[50] S.R.O., D. 1197/6/2/4A; L.J.R.O., B/V/6/Kinver, n.d.

[51] Below, educ.

[52] Hodgson, Queen Anne's Bounty, p. ccxcvii.

[53] Rep. Com. Eccl. Revenues, 485.

[54] Lond. Gaz. 26 Apr. 1872, p. 2073; 2 May 1873, p. 2180.

[55] L.J.R.O., B/V/6/Kinver, 1841.

[56] Ibid. B/C/5/Kinver, 1902.

[57] S.H.C. N.S. viii. 16.

[58] L.J.R.O., B/V/6/Kinver, 1701, 1705.

[59] Ibid., B/V/5/Kinver, 1772; B/V/6/Kinver, 1805; 5th Rep. Com. Char. 631; S.H.C. 4th ser. x. 15; W.S.L., notes on Kinver par., copy of conveyance.

[60] Lond. Gaz. 2 July 1869, p. 3754; 24 June 1870, p. 3116.

[61] Par. Church of St. Peter, Kinver (n.d., later 1970s), 13.

[62] H.W.R.O. (H.), E 12/S, Kinver ct. rolls 1387–1498, bdle. 1.

[63] Ibid., bdle. 22, ct. of 2 Oct. 1454; bdle. 24, ct. of 6 Oct. 1457.   [64] P.R.O., PROB 11/6, f. 42v.

[65] P.R.O., C 1/948, no. 38; ibid. E 301/40, no. 23; E 301/54, no. 15; Valor Eccl. (Rec. Com.), iii. 102.

[66] S.H.C. 1915, 142, 144.

[67] S.R.O., Tp. 1273/12, bk. of deeds and evidences, pp. 3–4.   [68] P.R.O., PROB 11/6, f. 42v.

a lamp endowed with a cottage and land let for 8s. a year.[69] In 1498 Thomas Taylor settled land to produce 12d. for an obit for his parents and himself.[70] In 1552 there was an obit endowed with a cow.[71]

Puritan influence was marked in the 17th century. There was a reader, John Cross, by 1620,[72] presumably supported from William Moseley's bequest of 1617. It was as a result of an approach by the people of Kinver that the puritan Feoffees for the Purchase of Impropriations intervened in 1630.[73] Cross, who was lecturing on Sunday afternoons in 1635,[74] had become curate by 1639.[75] The Samuel Smith who was curate in the earlier 1650s may have been the Presbyterian divine who was curate of Cressage, in Cound (Salop.), from 1638 to 1655.[76] Richard Moreton (1637–98) was curate from 1659 until his ejection in 1662; he then turned to medicine, eventually becoming a physician in ordinary to William III.[77]

Edward Barton, in addition to his gift to the curate in 1715, gave £20 a year to the schoolmaster provided that he helped the curate by acting as reader in the church every Sunday morning and afternoon.[78] In the earlier 1770s the curate was preaching two sermons every Sunday and reading prayers every Wednesday and Friday and on all holy days. The sacrament was administered on the first Sunday of the month and at the festivals; between 40 and 50 people received it on Sundays, and numbers were higher at the festivals. The schoolmaster was reading prayers twice on Sundays. Children were catechized from the last Sunday in April to the first Sunday in August.[79] By 1830 the curate was a non-resident pluralist and employed an assistant to serve Kinver. There were two services on Sundays and none at any other time; the sacrament was still administered every month and at the festivals.[80]

In 1837 a school-chapel was built at Halfcot by J. H. Hodgetts-Foley to provide a service every Sunday afternoon. Since the minister could not serve it without help, Foley agreed to make a regular payment to support an assistant. In 1851 the amount was £35.[81] The school closed in the 1880s, but the building was still used as a mission chapel in 1982. Known as St. Peter's chapel, it is built of pink sandstone; there is a bell dated 1837 in a frame by the south door.[82]

A parish magazine was started in the later 1880s.[83] The parish hall at the southern end of Vicarage Drive was opened in 1961.[84]

The church of ST. PETER, an invocation in use by 1472 and probably by the 14th century,[85] is built of pink sandstone with some dressings in grey stone. It consists of a chancel with side aisles, an aisled nave of four bays with a south porch, and a west tower.

Fragments of carved stone and a clasping buttress at the south-west corner of the nave survive from a late 12th-century church which appears to have been rebuilt in the earlier 14th century. Of that date are the tower, the south arcade of the nave, the wall of the south aisle with piscina and sedilia, some window glass,[86] and perhaps the roof of the nave and aisle. In the later 15th century the church was extended eastwards. A north chapel joined to the chancel by an arcade of two bays was built by John Hampton, who was buried there in 1472; his effigy survives in a damaged state. The chapel was known in 1472 as the chapel of St. Anne and St. Catherine. By 1678 it was known as the Foleys' chancel, and by the 18th century its maintenance was the responsibility of the Foleys. Fragments of original glass survive in one of its windows.[87] The extension of the chancel is probably contemporary with the chapel; beneath the east end there is a vestry of the same period approached by a stair against the south side. The south aisle was also extended eastwards by one bay and an arcade was built matching that on the north side of the chancel. The south chancel aisle contains the altar tomb of Sir Edward Grey, lord of Whittington and Enville (d. 1529), with brasses of himself, his wife, and their children.[88] Although c. 1800 the tomb was in the nave in front of the altar rails,[89] it seems originally to have been in the south chancel aisle, which was known as the Greys' chancel by the 1670s.[90] The font is of the 14th or 15th century.[91]

The pulpit dates from 1625; it stood on the north side of the nave by 1771 and was then a three-decker.[92] A gallery had been erected by Richard Willett at the west end of the church by 1696.[93] By 1708 a gallery had been erected by John Norris and John Cumber, but it had not been authorized and six parishioners petitioned for its removal.[94] There was a gallery for the grammar school by 1750.[95] A gallery was erected over the whole south nave aisle for the Hodgetts family and their tenants evidently in 1761; by 1834 another private gallery adjoined it on the

[69] S.H.C. 1915, 142.
[70] H.W.R.O. (H.), E 12/S, Kinver I, deed of 30 Aug. 1498.
[71] S.H.C. 1915, 142.
[72] Ibid. 141, 143. For a mention of the minister and deacon in 1600 see L.J.R.O., B/C/11, Eliz. Clark (1600).
[73] Above, manors and other estates (rectory).
[74] L.J.R.O., B/V/1/55, p. 7.
[75] S.R.O., D. 1197/1/1, burial of 9 Sept. 1639.
[76] S.H.C. 1915, 141, 143; below, Wombourne, church. For Smith the Presbyterian divine see D.N.B.; V.C.H. Salop. viii. 77.
[77] Calamy Revised, ed. A. G. Matthews, 357; D.N.B.
[78] S.R.O., D. 1197/6/2/4A; L.J.R.O., B/V/6/Kinver, 1732.
[79] L.J.R.O., B/V/5/1772.
[80] Rep. Com. Eccl. Revenues, 484–5; S.H.C. 4th ser. x. 15.
[81] W.S.L., Newspaper Cuttings, Kinver, unident. cutting of 4 May 1837; P.R.O., HO 129/379/2/3.
[82] For a view see above, pl. facing p. 145.
[83] The set in B.L. begins with vol. iv (Jan. 1891).

[84] Express & Star, 18 Sept. 1961.
[85] P.R.O., PROB 11/6, f. 42v.; above (lights).
[86] For the glass see T.B.A.S. lxviii. 56.
[87] Shaw, Staffs. ii. 263; T.B.A.S. lxviii. 56; lxx. 6; P.R.O., PROB 11/6, f. 42v.; S.R.O., D. 1197/1/2, burial of 13 Sept. 1678; L.J.R.O., B/V/6/Kinver, undated terrier of c. 1740.
[88] T.B.A.S. lxix. 8; Pevsner, Staffs. 165–6.
[89] Shaw, Staffs. ii. 264.
[90] S.R.O., D. 1197/1/2, burials of 14 Apr. 1676, 13 Oct. 1679. In the 18th cent., however, it was maintained by the parish: L.J.R.O., B/V/6/Kinver, undated terrier of c. 1740.
[91] Pevsner, Staffs. 164, giving it as 14th-cent.; T.B.A.S. lxviii. 19, giving it as 15th-cent.
[92] T.B.A.S. lxvii. 53; L.J.R.O., B/C/5/1771/Kinver.
[93] S.R.O., D. 801/2/2, deed of 5 May 1712; D. 1197/1/2, bur. of Ric. Willetts 31 Aug. 1696.
[94] L.J.R.O., B/C/5/1708/Kinver.
[95] S.R.O., D. 1197/4/1.

east.[96] By the end of the 18th century there were two galleries at the east end of the nave.[97] They were taken down in 1834, and the singers' gallery at the west end was rebuilt. At the same time the south porch, which evidently existed by 1771, was made into a vestry, and a north door, in existence by 1771, was blocked; a new entrance was made through the base of the tower. The architect was Josiah Griffiths of Quatford (Salop.).[98] An organ was installed, apparently in the west gallery, c. 1836.[99] A north aisle, designed by Thomas Smith of Stourbridge, was added in 1856–7. At the same time the pulpit was moved to the south side of the chancel arch; still a three-decker in 1834, it was probably at the time of the move that it was reduced to a two-decker. A vestry was formed in the south chancel aisle, with a door made in the south wall; the south porch became an entrance once more, although the entrance in the tower was retained.[1]

Sir Gilbert Scott (d. 1878) prepared a plan for restoring the church, and the work was carried out in stages by his son J. O. Scott. In 1882 the south gallery was removed. The organ, which by 1882 had been moved from the west gallery to the south chancel aisle, was moved into the east arch on the south side of the chancel; it thus became possible to enlarge the vestry. The south aisle and the porch were restored in 1884–5, and it was probably then that the font was moved from the north-west corner of the nave to a position by the south porch. The restoration was completed to mark Queen Victoria's jubilee of 1887; the work included the removal of the west gallery.[2] The box pews in the nave were removed c. 1900.[3] In 1954 H. T. H. Foley renounced all rights in the Foley chapel, which in 1956 was converted into a choir vestry.[4] In 1975–6 the north aisle, which had become unsafe, was rebuilt to the design of J. G. Smith of Kinver. At the same time the medieval nave roof, which had been covered with a wooden ceiling by 1852, was uncovered.[5]

In 1552 and 1553 the church possessed a silver chalice and paten, a copper-gilt cross, and a brass pyx.[6] In 1981 the plate included a silver chalice given by Jonathan Newey, curate 1662–1716, and his wife Mary, a silver flagon and lid given by John Cook of Stourton slitting mill in 1750, and two silver trays given by John Hodgetts in 1771.[7] There were three bells in 1552 and 1553.[8]

About 1713 the bells were recast.[9] A peal of six was cast by Abel Rudhall of Gloucester in 1746; one of them was recast by Thomas Rudhall in 1770–1 and again by John Rudhall in 1790. The peal was enlarged by two cast by Mears & Stainbank of Whitechapel, London, in 1920.[10] The church had a clock by 1745.[11]

Until 1846 the churchyard was owned by the Foleys; by 1743 the churchwardens paid 10s. a year rent for it.[12] It was enlarged in 1843, 1857, 1881, 1907, 1916, 1948, and 1957.[13] In 1980 it was replaced by Comber Ridge burial ground and garden of remembrance at the west end of Church Road.[14] Part of the churchyard north-west of the church was dedicated in 1950 as a garden of memory for those who died in the Second World War.[15] The lichgate was erected in 1922.[16] There is a scratch dial on the south wall of the church east of the porch.

The registers date from 1560.[17] The entries from 1560 to 1598 are a copy made in 1598. The registers are incomplete between 1636 and 1639 and between 1644 and 1653.

ROMAN CATHOLICISM. In 1628 the borough court ordered the landlords of Richard Cooke and William Jukes to secure from each of the two tenants 'pledges for his recusancy'.[18] William, John, and Anthony Hamerton of Dunsley Hall were listed as recusants in the later 1660s,[19] and in 1676 five papists were returned for Kinver parish.[20] In 1705 and 1706 Catherine Hamerton and her two daughters, all of Dunsley Hall, were the only papists in the parish.[21] There was stated to be none in 1767 and the earlier 1770s.[22]

In 1933 mass began to be celebrated occasionally in Kinver by a priest from the church of Our Lady and All Saints at Stourbridge, which in the late 1920s and early 1930s had provided mass once a quarter at Prestwood sanatorium just over the Kingswinford boundary. The church of St. Peter and the English Martyrs, a former National school building in the Holloway between Kinver Hill and Mill Lane, was opened in 1935. It was still served from Stourbridge in 1982.[23]

PROTESTANT NONCONFORMITY. Puritan influence was strong in Kinver by the 1620s,

[96] L.J.R.O., B/C/5/1761/Kinver; S.R.O., D. 1197/3/1/1.
[97] Shaw, Staffs. ii. 265.
[98] S.R.O., D. 1197/3/1/1, 4, 7; Staffs. Advertiser, 13 Sept. 1834; W.S.L., Staffs. Views, v. 78; L.J.R.O., B/C/5/1771/Kinver.
[99] Subscription board in vestry; S.R.O., D. 1197/3/1/1.
[1] S.R.O., D. 1197/3/6/1–3; Trans. Lichfield and S. Staffs. Arch. Soc. ii. 21, 24–5; subscription board in north aisle. For the pulpit in 1834 see D. 1197/3/1/1.
[2] L.J.R.O., B/C/5/1882/Kinver; S.R.O., D. 1197/3/10; H.W.R.O. (H.), E 12/S, Kinver XII, printed appeal notice 1887.   [3] Bennett, Kinver, 133.
[4] Lich. Dioc. Regy., B/A/2i/X, pp. 257–8; S.R.O., D. 1197/3/14.
[5] Par. Ch. of St. Peter, Kinver, 13–14; W.S.L., notes on Kinver par., extracts from vestry min. bk. 5 Aug. 1852.
[6] S.H.C. n.s. vi (1), 189; S.H.C. 1915, 141.
[7] T.B.A.S. lxxiii. 30–1, 34–5; R. Simms, Bibliotheca Staffordiensis, 327.
[8] S.H.C. n.s. vi (1), 189; S.H.C. 1915, 141.
[9] H.W.R.O. (H.), E 12/S, Kinver VI, bill in Chancery 26 Nov. 1716.
[10] Lynam, Church Bells, 17; Trans. Old Stafford Soc.

1952–3, 13; Jennings, Staffs. Bells, 84; S.R.O., D. 1197/4/1, 1770–1, 1790–1.
[11] S.R.O., D. 1197/4/1.
[12] S.R.O., D. 1197/4/1 and 2; H.W.R.O. (H.), E 12/S, vol. of 18th- and 19th-cent. plans, Kinver, no. 35; ibid. Prestwood estate surveys I; W.S.L., notes on Kinver par., extracts from vestry min. bk. 13 Apr. 1846.
[13] Lich. Dioc. Regy., B/A/2i/M, pp. 598–615; Q, pp. 23–4; S, pp. 423, 485–8; V, pp. 524–35, 577–82; X, pp. 118, 136, 315, 317–18; Orders in Council 1859–1923, pp. 417–19.
[14] Inf. from the vicar.
[15] H. Grainger, Hist. of Church of St. Peter, Kinver (1951).
[16] Plaque on gate.
[17] All except those in current use are in S.R.O., D. 1197/1.
[18] H.W.R.O.(H.), E 12/S, Kinver ct. rolls 1590–1629, ct. of 5 May 1628. A threat of removal was made in the case of Jukes.
[19] L.J.R.O., B/V/1/72, p. 42; Cath. Rec. Soc. vi. 310.
[20] W.S.L., S.MS. 33, p. 371; Staffs. Cath. Hist. xviii. 14.
[21] Staffs. Cath. Hist. xiii. 28–9, wrongly giving their home as Dursley (instead of Dunsley) Hall.
[22] Ibid. xvii. 26; L.J.R.O., B/V/5/1772.
[23] Archdioc. of Birmingham Dir. (1929; 1930; 1931; 1934; 1982).

and the curate was ejected in 1662.[24] In 1668 John Law of Kinver was accused of having had a child baptized by a dissenting minister.[25] The minister was probably the Presbyterian Joseph Eccleshall, who was ejected from the vicarage of Sedgley in 1662. He continued to live there until the Five Mile Act of 1665 forced him to move, and he settled in Kinver. He preached privately in both places but attended Kinver church. He had moved back to Sedgley by 1669, but he may have continued to preach in Kinver. He died in 1692.[26] The nonconformist Richard Cook, who was chaplain for a time to Philip Foley at Prestwood, afterwards lived in his native Kinver and was buried there in 1685.[27] Only two dissenters were returned for Kinver in 1676.[28] In 1699 the parish register recorded the burial of an Anabaptist from Bewdley (Worcs.) 'by their preacher'. It also recorded the baptism by a nonconformist of two sons of Joseph and Elizabeth Tunnerton in 1699 and 1702 and of the daughter of John and Mary Spencer in 1703.[29]

About 1720 there was a regular dissenting meeting served by itinerant preachers.[30] In the earlier 1770s there was a family of Presbyterians of middling rank, with two others of humbler standing, one Quaker and one Anabaptist; they all attended the parish church at times.[31] Four houses in Kinver were registered for protestant dissenters between 1802 and 1822 and one in Stourton in 1823.[32] A Baptist chapel was built at the junction of High Street and Stone Lane in 1814. It was taken over as an Anglican Sunday school in 1827, but in 1830 there was still a Baptist meeting and Sunday school in the parish.[33]

In 1834 the Baptist trustees resumed possession of the former chapel, to the dismay of the curate, George Wharton. He saw the action as part of an attempt to secure those workers with a dissenting background who had lately been attracted to Kinver by the prosperous state of the iron industry.[34] The building was let to the Primitive Methodists, who used it until 1839 or 1840. About 1845 they built a chapel at Gallowstree Elm, which was replaced in 1901 by a corrugated-iron chapel at Potter's Cross. In 1925 Christ Church, a brick chapel designed by Henry Harper & Son of Nottingham, was opened on an adjoining site; the iron chapel was then used as the Sunday school until 1960.[35]

In 1830 the Wesleyan Methodists were holding services at Kinver and in a cottage on the Gothersley road at Stourton. The services at Stourton soon ceased, but by 1835 there were services every Sunday at Kinver. They ceased that year but in 1839 were held at the Lock inn in Mill Lane. In 1846 services were held in one of the rock houses at Gibraltar. When the Primitive Methodist chapel became vacant in 1839 or 1840 the Wesleyans took it over, enlarging it in 1852; a Sunday school was started in 1843. On Census Sunday 1851 there were congregations of 66 in the afternoon and 110 in the evening, with 140 Sunday school children in the morning and 130 in the afternoon. In 1887 the chapel was replaced by Trinity chapel, built further north on the opposite side of High Street to the design of Isaac Meacham of Cradley Heath, in Rowley Regis; a schoolroom, also designed by Meacham, was built in 1899, part of the cost being met by the sale of the old chapel that year.[36] In 1982 the old chapel was occupied as a shop.

As a result of a bequest from F. I. Payne of Norton, Stourbridge, in 1960, a new Methodist church was built on the site of the iron building at Potter's Cross to replace both Christ Church and Trinity. Designed by S. A. Griffiths of Stourbridge it was opened in 1962. Christ Church became the Sunday school building.[37] The High Street buildings were being used as a youth centre in 1982.

EDUCATION. In 1511 a priest was engaged to teach grammar at Kinver. A group of 22 men, headed by Edward Grey and John Whorwood, agreed to pay him 8 marks a year until he was instituted to the chantry in Kinver church. He was allowed to take fees from his pupils.[38] By the time of the chantry's dissolution in 1548, the priest provided free education for children of the parish.[39] In 1555 the endowments of the former chantry included a school house,[40] presumably the building which survives in Dark Lane.

There was a schoolmaster in 1558,[41] and he was also acting as curate in 1563.[42] By 1571 the school had endowments consisting of land and houses; they were administered by a body of trustees which then included the schoolmaster.[43] There was an usher by 1604. The grammar school remained free for the children of parishioners.[44] In 1635 the school's property comprised a school building, a master's house with an adjoining orchard and garden, and houses and cottages in Kinver and Stourton. The income that year was £15 13s. 4d. The master also received £3 6s. 8d. as his share of the bequest of William Moseley of London made in 1617, and £6 13s. 4d. from the

[24] Above, church.
[25] A. G. Matthews, Cong. Churches of Staffs. 56.
[26] Calamy Revised, ed. A. G. Matthews, 179; Cal. S.P. Dom. Oct. 1683–Apr. 1684, 187; A. Gordon, Freedom after Ejection, 257; Matthews, Cong. Churches of Staffs. 87, 90.
[27] Calamy Revised, ed. Matthews, 132; S.R.O., D. 1197/1/2.
[28] W.S.L., S.MS. 33, p. 371.
[29] S.R.O., D. 1197/1/2.
[30] Matthews, Cong. Churches of Staffs. 129.
[31] L.J.R.O., B/V/5/1772.
[32] S.H.C. 4th ser. iii. 5, 22, 35, 58, 60.
[33] J. H. Mees, Story of a Hundred Years: Handbk. of Wesleyan Methodist Church Stourbridge Circuit (Stourbridge, 1928), 94 (copy in Stourbridge Libr.); S.H.C. 4th ser. x. 15.
[34] S.R.O., Tp. 1273/24/Kinver Sch., Geo. Wharton to Lord Stamford 10 May 1834.

[35] H. J. Haden, The Methodist Church, Kinver (1961; copy in W.S.L. Pamphs.). This gives c. 1845 for the second chapel, but none appears in the 1851 Religious Census; the chapel was registered in 1863: G.R.O. Worship Reg. no. 4515.
[36] Mees, Story of a Hundred Years, 93–101; Haden, Methodist Church, Kinver; P.R.O., HO 129/379/2/3. For Meacham see Kelly's Dir. Staffs. (1888).
[37] Haden, Methodist Church, Kinver.
[38] Copy of deed of 5 Jan. 1510/11 printed in Kinver Par. Mag. vii, no. 10 (copy in S.R.O., D. 3162/1/1).
[39] S.H.C. 1915, 142.
[40] Cal. Pat. 1554–5, 315.
[41] L.J.R.O., B/C/11, Ric. Atkys (1559).
[42] S.R.O., D. 1197/1/1, baptism of 19 Apr. 1563.
[43] S.R.O., D. 648/22/2.
[44] S.R.O., D. 3162/1/3.

rent for the tithes leased by the Feoffees for the Purchase of Impropriations in 1630.[45] In 1637 an official inquiry found that the trustees had leased property below its value; it was ordered that the leases were to be cancelled and future ones made by the master alone. The repair of the school building was to be charged on the parish.[46] In 1649 and 1658 the master was also curate.[47] Richard Bate, master from 1705, later became curate as well.[48] By 1726 the master's failure to make sound leases had caused property to fall into decay; the school and master's house were also out of repair. In 1728 the trustees, who were mostly local yeomen and tradesmen, were replaced by a body of gentry and ironmasters, who were empowered to withhold the master's income until the school's property had been repaired. The churchwardens were instructed to repair the school house. At least from the mid 18th century the trustees met irregularly.[49]

There was an usher in 1757, evidently responsible for teaching English; in the late 1770s he received £8 a year.[50] By c. 1790 only a few of the 20 boys then at the school received a classical education from the master, John Fox. Complaints were made about Fox's unwillingness to teach non-classical subjects more appropriate to a parish like Kinver. The number of pupils fell to five or six c. 1804, and the lack of boys suitable for classical instruction resulted in the cessation of teaching c. 1813. Fox also mismanaged the school's endowments. After his death in 1816 the income was again devoted to the repair of the property. As a temporary measure the trustees appointed a master at £20 a year to teach 16 boys the elements free.[51] A new school was built in 1820–1; it stood north-east of the 16th-century building in Dark Lane, which was thereafter used as the master's house.[52] In 1832 George Wharton was appointed master at a salary of £160; the teaching of classics was resumed, and the master was allowed to take his own pupils.[53] The school reopened with 22 free boys, and there were 28 later in the year; in 1833 the master also had 10 boarders. Wharton, who was also perpetual curate of Kinver from 1834, employed a writing master at £60 a year.[54] By 1835 only four free boys were taught Latin, and in 1842 the master was instructed not to teach history and classics unless requested to do so by parents.[55]

In 1844, as the consequence of a petition by parishioners, the school was reorganized to make it more responsive to the needs of the parish. An upper class offered a classical education free to boys of the parish; other subjects were offered for which boys paid 1 guinea a quarter. A lower class provided a commercial education for which the fee was 5s. a quarter. The lower class was to be taught by an usher or under-master at a salary of £30; he also took the 5s. fees. In 1845 there were 13 boys in the upper class and 41 in the lower.[56] The average income from the school's endowments in the earlier 1860s was £220 5s. 10d., out of which the master received an average of £119 0s. 6¾d. His fees averaged £48 3s. 6d., and his share of the income from Moseley's bequest averaged £46 6s. 8d. Out of his income the master paid a salary of £50 to an assistant in the upper school. The usher's income consisted of the salary of £30 and fees estimated at £40 in 1864.[57] Chemistry may have been taught by 1861, when Matthew Packer, a chemistry teacher, was living in Kinver; he was an assistant master at the school by 1871.[58] In 1878 there were only 18 boys in the school and it was decided to unite the upper and lower classes. Fees were set at £2 a year. In the following year the headmaster was allowed to employ a pupil teacher in place of the usher, with a salary of no more than £10; in the mid 1880s he was evidently employing former pupils. The number of boys had risen to 29 by 1891 and there were again two classes.[59] Girls were first admitted in 1901, and by 1907 there were 17 girls and 11 boys.[60] By 1904 there was an assistant mistress.[61]

In 1907 the Board of Education recommended that the school should close because it was too small. There was strong local opposition, but the school was closed in 1916. Its income was thereafter spent on grants to Kinver children attending secondary schools and to Kinver students at places of further education, including universities. Under a Scheme of 1977 the conditions were widened to include grants to primary schoolchildren, to young people starting a trade or profession, and to Edgecliff school for purposes not covered by public funds. The income in 1981–2 was £4,042.[62]

In 1982 the original school building became a private house, known as the Old Grammar School House. The older part is a later 16th-century timber-framed building with an upper floor jettied on all sides. One short length of walling at the rear is of brick with a lozenge pattern of dark headers and evidently survives from an earlier building. The plan is L-shaped; the east wing contained a single room on each floor, and the north end was formerly subdivided and perhaps housed the staircase. In the 1830s a new range was added on the east end, and the front of the building was refenestrated and rendered to match the new work.[63] The house was restored in

[45] L.J.R.O., B/V/6/Kinver; above, manors and other estates (rectory); church.
[46] P.R.O., C 93/16, no. 16.
[47] S.H.C. 1915, 143; below, chars. for the poor.
[48] Above, church.
[49] P.R.O., C 93/54, no. 8; S.R.O., D. 3162/2/1.
[50] S.R.O., D. 1197/4/1; Birmingham Univ. Libr., accts. of Kinver schoolmaster (photocopy in S.R.O. 1401).
[51] 5th Rep. Com. Char. 624–5; S.R.O., Tp. 1273/24/ Kinver sch., John Darwall to Lord Stamford 30 Apr. 1813.
[52] S.R.O., D. 891/3, nos. 1059–60; ibid. 4, p. 54; D. 1197/4/1.
[53] S.R.O., D. 3162/2/1; S.R.O., Tp. 1273/24/Kinver sch., regulations of 1832.
[54] S.R.O., Tp. 1273/24/Kinver sch., Geo. Wharton to

Lord Stamford 31 Oct. 1832 and A.G.M. of trust 20 Jan. 1834; L.J.R.O., B/A/3/Kinver.
[55] S.R.O., Tp. 1273/24/Kinver sch., A.G.M. of trust 9 Feb. 1835; S.R.O., D. 3162/2/1.
[56] S.R.O., D. 3162/2/1.
[57] S.R.O., D. 3162/4/2.
[58] P.R.O., RG 9/1985; RG 10/2928.
[59] S.R.O., D. 3579/1/2; D. 3579/1/3, pp. 33–4, 64.
[60] S.R.O., D. 3162/5/5.
[61] S.R.O., D. 3579/1/3, p. 175. In 1907 a Bd. of Educ. rep. mentioned two junior mistresses, but payments to only one were recorded then: S.R.O., D. 3162/5/5; D. 3579/1/3.
[62] S.R.O., D. 3162/5/5 and 7; Char. Com. files; inf. from Mr. J. W. King.
[63] S.R.O., D. 3162/2/1, 20 Feb. 1837.

the 1970s.[64] The building to the north-east was demolished *c.* 1965.[65]

Kinver was entitled to send two boys to Old Swinford Hospital School (Worcs.) from its foundation in 1670.[66] In 1717 Mary Newey provided an income for a charity school in accordance with the wishes of her late husband, Jonathan Newey, minister of Kinver. There is no evidence that the school was established.[67]

By 1819 there were a number of schools in the parish providing education for *c.* 100 children, of whom *c.* 40 were supported financially by wealthy parishioners.[68] One of the schools may have been the Church of England Sunday school, which in 1826 had an average attendance of between 120 and 150 children. From 1827 the former Baptist chapel at the junction of High Street and Stone Lane was used for the school. In 1834 the Baptists resumed possession.[69] A new school was built in 1835 in the Holloway between Church Hill and Mill Lane; the cost was met by donations and a government grant, and the site was given by J. H. Hodgetts-Foley.[70] In 1840, and probably earlier, the building was also being used as a day school.[71] In the later 1840s the school, then a National school, had 81 boys and 93 girls taught by a master and a mistress.[72]

In 1847 the archdeacon remarked on the need for a school 'at the lower part' of the village.[73] In 1851 a National school for boys and girls was built on a site given from the glebe at the corner of High Street and Vicarage Drive. The school in the Holloway became the infants' department.[74] By 1856 there was an average attendance at the newer school of 69 boys and 53 girls, paying between 4*d.* and 2*d.* according to age. The rest of the income came from contributions and an annual collection.[75] In 1861 the boys were moved into the Holloway building and the infants into the newer building.[76] The schools received a government grant by 1861.[77] In 1864 there was an average attendance of 100 boys, 67 girls, and 102 infants.[78]

A school board for Kinver was established in 1871 and accepted an invitation to take over the management of the National schools.[79] It built a separate girls' school in Vicarage Drive in 1873; the older building was kept for infants. In 1876

the board opened a new boys' school in Castle Street; the Holloway building was given back to H. J. W. Hodgetts-Foley in 1878 and was used as a Roman Catholic church from 1935.[80] In 1905–6 the schools had an average attendance of 101 boys, 127 girls, and 74 infants.[81]

Edgecliff secondary modern school (from 1970 Edgecliff comprehensive school) in Enville Road was opened in 1951. The infants then moved from Vicarage Drive into the boys' school in Castle Street, renamed Foley infants' school in 1955. A primary school occupied the buildings in Vicarage Drive and High Street until 1966, when as Brindley Heath junior school it moved to Fairfield Drive. The former girls' school was converted into a library in 1967, and the former infants' school was demolished in 1971. The primary school moved to a new site at Potter's Cross in 1974, and its former premises in Fairfield Drive were then occupied by the infants' school.[82] In 1982 the Castle Street school building and master's house were being converted into private dwellings.

A school-chapel was built at Halfcot in 1837 by J. H. Hodgetts-Foley, who also maintained it. In 1838 it had an attendance of 60 children.[83] Known as Prestwood school by the later 1840s it then had 23 boys and 36 girls under a mistress and was a National school.[84] It continued to be maintained by the Foleys until its closure *c.* 1885.[85] The building continued in use as a mission chapel.[86]

There have been a number of private schools in the parish. A girls' boarding school existed in 1755.[87] There were three academies, one of them a girls' boarding school, in 1834.[88] In 1851 there was a school run by Anne Forty in Forest House at Comber; there were three girl boarders. In 1861 there were 10 boarders, and Miss Forty had a German partner and two assistant teachers, one of them a teacher of French. The school was still running in 1864.[89] It had closed by 1868, but there was another girls' day school at Comber in 1871.[90] Two girls' schools were mentioned in the parish in 1872 and 1876.[91] There was again a girls' school in Forest House in 1896.[92] A preparatory school in Enville Road was run by a Madame Elgar in 1928; it still existed in 1932.[93]

[64] Inf. from Mr. and Mrs. E. Shirrmacher of the Old Grammar School House, who are thanked for their help. For a view see above, pl. facing p. 145.

[65] Local inf.

[66] T. R. Nash, *Collns. for Hist. of Worcs.* ii. 210–11.

[67] Below, chars. for the poor.

[68] *Digest of Returns to Sel. Cttee. on Educ. of Poor*, H.C. 224, p. 862 (1819), ix (2).

[69] S.R.O., Tp. 1273/5, Thos. Housman to Ld. Stamford 2 Jan. 1826; 24/Kinver sch., Wharton to Ld. Stamford 12 Mar., 10 May 1834, 15 Oct. 1835; above, prot. nonconf.

[70] S.R.O., Tp. 1273/24/Kinver sch., Wharton to Ld. Stamford 13 Dec. 1834, 15 Oct. 1835; P.R.O., ED 7/109/194; Bannister, King & Rigbeys, Stourbridge, undated draft deed reciting deed of 25 Mar. 1835 (ref. supplied by Mr. J. W. King); *Rep. Educ. Cttee. of Council, 1864–5* [3533], p. 511, H.C. (1865), xlii.

[71] S.R.O., D. 1197/7/2/3.

[72] Nat. Soc. *Inquiry, 1846–7*, Staffs. 6–7.

[73] S.R.O., D. 1197/3/4.

[74] S.R.O., D. 812/3/108; D. 1197/7/2/3; S.R.O., CEH/76/1; H.W.R.O. (H.), E 12/S, Kinver XII, deed of 17 June 1851; above, church.

[75] P.R.O., ED 7/109/94.

[76] S.R.O., CEH/76/1, scheme of management at beginning

of book; S.R.O., D. 812/3/113.

[77] P.R.O., ED 7/109/194; *Rep. Educ. Cttee. of Council, 1861–2* [3007], p. 589, H.C. (1862), xlii.

[78] S.R.O., CEH/76/1, 30 Mar. 1864.

[79] *Lond. Gaz.* 17 Feb. 1871, p. 587; S.R.O., CEH/76/1, 15 Feb., 28 Apr., 29 Aug. 1871, 25 Jan. 1873.

[80] *Kelly's Dir. Staffs.* (1884); P.R.O., ED 7/109/194; ED 7/113/194; S.R.O., CEH/76/1, 13 Jan., 21 May 1878; above, Roman Catholicism.

[81] *Public Elem. Schs. 1907* [Cd. 3901], p. 568, H.C. (1908), lxxxiv.

[82] Inf. from the head teachers (1982); S.R.O., CEH/76/2, pp. 234, 240; *Express & Star*, 27 July 1971; above, p. 128.

[83] P.R.O., HO 129/379/2/3; *S.H.C.* 4th ser. x. 15.

[84] Nat. Soc. *Inquiry, 1846–7*, Staffs. 6–7.

[85] *Kelly's Dir. Staffs.* (1884).

[86] Above, church.

[87] *Aris's Birmingham Gaz.* 24 Feb., 3 Mar. 1755.

[88] White, *Dir. Staffs.* (1834), 262.

[89] P.R.O., HO 107/2017; P.R.O., RG 9/1985; *P.O. Dir. Staffs.* (1864), calling her Emma Forty.

[90] P.R.O., RG 10/2928; *P.O. Dir. Staffs.* (1868).

[91] *P.O. Dir. Staffs.* (1872; 1876).

[92] *Kelly's Dir. Staffs.* (1896).

[93] Ibid. (1928; 1932).

In 1906 Hyde House at the Hyde was opened as Bethany, a home supported by voluntary contributions where crippled boys could be taught a trade. The founder and first governor was E. G. Hexall. By 1913 all 40 beds were taken. The home was closed *c.* 1918, and the house was demolished a few years later.[94]

An evening school was held four times a week in one of the National school buildings in 1856. It was still held in March 1861, when the average attendance was 17.[95]

CHARITIES FOR THE POOR. By will of 1595 John Jorden, merchant and skinner of London, left £10 for the poor of Kinver parish. His brother William added £10 and his parents Edward and Eleanor £2 each. In 1628 another brother Humphrey, having added £4 of his own money, invested the total of £28 in property in Kinver, the income to be distributed twice a year to the poor.[96] The benefactors were evidently members of the Jorden family of Dunsley. In the late 1780s there was an income of £3 15s. 4½d.[97] By the 1820s it had increased to £13.[98]

By will proved 1622 Roger Jeston, citizen and haberdasher of London and a native of Kinver, gave property in London, from which £5 a year was to be paid to the poor of Kinver; inhabitants of the borough were to receive £3 and other parishioners the rest.[99]

By deed of 1650 Thomas Keightley of Hertingfordbury Park (Herts.), a native of Kinver, gave an annual £5 from land in Bromsgrove (Worcs.), to be distributed to 20 poor people of Kinver parish.[1]

Roger Kimberley (d. 1658), minister and schoolmaster of Kinver, left £50, the income to buy Bibles and Catechisms for the poor of Kinver and, after that had been done, to be spent in other charitable ways. In 1659 the capital was laid out on a close in Compton then called Wall croft and later Bible meadow. It was let for £2 10s., a rent still paid by the owner of Pigeonhouse farm in 1982.[2]

Some years before 1690 Robert Bird, citizen and stationer of London and a native of Kinver, left £50, the income to be used for apprenticing poor boys of Kinver. In 1737 the terms of the charity were altered; every third year the money was to be paid instead as a marriage portion to a girl born in the parish. By 1812 the income was £2 16s., the capital having increased to £70 as a result of the accumulation of unspent money. With a fall in the number of applications for apprenticing by 1820, the charity was paid mainly to poor young women on their marriage.[3]

By deed of 1717 Mary Newey, widow of Jonathan Newey, minister of Kinver, sold three cottages in Whittington to trustees who raised the necessary £70 from £50 of parish stock, partly given by Longworth Crosse, and from a gift of £20 by Mary Newey herself. Of the income from the property 20s. was to be spent on a parish charity school in accordance with Jonathan Newey's wishes and the rest on the poor of Kinver parish. There is no evidence that the school was established; in the 19th century, and probably by 1758, the cottages were used as poorhouses.[4]

By deed of 1760 John Cook of Stourton slitting mill gave a house and garden at Stourton to produce an income which was to be distributed annually in 20 shilling loaves to 20 poor of the parish, preference being given to those of Stourton. By 1820 there was an income of £2, distributed in shilling loaves.[5]

By will of 1777 Margaret Comber left £50, the income to be given to the poor of Kinver parish. By 1820 it was distributed in religious books and in doles of 3s. or 4s.[6]

Under a Scheme of 1860 the above eight charities were united, later becoming known as Kinver Parochial Charities; the income was to be used in the education of poor children and in the distribution of gifts to the poor in cash or kind. By 1906 the income was £58 3s., of which £10 was spent on religious teaching in the Kinver board schools and the rest distributed to the poor. In the early 1980s the income was distributed with that from three other charities in sums of around £4 to some 70 people at Christmas.[7]

Kinver was one of the parishes which benefited from the charity of William Seabright of Wolverley (Worcs.), established by will of 1620. Under its terms 14 penny loaves of white or wheaten bread were distributed each Sunday to the poor of the parish. In the early 1980s the income was distributed with the Parochial Charities.[8]

By deed of 1659 George Brindley of Compton gave an annual 20s. from 3 a. in Kinver to buy 21 shilling loaves of muncorn bread; 20 loaves were to be distributed at Easter to 20 poor of the parish, and the remaining one was to be kept by the distributor. By 1820 all 21 loaves were given to the poor. They were still distributed in the late 1860s,[9] but the later history of the charity is obscure.

By will of 1699 John Grove, a clothier of Kinver, gave £20, the income to buy 20 shilling loaves for 20 poor of Kinver during Lent. The distribution was still made in 1820 but had ceased by the late 1860s.[10]

[94] H.W.R.O. (H.), E 12/S, Kinver III; inf. from Mr. D. M. Bills.

[95] P.R.O., ED 7/109/194; S.R.O., CEH/76/1, 3 Apr. 1861.

[96] S.R.O., D. 1197/6/1/1; 6/2/1.

[97] *Char. Dons. 1786–88*, 1144–5.

[98] *5th Rep. Com. Char.* 625–6.

[99] *Ibid.* 625.

[1] *5th Rep. Com. Char.* 626; *D.N.B.*; *V.C.H. Herts.* iii. 465.

[2] S.R.O., D. 1197/1/2, burial of 28 Sept. 1658; D. 1197/6/2/3A; *5th Rep. Com. Char.* 626–7; inf. from Mr. T. R. Brown of Pigeonhouse Farm.

[3] *5th Rep. Com. Char.* 627. In 1690 Bird's last surviving trustee appointed new trustees.

[4] *Ibid.* 627–8; S.R.O., D. 1197/6/1/4; above, local govt.

[5] H.W.R.O. (H.), E 12/S, Kinver, Compton Hallows, and Kingsley ct. bk. 1734–61, ct. of 22 Apr. 1760; ibid. Kinver copyhold estates 1831, W. Bright's schedule, openings 14 and 15; *5th Rep. Com. Char.* 629.

[6] *5th Rep. Com. Char.* 630.

[7] *Staffs. Endowed Chars.* 78; inf. from Mr. S. A. Harris, churchwarden (1983).

[8] S.R.O., D. 1197/6/3; *5th Rep. Com. Char.* 629–30; inf. from Mr. Harris.

[9] *5th Rep. Com. Char.* 628–9; *Char. Digest Staffs.* 28–9.

[10] S.R.O., D. 1197/1/2, burial of 26 Jan. 1698/9; *5th Rep. Com. Char.* 629; *Char. Digest Staffs.* 28–9.

By will proved 1715 Edward Barton of London left an annual £10 for the poor of Kinver parish; £6 was to be spent on clothing for six or more poor children attending Kinver grammar school, and £4 on Bibles and other religious books for the poor. The income was still received in the late 1780s but was apparently spent only on clothing.[11] Nothing further is known of the charity.

The bread charity of Mary Whorrell which had £1 income in the late 1780s may have been established by the Mary Worrall who died in 1693.[12] Nothing more is known of the charity.

A further four charities had been lost by the late 1780s: £5 given by Richard Willetts, £10 given by Humphrey Bate in 1685, £30 or £50 given by Edward Ford, and the rent every third year from a house given by a Mr. Lythall of Compton.[13]

By will proved 1886 Caroline Brindley left money to provide an annual distribution to the poor, although for a certain period the first charge on it was to be the maintenance of her grave. In the early 1980s the income was distributed with the Parochial Charities.[14]

By will proved 1900 Ellen Lee left £300 to Kinver parish council, the income to provide food and fuel for the poor of the parish aged 60 and over. In 1971–2 the income was £7.72, and £10 was distributed in £1 vouchers.[15]

By will proved 1923 John Johnson left £100, the income to be used for the maintenance of his tomb and the remainder distributed in bread or coal to Anglicans living in the parish. In the early 1980s the charity was distributed with the Parochial Charities.[16]

By will proved 1944 Walter Holdnall of Sutton Coldfield (Warws.) left his estate, including a bungalow on Church Hill, Kinver, to provide an almshouse for the aged poor of Kinver. The bungalow proved unsuitable and was sold in 1956. In the early 1980s the estate was worth £35,733 but no almshouse had been provided.[17]

PATSHULL

THE ancient parish of Patshull, 1,824 a. (739 ha.) in area,[18] forms a peninsula jutting into Shropshire, attached to Staffordshire on the east and south-east. It is predominantly agricultural, and Patshull park is a notable feature. In 1845 the parish was transferred from the southern to the northern division of Seisdon hundred.[19]

The terrain is undulating, rising to just over 500 ft. (152 m.) in the north-east on the Pattingham boundary. It drops to around 250 ft. (76 m.) on the south-east, where a stream[20] forms the boundary with Pattingham, and to 220 ft. (68 m.) at Lower Snowdon on the west, where Snowdon brook forms the county boundary. The upper reaches of Pasford brook in the centre of the parish were dammed in the 18th century to form ornamental pools. The underlying rock is sandstone and was formerly quarried. Two strips of Keuper Marl run north–south through the centre and the west of the parish.[21] The soil is loam.[22]

In 1086 the recorded population of Patshull was 19.[23] Nine people there were assessed for the subsidy of 1332, and the lord of the manor and 15 others for that of the mid 1520s.[24] The lord and 14 others appeared in the muster roll of 1539.[25] In 1563 there were stated to be 12 households.[26] The poll-tax assessment of 1641 listed 78 people,[27] and 13 households were assessed for hearth tax in 1666.[28] The Compton Census of 1676 recorded 60 people in the parish.[29] Fourteen people paid a tithe modus in 1698 and 15 in 1705.[30] The population of the parish was 160 in 1801 and had dropped to 132 by 1831 and 112 by 1851. It had risen to 194 by 1861, a reflection of the expansion of the establishment at Patshull House and of the number of workers on the estate after Lord Dartmouth's move there in 1853. It was 208 by 1871, and although it was down to 193 by 1881, it had reached 234 by 1891. It was 222 in 1901 and 1911, 185 in 1921, and 204 in 1931. It had dropped to 187 by 1951 and 154 by 1961. In 1971 it was 155.[31]

---

[11] S.R.O., D. 1197/6/2/4A; *Char. Dons. 1786–88*, 1144–5; L.J.R.O., B/V/6/Kinver, n.d.

[12] *Char. Dons. 1786–88*, 1146–7; S.R.O., D. 1197/1/2, burial of 29 Nov. 1693.

[13] *Char. Dons. 1786–88*, 1146–7; H.W.R.O. (H.), E 12/S, addenda to portfolios, list of benefactors to poor of Kinver *c.* 1700.

[14] S.R.O., reg. of chars.; inf. from Mr. Harris.

[15] Char. Com. files.

[16] Ibid.; inf. from Mr. Harris.

[17] Char. Com. files; S.R.O., D. 1197/6/7; *The Spectator*, 9 Apr. 1983, 18–19.

[18] *Census*, 1971. This article was written in 1979–80. Mr. P. Kemp of Burnhill Green Farm, Captain J. Matthews, Patshull estate manager, Mr. S. J. Ponder of Burnhill Green, and Mrs. Mary Shakespeare, matron of Patshull rehabilitation centre, are thanked for their help.

[19] S.R.O., Q/SO 35, ff. 25, 139v., 163v.

[20] It was probably known formerly as Gallows brook: below, Pattingham, introduction.

[21] T. H. Whitehead and others, *Memoirs of Geol. Surv., Country between Wolverhampton and Oakengates*, 119, 131, 135, 140, 147, 193; *V.C.H. Staffs.* i, map before p. 1; *Kelly's Dir. Staffs.* (1940); O.S. Map 6″, Staffs. LXI. NW. (1890 and 1924 edns.); S.R.O., D. 21/2/A/PC/2, p. 13, ref. to cutting of rock at Nore Hill 1733–4; S.R.O., D.(W.) 1778/V/1303, letters of 1849 and 1850 from Mic. Turnor to Lord Dartmouth urging the use of stone from a quarry on the Patshull estate; below, church.

[22] *Kelly's Dir. Staffs.* (1940).

[23] Below, econ. hist.

[24] *S.H.C.* x (1), 130–1; P.R.O., E 179/177/96.

[25] *S.H.C.* N.s. vi (1), 172.

[26] *S.H.C.* 1915, p. lxxi.

[27] H.L., Main Papers, box 178.

[28] *S.H.C.* 1923, 84.

[29] W.S.L., S.MS. 33, p. 371.

[30] L.J.R.O., B/V/6/Patshull.

[31] *V.C.H. Staffs.* i. 326; *Census*, 1911–71. For the increase after Lord Dartmouth's move see P.R.O., RG 9/1852.

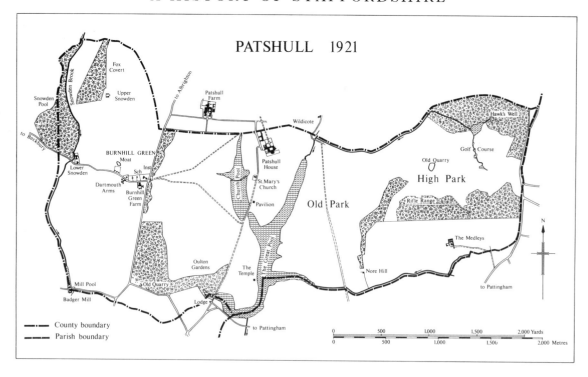

PATSHULL 1921

The name Patshull is thought to mean Paettel's hill.[32] It is not clear where the village of Patshull stood or even that there was such a village. Until the 18th century the manor house and the church 'stood low, near the water',[33] presumably the upper reaches of Pasford brook. They seem therefore to have been near the hamlet of Olton (formerly Oldington) which lay in the middle of the parish and existed by the mid 13th century. Burnhill Green (before the later 16th century simply Burnhill) in the west of the parish and Nore Hill (Nore before the 17th century) in the south were also inhabited places by the mid 13th century.[34] There is a moated site west of Burnhill Green.[35] Snowdon in the north-west corner, mentioned as a member of the manor in 1279, gave its name to a fishpool on the western boundary constructed probably in the mid 13th century.[36] Millhouse, probably lying east of the present Patshull House, and the Medleys in the south-east of the parish were inhabited places by 1327.[37] The parish was called a 'villula' in 1391.[38]

The pattern of settlement changed in the 18th century when the manor house and church were rebuilt and a new park laid out. In the petition for the rebuilding of the church in 1742 Sir John Astley, the lord of the manor, claimed that the new site, some ½ mile from the old, was nearer

and more convenient for the village of Patshull, where, according to the faculty for rebuilding, most of the parishioners lived. The convenience of the site seems in fact to have lain in its proximity to the new Patshull House. The subsequent creation of the park involved the demolition of many houses.[39] The settlements at Millhouse and Olton disappeared, although a farmhouse called Olton survived until the early 19th century.[40] The road pattern too was changed. The road from Burnhill Green to Pattingham formerly ran across the parish past Olton, Nore Hill, and the Medleys. A bridge called Forebridge, mentioned from the early 16th century and rebuilt in 1732–3, probably carried the road over Pasford brook east of Olton. About 1770 the road was stopped up by the new lord of the manor, Lord Pigot, and diverted to its more circuitous course to the south through Pattingham parish and across the dam of the Great Pool. The eastern end of the old road, however, survives as the access road to the Medleys. Another road, running south from Wildicote in Albrighton (Salop.), crossed the old Pattingham road near Nore Hill; that too was stopped up c. 1770.[41]

Burnhill Green has developed as the main centre of population in the parish. Already in the early 17th century it was a meeting place of juries

[32] Ekwall, *Eng. Place-Names.*
[33] Shaw, *Staffs.* ii. 283.
[34] W.S.L. 350A/40, ff. 18–19; Yates, *Map of Staffs.* (1775). Although the name Oldington continued into the 17th century the form Olton is found in 1374: B.L. Add. Ch. 43907; S.R.O., D.(W.) 1778/V/1366, cts. of 31 Mar. 1516, 21 Oct. 1608. For the name Burnhill Green see e.g. *S.H.C.* 1930, 80; 1931, 132; 1935, 90, 379. For Nore Hill see S.R.O., D.(W.) 1739/1, ff. 9 sqq. For open fields centring on Olton see below, econ. hist.
[35] *V.C.H. Staffs.* i. 365.
[36] *S.H.C.* vi (1), 141; viii (2), 127; below, econ. hist.

[37] *S.H.C.* vii (1), 251.
[38] L.J.R.O., B/A/1/6, f. 106.
[39] L.J.R.O., B/C/5/1742/Patshull; *S.H.C.* 4th ser. x. 18.
[40] Millhouse was mentioned in 1716 (S.R.O., D.(W.) 1739/1, f. 30), but no settlement of that name is shown by Yates, *Map of Staffs.* (1775). For Olton in the early 19th century see S.R.O., Q/RDc 14, map.
[41] S.R.O., Q/SO 16, ff. 46–7; Yates, *Map of Staffs.* (1775 and 1799). For Forebridge see e.g. S.R.O., D.(W.), 1778/V/1366, ct. of 20 Dec. 1509; S.R.O., D. 21/2/A/PC/2, p. 5. For a ref. to the Wildicote road in the 17th century see B.R.L., Keen 357, deed of 18 Jan. 1650/1.

for fixing boundaries within the manor,[42] and by 1775 there were a number of houses there.[43] The public house in Patshull mentioned in 1789 was probably a forerunner of the Dartmouth Arms at Burnhill Green, which was known as the Pigot's Arms by 1834 and was renamed *c.* 1870.[44] Burnhill Green Farm south of the Beckbury road is an 18th-century brick house with embattled parapets; presumably because of the castellated decoration it was known in the early 19th century as Castle Farm.[45] A school was opened in the later 1850s.[46] By 1861 there was a post office, kept in the late 19th and early 20th century by the master or mistress of the school.[47] The council houses on the Beckbury road date from the early 1920s and *c.* 1950.[48] The names Upper and Lower Snowdon were in use by 1861. Upper Snowdon was the former Snowdon; a house stood there until the later 20th century. Lower Snowdon is a group of cottages north of the Beckbury road.[49] Nore Hill is a farmhouse with a core dating probably from the 17th century, and the Medleys is one of *c.* 1800 with later additions.

The parish was crossed by the route between the south-west of England and Chester which was in existence by 1300 and continued in use until *c.* 1800. In the earlier 16th century it ran through Olton as Chester Way, but by 1762 it went through Burnhill Green. The Patshull stretch was turnpiked that year as part of the road running north from Highgate, in Enville, through Bobbington and Rudge (Salop.) and continuing from Burnhill Green to Kilsall, in Donington (Salop.), where it joined the Wolverhampton–Chester road. It was disturnpiked in 1877.[50]

Electricity was available by 1935. By the earlier 1950s the western part of Burnhill Green was supplied with water from a borehole sunk by Seisdon rural district council; the rest of the village was supplied from two springs in the grounds of Patshull House which also served the house and outlying farms.[51]

In the 18th century the parish wake was held in September.[52]

The earls of Dartmouth and their family played a prominent part in the life of the parish from the mid 19th century. They were active in the affairs of the church, and in 1901 a sharp drop in the offerings was recorded because of the family's long absence abroad.[53] The family took a close interest in the school at Burnhill Green, and in the mid and later 1940s the children were allowed to swim in the park.[54] The 5th earl's wife had started a clothing club and a lending library before leaving the area on the earl's death in 1891.[55] In 1904 their son, the 6th earl, built a village hall at Burnhill Green in their memory.[56]

The 5th earl was one of the chief supporters of the Volunteer movement in Staffordshire, and in 1860 he formed a Patshull company. It was made up almost entirely of his tenants and employees and was commanded by his uncle, Col. A. C. Legge; Lord Dartmouth was at first ensign to the company, but he took over the command later in 1860. The company was still in existence when he died in 1891. There was a rifle range in the park where in 1862 a shooting contest was held between the Patshull and the West Bromwich companies.[57] The 5th earl, who became the first president of the county cricket club in 1871 with his son Lord Lewisham as the first secretary, entertained the M.C.C. at Patshull in 1875 and 1876 after building a cricket pavilion in the park. The Patshull cricket club had been established by the 1890s, with the schoolmaster as secretary.[58] The earl was also interested in archery, and an archery ground below the new terrace formed part of his improvements at Patshull House.[59] An annual coursing meeting had become popular by the early 1870s, that held in 1873 being the most popular to date; Patshull park had been used for meetings by the Morfe club in 1827 and 1833, and a meeting was held there in 1849.[60] There was a golf course in the park in the early 20th century.[61]

In 1900 the duke and duchess of York (the future George V and Queen Mary) stayed at Patshull House for four days during a visit to Staffordshire; the 6th earl was then lord lieutenant. Queen Mary again stayed at Patshull in 1939.[62]

MANOR AND OTHER ESTATES. In 1066 *PATSHULL* was held by Brodor, a free man, with sac and soc. After the Conquest it passed to Robert de Stafford. In 1086 it was assessed at 3 hides.[63] The overlordship descended in the Stafford family and was held by Hugh, earl of Stafford, at his death in 1386.[64]

By 1086 Patshull was held of Robert de Stafford

[42] S.R.O., D.(W.) 1778/V/1366, cts. of 27 Oct. 1603, 15 Oct. 1604. Olton too was used, but for more local boundaries: ibid. ct. of 21 Oct. 1607. See also S.R.O., D. 3451/2/2, constables' accts. 1622, for a coroner's inquest at Burnhill Green.
[43] Yates, *Map of Staffs.* (1775); S.R.O., Q/RDc 14, map.
[44] S.R.O., D. 21/A/PC/2, p. 144; White, *Dir. Staffs.* (1834), 272; *P.O. Dir. Staffs.* (1868; 1872).
[45] Greenwood, *Map of Staffs.* (1820).
[46] Below, educ.
[47] Harrison, Harrod & Co. *Dir. Staffs.* (1861), 84; P.R.O., ED 7/109/242; *Kelly's Dir. Staffs.* (1884 and later edns.); O.S. Map 6″, Staffs. LXI. NW. (1890 and 1904 edns.).
[48] Inf. from Mr. S. J. Ponder.
[49] P.R.O., RG 9/1852; RG 10/2746; Yates, *Map of Staffs.* (1775); O.S. Map 1/50,000, sheet 127 (1974 edn.).
[50] Scott, *Stourbridge*, 170-1; *S.H.C.* v (1), 180; S.R.O., D.(W.) 1778/V/1365 (June 1533); S.R.O., Q/SO 12, f. 177v.; 2 Geo. III, c. 53; 36 & 37 Vic. c. 90.
[51] Seisdon R.D.C. *Rep. of M.O.H. for 1935*, 10; *1953*, 21 (copies in S.R.O., C/H/1/2/2/36).   [52] Shaw, *Staffs.* ii. 286.

[53] S.R.O., D. 21/A/PV/1; below, local govt.
[54] S.R.O., CEL/30/1.
[55] *Staffs. Advertiser*, 28 Sept. 1901.
[56] Inscription on hall; S.R.O., D. 1517/14/6-8.
[57] *Hist. of Volunteer Force of Staffs. 1859-1908* (Stafford, 1909), 2-3, 5, 20-1; F. Boase, *Modern Eng. Biog.* v. 21; *Wolverhampton Chron.* 22 Oct. 1862, p. 5; 25 Oct. 1865, p. 2; O.S. Map 6″, Staffs. LXI. NW. and NE. (1890 and 1924 edns.).
[58] *V.C.H. Staffs.* ii. 369; S.R.O., D. 564/9/3; *Kelly's Dir. Staffs.* (1896).
[59] S.R.O., D. 564/7/6, 4 Dec. 1881; D. 1517/4/12-13; S.R.O., Tp. 181/8.
[60] *Brit. Farmer's Mag.* ii. 129; *V.C.H. Salop.* ii. 184; *Staffs. Advertiser*, 15 Dec. 1849; *Wolverhampton Chron.* 3 Dec. 1873.
[61] O.S. Map 6″, Staffs. LXI. NE. (1924 edn.).
[62] *Staffs. Advertiser*, 21 and 28 July 1900; 14 Mar. 1936; *Staffs. Life*, Autumn 1954, 12.
[63] *V.C.H. Staffs.* iv. 6, 52.
[64] *S.H.C.* i. 148; v (1), 112; *S.H.C.* 1911, 373; *Bk. of Fees*, ii. 967, 974; *Feud. Aids*, v. 10; *Cal. Inq. p.m.* xvi, p. 171.

with several other manors in Staffordshire and Warwickshire by Hugh.[65] In 1166 Robert son of Otes of Loxley (Warws.), apparently Hugh's grandson, held a mesne lordship.[66] He was dead by 1179, with three daughters as his coheirs. One of them, Margaret, was the wife of William Bagot, and the mesne lordship of what was described in the 13th century as a knight's fee in Patshull passed to the Bagots of the Hyde in Coppenhall (in Penkridge). William's son Robert held it in 1242–3. He had been succeeded by William Bagot, probably his son, by 1250, and in 1255 William bought the reversion of the under-tenancy from Robert Mansel.[67]

It seems that for a time there was another mesne tenancy. A daughter of Robert son of Otes married Ralph de Mora, and in 1256 William Bagot sued their grandson Peter de Mora for quittance of the service claimed by Robert de Stafford for the tenement in Patshull and else-where which William held of Peter, described as 'medius'.[68]

Robert of Patshull, who witnessed a Patting-ham deed c. 1150,[69] held ⅔ knight's fee in Patshull of Robert son of Otes in 1166.[70] By 1188 he had been succeeded by Mansel of Patshull, who was still living in 1206.[71] Mansel's son Robert Mansel held Patshull in 1222.[72] His holding was given as 1 knight's fee in 1242–3 and as 3 hides in the mid 1250s.[73] At some date he granted Sir Ralph of Pitchford the reversion of the vill after his death,[74] but the grant was ineffective because of that to William Bagot.

As a result of the transaction in 1255 the Mansel tenancy passed to the Bagots of the Hyde. William Bagot settled the manor on members of his family in 1276 and was dead by 1300.[75] His son and heir, another William, still held it in 1316,[76] but by 1321 he had conveyed it to Kenilworth priory (Warws.); a mortmain licence was granted only in 1326.[77] The priory retained a lordship until the Dissolution,[78] and in 1632 the manor was said to be held of the heir of Ambrose Dudley, earl of Warwick (d. 1590).[79]

In 1333 the priory granted Patshull to William Shareshull (knighted shortly afterwards and chief justice of the King's Bench 1350–61), his wife Denise, and their issue. The rent was fixed at £40, but later the same year it was reduced to 10 marks and in 1338 to 1d. after Sir William and Denise had given the canons property else-where.[80] In 1333 John, son and heir of Ralph of Pitchford, remitted his rights in the manor to Sir William and Denise; in 1339 the three nieces and heirs of William Bagot did the same.[81] Sir William entered the Franciscan house at Oxford in 1369, dying there in 1370. Patshull passed to his second wife, also Denise, and on her death in 1376 to Sir William's grandson William Shareshull, knighted by 1385. He died childless in 1400 and Patshull passed to Richard Harcourt, husband of one of his nieces, then dead.[82] In 1405 Richard granted the manor to William Lee and his wife Joan, daughter of another niece.[83] In 1411 the Lees granted it for life to Roger Wylily, husband of a third niece.[84] By 1426 it was held for life by Richard Peshale of Patshull, Joan's uncle or cousin, who was still alive in 1439.[85] Joan died childless in 1451, and the manor passed to Thomas Astley, the son of Richard Harcourt's daughter Isabel and the husband of Joan Gresley, Henry VI's nurse.[86]

The manor then descended in the Astley family for over three centuries.[87] Thomas Astley was succeeded by his son, also Thomas (d. 1483–4), whose son William made a settlement of the manor in 1493.[88] William's brother Richard had succeeded by 1497.[89] Richard died in 1531 and was succeeded by his son Thomas.[90] Thomas's son Gilbert succeeded between 1556 and 1558 and died in 1587 with a son Thomas as his heir.[91] Thomas was succeeded in 1632 by his son Walter.[92] During the Civil War Walter, a papist, garrisoned his house for the king. 'Strongly fortified and moated about', it was successfully attacked in 1645, and Walter was captured.[93] His property was sequestrated, and he died in 1653. His son Richard, although an

[65] *V.C.H. Staffs.* iv. 32, 51–2.
[66] *S.H.C.* i. 148; W. Dugdale, *Antiquities of Warws.* (1730 edn.), ii. 678. *V.C.H. Staffs.* iv. 32, states that Rob. was Hugh's grandson; *S.H.C.* ii (1), 181, says that Hugh is supposed to have been Rob.'s ancestor. Neither gives a source.
[67] *S.H.C.* iv (1), 246–7; v (1), 112; n.s. xi. 124, 126, 128–9, 144; *Bk. of Fees*, ii. 967; *V.C.H. Staffs.* v. 139.
[68] *S.H.C.* iv (1), 134; *V.C.H. Warws.* iii. 131.
[69] *S.H.C.* 1939, 182.
[70] *S.H.C.* i. 148, 166–7. Erdeswick, *Staffs.* 364–5, misdates the evidence to the time of Hen. I, an error which appears to be the origin of John Huntbach's statement that Rob. de 'Heckstall' ('Pekdeshull' in Erdeswick) held Patshull in the time of Hen I: Shaw, *Staffs.* ii. 280.
[71] *S.H.C.* ii (1), 137; iii (1), 138.
[72] *S.H.C.* iv (1), 19, 197.
[73] *Bk. of Fees*, ii. 967; *S.H.C.* v (1), 112.
[74] W.S.L. 350A/40, ff. 18–19.
[75] *S.H.C.* vi (1), 75, 141; n.s. xi. 136; *S.H.C.* 1911, 130–1; *Feud. Aids*, v. 10.
[76] *S.H.C.* n.s. xi. 137–8; *S.H.C.* 1911, 64–5; *Feud. Aids*, v. 16.
[77] *S.H.C.* ix (1), 87; *S.H.C.* 1911, 372–3; *Cal. Pat.* 1324–7, 268–9.
[78] *S.H.C.* xiii. 71; P.R.O., C 142/52, no. 104.
[79] P.R.O., C 142/485, no. 79.
[80] W.S.L. 350A/40, ff. 20–1; B. H. Putnam, *Place in Legal Hist. of Sir Wm. Shareshull*, 162–3; *V.C.H. Staffs.* v. 30, 174.
[81] W.S.L., S.MS. 386 (2), f. 253v.; *S.H.C.* xi. 145–6; n.s.
xi. 140–1; *Cal. Close*, 1354–60, 623; Putnam, *Shareshull*, 5.
[82] Putnam, *Shareshull*, 8, 11–12, and App. I, pedigree; *V.C.H. Staffs.* v. 175 (which incorrectly gives Joan as another niece).
[83] W.S.L. 350A/40, f. 22. Snowdon Pool was excepted.
[84] *S.H.C.* xi. 220.
[85] *S.H.C.* xvii. 113; *Feud. Aids*, v. 22; Putnam, *Shareshull*, 241 (where the source for one of the statements should be given as W.S.L. 350A/40, ff. 22–3) and App. I, pedigree; W.S.L., S.MS. 386 (2), f. 262; *V.C.H. Staffs.* iv. 119.
[86] Putnam, *Shareshull*, 12 and App. I, pedigree; *S.H.C.* n.s. i. 53. For the early painting depicting the feats of arms of Thos.'s brother Sir John, a copy of which is at Patshull Ho., see Dugdale, *Warws.* i. 110 and pl. facing p. 111; Shaw, *Staffs.* ii. 284–5; *V.C.H. Warws.* iv. 174.
[87] For genealogical details see Shaw, *Staffs.* ii. 284.
[88] S.R.O., D.(W.) 1778/V/1366, ct. of 15 May 1486; *S.H.C.* xi. 253. A Thos. Astley was described as late of Patshull in 1478 and 1479: *S.H.C.* n.s. vi (1), 116, 120.
[89] Below, econ. hist. Although Ric. Astley was named as lord in 1516 and 1517 (S.R.O., D.(W.) 1721/1/6, un-numbered folios, 'A Booke of Informacions'; *V.C.H. Warws.* iv. 25), the manor court was held in the name of Thos. Astley in Oct. 1516 (S.R.O., D.(W.) 1778/V/1365).
[90] P.R.O., C 142/52, no. 104.
[91] S.R.O., D.(W.) 1778/V/1365, cts. of 9 Sept. 1556 (Thos. Astley) and 27 Sept. 1558 (Gilb. Astley); P.R.O., C 142/1226, no. 164.
[92] P.R.O., C 142/485, no. 79.
[93] *Cal. Cttee. for Money*, iii. 1415; Shaw, *Staffs.* i. 70; *V.C.H. Staffs.* iii. 105.

active royalist during the war, regained Patshull in 1654 under an entail made in 1616.[94] He was knighted for his loyalty and in 1662 was made a baronet.[95] He died in 1688 with an infant son John as his heir.[96] In 1765 Sir John sold his property in Patshull and Pattingham to Sir George Pigot, Bt., a nabob and owner of the Pigot diamond who was created Baron Pigot in 1766.[97] Sir John moved to Astley Castle (Warws.) but was buried at Patshull in 1772.[98]

Lord Pigot died in 1777, and the manor then descended with the Pigot baronetcy, passing to his brother Robert (d. 1796), Robert's son George (d. 1841), and George's son Robert.[99] In 1848 Sir Robert sold Patshull and Pattingham to William Legge, earl of Dartmouth, of Sandwell in West Bromwich. Lord Dartmouth's son Viscount Lewisham moved to Patshull the same year. Lord Dartmouth himself went to live there in 1853; he died there later that year and was buried in Patshull church.[1] The Patshull estate remained with the earls of Dartmouth until after the death of the 7th earl in 1958. He was succeeded by a cousin, and most of the estate passed in lieu of death duties to the Crown, still the owner in 1980. The house, gardens, and 230 a. adjoining were retained by the family, and the 7th earl's widow continued to live at the house until her death in 1963. During the Second World War part of the house became an orthopaedic rehabilitation centre, with the family occupying one wing. From 1966 the house was held on a repairing lease by the Wolverhampton area health authority and in 1980 was still occupied as a rehabilitation centre. In 1972 Patshull Properties Development Co. Ltd. was formed by members of the family to develop the 230 a. as Patshull Park recreation centre. The first stage was completed in 1980 with the opening of the Temple hotel.[2]

The manor house, still moated in the mid 17th century, evidently stood on the lower ground below the present Patshull House.[3] Sir Richard Astley was assessed for tax on 18 hearths in 1666.[4] In the 1680s the house was described as built of squared stone and was considered with its grounds 'the most accomplished and delicious mansion in the whole county'.[5] In 1698, however, it was thought 'old and low'. Sir Richard had planned to rebuild it but died too soon.[6]

Sir John began to build on a new site apparently in the mid or later 1730s.[7] His architect was James Gibbs (1682–1754), but Francis Smith of Warwick (1672–1738) supervised the building.[8] The layout is characteristic of Gibbs's country houses: a main block facing one way on the park and the other into a courtyard flanked by wings, originally detached,[9] beyond which there is a large walled forecourt. The main block is a plain square of seven bays with a rusticated ground floor. Because the site is on a slope, the ground floor is at basement level to the courtyard but at the back looks out on the gardens. It contains a vaulted central hall and cross passage with principal rooms on the garden front. The first floor, on ground level at the front, has an entrance hall and a saloon on the main axis. They rise up through a mezzanine of smaller rooms which is above the flanking rooms on the first floor. The uppermost floor contains a number of bedchambers with closets. Both the wings have large central doorways towards the courtyard in the manner of stables; the east wing contained kitchens and service rooms, and the archway on the west seems to have been a grand approach to the garden between rooms which were for domestic use.[10]

Francis Smith died in 1738; Gibbs towards the end of his life was in poor health and is unlikely to have continued the work on Patshull. By 1749 William Baker of Audlem (Ches.) was being paid for attendance, and in 1754 he started building the two pavilions which joined the wings to the main block. In 1757 Baker was paid for plans for the chapel, presumably that at the north end of Gibbs's west wing, and the stable. The north range which closed off the courtyard from the forecourt has been attributed to him,[11] and some of the plasterwork and fittings in the principal rooms on the west side of the main block are of his time.

Benjamin Wyatt, a builder of Sutton Coldfield, obtained designs for alterations to the saloon from his relative Lewis Wyatt in 1803,[12] but it is not known whether any work was carried out. By 1820 the loggia on the south front which existed c. 1800 had been remodelled.[13]

In 1850 Lord Dartmouth was considering proposals by W. L. Granville of London for the raising of the two corner pavilions and the

[94] Cal. Cttee. for Compounding, iv. 2921–2; Cal. Cttee. for Money, iii. 1415; W.S.L., S.MS. 339 (transcript of Royalist Composition Papers), i, ff. 31–46.
[95] G.E.C. Baronetage, iii. 255. S.R.O., D.(W.) 1778/V/1366, ct. of 25 Oct. 1661 styles him a knight.
[96] S.R.O., D.(W.) 1739/1, f. 24v.
[97] S.R.O., D. 802/29. For Pigot see D.N.B.; Complete Peerage, x, 520–1; V.C.H. Salop. iii. 255, 279–80; S.H.C. 1920 and 1922, 294. The statement in Pitt, Staffs. i. 188, that he used the diamond to buy Patshull is wrong; the diamond was sold by lottery under an Act of 1800.
[98] S.R.O., D. 802/29; D.(W.) 1739/3, 8 Feb. 1772.
[99] Burke, Peerage and Baronetage (1967), 1986–7.
[1] V.C.H. Staffs. xvii. 20; F. W. Hackwood, Hist. of West Bromwich (Birmingham, 1895), 62; S.R.O., D.(W.) 1778/V/1312.
[2] Inf. from Capt. J. Matthews and Mrs. Mary Shakespeare; Express & Star, 10 and 12 Sept. 1980.
[3] Shaw, Staffs. i. 70; above, p. 162. In 1370 Wm. Shareshull received a licence for an oratory 'apud Patyngham', perhaps an error for Patshull: L.J.R.O., B/A/1/5, f. 23v.
[4] S.H.C. 1923, 84.

[5] Plot, Staffs. 359.
[6] Journeys of Celia Fiennes, ed. C. Morris (1949 edn.), 228.
[7] C. Hussey, Eng. Country Houses, Early Georgian (1965 edn.), 18–19; W.S.L., S.MS. 237/Q, undated statement by the antiquarian Thos. Loxdale (d. 1742) that Sir John was rebuilding his house. Loxdale describes Sir John as M.P. for Salop.; he was elected in 1734: Trans. Salop. Arch. Soc. 4th ser. xii. 231.
[8] S.H.C. 1950–1, 118; Hussey, Eng. Country Houses, Early Georgian, 18–19. Sir John's bank account shows that in March 1738, immediately after Francis' death, Sir John paid £188 9s. 6d. to William Smith, Francis' brother: inf. from Dr. A. H. Gomme of Keele University.
[9] 'The offices are all out of doors': Soane Mus., London, memoir by Gibbs (ref. supplied by Mr. S. J. Ponder).
[10] W.S.L., Staffs. Views, vii. 137, 151; below, pl. facing p. 176.
[11] S.H.C. 1950–1, 117–18.
[12] Colvin, Brit. Architects, 937, 953.
[13] Shaw, Staffs. ii, plate facing p. 284 (in illuminated copies only); W.S.L., Staffs. Views, vii. 132; below, pl. facing p. 176.

c.1740 (James Gibbs)

c.1750 (William Baker)

19th century

feet

| 10 | 0 | | 50 | | 100 |

metres

| 10 | | 0 | | | 30 |

PLAN OF PATSHULL HOUSE

creation of a new terrace on the south.[14] It was probably William Burn who carried out those improvements; he is known to have worked at Patshull from the later 1850s.[15] In 1857 new kitchens were built at the north end of the west wing, and the dining room was moved to the south end of that wing.[16] Further work was carried out after Burn's death in 1870 by his nephew and partner J. McVicar Anderson.[17] The principal staircase, in the north-west corner of the main block, was rebuilt to a plan of 1876.[18] In 1882 the south and west fronts of the west wing were extended to provide for an enlarged dining room and for a billiard room which occupied the formerly recessed centre of the wing. A double flight of steps leads from the billiard room to the terraced garden; the doorway reproduces the design of the former archway in the west range, which had been filled in by 1875.[19] A porch, bridging the open area before the ground floor, was built in front of the main north doorway in

1894.[20] Undated 19th-century alterations include an intermediate floor in the chapel, the subdivision of the rooms on the uppermost floor to provide access passages, and a laundry at the north-east corner of the court. Minor alterations and additions continued into the early 20th century, the most notable being the creation of a boudoir with a bathroom at the south end of the east wing. Conversion to hospital use with staff flats has resulted in few structural alterations.

By the later 17th century the gardens next to the house were notably elaborate. There was an extensive arrangement of formal walks and enclosures with prospect mounds, statuary, knots, and waterworks. An unusual feature was an aviary, and Sir Richard's interest in fighting cocks was reflected in their portrayal amongst the statuary. Some of the features of the gardens may have been moved to the new house. About 1800 the statuary below the south front included two pillars surmounted by game cocks (perhaps those

[14] S.R.O., D.(W.) 1778/V/1317.
[15] Sessional Papers of R.I.B.A. 1869–70,126 (ref. supplied by Mr. A. G. Taylor of Staffs. C.C. Planning Dept.); S.R.O., D.(W.) 1805/3/12–14.
[16] Date on kitchen block; S.R.O., D. 1517/3/1.
[17] Sessional Papers of R.I.B.A. 1869–70,124 n.
[18] S.R.O., D.(W.) 1805/3/8, 30; inf. from Dr. Gomme.
[19] Kelly's Dir. Staffs. (1884); various schemes in S.R.O., D.(W.) 1805/3.
[20] Date over entrance to porch.

surviving in 1980 south-east of the churchyard), and part of the ironwork of the present north forecourt may also be re-used.[21] Both Sir Richard and Sir John spent large sums on landscaping, although in 1759 Sir John, whose wife had long lived apart from him, was described as living 'the life of a recluse amidst an infinite of most delightful scenes'.[22]

Soon after buying the estate Lord Pigot began extensive landscaping of the park, and it seems likely that his Huntingdonshire neighbour Lancelot Brown was consulted. By 1768 the southern end of the Great Pool, which may incorporate an earlier mill pool, had been begun. The work was continued by Sir Robert Pigot (d. 1796) and by his son George; by the end of the century they had extended the pools on either side of the house to form a Y-shaped lake. The landscaping extended into Pattingham parish with a cascade and an eel trap on Pasford brook. A Doric temple, in 1980 incorporated in the Temple hotel, was built on the west side of the lake. The woodland was thinned both to remove formal clumps and to create 'judicious openings'.[23] The major alterations to the grounds in the 19th century were south and west of the house. South of it William Burn replaced the 18th-century terrace and balustrade with terraces at two levels, and west of it he laid out small formal gardens leading down from the billiard-room steps.[24] On the lawn below the west wing are the remains of a canopied wellhead brought from Pepperhill in Albrighton (Salop.), after Lord Dartmouth had acquired that estate c. 1880.[25]

North-west of the house are extensive walled kitchen gardens with hot-houses of the 18th and 19th centuries, the former stables converted into living accommodation, the remains of an ice-house, and the site of the domestic gas and electricity plants in use by 1901.[26] Burn also designed lodges, farm buildings, and cottages for the estate.[27]

Before 1248 Robert Mansel granted his daughter Alice ½ virgate in Patshull formerly held by Robert Rufus. She was to pay 1d. rent and to have housebote and haybote in her father's wood of Patshull under the supervision of his forester. Alice gave the land with herself to the Augustinian canonesses of St. Leonard's priory ('White Ladies') just over the Shropshire boundary near Brewood; the nuns took over the payment of rent. Alice's gift was confirmed by her brother Hugh.[28] Nothing further is known of the property.

The estate known as Oldington farm by 1603 probably originated in the house, carucate, 4 a. of meadow, and 2 a. of wood in Olton which Richard of Oldington and his wife Joan conveyed to Richard's son John in 1336-7.[29] The estate passed from the Oldingtons to the Beckbury family, apparently their relatives, in 1387-8.[30] It had passed to the Kynnerton family by 1436 when John Kynnerton was living there.[31] In 1517 another John Kynnerton, who had been outlawed for murder, was succeeded by his son William, a Wolverhampton capper.[32] In 1537 William Kynnerton of Bewdley (Worcs.) and his wife Alice conveyed the farm to James Leveson of Wolverhampton, to whom they had mortgaged it in 1528.[33] It then descended in the Leveson and Leveson-Gower families with Great Wyrley, in Cannock.[34] It was held of the Astleys for a rent of 13d. and a heriot; William Leveson-Gower redeemed the heriot in 1672.[35] In 1718 John, Baron Gower, sold the farm to Sir John Astley, and it was later absorbed into the park.[36]

Patshull church had been annexed to Pattingham by 1342, and the great tithes remained part of Pattingham rectory until their commutation under the inclosure award of 1811.[37]

ECONOMIC HISTORY. In 1086 Patshull was apparently an arable area, as in the 20th century. Valued at 30s., the manor had land for 6 plough-teams; 2 were in demesne with 1 slave, and there were 12 villeins and 6 bordars with 4 teams.[38] Woodland, however, was extensive, ½ league in length and 4 furlongs in breadth; in the earlier 13th century the lord of the manor had a forester supervising his wood of Patshull.[39]

Three fields, probably open fields, were mentioned in 1405, Hill field, Gey field, and Wood field; they had meadow lying in them. Gey field apparently lay near the present church, which was built on part of Gay furlong in 1742-3.[40] In 1496-7 Richard Astley, lord of Patshull, inclosed 3 a. of common meadow and converted arable to pasture.[41] There were still open fields in the 16th and 17th centuries, apparently centring on the

[21] Plot, *Staffs.* 338-9, 359, 381, 387, and pl. facing p. 390; *Journeys of Celia Fiennes*, 228-30; Shaw, *Staffs.* ii. 285; below, pl. facing p. 176.
[22] Shaw, *Staffs.* ii. 283.
[23] D. Stroud, *Capability Brown* (1975 edn.), 235; S.R.O., Q/SO 16, ff. 46-7; Yates, *Map of Staffs.* (1775); Shaw, *Staffs.* i, map; ii. 283; above, p. 162; below, p. 169. For pools in the 17th cent. see B.R.L., Keen 357, 18 Jan. 1650/1; below, econ. hist.
[24] Plans in S.R.O., D. 1517/4; S.R.O., Tp. 181/8.
[25] D. H. Robinson, *The Wandering Worfe* (Albrighton, 1980), 90; W.S.L., Staffs. Views, vii. 152. It was broken when a branch from a tree fell on it in 1978.
[26] O.S. Map 6", Staffs. LXI. NW. (1904 edn.).
[27] S.R.O., D. 1517/5; D.(W.) 1805/3/12-14.
[28] W.S.L. 350A/40, ff. 17-18. Rob.'s charter was witnessed by Wm. of Wrottesley, who died between 1241 and 1248 (above, Tettenhall, manors and other estates), Alice's by Wm. and his son Hugh.
[29] *S.H.C.* xi. 88. For the name in 1603 see S.R.O., D. 593/C/8/2/16, f. 7.

[30] S.R.O., D. 593/H/14/1/4, f. 48. Ric. of Oldington was also known as Ric. of Beckbury: *S.H.C.* xi. 88.
[31] S.R.O., D. 593/H/14/1/4, f. 48; *S.H.C.* n.s. iii. 133.
[32] S.R.O., D.(W.) 1778/V/1365, ct. of 14 Oct. 1517; 1367, undated sheet endorsed 'Lewson Herriott'; P.R.O., C 1/531, no. 24.
[33] *S.H.C.* xi. 274, 276; S.R.O., D. 593/H/14/1/4, f. 48.
[34] S.R.O., D. 593/H/14/1/4, ff. 48-9; *V.C.H. Staffs.* v. 80.
[35] S.R.O., D. 593/A/2/7/1-4.
[36] S.R.O., D. 593/I/2/1B; D. 802/29/3; B.R.L., Keen 357; above, introduction.
[37] P.R.O., C 66/1318, mm. 6-7; P.R.O., REQ 2/2/141/3; L.J.R.O., B/V/6/Pattingham, 1673; S.R.O., Q/RDc 14; below, Pattingham, manor and other estates.
[38] *V.C.H. Staffs.* iv. 52.
[39] Ibid.; W.S.L. 350A/40, ff. 17-18.
[40] W.S.L. 350A/40, f. 22 (where Cegfeld should be Geyfeld: see W.S.L., S.MS. 386/2, f. 261); L.J.R.O., B/C/5/1742/Patshull.
[41] *Trans. R.H.S.* n.s. vii. 274; P.R.O., C 1/414, no. 32.

hamlet of Olton, whose fields had been mentioned in 1374.[42] In 1654 there were closes in Patshull field, and eight people were fined for inclosing part of the lord's waste.[43] Snowdon heath was mentioned from the 16th to the 18th centuries; *c.* 1600 Thomas Astley was accused of having 'nourished and increased' over 2,000 rabbits there to the detriment of the corn and grass on a neighbouring farm.[44] The only common land left at the end of the 18th century was the 350-a. Burnhill Green on either side of the Beckbury road; it was inclosed in 1811 under an Act of 1799.[45]

In the later 16th and earlier 17th century stock farming was widely practised, with sheep an important element. When George Wightwick, the minister of Patshull, died in 1640 his 15 cows and calves were valued at £32, his 150 sheep at £25, and his pigs at £3. The main crop mentioned during the period was wheat, with some barley, oats, rye, and peas; hemp was mentioned in 1583. George Wightwick's crops in 1640 were barley and dredge worth £15 13s. 4d., oats worth £2 10s., and peas and vetches worth £2 10s.[46]

By the 18th century the Patshull estate covered the whole parish and extended into Pattingham and northwards into Shropshire; the home farm stood just over the county boundary. Sir George Pigot, who held the estate from 1796 to 1841, was hailed by William Pitt, the agronomist, in 1817 as farming some 1,200 a. 'upon a magnificent scale'. He had adopted the Norfolk system of rotation, to which the light soil was well suited. The cattle were mostly Galloways and the sheep were Southdowns. The farm buildings were 'as commodious as possible', and water power was used for threshing.[47] There was also stock farming by tenants. At Burnhill Green farm in 1812 the retiring tenant offered for sale 23 Durham cows in calf, a Durham bull, and 250 Southdown sheep. At Nore Hill in 1814 the retiring tenant had 20 cows and 120 fat sheep for sale, and the tenant at the Medleys in 1816 had 411 New Leicester sheep and 61 pigs.[48]

Pigot practised a strict leasing policy. In 1811 he leased Burnhill Green farm and the adjoining Snowdon farm (which extended into Albrighton) on a yearly tenancy, with penalty rents if certain meadows or pastures were broken up without written consent, if any part were mown twice a year or more than once every two years without specified manuring, or if £50 a year were not spent on substantial improvements. Detailed conditions were made about cropping, manuring, and fallowing. Similar clauses were inserted

in two leases of other parts of the estate in Patshull and Pattingham in 1814 and 1816; the 1814 lease, of the Medleys farm, also required the tenant to insure the house and other buildings.[49]

The extension of the park in the later 18th century led to a drop in the number of farms. In the 1750s nine people besides the lord of the manor paid land tax; in 1851 there were two farms in the parish, Burnhill Green and the Medleys. The sale of the estate to Lord Dartmouth in 1848 had led by 1861 to an increase in the number of workers on the estate.[50] In 1866 his son and successor borrowed £4,000 to rebuild farms and erect cottages since Pattingham, the nearest village, was overcrowded already and could not contain the number of workers required for the improved cultivation of the district.[51] The chief crops in the late 19th century were wheat, barley, oats, and turnips.[52] Most of the land was still agricultural in 1979. Of the four farms recorded, two were over 200 ha. in area. Arable farming predominated, the chief crops being barley, wheat, and sugar beet. Cattle and pigs were the main stock.[53]

A park existed by the 14th century. A grant of free warren at Patshull was made to William Bagot in 1303 and to Sir William Shareshull and his wife in 1334.[54] In 1377 Sir William's grandson William Shareshull sued several people for breaking into his warren at Patshull and taking hares, rabbits, pheasants, and partridges. In 1394 he sued others for breaking into his park there and taking game.[55] In 1564 a former servant of Gilbert Astley claimed that Gilbert had promised him the keepership of the park at 26s. 8d. a year with a house for life.[56] By the earlier 17th century the park evidently occupied the north-eastern corner of the parish, as it did in 1775.[57] In the mid 18th century Sir John Astley walled it.[58] Lord Pigot, having bought the estate in 1765, at once set about the extension and landscaping of the park.[59]

There was a mill at Patshull in 1086 rendering 12d.,[60] but it is not possible to link it with any of the later mills. In the earlier 13th century William of Wrottesley, lord of Wrottesley in Tettenhall, gave his son Hugh a mill on the Hawk's Well stream near the Wrottesley boundary in the north-east of Patshull. By 1265 Hugh had leased the mill to William Bagot, lord of Patshull, for ½d. a year to be paid to the light of St. Mary at Patshull.[61] The Wrottesleys held a mill at Patshull in the later 15th century.[62] It formed part of the settlement made by Walter Wrottesley in 1545 on the occasion of his son

[42] S.R.O., D.(W.) 1778/V/1365, ct. of 17 Apr. 1464; 1366, cts. of 20 Dec. 1509, 21 Oct. 1607, 21 Oct. 1608; P.R.O., C 1/414, no. 32; B.R.L., Keen 357, 20 Mar. 1674/5; B.L. Add. Ch. 43907.
[43] S.R.O., D.(W.) 1778/V/1366, cts. of 17 Mar. and 9 Oct. 1654.
[44] Ibid. 1365, ct. of 1 Nov. 1519; W.S.L., S.MS. 339, i, ff. 41, 46; S.R.O., D.(W.) 1739/1, ff. 30v., 31v., 32v., showing the heath an inhabited area in the early 18th century; P.R.O., REQ 2/283/8.
[45] Pattingham and Patshull Inclosure Act, 39 Geo. III, c. 95 (Priv. Act); S.R.O., Q/RDc 14, pp. 1-2, 127-8.
[46] L.J.R.O., B/C/11.
[47] Pitt, *Staffs.* ii. 95-6; White, *Dir. Staffs.* (1834), 272.
[48] *Wolverhampton Chron.* 25 Nov. 1812; 9 Mar. 1814; 14 Feb. 1816.

[49] S.R.O., D. 564/3/4/13A and B and 15.
[50] S.R.O., D. 21/A/PZ/12-15; *S.H.C.* 4th ser. x. 18; above, introduction.
[51] R. W. Sturgess, 'Response of Agric. in Staffs. to the Price Changes of the 19th Cent.' (Univ. of Manchester Ph.D. thesis, 1965), 471. [52] *Kelly's Dir Staffs.* (1880; 1900).
[53] M.A.F.F., agric. returns 1979.
[54] *Cal. Chart. R.* 1300-26, 37; 1327-41, 310.
[55] *S.H.C.* xiv (1), 141; xv. 64.
[56] *S.H.C.* 1931, 152.
[57] S.R.O., D. 3548/1; Yates, *Map of Staffs.* (1775).
[58] Shaw, *Staffs.* ii. 283.
[59] Above, manor and other estates.
[60] *V.C.H. Staffs.* iv. 52.
[61] *S.H.C.* xi. 175; N.S. vi (2), 49, 73, 90, 140.
[62] P.R.O., C 140/80, no. 25.

John's marriage to Elizabeth, daughter of Thomas Astley, lord of Patshull. In 1551 John and Elizabeth conveyed the mill to Thomas Astley.[63] The site may be that of the present Golf House.

The hamlet of Millhouse, mentioned in 1327, was evidently associated with a mill known as Trill mill in the 16th and 17th centuries and described in 1623 as the mill of the lord of Patshull.[64] A water mill was held with Patshull manor by Richard Astley in 1656 and Sir John Astley in 1709,[65] and Patshull mill was mentioned in 1716.[66] It probably stood on Pasford brook east of Patshull House where existing pools were used in the landscaping of the later 18th century.[67]

A blade mill was held of the lord of Patshull by William Hardwick at the time of his death in 1608 or 1609.[68] It may be identifiable with the walk mill owned by Thomas Astley in 1623 and situated on Pasford brook at what was later the southern end of the Great Pool.[69]

Early in the 19th century, under the Inclosure Act of 1799, a stretch of Snowdon brook above the bridge at Badger Heath on the Shropshire boundary was straightened by agreement between Sir George Pigot and Joseph Green of Badger. By 1811 Green had dammed it to form a mill pool, with the Badger road running along the dam, and had built a corn and threshing mill on the Shropshire side of the road. Badgerheath mill remained in use until its demolition c. 1949.[70]

Before 1255 Robert Mansel granted Sir Ralph of Pitchford land for making a fishpond near the vill of Burnhill, presumably on Snowdon brook.[71] The grant was probably the origin of Snowdon Pool, a fishpond belonging to the lord of Patshull by the early 15th century. It lay on either side of the boundary north of the Beckbury road, which ran along the dam.[72] The pool was drained in the 1850s and planted with trees.[73]

In the late 17th century two large ponds in Sir Richard Astley's grounds were well stocked with fish.[74] Both the Great Pool and Church Pool in Patshull park provided fishing from the time of their formation in the later 18th century.[75] Angling formed a major feature of the Patshull Park development of the 1970s.

LOCAL GOVERNMENT. Robert Mansel held view of frankpledge by the mid 1250s,

paying 3s. for the right.[76] At least between 1486 and 1661 a court baron was usually held in either the spring or autumn each year. A view of frankpledge was recorded with the court baron three times in the 1590s, and a court leet was regularly held in the autumn in the late 17th century and during much at least of the 18th century.[77] A constable was still sworn at the leet in 1759, but by the late 17th century he presented his accounts to the parish.[78]

Two churchwardens were recorded in the 1550s, but by the early 17th century there was only one. A single churchwarden continued to be appointed until 1905; from then there were again two, Lord Dartmouth being appointed that year in addition to the existing warden.[79] A single overseer of the poor was being appointed by the late 17th century.[80] From 1750 he settled the constable's account and also that of the highway surveyor, who until then had evidently been responsible to the constable.[81]

In 1533 the manor court banned the harbouring of paupers coming from outside Seisdon hundred.[82] Two houses at Burnhill Green were used by the parish as poorhouses apparently from 1791.[83] A pound maintained by the parish was mentioned in 1709.[84] There was still a pound at Burnhill Green near the Dartmouth Arms in the early 1880s.[85]

In 1836 Patshull became part of Shifnal poor-law union.[86] It was assigned to Seisdon rural district in 1894,[87] and in 1974 it became part of South Staffordshire district.[88]

CHURCH. There was a church at Patshull by the reign of John when Mansel, the lord of the manor, presented his clerk Laurence. The advowson passed to Mansel's son Robert and then to Robert's son Hugh, who in 1272 granted it to the Augustinian priory of Laund (Leics.).[89] The church had become a dependent chapel of Pattingham church by 1342 when both were appropriated to Laund.[90] Patshull was served by a chaplain, who celebrated three times a week and on feast days and lived in a house provided by Laund. In 1352 the canons were ordered to repair the chancel and the house. By the later 1370s, however, the house was in ruin and the inhabitants of Patshull had no regular services. In 1391, following complaints by the inhabitants,

[63] S.H.C. N.S. vi (2), 271, 277.
[64] Above, introduction; S.R.O., D.(W.) 1778/V/1366, cts. of 20 Dec. 1509, 21 Oct. 1607, 9 Oct. 1654.
[65] P.R.O., IND 17187, p. 278; IND 17191, f. 146.
[66] S.R.O., D.(W.) 1739/1, f. 30v.
[67] Yates, Map of Staffs. (1775; 1799).
[68] S.R.O., D.(W.) 1778/V/1366, ct. of 6 Oct. 1609; W.S.L., M. 365; B.R.L., Keen 357, deeds of 8 June 1591, 22 May 1770, 19 and 20 Mar. 1781.
[69] B.R.L. 378054.
[70] S.R.O., D. 564/3/4/14; D. H. Robinson, The Wandering Worfe (Albrighton, 1980), 82.
[71] W.S.L. 350A/40, f. 18.
[72] Ibid. f. 22; Yates, Map of Staffs. (1775).
[73] S.R.O., D.(W.) 1778/V/1315; P.O. Dir. Staffs. (1860); O.S. Map 6", Staffs. LXI. NW. (1890 edn.).
[74] Journeys of Celia Fiennes, ed. C. Morris (1949 edn.), 230.
[75] Shaw, Staffs. ii. 285; O.S. Map. 6", Staffs. LXI. NW. (1904 edn.).   [76] S.H.C. v (1), 112.
[77] S.R.O., D.(W.) 1788/V/1365-7; D. 21/A/PC/1-2, 10; A/PK/1-8. The court baron was also variously referred to as

the great court and the little court, although both apparently transacted the same business.
[78] S.R.O., D.(W.) 1778/V/1366; D. 21/A/PC/1-2; A/PK/1-8.
[79] S.H.C. 1915, 200; S.R.O., Q/SR M. 1619, no. 13; S.R.O., D. 21/A/PC/1-26; A/PV/1; L.J.R.O., B/V/1/2, p. 17; Lich. Dioc. Ch. Cal. (1906 and later edns.).
[80] S.R.O., D. 21/A/PC/1-2; A/PO/69 and 74.
[81] S.R.O., D. 21/A/PC/1-2; A/PK/2; A/PS/1-6.
[82] S.R.O., D.(W.) 1778/V/1365.
[83] S.R.O., D. 21/A/PC/2, pp. 148 sqq.
[84] S.R.O., D. 21/A/PC/1.
[85] O.S. Map 6", Staffs. LXI. NW. (1890 edn.).
[86] 2nd Rep. Poor Law Com. H.C. 595, p. 546 (1836), xxix (1).
[87] Counties of Salop and Stafford (Shifnal and Seisdon) Conf. Order, 1894 (Local Govt. Bd. Order no. 31,917; copy in S.R.O., C/C/O/1).
[88] O.S. Map 1/100,000, Staffs. Admin. Areas (1974 edn.).
[89] S.H.C. iv (1), 197, 258-9.
[90] L.J.R.O., B/A/1/3, f. 60.

the bishop ordered the canons to repair the house and the vicar of Pattingham to find and support a chaplain.[91] A chaplain was living in Patshull in 1436.[92] By the late 15th century the prior was farming out the chapel with Pattingham church. In 1535 the chapel was described as annexed to the vicarage of Pattingham, to which it paid £1 6s. 8d. a year.[93]

Patshull had its own churchwardens by the 1550s[94] and its own registers from 1559. In 1563 its church, served by a curate, was described as independent.[95] By 1663 the patronage of what was described as a perpetual vicarage was held by Sir Richard Astley, and it thereafter descended with the manor. In the late 1970s the patron was Lord Dartmouth.[96] The living, having become a perpetual curacy as a result of a grant from Queen Anne's Bounty in 1722, was called a vicarage from 1868.[97]

An augmentation of £50 a year was granted by the committee for plundered ministers in 1652 for a curate yet to be chosen. It was probably never paid as Richard Bathoe, appointed in 1640, apparently remained curate until his death in 1663.[98] By the end of the 17th century the curate received £7 14s. 10d. for small tithes; after slight fluctuations the payment had by 1730 become a regular modus of £7 14s. He also received fees and Easter offerings. A grant of £200 was made from Queen Anne's Bounty in 1722 to meet a benefaction of £200 from Sir John Astley; between 1735 and 1741 the capital was used to buy land at Wheaton Aston in Lapley from which the curate received £17 10s. in 1741 and £30 in 1795.[99] When the church was rebuilt in the earlier 1740s the curate was given sole pasture rights in the new churchyard.[1] In 1786 a further £200 was granted from Queen Anne's Bounty, the minister 'being poorer than a day labourer'; Sir Robert Pigot was providing him with a house, a horse, and milk.[2] His income from modus, rent, and interest in 1795 was £41 14s. 10d.[3] His average income c. 1830 was £80 (gross and net).[4] By 1817 there was no house for the minister, and he was then given permission to live in Pattingham; an assistant curate appointed to serve Patshull in 1831 was allowed to live in Albrighton.[5] A vicarage house was built at Burnhill Green in 1924; in 1979 it was occupied by the diocesan youth officer, Patshull being served by the vicar of Pattingham from 1977.[6]

By 1830 the church was 'little more than a family chapel attached to the Hall', and in 1838

the archdeacon found the fabric 'shamefully neglected'. Richard Thursfield, perpetual curate from 1803, became vicar of Pattingham in 1819 and held both livings until his death in 1847. In 1830 he performed divine service at Patshull every Sunday at noon and celebrated communion six times a year there in alternation with Pattingham. An assistant curate was appointed for Patshull in 1831. In 1843 W. G. Greenstreet came as assistant curate of both Patshull and Pattingham, Thursfield being old and no longer resident in the area. Greenstreet succeeded him in both places in 1847 and continued to serve both until 1887 when he resigned Patshull. J. P. O'Connor, his curate and son-in-law, succeeded him there.[7]

By 1265 there was a light of St. Mary at Patshull.[8]

The present church of *ST. MARY* dates from 1743 and stands in the park south-west of Patshull House. Its predecessor stood ½ mile from the new site, probably further south at or near the former hamlet of Olton.[9] The body of the earlier church was rebuilt by Sir Richard Astley in the later 17th century, and it was reroofed in 1737.[10] Sir John Astley paid the cost of the new building and provided the site. Designed by James Gibbs in a Classical style and built of sandstone, the church consisted of a chancel with a Venetian east window, a nave with a pedimented Tuscan south porch, and a west tower with an ornamented parapet and a cupola. There was a statue, apparently of St. George, on the gable end of the chancel roof where there is now a cross.[11] The church was restored and enlarged in 1874 to designs by W. C. Banks of London and at Lord Dartmouth's expense. A three-bay north aisle was added with a vestry at the west end; a north porch was erected to correspond with that on the south, but it was non-functional, being backed by Sir Richard Astley's monument. In 1877 the top of the tower was remodelled by Banks to accommodate a new peal; the stone for the work came from a quarry in the north-east of Patshull park. Probably soon afterwards a statue of Charles II in a niche on the west side of the tower was removed to make way for a window; it was lying in the churchyard in 1979 and was destroyed soon afterwards.[12] It was perhaps in the 1870s that the pediment was removed from the south porch to allow a circular window to be inserted above the entrance.

Inside the church there are several monuments

[91] L.J.R.O., B/A/1/6, f. 106.
[92] *S.H.C.* N.S. iii. 133.
[93] P.R.O., SC 6/Hen. VIII/7312, m. 73d.; below, p. 177.
[94] Above, local govt.
[95] *S.H.C.* 1915, 200.
[96] L.J.R.O., B/A/3/Patshull; S.R.O., D. 802/29/2; D.(W.) 1778/V/1312; *Rep. Com. Eccl. Revenues*, 492; *Lich. Dioc. Dir.* (1978). For the grant of one turn in 1843 see Pattingham, church.
[97] *Lich. Dioc. Ch. Cal.* (1868; 1869).
[98] *S.H.C.* 1915, 200-1.
[99] L.J.R.O., B/V/6/Patshull; Hodgson, *Queen Anne's Bounty*, p. ccxcviii.
[1] L.J.R.O., B/C/5/1742/Patshull.
[2] Hodgson, *Queen Anne's Bounty*, p. ccxcviii; Pattingham ch., misc. bdle.
[3] L.J.R.O., B/V/6/Patshull.

[4] *Rep. Com. Eccl. Revenues*, 493.
[5] S.R.O., D. 21/A/PI/1-2.
[6] Inf. from Mr. P. Kemp.
[7] *S.H.C.* 4th ser. x. 18; Brighton, *Pattingham*, 40, 67-9; *Rep. Com. Eccl. Revenues*, 492; S.R.O., D. 21/A/PI/1-3.
[8] *S.H.C.* N.S. vi (2), 49.
[9] Shaw, *Staffs.* ii. 283; above, introduction.
[10] Plot, *Staffs.* 369; S.R.O., D. 21/127/A/PC/2, p. 28; PC/4.
[11] L.J.R.O., B/C/5/1742/Patshull; 1873/Patshull; Colvin, *Brit. Architects*, 340; transcript of diary of Ric. Wilkes of Willenhall by N. W. Tildesley of Willenhall (in poss. of Mr. Tildesley; made from original at Wellcome Inst. for Hist. of Medicine, London, MS. 5006), 6 Aug. 1743; above, pl. facing p. 177.
[12] *The Builder*, 4 Apr. 1874, p. 295, and 22 Dec. 1877, pp. 1277-8 (refs. supplied by Mr. S. J. Ponder); L.J.R.O., B/C/5/1873/Patshull; W.S.L., photographic colln., Patshull.

and memorials to Astleys, Pigots, and Legges. An alabaster table tomb, probably of Richard Astley (d. 1531) and his wife Joan, with effigies and figures has a later inscription wrongly attributing it. Behind it, filling a recess at the back of the north porch, is an elaborate alabaster monument to Sir Richard Astley (d. 1688); its central panel shows him at the head of a troop of horse.[13] In 1858 the church had box pews, and there was a pulpit and prayer desk on the north side of the chancel arch and a reading desk on the south side. They were all removed during the 1874 restoration except for the 18th-century pulpit, which was re-erected on a new base.[14] The font is probably of c. 1743.[15] The gilded wrought-iron screen, designed by Banks, was erected in 1893 as a memorial to Lord Dartmouth (d. 1891) by friends and neighbours.[16]

The plate in 1552 and 1553 consisted of a chalice, silver or silver-gilt, with a paten.[17] A paten of 1720 and a flagon and chalice of 1725, all silver-gilt, were given by Sir John Astley;[18] in 1979 they were in the Victoria and Albert Museum. There were three bells in 1552 and 1553. The present peal of six was cast in 1877 by Mears & Stainbank of London and given by Lord Dartmouth.[19]

The registers date from 1559 and are complete.[20]

ROMAN CATHOLICISM. In 1607 the minister of Patshull presented Thomas Astley's wife Margery as an obstinate recusant; a female servant of Thomas Astley was presented as a half recusant, going to church but refusing to receive communion.[21] From 1635 Walter Astley, son of Thomas and Margery, compounded for his estates, which had been sequestrated for recusancy, at £30 a year.[22] In 1635 there were 19 excommunicated recusants, headed by Walter Astley and his wife and a John Astley; 21 recusants were listed in 1641, headed by Walter and three other members of his family.[23] When Walter's house was captured in 1645, there was one 'Jesuit' priest there, perhaps two.[24] Walter's son Richard avoided sequestration as a papist in 1654 on the ground that there was no proof of his recusancy.[25] His first wife, Elizabeth Phillips, was returned as a recusant in 1657 with 17 others in Patshull and in 1665 with 11 others.[26] In 1678 Richard's arms were seized with those of other papists. By the beginning of 1679 he had taken the oaths of allegiance and supremacy, and orders were given for the return of his arms.[27] None the less he was included in a list of 'considerable'

PATSHULL CHURCH: ASTLEY MONUMENTS

Staffordshire papists in 1680.[28] His second wife, Henrietta Borlase, was a protestant, and their three chidren, including Richard's heir John, were baptized as Anglicans between 1685 and 1688. In 1704 Henrietta secured an Act of Parliament allowing John, though still a minor, to make a marriage settlement. In her petition she stated that John was the first protestant in that line of the Astley family and that she and his nearest protestant relatives thought that he should marry and be settled before he came of age.[29] Six papists at Patshull were returned in 1706, but in 1767 there was stated to be none.[30]

[13] T.B.A.S. lxx. 12-14; lxxi. 34; lxxv, 71, 76; lxxvi. 62, 74-5; Shaw, Staffs. ii. 285 and pl. facing p. 286 (reproduced above); Jnl. of Soc. for Army Historical Research, xxxviii (no. 153), 11-12.
[14] Lichfield Cathedral Libr., Moore and Hinckes drawings, ix, nos. 3 and 4; L.J.R.O., B/C/5/1873/Patshull; The Builder, 4 Apr. 1874, p. 295; S.R.O., D. 1517/20/2.
[15] T.B.A.S. lxviii. 23, ascribes it to the 17th century.
[16] Plaque on chancel arch; L.J.R.O., B/C/12/Patshull, 1893.
[17] S.H.C. N.S. vi (1), 190; S.H.C. 1915, 200.
[18] T.B.A.S. lxxiii. 24-7 (where the flagon and chalice are dated 1725 although described as given in 1723).
[19] S.H.C. N.S. vi (1), 190; S.H.C. 1915, 200; Lynam, Church Bells, 21; Jennings, Staffs. Bells, 35, 43-4, 102.

[20] All except those in current use are in S.R.O., D.(W.) 1739.   [21] Staffs. Cath. Hist. iv. 27.
[22] Ibid. xviii. 4.
[23] L.J.R.O., B/V/1/55, p. 17; Staffs. Cath. Hist. v. 16-17.
[24] V.C.H. Staffs. iii. 105. The term 'Jesuit' may simply mean popish.
[25] Cal. Cttee. for Compounding, iv. 2921.
[26] S.H.C. 4th ser. ii. 84-5; L.J.R.O., B/V/1/72, p. 45.
[27] S.R.O., D.(W.) 1721/3/291; Cal. S. P. Dom. 1679-80, 8, 84. These refs. have been supplied by Prof. A. G. Petti of Calgary Univ.
[28] Staffs. Cath. Hist. xviii. 13.
[29] S.R.O., D.(W.) 1739/1, ff. 23v., 24v.; MSS. of House of Lords, N.S. v. 351-2; Statutes of the Realm, viii. 276.
[30] Staffs. Cath. Hist. xiii. 34-5; xvii. 27.

PROTESTANT NONCONFORMITY. The only known place of worship for protestant dissenters was the house of Edward Hand, licensed for Congregational worship in 1672.[31] It was probably at Nore Hill, where the Hands lived in the 17th and early 18th century.[32]

EDUCATION. A schoolmistress lived with her parents at Nore Hill in 1841,[33] but it is not known that she taught in the parish. In the later 1840s there was no school in the parish and children attended a neighbouring one, presumably at Pattingham.[34] A school was opened in 1857 or 1858. It was at first held in the master's house but later moved into a converted granary. A husband and wife were master and mistress in 1860.[35] A building for boys, girls, and infants was erected on the Beckbury road at Burnhill Green in 1868 at Lord Dartmouth's expense; it consisted of a schoolroom and a classroom but was enlarged in 1894 by the addition of a second classroom. In 1877 the average attendance was 30 boys and 26 girls; school pence were 2d. or 1d. according to age.[36] A government grant was received from the later 1890s. Attendances averaged 49 c. 1894 and 60 c. 1899.[37] There were 43 pupils on the books in April 1928 and 38 in July 1950.[38] By 1965 the number of pupils had dropped to 11, and the school was closed that year.[39]

CHARITY FOR THE POOR. John Nicolls, Thomas Astley's bailiff, who died in 1608, gave £3 as a stock for the poor.[40] Its later history is unknown.

PATTINGHAM

THE ancient parish of Pattingham straddled the county boundary with Shropshire and consisted of two townships and manors, Pattingham in Staffordshire and Rudge in Shropshire. Each is a civil parish in its respective county. The present article is concerned primarily with the Staffordshire portion of the ancient parish. Certain topics common to both townships, such as ecclesiastical history, are treated here; otherwise the history of Rudge is reserved for the Shropshire *History*. In 1845 the Staffordshire portion was transferred from the southern to the northern division of Seisdon hundred.[41] The area remains predominantly rural, but there has been extensive residential development since the Second World War, mainly for people working in Wolverhampton.

Pattingham civil parish, 2,529 a. (1,023 ha.) in area,[42] lies on sloping ground, with the centre of Pattingham village by the church standing at 390 ft. (118 m.). In the north at Westbeech the land reaches 525 ft. (160 m.). It drops to 282 ft. (88 m.) on the south-eastern boundary, formed mainly by Black brook, and to below 200 ft. (61 m.) along Pasford brook on the western boundary. The north-western boundary is formed by a tributary of Pasford brook, probably once known as Gallows brook and possibly as Ball brook also.

Its confluence with Pasford brook is the southern end of the Great Pool in Patshull park, created in the later 18th century as part of the landscaping of the park; the cascade and eel trap to the south on Pasford brook are also part of that landscaping.[43] Copley brook, another tributary of Pasford brook, forms part of the south-western boundary. An oak tree once marked the boundary in the north-eastern corner of the parish, where the name Meer Oak survives. From there the northern boundary runs along the south side of Wrottesley Old Park following a track called Deers Leap.[44] There was evidently a boundary stone in the north-east giving its name to Whorestone field[45] and to Warstone Hill Road which runs north from the Wolverhampton road. The underlying rock is sandstone, and a notable feature in the south-east is the outcrop forming an escarpment along the 400-ft. (122 m.) contour from Dadnall Hill on the eastern boundary to the Clive and the south-western boundary. It is broken at Great Moor where Nurton brook flows through. The brook joins Black brook c. ½ mile to the south, and for much of that distance it flows along the lane leading south from Great Moor.[46] The sandstone has been quarried around Nurton and Great Moor in the east and Copley in the

[31] A. G. Matthews, *Cong. Churches of Staffs.* 92.
[32] P.R.O., C 2/Jas.I/H 25/19; S.R.O., D.(W.) 1739/1; L.J.R.O., B/C/11, Wm. Hande (1605); B.R.L., Keen 357.
[33] P.R.O., HO 107/1002.
[34] Nat. Soc. *Inquiry, 1846-7*, Staffs. 7.
[35] P.R.O., ED 7/109/242; ibid. RG 9/1852; *P.O. Dir. Staffs.* (1860).
[36] P.R.O., ED 7/109/242; Brighton, *Pattingham*, 69; *Kelly's Dir. Staffs.* (1896); S.R.O., D. 1517/14/2-4.
[37] *Rep. Educ. Cttee. of Council, 1894-5* [C. 7776-I], p. 993, H.C. (1895), xxvii; *Schs. in receipt of Parl. Grants, 1899-1900* [Cd. 332], p. 224, H.C. (1900), lxiv; S.R.O., D. 21/A/PV/1, 16 Apr. 1895.
[38] S.R.O., CEL/30/1, pp. 345, 500.
[39] Inf. from Mr. S. J. Ponder.
[40] S.R.O., D.(W.) 1739/1, f. 11.

[41] S.R.O., Q/SO 35, ff. 25, 139v., 163v. The present article was written mainly in 1979. The Revd. C. J. L. Walters, vicar of Pattingham, and others named in footnotes are thanked for their help.   [42] *Census*, 1971.
[43] D. H. Robinson, *The Wandering Worfe* (Albrighton, 1980), 92-3. There was a Gallows meadow near the brook: below, local govt. Diversions of 'Gallhouse' brook were mentioned in court rolls of both Patshull (1591: S.R.O., D.(W.) 1778/V/1366) and Pattingham (e.g. 1638; S.R.O., D.(W.) 1807/243). For Gallows brook in 1780 see S.R.O., D. 3451/8/8. For Ball brook in the late 1640s see S.R.O., D.(W.) 1807/264, 267; for Ball field nearby see below, econ. hist. Pasford brook no longer follows the boundary completely.
[44] For Meer Oak and Deers Leap see above, p. 11.
[45] Below, econ. hist.
[46] That stretch is marked as a ford on modern maps.

south-west. A patch of marl at Nurton Hill has been used for brick making.[47] There is a variety of soils.[48]

Evidence of early settlement is scanty. A gold torque found west of the church in 1700 has been dated to the Middle Bronze Age.[49] Tuters Hill to the north-west may be the site of a hillfort, the name meaning a look-out place.[50] The name Pattingham suggests settlement in the Anglo-Saxon period by the folk of Peatta.[51] There was a church by 1086.[52]

In 1086 the recorded population of Pattingham manor was 14.[53] Twenty-five people were assessed for the 1327 subsidy.[54] In 1343 at the manor court 16 free men and 127 neifs did fealty.[55] In the mid 1520s the taxpayers numbered between 39 and 57,[56] but the muster roll of 1539 listed only 28.[57] There were 74 households in the parish in 1563.[58] The poll-tax assessment of 1641 listed 204 people in Pattingham township.[59] In 1666 there were 73 people assessed for hearth tax and a further 41 too poor to pay.[60] The Compton Census of 1676 recorded 220 people in the parish.[61] There were 126 owing suit to the manor court in 1682, 178 in 1769, and 147 in 1789.[62] The population of Pattingham township was 750 in 1801 and 866 in 1821. It then declined to 817 in 1831 and 802 in 1841 but had risen to 939 by 1851. The drop from 959 to 924 between 1861 and 1871 was attributed to migration to Wolverhampton. Having risen to 955 by 1881 it steadily declined, to 859 in 1891, 779 in 1901, 775 in 1911, and 690 in 1921. It had risen to 708 by 1931. After the Second World War the population rose sharply, to 1,006 in 1951, 1,382 in 1961, and 1,981 in 1971.[63]

The village centre lies along High Street on either side of the church and continues south-west down the slope to Hall End, presumably the site of the manor house, and east around the crossroads at Newgate and along the Highgate part of the Wolverhampton road. Of the 126 people owing suit to the manor court in 1682, 65 were listed under the village; of the 147 in 1789, the village accounted for 100.[64] Most of the datable houses are of the 18th century and later. The Court House north of the later 18th-century vicarage is of the mid 18th century. The Elms in Clive Road, demolished in or after 1963, was built in the late 18th century and had a central block with pavilion-like wings.[65] Several houses

date from the early 19th century. Others were built between the two World Wars, notably in Clive and Westbeech Roads, and the large number built since the Second World War, most of them privately, are concentrated in the southern and south-eastern parts of the village.

Several roads radiate from the village linking it with outlying settlements, some of them single farms. Nurton on the Wolverhampton road in the north-east existed as Noverton in 1312.[66] Nurton bridge, carrying the road over Nurton brook, was mentioned from 1678.[67] The Hill, so called by 1392, was a settlement by 1428; it was either Dadnall Hill east of Nurton, a name in use by the mid 17th century, or Nurton Hill to the north-west, in use by the mid 18th century.[68] After the Second World War several houses were built along the ridge south of Dadnall Hill. Great Moor further south on Nurton brook was probably the place called Moor in 1229, which was a settled area by 1312. Great Moor was so called by 1514 and had a bridge by 1630.[69] Two large houses there date from the 18th century, and a farm to the east was being used as a slaughter house in 1979. Little Moor on the escarpment to the south-west was so named by 1338 and was a settlement by 1439.[70] The Clive further south-west and still on the escarpment was an inhabited place by 1312.[71] By the 1590s there was settlement at the Marsh in the low-lying area along Black brook below the escarpment where the name Rushy Marsh survives.[72] Copley on the south-western boundary was an inhabited place by 1314.[73] The manorial mill on Pasford brook on the western boundary existed by 1314 and was known as Basford or Pasford mill by 1717.[74] The nearby Pasford Farm existed by the early 19th century.[75] Hardwick to the north was a place name by the mid 12th century and a settlement by 1311. The farm disappeared c. 1820, after the death of John Plant whose stock and goods there were offered for sale in 1818.[76] Woodhouses to the east, presumably a clearing from woodland, was inhabited by 1311.[77] Tuters Hill south of Woodhouses was an area of waste in the mid 14th century. A house adjoined Tuters Hill common in 1653, and inclosure of the waste was then in progress. There were several houses there by the later 18th century.[78] The road through the area was extended westwards past Hardwick as the road to Patshull when the more northerly road

[47] T. H. Whitehead and others, *Memoirs of Geol. Surv., the Country between Wolverhampton and Oakengates*, 119, 135, 162–3; below, econ. hist.
[48] *Kelly's Dir. Staffs.* (1940).
[49] *N.S.J.F.S.* iv. 3.
[50] M. Gelling, *Signposts to the Past*, 147.
[51] Ekwall, *Eng. Place-names*.
[52] Below, church.
[53] Below, econ. hist.
[54] *S.H.C.* vii (1), 248–9.
[55] S.R.O., D.(W.) 1807/13B.
[56] P.R.O., E 179/96, 106.
[57] *S.H.C.* n.s. vi (1), 71.
[58] *S.H.C.* 1915, p. lxxi.
[59] H.L., Main Papers, box 178.
[60] *S.H.C.* 1923, 82–4.
[61] W.S.L., S.MS. 33, p. 371.
[62] S.R.O., D.(W.) 1778/V/1362; D.(W.) 1807/357; W.S.L. 447/28.
[63] *V.C.H. Staffs.* i. 326; *Census*, 1871, 1911–71.
[64] S.R.O., D.(W.) 1778/V/1362; D.(W.) 1807/357.

[65] Staffs. C.C. Planning Dept., Conservation Section photographs, 2245/63–249/63.
[66] S.R.O., D.(W.) 1807/2.
[67] S.R.O., D. 3451/6/1.
[68] S.R.O. D.(W.) 1807/38, 64, 277, 353.
[69] *S.H.C.* iv (1), 76; S.R.O., D.(W.) 1807/2, 100; D. 3451/2/2.
[70] S.R.O., D.(W.) 1807/4, 70.
[71] Ibid. 2.
[72] Ibid. 356; S.R.O., D. 3451/2/2; O.S. Map 1/25,000, SO 89/99 (1976 edn.).
[73] S.R.O., D.(W.) 1807/2.
[74] Below, econ. hist.
[75] R. Baugh, *Map of Salop.* (1808).
[76] Below, manor and other estates; S.R.O., D.(W.) 1807/1; *Wolverhampton Chron.* 4 Mar. 1818. It is shown by B.L. Maps, O.S.D. 213 (1814) and possibly by C. and J. Greenwood, *Map of Staffs.* (1820) but not by J. Phillips and W. F. Hutchings, *Map of Staffs.* (1832).
[77] S.R.O., D. 1807/1.
[78] Ibid. 20–1, 276, 278B; Yates, *Map of Staffs.* (1775).

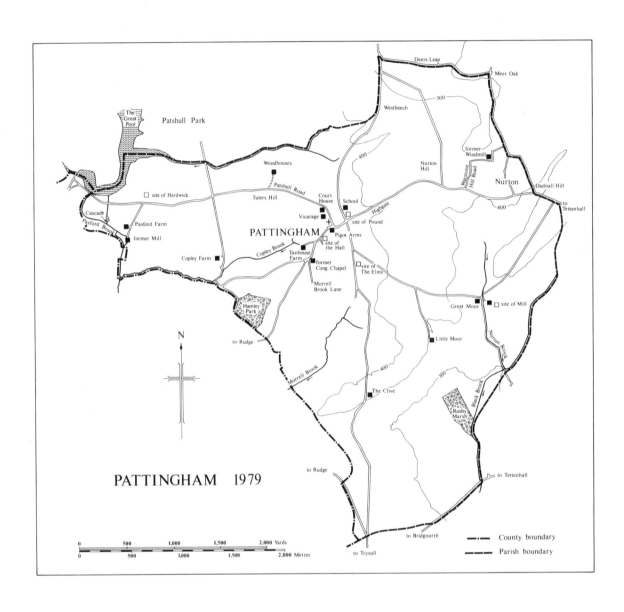

The Great Pool

Patshull Park

Deers Leap

Meer Oak

500

Westbeech

400

former Windmill

Nurton Hill

Wergstone Hill Road

Nurton

Dadnall Hill

to Tettenhall

Woodhouses

site of Hardwick

Patshull Road

Tuters Hill

Court House

School

Highgate

400

Cascade

Vicarage

site of Pound

Pasford Brook

Pasford Farm

former Mill

PATTINGHAM

Pigot Arms

site of the Hall

Copley Brook

site of The Elms

Copley Farm

Tanhouse Farm

former Cong. Chapel

Morrell Brook Lane

Great Moor

site of Mill

N

Hamley Park

Little Moor

Nurton Brook

to Rudge

Morrell Brook

400

300

The Clive

Rushy Marsh

Black Brook

PATTINGHAM 1979

to Rudge

to Tettenhall

to Bridgnorth

County boundary

Parish boundary

0   500   1,000   1,500   2,000 Yards
0   500   1,000   1,500   2,000 Metres

to Trysull

was stopped up *c.* 1770 in the course of the extension of the park in Patshull.[79] At Westbeech north of Pattingham village there were nine people owing suit to the manor court by 1682, the result probably of encroachment on the common there.[80]

There was mention of the New Inn in the parish in 1633 and 1653.[81] An inn called the London Prentice in 1759 stood opposite the church.[82] It may thus be identifiable with the Pigot Arms, which was so named by 1800[83] and is a remodelled 18th-century building. There were two inns in 1818, the Pigot Arms and the White Hart.[84] In 1841, and evidently 1834 also, there were three public houses besides the Pigot Arms (in 1834 the King's Arms): the Crown to the west of the churchyard, the Sow and Pigs (in 1871 the Red Lion) at the junction of High Street and Morrell Brook Lane, and the Roebuck on the corner of Newgate and Clive Road.[85] The sale of the Crown in 1888 and the closure of the Roebuck about the same time left the Pigot Arms as the only inn.[86] In 1979 there was a second inn, the Crown, further west along High Street.

In 1734 a meeting of 22 parishioners agreed to form an association for the prosecution of felons, the costs to be met by the churchwardens.[87] A policeman was living in Pattingham by 1841. There was a police station at the junction of the roads from Copley and Rudge by 1871. About 1960 it was replaced by one on the north side of Highgate, which was closed *c.* 1974.[88]

A post office was established in 1844.[89] By 1928 buses run by Wolverhampton corporation served Pattingham.[90] There was an electricity supply by the early 1930s.[91] Although water was supplied privately in the Tuters Hill area from 1928, there was no public supply until 1935 when one was provided by Wolverhampton corporation. Sewerage was provided in the earlier 1950s. Gas was available from 1966.[92]

There was mention of a wake day in 1610–11. In the mid 18th century the wake was held early in March, presumably in connexion with the feast of St. Chad, the patron of the church (2 March). In the early 19th century the open space opposite the east end of the church was used for bull and badger baiting and cock fighting.[93] Pattingham friendly society was established in a private house in 1800, meeting every fourth Saturday. By 1867 it met at the Pigot Arms, where it continued until at least 1914. The Victoria (later Loyal Victoria) Lodge of Odd

Fellows, established in 1844, met at the Roebuck by 1857 and was still meeting there in 1880; in 1979 the Odd Fellows were using the village hall. The British Oak Lodge of Free Gardeners was meeting at the Pigot Arms by 1879; it continued until at least 1894.[94] By 1896 there was a working men's club at Pear Tree House at the south-west end of the village. A new club house was built on an adjoining site *c.* 1957.[95]

The Pattingham Reading Rooms were mentioned in 1872, and by 1921 there was a reading room in part of the building which was formerly the Roebuck.[96] A village hall was opened in 1922 on a site given by Lord Dartmouth on the open space opposite the east end of the church. A new hall was built there in 1966.[97] A local history society was formed in 1967.[98]

There was a horticultural show every August in the 1880s and 1890s.[99]

MANOR AND OTHER ESTATES. Before the Conquest *PATTINGHAM* was held by Alfgar, earl of Mercia; in 1086 the 2 hides there were held by the king.[1] It appears that the overlordship passed to Hugh d'Avranches, earl of Chester (d. 1101), descending with the earldom of Chester until the death of Ranulph de Blundeville in 1232. It then passed to Hugh d'Aubigny, earl of Arundel and Sussex, son of Ranulph's sister Mabel. He died in 1243, and Pattingham, initially assigned as part of the dower of his widow Isabel, passed in 1244 to his sister Nichole and her husband Roger de Somery.[2] Roger died in 1273, and the overlordship descended to his son Roger (d. 1291), who was succeeded by his son John, created Lord Somery in 1308.[3] On John's death in 1322 Pattingham was assigned to his elder sister Margaret, wife of John de Sutton. The overlordship was still held by the Sutton family in the early 15th century.[4]

It seems likely that when Hugh d'Avranches gave Drayton Bassett to his daughter Geva on her marriage to Geoffrey Ridel, he gave her Pattingham also; certainly *c.* 1120 the church there was described as being of the lordship of her daughter Maud and Maud's husband Richard Basset.[5] About 1150 Richard's son Geoffrey Ridel granted Pattingham to his brother Ralph Basset in exchange for lands in Normandy. Ralph was dead *c.* 1160 and was succeeded by his son Ralph, who was dead by 1211, leaving a son Ralph, a minor; the manor was granted to his widow Isabel in

[79] S.R.O., Q/SO 16, ff. 46–7; above, Patshull, introduction.   [80] S.R.O., D.(W.) 1778/V/1362.
[81] L.J.R.O., B/C/11, John Bette (1633); *Pattingham Par. Reg.* (Staffs. Par. Reg. Soc. 1934), 144.
[82] S.R.O., D.(W.) 1807/346.   [83] S.R.O., D. 3451/8/3.
[84] Parson and Bradshaw, *Dir. Staffs.* (1818).
[85] White, *Dir. Staffs.* (1834), 273; L.J.R.O., B/A/15/ Pattingham, nos. 244, 267, 273, 333; Brighton, *Pattingham,* 20.
[86] *Kelly's Dir. Staffs.* (1884; 1888); S.R.O., D. 660/15/8.
[87] S.R.O., D. 3451/8/10.
[88] P.R.O., HO 107/1002; P.R.O., RG 10/2927; Staffs. C.C. Deeds, C. 824, HI 16; local inf. (1979).
[89] *P.O. Dir. Staffs.* (1845).
[90] *Kelly's Dir. Staffs.* (1928).
[91] Ibid. (1932); L.J.R.O., B/C/12/Pattingham, 1931.
[92] Seisdon R.D.C. *Reps. of M.O.H. 1928,* 9; *1934,* 9; *1935,* 10; *1946,* 3; *1953,* 18 (copies in S.R.O., C/H/1/2/2/36); local inf.

[93] S.R.O., D. 3451/2/2; S.R.O., Tp. 1322/1/39, 7 Mar. 1753; Brighton, *Pattingham,* 141.
[94] S.R.O., Q/RSf; Pattingham ch., bellringers' bk. 1852–1915; *Reps. Chief Registrar of Friendly Socs. 1876,* H.C. 429, p. 405 (1877), lxxvii.
[95] *Kelly's Dir. Staffs.* (1896); local inf. (1979).
[96] *P.O. Dir. Staffs.* (1872); O.S. Map 6″, Staffs. LXI. NE. (1924 edn.); local inf. (1979).
[97] Brighton, *Pattingham,* 154–6; *Seisdon R.D. Official Guide* (1973 edn.), 19.
[98] Inf. from the secretary.
[99] *Kelly's Dir. Staffs.* (1884 and edns. to 1896).
[1] *V.C.H. Staffs.* iv. 40.
[2] *Bk. of Fees,* i. 544; *Close R. 1242–7,* 252; *S.H.C.* ix (2), 17–18; *Complete Peerage,* i. 238; iii. 169.
[3] *S.H.C.* 1911, 152–7, 206, 353–4; *Feud. Aids,* vi. 9, 16.
[4] *Cal. Close, 1318–23,* 630; *1402–5,* 36; *S.H.C.* 1913, 48, 99.
[5] *S.H.C.* iii (1), 187; Dugdale, *Mon.* vi (1), 189.

dower.[6] The younger Ralph held the manor by 1236 and died between 1254 and 1257.[7] His heir was his son Ralph, who died fighting against Henry III at Evesham in 1265. In October the king granted the manor to William Bagot, but in November it was restored to Ralph's widow Margaret on account of the laudable service of her father Roger de Somery.[8] By 1275 the manor was held by her son Ralph, who was created Lord Basset of Drayton in 1295 and died in 1299. His son Ralph succeeded and, although a minor, received livery of his lands in 1300.[9] On his death in 1343 he was succeeded by his grandson, another Ralph Basset. Ralph died in 1390, and the manor passed under a settlement of 1340 to his brother-in-law Thomas de Beauchamp, earl of Warwick, by whom it was conveyed to Ralph's widow Joan in dower. When the estates of the earl of Warwick were confiscated in 1397, Pattingham was granted to Thomas, earl of Kent, but it was restored to Joan in 1398.[10] She died in 1402 and livery was granted to Richard Beauchamp, son of Thomas, earl of Warwick.[11] The manor descended with the earldom of Warwick until 1492 when it passed to the Crown on the death of Anne, countess of Warwick.[12]

The manor was leased by the Crown, and lessees included Sir John Giffard of Chillington, in Brewood, his son Thomas, and grandson John, from 1530 to 1578, and Walter Leveson of Lilleshall (Salop.) and Trentham from 1581 to 1589.[13] In 1590 the manor was sold to Rowland Watson of Chancery Lane, London. He was succeeded in 1595 by his son William, a minor.[14] Although he came of age in 1605, the manor courts were held in the name of his mother Jane until 1608. William Bailey was then granted the farm of the manor on account of her recusancy and held the courts until 1617, two years after William Watson's death. Watson was succeeded by his son, also called William, born posthumously in 1616. From 1618 until he reached his majority in 1637 courts were held by his mother Elizabeth in association with her successive husbands, Thomas Cornwallis and Thomas Stourton, as guardians.[15] In 1648 William Watson, then living at Monkton Farleigh (Wilts.), sold the manor to Clement Throckmorton of Haseley (Warws.). In the following year Throck-

morton compounded for two thirds of the manor which had been sequestrated on account of Watson's alleged recusancy. Throckmorton was still holding the manor court in 1663, but in 1664 Watson was again lord.[16]

William Watson lived until 1695, although between 1679 and 1686 the courts were usually held by his son Francis (d. c. 1690). In 1693 Elizabeth Watson, William's wife, held a court as lady of the manor, and she did so regularly from 1695 until her death in 1700. The manor passed to her grandson William, son of Rowland Watson.[17] In 1705 William Watson and his family were living at Rudge but had left the area by 1706.[18] In 1708 he was described as of Besford (Worcs.) and in 1709 of Pangbourne (Berks.).[19] In 1725 he conveyed the manor to Sir John Astley,[20] and the descent thereafter followed that of Patshull. Sir George Pigot owned over two thirds of the land in Pattingham in 1841. After the death of the 7th earl of Dartmouth in 1958 his property there passed to the Crown in lieu of death duties like most of the remainder of the Patshull estate.[21]

The manor house was presumably at Hall End at the south-western end of the village. A hall and chamber at Pattingham were mentioned in 1336. Repairs were made to the hall, chamber, and kitchen in the mid 15th century, and in 1477 work was carried out on the great chamber and the adjoining chamber and latrine. The gate ('porta') of the manor was mentioned in 1405 and a gatehouse in 1532.[22] Pattingham Hall at Hall End, demolished c. 1968, included a block of stone and brick, dating partly from the 17th century; a timber-framed wing, incorporating old materials, was added in 1935.[23]

There was a *RECTORY* manor by the earlier 14th century.[24] When the church was appropriated to Launde priory (Leics.) in 1342, the rectory was charged with the payment of ½ mark a year to the monks of Coventry, ½ mark to the vicars choral of Lichfield, and 4 marks to the fabric of Lichfield cathedral.[25] It had been leased by 1379 to John of Gaunt, duke of Lancaster, who in that year sublet it to his squire William Bagot for one year.[26] In 1405 Launde granted a further pension of 40s. charged on the rectory to the dean and chapter of Lichfield in recogni-

[6] S.H.C. ii (1), 156; iii (1), 188-9, 191, 193.
[7] Bk. of Fees, i. 544; Cal. Pat. 1247-58, 312; Cal. Chart. R. 1226-57, 474.
[8] Cal. Chart. R. 1257-1300, 58; Cal. Close (Suppl.), 1244-6, 47; Cal. Close, 1264-8, 130; Cal. Pat. 1258-66, 497-8.
[9] S.H.C. vi (1), 66; Cal. Pat. 1292-1301, 495.
[10] Cal. Inq. p.m. viii, p. 327; xvi, p. 388; S.H.C. xi. 148; Cal. Close, 1389-92, 205; 1396-9, 346, 360-1; Cal. Pat. 1396-9, 200, 215.
[11] Cal. Close, 1402-5, 36; Cal. Pat. 1401-5, 247-8.
[12] Complete Peerage, xii (2), 378-94; Cal. Pat. 1476-85, 65, 365; 1485-94, 13, 298; Cal. Inq. p.m. Hen. VII, iii, p. 198.
[13] S.R.O., D.(W.) 1807/118, 121, 124, 128-9, 131-2, 135-65; L. & P. Hen. VIII, v, p. 427; S.H.C. 1917-18, 335 n.; Cal. Pat. 1557-8, 22.
[14] S.R.O., D. 669; P.R.O., C 142/242, no. 30; C 142/354, no. 108.
[15] S.R.O., D.(W.) 1807/166-239; Cal. S.P. Dom. 1603-10, 407; P.R.O., C 142/354, no. 108. A single court was held in 1602 by Robert Watson and Charles Morgan as farmers of the manor.
[16] Cal. Cttee. for Compounding, iii. 2057; W.S.L., S.MS.

339 (transcript of Royalist Composition Papers), vi, pp. 212a-219; S.R.O., D.(W.) 1807/270-98.
[17] Wilts. Arch. Mag. xx. 92; S.R.O., D.(W.) 1807/304-51; P.R.O., C 5/168/86. Eliz. is incorrectly given as the wife of Rowland Watson in Wilts. Arch. Mag. xx. 92: see S.R.O., D.825.
[18] Below, Roman Catholicism.
[19] B.R.L., Keen 358; S.R.O., D. 825.
[20] P.R.O., Index of Fines, vol. xxxv, f. 223.
[21] L.J.R.O., B/A/15/Pattingham; inf. from Mr. D. Burton of Pasford Farm (1979).
[22] S.R.O., D.(W.) 1807/3, 48, 69, 72-3, 75, 93, 115; Warws. R.O., CR 895/8/23. The lord's dairy and granary were mentioned in 1311: S.R.O., D.(W.) 1807/2. The oratory of Wm. Shareshull licensed in 1370 was described as at Pattingham (L.J.R.O., B/A/1/5, f. 23v.), perhaps an error for Patshull, of which Shareshull was lord.
[23] Local inf. (1979); Dept. of Environment, List of Buildings. It was not owned by the lord of the manor in 1841; L.J.R.O., B/A/15/Pattingham, no. 282.
[24] Below, church.
[25] L.J.R.O., D 30/C 43.
[26] John of Gaunt's Reg. 1379-83, i (Camd. 3rd ser. lvi), 57; ii (Camd. 3rd ser. lvii), 314, 369.

The south front in the late 18th century

The north front

PATSHULL HOUSE

Pattingham: the church from the north-east and the east front of the vicarage house *c.* 1793

Patshull: the church from the south-east *c.* 1800

tion of their help in securing the appropriation of Hathersage church (Derb.).[27] About 1495 Launde leased the rectory to Richard Haughton for 80 years, with renewal every ten years. On the ground that the conditions of the lease had not been observed, the prior in 1506 granted a new 80-year lease to John Giffard, renewable every five years. Giffard was to pay £8 a year to Launde, pensions of 10s. and £5 to Coventry and Lichfield respectively, and one of 30s. to Brecon priory, apparently a survival from the original endowment of that priory by its founder, Bernard de Neufmarché. Besides paying 2 qr. of wheat a year to the vicar and certain fees, Giffard was responsible for the maintenance of the chancel of the church, the parsonage house, Patshull chapel, and all other property of the rectory except the books belonging to the church.[28] The prior's income from the rectory was given in 1535 as £1 2s. 6d. from glebe and £13 7s. 6d. from corn tithes; pensions were still due to Coventry, Lichfield, and Brecon.[29] The Crown retained the rectory after the dissolution of Launde in 1539[30] and leased it in 1581 to Edward Giffard of White Ladies, in Boscobel (Salop.), and his sons John and Thomas.[31] The Crown sold it with the advowson in 1588 to Edmund Downing and Miles Doding; it was still charged with the payment of a £5 pension to the dean and chapter of Lichfield.[32] By 1594 the rectory was held by Richard Broughton of the Inner Temple, who sold it that year to Rowland Watson, lord of Pattingham.[33] It thereafter descended with the manor[34] but was leased out. By 1646 it had been sequestrated from Sir Robert Wolseley, Bt., and the reversion was stated to lie with two other delinquents, William Watson and John Giffard of White Ladies; in 1655 John's widow Dorothy secured a grant of one third of the rectory, part of her dower and sequestrated from her for recusancy.[35] The rectory was held by lessees in 1672, and in the early 1680s the tenant was Thomas Southall of Pattingham.[36] The surviving great tithes of Pattingham township were commuted under the inclosure award of 1811,[37] and in 1839 the impropriator was assigned a rent charge of £194 12s. 10d. in place of tithes from Rudge.[38]

About 1150 Ralph Basset gave the nuns of St. Mary's priory, Brewood ('Black Ladies'), ½ virgate of his demesne in Pattingham and ½ virgate at Hardwick in free alms. The nuns exchanged the ½ virgate of the demesne early in the 13th century with Isabel, widow of Ralph Basset, for an assart at 'Chyltun', possibly in the Woodhouses area. By the beginning of the 14th century the nuns had leased out the Hardwick property along with land on the heath in Rudge granted to them in the later 12th century. In 1545 the Crown conveyed the property to George Tresham of Newton Parva (Northants.) and Edmund Twynyho.[39]

ECONOMIC HISTORY. There was land for 8 ploughteams in 1086; 3 villeins, a priest, and 10 bordars had 3 teams. The manor, which included woodland, was worth £3, the same value as before the Conquest.[40]

There were at least 6 open fields in the parish. Ball field, mentioned in 1311, lay north-west of Pattingham village in the Woodhouses area; by 1407 it had been divided into Netherball field and Overball field.[41] Merewall field, also Merewall (or Morrell) Brook field, south of the village was mentioned in 1338 and was probably the Mere field mentioned in 1314; it extended from Hamley park in the south-west over the brook to the Clive area.[42] East of the village between the Wolverhampton road and the road from Pattingham to Great Moor lay Wete (later Watt) field, mentioned in 1339.[43] It was bounded on the north by Stamberlow field, mentioned in 1358, which lay on Westbeech Hill on the east side of Westbeech Road and extended south towards the Wolverhampton road.[44] Whorestone field, mentioned in 1409, lay north-east of the village in the Nurton area on the north side of the Wolverhampton road.[45] West of Copley lay Nether (later Lower) field, mentioned in 1597.[46] The fields were inclosed piecemeal mostly during the 17th century,[47] but selions still remained in Lower field in 1701[48] and in Merewall Brook and Stamberlow fields in 1730.[49]

There was open meadow, called More meadow, along Morrell brook near the Clive. It was still open in the mid 17th century.[50] Doles in Duck meadow were mentioned in 1615 and 1646.[51]

The main areas of waste in the earlier 18th century were Westbeech common on the northern boundary, Clive common on the southern boundary, and Clifft common between Great Moor and Dadnall Hill on the east. At the end of the 18th century further waste was recorded at Copley

[27] L.J.R.O., D. 30/XXIII; *Cal. Pat.* 1405-8, 34.
[28] P.R.O., REQ 2/2/141; P.R.O., E 303/7/102. For the endowment of Brecon see Dugdale, *Mon.* iii. 259, 264.
[29] *Valor Eccl.* (Rec. Com.), iii. 100, 134, 136; iv. 164, 401 (giving the Brecon pension as 26s. 8d.); *List of Lands of Dissolved Religious Houses* (L. & I. Suppl. Ser. iii), ii, p. 89; iv, p. 253.
[30] *V.C.H. Leics.* ii. 12.
[31] P.R.O., E 310/24/133, no. 73.
[32] P.R.O., C 66/1318, mm. 1, 6-7, 9.
[33] *Handlist of Charters in John Rylands Libr.* i, ed. R. Fawtier, 84.
[34] L.J.R.O., B/V/6/Pattingham, 1673; E. A. Hardwicke, 'Manor and Par. of Pattingham' (TS. in W.S.L., 22/1/21), ff. 205, 211; *Rep. Com. Eccl. Revenues*, 492; *Kelly's Dir. Staffs.* (1940).
[35] *S.H.C.* 1915, 202; *Cal. Cttee. for Compounding*, v. 3180 (fuller details in the transcripts in W.S.L., S.MS. 339, iii, p. 257); *S.H.C.* N.S. v. 170-1.

[36] S.R.O., D. 3451/2/3, overseers' accts. 1672; P.R.O., C 5/168/86.
[37] S.R.O., Q/RDc 14; L.J.R.O., B/A/15/Pattingham.
[38] L.J.R.O., B/A/15/Rudge.
[39] *S.H.C.* 1939, 182-94 (identifying Chyltun as Chillington, in Brewood); *L. & P. Hen. VIII*, xv, p. 287; xx (1), pp. 415-16. For a holding at Woodhouses and 'Chilton' in Pattingham manor in 1341 see S.R.O., D.(W.) 1807/10. For 'Chilton' in 1314 see ibid. /2.   [40] *V.C.H. Staffs.* iv. 40.
[41] S.R.O., D.(W.) 1807/1, 56, 150, 184.
[42] Ibid. 2, 4, 134, 189, 209, 218.
[43] Ibid. 6, 150, 199, 309; L.J.R.O., B/V/15/Pattingham, nos. 375-6, 378, 390-1. It included Alcrofte furlong near Great Moor: S.R.O., D.(W.) 1807/158, 164A.
[44] S.R.O., D.(W.) 1807/34, 131, 140B, 184.
[45] Ibid. 51, 182C, 220.   [46] Ibid. 166A, 201, 266, 352.
[47] e.g. ibid. 236-8, 258, 279, 302C.
[48] Ibid. 306.   [49] W.S.L. 293-358/27.
[50] S.R.O., D.(W.) 1807/129-30, 145, 283C.
[51] Ibid. 200, 215.

Bank and Tuters Hill Bank.[52] Encroachment was marked in the 17th century: in 1651 the manor court imposed a pain of 39s. on any person erecting a cottage on the lord's waste and a further 39s. for every month during which the cottage remained.[53] In 1811 the surviving waste was inclosed under an Act of 1799; 104 a. of Clive common and of Clifft common were auctioned to defray the cost of inclosure.[54]

There was woodland 1 league in length and ½ league in breadth in 1086.[55] The lord's wood at Clifft was mentioned in 1315, and his grove at Tywall (later known as Tywall green) near Hardwick existed in 1405.[56] There was also woodland in a park, mentioned in 1312 and known as Armeley park by 1452; it lay on the south-western boundary in the area between the roads to Rudge and Copley.[57] In the mid 1470s the bailiff was accused of felling trees, including oak, in both Armeley park and Tywall green, and by 1578 there were only 30 a. of woodland at Armeley and 6 a. at Tywall.[58] A park keeper was mentioned in 1748.[59] By 1841 Armeley (later Hamley) park was reduced to 16½ a.[60] In 1979 it was 7 a. (2.8 ha.) in extent and was the only surviving woodland in the parish.[61]

Rye, peas, and oats were being grown in the parish in 1633,[62] and wheat in 1669.[63] In 1814 wheat and turnips were grown at Copley; there was also a store of barley there.[64] By 1840 a five-year Norfolk system of rotation which let clover lie a second year was practised in the parish.[65] Arable farming then predominated: in 1841 there were 1,968 a. of arable and only 459 a. of meadow and pasture.[66] Wheat, barley, and turnips were grown in the later 19th century, and there were several market gardeners by 1871.[67] In 1979 barley was the chief crop, and sugar beet, potatoes, and wheat were also grown.[68]

Sheep farming was recorded at Westbeech in the early 14th century, and a shepherd was then chosen at the manor court.[69] In 1605 a pain was laid on any inhabitant of the manor having more than 100 sheep for a yardland, 50 for a ½ yardland, 34 for a nook, and 6 for a cottage; the total number of sheep permitted was then 1,038.[70] In the early 19th century there was a flock of 128 sheep at Westbeech and one of 141, including 50 Leicester ewes in lamb, at Copley.[71] There were only a small number of sheep in 1979.[72]

Pigs were kept by the 14th century. Fines were imposed on people trespassing with pigs in Tywall green in 1315 and in the lord's park in 1354.[73] In 1355 pannage was paid by 35 people, each normally having 1 or 2 pigs, or 3 or 4 piglets. The total number of pigs then recorded was 161; in 1395 the same number of people paid pannage for 91 pigs.[74] Herds of 13 and 14 pigs were recorded in the later 16th century.[75] Stock kept by a farmer at Westbeech in 1813 included 4 fat pigs.[76] There were nearly 1,000 pigs in the parish in 1979.[77]

Bees were kept in the early 14th century, when hives were taken as mortuaries or heriots.[78] There was extensive poultry farming in 1979 when over 3,000 birds were recorded in the parish.[79]

In 1257 Ralph Basset was granted free warren in his demesne lands at Pattingham.[80] A warren east of the Clive and a warrener were recorded in the mid 14th century. The warren survived into the early 16th century.[81] A master of the game was mentioned in 1600, and in 1633 tenants on the manor were forbidden to take pheasants or partridges.[82] A fishery in Broadwell pool south-west of the village was leased out by the lord in the mid 15th century.[83] An eel trap on Pasford brook in Pattingham formed part of the landscaping of Patshull park, begun in the later 18th century; it remained in use until a few years before 1980.[84]

About 1341 holdings were small: 33 tenants each held a messuage and ½ virgate, 4 held a messuage and a few acres, 18 held cottages, and 12 held land only.[85] Most tenants were personally unfree: in 1343 there were 127 neifs on the manor and only 16 free men.[86] In 1623 there were some 40 messuages and 37 cottages in the manor, all copyhold. Copyholders paid heriots on ancient messuages only; their widows evidently enjoyed freebench then, and certainly by 1732.[87] Copyhold tenure was abolished under the Inclosure Act of 1799.[88] Inheritance by Borough English was recorded in 1534 and was mentioned as a custom in 1732.[89]

The manorial mill, mentioned in 1314, stood on Pasford brook and by 1403 was known as Basset's mill, a name still used in the mid 17th century. By 1717 it was known as Basford or Pasford mill. It continued in operation until the early 1940s but by then was grinding animal

[52] S.R.O., D.(W.) 1807/356; S.R.O., Q/RDc 14.
[53] S.R.O., D.(W.) 1807/274.
[54] 39 Geo III, c. 95 (Priv. Act); S.R.O., D. 3451/8/3, pp. 12–13, 22; S.R.O., Q/RDc 14.
[55] V.C.H. Staffs. iv. 40.
[56] S.R.O., D.(W.) 1807/2, 48.
[57] Ibid. 1–2; Warws. R.O., CR 895/8/23; Yates, Map of Staffs. (1775).
[58] S.R.O., D.(W.) 1807/91–2; P.R.O., E 310/24/133, nos. 23, 32.
[59] S.R.O., D.(W.) 1807/353.
[60] L.J.R.O., B/A/15/Pattingham, no. 216.
[61] M.A.F.F., agric. returns 1979.
[62] L.J.R.O., B/C/11, John Bette (1633).
[63] S.R.O., D.(W.) 1807/351.
[64] Wolverhampton Chron. 5 Jan. 1814.
[65] N.S.J.F.S. xiii. 46.
[66] L.J.R.O., B/A/15/Pattingham.
[67] P.O. Dir. Staffs. (1868); Kelly's Dir. Staffs. (1900); P.R.O., RG 10/2927.
[68] M.A.F.F., agric. returns 1979.
[69] S.R.O., D.(W.) 1807/2, 4.   [70] Ibid. 179.

[71] Wolverhampton Chron. 1 Dec. 1813, 5 Jan. 1814.
[72] M.A.F.F., agric. returns 1979.
[73] S.R.O., D.(W.) 1807/2, 18.
[74] Ibid. 19, 39.
[75] L.J.R.O., B/C/11, Wm. Barber (1559), John Pountney (1564).
[76] Wolverhampton Chron. 1 Dec. 1813.
[77] M.A.F.F., agric. returns 1979.
[78] S.R.O., D.(W.) 1807/1–2.
[79] M.A.F.F., agric. returns 1979.
[80] S.H.C. xv. 36.
[81] S.R.O., D.(W.) 1807/15, 21, 56, 107; L.J.R.O., B/A/15/Pattingham, nos. 448, 450.
[82] S.R.O., D.(W.) 1807/173, 233.
[83] Warws. R.O., CR 895/8/23.
[84] D. H. Robinson, The Wandering Worfe (Albrighton, 1980), 92–3.
[85] W.S.L., transcript of Pattingham ct. rolls, i, ff. 38–40.
[86] Above, introduction.
[87] B.R.L. 378054; S.R.O., D.(W.) 1807/356.
[88] S.R.O., D.(W.) 1807/354.
[89] Ibid. 356; B.R.L., Keen 358.

feed only. It ceased working when the bank of the mill stream collapsed during a flood. The building, probably of the mid 19th century, was used in 1979 as a store for Pasford farm.[90] An ordinance of 1380 required all tenants to use the lord's mill, and in 1605 it was forbidden to take corn out of the manor for grinding. In 1623, however, a customary recorded that copyholders were not required to use the manorial mill.[91] A mill was in use at Great Moor in the earlier 20th century, grinding only animal feed from c. 1914; it was powered by a channel diverted east from Nurton brook.[92] A few traces remained in 1979. About 1680 there was a windmill at Westbeech, which was still in operation in the early 19th century.[93] There was a windmill at Nurton Hill by 1841. It was still in operation in 1861 but had gone out of use by 1869.[94] The building survives as part of the adjoining house. Oatmeal mill near Tuters Hill, mentioned in 1765,[95] may have been a windmill.

In 1316 the Crown granted Ralph, Lord Basset, a Tuesday market and a fair at Pattingham on the vigil, feast, and morrow of the translation of St. Edward the Confessor (12–14 December).[96] By 1845 there was a cattle fair on the last Tuesday in April, and it was still held in the 1890s.[97]

There may have been iron working in 1341, when Jordan the bloomer was living in Pattingham.[98] There was a nailer there in 1598, and another in 1626; a whitesmith was mentioned in 1605.[99] In 1633 John Devy was presented at the manor court for setting up charcoal fires,[1] perhaps for use in iron smelting.

There was tanning by the late 16th century.[2] In the mid 17th century there was a tanhouse in Broadwell Lane, using water from the nearby Broadwell pool;[3] Tanhouse Farm still stood there in 1979. Francis Devey, a tanner, had hides and skins worth £149 at his death in 1724.[4] Leather sealers were appointed by the manor court in the mid 17th and earlier 18th century.[5]

A brickmaker was living in the manor in the early 18th century.[6] There were two brickyards in the mid 19th century. One was east of the Rudge road near the county boundary. The other

was at Nurton Hill, using the extensive marl; it continued until the early 20th century.[7] There was quarrying at Copley and in Hamley park before the 1880s; around Nurton and Great Moor quarrying was in progress in the later 19th century.[8]

Large numbers of Northumberland ploughs were made in Pattingham by a Mr. Rudge in the early 19th century.[9] James Harper, a blacksmith, produced agricultural implements in the village in the 1860s and 1870s, employing three men in 1871.[10] The Law family hired out threshing-machines from the early 1860s until c. 1945.[11]

LOCAL GOVERNMENT. By the mid 1250s the lord of Pattingham held view of frankpledge, paying ½ mark for it.[12] In 1293 Ralph Basset claimed twice-yearly view of frankpledge, sheriff's pleas, infangthief, outfangthief, gallows, waif, and assize of bread and ale.[13] Court rolls survive from 1311. From the 1520s to the mid 1630s the rolls are generally copies containing admissions and surrenders of land but not presentments or election of officers. Copies were again made from c. 1650 until 1799, when the last court was held, copyhold tenure being abolished by the Inclosure Act of that year. Rolls including presentments and elections survive from 1699 until 1781.[14] Two great courts were held annually, after Easter and Michaelmas, with small courts normally at intervals of between three and eight weeks in the 14th century. After the manor passed to the earl of Warwick in 1390 small courts were held less frequently, usually twice yearly with the great court. From the 1520s intermediate small courts were resumed. Customaries of 1623 and 1732 mention the lord's right to hold two leets a year and a court baron every three weeks; they also claimed probate of wills for the lord's court.[15] Between 1659 and 1758 courts were occasionally recorded as held in one of the hamlets or in the village. From 1760 they were held at the Court House, where the bailiff was living in 1783.[16]

From the later 14th century the reeve was normally chosen by the lord from two or three

[90] S.R.O., D.(W.) 1807/2, 46, 293B; D. 564/3/4/9; Staffs. C.C. Planning Dept., Ind. Arch. Survey; local inf. (1979).
[91] S.R.O., D.(W.) 1807/31, 179, 356; B.R.L. 378054.
[92] Local inf. (1979); Brighton, *Pattingham*, 160 (stating, in 1942, that it was not then in use); Soc. for Protection of Ancient Buildings, Watermill Survey 1967; *Wolverhampton and W. Midlands Mag.* (July 1975), 27 (photograph).
[93] Plot, *Staffs.* map; R. Baugh, *Map of Salop.* (1808).
[94] L.J.R.O., B/A/15/Pattingham, no. 87; P.R.O., RG 9/1852; S.R.O., D. 258/M/B/7.
[95] E. A. Hardwicke, 'Manor and Par. of Pattingham' (TS. in W.S.L., 22/1/21), f. 205.
[96] *Cal. Chart. R. 1300–26*, 315.
[97] *P.O. Dir. Staffs.* (1845); Brighton, *Pattingham*, 143; *Rep. Com. Market Rights and Tolls* [C. 5550], p. 203, H.C. (1888), liii; *Kelly's Dir. Staffs.* (1896).
[98] S.R.O., D.(W.) 1807/10.
[99] Ibid. 177C; *Pattingham Par. Reg.* (Staffs. Par. Reg. Soc. 1934), 7, 138.   [1] S.R.O., D.(W.) 1807/233.
[2] Ibid. 173; *Pattingham Par. Reg.* 6.
[3] S.R.O., D.(W.) 1807/242, 288, 350; L.J.R.O., B/A/15/ Pattingham, no. 200.
[4] W.S.L. 293–358/27.   [5] Below, local govt.
[6] S.R.O., D.(W.) 1807/333; W.S.L. 293-358/27, will of Ric. Tranter, 1721.

[7] *P.O. Dir. Staffs.* (1845); S.R.O., D. 3221/6; T. H. Whitehead and others, *Memoirs of Geol. Surv., the Country between Wolverhampton and Oakengates*, 139; O.S. Map 6", Staffs. LXI. NE. (1884, 1903, 1924 edns.).
[8] Whitehead, *Country between Wolverhampton and Oakengates*, 138–40, 205; O.S. Map 6", Staffs. LXI. SW. (1886 edn.); P.R.O., RG 9/1984; RG 10/2927.
[9] Pitt, *Staffs.* ii. 27.
[10] *P.O. Dir. Staffs.* (1854 and later edns.); P.R.O., RG 10/2927.
[11] Harrison, Harrod and Co. *Dir. Staffs.* (1861); *P.O. Dir. Staffs.* (1868; 1872; 1876); *Kelly's Dir. Staffs.* (1880 and later edns.); *Lond. Gaz.* 14 Nov. 1879, p. 6456 (ref. supplied by Mr. Peter Leigh of Pattingham); P.R.O., RG 10/2927; local inf. (1979).
[12] *S.H.C.* v (1), 114.
[13] *S.H.C.* vi (1), 249.
[14] S.R.O., D.(W.) 1807/1–335, 345–50, 360; S.R.O., D.(W.) 1778/V/1332–61; W.S.L. 293-358/27; above, p. 178.
[15] B.R.L. 378054; S.R.O., D.(W.) 1807/356. For examples of probate in the early 18th cent. see S.R.O., D.(W.) 1778/V/ 1363.
[16] S.R.O., D.(W.) 1807/293B (Copley, adjournment), 313 (Moor), 318 (Nurton), 321–2, 346 (houses in Pattingham, one by adjournment), 352 (Great Moor), 357.

candidates presented by the homage. Sometimes the steward granted exemption from serving, on the payment of a fine or because of age or poverty. The last recorded appointment was in 1417.[17]

A constable was chosen at the manor court in 1339. The election of a single constable or a pair was thereafter recorded at irregular intervals, but from 1461 there were always two until the last court in 1799. Appointment was at a Michaelmas court from the early 15th century and had become annual by the end of the century.[18] There was a change in the date of accounting from autumn to spring in 1592 or 1593. In April 1596, when two constables began office, they were described as 'chosen by the parishioners'. From 1608, however, they were chosen at the October leet and their accounts again began in the autumn. By 1689 their accounts were passed by the parish. About 1615 it was agreed that for every day and night when the constables went about the 'business of the king or of the parish' they should have 12d., with 6d. for day-time duty only.[19] A watchman was mentioned in 1561, and in 1688–9 the constables accounted for ale for the watch. In 1605 the court ordered every householder to keep a 'sufficient club' in his house and be ready to assist the constable when need arose.[20]

Two beadles were chosen by the court in 1353, and the election of one or two was recorded until the mid 15th century.[21] Ale tasters were mentioned in the earliest court rolls, and the election of two was noted from 1353 to 1735, annually from the late 15th century.[22] In the late 16th century weights and measures were taken to Wolverhampton by the constable to be checked by the clerk of the market there.[23] Leather sealers were appointed by the court in the mid 17th and earlier 18th century.[24]

A felon was hanged by the lord as late as 1421.[25] A gallows evidently stood in the Woodhouses area.[26] There was mention of a pillory in 1384 and of stocks in 1594; in the late 18th century the stocks stood outside the lichgate on the south side of the churchyard.[27] A pound on the north side of Newgate near the junction with Westbeech Road was demolished c. 1961.[28]

Courts were held by the rector in the earlier 14th century.[29]

Two churchwardens were recorded from 1552. In 1584 and 1591 they were elected in November, but from 1593 they were chosen at the Easter vestry meeting.[30] A clerk existed in 1591–2.[31] A

sexton was mentioned in 1682 when he was paid for rousing sleepers in church.[32] By 1650 two highway surveyors were elected at the vestry meeting; on five occasions in the 1670s the election was at Christmas. The surveyors worked under the constables.[33]

There were two overseers of the poor by the early 1620s, and their election at the vestry meeting was recorded from 1650. By the later 17th century one acted for Pattingham township and the other for Rudge. From 1706 until 1761 only one appointment was recorded each year, evidently that of the Pattingham overseer. In the later 18th century up to four were appointed.[34] By 1633 the parish was lending money, and apparently using the interest for the poor.[35] The poor were badged by 1685, and in 1742 the overseer bought red cloth for badges. Badging was still practised in 1748.[36] A parish poorhouse was built in 1642–3. Extensive repairs were made in 1685, most of the cost being met by two £5 legacies given for the purpose by Roger Devey and Sarah Cranage. It was referred to as the hospital in 1710. A new parish house was built in the mid 1720s and was presumably the building referred to as the workhouse from the 1730s. In 1763 and 1764 the overseer paid weekly allowances to the inmates. In the later 1760s the governor was paid a salary of £3 a year. The workhouse evidently stood near the vicarage house north of the church and seems to have gone out of use by 1793.[37]

Pattingham, including Rudge, became part of Seisdon poor-law union in 1836.[38] Pattingham civil parish was assigned to Seisdon rural district in 1894; Rudge, while remaining in Seisdon union, was assigned to Bridgnorth rural district.[39] In 1974 Pattingham civil parish became part of South Staffordshire district.[40]

CHURCH. The presence of a priest at Pattingham in 1086[41] indicates the existence of a church by then. The church was granted by Richard Basset and his wife Maud as part of the endowment of Launde priory (Leics.), a house of Augustinian canons which they founded c. 1120.[42] The advowson of the rectory remained with Launde, its right being confirmed in 1275 against Ralph Basset.[43] In 1284, when the rector, Philip of Cornwall (or of St. Augustine) was an absentee, the canons intruded John Danet as rector with

[17] S.R.O., D.(W.) 1807/2, 22, 26–31, 46, 57.
[18] Ibid. 4, 19, 21, 42, 50, 74, 80, 98, 100 sqq. In 1340 three were elected: ibid. 8.
[19] S.R.O., D. 3451/2/2; D. 3451/6.
[20] S.R.O., D.(W.) 1807/138A, 178; D. 3451/6/1.
[21] e.g. S.R.O., D.(W.) 1807/17–19, 21, 30, 76. The election was not recorded every year.
[22] Ibid. 2, 17, 95; D.(W.) 1778/V/1343–54. In 1390 three were elected: D.(W.) 1807/37.
[23] S.R.O., D. 3451/2/2, constables' accts. 1583–4, 1587–8, 1596–7.
[24] S.R.O., D.(W.) 1807/235, 275A; D.(W.) 1778/V/1343–54. [25] S.R.O., D.(W.) 1807/58.
[26] For Gallows meadow there in the late 18th cent. see ibid. 348–9; for Gallows brook see above, introduction.
[27] S.R.O., D.(W.) 1807/33; D. 3451/2/2, constables' accts. 1594; Shaw, Staffs. ii, pl. facing p. 279.
[28] O.S. Map 6″, Staffs. LXI. NE. (1884 and 1924 edns.); Staffs. C.C. Planning Dept., Arch. and Hist. Buildings Survey; local inf. (1979).

[29] Below, church.
[30] S.H.C. 1915, 201; S.R.O., D. 3451/2/1–2.
[31] S.R.O., D. 3451/2/2.
[32] Ibid. 2/3.
[33] Ibid. 2/1; 6/12, 14, 26.
[34] Ibid. 2/1–3; Salop R.O. 2028/BO/1/3/43–4.
[35] S.R.O., D. 3451/2/2–3.
[36] Ibid. 2/3; 5/1.
[37] Ibid. 2/1–3, 35; 5/1, 48; Shaw, Staffs. ii. 279; Brighton, Pattingham, 109.
[38] 3rd Ann. Rep. Poor Law Com. H.C. 546, p. 164 (1837), xxxi.
[39] Counties of Stafford and Salop (Tettenhall etc.) Conf. Order, 1894 (Local Govt. Bd. Order no. 31,893; copy in S.R.O., C/C/O/1).
[40] O.S. Map 1/100,000, Staffs. Admin. Areas (1974 edn.).
[41] V.C.H. Staffs. iv. 40.
[42] V.C.H. Leics. ii. 10; D. Knowles and R. N. Hadcock, Med. Religious Houses Eng. and Wales (1971 edn.), 163.
[43] S.H.C. vi (1), 66, 71.

the support of inhabitants including Basset. Danet came to Philip's house in Pattingham with the cellarer of Launde, and having bought provisions and a tun of wine at Bridgnorth, he 'made great feasts' which the prior attended. Danet then left. Philip evidently recovered the rectory after the Crown and the archbishop of Canterbury had intervened on his behalf.[44]

In 1342 the bishop appropriated the church to Launde. He stipulated the institution of a vicarage and the payment by the canons of 5 marks a year to the churches of Coventry and Lichfield.[45] Royal licence was granted in 1344.[46] The vicarage had been instituted by 1356,[47] and the advowson remained with Launde until the priory's dissolution in 1539. It was then held by the Crown until 1588 when it was sold with the rectory.[48] It probably passed to Rowland Watson, the lord of the manor, who bought the rectory in 1594; his grandson William held the advowson in 1638.[49] The Crown, however, presented in 1633, perhaps because of the Watsons' recusancy.[50] A John Holbrooke presented in 1677.[51] In 1705 William Watson's grandson William, although a papist, was described as patron, but in 1706 the advowson, lately held by him, was 'reputed to be sold'.[52] Samuel Butler of Halesowen (Worcs.) presented a vicar in 1709,[53] and in 1718 Joseph Butler of Pattingham granted the next presentation to two men who later the same year presented him in succession to John Butler.[54] John Hodgetts of Shut End, in Kingswinford, presented Joseph Honeybourne, his cousin by marriage, in 1755.[55] Thomas Murhall of Ash, in Whitchurch (Salop.), presented in 1780, William Yelverton Davenport of Davenport House, in Worfield (Salop.), and Thomas Dicken of Peatswood, in Tyrley, jointly in 1796, and George Bishton of Neach Hill, in Donington (Salop.), in 1819.[56] By 1830 the patronage was held by Sir Robert Pigot, the lord of the manor.[57] In 1843 he sold the next turn of both Pattingham and Patshull to John Fletcher of Liverpool, agreeing to put the vicarage house into good repair on the next voidance. In 1847 Fletcher presented his son-in-law, W. G. Greenstreet, who had been assistant curate in both places since 1843.[58] Pigot sold the advowson with the manor to the earl of Dartmouth in 1848.[59] In 1969 the 9th earl transferred the advowson to the bishop of Lichfield.[60]

The church was valued at £8 13s. 4d. in 1291.[61] In 1341 the rector had a house and a carucate of land together worth 5s. a year, rents of 52s., two

fishponds and a dovecot worth 20s., great tithes worth 20s., offerings and small tithes worth 26s. 8d., and perquisites of court worth 11s.[62] In 1535 the vicar received £6 1s. 6d. from small tithes and offerings, offerings of 1s. at Rudge chapel, £1 6s. 8d. from Patshull chapel, and a pension from the prior of Launde variously given as 8s. 10d. and £2.[63] By 1506 2 qr. of wheat were due from Launde as an augmentation; that or an equivalent was still due from the impropriator in the mid 19th century.[64] The vicarage was valued at 40 marks in 1604. In 1646 the committee for plundered ministers, finding it worth only £20, granted an augmentation of £50 out of the sequestrated rectory.[65] In 1723 the vicarage was worth £80, consisting of tithes, surplice fees, and a house and glebe worth £10. By 1776 the value had risen to £129 8s. 9d.[66] In 1830 the vicar's annual gross income was given as £300, although another assessment was £199 gross and £197 net. There was 1 a. of glebe. Owing to straitened circumstances the vicar, Richard Thursfield, then occupied only a small part of the vicarage house.[67] In 1839 he was assigned a rent charge of £75 in place of the tithes of Rudge and in 1843 a further £267 2s. for the tithes of the rest of the parish.[68] The vicarage house north of the church is a three-storeyed brick building of the later 18th century with an extension at the back of the 19th century. In the early 1950s it was divided into two, a porch on the front being replaced by a window.[69]

William Cooke, who was presented to the vicarage in November 1581, was described as curate the previous July while his predecessor as vicar was still alive.[70] There was another curate during the 1620s.[71]

By the mid 14th century a chantry endowed with ⅓ virgate in Pattingham had been founded to provide a chaplain celebrating four days a week for the souls of the Bassets, lords of the manor. In 1353 the prior of Launde as rector was accused in the manor court of having failed to find a chaplain since 1349; in 1356 both he and the vicar were presented for default in the matter.[72] In 1528 there was mention of the land of the Blessed Virgin in Pattingham. It was probably connected with the chantry served by the Lady priest, who was stated in 1549 to have been paid by the parishioners to sing mass in the parish church and pray for all Christian souls. His stipend came from a house in Stepple, in Neen Savage (Salop.), which the parishioners had bought for £10 and

[44] Cal. Inq. Misc. i, p. 385; Cal. Pat. 1281–92, 121, 140; Reg. Epist. J. Peckham (Rolls Ser.), ii. 674–5; S.H.C. vi (1), 136.
[45] L.J.R.O., B/A/1/3, f. 60; L.J.R.O., D 30/C 43; above, manor and other estates (rectory).
[46] Cal. Pat. 1343–5, 235.
[47] Below (chantry).
[48] Cal. Pat. 1550–3, 88; S.H.C. 1915, 201; above, p. 177.
[49] P.R.O., CP 43/221, f. 17.
[50] P.R.O., IND 17003, f. 19.
[51] L.J.R.O., B/A/3/Pattingham.
[52] Staffs. Cath. Hist. xiii. 35.
[53] Brighton, Pattingham, 60.
[54] L.J.R.O., B/A/3/Pattingham.
[55] K. C. Hodgson, Out of the Mahogany Desk, 21.
[56] L.J.R.O., B/A/3/Pattingham.
[57] S.H.C. 4th ser. x. 17.
[58] S.R.O., D. 564/1/3; Brighton, Pattingham, 67–8.

[59] S.R.O., D.(W.) 1778/V/1312; Lich. Dioc. Ch. Cal. (1857).
[60] Lich. Dioc. Regy., Reg. of Transfer of Patronage, f. 163.
[61] Tax. Eccl. (Rec. Com.), 243.
[62] Inq. Non. (Rec. Com.), 129.
[63] Valor Eccl. (Rec. Com.), iii. 100, 164.
[64] P.R.O., E 303/7/102; L.J.R.O., B/V/6/Pattingham.
[65] S.H.C. 1915, 202.
[66] L.J.R.O., B/V/6/Pattingham.
[67] S.H.C. 4th ser. x. 17; Rep. Com. Eccl. Revenues, 492–3.
[68] L.J.R.O., B/A/15/Rudge and Pattingham.
[69] Above, pl. facing p. 177; L.J.R.O., B/V/6/Pattingham; Pattingham ch., envelope labelled 'Vicarage Division Loan Arrangements'.
[70] S.H.C. 1915, 201; L.J.R.O., B/C/11, Rog. Hodson (1582).
[71] S.H.C. 1915, 201.
[72] S.R.O., D.(W.) 1807/17–18, 21.

which was worth 20s. a year: the last priest had left c. 1545.[73]

In 1760 the vicar, Joseph Honeybourne, moved to Wombourne, being licensed to hold the vicarage there in plurality on condition that he provided for a curate and at least 13 sermons a year at Pattingham.[74] In 1830 Richard Thursfield was holding morning and afternoon prayers on Sundays, with a sermon at the morning service, and he celebrated six times a year and on the festivals. Easter communicants numbered 20. There was catechism on Mondays.[75] In 1843, when Thursfield was old and ill and no longer resident, W. G. Greenstreet was appointed curate, and he served the parish as vicar from 1847 until his death in 1900; he was also incumbent of Patshull until 1877. A curate was appointed in 1853. Besides carrying out extensive work on the church fabric, Greenstreet introduced a parish magazine in 1869, surplices for the choir in 1871, and weekly celebrations in 1873. His son A. T. Greenstreet, appointed curate in 1887, succeeded him and remained at Pattingham until his retirement in 1920.[76]

In 1582 a house, cottage, and land at Fenhouse End apparently south of the village were settled by the lessee of the manor, Walter Leveson, for the benefit of the inhabitants of Pattingham parish. In 1613 William Bailey, the farmer of the manor, made a new settlement in return for a rent of 8s. 4d. and an entry fine of 8s. 4d. The trustees granted a lease of the property in 1625 at a rent of £4 13s. 4d. payable to the churchwardens, possibly an indication that the income was used for the benefit of the church, as it was by the early 18th century. After the inclosure award of 1811 the property consisted of seven cottages and of 21½ a. at Morrell Brook and Newgate. In 1822 the rent from the land was £53 2s. 8d. and from the cottages £12 10s. The church was still benefiting from the charity in 1979.[77]

The church of ST. CHAD, an invocation recorded in 1559,[78] is built of pink standstone and consists of a chancel with south chapel and north-east vestry, a two-bayed clerestoried nave with two north aisles and a south aisle and porch, and a west tower with a spire. The unusually small nave may retain the plan of the church which existed by 1086, but the earliest datable part of the present fabric is the north arcade of the nave of the later 12th century.[79] The chancel was rebuilt in the 13th century. Its seven lancet windows include two in the east wall surmounted by a quatrefoil and divided externally by a buttress; there are sedilia, a piscina, an aumbry, and a north doorway which was in use in 1725 but

was later blocked.[80] The tower and south aisle and chapel were added in the 14th century; the aisle flanks the tower. In 1599–1600 the tower was extensively repaired and a weathercock placed on it. In 1619–20 two windows were inserted 'to let out the sound of the leading bell'.[81] The church porch, presumably the south porch, was mentioned in 1608 and the north door of the church in 1656.[82] The font dates probably from c. 1660.[83] A gallery was erected at the east end of the nave in 1726, partly for singers. It was removed in 1746; by then there was also a west gallery.[84]

In 1856–7 the chancel was restored at Lord Dartmouth's expense by G. G. (later Sir Gilbert) Scott. Between 1863 and 1866 Scott restored the rest of the church, rebuilt the north aisle and south porch, and added a second north aisle and a north-east vestry. He reconstructed the roofs of the nave and the south aisle and inserted new tracery in the windows on the north, west, and south sides to match that in the chancel. Box pews and a two-decker pulpit were replaced, and the west gallery was removed. The cost was met by voluntary contributions, mainly from Lord Dartmouth and W. G. Greenstreet.[85] A spire was added to the tower in 1871, designed apparently by Scott; it was given by Lord Dartmouth as a memorial to his father (d. 1853).[86] An organ was installed in 1873.[87] An alabaster reredos, designed by Scott's son J. O. Scott and given by Lord Dartmouth, was erected in 1890.[88] A choir vestry was formed in 1954 in the north-west corner of the church.[89]

In 1552 and 1553 the church possessed a silver chalice and paten, a maslin cross, and two maslin candlesticks; two other maslin candlesticks had been sold with the consent of the parish.[90] The chalice and paten were remodelled in 1664 with a gift of £2 from Richard Whittington and Anne Copley and were still in the church in 1979.[91] There were five bells and a sanctus bell in 1552 and 1553. Five bells continued in use until the 1720s, though several were recast in the meanwhile; the sanctus bell was mentioned in 1617. In 1724 a peal of six was cast by Joseph Smith of Edgbaston (Warws.). Two bells cast by Mears & Co. of London in 1864 were added during the restoration. There was a clock by the end of the 16th century.[92]

The fittings include a royal coat of arms of 1710 at the west end of the nave and a benefaction board of 1710 in the vestry. In the tower are boards with the Commandments, the Creed, and the Lord's Prayer, all apparently dating from 1725–6.[93]

[73] S.R.O., D.(W.) 1807/116; S.H.C. 1915, 201; Cal. Pat. 1563–6, p. 64.
[74] Hodgson, Out of the Mahogany Desk, 22.
[75] S.H.C. 4th ser. x. 17.
[76] Brighton, Pattingham, 45, 48, 67–70; Nat. Soc. Inquiry, 1846–7, Staffs. 6–7; S.R.O., D. 660/26/5.
[77] Brighton, Pattingham, 104–7, 152; 9th Rep. Com. Char. 630–2; inf. from the vicar (1979). For Fenhouse as probably part of Merewall field in 1314 see S.R.O., D.(W.) 1807/2.
[78] L.J.R.O., B/C/11, Wm. Barber (1559).
[79] For an exterior view of the north aisle before it was rebuilt see above, pl. facing p. 177.
[80] S.R.O., D. 3451/2/35.
[81] Ibid. 2/2.
[82] Ibid. 2/2–3.
[83] Pevsner, Staffs. 219.
[84] L.J.R.O., B/C/5/1726/Pattingham; S.R.O., D. 3451/1/13.
[85] Brighton, Pattingham, 30–1, 34–6; L.J.R.O., B/C/5/1863/Pattingham; The Builder, 5 Aug. 1865, p. 558; Lich. Dioc. Ch. Cal. (1866), 84; Lichfield Cathedral Libr., Moore and Hinckes drawings, ix, nos. 1–2.
[86] Brighton, Pattingham, 51; Pevsner, Staffs. 219.
[87] Brighton, Pattingham, 36–8.
[88] Ibid. 47–8.
[89] Ch. of St. Chad, Pattingham (copy in W.S.L. Pamphs.).
[90] S.H.C. n.s. vi (1), 190; S.H.C. 1915, 201.
[91] T.B.A.S. lxxiii. 2, 12–13.
[92] S.H.C. n.s. vi (1), 190; S.H.C. 1915, 201; S.R.O., D. 3451/2/2–3, 33–5; Brighton, Pattingham, 31–2.
[93] S.R.O., D. 3451/2/35.

The registers date from 1559 and are complete.[94]

The churchyard contains memorials from 1661.[95] There is a cross, of which the octagonal shaft and the steps are medieval, with a 12th-century capital. There are two scratch dials on the south wall of the church.[96] Against the south wall is an angel bust from the Houses of Parliament, presented in 1934 by Geoffrey Mander, M.P. for Wolverhampton East.[97] Land was conveyed by the Patshull Estate Co. Ltd. in 1935 for the westward extension of the churchyard, consecrated in 1955.[98]

ROMAN CATHOLICISM.

Until the early 18th century several of the lords of the manor were Roman Catholics. John Giffard of Chillington, in Brewood, who farmed the manor from 1560 to 1578, was a notable recusant.[99] In 1608 the manor was farmed out by the Crown because of the recusancy of Jane Watson, who had held the courts during the minority of her son William and continued to do so after he came of age in 1605. William died in 1615, with a posthumous son William as his heir, and the manor continued to be farmed until 1617 or 1618. The elder William's widow, who then held the courts until her son came of age in 1637, appears as a recusant in the 1640s. At that time too the manor was sequestrated because of the younger William's recusancy, although in 1650 he claimed to be a protestant.[1] In 1705 his grandson, another William Watson, was living at Rudge and was listed as a papist along with his mother, two other members of the family, a Mr. Gibson (perhaps a priest), and six servants; by the following year he and his household had left the area.[2]

Pattingham, however, was not a Roman Catholic centre. In 1577 the only recusant returned was George Cockeram, who had a landed income of £100 a year; he was still returned as a recusant in 1607.[3] Two others were reported in that year, including Ursula Betts who was again listed as a recusant, with one other, in 1641.[4] Five were returned in 1657 and 1676.[5] Six were listed in 1679, four besides the Watson household in 1705, and three in 1730.[6]

About 1930 a mass centre was established at Pattingham through the initiative of the Wolverhampton branch of the Catholic Women's League. Mass was at first said at the Pigot Arms. About 1934 an upper room at Pattingham Stores was fitted up as a chapel dedicated to Our Lady and the English Martyrs and holding some 25 people. The owner eventually required the use of the premises, and c. 1957 the chapel was transferred to a private house at Upper Westbeech. At first Pattingham was served by a priest from the church of St. Mary and St. John in Wolverhampton, but in 1932 it became the responsibility of the priest at Tettenhall. The chapel was closed c. 1959.[7]

PROTESTANT NONCONFORMITY.

In 1698 the house of Richard Hill was registered for protestant dissenters.[8] There were frequent meetings of dissenters in Pattingham c. 1720 served by itinerant ministers.[9] A chapel was registered for Independents in 1843.[10] A Primitive Methodist chapel at the south-western end of the village was registered for worship in 1868.[11] In 1872 it was bought by S. S. Mander of Tettenhall, a leading member of Queen Street Congregational church, Wolverhampton, for use by that church, and Pattingham became one of the village stations run from Queen Street. After the chapel had been repaired, a church of eight members was formed; morning and evening services were held on Sundays, with a Sunday school in the afternoon. In 1877 there were nine members, and it was stated that 'the work here is especially arduous, but much needed, and there are signs of improvement'. In 1883 or 1884 six of the eight members seceded, and the chapel was closed. The closure was intended to be only temporary, but the cause was abandoned in 1887. The chapel was sold in 1894 and converted into cottages.[12] In 1979 the building was occupied as the West End Stores.

EDUCATION.

There was a schoolmaster at Pattingham in 1596 and 1605, and a schoolhouse was repaired by the parish in the later 1670s.[13] A new schoolhouse was built by subscription in 1684, a brick building on the south side of Newgate; the site is now crossed by Orchard Close. By the late 1720s there was a master's house attached.[14] The school remained a parochial responsibility: in 1707 the schoolmaster was nominated by trustees and the parishioners, and in 1725 the churchwardens carried out extensive repairs to the building.[15] It was described in 1676 as a grammar school and in the early 18th century as a free school where boys were taught the rudiments of grammar and English.[16] In 1725 William Plymley gave 2¼ a. to provide money for teaching poor children born in Pattingham and Rudge to

[94] All except those in current use are in S.R.O., D. 3451/1; they have been printed to 1812 by Staffs. Par. Reg. Soc. (1934).
[95] Brighton, Pattingham, 56.   [96] Ibid. 146.
[97] Inscription in situ.
[98] Lich. Dioc. Regy., B/A/2i/W, p. 556; X, p. 295.
[99] Above, manor and other estates; S.H.C. N.S. v. 127 sqq.
[1] Above, manor and other estates; Cal. Cttee. for Compounding, iii. 2059.
[2] Staffs. Cath. Hist. xiii. 35.
[3] S.H.C. 1915, 375, 386; Staffs. Cath. Hist. iv. 31.
[4] Staffs. Cath. Hist. iv. 31; v. 18.
[5] S.H.C. 4th ser. ii. 83; W.S.L., S.MS. 33, p. 371.
[6] B.R.L. 354851; Staffs. Cath. Hist. xiii. 35; L.J.R.O., B/V/5/Pattingham.
[7] Express & Star, 5 and 13 Jan. 1931; Cath. Dir. Archdioc.

of Birmingham (1931), 99; (1932), 98; (1933), 99; (1934), 105; (1935), 108; (1959), 125; inf. from the Revd. M. F. McGrath (1980), formerly parish priest at Tettenhall.
[8] S.H.C. 4th ser. iii. 111.
[9] A. G. Matthews, Cong. Churches of Staffs. 129.
[10] S.H.C. 4th ser. iii. 97.
[11] G.R.O., Worship Reg. no. 18475.
[12] Manual for Queen Street Chapel, Wolverhampton (1873 and later edns.; copies in S.R.O., D. 1206/1/26-36); H. A. May, Queen Street Cong. Church, Wolverhampton, 34, 114; S.R.O., D. 1206/1/41, 27 Mar., 28 June 1872; O.S. Map 6", Staffs. LXI. NW. (1883 edn.).
[13] S.R.O., D. 3451/2/2-3.
[14] Ibid. 2/37; 5/55; L.J.R.O., B/A/15/Pattingham.
[15] L.J.R.O., B/A/4/13; S.R.O., D. 3451/2/35.
[16] L.J.R.O., B/A/4/5, 14.

read English; a further 1½ r. was added by Thomas Mulliner in 1736. A new trust of 1790 declared the endowment to be for eight poor children at the free school.[17] The building had ceased to be used as a school by 1793, and it soon fell into decay; the master's house was used for lessons. By 1820 the master held the school land as his remuneration and taught the elements to eight boys, five from Pattingham and three from Rudge. When he died in 1821 the school was suspended to allow the accumulation of rent for the repair of the school building.[18]

In 1830–1 the school was repaired and enlarged by subscription and a grant from the National Society. It was reopened in 1831 as a National school. In 1834–5 it had an attendance of 64 boys and 52 girls under a master and a mistress. Although the attendance then fell, it had risen again to 55 boys and 46 girls by 1850.[19] By 1860 there was also an infants' school.[20] A bequest of £200 by Benjamin Matthews (d. 1856) for the National school became effective on his widow's death in 1874.[21] A new building in Westbeech Road was opened in 1875, with a teacher's house attached. The site was given by Lord Dartmouth, who also met the building costs above the amount raised by subscription.[22] There were three schoolrooms, one each for boys, girls, and infants, and two classrooms. The income in 1876 was mostly from voluntary contributions. The master augmented his salary by acting as organist and assistant overseer. The infants' school had its own mistress and was entirely the responsibility of Lord Dartmouth. The average attendance at the schools in 1875–6 was 40 boys, 43 girls, and 48 infants.[23] In 1880 total attendances averaged 159, and a government grant was then being paid.[24] In 1888 £201 stock was conveyed for the use of the school in fulfilment of the intentions of William Simmons.[25] Average attendance in 1894–5 was 188.[26] In the late 1970s the average attendance at the school, by then called St. Chad's C. of E. controlled primary school for juniors and infants, was 180; the building had been twice extended in recent years.[27]

A private school run by E. Curtis and his son was described in 1812 as having been in existence for many years; it was still open in 1815.[28] Another was opened in 1833 and soon had 52 boys and 28 girls.[29] A girls' boarding school existed in 1834 and 1851. In the later 1870s there was a school run by Mary Hawley.[30]

CHARITIES FOR THE POOR. William Wrottesley by deed of 1640 and Walter White by deed of 1702 settled land for the benefit of the poor. By deed of 1723 John Kirkham of Wombourne settled 3¾ a. for the poor. In 1746 the endowment comprised 5½ a. but had been reduced to 3¾ a. by 1823, when the land was let at £10 4s. 10d. By order of Chancery in 1856 the charities were formed into the Poor's Estate charity. In 1864–5 the income was £40 10s. 2d. of which £29 16s. 6d. was paid out in doles to 124 poor at Easter.[31] Several more gifts came to be amalgamated with the charity. Benjamin Matthews (d. 1856) left £300, the interest to be distributed in bread to the poor after his widow's death; she died in 1874. A further £100 was left in the same way for the maintenance of his family's tombstones, any residue to be applied to four widows and widowers of the parish; by 1908 the whole income was evidently distributed. Martha Simmons (d. 1878) left £200, the interest to be distributed among the poor of Pattingham not receiving parish relief. The charity was to take effect after the death of her brother William Simmons (d. 1895), who himself gave money for the poor which by 1909 had been invested in stock. By order of the Charity Commissioners in 1909 the charities were consolidated with the Poor's Estate charity.[32] In 1977 the income was £264, of which £85 was distributed in £5 doles to 17 married couples and £162 in £3 doles to 54 single people.[33]

In 1608 Thomas Wrottesley settled a rent charge of 20s. from land at the Clive for an annual distribution to the poor.[34] Nothing further is known of the charity.

About 1640 Henry Wood of Copley (d. 1648) gave £5 to the poor.[35] By 1681 Roger Bridgen had given £5, Thomas Allen £10, and Anne Wood of Copley £4; all three were lent out.[36] Those four charities were recorded in 1710 with others given by Walter Wrottesley (£23), Joan Devey (£3), Francis Dashfield (£5), George Sansome (£2), Gilbert Parker (£1), Martin Hardwick (£10), Hugh Hardwick (£1), Thomas Brown of Copley (£11), Benjamin Jorden, vicar of Pattingham (d. 1709; £10), Francis Taylor (£10 for bread), and Thomas Perry (£50 for bread). All had been lost by the later 1780s.[37]

John Perry of Rudge in 1775 left £10 for bread for the poor of Pattingham and Rudge not receiving parish relief, and Mary Taylor in 1775 left £10 10s. for the same purpose. By 1823 the

[17] S.R.O., D.(W.) 1807/349, 352.
[18] Brighton, Pattingham, 91, 116.
[19] S.R.O., D. 660/26/5; Educ. Enq. Abstract, H.C. 62, p. 883 (1835), xlii; Nat. Soc. Inquiry, 1846–7, Staffs. 6–7.
[20] P.O. Dir. Staffs. (1860).
[21] Brighton, Pattingham, 95.
[22] Ibid. 91–5; Pattingham ch., conveyance 23 Nov. 1874.
[23] P.R.O., ED 7/109/243.
[24] Rep. Educ. Cttee. of Council, 1879–80 [C.2562-I], p. 690, H.C. (1880), xxii.
[25] Brighton, Pattingham, 95–6.
[26] Rep. Educ. Cttee. of Council, 1894–5 [C.7776-I], p. 993, H.C. (1895), xxvii.
[27] Lich. Dioc. Dir. (1979); inf. from the vicar (1979).
[28] Wolverhampton Chron. 15 Jan. 1812; 27 Dec. 1815.
[29] Educ. Enq. Abstract, 883.
[30] White, Dir. Staffs. (1834), 273; (1851), 190; P.O. Dir. Staffs. (1876); Kelly's Dir. Staffs. (1880).
[31] S.R.O., D.(W.) 1807/249, 308, 345, 352; 9th Rep. Com. Char. 632–3; Pattingham ch., acct. of Pattingham Poor's Trust Property.
[32] Brighton, Pattingham, 112–13; S.R.O., D. 660/26/3; L.J.R.O., B/C/11/LII, ff. 113v.–118v.
[33] Char. Com. files.
[34] S.R.O., D.(W.) 1807/182B.
[35] S.R.O., D. 3451/2/2, anno 1640–1; Pattingham Par. Reg. (Staffs. Par. Reg. Soc. 1934), 143.
[36] S.R.O., D. 3451/2/3. The lending of money given for the poor occurs in the churchwardens' accts. by 1633–4: ibid. 2/2.
[37] Benefaction board in church; Char. Dons. 1786–8, 1146. For probable dates of death of the benefactors see Pattingham Par. Reg.

income was £1 10s.[38] Nothing further is known of the charity.

By will proved 1900 Jane Cartwright gave £1,000 for the maintenance of a vault and graves in Pattingham church, any surplus to be distributed among the poor. The bequest was illegal, and by order of the Charity Commissioners in 1914 the money was assigned entirely to the poor, particularly for medical expenses. In 1982 the income was £72, of which £65 was distributed in £1 grocery vouchers at Christmas.[39]

TRYSULL

TRYSULL was a chapelry of Wombourne until 1888 but for civil purposes was a parish by the 17th century. Consisting of the townships of Trysull and Seisdon it was 2,951 a. in area. In 1900 the extra-parochial Woodford Grange to the south-east became part of Trysull, and the area of the parish was thereby increased to 3,150 a. (1,275 ha.).[40] Although there has been residential development round both centres, the parish is still mainly rural.

The parish lies on the county boundary with Shropshire. That boundary once ran along Brantley (formerly Branford) Lane and the 2-mile ridge known as Abbot's (formerly Apewood) Castle Hill. The parish boundary there has remained unchanged, but since 1895 only the northern part of the ridge has marked the county boundary.[41] The parish boundary on the north-east follows Black brook nearly to its confluence with Smestow brook, which flows through the north-eastern part of the parish with the villages of Seisdon and Trysull on its banks. Until the extension of 1900 Smestow brook formed the whole of the south-eastern boundary. The brook was formerly called 'Tresel', a Celtic name descriptive of its meandering course. By 1576 it was called Smestow, an Old English name meaning a still pool. In the late 18th century, however, Trysull brook was still used as an alternative name.[42] The level of the ground along the brook between the two villages is around 250 ft. (76 m.), but it rises on either side. There is a sharp rise to over 300 ft. (91 m.) north of Trysull village, and the level reaches 400 ft. (122 m.) east of Seisdon. Abbot's Castle Hill is 456 ft. (139 m.) at its northern end, 417 ft. (127 m.) at Tinker's

Castle halfway along, and 375 ft. (114 m.) at its southern end. The hill, which falls away sharply on the Shropshire side, is an escarpment of the Bunter Pebble Beds. A ridge of sand and gravel runs across the north-east of the parish.[43] The soil is sandy loam.[44]

An intermittent ditch extends along the crest of Abbot's Castle Hill. It is most clearly defined on either side of Tinker's Castle, where in addition a hollow way and a road climb the face of the hill. The relationship between the county boundary and the ditch suggests that the ditch is of Anglo-Saxon or earlier date.[45] Seisdon probably means the hill of the Saxons,[46] evidently the 300-ft. hill at the west end of the village. About 1300 it was called Penn hill, a name derived from the Celtic penn, meaning a hill.[47] By the late 16th century it was called Round or Whitney hill.[48] Seisdon was evidently the meeting place of the hundred of the same name; 'le moustowe', meaning the meeting place, was mentioned as part of a boundary near Seisdon village in 1298,[49] and one of Seisdon's open fields was called Mustowe field.[50] The meeting place was associated with a 'plewe-stowe', a place used for sports or games:[51] land called Ploustowmere was recorded c. 1300, and Plewestowe green was mentioned in 1549.[52] The earliest evidence of settlement, however, comes from Domesday Book, which shows three villages or hamlets in 1066, Trysull, Seisdon, and 'Cocortone'.[53] 'Corcortone' was still inhabited in the late 13th century[54] but was subsequently abandoned. It probably lay in the area of the later Beeches farm in the south-west of the parish where land called Cockerton survived and

---

[38] Char. Dons. 1146; 9th Rep. Com. Char. 634.

[39] Brighton, Pattingham, 107-9; inf. from the vicar.

[40] Census, 1891, 1901, 1971. This article was written mainly in 1979-80. Mr. and Mrs. K. P. Ashbourne of the Manor House, Trysull, Mr. D. Farquharson of Wolmore Farm, Mr. and Mrs. J. A. Tonkinson of the Old Manor House, Seisdon, the Revd. A. C. Tapsfield, priest-in-charge of Trysull, and others named in footnotes are thanked for their help.

[41] Above, Bobbington, introduction. A definition of the Trysull part of the county boundary was ordered in 1236: Close R. 1234-7, 367; one was made in 1295: Cal. Inq. Misc. i, p. 462. For the name Branford Lane in 1660 see S.R.O., D. 593/A/2/19/18. Plot, Staffs. 397, gives the name of the hill as 'Abbots or rather Ape-wood Castle'; it was given as Aquar-descastel in 1295 and as Apeward and Apeis Castle in the 15th cent.: Cal. Inq. Misc. i, p. 462; W.S.L., S.MS. 201 (1), p. 233; W.S.L. 40/22/52.

[42] E. Ekwall, Eng. Place-Names; E. Ekwall, Eng. River Names; Charter of Wulfrun to the Monastery at 'Hamtun', ed. W. H. Duignan, 11; S.H.C. iii (1), 215-17; S.H.C. v (1), 179;

Erdeswick, Staffs. 346, 363, 367-8, 371; P.R.O., E 178/4984; S.R.O., D. 681/1; H.W.R.O. (H.), E 12/S, Kinver VIII, deed of 27 Sept. 1788.

[43] V.C.H. Staffs. i. 21 and map before p. 1; T. H. Whitehead and R. W. Pocock, Memoirs of Geol. Surv., Dudley and Bridgnorth, 5, 106, 110-11, 122, 129, 157, 171, 181.

[44] Kelly's Dir. Staffs. (1940).

[45] V.C.H. Staffs. i. 185, 192, 372; Staffs. C.C. Planning Dept., Sites and Monuments Rec. no. 1937.

[46] Ekwall, Eng. Place-Names.

[47] Eng. Place-Name Elements, ii (E.P.N.S. xxvi), 61; below, econ. hist.

[48] W.S.L. 40/52, nos. 7, 52; S.R.O., D. 740/1/19.

[49] S.R.O., D. 740/2/1; Eng. Place-Name Elements, ii. 44.

[50] Below, econ. hist.

[51] Eng. Place-Name Elements, ii. 67; Place-Names of Glos. iv (E.P.N.S. xli), 52; V.C.H. Glos. viii. 38.

[52] W.S.L. 40/6/52; S.R.O., D. 740/3/3, 6.

[53] Below, manors and other estates.

[54] S.H.C. 1911, 194.

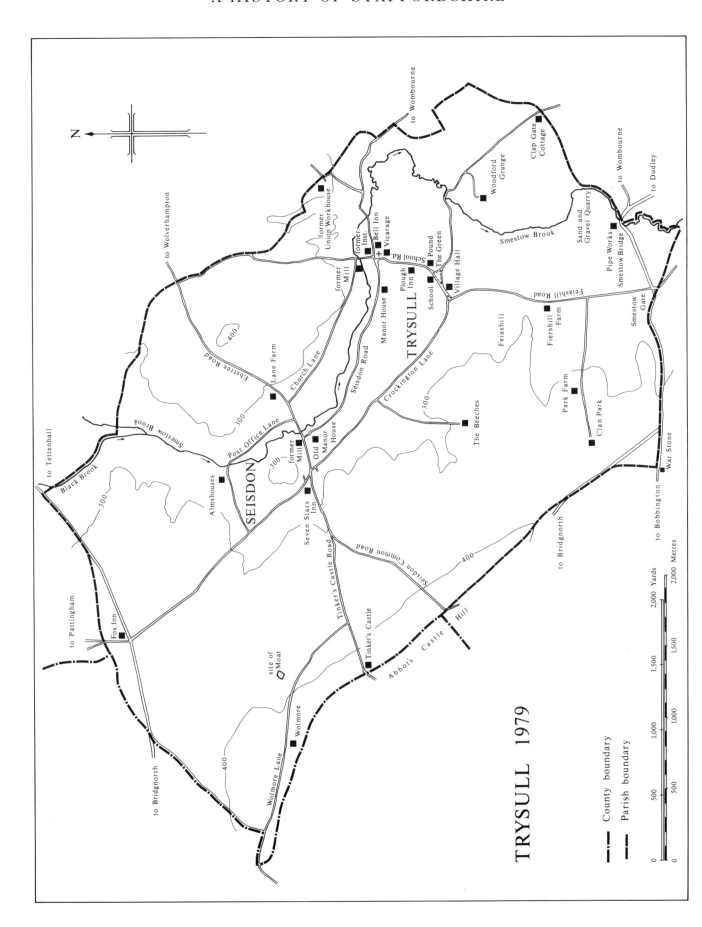

N

to Wombourne

to Wombourne

to Dudley

to Wolverhampton

Clap Gate
Cottage

Woodford
Grange

Sand and
Gravel Quarry

former
Union Workhouse

Bell Inn

former
Inst.

Vicarage

Smestow Brook

Pipe Works

Smestow Bridge

former
Mill

Pound

The Green

Manor House

School Rd

Village Hall

TRYSULL

Smestow
Gate

Feiashill Road

400

School

Feiashill

Fiershill
Farm

Lane Farm

Ebstree Road

Church Lane

Seisdon Road

Crockington Lane

300

Post Office Lane

Smestow Brook

300

The Beeches

Park Farm

Clan Park

to Tettenhall

Black Brook

former
Mill

Old
Manor
House

SEISDON

300

Almshouses

War Stone

Seven Stars
Inn

Tinker's Castle Road

Seisdon Common Road

400

to Bridgnorth

to Bobbington

to Pattingham

Fox Inn

site of
Moat

Tinker's Castle

Tinker's Castle

Abbots Castle Hill

2,000 Yards

2,000 Metres

1,500

1,500

1,000

1,000

500

500

0

0

Wolmore

to Bridgnorth

Wolmore Lane

400

TRYSULL 1979

County boundary

Parish boundary

Crockington (formerly Cockerton) Lane runs from Seisdon to the southern end of Trysull village.[55]

In 1086 the recorded population was 10 in Trysull and 2 in Seisdon.[56] In 1327 Trysull and Seisdon together had 15 people assessed for tax.[57] In the mid 1520s there were 28 assessed,[58] and 27 names appeared on the muster roll of 1539.[59] In 1563 there were 34 households.[60] The poll-tax assessment of 1641 listed 145 people in Trysull constablewick.[61] In 1666 there were 51 people assessed for hearth tax and a further 15 were too poor to pay.[62] The Compton Census of 1676 recorded 265 people in the parish.[63] In the earlier 1770s there were about 100 houses.[64] The population was just over 500 in 1801 and fluctuated somewhat during the 19th century. It reached its highest in 1861 with 610, including 39 inmates of the new union workhouse. In 1901 it was down to 568, including 15 in the newly added Woodford Grange.[65] In the 20th century the population rose steadily, to 574 in 1911, 597 in 1921, 604 in 1931, 748 in 1951, 866 in 1961, and 945 in 1971.[66]

The original settlement at Trysull was presumably around the church, in existence by the 12th century. By 1318 there was settlement at the Green south of the village, also known as Bent or Ben Green.[67] By the earlier 1770s settlement extended further south still along Feiashill Road as far as Fiershill Farm, itself in existence by 1722.[68] Common (later Park) Farm on the edge of Trysull common to the south-west evidently existed by 1735;[69] Clan Park to the west of it and the Beeches to the north existed by 1814.[70] Trysull village contained well over half the total population in the mid 19th century.[71] Council houses were built in Feiashill Road before and after the Second World War.[72]

In Seisdon settlement was concentrated by the 1770s along the later Post Office Road on both sides of Smestow brook,[73] and the position of the open fields suggests that that area was the ancient centre of the village. The house at the corner of Ebstree Road and the road to Trysull known as the Old Manor House dates from 1684.[74] Lanes Farm on Ebstree Road north-east of the village is dated 1746. Tinker's Castle, a house on the county boundary west of Seisdon, probably dates from the late 18th century; its cellar incorporates a rock dwelling. Council houses were built on the Pattingham road in the period between the two World Wars. A number of privately built houses have been erected in the later 20th century,

notably two estates at the crossroads formed by the Wolverhampton–Claverley and the Trysull–Pattingham roads; several council houses were also built there. The moated site near Wolmore 1¼ mile west of Seisdon existed c. 1300. Wolmore Lane, now a track serving Wolmore, was then 'le portsti' leading from Trysull towards Bridgnorth (Salop.).[75] The moated site was levelled c. 1965.[76] The farm buildings at Wolmore to the west on the other side of the lane include part of a 17th-century timber-framed range and an 18th-century barn and pigeon house.

Two major roads cross the parish. The Wolverhampton–Bridgnorth road runs through the north, and that stretch was apparently known as White Way in the late 13th century.[77] It was turnpiked in 1748 and disturnpiked in 1880.[78] The road from Dudley, which runs through the south and forms the parish boundary on the south-west, joins the first road near Shipley, in Claverley (Salop.). Smestow bridge, which carries the Dudley road over Smestow brook on the Trysull–Wombourne boundary, existed by 1300 and was the joint responsibility of Trysull and Wombourne parishes by 1647. The road was turnpiked in 1790, and by 1832 there was a tollgate, Smestow gate, at the junction with Feiashill Road.[79] The road from Wolverhampton to Claverley runs through Seisdon as Ebstree Road; the stretch between Seisdon and Tinker's Castle was called Seisdon Way in 1295.[80] Seisdon bridge, by which the road crosses Smestow brook, existed c. 1300. It was described in 1647 as a horse bridge and was then a parish responsibility. It was rebuilt by the county in 1826 as a three-arched carriage bridge of stone and brick, which is still in use.[81] Further upstream is a two-arched bridge of stone and brick carrying Post Office Road over the brook. The road which runs north from Trysull village to join the Seisdon–Wolverhampton road on the north-eastern boundary was mentioned in 1544.[82] A seven-arched horse bridge carrying it over Smestow brook was described in 1852 as of very rude construction and built at a very remote period. In times of flood the approaches quickly became impassable, and since the bridge had no parapet it was dangerous at all times; among many accidents at both the bridge and the ford beside it was one in 1848 when Lord Wrottesley and his horse fell off the bridge into the brook. The present three-span cast-iron bridge on brick piers was built by the county soon after 1852.[83]

[55] W.S.L., S.MS. 386/2, no. 227, giving Cokerton (misprinted by Shaw, *Staffs.* ii. 208, as Colverton); S.R.O., D. 548/A/PD/2; D. 740/1/3; S.R.O., Tp. 1273/11, 1623 survey; H. R. Thomas, 'Trysull and Seisdon', p. 5 (TS. in W.S.L.).
[56] Below, econ. hist.   [57] *S.H.C.* vii (1), 251–2.
[58] P.R.O., E 179/177/106.
[59] *S.H.C.* N.S. vi (1), 70.
[60] *S.H.C.* 1915, p. lxxii.
[61] H.L., Main Papers, box 178.
[62] *S.H.C.* 1923, 102–3.
[63] W.S.L., S.MS. 33, p. 371.
[64] L.J.R.O., B/V/5/1772/Trysull.
[65] *V.C.H. Staffs.* i. 327. The figure of 529 in 1801 evidently included Woodford Grange, which had a population of 14 in 1821.   [66] *Census*, 1901–71.
[67] S.R.O., D. 548/A/PD/1; D. 740/3/1; D. 3452/10/1, list of constables; Shaw, *Staffs.* ii. 208.
[68] Yates, *Map of Staffs.* (1775); S.R.O., D. 3452/10/1, list of constables.   [69] S.R.O., D. 3452/10/1, list of constables.

[70] B.L. Maps, O.S.D. 213.
[71] P.R.O., HO 107/2017; P.R.O., RG 9/1986; RG 10/2929.
[72] *Seisdon R.D.C. Yr. Bk. 1956–1957,* 22; *1964–1965,* 25.
[73] Yates, *Map of Staffs.* (1775).
[74] Below, manors and other estates.
[75] *V.C.H. Staffs.* i. 368; W.S.L. 40/52, nos. 5, 22; W.S.L. 674/35.
[76] Inf. from Mr. D. Farquharson.
[77] *Cal. Inq. Misc.* i, p. 462.
[78] Above, Tettenhall, introduction (communications).
[79] Below, Wombourne, introduction (communications). For the gate see J. Phillips and W. F. Hutchings, *Map of Staffs.* (1832).   [80] *Cal. Inq. Misc.* i, p. 462.
[81] Shaw, *Staffs.* ii. 208; S.R.O., Q/SR, E. 1647, no. 8; Q/SB, T. 1825; Q/SB, E. 1852, rep. on Trysull bridge.
[82] S.R.O., D. 593/A/2/19/11.
[83] S.R.O., Q/SB, E. 1852; W.S.L., Staffs. Views, xi. 70; W.S.L., H.M. 31/15, including list of county bridges 1864 (which, however, mentions 5 spans).

There are four inns in the parish, all long established. The Seven Stars at the crossroads at the west end of Seisdon village existed by 1714 when the justices held a monthly meeting there. When it was advertised for sale in 1812 it was described as 'well accustomed' and as having a large clubroom.[84] The Fox on the Wolverhampton–Bridgnorth road where it is crossed by the road from Pattingham is dated 1810. The Bell east of Trysull church and the Plough in School Road running south from the church were so named by 1851 and probably existed by 1834.[85] There was an inn called the Vine in Trysull village in the late 19th and early 20th century.[86]

There was a police officer in Trysull village by 1851.[87] A police station was built in Feiashill Road shortly after the Second World War,[88] but it had been closed by 1980.

The names Gibbet Bank north of Trysull village and Gibbethill Plantation north-west of Seisdon[89] presumably indicate the sites of gibbets.

Trysull village had a post office by 1845, and there was another at Seisdon from the later 1880s.[90] The parish lay on the route of buses running between Wolverhampton and Bridgnorth by 1908.[91] In 1896 Bilston urban district council laid water mains to Trysull village from the works at the Bratch in Wombourne.[92] Electricity was available by 1935.[93]

A parish wake was recorded in the mid 18th century, and in the earlier 19th century it was held on the Sunday nearest to 5 November.[94] There was a parish cricket club in the mid 1880s,[95] and in 1980 there was a cricket ground west of the Green. A Seisdon company of Volunteers was formed in 1860 with G. P. A. Pudsey of Seisdon as captain; it still existed in 1871.[96]

In 1798 Trysull and Seisdon each had a friendly society, that at Trysull being for women.[97] There were three friendly societies in 1876, the Union founded in 1865 and meeting at the Bell, a society founded in 1867, and Trysull Cottage Lodge of the United Order of Free Gardeners founded in 1870 and with 69 members meeting at the Plough.[98] A clothing club associated with the church by 1878–9 then had 34 depositors; there were 41 in 1889–90.[99] The Trysull Institute was mentioned in 1881 when a concert was held there.[1] An institute with a reading room, billiard room, and caretaker's house was built north of the church by B. H. Mander of the Manor House at the end of the century. It still existed c. 1950,[2] but by 1979 the building was a private club called Thatchers. The village hall west of the Green was built for the Women's Institute in 1935.[3]

Trysull and Seisdon have given their names to several administrative units. Seisdon hundred has already been mentioned. By 1224 there was a deanery of Trysull, approximating to Seisdon hundred; it was united with the deanery of Lapley in the late 13th century, but with the reorganization of the mid 19th century a separate Trysull deanery was again created.[4] Seisdon gave its name to a poor-law union in 1836, with a workhouse in Trysull from 1860,[5] and to a rural district in 1894; the district council met at the workhouse until c. 1930 when it moved to Wombourne.[6]

MANORS AND OTHER ESTATES. Before the Conquest *TRYSULL* was held by Turgot, a free man, with sac and soc. In 1086 the 2 hides there were held by William FitzAnsculf, lord of Dudley.[7] By the mid 13th century Trysull was held with half of Seisdon as 1 knight's fee, which was assessed at 3 hides. The overlordship descended with the barony of Dudley until the death of John, Lord Somery, in 1322. The barony was divided in 1323, the Trysull fee being assigned to John's elder sister Margaret and her husband, John de Sutton. It then descended in the Sutton (later Sutton or Dudley) family and was held by Lord Dudley in 1581.[8]

In 1086 Baldwin held Trysull of FitzAnsculf.[9] He also held Frankley (Worcs.), and about the mid 12th century the two manors were evidently held by Giles of Trysull. He was succeeded by his son Bernard, who was called both of Trysull and of Frankley and was still alive in 1206.[10] His son Simon, who was also known by both surnames, had succeeded by 1227 and died in 1232 or 1233, leaving a son.[11] A Thomas of Frankley was lord of a knight's fee in Trysull and Seisdon in 1242–3.[12] He was probably the Thomas of Trysull who was lord in 1251.[13] About that time a mesne lordship was created, and in 1254–5 it was held by Philip

[84] S.R.O., D. 571/A/PK/1, p. 1; D. 3452/1/1, f. [8]; *Wolverhampton Chron.* 19 Feb. 1812.
[85] White, *Dir. Staffs.* (1834), 291; (1851), 210; P.R.O., HO 107/1002.
[86] *Kelly's Dir. Staffs.* (1892; 1908).
[87] P.R.O., HO 107/2017.
[88] Staffs. C.C. Deeds, C. 552, H. 76/3.
[89] H. R. Thomas, 'Trysull and Seisdon' (TS. in W.S.L.), p. 4; O.S. Map 1/25,000, SO 89/99 (1976 edn.).
[90] *P.O. Dir. Staffs.* (1845); *Kelly's Dir. Staffs.* (1888).
[91] Above, p. 14; *Kelly's Dir. Staffs.* (1940).
[92] Seisdon R.D.C. *Rep. of M.O.H. for 1896*, 8 (copy in S.R.O., C/H/1/2/1/7).
[93] Ibid. 1935, 10 (copy in S.R.O., C/H/1/2/2/36).
[94] J. Ecton, *Thesaurus Rerum Ecclesiasticarum* (1742), 109; White, *Dir. Staffs.* (1834), 290.
[95] S.R.O., D. 3452/12/1, 1885–6.
[96] *Hist. of Volunteer Force of Staffs. 1859–1908* (Stafford, 1909), 4, 14.
[97] *S.H.C.* 4th ser. vi. 221.
[98] *Reps. of Chief Registrar of Friendly Socs. 1876*, H.C. 429, p. 410 (1877), lxxvii.

[99] S.R.O., D. 3452/12/1, 1878–9, 1889–90.
[1] Ibid. 1880–1.
[2] *Kelly's Dir. Staffs.* (1912), giving date of building as 1899, with later edns. giving it as 1896; *Seisdon R.D. Official Guide* (edn. of c. 1950), 24.
[3] Inscription on hall.
[4] *V.C.H. Staffs.* iii. 38, 92–3, 95–6; *S.H.C.* 1916, 190; *Reg. Pecham* (Cant. & York Soc.), ii. 154.
[5] Below, local govt.
[6] *Kelly's Dir. Staffs.* (1896 and later edns.).
[7] *V.C.H. Staffs.* iv. 54.
[8] *Bk. of Fees*, i. 543; ii. 968; *S.H.C.* v (1), 112; ix (2), 34, 44; *Complete Peerage*, xii (1), 115; *Cal. Fine R. 1430–7*, 132; P.R.O., C 142/127, no. 46; H.W.R.O. (H.), E 12/S, Bobbington and Enville, valor of lands of John Grey 1581.
[9] *V.C.H. Staffs.* iv. 54.
[10] *S.H.C.* i. 200; iii (1), 90, 130, 137, 214–15; *V.C.H. Worcs.* iii. 120.
[11] *S.H.C.* iv (1), 17, 52; *S.H.C.* 1921, 4; *Pat. R. 1225–32*, 523; *Close R. 1231–4*, 247.
[12] *Bk. of Fees*, ii. 968.
[13] *Cal. Chart. R. 1226–57*, 358.

of Frankley, apparently Simon's son. He was dead by 1276.[14] By the mid 1280s the mesne lordship had passed to the Walerand family, and it was claimed in 1323 by Alan, Lord Plugenet, whose great-grandmother had married into that family.[15] After Plugenet's death in 1325[16] the mesne lordship appears to have lapsed.

Thomas of Trysull was the terre tenant in 1254-5.[17] He was dead by 1272 and was succeeded by John of Trysull, who in 1291 held Trysull and half of Seisdon as a knight's fee.[18] In 1312 he conveyed what was called simply Trysull manor to William, son of John of Perton.[19] William of Perton, who succeeded to Perton, in Tettenhall, in 1331, died in 1360 with his son Sir John as his heir.[20] Sir John died in 1388 and was succeeded at Trysull by his nephew, John Barnhurst.[21] In 1396 Barnhurst conveyed the manor to Edmund Lowe.[22] The manor then descended with Whittington, in Kinver, and from the earlier 16th century with Enville also.[23] It became united with Seisdon manor in 1557. In 1633 the joint manor of Trysull and Seisdon, which had been mortgaged by Ambrose Grey of Enville, was bought by Sir Hugh Wrottesley.[24] It then descended in the Wrottesley family with Wrottesley in Tettenhall. In 1929 Lord Wrottesley put his property in the parish up for sale.[25]

The house of the lord of Trysull was described in 1535 as near the road to Kidderminster (Worcs.).[26] It is not clear that it is to be identified with the house on the Seisdon road at the west end of Trysull village which was known as the Manor House by 1860. By the 17th century that house was the home of the Barnsley family, who were living in the parish by the 16th century. William Barnesley (d. 1684) was succeeded by his son William (d. 1690) and he by his sister Elizabeth, wife of Robert Harriotts. Through her mother she was the second cousin of Samuel Johnson, who was brought to the house in 1711 while still an infant; he suffered from eye trouble, and Elizabeth arranged for him to be seen there by Dr. Thomas Attwood of Powick (Worcs.). She died in 1728, and her property passed to Wannerton Groome, another relative. He died at Trysull in 1748 and was succeeded by his son John. On John's death in 1799 the Trysull property passed to his widow Anna (d. 1803), who left to her husband's nephew Henry Jesson the option of buying the property. Jesson, a Wolverhampton surgeon, bought it in 1805 and was living there by 1811. He died in 1841, and his

younger son Henry, a barrister, lived there until his death in 1853. The elder son, the Revd. Cornelius Jesson, died in 1869, and the house, which had been let for many years, passed to a relative, Col. Thomas Smythe. He lived there from 1873 until his death in 1879. His daughters sold it in 1894 to B. H. Mander (d. 1912), whose widow was living there c. 1940. It was sold in 1947 to R. E. Probert, who sold it in 1949 to Major John Lees. It was bought from Major Lees in 1958 by Mrs. Ronald Lovatt, whose daughter Miss E. J. Lovatt sold it in 1978 to Mr. K. P. Ashbourne, the owner in 1980.[27]

The house, which is partly timber-framed and partly of stone and brick, is of several dates. The entrance hall and the cross wing at its east end are probably of the later 16th or early 17th century, and the kitchen, which has the date 1633 on its timber-framed gable, is probably the earliest extension. The west wing may also be 17th-century. In 1640 the house included a hall, a parlour, and seven chambers.[28] The drawing room and the adjacent main staircase were built in the mid 19th century, evidently for Henry Jesson the younger.[29] After 1894 the hall and the principal rooms on the south front were remodelled and the north-west corner was enlarged.[30] The range on the south side of the stable yard has a weathervane dated 1764 but has been much altered. The other stable buildings date probably from after 1894.

Before the Conquest *SEISDON* was held by four free men whose soc belonged to the king. In 1086 the 5 hides there were held by William FitzAnsculf.[31] By the 13th century, as already seen, the township had been divided. Half descended with Trysull and with it formed 1 knight's fee. The other half formed a separate ½ fee. The overlordship of each half followed the same descent in the barony of Dudley.

Walter held Seisdon of FitzAnsculf in 1086.[32] It is possible that in 1166 half of Seisdon was held by William de Offini, lord of Wombourne.[33] By the 13th century the ½ fee was held by the lords of Bradley, in Bilston. In 1227 Walter of Bradley claimed the moiety of a mill at Seisdon in succession to his father Geoffrey of Bradley, but a jury refused to uphold his claim.[34] Walter was succeeded by his son Reynold.[35] In 1291 Thomas of Bradley held half of Seisdon as ½ knight's fee,[36] and he or another Thomas, lord of Bradley, held it in 1323.[37] The lord of Bradley still held the estate in 1405.[38] By 1557 what was called Seisdon

[14] *S.H.C.* v (1), 112; *V.C.H. Worcs.* iii. 121.

[15] *Feud. Aids.* v. 10; *S.H.C.* ix (2), 34; *Cal. Close, 1318-23*, 630; W. Farrer, *Honors and Knights' Fees*, i. 110-11; *Complete Peerage*, x. 552-3.

[16] *Cal. Inq. p.m.* vi, p. 422.

[17] *S.H.C.* v (1), 112.

[18] *S.H.C.* iv (1), 203, 208; ix (2), 34.

[19] *S.H.C.* 1911, 80-1.

[20] *S.H.C.* 1917-18, 93.

[21] *Cal. Inq. p.m.* xvi, p. 293.

[22] *S.H.C.* xi. 202.

[23] *Feud. Aids*, v. 22; Shaw, *Staffs.* ii. 268; S.R.O., D. 1485/6/4/5; W.S.L. 40/22/52.

[24] *S.H.C.* n.s. vi (2), 298, 311. The manor was called Trysull and Seisdon in 1595: W.S.L. 40/33/52.

[25] S.R.O., index of gamekeepers' deputations; W.S.L. 39/47; White, *Dir. Staffs.* (1851), 209; W.S.L., Sale Cat. E/3/12; *Staffs. Advertiser*, 26 Oct. 1929.

[26] W.S.L. 40/26/52.

[27] A. L. Reade, *Johnsonian Gleanings*, i (priv. print. 1909), 22-4; A. L. Reade, *Reades of Blackwood Hill* (priv. print. 1906), 190; Shaw, *Staffs.* ii. 208-9; G. P. Mander, *Wolverhampton Antiquary*, 55-64; *P.O. Dir. Staffs.* (1860 and later edns.); *Kelly's Dir. Staffs.* (1884 and later edns.); *Hist. of Mander Brothers* (Wolverhampton, priv. print. 1955), family tree and p. 177; inf. from Miss E. J. Lovatt of Bagendon, Glos.

[28] L.J.R.O., B/C/11, Wm. Barnesley (1640).

[29] Reade, *Johnsonian Gleanings*, i. 23.

[30] Panelling in the study is dated 1907.

[31] *V.C.H. Staffs.* iv. 55.

[32] Ibid.

[33] Below, Wombourne, manors and other estates.

[34] *S.H.C.* iv (1), 52.

[35] *S.H.C.* 1928, 17.

[36] *S.H.C.* ix (2), 34.

[37] *Cal. Close, 1318-23*, 630; Shaw, *Staffs.* ii. 171.

[38] S.R.O., D. 740/3/2.

manor had passed from Thomas Leveson to his daughter Jane, wife of Richard Poulteney of Misterton (Leics.). In that year Jane and her husband sold it to Thomas Grey of Enville, lord of Trysull.[39]

The house at the corner of Seisdon Road and Ebstree Road now known as the Old Manor House was occupied by the Banton family as a farmhouse by the early 19th century. It was sold in 1930 by William Banton to T. W. Hartley. His widow married S. A. Grayson, who lived there until his death in 1980. Mr. J. A. Tonkinson and his wife, a daughter of T. W. Hartley, moved there later that year.[40] The first part of the house was built in 1684[41] and was a simple brick structure of two storeys with attics and basement. Originally there were only two rooms on each floor, but by the mid 18th century additions at the back had doubled the size of the house. In 1848[42] it was remodelled and enlarged by additions at each end.

Before the Conquest COCORTONE was held by three free men whose soc belonged to the king. In 1086 Baldwin held 1½ hide there of William FitzAnsculf. It was waste. The 'Cocretone' where ½ hide belonging to the royal manor of Kingswinford in 1086 was also waste has been identified as the same place.[43]

The rectorial tithes of Trysull and Seisdon were held by Dudley priory with those of the rest of Wombourne parish until its dissolution in 1540. They were then in the tenure of Fowke Lee under a 40-year lease of 1533.[44] In 1541 the Crown granted them to Sir John Dudley with the rest of the priory's possessions.[45] Later the same year Sir John sold them to Thomas Ridgeway of Shipley, in Claverley, who after a dispute bought out Lee's interest in 1542.[46] Ridgeway died in 1546 and left a life interest in the tithes to his widow Elizabeth. Later that year she married Edward Leveson of Perton, in Tettenhall, and they bought the reversionary interest also. Edward died in 1569 and Elizabeth in 1576.[47] Edward's heir was his nephew Walter Leveson of Lilleshall (Salop.) and Trentham, and the tithes then descended in the Leveson (later Leveson-Gower) family with Great Wyrley, in Cannock. They were worth £80 by the 1640s. After 1762 they were let to the tenants of the lands concerned, bringing in an average of £83 7s. 9½d. a year, and from c. 1769 Lord Gower sold them with the lands from which they arose.[48] By 1850 the owners of tithes from 1,639 a., over half the acreage of the parish, had merged the tithes with the land. A commutation award was made that

year assigning rent charges totalling £68 19s. 9d. to 16 owners of tithe from just over 1,100 a. The rest of the land was stated to be tithe free by prescription. In 1851 and 1852 the owners of the rent charges merged them in the freehold of the lands concerned.[49] A tithe barn stood in Whitnall field in Seisdon until it was removed to Shipley by the lessee of the tithes, apparently in the 17th century.[50]

Other property in Trysull formerly belonging to Dudley priory was retained by Sir John Dudley, but it returned to the Crown when, as duke of Northumberland, he was attainted in 1553. In 1554 and 1555 the Crown granted the estate, described as a messuage, with much of Northumberland's property to Edward Sutton, Lord Dudley. He made a settlement of it in 1580.[51]

In 1735 an estate in Seisdon was bought for £700 by the Blue Coat School at Wolverhampton. In 1820 it consisted of a farmhouse, cottages, and 80 a., mainly pasture, scattered throughout the parish. The school trustees bought the great tithes of the estate in 1805.[52] The trustees still owned an 80-a. estate in 1850,[53] but they no longer had property in the parish in 1980.[54]

ECONOMIC HISTORY. In 1086 Trysull manor had land for 3 ploughs. There were 2 ploughteams in demesne with 5 slaves, and 4 villeins and 1 bordar had a further 2 teams. At Seisdon the manor had land for 6 ploughs and there was 1 ploughteam in demesne with 2 servants. Trysull was valued at 30s. and Seisdon at 8s., the same values as before the Conquest; both included meadow, and Trysull had a mill.[55] 'Corcortone' manor had land for 2 ploughs but was waste in 1086; it may have been a recent addition to Kinver forest. Trysull and Seisdon were within the forest by the later 12th century.[56] By the 14th century assarts were being made around Seisdon.[57]

There were five open fields in Seisdon. Penn Hill field, mentioned c. 1300, lay west of Smestow brook; it is identifiable as the later Whitney (or Whitney Hill) field in that area.[58] Budbrook field, mentioned in 1338, lay north of the village and extended to the boundary with Pattingham and with Penn.[59] Pirre (later Perry) field, mentioned in 1427, lay near Smestow brook,[60] possibly south of the village. East of the village lay Mustowe field, recorded in 1518, when it included land called Newland; New Lunt (or

[39] S.R.O., D. 593/A/2/19/17.
[40] Inf. from Mr. and Mrs. Tonkinson; Parson and Bradshaw, *Dir. Staffs.* (1818); below, p. 191.
[41] The house is inscribed W/HE/1684 on the front.
[42] Inscription on the back.
[43] *V.C.H. Staffs.* iv. 38, 54.
[44] S.R.O., D. 593/A/19/2.
[45] *L. & P. Hen. VIII*, xvi, pp. 329–30.
[46] Ibid. p. 423; S.R.O., D. 593/A/2/19/3–7; P.R.O., C 1/1024/34–8.
[47] *L. & P. Hen. VIII*, xxi (2), p. 248; P.R.O., C 142/75, no. 69; S.R.O., D. 593/A/2/19/12, 14–16; D. 593/B/2/2/3; D. 593/C/6/1/6, 10.
[48] S.R.O., D. 593/B/1/26/13; D. 593/C/8/2/16; W.S.L., S.MS. 339 (transcript of Royalist Composition Papers), iv, pp. 140, 155, 169; *V.C.H. Staffs.* v. 80; above, Tettenhall,

manors and other estates (Perton).
[49] L.J.R.O., B/A/15/Trysull.
[50] S.R.O., D. 593/H/14/1/4, f. 53.
[51] *Cal. Pat.* 1554–5, 23; 1555–7, 37; *S.H.C.* xvii. 225.
[52] *4th Rep. Com. Char.* 357.
[53] L.J.R.O., B/A/15/Trysull.
[54] Inf. from Mr. J. L. H. Riches of Fowler, Langley & Wright, Bridgnorth.
[55] *V.C.H. Staffs.* iv. 54–5.
[56] Ibid. ii. 336, 343; iv. 54; *S.H.C.* i. 79; v (1), 138, 154, 180.
[57] B.R.L. 323678; W.S.L. 40/52, nos. 3, 9, 13–17.
[58] W.S.L. 40/52, no. 7; S.R.O., D. 593/A/2/19/9–10; D. 740/3/6; *S.H.C.* 1931, map in pocket.
[59] W.S.L. 40/52, no. 12; S.R.O., Tp. 1318, deed of 26 June 1464.
[60] S.R.O., D. 740/3/4, 6.

New Land) field was a separate field by the later 17th century.[61] At Trysull there appears to have been only one open field, mentioned c. 1300 and called Holloway field in 1458.[62] A parish meeting in 1699 made regulations for the management of the field of Trysull and the fields of Seisdon, including the appointment of a hayward for each township.[63] It seems that the regulations were the result of an agreement made in 1697 between Sir Walter Wrottesley and the 52 freehold tenants of his manor of Trysull and Seisdon to inclose, break up, and till the common and waste of the manor. Each freeholder was to receive an allotment in each of three new fields; the apportionment was to be by lot, except for the shares of three tenants who were assigned part of Blackley heath (presumably Blakeley common at Seisdon). The agreement also provided for alternate husbandry in a field called Hach field.[64] Although Mustowe and Perry fields were still mentioned in 1768,[65] the only open-field arable in the parish a few years later was 101 a. in Whitney, New Lunt, and Budbrook fields, which were inclosed in 1778 under an Act of 1773.[66]

In 1086 Trysull and Seisdon each had 4 a. of meadow.[67] There was open meadow on the north-eastern boundary in the late 13th century.[68] By the 14th century the making of the mill stream north of Smestow brook between Seisdon and Trysull had created extensive meadowland.[69] Doles in Ford meadow were mentioned in 1589.[70]

Waste north of Seisdon, later known as Blakeley heath or common, and waste in Trysull were mentioned c. 1300.[71] Plewestowe green in Seisdon was mentioned in 1549, and there was waste in Seisdon called the Green in 1552.[72] At Wolmore in the north-west of the parish waste was being rented to the inhabitants of Ludstone and Claverley (Salop.) in 1636.[73] There were 711 a. of common and waste in the parish in 1775 when they were inclosed under the Act of 1773. Most of the land lay on Trysull common along the western and southern boundary of the parish; there were smaller areas on Blakeley common north of Seisdon and on the Green south of Trysull village. Less than 1 a. of the Green survived as waste in 1980.[74]

Rye was being grown as a winter crop at Trysull in 1601. Crops at Seisdon in 1632 included barley, peas, rye, and wheat.[75] Flax and hemp were also grown in the parish. Mary Granger had flax, hemp, and yarn in her house

when she died in 1569, and in the late 18th century Richard Idiens was growing flax and hemp in both Seisdon and Trysull.[76] The Norfolk system of rotation, especially suited to the light sandy soil of the parish, had been adopted by the beginning of the 19th century. The chief crops then were barley, turnips, and wheat; oats, rye, peas, and potatoes were also grown.[77] At Seisdon in the mid 19th century Daniel Banton, who farmed 300 a. there, was the first in the county to use guano as a fertilizer; he also had a threshing machine which performed several operations at once.[78] In the early 1850s there was almost as much pasture as arable in the parish. Arable later came to predominate, and by 1979 there were 710½ ha. (1,758 a.) of arable and 331 ha. (820 a.) of pasture recorded in the parish. There was also a move towards smaller farms. Of the 12 or 13 farms in the early 1850s 7 had 200 a. or more. By 1979, of the 26 holdings recorded, 19 had under 50 ha. (123 a.) and only 1 over 200 ha.; 13 were worked part time.[79] The chief crops in the later 19th century were wheat, barley, oats, and roots.[80] Probably characteristic of the farms was the 120-a. Trysull Manor farm, of which 100 a. were arable in 1914; the farmer was then catering for the Black Country market, growing potatoes as well as rearing pigs and poultry.[81] In 1979 barley and sugar beet were the chief crops in the parish, but potatoes and wheat were also grown.[82]

There was market gardening in Trysull by the mid 19th century.[83] In 1979 there were 6½ ha. (16 a.) devoted to vegetables and fruit; there was also cultivation under glass then.[84]

Sheep were grazed on the extensive waste in the parish. Recorded in the early 14th century,[85] sheep farming was widespread by the earlier 16th century. Flocks of 80 existed at Seisdon and Trysull in the 1540s. Edmund Shenton of Seisdon had a flock of 260 worth over £30 and wool worth £9 in 1565, and at Trysull William Barnesley had a flock of 130 in 1571.[86] Smaller flocks often numbered between 50 and 70 sheep. The largest flock recorded in the 17th century was that of another William Barnesley of Trysull, who had 400 sheep worth £80 in 1640.[87] There were still large flocks in the early 19th century. One of 156 was recorded at Trysull in 1814, and in 1820, again at Trysull, 200 Leicesters were advertised for sale.[88] In 1871 four shepherds were living in the parish, three of them at Seisdon.[89] In 1979

[61] W.S.L. 40/52, nos. 25, 34; S.R.O., D. 740/1/27, 29.
[62] W.S.L., S.MS. 201 (i), p. 266; S.R.O., Tp. 1273/8, deed of 25 May 1458.
[63] S.H.C. 1931, 81.
[64] S.R.O., D. 740/5; W.S.L. 45/96/56.
[65] S.R.O., Tp. 1226, bdle XXXII.
[66] S.R.O., D. 548/A/PD/2; S.H.C. 1931, 78–9, 92; 1941, 16.
[67] V.C.H. Staffs. iv. 54–5.
[68] S.H.C. 1928, 17.
[69] W.S.L. 40/52, nos. 14, 16; S.R.O., D. 740/2/3.
[70] L.J.R.O., B/C/11, Rob. Sherwyn (1592).
[71] W.S.L. 40/52, nos. 1, 4; S.R:O., D. 740/1/18.
[72] Above, introduction; below, church.
[73] S.R.O., Tp. 1273/11, ct. of recognition and survey 1636.
[74] S.R.O., D. 548/A/PD/1; S.H.C. 1931, 91; inf. from S. Staffs. district council, clerk's dept.
[75] L.J.R.O., B/C/11, John Perry (1601), Jane Sheinton (1632).

[76] Ibid., Mary Granger (1568); S.R.O., Q/SO 18, f. 224; 19, ff. 49, 97, 145. [77] S.H.C. 1950–1, 235, 240.
[78] White, Dir. Staffs. (1851), 209–10; P.R.O., HO 107/2017.
[79] L.J.R.O., B/A/15/Trysull; M.A.F.F., agric. returns 1979.
[80] P.O. Dir. Staffs. (1868); Kelly's Dir. Staffs. (1940).
[81] Jnl. Royal Agric. Soc. of Eng. lxxv. 224–5.
[82] M.A.F.F., agric. returns 1979.
[83] P.R.O., HO 107/2017; P.R.O., RG 10/2929.
[84] M.A.F.F., agric. returns 1979.
[85] S.R.O., D.(W.) 1807/2; W.S.L. 40/52, nos. 3, 8; W.S.L., S.MS. 201 (i), p. 233.
[86] L.J.R.O., B/C/11, Ric. Shenton (c. 1540), John Taylor (1543), Edm. Shenton (1565), Wm. Barnesley (1571).
[87] Ibid., Agnes Dolman (1591), Thos. Shinton (1601), John Perry (1601), John Wedge (1614), Wm. Barnesley (1640).
[88] Wolverhampton Chron. 9 Feb. 1814; 8 Mar. 1820.
[89] P.R.O., RG 10/2929.

there were only a small number of sheep in the parish,[90] reflecting the decline in pastoral farming.

Edmund Shenton of Seisdon had 8 cows and 4 calves worth over £9 in 1565, and in 1571 the herd of William Barnesley of Trysull comprised 9 cows, 4 young steers, and 2 calves, worth £18 10s. Another William Barnesley had 9 cows, 12 one- and two-year olds, and 15 weaning calves, worth £61, in 1640.[91] The skins may have been used in tanning.[92] By the early 19th century cattle were probably kept for dairy purposes. Small herds were recorded then, and a farmer at Seisdon had a cheese press, vats, and dairy implements in 1814.[93] In 1979, out of 13 full-time farmers, 3 concentrated on livestock rearing and fattening and another on dairy produce; there were then some 425 cattle in the parish.[94]

In 1640 William Barnesley of Trysull had 18 pigs worth £10.[95] Small herds of between 10 and 20 were kept in the early 19th century.[96] In 1914 the farmer at Trysull Manor farm was noted for selling sucking pigs 'at wonderful prices' to the colliers of the Black Country.[97] In 1979 there were nearly 650 pigs recorded in the parish.[98]

Bees were kept by the earlier 16th century. Stephen Dolman of Seisdon bequeathed an after-swarm in his will of 1544, and in 1614 John Wedge of Trysull had 20s. worth of bees.[99]

In 1086 there was a mill at Trysull rendering 4s.[1] A mill was part of the manor in the earlier 14th century and was known as Heykeleye mill in 1356.[2] It was referred to as Heyclif mill in 1412 when it was one of several in the area attacked by rioters.[3]

There was a mill west of Trysull bridge in 1775.[4] A new mill was built there in 1854. It was evidently sold to the tenant by Lord Wrottesley in 1929, and it continued in use until c. 1950. Electricity was substituted for water power in 1940.[5] The disused building still stood in 1979.

There was a mill at Seisdon by the early 13th century,[6] and Seisdon mill was one of the mills attacked in 1412.[7] It probably stood on the site north of Seisdon bridge where there was a mill in 1775. A mill there was sold to the tenant by Lord Wrottesley in 1929. It continued in use until c. 1950, employing electricity instead of water power in its last years.[8] The disused building,

dating from the 19th century, survived in 1979. Mill House nearby is dated 1749.

In 1251 the Crown granted Thomas of Trysull a Tuesday market and a fair on the eve, feast, and morrow of Holy Trinity on his manor of Trysull. Both were recorded in 1254–5, and John of Trysull asserted his right to both in 1293.[9] Nothing further is known of either.

There was a nailer living in Trysull in 1538. Another nailer was churchwarden of Trysull in 1693.[10]

There was a tanhouse in Trysull in 1590; at his death that year the tanner, John Sherwine, left 348 tanned calves' skins there worth £166. In 1646 another tanner in Trysull, Stephen Dolman, left £125 worth of skins in his tanhouse.[11] A house in Seisdon was called the Tanhouse in the late 17th and early 18th century.[12]

There were two 'brick men', presumably brickmakers, named Price and Plant at Seisdon in the mid 1750s; a brick man named John Price was buried at Trysull in 1793.[13] By the 1930s a sand pit was being worked on the high ground above Trysull mill and another near Seisdon mill.[14] There was still extensive working at Trysull, Seisdon, and Smestow bridge in 1979. There was then also a pipe works at Smestow bridge.

LOCAL GOVERNMENT. Trysull and Seisdon, separate manors until the 16th century, were also separate townships which formed a parish for civil purposes by the 17th century.

No court records are known to survive for either manor.[15] Thomas of Trysull, lord of Trysull manor, paid 3s. for frankpledge in the mid 1250s.[16] In 1293 his successor, John of Trysull, claimed assize of bread and ale by reason of the market granted to Thomas in 1251.[17] There was mention of the Trysull manor court c. 1300; reference was also made about then to suit of court at Michaelmas and Easter. The court was again mentioned in 1473–4.[18] There was a single constable for both townships by the end of the 16th century, and he was accounting to the parish by the later 1670s.[19]

Two churchwardens were recorded in 1553

[90] M.A.F.F., agric. returns 1979.
[91] L.J.R.O., B/C/11, Edm. Shenton (1565), Wm. Barnesley (1571) and (1640).
[92] Below.
[93] Wolverhampton Chron. 10 Mar. 1813; 9 Feb., 16 Mar. 1814.
[94] M.A.F.F., agric. returns 1979.
[95] L.J.R.O., B/C/11, Wm. Barnesley (1640).
[96] Wolverhampton Chron. 9 Feb., 16 Mar. 1814; 10 Mar. 1819.
[97] Jnl. Royal Agric. Soc. of Eng. lxxv. 224–5.
[98] M.A.F.F., agric. returns 1979.
[99] L.J.R.O., B/C/11, Steph. Dolman (1544), John Wedge (1614).
[1] V.C.H. Staffs. iv. 54.
[2] S.H.C. xii (1), 150–1.
[3] S.H.C. xvii. 17–18; Procs. before J.P.s in 14th and 15th cents. ed. B. H. Putnam, 315.
[4] Yates, Map of Staffs. (1775); W.S.L., Staffs. Views, xi. 70.
[5] Sherlock, Ind. Arch. Staffs. 200; Staffs. Advertiser, 26 Oct. 1929; Seisdon R.D. Official Guide (edn. of c. 1950), 24; (1973 edn.), 25.
[6] S.H.C. iv (1), 52.
[7] S.H.C. xvii. 17–18, 26.

[8] Yates, Map of Staffs. (1775); W.S.L., Staffs. Views, viii. 162; O.S. Map 6″, Staffs. LXVI. NE. (1928 edn.); Staffs. Advertiser, 26 Oct. 1929; Seisdon R.D. Official Guide (edn. of c. 1950), 24; (1973 edn.), 25.
[9] Cal. Chart. R. 1226–7, 358; S.H.C. v (1), 112; vi (1), 248.
[10] W.S.L. 21/12/69; S.R.O., Tp. 1226, bdle XXXII, deed of 1 Feb. 1692/3.
[11] L.J.R.O., B/C/11, John Sherwine (1590), Steph. Dolman (1646).
[12] W.S.L. 40/53/52; S.R.O., D. 3452/10/1, list of constables.
[13] S.R.O., Tp. 1226/ADD/D10, Wombourne tithe bk., 1756; S.R.O., D. 3452/1/8.
[14] T. H. Whitehead and R. W. Pocock, Memoirs of Geol. Surv., Dudley and Bridgnorth, 157.
[15] Any existing in the late 19th century were presumably destroyed in the fire at Wrottesley Hall in 1897: S.H.C. n.s. vi (2), p. iii.
[16] S.H.C. v (1), 112.   [17] S.H.C. vi (1), 248.
[18] S.H.C. 1928, 15; Shaw, Staffs. ii. 208; W.S.L., S.MS. 386/2, no. 218A. The great leet mentioned in 1725 in connexion with the constable's oath (S.R.O., D. 3452/10/1, 20 May 1725) was not identified.
[19] S.H.C. 1935, 136; S.R.O., D. 3452/10/1.

TRYSULL: THE CHURCH FROM THE NORTH-EAST
in 1837 with the school on the right

ENVILLE: THE CHURCH FROM THE SOUTH-EAST IN 1837

View of Wombourne

Garden feature

Handel's Temple

The music room

Entrance to the hermitage

Interior of the hermitage

The grotto

The druids' temple

THE WODEHOUSE, WOMBOURNE: PROSPECTS AND GARDEN FEATURES IN 1773

and 1632, but by 1660 there was only one. From 1878 there were again two.[20] A single overseer of the poor officiated by the later 17th century; from 1825 to 1836 two were appointed. By the later 17th century the same person served both offices at once; in 1758 it was decided that the overseer should serve as churchwarden in the year following. The two offices and that of constable rotated by house. All three offices were served by Trysull township one year and by Seisdon the next in the later 17th and early 18th century. In 1713–14 it was agreed by the parishioners that the office of highway surveyor should be served by the constable; apparently in the 1720s it was decided that the churchwarden should be surveyor. In 1764 and 1765 two surveyors were appointed at a December meeting of the parishioners.[21]

A hayward of Trysull was mentioned in the mid 14th century.[22] In 1699 a hayward was chosen for each township at a parish meeting which also made regulations for the open fields.[23] The pound was a parish responsibility in the 1820s. By the early 1880s it stood on the east side of School Road north of the Green. The brick structure was restored c. 1970. It has been suggested that the building nearby used as a summer house was formerly the pinder's house.[24]

The parish clerk was for a time paid partly in kind: in 1704 he complained to the parish meeting that several of his neighbours had refused to allow him any eggs at Easter for sweeping the church. It was then decided to pay him 3s. a year out of parish funds in lieu of eggs. In 1830 he was appointed by the vicar and paid £3 and Christmas offerings.[25] In his will of 1725 John Rudge of Seisdon left 20s. rent for 'a civil, grave, and poor man' to patrol the church during the sermon in order to ensure that people stayed awake and dogs were kept out. The official was known as the nobbler by the earlier 1770s, and the 20s. was still paid in 1830.[26]

Besides the almshouses at Seisdon endowed by John Rudge[27] there was a poorhouse on Trysull Green by 1773, then occupied by two families. Though called an almshouse it appears to have been supported by the parish and not from an endowment. It was still in use in 1835, but it had been pulled down by 1843 when a school was built on the site.[28] The parish became part of Seisdon poor-law union in 1836.[29] The union workhouse was initially at Tettenhall, but a new workhouse was opened at Trysull in 1860 on the Penn road near the parish boundary. It was

closed in 1936, and after being used as an egg-packing station during the Second World War it stood derelict until its partial demolition c. 1965.[30] A children's home was opened by the union in Vine Cottage on the south side of the Green in 1918.[31]

Trysull was in Seisdon rural district until 1974 when it became part of South Staffordshire district.[32] The workhouse was used as the meeting place of the rural district council until c. 1930.[33]

CHURCH. There was a church at Trysull by the later 12th century. An inquisition at Stafford before Bishop Richard Peche (1161–82) established that 'the parish of Trysull and of Seisdon' belonged to Wombourne church. A chapel at Trysull was mentioned in Peche's confirmation of Wombourne church and its appurtenances as belonging to Dudley priory by grant of Guy de Offini. A similar papal confirmation in 1182 also mentioned the chapel.[34] It was served by a chaplain or curate until the late 19th century; his income was £10 c. 1710, £60 by 1826, £90 by 1858, £100 by 1869, and £150 by 1884.[35] The chapelry kept its own register of baptisms, marriages, and burials by 1558. In 1888 Trysull became a separate ecclesiastical parish under a perpetual curate presented by the patrons of Wombourne. It was endowed with £6,000 from the proceeds of the sale of part of the Wombourne glebe in 1878. The vicar of Wombourne also conveyed a house and 3 a. east of the church as the incumbent's house and glebe, and the Ecclesiastical Commissioners made a grant of £45 a year; a further grant of £694 18s. 9d. stock was made from Wombourne's funds in 1898.[36] The house was presumably the former Cecil Lodge which the vicar had bought in 1885 and into which the curate moved in 1886. A new house was built in School Road in 1961.[37] The advowson remained with the patrons of Wombourne, but from 1976 the living was held by a priest-in-charge.[38]

There was a chantry priest of the Blessed Virgin at Trysull church by 1472.[39] In 1534 Agnes Webb (or Penn) settled a house and land at Seisdon on trustees for the support of a priest in Trysull church who would pray for her soul and all Christian souls. The endowment became attached to Our Lady's chantry, and the trustees evidently appointed the chantry priest. By the Reformation the chantry had its own wardens.[40]

[20] S.H.C. 1915, 355; Shaw, Staffs. ii, p. *216; S.R.O., D. 3452/1/1, sub 1629; D. 3452/10/1; Trysull vicarage, Bk. of References, p. 22.
[21] S.R.O., D. 3452/8/1; ibid. 10/1.
[22] Shaw, Staffs. ii. 208.
[23] S.H.C. 1931, 81.
[24] S.R.O., D. 3452/8/1; O.S. Map 6″, Staffs. LXVI. NE. (1884 edn.); Trysull vicarage, envelope marked 'The Pound'.
[25] S.R.O., D. 3452/10/1; S.H.C. 4th ser. x. 27.
[26] S.R.O., D. 3452/8/1, Sept. 1818; D. 3452/11/1; L.J.R.O., B/V/5/1772/Trysull; F. W. Hackwood, Staffs. Customs, Superstitions and Folklore, 159.
[27] Below, chars. for the poor.
[28] L.J.R.O., B/V/5/1772/Trysull; S.R.O., D. 3452/8/1; below, educ.
[29] 3rd Ann. Rep. Poor Law Com. H.C. 546, p. 164 (1837), xxxi.
[30] S.R.O., D. 3268/ADD., rep. facing p. 16, and pp. 71, 93, 98; J. I. Langford, Towpath Guide to Staffs. and Worcs.

Canal, 117–18; inf. from Mrs. May Griffiths of Stonehedge, Giggetty Lane, Wombourne (1981).
[31] S.R.O., D. 1414/8A/6, pp. 190–1; O.S. Map 6″, Staffs. LXVI. NE. (1928 edn.).
[32] O.S. Map 1/100,000, Staffs. Admin. Areas (1967 and 1974 edns.).
[33] Kelly's Dir. Staffs. (1900); below, Wombourne, introduction.
[34] S.H.C. 1941, 56–7; Sir Christopher Hatton's Book of Seals, ed. C. Loyd and D. M. Stenton, p. 40.
[35] S.H.C. xvi. 27; S.H.C. 1915, 355–6; B.L. Harl. MS. 6826, f. 54v.; S.R.O., D. 3452/3/1; W.S.L., M. 915.
[36] Lond. Gaz. 8 May 1888, pp. 2611–12; 25 Oct. 1898, pp. 6216–17; Lich. Dioc. Regy., B/A/2i/T, pp. 205, 210.
[37] Trysull vicarage, Bk. of References, p. 37; inf. from the priest-in-charge (1979).   [38] Lich. Dioc. Dir. (1976; 1979).
[39] W.S.L. 40/21/52.
[40] P.R.O., E 315/123/308; E 315/522, f. 44; S.H.C. 1915, 355. A Geo. Webb was then curate of Trysull.

In his will of 1544 Stephen Dolman of Seisdon, besides leaving 8d. to the Lady altar, directed his son and heir Thomas to find a priest to pray in Trysull church for a year for the souls of Stephen, his wife, and his ancestors.[41] Thomas Barnsley of Seisdon, in his will of 1545, provided for a trental of masses at the Lady altar for his soul, those of his father and mother, and all Christian souls.[42] Certain lands in Trysull and Penn were described in 1562 as given for lights in the churches there.[43]

In 1652, a few months after the appointment of a new vicar and curate for Wombourne and Trysull, a day of thanksgiving for 'the settlement of a ministry' was held at Trysull by wish of the people there.[44] By will proved 1728 Elizabeth Harriotts of Trysull left £100, the interest to be paid to the curate for reading divine service morning and evening on at least Wednesdays and Fridays; if the curate refused, the schoolmaster, provided he was in orders, was to be offered the duty.[45] In the earlier 1770s there were two services and sermons every Sunday, with prayers occasionally on saints' days. Holy communion was celebrated six times a year, and between 40 and 80 people received the sacrament each time.[46] In 1830 the curate at Trysull and the curate at Wombourne served the two churches alternately. There were still two services on Sunday, with communion six times a year; there were no services on other days. Communicants numbered 18.[47] In 1878 C. W. Fullmer, soon after coming to Trysull as curate, started cottage lectures during the winter at Seisdon. It was the first of several ventures, not all of them successful, which he launched before his departure in 1887.[48] There was a parish library by 1879, apparently newly established. By then offertory collections were taken, of which one third was used for charity. There was a parish room by 1887.[49]

The church of *ALL SAINTS*, an invocation which was in use by 1544 and whose antiquity is suggested by the date of the wake,[50] consists of a chancel, a nave of four bays with north and south aisles and south porch, and a west tower with north vestry. The tower arch and a blocked north door may survive from the 12th-century church. The north aisle was added in the 13th century. A weathered sculpture, thought to be of a bishop, was formerly outside the church in a niche over the north door; it was moved to its position over the vestry door in 1905.[51] The south aisle was added c. 1300. The chancel east window is a little later, perhaps an indication of the enlargement of

an earlier building which was destroyed in the 19th century; the window contains some 14th-century glass. The tower was rebuilt in the 15th century. There are two 15th-century roof trusses in the nave. The font and the screen date from the 15th or early 16th century. There was formerly a three-decker pulpit, probably dating from the early 17th century since the present pulpit incorporates Jacobean work.[52] By the earlier 19th century the church had a south porch, a south chancel door, and a west gallery with an organ.[53] In 1843 and 1844 the north aisle was extended eastwards by one bay and the south aisle was rebuilt to incorporate a former south chapel; a vestry was built in the angle between the tower and the north aisle, replacing the vestry in the base of the tower. The architect was Robert Ebbels, who had lived in Trysull until 1841 and then moved to Tettenhall Wood.[54] In or soon after 1855 the pulpit was moved from the south side of the nave to the north side of the chancel arch and the reading desks were rearranged, again to Ebbels's design.[55] The church was restored in 1889. A new organ was installed at the east end of the north aisle and the gallery removed. The box pews were replaced by pitchpine seats.[56] By 1897 the pulpit had been moved to the south side of the chancel arch to allow more space for choir stalls behind the organ.[57] In that year the tower was restored. The rehanging of the bells meant that they had to be rung from the ground floor, and as a result the west door could no longer be used as the main entrance; a new south porch was therefore built. The architect was F. W. Simon of Edinburgh. The work was carried out in memory of John Baker of Seisdon and paid for by his deceased widow's trustees.[58] Dormer windows were installed on the south side of the nave roof at some time before 1934.[59]

In 1552 and 1553 there were two parcel gilt chalices with patens. The present plate includes a silver chalice and paten of 1628; a silver chalice, paten, and bread plate of 1637 given, like a duplicate set at Wombourne, by John Wollaston of London, the patron of Wombourne; a silver almsdish of 1718 given by John Rudge of Seisdon; a pewter flagon of the reign of George I; and a silver flagon of 1756 given by Margaret, Ann, and Letitia Pudsey.[60]

In 1552 there were four bells, two little sacring bells, and a lich bell; by the next year one of the four bells had gone. In 1700 the existing bells were recast as a peal of five by Abraham Rudhall of Gloucester; the treble and third bell were recast by W. and J. Taylor of Oxford in 1844.

[41] L.J.R.O., B/C/11, Steph. Dolman (1544).
[42] Ibid., Thos. Barnesley (1546).
[43] *Cal. Pat.* 1560–3, 259–60.
[44] Below, Wombourne, church.
[45] A. L. Reade, *Reades of Blackwood Hill*, 195.
[46] L.J.R.O., B/V/5/1772/Trysull.
[47] *S.H.C.* 4th ser. x. 27.
[48] Trysull vicarage, Bk. of References; *Lich. Dioc. Ch. Cal.* (1878).
[49] S.R.O., D. 3452/12/1.
[50] L.J.R.O., B/C/11, Steph. Dolman (1544); above, introduction.
[51] Shaw, *Staffs.* ii. 209; S.R.O., D. 3452/3/1, 28 Apr. 1905; D. 3452/4/11; above, pl. facing p. 192.
[52] Pevsner, *Staffs.* 286–7; S.R.O., D. 3452/4/11.

[53] Trysull ch., plan of 1837; S.R.O., D. 3452/4/1.
[54] S.R.O., D. 3452/4/1; W.S.L., Staffs. Views, xi. 68; Trysull vicarage, Bk. of References, and drawings of 1842; Colvin, *Brit. Architects*, 279.
[55] S.R.O., D. 3452/4/12; *Trans. Lich. and S. Staffs. Arch. Soc.* ii. 20.
[56] S.R.O., D. 3452/4/3–4, 8–9; *Lich. Dioc. Ch. Cal.* (1890), 159–60.
[57] S.R.O., D. 3452/4/5.
[58] Ibid.; D. 3452/5/1, 4 Dec. 1896; Trysull vicarage, Bk. of References, 13 June 1897; *Lich. Dioc. Mag.* (1897), 109; *Kelly's Dir. Staffs.* (1900).
[59] L.J.R.O., B/C/12/Trysull.
[60] *S.H.C.* n.s. vi (1), 189; *S.H.C.* 1915, 355; *T.B.A.S.* lxxiii. 2, 10–13, 24–5, 30–1.

The peal was enlarged to six in 1897, and at the same time a clock was replaced.[61]

In 1662 the rails of the churchyard were repaired and a new wooden stile was made.[62] By 1837 the churchyard was walled, with a north-west lichgate and an opening on the north side. By 1847 the present gate in front of the tower was in use.[63] Extensions of the churchyard were consecrated in 1896, 1920, and 1951.[64]

The registers, dating from 1558, are complete, though damaged at the beginning.[65]

There may have been a chapel at Seisdon by the later 12th century: the confirmation by Bishop Peche of the Offini gift to Dudley priory mentioned the chapels of Trysull and Seisdon. The papal confirmation of 1182, however, mentioned only Trysull.[66] In 1545 there was a field in Seisdon called Chapel field; it was bounded by a road called Church Way, perhaps the present Church Lane which runs between Seisdon and Trysull north of Smestow brook.[67] In 1552 the lord of the manor granted Thomas Dolman a lease of what was described as a tenement or chapel on waste called the Green in Seisdon, with land adjoining to make a garden; in 1623 the property was held by Walter Dolman.[68]

NONCONFORMITY. In the earlier 1770s the curate stated that there were a few Methodists in the chapelry 'of the lower rank, without any tabernacle, preacher, or teacher'.[69] A meeting house at Seisdon belonging to Samuel Buttle was registered for protestant dissenters in 1813.[70] In 1882 'itinerant dissenters' held several meetings in a cottage on Sunday evenings at the same hour as the prayer meeting held by the curate; attendance at the Anglican meetings was slightly reduced.[71]

EDUCATION. By the late 1680s there was a schoolmaster teaching boys in Trysull parish, and in 1694 a master was licensed to teach in the school there.[72] In 1707 the school was endowed with land at Trimpley, in Kidderminster, bought with £200 given by Thomas Rudge of Westminster. The income was used for teaching the elements and the catechism to 18 poor children of the parish, both boys and girls. They were chosen at regular meetings of the trustees; 11 of the 18 pupils were dismissed in 1708 for truancy and another eleven were elected in their place. Up to

20s. a year from the Trimpley land was available for books, paper, and ink for pupils whose parents could not afford them.[73] Books, mostly bibles and prayer books, were given to pupils and past pupils out of the annual 5s. income from £5 left for that purpose by Elizabeth Barnesley of Trysull (d. 1697); the distribution was first recorded in 1703. A further £10 given for the same purpose by Thomas Hickmans of Seisdon (d. 1704) produced an additional 10s. In 1712 the capital of both gifts was used to buy more land at Trimpley for the poor of Trysull, and the annual 15s. was reserved out of the rents. Bibles were still distributed in the mid 19th century, and by the mid 1880s the money was used to buy books for the Sunday school.[74]

A schoolroom was built in the 18th century west of the church.[75] In 1716 a parish meeting agreed that the overseer of the poor should pay 1s. a year to John Ketley, the schoolmaster, for the school to use the 'little house of ease' beside the churchyard.[76] In the earlier 1770s the curate described the schoolroom as out of repair; the school's revenues were 'preserved and employed with less care' than they should have been and its statutes not properly observed. The master then received a salary of £9 10s., the amount of the rent from the school's land at Trimpley.[77] From the later 1790s he also received £1 10s. a year from the gift of Thomas and Samuel Peach for teaching two poor children.[78] In 1818 he received 6s. a week out of the Trimpley rent and the Peach gift and taught 11 poor boys and girls, providing them with stationery. The master was then teaching a further 10 children, presumably for fees.[79] There was a Sunday school by 1817.[80]

In 1843 a new school was built on the east side of Trysull Green on land given by Lord Wrottesley, formerly the site of the poorhouse. A master's house adjoining the school, part of the original plan, was not built until the mid 1860s.[81] In the later 1840s there were 21 boys and 18 girls at the school.[82] By 1851 besides the master there was a schoolmistress paid by the parish.[83] John Turner (d. 1854) left £100 for teaching poor children at the school; in 1856 his trustees elected seven additional free scholars and subsequently filled vacancies among them.[84] In 1864–5 there were 16 free pupils; in addition there were 10 boys, 27 girls, and 18 infants paying 2d. a week and 1 boy and 1 girl who were taught writing and who paid 4d.[85]

In 1873 a committee elected by subscribers

[61] S.H.C. n.s. vi (1), 189; S.H.C. 1915, 355; Lynam, Church Bells, 29; S.R.O., D. 3452/10/1, 19 Feb. 1699/1700; Lich. Dioc. Mag. (1897), 109; Trysull vicarage, Bk. of References, 13 June 1897. There was a clock by 1881: S.R.O., D. 3452/12/1.
[62] S.R.O., D. 3452/1/1 sub 1662.
[63] W.S.L., Staffs. Views, xi. 66, 68.
[64] Lich. Dioc. Regy., B/A/2i/U, pp. 19, 125; 2i/W, pp. 3, 13; 2i/X, p. 198; Lich. Dioc. Mag. (1896), 133; Trysull vicarage, misc. bdle.
[65] All except those in current use are in S.R.O., D. 3452/1.
[66] S.H.C. 1941, 57; B.L. Harl. MS. 3868, ff. 275–6; Sir Christopher Hatton's Book of Seals, p. 40.
[67] S.R.O., D. 740/3/5.
[68] W.S.L. 40/27/52; S.R.O., Tp. 1273/11, 1623 survey.
[69] L.J.R.O., B/V/5/1772/Trysull.
[70] S.H.C. 4th ser. iii. 29.
[71] Trysull vicarage, Bk. of References, p. 32.
[72] L.J.R.O., B/A/4/7, 22.

[73] 5th Rep. Com. Char. 636–7; Staffs. Endowed Chars. 124; S.R.O., D. 3452/11/3; Trysull vicarage, Bk. of References, p. 26.
[74] 5th Rep. Com. Char. 633; S.R.O., D. 3452/10/1.
[75] 5th Rep. Com. Char. 634; above, pl. facing p. 192.
[76] S.R.O., D. 3452/10/1.
[77] L.J.R.O., B/V/5/1772/Trysull; 5th Rep. Com. Char. 637.
[78] S.R.O., D. 3452/10/1; below, chars. for the poor.
[79] 5th Rep. Com. Char. 637; Digest of Returns from Sel. Cttee. on Educ. of Poor, H.C. 224, p. 869 (1819), lx (2); S.R.O., D. 3452/11/3. [80] S.R.O., D. 3452/10/1.
[81] Staffs. Endowed Chars. 123; Trysull ch., sch. plan 1842, photograph, and specification for house; O.S. Map 6", Staffs. LXVI. NE. (1884 edn.).
[82] Nat. Soc. Inquiry, 1846–7, Staffs. 12–13.
[83] P.R.O., HO 107/2017.
[84] Staffs. Endowed Chars. 125; S.R.O., D. 3452/11/3.
[85] P.R.O., ED 7/110/331.

was appointed to run the school as a public elementary school for the poorer children of the parish; it was supported by a government grant as well as by subscriptions. Daily reading of the Bible was to be an essential feature of the curriculum. In the mid 1870s the average attendance was 85.[86] The school building was abandoned after storm damage in 1895, and a new school on the north side of the Green was opened in 1896; the cost of nearly £3,000 was met by a bequest from Eliza Baker of Bromsgrove (Worcs.), formerly of Seisdon.[87] At the end of the century attendance averaged 110.[88] The school became controlled in 1951.[89] By the late 1970s it was called All Saints' C. of E. controlled primary school for juniors and infants and had an average attendance of 68.[90]

In 1833 there were three private schools in the parish teaching 28 boys and 31 girls. In the 1890s the former mistress of the free school was running a girls' school there.[91]

CHARITIES FOR THE POOR. By will dated 1725 John Rudge of Seisdon gave to the poor of Seisdon and Trysull a building which he had erected in Budbrook field in Seisdon; it was divided into three dwellings, each with a garden. No more than two of 'the poorest and greatest objects of charity' in the parish were to occupy each house. He also left £4 10s. rent from lands in Seisdon to provide 30s. for each house, 10s. of which was for coal and 20s. for bread. The almspeople were obliged to attend Trysull church on Sundays, having the right to a seat given by Rudge behind the north door. It became the usual practice to assign the houses to widows. In 1897 the property was rebuilt with money left by Eliza Baker, whose trustees spent a further £100 on a field near the churchyard, the rent to be divided among the almspeople.[92]

By will dated 1591 Agnes Dolman left 40s. for the poor of Trysull parish, to be used as decided by the churchwardens and some of the substantial inhabitants. By will dated 1646 Stephen Dolman gave £10 for the poor, to be used at the discretion of Thomas Dolman and William Barnesley.[93] Nothing further is known of either gift.

In 1620 money collected from inhabitants of Trysull was used to buy land at Bulwardine, in Claverley, for the poor. In 1821 the endowment consisted of 11 a. let for £15 a year, which was divided equally between the poor of Trysull and Seisdon.[94]

By will proved 1697 Henry Wheeler left the reversion of an annual 20s. from land at Orton, in Wombourne, to the poor of Trysull. Payments, recorded from December 1701, were divided equally between the poor of Trysull and Seisdon.[95]

In 1712 two closes at Trimpley, in Kidderminster, were bought with gifts of £5 from William Barnesley (d. 1684), 40s. from Margaret Pudsey (d. 1687), £5 from Elizabeth Barnesley (d. 1697), and £10 from Thomas Hickmans (d. 1704). From the income 15s. was to be spent on books under the wills of Elizabeth Barnesley and Hickmans, and the rest on relief of the poor. In 1820 the amount spent on poor relief was £3 7s.[96]

By deed of 1716 Mary Poulton or Andrewes (d. 1718) demised a cottage and nearly 3 a. of land in Seisdon for 1,000 years at a peppercorn rent for the benefit of the poor. Under the inclosure award of 1775 part of Trysull Green was added to the endowment. The income in 1820 was £6 15s.[97]

By 1722 John Ketley had given an annual 12s. from land in Trysull to buy 12 penny loaves of wheat bread for distribution on the first Sunday in each month to 12 poor children present at the sermon, to the sick, or to the poor.[98]

John Strafford (d. by 1722) bequeathed £2 for the poor of Trysull, the interest to buy 12 twopenny loaves of white bread for the 12 poorest families of Seisdon at Christmas. It was apparently still paid in 1820,[99] but nothing further is known of it.

By will dated 1725 John Rudge of Seisdon left a rent charge of 40s. from his lands in Seisdon for the poor of the parish other than those in the almshouse which he had founded. Half was to be distributed quarterly in sixpenny loaves and the other half in shoes and stockings.[1]

In 1753 a small estate in Seisdon, called Shinton's meadow and garden, was bought for the poor with money raised from the rents and the sale of timber from the poor's land at Bulwardine. The income in 1820 was £1 10s.[2]

Thomas Peach (d. 1740) left £40, half the income from which was to be distributed to the poor at Christmas and half used for teaching two poor children chosen by Samuel Peach, his executor, and Samuel's heirs. In the later 1780s no land had yet been bought and there was no income. The bequest was augmented by Samuel Peach, who endowed the charity with £100 stock. In the late 1790s the poor received £1 10s. a year, distributed equally between the inhabitants of Trysull and Seisdon.[3]

[86] Staffs. Endowed Chars. 124; Rep. of Educ. Cttee. of Council, 1874-75 [C. 1265-I], p. 405, H.C. (1875), xxiv.
[87] Lich. Dioc. Mag. (1896), 133; Kelly's Dir. Staffs. (1900).
[88] Schs. in receipt of Parl. Grants, 1899-1900 [Cd. 332], p. 226, H.C. (1900), lxiv.
[89] Trysull ch., Min. of Educ. Order, Nov. 1951.
[90] Lich. Dioc. Dir. (1979).
[91] Educ. Enq. Abstract, H.C. 62, p. 889 (1835), xlii; P.O. Dir. Staffs. (1876); Kelly's Dir. Staffs. (1892; 1896).
[92] 5th Rep. Com. Char. 634-5; S.R.O., D. 3452/11/1; Char. Dons. 1786-8, 1146-7; Trysull vicarage, Bk. of References. The building carries a date stone of 1896.
[93] L.J.R.O., B/C/11, Agnes Dolman (1591), Steph. Dolman (1646).
[94] 5th Rep. Com. Char. 631-2; S.R.O., D. 3452/10/1.
[95] L.J.R.O., B/C/11, Hen. Wheeler (1697); 5th Rep. Com.

Char. 635; S.R.O., D. 3452/10/1; Char. Dons. 1786-8, 1146-7.
[96] 5th Rep. Com. Char. 633; S.R.O., D. 3452/1/1; above, educ.
[97] 5th Rep. Com. Char. 633; S.R.O., D. 548/A/PD/1; D. 3452/1/1; ibid. 10/1.
[98] Trysull vicarage, Bk. of References, p. 24 (transcript from char. boards), wrongly calling him Thomas; 5th Rep. Com. Char. 635.
[99] Trysull vicarage, Bk. of References, p. 25 (transcript from char. boards); 5th Rep. Com. Char. 634; S.R.O., D. 3452/10/1.
[1] S.R.O., D. 3452/11/1; 5th Rep. Com. Char. 634.
[2] 5th Rep. Com. Char. 632; S.R.O., D. 3452/10/1.
[3] 5th Rep. Com. Char. 635; S.R.O., D. 3452/1/8; ibid. 10/1.

By the 1860s the Bulwardine, Trimpley, Andrewes, and Shinton charities had been united and produced an annual £37 rent and £2 10s. interest from stock.[4] Under a Scheme of 1921 the Rudge, Wheeler, Ketley, and Peach charities were added to form the Trysull and Seisdon Charities. In the early 1980s the income was some £2,000; some £1,500 was spent on the maintenance of the almshouses and the rest in gifts at Christmas to the almspeople and other parishioners.[5]

WOMBOURNE

THE ancient parish of Wombourne[6] developed round three centres, Wombourne village and the smaller settlements of Orton and Swindon. Despite extensive industrial and residential development, particularly since the 1950s, the area remains largely agricultural. The ancient parish, 4,360 a. in size, was divided in 1896 into two civil parishes, Wombourne (including Orton) and Swindon. Wombourne was increased from 1,434 a. to 3,399 a. in 1934 by the addition of part of Penn and to 3,410 a. (1,370 ha.) in 1965 by the transfer of a small part of Wolverhampton borough. Swindon has remained 1,783 a. (723 ha.) in area.[7] This article deals only with the area covered by the ancient parish.

The terrain is undulating. It rises to 533 ft. (163 m.) near the north-eastern boundary above the escarpment of Orton Hill and to 357 ft. (112 m.) on the south-western boundary. The level drops to its lowest along Smestow brook in the south, the ground lying at 207 ft. (63 m.) at the southern end of Church Road in Swindon and 204 ft. (62 m.) at Hinksford on the south-eastern boundary. Smestow brook forms a short stretch of the western boundary north of the hamlet of Smestow and part of the south-eastern boundary. A tributary, Wom brook, gives the parish its name, which is Old English and means the winding stream.[8] The brook rises on Penn common and enters the parish near Wodehouse mill to flow through a valley south of Wombourne village. It is forded in Giggetty Lane. It was mentioned as Wombourne brook in 1322.[9] The stretch in the Wodehouse area was called Lude or Lyde brook in the Middle Ages[10] and the name Lyd brook is now given to a tributary which rises near Lloyd House in Penn and joins Wom brook near Wodehouse mill. The stretch running through Wombourne village was formerly known as Bate brook.[11] Small brook, which flows south-west through the village along High Street to join Wom brook below Walk Lane, was mentioned in 1416; it is now piped through the built-up area.[12] A little to the west of Giggety Lane Wom brook is joined by a stream which rises in the Goldthorn Hill area of Wolverhampton, flows through Lower Penn, and then follows the Staffordshire and Worcestershire Canal south through Wombourne parish.[13] The underlying rock is sandstone; there is some boulder clay north of Wombourne village, and a ridge of sand and gravel runs south-east from Swindon through Hinksford.[14] The soil is light loam.[15]

Prehistoric settlement in the area is suggested by post-Mesolithic flint artifacts found at Greensforge farm in the south-east corner of the ancient parish and Smallbrook farm north-east of Wombourne village, a stone axe of Neolithic or Bronze Age date from Greenhill nurseries south of the village, and a flint arrowhead of the Early Bronze Age found at the Blakeley end of Giggetty Lane.[16] A Roman road running from a camp at Ashwood just over the Kingswinford boundary near Greensforge farm passed through the south-west of the parish to Bridgnorth and Wales; on Chasepool common there is the site of a marching camp.[17] Pottery of the late 2nd century has been found at the farm,[18] and to the south-west the remains of another camp straddle the boundary with Kinver.[19] The antiquary Richard Wilkes (d. 1760) recorded three barrows on Wombourne common south-west of the village and another, known as Soldiers' Hill, about ½ mile north of them. He used them as evidence that the battle of Tettenhall was fought there; that suggestion may be responsible for the name Battlefield for the area on the Stourbridge road east of the village, in use by 1841.[20]

In 1086 the recorded population of Wombourne was 26 and that of Orton 11; Swindon may have been included under Himley.[21] In 1327

[4] Char. Digest Staffs. 56–7.
[5] Char. Com. files; inf. from the clerk of the charities (1983).
[6] Wombourne has been spelled both with and without a final 'e'. The 'e' is now used by local government and the Post Office. The Ordnance Survey omitted the 'e' on some maps until recently when it adopted the spelling with the 'e' for all its maps. This article was written mainly in 1980–1. Mrs. May Griffiths of Stonehedge, Giggetty Lane, the Revd. S. Huyton, vicar of Wombourne, Mr. J. W. Phillips of the Wodehouse, and others named in footnotes are thanked for their help. Much help was also received from the late Miss Dorothy Shaw-Hellier of the Wodehouse.
[7] Census, 1901, 1951, 1971; Kelly's Dir. Staffs. (1940).
[8] Ekwall, Eng. Place-names.
[9] S.H.C. 1928, 33.   [10] Ibid. 11, 23, 26–8, 30, 47.
[11] L.J.R.O., B/V/6/Wombourne, 1635, 1679, 1682, 1698; B/A/15/Wombourne, no. 441.
[12] Wombourne Compass (Sept. 1975; in poss. of Mrs. May Griffiths); S.H.C. 1928, 65.

[13] A. Dunphy, 'A Geography of Parishes of Wombourne and Lower Penn' (Dudley Teachers' Centre, 1972; copy in Wolv. C.L.), 4; J. I. Langford, Towpath Guide to Staffs. and Worcs. Canal, 115–16, 120.
[14] Dunphy, 'Wombourne and Lower Penn', 2–3, 5; T. H. Whitehead and R. W. Pocock, Memoirs of Geol. Surv., Dudley and Bridgnorth, 151–3.
[15] Kelly's Dir. Staffs. (1940).
[16] Trans. Salop. Arch. Soc. lix. 205; N.S.J.F.S. iv. 44; Wolverhampton Mag. Feb. 1972, 31.
[17] Trans. Salop. Arch. Soc. lvi. 237; Staffs. C.C. Planning Dept., Sites and Monuments Rec. 214, 1411, 1720.
[18] Birmingham Univ. Dept. of Extra-mural Studies, W. Midlands Arch. News Sheet, xv. 18.
[19] Staffs. C.C. Planning Dept., Sites and Monuments Rec. 1720.
[20] Shaw, Staffs. i, Gen. Hist. p. 38; P.R.O., HO 107/1002. For the battle see above, Tettenhall, introduction.
[21] Below, econ. hist. For Swindon see below, manors and other estates.

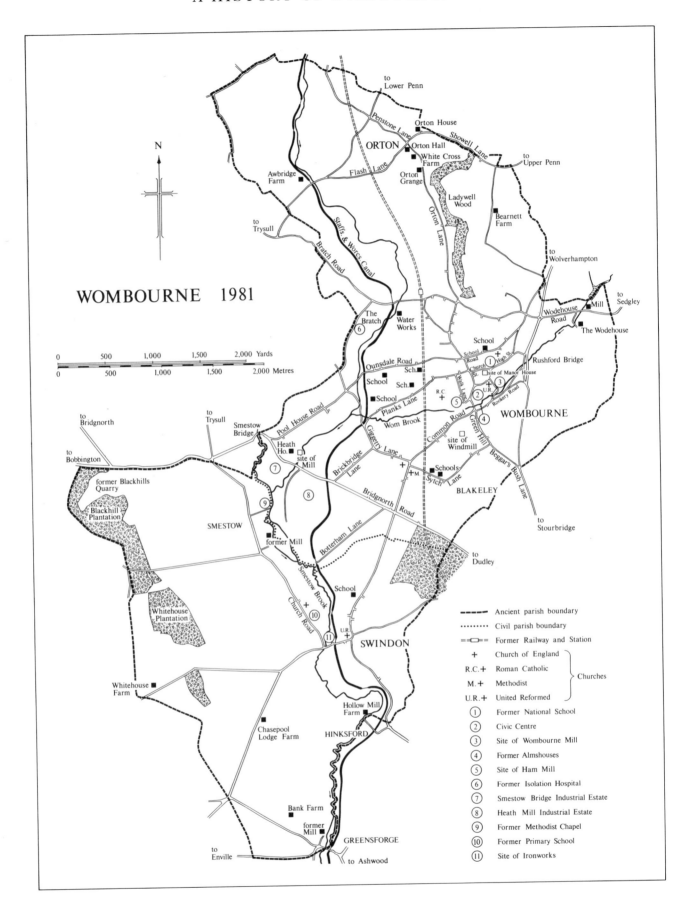

WOMBOURNE 1981

N

to Lower Penn

Penstone Lane

Orton House

ORTON   Orton Hall

Showell Lane

to Upper Penn

White Cross Farm

Flash Lane   Orton Grange

Ladywell Wood

Bearnett Farm

Awbridge Farm

Orton Lane

to Trysull

Staffs & Worcs Canal

Bratch Road

to Wolverhampton

Mill   to Sedgley

Wodehouse Road

The Bratch   Water Works

The Wodehouse

6

School

School Road   High St.

Ounsdale Road   Sch.   1   Church St.   Rushford Bridge

School   Sch.   U.R.   site of Manor House

School   R.C.   2   3

Planks Lane   5   WOMBOURNE

Wom Brook   Rookery Road

to Bridgnorth   to Trysull   4

Smestow Bridge   Pool House Road   site of Windmill   Green Hill

Heath Ho.   site of Mill   Common Road   Beggar's Bush Lane

to Bobbington   7   Brickbridge Lane   M   Schools   BLAKELEY

Gigetty Lane   Sytch Lane

former Blackhills Quarry   9   8   Bridgnorth Road   to Stourbridge

Blackhill Plantation   SMESTOW   Botterham Lane   to Dudley

former Mill

Whitehouse Plantation   School

Smestow Brook

Church Road   10

Whitehouse Farm   11   U.R.   SWINDON

Hollow Mill Farm

Chasepool Lodge Farm   HINKSFORD

Bank Farm

former Mill

to Enville   GREENSFORGE   to Ashwood

Scale:
0   500   1,000   1,500   2,000 Yards
0   500   1,000   1,500   2,000 Metres

Legend:
— — —   Ancient parish boundary
· · · · ·   Civil parish boundary
= ▭ =   Former Railway and Station
+   Church of England ⎤
R.C. +   Roman Catholic   ⎥
M. +   Methodist   ⎬ Churches
U.R. +   United Reformed ⎦

1   Former National School
2   Civic Centre
3   Site of Wombourne Mill
4   Former Almshouses
5   Site of Ham Mill
6   Former Isolation Hospital
7   Smestow Bridge Industrial Estate
8   Heath Mill Industrial Estate
9   Former Methodist Chapel
10   Former Primary School
11   Site of Ironworks

Wombourne had 18 people assessed for tax and Orton 15.[22] The muster roll of 1539 contained 17 names for Wombourne, 6 for Orton, and 4 for Swindon.[23] In 1563 the parish had 37 households.[24] An assessment in 1609 listed 26 ratepayers in Wombourne, over 15 in Orton, and 16 in Swindon.[25] The poll-tax assessment of 1641 listed 125 people in Wombourne and 44 in Orton.[26] In 1666 Wombourne constablewick had 37 people assessed for hearth tax and 23 others too poor to pay; in Orton constablewick 18 were assessed with 9 too poor.[27] The Compton Census of 1676 returned 386 people in the parish.[28] In the earlier 1770s the number of houses in the parish was given as 'pretty near 400'.[29] In 1801 the population was 1,170; although it had dropped to 1,136 by 1811 it had reached 1,478 by 1821 and rose steadily to reach 2,236 in 1861. It had dropped to 2,080 by 1871 owing to the decline of nailing and continued to fall, reaching 1,856 in 1901 (1,411 in Wombourne civil parish and 445 in Swindon). Although Swindon's population continued to fall until after 1921, Wombourne's increased during the early 20th century. Wombourne had a population of 1,569 and Swindon one of 442 in 1911; the figures were 1,670 and 422 in 1921 and 1,989 and 486 in 1931. The area of Penn added to Wombourne in 1934 had a population of 480 in 1931 and has remained thinly populated. On the other hand the growth of Wombourne, particularly from the 1950s, was reflected in a sharp rise in the total population. In 1951 Wombourne's population was 3,838 and Swindon's 537. Wombourne's was 9,974 in 1961 and 12,069 in 1971, and Swindon's 578 in 1961 and 748 in 1971.[30]

Wombourne township covered the central part of the parish. The village occupies a slope rising northwards from Wom brook. The centre lies round an open space which may once have been a village green. There are references to a green in Wombourne in the 13th and 14th centuries.[31] By 1771, however, the space in the village was known as Dovehouse Close and was in private ownership. From 1901 it was occupied by Wombourne Cricket Club (since 1909 Wombourne Cricket, Tennis, and Bowling Club).[32] The church on the north side was founded before 1086.[33] The hamlet of Woodhouse ¾ mile northeast of the village existed by the late 13th century, evidently as a result of assarting, and it had its own open fields; four people there were assessed for tax in 1327.[34] By the early 17th century Heath

forge west of the village was in operation.[35] The nearby Heath House is a three-storey brick house of the early 18th century; it has an east front of four bays and on the west a front of three bays with low flanking buildings which make a small courtyard against the hill slope. The interior retains a fine staircase, a richly panelled room, and other original fittings. About the mid 17th century a house was built at or near Ounsdale in the hollow on the Sedgley–Bridgnorth road ¾ mile west of the village.[36] By 1775 settlement was concentrated along the present Gravel Hill, Maypole Street (where there was a house called the Maypole c. 1750), and Windmill Bank and eastwards along Church Street, High Street, and Withymere Lane. There was also settlement to the south-west on the edge of Wombourne common in the areas known by the 19th century as Giggetty (at first Giggatree) and Blakeley.[37]

With the growth of nailing in the parish in the early 19th century Wombourne village became populous.[38] By 1816 the industry was concentrated in and around the village; by 1841 Blakeley too was a nailing centre.[39] The population of Wombourne township was 1,220 in 1841 and some 1,530 in 1861; thereafter it fell with the decline of nailing.[40] Greenhill House south of the village was built c. 1830,[41] and there were other large houses to the south-east by the 1880s.[42] In the period between the two World Wars there was council and private building of houses north of the village, in Rookery Road to the south-east, and in Sytch Lane to the south.[43] About 1930 Seisdon rural district council moved its meeting place from the union workhouse in Trysull parish to Gravel Hill House in Wombourne village. New offices with a magistrates' court were opened on the opposite side of Gravel Hill in 1968; in 1977 the offices became a civic centre, the new South Staffordshire district council having built its offices in Codsall.[44] From the 1950s Ounsdale, Giggetty, and the Bridgnorth Road area to the south became industrialized. Extensive housing estates, council and private, were built north and west of the village, up Green Hill and over the grounds of Greenhill House, in the area south of Pool House Road, at Giggetty and Blakeley, and at Brickbridge north of Bridgnorth Road. Between 1951 and 1960 alone 1,870 dwellings were built.[45] In the 1960s and 1970s a park was laid out along Wom brook from Battlefield to Bridgnorth Road.[46]

[22] S.H.C. vii (1), 253–4.
[23] S.H.C. N.S. vi (1), 65, 67–8.
[24] S.H.C. 1915, p. lxxii.
[25] S.R.O., Tp. 1226/ADD/L/2, lewn made 30 Dec. 1609.
[26] H.L., Main Papers, box 178.
[27] S.H.C. 1923, 86, 112–13.
[28] W.S.L., S.MS. 33, p. 371.
[29] L.J.R.O., B/V/5/1772.
[30] V.C.H. Staffs. i. 327; Census, 1871, 1911–71.
[31] S.H.C. 1928, 14, 24, 28–9; S.H.C. 4th ser. vi. 8.
[32] S.R.O. 3279/20/1–2; W.S.L., D. 691/6; below, p. 201.
[33] Below, churches.
[34] S.H.C. 1928, 16–18, below, pp. 204, 216.
[35] Below, p. 213.
[36] S.R.O., Tp. 1226, bdle. III, no. 24; XXXII, deed of 26 May 1648; XLI, deed of 23 Mar. 1640/1; folder 1/ii.
[37] Yates, Map of Staffs. (1775); S.R.O., Tp. 1322, map; D.C.L., R. H. Wyatt's plan of Wombourne par. 1816.

[38] A. G. Matthews, Cong. Churches of Staffs. 230.
[39] Below, econ. hist.
[40] P.O. Dir. Staffs. (1845; 1864; 1872).
[41] S.R.O., Q/RDc 71, showing no house at Greenhill in 1825; J. Phillips and W. F. Hutchings, Map of Staffs. (1832), showing the house; White, Dir. Staffs. (1834), 293.
[42] O.S. Map 6″, Staffs. XLVII. NW. (1889 edn.).
[43] O.S. Map. 6″, Staffs. XLVII. NW. (prov. edn. with addns. of 1938); J. N. Williams, By Rail to Wombourne (Wolverhampton, 1977 edn.), 25.
[44] Kelly's Dir. Staffs. (1928; 1932; 1936), sub Trysull; Wolverhampton Mag. Feb. 1972, 30; inf. from Mrs. May Griffiths; below, social and cultural activities.
[45] Below, econ. hist.; Dunphy, 'Wombourne and Lower Penn', 27.
[46] Wombourne Compass (Sept. 1970 and Apr. 1971; in possession of Mrs. Griffiths); inf. from the Chief Planning Officer, S. Staffs. District Council.

The township of Orton covered the northern part of the ancient parish and also a tongue of land extending along the western boundary from the Bratch to Smestow bridge; it included most of Bratch common.[47] It was known as Overton until the later 16th century when the present form of the name came into use.[48] Settlement centred on the crossroads formed by the road from Lower Penn to Wombourne (Penstone, formerly Pound, Lane and Orton Lane) and the road from Trysull to Upper Penn and Wolverhampton (Flash Lane and Showell Lane). Orton Grange in Orton Lane has a cross wing dated 1685 and a three-storeyed 18th-century block on the site of the main range. White Cross Farm to the north was built in 1730 and Orton Hall Farm further north still in 1754. Orton House in Showell Lane also dates from the 18th century.[49] By 1775 there was settlement at the Bratch on the northern edge of Bratch common.[50] In 1841 the population of Orton was 169 and in 1891, after some fluctuation, again 169.[51] A number of large houses were built in Orton Lane in the years between the two World Wars and later, and a private estate was built on the west side after the Second World War. The single-storeyed Orton Manor at the crossroads was built in 1976 on the site of some cottages.[52] There are houses of the inter-war period and later in Penstone Lane near the Lower Penn boundary; Dimmingsdale pumping station just over the boundary was opened by Wolverhampton corporation in 1932.[53] Several houses were built at the Bratch in the inter-war period. A well with curative properties cut into the sandstone outcrop in Ladywell Wood on Orton Hill was presumably sacred to the Virgin Mary in the Middle Ages and may be the 'Wodewell' near Orton mentioned in the 13th century. In the late 19th century it was described as 'a favourite resort of local pleasure seekers, who go to drink of the cooling and delicious beverage and ruralize in the adjacent wood'.[54]

The southern part of the parish was covered by the township of Swindon, a name meaning 'swine hill'. The settlement, or its site, was first mentioned in 1166, but in 1086 an estate there may have been part of the smaller of two estates in Himley. Chasepool in the south-west was mentioned in 1086 when it was within the forest and was waste; earlier, however, it had evidently been a cultivated area. It remained an extensive waste until its inclosure in 1796.[55] Swindon was an inhabited area in the early 14th century.[56] The bridge over Smestow brook in the centre of the

village existed by 1435.[57] Ashwood bridge on the boundary with Kinver and Kingswinford was the responsibility of Kinver and Kingswinford parishes in the later 1540s. It was converted from a horse bridge into a cart bridge by Lord Dudley in the earlier 17th century and was considered to be partly in Wombourne and partly in Kingswinford later in the century.[58] Two forges on Smestow brook were in operation in the 17th century, in Swindon village and at Greensforge on the southern boundary.[59] There was an inn at Swindon, the Cock, by the early 18th century.[60] The hamlet of Smestow nearly a mile north of Swindon village existed as a nailers' settlement by 1816, and there was then some nailing in Swindon also.[61] The population of the township was 419 in 1841 and some 500 in 1851. Swindon forge was enlarged in the 1850s, and the population was some 540 in 1861, with most of the ironworkers living at Smestow. Thereafter the population of Swindon township declined until the 1920s, after which it rose steadily. The growth was reflected in council and privately built housing, notably after 1945. In 1980 a large private estate was being laid out over the site of the forge, closed and demolished a few years before.[62]

COMMUNICATIONS. The stretch of the road between Stafford and Worcester which runs east of Wombourne village was mentioned in the 13th century.[63] It was turnpiked in 1761 as part of the road between Wolverhampton and Stourbridge and disturnpiked in 1882.[64] It crosses Wom brook at Rushford bridge, a name suggesting that there was once a ford there.[65] The present bridge evidently dates from 1801 when what was then called Wombourne bridge (and later Wombourne upper bridge) was built as a one-arch bridge of stone and brick at the joint expense of the turnpike trust and the county.[66] Its present appearance suggests that later in the 19th century a causeway was made on either side and the level of the road raised. The stretch of road north and south of the bridge became a side road when a dual carriageway was opened to the east in the 1960s.[67] The Red Lion inn south of the bridge existed by 1816.[68]

By the 13th century the road between Dudley and Bridgnorth ran along the present Wodehouse Road, School Road, Ounsdale Road, and Pool House Road to cross Smestow brook at Smestow bridge and a nearby ford.[69] By the mid 17th century the bridge was the joint

[47] D.C.L., Wyatt's plan of Wombourne.
[48] See e.g. S.H.C. xiii. 287; xiv (1), 214; N.S. iii. 45; 1929, 107.
[49] S.R.O., D. 691/3.
[50] Yates, Map of Staffs. (1775).
[51] P.O. Dir. Staffs. (1845; 1860; 1864; 1872); Kelly's Dir. Staffs. (1884; 1892).
[52] Date on house; inf. from Mrs. Griffiths.
[53] O.S. Map 6", Staffs. LXI. SE., LXVII. NW. (prov. edn. with addns. of 1938); B. L. McMillan, Hist. of Water Supply of Wolverhampton 1847–1947 (Wolverhampton, 1947), 49.
[54] The Antiquary, xxii. 162; W.S.L., S.MS. 386/2, no. 227.
[55] Below, manors and other estates; econ. hist.
[56] S.H.C. x (1), 130; S.H.C. 1911, 74–5.
[57] W.S.L. 55/152/52.
[58] S.H.C. 1948–9, 81; S.R.O., Q/SR, E.1647, no. 8; D.C.L., Himley manorial, ct. of 26 Apr. 1683.

[59] Below, econ. hist.
[60] Lond. Gaz. 31 Mar.–3 Apr. 1707, 14–16 Feb. 1711/12.
[61] Below, econ. hist.
[62] P.O. Dir. Staffs. (1845; 1860; 1864); below, econ. hist.
[63] S.H.C. 1928, 17.
[64] 1 Geo. III, c. 39; 42 & 43 Vic. c. 46.
[65] For land in that area called Riseford in 1316 see S.H.C. 1928, 25.
[66] S.R.O., Q/SB, E. 1801; W.S.L., H.M. 31/15, printed list of county bridges 1864. For Wombourne nether bridge in Gravel Hill south of the village, rebuilt by the county in 1830, see S.R.O., Q/SO 30, ff. 102, 177, 194, 239, 295.
[67] Inf. from Mrs. May Griffiths.
[68] S.R.O., D. 2/1.
[69] S.H.C. 1928, 10, 17, 23, 27–8, 47, 54; S.R.O., Tp. 1226, bdle. I, no. 41; D.C.L., Wyatt's plan of Wombourne; W.S.L., S.MS. 386/2, no. 227.

responsibility of Wombourne and Trysull.[70] The present two-arch bridge is of stone and brick. Wodehouse Road was turnpiked in 1793 as part of the road from Sedgley.[71] The present Dudley–Bridgnorth road running south-west of Wombourne village to Smestow bridge formed part of the main London–Holyhead road by 1675, but in the early 18th century a new route through Wolverhampton and Tettenhall came to be favoured by travellers.[72] The road through Wombourne, however, was turnpiked in 1790; it was disturnpiked in 1876.[73]

The Staffordshire and Worcestershire Canal was opened through the west of the parish in 1770. The lock at Awbridge may represent James Brindley's first attempt at combining a lock and a bridge on a public road. The bridge is unusual in having a balustrade of nine brick pillars supporting the sandstone coping. At the Bratch there is a complex flight of three locks which seems to have replaced an earlier staircase. There is a two-storey house for the lock keeper and a tall octagonal toll house. The two locks at Botterham are an early example of a staircase.[74]

The Wolverhampton and Kingswinford Railway was begun in 1913; the contractors' headquarters was in Planks Lane, Wombourne, until work was stopped during the First World War. The line was opened in 1925, with a station north of Bratch Road. Passenger services were withdrawn in 1932, and the station was closed for goods in 1964. The line was closed in 1965 and the track lifted in 1967–8. The station was used as offices by an industrial roofing firm from 1965 until 1972. It then became derelict, but in 1980 it was being restored as an information centre and warden's office for the South Staffordshire district council's Kingswinford Branch Railway Walk.[75]

Wombourne was on the route of a Stourbridge–Wolverhampton omnibus by 1845.[76]

SOCIAL AND CULTURAL ACTIVITIES. Wombourne wake is said to have been held originally in connexion with the feast of St. Benedict Biscop (12 January). By 1834 the wake was celebrated on the last Sunday in October.[77] The change of date may have occurred by 1808: a wake was then held at Swindon in late October or November, and in October 1816 a two-day meeting for pony races was held at Wombourne.[78] In the early 1780s there was mention of public merriment and dancing at Wombourne at Whitsuntide.[79] In the late 1760s Sir Samuel

Hellier was planning music meetings in September in the church.[80] By 1770 he had formed a Wombourne Band which included strings, woodwind, and brass.[81]

There was a cricket club by 1867, when the Wombourne Mutual Improvement Society sought to affiliate itself to the club. The proposal must have been rejected as the society rented its own cricket field that year at Sodom, the name then used for the east end of the village. The venture was not a success and was abandoned the following year; nor is anything further known of the club. In 1874 the society established its own cricket club, run separately from the society from 1875. Tennis and bowling were added to the club's activities in 1907, and from 1909 it was known as the Wombourne Cricket, Tennis, and Bowling Club. At first the club played on a field on the Wodehouse estate; in 1901 it moved to its present ground in the centre of the village, which was rented to it by Col. T. B. Shaw-Hellier. In 1945 Evelyn Shaw-Hellier transferred the site to the county council to ensure a permanent ground for sport in the village. A clubhouse was built on the site of the Manor House north-east of the ground in 1969 and extended in 1972 and 1980.[82] Wombourne Hockey Club was established in 1910. It used the ground in the centre of the village until 1965 when it moved to a ground on Wobaston Road in Pendeford, in Tettenhall.[83]

The Wombourne Reading Association was established by the vestry in 1854 to provide books and periodicals, a reading room, and the opportunity for mutual improvement.[84] It is probably identifiable with the mechanics' institute which was established in the same year, meeting in a house in Main Street.[85] The association still functioned as a parish lending library in 1867.[86] The Wombourne Mutual Improvement Society was established in 1863 with the same aims as those of the reading association but under separate management. Books and periodicals were to be made available every weekday evening at the National school in School Road, and there were to be regular social evenings there during the winter. The society moved into rented rooms in 1866; from 1867 it met in a house in Church Street, formerly the National school.[87] Money was raised by subscription and by holding bazaars and concerts. The proposal to have a German Tree at Easter 1870 was rejected but a bazaar with a Christmas Tree was held later in the year. Performers at concerts included a Madame Budersdorff in 1871 and George

[70] S.R.O., Q/SR, E. 1647, no. 8.   [71] 33 Geo. III, c. 167.
[72] E. Bowen, *Britannia Depicta* (1720), 126; *V.C.H. Staffs.* ii. 278 (where n. 2. should read 'E. Bowen' instead of 'J. Owen').
[73] 30 Geo. III, c. 102; 39–40 Vic. c. 39.
[74] J. I. Langford, *Towpath Guide to Staffs. and Worcs. Canal*, 117–20, 125; Brook, *Ind. Arch. W. Midlands*, 144; Sherlock, *Ind. Arch. Staffs.* 205; above, pp. 13–14; above, pl. facing p. 80.
[75] J. N. Williams, *By Rail to Wombourne* (Wolverhampton, 1977 edn.), 20–4, 31, 35, 42; C. R. Clinker, *Clinker's Reg. of Closed Passenger Stations and Goods Depots*, 146; Dunphy, 'Wombourne and Lower Penn', 22–3; inf. from the Chief Planning Officer, S. Staffs. District Council (1980).
[76] *P.O. Dir. Staffs.* (1845).
[77] Below, churches; White, *Dir. Staffs.* (1834), 292.
[78] *Trial of Wm. Hawkeswood* (Stafford, 1808; copy in

W.S.L. Pamphs. *sub* Wombourne); *Wolverhampton Chron.* 23 Oct. 1816.
[79] S.R.O., Tp. 1226/ADD/K1, 23 July 1781; K2, 23 May 1782.
[80] Ibid. K1, 1 Sept. 1768, 14 Feb. 1769; below, educ.
[81] S.R.O., Tp. 1226/ADD/K1, 15 Feb. 1770.
[82] Wombourne Mutual Improvement Soc. Min. Bk. 1863–76 (in possession of Mrs. May Griffiths), 19 Feb., 16 Apr. 1867, 11 Mar. 1868, 13 Feb., 24 Apr. 1874, 20 Apr. 1875; inf. from the club chairman.   [83] Inf. from the club secretary.
[84] Mutual Improvement Soc. Min. Bk., rules of the assoc. at back of bk.
[85] *White's Dir. South Staffs. 1855*, 557; P.R.O., HO 107/2017(2).
[86] Mutual Improvement Soc. Min. Bk., 1 and 18 Oct. 1867.
[87] Ibid., rules at beginning of bk., 3 Dec. 1866, 23 Nov., 4 Dec. 1867.

Grossmith, as an entertainer and singer of light opera, in 1875.[88] The society was renamed the Wombourne Literary Institute in 1875. In 1905 Harriet Shaw-Hellier conveyed the house in Church Street to trustees for permanent use as a village institute for men and boys.[89] It still met, as the Men's Institute, in the late 1930s; from 1973 the building was used by the Wombourne Volunteer Bureau, formed that year.[90]

There was a choral society in the later 1860s.[91]

A branch of the Women's Institute was formed in 1921, meeting in a hut in Planks Lane. The Institute opened a hall in High Street in the mid 1930s for use as a village hall.[92] A branch library was opened in Windmill Bank in 1960.[93] A youth and community centre south of the library was opened in 1964.[94] A civic centre with dining and ballroom facilities was opened by the parish council in 1977 in the former rural district council offices.[95]

Annual shows of gooseberries and carnations were held at Wombourne by 1813.[96] The Wombourne Cottagers' Horticultural Society held annual flower and vegetable shows in the earlier 1870s. At the show in 1874 it engaged the Wombourne Rifle Band to play.[97] From the early 1920s to the late 1960s there was an annual flower show; at first it was held on the cricket ground in the centre of the village, but after a few years it moved to a field in Gilbert Lane east of the village.[98]

The Botterham Friendly Union Society, established in 1856, was meeting at the Boat inn, Botterham, in 1876. The Mount Pleasant Lodge of the United Order of Free Gardeners, established in 1872, met at the Vine inn, Wombourne, in 1876; it then had a membership of 92.[99]

MANORS AND OTHER ESTATES. In 1086 William FitzAnsculf, lord of Dudley, held 7 hides in *WOMBOURNE*, which Turstin had held in 1066 with sac and soc, and 3 hides in *ORTON*, which had been held in 1066 by Ultan, a free man. The overlordships then descended with the Dudley barony. When the barony was divided in 1323 after the death of John, Lord Somery, Wombourne and Orton fell to Somery's elder sister Margaret and her husband, John de Sutton. The overlordships then descended in the Sutton (later Sutton or Dudley) family, from 1440 lords Dudley; that of Wombourne was still held by them in 1432, while that of Orton

was held by Edward Sutton, Lord Dudley, in 1581.[1]

Ralph held Wombourne of FitzAnsculf in 1086. Guy de Offini was lord in the mid 12th century. His son William had succeeded him by 1166, and William's son Richard was lord by 1212.[2] Richard (d. 1222) granted the manor to Alan, son of Walter of Orton, on his marriage to Richard's daughter Maud; it was to be held of Richard and his heirs at a rent of 6 marks.[3] In 1235-6 the manor was held with Swindon and with Oxley in Bushbury as 1 knight's fee.[4] Alan of Orton was alive in 1240[5] but seems to have died soon afterwards. His widow Maud made several grants as lady of Wombourne,[6] but in 1243 Walter of Orton, possibly Alan's nephew, held Wombourne, Swindon, and Oxley with Orton as 2 knights' fees.[7] The manor then descended with Orton at least until 1339.[8]

A Walter held Orton of FitzAnsculf in 1086.[9] It has been suggested that 1 of the 3 knights' fees held of the Dudley barony in 1166 by William de Offini, lord of Wombourne, consisted of Orton, Oxley, Bradley in Bilston, and half of Seisdon in Trysull, and that the Orton family, who later held Orton, were subtenants of William and his heirs.[10]

A Gilbert of Orton occurs as lord of Orton in 1176; he was succeeded by his son Walter, probably by the 1190s.[11] In 1235-6 Orton was held with Bradley in Bilston as 1 knight's fee.[12] The Walter of Orton who held Wombourne and Orton in 1243 was probably the son or grandson of his namesake.[13] He died between 1259 and 1268 and was succeeded by his son William.[14] William was still alive in 1295 but by 1300 had been succeeded by his son Thomas.[15] In 1339 he or another Thomas of Orton, styling himself lord of Orton, held what was described as the fee of Orton and Wombourne.[16] The Orton family disappeared after 1339 and its estates were broken up, although the nature and date of the division is not clear. By the 17th century there were three so-called manors which all came into the possession of the Wrottesleys of Wrottesley, in Tettenhall.

An estate which was called the manor of Wombourne by the 16th century passed to Sir Roger Hillary of Bescot in Walsall, chief justice of Common Pleas. At his death in 1356 he held of the Dudley barony a messuage and 20s. rent from free tenants in Wombourne, Seisdon, Trysull, and Upper Penn.[17] The property descended with

[88] Mutual Improvement Soc. Min. Bk., 15 and 16 Mar., 28 Oct., 16 Dec. 1870, 11 Oct., 5 and 22 Dec. 1871, 9 Apr., 4 June 1875; *D.N.B.* 1912-21.
[89] Mutual Improvement Soc. Min. Bk., 1 Oct. 1875; copy of deed of conveyance (in poss. of Mrs. May Griffiths).
[90] *Kelly's Dir. Staffs.* (1940); *Wombourne Compass* (June 1971; copy in poss. of Mrs. Griffiths); inf. from Mrs. Griffiths.
[91] S.R.O., D. 3710/3/41/1.
[92] Wombourne ch., vestry mins. 1835-1941, 17 Feb. 1941; inf. from Mrs. Griffiths.
[93] Inf. from Mr. G. L. King, deputy divisional librarian.
[94] Inf. from Mrs. Griffiths.
[95] *Express & Star*, 30 May 1977.
[96] *Wolverhampton Chron.* 28 July 1813.
[97] Mutual Improvement Soc. Min. Bk., 18 Aug. 1873, 7 and 31 Aug. 1874. [98] Inf. from Mrs. Griffiths.
[99] *Reps. Chief Registrar of Friendly Socs. 1876*, H.C. 429, pp. 393, 416 (1877), lxxvii.
[1] *V.C.H. Staffs.* iv. 54; *Complete Peerage*, xii (1), 114-15;

S.H.C. ix (2), 52-3; *Cal. Fine R.* 1430-7, 132; H.W.R.O. (H.), E 12/S, Bobbington and Enville, valor of lands of John Grey 1581.
[2] *S.H.C.* i. 198-9; *V.C.H. Staffs.* xvii. 15.
[3] *S.H.C.* iii (1), 220. [4] *Bk. of Fees*, i. 543.
[5] W.S.L., S.MS. 386/2, no. 214.
[6] See e.g. *S.H.C.* 1928, 13-14.
[7] Ibid. 1911, 400.
[8] *Cal. Close*, 1318-23, 630; B.L. Add. Ch. 47249.
[9] *V.C.H. Staffs.* iv. 54.
[10] *S.H.C.* iii (1), 221; v (1), 178.
[11] *S.H.C.* i. 80; iii (1), 215, 219.
[12] *Bk. of Fees*, i. 543. [13] Ibid. ii. 968.
[14] *S.H.C.* n.s. vi (2), 39; *S.H.C.* 1911, 140. For the relationship see *S.H.C.* iv (1), 203.
[15] *S.H.C.* vii (1), 66; *S.H.C.* 1911, 238.
[16] *Feud. Aids*, v. 16; B.L. Add. Ch. 47249.
[17] *Cal. Inq. p.m.* x, p. 280; *V.C.H. Staffs.* xvii. 171; B. H. Putnam, *Place in Legal Hist. of Sir Wm. Shareshull*, 138.

his estate at Goscote, in Walsall, at least until 1411 and was later assigned to John Gibthorp, who was dead by 1421 with his daughter Elizabeth as his heir.[18] In 1428–9 lordship was apparently exercised by Sir Robert Babthorpe (d. 1436), sheriff of Staffordshire in 1414–15 and a leading officer of the royal household.[19] At some date Elizabeth's husband William Babington (d. 1474) of Chilwell, in Attenborough (Notts.), was lord.[20] Their son John died in 1501 and was succeeded by his sister Etheldena (or Ethelneda) Delves; when she died in 1504 her estates passed to her elder daughter Ellen, wife of Sir Robert Sheffield of Butterwick (Lincs.).[21] Sir Robert was holding the manor of Wombourne in 1515. He died in 1518 and was succeeded by his son Sir Robert (d. 1531), whose son Edmund, later Baron Sheffield, was lord of Wombourne in 1538–9.[22] Wombourne was sold to Gilbert Wakering of Yieldfields Hall in Bloxwich by one of Edmund's successors, probably Edmund, Lord Sheffield, who sold land at Essington and Bloxwich to Wakering in 1587.[23] Wakering was lord of Wombourne in 1601. He was knighted in 1604 and died in 1616.[24] His nephew and successor John Wakering sold the manor in 1619 to John Woodhouse of the Wodehouse. In 1641 Woodhouse and John Huntbach of Seawall, in Bushbury, sold it to Walter Wrottesley (later Sir Walter Wrottesley, Bt.) of Wrottesley.[25]

The manor of Orton seems to have been acquired by Sir William Shareshull, lord of Shareshill and Patshull, by 1342. In 1344 he settled it for life on a relative, Nicholas Shareshull (d. 1350).[26] It is not clear whether the manor reverted to Sir William since it was said in 1372 to have been occupied by a Richard de Everdon.[27] Richard may have been the father of John le lordeson or John *filius domini* who witnessed grants in the 1360s and 1370s.[28] Sir William Shareshull's grandson, another Sir William Shareshull, had recovered the manor by his death in 1400.[29] In 1401, however, it was claimed by John Everdon,[30] who may have been John le lordeson. John Everdon was styled lord of Orton in 1414 or 1415, and William Everdon, who granted a lease of property at Wombourne in 1437, was called lord in 1439 or 1440. When in 1462 Humphrey, Roger, and Thomas Everdon granted a 101-year lease of property in Wombourne, they demanded heriot from the tenants and suit at their court whenever it should be held

at Orton. Simon Everdon, chaplain, was called lord of Orton in 1505 or 1506.[31] The manor may eventually have passed to the Greys of Enville. In 1538 George Acworth conveyed to Thomas Grey of Enville what were described as the manors of Orton and Wombourne, with land and rent in Orton, Wombourne, and Trysull.[32] Grey called himself lord of Wombourne and lord of Orton.[33] In 1574 or 1575 his son John bought from Edward Hussey what was called the manor of Wombourne and Orton.[34] That manor, described in 1527 as the manors of Wombourne and Orton and then held by Humphrey Rugeley and his wife Margaret, had been sold to Hussey's father Richard in 1562 by Margaret Rugeley, probably Humphrey's widow, and Francis Rugeley.[35] In 1620 Ambrose Grey of Enville was holding courts for his manor of Orton and Wombourne.[36] In 1633 the manor, which Ambrose had mortgaged, was bought by Sir Hugh Wrottesley.[37]

A third manor seems to have derived from what was called in 1356 the fee of Orton, Wombourne, and Lower Penn, apparently held then or earlier by William of Penn, son of Hugh Buffery of Penn.[38] In 1402 John Buffery of Lower Penn was holding courts at Wombourne.[39] In 1434 John Buffery of Codsall granted lands in Penn, Orton, and Wombourne to his son-in-law John Burnett of Penn at a rent of 20s.[40] It was later stated that Buffery was lord of Wombourne and Orton and that on his death the lordship passed to his daughter Jane and her husband, John Burnett. In 1514 or 1515 Thomas Burnett of Lower Penn granted his lands and manorial rights in Wombourne and Orton to his son Robert in tail.[41] In 1593 Robert's son Thomas Burnett of Lower Penn settled the reversion of his manors of Wombourne and Orton on his grandson Thomas Burnett. The elder Thomas died in 1599, and lands and rents in Wombourne and Orton known as the manor of Wombourne or Burnett's manor passed to his grandson.[42] In 1608 the grandson sold the manor of Wombourne and Orton, with 20s. rent and 300 a. of heath in Wombourne and Orton, to Hugh, later Sir Hugh, Wrottesley of Wrottesley.[43]

After the purchases made by Sir Hugh and Sir Walter Wrottesley the lordship of what was known as the manor of Wombourne and Orton[44] descended with Wrottesley. In 1816 Sir John Wrottesley owned 117 a. in the townships of

[18] P.R.O., C 137/36, no. 36; S.R.O., D. 260/M/F/1/5, f. 172v.; B.L. Harl. MS. 506, p. 332; Cal. Close, 1402–5, 216; S.H.C. xvii. 133–5, 178; V.C.H. Staffs. xvii. 171, 173.

[19] S.R.O., Tp. 1226, folder 5, excerpts from rentals; R. Somerville, Hist. of Duchy of Lancaster, i. 563; J. S. Roskell, Commons in Parl. of 1422, 219.

[20] Shaw, Staffs. (1976 edn.), ii, Addns. I, p. 312; Collectanea Topographica et Genealogica, viii. 319; Topographer and Genealogist, i. 260–2; J. C. Wedgwood, Hist. of Parl.: Biographies 1439–1509, 32.

[21] Topographer and Genealogist, i. 262–4; Cal. Inq. p.m. Hen. VII, ii, p. 573; Shaw, Staffs. (1976 edn.), ii, Addns. I, p. 312.

[22] S.R.O., Tp. 1226, folder 5, excerpts from rentals; D.N.B. s.v. Sheffield, Sir Rob.; P.R.O., PROB 11/19, ff. 115v.–116; V.C.H. Staffs. xvii. 173–4 (wrongly giving the elder Sir Rob.'s date of death as 1517).

[23] Shaw, Staffs. ii. 211; S.H.C. xv. 177–8.

[24] S.R.O., Tp. 1226, folder 6, Huntbach's notes; V.C.H. Staffs. xvii. 179.

[25] Shaw, Staffs. ii. 211; S.R.O., Tp. 1226, folder 5, deed of 1641.

[26] S.H.C. xii (1), 10; xiv (1), 131–2; Putnam, Shareshull, 6, 8, and App. I, pedigree.

[27] S.H.C. xiv (1), 131–2.

[28] Shaw, Staffs. ii. 220.

[29] Putnam, Shareshull, 8, 11.

[30] Cal. Close, 1399–1402, 362.

[31] Shaw, Staffs. ii. 215, 229; S.H.C. 1928, 45, 49.

[32] S.H.C. xi. 278.

[33] P.R.O., C 1/1319, nos. 71–2.

[34] W.S.L., D. 1933, vol. 5, f. 21; V.C.H. Salop. viii. 202.

[35] S.H.C. xi. 266; xiii. 220–1.

[36] S.R.O., Tp. 1226, folder 6, Huntbach's notes, copy of ct. roll 1620.

[37] S.H.C. N.S. vi (2), 298, 311.

[38] S.H.C. x (2), 45; xiv (1), 105.

[39] B.L. Add. Ch. 62561.

[40] S.R.O., D. 593/B/1/17/13/3.

[41] S.H.C. N.S. iii. 17 n.

[42] S.R.O., Tp. 1226, bdle. I, nos. 8, 11.

[43] S.H.C. N.S. iii. 17.

[44] See e.g. W.S.L. 574/38; White, Dir. Staffs. (1851), 210.

Wombourne and Orton, of which 7 a. was in demesne; he also owned 21 a. in Swindon.[45] The estate was much the same size in 1929, when Lord Wrottesley put his property in the parish up for sale.[46]

There were tenants with the surnames *de aula, en le Hale*, atte Halle, and similar variants at Wombourne in the later 13th and earlier 14th century.[47] The name presumably refers to a manor house in or near the village; the site is unknown. The Thomas del Halle, gentleman, who was living at Orton in 1425 may have occupied the manor house there, but the name is more likely by that date to have been a patronym.[48] A manor house at Orton was held by tenants of the Greys at least between the 1580s and 1620s.[49]

The estate which takes its name from the house known as *THE WODEHOUSE* originated between 1176 and 1189 when the lord of Wombourne, William son of Guy de Offini, granted William the cook land in Wombourne formerly held by Roger Brown. Between 1194 and 1206 the tenant in chief, Ralph de Somery, granted William the cook two assarts, one bordering the fields of Wombourne and the other adjoining the present Wodehouse Road. In or before 1206 William's son Nicholas acquired from Bernard of Frankley, lord of Trysull, another assart in Wombourne or Trysull. Between 1224 and 1241 Alan of Orton, lord of Wombourne, granted or confirmed to Nicholas an assart on 'Ouhul', the later Owen Hill, which Nicholas had enclosed. All three grants were in return for cash payments and money rents. Nicholas was succeeded by his son William some time between 1241 and 1243. William, known as William Wood, married Sibyl, daughter of Walter of Bradley, lord of Bradley in Bilston; he acquired more land in Wombourne and bought freedom from suit of court at Trysull. He was still alive in 1272 and was succeeded by his son Walter, who became known as Walter Woodhouse (de la Wodehouse or atte Wodehouse). Walter was succeeded by his son Thomas, probably before 1290. Thomas's son William succeeded him, apparently between 1313 and 1315. William's son William had evidently succeeded by 1336.[50]

The descent is then obscure. In the 1320s and 1330s there were at least three or four households of the Woodhouse family in Wombourne. A Thomas Woodhouse occurs in 1379 and 1384.[51] A Thomas Woodhouse the younger is found in 1391, in 1401, when he was described as of Orton,

and in 1403; he was probably the Thomas Woodhouse who was alive in 1438. A John Woodhouse, son of the late Thomas Woodhouse, occurs in 1442 and, as John Woodhouse of the Wodehouse, in 1457.[52] A John Woodhouse held the Wodehouse in 1479. He was succeeded in 1523 by his son Stephen (d. 1527 or 1528). The Wodehouse then passed to Stephen's son Benedict.[53] Benedict died in 1586 and was succeeded by his son Walter (d. 1610). Walter was followed by his son Francis (d. 1643) and he by his son John (d. 1651).[54]

Edward, John's son and heir, and the first of the family to style himself gentleman, died in 1688 leaving his estate encumbered with mortgages and legacies.[55] In the 1690s his son and heir John mortgaged the property.[56] John and his brother and heir both died unmarried in 1702, with four sisters and the son of a fifth as their heirs. In 1703 the mortgagees began proceedings to foreclose.[57]

By 1708 the Wodehouse estate had passed to Samuel Hellier, a London brewer and the son-in-law of one of the mortgagees. He leased the house and land, and although he built a family vault in Wombourne church and was buried there in 1727, he does not appear to have lived at the Wodehouse. His son and heir Samuel settled there, dying in 1751. He was succeeded by his son, another Samuel, who came of age in 1757.[58] He was high sheriff of Worcestershire in 1762 and was knighted that year when he presented the county's loyal address to George III on the birth of the Prince of Wales. He died unmarried in 1784.[59]

He left his property to his friend and man of business the Revd. Thomas Shaw, minister of St. John's, Wolverhampton, and perpetual curate of Tipton and of Claverley (Salop.). In accordance with the terms of the will Shaw moved into the Wodehouse and in 1786 changed his name to Shaw-Hellier.[60] He died in 1812, leaving his lands in trust for his grandson Thomas Shaw-Hellier, the eldest son of his elder son, James. James, one of the trustees, was to have the Wodehouse, its contents, and its grounds rent-free for life, with an annuity, and was to draw a salary for continuing to manage the family's coal and ironstone interests.[61] In 1816 the Shaw-Hellier trustees held 267 a. in the parish, of which 234 a. lay in Wombourne township.[62] James died in 1827 and Thomas in 1870. Thomas's successor, his son Col. Thomas Bradney Shaw-Hellier, was commandant of the Royal Military

---

[45] S.R.O., D. 2/1.
[46] W.S.L., Sale Cat. E/3/12.
[47] *S.H.C.* 1928, 18, 20, 22, 24.   [48] *S.H.C.* xvii. 103.
[49] W.S.L., D. 1933, vol. 5, ff. 21–2; S.R.O., Tp. 1273/11, 1623 survey.
[50] *S.H.C.* 1928, 10–19, 24–6, 33–4. For Owen Hill see S.R.O., Tp. 1226, bdle. XXXII, 28 Feb. 1658/9.
[51] *S.H.C.* vii (1), 254; x (1), 130; *S.H.C.* 1928, 39, 41. The pedigree in Shaw, *Staffs.* ii. 216, seems to be largely conjectural for the mid 14th and the later 15th cent.
[52] *S.H.C.* 1928, 40–3, 46–9; Shaw, *Staffs.* ii. 216.
[53] *S.H.C.* 1928, 51–2, 54–6; Shaw, *Staffs.* ii. 216; S.R.O., Tp. 1226/43, will of John Woodhouse 1523.
[54] *S.H.C.* v (2), 327; *S.H.C.* 1928, 57–8; S.R.O., D. 3710/1/1.
[55] S.R.O., Tp. 1226, bdle. IX, nos. 15–16; P.R.O., C 7/377, no. 106; C 8/527, no. 5.

[56] S.R.O., Tp. 1226, bdle. IX, nos. 18–30; P.R.O., C 7/377, no. 106; C 7/604, no. 49.
[57] S.R.O., D. 3710/1/1; P.R.O., C 7/377, no. 106; Burke, *Ext. & Dorm. Baronetcies* (1838), 573–4.
[58] W.S.L. 45/88/56; P.R.O., C 7/362, no. 2; C 7/376, no. 20; S.R.O., D. 3710/1/10; S.R.O., Tp. 1226, bdle. XXXII, 20 Oct. 1708, 23 June 1717.
[59] W. A. Shaw, *Knights of Eng.* ii. 291; M. Wyndham, *Chronicles of the Eighteenth Century*, ii, chap. ix; S.R.O., D. 3710/1/10; S.R.O., Tp. 1226/ADD/K16, printed copy of Hellier inscription for Wombourne ch.
[60] *S.H.C.* 4th ser. vi. 137–8; *Lond. Gaz.* 15–18 July 1786, p. 321; A. A. Rollason, 'Antiquarian Notes', *Dudley Herald*, 11 Feb. 1911; W.S.L. 45/88/56.
[61] *Staffs. Advertiser*, 18 July 1812; W.S.L. 45/88/56; *Dudley Herald*, 11 Feb. 1911.
[62] S.R.O., D. 2/1.

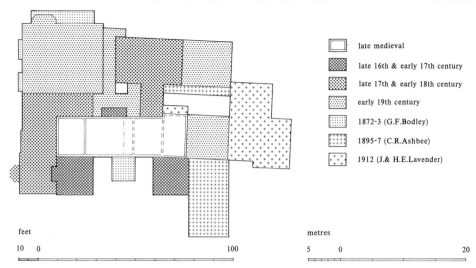

late medieval

late 16th & early 17th century

late 17th & early 18th century

early 19th century

1872-3 (G.F.Bodley)

1895-7 (C.R.Ashbee)

1912 (J.& H.E.Lavender)

feet

10   0   100

metres

5   0   20

PLAN OF THE WODEHOUSE, WOMBOURNE

School of Music 1883–93.[63] During part of that time the Wodehouse was occupied by the Hon. P. J. Stanhope, Liberal M.P. for Wednesbury 1886–92 and later Baron Weardale.[64] Towards the end of his life Col. Shaw-Hellier went to live in Sicily where he died in 1910. He was succeeded by his nephew Evelyn Shaw-Hellier, formerly Simpson, who was living at the Wodehouse by 1903 and took the name and arms of Shaw-Hellier in 1909. Evelyn Shaw-Hellier died in 1922 and was succeeded by his elder daughter Evelyn Mary Penelope Shaw-Hellier.[65] She died in 1975, and her sister Dorothy continued to live at the Wodehouse until her death in 1981. The estate passed to the Phillips family, Mr. J. W. Phillips being Miss E. M. P. Shaw-Hellier's first cousin twice removed.[66] He was living at the Wodehouse in 1982.

The house known by the later 13th century as the Wodehouse seems to have existed by the early 1240s.[67] The core of the present house is a late-medieval timber-framed house of which the hall and parlour end survive. The existence of a spere truss at the east end of the hall implies that there were formerly service rooms beyond it. The present kitchen block to the north, although structurally probably of the early 18th century, is likely to be on the site of its medieval predecessor. By the mid 17th century gabled wings had been added to each end of the south side, and subsequently a block was added alongside the west front. In 1666 the house was assessed at six hearths.[68] In 1688 it contained two parlours, a hall, a kitchen, a brewhouse, a bakehouse, two

butteries, a dairy, and a pantry, with eight chambers on the first floor.[69] Internal refitting in the earlier 18th century included the panelling of several rooms and the insertion of a new staircase within the medieval parlour, probably in the 1740s when extensive work was done on the house.[70] William Baker prepared plans for Samuel Hellier in 1758 and 1759,[71] perhaps for alterations to the house; if so, nothing seems to have been done. In 1767 James Gandon, a friend of Hellier, proposed the rebuilding of everything west of the hall,[72] and by 1769 Joseph Pickford had produced plans for alterations or additions.[73] Nothing came of either scheme. In 1800 John Plaw published designs for a neo-classical villa on the site of the existing house,[74] but when work was carried out a few years later it was the addition of dining and drawing rooms to the north front and the replacement of the straight gables by a Jacobean roof line of tall chimneys and Flemish gables. In 1872–3 G. F. Bodley remodelled the south and west fronts for T. B. Shaw-Hellier, adding a porch and square bay windows; he also redecorated the drawing room.[75] Soon afterwards the name of the house, which since the 17th century had been spelled 'Woodhouse' or 'Woodhouses', was given the archaic spelling 'Wodehouse' which it has retained.[76] In 1895–7 Shaw-Hellier employed C. R. Ashbee to add a billiard room above the kitchen and a chapel against the east end of the south front. Ashbee also rebuilt the chimneys, replaced two gables by a parapet with the motto 'Domum Dulce Domum' instead of balusters, and remodelled

[63] Staffs. Advertiser, 7 July 1827; Staffs. and some neighbouring records: historical, biographical, and pictorial [1910], 204.
[64] J. Parkes, Hist. of Tipton (Tipton, 1915), 45; Kelly's Dir. Staffs. (1888; 1892); Complete Peerage, xiii. 60.
[65] Burke, Land. Gent. (1952), 1203; F. MacCarthy, The Simple Life: C. R. Ashbee in the Cotswolds, 158–60; Kelly's Dir. Staffs. (1904; 1908).
[66] Wombourne Compass (Apr. 1975; copy in poss. of Mrs. May Griffiths); Express & Star, 6 July 1981; inf. from Mr. Phillips.   [67] S.H.C. 1928, 13–14.
[68] S.H.C. 1923, 112.
[69] L.J.R.O., B/C/11, Edw. Woodhouse (1691).
[70] S.R.O., Tp. 1322/2, 30 Nov. 1743, 15 Jan. 1744/5, 21 Dec. 1745, 3 and 29 Jan. 1745/6, 11 Dec. 1752.

[71] S.H.C. 1950–1, 128.
[72] Signed and dated plan at the Wodehouse; Life of James Gandon, ed. M. Craig, 21.
[73] S.R.O., Tp. 1226/ADD/K4, 18 Feb. 1769. An unsigned plan at the Wodehouse may be by Pickford.
[74] J. Plaw, Sketches for Country Houses, Villas and Rural Dwellings (1800), plates 29–31.
[75] Photographs at the Wodehouse of the exterior before and after Bodley's alterations; R.I.B.A., Drawings Colln., note by Ashbee on his drawing of the west front; above, pl. facing p. 16.
[76] Dirs. up to and including P.O. Dir. Staffs. (1876) give 'Woodhouse', while those from Kelly's Dir. Staffs. (1880) give 'Wodehouse'. For 'Woodhouses' see e.g. S.R.O. 3279/18; S.R.O., D. 260/M/F/4/11; S.R.O., Tp. 1322/1–2, passim.

the other gables.[77] In 1912 a service wing was added on the east by J. and H. E. Lavender of Wolverhampton and the chapel and billiard room were divided to form smaller rooms.[78]

In 1710 the outbuildings consisted of two ranges east and south-east of the house and a dovecot north of it. The dovecot still stood in 1784.[79] The only surviving major building is a large two-storeyed stable block east of the house. It incorporates some 18th-century walling and woodwork, part of a coach house built in 1743,[80] but it seems to be mostly of the mid or later 19th century. The northern half houses a music room designed probably for T. B. Shaw-Hellier.

The gardens west of the house are terraced down to a small lake which existed by 1710[81] and was formed by damming Wom brook. A causeway to the house runs across the dam and divides the lake from a pool which lies downstream. The arrangement may be 17th-century in origin but probably dates mainly from the 18th century. In the later 18th century the grounds of the house included three pools and a waterfall along Wom brook; the present lake by the house is apparently what was then known as Middle Pool.[82]

Samuel Hellier (d. 1751) greatly enlarged the gardens and was making extensive alterations to them at the time of his death.[83] The work continued, probably along the lines which he had laid down. In 1754 an octagon was built and a yew tree planted 'in the centre of the intended visto in the line of the walk'.[84] In 1763 Sir Samuel Hellier began the transformation of the 7-a. wood on the steep slope east and north-east of the house into a pleasure ground.[85] By 1767 the buildings and monuments there included a root house, a grotto, a hermitage with several rooms and a life-size model of a hermit called Father Francis, and a music room equipped with an organ.[86] Handel's Temple, built in memory of the composer, was completed in 1768 to a design by Gandon.[87] A druids' temple had been constructed by 1773, perhaps inspired by the visit to Stonehenge which Sir Samuel made with Thomas Shaw in 1768.[88] Walks were cut through the wood to give access to the various monuments; boards beside the paths had appropriate verses painted on them.[89] Walls of some tenants' houses which could be seen from the pleasure ground were whitewashed to improve their appearance, and

some had trompe-l'oeil windows painted on them.[90] The wood rapidly became a tourist attraction for what Sir Samuel called 'people of consequence' and for 'tag rag and rabble'; eventually only 'such who come in coaches and appear as people of fashion' were admitted.[91] It is unlikely that the pleasure ground survived its creator's death in 1784 for long. Many of the structures seem to have been badly built or made of flimsy materials,[92] and nothing of them remains visible.[93] Interest turned to other parts of the grounds where there was much specimen planting in the 19th and early 20th century.

In the 19th century the owners of the house in Penn known as the Lloyd were among the largest landholders in Wombourne. Their property in the parish consisted of estates which had been built up by two Wombourne families, the Marshes and the Smiths.

The Marsh family was established in the parish by the earlier 16th century.[94] John Marsh and his son John, both described as yeomen, held land in Wombourne and Orton in the 1660s and 1670s. William Marsh (d. 1709), apparently the first of the family to style himself gentleman, acquired more property in both places.[95] In 1745 his son John owned the house at Wombourne in which he lived, with its farmland in Wombourne and Orton, another farm in Wombourne, and a farm and other land in Orton.[96] He bought another farm in Orton in 1747.[97] He died in 1763. His son John had bought land in Wombourne in the 1750s[98] and consolidated part of his holding there in 1765 by an exchange of land with Sir Samuel Hellier.[99] In 1771 he bought the Lloyd in Penn, to which he had moved by 1781.[1] He continued to buy property in Wombourne, including, in 1792, Mill Lane farm.[2] He died in 1796. In 1816 his son Richard Bayley Marsh of the Lloyd owned 396 a. in Wombourne parish, of which 163 a. lay in Wombourne township and 233 a. in Orton township.[3]

In 1816 the Marsh property included two large houses, one at Wombourne and the other at Orton. The house at Wombourne stood at the junction of Church Street and High Street; it was known as Old Hall and later as the Manor House and was demolished c. 1968.[4] It was John Marsh's home in 1771[5] and was apparently the house in which his father had been living in 1745;

[77] Ground plan and sketch design at the Wodehouse for billiard-room gable; R.I.B.A., Drawings Colln., drawing of west front; drawing of south front exhibited at Royal Academy in 1898 and illustrated in *Archit. Rev.* iv, supplement. Mr. A. Crawford of the Victorian Soc. is thanked for his help.

[78] Signed and dated drawings at the Wodehouse.

[79] Map of Woodhouse estate 1710 at the Wodehouse; S.R.O., Tp. 1226/ADD/K1, 6 July 1784.

[80] S.R.O., Tp. 1322/2, 30 Nov. 1743.

[81] Map of Woodhouse estate 1710.

[82] S.R.O., Tp. 1226/ADD/K1, 23 Jan. 1769; K16, undated survey of Woodhouse estate.

[83] S.R.O., Tp. 1322/1/39, 9 and 30 Jan. 1750/1, 10 July, 3 Aug. 1751, 16 Feb. 1751/2, 13 May, 18 Nov. 1752.

[84] Ibid. 10 Apr. 1754.

[85] S.R.O., Tp. 1226/ADD/K16, acct. of work to be done in 1763 and undated survey of Woodhouse estate.

[86] Ibid. K1, 3 and 31 Jan., 28 Mar., 14 Apr., 1 June, 7 July 1767, 20 and 30 Apr., 5 May, 2 June 1768, 23 Feb., 4 Mar., 1 June 1769, 4 Oct. 1781; K2, 14 Jan., 19 Apr., 16 May 1782. For the buildings and monuments see above, pl. facing p. 193.

[87] S.R.O., Tp. 1226/ADD/K1, 15 and 26 Mar., 20 Apr., 17 May 1768; Colvin, *Brit. Architects*, 327. For Sir Samuel as a music lover see e.g. Tp. 1226/ADD/K1, *passim*.

[88] Above, pl. facing p. 193; S.R.O., Tp. 1226/ADD/K1, 22 Aug. 1768.

[89] S.R.O., Tp. 1226/ADD/K1, 15 Mar. 1768.

[90] Ibid. 2 June 1768, 5 June 1770, 21 May 1772.

[91] Ibid. 27 June, 7 and 28 July 1767, 20 Apr., 25 May, 1 June 1769, 5 June 1770, 21 May 1772.

[92] See e.g. ibid. 20 Apr. 1768, 1 July 1770, 17 June 1773.

[93] Inf. from Mr. Phillips.

[94] *S.H.C.* n.s. vi (1), 65, 68; 4th ser. viii. 128. For dates of death given in this para. see, unless otherwise stated, S.R.O., D. 3710/1/10.

[95] S.R.O. 3279/27-8, 38.

[96] Ibid. 18.

[97] Ibid. 24/3.

[98] Ibid. 16/4; ibid. 40.

[99] Ibid. 17.

[1] Ibid. 2/8; 5/16; S.R.O., Tp. 1226/ADD/K1, 23 July 1781.

[2] S.R.O. 3279/19/4-6 (Mill Lane farm); 20/1-2; 21/1.

[3] Shaw, *Staffs.* ii, p. *221; S.R.O., D. 2/1.

[4] S.R.O., D. 2/1; D. 691/6; local inf. (1980).

[5] S.R.O., 3279/20/1-2.

it was probably the house in Wombourne township, with three hearths and one hearth stopped up, on which John Marsh was taxed in 1666.[6] The house at Orton, later known as Orton Grange, is dated 1685[7] and was probably the house at Orton in which William Marsh was living in 1700 and from which he later moved back to Wombourne.[8]

The Smith property lay almost entirely in Wombourne township. In 1818 R. B. Marsh bought the 353 a. in the parish which belonged to William Tennant of Little Aston Hall in Shenstone; the estate had descended to Tennant from John Smith, one of the cursitors of Chancery (will dated 1751). All but 6 a. lay in Wombourne township, and it included the houses later known as Mill House, Smallbrook Farm, Walk House, and Wombourne Farm.[9] Smith and his father John, of Lincoln's Inn (will dated 1708), had acquired various properties in the parish,[10] but the family had lived at Wombourne at least since the later 16th century. Edward Smith (d. 1679), father of the elder John, had been styled gentleman and had been a prominent figure in the parish. He was elected parish registrar in 1654. His house was taxed at six hearths in 1666, more than any in the parish save the Wodehouse and the vicarage.[11]

In 1899 Harriet Bradney-Marsh, owner of the Lloyd estate, married Col. Shaw-Hellier of the Wodehouse,[12] and in 1901 the Lloyd estate was sold by auction and broken up. The 852 a. in Wombourne included houses and land in and around the village, notably the Manor House, Arbour Tree House, and Waverley House, and Mill House farm, Mill Lane farm, Smallbrook farm, Walk House farm, and Wombourne farm. Further north was Orton Grange farm.[13] Some of the property was acquired by Col. H. H. Ward of Bearnett House in Penn, who already owned land in Wombourne. His estate later passed to Commander Melvill Hensman of Eashing, in Godalming (Surr.). In 1924 Hensman sold it by auction, and it was broken up. It then covered virtually all the parish north of the Bratch and amounted to 852 a.; it included New and Awbridge farm at Orton, Orton Grange farm, Orton Hall farm, and a farm which had been formed by merging White Cross (or Fox Hall) farm and Bearnett farm.[14]

SWINDON was not mentioned by name in Domesday Book. The settlement, or its site, was apparently included in the smaller of two estates in Himley held in 1086 of William FitzAnsculf.[15] It was first mentioned in 1166, when it was held of Gervase Paynel, lord of Dudley, and the overlordship then descended with the Dudley barony.[16]

In the 13th century a mesne lordship was held by the lords of Orton. It was last mentioned in 1323, when Swindon was said to be held of Thomas of Orton as $\frac{1}{5}$ knight's fee.[17]

The terre tenant of Swindon in 1086 was evidently Gilbert, who held of FitzAnsculf 1 hide in Himley and also the Berkshire manor of Englefield.[18] By 1166 there was a manor of Swindon, held by Ellis Englefield, son of Ansculf Englefield and lord of Englefield.[19] Swindon then descended with Englefield, probably as a sub-manor of Himley.[20] Ellis's successor was probably the William Englefield mentioned before 1184. Another William Englefield became lord, apparently in the earlier 1190s, and was alive in 1197.[21] He was succeeded before 1217 by Alan Englefield, who died in 1226 or 1227.[22] Alan's successor was his son William, who held Swindon as $\frac{1}{3}$ knight's fee in 1243[23] and was still alive in 1258. He was succeeded by his son John (d. c. 1276), who was followed by his son William (d. before 1281). William's successor was Roger Englefield.

The Englefields' main interests lay in Berkshire and Oxfordshire, and it is possible that in the mid 13th century a younger son was settled on their Staffordshire lands. In the earlier 1270s dower rights in the Himley and Swindon property were claimed by Joan, widow of an Alan Englefield and later the wife of John de Eton; Alan was presumably a younger son and was probably the Alan Englefield who was a verderer of Kinver forest in 1271.[24] In the 1270s the Swindon property seems to have consisted of some 13 messuages, $6\frac{1}{2}$ virgates, and 15s. rent.[25] In 1284–5 John de Eton and William Beresford held two thirds of Roger Englefield's manor of Himley, which presumably included Swindon, and William de Baylol held the remaining third. In 1291 Eton and Beresford were holding the manor jointly, and in 1306 Roger mortgaged all his property in Himley and Swindon to Beresford.[26]

About 1316 Roger demised land and rent in Himley and rent and services worth 33s. in Swindon to the tenant in chief, John, Lord Somery, for life, with reversion to Roger and his heirs. After Somery's death in 1322 Roger's son Philip took possession of the property. He was ejected by the keepers appointed by the Crown to take custody of Somery's lands but in 1323 obtained a writ ordering them to restore Himley and Swindon to him.[27]

By 1346 what was described as the manor of Himley, or Himley and Swindon, had passed to John, son of Margaret de Sutton and lord of Dudley.[28] It then descended in the Sutton (later Sutton or Dudley) family, from 1440 lords

[6] *S.H.C.* 1923, 112.
[7] S.R.O., D. 2/1; D. 691/6.   [8] S.R.O. 3279/27–8.
[9] Ibid. 22/4; D. 2/1; D. 691/4, 6; *Wolverhampton Chron.* 17 May 1815.   [10] S.R.O. 3279/38.
[11] S.R.O., D. 3710/1/1; *S.H.C.* 1923, 112.
[12] *Staffs. and some neighbouring records*, 204.
[13] S.R.O., D. 691/4, 6.
[14] Ibid. 3.   [15] *V.C.H. Staffs.* iv. 54.
[16] *S.H.C.* i. 151, 197; *Bk. of Fees*, i. 543; ii. 968.
[17] *Bk. of Fees*, ii. 968; *Cal. Inq. p.m.* vi, p. 260.
[18] *V.C.H. Staffs.* iv. 54; *V.C.H. Berks.* iii. 405–6.
[19] *S.H.C.* i. 49, 51, 151, 197; *V.C.H. Berks.* iii. 406.

[20] For the rest of the para. see, unless otherwise stated, *V.C.H. Berks.* iii. 406.   [21] B.L. Add. Ch. 20592.
[22] *Rot. Litt. Claus.* (Rec. Com.), i. 300; *S.H.C.* iv (1), 55–6.
[23] *S.H.C.* 1911, 400.
[24] *S.H.C.* iv (1), 191, 195, 204; v (1), 140; vi (1), 70–1.
[25] Ibid. iv (1), 195; vi (1), 70–1.
[26] *Bk. of Fees*, v. 10; *Cal. Inq. p.m.* ii, pp. 494, 496; *S.H.C.* vii (1), 149.
[27] *Cal. Inq. p.m.* vi, p. 260; *Cal. Close*, 1323–7, 9.
[28] *Cal. Pat.* 1345–8, 252–3, stating that he had mortgaged the manor to the late Adam de Peshale. Peshale was killed early in 1346: *S.H.C.* 1917–18, 85.

Dudley. After Sir John Sutton's death in 1359 his widow Isabel held the manor of Swindon with that of Himley in dower until her death in 1397; in 1401 it was delivered to her great-grandson, another John Sutton.[29] In the 15th century and later Swindon formed a sub-manor of Himley.[30] Himley, including Swindon, was one of the properties acquired from John, Lord Dudley, by his cousin Sir John Dudley, later duke of Northumberland; the date was probably 1537, when Sir John took possession of Dudley castle.[31] After Northumberland's attainder in 1553 Himley manor remained with the Crown until 1555, when it was granted to Edward, Lord Dudley, with its appurtenances in Wombourne and Swindon.[32] He died in 1586, and Swindon passed to his son Edward.[33] On the death of Edward, Lord Dudley, in 1643 the estates passed to his granddaughter Frances, *suo jure* Baroness Dudley. She was the wife of Humble Ward, who in 1644 was created Baron Ward. Their son Edward succeeded his father as Lord Ward in 1670 and became Lord Dudley and Ward on the death of his mother in 1697. Swindon then descended with the Ward barony.[34] In 1816 Viscount Dudley and Ward owned 850 a. in the parish, of which 72 a. lay in Wombourne township and 778 a. in Swindon township; 184 a., mostly in Swindon, were in demesne.[35] A further 456 a. in Swindon, part of the glebe, was bought in 1878.[36] In 1947 William Humble Eric Ward, earl of Dudley, sold his Himley estate, which then included over 1,600 a. in Wombourne and Swindon.[37]

In 1240 or 1241 Master Richard Black granted a virgate, 7 a., and an assart in Wombourne to Halesowen abbey (Worcs.) at a clove rent. Alan of Orton confirmed the grant as lord of Wombourne.[38] The assart was probably the 2-a. assart held by the abbey in 1254-5.[39] Alan granted the abbey another virgate in Wombourne for a 6d. rent. By 1243 a weaver, Randal of Wombourne, had given 12½ a. at Wombourne in free alms. William Englefield granted ½ virgate at Swindon, also in free alms.[40] In 1425 the abbey was holding a court for its manor of *WOMBOURNE AND SWINDON*,[41] and in 1535 it received 44s. 8d. rent from its property there.[42]

Halesowen abbey was dissolved in 1538, and its estates, including what were described as the manors of Wombourne and Swindon, were granted to Sir John Dudley, later duke of

Northumberland, attainted in 1553.[43] In 1563 the Crown granted land at Swindon formerly belonging to the abbey to Cecily Pickerell of Norwich in satisfaction of a debt which had been owed to her deceased husband John by the late Edward, duke of Somerset. In 1564 it sold Halesowen land at Wombourne and what was then described as the manor of Wombourne and Swindon to two speculators, William Grice and Anthony Forster.[44] They immediately sold it to Richard Whorwood of Lutley, in Enville, who in 1565 sold it to his relative by marriage William Uvedale.[45] In 1577 William Uvedale, son and heir of William Uvedale of Bromley in Kingswinford, sold it to Walter James of Staple Inn, and in 1592 James, then described as of Corbyn's Hall in Kingswinford, sold it with some land and a mill in Swindon which had belonged to Halesowen abbey to Edward Jorden of Dunsley, in Kinver.[46] Edward was dead by 1616. His son Humphrey died in 1640 and Humphrey's son Edward in 1667. In 1677 Edward's son Edward sold the manor to Edward, Lord Ward.[47] It was then absorbed into the Ward estate.

In 1086 William FitzAnsculf's lands included 1 hide at *CHASEPOOL*. The property had evidently once been cultivated, but by 1086 it had been taken into the king's forest and was waste.[48] By the 1220s one of the hays of Kinver forest took its name from Chasepool. The Crown granted John, Lord Dudley, leases of the herbage, pannage, and other perquisites of Chasepool hay from 1454, and in 1484 he was appointed bailiff of the hay. Edward, Lord Dudley, John's grandson and heir, was made lieutenant of the forest for life in 1487. He died in 1532, and later that year Thomas, duke of Norfolk, was appointed lieutenant of the forest and of Chasepool hay.[49] The hay was later held by the duke of Northumberland and reverted to the Crown on his attainder in 1553. In 1555 it was granted in tail to Edward, Lord Dudley.[50] Chasepool was inclosed in 1796,[51] and by 1816 Lord Dudley had three farms there: Greensforge farm (158 a.), Chasepool Lodge farm (249 a.), and Whitehouse farm (188 a.). A further 157 a. was mainly plantation.[52] The property descended with Swindon until its sale in 1947 as part of Lord Dudley's Himley estate.[53]

There was a lodge at Greensforge by 1600;[54] it was then occupied by Thomas Green, and the name Greens Lodge was used for the house in the 17th and early 18th century. Another name

[29] *Cal. Close*, 1399-1402, 251; *S.H.C.* ix (2), 55, 57-8, 62.

[30] See e.g. S.R.O., D. 593/O/3/3; D.C.L., Himley and Swindon manorial.

[31] *S.H.C.* ix (2), 94-5; *Complete Peerage*, iv. 481.

[32] *Cal. Pat.* 1555-7, 35; *Complete Peerage*, iv. 482.

[33] P.R.O., C 142/234, no. 74.

[34] *Complete Peerage*, iv. 482-4, 487-91; xii (2), 342-4.

[35] S.R.O., D. 2/1.   [36] Below, churches.

[37] W.S.L., Sale Cats. E/1/16, E/4/25; *Staffs. Advertiser*, 19 Jan. 1947.

[38] W.S.L., S.MS. 386/2, no. 214; *Close R.* 1237-42, 247, 346.

[39] *S.H.C.* v (1), 111.

[40] W.S.L., S.MS. 386/2, nos. 214, 224.

[41] D.C.L., Wombourne and Swindon manorial.

[42] *Valor Eccl.* (Rec. Com.), iii. 206.

[43] *S.H.C.* xii (1), 186; *L. & P. Hen. VIII*, xiii (2), p. 191;

Complete Peerage, ix. 722-6.

[44] *Cal. Pat.* 1563-6, pp. 63, 65.

[45] H.W.R.O. (H.), E 12/S, Wombourne, deed of 19 Sept. 1565; D.C.L., D/DE/I/2, deed of 20 Mar. 1564/5; *S.H.C.* iii (2), 149.

[46] D.C.L., D/DE/I/2, deeds of 26 Oct. 1577, 28 Oct. 1592; *S.H.C.* xvi. 127. For James see *S.H.C.* 1928, 134; G. P. Mander, *Wolverhampton Antiquary*, i. 377-8.

[47] D.C.L., D/DE/I/2, deed of 17 Jan. 1676/7; S.R.O., D. 1197/1/1, baptisms 29 Mar. 1576. 20 Sept. 1612, 6 June 1639, burials 25 Feb. 1615/16, 4 Aug. 1640; 1/2, burial 4 Sept. 1667.

[48] *V.C.H. Staffs.* iv. 54.

[49] Ibid. ii. 343-6; *L. & P. Hen. VIII*, v, p. 400.

[50] *Cal. Pat.* 1555-7, 35; P.R.O., E 101/150/32, m. 3.

[51] Below, econ. hist.

[52] S.R.O., D. 2/1, Swindon ff. 102, 105, 112, 114.

[53] W.S.L. 298/80.

[54] D.C.L., D/DE/IV/3, deed of 11 July 1600.

used in the early 18th century was Swin Lodge.[55] In 1612 Edward, Lord Dudley, gave the house to his illegitimate son, the industrialist Dud Dudley (1599–1684).[56] Dudley was probably living there in the early 1620s, and he was still there in 1674, when he was working the nearby forge.[57] The house stood near Greensforge mill,[58] probably on the site of Greensforge House (later known as Bank Farm), a brick building dating from the 19th century. Chasepool Lodge Farm existed by the late 1640s as a lodge for the warren that had been laid out over the northern part of Chasepool.[59] It was rebuilt in the late 18th or early 19th century. It was demolished in 1969 and a new house was built to the east.[60] Whitehouse Farm is a brick building which dates from the 19th century.

After the grant of Wombourne church to Dudley priory c. 1150, the *RECTORY* remained with the priory until its dissolution in 1540. The church, with Trysull chapel, was valued in 1291 at £10 13s. 4d.[61] In 1535 the great tithes of Wombourne and Trysull were worth on average £10 a year.[62] In 1541 the Crown granted the rectory with the rest of the priory's possessions to Sir John Dudley,[63] and the great tithes of Wombourne and Orton townships then descended with Woodford Grange, passing in 1576 to the Wrottesleys of Wrottesley, in Tettenhall.[64] By 1840 some of the tithes had been merged by the owners of the land from which they were due. Most of the remaining tithes in Wombourne and Orton townships were owned by Lord Wrottesley, but those from 4 a. in Wombourne were owned by John Hill of Wombourne, Thomas Lane of Wombourne, and William Phillips of Enville. In 1840 Hill was granted a rent charge of 7s. 6d. in lieu of his tithes, Lane 3s., and Phillips 1s. Lord Wrottesley was granted a rent charge of £193 10s. in lieu of his tithes in Wombourne township, but the sum was found to be below the average paid and in 1842 was increased to £206 13s. 7d. In 1841 Lord Wrottesley was granted £180 in lieu of the great tithes of Orton.[65]

In 1360 Sir William Shareshull was licensed to grant Dudley priory 15s. rent in Wombourne in exchange for rent in Shareshill.[66] In 1535 the priory had a house and land in Wombourne worth 10s. a year.[67] The property evidently passed to Sir John Dudley in 1541, back to the Crown on his attainder in 1553, and to Edward Sutton, Lord Dudley, in 1554. Lord Dudley's son

Edward, Lord Dudley, sold a house and land in Wombourne to Thomas Bache of Wombourne in 1597.[68]

At the time of its suppression in 1525 Sandwell priory in West Bromwich owned property in Wombourne. The property then evidently descended with the Sandwell estate and passed to Robert Whorwood in 1569.[69]

The curacy of Bilston had glebe in Wombourne and Orton; the estate was nearly 80 a. in extent in 1816.[70]

ECONOMIC HISTORY. AGRICULTURE. Much of the parish consists of light, easily worked soil, and by 1086 cultivation was extensive. There was land for 8 ploughteams at Wombourne. Two teams were in demesne with 8 slaves; 14 villeins, a priest, and 3 bordars had a further 4 teams. With meadow and two mills Wombourne was worth £3, the same value as before the Conquest. At Orton there was land for 4 teams in 1086. Two teams were in demesne with 2 slaves, and there were 7 villeins and 2 bordars with a further 2 teams. With meadow the manor was worth 40s., the same value as before the Conquest.[71] Chasepool in the south-west, with land for 2 teams, lay within the forest and was waste; by the later 12th century the rest of the parish too lay within Kinver forest.[72] Assarting was common in the 13th century.[73]

There were at least three open fields at Wombourne in the Middle Ages. Pottelith, later Putley, field was mentioned in the 13th century. It lay north and east of Wombourne village.[74] Churchill field, mentioned in 1642, is possibly to be identified as Putley field, which was also known as Hill field in 1649.[75] Putley field still existed in the early 18th century.[76] Baggeridge field south-east of the village was mentioned in 1317.[77] Land there was described in 1587 as bounded by Himley park, and Park field, which was named as one of Wombourne's three open fields in 1621, may be the same field.[78] Woodhill field, mentioned in 1647, 1649, and 1688,[79] was probably another name for Baggeridge field, as was Woodside field mentioned in 1666.[80] The name Baggeridge field was still in use in 1693 and Park field in the early 18th century.[81] Holendene field, which lay on the west side of Wombourne at Ounsdale, existed by 1316. It was mentioned as Hounden field in 1483.[82] Another open field, Blakeley field, lying south and south-west of

[55] D.C.L., D/DE/II, deed of 5 Dec. 1639; D/DE/IV/3, deeds of 14 Feb. 1710/11, 30 July 1716.
[56] *D.N.B.*; D.C.L., D/DE/II, deed of 5 Dec. 1639.
[57] H.W.R.O. (H.), E 12/S, Wombourne, deed of 31 Aug. 1674; below, econ. hist. (industries).
[58] H.W.R.O. (H.), E 12/S, Wombourne, deed of 31 Aug. 1674.
[59] Below, econ. hist.
[60] W.S.L., Sale Cat. E/4/25; local inf.
[61] *Tax. Eccl.* 243.
[62] *Valor Eccl.* iii. 104.
[63] *L. & P. Hen. VIII*, xvi, p. 329.
[64] Ibid. p. 465; *S.H.C.* n.s. vi (2), 279–80; below, Woodford Grange.
[65] L.J.R.O., B/A/15/Wombourne.
[66] *Cal. Pat.* 1358–61, 470–1.
[67] *Valor Eccl.* iii. 104.
[68] Above, p, 190; *Cal. Pat.* 1554–5, 23; 1555–7, 35; *S.H.C.* xvii. 225; B.R.L., Keen 394A.

[69] P.R.O., C 142/76, no. 35; *Cal. Pat.* 1566–9, p. 409; *S.H.C.* xiii. 274; *V.C.H. Staffs.* xvii. 18.
[70] S.R.O., D. 2/2.
[71] *V.C.H. Staffs.* iv. 54.
[72] Ibid.; *V.C.H. Staffs.* ii. 343–4; *S.H.C.* v (1), 180.
[73] *S.H.C.* v (1), 111–12; *S.H.C.* 1928, 10, 14, 22–3.
[74] *S.H.C.* 1928, 18, 26; S.R.O., Tp. 1226, bdle. XXXII, deed of 16 Feb. 1646/7.
[75] W.S.L., M. 476.
[76] S.R.O., Tp. 1226, bdle. XXXII, draft deed n.d.
[77] *S.H.C.* 1928, 28–9; B.R.L., Keen 394A; S.R.O., Tp. 1226, bdle. XXXII, deed of 16 Feb. 1646/7.
[78] B.R.L., Keen 394A and B.
[79] W.S.L., M. 476; B.R.L., Keen 394F.
[80] S.R.O., Tp. 1226, parcel F.
[81] L.J.R.O., B/V/6/Wombourne; S.R.O., Tp. 1226, bdle. XXXII, draft deed n.d.
[82] B.R.L., Keen 394A; S.R.O. 3297/22/4; W.S.L., S.MS. 36, no. 14.

Wombourne village, was mentioned in 1612. It still existed in 1698, and in the mid 18th century there were still open-field strips in Planks and Minifarm fields south of Planks Lane.[83]

Orton had at least three open fields, one of them apparently shared with Wombourne for a time. Selions in 'Slouthm' field were mentioned in 1419.[84] Chapel field existed by the mid 16th century; it lay north-west of Orton hamlet with selions on Ebstree Hill. It was still open in 1745.[85] Nether field, mentioned in 1607,[86] was possibly the same field as Low field, mentioned in 1681.[87] Low field lay south of Orton and adjoined Wombourne's Putley field.[88] The Putley field which was mentioned in 1666 and 1702 as one of Orton's three open fields was apparently Low field under another name.[89] Low field was still open in 1745.[90] Loming or Lawning field to the west was mentioned from 1623. By 1698 it was known as Lane End field, but the name Lawning field was again used in the early 18th century. It was still open in 1737.[91]

There were two open fields at Woodhouse by the earlier 14th century, Wheat field and Wood field.[92] There was an Old field in 1442, the name Old possibly being a variant of Wood.[93] Both Old and Wheat fields were mentioned in 1521.[94]

A field at Swindon was mentioned in 1338.[95] There was a field called Middle field in 1366; the name suggests that there were other fields at that date, and Hinksford field was named in 1412.[96] In 1628 the three fields of Swindon were Middle, Hinksford, and Liddiatt fields.[97] Hinksford field was mentioned in 1670 and Middle field in 1675. Liddiatt field was still open in 1708.[98] Butts in Greenhill field in Swindon were mentioned in 1765.[99] A decision by the manor court in 1676 to transfer the duties of the hayward to the headborough of Swindon[1] may suggest a reduction in the extent of the open fields.

Temporary inclosure of the waste for cultivation was in progress in the early 17th century. In 1612 Hugh Wrottesley of Woodford Grange secured permission from the freeholders to plough up for periods of three years until 1644 some 40 a. of common in Orton called the Bratches.[2]

There were 4 a. of meadow in Wombourne in 1086 and another 4 a. in Orton.[3] Common meadow survived in Wombourne in 1612 when a dole of meadow near Blakeley field was mentioned.[4] Doles in Adams meadow in Orton were mentioned in 1607, and New meadow in Orton was still open in 1729.[5] A dole meadow in Swindon was mentioned in 1670.[6]

The main area of waste in the parish lay in Swindon. Chasepool common west of Smestow brook was waste in 1086 and lay in the forest.[7] Pasture rights there were recorded in 1613 and 1648.[8] Swindon heath, east of Smestow brook, was mentioned in 1676.[9] Parts of Chasepool common had been inclosed by 1624 when crops were being grown there, but some 1,500 a. of Chasepool and Swindon commons remained in 1796 when most was inclosed under an Act of 1793. The remaining 33½ a. of Swindon common was inclosed in 1825 under an Act of 1808.[10] In the early 17th century there was waste in Orton called the Bratches.[11] Wombourne common, lying south and south-west of the village and adjoining Swindon common,[12] was partly inclosed by 1812: a plot of 50 a. was then advertised for sale.[13] Some 420 a. of common in Wombourne and Orton, including Bratch heath, were inclosed in 1825 under the 1808 Act.[14]

Rye, barley, peas, and oats were grown in the parish in the 1590s. At Orton in the autumn of 1615 a farm had growing wheat worth £18, and crops in the barn consisted of barley (£9), rye (£8), peas (20s.), and oats (20s.). The same crops were grown by Walter Woodhouse and by John Bird of Swindon in the mid 1630s and by John Faulkner of Swindon in 1699.[15]

Goats were kept in the mid 1250s,[16] and sheep farming was practised by the 14th century. There were two shepherds at Orton in 1327, and the theft of 20 sheep there was recorded in 1386.[17] In the later 16th and the 17th century flocks of 80 sheep and over were not uncommon. John Bate of Orton had a flock of 113 sheep worth £13 c. 1570 and William Smith of Wombourne had a flock of 80 worth £10 and a stock of wool worth £3 15s. in 1581. Robert Smith of Orton had 120 sheep and 40 lambs worth £28 in 1603, and at Wombourne John Smith had 130 sheep and lambs worth £53 in 1638.[18] The extensive waste at Chasepool in Swindon provided pasture for sheep. Walter Wrottesley had a sheepcot at Chasepool in 1598, and in 1613 a lease of Greens Lodge included pasturage for 600 sheep on the

[83] L.J.R.O., B/V/6/Wombourne; S.R.O., Tp. 1322, map.
[84] S.H.C. 1928, 44-5.
[85] S.H.C. 1915, 355; W.S.L. 55/164/52; S.R.O. 3279/24/3; 3279/29.
[86] W.S.L. 55/161/52.
[87] S.R.O., D. 740/8/18.
[88] Ibid.; S.R.O. 3279/29; S.R.O., D. 2/2, Orton f. 45; D.C.L., R. H. Wyatt's plan of Wombourne par. 1816.
[89] S.R.O., Tp. 1226, parcel F; B.R.L., Keen 355C.
[90] S.R.O. 3297/24/3.
[91] S.R.O., Tp. 1273/11, 1623 survey; S.R.O. 3279/27-9; S.R.O., D. 740/8/7; L.J.R.O., B/V/6/Wombourne; B.R.L., Keen 355B.
[92] S.H.C. 1928, 33-4.   [93] Ibid. 47-9.
[94] Ibid. 53.
[95] P.R.O., E 32/281, m. 6d.
[96] W.S.L. 55/52, nos. 148, 151.
[97] W.S.L. 14/52, no. 1.
[98] D.C.L., D/DE/I/2; D/DE/III, ct. of 1675 and doc. recording pains 1708.
[99] D.C.L., D/DE/I/4.
[1] D.C.L., D/DE/III.

[2] S.R.O., D. 740/8/7.
[3] V.C.H. Staffs. iv. 54.
[4] L.J.R.O., B/V/6/Wombourne.
[5] S.R.O., D. 740/8/4; S.R.O. 3279/29.
[6] D.C.L., D/DE/I/2.
[7] Above.
[8] D.C.L., D/DE/II; W.S.L. 55/165/52.
[9] D.C.L., Wombourne and Swindon manorial.
[10] L.J.R.O., B/C/11, John Parker (1624); S.R.O., Q/RDc 53 and 71; S.H.C. 1941, 17-18.
[11] Above.
[12] S.H.C. 1928, 49-50; D.C.L., D/DE/III, ct. of 28 Mar. 1575; S.R.O. 3297/22/4.
[13] Wolverhampton Chron. 8 Apr. 1812.
[14] S.R.O., Q/RDc 71; S.H.C. 1941, 18.
[15] L.J.R.O., B/C/11, Wm. Birde (1591), Ric. Smith (1593), Fra. Lee (1615), Wal. Woodhouse (1635), John Bird (1636), Wm. Faulkner (1700).
[16] S.H.C. v (1), 112.
[17] Ibid. vii (1), 255; xiii. 200.
[18] L.J.R.O., B/C/11, John Bate (1571), Wm. Smith (1582), Rob. Smith (1603), John Smith (1638).

waste.[19] John Bird of Swindon had a flock of 96 sheep and 32 lambs worth nearly £29 in 1636, and in 1667 John Tongue of Swindon had 180 sheep worth £41.[20] In the 1720s some 25 flocks were recorded in Wombourne and Orton, some of them small, others with up to 400 sheep and 100 lambs.[21] At the end of the 18th century the agronomist William Pitt referred to flocks of a mixed breed at Wombourne and Swindon. He thought that they were bred with little attention, although they produced tolerably fine wool for use in making cloth.[22]

Sheep may have been kept for their milk in the 17th century. In 1631 Thomas Green of Wombourne, who had butter and cheese in his house, had a flock of sheep worth £30 and probably numbering over 100 but only 6 cows. At Swindon in 1667 John Tongue had 13 cheeses and a cheese press in his house; besides his large flock of sheep, noted above, he had only 2 cows.[23]

John Bate of Orton had 5 cows and 5 young beasts worth over £7 c. 1570, and at Swindon in 1579 John Horwood had 4 cows, 5 young beasts, and 2 yearlings worth £9 10s. Larger herds were those of Francis Lee of Orton, who had 7 cows, 2 yearling calves, and weaning calves, together worth £21 in 1615; of Edward Woodhouse, who had 8 cows, a bull, 4 weaning calves, and 4 yearlings, together worth £26 6s. 8d. in 1688; and of Thomas Meredith of Wombourne, who had 4 cows and 12 yearlings worth £37 in 1696.[24]

Pigs, whose presence at Swindon is indicated by the place name, were not a major item of stock in the later 16th and earlier 17th century. Herds of 6 or fewer were usual,[25] although in 1615 Francis Lee of Orton had 10 pigs worth £4 and in 1696 Thomas Meredith of Wombourne had 15 worth over £10.[26]

Geese and hens were commonly kept in the later 16th and earlier 17th century. Among the largest flocks recorded then were those of William Rudge of Wombourne, worth 12s. in 1604, and of Francis Lee of Orton, worth 16s. in 1615.[27]

About 1840 there were some 1,100 a. of arable land and 206 a. of meadow or pasture in Wombourne. The balance was similar in Orton, where there were 929 a. of arable land and 133 a. of meadow or pasture. In 1979 crops were grown on 517.1 ha. (1,277½ a.) of the 719.6 ha. (1,778 a.) of farming land returned for Wombourne and Orton; the land was divided among 19 farmers, 15 of them with holdings of less than 50 ha. and only one having over 200 ha.[28] At Swindon there

were 560 a. of arable in the late 18th century; the acreage was considerably increased when land inclosed from Chasepool and Swindon commons in 1796 was brought into cultivation. In 1979 crops were grown on 301.3 ha. (744½ a.) of the 462.2 ha. (1,144½ a.) of farming land returned for Swindon; the land was divided among 10 farmers, 6 of them with holdings of less than 50 ha. and none with more than 200 ha.[29]

Turnips were grown in Wombourne as early as 1726, and land inclosed from the common in Swindon was given over to turnips and barley by the mid 1830s.[30] A five-year Norfolk system of rotation which let clover lie a second year was general in the parish by the earlier 19th century.[31] Barley and wheat were the chief crops in the later 19th century, although swedes, mangolds, and potatoes were grown at Wodehouse Mill farm in the early 20th century.[32] Barley was predominant in 1979, and sugar beet, potatoes, and wheat were also grown.[33]

With the light and sandy soil suited to producing vegetables early in the year, market gardens and nurseries were well established by the early 19th century, presumably supplying the nearby Black Country towns.[34] In 1815 large numbers of fruit trees were advertised for sale by a nurseryman, John Pilsbury; in 1816 George Pilsbury had two nurseries, one in Mill Lane and another at Beggar's Bush south-east of Wombourne village near the Himley boundary.[35] A market gardener named John Pilsbury was living in Gravel Hill in 1851.[36] Horticulture was still important in 1979: of farms which then made returns 4 out of 19 in Wombourne and 2 out of 10 in Swindon were engaged in it full time. The chief vegetables grown were parsnips, carrots, cabbages, and lettuces.[37] In 1981 there was a nursery at Beggar's Bush and another at Orton.

Livestock in 1979 comprised some sheep and pigs, mainly in Swindon, over 300 head of cattle in Wombourne and Swindon, and nearly 1,700 birds in Wombourne.[38]

The Stewponey Association for the Improvement of the Labouring Classes was letting 42 a. in Wombourne to the poor in 1845. By 1851 the land was held as 120 allotment gardens and in 1853 there were 164. The land was leased to the association by the Revd. William Dalton of the Lloyd in Penn; he took it back in 1872.[39]

The wood of Chasepool was mentioned in 1225. The king made a grant of 60 oaks from it in 1227, and further grants were made in the later

[19] S.H.C. N.S. vi (2), 289–90; D.C.L., D/DE/II.
[20] L.J.R.O., B/C/11, John Bird (1636), John Tongue (1667).
[21] S.R.O., Tp. 1226/ADD/D10, Wombourne tithe bks. 1726 and 1727.
[22] Pitt, Agric. Staffs. (1796 edn.), 141. For fulling in the parish, see below, industries.
[23] L.J.R.O., B/C/11, Thos. Green (1631), John Tongue (1667).
[24] Ibid. John Bate (1571), John Horwood (1579), Fra. Lee (1615), Edw. Woodhouse (1688), Thos. Meredith (1696).
[25] Ibid. Wm. Marsh (1578), John Green (1591), Rob. Smith (1603), John Bird (1636), Sam. Downing (1677).
[26] Ibid. Fra. Lee (1615), Thos. Meredith (1696).
[27] Ibid. Wm. Rudge (1604), Fra. Lee (1615).
[28] L.J.R.O., B/A/15/Wombourne and Orton; M.A.F.F.,

agric. returns 1979 (covering Wombourne civil par. as enlarged in 1934).
[29] S.R.O., D. 695/4/30/1; M.A.F.F., agric. returns 1979.
[30] S.R.O., Tp. 1226/ADD/D10, Wombourne tithe bks. 1726, 1727, and 1756; White, Dir. Staffs. (1834), 293.
[31] N.S.J.F.S. xiii. 46.
[32] P.O. Dir. Staffs. (1868; 1876); S.R.O., Tp. 1273/53, Wodehouse Mill Farm sale cat. 1901.
[33] M.A.F.F., agric. returns 1979.
[34] Pitt, Staffs. i. 187; V.C.H. Staffs. vi. 107.
[35] Wolverhampton Chron. 22 Feb. 1815; S.R.O., D. 2/2, Wombourne ff. 8, 25; D.C.L., Wyatt's plan of Wombourne.
[36] P.R.O., HO 107/2017(2).
[37] M.A.F.F., agric. returns 1979.   [38] Ibid.
[39] H.W.R.O. (H.), E 12/S, Stewponey Becher Club II, ann. reps. of the assoc.; White, Dir. Staffs. (1851), 192, 210. For the association see above, Kinver, econ. hist.

13th and the mid 14th century.[40] Land called Hungerwall, on the high ground north and west of Chasepool Lodge, presumably derives the first part of its name from an Old English word meaning a wood on a steep hillside.[41] The area was evidently still well wooded in the mid 16th century but was being given over to arable farming in the 17th century.[42] After the inclosure of Chasepool common in 1796 parts of it were planted with trees, and in 1979 there were 34 ha. (84 a.) of woodland there.[43] Putley wood in Orton was mentioned in 1262 and Putley grove a few years later.[44] Baggeridge Wood straddling the Wombourne-Himley boundary was mentioned in 1295.[45] There were oaks growing on Birch Hill near Woodhouse in the early 16th century.[46] The main area of woodland in Wombourne and Orton c. 1840 lay along Orton Hill at the present Ladywell Wood and Bullmeadow Coppice and south of Blakeley along the Himley boundary.[47] By 1979 there were only 2.3 ha. (6 a.) of woodland remaining.[48]

An abandoned fish pond below Rufford, evidently Rushford on Wom brook, was mentioned in the later 13th century.[49] In 1393 a fishery in both Kingswinford and Wombourne parishes, and presumably on Smestow brook, was stated to be stocked with trout, roach, perch, tench, bream, and eels.[50] A fishery in Wombourne was mentioned in 1432.[51]

A warren on the northern part of Chasepool common was leased by William Ward of Himley in 1639. By the late 1640s it was at least 200 a. in extent and the warrener lived in a lodge. The warren still existed in 1704 but had been abandoned by 1711 when the land was leased for tillage. In 1716, however, it was let to Henry Maneer, a Wolverhampton furrier, for the making of a new warren.[52]

MILLS. There were two mills at Wombourne in 1086, together worth 4s.[53] Two mills on Wom brook were described in 1483 as the mill of Wombourne and the mill of the lord of Dudley;[54] their sites may have been those of the two mills working in the 19th century. There was a mill on the stretch of the brook in the village in 1664.[55] The mill which stood in Mill Lane in the early 19th century was evidently a corn and blade mill by 1758; by 1816 it was a blade mill only.[56] A mill

known as Ham mill stood west of Gravel Hill in 1815; the miller there in 1840, George Prior, was still recorded as a miller in Wombourne in 1860.[57] The sites of the two mills form part of the park laid out along Wom brook in the 1960s and 1970s.

Ludes mill is mentioned in 1458; it probably stood on Wom brook in the Woodhouse area.[58] There was a fulling mill on Wom brook at Woodhouse in 1570. It may have become a corn mill: a malthouse converted from a water corn mill stood at Woodhouse in 1672, and there was again a corn mill there in 1693.[59] A corn mill at Woodhouse was burnt down in 1814. It was rebuilt in 1840 and was grinding corn for cattle feed when it ceased operation c. 1976.[60] The adjoining farmhouse dates from the earlier 18th century.

There was a mill in Orton called Trill mill in 1294; it was then worth an annual 20s. to the lord of Wrottesley. It is probably to be identified as Caldewall mill in Orton, mentioned in 1362. Trill mill was still held by the Wrottesley family c. 1501.[61]

Soon after 1551 William Barnesley built a mill on land given by Thomas Grey as lord of Wombourne and Orton.[62] It was probably Hackley mill in Orton, which was mentioned in 1562 and 1581. In 1623 a water mill in the manor of Wombourne and Orton, recently held by Thomas Barnesley, was in the tenure of Hugh (later Sir Hugh) Wrottesley.[63] He became lord of the manor in 1633; in 1648 a tenant surrendered Hackley mill to his son Sir Walter.[64] The mill in the manor of Wombourne and Orton which William Wollaston bought from John Grey in 1584 seems to have been a second mill. It was presumably the mill which Wollaston sold to Hugh (later Sir Hugh) Wrottesley in 1601.[65] It may be the mill which became Heath forge.

Heath forge was advertised for letting in 1814, and proposals were invited for its conversion into a corn mill or for another purpose. It was called a mill in 1820 but was still occupied by iron-masters.[66] Its conversion into a corn mill evidently dates from 1827 when it was remodelled or rebuilt by Sir John Wrottesley. It stopped working c. 1930.[67] The four-storey brick building still stood in the later 1970s[68] but was subsequently demolished.

[40] Rot. Litt. Claus. (Rec. Com.), ii. 80, 196; Close R. 1268-72, 199, 305; P.R.O., E 32/313.
[41] D.C.L., D/DE/IV/3, deeds of 3 Oct. 1650, 14 Feb. 1710/11, 5 Aug. 1778; Eng. Place-Name Elements, i (E.P.N.S. xxv), 233.
[42] P.R.O., REQ 2/24/44; above.
[43] White, Dir. Staffs. (1834), 293; M.A.F.F., agric. returns 1979.
[44] S.H.C. v (1), 139, 144; W.S.L., S.MS. 201 (i), p. 266.
[45] S.H.C. 1928, 23.   [46] Ibid. 54.
[47] L.J.R.O., B/A/15/Wombourne and Orton.
[48] M.A.F.F., agric. returns 1979.
[49] Cat. Anct. D. iii, C 3031; S.H.C. 1928, 13-14, 25; W.S.L., S.MS. 386/2, no. 214.
[50] S.H.C. xv. 61-2.
[51] Ibid. xvii. 146.
[52] D.C.L., D/DE/IV/3; H.W.R.O. (H.), E 12/S, Staffs. legal papers, draft articles of agreement 1704.
[53] V.C.H. Staffs. iv. 54.
[54] W.S.L., S.MS. 36, no. 14.
[55] B.R.L., Keen 394E, which refers to a mill on Bate brook, a name given to the stretch of Wom brook in the village

(above, introduction).
[56] Below, p. 214.
[57] S.R.O. 3279/22/4; L.J.R.O., B/A/15/Wombourne, no. 451; P.O. Dir. Staffs. (1860).
[58] B.R.L., Keen 394A. For Wom brook as Lude or Lyde brook see above, introduction.
[59] S.R.O., Tp. 1226, bdle. IV, no. 19; bdle. XXXII, deed of 21 May 1672; P.R.O., C 7/377/106.
[60] Wolverhampton Chron. 27 Apr. 1814; Sherlock, Ind. Arch. Staffs. 204-5; local inf. (1981).
[61] S.H.C. N.S. vi (2), 70, 251; Cal. Close, 1360-4, 445.
[62] P.R.O., C 1/1319, no. 71.
[63] John Rylands Univ. Libr. of Manchester, Ryl. Ch. 130; H.W.R.O. (H.), E 12/S, Bobbington and Enville, valor of lands of John Grey 1581; S.R.O., Tp. 1273/11, 1623 survey.
[64] S.R.O., D. 740/8/13; above, manors and other estates.
[65] S.H.C. xv. 159; W.S.L., D. 1933, vol. 1506/34, p. 64.
[66] Wolverhampton Chron. 19 Jan. 1814; D.C.L., S.C. 10.
[67] Sherlock, Ind. Arch. Staffs. 204; A. Dunphy, 'A Geography of Parishes of Wombourne and Lower Penn' (Dudley Teachers' Centre, 1972; copy in Wolv. C.L.), p. 15b.
[68] Brook, Ind. Arch. W. Midlands, 144.

There was a mill at Smestow in 1816, and in 1839 it was stated to have been recently repaired. By 1972 the building was used for storage.[69]

By the mid 16th century there was a corn mill on Smestow brook at Swindon converted from a fulling mill formerly owned by Halesowen abbey. It was turned into a forge in the mid 17th century.[70]

Hollow mill on the west bank of Smestow brook at Hinksford was mentioned in 1678.[71] In 1721 it was being used to grind timber for dye stuffs.[72] It had been converted into a forge by 1779 and was still used as such in 1816.[73] By 1851 there was a miller at Hinksford,[74] presumably working Hollow mill as a corn mill. It was disused by the early 20th century.[75] Some of the buildings, but not the mill itself, survived in 1980 as Hollow Mill Farm, then occupied by a riding school.

There was a corn mill at Greensforge further south on Smestow brook before 1602; by then it had been converted into a hammer mill. One of the blade mills near the site of the hammer mill had been turned into a corn mill by 1733.[76] It was rebuilt in the late 19th century, and it then continued to be used as a corn mill until c. 1925.[77]

There was a windmill in Wombourne by 1358.[78] Kenes mill which existed in 1458 may be identifiable with Kems mill, which stood near Cockshoot Hill south-east of Swindon in the early 18th century and was presumably a windmill.[79] There was a windmill in Blakeley field south of Wombourne in 1612; it was held by John Smith and was known as Hills mill in 1635.[80] It was evidently rebuilt on the same or a nearby site west of Green Hill by Edward Smith before 1655. He still held it in 1674, and it was presumably the mill known as Mr. Smith's mill in 1729.[81] At some date there was evidently a windmill at the top of Windmill Bank in Wombourne village; the road was so named by 1816, but no mill existed then.[82] In 1840 there was a windmill between the present School Road and Withymore Lane.[83]

INDUSTRIES. Ironmaking was in progress in the parish by the late 16th century and continued until 1976. Land at Woodhouse beside the

Wombourne–Sedgley road was leased in 1580 to Nicholas Smith of Sedgley, a 'branner', as the site for a bloomsmithy and a 'bransmithy'.[84] Two smithies in the Pool House road area were mentioned c. 1585.[85] By the earlier 17th century there were three forges in the parish, Greens, Heath, and Swin.[86]

A newly built hammer mill on Smestow brook at Greensforge was mentioned in 1602; it replaced a corn mill.[87] It was one of several ironworks which Thomas Foley transferred to his son Philip in 1669.[88] Dud Dudley was working there in 1674.[89] In 1675 Philip Foley leased the forge to Sir Clement Clerke and John Forth and in 1676, after that partnership had broken up, to Henry Cornish, John Langworth, and Thomas Sergeant. In 1681 it was leased to John Wheeler and Richard Avenant.[90] By 1708 the forge had been pulled down.[91]

Heath forge at the confluence of Wom and Smestow brooks may have been the hammer mill in Wombourne which was converted from a corn mill c. 1600 and may also be identifiable as the mill sold to Hugh Wrottesley in 1601.[92] Sir Walter Wrottesley owned Heath forge in 1650 when it was in the tenure of Thomas Foley.[93] It passed to Philip Foley in 1669 and was included in the leases of 1675, 1676, and 1681.[94] Ironworking there had probably ceased by 1814.[95]

There was a forge on Smestow brook at Swindon by the 1620s.[96] It may have been the forge there occupied by a Mr. Lidiat in 1636; sparks from it then caused a fire which burnt down seven houses and other buildings.[97] In 1647 the corn mill at Swindon was leased by the Jordens of Dunsley in Kinver to Thomas Foley, who converted it into a forge. He bought it from the Jordens in 1668; timber, charcoal, coals, pig-iron, and other materials were then stored on land adjoining it.[98] It too passed to Philip Foley in 1669 and was included in the three subsequent leases.[99] The forge was being worked in the 1730s by Francis Homfray of Old Swinford (Worcs.) (d. 1737).[1] By 1756 it was worked by his son Francis of Wollaston Hall, in Old Swinford, who still occupied it in 1768.[2] It was leased in 1788 to Francis and his sons Jeston and Francis and evidently sold in 1790 to the sons. The third

[69] S.R.O., D. 2/2, Wombourne f. 26; D.C.L., Wyatt's plan of Wombourne; Staffs. Advertiser, 2 Mar. 1839; Dunphy, 'Wombourne and Lower Penn', p. 15b.
[70] Above, p. 208; below, industries.
[71] D.C.L., D/DE/IV/4.
[72] M. W. Flinn, Men of Iron, 26.
[73] D.C.L., D/DE/I/5, deed of 9 Aug. 1782; S.R.O., D. 2/2, Swindon f. 60.
[74] P.R.O., HO 107/2017(2).
[75] J. I. Langford, Towpath Guide to Staffs. and Worcs. Canal, 129. [76] Below, industries.
[77] Brook, Ind. Arch. W. Midlands, 146; Soc. for Protection of Ancient Buildings, Watermill Survey (1967).
[78] S.H.C. xii (1), 155.
[79] B.R.L., Keen 394A; H.W.R.O. (H.), E 12/S, Himley estate rental 1704–9; D.C.L., D/DE/III, doc. recording pains 1723; D.C.L., Wyatt's plan of Wombourne; S.R.O., D. 2/2, Swindon f. 58.
[80] L.J.R.O., B/V/6/Wombourne.
[81] W.S.L. 55/173/52; B.R.L., Keen 394G; S.R.O., D. 3279/22/4, plan of Wm. Tennant's estate, nos. 657–9.
[82] S.R.O., D. 2/2, Wombourne f. 20.
[83] L.J.R.O., B/A/15/Wombourne, no. 16; P.R.O., HO 107/2017(2).

[84] S.R.O., Tp. 1226, folder 1.
[85] Ibid. bdle. I, no. 41.
[86] V.C.H. Staffs. ii. 114.
[87] H.W.R.O. (H.), E 12/F/VI/KAc/58; ibid. E 12/S, Wombourne, deed of 19 June 1602.
[88] Business Hist. xiii. 22.
[89] Above, manors and other estates.
[90] Business Hist. xiii. 29, 31.
[91] H.W.R.O. (H.), E 12/S, Wombourne, deed of 17 Jan. 1707/8.
[92] V.C.H. Staffs. ii. 113; above (mills).
[93] H.W.R.O. (H.), E 12/F/VI/KAc/2.
[94] Business Hist. xiii. 22, 29, 31.
[95] Above, mills. [96] V.C.H. Staffs. ii. 114.
[97] Shaw, Staffs. ii, p. *216.
[98] P.R.O., CP 25(2)/486/23 Chas. I Mich. no. 17; D.C.L., D/DE/I/2.
[99] Business Hist. xiii. 22, 29, 31.
[1] H.W.R.O. (H.), E 12/F/P7; H. S. Grazebrook, Collns. for Genealogy of Noble Families of Henzey, Tittery, and Tyzack (Stourbridge, 1877), 53 n.
[2] S.R.O., Tp. 1226/ADD/D10, Wombourne tithe bk. 1756; H.W.R.O. (H.), E 12/S, Wombourne, deed of 21 June 1768.

Francis was working the forge at his death in 1809, and in 1811 it was advertised for sale by auction.[3] In 1816 it was stated to have been lately owned and occupied by Thomas Homfray.[4] It was later run by P. Homfray and R. Shinton, who dissolved their partnership in 1820.[5] In 1834 it was owned by George and Edward Thorneycroft of Wolverhampton and produced bar iron and wire rods. Output was apparently on a small scale: in 1841 there were only two forgemen, one iron roller, and one furnacer living in Swindon.[6] The forge was acquired by Eli Richards, Joseph Shaw, and Richard Brown in 1852. Brown and Shaw died in 1854, and Richards became a bankrupt in 1855. By 1859 the works had been taken over by J. Watkins; from 1862 it was run by William Watkins & Co. New equipment was installed and the works extended; by 1859 there were 13 puddling furnaces, and in 1862 there were 12 with 4 rolling mills.[7] As a consequence the number of iron workers living in Wombourne parish increased considerably. In 1861 there were 48, of whom 32 were puddlers and the remainder rollers, shinglers, and forgemen. Most of the workers lived at Smestow and Blakeley.[8] In 1866 the forge was leased to E. P. and W. Baldwin, the owners from 1899.[9] The number of iron workers in the parish had increased to 73 by 1871, nearly half of them described as labourers; the 17 puddlers were the most numerous group of skilled workers.[10] In 1873 the works comprised 12 puddling furnaces and 2 mills and produced sheet iron.[11] From 1945, when the company became Richard Thomas & Baldwin Ltd., production concentrated on rolling silicon sheets for the electrical engineering industry. The works was closed in 1976,[12] and the buildings were subsequently demolished.

By 1779 Hollow mill at Hinksford was being worked as a forge. It became a corn mill some time between 1816 and 1851.[13]

There was a blade mill at Greensforge by 1657.[14] In 1708 there were two blade mills there. By 1733 one of them had been converted into a corn mill; the other was still working as a blade mill in 1816 and possibly in 1841, when a scythegrinder was living at Greensforge.[15] A blade mill at Woodhouse was mentioned in 1688 and 1693.[16] There was a scythegrinder in

Wombourne in 1695,[17] and there were two in Swindon in 1710.[18] The mill in Mill Lane, Wombourne, was evidently a blade as well as a corn mill by 1758, and by 1816 it was a blade mill only[19] It was probably the old-established scythe manufactory in Wombourne mentioned in 1835, and in 1840 it was occupied by a scythemaker named Thomas Meredith. In 1841 five scythesmiths and grinders were living in Wombourne village. Meredith was still making scythes in 1851.[20]

There was a nailer at Wombourne in 1601, and several other nailers were living there during the 17th century.[21] There was one at Orton in 1658.[22] Nailing was widespread in the parish by the early 19th century. There were 18 nailshops in Wombourne in 1816, some of them in the centre of the village, others in Rookery Road, Battlefield Lane, and Blakeley Lane (later the northern part of Common Road); there were also two nail warehouses in Rookery Road and Blakeley Lane. There were two other nailshops at Orton and the Bratch and four at Swindon. Smestow had five nailshops, three of them in Chapel Lane.[23] There were 174 nail workers in the parish in 1841, most of them living in and around Wombourne village. There were 33 nailers at Blakeley, 18 at Swindon, and 6 at Smestow.[24] By 1851 the number of nailers in the parish had risen to 242, still concentrated in Wombourne village.[25] There followed a decline, although there were still 186 at work in 1861; of these 60 were nail forgers and 4 horse-nail forgers.[26] By 1871 the figure had slumped to 87, of whom 8 were horse-nail forgers, and in 1889 it was stated that there were no nailers remaining.[27] In 1980 two rows of nailers' cottages survived in Rookery Lane and Giggetty Lane, and nailshops in Blakeley had been converted into sheds, garages, and kitchens.[28]

There may have been a fulling mill at Swindon in the mid 13th century: land there once held by William the fuller was then mentioned in a grant by William Englefield to Halesowen abbey. The mill of Swindon was mentioned in 1303–4, and the abbey had a fulling mill on Smestow brook there in 1465. It had been converted into a corn mill by the mid 16th century.[29] About 1540 a tenter for drying woollen cloth was erected in Swindon; the owner planned to build a fulling

[3] S.R.O., D. 695/8/6, sched. of deeds relating to Swindon ironworks; *Wolverhampton Chron.* 6 Mar. 1811; above, Kinver, econ. hist. (iron: Hyde and Gothersley mills).
[4] S.R.O., D. 2/2, Swindon.
[5] D.C.L., Salter and Camm, deed of 4 Feb. 1820.
[6] White, *Dir. Staffs.* (1834), 293; P.R.O., HO 107/1002.
[7] S.R.O., D. 695/8/6; R. Hunt, *Memoirs of Geol. Surv., Mineral Statistics of U.K. 1859*, 50; *1861*, 84; *1862*, 59.
[8] P.R.O., RG 9/1986.
[9] Brochure for Swindon Flower Festival, 1978 (copy in W.S.L. Pamphs. *sub* Wombourne).
[10] P.R.O., RG 10/2929.
[11] Brook, *Ind. Arch. W. Midlands*, 144.
[12] Brochure for Swindon Flower Festival.
[13] Above, mills.
[14] D.C.L., D/DE/IV/3.
[15] H.W.R.O. (H.), E 12/S, Wombourne, deeds of 17 Jan. 1707/8, 23 July 1733; S.R.O., D. 2/2, Swindon f. 62; D.C.L., Wyatt's plan of Wombourne; P.R.O., HO 107/2017(2).
[16] L.J.R.O., B/C/11, Edw. Woodhouse (1688); P.R.O., C 7/377/106.
[17] L.J.R.O., B/C/11, John Downing (1695).

[18] H.W.R.O. (H.), E 12/S, Wombourne, deed of 23 Jan. 1716/17.
[19] Ibid. Kingsley Manor, deeds of 2 and 3 Dec. 1789; S.R.O., D. 2/2, Wombourne f. 8; D.C.L., Wyatt's plan of Wombourne.
[20] Pigot, *Nat. Com. Dir.* (1835); L.J.R.O., B/A/15/Wombourne, no. 88; P.R.O., HO 107/1002, 2017(2); White, *Dir. Staffs.* (1851), 211.
[21] W.S.L. 55/159/52; B.R.L., Keen 394c; S.R.O., Tp. 1226, bdle. XXXII, deed of 26 May 1648; bdle. XLI, deed of 23 Mar. 1640/1; L.J.R.O., B/C/11, Thos. Cartwright (1616), John Deens (1698). [22] W.S.L. 66/47.
[23] S.R.O., D. 2/2; D.C.L., Wyatt's plan of Wombourne.
[24] P.R.O., HO 107/1002.
[25] P.R.O., HO 107/2017(2). [26] P.R.O., RG 9/1986.
[27] P.R.O., RG 10/2929; *V.C.H. Staffs.* ii. 24 (where the date 1888 is given instead of 1889).
[28] Dunphy, 'Wombourne and Lower Penn', 17.
[29] *S.H.C.* 1928, 13; W.S.L., S.MS. 201(i), pp. 263–4; H.W.R.O. (H.), E 12/S, Kinver VI, rents of waste of Kinver forest temp. Edw. I; D.C.L., D/DE/III, ct. of 3 July 1425 and endorsement; B.L. Add. Ch. 42618.

mill there but died before he had done so.[30] There was a fulling mill at Woodhouse in 1570.[31] A clothier was living at Swindon in 1687.[32]

There was malting at Woodhouse by 1672 when, as seen above, the corn mill had been converted into a malthouse. There were four maltsters in the parish in 1834, two in Wombourne and one each in Orton and Swindon; the malthouses in Wombourne stood in the present School Road and Gravel Hill.[33] By 1861 there was a malthouse in Walk Lane; floor malting was still carried on there in 1970. By 1977 it was derelict, and in 1979 flats were built on the site.[34]

Dud Dudley claimed that the first use of pit coal in the making of glass was in the 1620s near his house, Greens Lodge.[35] Land called Glass House Piece lay on the east side of Beggar's Bush Lane south of Rookery Lane in 1816, and there was a glazier's shop in High Street, Wombourne in 1840.[36] A glassmaker was living in Wombourne village in 1851.[37]

A sand deposit at Beggar's Bush was being worked in the late 1780s;[38] the nearby Sandy Hole Lane running south from Rookery Lane was mentioned in 1840.[39] In the early 1880s there were sand pits on the east side of the Staffordshire and Worcestershire Canal near Bumblehole lock north of Ounsdale, at Ounsdale itself, and south of Giggetty.[40] Two other pits were worked in the 1880s at Bullmeadow Coppice in Orton and east of Hinksford Lane near the present Hinksford Gardens.[41] Moulding sand was still dug at Ounsdale in 1916 and at Bumblehole lock and Giggetty in 1921.[42] The pit at Bullmeadow Coppice was disused by 1913;[43] that near Hinksford Gardens was still being worked in 1947.[44] The other main deposit of sand dug in the parish was at Blackhill Plantation on the boundary west of Smestow: a pit there was worked in the 1880s.[45] In 1935 the earl of Dudley developed the site as a sand and gravel quarry called Blackhill Quarry; it covered 21 a. in 1947.[46] In that year the quarry was conveyed to Blackhills (Swindon) Sand and Gravel Co. which held it until 1963 when it was bought by Hoveringham Group Ltd. of Nottingham. By the early 1970s the quarry had been worked out, and by 1980 part of the site had been made into a golf course.[47] There were sand merchants at Ounsdale and Swindon in the 1880s, and four companies dealing in sand were in business in 1940, two at Ounsdale, one at the Bratch, and one at Orton. The sand was used for moulding, for pig-iron beds, and for building.[48]

In the 20th century, and particularly since the 1950s, the western part of the parish has become industrialized. Two factories were opened in the period between the two World Wars. In 1926 Joseph Timms from Sedgley began to make safes and strong boxes in premises off the east end of High Street. In 1938 he moved to the Giggetty end of Planks Lane where in 1981 the Guardian Safe Works was producing steel furniture as well as safes.[49] Ferro (Great Britain) Ltd., a subsidiary of the Ferro Corporation of Cleveland, Ohio, opened a factory on the high ground west of the canal at Ounsdale in 1935. The company originated in 1929 as a sales organization for vitreous enamels made in the corporation's factory at Rotterdam; it operated from the managing director's house in Ounsdale Road. The Wombourne factory was at first small but expanded after the Second World War; ceramic colours and pigments for plastics were added to the products, and an engineering section was established to serve the enamelling industry. Later a chemical plant was opened to supply the plastics industry. About 1955 the 'top-hat' intermittent electric kiln for firing pottery was designed at the factory.[50] After the Second World War two industrial estates were created south of Bridgnorth Road to accommodate overspill industry from Wolverhampton. The smaller, Smestow Bridge, dates from 1954, and by the early 1970s it housed a steel stockholding firm and a firm making spring washers. The second and larger, Heath Mill, by the early 1970s housed firms making a range of equipment for both industrial and domestic use; there was also a bakery. At Ounsdale in the early 1970s, besides Ferro, there were firms making copper products, sheet metal work, and hose connexions and also a plant hire firm; at Brickbridge on Bridgnorth Road was the headquarters of another plant hire firm with interests in sand and gravel working outside the parish.[51]

LOCAL GOVERNMENT. Wombourne parish included Trysull for ecclesiastical purposes until 1888, but in civil matters the two places were distinct; each had its own parish meeting and parish officers. A select vestry was established for Wombourne at the end of 1824 and continued until 1836.[52] Swindon became a separate civil

[30] P.R.O., C 1/1319, no. 71.
[31] Above, mills.
[32] Salop. R.O. 4001/Mar/1, toll bks. (ref. supplied by Dr. P. R. Edwards of the Froebel Inst., Roehampton).
[33] White, *Dir. Staffs.* (1834), 293; L.J.R.O., B/A/15/ Wombourne, nos. 26, 381.
[34] P.R.O., RG 9/1986; Sherlock, *Ind. Arch. Staffs.* 75; *Wombourne Compass* (Nov. 1970; copy in possession of Mrs. May Griffiths); Brook, *Ind. Arch. W. Midlands*, 144; *Wolverhampton Chron.* 19 Oct. 1979.
[35] D. R. Guttery, *From Broad-glass to Cut Crystal*, 5; Dud Dudley, *Mettallum Martis* (1665), 35; *V.C.H. Staffs.* ii. 225 (where the house is wrongly said to be in Kingswinford); above, manors and other estates.
[36] S.R.O., D. 2/2, Wombourne f. 9; D.C.L., Wyatt's plan of Wombourne; L.J.R.O., B/A/15/Wombourne, no. 100b.
[37] P.R.O., HO 107/2017(2).
[38] W.S.L. 21/39.
[39] L.J.R.O., B/A/15/Wombourne, no. 161a.

[40] O.S. Map 6", Staffs. LXVI. NE. (1884 edn.).
[41] O.S. Map 1/2,500, Staffs. LXVI. 16 (1882 edn.), LXVII. 1 (1887 edn.).
[42] S.R.O., D. 691/1, 6; O.S. Map 1/2,500, Staffs. LXVI. 8 (1923 edn.).
[43] O.S. Map 1/2,500, Staffs. LXVII. 1 (1919 edn.).
[44] D.C.L., D/DE/IV/14.
[45] O.S. Map 6", Staffs. LXVI. NE. (1884 edn.), SE. (1887 edn.).
[46] D.C.L., D/DE/IV/4; inscription on surviving building.
[47] Inf. from Hoveringham Group Ltd. (1981).
[48] *Kelly's Dir. Staffs.* (1880; 1884; 1888; 1940); T. H. Whitehead and R. W. Pocock, *Memoirs of Geol. Surv., Dudley and Bridgnorth*, 181.
[49] *Wombourne Compass* (May 1972).
[50] Ibid. (Jan. 1972); *V.C.H. Staffs.* ii. 42.
[51] Dunphy, 'Wombourne and Lower Penn', pp. 17, 18b.
[52] S.R.O., D. 3710/4/1; Wombourne ch., vestry mins. 1835–1941.

parish in 1896. Wombourne civil parish was enlarged in 1934 by the addition of part of Penn parish.[53]

Walter of Orton, lord of Wombourne and Orton, held view of frankpledge by the mid 1250s, paying 5s. for the right.[54] His son William held Michaelmas and Easter great courts each year at Wombourne as well as his courts baron.[55] John Buffery was holding two great courts each year at Wombourne in the early 15th century.[56] Sir Robert Babthorpe's bailiff paid the steward for holding a court at Wombourne in 1428-9, and in 1601 Gilbert Wakering held a court baron there for his manor of Wombourne.[57] Suit at the court of Humphrey, Thomas, and Roger Everdon at Orton was mentioned in 1462.[58] Lord Dudley had view of frankpledge for his manor of Swindon in 1597 and 1602.[59] Spring and autumn courts leet for Himley and Swindon were being held in 1662-3, and at least from 1675 two courts were generally held each year. From 1745 there was an annual court in October; it was still held in 1821.[60] Three-weekly courts baron for Himley and Swindon were being held in 1645-6.[61] The abbot of Halesowen was holding a court for his manor of Wombourne and Swindon by 1425. Courts baron were held until 1677, when the manor was bought by Edward, Lord Ward, and absorbed into the manor of Swindon.[62]

In the mid 1250s Walter of Orton paid 5s. for sheriff's aid and 20d. for hundred aid.[63] Frithfee was due from lands at Wombourne in 1309, and in 1518-19 a tenant in Wombourne had to pay a due known as frith and stuff in addition to chief rent to the lord and suit to hundred and manor courts. From at least 1826 until 1835 the vestry paid a biennial rent of 17s. 6d. for 'Sheriff's Tooth and Frith Silver'.[64]

A constable of Wombourne existed in the late 1430s and a constable of Orton in 1605.[65] There was a single constable for Wombourne and Orton in 1662, but in 1666 the two places were separate constablewicks.[66] A headborough for Swindon was appointed by the manor court in 1638, and the court was still appointing in 1821.[67] By 1825 the vestry was settling the bills of the constables of Wombourne and Orton and of the Swindon headborough, and it was still doing so in the mid 1830s. In 1827 it ordered a constable's staff to be delivered to the headborough of Swindon for the use of that liberty.[68] In 1676 the manor court decided that the headborough should take over the hayward's duties.[69]

In 1732 stocks at Swindon were the responsibility of the headborough.[70] At Wombourne stocks stood outside the entrance to the church-yard and were still there in 1837.[71] In the mid 18th century a pound stood on the north-east corner of Windmill Bank and Church Street.[72] In 1827 the vestry built a pound in the garden of the poorhouse in Rookery Lane. The vestry appointed the Wombourne highway surveyor as keeper in 1887.[73] There had evidently been a pound in Orton before the early 19th century: Penstone Lane was then known as Pound Lane, with land called Pound leasow and Pound meadow lying on either side of it north-east of the hamlet.[74]

Two churchwardens were recorded for Wombourne from the mid 16th century.[75] From 1870 sidesmen were appointed by the vestry to help the churchwardens suppress unseemly behaviour at the west end of the church, especially during the afternoon and evening services.[76] A parish clerk was mentioned in 1698; in 1830 he was appointed by the vicar.[77]

A surveyor of the highways for Swindon was mentioned in 1732 when the manor court fined him and the headborough for the non-repair of Swindon bridge.[78] A surveyor for Wombourne liberty and another for Orton existed in 1813.[79] From 1836 until 1883 the vestry appointed two surveyors each for Wombourne, Orton and Swindon; from 1879 a paid collector of highway rates was also appointed under the Highways and Locomotives (Amendment) Act of 1878. From 1884 until 1894 two paid surveyors were appointed, one for Wombourne and one for Swindon.[80]

In 1648 the churchwardens were acting as overseers of the poor.[81] Two overseers were recorded from 1785, described in 1826 as for Wombourne and for Orton and Swindon; two sets of three were appointed in 1827, and the number increased from 1831, reaching twelve for Wombourne and seven for Orton and Swindon in 1836. A paid assistant overseer was also appointed from 1830. The vestry was employing a parish surgeon by 1827, and from 1828 it subscribed to the Dudley General Institution for the Relief of Ruptures.[82] In 1836 the parish became part of Seisdon poor-law union.[83]

[53] Above, introduction. [54] S.H.C. v (1), 111.
[55] S.H.C. 1928, 16, 20-1. [56] B.L. Add. Ch. 62561.
[57] S.R.O., Tp. 1226, folder 5, excerpts from rentals; folder 6, Huntbach's notes.
[58] Shaw, Staffs. ii. 215.
[59] S.H.C. xviii (1), 12-13, 20-1.
[60] D.C.L., Himley and Swindon manorial.
[61] D.C.L., Kingswinford ct. rolls, vol. i, p. 347.
[62] D.C.L., Wombourne and Swindon manorial; S.R.O., Tp. 1226, folder 5, ct. roll 9 June 1651; above, manors and other estates. [63] S.H.C. v (1), 111.
[64] S.H.C. 1928, 24 (calling it 'frithfen'); Shaw, Staffs. ii. 215; S.R.O., D. 3710/4/1; Wombourne ch., vestry mins. 1835-1941.
[65] Shaw, Staffs. ii. 215; S.H.C. 1940, 225.
[66] S.H.C. 1923, 86, 112-13; S.H.C. 4th ser. ii. 63.
[67] D.C.L., Kingswinford ct. rolls, vol. i, p. 388; D.C.L., D/DE/III.
[68] S.R.O., D. 3710/4/1; Wombourne ch., vestry mins. 1835-1941, 22 Mar. 1836.
[69] Above, econ. hist. [70] D.C.L., D/DE/II.

[71] S.R.O., Tp. 1226/ADD/K1, 21 Apr. 1770; above, pl. facing p. 81. [72] S.R.O., Tp. 1322, map.
[73] S.R.O., D. 3710/4/1, 24 July, 13 Nov. 1827; Wombourne ch., vestry mins. 1835-1941, 14 Apr. 1887; O.S. Map. 6", Staffs. LXVII. NW. (1921 edn.).
[74] S.R.O., D. 2/1, f. 89; S.R.O., Q/RDc 71; L.J.R.O., B/A/15/Wombourne: Orton, nos. 12, 44a.
[75] S.H.C. 1915, 354; Wombourne ch., churchwardens' accts. 1768-1938.
[76] Wombourne ch., vestry mins. 1835-1941, 21 Apr. 1870, 4 Apr. 1872 sqq.
[77] L.J.R.O., B/V/6/Wombourne; Wombourne ch., churchwardens' accts. 1768-1938; S.H.C. 4th ser. x. 34.
[78] D.C.L., D/DE/II.
[79] Wolverhampton Chron. 10 Nov. 1813.
[80] S.R.O., D. 3710/4/1.
[81] Shaw, Staffs. ii, p. *217.
[82] S.R.O., D. 3710/4/1; Wombourne ch., vestry mins. 1835-1941, 22 and 25 Mar., 28 June 1836.
[83] 3rd Ann. Rep. Poor Law Com. H.C. 546, p. 164 (1837), xxxi.

The two almshouses built in Rookery Road in 1716 seem to have become a parish poorhouse by the late 18th century. They were owned and maintained by the churchwardens in the early 19th century. In 1828 there was mention of the upper and the lower poorhouse. The almshouses were later leased out, presumably after the establishment of the union with its workhouse, and the income was eventually used to establish a new charity.[84]

In 1896 Swindon became a separate civil parish.[85] Both it and Wombourne civil parish remained in Seisdon rural district until 1974 when they became part of South Staffordshire district.[86] The rural district council moved its meeting place from Trysull to Wombourne c. 1930; its offices and those of South Staffordshire district council remained there until 1976.[87]

PUBLIC SERVICES. After a meeting of parishioners in 1857 a drain was made down the centre of the road from the top of Windmill Bank to Wom brook. In 1874 a parochial committee was set up to consider the water supply of Wombourne, and a general meeting in 1875 instructed the inspector of nuisances of Seisdon union rural sanitary authority to inspect wells which were thought to be impure or were inadequately supplied.[88] Under an Act of 1893 a waterworks was built beside the canal at the Bratch by Bilston urban district council to supply the Wombourne area as well as Bilston. Pumping began in 1896 and houses in Wombourne village were connected to the mains in 1897–8. The works was taken over by Wolverhampton corporation in 1959. The buildings are of red brick with decoration in red, buff, and blue bricks and include a castellated engine house with four corner turrets. The two steam engines remained in operation until 1960 when they were replaced by electric plant; they were named Victoria and Alexandra when the works was formally opened in 1897, the year of Queen Victoria's diamond jubilee.[89] At Swindon a village well at the southern end of Church Road continued in use until 1902.[90]

In 1894 Seisdon union rural sanitary authority converted some cottages on the Wombourne side of Bratch Common Road into an isolation hospital, which was enlarged in 1897; in the early 1920s it had 24 beds. It remained in use until some time during the Second World War.[91]

Electricity and gas were generally available by the 1930s. A sewerage scheme for Wombourne village was brought into use in 1939. Extensions to the sewage disposal works south of Bridgnorth Road near Heath House were officially opened in 1962.[92]

In 1831 the vestry gave the overseers permission to appoint a paid watchman.[93] There was a police officer living in Wombourne village by 1851.[94] In 1862 the vestry appointed two constables for Wombourne, one for Orton, and one for Swindon, each with a staff and a pair of handcuffs; the appointment was repeated for Wombourne in 1865.[95] The sub-divisional police station in High Street was opened in 1971, replacing a station in School Road.[96]

A fire brigade was formed by the parish council in 1898.[97] In 1968 a fire station was opened in Giggetty Lane. An ambulance was garaged there from 1971 until an ambulance station was opened on an adjoining site in 1973.[98]

There was a post office at Wombourne by 1845 and another at Swindon by 1884.[99]

CHURCHES. There was a church at Wombourne by 1086. By the later 12th century it had a chapel at Trysull which remained a dependency until 1888. Chapels were opened at Swindon and Blakeley in the 19th century.

The presence of a priest at Wombourne in 1086[1] indicates the existence of a church by then, and the present invocation to St. Benedict Biscop, if original, suggests a pre-Conquest foundation. No other example of the invocation is known, and the Wombourne invocation is given simply as St. Benedict in 1405 and in various sources before the late 19th century. The parish wake, however, is said to have been held in connexion with the feast of St. Benedict Biscop (12 January) before the 19th century.[2]

About 1150 the church was given to Dudley priory by Guy de Offini, his wife Christine, and his son and heir William. The grant was confirmed by Walter, bishop of Coventry (1149–59). Further confirmations were made by Bishop Richard Peche (1161–82) and in 1182 by the pope.[3]

[84] Below, chars. for the poor; Wombourne ch., churchwardens' accts. 1768–1938, levy for almshouses 1802, 1804, 1806; S.R.O., D. 2/1, f. 55; S.R.O., Q/RDc 71.
[85] County of Stafford (Swindon) Conf. Order, 1895 (Local Govt. Bd. Order no. 33,251; copy in S.R.O., C/C/O/1).
[86] O.S. Map 1/100,000, Staffs. Admin. Areas (1967 and 1974 edns.).
[87] Above, pp. 86, 199.
[88] Wombourne ch., vestry mins. 1835–1941, 6 and 25 Mar., 25 Apr. 1856, 25 Mar. 1857, 2 Nov. 1874, 7 June 1875.
[89] B. L. McMillan, Hist. of Water Supply of Wolverhampton 1847–1947 (Wolverhampton, 1947), 41; Seisdon R.D.C. Rep. of M.O.H. for 1897, 7–8 (copy in S.R.O., C/H/1/2/1/8); Wombourne Official Guide [1965], 30–1; Sherlock, Ind. Arch. Staffs. 205–6; above, pl. facing p. 81.
[90] Plaque on well.
[91] Seisdon Union R.S.A. Rep. of M.O.H. for 1894, 8 (copy in S.R.O., C/H/1/2/1/5); Seisdon R.D.C. Rep. of M.O.H. for 1897, 7 (copy in S.R.O., C/H/1/2/1/8); 1921, 5–6; 1938, 3; 1945, 9 (copies in S.R.O., C/H/1/2/2/36); O.S. Map 6", Staffs. 1/2,500 LXVI. 8 (1903 edn.).

[92] D.C.L., D/DE/IV/4; Seisdon R.D.C. Reps. of M.O.H. for 1935, 10; 1938, 9; 1961, 21 (copies in S.R.O., C/H/1/2/2/36); Kelly's Dir. Staffs. (1940).
[93] S.R.O., D. 3710/4/1, 21 June 1831.
[94] P.R.O., HO 107/2017(2).
[95] Wombourne ch., vestry mins. 1835–1941, 7 Apr. 1862, 5 June 1865.
[96] Plaque in entrance; inf. from the police station (1981).
[97] Salop. R.O. 1305/143, 146.
[98] Inf. from Mrs. May Griffiths; Wombourne Compass (Apr. 1973; copy in poss. of Mrs. Griffiths).
[99] P.O. Dir. Staffs. (1845); Kelly's Dir. Staffs. (1884).
[1] V.C.H. Staffs. iv. 54.
[2] L.J.R.O., B/A/1/7, f. 60 (1405); B/C/11, Humph. Woodhouse (1557), Chris. Elyats (1558); J. Ecton, Thesaurus Rerum Ecclesiasticarum (1742), 109; P.R.O., HO 129/379/3/2 (1851); F. Arnold-Forster, Studies in Church Dedications (1899), ii. 56, 60. Lich. Dioc. Dir. first gives the dedication to St. Benedict Biscop rather than St. Benedict in the 1936 edn.
[3] S.H.C. 1941, 55–7; Sir Christopher Hatton's Book of Seals, ed. L. C. Loyd and D. M. Stenton, p. 40.

A vicarage was ordained in 1275.[4] The patronage remained with Dudley priory until its dissolution in 1540. In 1541 the Crown granted the patronage with the rest of the priory's possessions to Sir John Dudley, later duke of Northumberlend.[5] It reverted to the Crown on his attainder in 1553 and evidently passed to Edward, Lord Dudley, who in 1554 and 1555 was granted much of Northumberland's property.[6] On a vacancy in 1555, however, John Grainger and John Shenton, both of Trysull, presented, the prior and convent of Dudley having made a grant of that turn shortly before the Dissolution.[7] Lord Dudley presented in 1561,[8] and his son Edward, Lord Dudley, still held the patronage in 1602.[9] He sold it to Nicholas Paston of Kingswinford, who died in 1622 or 1623, leaving it to his nephew, also Nicholas Paston.[10] After the death of the second Nicholas in 1623 the patronage passed to his daughter Margaret, wife of John Hodgetts.[11] In 1630 John and Margaret Hodgetts conveyed it to John Wollaston, a native of Tettenhall and lord mayor of London in 1643-4.[12] Wollaston died in 1658, leaving the patronage to a group of trustees. Failure to observe his instructions about the appointment of new trustees led to disputes over the patronage in the 1690s, 1750s, and 1790s, but in 1980 it remained in the hands of his trustees.[13]

When the vicarage was ordained in 1275 it was endowed with the altarage of Wombourne and Trysull, tithe of hay from both places, tithe of corn from Swindon, half the tithe of corn from Himley, and mortuaries.[14] Glebe was mentioned in 1318.[15] When the aged William Wylnale resigned the vicarage in 1426, the bishop assigned him a pension of 5 marks, to be paid by the monks of Dudley and charged on the vicarage.[16] By 1535 the vicar's gross income was £13 8s. 4d., from glebe, tithes, and Easter offerings.[17] In 1604 the vicarage was stated to be worth £26.[18] The glebe in 1612 consisted of a house, 28 a. in the fields, and a dole of meadow, worth in all £3 6s. 8d.[19] The vicar's income in 1646 was £30, and he was granted £60 a year from the impropriated tithes of Trysull, sequestrated from Sir Richard Leveson; although there was some initial delay in its payment, it was still being paid in the 1650s.[20] By 1698 the vicar received the great tithes of Swindon and the small tithes of Wombourne, Orton, Trysull, and Seisdon; all were paid in kind except tithes of cows and calves in Wombourne and Orton and

tithe of hay in Trysull and Seisdon. There had been further commutation by 1735.[21] The value of the living in 1735 was £49.[22] When Trysull common was inclosed in 1775 the vicar was allotted 92 a. (later Clan Park farm) in lieu of tithe. In 1796 on the inclosure of common in Swindon he was allotted 234 a. in Swindon instead of tithes there; after a lawsuit he was assigned a further 200 a. there in lieu of the tithes of Chasepool, the land having been allotted in 1796 to the impropriator.[23] His average gross income around 1830 was £643 (£608 net).[24] The vicarial tithes of Wombourne township were commuted for a rent charge of £95 13s. 4d. in 1840 and those of Orton for one of £100 13s. 4d. in 1841.[25] In 1878 Clan Park farm and 456 a. of glebe in Swindon were sold to the earl of Dudley, already the tenant.[26] The gross average income of the vicarage between 1884 and 1887 was £1,126 5s. 4d., consisting of £890 16s. 4d. interest from the proceeds of the 1878 sale, £177 17s. 9d. tithe-rent charge, £48 11s. 3d. rent from the remaining 33 a. of glebe, and £9 from surplice fees; from the income payments were made to the vicar of Swindon and the curate of Trysull.[27] In 1888 Trysull was made a separate parish with an endowment of £6,000 from the capital of the 1878 sale, and the annual payment ceased. In 1898 an endowment of £6,250 was granted to Swindon in place of the annual payment, and the Trysull endowment was increased.[28]

In 1612 there was a vicarage house with a kitchen, a barn, and a 2-a. garden. In 1690 the house consisted of a hall, parlour, kitchen, and buttery, each with a chamber above, two garrets, and a study containing books worth £20. It was probably the vicarage house of timber and brick which stood east of the church in 1830.[29] A new house was built in 1840 on a site in School Road north-east of the church.[30] It was rebuilt on an adjoining site in the early 1950s.[31]

There was a curate at Wombourne in the earlier 1530s as well as one at Trysull.[32] A curate of Wombourne was recorded in 1617, 1637, 1638, and 1640,[33] but the curate at Trysull may have been meant. In 1812 the vicar, T. P. Foley, who was also rector of Old Swinford (Worcs.), appointed James Bevan to serve as his curate at Wombourne at £65 a year; in 1830 Bevan had £60, fees, and the vicarage house. Bevan was also perpetual curate of Tipton by 1834, though living in Wombourne and not officiating at Tipton.[34] In the early 1860s Wombourne had its

[4] L.J.R.O., B/C/4, p. 9.
[5] L. & P. Hen. VIII, xvi, p. 329.
[6] Cal. Pat. 1554-5, 23; 1555-7, 37.
[7] L.J.R.O., B/A/1/15, f. 13v.   [8] Ibid. 5, f. 32v.
[9] S.H.C. ix (2), 108-9; xviii (1), 20-1.
[10] S.R.O., D. 695/4/30/1.
[11] P.R.O., C 60/496, no. 20; C 142/416, no. 26.
[12] P.R.O., CP 25(2)/485/6 Chas. I Mic. no. 45. For Wollaston see above, Tettenhall, introduction.
[13] L.J.R.O., B/A/3/Wombourne; Lich. Dioc. Dir. (1980).
[14] L.J.R.O., B/C/4, p. 9.   [15] S.H.C. 1928, 30.
[16] L.J.R.O., B/A/1/9, ff. 153v.-154.
[17] Valor Eccl. (Rec. Com.), iii. 100.
[18] S.H.C. 1915, 256.
[19] L.J.R.O., B/V/6/Wombourne.
[20] S.H.C. 1915, 356; W.S.L., S.MS. 339 (transcript of Royalist Composition Papers) iv, pp. 140, 149, 151, 155, 157, 169, 175; S.R.O., D. 593/B/3/11.
[21] L.J.R.O., B/V/6/Wombourne.

[22] Return made by Governors of Bounty of Queen Anne (1736), 102.
[23] S.R.O., D. 548/A/PD/1; D. 695/4/30/1; D. 3710/2/52/3; S.R.O., Q/RDc 53A.   [24] Rep. Com. Eccl. Revenues, 508-9.
[25] L.J.R.O., B/A/15/Wombourne.
[26] S.R.O., D. 3710/2/53.
[27] Lond. Gaz. 8 May 1888, p. 2611; Return relating to Glebe Lands in Eng. and Wales, H.C. 307, p. 68 (1887), lxiv.
[28] For Trysull see above, Trysull, church; for Swindon see below.
[29] L.J.R.O., B/C/11, John Dolman (1690); B/V/6/Wombourne; S.H.C. 4th ser. x. 34.
[30] White, Dir. Staffs. (1851), 210.
[31] S.R.O., D. 3710/2/45-6.
[32] S.H.C. 4th ser. viii. 127-8.
[33] L.J.R.O., B/C/11, Wm. Griffyn (1617); Shaw, Staffs. ii, pp. *216-17.
[34] L.J.R.O., B/A/3/Wombourne, 1812; S.H.C. 4th ser. x. 34; White, Dir. Staffs. (1834), 293, 403.

own assistant curate distinct from those serving Trysull and Swindon.[35] A house in Common Road on the Wombourne Park estate was bought for the curate in 1957 and later replaced by one on the Pool House estate.[36]

There was evidently a chantry of St. Mary in the church by 1342 when Adam the mercer of Wombourne assigned to St. Mary of Wombourne a rent of 2 farthings. John Woodhouse left 3s. 4d. to Our Lady's service in his will proved in 1523 as well as money to provide tapers for St. Mary's altar. His son Stephen left 3s. 4d. to Our Lady of Wombourne in his will proved in 1528. The chantry seems to have been that founded by John Bloxwich and endowed, probably in the 1530s, by Agnes Webb (or Penn) with lands worth £1 17s. 6d. a year. In 1548 the endowments of the chantry included a cow and three sheep. The priest's stipend was then £1 14s. 10d. In 1553 the endowments were listed as a house and lands in Wombourne, Our Lady Acre in Chapel field in Orton, and lands in Rushall and Walsall. The last priest received a pension of 53s. 4d. in 1548, and in his will of 1564 he expressed a wish to be buried in the Lady aisle of Wombourne church. Another chantry was stated in 1546 to have been founded by Richard Hurst, and the priest's stipend was then £1 13s. 4d.[37] In 1487 a house and croft called Fordplace and land in Wombourne, formerly the property of the deceased John Wilmyns, were settled to secure prayers for John, his parents, and benefactors, evidently in fulfilment of his wishes.[38]

Puritan influence was marked around the mid 17th century after John Wollaston's purchase of the patronage. The two vicars presented by him, Ithiel Smart (1632–52) and Thomas Willesby (1652–62), were educated at Emmanuel College, Cambridge; the three curates appointed between 1638 and 1652 were also from Emmanuel and included Smart's nephews Nathaniel and Ezekiel.[39] Wombourne was one of the places to which William Pinson, a Wolverhampton attorney, was accused of resorting in the mid 1630s to hear preaching by 'inconformable ministers', instead of attending his parish church.[40] Smart recorded in the parish register that he was absent from Wombourne from 1642 to 1648 'by reason of the wars'.[41] He signed the Testimony in 1648.[42] The puritanism evidently divided the parishioners. In 1650 one of the churchwardens and two other men pulled down the pulpit and reading desk erected in 1633. The following Sunday afternoon the brother of one of them occupied the reading pew and forcibly kept

out the preacher who had been appointed to officiate by Smart and who had already preached in the morning.[43] Smart moved to Ashby De La Zouch (Leics.) in May 1652. His successor Thomas Willesby and a new curate arrived in June; in October a day of thanksgiving for 'the settlement of a ministry' was held at Trysull by the wish of the people there. The Presbyterian divine Richard Baxter, then lecturer at Kidderminster (Worcs.), and Samuel Smith, curate of Kinver, prayed and preached.[44] Willesby was a member of Baxter's Worcestershire Voluntary Association by 1655. He was deprived in 1662; in 1669 he was holding a conventicle in his house in Birmingham. By his will proved in 1683 he left 40s. to buy bibles and copies of Baxter's *Call to the Unconverted* for the poor of Wombourne and Trysull.[45]

By 1767 there was a morning and afternoon service on Sunday. The afternoon service was supported by the parishioners' subscriptions, and some at least regarded it as a lectureship in their gift rather than that of the vicar. They enforced their view for a few years, but by 1772 the duty was performed by the curate who had been the vicar's choice in 1767.[46] In the earlier 1770s holy communion was celebrated four times a year, and there were 80 or more communicants.[47] In 1825, however, the inhabitants petitioned for an afternoon service,[48] and by 1830 there were two services on Sunday, Wombourne and Trysull churches being served alternately by the curate at Wombourne and the curate at Trysull. Holy communion was then celebrated four times a year, and communicants numbered between 30 and 40. There was occasional catechism. Although there was no parochial library, the curate lent out books.[49] By 1871 an offertory collection was taken from communicants on the first Sunday of the month and at festivals. It was extended that year to the whole congregation. It was taken fortnightly by 1916 and that year became weekly.[50] A surpliced choir was introduced at Easter 1872, surplices for eight men and fourteen boys being presented by T. B. Shaw-Hellier of the Wodehouse.[51]

A parish magazine was started in 1886 in place of a parish almanac; from 1970 to 1979 it took the form of a newspaper, the *Wombourne Compass*.[52]

A church was opened at Swindon in 1854.[53] A mission room was opened at Blakeley in 1890 on a site in Chapel Street given by Thomas Barrow of Himley (d. 1879).[54] It was replaced in 1957 by the mission church of the Venerable Bede in Giggetty Lane, designed by B. A. Miller of

[35] *Lich. Dioc. Ch. Cal.* (1862).
[36] S.R.O., D. 3710/2/47–9; inf. from Mrs. May Griffiths.
[37] *S.H.C.* 1915, 354–6; 1928, 36, 54–5; *Cal. Pat.* 1560–3, 406–7; 1563–6, pp. 64, 455; S.R.O., Tp. 1226, bdle. I, no. 32; Tp. 1226/43, will of John Woodhouse 1523; S.R.O., D. 1287/1/2, survey of Walsall manor, 1576, m. 10.
[38] *S.H.C.* 1928, 52.
[39] Ibid. 1915, 356; Shaw, *Staffs.* ii, pp. *216–17.
[40] A. G. Matthews, *Cong. Churches of Staffs.* 9–11; G. P. Mander, *Wolverhampton Antiquary*, i. 260–3.
[41] S.R.O., D. 3710/1/1, following entries for 1647.
[42] *Calamy Revised*, ed. A. G. Matthews, 557.
[43] S.R.O., Q/SR A.1650/1, no. 5; Shaw, *Staffs.* ii, p. *216; *Cal. S.P. Dom.* 1650, 247.
[44] Shaw, *Staffs.* ii, p. *217; *D.N.B.* s.v. Baxter.
[45] *Calamy Revised*, 531; Matthews, *Cong. Churches of*

Staffs. 28 n., 88; W. A. Shaw, *Hist. of Eng. Church 1640–60*, ii. 153, 455.
[46] S.R.O., Tp. 1226/1/14, 28 Oct. 1767; Tp. 1226/ADD/K1, 4 June, 7 July, 18 Aug., 28 Sept. 1767, 22 Aug. 1768, 22 Jan. 1769, 21 Apr., 30 July 1770, 30 Apr., 7 May, 6 Aug. 1772.
[47] L.J.R.O., B/V/5/1772.
[48] S.R.O., D. 3710/4/1, 20 Sept. 1825.
[49] *S.H.C.* 4th ser. x. 34.
[50] S.R.O., D. 3710/4/1, 13 Apr. 1871, 4 Apr. 1872, 18 May 1916, 12 Apr. 1917.
[51] Ibid. 4 Apr. 1872.
[52] Trysull vicarage, Bk. of References, p. 37. There is a set of *Wombourne Compass* in the possession of Mrs. May Griffiths.   [53] See below.
[54] *Lich. Dioc. Ch. Cal.* (1891), 161; O.S. Map 1/2,500, Staffs. LXVI. 12 (1903 edn.); P.R.O., C 54/18516.

Liverpool. The site and £1,000 were given by Miss E. M. P. Shaw-Hellier.[55] The 1890 building still stood in 1980, adapted as a house.

The church of *ST. BENEDICT BISCOP* is built of pink sandstone and consists of a chancel with a north vestry and organ chamber, a four-bay nave with north and south aisles, a north side chapel, a south porch, and a west tower with a spire. Nothing is known of the appearance of the church which existed by 1086. In 1234, after a fire, the king granted the vicar 10 trees from Kinver forest for making rafters.[56] At some stage a church consisting of a chancel and a nave had a three-bay north aisle added, mentioned as the Lady aisle in 1564 and probably existing by 1342;[57] a blocked doorway survives at its west end. The tower and spire date from c. 1400. There was a porch in 1639 when a gate was made for it 'and rails done about it at the top that idle and vagrant people might not lodge therein as in former times'. It had been demolished by 1830.[58] There was a west gallery by 1736 when Edward Sherwin built a north extension to it to provide himself with a family pew.[59] In 1761 a faculty was granted for the erection of a north gallery containing four family pews and a fifth pew for the singers.[60] An organ built by Abraham Adcock of London was installed in the west gallery by Sir Samuel Hellier in 1767. At the same time work was carried out on the spire and Hellier gave a dragon weathervane.[61] In 1782–3 'the back oile', presumably the north aisle, was rebuilt, still with a gallery.[62] A new north gallery was erected in 1814–15; at the same time a vestry room was built in the tower, a new pulpit and reading desk were installed, and the church was repewed.[63] It was probably then that the singers were moved to the west gallery.[64]

The east end was rebuilt in 1840–1 to the design of Robert Ebbels, then of Tettenhall Wood: north and south transepts were added with a shallow sanctuary, and extra pews and seats were installed in the transepts and the crossing. A south porch was also added. The cost was met by subscriptions and by grants from the Diocesan Church Building Society and the Incorporated Society for the Building and Enlarging of Churches.[65] A font, which had been lacking in 1830, had been installed by 1841.[66]

In 1866–7 the church was largely rebuilt to the design of G. E. Street in a late 13th-century style; only the tower and the walls of the north aisle and of the north transept were left. The new parts included the chancel with a north vestry and an organ chamber, and a south aisle with a south porch. The spire was partially taken down and was rebuilt 4 ft. higher; the dragon on the top, being found too heavy, was replaced with a cross and new vane and at some date was re-erected on the stables at the Wodehouse, where it survived in 1981. The galleries were removed, and the box pews were replaced with benches. The two-decker pulpit in the south-east corner of the nave was replaced with a new pulpit on the north side of the chancel arch, later moved to the south side. The font was moved from the north side of the chancel arch to the west end by the porch. Much of the cost was met by subscription, a grant from the Diocesan Church Building Society, and a loan from the Public Works Loan Commissioners.[67] A new organ by Bevington & Sons of Soho, London, was installed in 1870.[68] In 1954 the north transept, then used as a choir vestry, was converted into a side chapel; the base of the tower became the choir vestry, which was extended eastward in 1963.[69]

The plate includes a silver chalice and paten, probably those mentioned in 1552, when there was also a maslin cross. A silver chalice, paten, and bread plate dating from 1637 were the gift of John Wollaston and are duplicates of those which he gave to Trysull. A silver repoussé dish, thought to be Portuguese and possibly 16th-century, was given in 1701 by the Revd. Edward Smith, son of Edward Smith of Wombourne. A pewter tankard with lid is dated 1740. A silver-gilt flagon, dish, christening bowl, chalice, and paten are dated 1812 and were bought with money left for the purpose by Sir Samuel Hellier (d. 1784).[70]

There were four bells and two sacring bells in 1552 and 1553.[71] A peal of six cast in 1744 by Henry Bagley of Chacombe (Northants.) was, in part at least, the gift of Samuel Hellier of the Wodehouse. Two trebles were given by T. B. Shaw-Hellier in 1890. The bells were retuned and rehung in 1953 to commemorate the coronation of Elizabeth II.[72] A clock was repaired in 1634. A clock with chimes was installed in 1888 to mark Queen Victoria's golden jubilee.[73]

The monuments include one to R. B. Marsh (d. 1820) by Sir Francis Chantrey.[74]

The churchyard was mentioned in 1316.[75] A new gate was erected in 1633, and in 1634 the churchyard was newly fenced.[76] It had a wall by the late 17th century.[77] New lich gates were

[55] S.R.O., D. 3710/2/62–7; *Wombourne Compass* (May 1970).
[56] *Close R.* 1231–4, 427.
[57] Above (chantry of St. Mary).
[58] Shaw, *Staffs.* ii, p. *217; *S.H.C.* 4th ser. x. 34.
[59] L.J.R.O., B/C/5/Wombourne.
[60] Ibid.
[61] S.R.O., D. 3710/3/1; S.R.O., Tp. 1226/ADD/K1, 25 Dec. 1766 to 1 June 1767.
[62] Wombourne ch., churchwardens' accts. 1768–1938; S.R.O., Tp. 1226/ADD/K1, 16 Nov. 1780; K2, 21 Sept., 7 Oct., 28 Nov. 1782.
[63] Wombourne ch., churchwardens' accts. 1768–1938; S.R.O., D. 3710/3/2; *Staffs. Advertiser*, 3 May 1815.
[64] S.R.O., D. 3710/3/29.
[65] Ibid. 3/3, 22–30, 39; W.S.L., Staffs. Views, xii. 135. For a view of 1837 see above, pl. facing p. 81.
[66] *S.H.C.* 4th ser. x. 34–5.
[67] L.J.R.O., B/C/5/Wombourne; S.R.O., D. 3710/2/1, p. [1]; ibid. 3/4; ibid. 3/41/1–5; *Staffs. Advertiser*, 24 Aug. 1867. Inf. on the removal of the dragon has been supplied by Mrs. Griffiths.
[68] *Lich. Dioc. Ch. Cal.* (1871), 76; S.R.O., D. 3710/3/42.
[69] S.R.O., D. 3710/3/14–16.
[70] *T.B.A.S.* lxxiii. 2–3, 6–7, 10–11, 32–3, 40–1; *Trans. Lich. and S. Staffs. Arch. and Hist. Soc.* iii. 20–1; *S.H.C.* vi (1), 190; S.R.O., Tp. 1226, bdle. XXXII, excerpts from wills of Sir Sam. Hellier. The chalice was described as partly gilt in 1553: *S.H.C.* 1915, 354.
[71] *S.H.C.* n.s. vi (1), 190; *S.H.C.* 1915, 354.
[72] Lynam, *Church Bells*, 37 and pl. 121; *Trans. Old Stafford Soc.* 1952–3, 15; S.R.O., D. 3710/3/5, 13.
[73] Shaw, *Staffs.* ii, p. *216; plaque in base of tower.
[74] Pevsner, *Staffs.* 327.
[75] *S.H.C.* 1928, 25–6.
[76] Shaw, *Staffs.* ii, p. *216.
[77] S.R.O., Tp. 1226, folder 1/ii.

erected in 1767.[78] In 1830 there was a wall on the south with hedges on the other three sides, and in 1860 a meeting of ratepayers resolved to build a wall on the east side in consideration of an addition there from the vicarage garden.[79] The churchyard was extended in 1883 by the addition of 1,752 sq. yds. given by the Revd. John Bradney-Marsh of the Lloyd.[80] In 1901 John Roderick and J. B. Clarke of Birmingham, owners of the Lloyd estate, gave 1½ a. extending north from the churchyard to School Road; the land was to be added to the churchyard as required and in the mean time to be used as a public recreation ground. It was consecrated as part of the churchyard in 1952.[81] A cross was erected in 1913 at the expense of the vicar, E. P. Nicholas, to commemorate the formation of a branch of the Church of England Men's Society.[82]

The registers begin in 1570 and are complete.[83]

In 1838 it was stated that a chapel of ease was needed at Swindon.[84] One was consecrated in 1854. The cost of building it was met by subscription and grants from the Lichfield Diocesan Church Extension Society, the Corden Fund, and the Incorporated Building Society; the last was made on condition that 350 free seats were provided for the poorer inhabitants.[85] In 1867 a district chapelry was assigned covering the township of Swindon.[86] The living, at first a perpetual curacy and a vicarage from 1868, was in the gift of the vicar of Wombourne, W. J. Heale, for his life; on his death in 1897 the patronage passed to the patrons of Wombourne, who still held it in 1980.[87] Under an agreement of 1866 the incumbent of Swindon was paid £100 a year by the vicar of Wombourne, although by 1884 Heale was paying an extra £70 and by 1888 £90.[88] In 1898 Swindon was assigned instead £6,250 stock out of Wombourne's funds.[89] The vicarage house north-west of the church dates from 1973, one of several houses built over the site of the 19th-century vicarage.[90]

The church of *ST. JOHN THE EVANGELIST* is a building of pink sandstone standing on the hill north of the village. Designed by William Bourne,[91] it consists of a chancel, nave, five-bay north aisle, south porch, and a west turret with a bell. The organ chamber on the north side of the chancel contains an organ of 1872 made by Nicholson & Son of Walsall and presented by T. B. Shaw-Hellier.[92] A vestry has been formed at the west end by screening off a bay of the aisle and the adjoining half of the nave. The Lady chapel at the east end of the aisle was dedicated in 1972 in memory of Lilian May, wife of the vicar V. J. Crane.[93] The lich gate was dedicated in 1885.[94]

ROMAN CATHOLICISM. Edward Powell, a hammerman, and his wife Mary were returned as recusants in Wombourne in 1665 and as popish recusants in 1679. Thomas Wheeler and his wife Eleanor were recorded with the Powells as recusants c. 1670.[95] In 1706 the only papists mentioned were Elizabeth Banton and her three daughters, all poor.[96]

With the growth of Wombourne after the Second World War a place of Roman Catholic worship became necessary. From 1952 mass was said every Sunday in the British Legion Hall in Maypole Street by a priest from St. Michael's, Merry Hill, Wolverhampton. The church of St. Bernadette in Rennison Drive was opened in 1961. Designed in a modern style by C. V. Mason of Mason & Richards, Wolverhampton, it is of brick and has a thin fibre-glass spire. A resident priest was appointed in 1962, living first in Giggetty Lane; in 1965 a presbytery was built adjoining the church on the north.[97]

PROTESTANT NONCONFORMITY. In 1672 Ithell Bates's house at Orton was licensed for Congregationalist worship,[98] and three nonconformists in Wombourne parish were returned in 1676.[99] Around 1720 there was a dissenting meeting served by itinerant preachers.[1] In 1778 a house in the possession of Jacob Cartwright was registered for protestant dissenters.[2] A Congregationalist report in 1825 stated that repeated efforts had been made during the previous fifty years at Wombourne 'by every body of protestant dissenters' but that all had failed.[3]

It seems, however, that from c. 1813 Congregationalist services and occasional preachings were held in Wombourne at the house of Mr. and Mrs. Stephens, members of Queen Street chapel, Wolverhampton. Later the meeting was moved to a house at the top of Windmill Bank and finally to a house near Mill Lane. About 1835 a barn on the corner of Gravel Hill and Rookery Road, which was used for a day school, was taken over for Sunday worship, and a Sunday school too was started. The cause flourished, and in

---

[78] S.R.O., Tp. 1226/ADD/K1, 10 Mar. to 7 July 1767, 21 Apr. 1770; Wombourne ch., churchwardens' accts. 1768–1938.

[79] *S.H.C.* 4th ser. x. 34; Wombourne ch., vestry mins. 1835–1941, 23 Feb. 1860; churchwardens' accts. 1768–1938, 1860.

[80] Lich. Dioc. Regy., B/A/2i/S, p. 647; Wombourne ch., vestry mins. 1835–1941, 17 Apr. 1883.

[81] S.R.O., D. 3710/8/2; L.J.R.O., B/A/2i/X, p. 453.

[82] L.J.R.O., B/C/12/Wombourne; inscription on cross.

[83] All except those in current use are in S.R.O., D. 3710/1.

[84] *S.H.C.* 4th ser. x. 34.

[85] L.J.R.O., B/A/2i/P, pp. 154–66; plaque in church porch.   [86] *Lond. Gaz.* 1 Jan. 1867, p. 5.

[87] *P.O. Dir. Staffs.* (1872); L.J.R.O., B/A/3/Swindon; *Lich. Dioc. Ch. Cal.* (1898), 67; ibid. (1899); *Lich. Dioc. Dir.* (1980).

[88] *Lond. Gaz.* 8 May 1888, p. 2611; W.S.L., M.915; S.R.O., D. 3710/2/59.

[89] *Lond. Gaz.* 25 Oct. 1898, pp. 6216–17.

[90] Inf. from the vicar (1981); O.S. Map 6″, Staffs. LXVI. SE. (1887 edn.).

[91] National Monuments Record, Goodhart-Rendel index.

[92] Plate on organ; *Kelly's Dir. Staffs.* (1880).

[93] Plate *in situ*.

[94] *Lich. Dioc. Mag.* (1885), 108.

[95] L.J.R.O., B/V/1/72; B.R.L. 354851, p. 10; *Cath. Rec. Soc.* vi. 310 (giving Powell's occupation).

[96] *Staffs. Cath. Hist.* xiii. 55.

[97] *Cath. Dir. Archdioc. Birmingham* (1963), 155, 205; *Wombourne Compass* (June 1975; copy in possession of Mrs. May Griffiths).

[98] A. G. Matthews, *Cong. Churches of Staffs.* 92.

[99] W.S.L., S.MS. 33, p. 371.

[1] Matthews, *Cong. Churches of Staffs.* 129.

[2] *S.H.C.* n.s. iii. 126.

[3] Matthews, *Cong. Churches of Staffs.* 230.

1837 a 21-year lease of the barn was taken; it was plastered and ceiled, and a pulpit and forms were installed. In 1851 a chapel was opened in Mill Lane close to its junction with High Street. It is a building of brick with stone dressings; the north-west turret originally had a spire. The chapel was designed free of charge by George Bidlake, then a young man starting architectural practice in Wolverhampton. Attendances in 1850–1 averaged 60 in the afternoon and 150 in the evening, with 100 Sunday school children in the morning and 90 in the afternoon. In 1870 a vestry and schoolroom were added and the area in front of the chapel was opened to High Street by the demolition of three cottages. In 1872 an organ was bought from Penn parish church and installed in a gallery; it was replaced in 1914. Membership, which was 16 in 1851, was 34 in 1873 and reached 55 towards the end of the century. The schoolroom was enlarged in 1925 and rebuilt in 1957. A resident minister was appointed in 1951. In the late 1970s Wombourne United Reformed church had a membership of 68.[4]

At Swindon a house was registered for Congregationalist worship in 1815. A chapel was opened in 1820, and soon afterwards a Sunday school was established. A gallery was added in 1834. Thomas Taylor, one of the original trustees, left £45 to provide an income for the support of preaching at Swindon. On Census Sunday 1851 the congregation at the chapel, then called Ebenezer, numbered 40 in the afternoon and 47 in the evening; there were 40 Sunday school children in the morning and 43 in the afternoon. In 1873 the membership was 8. The chapel was renovated in the late 1870s, and a schoolroom was built in 1886. In the late 1970s Swindon United Reformed church had a membership of 14.[5]

In 1850 a house at the Bratch was registered for Congregationalist worship.[6] The meeting evidently failed to survive.

By 1829 Wesleyan Methodists were worshipping in a cottage in Common Lane, Blakeley, belonging to Samuel Evans. A chapel was built in 1850 on a nearby site given by Job Taylor of Stourbridge in what became Chapel Street. On Census Sunday 1851 the congregation numbered 30 in the afternoon and 58 in the evening, with 24 Sunday school children in the morning and 12 in the afternoon. A new chapel with a schoolroom and vestries was built nearby in Common Lane in 1894. The schoolroom was rebuilt in 1966 as a two-storeyed building; it was extended in 1980 when the chapel too was remodelled.[7]

There was a Primitive Methodist preaching house in Grettons Row off School Road in Wombourne in 1851. On Census Sunday that year there were congregations of 17 in the morning, 20 in the afternoon, and 24 in the evening.[8] By the mid 1860s Primitive Methodists were holding services in a cottage at Smestow off the present Chapel Lane. They built a chapel in the lane in 1866. A hall for the Sunday school was built on the opposite side of the lane in 1938 in memory of Thomas Lamb (d. 1931), who was superintendent of the school for some 60 years; the land was given by his son-in-law, William Mallett. By the late 1960s there was no longer support for a Sunday school, and the hall was sold. The chapel was closed in 1973 and later sold.[9] Both buildings were derelict in 1980.

A house at Blakeley was registered for the Latter Day Saints by George Boddison in 1849. On Census Sunday 1851 there were congregations of 21 in the afternoon and 22 in the evening; Boddison stated that the morning congregation averaged 13. In 1855 he registered a building at the 'lower end' of Wombourne for the Latter Day Saints; it had ceased to be used for worship by 1876.[10]

A non-denominational group was meeting on Sunday evenings in a house in Wombourne by 1851. Attendance averaged 30. Services were described as 'conducted by friends of the neighbouring towns, Wombourne and Wolverhampton'.[11]

The International Bible Students' Association registered an assembly room in Planks Lane, Wombourne, in 1924. The registration was cancelled in 1928.[12]

EDUCATION. In 1638 Nathaniel Smart, the new curate, was licensed to teach school in Wombourne parish.[13] The parish was entitled to send one boy to Old Swinford Hospital School (Worcs.) from its foundation in 1670.[14] In 1766 a group of parishioners, including Sir Samuel Hellier of the Wodehouse, established a charity school at Wombourne for 20 children. It was supported by subscription, and the boys and girls were chosen by the subscribers. The children were provided with uniforms designed by Hellier, whose bailiff's brother was appointed schoolmaster. Apparently it was decided that boys sent to Old Swinford Hospital School should be chosen from pupils at the charity school. A schoolroom was planned but was never built. The school was at work by January 1767, but

[4] D. Joseph, *The First Hundred Years: the Story of Wombourne, Staffs., Cong. Church* (1951; copy in W.S.L.); H. A. May, *Queen St. Cong. Church, Wolverhampton*, 107–9; *Manual for Queen St. Chapel, Wolverhampton* (1873), 10, 31–2 (copy in S.R.O., D. 1206/1/26–36); (1926), 49; (1927), 56; *S.H.C.* 4th ser. iii. 85; L.J.R.O., B/A/15/Wombourne; P.R.O., HO 129/379/3/2; inscriptions on buildings; *United Reformed Ch. Yr. Bk.* (1980), 72.
[5] *S.H.C.* 4th ser. iii. 35; Matthews, *Cong. Churches of Staffs.* 181; May, *Queen St. Cong. Ch.* 106 (following *Manual of Queen St. Chapel* (1873), 32, by giving 1819 for the introduction of 'the preaching of the gospel' in Swindon); P.R.O., HO 129/379/3/2; *Manual of Queen St. Chapel* (1923), 11; *United Reformed Ch. Yr. Bk.* (1980), 72.
[6] *S.H.C.* 4th ser. iii. 102.
[7] J. H. Mees, *Story of a Hundred Years: Handbk. of Wesleyan Methodist Church Stourbridge Circuit* (Stourbridge, 1928), 117–21 (copy in Stourbridge Libr.); C. Anderson, *150 years of Methodism in Wombourn* (1980; copy in W.S.L. Pamphs. *sub* Wombourne); P.R.O., HO 129/379/3/2; inscriptions on Common Lane buildings; inf. from members of the church (1980).
[8] P.R.O., HO 129/379/3/2. For Grettons Row see P.R.O., RG 9/1986.
[9] Inf. from Mrs. F. Lamb, Smestow (1980); date on chapel.
[10] *S.H.C.* 4th ser. iii. 101; P.R.O., HO 129/379/3/2; G.R.O., Worship Reg. no. 6482.
[11] P.R.O., HO 129/379/3/2.
[12] G.R.O., Worship Reg. no. 49509.
[13] L.J.R.O., B/A/4/18.
[14] T. R. Nash, *Collns. for Hist. of Worcs.* ii (1782), 210–11.

there were frequent disputes among the subscribers and it was eventually closed in 1770.
Hellier blamed the failure on the meanness of
his fellow parishioners, claiming that they
expected him to support it unaided; the others
apparently suspected that he saw the school
mainly as a source of choristers for musical
performances which he planned should be held
at the church.[15] A Sunday school was opened in
1805. It was stated in 1818 that 'the poorer
classes are very thankful for the instruction
afforded their children' there; they were, however, 'desirous of possessing more sufficient
means of education'.[16]

A National school was built in 1833 west of
Wombourne church in Church Street, the expense being met by Sarah Dalton of the Lloyd in
Penn. There was a mistress in 1835 and a master
in 1841.[17] By 1845 the school had both a master
and a mistress, and there was an average attendance of 49 boys and 52 girls in the later 1840s.[18]
An infants' school was opened in part of the
almshouses in the early 1850s.[19] The National
school was rebuilt in 1860 on land given from the
glebe on the north side of the present School
Road; nearly half the £1,400 cost of erection was
met by a government grant, and the remainder by
subscriptions and a grant from the National
Society. The staff consisted of a master and
mistress, who were husband and wife, and an
infants' mistress, and a house was provided. The
school was supported by subscription and school
pence of 2d. and 6d.; the higher rate was paid by
those in an upper class where more advanced
subjects were taught.[20] The school received a
government grant by 1869–70.[21] There was an
average attendance of 116 in the mid 1870s and
185 in the mid 1880s.[22] The average attendance
in 1905–6 was 311, of whom 107 were infants.[23]
The school became controlled in 1951. A new
school building was officially opened in 1974, and
the old school was then demolished. In the late
1970s average attendance at the school, by then
St. Benedict Biscop C. of E. controlled first
school, was 213.[24]

Although the need for a school in Swindon was
voiced in the later 1840s, it was only in 1864 that
one was built, south of St. John's church. It was
supported mainly by subscription and school
pence. Children paid 4d., 2d., or 1d. a week, the
different rates being determined by their parents'
income and the number of children sent from a

family.[25] By 1872 the school received a government grant.[26] There was an average attendance of
56 in 1867, 53 in 1884–5, and 95 in 1892.[27] The
building, which originally consisted of a schoolroom and a classroom, was enlarged in 1893.[28] In
1905–6 the school had an average attendance of
84, of whom 24 were infants.[29] It moved to new
premises in Wombourne Road in 1968.[30] In the
late 1970s average attendance at what was then
St. John's C. of E. controlled primary school was
115.[31] The old school building was then used as a
photographic studio.

The development of the area since the Second
World War is reflected in the number of new
schools.[32] In 1980 there were three secondary
schools: Ounsdale high, formerly Ounsdale
secondary, in Ounsdale Road (1956); Westfield
middle in Ounsdale Road (1976); and Blakeley
Heath middle in Sytch Lane (1976). Both Westfield and Blakeley Heath were previously
primary schools opened c. 1955 and in 1960
respectively. There were three new primary
schools in 1980: Westfield first, formerly Westfield infants', in Planks Lane (1963); Blakeley
Heath first in Sytch Lane (1976), replacing the
former primary school; and St. Bernadette's
Roman Catholic junior mixed and infants (aided)
in Lindale Drive (1969). Cherry Trees special
school in Giggetty Lane was opened in 1969; the
adjoining Brookside residential hostel for handi-
capped children was opened about the same time,
although separately organized.

There were four private day schools in Wombourne in 1833, teaching 40 boys and 51 girls; one
school had started in 1821, and another in 1828.[33]
Two private schools were mentioned in 1835.
One, run by Thomas Hill, was held in a barn
at the corner of Gravel Hill and Rookery Road;
the building was taken over by the Congregationalists in 1837, but Hill was still teaching
in Wombourne c. 1841. The other school was run
by Elizabeth Pilsbury; in 1851 she was running a
dame school in Upper Street (the present Church
Street and its High Street continuation).[34]

A night school, run by the Wombourne
Mutual Improvement Society, was held at the
National school twice a week during the winter of
1863–4, each student paying 1d. an evening. It
was held in the following winter also but seems to
have ceased because of poor attendance.[35] An
evening institute was held in Ounsdale school
from the later 1950s.[36]

[15] S.R.O., Tp. 1226/ADD/K1, 25 Dec. 1766, 3, 11, 15, and
31 Jan., 17 and 28 Feb., 28 Mar., 21 May, 1, 4, and 27 June, 28
July, 8 Aug. 1767, 5 and 28 Jan., 17 May, 4 Sept. 1768, 26
Jan., 1 and 8 Apr., 1, 10, and 29 June, 10 July 1769, 10 and
24 Feb., 8 Mar., 21 Apr., 5 and 23 June, 1 July 1770.
[16] Digest of Returns to Sel. Cttee. on Educ. of Poor, H.C.
224, p. 871 (1819), ix (2); White, Dir. Staffs. (1834), 292.
[17] Pigot, Nat. Com. Dir. (1835), 440–1; L.J.R.O., B/A/15/
Wombourne, no. 22; P.R.O., HO 107/1002. For Sarah
Dalton see S.R.O. 3279/14/1, 3.
[18] Nat. Soc. Inquiry, 1846–7, Staffs. 12–13; P.O. Dir.
Staffs. (1845).   [19] Wombourne Compass (May 1975).
[20] Lich. Dioc. Ch. Cal. (1861), 124; P.R.O., ED 7/110/368.
[21] Rep. Educ. Cttee. of Council, 1869–70 [C. 165], p. 645,
H.C. (1870), xxii.
[22] Rep. Educ. Cttee. of Council, 1874–5 [C. 1265-I], p. 406,
H.C. (1875), xxiv; 1884–85 [C. 4483-I], p. 627, H.C.
(1884–5), xxiii.
[23] Public Elem. Schs. 1907 [Cd. 3901], p. 575, H.C. (1908),
lxxxiv.

[24] S.R.O., surv. of school records, 1965; Wombourne
Compass (Sept. 1974; Jan. 1975); Lich. Dioc. Dir. (1980).
[25] Nat. Soc. Inquiry, Staffs. 13; P.R.O., ED 7/110/315.
[26] P.O. Dir. Staffs. (1872).
[27] P.R.O., ED 7/110/315; Rep. Educ. Cttee. of Council,
1884–85, 625; Kelly's Dir. Staffs. (1892).
[28] P.R.O., ED 7/110/315; Kelly's Dir. Staffs. (1896); inscription on building.   [29] Public Elem. Schs. 1907, 572.
[30] Inf. from the headmistress (1980).
[31] Lich. Dioc. Dir. (1980).
[32] This para. is based on information from the respective
head teachers.
[33] Educ. Enquiry Abstract, H.C. 62, p. 893 (1835), xlii.
[34] Pigot, Nat. Com. Dir. (1835), 440–1; (1841), 59; P.R.O.,
HO 107/2017 (2); above, prot. nonconf.
[35] Wombourne Mutual Improvement Soc. Min. Bk.
1863–76 (in possession of Mrs. May Griffiths), 23 Oct. 1863,
13 Oct. 1864.
[36] Wombourne Official Guide [1965], 31–2; inf. from Mrs.
May Griffiths.

CHARITIES FOR THE POOR. By deed of 1715 land in Rookery Road was given by John Smith, a cursitor of Chancery and owner of property in Wombourne, to a group of parishioners as the site for two almshouses. Two or more poor parishioners were to be chosen to live in the houses; they were not to teach school or sell liquor.[37] The building was erected in 1716.[38] The charity appears to have ceased by the late 1780s,[39] the almshouses becoming a poorhouse for the parish; in the 1850s part of the building was used as an infants' school.[40] In 1859 the building was conveyed to the vicar and church-wardens, who divided it into three dwellings and leased them out, using the rents for the benefit of the poor.[41] By 1886 the income consisted of £14 19s. rent from the cottages, 12s. rent from a garden, and interest from £87 4s. 1d. stock. A Scheme of 1886 directed that the income from the capital was to be applied in the establishment or enlargement of a village institute or reading room, open to the poor of the parish; the remaining income was to be used for the benefit of the poor not receiving parish relief. A further £50 was added to the capital in 1912 by the sale of land.[42] The almshouses were sold c. 1975 and the proceeds invested. In 1982 the money from the sale was still being allowed to accumulate, although there was also an income from earlier stock of £3.88, all of which was distributed to the poor in groceries.[43]

By deed of 1912 six houses in Windmill Bank known as the Fold Houses were vested in the Lichfield Diocesan Trust for use as almshouses in fulfilment of the wish of the late Revd. Thomas Hill of North Somercoates (Lincs.) (d. 1912), himself following the intentions of his aunt. In the choice of almspeople preference was to be given to former employees of Hill's family. In 1952 the almshouses were sold to Wombourne Village Community Council and the proceeds invested in stock. In 1982 there was an income of £110.33, all of which was distributed to aged and sick members of the Church of England.[44]

Walter Woodhouse of Wombourne (d. 1634) gave during his lifetime £20 to be invested in land for the benefit of the poor. The £20 was held by his brother Edward, who paid out the yearly interest. In 1687 he converted the payment into a rent charge of 20s. from meadow apparently on the boundary of Wombourne and Trysull parishes, to be distributed among the poor on St. Thomas's day (21 December). In 1820 payments were four years in arrears, and the charity had lapsed by the late 1860s.[45]

In 1634 Francis Woodhouse of the Wodehouse gave £6 to provide an income for the poor of the parish. The gift was the beginning of a parish stock which was lent out on bond, with the interest paid to the poor. The stock was increased to £10 in 1635 by a legacy of £2 from Walter Woodhouse and £2 collected among the parishioners. In 1640 and 1642 two further sums of £2 were given. Money was still being lent out in 1650.[46]

By deed of 1647 Edward Bird of Swindon gave a rent charge of 20s. from meadow in Kinver in trust to be distributed on Lady Day among the poor of the parish. Subsequently a penalty of 2s. for every day that payment was delayed was imposed on the tenant of the land and added to the distribution. In 1810 arrears of £9 10s. were distributed in sums of up to 5s.; the income was then allowed to accumulate, and in 1820 £11 5s. remained undistributed. In the late 1860s the charity was paid out in clothing.[47] The charge was redeemed in 1901, and the proceeds invested in stock. In 1982 there was an income of £1, which was distributed to the poor in groceries.[48]

Sir Samuel Hellier (d. 1784) left £100, the income to be distributed among the poor of the parish after annual payments had been made to maintain his vault (5s.) and the organ (2 guineas) in Wombourne church and to the organist (1 guinea). The legacy was not invested until 1819 when it was laid out in stock. In 1982 there was an income of £3.20, of which £3.15 was spent on the organ and organist, leaving only 5p for the poor.[49]

A bread charity for the poor was being distributed in the late 1780s. The original endowment of £3 had been lost for some time, and the 3s. charity was paid out of the poor rate.[50]

By will proved 1892 W. H. Hill of Walsall left £600, the income to be distributed among the poor of Wombourne parish. In 1982 there was an income of £21.06, all of which was distributed to the poor in groceries.[51]

---

[37] S.R.O., D. 3710/6/5; above, manors and other estates.
[38] Tablet on building.
[39] It is not listed in *Char. Dons. 1786–88* or in *5th Rep. Com. Char.*
[40] Above, local govt.; educ.
[41] W.S.L., M. 915.
[42] S.R.O., D. 3710/6/7–8.
[43] *Wombourne Compass* (May 1975); *Wolverhampton and W. Midlands Mag.* (July 1976), 17; inf. from Mrs. Barbara Webb, churchwarden.

[44] S.R.O., D. 3710/6/21, 24–5; inf. from Mrs. Webb.
[45] *5th Rep. Com. Char.* 638; *Char. Digest Staffs.* H.C. 91(5), pp. 66–7 (1868–9), xlv(3); S.R.O., D. 3710/6/5.
[46] Shaw, *Staffs.* ii, pp. *216–17.
[47] *5th Rep. Com. Char.* 637–8; *Char. Digest Staffs.* 66–7.
[48] S.R.O., D. 3710/6/2–3; inf. from Mrs. Webb.
[49] *5th Rep. Com. Char.* 638–9; above, manors and other estates; inf. from Mrs. Webb.
[50] *Char. Dons. 1786–88*, ii. 1146–7.
[51] S.R.O., D. 3710/7/17; inf. from Mrs. Webb.

WOODFORD GRANGE

WOODFORD Grange, formerly an extra-parochial place of 199 a. (80 ha.), was added to Trysull parish in 1900.[52] It became extra-parochial apparently because it was a self-contained area with little or no population, belonging to a monastic house and tithe free. Smestow brook formed its western boundary separating it from Trysull. The land rises from 250 ft. (76 m.) along the brook to 300 ft. (91 m.) along the boundary with Wombourne in the east and south-east. Woodford marks the southern limit of boulder clay on the east side of Smestow brook, and sand deposits on the southern boundary were being worked by 1980.[53]

William son of Guy de Offini, lord of Wombourne, gave land and meadow at Wood-ford to Dudley priory (Worcs.) in the later 12th century. During the same period Bernard son of Giles of Trysull freed a virgate at Woodford belonging to Trysull church from all foreign service in return for a rent of 12d. from the priory; the church as a dependency of Wombourne belonged to the priory.[54] A grange was established, and there may have been a monk living at Woodford in 1272.[55] In 1285 the priory was licensed to assart heath in Kinver forest adjoining what was then described as Woodford manor.[56] In 1291 the priory had 2 carucates in Woodford worth 32s. a year, stock worth £1 a year, and 11s. 6d. rent.[57] By the early 1420s the manor included a messuage and 80 a. of arable, worth 40s. a year, and it was held by tenants by the mid 1480s.[58] The priory retained the manor until its dissolution in 1540. In the early 1540s the tenant had a house, 79 a. of arable divided into 8 closes, each with heath and moor attached, and 1 a. of meadow; the rest of the estate was woodland.[59]

In 1541 the Crown granted Woodford to Sir John Dudley, later duke of Northumberland, who leased it in 1541–2 to Hugh Lee, clerk at the royal armoury at Greenwich.[60] In June 1554, following the attainder of the duke in 1553, the Crown sold Woodford to Thomas Reeve and George Cotton, both of London, who conveyed it to Edward Leveson and Humphrey Dickins in July. In the same month Leveson and Dickins granted Woodford and its tithes to Hugh Lee, still the tenant.[61] Lee was living at Woodford in 1559 and evidently died there in 1576.[62] His heir was his grandson Hugh, aged 6, the son of Walter Wrottesley of Wrottesley, in Tettenhall, who had married Lee's daughter and heir Mary in 1568. Hugh was living at Woodford Grange in 1599 and 1612.[63]

The estate then descended in the Wrottesley family with Wrottesley manor. In the mid 17th century the house may have been used as a dower house: Sir Walter Wrottesley (d. 1659) in his will of 1647 gave his wife the choice of living at Woodford or in the gatehouse at Wrottesley after his death.[64] The house was assessed at six hearths in 1666, and it probably stood on or near the site of the present Woodford Grange. There was a second house in 1666, assessed at a single hearth, at Clapgate on the boundary with Wombourne.[65] It may have been the Woodford Gate where Oliver Cartwright, a nailer and farmer, was living in 1669; a William Cartwright was living at Clapgate in 1673.[66] A house at Clapgate was burnt down in 1757. It had been rebuilt by the early 19th century and was known as Woodford Cottage by the 1860s.[67] In the early 19th century Woodford Grange farm was mainly arable, but it also supported sheep.[68] In 1841 there were still only the two households, both farming there and together numbering 14 people.[69] There were 15 inhabitants in 1901.[70] When Lord Wrottesley put the property up for sale in 1929, the 302-a. Woodford Grange farm, extending into Trysull, was predominantly arable; Woodford Cottage (later Clap Gate Cottage) had a 5-a. small-holding.[71] In 1966 Aubrey Wright, who had owned Woodford Grange for some 18 years, sold it with 25 a. to Mr. P. G. Bannister, the owner in 1981.[72]

[52] County of Stafford (Trysull and Seisdon) Conf. Order, 1899 (Local Govt. Bd. Order no. 40,311; copy in S.R.O., C/C/O/1). This article was written in 1981.
[53] T. H. Whitehead and R. W. Pocock, *Memoirs of Geol. Surv., Dudley and Bridgnorth*, 156, 181.
[54] *S.H.C.* iii (1), 214–17; above, Trysull, church.
[55] *S.H.C.* iii (1), 215–16; v (1), 160.
[56] *Cal. Pat.* 1281–92, 197.
[57] *Tax. Eccl.* (Rec. Com.), 251.
[58] P.R.O., SC 6/988/6; W.S.L., S.MS. 201 (i), p. 235.
[59] P.R.O., LR 2/184, f. 176v.
[60] *L. & P. Hen. VIII*, xvi, pp. 329–30; *S.H.C.* N.S. vi (2), 279–80; *Cal. Pat.* 1553–4, 125.
[61] *Cal. Pat.* 1553–4, 458; *S.H.C.* N.S. vi (2), 280 (giving Reeve as Rees and Cotton as Colton).
[62] *S.H.C.* 1938, 152; S.R.O., D. 3710/1/1.

[63] P.R.O., C 142/179, no. 67; *S.H.C.* N.S. vi (2), 279, 287; above, p. 210.
[64] *S.H.C.* N.S. vi (2), 333.
[65] *S.H.C.* 1923, 113; W.S.L., Staffs. Views, xii. 150; *Tettenhall Par. Reg.* i (Staffs. Par. Reg. Soc. 1930), 162.
[66] L.J.R.O., B/C/11, Oliver Cartwright (1669); S.R.O., D. 3710/1/1, bapt. 16 Feb. 1672/3.
[67] *Public Advertiser*, 21 July 1757; D.C.L., map 831; Harrison, Harrod & Co. *Dir. Staffs.* (1861).
[68] *Wolverhampton Chron.* 11 Oct. 1815.
[69] P.R.O., HO 107/1002.
[70] *Census*, 1901.
[71] W.S.L., Sale Cat. E/3/12, pp. 22–4; O.S. Map 1″, sheet 130 (1954 edn.). The farm was not sold: *Staffs. Advertiser*, 26 Oct. 1929.
[72] Inf. from Mr. Bannister.

INDEX

Abbot's (formerly Apewood) Castle Hill, 64, 185

Abetot:
Rog. d', 129
Urse d', 129

Acton Burnell (Salop.), 133

Acworth, Geo., 203

Adam, abbot of Evesham, 26

Adam the mercer, 219

Adams:
T. B., 9
his w., 9
and see Addams

Adcock, Abraham, 220

Addams, Thos., 40

Addenbrooke:
J. A., 61
John, 46

Adelaide, queen of William IV, 62

aero-engineering, 36

Agatha, Wm. s. of, *see* Claverley

agricultural engineering, 36

Agriculture, Fisheries, and Food (formerly Agriculture and Fisheries), Ministry of, 8

Aingworth, Wm., 112

Air Ministry, 65, 67, 70, 73

Air Training Corps, 14

airfields, *see* Bobbington, Halfpenny Green; Tettenhall, Pendeford *and* Perton

Aiton:
Hugh, 99*n*
John, 99
fam., 99

Albrighton (Salop.), 46, 87, 90, 122, 168, 170
Beamish Hall, 103
Pepperhill, *q.v.*
Wildicote, *q.v.*

Albrighton Hunt, 95

Aldersley, *see* Tettenhall

Aldersley Engineers Ltd., 36

Aldersley Junction, *see* Bushbury

Alfgar, earl of Mercia, 53–4, 129, 175

Alfred, priest, 136

Alice, Princess, dowager dchss. of Gloucester, 75

Allen:
Sampson, 93
Thos., 184
fam., 34

Almar, Domesday tenant, 12, 23

Alric, pre-Conquest tenant, 96

Alton, in Farley, 83

Alveley (Salop.), 106

Amblecote, Denis of, 51

Amblecote, **49–64**
agric., 54–5
Amblecote Bank, 49, 51, 54, 56–7, 63

Amblecote Fm., *see* Amblecote, Amblecote Ho.

Amblecote Hall, 49, 51, 54–5, 57

Amblecote Ho. (formerly Amblecote Fm.), 54

Babylon, 51

Bacca Box or Box Hill, *see* Amblecote, Tobacco Box Hill

bridge, 52

canal, *see* Amblecote, communications

chars. for the poor, 64

ch., 53, 62–4, *64*

Coalbournbrook, 49, 52–3, 55, 57–61, 63, 127, *144*

Coalbournhill, 51, 61

Colliers Ho., 56

communications:
canal, 49, 52–3
rlys., 49, 53
rds., 49, 52
trams, 53

Corbett Hosp., 62

council housing, 52, 62

cricket, 53

Crown clay works, 57

curate, *see* Grier

Dennis, 51, 56, 58–9

Dennis glassworks, 59, *64*

Dennis Ho. (later Hall), 51, 59, 62–3

Dennis Pk., 51

econ. hist., 54–61

educ., 53, 63–4, *64*

Fimbrell glassho., 58–9

fishery, 55

fords, 52

gasworks, 62–3

Harrington Ho. (formerly Holloway End Ho.), 58, 62

High Ho., 64

the Hill, 51, 58, 62–3

Holloway End, 49, 52, 57–8, 62–3

Holloway End Ho., *see* Amblecote, Harrington Ho.

Hoo glassho., 58

hosp., *see* Amblecote, Corbett Hosp.

inds., 49, 51–3, 55–61, *64*, *144*

inns:
Birch Tree, 51
Fish, 51, 53
Green Dragon, *see* Amblecote: inns, Royal Oak (1718)
Holly Bush, 52
Pear Tree, 51
Royal Oak (1718; later Green Dragon), 51, 60
Royal Oak (20th cent.), 64

inst., 53

John Bradley Rolling Mills, 61

librs., 53

local govt., 61–2

man., 53–4, 61

mills, 49, 54–5, 60

nonconf., 63

pk., 55

Penfield, 52–4

Peter's Hill, 51–3, 64

the Platts, 49, 51–2, 57–60

pop., 49, 51, 54

post office, 62

pound, 61

public services, 62

rlys., *see* Amblecote, communications

rds., *see* Amblecote, communications

Royal forge, 60–1

social and cultural activities, 53

Stamford Ho., 63

stepping stones, 52, 55

stocks, 61

Stourbridge ironworks, 53, 60–1

Stourbridge War Memorial athletic ground, 53

streets:
Amblecote Lane, *see* Amblecote: streets, Vicarage Rd.
Bagley St., 52
Bagleys Rd., 49
Brettell Lane, 51–3, 61–3
Collis St., 51, 53, 61
Dennis St., 51
High St., 61–4
Hill St., 51, 64
Hillfields Rd., 52–3
the Holloway, 62
Hollybush Rd., 52
King William St., 51, 53, 63–4
Old Wharf Rd., 51–2, 61
Penfield Rd., 57
Peter's Hill Rd., 64
Piper Place, 52
Platts Crescent, 51
Platts Rd., 61
Queen's Crescent, 62
School Drive, 63–4
Stamford Rd., 51, 57
Stamford St., 52
Trinity Rd., 52
Vale St., 51
Vicarage Rd. (formerly Amblecote Lane), 49, 51–4, 57, 62–4
Villa St., 51
Withymoor Lane, 54

Titan works, 61

tithes, 54

Tobacco Box Hill (later Box Hill and Bacca Box), 51–2

trams, *see* Amblecote, communications

Amblecote (*cont.*):
urban dist., 49, 52–3, 61–2
vicars, *see* Boldero; Moore
water supply, 62
Withymoor, 51, 55–8, 63
Amblecote Glass Co. Ltd., 58
Amblecote Training School, 64
Amesbury (Wilts.), *see* Stonehenge
Amies, H. J., 68
Amphlett:
(formerly Dunne), Chas., 104
Chas., 69, 104
Eliz., *see* Wollaston
Revd. Geo., 104
Jos., 104, 111
Jos., his s., 104
Leila, 104
fam., 69, 111
Anderson, J. McVicar, 166
Andrewes, *see* Poulton
Anglesey, *see* Holyhead
Anslow, Hen., 80
Anson, Jervis, 31
Apewood Castle Hill, *see* Abbot's
Castle Hill
Apley (in Stockton, Salop.), 71, 74
Archer, Edw., curate of Enville, 114–
15
Arkle:
Geo., 132
fam., 132
Arley, Upper (Staffs., later Worcs.),
105
Arnold, Thos., and his w. Marg., 97
Arnott, Thos., 148
Arts, Manufactures, and Commerce,
Society for the Encouragement of,
59
Arundel and Sussex:
ctsses. of, *see* Aubigny; Mabel
earl of, *see* Aubigny
Ash (in Whitchurch, Salop.), 181
Ashbee, C. R., 205
Ashbourne, K. P., 189
Ashby De La Zouch (Leics.), 219
Ashwood, John, 82
Ashwood, *see* Kingswinford
Astley:
Eliz., m. John Wrottesley (d. 1578),
41, 169
Eliz., *see* Phillips
Gilb., 164, 168
Henrietta, *see* Borlase
Isabel, *see* Harcourt
Joan, *see* Gresley
Joan, w. of Ric., 171
Sir John (fl. mid 15th cent.), 164*n*
Sir John (d. 1772), 162, 165, 167–71,
176
Margery, w. of Thos. (d. 1632), 171
Ric., 164, 167, 171
Sir Ric., 164–7, 169–71, *171*
Thos. (fl. mid 15th cent.), 164
Thos. (d. 1483–4), 164
Thos. (d. between 1556 and 1558),
164, 169
Thos. (d. 1632), 164, 168–9, 171–2
Thos. (fl. 1707), 29
Wal., 164, 171
Wm., 164
fam., 167, 171
Astley (Worcs.), Woodhampton in, 104
Astley castle (Warws.), 165
Aston (in Claverley, Salop.), 71
Aston (Warws.), *see* Erdington
Aston, Little, *see* Shenstone
Aston, Wheaton, *see* Lapley
Atkys, Ric., 139–40
Attenborough (Notts.), *see* Chilwell
Attwood, Dr. Thos., 189; *and see*
Atwood
Atwell, Ric., 134
Atwood:
Edw., 129
John, 129
and see Attwood; Wood

Aubigny:
Hugh d', earl of Arundel and Sussex,
175
Isabel d', his w., 175
Mabel d', ctss. of Arundel and
Sussex, *see* Mabel
Nichole d', m. Rog. de Somery
(d. 1273), 175
Audlem (Ches.), 97, 165
Audnam, *see* Kingswinford
Autherley Junction, *see* Bushbury
Avenant, Ric., 113, 145, 213
Avranches, Hugh d', earl of Chester,
175
Awbridge, *see* Wombourne

Babington:
Eliz., *see* Gibthorp
Etheldena (or Ethelneda), m. ——
Delves, 203
John, 203
Wm., 203
Babthorpe, Sir Rob., 203, 216
Bache, Thos., 209
Bacun, Ric. atte, 122*n*
Badger (Salop.), 169
badger baiting, 175
Bagley:
Dudley, 55
Hen., 220
Bagot:
Hervey, 26
Marg., *see* Margaret
Millicent, *see* Stafford
Rob., 164
Wm. (fl. 1179), 164
Wm. (d. by 1300), 164, 168, 176
Wm., his s., 164, 168
Wm. (fl. 1379), 176
fam., 164
Bailey:
Wm. (fl. 1608–17), 176, 182
Wm. (fl. 1851), 79
Baker:
Eliza (? w. of John), 196
John, 194
Wm., 97, 99, 165, 205
Baker's of Wolverhampton (nursery-
man), 85
Baldwin, Domesday tenant, 188, 190
Baldwin, E. P. and W., 214
Ball brook, *see* Gallows brook
Ballincolig Royal Gunpowder Mills
Co., 36
Banks:
Edw., 88
W. C., 170–1
Bannister, P. G., 225
Bannockburn, battle of, 67
Banton:
Daniel, 191
Eliz., 221
Wm., 190
fam., 190
Baptists, 157
Baring-Gould, Revd. Sabine, 126
Barnesley:
Eliz. (d. 1697), 195–6
Eliz., m. Rob. Harriotts, 189, 194
Thos. (d. probably 1545), 194
Thos. (fl. 1623), 212
Wm. (fl. 1550s), 212
Wm. (d. probably 1571), 191–2
Wm. (d. probably 1640), 191–2
Wm. (fl. 1646), 196
Wm. (d. 1684), 189, 196
Wm. (d. 1690), 189
fam., 189
Barney, Ric., 61
Barnhurst:
Hen. of, 20
Joan, m. —— Milston, 20
John (several of this name 1337–
1463), 20, 24, 189
Ric., 20
Wm. s. of Alf. of, 20

Barnhurst, *see* Tettenhall
Barrar, Elijah, 59
Barre, Isabel, m. Humph. Stafford,
earl of Devon, 104
Barrett:
Anne, m. 1 Wm. Hickman, 2 ——
Barrett, 83
Anne, m. Wal. Mansell, 83
Nat., 83
Wm., 83, 88, 90
Barrow, Thos., 219
barrows, 3, 197
Barton, Edw., 154–5, 161
Barton Hall, *see* Tatenhill
basket making, 86
Basset:
Isabel, w. of Ralph (d. by 1211), 175,
177
Joan, w. of Ralph, Baron Basset (d.
1390), 176
Marg., *see* Somery
Maud, *see* Ridel
Ralph (d. *c.* 1160), 175, 177
Ralph (d. by 1211), 175
Ralph (d. 1254 × 1257), 175–6
Ralph (d. 1265), 176
Ralph, Baron Basset (d. 1299), 176,
178–81
Ralph, Baron Basset (d. 1343), 176,
179
Ralph, Baron Basset (d. 1390), 176
Ric., 175, 180
fam., 181
Batchelor:
Benj., 58–9
Elijah, 59
Eliz., w. of Humph., 59
Humph., 58–9
Thos. (fl. 1690s), 58–9
Thos. (fl. 1749), 59
Bate:
Hen., 64
Humph., 161
John, 210–11
Ric., 147
Ric., curate of Kinver, 154, 158
Thos. (fl. 1619), 150
Thos. (fl. 1821), 146
fam., 34
Bate Brook, *see* Wom brook
Bateman & Corser, 43
Bates:
Geo., 60
Ithel, 221
Bath and Wells, bp. of, *see* Burnell
Bathoe, Ric., curate of Patshull, 170
Batson, Jas., 64
Baxter, Ric., Presbyterian divine, 219
Bayliss, Sam., 22
Baylol, Wm. de, 207
Beamhurst, *see* Checkley
Beamish Hall, *see* Albrighton
bear baiting, 80
Beare, Leonard, 58; *and see* Tompson
Beauchamp:
Ric., earl of Warwick, 176
Thos. de, earl of Warwick, 176
Becher, Canon John, 128
Beck, F. T., 27, 40
Beckbury:
Ric. of, *see* Oldington
fam., 167
Becket, John, 30
Beckingham:
Cath., 69
John Chas., 69
Bedford:
Thos., 81
Thos. Stubbs, 81
bee keeping, 32, 109–10, 178, 192
Beiston, Thos., curate of Tettenhall, 40
Belgium, 83
Beneit, Ric., 143
Bengal, *see* India
Bennett:
Fra., 147

Jas., 153
Wm., 147
Mrs., 147
Bennitt, Wm., 123
Bentley, And., 145
Beresford, Wm., 207
Berkshire, 207; *and see* Englefield; Pangbourne
Bernard, King & Sons, 36, 150
Berry, John, 58
Bescot, *see* Walsall
Besford (Worcs.), 176
Betts, Ursula, 183
Bevan, Revd. Jas., 218
Bevington & Sons, 220
Bewdley (Worcs.), 57-8, 88, 157
Bible Students' Association, International, 222
Bidlake, Geo., 44, 222
Bigoe, Abraham, 58
Bilbrook, *see* Codsall; Tettenhall
Bilston (in St. Peter's, Wolverhampton), 17-18, 77, 79, 89, 147
  Bradley, 189, 202, 204
  ch., 209
  urban dist. council, 188, 217
Bird:
  Edw., 224
  John (fl. 1625), 124
  John (fl. mid 1630s), 210-11
  Ric., 124, 139
  Rob., 160
  Thos., 140
  fam., 124
Birmingham:
  Brian s. of Wm. s. of Peter of, 105
  Edw., 113
  Sir Fulk, 96, 111, 113
  Hen. of, *see* Morfe
  Sir John, 96, 106, 113
  Peter of (Peter s. of Wm. of Birmingham), 105
  Rog. s. of Wm. s. of Peter of, *see* Morfe
  Wm. of, 96, 105, 111, 113
  Wm. s. of Peter of, 105
  fam., 96, 105, 113
Birmingham, 9, 27, 34, 43, 95-6, 128, 147, 221
  Handsworth, *q.v.*
  ind., 35, 132, 147
  Norton, King's, *q.v.*
  prot. nonconf., 219
  Small Heath, 147
Birmingham and Liverpool Junction Canal, *see* Shropshire Union Canal
Birmingham Canal, 14*n*
Birmingham Roman Catholic archdiocese, 43
Bishopsbourne (Kent), 69
Bishton, Geo., 181
Bissell, Job, 94
Bissill:
  Eileen, *see* Grey
  J. P., 97
Black, Master Ric., 208
Black brook, 1, 38, 172-3, 185
Black Country, 191-2, 211
Black Ladies, *see* Brewood
Black Prince, *see* Edward
Blackheath, *see* Rowley Regis
Blackhills (Swindon) Sand and Gravel Co., 215
Blacklands, *see* Bobbington
blade mills, 55, 112, 147-8, 169, 214
Blakelands, *see* Bobbington
Blakeley (formerly Blakeway) Green, *see* Tettenhall
Blomfield, A. W. (later Sir Arthur), 75
bloomer, Jordan the, *see* Jordan
Bloxwich, John, 219
Bloxwich (in Walsall), 90, 203
  Yieldfields Hall, 203
Blundel:
  Wal., 93

fam., 93
Blundeville, Ranulph de, earl of Chester, 175
Bobbington, **64-76**, 105
  agric., 71-2
  airfield, *see* Bobbington, Halfpenny Green
  Bannockburn, 65, 67
  Blacklands (formerly Blakeland), 68-9, 72
  Blakelands, 65, 69, 72
  Bobbington fm., *see* Bobbington, College fm.
  Bobbington Hall, 65, 68, 72
  Bobbington Ho. Fm., 65, 76
  Bobbington Mill Fm., 73
  Broadfields, 71, 73
  Broadfields Fm., 76
  chars. for the poor, 76
  ch., 67, 73-5
  College (formerly Bobbington) fm., 69, 72, 74
  council hos., 65
  Crab Mill Fm., 73
  curates, *see* Bradley; Brown; Darbey; Downing; Morten; Shokeborough
  econ. hist., 71-3
  educ., 75-6, 117
  electricity, 67
  the Fieldhouse, *see* Bobbington, Whittimere
  friendly socs., 67
  Gospel Ash, 75
  Gospelash Fm., 67
  Halfpenny Green, 65, 67, 71, 75
    airfield, 14, 65, 67, 75-6
  Hay Fm., 65, 69, 72
  the Hill, *see* Bobbington, Whittimere
  History Group, 67
  inds., 73
  inns:
    Red Lion, 65, 67
    Royal Oak, 65, 67
    Six Ashes, 67
  Leaton, 70
    Leaton Hall, 64, 70, 72
  the Lee, 70
  local govt., 73
  man., 67-8, 73
  Manor fm., 68, 72
  Mill Fm., 65
  mills, 72-3
  nonconf., 75, 116
  pop., 65, 71
  post office, 67
  public services, 67
  Rickthorn, 65
  rds., 65, 67
    Brantley Crescent, 65
    Chester Way, *see* Bobbington: rds., Gospelash Rd.
    Church Lane, 65, 67, 73
    Commonside, *see* Bobbington: rds., Gospelash Rd.
    Crab Lane, 73
    Gospelash Rd. (formerly Chester Way and Commonside), 65, 67, 73, 75-6
    Naylors Lane, 73
    Six Ashes Rd., 65, 67
  Salters Pk. fm. (formerly Saltershill), 71, 73
  Saltershall fm., 72
  sewerage, 67
  Six Ashes, 64, 67, 73
  social and cultural activities, 67
  Thom (Tom) Street, 65
  tithes, 71
  Tuckhill, 64-5, 70, 72
  War Stone, 64
  water supply, 67
  White Cross, 75
  Whittimere, 64-5, 71-3
    the Fieldhouse, 71
    the Hill, 71

    the Scholle, *see* Bobbington: Whittimere, Whittimere fm.
    Upper Whittimere, 65, 71
    Whittimere fm. (formerly the Scholle and Whittimere Hall), 70-3
  woodland, 72
  Yew Tree Fm., 75
Bobbington Bulletin, 67
Boddison, Geo., 222
Bodley, G. F., 205
Boldero, J. S., vicar of Amblecote, 63
Bolland, C. P., 69
Bolton:
  S. F., 147
  Thos. (ironmaster), 80
  Thos. (lawyer), 146
Boningale (Salop.), 3, 87
Bookham, Great (Surr.), 16
Booth:
  Eliz., *see* Wilkes
  Geo., earl of Warrington, 97
  Geo., 68
  Godfrey, 68
  John Wilkes, 20
  Junius Brutus, 20
  Mabel Janet, 64
  Lady Mary, m. Harry Grey, earl of Stamford (d. 1768), 97, 99
Bordesley abbey (Worcs.), 136, 153
Borlase, Henrietta, m. Sir Ric. Astley, 171
Borough English, 178
Boscobel (Salop.), 5
  White Ladies, 167, 177
Boston, barons, *see* Irby
Botetourt:
  Joan, *see* Somery
  Sir John, 67, 103
Boulton, Matt., 58
Boulton Paul Aircraft Ltd., 12, 14, 36
Bourne, Wm., 221
Bowen:
  Thos., 68-9, 75
  fam., 69
Bowland, Humph., 130
Bowles:
  Bridget, m. —— Downing, 113
  Hen., rector of Enville, 113
  Thos., rector of Enville, 113
  Wm., rector of Enville, 113-14
Bradeney, Sam., 31
Bradley:
  Edw., 59
  Edw. ('Cuthbert Bede'), curate of Bobbington, 67
  Geof. of, 189
  Hannah, w. of Joshua, 60
  Hen., 61
  John (fl. 1714), 59
  John (d. 1816), 60-1
  Joshua, 60
  Reynold of, 189
  Ric. (fl. 1712-18), 139
  Ric. (fl. later 18th cent.), 59
  Sibyl of, m. Wm. Wood, 204
  Thos. of (? two of this name), 189
  Thos., 58
  Wal. of, 189, 204
Bradley, John, & Co., 60-1, 146
Bradley, John, & Co. (Stourbridge) Ltd., 61
Bradley, Littywood in, 24
Bradley, *see* Bilston
Bradley, North (Wilts.), *see* Southwick
Bradney (in Worfield, Salop.), 68
Bradney-Marsh:
  Harriet, m. T. B. Shaw-Hellier, 202, 207
  Revd. John, 221
Bradninch (Devon), 103
Brantley brook, 64, 72-3
Braunston (Leics.), 68
Brauntley, Isabel, 115
Brecon priory, 177

Brettell:
John, 143
Thos., 107
Thos., his s., 107
Brettle, Thos., 131
Brewood, 3, 23, 46
Black Ladies, 177
Chillington, 33, 87, 89, 176, 183
Coven, 3
Gunstone, 113
Brewood forest, 11, 29, 84
brickmaking, 35, 73, 86, 111–12, 148–9, 179, 192
firebricks, 57, 59, 63
Bridgen, Rog., 184
Bridges, John, 141
Bridgnorth (Salop.), 13–14, 69, 73, 127, 181, 187, 197, 200–1
coll., 71, 74
peculiar, 73
rural dist., 180
Brierley Hill, see Kingswinford
Brierley Hill Gas Co., 152
Brigg:
Humph., 71
Moreton, 71
Brindley:
Caroline, 161
Geo., 143, 146, 160
Hester, w. of Ric., 143
Jas., 13, 127, 201
John, 146
Ric., 143, 146
fam., 123, 146
Bristol, 57
British Association for the Advancement of Science, 5
British Lens & Wall Glazing Co., 59
Broadwaters (in Kidderminster, Worcs.), 145–6
Brodor, pre-Conquest tenant, 83, 163
Bromley, see Kingswinford
Bromsgrove (Worcs.), 160, 196
Bromwich, West, 57
Sandwell, 165, 209
Volunteers, 163
Brook:
Allan, 82
Thos., 93
Brooke:
Benj., 124
Edw., 68–9
John (fl. 15th cent.), 68
John (d. 1543), 68
John (d. 1640), 68, 90
Revd. John, 69
Leigh, 69
Ralph, 68
Ric. (fl. 15th cent.), 68
Ric. (d. 1677), 69
Revd. Ric., 69
Thos., 68
fam., 68
and see Townshend
Brookes, Thos., 31–2
Brookes, Ric., 177
Broughton (in Claverley, Salop.), 68
Brown:
Gilb., 144
John, curate of Bobbington, 74
Lancelot, 167
Ric., 214
Rog., 204
T. R., 134
Thos., 184
Wm., 146–7
fam., 136
Bruford, Mary, 48
Buckinghamshire, see Stoke Poges
bucklemaking, 35, 112
Budersdorff, Madame, 201
Buffery:
Hugh, 203
Jane, m. John Burnett, 203
John (? two of this name), 203, 216
Wm., see Penn

bull baiting, 14, 53, 80, 127, 175
Bulwardine, Ric., 71
Bulwardine (in Claverley, Salop.), 196
Bunn, S. W., 147
Buraston, Miss, 117
Burdun, Ric., 85
Burgess:
Geo., 124, 144
Geo., his s., 144
fam., 124
Burgh, Ralph de, 33
Burgoyne, Sir John, 5
Burn, Wm., 166–7
Burne-Jones, Sir Edw., 9
Burneford, Ric., 147
Burnell:
Edw., 133
Sir Hugh, 133
Hugh, Baron Burnell, 67
Joyce, his w., 67
Maud, m. 1 John Lovel, Baron Lovel, 2 John de Haudlo, 133
(formerly Haudlo), Sir Nic., 133
Phil., 133
Rob., bp. of Bath and Wells, 132–3
Burnett:
Jane, see Buffery
John, 203
Rob., 203
Thos. (fl. 1514 or 1515), 203
Thos. (d. 1599), 203
Thos. (fl. 1608), 203
Burnhill Green, see Patshull
Bury, John atte, 122
Bushbury, 1, 17, 22–3
Aldersley Junction, 14n
Autherly Junction, 13–14
Essington, q.v.
Ford Mill fm., 28
Gorsebrook, 81
Moseley, 5
Oxley, 13, 79, 202
Seawall, 203
Butler:
Eliz., see Wrottesley
John, 181
Jos., 181
Sam., 181
Sir Wm., 27
Butterwick (Lincs.), 203
Buttle, Sam., 195
Buxton, Thos., curate of Tettenhall, 40

Caen (Calvados), 42
Cambridge university:
Emmanuel Coll., 219
Trinity Coll., 24
Cambridgeshire, see Milton
Campbell:
Capt. H. J. M., 107
Hugh Montgomery, 107
Mary, see Hale
Cannock forest, 30
Canterbury, abp. of, 181; and see Pole; Walter
capping, 167
Careswell, Edw., 69, 74, 76
his w., 74
Caroline, queen of George IV, 95
Carr:
R. S., 81
Thos., 44
Carter:
Cath., m. John Hamerton, 134, 153, 156
Thos., 35
Wm., 134
Cartwright:
Jacob, 221
Jane, 185
Oliver, 225
Wm., 225
Castlecroft, see Tettenhall
Castrey & Gee, 58

Caswell:
Eleanor, m. Paul White, 146
Jeremiah, 146
Catherine II, empress of Russia, 98
Catteroll (Catheralle), John, 148
Cavendish, Lord Geo., 68
Chacombe (Northants.), 220
chainmaking, 35
Chamberlayne:
John, 83
Ric., 83
Rob., 83
Chambers, Sir Wm., 97
Chandler (or Chandless), Ric., 88
Channel Islands, see Jersey
Chantrey, Sir Fra., 220
Chapel Ash, see Wolverhampton
chaplain, Wm. the, see William
Chapman, Thos., 37
Charles I, 141
Charles II, 5, 126, 137, 170
Chasepool, see Wombourne
Chasepool hay, see Kinver forest
Chebsey, 154
Checkhill, see Kinver
Checkley, Beamhurst in, 39–40
Chenvin, king's thegn, 81
Chertsey (Surr.), Sandgates in, 16, 18
Cheshire, see Audlem; Chester; Combermere abbey; Woodhey
Chester:
earldom, 175
earls of, see Avranches; Blundeville
Chester, 13, 80, 126, 163
Chillington, see Brewood
Chilwell (in Attenborough, Notts.), 203
Chishull, John, bp. of London, 16, 40
Christ Church, see Oxford, university
Christian Science, 63
Church Commissioners, see Ecclesiastical Commissioners
Church of England Men's Society, 221
Churches, Incorporated Society for the Building and Enlarging of, 220–1
Churchill (Worcs.), 52, 70, 126
Five Ways, 127
'Cippemore', see Enville
Civil Resettlement Unit, 11
Civil War, 11, 27, 33, 83, 131–2, 164–5, 219
Clam brook, see Mill brook
Clare:
Leonard, 55
Nic. le, 7
Ric., 7
Rob., 55
Claregate, see Tettenhall
Clarence, duke of, see Plantagenet
Clarke:
J. B., 221
John, 139–40
Claverley, Wm. of (? Wm. s. of Agatha), 71
Claverley (Salop.), 68, 73–5, 187, 191, 204
Aston, q.v.
Broughton, q.v.
Bulwardine, q.v.
Gatacre Pk., 69–70
man., 71, 73
rectory, 71
Shipley, q.v.
clay working, 56–7, 59
clementing, see folk customs
Clent (Staffs., later Worcs.), 126
Cleobury:
Ric. of, 129
Ric. s. of Ric. of (? another), 129
Clerke, Sir Clement, 145, 213
Cleveland (Ohio, U.S.A.), 215
Cliffe, Wastel, 57
Clifton (Glos.), 5
Clive, the, see Pattingham
cloth industry, 55, 112, 140, 148, 160, 169, 214–15
coal mining, 11, 52–3, 55–7, 204

Coalbourn brook, 49, 53, 55
Coalbournbrook, *see* Amblecote
cock fighting, 127, 175
Cockeram, Geo., 183
Cocks, Kath., m. Geo. Harry Grey, earl of Stamford and Warrington (d. 1883), 96, 116; *and see* Cox
'Cocortone' ('Cocretone'), *see* Trysull
Codsall, Wm. of, 81
Codsall, 1, 12, 17, 33, 38, 40, **76–90**, 203
    agric., 84–5
    Bilbrook, 79–80, 84, 86
        Bilbrook Ho., 79
        ch., 87
        and see Tettenhall
    the Birches, 79, 81–2, 84–5
    Brabourne, 77
    chars. for the poor, 80, 90
    ch., 39, 41, 86–90
    Clifton Ho., *see* Codsall, Manor Court
    Codsall Hall (formerly New Hall and Upper Ho.), 81
    Codsall Hall fm., 85
    Codsall Ho. (formerly Hall Ho., Lower Ho., and Old Hall), 81, 90
    Codsall Lanes, 77
    Codsall Wood, 76, 79–81, 84–6, 89
        ch., 87
        prot. nonconf., 88
        sch., 90
    council housing, 77
    curates, 87; *and see* Webb
    Dam Mill, 76–7, 79, 82, 84–5; *and see* Tettenhall
    Dead Woman's Grave, 79
    econ. hist., 84–6
    educ., 79, 81, 89–90
    electricity, 80
    fire stn., 80
    the Firs, 77
    Flemmyng Ho., 77
    Greenhills, 80
    Hall Ho., *see* Codsall, Codsall Ho.
    Heath Ho., 79
    the Hollies, 80
    Husphins Fm., 79
    inds., 85–6
    inns, 79
        Bull (Codsall village), 77
        Bull (Holyhead Rd.), 79–80
        Cross Guns, 79
        Crown, 77, 79
        Foaming Jug, 80
        Giffard Arms, 79
        Holly Bush, 77
        Lord Nelson, 77
        Old Giffard's Arms, 79
        Wheel, 77
    Kingswood, 3, 29, 76, 80, 84–6
        ch., 87
        prot. nonconf., 88
        sch., 89
        and see Tettenhall
    librs., 81
    local govt., 86
    Lower Ho., *see* Codsall, Codsall Ho.
    man., 81–2, 86
    Manor Court (formerly Clifton Ho.), 77
    Merridale Ho., *see* Codsall, Moatbrook Ho.
    Merriden, 77
    mills, 12, 85
    Moatbrook, 77
    Moatbrook (formerly Merridale) Ho., 77
    Moor Hall, 79, 82
    the Mount, 77
    New Hall, *see* Codsall, Codsall Hall
    Oaken, 17, 76, 79, 86
        agric., 84–5
        char. for the poor, 90
        Dower (formerly Oaken) Ho., 79, 83–4

    grange, 83, 85
    man., 83–4, 86
    Manor Ho., 79
    mill, 85
    Oaken green, 79
    Oaken Ho., *see* Codsall: Oaken, Dower Ho.
    Oaken Lanes, 79
    Oaken Lawn, 80, 84
    Oaken Manor, 79
    Oaken Pk. Fm., 80, 85
    pk., 80, 85
    pop., 76
    post office, 80
    prot. nonconf., 88
    Rom. Cath., 88
    sch., 90
    tithes, 82, 87
    water supply, 80
    woodland, 85
    observatory, 5
    Old Giffards, 79
    Old Hall, *see* Codsall, Codsall Ho.
    the Old Workhouse, 86
    pk., 85
    Park Ho., 79
    Pendrell (formerly Pendryl) Hall, 79, 87
    police, 80
    poor relief, 86
    pop., 3, 76, 79
    post offices, 80
    pound, 86
    prebend, *see* Tettenhall, coll.
    prot. nonconf., 88
    public services, 80
    rly., 14, 80, 84
    rds. and streets, 80
        Bakers Way, 77, 81
        Birches Ave., 90
        Birches Rd., 79
        Broadway, 89
        Chapel Lane, 89
        Chillington Drive, 89
        Church Lane, 89
        Church Rd., 77, 80–1, 89
        County Lane, 76, 80, 85
        Duck Lane, 80
        Elliots Lane, 77, 81, 90
        Heath Ho. Lane, 79–80
        Histons Hill, 77, 81, 89
        Hollybush Lane, 79
        Holyhead Rd., 76, 79, 86
        Husphins (formerly Stocking) Lane, 79
        Middle Lane, 88
        Mill Lane, 90
        Moat Brook Ave., 77
        Moatbrook Lane, 77
        Oaken Lane, 79
        Oaken Lanes, 77
        Sandy Lane, 77, 80, 85
        Shop Lane, 85
        Slate Lane, 77
        Station Rd., 77, 86
        Stocking Lane, *see* Codsall: rds. and streets, Husphins Lane
        Strawmoor Lane, 79–80
        Whitehouse Lane, 79, 87
        Wilkes Rd., 77
        Wolverhampton Rd., 77, 80, 86, 88, 90
        Wood Rd., 77
    Rom. Cath., 43, 88, 90
    the Shrubbery, 77
    social and cultural activities, 80–1
    Springfield Ho., 79
    the Stockings, 79, 82
    stocks, 86
    stone (as building material), 42–4, 85–6, 88
    Strawmoor Fm., 80
    sulphur spring, 79
    the Terrace, 79
    tithes, 19, 82, 87
    Upper Ho., *see* Codsall, Codsall Hall

    wake, 80
    water supply, 80
    Wheatstone Pk., 77
    Wood Hall, 82
    woodland, 84–5
Cole:
    Cath., w. of Rob., 104
    Jos., 64
    Rob., 104
Collier, Ric., 56
Collings, John, 112
Collins, Wm., 86
Collis:
    G. R., 132
    Wm. Blow, 51
Colombyne, John, rector of Enville, 114
Colwich, Great Haywood in, 13
Comber:
    Marg., 160
    Thos., 139
    Thos. the, *see* Thomas
    and see Cumber
Combermere abbey (Ches.), 137
Compower Ltd., 79
Compson, Thos., 57
Compton:
    John s. of Wm. of, 34
    Rob. s. of Wm. of, 122
    Sir Wm., 25
Compton, *see* Kinver; Tettenhall
Compton brook, 144
Congregationalism, 5, 8, 43–4, 88–9, 172, 183, 221–2
Coningsby (Lincs.), 62
Connolly:
    Henrietta, w. of Louis, 88
    Louis, 88
Conservative party, 11, 18, 22
Cook:
    John, 145, 156, 160
    Nic. s. of Wm. the, *see* Nicholas
    Ric., 157
    Thos., 145
    Wm. the, *see* William
Cooke:
    Ric., 156
    Wm., vicar of Pattingham, 181
Coote, Diana, *see* Newport
Cope, Wm. Hen., 57
Copley, Anne, 182
Copley, *see* Pattingham
Copley brook, 172
Coppenhall (in Penkridge), the Hyde in, 164
Corbett:
    Chas., 69
    Edw. (d. 1719), 69
    Edw. (d. 1752), 69
    Hannah, 69, 75
    John, 62
    Mary, w. of Edw. (d. 1752), 69
    Mary (d. 1792), 69, 75
    Rog., 69
    Mrs., 69
    fam., 69
Corbyn:
    Cath., *see* Morfe
    John, 106
Corden Fund, 221
Corngreaves, *see* Rowley Regis
Cornish, Hen., 145, 213
Cornwall (or St. Augustine), Phil. of, rector of Pattingham, 180–1
Cornwallis:
    Eliz., *see* Watson
    Thos., 176
Cotton, Geo., 225
Coughton:
    Sim. of (also Sim. de Verdun), 26
    Wm. of, 26
Coughton (Warws.), 83, 130
Cound (Salop.), *see* Cressage
Courtenay, Frances, m. Sir John Wrottesley (d. 1787), 83
Coven, *see* Brewood
Coventry, bps. of, *see* Lichfield

Coventry and Lichfield, bps. of, *see* Lichfield
Coventry priory, 153, 176–7
Cox:
　Eliz., 76
　Frances, w. of Thos. (d. 1621), 106
　Fra., 106
　J., 76
　John, 106
　Thos. (d. by 1615), 109
　Thos. (d. 1621), 106, 109
　Thos., ? his father, 106
　Wm., 75–6
　fam., 106
　and see Cocks
Cradley (in Halesowen, Worcs.), 55, 57
Cradley Heath, *see* Rowley Regis
Cranage, Sarah, 180
Crane:
　Lilian May, wife of V. J., 221
　V. J., vicar of Swindon, in Wombourne, 221
Creed, Ric., 98
Cressage (in Cound, Salop.), 155
Cresswell:
　John, 31–2
　Ric. (fl. 1524), 20
　Ric. (d. 1559), 19, 21
　Ric. (d. 1612), 19, 21
　Ric. (d. 1625), 21
　Ric. (d. 1708), 21, 39, 46
　Ric. (d. 1723), 21
　Ric. (d. 1743), 17, 19, 21, 34
　fam., 19–21, 46
cricket, 14, 53, 81, 95–6, 128, 163, 188, 201
Crimean War, 5
Croffts, Thos., and his w. Anne, 46
Croft, John, 46
Cronkhall, Ric., 40
Cronkhall, *see* Tettenhall
Cross, John, curate of Kinver, 155
Crosse, Longworth, 160
Crowley, Ambrose, 60
Crown House Ltd., 59
Croxden abbey, 83, 86
Croydon (Surr.), 42
Crump, John Herb., 68
Cumber, John, 155; *and see* Comber
Curtis, E., 184
　his s., 184
Curzon:
　Dame Mary, 25*n*
　Mary, m. Edw. Sackville, earl of Dorset, 25
'Cuthbert Bede', *see* Bradley
Cynefares Stane, *see* Wolverley, Vale's Rock
Cynibre, *see* Kinver

Dadnall Hill, *see* Pattingham; Tettenhall
Dalton:
　Sarah, 223
　Revd. Wm., 211
Dam Mill, *see* Codsall; Tettenhall
Damer:
　Lady Caroline, 68
　Jos., Baron Milton, later earl of Dorchester, 68
　Lionel, 68
Danet, John, rector of Pattingham, 180–1
Danynell, John, 81
Darbey, Wm., curate of Bobbington, 74
Dartmouth:
　ctsses. of, *see* Finch; Wynn-Carrington
　earls of, *see* Legge
Dashfield, Fra., 184
Davenport:
　H. T., *see* Hinckes
　Jane Mary, 123
　John, 22
　Wm. Yelverton, 181

David, prince of Gwynedd, 15
　Emma, his w., *see* Emma
Dawncraft (boat hire business), 127
de Houx:
　——, 58
　fam., 58
Delves:
　Ellen, m. Sir Rob. Sheffield, 203
　Etheldena, *see* Babington
Dema Glass Ltd., 59
Dene:
　John de (fl. 14th cent.), 82
　John (fl. 15th cent.), 82
　Martin de, 82
　Ric., 82
　and see Wood, otherwise Dene
Dent, Wm., 81
Derby, Dorothy, *see* Persehouse
Derby Stakes, 124
Derbyshire, *see* Hathersage; Somersall Herbert
Despenser, Hugh le, 67
Devey:
　Fra., 109, 179
　Joan, 184
　Rog., 180
　and see Devy
Devon:
　ctss. of, *see* Barre
　earl of, *see* Stafford
Devon, *see* Bradninch
Devy, John, 179; *and see* Devey
Deysse, Thos., 109
Dicken, Thos., 181
Dickins (Dicones, Dykon):
　Hugh, 70
　Humph., 70
　Humph. (? another), 225
　John (fl. 1379), 70
　John (fl. 1496), 70
　John (d. 1679), 70
　John (d. 1760), 70
　Martha, w. of Tomyns the younger, 72
　Thos. (fl. 15th cent.), 70
　Thos. (d. 1674), 68, 70, 72
　Thos. (d. 1710), 70
　Tomyns, 68, 117
　Tomyns, his s., 72
　Wm. (fl. 1377), 70
　Wm., father of John (fl. 1379), 70
　Wm. (fl. 16th cent.), 70–1
　fam., 69–71
Dimmock, E. B., 147
Dippons, the, *see* Tettenhall
Dixon, Oliver, 59
Dobson, Mary, 46
Dodderhill (Worcs.), *see* Impney
Dodford priory (Worcs.), 137
Doding, Miles, 177
Dole, Adam s. of Rob., 83
Dolman:
　Agnes, 196
　Steph. (d. ? 1554), 192, 194
　Steph. (d. ? 1648), 196
　Thos. (fl. 16th cent.), 194–5
　Thos. (fl. 1648), 196
　Wal., 195
Don Everall Aviation Ltd., 14
Donington (Salop.), 26
　Kilsall, *q.v.*
　Neach Hill, 181
Dorchester, earl of, *see* Damer
Dorset:
　ctss. of, *see* Curzon
　earls of, *see* Sackville
Dorset, 31
Downing:
　Bridget, *see* Bowles
　Edm., 177
　Hen., curate of Bobbington, 74
　Hen. Bowles, rector of Enville, 113
　Isaac, 68
　John, rector of Enville, 106, 113
　John, his grds., rector of Enville, 113
　T. L., 146

Dowty Group Ltd., 36
Draper:
　Geo., 146
　Geo., his s., 146
Drayton Bassett, 175
Droitwich (Worcs.), 119
Ducat Heating Co., 51
Dudley:
　Ambrose, earl of Warwick, 83, 130, 134, 164
　Anne, *see* Whorwood
　Dud, 209, 213, 215
　Sir John, later duke of Northumberland, 190, 208–9, 218, 225
　fam., *see* Sutton
Dudley:
　Baroness, *see* Sutton
　barons, 207–8; *and see* Sutton; Ward
　barony, 23, 96, 188–9, 202
　earls of, *see* Ward
Dudley (Worcs., later Staffs.), 35, 40, 52, 95, 146, 152, 187, 200–1, 207
　boro., 61–2
　castle, 208
　General Institution for the Relief of Ruptures, 216
　man., 23, 103, 188, 202, 212
　Netherton, *q.v.*
　pk., 55
　priory, 190, 193, 209, 217–18, 225
Dudley and Ward:
　Baron, *see* Ward
　Vct., *see* Ward
Dugdale, Sir John, 94
Dunclent, Thos., 96
Dunne:
　Ann, 104
　Chas., *see* Amphlett
Dunsley, Gilb. of, 134
Dunsley, *see* Kinver
Dunstall, *see* Wolverhampton
Dunston (in Penkridge), Dunston Hall in, 18
Durham, bp. of, *see* Talbot
Durdent, Wal., bp. of Coventry, 217
Dutch troops, 11
Dykon, *see* Dickins
Dyson:
　Gravenor, 107
　Hen., 107

Eardington, Alan of (also Alan de Haya), 23; *and see* Erdington
Eardington (Salop.), 23
Eashing (in Godalming, Surr.), 207
Eastham (Worcs.), 101
Eaton, John, 149
Ebbels, Rob., 41, 194, 220
Eccleshall, Jos., vicar of Sedgley, 157
Eccleshall, 58
Ecclesiastical (later Church) Commissioners, 39–40, 42–4, 62, 81, 87, 154, 193
Edgar, King, 18, 39
Edgbaston (Warws.), 5, 89, 182
Edinburgh, 194
Education, Board of, 158
Edward the Confessor, 24
Edward I, 126
Edward II, 129; as Prince of Wales, 129
Edward III, 16, 26, 83
Edward IV, 96
Edward, Prince of Wales (the Black Prince), 26
Edwin, earl of Mercia, 129
Edwin, pre-Conquest tenant, 107
Egginton, John, 79
Elcock, John, 117
Elfhild, Anglo-Saxon landowner, 26
Elgar, Madame, 159
Elizabeth I, 25, 141
Elizabeth II, 220
Elwell:
　Chas. John, 9
　Paul, 9
　Thos., 9

Emma, dau. of Geof., count of Anjou, m. David, prince of Gwynedd, 15
Emmanuel College, see Cambridge university
engineering, see aero-engineering; agricultural engineering
England:
  G. P., 41
  R. A., 70
Englefield:
  Alan (d. 1226 or 1227), 207
  Alan (fl. 1271), 207
  Ansculf, 207
  Ellis, 207
  Joan, w. ? of Alan (fl. 1271), m. 2 John de Eton, 207
  John, 207
  Phil., 207
  Rog., 207
  Wm. (fl. before 1184), 207
  Wm. (fl. 1190s), 207
  Wm. (fl. mid 13th cent.), 207–8, 214
  Wm. (d. before 1281), 207
Englefield (Berks.), 207
Ensell, Geo., 59
Enville:
  Alice, w. of Wm. of (d. by 1279), 29n
  And. of, 96
  Joan, ? m. —— Lowe, 96
  Joan, w. of ? Wm. (d. ? 1286 or 1287), 96n
  John of, 96
  Margery, w. of John of, 96
  Ralph of (fl. 12th cent.), 96
  Ralph of (d. 1354 or 1355), 96
  Ric. of (fl. 12th cent.), 96
  Ric. of (d. ? 1276), 96
  Ric. of (fl. 14th cent.), 96
  Wm. of (fl. 12th cent.), 96
  Wm. of (d. by 1279), 96n
  Wm. of (d. ? 1286 or 1287), 96
Enville, 56, **91–118**, 209
  agric., 107–11
  almshos., 113
  assoc. for prosecution of felons, 95
  Bar green, 91, 108–9, 115
  Blundies, 93, 108
  Blundies fm., 93, 110
  Bradbury's Fm., 94
  Camp fm., 94
  chars. for the poor, 117–18
  cherries, 96
  ch., 113–16, *113*, *192*
  'Cippemore', 93, 107, 109
  the Cottage, 95
  council hos., 93
  Coxgreen, 91, 106–7, 110
  cricket, 95–6, 128
  Crump Hillocks fm., 104
  curates, 114; and see Archer; Evans
  econ. hist., 107–12
  educ., 116–17, *145*
  electricity, 95
  Enville Hall, 91, 93, 95–9, *96*, *98*
    est., 62, 68, 104–7, 110, 112, 142
    gardens, 95, *96*, 99–100
    pk., 98–101, *100*, *101*, 110
  fair, 111
  Four Ashes, 74, 104, 109, 111–12, 116–17
  friendly socs., 96
  gasworks, 95
  Gilbert's Cross, 94, 112
  golf course, 96
  Greenage, see Enville, Groundwyns
  Greenwich Pool, 94
  Groundwyns (otherwise Greenage), 94, 114
  Grove fm., 94, 104
  Hay Ho., see Enville, Toys Fm.
  Highgate common, 94, 96, 109–10, 112
  Highgate Fm., 94
  Hillhouse (formerly the Hull), 93
  the Hollies, 91, 107, 114, 116–17
  Home fm., 99, *102*, 111

Hoo, 93, 101, 108–11
Hoo Fm., 93, 111
Hoo, Over, 93
the Hull, see Enville, Hillhouse
inds., 111–12
inns:
  Cat, 91, 94
  Cock, 93
  Crown, 91
  Stamford Arms, 95
  Swan, 91
Lady Dorothy's Cottage, 117, *145*
Leigh Ho., 91, 99, 101, 103
Little Morfe Fm., 93
local govt., 112–13
Lutley, 94, 108, 114
  agric., 108–9, 111
  chap., 115
  Lutley Fm., 104
  Lutley Mill fm., 104
  man., 73, 91, 103–5, 112
  mills, 111
Lyndon, 93, 99, 108–9, 112, 115
Lyndon Fm., 99, 103, *112*
Lyons, 94
man., 96–103, 111–13
Mere, 94, 108, 111–12
  est., 104–5, 110
  the Mere, 105, 112
  Mere fm., *33*, 105, 110, 112
  Mere Hall (formerly Mere Ho.), 105
mills, 108, 111–12
Moos Cottage, 117
Morfe, 91, 93, 107–9, 111, 114
  chap., 106, 115
  man., 105–7, 111–12
  Morfe Hall Fm., 93, 111
  Morfe Ho. Fm., 93, 111
  Morfeheath Fm., 94, 96, 111
Newhouse fm., 94, 110
No Man's Green, 91, 109
nonconf., 116
Over Hoo, see Enville, Hoo, Over
Philleybrook, 94, 109
Philleybrook Hall fm., 94, 110–11
police, 95
Poolhouse Fm., 94
poor relief, 113
pop., 91, 107
post office, 95
pound, 112
public services, 95
race horses, 95
rectors, 113–14; and see Bowles; Colombyne; Downing; Garbett; Jesson; Payne; Price; Southall; Watts; Wilkes
rectory, 112, 114
rds., 94–5
  Blundies Lane, 91, 93, 95
  Brookside, 93
  Browns Lake, 93
  Chester Rd., 91, 93–4, 113
  Legh Lane, 91–2, 98–9
  Mere Lane, 94, 105
  Mill Lane, 99
  Morfe Lane, 93–4
  Pouchers Pool Rd., 111
Sampson's Cave, 93
the Sheepwalks, 93, 110–11
social and cultural activities, 95–6
Stamford Ho., 95
stocks, 112
Swinford Cottage, 116
tithes, 109, 114
Toys Fm. (formerly Hay Ho.), 94, 111
Upper Falcon Fm., 93
wakes, 95
the Walls, 93
warreners' lodges, 99, 111
warrens, 111
water supply, 95
West Cottage, 114
Woodcock Hill, 112

Woodhouse, 94
woodland, 91, 98–9, 106, 109
Enville and Kinver Farmers' Club, 140
Enville hunt, 95
Erdington:
  Alan of, 23
  Giles of, dean of Wolverhampton, 23, 81
  and see Eardington
Erdington (in Aston, Warws.), 23
Essex, see Pyrgo (in Havering-atte-Bower)
Essington, in Bushbury, 203
Estepona (Spain), 124
Ethelred, King, 25
Eton:
  Joan de, see Englefield
  John de, 207
Evans:
  John, curate of Enville, 114, 116
  John, 9
  Nancy, 122
  Sam., 222
  Sarah, 122
  Thos., archdeacon of Worcester, 117
Everdon:
  John (? John le lordeson) (fl. 15th cent.), 203
  John (fl. 16th cent.), 134, 144
  Humph., 134, 144, 203, 216
  Ric. de, 203
  Rog., 203, 216
  Sim., 203
  Thos., 134, 144, 203, 216
  Wm., 134, 144, 203
Everest Frozen Foods, 73
Evesham abbey (Worcs.), 26–7
Evesham, battle of, 26, 176
Eveson, L. W., 69

Faddiley (Ches.), see Woodhey
Fairbanks:
  Emma, 90
  Maryann, 90
Fareley:
  Hen., 83
  Ric., 83
Farley, see Alton
Farmer, Thos., 46
Faulkner:
  John, 210
  Judith, w. of Thos., 31
  Thos., 31
Feckenham (Worcs.), 142
Felkin, Ellen Thorneycroft, see Fowler
Fellows, M., 132
Feoffees for the Purchase of Impropriations, 136, 153–4, 158
Fernyhough, Revd. Wm., 3
Ferrers:
  Eliz., Baroness Ferrers of Groby, 16
  Eliz., see Wrottesley
  Hen., Baron Ferrers of Groby, 16
  Sir Humph. (d. 1554), 16
  Sir Humph. (d. 1608), 16
  Sir Humph. (d. 1633), 16
  Sir John (d. 1512), 16
  John (d. 1576), 16
  Sir John (d. 1633), 16
  John (d. 1680), 16
  Thos., 16
  Sir Thos., 16
  Wm., Baron Ferrers of Groby, 16, 27
Ferro Corporation, 215
Ferro (Great Britain) Ltd., 215
Fieldhouse:
  Benj., 153
  Rog., 71
  Wm. s. of Ric. of the, 71
  Wm., 71
Finch:
  Lady Augusta, m. Wm. Wal. Legge, earl of Dartmouth, 163
  John, 131, 145
Finchfield, see Tettenhall
Finnemore, Wm., 147

firebricks, *see* brickmaking
Firmstone, H. O., 146
Fitton:
  Anne, 25
  Mary, m. 1 Wm. Polwhele, 2 John
    Lougher, 25
FitzAnsculf, Wm., 23, 53, 96, 105, 107,
  188–90, 202, 207–8
FitzBernard, Thos., 129
Fitzherbert, Nic., 82
FitzPeter, Geof., 129
FitzPhilip:
  Emma, *see* Leaton
  Gilb., 70
  John, 21, 67, 70, 72, 74, 129, 143, 153
    his w., 72
  and see John son of Philip
Fladbury (Worcs.), *see* Throckmorton
Fleeming (Flemyng):
  Hen., 17
  Humph., 16–17
  John (d. 1740), 17
  John (d. 1764), 17
  John (d. 1810), 17
  Thos. (fl. 1586–90), 17
  Thos. (d. 1658), 17
  Wal., 46
  fam., 17
Fleming, Rog., 33–4
Fleming, Jos., & Co., 58
Flemyng, *see* Fleeming
Fletcher:
  John, 181
  R. J., 133
Foley:
  Edw., 130
  Eliza Maria, *see* Hodgetts
  Eliz., m. John Hodgetts, 130
  H. T. H., 156
  John, 158
  John Hodgetts, *see* Hodgetts-Foley
  P. H., 134, 152
  Paul, 130
  (formerly Hodgetts-Foley), Paul
    Hen., 130
  Phil., 130, 133–4, 139, 141–5, 147,
    153, 157, 213
  Ric., 135, 145–6
  T. P., vicar of Wombourne, 218
  Thos., 54, 130, 133, 135–6, 141, 143,
    145–6, 213
  Wm. (d. 1735), 130
  Wm. (d. 1755), 130, 145, 150
  fam., 16 *n*, 131, 136–7, 141, 144, 148,
    153, 155–6
folk customs:
  clementing, *33*, 96
  gooding, 67
  well dressing, 14
Folkes, H. J., 153
Ford, Edw., 161
Foresters, Ancient Order of, 15, 129
Forster, Ant., 208; *and see* Foster
Forth, John, 145, 213
Forty, Anne, 159
Foster:
  Jas., 61–3, 132
  Wm., 53, 61
  Wm. Hen., 61
  Wm. Orme, 53, 61, 132
  fam., 60
  and see Forster
Four Ashes, *see* Enville
Fowke:
  Ant., 113
  John, 113
Fowler:
  Cath., 47
  Chas., 23, 39
  Dorothy, w. of Ric., 23
  Dorothy (d. 1791), 47
  Ellen, *see* Thorneycroft
  Ellen Thorneycroft, m. A. L. Fel-
    kin, 5
  Hen. Hartley, Vct. Wolverhampton,
    5, 8

Jas., 23
Ric. (d. 1752), 23
Ric., *see* Fowler-Butler
Sibyl, *see* Lee
Thos. (d. 1796), 23
Thos. (d. 1851), 23
Thos. Leversage, 23
Wal. (d. 1647), 23
Wal. (d. 1668), 23
Wal. (d. 1711), 23, 46
fam., 41
Fowler-Butler:
  Caroline Anne, w. of Lt.-Col. Ric.,
    23
  (formerly Fowler), Ric., 23
  Lt.-Col. Ric., 23
  Ric. Owen Wynne, 23
  Maj.-Gen. Rob. Hen., 23
Fox, Col. Thos., 131
Fox Earth, Marg. of the, *see* Margaret
Foxall, John, 32
France, 24; *and see* Caen; Lorraine;
  Normandy; Paris Exhibition
  (1878)
Frankley, Phil. of, 188–9; *and see* Try-
  sull (or Frankley)
Frankley (Worcs.), 188
Free Foresters cricket club, 95
Free Gardeners, United Order of, 15,
  67, 175, 188, 202
Freman:
  Hervey, 83
  Ralph, 83
Friends, Society of (Quakers), 88
Fryer:
  John (d. 1780), 34
  John (fl. 1828), 34
  Mary, 17
  Ric. (d. 1774), 34
  Ric. (d. 1846), 17, 34
  Wm. Fleeming, 17, 81–2
  fam., 17
Full Gospel Church, 63
fuller, Wm. the, *see* William
Fullmer, C. W., curate of Trysull, 194

Gabert, Revd. Geo., 74
Gailey, *see* Penkridge
Gallows (? also Ball) brook, 172
Gamage (Gamages):
  Matt. de, 15
  Wm. de, 16
Gandon, Jas., 205–6
Garbett, Ric., rector of Enville, 109,
  114
Garret, Ric., 46
Garter, Knights of the, 26
Gaskell:
  Frank, 79, 82, 87
  fam., 82
Gatacre Park, *see* Claverley
Gaunt, John of, duke of Lancaster, 176
Gaunt & Hickman, 36
Gentlewoman's Journal, 79
George III, 204
George IV, 95; as Prince of Wales,
  204
George V, as duke of York, 163
Gerard, Sir Gilb., 131
Germany, 59
Geva, dau. of Hugh d'Avranches, earl
  of Chester, m. Geof. Ridel, 175
Gibbons, Benj., 69
Gibbs, Jas., 165, 170
Gibson, ——, 183
Gibthorp:
  Eliz., m. Wm. Babington, 203
  John, 203
Giffard:
  Dorothy, 177
  Edw., 177
  Sir John (d. 1556), 89, 176–7
  John (d. 1613), 176, 183
  John (d. by 1647), 177
  Sophia, m. John, Baron Wrottesley
    (d. 1867), 83

T. W., 33
Thos. (d. 1560), 176
Thos. (fl. 1581), 177
W. T. C., 87
Giggetty, *see* Wombourne
Gilbert, Domesday tenant (? two of this
  name), 96, 207
Gilbert, Thos., 42
Gillett & Johnston, 42
Girls' Friendly Society, 124
glassmaking, 52, 56–60, *64*, 134, *144*,
  149, 215
Glodoen, Domesday tenant, 26
Gloucester:
  dchss. of, *see* Alice
  duke of, *see* William
Gloucester, 75, 116, 156, 194
Gloucestershire, *see* Bristol; Clifton;
  Gloucester; Tewkesbury abbey
Godalming (Surr.), *see* Eashing
Godwin, pre-Conquest tenant, 23
Goldthorn Hill, *see* Wolverhampton
gooding, *see* folk customs
Gorsebrook, *see* Bushbury
Goscote, *see* Walsall
Gower:
  Baron, *see* Leveson-Gower
  Earl, *see* Leveson-Gower
Grafton (Worcs.), 104
Grainger, John, 218; *and see* Granger
Graiseley, *see* Wolverhampton
Graiseley brook, 1, 9, 29
Granger:
  Hen., 44, 47
  Mary, 191
  Rob., 25
  and see Grainger
Granville, W. L., 165
Gravenor:
  Edw. (d. *c.* 1580), 107
  Edw. (d. 1654), 107, 116–17
  John (fl. 1550s), 107
  John (d. by 1621), 107
  Nic., 71
  Wm. (d. 1544), 71–2
  Wm. (d. before 1550), 107
  and see Grosvenor; Grovenor
Gray & Ormson, 100
Grayson, S. A., 190
  his w., *see* Hartley
Grazebrook:
  Eliz., w. of T. W., 132
  Fra., 132
  O. F., 132
  T. W., 132
Greasley, Wm., 90
Great Haywood, *see* Colwich
Green:
  Edw., 153
  Jos., 169
  Maud of the, *see* Maud
  Sim. of the, *see* Simon
  Thos. (fl. 1600), 208
  Thos. (fl. 1631), 211
  Thos. in the, *see* Thomas
Greene, Edw., 35
Greensforge, *see* Wombourne
Greenstreet:
  A. T., vicar of Pattingham, 182
  W. G., curate of Patshull and vicar of
    Pattingham, 170, 181–2
Greenwich (Kent), 225
Gresley, Joan, m. Thos. Astley, 164
Gretton, Mrs., 76
Grey:
  Ambrose, 54, 56, 97, 104, 112, 189,
    203
    his w., 115
  Anne, w. of Edw., 115
  Anne, w. of Humph., 135
  Booth, 99
  (formerly Lambert), Cath., *see* Payne
  Lady Dorothy, 116–17
  Sir Edw., 97, 106, 135, 142, 144, 155,
    157
  Edw., 115

Eileen, m. 1 Wm. Hen. Leicester Stanhope, earl of Harrington, 2 J. P. Bissill, 54, 97, 114, 135
Eleanor, *see* Lowe
Fra., 97
Geo., 106
Geo. Harry, earl of Stamford, later earl of Stamford and Warrington (d. 1819), 57, 63, 93, 95, 97, 109–10, 113, 116–17, 122, 125, 138, 141, 145
Geo. Harry, earl of Stamford and Warrington (d. 1845), 55, 62, 95, 110, 113, 136
Geo. Harry, earl of Stamford and Warrington (d. 1883), 52–4, 95–7, 97, 99–100, 105, 107, 110–12, 114, 116, 128, 134–5, 142–3
Harry, earl of Stamford (d. 1739), 93, 97, 116, 118
Harry, earl of Stamford (d. 1768), 97, 97, 99, 103, 107, 112–13, 115, 117
Hen. (fl. 15th cent.), 106
Hen. (d. 1687), 54, 56, 94, 97, 117, 135–6, 145
Hen., Baron Grey of Groby, 97
Hen., earl of Stamford, 97
(formerly Lambert), Sir Hen. Foley, 97
Humph., 135
Jane, w. of John (d. 1594), 97
John (fl. 15th cent.), 106
John (d. 1594), 56, 68, 97, 106, 111, 144, 203, 212
John (d. 1709), 56, 97, 136
Sir John Foley, 62, 97
Kath., ctss. of Stamford and Warrington, *see* Cocks
Mary, m. Sir Wal. Wrottesley (d. 1659), 225
Mary, w. of Hen. (d. 1687), 115
Mary, ctss. of Stamford, *see* Booth
Reynold, Baron Grey of Ruthin, 135
Rob., 135
Rob., his s., 106
Thos. (d. 1559), 97, 110, 115, 135, 190, 203, 212
Thos. (fl. later 16th cent.), 109
Thos. (d. before 1690), 115
Thos., earl of Stamford, 97
Wm., 106
fam., 54, 68, 110, 116, 135–6, 151, 155, 203
Grice, Wm., 208
Grier, J. W., curate of Amblecote, 53, 62
Griffiths:
    J., 60
    Josiah, 156
    S. A., 157
    fam., 60
Groome:
    Anna, w. of John, 189
    John, 189
    Wannerton, 189
Grossmith, Geo., 201–2
Grosvenor:
    (otherwise Gravenor), John, 71
    Jonas, 7
    Wm., 82
    and see Gravenor; Grovenor
Grove:
    Edm. Wells, 124
    Edw., 34
    Jas. Amphlett, 104, 110–11
    John (d. 1699), 160
    John (fl. 1724), 51
    John (fl. 1744), 34
Grovenor, Ric., 61; *and see* Gravenor; Grosvenor
Grylls, Mary Rosalie, m. Sir Geof. Mander, 18
Guest, Thos., 61
Gunstone, *see* Brewood

Gutheresburn, *see* Kinver forest
Gwynedd, prince of, *see* David

Hackett:
    Thos., 148
    Wm., 89
Hagley:
    Phil. of, 103
    Rob. of, 103
    Rog. of, 103
    Wm. of, 103
Hagley (Worcs.), 57, 61, 99, 103
Hale:
    Corbett, 107, 117
    John (d. 1710), 107
    John (d. 1745), 107
    John (d. 1808), 107
    Mary, m. Hugh Montgomery Campbell, 107
    Mary, w. of Corbett, 107
    Polly, w. of John (d. 1808), 107, 110
    Thos. (fl. 1586–1606), 107
    Thos. (d. 1627), 107
    Thos. (d. 1630 or 1632), 107
    fam., 106
Halesowen (Worcs.), 113, 181
    abbey, 208, 214, 216
    and see Cradley; the Leasowes
Halfcot, *see* Kinver
Halfpenny Green, *see* Bobbington
Halidon Hill, battle of, 26
Hall (Halle):
    Hen., 57
    John, 57
    Thos. del, 204
Hall, John, & Co. (of Stourbridge) Ltd., 54, 57
hall gate, Wm. at the, *see* William
Halle, *see* Hall
Hallen, Benj., 124
Halling (Kent), 25
Hamerton:
    Ant., 156
    Cath., *see* Carter
    Cath., *see* Whorwood
    John (d. 1669), 134, 156
    John, his s., 134
    Wm., 130, 134, 153, 156
Hampshire, *see* Hinton
Hampton:
    Bevis, 129
    John de (fl. 1325–7), 26
    John (d. 1433), 129, 131, 141–2
    John (d. 1472), 129, 141–2, 154–5
    Ric., 129
Hancox fam., 124
Hand:
    Edw., 172
    Thos., 44, 47
    fam., 172
Handel, G. F., 206
Handsworth (Staffs., later Birmingham), Soho manufactory in, 58
Harbridge Crystal Glass Co., 60
Harcourt:
    Ellen, 117
    Isabel, m. —— Astley, 164
    Jane, 117
    Ric., 164
Hardware, Chas., 86
Hardwick:
    Hugh, 184
    Martin, 184
    Wm., 169
Hardwick, *see* Pattingham
Harley:
    Thos., 77
    Thos., his s., 77
Harper, Jas., 179
Harper, Hen., & Son, 157
Harrington:
    ctss. of, *see* Grey
    earl of, *see* Stanhope
Harriotts:
    Eliz., *see* Barnesley
    Rob., 189

Harris, Peter, 57
Harris & Pearson, 57
Harris, J. Seymour, & Partners, 89
Harrison, Ric., curate of Tettenhall, 40
Harrison, Arthur, & Co., 60
Hart, John, 57
Hartley, T. W., 190
    his w., m. 2 S. A. Grayson, 190
    his dau., *see* Tonkinson
Hartshorn, Geo., 145
Harwale, John, 140
Haseley (Warws.), 176
Haselwall, Wm. de, 71
Hastings:
    Ferdinand, 68
    Sir Hen., 68
Hathersage (Derb.), 177
Hatherton (in St. Peter's, Wolverhampton), 82
Hatton, Wm. (? two of this name), 147
Haudlo:
    John de, 133
    Maud, *see* Burnell
    Sir Nic., *see* Burnell
    fam., 132
Haughton:
    John, 74
    Ric., 177
Haughton (in Shifnal, Salop.), 71
Havering-atte-Bower (Essex), *see* Pyrgo
Hawkes, Edw., 111
Hawk's Well stream, 168
Hawley, Mary, 184
Hawys, Thos., 139
Hay, Wm. atte, 69
Haya, Alan de, *see* Eardington
Haycock, Edw., 41
Hayward:
    John, 83
    John, s. of Wm., 16
    Revd. John, 16
    Rob., 83
    Wm., 16
Haywood, Great, *see* Colwich
Hazelwood, Thos., 140, 148
Heale, W. J., vicar of Wombourne, 221
Heath, Thos., 148
Heiton, And., 98
Helgot, Domesday tenant, 67
Helgor, Phil. s. of, *see* Philip
Hellier:
    Sam. (d. 1727), 19, 21, 204
    Sam. (d. 1751), 204, 206, 220
    Sir Sam., 201, 204–6, 220, 222–4
    and see Shaw-Hellier
Hellman, *see* Hillman
Heming, Sam., 63
Henry III, 67–8, 123, 129, 131, 153, 176
Henry VI, 164
Henry VIII, 141
Hensman, Commander Melvill, 207
Henzey:
    Edw., 58
    Jacob, 58
    John, 59
    Joshua, 51, 60
    Thos., 59
Hepham:
    Hugh de, 67, 71
    Joan de, *see* Wauton
Herbert, Baron, *see* Somerset
Hereford diocese, 73
Herefordshire, *see* Rolstone; Stoke Edith
Hertfordshire, Hertingfordbury Park in, 160
Hewett:
    John, 74
    Wm., 74
Hexall, E. G., 160
Heygreve:
    Emma of, 136
    Felice of, 136
    Rob. of, 136

Hickman:
  Sir Alf., 11, 18, 22
  Anne, see Barrett
  Edw., 8
  Ethel Marg., w. of V. E., 22
  John, 83
  M. J., 68
  Nathan, 83
  (formerly Hickmans), Ric., 83
  Rog., 83, 88
  Col. T. E., 18
    his w., 18
  V. E., 22
  Wm., 83
Hickmans:
  Ric., see Hickman
  Thos., 195-6
Higgs:
  John, 33
  Rog., 112
  Thos., 33, 43
Hill:
  Charlotte, 45
  Fra., vicar of Tettenhall, 39
  John, 209
  Peter, 51
  Ric., 183
  Ric. s. of Ric. of the, 71
  Thos. (fl. 1762-1815), 51, 59-60, 63
  Thos. (fl. 1821-31), 146
  Thos. (fl. 1835-c. 1841), 223
  Revd. Thos., 224
  W. H., 224
  Waldron, 59-60
  Wm., 45
  Mrs., 45
  fam., 224
  and see Hull
Hill, Messrs., 42
Hill, Hampton & Co., 57, 59
Hill, Hampton, Harrison & Wheeley, 59
Hill, Waldron, Littlewood & Hampton, 59
Hillary, Sir Rog., 202
Hillman (Hellman):
  John, 124, 139
  Revd. John, 90
  Thos., 124, 139
  fam., 124, 139
Himley, 207-9, 212, 216, 218-19
Hinckes:
  (formerly Davenport), H. T., 22
  Revd. Josiah, 18, 22
  Peter, 20, 22
  Peter Tichborne, 18, 20, 22
  Theodosia, 10, 17, 22
  Wm., 31
  fam., 20
Hinckes Trust Estate, 17
hingemaking, 9, 31, 35-6
Hinksford, see Wombourne
Hinnington (in Shifnal, Salop.), 29
Hinton (Hants), 83
Hodgetts:
  Eliza Maria, m. Edw. Foley, 130, 134
  Eliz. (d. ? 1690), 109
  Eliz., w. of John Hodgetts (d. 1800), 146
  Eliz., see Foley
  John (fl. 1623-30), 218
  John (d. 1789), 123, 130, 144, 146-7, 149, 156, 181
  John (d. 1800), 123, 146
  Marg., see Paston
  Thos., 145
  Wm., 123
  fam., 155
Hodgetts-Foley:
  H. J. W., 130, 159
  (formerly Foley), John Hodgetts, 128, 130, 133, 136, 144, 146, 155, 159
  Paul Hen., see Foley

Hodgson:
  Hen., 146
  John, vicar of Kinver, 154
Hodson:
  Lawr., 9
  Wm., 9
Holand, Thos. de, earl of Kent, 176; and see Holland
Holbrooke, John, 181
Holdnall, Wal., 161
Holland, Norman, 69; and see Holand
Hollins fam., 132
Holmer, Wm., 107
Holt:
  John, 134
  Mary, m. G. W. Wainwright, 134
Holyhead (Ang.), 201
Homfray:
  Fra. (d. 1737), 60, 146, 213
  Fra., his s., 145-6, 213
  Fra. (d. 1809), 146, 213-14
  Jeremiah, 146
  Jeston, 145-6, 213
  Mary, w. of Fra. (d. 1737), 146
  P., 214
  Thos., 146, 214
Honeybourne, Jos., vicar of Patting-ham, 181-2
Hope:
  Humph., 140
  John, 98
  Thos. (fl. earlier 19th cent.), 35
  Thos. (fl. later 19th cent.), 35-6
Hopkins:
  Eliza, 64
  Maria, 64
Horewood, see Whorwood
Horewood, see Kinver, Compton
Horwood, John, 211
Hospitallers, Knights, 137
Housman, Revd. Thos., 128
Houx, see de Houx
Hoveringham Group Ltd., 215
Howard:
  Sir Geo., later Field Marshal, 16
  Marg., m. Sir Ric. Leveson (d. 1661), 25
  Mary, 16
  Thos., duke of Norfolk, 208
  Gen. Thos., 16
  Wm., Baron Howard of Effingham, 25
Howard-Vyse (formerly Vyse), Ric. Wm. Howard, 16
Howe, Wm., otherwise John Wood, 125
Hugelin, chamberlain of Edward the Confessor, 24
Hugh, Domesday tenant, 83, 164
Hugh son of Peter, 105
Hull, Wm. de la, 93; and see Hill
Hulton, Nat., 68
Hunt, John, 146-7
Hunta, pre-Conquest tenant, 26
Huntbach, John, 203
Huntingdonshire, 167
Hurcott Hall, see Kidderminster
Hurech, Peter de, 135
Hurst, Ric., 219
Hussey:
  Edw., 203
  Ric., 203
Hyde:
  Felicity atte, 123n
  Rog. atte, 123n
  Wal. atte, 123n
Hyde, the, see Coppenhall; Kinver

Idiens, Ric., 191
Impney (in Dodderhill, Worcs.), 62
Incorporated Society for the Building and Enlarging of Churches, see Churches
India, 21
  Bengal, 21
  sec. of state for, 5
Inkberrow (Worcs.), 107

Insall, John, 148
International Bible Students' Associa-tion, see Bible Students' Association
Irby:
  Florance Geo. Hen., Baron Boston, 130, 135
  Frederick, Baron Boston, 130, 135
Ireland, 126n
iron industries, 35-6, 52-3, 59-61, 119, 145-8, 144, 157, 179, 213-14
  ironmasters, 8, 11, 17, 21, 33, 57, 62, 158
  ironstone mining, 60, 204
Ironworks in Partnership, 145
Islington (Mdx.), 34
Iverley, Nic. of, 126
Iverley, see Kinver
Iverley hay, see Kinver forest

James, Wal., 71, 208
japanning, 8
Jennings, Homer & Lynch, 43
Jersey (Channel Islands), 14
Jesson:
  Cornelius, rector of Enville, 114, 116, 189
  Hen., 114, 189
  Sarah, see Wilkes
Jeston, Rog., 160
Jevon, Humph., 110
John, King, 16, 129, 131, 153
John le lordeson, see Everdon
John son of Philip, 68, 74, 129, 131, 142-3, 153
  John, his s., see FitzPhilip
  Parnel, w. of John son of Philip, 68, 131
Johnson:
  John, 161
  Sam. (lexicographer), 189
Johnstone, A., 82
Jones & Attwood, 61
Jordan the bloomer, 179
Jorden:
  Benj., vicar of Pattingham, 184
  Edw. (d. by 1616), 136, 160, 208
  Edw. (d. 1667), 124, 139, 208
  Edw., his s., 208
  Eleanor, w. of Edw. (d. by 1616), 160
  Humph., 147, 160, 208
  John, 160
  Wm., 160
  fam., 124, 160, 213
Jukes:
  Marg., w. of Sam. the younger, 144
  Sam., 144
  Sam., his s., 144
  Thos., 125, 145
  Wm., 156

Keene, Hen., 99n
Keightley, Thos., 160
Keir, Jas., 58
Kempe, C. E., 18
Kemsey, Revd. Matt., 87
Kenilworth, Dictum of, 26
Kenilworth priory (Warws.), 164
Kensford (Som.), 83
Kent, earl of, see Holand
Kent, see Bishopsbourne; Greenwich; Halling; Orpington; Saltwood
Ketley:
  John, 195-6
  Ric., 139
Kettle, John, 147
Kettleby, Ric., 135
Key, John, 116
keystamping, 35-6
Kidderminster (Worcs.), 52, 126-7, 143, 147, 219
  Broadwaters, q.v.
  Hurcott Hall, 141
  Park Hall, 145
  Stourport, q.v.
  Trimpley, q.v.
Kilsall (in Donington, Salop.), 163

Kimberley:
Eliz., w. of Wm., 144
Rog., curate of Kinver, 160
Wm., curate of Kinver, 144
King:
Ernest, 70
Jos., 55, 57
Wm., 51, 54–5, 57, 63
fam., 70
Kingsley, see Tettenhall
King's Norton, see Norton, King's
Kingswinford, 53, 58, 64, 127, 143, 190, 212, 218
Ashwood, 3, 64, 118–19, 197, 200
Ashwood Lane, 147
Ashwood Lodge, 145
Audnam, 132
Brierley Hill, 43, 51–2, 61, 118, 152
inds., 57, 134
Bromley, 208
Corbyn's Hall, 71, 208
inds., 52, 56–60, 134
Prestwood, 118, 123, 127, 130–1, 142, 149, 156–7
rural dist., 152
Shut End, 69, 130, 181
Wall Heath, 53, 145
Wordsley, 52, 58, 95, 134, 140
Dial glassho., 60
White Ho. Works, 59
Kingswinford Branch Railway Walk, 201
Kingswood, see Codsall; Tettenhall
Kinver, Phil. of, see Philip son of Helgot
Kinver, 17, 56, 107–8, **118–61**, 224
agric., 137–41
Astle's Rock, 122
Barratt's Coppice, 125, 142, 149–50
Bathpool Cottages, see Kinver: Whittington, Whittington Old Ho.
Battlestone, see Kinver, Boltstone
Bethany, see Kinver, the Hyde
Boltstone (or Battlestone), 119
boro., 137, 143, 148–50, 153
Bott's Fm., 125
bridges, 121, 124–5, 127, 148, 200
Brindley (formerly Union) Hall, 123
the Britch, 122
Brown's Fm., 122
Bum Hall, see Kinver: Iverley, Iverley Ho. fm.
the Burgesses, 119
buses, see Kinver, communications
canals, see Kinver, communications
chars. for the poor, 160–1
Checkhill, 137, 140, 142, 149–50
Checkhill Fm., 142
common, 114, 123, 127–8, 137–9, 142, 148
ind., 147–8
mills, 142, 144
ch., 125, 136, 153–7
Church Hill Ho., 121
cinema, 128
Clambrook (later Clanbrook), 121
Clifford Cottage, 151
Comber, 121–2, 142, 148, 159
Comber Ridge burial ground, 149, 156
communications:
buses, 127
canals, 127
rds., 126–7
trams, 53, 127–8
Community Assoc., 128
Compton, 114, 118–19, 122–3, 133, 136, 148–9, 151–2, 160–1
agric., 137–40
Compton Ct. Fm., 122
Compton Hall (later Compton Hall Fm.), 133–4
Compton Hall fm., 139
Compton Hallows (formerly Horewood) man., 132–4, 144, 151

Compton Ho., 123
Compton Park fm., 141–2
Horewood (Whorwood), 126, 141–2; man., see Kinver: Compton, Compton Hallows
Lower Compton, 122
mill, 144
pk., 141, 144
tithes, 62, 136
Upper Compton, 122
woodland, 118, 142
Copton hill, 148
council hos., 121–2
cricket, 128
curates, 151, 154–5; and see Bate; Cross; Kimberley; Moreton; Newey; Smith; Wharton; White
Cynibre, 119, 141
Dunsley, 124, 135, 137, 148–9, 152–3
agric., 138–40
Dunsley Hall, 134–5, 156
Dunsley Hill, 124
Dunsley Ho., 124
Dunsley Manor, 124
Dunsley Manor Fm., 124
Dunsley Villa, 124
the Hill, 124
man., 134–5
econ. hist., 137–49
Edge View, 128, 152
educ., 117, 136, 145, 147, 155, 157–61
Edward Marsh Centre, 128
fairs, 143
fire precautions, 153
fisheries, 142–3
Flatheridge, 142
Forest Ho., 159
friendly socs., 128–9
Gallowstree Elm, 121, 150, 157
Giant's Well, 151–2
gibbet, 125
Gibraltar, 124–5, 157
Gothersley, 123, 146–7
Gothersley (formerly Stourton Fields) man., 134–5
Gothersley Ho., 147
Sheeps Way, 139
Greyfields, 122
Greyfields Ct., 122
gumblestool, 149
Halfcot, 123–4, 136, 142–3, 149–50
agric., 138–40, 142
bridge, 127, 148
mills, 143–4
school-chapel, 145, 155, 159
wire mill, 147
Hampton Lodge (formerly Hampton Ho.), 123
Haygreve, 136
Heathlands, 121
High Down fm., 126
High Grove (formerly High Greaves) fm., 136
High Ho., 126
High Ho. Fm., see Kinver, High Lodge Farmhouse
High Lodge, 126
High Lodge Farmhouse (formerly High Ho. Fm.), 126
High Pk. Fm., 125
Hill fm., 140
Hill Ho., 121
hillfort, 119, 122, 141
Historical Soc., 128
the Hole, 152
Holy Austin Rock, 112, 122, 151
Horewood, see Kinver, Compton
horse racing, 95, 127–8
hosps., 152
the Hyde, 123, 127, 144, 149
agric., 134–40
corn mill, 144
Hyde Ho. (later Bethany), 146, 160
ind., 119, 144, 146, 148

inds., 119, 131–2, 140, 145–9, 144, 151, 153, 157, 160
inns, 150
Anchor, 125
Cock, 121
Cross, 121
Crown, 126–7
Fox, 121
George and Dragon, 121
Green Dragon, 121
Lock, 121, 129, 157
Plough, 121
Red Lion, 121
Rock tavern, 123
Stag, 129
Stewponey and Foley Arms, 124, 127–8, 129, 140, 150–1
Swan, 121, 128
Talbot, 125
Unicorn, 121
White Hart, 121, 128, 128, 150, 153
Whittington Inn, 125 and n
Windsor Castle, 125
Iverley, 52, 118, 126–7, 137, 142, 148–9, 152
agric., 138–40
Iverley Hay fm. (formerly Nash's fm.), 126
Iverley Ho. (formerly Bum Hall) fm., 126, 139
Iverley Park fm. (formerly Tristram's fm.), 126
Kinver common, 126, 138–9, 142
Kinver Edge, 118–19, 122–3, 128, 128, 138, 149
Kinver Edge Fm., 122, 128
Kinver Hill (formerly the Overend), 121, 139, 141, 148–9
Lady Well pool, 152
libraries, 128, 140
Light Operatic Soc., 128
local govt., 149–51
Lodge Fm., 122
the Lydiates, 122
Mag-a-Fox Hole, see Kinver, Nanny's Rock
man., 21, 129–36, 140–1, 143–4, 149–50, 153
mkts., 143
mills, 127, 142–5
Nanny's Rock (formerly Mag-a-Fox Hole), 122
Nash's fm., see Kinver: Iverley, Iverley Hay fm.
Navigation Cut, 127, 144
New Wood, 127, 142
New Wood fm., 124
Newtown, 124
No Man's Green, 118; and see Enville
Old Grammar Sch. Ho., 145, 158
the Overend, see Kinver, Kinver Hill
pk., 141–2
Park Fm., 125, 133
Penhole, 121
Pigeonhouse fm., 122, 134, 160
police, 152
poor relief, 151
pop., 119, 121–6, 137, 140, 143
post offices, 153
Potter's Cross, 121, 152, 157, 159
Potter's Cross Fm., 121
pounds, 150–1
Prestwood water works, 152
prot. nonconf., 156–7
public services, 151–3
Quarry hill, 148
rector, see Romsley
rectory, 136–7
rds. and streets:
the Acre, 153
Bacons Lane, see Kinver: rds. and streets, Beacon Lane
Bannut Tree Rd., 123, 137, 152
Beacon (formerly Bacons) Lane, 122

Kinver (*cont.*):
 rds. and streets (*cont.*):
  Brockley's Walk, 121
  Castle St., 121, 159
  Chester Rd., 126
  Church Hill, 121, 151, 161
  Church Rd., 149, 156
  Comber Rd., 128, 152
  Compton Lane, *see* Kinver: rds. and streets, Herons Gate Rd.
  Compton Rd., 140, 151; *and see* Kinver: rds. and streets, Wigley Lane
  Cookley Lane, 125–6
  County Lane, 119
  Dark Lane, 121, 125, 157–8
  Dunsley Rd., 124, 127
  Enville Rd., 121–2, 126, 159
  Fairfield Drive, 149, 153, 159
  Foley St., 121
  Foster St., 121, 128
  Gibbet Lane, 125, 127, 138, 152
  Gipsy Lane, 119
  Gothersley Lane, 152
  Heath Drive, 152
  Herons Gate Rd. (formerly Compton Lane), 122, 139
  High St., 119, 121, 126, 128, *128*, 143, 148–9, 152–4, 157, 159
  the Holloway, 121, 156, 159
  Horse Bridge Lane, 125, 144, 151
  Hyde Lane, 122, 144
  Hyperion Rd., 124
  James St., 121
  Meddins Lane, 122, 140
  Mill Lane, 121, 127, 129, 144, 147, 150, 152–3, 157
  Nailers Row, 148
  Sandy Lane, 122
  Sheepwalks Lane, 122–3, 152
  Stone Lane, 121–2, 137, 148, 151, 157
  Stourton St., 123
  Sugarloaf Lane, 126–7, 139
  Swan Lane, *see* Kinver: rds. and streets, Vicarage Drive
  Vicarage Drive (formerly Swan Lane), 128, 151–2, 154–5, 159
  White Hill, 122
  Whittington Hall Lane, 125, 136, 152
  Wigley Lane (later Compton Rd.), 123
  Windsor Holloway, 125, 152
  and see Kinver, communications
 rock hos., 118, 121–3, 125
 Rockmount (formerly the Stone Ho.), 121, 126
 Roman camp, 197
 Rom. Cath., 156
 Round Hill fm., 125, 152
 sewage works, 152
 social and cultural activities, 127–9
 Stapenhill, 123–4, 138, 143, 148–9
  Stapenhill fm., 139
 Start's Green, 119*n*
 Stewponey, 52, 124, 127, 149; *and see* Kinver, inns
 the Stone Ho., *see* Kinver, Rockmount
 Stonelane Fm., 121
 Stourton, 123, 126–8, 142, 148–9, 153, 157, 160
  agric., 137–40
  ind., 145–6
  man., 129–32, 150
  mill, 144
  Stourton Castle, 123, *129*, 130–2, 145
  Stourton Ct., 123
  Stourton Hall, 123, 146, 153
 Stourton Fields fm., *see* Kinver: Gothersley, Gothersley fm.
 Sugarloaf fm., 126, 139
 tithes, 62, 136–7
 town hall, 149–50

trams, *see* Kinver, communications
Tristram's fm., *see* Kinver: Iverley, Iverley Pk. fm.
Union Hall, *see* Kinver, Brindley Hall
Vale Head Fm., 123
vicar, *see* Hodgson; Smith
warrens, 142
water supply, 151–2
White Hill Fm., 121
Whittington, 125–6, 136–7, 142, 146, 149, 151–2, 160
 agric., 138–9
 ind., 145, 148
 man., 135–6, 141, 151
 mills, 142, 144
 Whittington Hall (later Whittington Manor Fm.), *65*, 135–6
 Whittington Lower Fm., 125
 Whittington Manor Fm., *see* Kinver: Whittington, Whittington Hall
 Whittington Old Ho. (formerly Bathpool Cottages), 125
Whorwood, *see* Kinver, Compton
woodland, 141–3
Kinver and District Horticultural Society, 128
Kinver Benefit Building Society, 121
Kinver Crystal Glass Co., 149
Kinver forest, 9, 21, 29, 54, 71, 96, 107, 129, 131, 136–8, 142, 144, 190, 207–9, 220, 225
 Chasepool hay, 208
 Gutheresburn, 123
 Iverley hay, 96, 126, 137, 142
Kinver Gas Light Co., 152
Kinver Light Railway, 53, 127–8
Kirkham, John, 184
Knight:
 Edw., 145
 John, 145
 John, his s., 145
 fam., 145
Knocker, Thos., 72
Kynnerton:
 Alice, w. of Wm., 167
 John (fl. 1436), 167
 John (fl. 16th cent.), 167
 Wm. (? two of this name), 167

Lafargue, Peter, 118
Lamb, Thos., 222
Lambert, *see* Grey
Lambeth, Sergeant, 126*n*
Lancaster:
 duchy of, 130
 duke of, *see* Gaunt, John of
Lancashire, 30–1, 79; *and see* Liverpool; Warrington
Lane, Thos., 209
Lane Green, *see* Tettenhall
Langriville (Lincs.), 62
Langworth, John, 145, 213
Lapley, Wheaton Aston in, 170
Lapley deanery, 188
Latter Day Saints (Mormons), 222
Launde priory (Leics.), 169–70, 176–7, 180–1
Laurence, rector of Patshull, 169
Lavender, J. and H. E., 206
Lavender, Twentyman & Percy, 43
Law:
 John, 157
 fam., 179
Lawley, Sir Fra., 131
Leamington (Warws.), 48
Leasowes, the (in Halesowen, Worcs.), 99
leather working, 112, 148, 179–80, 192
Leathersellers' Company, 154
Leaton:
 Emma of, m. Gilb., s. of John Fitz-Philip, 70
 Wm. of, 70

Leaton, *see* Bobbington
Lee:
 Anne, 21
 Ellen, 161
 Fowke, 190
 Fra., 211
 Hugh de la (fl. 14th cent.), 70
 Hugh (d. 1576), 225
 J. F., 146
 Mary, m. Wal. Wrottesley, 225
 Ric., 111–12
 Ric., prebendary of Wolverhampton, 40
 Rowland, bp. of Coventry and Lichfield, 23
 Sibyl, m. —— Fowler, 23
 Thos. Grosvenor, 128
 Wm. de la (fl. 14th cent.), 70
 Wm. (fl. 15th cent.) and his w. Joan, 164
 fam., 63, 128
Leek, Westwood in, 22
Lees:
 John, 31–2
 Maj. John, 189
Legge:
 Col. A. C., 163
 Augusta, ctss. of Dartmouth, *see* Finch
 Gerald Humphry, earl of Dartmouth, 170, 181
 Humphry, earl of Dartmouth, 165
 Ruperta, ctss. of Dartmouth, *see* Wynn-Carrington
 Wm., earl of Dartmouth (d. 1853), 161, 165, 168, 181–2
 Wm., earl of Dartmouth (d. 1958), 165, 176
 Wm. Heneage, earl of Dartmouth, 163, 169, 175
  as Vct. Lewisham, 163
 Wm. Wal., earl of Dartmouth, 163, 165, 167–8, 170–2, 182, 184
  as Vct. Lewisham, 165
 fam., 163, 165, 171
Leicestershire, 125*n*; *and see* Ashby De La Zouch; Braunston; Launde priory; Loughborough
Leigh:
 Ann, 106
 John (fl. 15th cent.), 101
 John (fl. 16th cent.), 101
 John (d. 1642), 101
 John (d. by 1645), 101
 John (d. 1700), 101
 John (fl. 1739), 101
 Mary, w. of Ric. (d. 1650), 106
 Ric. (d. before 1577), 101
 Ric. (d. 1650), 101
 Ric. (d. 1674 or 1675), 101
 Ric. (fl. 1692–1725), 106
 Revd. Ric., 101, 103
 Ric., his s., 106
 Rob., 101
 Thos. (d. ? 1629), 101, 112
 Thos. (d. 1692), 106
 Thos. (fl. 1741), 103
 Wm., 101
Leo, chaplain of Bobbington, 74
Leo son of Leo, 132
Leveson:
 Edw., 19, 25, 41, 190
 Edw. (? another), 225
 Eliz., *see* Ridgeway
 Jas., 20, 25, 31, 82, 167
 Jane, m. Ric. Poulteney, 190
 Sir John, 25
 Marg., *see* Howard
 Ric. (fl. 1411), 106
 Sir Ric. (d. 1560), 25
 Vice-Admiral Sir Ric. (d. 1605), 25
 Sir Ric. (d. 1661), 25, 39, 218
 Thos., 190
 Wal., 13
 Sir Wal., 25, 176, 182, 190
 fam., 167, 190

Leveson-Gower:
    Geo. Granville, duke of Sutherland, 82
    Granville, Earl Gower, later marquess of Stafford, 19, 82, 190
    John, Baron Gower, 167
    Wm., 41, 167
    fam., 19–20, 37, 41, 82, 167, 190
    and see Sutherland-Leveson-Gower
Lewisham, vcts., see Legge
Ley, John, 140
Liberal party, 5, 18
Lichfield (formerly Coventry, Coventry and Lichfield, Lichfield and Coventry), bps. of, 39, 42, 87, 153, 170, 181, 218; and see Durdent; Lee; Nonant; Overton; Peche; Smith; Stretton
Lichfield, 16
    cathedral, 176
        dean and chapter, 153–4, 176–7
        vicars choral, 176
Lichfield and Coventry, bp. of, see Lichfield
Lichfield diocese, 73
    Diocesan Board of Patronage, 154
    Diocesan Church Building Society (later Diocesan Church Extension Society), 62, 220–1
    Diocesan Trust, 224
Lidiat, ——, 213
Lilleshall (Salop.), 25, 176, 190
Lillywhite, F. W., 95
limestone burning, 10, 30, 35
Lincoln, Abraham, 20
Lincoln, bp. of, see Smyth
Lincoln College, see Oxford, university
Lincolnshire, 117; and see Butterwick; Coningsby; Langriville; Somercoates, North
Little Aston, see Shenstone
Littlewood:
    Benj., 58, 146
    Revd. H. C., 146
    Thos., 58
    fam., 146
Littlewood & Berry, 58
Littlewood, King & Co., 55
Littywood, see Bradley
Liverpool, 36, 42, 88, 98, 132, 181, 220
Lloyd, Humph., 30
Lloyd, the, see Penn
lockmaking, 8–9, 35, 60, 73, 86, 112
London, bp. of, see Chishull
London, 13, 57, 94, 125, 201
    as address, 16, 33, 42, 68, 83, 98, 100, 103, 105–6, 125, 136, 149, 154, 160–1, 165, 170–1, 182, 194, 204, 220, 225
    Chancery Lane, 176
    Croydon, q.v.
    Greenwich, q.v.
    Inner Temple, 177
    Islington, q.v.
    Lincoln's Inn, 207
    lord mayor, 5
    Poultry Counter, 101
    Putney, q.v.
    Richmond, q.v.
    Shadwell, q.v.
    Soho, q.v.
    Staple Inn, 208
    Victoria and Albert Museum, q.v.
    Wapping, q.v.
    Westminster, q.v.
    Whitechapel, q.v.
    Wood St. Counter, 101
Longmeadow brook, 34
Longmore:
    Agnes, m. John Moseley, 105
    Hen., 105
    Thos., 139
Longnor (Salop.), 26
Lorraine, 57–8
lost villages, see Enville, 'Cippemore';

Tettenhall, Wrottesley; Trysull, 'Cocortone'
Loughborough (Leics.), 42, 63, 116
Lougher:
    John, 25
    Mary, see Fitton
Lovat, Ralph, 46
Lovatt:
    Miss E. J., 189
    Mrs. Ronald, 189
Lovel:
    Fra., Vct. Lovel, 133
    John, Baron Lovel (d. 1314), 133
    John, Baron Lovel (d. 1465), 133
    Maud, see Burnell
    Wm., Baron Lovel, 133
Loveridge, Sam., 8
Lowe:
    Adam, 135
    Alice, w. of Humph., 106
    Constance, 97
    Edm., 106, 135, 144, 189
    Edw. atte, 68
    Eleanor, w. of Edm., 135
    Eleanor, w. of Ric. (d. by 1479), 96–7
    Eleanor, m. Rob. Grey, 106, 135
    Eliz., 97
    Humph., 135
    Joan, see Enville
    John (fl. 1684), 139
    John (fl. 18th cent.), 12
    Ric. (d. by 1479), 96–7
    Ric. (fl. 19th cent.), 85
    Rog., 96
    Thos., 96, 135
    Wm. (fl. 1324), 136
    Wm. (fl. 15th cent.), 96
    fam., 68
Loxley (Warws.), 164
Luce, Ric., 140
Ludlow (Salop.), 70
Ludstone (Salop.), 191
Lutley:
    John, 103
    Phil. (several of that name 1183–c. 1369), 103, 111, 114
    Wm. of, 103
Lutley, see Enville
Lycett:
    Ann, w. of Dr. John, 48
    Dr. John, 48
Lyd brook, 197
Lye, the (in Old Swinford, Worcs.), 57
Lythall, ——, 161

Mabel, sister of Ranulph Blundeville, earl of Chester, m. Wm. d'Aubigny, earl of Arundel and Sussex, 175
McAlpine, Sir Alf., & Son Ltd., 18
Madstard, Alice, 54
Maitland, Mrs. R. J. L., 83
Mallett, Wm., 222
malting, 215
Man, Isle of, 14
Mander:
    B. H., 188–9
        his w., 189
    C. B., 9
    Sir Chas., 9, 11
    G. P., 9
        his w., 9
    Sir Geof., 17–18, 183
    Mary Rosalie, see Grylls
    S. S., 44, 89, 183
    Theodore, 10, 18
Mander Bros., 9, 18
Maneer, Hen., 212
Mansel, see Patshull, Mansel of
Mansel:
    Alice, 167
    Hugh, 167, 169
    Rob., 164, 167, 169
Mansell:
    Anne, see Barrett
    Sir Rob., 56

Wal., 83
Mareford:
    Thos. of, 11
    Wm. of, 11
Margaret, dau. of Robert son of Otes, m. Wm. Bagot, 164
Margaret of the Fox Earth, 122
market gardening, 32, 84–5, 178, 191, 211
Marks, Phil., 64
Marrian, Wm., 73
Marsh:
    A. E., 134–5
    Alf., 134–5
    E. E., 69, 134–5
    John (fl. 17th cent.), 206–7
    John, his s., 206
    John (d. 1763), 206
    John (d. 1796), 206
    Ric. Bayley, 206–7, 220
    Wm., 206–7
    fam., 206
Marsh & Baxter Ltd., 134
Marston, Ric., 145
Martyrs Memorial Trust, 74
Mary I, 40, 141
Mary, queen of George V, 163; as dchss. of York, 163
Marylebone Cricket Club, 95, 163
Mase, Ric., 88
Mason, C. V., 221
Mason & Richards, 221
Mason Richards Partnership, 86
Massen, R. H., 31
Matthews:
    Revd. A. G., 5
    Benj., 184
    John, 85
Maud of the green, 139
Mawson, T. H., 18
Maybury, Jos., 147
Meacham, Isaac, 157
Mears, Thos., 42
Mears & Co., 182
Mears & Stainbank, 156, 171
Medleys, the, see Patshull
Meeke, Edw., 147
Meer Oak, see Tettenhall
mercer, Adam the, see Adam
Mercia, earls of, see Alfgar; Edwin
Mere:
    Humph., 105
    Phil. atte, 105
    Rog. atte, 105
    Thos. atte, 105
    fam., 104–5
Mere, see Enville
Meredith:
    Thos. (fl. 1696), 211
    Thos. (fl. 1841–51), 214
Merry Hill, see Wolverhampton
Methodism, 43, 88–9, 157, 195
    Primitive, 44, 88–9, 157, 183, 222
    New Connexion, 63
    Wesleyan, 5, 43–4, 63, 75, 88–9, 116, 157, 222
Michell, John, 32
Middlesex, see Islington; Shadwell; Wapping; Whitechapel
Middleton, Sir Thos., 146
Mill (or Clam) brook, 91, 118, 138, 144
Miller:
    B. A., 42, 88, 219
    Sanderson, 99
Milston, Joan, see Barnhurst
Milton, Baron, see Damer
Milton (Cambs.), 96
Minors, Jeremiah, 59
Moat brook, 1, 12, 29, 33–4, 76, 79, 84–5
moated sites, 25, 27, 33, 82, 162, 187
Monkton Farleigh (Wilts.), 176
Montfort, Sim. de, 26
Montgomery, Rog. de, earl of Shrewsbury, 71
Moor, see Pattingham

Moore:
  E. G. J., vicar of Amblecote, 53
  Hen., archdeacon of Stafford, 22
  Rebecca, w. of Hen., 22
Mora:
  Peter de, 164
  Ralph de, 164
Moreton:
  Caleb, 57
  Ric., curate of Kinver, 155
Morfe:
  Cath., m. John Corbyn, 106
  Hen. of (formerly Hen. of Birming-
    ham), 105–6
  Hen. (d. 1296 × 1302), 106
  Hen. (d. by 1330), 106
  Hen. (d. by 1332), 106, 111
  Hen. (d. 1408 × 1411), 106
  Hugh of, 105
  Joan, w. of Hen. (d. by 1332), 106,
    111
  John, 106
  Rog. of (? Rog. s. of Wm. s. of Peter
    of Birmingham), 105
Morfe, see Enville
Morfe club, 163
Morgan:
  Chas., 176n
  John, 69
  Wm. de, 9
Mormons, see Latter Day Saints
Morrell brook, 177
Morris:
  Fra., 46
  Sir John, 9
  Wm., 9, 18
Morris & Co., 9, 18
Morse Code, 5
Morten, Humph., curate of Bobbing-
  ton, 74
Mortimer, Hen., 129
Moseley:
  Acton, 70, 105
  Adam, 35
  Agnes, see Longmore
  Anne, w. of Rowland, 74
  Ant., 74
  Cath., 74
  Eliz., w. of Nic., 74
  Jas., 70
  Jas., his s., 70
  John (d. 1511 × 1513), 105
  John (fl. 1543–68), 105, 111
  Mic. (d. 1592 or 1593), 104–5
  Mic. (fl. 1626), 116
  Nic. (d. by 1568), 105, 111
  Nic. (fl. 1590s to 1638; ? two of this
    name), 74, 105
  Nic. (fl. 1641), 133
  Rowland, 74
  Thos., 125
  Wal. (d. 1656), 105
  Wal. (d. 1712), 105
  Wal. (fl. 19th cent.), 105, 110–11
  Wal. Acton, 105, 111
  Wal. Hen., 68, 70
  Wal. Mic., 105
  Wm. (d. 1617), 125, 154–5, 157–8
  Wm. (d. 1869), 68–72
  Wm. Hen., 70, 74
  fam., 68–9, 72, 125
Moseley, see Bushbury
Mott:
  John, 16
  Wm., 16
Mountford, Wm., 84
Mountrath, ctss. of, see Newport
Mulliner:
  Rog., 31
  Thos., 184
Mulne, Wm. s. of Hen. atte, 34; and see
  Mylne
Murdak:
  Gillian, w. of Sir Thos., m. 2 Sir John
    de Vaux, 131
  Sir Thos., 131

Murhall, Thos., 181
Music, Royal Military School of, 204–5
Myatt, J. F., 43
Mylne, Rob., 97–8; and see Mulne
Mytton:
  John, 103
  Wm., 67, 70

nailing, 35, 57, 60, 73, 86, 112, 148, 151,
  153, 179, 192, 199, 214, 225
Nash, Thos., 126
Nash, Isaac, & Sons, 146
Nashe, Ric., 143
National Coal Board, 79
National Society, 44, 184, 223
National Trust, 18, 128
Neach Hill, see Donington
Neale, Benedict, 145
Neen Savage (Salop.), see Stepple
Nelsonic Crimson Oaks (friendly soc.),
  128
Netherland, the, see Dutch troops;
  Rotterdam
Netherton (in Dudley, Worcs.), 132
Netherton, see Tettenhall
Nettlefold & Chamberlain, 147
Neufmarché, Bernard de, 177
Neve:
  Chas., 16–17
  Edw. John, 17
  John, 17
Neville:
  Anne, ctss. of Warwick, 176
  Ric., earl of Warwick, 27
Newbridge, see Wolverhampton
Newbrough:
  John, 60
  Mary, his w., 60
Newcastle upon Tyne, 56
Newey:
  Jonathan, curate of Kinver, 153, 156,
    159–60
  Mary, his w., 156, 159–60
Newport, Diana, m. Algernon Coote,
  earl of Mountrath, 67
Newport (Salop.), 13
Newton Parva (Northants.), 177
Nicholas s. of Wm. the cook, 204
Nicholas, E. P., vicar of Wombourne,
  221
Nicholls:
  Thos., 70
  fam., 71
  and see Nicolls
Nicholson, J., 63
Nicholson & Son, 221
Nicolls, John, 172; and see Nicholls
Nock, John, 140
Nonant, Hugh de, bp. of Coventry,
  24
Nore Hill, see Patshull
Norfolk, duke of, see Howard
Norfolk, see Norwich
Normandy, 15–16, 175
Norris:
  John, 155
  Mary, 117
  Sarah, 117
North Bradley, see Bradley, North
North Somercoates, see Somercoates,
  North
Northamptonshire, see Chacombe;
  Newton Parva
Northfield (Worcs.), see Weoley castle
Northumberland, duke of, see Dudley
Northumberland, see Newcastle upon
  Tyne
Northwood, see Tettenhall
Norton (in Old Swinford, Worcs.), 157
Norton, King's (Worcs., later Birming-
  ham), 117
Norwich, 208
Nottingham, 157, 215
Nottinghamshire, see Chilwell; Not-
  tingham
Nurthall, John, 136

Nurton, see Pattingham
Nurton brook, 172, 179

Oaken:
  Nic. of, 83
  Nic. s. of Adam of (? the same), 85
Oaken, see Codsall
O'Connor, J. P., vicar of Patshull, 170
Odd Fellows, Independent Order of,
  15, 175
Offini:
  Christine, w. of Guy de, 217
  Guy de, 193, 202, 217
  Maud de, m. Alan s. of Wal. of Orton,
    202
  Ric. de, 202
  Wm. de, 189, 202, 204, 217, 225
Ohio (U.S.A.), 3; and see Cleveland
Old Swinford, see Swinford, Old
Oldberrow (Worcs.), 26
Oldington:
  Joan, w. of Ric. of, 167
  John of, 167
  Ric. of (also Ric. of Beckbury), 167
    and n
Oliver:
  Edw., 150
  Ric., 131
Olton, see Patshull
Onions, Thos., 32
Orme, Wm., 53, 61
Orpington (Kent), 70
Orton:
  Alan s. of Wal. of, 202, 204, 208
  Gilb. of, 202
  Maud, see Offini
  Thos. of (? two of this name), 202,
    207
  Wal. of (fl. c. 1190), 202
  Wal. of (d. 1259 × 1268), 202, 216
  Wm. of, 202, 216
  fam., 202
Orton, see Wombourne
Osland, Hen., 88
Otes, Rob. s. of, see Robert
Ould, Edw., 9, 18
Overton:
  Mary, w. of Wm., 135
  Wm., bp. of Coventry and Lichfield,
    135
Overton, see Wombourne, Orton
Owen:
  H., 31
  Hen., 47
  Wm., 31
Oxford, bp. of, see Talbot
Oxford, 194
  Franciscan friary, 164
  university:
    Christ Church, 69
    Lincoln Coll., 28
Oxford, Worcester, and Wolverhamp-
  ton Railway, 53
Oxfordshire, 207; and see Oxford
Oxley, see Bushbury

Packer, Matt., 158
Pain, Domesday tenant, 53
Palmer:
  And., 35
  Geo., 113
  Hen., 113
Palmers Cross, see Tettenhall
Pangbourne (Berks.), 176
Paris Exhibition (1878), 59
Park Hall, see Kidderminster
Parker:
  Gilb., 184
  Wm. the, see William
Parkes:
  C., 133
  Jos., 146
  Thos., 146
  fam., 146
Parliament, Houses of, 183
Parrish, Jas., 111

Parsons, Alf., 18
Pasford brook, 161–2, 167, 169, 172, 178
Paston:
　Marg., m. John Hodgetts, 218
　Nic. (d. 1622 or 1623), 218
　Nic. (d. 1623), 218
Patshull, Mansel of, 164, 169
Patshull, 3, **161–72**
　agric., 167–8
　Burnhill Green, 162–3, 168–70, 172
　Burnhill Green (formerly Castle) Fm., 163, 168
　char. for the poor, 172
　Chester Way, 163
　ch., 163, 165, 169–71, *171*, 177, *177*, 181
　cricket, 163
　curates, 170–1; *and see* Bathoe; Greenstreet; Thursfield; Wightwick
　Dartmouth (formerly Pigot's) Arms, 163
　econ. hist., 167–9
　educ., 163, 172
　electricity, 163
　fishing, 169
　Golf Ho., 169
　ind., 169
　libr., 163
　local govt., 169
　Lower Snowdon, *see* Patshull, Snowdon
　man., 161, 163–7, 169
　the Medleys, 162–3, 168
　Millhouse, 162, 169
　mills, 168–9
　Nore Hill, 162–3, 168, 172
　Oldington fm., 167
　Olton (formerly Oldington), 162–3, *163 n*, 167–8, 170
　pk., 3, 161–3, 165, 167–9, 172
　Patshull Ho., 161–3, 164 *n*, 165–6, *166*, *176*
　Pigot's Arms, *see* Patshull, Dartmouth Arms
　poor relief, 169
　pop., 161, 167
　post office, 163
　pound, 169
　prot. nonconf., 172
　rector, *see* Laurence
　rds., 163
　Rom. Cath., 171
　Snowdon:
　　Lower Snowdon, 163
　　Snowdon fm., 168
　　Snowdon heath, 168
　　Snowdon Pool, 164 *n*, 169
　　Upper Snowdon (formerly Snowdon), 163
　stone quarrying, 161
　Temple hotel, 165, 167
　tithes, 167, 170
　Upper Snowdon, *see* Patshull, Snowdon
　vicar, *see* O'Connor
　village hall, 163
　wake, 163
　water supply, 163
　woodland, 167
Patshull Estate Co. Ltd., 183
Patshull Properties Development Co. Ltd., 165
Pattingham, 3, 11, 164, 167–8, 170, **172–85**
　agric., 177–8
　Armeley pk., *see* Pattingham, Hamley pk.
　assoc. for prosecution of felons, 175
　Broadwell pool, 178–9
　buses, 175
　chars. for the poor, 184–5
　ch., 172, 177, *177*, 180–3
　Clifft, 178
　Clifft common, 177–8

the Clive, 172–3, 177, 184
Clive common, 177–8
Copley, 173, 177–9, 179 *n*, 184
Copley Bank, 177–8
Court Ho., 173, 179
Dadnall Hill, 172–3, 177; *and see* Tettenhall
econ. hist., 177–9
educ., 183–4
electricity, 175
the Elms, 173
fairs, 179
Fenhouse End, 182
fishery, 178
friendly socs., 175
gallows, 180
gas, 175
Great Moor, *see* Pattingham, Moor
Hall End, 173, 176
Hamley (formerly Armeley) pk., 178–9
Hardwick, 173, 177–8
Highgate, 173, 175
hist. soc., 175
horticultural show, 175
inds., 179
inns:
　Crown (19th cent.), 175
　Crown (20th cent.), 175
　King's Arms, *see* Pattingham: inns, Pigot Arms
　London Prentice, 175
　New Inn, 175
　Pigot Arms (also King's Arms), 175, 183
　Red Lion, *see* Pattingham: inns, Sow and Pigs
　Roebuck, 175
　Sow and Pigs (later Red Lion), 175
　White Hart, 175
Little Moor, *see* Pattingham, Moor
local govt., 179–80
man., 10–11, 175–6, 179–81
mkt., 179
the Marsh, 173
mills, 178–9
Moor, 173, 179 *n*
　Great Moor, 172–3, 177, 179 *and n*
　Little Moor, 173
Morrell Brook, 182
Newgate, 173, 175, 180, 182–3
Nurton, 177, 179 *and n*
Nurton Hill, 173, 179
Pasford fm., 173, 179
Pattingham Hall, 176
Pattingham Stores, 183
Pear Tree Ho., 175
pillory, 180
police, 175
poor relief, 180
pop., 173, 175, 177
post office, 175
pound, 180
prot. nonconf., 183
reading rooms, 175
rectors, 181; *and see* Cornwall; Danet
rectory, 176–7
rds. and streets:
　Broadwell Lane, 179
　Clive Rd., 173, 175
　High St., 173, 175
　Morrell Brook Lane, 175
　Orchard Close, 183
　Warstone Hill Rd., 172
　Westbeech Rd., 173, 177, 184
Rom. Cath., 176, 183
sewerage, 175
stocks, 180
Tanhouse Fm., 179
tithes, 177, 181
Tuters Hill, 173, 175, 179
Tuters Hill Bank, 178
Tywall green, 178
Upper Westbeech, *see* Pattingham, Westbeech

vicars, 170, 181; *and see* Cooke; Greenstreet; Honeybourne; Jorden; Thursfield
village hall, 175
wake, 175
warren, 178
water supply, 175
West End Stores, 183
Westbeech, 172, 175, 178–9
　common, 177
　Upper Westbeech, 183
Westbeech Hill, 177
Woodhouses, 173, 177, 180
woodland, 178
working men's club, 175
Payne:
　Cath., m. Sir Hen. Foley Lambert (later Grey), 53, 97
　F. I., 157
　Hen., rector of Enville, 97, 114
Paynel, Gervase, 103, 105, 207
Peach:
　Sam., 195–6
　Thos., 195–6
Pearson:
　Edw., 21
　G. J. H., 21
　Geo., 57
　John, 21
　Thos., 21
　Lt.-Gen. Thos. Hooke, 21
　fam., 5, 8, 34
Pearson, E. J. and J., Ltd., 57
Peatswood, *see* Tyrley
Peche, Ric., bp. of Coventry, 193, 217
Pedmore (Worcs.), 113
Pendeford:
　John of, 23, 33
　Rob. (fl. ? 1220s), 23
　Rob., his s., 23
Pendeford, *see* Tettenhall
Pendeford brook, 1
Penderel fam., 137
Penk, river, 1, 3, 12–13, 15, 29, 33–4, 76, 85
Penkridge, 154
　Coppenhall, *q.v.*
　Dunston, *q.v.*
　Gailey, 13
　Pillaton, 28
　Rodbaston, 82
　Stretton, *q.v.*
Penn:
　Agnes, *see* Webb
　Fra., 147
　Wm. of (fl. 14th cent.), s. of Hugh Buffery, 203
　Wm. (d. 1642), 139–40
Penn, 1 *n*, 9 *n*, 14, 33, 194, 197, 199, 203
　Bearnett Ho., 207
　ch., 222
　common, 197
　Dimmingsdale pumping stn., 200
　the Lloyd, 206–7, 211, 221, 223
　Lower Penn, 197, 203
　Upper Penn, 202
Pennocrucium, *see* Stretton
Pentecostalists, 44
People's Refreshment House Association, 10
Pepperhill (in Albrighton, Salop.), 167
Perot, John, 154
Perrott:
　Rog. (fl. 1552), 56
　Rog. (? another), 54
Perry:
　Edw., 8
　F. C., 17–18
　Helen, 18, 40, 47
　Jas. (d. 1837), 17
　Jas., educ. reformer, 90
　Jane Marg., 40
　John, 184
　T. J., 17
　Thos. (fl. before 1710), 184
　Thos. (fl. 1837–43), 17

Perry (cont.):
  the Misses, 90
  Mrs., 90
Persehouse:
  Alex., 82, 89
  Dorothy, m. —— Derby, 89
  Edw., 82
  Mary, see Wood, otherwise Dene
  Peter, 82
  Ric., 82
  Wm., 82
Perth (Scotland), 98
Perton:
  John of (d. by 1193), 24
  John of (d. 1257), 24
  John (d. 1331), 24
  Sir John (d. 1388), 10, 24–5, 33, 189
  John, his s., 24
  Leo (or Lionel), 24
  Ralph, 24
  Ranulph, 24, 34
  Wm. of (d. 1279 or 1280), 24
  Wm. of (d. 1360), 24, 189
  Wm. (fl. 1419), 24
  fam., 34
Perton, see Tettenhall
Peshale:
  Adam de, 207 n
  Sir Adam de, 67
  Joyce, his w., 67
  Ric., 164
Peter, Hugh s. of, see Hugh
Peter son of William, see Birmingham
Philip, John s. of, see John
Philip son of Helgot (also Philip of
    Kinver), 67, 129, 135, 153
Philley brook, 64, 91, 111
Phillips:
  Eliz., m. Sir Ric. Astley, 171
  J. W., 205
  Wm., 209
  fam., 205
Phipson, J. W., 147
Pickerell:
  Cecily, w. of John, 208
  John, 208
Pickford, Jos., 205
Pidcock:
  John (d. 1791), 59–60
  John (d. 1834), 57, 60
  John Henzey, 57
  the Misses, 60
Pigot:
  George, Baron Pigot, 162, 165,
    167–8
  Sir Geo., 165, 167–9, 176
  Sir Rob. (d. 1796), 165, 167, 170
  Sir Rob. (d. 1891), 165, 181
  fam., 171
Pigot diamond, 165
Pillaton, see Penkridge
Pilsbury:
  Eliz., 223
  Geo., 211
  John (? two of this name), 211
Pinson, Wm., 219
pipe making, 192
Piper, Harold, 52
Pitchford:
  John of (fl. 1333), 164
  John (d. 1634), 109, 112
  Sir Ralph of, 164, 169
Pitman:
  Jas., 55
  Jos., 55
Pitt, Wm., agronomist, 3, 5, 30–2, 35,
    168, 211
Plant:
  John, 173
  ——, 192
Plantagenet:
  Geo., duke of Clarence, 129, 131
  Marg., m. Sir Ric. Pole, 131
Platte fam., 49
Plaw, John, 205
Plot, Rob., 3, 56–7, 118

Plugenet, Alan de, Baron Plugenet, 189
Plymley, Wm., 183
Pole:
  Marg., see Plantagenet
  Reginald, cardinal and abp. of
    Canterbury, 131
  Sir Ric., 131
  Wm., chantry priest, 154
Polwhele:
  Mary, see Fitton
  Wm., 25
  Wm., his s., 25
Poole:
  Esdras, 148
  R., 68
Pope, John, & Sons, 99
pottery making, 57
Poulteney:
  Jane, see Leveson
  Ric., 190
Poulton (or Andrewes), Mary, 196
Powell:
  Edw. and his w. Mary, 221
  John, 153
  Wm., 149
Powick (Worcs.), 189
Pratt:
  Frances, 65
  Revd. Hen., 70
  Hugh, 70
  John (d. 1678), 70
  John (d. 1742), 70
  Revd. John, 70
  Ric., 109
  Thos., 70, 72
  Wm. (fl. 1646), 70
  Wm. (fl. 1695), 65
  Wm. (fl. 1718), 70
  Wm. (fl. 1742), 70
prehistoric remains, 3, 64, 118–19, 173,
    197
Pre-Raphaelites, 18
Presbyterianism, 88, 155, 157, 219
  Presbyterian Church of England,
    44
Prestwood, see Kingswinford
Price:
  Job, 44
  John, 192
  Nancy, 126
  Thos., rector of Enville, 114
Prior, Geo., 212
Pritchard, T. F., 99
Probert, R. E., 189
Public Works Loan Commissioners,
    220
Pudsey:
  Ann, 194
  G. P. A., 188
  Letitia, 194
  Marg. (d. 1687), 196
  Marg. (fl. 1756), 194
puritanism, 40, 115, 136, 155, 219
Purslow, Roland, 21
Putney (Surr.), 83
Pyrgo (in Havering-atte-Bower, Essex),
    97

Quakers, see Friends, Society of
Quatford (Salop.), 156
  coll., 71
Queen Anne's Bounty, 39, 74, 87, 154,
    170

Ralph, Domesday tenant, 202
Raybold, Jas., 147
Rechabites, Independent Order of, 15
Reeve, Thos., 225
Rice, Wm., 134
Richard I, 15, 24, 129, 137
Richard the shepherd, 30
Richards:
  Eli, 214
  Rob., 55
  fam., 55

Richardson & Smith, 58
Richardson, Mills & Smith, 58
Richmond:
  Mary, w. of Thos., 90
  Thos., 90
Richmond (Surr.), 99 n
Rickman, Thos., 22
Rickthorn:
  Bertram s. of Bertram of, 71
  Thos. (fl. 1574), 73
  Thos. (fl. 1620), 73
Ridel:
  Geof., 175
  Geof., his grds., 175
  Geva, see Geva
  Maud, m. Ric. Basset, 175, 180
Ridgeway:
  Eliz., w. of Thos., m. 2 Edw. Leve-
    son, 25, 41, 190
  Thos., 190
Roaf, Revd. John, 8, 44
Robbins, Thos., 103; and see Robins
Robert son of Otes, 164
Robins:
  Benj., 125
  John, 140
  Wm., 146
  fam., 135
  and see Robbins
Robinson, Geo., 16
Robson, Mary, 46
rock houses, 49, 93, 112, 118, 121–3,
    125, 151, 157, 187
Rodbaston, see Penkridge
Roderick, John, 221
Roger, Domesday tenant, 107
Rogers:
  Anne, see Tittery
  Eliza, 76
  Phoebe, 44, 47
  Sam. (poet), 51
  Thos. (d. 1680), 58
  Thos., his s., 58
  Thos., s. of the latter, 51, 58
Rolstone (Herefs.), 81
Roman rds., 3, 64–5, 119, 197
  Watling Street, 3
Romano-British remains, 3, 119, 197
Romsley, Leo of, rector of Kinver, 132,
    141
ropemaking, 61, 86
Rotterdam (the Netherlands), 215
Roughton (in Worfield, Salop.), 17
Round, J. H., 5
Rowley Regis, 147
  Blackheath, 53
  Corngreaves, 57
  Cradley Heath, 157
Royal Academy, 81
Royal Air Force, 11
Royal Astronomical Society, 5
Royal Doulton Group, 59
Royal Navy, 46
Royal Show, 14
Royal Society, 5
Rudge:
  John, 193–4, 196
  Thos., 195
  Wm. (d. 1604), 211
  Wm. (fl. 1712), 44
  ——, 179
Rudge (Salop.), 19, 163, 172, 176–7,
    180–1, 183–4
Rudhall:
  Abel, 156
  Abraham, 75, 116, 194
  John, 156
  Thos., 156
Rufus, Rob., 167
Rugby (Warws.), 34
Rugeley:
  Fra., 203
  Humph., 203
  Marg., w. of Humph., 203
Rushall, 219
Ruskin, John, 18

Russel, Revd. Paul, 43
Russell:
  Eliz., 47
  Nic., 106
Russia, 98
Ryce:
  John, 71
  Wm., 71
Ryland, John, 147

Sackville:
  Edw., earl of Dorset, 25
  Mary, ctss. of Dorset, *see* Curzon
  Ric., earl of Dorset, 25
St. Augustine, Phil. of, *see* Cornwall
St. Joseph of Tarbes, Sisters of, 43, 46
St. Thomas's priory near Stafford, 23, 33
Salisbury, bp. of, *see* Talbot
Saltwood (Kent), 16
sand working, 35, 58, 73, 86, 148-9, 192, 215, 225
Sandwell, *see* Bromwich, West
Sansome, Geo., 184
Saxton, Chris., 91, 118
Scale, John, 146
Scotland, *see* Edinburgh; Perth
Scott:
  Sir Gilb., 115, 156, 182
  J. O., 156, 182
  John, 55
  Wm., 55
Scott, Jones & Co., 57-8
Scott, Keir, Jones & Co., 58
scythegrinding, 35, 60, 86, 112, 134, 139, 147, 214; *and see* blade mills
Seabright, Wm., 160
Seawall, *see* Bushbury
Sedgley, 23, 82, 157, 201, 213, 215
Sedlescombe (Suss.), 70
Seisdon, in Trysull, 185, 187-8, 193-6, 202
  agric., 190-2
  almsho., 196
  chap., 195
  hundred, 1, *1*, 17, 76, 161, 169, 172, 185
  inds., 192
  local govt., 192-3
  man., 189-90
  mill, 192
  Mill Ho., 192
  Old Manor Ho., 190
  poor-law union, 37, 73, 86, 113, 151-2, 180, 193, 216
  pop., 187, 190
  rural district, 11, 38, 73, 81, 86, 113, 151-2, 163, 169, 180, 188, 193, 199, 217
  rural sanitary authority, 217
  tithes, 190, 218
  Volunteers, 188
  workho., 37, 187-8, 193
Sergeant, Thos., 145, 213
Severn, river, 1, 13, 52, 127
Seymour:
  Edw., duke of Somerset, 208
  John, 71
Shadwell:
  Dorothy, *see* Whorwood
  Edw., 103, 116
  Hugh, 133
  John (d. 1653), 103
  John (fl. 1666), 103
  Lancelot (d. 1713), 69, 103
  Lancelot (fl. 1730s and 1740s), 103
  Thos. (d. *c.* 1553), 103
  Thos. (fl. 1659), 116
  Thos. (d. 1682 or 1683), 103
  Thos. (d. 1692), dramatist, 103
  Thos. (d. 1731), 103
  fam., 69, 103, 122
Shadwell (Mdx.), 154
Shakespeare, Wm., 25
Shareshill, 203, 209

Shareshull:
  Denise, first w. of Sir Wm. (d. 1370), 164, 168
  Denise, second w. of Sir Wm. (d. 1370), 164
  Nic., 203
  Sir Wm. (d. 1370), 164, 168, 203, 209
  Sir Wm. (d. 1400), 164, 165*n*, 168, 203
Shaw:
  Jos., 214
  Mrs. M. L., 89
  Revd. Thos., *see* Shaw-Hellier
Shaw-Hellier:
  Dorothy, 205
  (formerly Simpson), Evelyn, 205
  Evelyn Mary Penelope, 201, 205, 220
  Harriet, *see* Bradney-Marsh
  Jas., 204
  (formerly Shaw), Revd. Thos., 204, 206
  Thos., 21, 204
  Col. Thos. Bradney, 201, 204-7, 219-21
sheep farming, 31-2, 54, 72, 109-10, 139-40, 168, 178, 191-2, 210-11, 225
Sheepwalks, the, *see* Enville
Sheffield:
  Edm., Baron Sheffield (d. 1549), 203
  Edm., Baron Sheffield (d. 1646), 203
  Ellen, *see* Delves
  Sir Rob. (d. 1518), 203
  Sir Rob. (d. 1531), 203
Sheldon:
  John, vicar of Tettenhall, 39
  Marg., *see* Whorwood
  Wm., 130
Shelsley Walsh (Worcs.), 113
Shelton, John, 34
Shenstone, Wm., 99
Shenstone, Little Aston Hall in, 207
Shenton:
  Edm., 191-2
  John, 218
shepherd, Ric. the, *see* Richard
Sheriff Hales (Salop.), 41
Sherwin, Edw., 220
Sherwine, John, 192
Shifnal (Salop.), 69, 144; *and see* Haughton; Hinnington
Shifnal poor-law union, 169
Shinton, R., 214
Shipley (in Claverley, Salop.), 187, 190
Shokeborough, Benedict, curate of Bobbington, 74
Shrewsbury, earl of, *see* Montgomery
Shrewsbury, 13-14, 41, 99, 147
Shropshire:
  K. J., 82
  R. G., 82
Shropshire, 31, 64, 70, 146, 161, 168, 185; *and see* Acton Burnell; Albrighton; Alveley; Apley; Ash; Aston; Badger; Boningale; Boscobel; Bradney; Bridgnorth; Broughton; Bulwardine; Cressage; Donington; Eardington; Haughton; Hinnington; Kilsall; Lilleshall; Longnor; Ludlow; Ludstone; Newport; Pepperhill; Quatford; Roughton; Rudge; Sheriff Hales; Shifnal; Shipley; Shrewsbury; Sidbury; Spoonhill; Stepple; Wildicote; Worfield
Shropshire Union Canal (formerly Birmingham and Liverpool Junction Canal), 14, 36
Shuffrey, L. A., 18
Shut End, *see* Kingswinford
Sicily, 205
Sidbury (Salop.), 19, 21
Siddaway:
  John, 61
  Thos., 61

Silvester:
  Eliz., 55
  John, 55
Simcox, Marg., 84
Simmons:
  Martha, 184
  Wm., 184
Simon of the green, 139
Simon, F. W., 194
Simpson, Evelyn, *see* Shaw-Hellier
Six Ashes, *see* Bobbington
Skey, Sam., 58
Small brook, 197
Small Heath, *see* Birmingham
Smallman:
  Ric. (fl. 1671), 149
  Ric. (fl. 1855-6), 116
  Wm., 149
  fam., 149
Smart:
  Ezekiel, curate of Wombourne, 219
  Ithiel, vicar of Wombourne, 219
  Nat., curate of Wombourne, 219, 222
Smestow, *see* Wombourne
Smestow brook, 1, 7, 9-11, 13-14, 21, 29, 34, 38, 118, 123, 142, 147-8, 185, 187, 191, 197, 200, 212-14, 225
  as Trysull brook, 185
Smethwick, 99, 147
Smirke, Sir Rob., 132
Smith:
  Edw., 207, 213, 220
  Revd. Edw., 220
  Fra., 5, 165
  J. G., 156
  John (fl. 1630s), 210, 213
  John (fl. 1708), 207
  John, his s., 207, 224
  Jos. (fl. 1724), 182
  Jos. (fl. 1759), 147
  Nic., 213
  Ric., 27, 47
  Rob., 210
  Sam., curate of Kinver, 155, 219
  Thos., 98, 156
  Wm., bp. of Coventry and Lichfield, 153
  Wm. (fl. 1581), 210
  Wm. (d. 1645), 83
  Wm., his s., 83
  Wm. (d. 1724), 27, 47
Smyth, Wm., bp. of Lincoln, 28
Smythe, Col. Thos., 189
Snelson:
  J., 71
  J. J., 71
Sneyd's brook, 91, 93, 111
Snowdon, *see* Patshull
Snowdon brook, 161, 169
soapmaking, 86
Society for the Encouragement of Arts, Manufactures, and Commerce, *see* Arts
Soho (in Westminster), 220
Soho manufactory, *see* Handsworth
Solmore, John, 56
Solomcoates, North (Lincs.), 224
Somerford, Marg., 89
Somers:
  Chas., Earl Somers, 17
  John, Baron, later Earl, Somers, 17
Somersall Herbert (Derb.), 82
Somerset, Chas., Baron Herbert, later earl of Worcester, 129-30
Somerset, duke of, *see* Seymour
Somerset, *see* Kensford
Somery:
  Joan de, m. Thos. Botetourt, 67, 72, 103
  John de, Baron Somery, 23, 67, 96, 103, 175, 188, 202, 207
  Marg. de, m. Ralph Basset (d. 1265), 176

Somery (*cont.*):
Marg. de, m. John de Sutton (fl. 1323), 23, 96, 103, 105, 175, 188, 202, 207
Nichole de, *see* Aubigny
Ralph de, 204
Rog. de (d. 1273), 175-6
Rog. de (d. 1291), 175
South Staffordshire district, 38, 73, 86, 113, 151, 169, 180, 193, 201, 217
offices, 85-6
South Staffordshire Golf Club, 14
South Staffordshire Mines Drainage Commissioners, 55
South Staffordshire Water Works Co., 67, 95
Southall:
Geo., rector of Enville, 113
John, 75
Thos., 177
Southwick (Southwycke):
Hen., canon of Tettenhall, 19, 41
Hen. (d. 1650 or 1700), 46
Thos., 46
Southwick (in North Bradley, Wilts.), 24
Spain, *see* Estepona
Sparkes, Sherington, 69
spectacle-frame making, 7, 36, 112
Spencer, John, and his w. Mary, 157
Spink, Geo., 15
Spittle brook, 91, 108, 112, 118, 137-8, 142, 144, 147
Spoonhill (in Much Wenlock, Salop.), 131
Sprenchose, Rog., 26
Springfield Brewery Co. Ltd., 9
Stafford:
Cecily de, 61
Eliz., w. of Sir Nic., 27
Hugh, earl of Stafford, 163
Sir Humph. (d. 1413), 24
Sir Humph., his s., 24, 103-4
Humph. (fl. 1469), 104
Humph., earl of Devon, 104
Isabel, ctss. of Devon, *see* Barre
Millicent de, m. Hervey Bagot, 26
Nic. de, 26
Nic. de, baron of Stafford, 26
Sir Nic., 27
Rob. (d. probably 1088), 26-7, 83, 163
Rob. (d. *c.* 1193), 26, 164
Sir Wm. de, 54-5
fam., 83, 163
Stafford:
barons of, *see* Stafford
barony, 26, 67
earls of, *see* Stafford
marquess of, *see* Leveson-Gower
Stafford, archdeacons of, 159, 170; *and see* Moore
Stafford, 7*n*, 13, 125, 127; *and see* St. Thomas's priory
Staffordshire and Worcestershire Canal, 1, 9-10, 13-14, 33, 35, 52, 123, 125, 127, 152, 201, 215
Staffordshire county council, 32, 81, 94
Staffordshire Record Society (formerly William Salt Archaeological Society), 5
Staffordshire, Wolverhampton, and Dudley Joint Committee for Tuberculosis, 152
Stamber Mill (in Old Swinford, Worcs.), 57
Stamford:
ctsses. of, *see* Booth; Grey
earls of, 109; *and see* Grey
Stamford and Warrington:
ctss. of, *see* Cocks
earls of, *see* Grey
Standon, John, 116
Stanford brook, 34
Stanhope:
Eileen, *see* Grey

P. J., Baron Weardale, 205
Wm. Hen. Leicester, earl of Harrington, 97
Stanley, Alex., 7
Stephens, ——, and his w., 221
Stepple (in Neen Savage, Salop.), 181
Stevens, Jos., 57, 59
Steward, Fra., 81, 84
Stewponey, *see* Kinver
Stewponey Agricultural Society, 128, 140
Stewponey Association for the Improvement of the Labouring Classes, 55, 140, 211
Stewponey Becher Club, 128
Stockton (Salop.), *see* Apley
Stockwell End, *see* Tettenhall
Stoke Edith (Herefs.), 130
Stoke Poges (Bucks.), Stoke Place in, 16
Stokes:
Fra. Smith, 17
Geo., 147
John (d. 1724), 17
John (d. 1752), 17
John (d. 1786), 17
Nancy, 17
Wm. (d. 1779), 17
Wm. (d. 1784), 17
Wm. Smith, 17
fam., 147
Stone, Chas., 74
stone quarrying, 25, 34-5, 42-4, 85-6, 148, 161, 179
Stonehenge (in Amesbury, Wilts.), 206
Stour, river, 1, 49, 51-5, 57, 60, 118-19, 121, 123-5, 127, 137-8, 142-4, 146, 148
Stour Valley Partnership, 145
Stourbridge (in Old Swinford, Worcs.), 49, 51-2, 55-6, 61-2, 95, 125, 128, 146, 153
as address, 36, 51, 55, 60, 64, 98, 107, 150, 156-7, 222
boro., 61
coaches, 94
fire brigade, 153
grammar sch., 63
heath, 131
improvement commissioners, 62
inds., 55, 57, 60, 62
omnibuses, 201
prot. nonconf., 63
rlys., 53
rds., 52, 62, 127
Rom. Cath., 156
trams, 53
Stourbridge and District Water Board (formerly Stourbridge Water Works Co.), 62, 152
Stourbridge Canal, 51-3, 127, 149
Stourbridge Cricket Club, 53
Stourbridge Football Club, 53
Stourbridge Gas Co., 62
Stourbridge Lawn Tennis Club, 126
Stourbridge Main Drainage Board, 152
Stourbridge poor-law union, 61
Stourbridge Rugby Football Club, 124
Stourbridge Water Works Co., *see* Stourbridge and District Water Board
Stourport (in Kidderminster, Worcs.), 13, 57, 127
Stourton:
Adam of, 123
Eliz., *see* Watson
John of, 123
Thos., 176
Wal. of, 123
Stourton, *see* Kinver
Strafford, John, 196
Strangeways:
Eleanor, 104, 111
Sir Giles, 104, 108
Hen., 104
Street:
A. E., 42

G. E., 42, 220
Stretton, Rob., bp. of Coventry and Lichfield, 153
Stretton (in Penkridge), Pennocrucium in, 3
strolling players, 128
Stuart fam., 81
Stubbs:
John, 81
Ric., 81
Sam., 81
Studley Ct., *see* Swinford, Old
Stukeley, Sir Thos., 83
Surrey, *see* Bookham, Great; Chertsey; Croydon; Eashing; Putney; Richmond
Sussex, *see* Sedlescombe
Sutherland, dukes of, *see* Leveson-Gower; Sutherland-Leveson-Gower
Sutherland-Leveson-Gower, Geo. Granville Wm., duke of Sutherland, 87
Sutton (sometimes Sutton or Dudley):
Edw., Baron Dudley (d. 1532), 97, 105-6, 130, 208
Edw., Baron Dudley (d. 1586), 188, 190, 202, 208-9, 218
Edw., Baron Dudley (d. 1643), 54, 200, 208-9, 216, 218
Frances, Baroness Dudley, m. Humble Ward, Baron Ward, 208
Isabel, w. of Sir John (d. 1359), 208
John de (fl. 1323), 23, 96, 103, 105, 188, 202
Sir John (d. 1359), 207-8
John (d. 1406), 208
Sir John, later Baron Dudley (d. 1553), 97, 208
Marg. de, *see* Somery
fam., 23, 105, 175, 188, 202, 207
Sutton Coldfield (Warws.), 147, 161, 165
Swan, J. A., 27
Swanson, J. L., 18
Swift, John, 62
Swindley, Ann, 14
Swindon, *see* Wombourne
Swinford, Old (Worcs. portion), 49, 52-3, 61-2
as address, 60, 126, 145-6, 213
char. for the poor, 64
Hosp. Sch., 54, 159, 222
ind., 58
the Lye, *q.v.*
man., 55
Norton, *q.v.*
rector, 54, 218
Stamber Mill, *q.v.*
Stourbridge, *q.v.*
Studley Ct., 136
Wollaston, *q.v.*

Talbot:
Mary, w. of Wm. (d. 1686), 135
Wm. (d. 1686), 131, 135-6, 153
Wm., bp. of Oxford, Salisbury, and Durham, 136
Tamworth, 16
Tarratt, Jos., 79
Tatenhill, Barton Hall in, 23
Taylor:
Brian, 69
Fra., 184
Geo., 145
Job, 222
John (fl. 1739), 33
John, his s., 33
John (fl. late 18th cent.), 58
Mary, 184
Thos. (fl. 1498), 155
Thos. (fl. 19th cent.), 222
Taylor, John, & Co., 42, 63, 116
Taylor, W. and J., 194
Telford, Thos., 13

Tennant, Wm., 207
Testimony to the Truth, 219
Tetbury, John of, 26
Tettenhall, **1–48**
  agric., 28–32
  Aldersley, 1, 13, 16–18, 22, 36–7
    agric., 28–30, 32
    Aldersley Lower Fm., 19–20
    Aldersley Upper Fm., 19–20
    chs., 40–2
    sch., 45
  almsho., 46
  amateur dramatic soc., 15
  assoc. for prosecution of felons, 38
  Barnhurst, 1, 12–13, 18, 37
    agric., 28–9
    ch., 41
    fm., 19–21, 31–3, 39, *65*
    gunpowder warehouse, 36
    schs., 41, 45
  Bilbrook, 1, 12, 14, 18, 20, 28, 37, 40, 46
    agric., 29–30
    Bilbrook Manor Ho., 12, 40
    ch., 40–1
    green, 12, 30
    ind., 35
    prot. nonconf., 43
    schs., 45
    tithes, 19
    and see Codsall
  Blakeley (formerly Blakeway) Green, 1, 13
  bridges, 13–14
  Brych Ho., 37, 46–7
  buses, *see* Tettenhall, communications
  canals, *see* Tettenhall, communications
  Castlecroft, 10, 34, 38
    ch., 43
    schs., 45
  the Cedars, 14
  cemetery, 38
  chars. for the poor, 46–8
  chs., 3, 7, 39–43, *81*, 87
  Claregate, 1, 7, 43
  coll., 18–20, 28, 36–7, 39
    buildings, 7
    canons, 3; *and see* Southwick; Wollaston
    peculiar jurisdiction, 16, 39, 44, 86
    prebends, 36; Bovenhill (formerly Compton), 19–21, 32, 37, 39, 41; Codsall, 19, 37, 82, 87; Pendeford, 19, 21, 32, 37, 40; Perton, 19–20, 37, 39, 82; Wrottesley, 19, 37
  communications:
    airfields, *see* Tettenhall: Pendeford *and* Perton
    buses, 14
    canals, 1, 9–10, 13–14, 33, 35–6
    rlys., 14
    rds., 13, *80*
    trams, 14
  Compton, 1, 9–10, 13–15, 21, 28, 36–7, 40, 42–3
    agric., 30–2
    Compton Hall, 9–10, *17*
    inds., 31, 35–6
    mill, 32, 34
    post office, 39
    prot. nonconf., 43–4
    schs., 44–5
  copyhold tenure, 21, 32
  council housing, 9–10, 13, 22, 38
  Court Oak, 36
  Cranmoor, *see* Tettenhall, Wrottesley
  cricket, 14
  Cronkhall, 12, 15, 20, 29–30
  Cuckolds Corner, 9
  curates, 39–40; *and see* Beiston; Buxton; Harrison

Dadnall Hill, 1, 10–11, 35; *and see* Pattingham
Dam Mill, 1, 12, 15, 29; *and see* Codsall
Danes Court, 8, 14
Danesbury Ho., 7, 43
the Deeps, 28
the Dippons, 9
Dippons Fm., 8, 17, 29
drill halls, 14–15, 38–9, 44, 46
driving club, 15
econ. hist., 28–36
educ., 7, 11, 22, 40–6
Eynsham Ho., 40
Finchfield, 1, 9, 15, 35, 38
  ch., 43
  prot. nonconf., 44
  schs., 45
fire brigades, 39
fisheries, 33
free warren, 33
friendly socs., 15
Glen Bank, 44
golf, 14
Gorsty Hayes Cottage, 7, 43
greens, 30
  Lower Green, 5, 7, 15, 30, 36, 39
  Upper Green, 5, 7–8, 30, 33, 36 *and n*, 38
  and see Tettenhall: Bilbrook, Perton, *and* Wrottesley
the Hall, 8, 45
Harewood, *see* Tettenhall, Perton
the Hollies, 11
inds., 9, 25, 30–1, 33–6, 38
inns, 10–11, 15, 17, 36
  Angel, 15
  Blue Boar, *see* Tettenhall: inns, King's Head
  Crown (at Wergs), 12
  Crown, *see* Tettenhall: inns, Old Rose and Crown
  Field Ho., 10
  Holly Bush (site of Tettenhall Towers), 21
  Holly Bush (Trescott), 11
  Junction, 12
  King's Head (formerly Blue Boar), 8
  Mermaid, 10, 15
  Mitre, 36
  Old Rose and Crown (formerly Rose and Crown, and probably Crown, later Rock Villa and Rock Hotel), 15, 36, 38
  Prince of Wales, 8
  Rock Villa (later Rock Hotel), *see* Tettenhall: inns, Old Rose and Crown
  Rose and Crown, *see* Tettenhall: inns, Old Rose and Crown
  Rose and Crown (another), 36
  Swan, 9, 15, 36
  Woodman, 12
  Wrottesley's Arms, 15, 36
insts., 15
King's Tettenhall, *see* Tettenhall: Tettenhall Regis, man.
Kingsley, 21–2, 35–6
Kingsley Wood, *see* Tettenhall: Tettenhall Wood, common
Kingswood, 3, 11–13, 18*n*, 19, 30, 37, 40
  common, 11, 29, 39
  Kingswood Bank Fm., 11
  Kingswood Ho., 11
  prot. nonconf., 37
  sch., 45
  and see Codsall
labour services, 32
Lane Green, 12, 30, 33, 38
librs., 15, 45
local govt., 36–8
Long Lake, 38
Lower Green, *see* Tettenhall, greens

Macmillan Home for Continuing Care, 10
Manor Ho., 8
mans., *see* Tettenhall: coll. (prebends), Kingsley, Pendeford, Perton, Tettenhall Clericorum, Tettenhall Regis, *and* Wrottesley
Meer Oak, 10–11
mills, 5, 13, 32–4, 43
the Mount, 9, *17*
Mount Pleasant, 45
Netherton, 10
New Ho., 8
New Ho. fm., 5, 30–2, 35
New Village, 8
Northwood, 10
Palmers Cross, 12, 31–2, 45
pks., *see* Tettenhall: Perton *and* Wrottesley
pears, 10, 30–2
Pendeford, 1, 3, 5, 12–15, 20, 37–8, 201
  agric., 29–32
  airport, 14
  ch., 41–2
  free warren, 33
  inds., 30, 35–6
  man., 23–4, 28, 36–7
  mills, 5, 13, 33–4, 43
  Pendeford Fm., 23
  Pendeford Hall, 13, 23–4
  Pendeford Mill fm., 30–1
  prebend, *see* Tettenhall, coll.
  schs., 41, 45
  woodland, 33
Perton, 1, 3, 10–11, 15, 37
  agric., 28–32
  airfield, 11, 17, 43
  ch., 42–3
  free warren, 33
  green, 10
  Harewood, 29
  inds., 35
  man., 10, 24–6, 30, 32, 36–7
  mill, 34
  pk., 33
  Perton Grove, 10
  Perton Hall, 5, 10, 25, 27
  Perton Mill Fm., 34
  prebend, *see* Tettenhall, coll.
  sch., 45
police, 37–9
poor relief, 37
pop., 3, 7–12
post offices, 15, 39
pounds, 36
prot. nonconf., 5, 43–5
public services, 38–9
rack rents, 32
rlys., *see* Tettenhall, communications
Red Hill Lodge, 43
Red Ho., 8
rds. and streets:
  Aldersley Rd., 7, 13, 20, 38
  Ash Hill, 10
  Barnhurst Lane, 36, 45
  Bennett's Lane, 38
  Bilbrook Rd., 12, 40, 45
  Bridgnorth Rd., 9–11, 13
  Broxwood Pk., 43
  Castlecroft Ave., 43
  Castlecroft Rd., 9, 44
  Chester Ave., 45
  Church Hill, 7
  Church Hill Rd., 40
  Church Rd., 8, 42–3
  Clifton Rd., 36, 45
  Codsall Rd., 1, 12
  Compton Holloways, *see* Tettenhall: rds. and streets, the Holloway
  Compton Rd. West, 9, 28–9
  Coppice Lane, 28, 38
  Deers Leap, 11
  Finchfield Hill, 9–10, 13, 45

Tettenhall (*cont.*):
 rds. and streets (*cont.*):
  Finchfield Rd. West, 45
  Gainsborough Drive, 45
  Grange Rd., 8, 43
  Green Lane, 34
  Grotto Lane, 40
  Henwood Rd., 7, 9–10, 38, 44
  High St., 7, 37, 39
  the Holloway (formerly Compton Holloways), 8–9, 15, 35–6
  Jenny Walkers Lane, 10
  Keepers Lane, 12
  Knights Ave., 12
  Lane Green Rd., 12
  Limes Rd., 8
  Lothians Rd., 7
  Lower St., 5, 7, 35–6, 38–40, 42, 44
  Malthouse Lane, 7
  Manston Drive, 45
  Martham Drive, 45
  Meadow View, 13–14
  Moors Lane, 43
  Mount Rd., 8, 43
  Nursery Walk, 8
  Oak Hill, 9, 43
  Old Hill, 3, 7, 14–15, 18, 38, 43–4
  Ormes Lane, 8, 44
  Pattingham Rd., 11
  Pendeford Ave., 12, 34, 41
  Penk Rise, 1
  Perton Rd., 10
  Redhouse Rd., 7–8
  Regis (formerly Waterworks) Rd., 7–8, 38–9, 45
  Ryefield, 45
  Sandy Lane, 7, 35, 43, 46
  School Rd., 8–9, 15, 45
  Shaw Lane, 45
  Stockwell Rd., 14
  the Terrace, 10
  Tinacre Hill, 10–11, 18
  Tyninghame Ave., 12
  Upper Green, 13, 15, 32, 39
  Upper Street, 7, 13, 15
  Waterworks Rd., *see* Tettenhall: rds. and streets, Regis Rd.
  Wergs Hall Rd., 12
  Wergs Rd., 5, 8, 12, 14, 30, 39
  Wightwick Bank, 10, 18
  Windermere Rd., 12, 45
  Windmill Crescent, 45
  Windmill Lane, 10, 34, 43
  Wobaston Rd., 12, 201
  Wood Rd., 8–9, 15, 43
  Woodcote Rd., 45
  Woodland Ave., 38
  Woodthorne Rd., 7, 12–13
  Woodthorne Rd. South, 45
  Wrottesley Park Rd., 11
  Wrottesley Rd., 1, 7, 13–14, 37
  Yew Tree Lane, 1
  and see Tettenhall, communications
 Rock Ho., 43
 Rom. Cath., 43, 46
 sewage works, 21, 23, 28, 38
 social and cultural activities, 14–15
 stocks, 36–7
 Stockwell End, 7–8, 14, 35, 44
 Tettenhall Clericorum, 3, 7, 12*n*, 37–8
  agric., 28–9
  man., 18–21, 32, 36
 Tettenhall Regis, 3, 15, 37–8, 43
  agric., 11, 28–30, 32
  man. (otherwise King's Tettenhall), 9, 15–19, 27, 32, 36, 39–40, 83
 Tettenhall Towers, 5*n*, 8, 21–2, 22, 23, 39
 Tettenhall Wood, 1, 5, 8–9, 14–15, 32, 36–9
  as address, 46–7, 194, 220
  chars. for the poor, 47–8

 ch., 42–3
 common (formerly Kingsley Wood), 7–8, 14, 29, 31, 35
 inds., 34–6, 38
 prot. nonconf., 5, 43–4
 schs., 42, 45
 Tettenhall Wood Ho., 8, 22
 tithes, 19–20, 39–40, 43, 82
 trams, *see* Tettenhall, communications
 Trescott, 3, 10–11, 15, 37, 46
  agric., 28–9, 32
  ch., 42–3
  ind., 35
  man., 24–6, 36
  Old Trescott Fm., 11
 urban dist., 1, 3, 22, 38, 47
 Upper Green, *see* Tettenhall, greens
 vicars, *see* Hill; Sheldon; Wollaston
 wake, 14
 water supply, 33, 38
 Wergs, 1, 5, 12–13, 33, 36–7, 47
  agric., 28, 30
  Hall, 17–18
  mill, 34
  sch., 45–6
 Westacre, 10
 Wightwick, 1, 10, 13–15, 17, 37, 46–7
  agric., 28–32
  ch., 42
  ind., 35
  man., 18
  mill, 34
  sch., 45
  tithes, 19
  Wightwick Hall (Tinacre Hill), 11, 18, 22, 45
  Wightwick Hall (Wightwick Bank), 18
  Wightwick Manor, 16, 18
  Wightwick Mill Fm., 34
 Woodfield Heights, 8
 woodland, 32–3
 Woodthorne, 5, 8
 workho., 14, 37
 Wrottesley, 1, 3, 11, 14–15, 19, 37
  agric., 28–32
  civil par., 1, 3, 30, 32–3, 38, 47
  Cranmoor, 1, 33
  fishery, 33
  free warren, 33
  graveyard, 40
  green, 11, 30
  man., 10–11, 26–8, 34, 36
  pks., 1, 3, 14, 32–3
  prebend, *see* Tettenhall, coll.
  woodland, 32–3
  Wrottesley Hall, 11, 27–8, 32
  Wrottesley Lodge Fm., 33
Tettenhall, battle of, 3, 197
Tettenhall Club, 32
Tettenhall College, formerly Tettenhall Proprietory School, 21–2, 45
Tettenhall Wood, *see* Tettenhall
Tettenhall, Wrottesley, and Codsall joint cemetery board, 38
Tewkesbury abbey (Glos.), 129
Thomas in the Green, 7
Thomas the comber, 148
Thomas, Wm., 84–5
Thomas, Ric., & Baldwin Ltd., 214
Thompson:
 Sir Edw., 69–70
 John (fl. 1799), 146
 John (fl. 1846–56), 147
 and see Tompson
Thorneycroft:
 Edw., 147, 214
 Ellen, m. Hen. Hartley Fowler, Vct. Wolverhampton, 5*n*
 Florence, 21
 G. B., 47
 Geo., 147, 214
 Thos., 5*n*, 15, 21–2, 39, 42, 47
  his w., 21
 fam., 43

Throckmorton:
 Clement, 176
 Marg., *see* Whorwood
 Rob., 134
 Thos., 83, 130, 134
Throckmorton (in Fladbury, Worcs.), 134
Thursfield, Ric., curate of Patshull and vicar of Pattingham, 170, 181–2
tilemaking, 35
Timmings:
 C. H., 147
 Thos., 147
Timmis & Co., 57
Timms, Jos., 215
Tinker's Castle, *see* Trysull
Tinley, R. C., 95
Tipton, 69, 94, 204, 218
Titley, Ric., 147
Tittery:
 Anne, *see* Tompson
 Anne, m. Thos. Rogers, 58
 Daniel, 58
 Daniel, his s., 58
Tomkins, Fra., 46
Tompson, otherwise Beare:
 Anne, 58
 Anne, m. Daniel Tittery, 58
 fam., 58
 and see Thompson
Tongue, John, 211
Tonkinson, J. A., and his w. (née Hartley), 190
Tonks, Wm., 89
Townshend (later Brooke), Geo., 69
Toy:
 Edw., 111
 Humph., 111
 John, 111
 Steph., 111
 fam., 111
Tranter:
 Thos. (fl. 1604), 35
 Thos. (fl. 1636), 35
 Thos. (fl. 1690s), 35
 Wm., 35
Tredington (Worcs., later Warws.), 96
Trench brook, 127
Trent, river, 1
Trent and Mersey Canal, 13
Trentham, 25, 39, 176, 190
Trescott, Rog. s. of Nic. of, 34
Trescott, *see* Tettenhall
Tresham, Geo., 177
Trimpley (in Kidderminster, Worcs.), 195–6
Trinity College, *see* Cambridge university
Tristram, Wm., 126
Trysull:
 Giles of, 188
 John of, 189, 192
Trysull (or Frankley):
 Bernard of, 188, 204, 225
 Sim. of, 188–9
 Thos. of, 188–9, 192
Trysull, 41, **185–97**, 202–4, 218–19, 225
 agric., 190–2
 Beeches fm., 185, 187
 Bent (or Ben) Green, *see* Trysull, Trysull Green
 Blakeley common, 191
 bridges, 187, 192
 buses, 188
 Cecil Lodge, 193
 chars. for the poor, 196–7
 children's home, 193
 ch., 192, 193–5, 209, 218–19, 225
 Clan Park fm., 187, 218
 'Cocortone' ('Cocretone'), 185, 187, 190
 Common Fm., *see* Trysull, Park Fm.
 council hos., 187
 cricket, 188
 curates, 193–5; *and see* Fullmer; Webb

econ. hist., 190-2
educ., *192*, 194-6
electricity, 188
fair, 192
Fiershill Fm., 187
friendly socs., 188
gibbets, 188
inds., 192
inns:
  Bell, 188
  Fox, 188
  Plough, 188
  Seven Stars, 188
  Vine, 188
insts., 188
Lanes Fm., 187
libr., 194
local govt., 192-3
man., 188-9, 192
Manor Ho., 189
mkt., 192
mills, 192
Old Manor Ho., 187
Park (formerly Common) Fm., 187
police, 188
poor relief, 193
pop., 187, 190
post offices, 188
pound, 193
prot. nonconf., 195
rds., 187
  Brantley (formerly Brandford)
    Lane, 185
  Church Lane, 195
  Crockington (formerly Cockerton)
    Lane, 187
  Ebstree Rd., 187, 190
  Feiashill Rd., 187-8
  Post Office Rd., 187
  School Rd., 188, 193
  Seisdon Rd., 190
  Seisdon Way, 187
  White Way, 187
  Wolmore Lane, 187
Seisdon, *q.v.*
Tinker's Castle, 185, 187
tithes, 190, 209, 218
Trysull common, 191
Trysull Green (formerly Bent or
  Ben) Green, 187, 191, 193,
  195-6
Trysull Manor fm., 191-2
Vine Cottage, 193
wake, 188
water supply, 188
Wolmore, 187, 191
Women's Inst., 188
Trysull brook, *see* Smestow brook
Trysull deanery, 188
Tuckhill, *see* Bobbington
Tuk:
  John, 70
  Ric., 70
Tunck, Fra., 46
Tunnerton, Jos., and his w. Eliz., 157
Turgot, pre-Conquest tenant, 188
turkeys, 32, 109-10
Turner:
  Hen., 145, 147
  Jacob, 145
  John, 195
Turstin, pre-Conquest tenant, 202
Turton, John, 147
Tuters Hill, *see* Pattingham
Twentyman, Lt.-Col. H. E., 12, 40
Twynyho, Edm., 177
Tyrel:
  Cath., w. of Sir Hugh the younger,
    129
  Sir Hugh, 129
  Sir Hugh, his s., 129
  John, 129
Tyrer:
  Thos., 113
  Wm., 153
Tyrley, Peatswood in, 181

Tyzack:
  Paul, 58
  Zachariah, 58

Ulstan, pre-Conquest tenant, 23
Ultan, pre-Conquest tenant, 202
Underhill, Hen., 10
Unifurnaces Ltd. (later Unifurnaces
  (Overseas) Ltd.), 70
United Reformed Church, 43-4, 222
Upper Arley, *see* Arley, Upper
Upper Stour Valley Main Sewerage
  Board, 135, 152
Uvedale:
  Wm., 208
  Wm., his s., 208

Vale's Rock, *see* Wolverley
Vaux:
  Gillian de, *see* Murdak
  Sir John de, 131
Veall, J. B., 89
Verdun:
  Bertram de, 83
  Sim. de, *see* Coughton
  Wm. de, *see* Wrottesley
Victoria, Queen:
  jubilee of 1887, 156, 220
  jubilee of 1897, 217
Victoria and Albert Museum, 171
Viles, Edw., 79
Volunteers, 14, 44, 46, 128, 163, 188
Vyse, *see* Howard-Vyse

Wainwright:
  G. W., 134
  Mary, *see* Holt
Wakering:
  Sir Gilb., 203, 216
  John, 203
Waldron, Wm., 57, 59-60
Walerand fam., 189
Wales, Princes of, *see* Edward II;
  Edward, the Black Prince; George
  IV
Wales, 24, 126, 197; *and see* Brecon
  priory; Holyhead
Walhouse, John, 82
Walker:
  Jos., 42
  Wm. the, *see* William
Wall Heath, *see* Kingswinford
Walsall, 17, 67, 219, 221, 224
  Bescot, 202
  Bloxwich, *q.v.*
  Goscote, 203
  Reynolds Hall, 82
Walter, Domesday tenant (? two of this
  name), 189, 202
Walter, Hubert, abp. of Canterbury,
  15-16
Wannerton:
  Elias, 73
  Thos., 147
Wapping (Mdx.), 154
War Office, 5
Ward:
  Edw., Baron Dudley and Ward, 56,
    208, 216
  Frances, *see* Sutton
  Col. H. H., 207
  Hen., 82
  Humble, Baron Ward, 208
  John, Vct. Dudley and Ward, 208
  Wm. (fl. 1639), 212
  Wm., earl of Dudley, 68
  Wm. Humble, Baron Ward, 62
  Wm. Humble Eric, earl of Dudley,
    208, 215
  fam., 82
Ward:
  Baroness, *see* Sutton
  barons, *see* Ward
  barony, 208
Warham:
  Jane, w. of Wm. (fl. 1635), 71-2

Wm. (fl. 1635), 71
Wm. (fl. 18th cent.), 71
Warren, Benj., 144
Warrington, earl of, *see* Booth
Warrington (Lancs.), 27
Warwick:
  ctss. of, *see* Neville
  earldom, 176
  earls of, *see* Beauchamp; Dudley;
    Neville
Warwick, 165
Warwickshire, 164; *and see* Astley
  castle; Birmingham; Coughton;
  Coventry priory; Edgbaston; Erd-
  ington; Haseley; Kenilworth
  priory; Leamington; Loxley;
  Rugby; Sutton Coldfield; Tred-
  ington; Warwick
Watkins:
  J., 214
  John, and his w., 106
Watkins, Wm., & Co., 214
Watling Street, *see* Roman roads
Watson:
  Eliz., w. of Wm. (d. 1615), m. 2 Thos.
    Cornwallis, 3 Thos. Stourton,
    176, 183
  Eliz., w. of Wm. (d. 1695), 176
  Fra., 176
  Jane, w. of Rowland, 176, 183
  Rob., 176*n*
  Rowland (d. 1595), 176-7, 181
  Rowland, s. of Wm. (d. 1695), 176
  Wm. (d. 1615), 176, 181, 183
  Wm. (d. 1695), 176-7, 183
  Wm., his s., 176, 181, 183
Watt, Jas., 58
Watts, Abigail, w. of ——, rector of
  Enville, 117
Wauton:
  Joan de, m. Hugh de Hepham, 67
  John s. of John de, 67
Weardale, Baron, *see* Stanhope
Webb:
  (or Penn), Agnes, 193, 219
  Chas., 136
  Edw. (fl. 19th cent.), 58
  Edw. (fl. 1911), 136, 143
  Geo., curate of Trysull, 193*n*
  Jane, w. of Wm., 148
  Jos., 58-9
  Maj. M. J., 136
  Nic., curate of Codsall, 86-7
  Thos., 59-60
  Thos. (? another), 145
  Thos. Wilkes, 59
  W. H., 136
  Wm., 147
Webb, Edw., & Sons, 140
Webb, Thos., & Corbett Ltd. (later
  Webb Corbett Ltd.), 59-60
Webb, Thos., & Sons, 59
Webb's Crystal Glass Co. Ltd., 59
Webster, John, 147
Wedge, John, 192
Wedgwood, Josiah, 98
Wednesbury, 77, 205
Wednesfield, in St. Peter's, Wolver-
  hampton, 3
well dressing, *see* folk customs
Wenlock, Much (Salop.), *see* Spoonhill
Wenman:
  Wm., 81
  Wm., his s., 81
Weoley castle (in Northfield, Worcs.),
  103
Wergs, *see* Tettenhall
Wesley, John, 43, 63
West Bromwich, *see* Bromwich, West
West Midlands, county of, 32, 62
Westbeech, *see* Pattingham
Westminster, 88, 90, 195
  abbey, 24
  and see Parliament, Houses of; Soho
Weston under Lizard, 67
Westwood, *see* Leek

Wharton:
Geo., curate of Kinver, 157–8
Thos., curate of Kinver, 128
Wheaton Aston, see Lapley
Wheeler:
Sir Chas., 81
Hen., 196
John, 145, 213
Ric., 145
Thos., and his w. Eleanor, 221
Wheeley, W. S., 59
Wheeley, Messrs., 53
Whichcot:
John, 97
John, his s., 97
Whitchcote, ——, widow of Dr., 154
Whitchurch (Salop.), see Ash
White:
Eleanor, see Caswell
Paul, curate of Kinver, 146
Thos. (fl. 1716), 143–4
Thos. (fl. 1816), 77
Wal., 184
White Ladies, see Boscobel
Whitechapel (Mdx.), 42, 156
Whitehouse:
Frank, 69
Jas., 35
Whitehouse, Jas., & Sons, 35
Whitmore:
Revd. Geo., 75
Thos. (fl. 1738), 71
Thos. (fl. 1862), 74
Wm. (fl. 1565), 71
Sir Wm. (fl. 1628), 71, 74
Wm. (fl. 1718), 74
fam., 71, 74
Whittimere, see Bobbington
Whittington:
Peter of, 135
Ric., 182
Sir Wm., 135
Sir Wm., his s., 135
Whittington, see Kinver
Whittington Patent Horse Nail Co.
Ltd., 145
Whorrell, Mary, 161; and see Worrall
Whorwood (formerly Horewood):
Anne, m. Ambrose Dudley, 83, 130, 134
Anne, w. of Gerard, 130, 133
Cath., w. of Sir Wm., m. 2 Wm.
Hamerton, 130–1, 134
Dorothy, w. of Edw., m. 2 Hugh
Shadwell, 133
Edw., 133
Fra., 104
Gerard, 113, 130–1, 133, 146
John (fl. 1386–7), 96, 133
John (fl. 15th cent., several of this
name), 133
John (d. 1527), 113, 133, 157
John, his s., 133
John (d. ? 1669), 130–1, 133–4, 136,
139, 144, 146, 153
Marg., w. of Wm., m. 2 Wm. Shel-
don, 83, 130
Marg., m. Thos. Throckmorton, 83,
130, 134
Ric., 104, 208
Rob., 209
Sir Thos., 83, 96, 113, 130–1, 133–4,
136
Wm. (d. 1545), 83, 130, 136, 143, 153
Wm. (fl. 1590), 104
Sir Wm. (d. 1653 × 1657), 130–1,
133–4, 144
Wortley, 113, 130–1, 145, 149, 153
fam., 96, 106, 113, 130, 133
and see Horwood
Whorwood, see Kinver: Compton,
Horewood
Wifare, pre-Conquest tenant, 67
Wightwick:
Alex., 18
Eliz., 16

Fra. (d. 1616), 18
Fra. (d. 1692), 16, 18
Fra. (d. c. 1697), 16, 18
Fra. (d. 1714), 16, 18, 46
Fra. (d. 1715), 18
Fra. (d. 1843), 16, 18
Geo., curate of Patshull, 168
Hancox, 18
Humph., 18
Jas., 16, 18
John, 16, 18
Matt., 46
Winifred, 16
fam., 10, 18, 41
Wightwick, see Tettenhall
Wilbraham, Sir Thos., 68
Wilcox:
Hen., 111
John (fl. 1558), 109
John (fl. 1666), 103
Wildicote (in Albrighton, Salop.), 162
Wilkes:
Barnet, 20
Bernard, 20
Edw., 20
Eliz., w. of Wm. (d. 1734), 20
Eliz., m. —— Booth, 20
Geo., 20
Hen., 19
Israel, 16
John (fl. 15th cent.), 19
John (18th-cent. politician), 20
Ric. (fl. 1444), 19
Ric. (fl. 1507), 19
Ric. (fl. 1576), 20
Ric. (d. 1655), 20
Ric. (fl. 1750), 20
Ric. (d. 1760), antiquary, 119, 147–8,
197
Ric. (d. 1797), 113–14
Ric., rector of Enville, 114, 116
Rog. (fl. 1385–98), 19
Rog. (fl. 1410–18), 19
Sarah, m. Hen. Jesson, 114
Thos. (d. by 1507), 19–20
Thos. (d. ? by 1569), 20
Thos. (d. 1612), 20
Thos. (d. 1694), 20
Wm. (fl. 1398–1411), 19
Wm. (d. by 1507), 19
Wm. (d. 1521), 20, 40
Wm. (d. 1726), 20
Wm. (d. 1734), 20
Wm., his s., 20
Wm. (fl. 1729–37), 16
fam., 16, 19
Willenhall (in St. Peter's, Wolver-
hampton), 19
Willesby, Thos., vicar of Wombourne,
219
Willett (Willetts):
John (fl. 1573), 143
John (? another), 143
Marg., 143
Ric. (fl. 1573), 143
Ric. (fl. 17th cent.), 155
Ric. (? another), 161
William I, 24, 26
William II, 131
William III, 155
William, Prince, duke of Gloucester,
75
William at the hall gate, 81
William s. of Agatha, see Claverley
William the chaplain, 33
William the cook, 204
Nic., his s., see Nicholas
William the fuller, 214
William the parker, 55
William the walker, 148
William Salt Archaeological Society,
see Staffordshire Record Society
Williams:
Benj., 145
Jas., 145
Williams, Jas., & Co., 145

Willoughby, Rob., Baron Willoughby
de Broke, 24–5
Wilmyns, John, 219
Wilson:
Geo., 127
Ralph, 127
Wiltshire, 31; and see Monkton Far-
leigh; Southwick; Stonehenge
Windham, Thos., 83
Witley, Great (Worcs.), Witley Ct. in,
62
Wodehouse, the, see Wombourne
Wollaston:
Edw., 5
Eliz., m. Jos. Amphlett, 104
Hen., canon of Tettenhall, later vicar
of Tettenhall, 39
Hen. (d. 1720), 104, 111–13
Hen., his s., 112
Sir John, 5, 46, 194, 218–20
Thos., 104
Wm. (d. 1595), 46
Wm. (fl. 1584–1601), 212
Wollaston (in Old Swinford, Worcs.),
49, 52–6, 62, 127
Hall, 145, 213
Wolmore, see Trysull
Wolseley, Sir Rob., 177
Wolverhampton, Vct., see Fowler
Wolverhampton, 1, 3, 5, 7, 14–15, 25,
30, 35, 46, 76–7, 80, 84, 140, 172–3,
180, 222
as address, 10, 12–13, 16–17, 20, 25,
27, 33–4, 36–7, 40, 43–4, 77,
79–82, 84–6, 88–9, 135, 140,
167, 189, 206, 212, 219, 221
Blue Coat Sch., 190
boro., 38, 47, 197
buses, 14, 95, 188, 201
Chapel Ash, 113
chs.:
St. John's, 35, 204
St. Mary's, 22, 42
Cistercian monastery, 15–16
coll., 25–6, 81
deans, 33, 81–2, 85; and see
Erdington
deanery manor, 86
prebendary, see Lee
corp., 10, 12–14, 21–3, 28, 32–3, 38,
175, 200, 217
Dunstall, 18
Goldthorn Hill, 38, 197
Graiseley, 17
Horseley Fields, 36
inds., 5, 8–9, 18, 21–2, 79, 167,
214–15
M.P.s, 5, 11, 17–18, 183
Merry Hill, see Wolverhampton,
Rom. Cath.
Newbridge, 14
prot. nonconf., 88–9, 222
Queen St. Cong. ch., 8, 44, 89, 183,
221
rds., 13, 52, 127, 187, 200–1
Rom. Cath.:
ch. of St. Mary and St. John, 43,
88, 183
St. Michael's ch., Merry Hill, 221
water supply, 38, 175
Wolverhampton, St. Peter's parish, 46;
and see Bilston; Hatherton;
Wednesfield; Willenhall
Wolverhampton and Dudley Breweries
Ltd., 18
Wolverhampton and Kingswinford
Railway, 14, 201
Wolverhampton area health authority,
165
Wolverhampton Aviation Ltd., 14
Wolverhampton Cricket Club, 14
Wolverhampton Waterworks Co., 8,
38, 80
Wolverley, Ric., 149
Wolverley (Worcs.), 119, 144, 160
Vale's Rock (? Cynefares Stane), 119

Wom brook, 197, 199–200, 206, 212–13, 217
  as Bate brook, 197, 212 *n*
Wombourne, Randal of, 208
Wombourne, **197–224**
  agric., 209–12
  almshos., 224
  ambulance stn., 217
  Arbour Tree Ho., 207
  Awbridge, 201
  Awbridge fm., 207
  Bank fm., *see* Wombourne, Greensforge Ho.
  Battlefield, 197, 199
  Bearnett fm., 207
  Beggar's Bush, 211, 215
  Birch Hill, 212
  Blackhill Plantation, 215
  Blakeley, 197, 199, 209, 214, 219, 222
  Botterham, 201–2
  the Bratch, *80*, *81*, 200–1, 210, 214–15, 217, 222
  Brickbridge, 199, 215
  bridges, 200–1, 216
  British Legion Hall, 221
  Bullmeadow Coppice, 215
  Bumblehole, 215
  canal, *see* Wombourne, communications
  chars. for the poor, 224
  Chasepool, 197, 208–12, 218
  Chasepool Lodge fm., 208–9
  chs., *81*, 182, 193, 204, 217–21, 224
  Cockshoot Hill, 213
  communications:
    canal, *80*, 201
    omnibuses, 201
    rly., 201
    rds., 200–1
  Cottagers' Horticultural Soc., 202
  council housing, 199–200
  Cricket, Tennis, and Bowling Club, 201
  Ebstree Hill, 210
  econ. hist., 209–15
  educ., 201, 221–3
  electricity, 217
  fire brigade, 217
  fisheries, 212
  flower show, 202
  Fox Hall fm., *see* Wombourne, White Cross fm.
  friendly socs., 202
  gas, 217
  Giggetty, 199, 215
  Gravel Hill Ho., 199
  green, 199
  Greenhill Ho., 199
  Greensforge, 213–14
    Greens (also Swin) Lodge, 208–10, 215
    Greensforge fm., 197, 208–9
    Greensforge Ho. (later Bank Fm.), 209
  Guardian Safe Works, 215
  Heath forge, 212–13
  Heath Ho., 199
  Heath Mill ind. est., 215
  Hinksford, 197, 213
  Hockey Club, 201
  Hollow Mill Fm., 213
  hosp., 217
  inds., 146, 199, 213–15
  inns:
    Boat, 202
    Cock, 200
    Red Lion, 200
    Vine, 202
  Ladywell Wood, 200, 212
  librs., 201–2
  Literary Inst., *see* Wombourne, Mutual Improvement Soc.
  local govt., 215–17
  Manor Ho. (formerly Old Hall), 201, 206–7

  mans., 202–8, 216
  the Maypole, 199
  Men's Inst., *see* Wombourne, Mutual Improvement Soc.
  Mill Ho. fm., 207
  Mill Lane fm., 206–7
  mills, 212–13
  Mutual Improvement Soc. (later Literary Inst. and Men's Inst.), 201–2, 223
  New fm., 207
  Old Hall, *see* Wombourne, Manor Ho.
  Orton (formerly Overton), 134, 196–7, 200, 206–7, 217, 219
    agric., 210–12
    inds., 214–15
    local govt., 216
    mans., 202–4, 207, 216
    mills, 212
    Orton Grange, 200, 207
    Orton Hill, 197, 200, 212
    Orton Ho., 200
    Orton Manor, 200
    pop., 197, 199–200, 209
    prot. nonconf., 221
    tithes, 209, 218
  Ounsdale, 199, 209, 215, 223
  Owen Hill, 204
  pk., 199
  police, 217
  Pool House housing est., 219
  poor relief, 216–17
  pop., 197, 199–200, 209
  post offices, 217
  pounds, 216
  prot. nonconf., 221–2
  public services, 217
  rly., *see* Wombourne, communications
  Reading Assoc., 201
  rectory, 209
  Rifle Band, 202
  rds. and streets:
    Battlefield Lane, 214
    Beggar's Bush Lane, 215
    Blakeley Lane (part of the later Common Rd.), 214
    Bratch Common Rd., 217
    Bratch Rd., 201
    Bridgnorth Rd., 199, 215
    Chapel Lane, 214, 222
    Chapel St., 219, 222
    Church Rd., 197, 217
    Church St., 199, 201, 216, 223; *and see* Wombourne: rds. and streets, Upper St.
    Common Lane, 222
    Common Rd., 219; *and see* Wombourne: rds. and streets, Blakeley Lane
    Flash Lane, 200
    Giggetty Lane, 197, 214, 217, 219, 221, 223
    Gilbert Lane, 202
    Gravel Hill, 199, 211, 215, 221
    Green Hill, 213
    Grettons Row, 222
    High St., 197, 199, 202, 215, 217, 222; *and see* Wombourne: rds. and streets, Upper St.
    Hinksford Gardens, 215
    Lindale Drive, 223
    Main St., 201
    Maypole St., 199, 221
    Mill Lane, 211–12, 214, 221–2
    Orton Lane, 200
    Ounsdale Rd., 200, 215, 223
    Penstone (formerly Pound) Lane, 200, 216
    Planks Lane, 201–2, 210, 215, 222–3
    Pool House Rd., 199–200, 213
    Pound Lane, *see* Wombourne: rds. and streets, Penstone Lane
    Rennison Drive, 221

    Rookery Rd., 199, 214, 216–17, 221, 224
    Sandy Hole Lane, 215
    School Rd., 200–1, 215, 217–18, 221, 223
    Showell Lane, 200
    Sytch Lane, 199, 223
    Upper St. (later Church St. with High St.), 223
    Walk Lane, 215
    Windmill Bank, 199, 202, 213, 216–17, 221, 224
    Withymere Lane, 199
    Wodehouse Rd., 200–1, 204
    Wombourne Rd., 223
    and see Wombourne, communications
  Rom. Cath., 221
  Rushford, 200, 212
  sewage works, 217
  Smallbrook fm., 197, 207
  Smestow, 213–14, 222
  Smestow Bridge ind. est., 215
  social and cultural activities, 201–2
  Sodom, 201
  Soldiers Hill, 197
  stocks, 216
  Swindon, 116, 197, 200–1, 204, 217, 224
    agric., 210–11
    ch., 221
    educ., 223
    inds., 213–15
    local govt., 216–17
    mans., 207–8, 216
    mills, 213
    pop., 199–200
    prot. nonconf., 222
    tithes, 218
    vicar, *see* Crane
  tithes, 209, 218
  vicars, 193–4, 218; *and see* Foley; Heale; Nicholas; Smart; Willesby; Wylnale
  Village Community Council, 224
  Volunteer Bureau, 202
  wake, 201
  Walk Ho., 207
  warren, 212
  water supply, *81*, 188, 217
  Waverley Ho., 207
  White Cross (or Fox Hall) fm., 200, 207
  Whitehouse fm., 208–9
  the Wodehouse, *16*, 201, *203*, 204–5, *206*, 220
  Wodehouse Mill fm., 211
  Wombourne common, 197, 199
  Wombourne fm., 207
  Wombourne Park housing est., 219
  Women's Inst., 202
  Woodhouse, 199, 210, 212–15
  woodland, 211–12
Wombourne Compass, 219
Wood:
  Anne, 184
  Chris., 79
  Hen. (d. 1648), 184
  Hen. (d. 1775), 81
  Hen., ? his s., 79, 81
  John, *see* Howe, Wm.
  Ric., 71
  Sibyl, *see* Bradley
  Wal., *see* Woodhouse
  Wm. (fl. 1240s × 1272), 204
  Wm. at the (fl. 14th cent.), 79
  Wm. (fl. ? 15th cent.), 71
  and see Attwood; Atwood
Wood, otherwise Dene:
  Edw., 82
  Mary, m. Alex. Persehouse, 82
  Ric., 82
  Wal., 82
  Wm., 82
  and see Dene
Woodall, Wm., 79

Woodford Grange, 187n, **225**
  Clapgate, 225
Woodhampton, *see* Astley
Woodhey (in Faddiley, Ches.), 68
Woodhouse:
  Benedict, 204
  Edw., s. of Fra., 224
  Edw. (d. 1688), 204, 211
  Fra., 204, 224
  John (fl. 15th cent.), 204
  John (d. 1523), 204, 219
  John (d. 1651), 203-4
  John (d. 1702), 204
  Steph., 204, 219
  Thos. (d. ? c. 1314), 204
  Thos. (several of this name 14th–15th cent.), 204
  Thos. (fl. 20th cent.), 70
  (formerly Wood), Wal., 204
  Wal. (d. 1610), 204
  Wal. (d. 1634), 210, 224
  Wm., 204
  Wm., his s., 204
  fam., 204
Woodhouse, *see* Wombourne
Woodhouses, *see* Pattingham
Woodyatt, T. M., 121n, 147
wool trade, 21, 25, 31
Worcester, archdeacon of, *see* Evans
Worcester, bps. of, 62, 142
Worcester, earl of, *see* Somerset
Worcester, 94, 103, 106, 127, 131, 134, 200
  cathedral, 114
Worcester, battle of, 126, 137
Worcester diocese, 62, 129
Worcestershire, 49, 129, 138, 204; *and see* Arley, Upper; Astley; Besford; Bewdley; Bordesley; Broadwaters; Bromsgrove; Churchill; Clent; Cradley; Dodford priory; Droitwich; Dudley; Eastham; Evesham abbey; Feckenham; Frankley; Grafton; Hagley; Halesowen; Impney; Inkberrow; Kidderminster; the Leasowes; the Lye; Netherton; Norton; Norton, King's; Oldberrow; Pedmore; Powick; Shelsley Walsh; Stourbridge; Stourport; Swinford, Old; Throckmorton; Tredington; Trimpley; Weoley castle; Witley, Great; Wolverley

Worcestershire Agricultural Society, 110
Worcestershire Voluntary Association, 219
Wordsley, *see* Kingswinford
Worfield (Salop.), 68
  Bradney, *q.v.*
  Davenport Ho., 181
  Roughton, *q.v.*
World Wars:
  First, 83, 100, 152, 201
  Second, 11, 41, 64, 100, 128, 152, 156, 165, 193
Worrall, John, 140; *and see* Whorrell
Wright:
  Ann, 45
  Ann, her dau., 45
  Aubrey, 225
Wrottesley:
  Adam of, 26
  Arthur, Baron Wrottesley, 40
  Chas., 83, 90
  Dorothy, w. of Ric. (d. 1521), 41
  Eliz., w. of John (d. 1402), m. 2 Sir Wm. Butler, m. 3 Wm., Baron Ferrers of Groby, 27
  Eliz., *see* Astley
  Frances, w. of Sir John (d. 1726), 25, 46
  Frances, *see* Courtenay
  Maj.-Gen. Geo., 5
  Henrietta, 46
  Sir Hugh (d. 1275 or 1276), 26, 167n, 168
  Sir Hugh (d. 1381), 5, 20, 26-7, 30, 32, 34, 103
  Hugh (d. ? 1385), 26
  Hugh (d. 1463 or 1464), 27
  Sir Hugh (d. 1633), 27, 189, 203, 210, 212, 225
  Joan, w. of Sir Wm. (d. 1319 or 1320), m. 2 John of Tetbury, 26
  John (d. 1402), 26-7
  John (d. 1578), 27, 41, 169
  Sir John (d. 1726), 83
  Sir John (d. 1787), 27
  Sir John, later Baron Wrottesley (d. 1841), 19, 27, 30, 82, 203-4, 212

  John, Baron Wrottesley (d. 1867), 5, 39, 42-3, 87, 187, 195, 209
  Mary (d. 1711), 46
  Mary, *see* Grey
  Mary, *see* Lee
  Ric., 27, 41
  Sophia, *see* Giffard
  Thos., 184
  Thomasine, w. of Sir Wal. (d. 1463 or 1464), 27
  Victor Alex., Baron Wrottesley, 27, 83-4, 189, 192, 204, 225
  Sir Wal. (d. 1473), 27
  Wal. (d. 1562 or 1563), 19, 25, 27, 39, 82, 87, 104, 168
  Wal. (d. 1630), 27, 46, 82, 88, 90, 104, 210, 225
  Sir Wal. (d. 1659), 27, 39, 87, 203, 212-13, 225
  Sir Wal. (d. 1686), 19, 25, 27, 31, 41, 47
  Wal. (fl. before 1710), 184
  Sir Wal. (d. 1712), 27, 47, 191
  Wm. of (also Wm. de Verdun), 26, 167n, 168
  Sir Wm. (d. 1313), 26
  Sir Wm. (d. 1319 or 1320), 26, 34
  Wm. (fl. 1640), 184
  fam., 5, 19, 26-7, 34, 36, 39, 41-2, 82, 87, 168, 209, 212
Wrottesley, barons, 39, 42, 87
Wrottesley, *see* Tettenhall
Wulfgeat, 26
Wulfrun, the Lady, 25
Wyatt:
  Benj., 165
  John, 60
  Lewis, 165
  Wm., 40
Wylily, Rog., 164
Wylnale, Wm., vicar of Wombourne, 218
Wynn-Carrington, Lady Ruperta, m. Wm. Legge, earl of Dartmouth (d. 1958), 165
Wyrley and Essington Canal Co., 44

York:
  dchss. of, *see* Mary
  duke of, *see* George V
Young, Arthur, agronomist, 3
Young, Alan, & Partners, 40
Young & Son, 61